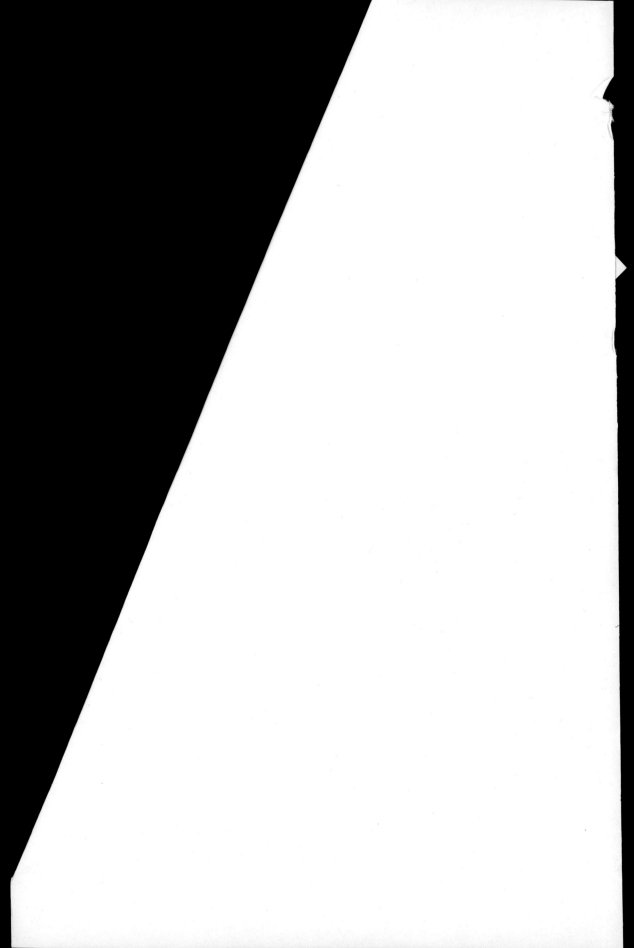

University Casebook Series

REAL ESTATE TRANSACTIONS

Cases and Materials on
Land Transfer, Development
and Finance

By

PAUL GOLDSTEIN

Stella W. and Ira S. Lillick Professor of Law
Stanford University

GERALD KORNGOLD

Professor of Law
Case Western Reserve University

THIRD EDITION

Westbury, New York
THE FOUNDATION PRESS, INC.
1993

Library of Congress Cataloging-in-Publication Data

Goldstein, Paul, 1943–
    Real estate transactions : cases and materials on land transfer,
development and finance / by Paul Goldstein and Gerald Korngold. —
3rd ed.
        p.   cm. — (University casebook series)
    Includes index.
    ISBN 1–56662–064–3
    1. Vendors and purchasers—United States—Cases. 2. Conveyancing—
United States—Cases. I. Korngold, Gerald. II. Title.
III. Series.
KF665.A4G65   1993
346.7304'38—dc20
[347.306438]   93–14767

 TEXT IS PRINTED ON 10% POST
CONSUMER RECYCLED PAPER

Goldstein & Korngold Real Est.Trans. 3rd Ed. UCS
1st Reprint—1995

To Jan
P.G.

To Alice
G.K.

*

PREFACE

Real estate transactions have changed dramatically over the last thirty years. Federal income tax law has created new incentives for residential ownership as well as new opportunities, and pitfalls, for commercial real estate investment. The growth of title insurance has increased the security and efficiency of real estate transactions and contributed to the evolution of a national market for real estate finance. Because title policies are backed by large, resourceful institutions and generally follow nationally uniform standards, title insurance has drawn major institutional lenders and sophisticated financing schemes into every corner of the country. The federal government and the secondary mortgage market have played an increasingly important role in nationalizing and systematizing real estate finance. The savings and loan crisis has constrained the capital for real estate development, and government's response to the crisis has altered the structure and conduct of transactions. Increased federal and state environmental regulation influences virtually every real estate sale, exposing the parties to potentially devastating liability. The civil rights and consumer movements have also left their mark, principally on residential real estate sales.

Some of these changes, such as the spread of title insurance, have taken work away from lawyers. Other changes, because they implicate a wide and complex range of legal issues, have magnified and complicated the real estate lawyer's role. It is no longer sufficient to know the law on conveyancing, title and mortgages. The real estate lawyer today must also grasp at least the basics of federal income taxation, personal property security, environmental regulation, bankruptcy and products liability law. He or she must also have a feel for the informal legal culture created by the many nongovernmental institutions and individuals involved in real estate transactions—brokers, title companies, surveyors, appraisers, lenders and their various trade associations.

This book encompasses emergent, as well as traditional, fields of real estate law. Part One covers the basic elements of real estate transactions, using the residential transaction as a vehicle for exposing the fundamentals of real estate conveyancing, title assurance, secured financing and federal income taxation. Part Two covers commercial real estate transactions, exploring contemporary innovations in tax, financing and leasing techniques and examining current issues related to distressed properties and environmental regulation; it concludes with materials on the assembly and operation of shopping centers.

Although real estate transactions have become increasingly subject to nationalizing influences, real estate law remains in many respects the creature of local rules. As a consequence, one message should be emphasized here: no real estate lawyer can safely ignore applicable state law when counselling on any transaction, large or small.

v

PREFACE

Real estate law is a happy blend of practical insight and academic perspective, a mix that we have tried to convey in the pages that follow. Colleagues in practice and in academe have provided helpful comments for the preparation of the third edition. We are particularly grateful to Todd Davis for his help with the environmental law materials, Edward Hurtuk, Charles Daroff and Zachary Paris for their insights on new developments in real estate law, and Leon Gabinet for his comments on the tax materials. We also appreciate Bob Lawry's comments on professional responsibility issues and Morris Shanker's comments on bankruptcy.

Many law teachers who used the second edition of this casebook have been generous with their suggestions for the third edition. For their thoughtful comments, we are indebted to Professors Pamela W. Bray, John D. Briggs II, Alex Johnson, John W. Larson, Carl H. Lisman, John R. Nolon, Patrick A. Randolph, Jr., Peter W. Salsich, Jr., M. John Schubert, John M. Tyson, G. Graham Waite, Robert Weiler and Alan M. Weinberger.

We also appreciate the patient and careful work of student assistants—Mary Percifull, Deborah Peters, and Kimberly Mack—in performing research, checking citations and proofreading the manuscript. Their work was supported by the Case Western Reserve University School of Law. We also acknowledge the support of the faculty summer research fund of Case Western Reserve University School of Law.

We are indebted to Ellie Ettinger and Lynne Anderson for their superb secretarial and organizational support. The staffs of the Robert Crown Law Library at Stanford and of the law library at Case Western Reserve were, as ever, kind and efficient in helping us to locate sources.

A Note on Style. Most of the cases and other materials appearing in these pages have been edited. The deletion of sentences and paragraphs is indicated by ellipses; the deletion of citations is not indicated. Most footnotes have been excised. The remaining footnotes retain their original numbering. Authors' footnotes are lettered.

P.G.
G.K.

Stanford, California
Cleveland, Ohio
June, 1993

SUMMARY OF CONTENTS

SUMMARY OF CONTENTS

TABLE OF CONTENTS

TABLE OF CASES

Principal cases are in italic type. Non-principal cases are in roman type. References are to Pages.

TABLE OF CASES

REAL ESTATE TRANSACTIONS

Cases and Materials on
Land Transfer, Development
and Finance

*

Part One

BASIC ELEMENTS OF THE REAL ESTATE TRANSACTION

I. ARRANGING THE DEAL

A. AN INTRODUCTION TO THE CONVEYANCING INDUSTRY

PAYNE, A TYPICAL HOUSE PURCHASE TRANSACTION IN THE UNITED STATES *

30 The Conveyancer (n.s.) 194–195; 199–211; 218 (1966).

A year or two ago, when I was privileged to visit London and talk shop with English conveyancers, I received confirmation of a long-held suspicion that English and American lawyers are rapidly losing the capacity to communicate effectively with each other. Since we both practise in common law jurisdictions, it would be thought that our procedures would be sufficiently alike to permit us to discuss them in language reasonably intelligible on both sides. But, in fact, this is not the case. The land law in the two countries has shown great divergence, the organization of the legal profession is somewhat different and American practise is in large part the result of our unique system of recording. In addition, dissimilar development in ancillary institutional growth, as in the case of the credit structure has been influential to produce unlike procedures. . . .

With this in mind, I shall undertake in this essay to describe step by step, in words which I hope will be intelligible to the English reader, a reasonably simple and uncomplicated American land transfer. For this purpose I have chosen the purchase of a house, not merely because it is the commonest of all real estate transactions, but also because it illustrates significant contemporary trends in American conveyancing. . . .

Normally, the *first* step in a house-buying venture is to consult a real estate agent. He will know what property is for sale in the local market and what price is being asked. Then will follow the conventional searching and haggling, culminating in a parol understanding as to the amount of the purchase price (frequently expressed merely in terms

---

* Reprinted by permission of Sweet & Maxwell, Ltd.

of the amount of the required down payment and the anticipated monthly mortgage amortisation payments) and the time when occupancy can be given.

Second: At this point the reasonable and prudent buyer will employ his own attorney to draft a proper contract and steer him through the legal and financial shoals which lie ahead. He will know that the contract he is about to sign will have predominate influence upon what is to follow and should clearly and explicitly express the rights and responsibilities of both parties. As a matter of fact it is much more probable that the buyer is somewhat unreasonable and not very prudent, and will, instead, sign a printed form supplied by the real estate agent. In this he will be flying in the face of fortune and may suffer bitter regrets when he finds that the contract holds him to a bad bargain, does not express the intention of the parties or is unenforceable for indefiniteness. But sign it he will, for the American lay public is not yet convinced that a lawyer is needed at this juncture and prefers to thrust itself into the hands of the real estate agent. This is somewhat anomalous, for certainly the reputation of these agents is not above reproach and obviously they are the creatures of the seller. Nevertheless, they seem to have obtained the confidence of those who deal with them, in part, I surmise, because the buyer is at this point generally pretty well confused and worn out and also, in part, because the agent purports to render his services "free."

The contract which the parties have signed may in at least three respects differ from its English counterpart. In the first place, it will seldom contain a legal description of the property, but rather some general identification, such as "2020 Main St." or the like. This may lay the ground for much future disagreement between the parties as to what was in fact bargained for, but the agent is generally anxious to close the contract and does not pay much attention to legal niceties. Secondly, the agreement as signed will not contain what the English lawyer would feel to be vital, that is, a description of the nature of the title evidence to be offered by the vendor. The reason for this omission will become apparent later when we consider the recording system and for the moment it is enough to say that the vendee will expect, not a title proved by certain identifiable muniments, but, rather, a "good and marketable title" as established by the public records. This sort of title the vendee will demand in any event and if the title actually proffered fails to meet this definition he will simply withdraw from the contract and demand the return of his deposit. The vendor and the real estate agent, on the other hand, assume that the title is good and marketable. If they are correct in this assumption, they can enforce the contract and, if not, they feel that they will suffer no out-of-pocket loss. This assumption, although ordinarily indulged in, lacks justification in many cases and in others results in expensive disagreements. For example, the good and marketable title of the law is one that is entirely unencumbered. Now suppose the property in question is crossed by a perfectly visible telephone-line easement or is subject to a restrictive covenant. Was it the intention of the parties to except these encumbrances? This sort of question ought to have been answered by the specific terms of the contract, but seldom is. Where the buyer continues to desire performance of the contract little difficulty arises. But suppose, to the contrary, he wants to rescind. Can he seize upon this defect as grounds for breach? Is there any contract at all, and, if so, what are its terms? Finally, the contract may be vague as to the exact consideration to be paid, particularly when a house already encumbered by a mortgage is the subject-matter. For example, it is not uncommon to find such expressions as "in consideration of $14,000, subject to an existing mortgage," or the like.

Third: For our purposes here I will assume that the buyer has agreed to pay $14,000 (£5,000) for the house. He expects to pay down 3 per cent.[16] (the minimum permitted by F.H.A.) and to obtain the remainder of the purchase price by giving a mortgage. The loan will be liquidated by level monthly payments, covering principal and interest, over a period of approximately thirty years. He will plan to buy a freehold, as outside Maryland, Pennsylvania and Ohio little American residential property is subject to a term running more than one year. After he has signed the contract, the buyer will require two things, credit and the assurance that the seller has a good title to convey. These two needs are closely linked for, if a mortgage is to be given, the mortgagee will also demand proof of title. It is entirely possible that the buyer will now himself solicit credit directly from some lender and that he may also employ his own attorney for the purpose of protecting his interests. However, this would not be the typical transaction which we are now describing. Instead, at some point in the negotiations he will have been assured by the real estate agent that he, the agent, will "take care of everything," including all details as to the loan, drafting of instruments, and closing, and that the buyer will have nothing to do except come to a designated office at an appropriate time and sign the necessary papers. This offer will have been accepted with alacrity, as the buyer at that point was uncertain as to how he should proceed and wanted, above all, to avoid any unnecessary trouble. If this arrangement is to proceed, however, he will now have to sign an application for a mortgage and make a deposit sufficient to cover all anticipated closing costs.

Fourth: Prior to this time the real estate agent will have obtained some sort of informal commitment for the necessary loan. Since credit is the lifeblood of the real estate market, every agent must be in a position to assist buyers in obtaining financing. This results in close relations between lending institutions and the realtors. This relation

---

16. It is common for borrowers to pay down only the absolute minimum required. If a borrower can make a larger down payment he may prefer what is called a "conventional" mortgage, which is one not backed by an F.H.A. guarantee. The advantage of the conventional mortgage is an appreciable saving, since no mortgage guarantee premium is necessary (½ per cent. of the principal per year) and closing charges are smaller. However, such conventional mortgages are unacceptable by some lenders, generally those dealing in the national mortgage market.

may range from *ad hoc* negotiation in each transaction to something like organic union, but there are few, if any, substantial real estate firms which cannot offer this service. In the case we are now considering, since credit has already been promised, the agent will forward the application for the loan to the lending institution. There it will be processed to determine whether the lender is a good risk and a credit report will be obtained. An appraisal will also be ordered. ...

Fifth: With the investigation of title comes the most involved and time-consuming part of the transfer process. Three principal types of title assurance, each exclusive of the other, are used. None of these can be understood, however, without some preliminary grasp of the American recording system and the theories of title which have depended upon it. Unlike the mother country, the American colonist from the very beginning rejected the system of proof by muniments of title and, instead, provided for registration of assurances. The American recording statutes ordinarily provide that all documents relating to land titles may be recorded in the county courthouses. There they are entered seriatim and *in extenso* in large folio volumes. These records are open to public inspection and access to the contents is made possible through name (and sometimes tract) indices. Registration is voluntary, but a failure to register may result in an innocent purchaser for value obtaining priority. As a consequence, registration is almost universal. The legal effect of registration is simply to give notice, as the record is not self-proving and a recorded instrument may be entirely ineffective. In good theory, the records should not be relied upon to prove title. However, Americans are notoriously lax in preserving actual deeds and the records must be searched in any event to eliminate the possibility of adverse conveyances. As a consequence, we deduce title from the documents found in the courthouse. This is done by starting with the present owner and, using the indirect or grantee index, taking a "chain of title" back to a grant from the sovereign. The title is then "back tracked" through the indices to determine whether any adverse interests have been created. Tracing title back to the state is, in conventional American theory, the only way in which a good marketable title can be established. However, as in some of the older sections of the country the original grants are found more than three centuries ago, it is no longer practical in these areas to make a full search of title and searches are limited to some conventional period, say sixty years. The system which I have described involves a direct search of the records by the examining attorney and culminates in the attorney giving his client a written statement, called a "certificate of title," to the effect that he has made the examination and that, on the basis of what he has found, the fee simple is vested in the vendor free and clear of any encumbrances other than those noted as exceptions. This system of direct examination still prevails in some places but is excessively laborious because the books which must be examined are quite numerous and unwieldy and indices are so primitive that most of the examiner's time must be spent in separating the relevant from the irrelevant. These objections have led to its being superseded in many areas by the system of examining abstracts.

Where abstracts are used a lay individual or corporation makes a "take-off," or copy of all of the public records, and then re-indexes them so as to make the contents readily available. This constitutes the "title plant." When an abstract is ordered the abstractor assembles all of the pertinent records, and abstracts, or abbreviates their content. He then "certifies" this abstract on its face as containing a reference to all instruments of record pertaining to the particular title and sells it to the purchaser of the abstract. It is then examined by an attorney, who certifies the title to his client in the same fashion as the attorney who has made a direct examination. Once the abstract has been prepared, it is passed down from seller to buyer, being merely brought up to date by addenda at the time of each transfer. A fee is charged at the time of each up-dating but a complete new examination of the original records is eliminated. However, it is customary, despite much adverse criticism, for the attorney for the buyer or mortgagee to make a complete re-examination of the abstract upon each transfer and to charge his client as though no previous examination had been made.

Whether the title is established by direct search or by the examination of an abstract, the attorney for the vendee or mortgagee may demand, as additional security, that a certificate of title insurance be obtained from a national company. This kind of insurance is issued by a corporate insurer on the basis of a certificate furnished to it by the local attorney. It has three principal advantages—the substitution of contract for tort liability, the replacement of a mortal individual assurer by an immortal corporation and some additional protection against defects of title not appearing on the record. It simply supplements other modes of title assurance, at somewhat greater cost, and does not interfere with the conventional relationship between attorney and client.

The third major method of establishing title is by local title insurance. A company issuing this kind of a policy maintains a title plant substantially like that of the abstractor. When a title policy is ordered it assembles its records and then makes an examination by its own salaried staff. On the basis of this examination it issues a policy and this policy is used by the vendee or mortgagee in lieu of the conventional attorney's certificate. This form of insurance, then, displaces the independent attorney from the principal work in the title transaction and local title companies are in direct competition with the Bar.

The protection afforded by the attorney's certificate runs only to his client. In theory both the vendee and the mortgagee should insist that they receive attorneys' certificates, but in practice this is seldom done, the vendee feeling that he has sufficient protection if the mortgagee will accept the title. In similar fashion, title insurance companies will issue owners' or mortgagees' or combined policies. But ordinarily only the mortgagee asks for and obtains such a policy, since the mortgagor is unwilling to pay the additional cost for combined owner-mortgagee coverage.

I have described above the three basic forms of establishing title, and, obviously, all three are not employed simultaneously. Despite the very great expansion of local title insurance during the post-Second World War period, especially in large urban areas, it is probable that the abstract system is still the most prevalent in the United States and I will, for that reason, assume its use in the typical house-buying transaction. When the mortgagee's attorney has been instructed to prepare for closing, his first step will be to get in touch with the vendor and arrange to have the abstract brought up to date. When he has received the abstract from the abstract company he will examine it and make an informal judgment as to whether curative action is required. If such action is needed, he will notify the vendor what his requirements are. Thereafter, if the vendor fails to take proper curative action, the attorney may advise his client to refuse to complete the contract. We will assume in this case, however, that the title is acceptable. Some time during the course of examination the attorney will have ordered a survey. When he has before him the accepted abstract and the plat of survey he will then make an application for a title insurance "binder." As soon as the binder is received he will notify the mortgagee to set a date for closing and will then prepare a note (or bond) and mortgage for execution by the mortgagor. If he has been requested to do so by the vendor, he will also prepare a deed. In addition, either he or the mortgagee will prepare a closing statement.

Sixth: The function of the closing is to bring all interested parties together and to permit them to execute and deliver the necessary documents simultaneously with the payment of the purchase price and the settlement of the costs of the transactions. The latter are conventionally known as closing costs, although they are generally incurred prior to the time when the closing actually takes place. A closing may be held at any convenient place—the office of the mortgagee's attorney, mortgagee's place of business, real estate agent's office or elsewhere. When the parties have assembled it is first customary to check the closing statement. The vendor (and his wife, if necessary) will then execute the deed and will receive the adjusted purchase price by cheque drawn by the mortgagee. At the same time the vendee (and his wife, if necessary) will execute the bond (or note) and mortgage. He will then or later receive a cheque for any amount he has paid to the mortgagee in excess of the actual closing charges.

Seventh: Following the closing the mortgagee's attorney will send the deed and mortgage to the courthouse for the attachment of revenue stamps and recording and will pay the necessary fees. When the instruments are returned from the courthouse he will send the deed to the vendee and the abstract, mortgage, note (or bond) and a certificate of title to the mortgagee. In the meantime he will have sent to the title insurance company a final certificate of title and an application for a mortgagee policy. His certificate will show that title is vested in the mortgagor and that the mortgage is a valid first lien against the property. ...

In summary, it now appears that the typical American land transfer is not too slow to meet ordinary functional demands but is unduly expensive and fails to give the parties optimum protection. To the Englishman first coming into contact with the system employed I suspect that at least six of its characteristics would seem most striking: (1) the cumbersomeness imposed upon the entire transaction by the mechanical defects in the system of recording; (2) the excessive duration of search resulting from the failure of American legislatures to limit the duration of interests in land and notice thereof; (3) the lack of adequate protection afforded vendee-mortgagors when land is purchased and a mortgage given; (4) the very high cost when compared to similar costs in England; (5) the lack of a contract of sale adequate to provide full protection to both buyer and seller; and (6) the appearance of only one lawyer in the transaction, with attendant ethical and practical problems arising out of conflicts of interests and lack of proper representation. These characteristics will also lead him to think that the system is inefficient and far from fair. He will ask himself how a country like the United States, which lays great store by the efficiency of its institutions, can tolerate a device so faulty in its workings and so partial in the results achieved.

WHITMAN, HOME TRANSFER COSTS: AN ECONOMIC AND LEGAL ANALYSIS *

62 Georgetown Law Journal 1311, 1329–1340 (1974).

The 1971 HUD/VA Report provides a data base which can be helpful in assessing whether title-related closing costs are excessive. The survey disclosed an enormously wide variation in average costs, ranging from $56 in North Dakota to $480 in New York. The average of the five lowest cost states was $84, and of the five highest cost states, $418. The geographic distribution of the cost spectrum is instructive. Seven of the ten highest cost states are located in the Middle Atlantic area, while all but one of the 20 lowest cost states are in the Midwest, New England, or the Rocky Mountain States.

REASONS FOR GEOGRAPHIC COST VARIATIONS

Professional field observations and discussions with title practitioners yield a variety of explanations for the wide range in closing costs. The most obvious is that the high-cost jurisdictions are generally areas of dense population, with high wage rates and living costs. Because of the labor-intensive nature of title work, areas characterized by high labor costs could be expected to have higher title costs, but the differences which now exist are far too great to be explained by labor costs alone.

* Reprinted with permission of the publisher; Copyright © 1974 by the Georgetown Law Journal.

Goldstein & Korngold Real Est.Trans. 3rd Ed. UCS—2

Undoubtedly, mere cost figures are deceptive, since the services provided are not necessarily comparable among the jurisdictions in question. For example, title insurance is considerably less widely used in New England than in Middle Atlantic States, largely because of the presence of many large lenders in New England who do not customarily sell their mortgage loans on the secondary market and who are therefore willing to accept the title opinions of attorneys, without more, as adequate title evidence. Similarly, in some areas lending institutions and real estate brokers provide closing services without charge. The absence of title insurance or closing charges necessarily lowers the overall costs of title transfer and provides an explanation for at least some degree of cost differentials.

The underlying reasons for cost variations, however, are not so easily explained. Because costs in the Midwest tend to be significantly lower than in other areas, midwestern practice is worthy of special attention. That practice is characterized by its use of the abstract, a technique which provides significant savings. ...

Two other factors allegedly contribute to lower title costs in the Midwest. The first is the prevalence of the government survey system, resulting in land descriptions which are simpler, more accurate, and more readily reproducible than those which prevail in the East. While this factor has some pertinence, its importance should not be overemphasized; the majority of residential property transfers in all parts of the nation probably rely on references to recorded subdivision plats, rather than either government survey descriptions or metes and bounds.

A second factor is the relative age of the public land records. Some eastern attorneys argue that their task is more difficult than that of midwestern or Pacific coast title searchers because the history of land titles in the East is simply much longer. The factual assertion is correct but is relevant to the difficulty of title searching only if searches are made back to the sovereign. In reality few attorneys of any jurisdiction search beyond 60 years on a normal basis. Some title insurers do so, but for established companies, cases in which full historical searches must be made are extremely rare, since the great majority of searches will be for parcels whose base titles have been previously examined.

Marketable title statutes were thought by HUD analysts to have a significant bearing on the cost of title proof. In principle, these statutes permit a reduction of the search period from the conventional 60 years to some lesser period. Unfortunately, most of the statutes embody a statutory period that is still too long and contain such a range of exceptions that their actual impact on search periods is probably slight or negligible. Moreover, they frequently are found in the same states in which the abstract system predominates. Although the HUD analysts ultimately concluded that the statutes' impact on costs was significantly beneficial, the statutes' contribution to efficiency and low costs probably is small compared to the contribution of the abstract system itself.

Title practitioners from high-cost states often offer one additional justification for the high fees they charge—that the "client" receives a degree of personal service and representation which is not generally available in lower cost areas. For example, in New York and New Jersey it is common for three attorneys, representing the buyer, seller, and lender respectively, to participate in the transfer of residential property. Under this system, the buyer, who is most in need of representation, truly appears to receive it, although at an exceedingly high cost. By contrast, in most southern Atlantic seaboard states, one attorney not formally representing any party usually handles the entire transaction. In a questionable situation the attorney's true allegiance would probably lie with the lender, broker, or developer if one of these referred the case to him, yet the buyer often assumes that the attorney is "his" lawyer, and counsel rarely disabuses him of this view.[106] Both the New York/New Jersey and the southern Atlantic systems are fundamentally defective, for neither permits the home buyer to make an intelligent choice concerning the extent of personal representation he wishes to obtain. Instead, the degree of personal representation is likely to depend on local custom and on the predilections of the individual attorney.

A major factor in the inefficiency of present real estate transfers is the concept that attorneys should search titles and conduct closings. The use of legally trained professionals to perform these routine tasks constitutes an enormous waste of skill and causes increased overall costs to parties. By contrast, on the Pacific coast all of the routine aspects of transfer are handled by title and escrow companies. The most reasonable system would be one in which laymen conducted the mechanical work of title transfers, but under which each party could determine his own need for legal representation. Indeed, counseling and negotiation arguably are not title-related closing services at all and should not be included in an analysis of closing costs.

An unfortunate practice found with great frequency throughout the nation except on the Pacific coast and in New England is the requirement that surveys accompany land title transfers even when there is no reasonable ground for believing that a survey is necessary. Many title companies and lenders commonly require a new survey for every transaction, even if the parcel is in a platted subdivision and a survey is available from a previous transaction involving the same land. In such cases, the only significant function of the new survey is to ascertain that there are no improvements which encroach upon the parcel's boundaries. A visual check of the boundaries by a nonsurveyor could satisfy this function at a much lower cost in the great majority of cases. Indeed, at least one surveyor has admitted relying on an old survey and

106. Whitman, Transferring North Carolina Real Estate, Part II: Roles, Ethics, and Reform, 49 N.C.L.Rev. 593, 605 (1971) (only 37 percent of North Carolina attorneys surveyed customarily explained to buyers that they represented another party). ...

a visual inspection but charging as though a new survey were performed. Since survey charges commonly run from $40 to $60 or more, requiring an actual survey only where a visual inspection indicated its necessity would produce a significant savings.

Another significant source of inefficiency in the eastern, southern, and Pacific coast practice is the use of outside closing agents. In cases in which a new loan is being made, lending institutions can most economically perform closings. The process by which a lender transmits instructions, documents, and checks to an attorney, title company, or escrow company is cumbersome, time-consuming, and error-producing. In the Midwest and Mountain States, especially outside metropolitan areas, lenders commonly handle closings without outside assistance and often do not charge for the service. There can be no doubt that net savings are achieved by this method.

THE OPERATION OF MARKET FORCES

The institutional changes needed to reduce title costs in a specific jurisdiction are easily listed; however, change occurs with glacial speed, if at all. The explanation for the persistence of the status quo may be found in the nature of the market for title and closing services. Since there are many buyers and sellers of title services, an observer might assume that the forces of supply and demand are functioning to allocate resources and set prices most efficiently. Ironically, a comparison of the characteristics of the market for title services with the characteristics classically thought to be necessary for a perfectly competitive market points up a number of critical shortcomings in the title services market.

Buyer Knowledge Is Grossly Inadequate. The purchasers of title services are usually buyers and occasionally sellers of homes. They are typically laymen, inexperienced in coping with the processes by which titles are assured and transferred. Even the individual who has previously bought or sold several homes is not likely to be knowledgeable about the jurisdiction's laws and systems. More specifically, the buyer, unaware of the frequency and significance of myriad title defects which may be disclosed by a careful search of the records, does not appreciate the need for a title search, does not understand the added protection offered by title insurance, and does not comprehend the methods by which title searches, title insurance, and closing services are priced. Further, the typical buyer is unaware of the differences in coverage between various lawyers' title certificates or between different forms of title insurance policies. The buyer neither understands the necessity for a survey nor is aware that less costly, acceptable substitutes for a survey are available. He does not know that many different suppliers of title services exist, that some of them offer less costly overall packages of services than others, or that there is a possibility of claiming a reduced rate for title insurance from the company which wrote the policy when the parcel was transferred previously. The foregoing list is not exhaustive but indicates the layman's inability to cope with the complexities of the process he faces.

Sellers Do Not Act Independently. There is considerable outright collusion among sellers of title services, often under color of law. Minimum fee schedules for attorneys recently have been investigated by the Justice Department, attacked by private litigants, and abolished in a number of jurisdictions. However, even when the schedules are abolished, departure from the fees they had listed is likely to occur slowly. Title insurance companies engage in formalized price fixing under the sponsorship of rating bureaus in many states. In other states, the presence of a few very large title insurers permits strong price leadership, and most smaller firms are unwilling to depart from the established rates. These tendencies are sometimes reinforced by state insurance commissioners who are willing to acquiesce in rates for all companies at levels which permit profitable operation of even the most inefficient companies. Among other suppliers of title-related services, such as surveying, tax service, and pest inspection companies, there are discernible but less egregious tendencies toward the establishment of "going rates" from which few competitors depart.

Another form of lack of independence results from the interrelationships which commonly exist among firms which supply various title services. For example, in jurisdictions where the "approved attorney" system of title insurance is employed, title companies must largely rely upon attorneys to direct business to them. The companies compensate the attorneys by paying commissions and by providing free services, entertainment, meals, and other promotional activities. Similarly, in jurisdictions in which title insurers perform their own title searches, real estate brokers and salesmen, lenders, and builders provide referrals to title companies and receive similar inducements.

Finally, the choice of attorneys in those jurisdictions in which attorneys perform title services is often in the hands of the real estate broker, builder, or lender. It is fairly common for this relationship to take the form of a specific "tying arrangement." In other cases, the choice is theoretically left to the home buyer, but because of his lack of knowledge of the market and of the services involved, the buyer is an easy mark for "steering" by the broker or lender. Where the referring entity is a lending institution, the attorney may be a member of its board of directors, or may perform non-title work at a reduced charge in return for profitable referrals. Reduced-cost legal work is often performed for real estate brokers on the same basis. The developer of new homes may persuade an attorney to do his base title work at a low rate or without charge in return for a promise to refer all home buyers to the same title attorney.

The problems of lack of knowledge by buyers and lack of independence by sellers of title services are interrelated; the naivete of laymen permits collusive practices and rebates among sellers to flourish, while sellers make virtually no effort to help buyers understand the nature of the services involved and the ways costs might be reduced. Consequently, it is not surprising that prices remain high and that industry interest in efficiency and reform is meager. Since the consumers who pay for title services generally do not shop for or select the suppliers of services, standard rates or fees are easy to maintain. In the absence of price competition, providers are relatively unconcerned with costs. Their principal means of expanding business is to compete for the favor of other real estate professionals who supply them with referrals, a process which tends to raise rather than lower costs to consumers. The providers may give lip service to such concepts as modernization or computerization of title records, but probably will take little action to effectuate these reforms, for the reforms promise no significant economic benefit. On the contrary, better records systems might produce pressure from the public for lower prices. The gross income of providers has steadily risen because many title services are priced as a percentage of the selling price of the property. From the providers' point of view price competition is neither necessary nor desirable, and improvements in efficiency have a very low priority.

These anticompetitive features do not characterize the market for title services everywhere; rather, they tend to prevail where costs to consumers are highest. The reasons for the appearance of anticompetitive features in some markets and not in others are complex. Generally, they can be traced to local law, custom, and the presence of greater or less cupidity on the part of the suppliers of title services. Where anticompetitive features do exist, it is difficult to see any simple method of reform which will make the market more competitive. The prospect of educating consumers in the mysteries of title services is not promising. Lenders, brokers, and builders may be forbidden to require that title services be rendered by a particular provider, but it is probably impractical to prohibit referrals, which have nearly the same effect. Complete restructuring of the market is needed to provide the price competition which is now lacking and to provide incentives for sellers of title services to implement more efficient techniques.

NOTES

1. *The Cost of Conveyancing Services.* Many professionals and specialists participate in residential sales. Among the more evident are brokers, lawyers, loan officers, appraisers, title assurance personnel, surveyors, house inspectors and escrow agents. Other participants stay in the background. There are, for example, the many brokers who may have shown a house with no success, and the many bureaucrats who administer the recording system.

All of these participants must be paid. According to a 1972 study, prepared by the United States Department of Housing and Urban Development and the Veterans Administration from a nationwide sample of more than 50,000 FHA and VA loan applications, total settlement costs averaged roughly 10% of the contract sales price— $1,937 on the sale of a $19,397 home. Department of Housing & Urban Development and Veteran's Administration, Mortgage Settlement Costs: Report to Sen. Comm. on Banking, Housing & Urban Affairs 35 (Comm. Print 1972). The study's breakdown of average total settlement costs reveals that brokers' fees accounted for 3.2% ($626) of sales price;[a] prepaid items such as insurance and taxes, for 1.5% ($299); loan discount payment for 2.3% ($454); and loan origination fee for 1% ($178). Title related costs (title examination, title insurance, attorneys' fees, closing fees) amounted to $254, or 1.3% of sales price—about 12% of total settlement costs.

The 1972 HUD report is the most recent comprehensive study of the cost of conveyancing. Other studies have focused on particular conveyancing costs. See, e.g., Wachter, Residential Real Estate Brokerage: Rate Uniformity and Moral Hazard, 10 Res.L. & Econ. 189 (1987). One recent study of the cost of brokers, lenders, and attorneys in Canadian real estate transactions concluded that "[i]n some instances, it is conceivable that closing costs could raise the effective price of a house sufficiently to necessitate looking for a less expensive housing unit that is less suited to the needs of the household." Goldberg & Horwood, The Costs of Buying and Selling Houses: Some Canadian Evidence, 10 Res.L. & Econ. 143, 144 (1987).

For an excellent analysis of the different roles played in a land transaction, see Johnstone, Land Transfers: Process and Processors, 22 Val.U.L.Rev. 493 (1988).

2. *The Quality of Conveyancing Services.* Nationwide disparities in settlement costs are often cited as evidence that costs in many places are too high. If a sale can be closed in Louisiana at 6% of the sales price, why should it cost twice that much in Pennsylvania? One answer is that higher prices may signify higher quality—more complete title searches, more accurate and frequent surveys and independent legal advice to each party involved.

Consider the plight of the homebuyer who has just received a preliminary title report. If, as often happens, the buyer has no lawyer, whom can he turn to for advice on the legal effect of the exceptions listed in the title report? The seller's lawyer may be willing to advise the buyer—*if* the seller has a lawyer and *if* the lawyer is not bothered by the ethical implications of his or her consequently divided loyalties. In locales where neither buyer nor seller is represented by counsel, the buyer will naturally turn for advice to the broker (even though the broker is the seller's agent, may lack the expertise to understand title exceptions, and has an overriding interest in seeing the deal closed so that his commission will be paid). Institutional lenders, when they are involved, typically have a larger financial stake in the house than the buyer and can generally be relied on for their own well-informed opinion on title. But, what if the exception appears in the homeowner's title policy and not in the lender's? What if no institutional lender is involved and the sale is being financed by the seller, whose main interest is in seeing the deal closed?

a. Because the breakdown is of *average* settlement costs, the underlying computations valued instances in which no fee was paid at $0. Thus, $626 is not the average commission paid by all sellers who incurred broker charges. The average fee, where a fee was charged, was $1,019.

In light of the tradeoffs between cost and quality, consumers probably want to know not how far settlement costs can be reduced but, rather, how far they can be reduced without sacrificing acceptable levels of quality. What governmental steps, if any, should be taken to restructure the conveyancing industry so that an array of costs and services will be available to satisfy the interests of both cost-conscious and quality-conscious consumers?

3. *RESPA.* The Real Estate Settlement Procedures Act, 12 U.S.C.A. § 2601 *et seq.,* enacted in 1974 and substantially amended a year later, sought to lower conveyancing costs by increasing the price information available to residential buyers. The Act requires lenders to give residential mortgage borrowers an itemized estimate of projected closing costs and a HUD-prepared booklet describing the nature and purpose of each closing cost and the choices available to consumers "in selecting persons to provide necessary services incident to a real estate settlement." 26 U.S.C.A. §§ 2603, 2604.

The Act also introduced incentives to modernize "local recordkeeping of land title information" and rules reducing "the amounts home buyers are required to place in escrow accounts established to insure the payment of real estate taxes and insurance" and outlawing covert economic arrangements between conveyancing firms—"No person shall give and no person shall accept any fee, kickback, or thing of value pursuant to any agreement or understanding, oral or otherwise, that business incident to or a part of a real estate settlement service involving a federally related mortgage loan shall be referred to any person." 12 U.S.C.A. §§ 2601(b), (3), (4); 2607(a).

Congress in 1990 amended RESPA to add two new objects of disclosure: escrow accounts and the transfer of mortgage servicing arrangements. 12 U.S.C.A. §§ 2605, 2609.

For a detailed chronicle of events surrounding passage of RESPA, see D.B. Burke, Jr., American Conveyancing Patterns 133–199 (1978). See generally, P. Barron, Federal Regulation of Real Estate and Mortgage Lending (3d ed. 1992); Hirschler, RESPA Revised and Revisited, 11 U.Rich.L.Rev. 571 (1977); Field, RESPA in a Nutshell, 11 Real Prop., Probate & Trust J. 447 (1976).

4. *Does RESPA Work?* RESPA directed the Secretary of Housing and Urban Development to report to Congress "on whether, in view of the implementation of the provisions of this chapter imposing certain requirements and prohibiting certain practices in connection with real estate settlements, there is any necessity for further legislation in this area." 12 U.S.C.A. § 2612. HUD's Report, submitted to Congress on September 10, 1981, observed that, even with the disclosures required by the Act, consumers continued to be poorly informed about the costs and consequences of available closing services. The Report concluded that many RESPA regulations, including those against kickbacks and unearned fees, should be scrapped and replaced by a mandatory program for "lender packaging" of settlement services for resale to consumers. Among the services that might be included in the lender

package would be title search, title insurance, surveys, credit reports, legal services and mortgage insurance.

The Report's recommendations are reprinted in P. Barron, Federal Regulation of Real Estate: The Real Estate Settlement Procedures Act § 5.08 (Supp.1982).

The problem with reform efforts like those embodied in RESPA and proposed in the 1981 HUD Report is that they only scratch the surface. It seems idle to hope that one of RESPA's key objects—more and better information for consumers—will lower settlement costs. Buyers and sellers defer, and probably will continue to defer, to advice from real estate specialists—brokers, lawyers and mortgage lenders. Because time is so often essential in residential transactions, buyers are not likely to jeopardize a deal by taking the time to shop and compare settlement prices. Also, the buyer or seller who *does* take the time to comparison shop will find substantial uniformity in the prices quoted by title companies, brokers and others providing closing services. Rate regulation of title insurers and the absence of any real price competition among brokers makes price disclosure at best a futile gesture in the direction of reducing costs.

For a thoughtful analysis of the 1981 HUD Report, see Patterson, Federal Regulation of the Real Estate Settlement (Closing) Process: HUD's Report to Congress, 16 Real Prop., Probate & Trust J. 806 (1981). For other thoughtful and critical views on RESPA generally, see Stoppello, Federal Regulation of Home Mortgage Settlement Costs: RESPA and its Alternatives, 63 Minn.L.Rev. 367 (1979); Wallace, "Explicit Pricing," Fraud, and Consumer Information: The Reform of RESPA, 12 Rutgers L.J. 183 (1981).

B. LAWYERS

AMERICAN BAR ASSOCIATION, CODE OF PROFESSIONAL RESPONSIBILITY (1975) *

CANON 5 [b]

A Lawyer Should Exercise Independent Professional Judgment on Behalf of a Client

ETHICAL CONSIDERATIONS

Interests of Multiple Clients

EC 5–14 Maintaining the independence of professional judgment required of a lawyer precludes his acceptance or continuation of employ-

---

* Excerpted from The Model Code of Professional Responsibility, as amended February, 1979, Copyright, American Bar Association.

b. "The Canons are statements of axiomatic norms, expressing in general terms

the standards of professional conduct expected of lawyers in their relationships with the public, with the legal system, and with the legal profession. They embody the general concepts from which the Ethi-

ment that will adversely affect his judgment on behalf of or dilute his loyalty to a client. This problem arises whenever a lawyer is asked to represent two or more clients who may have differing interests, whether such interests be conflicting, inconsistent, diverse, or otherwise discordant.

EC 5–15 If a lawyer is requested to undertake or to continue representation of multiple clients having potentially differing interests, he must weigh carefully the possibility that his judgment may be impaired or his loyalty divided if he accepts or continues the employment. He should resolve all doubts against the propriety of the representation. A lawyer should never represent in litigation multiple clients with differing interests; and there are few situations in which he would be justified in representing in litigation multiple clients with potentially differing interests. If a lawyer accepted such employment and the interests did become actually differing, he would have to withdraw from employment with likelihood of resulting hardship on the clients; and for·this reason it is preferable that he refuse the employment initially. On the other hand, there are many instances in which a lawyer may properly serve multiple clients having potentially differing interests in matters not involving litigation. If the interests vary only slightly, it is generally likely that the lawyer will not be subjected to an adverse influence and that he can retain his independent judgment on behalf of each client; and if the interests become differing, withdrawal is less likely to have a disruptive effect upon the causes of his clients.

EC 5–16 In those instances in which a lawyer is justified in representing two or more clients having differing interests, it is nevertheless essential that each client be given the opportunity to evaluate his need for representation free of any potential conflict and to obtain other counsel if he so desires. Thus before a lawyer may represent multiple clients, he should explain fully to each client the implications of the common representation and should accept or continue employment only if the clients consent. If there are present other circumstances that might cause any of the multiple clients to question the undivided loyalty of the lawyer, he should also advise all of the clients of those circumstances.

cal Considerations and the Disciplinary Rules are derived.

"The Ethical Considerations are aspirational in character and represent the objectives toward which every member of the profession should strive. They constitute a body of principles upon which the lawyer can rely for guidance in many specific situations.

"The Disciplinary Rules, unlike the Ethical Considerations, are mandatory in character. The Disciplinary Rules state the minimum level of conduct below which no lawyer can fall without being subject to disciplinary action."

DISCIPLINARY RULES

DR 5–105 Refusing to Accept or Continue Employment if the Interests of Another Client May Impair the Independent Professional Judgment of the Lawyer.

(A) A lawyer shall decline proffered employment if the exercise of his independent professional judgment in behalf of a client will be or is likely to be adversely affected by the acceptance of the proffered employment, or if it would be likely to involve him in representing differing interests, except to the extent permitted under DR 5–105(C).

(B) A lawyer shall not continue multiple employment if the exercise of his independent professional judgment in behalf of a client will be or is likely to be adversely affected by his representation of another client, or if it would be likely to involve him in representing differing interests, except to the extent permitted under DR 5–105(C).

(C) In the situations covered by DR 5–105(A) and (B), a lawyer may represent multiple clients if it is obvious that he can adequately represent the interest of each and if each consents to the representation after full disclosure of the possible effect of such representation on the exercise of his independent professional judgment on behalf of each.

(D) If a lawyer is required to decline employment or to withdraw from employment under a Disciplinary Rule, no partner, or associate, or any other lawyer affiliated with him or his firm, may accept or continue such employment.

W. FISHER, WHAT EVERY LAWYER KNOWS
41–42 (1974).

It is often said that a lawyer may properly represent conflicting interests if the parties consent to his doing so, that is, if the client is aware of the conflict and nevertheless consents. This is ordinarily true. But the application of the rule is not as easy as it may seem. How far does the consent go? Is its scope wide enough to permit the lawyer, in discussing the subject with one of the clients involved, to disclose the normally confidential matters of the client? May he discuss the moral aspects of the problem, pointing out that one client is in a better ethical position than the other? May he disclose every weakness of both sides? Does the client in consenting realize how far he is relinquishing a devoted servitor and receiving in exchange an impartial judge who is well likely to decide points against him? Would he be satisfied that the lawyer would be impartial as between the opposing clients if he knew the extent of the lawyer's relationship with the other client? Maybe he is his drinking companion or heavily indebted to him. Does each client realize how far the outcome may differ from what he expects? In short, does he realize what he is consenting to? For the consent to be genuine each consenting party must be fully informed as to the nature of the conflict of interest and the extent of its possible adverse effect on himself.

Still there are situations where it may be appropriate for the lawyer to accept a consent, even given rather casually, to represent two clients with different interests. Of course the lawyer will not venture into this thicket unless he feels certain that under the particular circumstances he can represent each client fully and fairly. That may well be true of some standardized situations whose scope is widely understood, e.g., where the one client is buying the other's house, and says to him: "I am well acquainted with your regular lawyer and know his high reputation. I want to save money and time and avoid delay by having him represent both of us in this sale." Title questions may arise that are not understood, but they are within a definite range. The parties expect to give and receive a good title, upon customary terms. If special questions arise, either of title or terms, they can be discussed with both parties. The question will be of a well-defined class. It may turn out that one party or both will be disappointed if the lawyer raises issues that burden one or the other with unexpected expenses or that cause the deal to fall through; but there will be no feeling of disappointment with the lawyer's role. He was expected to raise such issues. Once raised, there were no practical alternatives to what had to be done about them; they had to be dealt with on lines established by real estate law or custom. Both clients understood this when they consented to be represented by the same lawyer. So the disappointed client does not blame the lawyer, for he knows that he had consented to have the lawyer do just what was done.

IN RE LANZA

Supreme Court of New Jersey, 1974.
65 N.J. 347, 322 A.2d 445.

PER CURIAM.

The Bergen County Ethics Committee filed a presentment with this Court against respondent, Guy J. Lanza, who has been a practicing member of the bar of this State since 1954.

The Committee specifically found that respondent's conduct violated DR 5-105. This Disciplinary Rule forbids an attorney to represent adverse interests, except under certain very carefully circumscribed conditions.

In April or May of 1971, Elizabeth F. Greene consulted respondent with respect to the sale of her residence property in Palisades Park,

New Jersey. Mr. Lanza agreed to act for her. In due course a contract, apparently prepared by a broker, was signed by Mrs. Greene as seller as well as by the prospective purchasers, James and Joan Connolly. The execution and delivery of the contract took place in Mr. Lanza's office, although he seems to have played little or no part in the negotiation of its terms. By this time he had agreed with the Connollys that he would represent them, as well as Mrs. Greene, in completing the transaction. The testimony is conflicting as to whether or not Mrs. Greene had been told of this dual representation at the time she signed the contract. Mr. Lanza says that she had been told, but according to her recollection she only learned of this at a later date from Mrs. Connolly. In any event it is quite clear that respondent agreed to act for the purchasers before discussing the question of such additional representation with Mrs. Greene.

The contract as originally drawn provided for a closing date in late July, 1971. At Mrs. Greene's request this date was postponed to September 1. A short time later, circumstances having again changed, Mrs. Greene found that she would now prefer the original date. This proved satisfactory to the purchasers but Mr. Connolly told Mrs. Greene that at this earlier date he would not have in hand funds sufficient to make up the full purchase price of $36,000. Of this sum he would lack $1,000. He suggested, however, that the parties might close title upon the earlier date if Mrs. Greene would accept, as part of the purchase price, a check for $1,000 postdated approximately 30 days. Mrs. Greene was personally agreeable to this. She consulted respondent who advised her that he saw no reason why she should not follow this course.

The closing accordingly took place late in July and in accordance with the foregoing arrangement, Mrs. Greene received, as part of the purchase price, Mr. Connolly's check in the sum of $1,000 dated August 31, 1971. Shortly after this latter date she deposited the check for collection and it was returned because of insufficient funds. When questioned, Mr. Connolly said that after he and his wife had taken possession of the property they discovered a serious water condition in the cellar. He added that Mrs. Greene had made an explicit representation that the cellar was at all times dry. For this reason he refused to make good the check, saying that it would cost him $1,000 to rectify the condition in the cellar. Mrs. Greene denied that she had ever made any representation whatsoever. She immediately got in touch with respondent who did nothing effective on her behalf. She then retained other counsel and has subsequently initiated legal proceedings against the Connollys.

We find respondent's conduct to have been unprofessional in two respects. In the first place, the way in which he undertook the dual representation failed to meet the standards imposed upon an attorney who elects to follow such a course. In the second place, after the latent conflict of interests of the two clients had become acute, he nevertheless continued to represent both parties. At that point, rather than going forward with the matter as he did, he should have withdrawn altogether.

Mr. Lanza first undertook to act for the seller, Mrs. Greene. This immediately placed upon him an obligation to represent her with undivided fidelity. Despite this obligation, he later agreed, without prior consultation with Mrs. Greene, to represent Mr. and Mrs. Connolly, whose interest in the matter was of course potentially adverse to that of his client. He should not have undertaken to represent the purchasers until he had initially conferred with Mrs. Greene. He should have first explained to her all the facts and indicated in specific detail all the areas of potential conflict that foreseeably might arise. He should also have made her aware that if indeed any of these contingencies should thereafter eventuate and not prove susceptible of ready solution in a manner fair and agreeable to all concerned, it would then become his professional duty immediately to cease acting for all parties. Only after such a conference with his client, and following her informed consent, would he have been at liberty to consider representing the purchasers. They, too, were entitled to the same explanation as is set forth above, as well as being told of respondent's existing attorney-client relationship with the seller.

The second instance of misconduct arose after respondent learned that the purchasers would not be able to pay the full purchase price in cash at the time of closing title. At that point adequate representation of the seller required that her attorney first strongly insist on her behalf that cash be forthcoming. Failing this, and if the seller persisted in her wish to close upon the earlier date, her attorney should have vigorously urged the execution and delivery to her of a mortgage from the purchasers in the amount of $1,000, or of other adequate security, in order to protect her interest pending receipt of the full cash payment. We think it fair to assume that had respondent not found himself in a position of conflicting loyalties, his representation of the seller would have taken some such course. Had the purchasers persisted in their unwillingness to pay the full amount in cash at the time of closing and had they also refused to execute and deliver a mortgage or other security, respondent should have immediately withdrawn from the matter, advising both parties to secure independent counsel of their respective choosing. At that point in time it would have clearly been impossible for any single attorney adequately and fairly to represent both sides.

This case serves to emphasize the pitfalls that await an attorney representing both buyer and seller in a real estate transaction. The Advisory Committee on Professional Ethics, in its Opinion 243, 95 N.J.L.J. 1145 (1972) has ruled that in all circumstances it is unethical for the same attorney to represent buyer and seller in negotiating the terms of a contract of sale. Here the respondent did not enter into these negotiations so he does not come under the ban of this rule. Canon 6 declared, however, that "[i]t is unprofessional to represent conflicting interests, except by express consent of all concerned given after a full disclosure of the facts." DR 5–105 is at least as strict in the requirements it lays down and in subparagraph (C) carries forward the injunction quoted above by prohibiting multiple representation unless "each [party] consents to the representation after full disclosure of the facts and of the possible effect of such representation on the exercise of his [the attorney's] independent professional judgment on behalf of each."

The extent of the necessary disclosure is what is important. As Opinion 243, supra, makes clear, this is a question that must be conscientiously resolved by each attorney in the light of the particular facts and circumstances that a given case presents. It is utterly insufficient simply to advise a client that he, the attorney, foresees no conflict of interest and then to ask the client whether the latter will consent to the multiple representation. This is no more than an empty form of words. A client cannot foresee and cannot be expected to foresee the great variety of potential areas of disagreement that may arise in a real estate transaction of this sort. The attorney is or should be familiar with at least the more common of these and they should be stated and laid before the client at some length and with considerable specificity. Of course all eventualities cannot be foreseen, but a great many can. Here respondent was representing Mrs. Greene, a seller of property. Generally a seller who has entered into a mutually binding contract of sale is principally interested in securing the full purchase price to which he or she is entitled. As counsel experienced in this field of practice well know, to allow a purchaser to take possession of the premises in question before the entire consideration has been received, either in the form of cash or purchase money mortgage, will often prove contrary to the seller's best interests. So it was here.

For the reasons set forth above, we deem respondent's conduct to merit censure. He is hereby reprimanded.

For reprimand: Chief Justice HUGHES and Justices JACOBS, HALL, MOUNTAIN, SULLIVAN, PASHMAN and CLIFFORD–7.

Opposed: None.

PASHMAN, J. (concurring).

. . .

It is virtually impossible for one attorney in any manner and under any circumstances to faithfully and with undivided allegiance represent both a buyer and seller. This concurrence, therefore, stands for the position of the majority and further holds that dual representation in a buyer-seller situation should be totally forbidden. The reasons for this seem to me fairly obvious. In this type of transaction, it is most certainly in the public interest to safeguard and protect both parties from any abuses, whether they be ill-advised or inadvertent. The potential conflict in home buying or selling may never come to fruition. However, when it does surface, both sides explode in anger and accusations. The attorney will then withdraw, leaving the situation no better than when it occurred and, for that matter, probably a bit worse. This is not fair to either party.

It is my contention that neither buyer nor seller can ever possibly fully appreciate all the complexities involved. That is precisely the reason why full disclosure and informed consent are illusory. What most people typically do is rely upon the representation of their attorney when he reassures them that everything will be properly handled. However, the attorney is, unfortunately, not a clairvoyant who can foresee problem areas, although he realizes that there is certainly the potential for genuine conflict. Even where his motives are of the highest, as they usually are, and in good faith believes that he can effect a meeting of the minds, he really is not sure. Because of that dangerous uncertainty, I believe attorneys would, generally, welcome this prohibition against potential conflict.

Numerous situations like the present instance require affirmative legal action and demand an attorney's undivided loyalty. If two separate attorneys were individually retained, both parties would be sure that they were receiving the best possible legal attention. If and when a conflict developed, they would be duly represented, instead of deserted. The inconvenience in retaining separate attorneys is minimal when weighed against the dangers involved, and the cost differential in the final analysis would be inconsequential.

. . .

NOTES

1. *The Lawyer's Role in Residential Transactions.* According to a pamphlet published by the American Bar Association's Special Committee on Residential Real Estate Transactions, there is plenty for each party's lawyer to do. Seller's lawyer should oversee negotiations to modify the broker's form of listing agreement. "The objections to form contracts are that they may be inappropriate to the particular transaction, badly drawn initially or incorrectly filled in. Any seller signing such a contract should have it approved by the seller's attorney before signing." Residential Real Estate Transactions: The Lawyer's Proper Role—Services—Compensation 3 (1978).

In preliminary negotiations between buyer and seller, "a great deal of trouble can be avoided if both the buyer and the seller consult their own lawyers during the course of the negotiations." For example, "they should consider such problems as the mode of paying the purchase price and the tax consequences resulting therefrom, the status of various articles as fixtures or personal property, the time set for occupancy and the effect of loss by casualty pending the closing." pp. 4–5. The contract of sale must be drafted, with careful attention paid to the financing contingency. And, since standard forms will typically be used, "any insertion should be carefully checked by the buyer's and seller's attorneys."

The buyer's lawyer "should inform the buyer of the limitations, if any, which impair the title." p. 6. One lawyer may have to obtain and record affidavits to cure defective title. Lawyers for the other parties would then review the affidavits for sufficiency. The deed and mortgage or deed of trust must be prepared, and the buyer advised "as to the tax and other effects of the manner in which title is taken." p. 7. Finally, one of the lawyers should draft a closing statement and, "as a part of the closing, arrangements must be made for insurance, taxes, and other incidents of ownership. Instruments must be recorded and a final check of title made." p. 8.

2. The ideal world envisioned by the ABA pamphlet, in which each party is individually represented by counsel, is not commonly realized in practice. The parties may perceive the residential sale to be sufficiently complex, and their investment sufficiently large, to warrant one lawyer, but not large enough to warrant two. And they may also suspect that the price of two lawyers will be more than twice the price of one. Time must be spent, and bills rendered, for the resolution of conflicts or potential conflicts that a single lawyer would probably glide over.

What would happen if lawyers followed the rule proposed in Justice Pashman's *Lanza* concurrence, allowing attorneys to represent no more than one party to a residential sale? Is it likely that each party would secure individual counsel? Is it likely that some or all parties would go without any legal advice at all? Is Pashman saying that no representation is preferable to representation shared with a potential adversary?

According to a recent study of 132 home purchasers in Columbus, Ohio, less than half the buyers retained their own lawyers and a quarter of that number first met the lawyer at or shortly before closing. Braunstein & Genn, Odd Man Out: Preliminary Findings Concerning the Diminishing Role of Lawyers in the Home–Buying Process, 52 Ohio St.L.J. 469 (1991). Lawyers interviewed for the study indicated that the use of title insurance rather than title opinions accounted for the decline in lawyer representation of buyers. Would buyers be better off if they had lawyers? The study's preliminary results indicated no: purchasers currently using lawyers are no better informed, satisfied, or likely to avoid disputes than purchasers not retaining lawyers. Id. at 471–472.

3. *Multiple Representation: The Duty to Disclose.* What amount of disclosure would *Lanza* require for informed consent? If you were the lawyer in that transaction, what would you have disclosed to Mrs. Greene and the Connollys? Would you have anticipated the specific problem that subsequently arose? Would you have felt comfortable referring to the problem in general terms—"Disagreements may arise between you about how payment is to be made"—or still more generally—"Disagreements may arise with respect to the details of closing"? Form of payment is one of the more easily disclosed areas of dispute in residential sales. How would you have explained the harder, more

intricate questions that arise in determining whether seller's title is marketable?

Buyers who are financing their purchase through an institutional lender sometimes agree to be represented by the lender's lawyer. Is the lawyer in this situation under a duty to describe important provisions of the loan instrument to the buyer-borrower? Say the note restricts the borrower's statutory right to redeem or waives the protection of antideficiency rules. Must the lender's lawyer disclose the effect of these clauses, the lender's relative willingness to delete them, and the willingness of competing lenders to exclude these clauses?

For an excellent analysis of the conflict issue, see McMunigal, Rethinking Attorney Conflict of Interest Doctrine, 5 Geo.J.Leg. Ethics 823 (1992). See also, Note, One For All Is Worth Two in the Bush: Mixing Metaphors Creates Lawyer Conflict of Interest Problems in Residential Real Estate Transactions, 56 U.Cinn.L.Rev. 639 (1987).

4. *The Model Rules.* The Model Rules of Professional Conduct, adopted by the American Bar Association in 1983, provide in part that:

(a) A lawyer shall not represent a client if the representation of that client will be directly adverse to another client, unless:

(1) the lawyer reasonably believes the representation will not adversely affect the relationship with the other client; and

(2) each client consents after consultation.

(b) A lawyer shall not represent a client if the representation of that client may be materially limited by the lawyer's responsibilities to another client or to a third person, or by the lawyer's own interests, unless:

(1) the lawyer reasonably believes the representation will not be adversely affected; and

(2) the client consents after consultation. When representation of multiple clients in a single matter is undertaken, the consultation shall include explanation of the implications of the common representation and the advantages and risks involved.

Model Rules, Rule 1.7. A comment to Rule 1.7 directs the lawyer who is weighing multiple representation to evaluate "the likelihood that a conflict will eventuate and, if it does, whether it will materially interfere with the lawyer's independent professional judgment in considering alternatives or foreclose courses of action that reasonably should be pursued on behalf of the client."*

How would, and should, the New Jersey Supreme Court have decided *Lanza* under Rule 1.7? Compare Rule 2.2 which permits a lawyer to act as an intermediary between clients under closely prescribed conditions.

For an extensive analysis of the multiple representation issue under both the Code and Model Rules, see Comment, Conflicts of Interest in Real Estate Transactions: Dual Representation—Lawyers Stretching the Rules, 6 West. New England L.Rev. 73 (1983).

5. *Individual Representation Is No Guarantee of Good Representation.* A survey of eight law firms, conducted by the Wall Street Journal to determine the ability of lawyers to spot defects in a simulated residential sales contract, produced some unsettling results. In the judgment of the Journal's panel of real estate experts, none of the eight attorneys spotted every defect he or she should have. Two of the lawyers did "dangerously bad" jobs and four got "low marks" on either or both of the major problem areas. Lancaster, Rating Lawyers, Wall St. J., July 31, 1980 at 1.

These survey results should, however, be kept in perspective. The survey was "admittedly unscientific." Six of the eight firms were "advertised as, or appeared to be," legal clinics. More important, the survey was conducted in California where lawyers only rarely represent parties to residential transactions and thus have little of the experience that is so common to general practitioners in other parts of the country. (Inexperience does not, however, excuse bad advice. As one member of the panel observed, the correct approach for several of these attorneys would have been to refer the client to a real estate specialist.)

6. *Malpractice.* A study of 18,486 malpractice claims conducted by the National Legal Malpractice Data Center between 1981–83, revealed that real estate practice generated a greater proportion of legal malpractice claims—24.9% of all claims—than any other field. (Personal injury litigation was a close second at 24.0%.) At the low end of recoveries, 72.6% of all real estate claims were concluded for an amount between $0 and $1,000 and 9.9% for between $1,001–$5,000; at the high end, 1.3% of claims were concluded for between $50,001–$100,000 and 3.7% for over $100,000. Gates, The Newest Data on Lawyers' Malpractice Claims, 70 A.B.A. J. 78 (April 1984).

What are the most common causes of client complaint? In the view of an experienced practitioner, one is that the lawyer counselled outside his or her area of expertise. Another problem is failure to advise clients of business risks—for example, not advising a landlord-client against signing a lease with the shell subsidiary of a creditworthy parent corporation that has not itself signed or guaranteed the lease. Malpractice liability may also arise out of the joint representation of clients with conflicting interests, such as buyer and seller, landlord and tenant, or mortgagor and mortgagee, or acting as an escrow agent or real estate broker in addition to representing one or more of the clients to a transaction. Blumberg, Avoiding Malpractice in Real Estate Law Practice, 2 Calif.Real Prop. J. 1 (Summer 1984).

To prevail in a malpractice action, the victim must show that the attorney failed to exercise the degree of care and skill commonly possessed by an ordinary member of the legal community and that the negligence was the proximate cause of the injury. See Logalbo v. Plishkin, Rubano & Baum, 163 A.D.2d 511, 558 N.Y.S.2d 185 (1990), appeal dismissed, 77 N.Y.2d 940, 569 N.Y.S.2d 613, 572 N.E.2d 54 (1991) (oral notice of cancellation of contract of sale by buyers' attorney was legal malpractice as a matter of law when contract expressly required written notice of cancellation within a specified period of time; "[t]he state of the law on the exercise of an option to cancel a real estate contract requiring that written notice be given within a specified time is clearly defined and firmly imbedded in our jurisprudence so as to be beyond doubt or debate").

An unrepresented party to a real estate transaction will sometimes pursue a malpractice action against an attorney for one of the other parties. The traditional rule has barred liability in the absence of privity. See, e.g., Noth v. Wynn, 59 Ohio App.3d 65, 571 N.E.2d 446 (1988) (lender's attorney did not owe duty to buyers to disclose restriction on purchased property). However, many courts allow recovery if the injured party was a third party beneficiary of the attorney-client relationship. See Crossland Savings FSB v. Rockwood Insurance Co., 700 F.Supp. 1274 (S.D.N.Y.1988) (issuer of surety bonds may take advantage of opinion letter addressed to borrower where it was understood that surety was also to benefit from the letter). Some courts go further, permitting recovery by individuals who the lawyer knew relied upon his work. See, e.g., Collins v. Binkley, 750 S.W.2d 737 (Tenn.1988) (seller's attorney liable to buyer for approving deed that failed to contain language required for recordation). Is such expanded attorney liability appropriate? Will it encourage or discourage parties from retaining their own counsel? What effect will such liability have on the cost of legal services? Which parties to the transaction will ultimately bear the increased costs due to expanded liability of the attorney?

7. *Unauthorized Practice.* According to an American Bar Foundation study, in the estimated 5.5 million residential purchases made every year, there is only a 40% probability that the purchaser will consult a lawyer. "When a lawyer is not contacted the most frequently mentioned sources of advice and help are real estate brokers, financial institutions and title companies." Curran, Survey of the Public's Legal Needs, 64 A.B.A. J. 848, 850 (1978). Because residential transactions are pervaded by legal issues and heavily papered with legal instruments, the work performed by these nonlawyers unavoidably borders on the practice of law.

Brokers have been a main target of unauthorized practice charges, chiefly in connection with their preparation of sales contracts. In one major case, State Bar of Arizona v. Arizona Land Title & Trust Co., 90 Ariz. 76, 366 P.2d 1 (1961), the Arizona Supreme Court took an unusually hard line, ruling that realtors may not advise or assist in the preparation of documents that affect, alter or define legal rights. The court's proscription encompassed even the filling in of blanks on printed forms.

The realtors petitioned for a rehearing, but ultimately enjoyed greater success through another route, obtaining 107,420 signatures on an initiative petition to amend the state constitution to give real estate brokers and salespeople the right "to draft or fill out and complete without charge ... preliminary purchase agreements ... deeds, mortgages, leases ... contracts of sale." The proposed amendment passed by a margin of almost 4 to 1. But the victory was not costless. In 1976 an Arizona appellate court ruled that the constitutional amendment created not only new rights, but also new duties, and held that a broker breached his duty to seller by failing to explain the possible consequences of accepting from buyer a promissory note in which one key phrase—"This note is secured by a mortgage on real property"—had been stricken. The action was precipitated by the buyer's default on the note. Morley v. J. Pagel Realty & Insurance, 27 Ariz.App. 62, 550 P.2d 1104 (1976).

Charges of unauthorized practice against title companies stem largely from their involvement in closings—preparing deeds and title reports and obtaining affidavits to clear title. Indeed, the defendants in the main case consolidated in *Arizona Land Title & Trust* were five title companies. In several parts of the country, title companies and bar associations have worked out their differences through treaties.

For background on unauthorized practice in Arizona and elsewhere, see Marks, The Lawyers and the Realtors: Arizona's Experience, 49 A.B.A. J. 139 (1963); Riggs, Unauthorized Practice and the Public Interest: Arizona's Recent Constitutional Amendment, 37 So.Cal.L.Rev. 1 (1964); Note, 19 De Paul L.Rev. 319 (1969).

New Jersey allows brokers and title companies to play only a limited role in documenting agreements and conveyances. While brokers are generally prohibited from drafting contracts of sale, they may prepare residential contracts of sale if a clause is conspicuously displayed on the first page permitting attorney review and cancellation of the contract by either side within three days of execution after attorney review. New Jersey State Bar Ass'n v. New Jersey Ass'n of Realtor Boards, 93 N.J. 470, 461 A.2d 1112 (1983). Recently, the Committee on the Unauthorized Practice of the Law appointed by the New Jersey Supreme Court, issued an advisory opinion that finds certain activities to constitute the unauthorized practice of law: the ordering of a title search and abstract by brokers; the retention by title companies and brokers of attorneys to prepare conveyance documents; the removal by title companies of exceptions from a title policy where a legal opinion is required; and "the practice of title companies in conducting closings or settlement without the presence of attorneys.". Opinion No. 26, 130 N.J.L.J. 882, Mar. 16, 1992. Will this ruling protect consumers, attorneys, or both? See Lambert & Moss, Lawyers Ruled Indispensable in New Jersey, Wall Street Journal, May 20, 1992, p. B3.

8. *What Constitutes Unauthorized Practice?* The real question, of course, is what constitutes the practice of law? The general principle,

followed everywhere, is that, aside from court appearances and preparation of pleadings, law practice consists of giving advice or drafting instruments affecting legal rights. More specific tests vary from state to state.

The "Incidental" Test. A nonlawyer may perform some legal tasks if they are minor and only incidental to the main service being offered. For example, the principal job of brokers is to bring buyers and sellers together; their incidental job is to keep them together. Because the contract of sale serves that collateral purpose, some states allow brokers to fill in the blanks in sales contracts. The obvious problem with this test is that it is totally unrelated to the client's need for expert and independent legal advice.

The "Simple-Complex" Test. Nonlawyers may perform simple legal tasks; only lawyers may perform complex ones. The problem with this test is that, while there certainly are complex legal tasks, it is hard to find a simple one. Advising a husband and wife to take title as joint tenants might appear to be a simple matter. In fact it is quite complex, implicating their motives, income, family plans and estate plans.

The "Personal Representation" Test. While a nonlawyer may not give legal advice to others, he may perform legal services for himself. The problem in applying this test arises when the services take the form of an opinion that is then justifiably relied on by a third party. For example, a title company's title examination and report serve as more than the basis for the company's decision to insure title. It will unavoidably affect the buyer's decision to proceed with the purchase on the assumption that title is in fact clear.

See generally, Payne, Title Insurance and the Unauthorized Practice of Law Controversy, 53 Minn.L.Rev. 423 (1969).

9. *Anticompetitive Practices Among Lawyers.* Longstanding anticompetitive practices of the bar have doubtless increased the cost of residential closings. Some of these practices have recently come under attack. In Goldfarb v. Virginia State Bar, 421 U.S. 773, 95 S.Ct. 2004, 44 L.Ed.2d 572 (1975), the Court ruled that a minimum fee schedule for lawyers' title examinations, published by the Fairfax County Bar Association and enforced by the Virginia State Bar, violated section 1 of the Sherman Act. The Goldfarbs, after contracting to buy a house in Fairfax County, sought to obtain a title insurance policy. Under the state bar's unauthorized practice rules, only a lawyer could perform the title examination necessary for a title insurance policy to issue. The first lawyer contacted by the Goldfarbs quoted them precisely the fee suggested by the Fairfax County Bar Association schedule—1% of the contract price. The Goldfarbs then tried but failed to find a lawyer to examine title for a lower fee. Of the nineteen lawyers who replied to the Goldfarbs' letters requesting fee information, "none indicated that he would charge less than the rate fixed by the schedule; several stated that they knew of no attorney who would do so."

The Supreme Court found that "respondents' activities constitute a classic illustration of price fixing," and rejected the bar association's multifaceted defense that the fee schedule was merely advisory; that its effect on interstate commerce was only incidental and remote; that, as a learned profession, law was not "trade or commerce" subject to antitrust regulation; and that, as state action, bar-enforced fee schedules were immune from antitrust regulation. The court ruled that the fee schedule was not advisory because it "was enforced through the prospect of professional discipline from the State Bar, and the desire of attorneys to comply with announced professional norms." The national scope of real estate finance, and lenders' universal requirement that title be examined, sufficiently implicated fee structures in interstate commerce. The court answered the "learned profession" defense by noting that "the examination of a land title is a service; the exchange of such a service for money is 'commerce' in the most common usage of that word." The Court's answer to the state action defense was that the state bar "has voluntarily joined in what is essentially a private anticompetitive activity."

A subsequent decision striking down a ban on lawyer advertising may introduce new competitive elements into the pricing of legal services, possibly reducing overall closing costs. Bates v. State Bar of Arizona, 433 U.S. 350, 97 S.Ct. 2691, 53 L.Ed.2d 810 (1977) (the "ban on advertising serves to increase the difficulty of discovering the lowest-cost seller of acceptable ability." As a result, "attorneys are isolated from competition and the incentive to price competitively is reduced.") See generally, Branca & Steinberg, Attorney Fee Schedules and Legal Advertising: The Implications of Goldfarb, 24 U.C.L.A. L.Rev. 475 (1977).

Arrangements between lawyers and other conveyancing professionals and institutions have also been attacked. See, for example, Blair & Jernigan, "Sweetheart" Arrangements Between Lenders and Their Title Lawyers—Are They Really? 37 Wash. & Lee L.Rev. 343 (1980); Roussel, Pera & Rosenberg, Bar-Related Title Insurance Companies: An Antitrust Analysis, 24 Vill.L.Rev. 639 (1979); Marcotte, Kickbacks to Lawyers Rapped, A.B.A.J., Nov. 1, 1986, p. 30. Problems may also arise when an attorney attempts to fill the role of other conveyancing professionals. See, e.g., Mortland, Attorneys As Real Estate Brokers: Ethical Considerations, 25 Real Prop. Probate & Trust J. 755 (1991).

It remains to be seen whether bar practices will prevail against antitrust attacks on yet another front: state bar rules on unauthorized practice that effectively define the scope of the bar's monopoly. A former head of the Justice Department's Antitrust Division has challenged statements of principles and treaties between the organized bar and other professional associations: "As a general rule, two competitors may not agree with each other to allocate markets, or bids, or even functions. ... At the least, this traditional antitrust principle raises some questions about the legal effect of such 'statements of principles.'" 63 A.B.A. J. 299 (1977). See Virginia State Bar v. Surety Title Ins. Agency, Inc., 571 F.2d 205 (4th Cir.1978).

C. BROKERS

OWEN, KICKBACKS, SPECIALIZATION, PRICE FIXING, AND EFFICIENCY IN RESIDENTIAL REAL ESTATE MARKETS *

29 Stanford Law Review 931, 944–49 (1977).

1. THE FUNCTION OF THE BROKERAGE INDUSTRY

The real estate broker's function is to provide information about the housing market to buyers and sellers who have no other source of expert knowledge about conditions in the housing market. Because brokers are the primary contact with the real estate market for most homebuyers, their clients often rely on them to provide other information about the home buying process. Thus, brokers have a unique capacity to influence their clients' purchases of other conveyancing services, such as title insurance and escrow services which the home-buyer typically views as oppressively complicated formalities. Because parties in a residential real estate transaction frequently feel great pressure to complete the transaction quickly, they often turn to the broker to recommend or obtain the necessary ancillary conveyancing services. A common practice among brokers is to supply clients with standard purchase agreement forms, sometimes preprinted with the names of particular firms for title insurance, escrow and other services.

2. THE MARKET STRUCTURE OF THE BROKERAGE INDUSTRY

In California, real estate brokers must meet certain educational requirements, pass an examination and be licensed by the state. Apparently these requirements are not significant barriers to entry into the industry, however. There are over 178,000 full- and part-time brokers active in California, and few firms control over 10 percent of any local market. An unconcentrated industry, such as the California brokerage services industry, normally presents few opportunities for collusion and should be characterized by competition both in the quality of service and in price.

Quality-of-service competition. Despite the great number of brokers, however, the California brokerage industry is not perfectly competitive. Brokers pool information about the housing market by forming local "multiple listing service" (MLS) organizations through which each member gains access to information available to other members.

Before the advent of MLS organizations, brokers in California would compete for business by attempting to offer higher quality service in

---

the form of more information about the housing markets, and those brokers who worked harder or more efficiently had more information about the housing market than others. Under the terms of most MLS agreements, brokers pool information and agree to split commissions between the listing and selling brokers according to various formulae. Because MLS systems substantially reduce the possibility that one member of an MLS organization will be able to supply a client with useful information that other members do not have, their widespread use has eliminated a considerable amount of quality-of-service competition in the brokerage industry.

Price competition. Even if MLS organizations stifle competition in quality of service, a number of factors suggest that competitive pricing still may occur in the brokerage industry. First, coordination of pricing in an industry with a structure as atomistic as the California brokerage industry is difficult. There are no obvious mechanisms for price collusion, such as the requirement that rates be public.

Second, consumers are likely to be more sensitive to brokerage fees than to fees for other conveyancing services. On a $40,000 home purchase, brokerage fees average $2,400, 10 times the fees for title insurance. Finally, the time costs involved in shopping for brokerage services are not as high as for other conveyancing services. Unlike title insurance, which often may have to be obtained quickly in order to avoid jeopardizing a preliminary purchase agreement, the broker is chosen when the consumer first decides to buy or sell a house. Because an instant decision is unnecessary at that time, the prospective seller or buyer might take more time to shop for the right broker.

Despite the pressures on brokers to reduce prices in order to increase sales, little evidence demonstrates that they do so. Approximately 75 percent of all residential real estate transactions in California involve a brokerage fee of exactly 6 percent. In some local areas the figure may be even higher. Eighty-five percent of new residential listings in San Francisco for the week of May 31, 1976, specified 6 percent brokerage fees; the remainder specified a 7 percent fee or a sliding scale of fees that depended upon the size of the transaction.

Avoidance of competition. The California brokerage industry apparently maintains uniformity of prices by price fixing and collusion. Price fixing is a phenomenon that is difficult to explain in unconcentrated industries, although it appears that the mechanism for price fixing activities among brokers is the coordination provided by local MLS organizations. Because the information provided by the MLS is very useful to buyers and sellers, and is generally unavailable elsewhere, brokers outside the MLS organization rarely can compete with members. For example, over 80 percent of all urban California residential purchases involve an MLS member.

Nor is it surprising that so many brokers belong to MLS organizations. Without access to the MLS system, most brokers could not stay in business, for the information provided is the broker's most valuable asset. Thus, brokers have strong incentives to do whatever is necessary to maintain their membership in an MLS organization.

The MLS structure has a built-in device for detecting secret price cutting. Each MLS member always knows what other members are charging because commissions are split between the listing and selling brokers. Furthermore, MLS organizations have a number of methods of enforcing adherence to uniform prices among their members. The most blatant method is to threaten members who depart from fixed prices with expulsion. More subtle influences also operate. For example, MLS members simply may be less anxious to sell homes listed by brokers who charge less than the fixed rate.

NOTES

1. *Structure of the Residential Brokerage Industry.* An extensive, nationwide study by staff members of the Federal Trade Commission confirms several of the observations made in the Owen study excerpted above. According to the staff report, approximately 80% of home sales were negotiated through a broker. Of all homes sold through brokers, about 90% were listed with a local multiple listing service. "Our investigation indicates that while there is some variation in commission rates contracted for and paid in every local community surveyed, commission rates in all markets do tend to be roughly uniform from sale to sale." A 1979 survey revealed that "85 percent of the sellers surveyed alleged they were quoted a commission rate either of 6 or 7 percent by the broker whom they used, and ultimately 78 percent paid either 6 or 7 percent." Staff Report by the Los Angeles Regional Office of the FTC, The Residential Real Estate Brokerage Industry, 15, 19 (December 1983).

The Staff Report also sought to solve the puzzle of relatively uniform prices in a highly atomized industry. Interdependency among brokers, facilitated by the multiple listing service, appeared to be the cause. In the typical multiple listing service, a broker who has obtained an exclusive listing from a seller submits the listing to the service. At this point, every other member of the service is free to try to sell the property by procuring a buyer. The commission from such "cooperative" sales is divided between the listing and the cooperating broker. "Many observers believe that most firms, and especially small firms and new entrants, are dependent upon the MLS and cooperative sales and cannot take any risks that might lessen the cooperation they will receive."

Specifically, while "brokers might attract many listings by advertising low commission fees, those brokers might encounter problems in cooperatively selling their listings. Cooperating brokers usually are compensated by the listing broker's splitting his or her commission with the cooperating brokers. 'Discount' or 'alternative' brokers may offer potential cooperating brokers substantially less compensation than that provided by 'traditional' brokers. For this reason (and also because a cooperating traditional broker who charges the higher prevailing commission rate will be a competitor of the listing discount broker for future listings) many traditional brokers are alleged to quite understandably steer potential buyers to homes listed by brokers charging the prevailing commission rate and offering the prevailing split." As a result, price competition may become "a potentially unsuccessful competitive strategy and it is our belief that is the most important factor explaining the general uniformity of commission rates in most local markets." Staff Report 17–19.

2. *Licensing.* All fifty states license real estate brokers and salespeople through laws covering practically every activity performed for a fee in connection with a real estate transaction. (Lawyers, when performing legal work, are typically exempted.) Applicants are tested on subjects ranging from reading, writing and arithmetic to applicable real property law and the practical aspects of deeds, mortgages, contracts and agency. In a few states they are tested on ethics and the basic principles of land economics and appraising. Some states require relevant work experience and some require that the applicant successfully complete a real estate course approved by the state.

Licenses may be revoked for such delicts as fraud, deceptive advertising, untrustworthiness or incompetence (N.Y.Real Prop.Law § 441–c(1)); acting for more than one party without the knowledge or consent of all, or commingling funds (Cal.Bus. & Prof.Code § 10176(d), (e)); acting in the dual capacity of broker and undisclosed principal, charging an undisclosed commission for a principal, or not giving a copy of the purchase and sale agreement to buyer and seller (Mass.Gen.Laws Ann. ch. 112, § 87AAA(b), (f), (i)).

3. *Real Estate Boards and Associations.* Most brokers belong to local, state and national groups that lobby actively on their behalf, oversee their professional conduct and provide or support marketing facilities. The main locus of day-to-day activities is the local real estate board, a voluntary association offering market and industry information to its members. Local boards belonging to the National Association of Realtors, the largest national organization of real estate professionals, enforce the Association's Code of Ethics through grievance and hearing committees. Membership in a local board may also be a prerequisite to participation in a multiple listing service.

4. *Trends in the Brokerage Industry.* Brokerage firms, traditionally small and independent, have recently begun to expand nationwide through branches, referral networks and franchise operations. The growth of brokerage chains has been more than geographic. The giants have also expanded their services to include home finance, insurance, and escrow and other closing services. Some small independents have responded by forming cooperative networks in which a relocating seller is referred by her hometown broker to a cooperating broker in the locale to which she is moving. Other local brokers have joined national franchising operations, receiving in return for payment of an initial fee

and percentage of gross revenues, the benefits of advertising, name recognition, training, and office management expertise.

Computer technology has doubtless spurred these developments, fostering nationwide listing networks through which a potential buyer, sitting at a terminal in an office on one side of the country, can summon up all current listings in a locale on the other side of the country. The same computer-communications technologies have also helped to nationalize and shorten the otherwise local and protracted search for financing. Several computer-based networks now give brokers continuously updated lists of mortgage lenders and itemize the availability and terms of their loans. Some networks will evaluate the borrower's creditworthiness, process the loan documents and even commit the funds.

5. *Antitrust Violations.* Broker groups have employed price fixing and exclusionary practices to restrict competition in the conveyancing industry. Mandatory commission schedules were the earliest form of price fixing. In United States v. National Ass'n of Real Estate Boards, 339 U.S. 485, 70 S.Ct. 711, 94 L.Ed. 1007 (1950), the United States Supreme Court held that these schedules violated section 3 of the Sherman Act. Local boards subsequently confined themselves to recommending "fair and reasonable" rates. These recommendations came under Justice Department attack in a flurry of actions brought in the early 1970's. See, for example, United States v. Prince George's County Bd. of Realtors, Inc., 1971 Trade Cas. ¶ 73,393 (D.Md.1970); United States v. Long Island Bd. of Realtors, Inc., 1972 Trade Cas. ¶ 74,068 (E.D.N.Y.1972). As a result, real estate boards entirely dropped recommended rate schedules. Yet, six months after one New Jersey board discontinued its fee schedule, rates had not budged from the previous 6% rate. Wall St.J., March 13, 1973, p. 1, col. 5.

Exclusionary practices arise mainly in connection with access to multiple listing service facilities and have been attacked from three quarters: federal antitrust law, state antitrust statutes and common law doctrine. See generally, Trombetta, The MLS Access Issue: A Rule of Reason Analysis, 11 Seton Hall L.Rev. 396 (1981); Erxleben, In Search of Price and Service Competition in Residential Real Estate Brokerage: Breaking the Cartel, 56 Wash.L.Rev. 179 (1981); Austin, Real Estate Boards and Multiple Listing Systems as Restraints of Trade, 70 Colum.L.Rev. 1325 (1970).

To blunt these and other charges of anticompetitive conduct, the National Association of Realtors in 1971 adopted "14 Points for Multiple Listing Services" aimed at curbing the more excessive practices. Among the fourteen points, a multiple listing service was not permitted to: "Fix, control, recommend, suggest or maintain commission rates or fees for services to be rendered by members;" "Make any rule prohibiting or discouraging cooperation with nonmembers;" "Prohibit or discourage a member from accepting a listing from a seller (owner) preferring to give an 'office exclusive;'" "Refuse any exclusive listing submitted by a member on the basis of the quality or price of the listing." Like all other NAR regulations, the 14 Points bind only Association members.

Federal antitrust actions were for many years hobbled by the belief that the local nature of broker activities insulated them from federal jurisdiction. The United States Supreme Court reinforced this belief in United States v. National Association of Real Estate Boards, above, when it noted that, since jurisdiction in the case rested on defendant's activities in the District of Columbia, the "fact that no interstate commerce is involved is not a barrier to this suit."

Thirty years later the Court took a different view, holding 8–0 that to "establish the jurisdictional element of a Sherman Act violation it would be sufficient for petitioners to demonstrate a substantial effect on interstate commerce generated by respondents' brokerage activity." The effect need not be direct.

> Brokerage activities necessarily affect both the frequency and the terms of residential sales transactions. Ultimately, whatever stimulates or retards the volume of residential sales, or has an impact on the purchase price, affects the demand for financing and title insurance, those two commercial activities that on this record are shown to have occurred in interstate commerce. Where, as here, the services of respondent real estate brokers are often employed in transactions in the relevant market, petitioners at trial may be able to show that respondents' activities have a not insubstantial effect on interstate commerce.

McLain v. Real Estate Board of New Orleans, Inc., 444 U.S. 232, 242, 246, 100 S.Ct. 502, 509, 511, 62 L.Ed.2d 441, 451, 453 (1980). See Stoppello, Sherman Act Extends to Activities of Real Estate Brokers: Federal Regulation of Brokers May Be on the Way, 9 Real Estate L.J. 151 (1980); Mann, The Applicability of Antitrust Law to Activities of Real Estate Boards: Before and After *McLain*, 18 Hous.L.Rev. 317 (1981).

For a survey of several other areas in which broker practices are subject to antitrust attack, see Jennings, Real Estate Transactions: More Antitrust Litigation is on its Way, 10 Real Est.L.J. 52 (1981); Epley & Parsons, Real Estate Transactions and the Sherman Act: How to Approach an Antitrust Suit, 5 Real Est.L.J. 3 (1976).

6. *Brokers and Housing Discrimination.* As gatekeepers to their communities, real estate brokers contributed to racially discriminatory patterns of home ownership. Probably the most notorious practice was blockbusting, in which brokers stimulated sales by representing to fearful home owners that the racial composition of their neighborhood was about to change and real estate values about to plummet. State and local governments have enacted criminal and civil prohibitions against blockbusting. The practice has also been outlawed by Title VIII of the Civil Rights Act of 1968. Title VIII provides in part that it shall be unlawful "For profit, to induce or attempt to induce any person

to sell or rent any dwelling by representations regarding the entry or prospective entry into the neighborhood of a person or persons of a particular race, color, religion, sex, or national origin." 42 U.S.C.A. § 3604(e). Is it possible that by prohibiting brokers from encouraging sales in the face of racial change, section 3604(e) may inadvertently spur brokers to *discourage* sales to minority group members, directly contravening the overriding purposes of Title VIII?

Title VIII of the 1968 Civil Rights Act has also been interpreted to prohibit racial steering, another discriminatory practice, in which the broker directs white buyers to white neighborhoods, and minority buyers to minority or mixed neighborhoods. Some support has also been found in the 1866 Civil Rights Act, 42 U.S.C.A. § 1982. See Zuch v. Hussey, 394 F.Supp. 1028 (E.D.Mich.1975). As late as 1950, the National Association of Realtors (then called the National Association of Real Estate Boards) expressly encouraged racial steering. The Association's Code of Ethics, Article 34, provided that "A realtor should never be instrumental in introducing into a neighborhood ... members of any race or nationality, or any individual whose presence would be clearly detrimental to property values in that neighborhood." Today the Association endorses the principle that brokers "have the responsibility to offer equal service to all clients and prospects without regard to race." National Association of Realtors, Realtors' Guide to Practice Equal Opportunity in Housing 5 (1973).

Apart from general statutory sanctions, a broker who participates in racially discriminatory practices may lose her license. In a small number of states, licensing statutes specifically make discriminatory practices a ground for suspension or revocation. Other states discipline brokers on more general and traditional grounds. In New York, the Secretary of State has disciplined brokers on the ground that discriminatory practices constitute "untrustworthy" behavior. See, for example, Kamper v. Department of State, 22 N.Y.2d 690, 291 N.Y.S.2d 804, 238 N.E.2d 914 (1968). By contrast, Wisconsin's Supreme Court has held discrimination not to constitute "incompetency," "improper dealing," or "untrustworthiness" as those terms are used in the state's license revocation statute. Ford v. Wisconsin Real Estate Examining Board, 48 Wis.2d 91, 179 N.W.2d 786 (1970). See generally, Suspension or Revocation of Real Estate Broker's License on Ground of Discrimination, 42 ALR3d 1099.

For a detailed, but somewhat dated, description of broker practices, see R. Helper, Racial Policies and Practices of Real Estate Brokers (1969). On blockbusting, see Note, Blockbusting, 59 Geo.L.J. 170 (1970). On steering, see Note, Racial Steering: The Real Estate Broker and Title VIII, 85 Yale L.J. 808 (1976).

7. *Bibliographic Note.* For an excellent treatise covering the field generally, see D.B. Burke, Jr., Law of Real Estate Brokers (1982).

1. SELLER'S AND BUYER'S LIABILITY TO BROKER

NATIONAL ASSOCIATION OF REALTORS, CODE OF ETHICS (1991)

Article 4

To prevent dissension and misunderstanding and to assure better service to the owner, REALTORS ® should urge the exclusive listing of property unless contrary to the best interest of the owner.

GALBRAITH v. JOHNSTON

Supreme Court of Arizona, 1962.
92 Ariz. 77, 373 P.2d 587.

STRUCKMEYER, Justice.

Plaintiff, L.B. Galbraith, a real estate broker doing business as L.B. Galbraith & Co. brought this action against J.B. Johnston and Virgie Mae Johnston, his wife, for a commission on the sale of real property allegedly due pursuant to the terms of a written real estate listing. The defendants thereafter joined in the action a second real estate broker, Joe J. Paterno asserting that Paterno's activities were the procuring cause of the sale. At the trial a jury returned a verdict in favor of Paterno and in favor of defendants against plaintiff. Judgments were entered accordingly and plaintiff appealed.

Prior hereto defendants were the owners of a farm near Stanfield, Arizona, consisting of approximately 400 acres devoted to the growing of cotton which they listed for sale with various real estate brokers. On August 24th, 1956, they entered into a written listing with plaintiff to sell for $160,000. Alternatively the listing provided that defendants would accept $142,800 net, if their equity was paid in cash. At defendants' insistence a nonexclusive listing was agreed upon. To accomplish this a printed form designed for use as an exclusive listing was modified by adding the words, "None (sic) Exclusive Listing" immediately following the printed body of the agreement. Certain portions of the printed body were stricken. In its pertinent parts the listing provided:

"For and in consideration of your listing my property, and your efforts to find a purchaser, I hereby appoint you my Agent, and hereby grant you the right to sell my property described herein for a period of ... days from date hereof, and thereafter shall remain an open listing until cancelled in writing by me, on the terms set forth here in or upon any other price, terms or exchange to which I may consent. I agree to pay you 5% of the selling price for your services, if sold or exchanged by you while this contract is in force, or if sold within one (1) year after the expiration of this listing to anyone with whom you had negotiation prior to expiration.

. . .

"None Exclusive Listing"

Following receipt of this listing plaintiff advertised the property for sale. In September of 1956, one C.L. Kenworthy, after reading one of these advertisements contacted plaintiff's office and inquired about the property. One of plaintiff's salesmen took Kenworthy and his wife to see the farm and spent about an hour showing it to them. After being shown the farm Kenworthy told plaintiff's salesman that he liked the Johnston farm. During the next few weeks plaintiff contacted Kenworthy several times in regard to the property, but no agreement of sale was reached.

On October 8th, 1956, defendants informed plaintiff in writing that they were taking their farm off the market. Other real estate brokers who had been given listings were similarly informed. Plaintiff, however, continued to negotiate with Kenworthy after receipt of the letter, at least through the remainder of October since Kenworthy seemed to have a sincere interest in purchasing the farm.

In the early part of November, 1956, Paterno called upon defendant, J.B. Johnston, at his residence and was given an oral listing to sell the farm at a price of $150,000. Paterno thereafter in turn advertised the property for sale. As a result in the latter part of November he received an inquiry by telephone from Kenworthy. Paterno then made arrangements to meet Kenworthy and show him the farm. After showing the farm Paterno discussed the terms of his listing and on November 30th, 1956, a "purchase contract and receipt" agreement was drawn up whereby Kenworthy offered to purchase for $150,000. This agreement which also provided for the payment of a commission by defendants of $7,500 to Paterno was thereafter accepted by defendants.

Three days after the purchase contract had been signed by defendants, plaintiff called upon J.B. Johnston and asked if he could start working on the sale of the farm again. At this time Johnston told plaintiff the farm had been sold to Kenworthy. Plaintiff informed Johnston that Kenworthy had been his prospect and thereafter instituted this action.

Plaintiff's claim for relief was based on the written listing of August 24th, 1956, particularly that portion in which defendant J.B. Johnston agreed to pay him 5% of the selling price, "... *if sold within one (1) year after the expiration of this listing to anyone with whom you* [Galbraith] *had negotiation prior to expiration.*" The trial judge, prior to the introduction of any evidence ruled that plaintiff in order to recover must prove that he was the procuring cause of the sale. Although plaintiff voiced his objection to this ruling initially and at various stages of the trial, the court adhered thereto being of the opinion that a broker before being entitled to a commission had to show he was the efficient, procuring cause of the sale. The question as to whether Galbraith or Paterno was the procuring cause was submitted by special interrogatories to the jury and answered in favor of Paterno.

The dispositive issue on this appeal relates to the propriety of the trial court's ruling that only the broker who is the procuring cause is entitled to a commission.

Provisions in exclusive listings whereby the owner of real property agrees to pay a commission to the broker if the property is sold to one [with] whom the broker has had negotiations prior to the expiration of the listing have been enforced irrespective of the fact that the broker is not the effective, efficient and procuring cause of the sale. The purpose of such a provision is to protect the broker where he has negotiated with a prospect but the sale has not been consummated until after the listing has expired. Although a provision, as in the instant case, is usually found in an exclusive listing, unless there is a valid reason why a prospective seller of real property may not agree to be bound to the same conditions in a nonexclusive listing, the trial court must be held to have erred.

It is true that generally a real estate broker who along with other brokers is given a listing for the sale of real property on a nonexclusive basis must in order to be entitled to a commission from the seller of property prove that he was the procuring cause of the sale.

But patently a prospective seller may obligate himself by contract to the possibility of payment of an additional commission. . . .

. . .

This Court has repeatedly ruled that parties have a legal right to make such contracts as they desire provided only that it is not for an illegal purpose or against public policy. A party cannot complain of the harshness of the terms nor expect a court to relieve him of the consequences.

While fully recognizing the foregoing, defendants assert that the failure to fill in blanks on the printed form along with the deletion of specific words and the addition of others shows an intent that plaintiff could earn a commission only by being the procuring cause of the sale. Significantly, however, no deletion was made of the clause "or if sold within one (1) year after the expiration of this listing to anyone with whom you had negotiation prior to expiration." This clause, although it could have been eliminated had the parties so intended, remained as an integral part of the contract. It is clear, concise and unambiguous and no rule of construction now permits a court to superimpose a contrary subjective intent. A contract which is clear and unambiguous must be interpreted according to its terms.

The fact that there was here intended a nonexclusive listing does not of itself raise an ambiguity. An exclusive listing gives the broker an exclusive right to sell the property for a specified period and an additional right that, if a sale is made by another during that period, the seller becomes obligated for a commission to the broker with whom the listing is given. It is not that the broker has by procuring the sale earned a commission but that the parties contracted for payment of a commission irrespective of whether he was the procuring cause. Under the terms of the contract in this case Galbraith earned a commission if the sale was made to a person with whom he negotiated prior to the expiration of the listing. While the contract may not be the customary one for a nonexclusive listing, no inconsistency leading to an ambiguity exists and hence it must be construed according to its plain terms.

Defendants in their amended answer raised certain affirmative defenses which were not litigated because of the trial court's initial ruling. No opinion is now expressed as to such defenses. We simply remand this cause for proceedings consistent with the views herein expressed. The judgment in favor of J. B. Johnston and Virgie Mae Johnston against L. B. Galbraith is ordered reversed.

Judgment reversed.

BERNSTEIN, C. J., UDALL, V. C. J., JENNINGS, J., and ROBERT E. McGHEE, Judge of Superior Court, concurring.

TRISTRAM'S LANDING, INC. v. WAIT

Supreme Judicial Court of Massachusetts, 1975.
367 Mass. 622, 327 N.E.2d 727.

TAURO, Chief Justice.

This is an action in contract seeking to recover a brokerage commission alleged to be due to the plaintiffs from the defendant. The case was heard by a judge, sitting without a jury, on a stipulation of facts. The judge found for the plaintiffs in the full amount of the commission. The defendant filed exceptions to that finding and appealed.

The facts briefly are these: The plaintiffs are real estate brokers doing business in Nantucket. The defendant owned real estate on the island which she desired to sell. In the past, the plaintiffs acted as brokers for the defendant when she rented the same premises.

The plaintiffs heard that the defendant's property was for sale, and in the spring of 1972 the plaintiff Van der Wolk telephoned the defendant and asked for authority to show it. The defendant agreed that the plaintiffs could act as brokers, although not as exclusive brokers, and told them that the price for the property was $110,000. During this conversation there was no mention of a commission. The defendant knew that the normal brokerage commission in Nantucket was five per cent of the sale price.

In the early months of 1973, Van der Wolk located a prospective buyer, Louise L. Cashman (Cashman), who indicated that she was interested in purchasing the defendant's property. Her written offer of $100,000, dated April 29, was conveyed to the defendant. Shortly thereafter, the defendant's husband and attorney wrote to the plaintiffs that "a counter-offer of $105,000 with an October 1st closing" should be made to Cashman. Within a few weeks, the counter offer was orally accepted, and a purchase and sale agreement was drawn up by Van der Wolk.

The agreement was executed by Cashman and was returned to the plaintiffs with a check for $10,500, representing a ten per cent down payment. The agreement was then presented by the plaintiffs to the defendant, who signed it after reviewing it with her attorney. The down payment check was thereafter turned over to the defendant.

The purchase and sale agreement signed by the parties called for an October 1, 1973, closing date. On September 22, the defendant signed a fifteen day extension of the closing date, which was communicated to Cashman by the plaintiffs. Cashman did not sign the extension. On October 1, 1973, the defendant appeared at the registry of deeds with a deed to the property. Cashman did not appear for the closing and thereafter refused to go through with the purchase. No formal action has been taken by the defendant to enforce the agreement or to recover damages for its breach, although the defendant has retained the down payment.

Van der Wolk presented the defendant with a bill for commission in the amount of $5,250, five per cent of the agreed sales price. The defendant, through her attorney, refused to pay, stating that "[t]here has been no sale and consequently the 5% commission has not been earned." The plaintiffs then brought this action to recover the commission.

In the course of dealings between the plaintiffs and the defendant there was no mention of commission. The only reference to commission is found in the purchase and sale agreement signed by Cashman and the defendant, which reads as follows: "It is understood that a broker's commission of five (5) per cent on the said sale is to be paid to ... [the broker] by the said seller." The plaintiffs contend that, having produced a buyer who was ready, willing and able to purchase the property, and who was in fact accepted by the seller, they are entitled to their full commission. The defendant argues that no commission was earned because the sale was not consummated. We agree with the defendant, and reverse the finding by the judge below.

1. The general rule regarding whether a broker is entitled to a commission from one attempting to sell real estate is that, absent special circumstances, the broker "is entitled to a commission if he produces a customer ready, able, and willing to buy upon the terms and for the price given the broker by the owner." Gaynor v. Laverdure, 362 Mass. 828, 291 N.E.2d 617 (1973), quoting Henderson & Beal, Inc. v. Glen, 329 Mass. 748, 751, 110 N.E.2d 373 (1953). In the past, this rule has been construed to mean that once a customer is produced by the broker and accepted by the seller, the commission is earned, whether or not the sale is actually consummated. Furthermore, execution of a purchase and sale agreement is usually seen as conclusive evidence of the seller's acceptance of the buyer.

Despite these well established and often cited rules, we have held that "[t]he owner is not helpless" to protect himself from these consequences. "He may, by appropriate language in his dealings with the broker, limit his liability for payment of a commission to the situation where not only is the broker obligated to find a customer ready, willing and able to purchase on the owner's terms and for his price, but also it is provided that no commission is to become due until the customer actually takes a conveyance and pays therefor." Gaynor v. Laverdure, supra, at 835, 291 N.E.2d at 622.

In the application of these rules to the instant case, we believe that the broker here is not entitled to a commission. We cannot construe the purchase and sale agreement as an unconditional acceptance by the seller of the buyer, as the agreement itself contained conditional language. The purchase and sale agreement provided that the commission was to be paid "on the said sale," and we construe this language as requiring that the said sale be consummated before the commission is earned.

. . .

In two of the more recent cases where we were faced with this issue, we declined to follow the developing trends in this area, holding that the cases presented were inappropriate for that purpose. See LeDonne v. Slade, 355 Mass. 490, 492, 245 N.E.2d 434 (1969); Gaynor v. Laverdure, 362 Mass. 828, 291 N.E.2d 617. We believe, however, that it is both appropriate and necessary at this time to clarify the law, and we now join the growing minority of States who have adopted the rule of Ellsworth Dobbs, Inc. v. Johnson, 50 N.J. 528, 236 A.2d 843 (1967).[6]

In the *Ellsworth* case, the New Jersey court faced the task of clarifying the law regarding the legal relationships between sellers and brokers in real estate transactions. In order to formulate a just and proper rule, the court examined the realities of such transactions. The court noted that "ordinarily when an owner of property lists it with a broker for sale, his expectation is that the money for the payment of commission will come out of the proceeds of the sale." Id. at 547, 236 A.2d at 852. It quoted with approval from the opinion of Lord Justice Denning, in Dennis Reed, Ltd. v. Goody, [1950] 2 K.B. 277, 284–285, where he stated: "When a house owner puts his house into the hands of an estate agent, the ordinary understanding is that the agent is only to receive a commission if he succeeds in effecting a sale .... The common understanding of men is ... that the agent's commission is

---

6. Both Kansas and Oregon have adopted the *Ellsworth* rule in its entirety. See Winkelman v. Allen, 214 Kansas 22, 519 P.2d 1377 (1974); Brown v. Grimm, 258 Or. 55, 59–61, 481 P.2d 63 (1971). Additionally, Vermont, Connecticut and Idaho have cited the case with approval. See also Potter v. Ridge Realty Corp., 28 Conn. Supp. 304, 311, 259 A.2d 758 (1969); Rog-

ers v. Hendrix, 92 Idaho 141, 438 P.2d 653 (1968); Staab v. Messier, 128 Vt. 380, 384, 264 A.2d 790 (1970). Other States and the District of Columbia also have similar, but more limited, rules which were adopted prior to the *Ellsworth* case. See generally Gaynor v. Laverdure, 362 Mass. 828 n. 2, 291 N.E.2d 617 (1973).

payable out of the purchase price. ... The house-owner wants to find a man who will actually buy his house and pay for it. He does not want a man who will only make an offer or sign a contract. He wants a purchaser 'able to purchase and able to complete as well.' " Id. at 549, 236 A.2d at 853.

The court went on to say that the principle binding "the seller to pay commission if he signs a contract of sale with the broker's customer, regardless of the customer's financial ability, puts the burden on the wrong shoulders. Since the broker's duty to the owner is to produce a prospective buyer who is financially able to pay the purchase price and take title, a right in the owner to assume such capacity when the broker presents his purchaser ought to be recognized." Id. at 548, 236 A.2d at 853. Reason and justice dictate that it should be the broker who bears the burden of producing a purchaser who is not only ready, willing and able at the time of the negotiations, but who also consummates the sale at the time of closing.

Thus, we adopt the following rules: "When a broker is engaged by an owner of property to find a purchaser for it, the broker earns his commission when (a) he produces a purchaser ready, willing and able to buy on the terms fixed by the owner, (b) the purchaser enters into a binding contract with the owner to do so, and (c) the purchaser completes the transaction by closing the title in accordance with the provisions of the contract. If the contract is not consummated because of lack of financial ability of the buyer to perform or because of any other default of his ... there is no right to commission against the seller. On the other hand, if the failure of completion of the contract results from the wrongful act or interference of the seller, the broker's claim is valid and must be paid." Id. at 551, 236 A.2d at 855.

Accordingly, we hold that a real estate broker, under a brokerage agreement hereafter made, is entitled to a commission from the seller only if the requirements stated above are met. This rule provides necessary protection for the seller and places the burden with the broker, where it belongs. In view of the waiver of the counts in quantum meruit, we do not now consider the extent to which the broker may be entitled to share in a forfeited deposit or other benefit received by the seller as a result of the broker's efforts.

We recognize that this rule could be easily circumvented by language to the contrary in purchase and sale agreements or in agreements between sellers and brokers. In many States a signed writing is required for an agreement to pay a commission to a real estate broker. See Restatement 2d: Contracts, 418, 420 (Tent. drafts Nos. 1–7, 1973). Such a requirement may be worthy of legislative consideration, but we do not think we should establish such a requirement by judicial decision. Informal agreements fairly made between people of equal skill and understanding serve a useful purpose. But many sellers, unlike brokers, are involved in real estate transactions infrequently, perhaps only once in a lifetime, and are thus unfamiliar with their legal rights. In such cases agreements by the seller to pay a commission even though the purchaser defaults are to be scrutinized carefully. If not fairly made, such agreements may be unconscionable or against public policy.

Exceptions sustained.

Judgment for the defendant.

NOTES

1. *Forms of Listing Agreement.* There are four basic types of listing agreement: exclusive right to sell; exclusive agency; open; and net. The exclusive right to sell listing is the most favorable to the listing broker, giving him the right to a commission if the property is sold by anyone, even the owner, during the term of the listing agreement. An exclusive agency listing entitles the broker to a commission if he or any other broker sells the property, but not if the property is sold through the efforts of the owner. In an open or nonexclusive listing, the seller agrees to pay a commission only if the broker is the first to procure a buyer; if the property is sold through the efforts of the seller or anyone else, the broker has no claim. In a net listing, the seller agrees to accept a specified price for the property and the broker receives any amount paid over that price.

2. *Interpreting the Listing Agreement.* Sellers typically list their homes through form agreements drafted by broker associations. As a result, disputes over the seller's duties to the broker turn principally on contract interpretation and on judicial estimates of relative bargaining power. Three interpretational questions recur.

One question concerns the type of listing agreement broker and seller made. If the agreement is ambiguous, a court will generally construe it against the broker on the grounds of superior bargaining position and responsibility for selecting the form of listing agreement. For example, in Holiday Homes of St. John, Inc. v. Lockhart, 678 F.2d 1176 (3d Cir.1982), the form agreement specified an "Exclusive Right to Sell Basis," but also provided that the commission would be payable only upon the broker's procurement of a ready, willing and able buyer. The court seized on this ambiguity to hold that an exclusive right to sell agreement had not been created. As a general rule an open listing will be found unless exclusivity is clearly indicated. Similarly, where there is doubt, an agreement will be held to create an exclusive agency, rather than an exclusive right to sell, listing. See Bourgoin v. Fortier, 310 A.2d 618 (Me.1973).

Second, when has a "sale" occurred, perfecting the broker's right to a commission under an exclusive right to sell listing? An exchange of property usually constitutes a sale for these purposes. See Donlon v. Babin, 44 So.2d 134 (La.App.1950). But what if the house is taken by eminent domain while the listing agreement is in effect? See, e.g., Lundstrom, Inc. v. Nikkei Concerns, Inc., 52 Wash.App. 250, 758 P.2d 561 (1988) (no commission awarded). If the house is leased, not sold, during the term of the listing agreement? Leased with an option to purchase that is later exercised? Taken off the market? Listing agreements sometimes provide that seller's withdrawal of the property from the market during the listing period is equivalent to a sale, entitling the broker to a commission based on the listing price. While the provision might seem unfair to the seller who withdraws because she cannot get an offer close to her listing price, it has been upheld against charges that it is a penalty. See Blank v. Borden, 11 Cal.3d 963, 115 Cal.Rptr. 31, 524 P.2d 127 (1974).

The third question, which arises in open listing agreements, is whether one broker rather than another was the "procuring cause" of the sale and thus entitled to the commission. There are few reasoned rules on the point, but colorful metaphors abound. See, for example, Vincent v. Weber, 42 O.O.2d 347, 232 N.E.2d 671 (1965) (the broker must establish that she was the primary, proximate and procuring cause, not merely the one who "planted the seed from which the harvest was reaped").

3. Ellsworth Dobbs, Inc. v. Johnson, 50 N.J. 528, 236 A.2d 843 (1967), relied on in Tristram's Landing, Inc. v. Wait, is a modern landmark, adjusting legal rules to customary broker and seller expectations about when the broker's commission becomes due. The court recognized that the seller's reasonable expectation is that the commission will be paid out of the sale proceeds, and that this expectation is reinforced by the common broker practice of not requesting the commission until the closing. *Ellsworth Dobbs'* interpretational presumption—no closing, no commission—has since been widely followed by courts that have considered the issue, although some recent decisions follow the traditional rule of awarding a commission on the procurement of a ready, willing, and able buyer even if the deal does not close. See, e.g., Ladd v. Coldwell Banker, 167 A.D.2d 676, 563 N.Y.S.2d 255 (1990); Sticht v. Shull, 543 So.2d 395 (Fla.App.1989).

Ellsworth Dobbs announced a second rule that has, by contrast, won few adherents. The rule is one of contract illegality rather than interpretation. According to the court, whenever "there is substantial inequality of bargaining power" between broker and seller, a clause entitling the broker to a commission on the contract signing is "so contrary to the common understanding of men, and also so contrary to fairness, as to require a court to condemn it as unconscionable." 50 N.J. at 555, 236 A.2d at 857.

4. *Ellsworth Dobbs and Tristram's Landing Applied.* Like many other pioneering decisions, *Ellsworth Dobbs* and *Tristram's Landing* are short on implementing details. Consider, for example, a sales contract requiring buyer to pay 10% down on closing, and requiring seller to take back a note and mortgage under which buyer will pay the remainder of the purchase price over ten years (a not uncommon form of purchase money financing). At what point does the broker become entitled to a commission: At closing? Or ten years hence, after all

financing risk is past? What if a ten-year installment land contract is used as the financing device?

Ellsworth Dobbs and *Tristram's Landing* do not completely relieve seller from liability for the commission on an aborted sale. Instead, they allocate liability according to fault. If it was the seller's fault that the sale did not go through, the seller remains liable for the commission. If it was the buyer's fault, seller has no liability. Who should bear the risk when, through the fault of no one, the sale fails to close? In Hecht v. Meller, 23 N.Y.2d 301, 296 N.Y.S.2d 561, 244 N.E.2d 77 (1968), broker was awarded her commission even though the property had been substantially destroyed by fire before the closing and the contract of sale had been rescinded. The court rested its decision on the traditional view that a broker's right to a commission attaches when she procures a ready, willing, and able buyer. Would a court following *Ellsworth Dobbs* and *Tristram's Landing* reach a different result?

5. *Does a Broker Have Any Rights Against a Buyer?* Because their contract is with the seller, residential brokers have in the past had few routes to recovery against buyers who have maneuvered them out of their commissions or prevented the deal from closing. Third party beneficiary theory, tortious interference with contractual relations and the emerging tort of unlawful interference with prospective economic advantage have been the main grounds for relief.

In Harris v. Perl, 41 N.J. 455, 197 A.2d 359 (1964), plaintiff broker had shown a house to defendant buyer. During negotiations between buyer and seller, seller conveyed the property to a bank to satisfy an earlier obligation to the bank that had been secured by the property. Learning of the transfer, and that the bank had not engaged a broker to sell the house, buyer purchased the property directly from the bank. Broker sued buyer for her lost commission and won, the court observing that she was "not a meddlesome interloper," and that when buyer "accepted plaintiff's services, it was with the obligation which all decent men would recognize—that they would not line their purse with the money value of those services ... the law protects not only contracts but also the reasonable expectations of economic gain." Before your sympathy for the broker leads you to the same conclusion, remember that Article 6 of the Realtor's Code of Ethics recommends that brokers "urge the exclusive listing of property," and that under a typical exclusive listing the seller's transfer to the bank would have constituted a "sale" entitling the broker to a commission from the seller.

Even though tort actions traditionally lay against only outrageous buyer shenanigans, the broker was nonetheless well protected. Broker actions against less culpable buyers were unnecessary, for the seller was in any event liable for the commission at the moment broker presented a ready, willing, and able buyer. But with more recent decisions, like *Ellsworth Dobbs* and *Tristram's Landing*, brokers, to recover, must look to the defaulting buyer, whether the default was willful or not. *Ellsworth Dobbs* sought to protect the broker in these situations by enlarging the occasions for buyer liability: "when a prospective buyer solicits a broker to find or to show him property which he might be interested in buying, and the broker finds property satisfactory to him which the owner agrees to sell at the price offered, and the buyer knows the broker will earn a commission for the sale from the owner, the law will imply a promise on the part of the buyer to complete the transaction with the owner."

At least one state has followed *Ellsworth Dobbs'* implied promise theory and two have rejected it. Compare Donnellan v. Rocks, 22 Cal.App.3d 925, 99 Cal.Rptr. 692 (1972), with Rich v. Emerson-Dumont Distributing Corp., 55 Mich.App. 142, 222 N.W.2d 65 (1974); Professional Realty Corp. v. Bender, 216 Va. 737, 222 S.E.2d 810 (1976). *Ellsworth Dobbs* itself was limited by the New Jersey Supreme Court in Rothman Realty Corp. v. Bereck, 73 N.J. 590, 376 A.2d 902 (1977). Buyers there suffered a sudden stock market reversal making it impossible for them to come up with the cash needed to close the purchase of a house. The court recognized that buyers' "implied promise to the broker did not encompass a failure to close where they had acted in good faith, and the inability to consummate the deal ... was due to a circumstance beyond their control." The court distinguished *Ellsworth Dobbs* on the ground that the buyer there was engaged in a commercial enterprise; the "bargaining power and expertise of such buyers are far superior to those of the average home purchaser." 73 N.J. at 602, 376 A.2d at 908.

Does the expansion of tort theory, as in *Harris,* and of implied contract theory, as in *Ellsworth Dobbs,* point to an emerging fiduciary tie between broker and buyer? Would such a tie necessarily dilute the broker's fiduciary duties to the seller?

2. BROKER'S DUTIES TO SELLER AND TO BUYER

NATIONAL ASSOCIATION OF REALTORS, CODE OF ETHICS (1991)

Article 7

In accepting employment as an agent, REALTORS ® pledge themselves to protect and promote the interests of the client. This obligation of absolute fidelity to the client's interests is primary, but it does not relieve REALTORS ® of the obligation to treat fairly all parties to the transaction.

**GROHMAN, A REASSESSMENT OF THE SELLING REAL
ESTATE BROKER'S AGENCY RELATIONSHIP WITH
THE PURCHASER**

61 St.John's Law Review 560, 560–563, 584–588 (1987).

I. INTRODUCTION

Real property sellers have traditionally utilized real estate broker-age services to sell their properties. Typically, the seller and broker enter into a listing agreement which expressly authorizes the broker to act as the seller's exclusive agent in selling the specified property. This broker is commonly referred to as a listing broker. One of the listing broker's responsibilities is to inform others of the seller's desire to convey the property. The listing broker often accomplishes this by registering the property with a multiple listing service ("MLS"). This service aids the listing broker in informing other MLS members of the pertinent facts regarding the property and the sale. As a result, access to the MLS is one of the most important services a broker could offer to a client. Usually, when a cooperating MLS member, working with a potential purchaser, prepares to make an offer on the listed property, the cooperating or selling broker is deemed a subagent of the listing broker. Generally, subagents are in a fiduciary relationship with their principals. As a result, they owe their principal—the seller—the same duties as those which an agent owes the principal.

Without expressly agreeing to retain a broker as their agent, pur-chasers may also utilize a broker's services to locate property which they may opt to purchase. The real estate broker, in many cases, is the purchaser's sole source of expertise and material information regarding real property purchases. Often, this broker is not the same as the seller's listing broker. First, the broker will attempt to interest the purchaser in property listed with his office. If successful, he will not have to share the sales commission with an outside broker. If unsuc-cessful, the broker will try to interest the purchaser in property listed with the MLS. If successful in this attempt, the broker will be referred to as the "selling" or "cooperating" broker for that property even though another broker's office had originally listed it. As a result, the brokers will share the commission. Once the buyer has located a property in which he is interested, the selling broker normally aids the buyer in determining the terms of his offer and then assists the buyer in presenting the offer to the seller, usually through the listing broker.

A clear distinction exists between the listing broker and the selling broker. It is the seller of real property who usually initiates the relationship with the listing broker. It is the purchaser who typically initiates the relationship with the selling broker. For some time, federal courts, state courts, professional real estate organizations, sell-ers, and purchasers have questioned the status of the selling broker's relationship and his duties to the real estate purchaser. Absent a specific contractual relationship, case law generally concludes and authors opine that the selling broker is the seller's subagent and not the purchaser's agent. Therefore, he has little, if any, fiduciary obligation to the purchaser. The real estate broker's primary obligation to the purchaser is to deal honestly and fairly with him. This obligation, rather than emanating from an agency relationship, arises, at least partially, from the position of public trust which brokers occupy, and is supported by their virtual monopoly in real estate sales. As a result, the purchaser, without an attorney, is the least protected and most vulnerable party in a real estate transaction. ...

IV. AVAILABLE ALTERNATIVES

A. *Mandatory Duty to Disclose Subagency to Purchaser*

One of the reactions to the assertion that the current system misleads the real property purchaser is to proffer the idea that the selling broker must advise the purchaser that he will be acting solely as the seller's agent. Such a proposition would prove fruitless for two reasons.

First, brokers are reluctant to disclose such information to purchasers. Psychologically, it is to the broker's and seller's advantage to get the buyer committed in writing as soon as possible. Advising the purchaser in advance that neither broker represents him most likely would encourage him to seek alternative representation and delay the process. This is the antithesis of the sales concept. It is unlikely that many brokers would encourage such activity. Disclosures probably would be infrequent. This presumption follows from the brokers' past failures in being open with purchasers and sellers where it appears that such openness in disclosure would be contrary to the brokers' best interests. For example, brokers have failed to disclose to real estate participants how negotiable real estate commissions might be. Also, they have failed to advise the parties about each participant's role in the real estate transaction. Consequently, the purchaser is virtually unaware that the person upon whom he is relying may actually have interests adverse to his. So, too, brokers frequently fail to show prospective purchasers homes listed with other brokers who discount their commissions. There is little reason, therefore, to believe that brokers would be any more informative in disclosing their subagency relationship than they are presently in disclosing other information.

Second, a mere revelation that a subagency relationship exists still fails to provide the purchaser with what he needs. It is necessary to recognize that an agency relationship exists and this will provide the purchaser with the same advocacy and protection that the seller receives.

B. *Dual Agency*

Another response to the problem is to propose the dual agency theory whereby the selling broker would be the agent for both the seller and the buyer. Again, this theory is unlikely to provide adequate protection for purchasers.

First, in all but the most basic transactions, there are conflicts inherent in a dual agency. The dual agent owes both principals the same degree of care and duty as if he represented each alone. He must, as to both, act loyally, act in good faith and fairly, and openly and fully disclose all relevant facts known to him or which he should have discovered in carrying out his duties. In many real estate dealings this is an impossibility because of the contrasting motivations of the seller and purchaser, and the selling broker's duty to disclose to each. Likewise, he would have to disclose to the purchaser the seller's need for sale proceeds.

Moreover, where there are conflicts between the two principals, the dual agent must obtain the consent of each principal before embarking on the dual agency. The basic principle underlying this requirement is "to prevent the agent from putting himself in a position in which to be honest must be a strain on him, and to elevate him to a position where he cannot be tempted to betray his principal." Defining the selling agent as a dual agent in a transaction that is fraught with inherent conflicts, places a strain on him to be honest and enhances the difficulty of not betraying his principal, even though he may betray the principal negligently. The broker's falling prey to such temptation has resulted in courts referring to it without citation.

Unfortunately, because of the nature of agency relationships, one can infer such a relationship in many transactions solely from the parties' actions. Therefore, the agent may have acted already without obtaining the necessary consents. Doing so gives each principal who did not have prior knowledge of the dual representation the right to void the agency and the transaction. As a result, a broker acting in this fashion may have already breached his fiduciary obligations and lost his right to a commission by the time he attempts to obtain each party's consent. It is important to note that the primary exception to the general dual agency rule is where the broker acts as a middleman.

A third problem with the dual agency theory is that the dual agent must withdraw from representing the principals when a conflict between the two arises because he is unable to represent adequately each principal's interests. By the selling dual agent's withdrawal from the agency, the purchaser loses the affirmative representation he sought and expected. The seller, on the other hand, may still have the listing broker acting as his agent. Therefore, such a theory fails to remedy the inequities inherent in the current system.

C. *Purchaser's Agent*

Another way to deal with the question is to recognize that elements already exist in the typical relationship between a purchaser and a selling broker which make the selling broker the purchaser's agent. As a result, the purchaser has the agent that he needs and that both he and the seller already expect him to have. The purchaser's agent would be better able to serve the purchaser without fear of conflicts of interest or fear of losing his right to reimbursement for failure to obtain the necessary consents for dual agency. The agent would no longer be faced with the problem of trying to determine what to disclose and when to withdraw when conflicts arise in dual agencies. The purchaser then has an agent who will assist him in determining the best price at which he can obtain the property, in determining the most favorable terms under which the seller is willing to convey, in deciding what inspections to have, and, generally, in taking all usual steps inherent in the prudent purchase of real property.

In recognizing and applying agency principles to the selling broker-purchaser relationship, the law would balance inequities inherent in the existing system. Presently, the seller knows the most about his property. The broker is expert in comparing the property in question with similar properties and in discovering material information about the property for sale. The typical purchaser not only does not have the seller's information about his home, but, also, is without the broker's general expertise. Presumably, the purchaser represented by a broker should fare better in negotiations for the purchase of property.

HAYMES v. ROGERS

Supreme Court of Arizona, 1950.
70 Ariz. 257, 219 P.2d 339, rehearing, 70 Ariz. 408, 222 P.2d 789.

DE CONCINI, Justice.

Kelley Rogers, hereinafter called appellee, brought an action against L. F. Haymes, hereinafter referred to as appellant, seeking to recover a real estate commission in the sum of $425. The case was tried before a jury which returned a verdict in favor of appellee. The said appellant owned a piece of realty which he had listed for sale with the appellee, real estate broker, for the sum of $9,500. The listing card which appellant signed provided that the commission to be paid appellee for selling the property was to be five (5%) per cent of the total selling price. Tom Kolouch was employed by the said appellee as a real estate salesman, and is hereafter referred to as "salesman".

On February 4, 1948, the said salesman contacted Mr. and Mrs. Louis Pour, prospective clients. He showed them various parcels of real estate, made an appointment with them for the following day in order to show them appellant's property. The salesman then drew a diagram of the said property in order to enable the Pours to locate and identify it the next day for their appointment. The Pours, however, proceeded to go to appellant's property that very day and encountering the appellant, negotiated directly with him and purchased the property for the price of $8,500. The transcript of evidence (testimony) reveals that the appellant knew the Pours had been sent to him through the efforts of appellee's salesman but he did not know it until they verbally agreed on a sale and appellant had accepted a $50 deposit. Upon learning that fact he told the Pours that he would take care of the salesman.

Appellant makes several assignments of error and propositions of law. However we need only to consider whether the trial court was in error by refusing to grant a motion for an instructed verdict in favor of the defendant.

One of the propositions of law relied upon by the appellant is as follows: "The law requires that a real estate broker employed to sell land must act in entire good faith and in the interest of his employer, and if he induces the prospective buyer to believe that the property can be bought for less, he thereby fails to discharge that duty and forfeits all his rights to claim commission and compensation for his work."

There is no doubt that the above proposition of law is correct. A real estate agent owes the duty of utmost good faith and loyalty to his principal. The immediate problem here is whether the above proposition is applicable to the facts in this instance. The question is, is it a breach of a fiduciary duty and a betrayal of loyalty for a real estate broker to inform a prospective purchaser that a piece of realty may be purchased for less than the list price? We believe that such conduct is a breach of faith and contrary to the interests of his principal, and, therefore, is a violation of the fiduciary relationship existing between agent and principal which will preclude the agent from recovering a commission therefrom.

The facts here are clear and undisputed. The salesman informed the purchasers that he had an offer of $8,250 for the property from another purchaser which he was about to submit to appellant. He further told them he thought appellant would not take $8,250 but would probably sell for a price between $8,250 and $9,500 and that they in all probability could get it for $8,500. The agent was entirely without justification in informing the purchasers that the property might be bought for $8,500, since that placed the purchasers at a distinct advantage in bargaining with the principal as to the purchase price of the realty. As a general rule an agent knows through his contacts with his principal, how anxious he is to sell and whether or not the principal will accept less than the listed price. To inform a third person of that fact is a clear breach of duty and loyalty owed by the fiduciary to his principal. Such misconduct and breach of duty results in the agent's losing his right to compensation for services to which he would otherwise be entitled.

. . .

This determination makes a consideration of the other grounds for appeal unnecessary. Under the circumstances the court should have directed a verdict for the defendant, appellant.

Judgment reversed.

LA PRADE, C.J., and STANFORD and PHELPS, JJ., concur.

UDALL, Justice (dissenting).

I dissent for the reason that as I construe the record in the instant case the facts do not disclose such bad faith or gross misconduct on the part of the broker as to disentitle him to compensation.

There is no disagreement between us as to the high standard which the law prescribes must be maintained in dealings between an agent and his principal. The difficulty comes in applying the law to the facts of this case.

The great majority of the reported cases denying a brokerage fee involve instances where (1) the agent acts adversely for the purpose of securing a secret profit for himself or otherwise advancing his own welfare at the expense of that of his employer; (2) an agent disclosing the necessitous circumstances of his principal; (3) the agent is guilty of fraud or dishonesty in the transaction of his agency; (4) his conduct is disobedient or constitutes a wilful and deliberate breach of his contract of service; or (5) where he withholds information from his principal which it is his duty to disclose.... I submit, however, that the facts before us do not place the conduct of this broker within any of the prohibitions above enumerated and I have been unable to find a single case where the courts have denied compensation under a factual situation comparable to that presented by this record.

. . .

An analysis of the testimony before us, when taken as it must be in the light most favorable to a sustaining of the judgment, shows but four questionable matters. First, the agent advised his principal, before the Pours came onto the scene, that in his opinion the listed sales price of $9500 was excessive. This statement was made after repeated efforts to sell to others at the list price had failed. I can see nothing improper in this. Second, the agent advised Pour (the ultimate purchaser whom he had procured) that his principal, the owner, then had on his desk for acceptance or rejection an offer of $8,250 which offer, in his opinion, the seller would not accept. There may have been some impropriety in this disclosure of his principal's business but I cannot read into this slip such gross misconduct as to warrant denying him compensation. Third, complaint is made that the broker failed to exert his best efforts to effect a sale to the Pours at the list price of $9500. In my opinion there is no merit to this contention because it is clear that the broker did advise the prospective purchasers that the owner's asking price was $9500 and it further appears that appellant perfected the sale with the Pours the evening of the first day they were contacted and before the broker's salesman had an opportunity to keep an appointment for the following day at 1:00 p.m., when he was to show them the property in question. It is unthinkable to believe that any purchaser would buy property without first seeing it. The majority evidently do not base the reversal upon any of these derelictions so finally we consider what is urged as the broker's most serious breach of duty to act in good faith and for the interest of the appellant, to wit, his unauthorized statement that the owner might accept less than the list price. To keep the record straight I quote from the cross-examination of salesman Tom Kolouch:

"Q. And you also told them at that time that you were pretty sure if they would offer $8500 for the property that they would get it? A. I told them they might try $8500. I didn't tell them for sure they would get it because I wasn't setting a price on the other man's property. Q. And you told them if they would offer $8500 that they might get the property? A. They might have, yes. Q. And there wasn't anything said at that time about their offering $9500 for the property? A. I told them the price was $9500 on our list." and the following is Mr. Pour's version of the matter: "Q. He told you to go out there and offer $8500 for the property? A. No, he told me it was listed for more, but he didn't think this offer would go through, and if I met somewhere in between I might get it."

. . .

In effect, as I view it, all the appellee intended by his statements to the Pours was to hold their interest in the property until he could show it to them and the parties could be brought together. I understand it to be the law that the ultimate duty of the broker toward his principal is to procure a purchaser ready, willing and able to purchase upon terms agreed upon by the owner and the purchaser. How then can it be said that the effort of the broker in the instant case in attempting to interest a purchaser and bring the purchaser and owner together by stating that the property might possibly be purchased for less than the quoted price (something which every prospective purchaser would be justified in assuming and which is a hope in the mind of every buyer) amounted to a breach of his duty to act for his principal's best interest? Will not the court's opinion be construed as holding that if a broker states to a purchaser or even indicates in any manner that property might be acquired for less than the listed price his right to a commission is thereby forfeited? If such be the declared law of this state it will certainly give a wide avenue of escape to unscrupulous realty owners from paying what is justly owed to agents who have been the immediate and efficient cause of the sale of their property.

It would be a most naive purchaser who would not know or assume without being told that the owner of realty might sell for less than the original asking price. In my opinion this broker's conduct does not disclose such bad faith or gross misconduct on his part as to warrant a forfeiture of all right to a commission. Particularly is this true where, as here, it is shown that the owner primarily refused to pay the usual 5% commission and thus brought on the lawsuit, because the broker would not agree to split the fee with him. Certainly the appellee was the procuring cause of the sale to the Pours as he put them in touch with the owners. The case was fairly tried to a jury and by their verdict it is apparent they found no evidence of bad faith or gross misconduct on the part of appellee. To me it seems erroneous for this court to now declare that the conduct heretofore enumerated, as a matter of law is such as to warrant denying all compensation to the broker.

I would affirm the judgment as entered by the learned trial court.

Opinion on Rehearing

DE CONCINI, Justice.

In our former opinion, June 12, 1950, 70 Ariz. 257, 219 P.2d 339, we held that as a matter of law there was bad faith shown on the broker's part which precluded him from recovery of his commission. In the light of the motion for rehearing and a re-examination of the evidence and instructions we are constrained to change our view.

. . .

The evidence in this case presents a close question as to good or bad faith on the part of the broker. The trial court should have submitted that matter for the jury to decide. This court has held in negligence cases where the question is close or is in the "shadow zone" that the trial court should not as a matter of law decide those things but rather submit the question to the jury. We feel that while the facts are not analogous, yet the principle of law is the same and decline to decide what is bad faith as a matter of law because that is within the province of the triers of fact. The appellant is entitled to have the jury weigh the evidence and inferences therefrom as to whether or not appellee acted in bad faith in the light of the foregoing.

We wish to reiterate that a broker or salesman owes the utmost good faith to his principal as does any other person acting as agent or in a fiduciary capacity. If an agent betrays his principal, such misconduct and breach of duty results in the agent's losing his right to compensation for services to which he would otherwise be entitled.

In this case the appellant sold the property to a purchaser who he knew was sent to him by the appellee's salesman. Therefore, in the absence of bad faith the broker is entitled to his commission when he is the procuring cause of sale.

Judgment is reversed and the case remanded for a new trial with directions to submit the question of bad faith on the part of the appellee to the jury.

Judgment reversed.

LA PRADE, C.J., and UDALL, STANFORD and PHELPS, JJ., concurring.

HOFFMAN v. CONNALL

Supreme Court of Washington, 1987.
108 Wash.2d 69, 736 P.2d 242.

ANDERSEN, Justice.

FACTS OF CASE

At issue in this case is whether a real estate broker [1] is liable for innocently misrepresenting a material fact about real estate to a buyer.

In January 1983, Bryan G. and Connie J. Connall, hereinafter referred to as the sellers, signed a listing agreement with Cardinal Realty, Inc. and Charles Huggins, an associate broker with Cardinal Realty. The sellers wanted to sell 5 acres of land north of Spokane. A few days after signing the listing agreement, one of the sellers showed the property to the Cardinal broker. The seller pointed to a stake or piece of pipe as the southeast corner of the property, and the broker saw that the stake lined up with an old fence line to apparently form the east boundary. The sellers had built a new fence approximately 6" inside the old fence line and a corral and horse shed stood just inside the new fence. The seller insisted that his corral was inside the property line.

The seller then showed the broker a wooden stake, which he said marked the southwest corner of the property. The broker saw that the stake was in line with a row of poplar trees that evidently formed the west boundary. To the north of the trees was a pole that apparently was near the northwest corner. The seller could not find the stake marking the northwest corner of the property, and the two men felt they were close to but could not exactly locate the northeast boundary.

The broker later stated that the seller "was very emphatic about what he bought and where he built", and never gave the broker any indication that the boundaries he pointed out were incorrect. The seller told the broker that the property had been surveyed before he and his wife bought it. The broker did not verify that statement.

James and Verna Hoffman, the buyers herein, read about the property in the newspaper. The property's improvements—corral, cattle chute, barn and shed—were important to the buyers because they owned a horse and wanted to get involved with 4–H horse activities. They called the broker and visited the property with him. He pointed out the fence as the east boundary, and the pole as the northwest boundary. He gave an approximate indication of the northeast corner but could not find the marker for the southwest corner. The broker later testified that in telling the buyers about the property, "there was no doubt in my mind of where the proper property line was". The broker did not recommend that the buyers obtain a survey.

---

1. As have the parties, we use the term "broker" herein to include real estate agents and salespeople.

The buyers bought the property on February 28, 1983. In May 1983 a neighbor told them that a recent survey showed that their east fence encroached upon his property. The buyers had their own survey done and discovered that their east-side improvements encroached upon their neighbor's property by 18 to 21 feet. The encroachment consisted of the fence built by the sellers and part of the corral, cattle run and horse shed. The buyers discovered it would cost almost $6,000 to move the improvements onto their own property.

On September 18, 1984, the buyers brought an action for damages against the sellers and the broker, alleging that they misrepresented the true boundary lines. Following a bench trial, the trial court found as a fact that there was nothing to give the broker or the sellers notice that anything was wrong with the property lines. The court concluded that the broker did not breach the standard of care of a reasonably prudent real estate broker, and that the sellers were not liable since they were unaware of any problem with the boundaries as represented. A judgment of dismissal was thereupon entered against the buyers.

The Court of Appeals reversed, holding that an owner of realty who innocently misrepresents its boundaries is liable to the purchaser. The court then extended liability for innocent misrepresentation to an owner's real estate agent and, in the alternative, held that the broker breached his duty to take reasonable steps to avoid disseminating false information to buyers. The seller did not appeal the Court of Appeals decision. Thus, the question of the *owner's* liability is not before this court. The broker and the real estate company sought review of the Court of Appeals decision and we granted review pursuant to RAP 13.4(b).

Two principal issues are presented.

ISSUES

ISSUE ONE. Should a real estate broker be held liable for innocently misrepresenting a material fact to a buyer of real property?

ISSUE TWO. Was the broker negligent in failing to verify the sellers' statements concerning the property's boundaries?

DECISION

ISSUE ONE.

CONCLUSION. A real estate broker is held to a standard of reasonable care and is liable for making "negligent", though not "innocent", misrepresentations concerning boundaries to a buyer.

The Restatement (Second) of Torts defines the tort of innocent misrepresentation as follows:

Misrepresentation in Sale, Rental or Exchange Transaction

(1) One who, in a sale, rental or exchange transaction with another, makes a misrepresentation of a material fact for the purpose of inducing the other to act or to refrain from acting in

reliance upon it, is subject to liability to the other for pecuniary loss caused to him by his justifiable reliance upon the misrepresentation, even though it is not made fraudulently or negligently.

Restatement (Second) of Torts § 552C(1) (1977).

The Restatement, however, leaves open the question of whether such a cause of action lies against real estate brokers. While the Court of Appeals in *Hoffman* was the first Washington court to apply § 552C to brokers, prior established Washington case law recognizes a cause of action against *owners* who innocently misrepresent the boundaries of their property to a purchaser. Owners are liable for such misrepresentations because they are presumed to know the character and attributes of the land which they convey.

We recognize that some jurisdictions have agreed with the viewpoint of the Court of Appeals in this case and have held real estate brokers liable for making innocent misrepresentations on which buyers justifiably rely.[7] Courts that so hold do so because of their belief that the innocent buyer's reliance tips the balance of equity in favor of the buyer's protection. The courts justify placing the loss on the innocent broker on the basis that the broker is in a better position to determine the truth of his or her representations.

This approach has been criticized for imposing a standard of strict liability for all misrepresentations that a broker might make or communicate, however innocent, in a real estate transaction.[9] Another commentator observes the obvious—that there is a problem with subjecting brokers to liability for innocent misrepresentations without imposing a corresponding duty of inspection for defects, and that without such a duty, a broker may be tempted to provide less information to a buyer, fearing that his or her chances of exposure to liability for innocent misrepresentations will multiply with the quantity of information provided.

At the other end of the spectrum from liability for innocent misrepresentation is the view that a real estate broker is an agent of the seller, not of the buyer, and is protected from liability under agency law. Thus, an agent would be permitted to repeat misinformation from his principal without fear of liability unless the agent knows or has reason to know of its falsity. This principle has been upheld by approximately half the jurisdictions that have addressed the issue of broker liability for innocent misrepresentations. The Supreme Court of Vermont recently reaffirmed this rule, holding that "[r]eal estate brokers and agents are marketing agents, not structural engineers or contractors. They have no duty to verify independently representa-

---

7. Note, *Realtor Liability for Innocent Misrepresentation and Undiscovered Defects: Balancing the Equities Between Broker and Buyer,* 20 Val.U.L.Rev. 255, 260 (1986).

9. Fossey & Roston, *The Broker's Liability in a Real Estate Transaction: Bad News and Good News for Defense Attorneys,* 12 U.C.L.A.—Alaska L.Rev. 37, 40 (1982–1983) * * *

tions made by a seller unless they are aware of facts that 'tend to indicate that such representation[s are] false.' " [14]

A recent decision of our Court of Appeals declared a middle ground that we find persuasive. At issue in *Tennant v. Lawton*, 26 Wash.App. 701, 615 P.2d 1305 (1980) was a broker's liability for misrepresenting that a parcel of land could support a sewage system and thus was "buildable". The *Tennant* court echoed the Vermont court in holding that a broker is negligent if he or she repeats material representations made by the seller and knows, or reasonably should know, of their falsity. The court went on, however, to hold that a broker has a limited duty toward a purchaser of real property.

> The underlying rationale of [a broker's] duty to a buyer who is not his client is that he is a professional who is in a unique position to verify critical information given him by the seller. His duty is to take reasonable steps to avoid disseminating to the buyer false information. The broker is required to employ a reasonable degree of effort and professional expertise to confirm or refute information from the seller which he knows, or should know, is pivotal to the transaction from the buyer's perspective.

(Citations omitted.) *Tennant*, at 706, 615 P.2d 1305; *see also McRae v. Bolstad*, 32 Wash.App.173, 646 P.2d 771 (1982); *aff'd*, 101 Wash.2d 161, 676 P.2d 496 (1984).

We perceive no persuasive reason to hold real estate brokers to a higher standard of care than other professionals must satisfy. We have held that lawyers must demonstrate " 'that degree of care, skill, diligence and knowledge commonly possessed and exercised by a reasonable, careful and prudent lawyer in the practice of law in this jurisdiction.' " Chiropractors and other drugless healers owe their patients a duty to exercise reasonable care in diagnosing and treating them. RCW 7.70.040(1) requires physicians and surgeons to adhere to a standard of reasonable prudence.

Of relevance in this connection is RCW 18.85.230(5), which provides that a real estate license may be suspended or revoked if the holder is found guilty of

> *[k]nowingly committing*, or being a party to, any material fraud, misrepresentation, concealment, conspiracy, collusion, trick, scheme or device whereby any other person lawfully relies upon the word, representation or conduct of the licensee; ...

(Italics ours.) Under this statute, a broker is only guilty of *knowingly committing* a misrepresentation. Consistent with this reading is one that would similarly find liability only when a broker is a *knowing party* to a misrepresentation.

14. *Provost v. Miller,* 144 Vt. 67, 69–70, 473 A.2d 1162 (1984), quoting *Lyons v. Christ Episcopal Church,* 71 Ill.App.3d 257, 259–60, 27 Ill.Dec. 559, 561, 389 N.E.2d 623, 625 (1979).

Absent a legislative directive to the contrary, we do not consider it appropriate to impose liability on a real estate broker without a similar requirement of knowledge. Knowledge, or any reasonable notice, that the boundaries pointed out by the seller were incorrect is absent in this case, as the trial court found in its findings of fact. The following findings by the trial court are illustrative:

> There was no evidence on the property which suggested to [the broker] he should investigate the boundary lines further.

> There was nothing in the surrounding circumstances that would have put [the broker] ... on notice that there may have been something wrong with the property lines.

This broker was thus not the guarantor of the seller's representations. If the buyers had wanted full protection against potential defects or misrepresentations, they could have purchased appropriate title insurance. ...

While a broker must be alert to potential misrepresentations made by a seller, we decline to hold that a broker must guarantee every statement made by the seller. Nor, however, can a broker relay false information to a buyer without fear of liability. The trial court did not err in concluding as follows:

> A real estate broker must take reasonable steps to avoid disseminating false information to buyers. The broker is required to make reasonable efforts and use his [or her] professional expertise to confirm or refute information from a seller which he [or she] knows is pivotal to the buyer.

> A real estate broker must exercise the degree of care that a reasonably prudent broker would use under all of the circumstances.

In short, a real estate broker must act as a professional, and will be held to a standard of reasonable care. If a broker willfully or negligently conveys false information about real estate to a buyer, the broker is liable therefor. We decline, however, to turn this professional into a guarantor. Real estate agents and brokers are not liable for innocently and nonnegligently conveying a seller's misrepresentations to a buyer.

ISSUE TWO.

CONCLUSION. The broker did not breach the standard of care of a reasonably prudent broker.

In *Tennant*, the court found that the real estate broker failed to exercise due care to verify the "critical contingency" of an approved septic tank site on the property. When the broker asked the owner for evidence of an approved percolation site evaluation for the property, the owner produced two applications for perc hole permits and asked the broker to see if they had expired. The broker reported that the applications had expired and promised to renew them. The applications stated on their face that they were for adjoining 2½-acre parcels rather than the 6–acre parcel at issue. The broker neglected to read them, to renew them, or even to check on the site evaluation, even though the buyers had made an approved septic tank site an express condition of their offer. While the broker in *Tennant* acted without malice or fraudulent intent,

> she failed to take the simple steps within her area of expertise and responsibility which would have disclosed the absence of any health district approved site on the subject property. This failure constituted negligence as a matter of law which resulted in damages to the Tennants.

Tennant, at 707–08, 615 P.2d 1305.

In the present case, the improvements on the property were important to the buyers because they wanted to raise and ride horses. The broker saw markers for some of the boundaries when he walked the property with the seller, but could not locate all of the boundaries with certainty. Trees and other physical features on the land supported the sellers' representations regarding the boundaries, however, and the broker testified that the seller assured him that the improvements were inside the property line. The trial court accepted this testimony, as it was entitled to do as the fact finder in a bench trial, and expressly found that "there was absolutely nothing, I think, that would have put [the broker] ... on notice that there may have been something wrong with the property line that imposed a duty to ... do anything further than [he] did do in this case."

The trial court is sustainable in its view that, contrary to the broker in *Tennant*, the broker in this case had no notice that anything was wrong with the boundaries as represented by the sellers. While hindsight suggests that the broker would have done well to check on the alleged survey, there was no testimony that such a check was the prevailing practice in the real estate business. Moreover, natural and man-made boundaries reinforced the sellers' representations concerning the legal boundaries. Accordingly, the trial court did not err in finding and concluding that the broker in this case was not negligent.

Our resolution of these issues disposes of the other issues raised. The Court of Appeals decision overturning the trial court's decision on the broker's liability is incorrect.

Reversed.

PEARSON, C.J., and UTTER, BRACHTENBACH, CALLOW, DURHAM, JJ., and CUNNINGHAM, J. Pro Tem., concur.

DORE, Justice (dissenting).

Contrary to the majority, I believe that a broker should be liable for any material misrepresentation he or she makes which induces buyers to act to their detriment. Furthermore, even applying the majority's far more lax standard of care, I would find the broker liable in this case. Therefore, I dissent.

LIABILITY FOR "INNOCENT" MISREPRESENTATIONS

. . .

Brokers possess more knowledge than buyers about the attributes of the property to be sold, and innocent buyers should be able to rely on representations made by the broker. I would follow the increasing trend of state courts to impose liability on real estate brokers for any kind of misrepresentation. . . .

In this case, both the majority and I conclude that the broker made a material misrepresentation which induced the Hoffmans to purchase the land, and that as a result, the Hoffmans incurred significant damages. The broker represented the property line to be located some 20 feet from where it actually was; consequently the corral, cattle run and horse shed all had to be moved so as not to encroach on their neighbor's land. Even if the majority is correct and this misrepresentation was innocently, and not negligently, made—a conclusion I dispute—I would still hold the broker liable. Between innocent purchasers, who may justifiably rely on the broker's knowledge and expertise, and a broker, who is in a far better position to check the accuracy of any purported boundary lines, I believe the broker should be liable for any misrepresentation as to the boundary's location. Equity demands such a result.

THE TENNANT APPROACH

The majority cites *Tennant v. Lawton*, 26 Wash.App.701, 615 P.2d 1305 (1980) for the proposition that the rule of law should be "that the broker is liable because of material representations of the principal if he repeats them and knows, or reasonably should know, of their falsity." *Tennant*, at 706, 615 P.2d 1305. While I note in passing that this decision is in conflict with our earlier decision in *Lawson v. Vernon*, [38 Wash. 422, 80 P. 559 (1905),] I believe that even following the rule set forth in *Tennant*, the broker in this case should still be liable.

The broker in this case testified that Mr. Connall was emphatic about the boundary of his property and that an earlier survey had indicated that his property ended just to the east of where he built his fence. Report of Proceedings, at 167–68. Nevertheless, an expert witness testified that any such survey would be a public record, and that no survey had been made of this property. Report of Proceedings, at 25. While under the standard of care propounded by the majority, a reasonably prudent broker would not be required to verify the accuracy of Connall's comments by a detailed investigation of the survey that Connall believed had been completed, the broker should at least verify the existence of the survey. This he did not do, and this failure, even under the majority's standard of care, was a breach of the duty "to take reasonable steps to avoid disseminating to the buyer false information." *Tennant*, at 706, 615 P.2d 1305. Thus, even under the majority's more lax standard of care, the broker was negligent, and therefore, liable for the damages to the Hoffmans.

. . .

GOODLOE, J., concurs.

NOTES

1. What facts bearing on bad faith should the jury have considered on the Haymes v. Rogers remand? Since the broker's commission is typically tied to the sales price, should it not be presumed that the broker's negotiations on price are in the seller's best interest? Outside the five recurrent fact situations identified in Justice Udall's dissent, what facts could possibly rebut this presumption? Should the jury be permitted to consider the possibility that a broker, interested only in a commission, will favor a sure deal at a lower price over the risk of no deal at the listing price? Does and should the broker's fiduciary obligation to the seller change with the kind of listing agreement involved? For example, should a higher duty be imposed under an exclusive right to sell listing than under an exclusive agency or open listing?

The usual remedy for breach of fiduciary duty is to deprive the broker of the entire sales commission, ostensibly as a penalty to deter serious breaches of trust. Would it make more sense in borderline cases like *Haymes* to limit the seller to damages suffered from the breach? Compare Cogan v. Kidder, Mathews & Segner, Inc., 97 Wash.2d 658, 648 P.2d 875 (1982), in which the broker's failure to inform the seller that, acting as a dual agent, it also represented the buyer, was held to bar the broker from recovering the agreed-upon $19,000 commission, even though the nondisclosure caused the seller at most $660 damages.

2. *Self-Dealing.* The rules on broker self-dealing are fairly clear. A broker cannot, without the seller's informed consent, purchase the property himself, split a commission, or take a rebate from buyer or buyer's broker. See, for example, Ornamental and Structural Steel, Inc. v. BBG, Inc., 20 Ariz.App. 16, 509 P.2d 1053 (1973). Litigation frequently centers on the broker's duty of disclosure when he has some pre-existing business or family relationship with the buyer. The general rule is to require full disclosure, even if the broker does not stand to profit from the relationship, and even if disclosure would not alter the seller's decision to list or sell. See, for example, Thompson v. Hoagland, 100 N.J.Super. 478, 242 A.2d 642 (App.Div.1968).

3. *Broker as "Middleman."* The broker who functions only as an intermediary—bringing the parties together, but without discretion to negotiate terms or perform other services—can act for both the buyer and seller without being held to a fiduciary duty to either. According to one landmark case, "If A. is employed by B. to find him a purchaser for his house upon terms and conditions to be determined by B. when

he meets the purchasers, I can see nothing improper or inconsistent with any duty he owes B. for A. to accept an employment from C. to find one who will sell his house to C. upon terms which they may agree upon when they meet." Knauss v. Gottfried Krueger Brewing Co., 142 N.Y. 70, 75, 36 N.E. 867, ___ (1894). See also Batson v. Strehlow, 68 Cal.2d 662, 68 Cal.Rptr. 589, 441 P.2d 101 (1968). Was a middleman defense available under the facts of Haymes v. Rogers?

4. *Cooperating Brokers and Misled Buyers.* As Professor Grohman's article indicates, traditional doctrine which holds a selling broker to be the subagent of the listing broker, owing a fiduciary duty only to the seller, contradicts the expectations of typical buyers and sellers. According to the F.T.C. Staff Report described at page 32 above, "where two brokers were involved, 74 percent of the sellers and 71 percent of the buyers believed the cooperating broker (the broker working directly with the buyer) was, in some sense, 'representing' the buyer." Staff Report, page 22.

The rule treating the selling broker as the listing broker's subagent was affirmed in Stortroen v. Beneficial Finance Co. of Colorado, 736 P.2d 391 (Colo.1987). The court there rejected seller's claim that the selling broker was buyer's agent, and held that a notice of acceptance of the sales contract given by buyer to the broker bound the seller. The court stated that a contrary rule would open the door to finding that the broker was the dual agent of both parties, with the complications that such arrangements create. Moreover, the court ruled that the buyer could lose rights against the seller based on the broker's misrepresentations if the broker was no longer considered to be the seller's agent. The facts of the case were unusual in that it was the seller, not the buyer, who sought to treat the selling broker as the buyer's agent.

A few courts have rejected the general rule. The Alabama Supreme Court took this innovative approach in Cashion v. Ahmadi, 345 So.2d 268 (Ala.1977), where the buyer, on discovering a periodic water problem in the basement, abandoned the house and sued the seller and the two real estate firms that had brokered the transaction, claiming that all had known of the defect. Affirming the lower court judgment for the seller and the listing broker on strict *caveat emptor* grounds, the court reversed the judgment for the cooperating broker, holding that, as to him, a jury could find an agency relationship with the buyer and, consequently, a duty to disclose knowledge of the defect. Among the facts to be considered on remand were whether the broker's statements indicated a belief that he was primarily representing buyer or seller. For a thoughtful comment on *Cashion,* see Payne, Broker's Liability for Nondisclosure of Known Defects in Sale Property—Caveat Emptor Still Applies, 6 Real Est. L.J. 341 (1978).

In addition to the alternatives suggested in the Grohman excerpt, some states have passed legislation or implemented regulations requiring brokers to submit a disclosure statement to the parties indicating whether the broker will function as the agent of buyer or seller. See, e.g., N.Y. Real Prop. Law § 443. Will such disclosure be adequate to protect buyers?

See generally, Wolf & Jennings, Seller/Broker Liability In Multiple Listing Service Real Estate Sales: A Case For Uniform Disclosure, 20 Real Est.L.J. 22 (1991).

5. *Does Buyer Have Any Rights Against a Broker?* Courts generally hold that, whether or not there is an MLS arrangement, the listing broker owes no fiduciary duty to the buyer. See, e.g., Richard Brown Auction & Real Estate, Inc. v. Brown, 583 So.2d 1313 (Ala.1991) (no duty to disclose title defects); Andrie v. Chrystal–Anderson & Associates Realtors, Inc., 187 Mich.App. 333, 466 N.W.2d 393 (1991), appeal denied, 439 Mich. 899, 478 N.W.2d 652 (1991) (no duty to convey buyer's offer to seller). Many of the cases where the buyer seeks to hold the broker liable involve defects in the property.

Despite the general rule, courts have found liability by the listing broker to the buyer on various theories. One approach is to find that an agency relationship did exist between the broker and the buyer, creating a fiduciary relationship. This might occur in a Multiple Listing Service situation, as described in Note 4, or in other cases as well. See, e.g., Lewis v. Long & Foster Real Estate, Inc., 85 Md.App. 754, 584 A.2d 1325, cert. denied, 323 Md. 34, 591 A.2d 250 (1991) (question for jury whether agency relationship arose between buyer and broker).

Even where the broker is not found to be the buyer's agent, the broker may become liable to buyer under other theories. Under fraud doctrine, a broker will be liable to a buyer for concealment of material information, see, e.g., Roberts v. Estate of Barbagallo, 366 Pa.Super. 559, 531 A.2d 1125 (1987) (presence of hazardous urea formaldehyde foam insulation concealed by broker), or failure to disclose known information materially affecting the property which could not be discovered with ordinary diligence, see, e.g., Gray v. Boyle Investment Co., 803 S.W.2d 678 (Tenn.App.1990) (failure to disclose that property was undergoing foreclosure and only notice was published in trade papers which buyer is not expected to read). Legislation in California requires brokers involved in residential sales to "conduct a reasonably prudent competent and diligent visual inspection" and to disclose to the buyer facts uncovered by the investigation which materially affect the "value or desirability of the property." Cal.Civ. Code § 2079.

Other theories are available to the buyer who is unable to meet the requirements of common law fraud. One theory is to impose a constructive trust for buyer's benefit on any gains from broker self-dealing. See, for example, Harper v. Adametz, 142 Conn. 218, 113 A.2d 136 (1955). Another is to imply a private right of action for damages against a broker violating the disclosure and self-dealing provisions of the state broker licensing statute. See Sawyer Realty Group, Inc. v. Jarvis Corp., 89 Ill.2d 379, 59 Ill.Dec. 905, 432 N.E.2d 849 (1982). At least one court has found the broker liable to buyers under "a general duty not to negligently cause them harm." Gerard v. Peterson, 448 N.W.2d 699 (Iowa App.1989) (broker responded to buyers' question by stating that a mortgage contingency clause was not necessary in sales contract). After a deal has collapsed, a buyer may recover any earnest money held by the broker. See, e.g., Mader v. James, 546 P.2d 190 (Wyo.1976).

Hoffman v. Connall addresses the difficult problem of innocent misrepresentations by the broker. While courts agree that a knowing misrepresentation subjects a broker to liability, they differ on innocent misrepresentations. Did the *Hoffman* court strike the right balance? Will buyer be adequately compensated? Will such misrepresentations be more or less likely to occur if a court were to chose a different rule? How does the court view the role of the broker in a real estate transaction?

In addition to the articles cited in *Hoffman*, see generally Note, Potential Liability for Misrepresentations in Residential Real Estate Transactions: Let the Broker Beware, 16 Ford.Urb.L.J. 127 (1988).

6. *Net Listing Agreements.* Net listing agreements, in which the seller authorizes sale at a specified price, allowing the broker to retain as commission the difference between that price and the price at which the property is in fact sold, harbor serious potential for broker abuse. They have been regulated accordingly. A rule promulgated by New York's Secretary of State, 19 NYCRR 175.19 (1962), flatly prohibits net listing agreements, presumably to "prevent overreaching and unfair dealing." Express Realty Co. v. Zinn, 39 Misc.2d 733, 241 N.Y.S.2d 954, 956 (Nassau Cty.Dist.Ct.1963).

In states where they are permitted, net listing agreements inevitably complicate the already thorny conceptual issues raised by broker self-dealing. On the one hand, if the broker buys the land for herself, it can be argued that there has been no self-dealing because the broker is only capturing the land's surplus value, which she would have received in any event had the land been sold to an unrelated person. On the other hand, it is difficult to rest liability on the fact that the broker lured the seller into a net listing agreement: no fiduciary duties can precede the listing agreement because, until the agreement is made, no principal-agent relationship exists between the seller and the broker. Judicial efforts to escape this conundrum have not been entirely successful. Compare Allen v. Dailey, 92 Cal.App. 308, 268 P. 404 (1928), with Loughlin v. Idora Realty Co., 259 Cal.App.2d 619, 66 Cal.Rptr. 747 (1st Dist.1968).

II. PERFORMING THE CONTRACT

A. RISK OF LOSS

SKELLY OIL CO. v. ASHMORE, Supreme Court of Missouri, 1963, 365 S.W.2d 582, 587, HYDE, J: It is stated in 3 American Law of Property, § 11.30, p. 90, that in the circumstances here presented at least five different views have been advanced for allocating the burden of fortuitous loss between vendor and purchaser of real estate. We summarize those mentioned: (1) The view first enunciated in Paine v. Meller (Ch. 1801, 6 Ves.Jr. 349, 31 Eng. Reprint 1088, 1089) is said to be the most widely accepted; holding that from the time of the contract of sale of real estate the burden of fortuitous loss was on the purchaser even though the vendor retained possession. (2) The loss is on the vendor until legal title is conveyed, although the purchaser is in possession, stated to be a strong minority. (3) The burden of loss should be on the vendor until the time agreed upon for conveying the legal title, and thereafter on the purchaser unless the vendor be in such default as to preclude specific performance, not recognized in the decisions. (4) The burden of the loss should be on the party in possession, whether vendor or purchaser, so considered by some courts. (5) The burden of loss should be on the vendor unless there is something in the contract or in the relation of the parties from which the court can infer a different intention, stating "this rather vague test" has not received any avowed judicial acceptance, although it is not inconsistent with jurisdictions holding the loss is on the vendor until conveyance or jurisdictions adopting the possession test.

SANFORD v. BREIDENBACH

Court of Appeals of Ohio, 1960.
111 Ohio App. 474, 15 O.O.2d 179, 173 N.E.2d 702.

HUNSICKER, J. Three appeals, all arising from the same judgment below, have been submitted on the same briefs and arguments; the details of which are hereinafter set out at length.

On January 14, 1959, James R. Sanford and Bianchi R. Sanford, his wife, herein known as "Sanford," agreed in writing to sell to Frederic (herein impleaded as "Frederick") R. Breidenbach, herein known as "Breidenbach," certain lands in the village of Hudson, Summit County, Ohio, upon which lands was an 8-room, 1½ story, house and separate outbuilding. The agreed purchase price was $26,000. According to the terms of the contract, possession of the premises was to be delivered on transfer of the title, although Breidenbach did receive two keys to the house prior to its destruction by fire. He did enter the house with certain others, preparatory to having the heating system changed from oil heat to gas, to plan the location of furniture, and to show the new home to friends. Breidenbach also checked the oil tank to see if there was fuel to heat the house.

The written contract to purchase these premises had, on the reverse side thereof, the following provisions:

"The following paragraphs are an essential part of the contract on the reverse side hereof.

"January 14, 1959.

"1. A proper legal agreement signed by all owners concerned shall be furnished by the sellers giving permanent [*sic*] permission to use of the present septic system by the purchasers and their successors and assigns.

"2. It is understood that legal agreements covering driveway easement, easement for water line, etc., are in effect covering the thirty-acre properties. Said agreements shall be submitted to the purchasers for their approval prior to deposit of funds in escrow."

The parties who had signed the contract on its face also signed these provisions at the end thereof.

On February 16, 1959, while the papers necessary to a transfer of title were being prepared, the 8-room house on the lands was totally destroyed by fire. Breidenbach immediately instructed the Evans Savings Association, that was to loan him a part of the money needed to buy the home, not to file the deed for record. This deed, transferring the premises from Sanford to Breidenbach, had been prepared and placed in escrow with the Evans Savings Association pending a title search.

When Breiderbach executed the contract of purchase, he secured from Northwestern Mutual Insurance Company a policy of insurance to protect him against loss in the event the 8-room house was destroyed by fire. The amount of this insurance was $22,000.

Sanford had maintained insurance on these premises in the sum of $20,000. The agent from whom Sanford purchased insurance, in accord with standing instructions from Sanford, renewed this insurance coverage on December 26, 1958. On learning that the premises were being sold, this agent, through his employee, cancelled this policy without authority from Sanford, and without notice to Sanford. There seems to be no great question herein that the terms of such policy were in full force and effect at the time of the fire.

On April 29, 1959, Sanford brought an action in the Common Pleas Court of Summit County, Ohio, against Breidenbach, Northwestern Mutual Insurance Company, and Hudson Village Real Estate Co., Inc. Breidenbach had deposited, with the real estate company, $12,000 as a partial payment for the premises. This sum has been, by arrangement of the parties, placed in escrow with a third party, and the real estate company is to all intents and purposes no longer involved herein. The principal relief sought by this action was specific performance of the contract to purchase the lands of Sanford.

Breidenbach, by way of cross-petition, brought Insurance Company of North America into the action by alleging that such company had insured the Sanford home against fire, and that such company should be made responsible for the loss suffered by Sanford, or, if the premises are decreed to be the property of Breidenbach, then his interest in the proceeds of the policy should be declared.

The Insurance Company of North America says, by way of answer, that it did, on December 26, 1958, renew the policy of insurance on these premises, but that, by agreement between the company and the insured, it was cancelled on January 26, 1959. It further alleged that Breidenbach never had any interest in such policy. As stated above, there seems to be no question now that this policy was in full force and effect at the time of the fire. The attempted cancellation of such policy was of no force or effect.

After a trial of the issues herein, the court determined that Sanford was not entitled to specific performance, but that he should recover from each insurance company for the loss of the premises.

The judgment against Northwestern Mutual Insurance Company is $11,523.81, being $22/42$ of the loss, and the judgment against Insurance Company of North America is $10,476.19, being $20/42$ of the loss. The court added the amounts of the two policies, and then proportioned the loss in accord with the ratio which each policy bears to such total.

. . .

We shall first direct our attention to the question of whether Sanford is entitled to specific performance, and shall therein consider whether Breidenbach was, under the doctrine of equitable conversion, the owner of the premises at the time the house was destroyed by fire. After a disposition of those questions, we shall then pass to the matter of the liability of the two insurance companies.

"A decree for the specific performance of a contract is not a matter of right, but of grace, granted on equitable principles, and rests in the sound discretion of the court." 37 Ohio Jurisprudence, Specific Performance, Section 20, at pp. 24 and 25, and authorities there cited.

The rule above set out is so well known that no authorities need be cited, and it is such rule that must be applied in the instant case. We have a contract herein for the sale and purchase of real property, which made definite mention of a septic tank easement. The easement is, by the language used by the parties, an essential part of the contract. At the time of trial, August 3, 1959, a satisfactory septic tank easement had not been submitted to the purchaser, Breidenbach. The septic tank agreement submitted in May, 1959, provided that under certain conditions the right to use this facility terminated, whereas the provision of the contract made no such exception.

It is apparent, therefore, that at the time when specific performance was sought in the trial court, one of the material parts of the agreement had not been complied with, and hence we had an uncompleted contract.

There are many cases where specific performance has been granted, even though there has been a failure to perform on the part of the one seeking to enforce the contract; yet the general rule is stated in 4 Pomeroy's Equity Jurisprudence, 1050, Section 1407, to be as follows:

"The doctrine is fundamental that either of the parties seeking a specific performance against the other must show, as a condition precedent to his obtaining the remedy, that he has done or offered to do, or is then ready and willing to do, all the essential and material acts required of him by the agreement at the time of commencing the suit, and also that he is ready and willing to do all such acts as shall be required of him in the specific execution of the contract according to its terms. . . ."

Some of the authorities have determined that literal and exact performance is not always necessary; but in the instant case we are dealing with real property, and when a deed is given in pursuance of a contract, there is a merger of the agreement into the deed, and an action cannot thereafter be maintained on such contract.

We therefore determine that specific performance cannot be decreed under the facts of this case.

Sanford insists that, even though specific performance may not lie, Breidenbach is to be considered in equity the owner of the premises; and, under the doctrine of equitable conversion, the loss, if any has ensued as a result of the destruction of the house by fire, must be placed upon Breidenbach and his insurer, Northwestern Mutual Insurance Company.

. . .

In general, the rule under the doctrine of equitable conversion is that a contract to sell real property vests the equitable ownership of the property in the purchaser; and thus, where there is any loss by a destruction of the property through casualty during the pendency of the contract (neither party being guilty of causing the destruction), such loss must be borne by the purchaser.

. . .

The better rule in cases such as that now before us, we believe, is that equitable conversion by the purchaser, in a contract to convey real property, does become effective in those cases in which the vendor has fulfilled all conditions and is entitled to enforce specific performance, and the parties, by their contract, intend that title shall pass to the vendee upon the signing of the contract of purchase. The case before us does not meet any of these requirements.

In 4 Pomeroy's Equity Jurisprudence (5 Ed.), Section 1161a, the author, quoting from "Chafee and Simpson, Cases on Equity," gives five rules concerning the risk of loss in contracts for the sale of real estate.

One of such rules, which we believe sustains our position herein, is stated by the author as follows:

" 'That the risk of loss should be on the vendor until the time agreed upon for the conveyance of the legal title, and thereafter on the purchaser, unless the vendor is then in such default as to be unable specifically to enforce the contract.' "

It is hence our judgment that, since Sanford could not specifically enforce the contract of sale, and there was no intention expressed in the contract of purchase that the risk of loss should be on the vendee when the contract was executed by the parties, there is no basis to claim that equitable conversion existed, thereby placing the burden of loss by fire upon Breidenbach.

We now pass to the question of the liability of the respective insurance companies. As we have heretofore stated, Sanford had fire loss coverage in the amount of $20,000, with Insurance Company of North America as the insurer; Breidenbach, in order to protect whatever interest he had in such premises, secured a policy with a fire loss coverage of $22,000 with Northwestern Mutual Insurance Company.

It is our heretofore stated judgment that the policy of Insurance Company of North America is a valid and subsisting contract to indemnify Sanford for the loss he might sustain, if, as a result of fire, the house described in the policy was destroyed. This contract of insurance was not cancelled by the unilateral action of the agent for Insurance Company of North America.

At the time of the loss, Sanford was the owner of the premises, and hence the risk of loss must, in this case, fall upon him. With this view of the matter, it follows naturally that his insurer must respond under the terms of the policy for the face amount thereof.

Since we have determined that Sanford and not Breidenbach was the owner of the premises at the time of the fire, what, if any, interest did Breidenbach have in these premises?

It is true that he could have waived any defect in the title or a failure to give a septic tank agreement and insisted that the contract of sale be completed by a delivery to him of a deed to the lands. He did not, however, choose this course of action, but, since the subject matter of the contract was destroyed, he refused to accept delivery of a deed to the land. We have said, in effect, that he had a legal right to take this position.

Up to the moment when Breidenbach refused to complete the contract of purchase, he had an insurable interest in the premises. The contract of insurance with Northwestern Mutual Insurance Company insured Breidenbach and his legal representatives for loss by fire and other casualty; it did not insure Sanford or any other person except those "named in the policy." This policy which Breidenbach purchased was for his protection in the event he suffered a loss. Breidenbach did not suffer a loss: first, because all of the money he deposited in escrow, as a part of the purchase price for the premises, has been, or will be, returned to him under an agreement to that effect, made by the parties and Hudson Village Real Estate Company, Inc., the realtor herein; and, second, because by the judgment of this court he is not required to perform his contract. Inasmuch as Breidenbach suffered no indemnifiable loss in this matter, his insurer need not respond by way of money payment under the policy of insurance.

We do not believe that Section 3929.26, Revised Code, which covers the situation where there is more than one policy of insurance on the same property, is applicable to the facts of this case.

There can be no apportionment of loss between insurers in this case, because there was no loss applicable to an insurable interest held by Breidenbach which inured to the benefit of Sanford. The interest of Breidenbach in the property, we have indicated above, ceased, or was not effective, at the time of the loss; hence the insurance ended at the same moment. There being no loss to Breidenbach, and no interest of Sanford to be protected by the Northwestern Mutual Insurance Company policy, there can be no pro rata division of the proceeds of that policy.

We therefore determine herein, as to cause No. 4976, that specific performance must be denied and the petition dismissed, at the costs of the appellant.

In case No. 4970, the judgment entered against Northwestern Mutual Insurance Company is reversed and held for naught, and the appellant therein may go hence with its costs.

As to case No. 4977, which we consider herein as an appeal on questions of law only, we modify the judgment entered on December 15, 1959, by finding that Insurance Company of North America shall pay to Sanford, by reason of the destruction of the dwelling house situated on the premises described in the petition filed in the trial court, the sum of $20,000, with interest at the rate of 6% per annum from March 16, 1959.

Judgments accordingly.

DOYLE, P.J., and GRIFFITH, J., concur.

NOTES

1. Sanford v. Breidenbach explored three factors shaping the contemporary land sale contract: conditions, remedies and risk of loss. The factors are interrelated. For example, courts are reluctant to order specific performance of heavily conditioned contracts. And, as

the number and flexibility of conditions increase, and the buyer's chances of getting specific performance decrease, the argument for equitable conversion also diminishes and, with it, the argument that buyer should bear the risk of loss from fortuitous destruction.

Sanford also touched on a fourth factor shaping the land sale contract: the statute of frauds. The statute of frauds is closely connected to the other three factors. For example, if a contract only barely complies with the statute of frauds and is not complete in all material respects, courts will often refuse to specifically enforce it. Thus, in Phillips v. Johnson, 266 Or. 544, 514 P.2d 1337 (1973), the Oregon Supreme Court upheld the trial court's specific enforcement of an earnest money receipt even though questions existed concerning the accuracy with which the instrument described the parcel to be conveyed and whether the instrument was anything more than an "agreement to agree." The court held, however, that the terms by which seller agreed to finance the purchase were too ambiguous to be specifically enforced. The court further held that since the instrument gave buyer an election to purchase outright for cash, the contract could be enforced on the condition that buyer made this election.

For excellent practical overviews of the elements of a residential land sale contract, see Yzenbaard, Drafting the Residential Contract of Sale, 9 Wm. Mitchell L.Rev. 37 (1983); Scheid, Buying Blackacre: Form Contracts and Prudent Provisions, 23 John Marshall L.Rev. 15 (1989).

2. *Allocation of Risk of Loss.* Equitable conversion, though it has suffered substantial inroads, continues to represent the majority rule in the United States for allocating risk of loss from destruction during the executory period. The rule may have made some practical sense under early, agrarian conditions when land, not buildings, was presumed to be the real object of any sale. Fortuitous destruction of the improvements would not excuse the buyer from performance for he would still get what he bargained for.

There is a growing trend in the United States today to replace the rule of equitable conversion with a rule that allocates risk of loss to the party—whether seller or buyer—who is in possession at the time the premises are destroyed. The technical rationale for this newer, minority rule is almost as formalistic as the rationale for the majority rule: "the purchaser in possession is substantial owner of the property and should bear the burdens of ownership, while the purchaser out of possession is not substantial owner." 3 American Law of Property § 11.30 (A.J. Casner, ed. 1952). The better reason for the minority rule is that the party in possession is best placed to guard against the hazards of destruction, to insure the premises, and to conserve any evidence bearing on destruction.

The most striking aspect of both the majority and minority rules is that there should be any need for them at all. They are rules of implication, not rules of law, and can be easily altered by contract terms expressly allocating the risk of loss. ("Buyer shall not be obligated to perform if, during the executory period and before Buyer takes possession, the premises are substantially or entirely destroyed by natural causes or if, during the executory period, and without regard to whether Buyer is in possession, the premises are substantially or entirely taken by eminent domain.") Since buyer and seller can shift the risk of loss in their contract, and can insure against the risk, the question to consider in devising a rule today is whether, in the usual case, buyer or seller is better placed to raise risk of loss as a bargaining point and to obtain casualty coverage. Why do you suppose residential buyers and sellers, and their lawyers and brokers, are so reluctant to address and resolve the question of executory period losses? Even if the issue is raised, will the drafted language be adequate to express the parties' intent? See Bryant v. Willison Real Estate Co., 177 W.Va. 120, 350 S.E.2d 748 (1986) (clause stating that "the owner is responsible for said property until the Deed has been delivered to said purchaser" placed risk on seller despite "as is" clause and provision requiring the buyer to insure). See generally, McDowell, Insurable Interest in Property Revisited, 17 Cap.U.L.Rev. 165 (1988).

For background on equitable conversion and allocation of risk of loss during the executory interval, see Dunham, Vendor's Obligation as to Fitness of Land for a Particular Purpose, 37 Minn.L.Rev. 108 (1953); Hume, Real Estate Contracts and the Doctrine of Equitable Conversion in Washington: Dispelling the Ashford Cloud, 7 U. Puget Sound L.Rev. 233 (1984); Note, Equitable Conversion and its Effect on Risk of Loss in Executory Contracts for the Sale of Real Property, 22 Drake L.Rev. 626 (1973); Lewis & Reeves, How the Doctrine of Equitable Conversion Affects Land Sale Contract Forfeitures, 3 Real Est.L.J. 249 (1975).

3. *U.V.P.R.A.* The Uniform Vendors and Purchasers Risk Act alters the traditional rule by shifting the risk of loss from destruction or condemnation from seller to buyer only if the buyer has taken possession or title. If the reason behind assigning the risk of loss to the buyer in possession is that he is best placed to guard against hazards, to insure, and to conserve evidence bearing on destruction, does it not follow that seller should bear the risk of loss when *she* is in possession, even though the buyer has title? Or is the reasoning that, having taken possession or title, the buyer is too far committed to the transaction to be allowed to back out because of fortuitous destruction? Can the U.V.P.R.A. rule be easily applied? Had "possession" passed in Sanford v. Breidenbach? See also Caulfield v. Improved Risk Mutuals, Inc., 66 N.Y.2d 793, 497 N.Y.S.2d 903, 488 N.E.2d 833 (1985) (risk of loss passed when deed was placed in escrow).

The brain child of Professor Samuel Williston, the U.V.P.R.A. was promulgated by the National Conference of Commissioners on Uniform State Laws in 1935. At last count, the Act has been adopted in twelve states: California (Civ.Code § 1662); Hawaii (Rev.Stat. § 508–1); Illinois (Ann.Stat. ch. 29, §§ 8.1–8.3); Michigan (Comp.Laws Ann. §§ 565.-701–565.703); Nevada (Nev.Rev.Stats. 113.030–113.050); New York (Gen.Oblig.Law § 5–1311); North Carolina (Gen.Stat. §§ 39–37 through

39–39); Oklahoma (Stat.Ann. tit. 16 §§ 201–203); Oregon (Rev.Stat. §§ 93.290–93.300); South Dakota (Comp.Laws Ann. §§ 43–26–5 through 43–26–8); Texas (VTCA Property Code § 5.007); Wisconsin (Stat.Ann. § 706.12).

With three exceptions, these statutes almost literally track the language of the original Act. The Illinois version differs in one detail— assigning special consequence to passage of title through escrow. The New York Act makes two changes. It expressly provides that its terms are not intended to deprive the seller or buyer of any right to recover damages against the other for breach of contract occurring prior to the destruction or condemnation. Second, it provides that if buyer has taken neither possession nor title, and an "immaterial part" is destroyed or taken, neither seller nor buyer "is thereby deprived of the right to enforce the contract; but there shall be, to the extent of the destruction or taking, an abatement of the purchase price." Eminent domain takings are not covered by the North Carolina version of the statute.

4. *U.L.T.A.* The Uniform Land Transactions Act, approved in 1975 by the National Conference of Commissioners on Uniform State Laws, represents a comprehensive effort to harmonize, simplify and modernize state law governing land transactions. The U.L.T.A. regulates contract conditions, remedies and formalities (Article 2) and secured transactions (Article 3). The U.L.T.A. is frankly modeled on the Uniform Commercial Code. However, the U.L.T.A. has not had the enthusiastic reception enjoyed by the U.C.C. No jurisdiction has adopted the U.L.T.A. Recognizing the difficulties with the statute, in 1985 the National Conference of Commissioners on Uniform State Laws promulgated a new statute, the Uniform Land Security Interest Act, which is essentially Article 3 of U.L.T.A. The recent emphasis of the National Conference has been on the adoption of the U.L.S.I.A. rather than the U.L.T.A Nevertheless, the U.L.T.A. has had some influence on the courts. See, e.g., Kuhn v. Spatial Designs, Inc., at page 126. For an analysis of some of the problems of the U.L.T.A., see Bruce, Mortgage Law Reform Under the Uniform Land Transactions Act, 64 Geo.L.J. 1245 (1976). On the U.L.S.I.A., see Platt, The Uniform Land Security Interest Act: Vehicle For Reform of Oregon Secured Transaction Law, 69 Or.L.Rev. 847 (1990).

U.L.T.A. § 2–406, dealing with destruction of premises, modifies the approach taken by the U.V.P.R.A. Section 2–406(c)(2) adopts the Illinois rule on sales closed through escrow, and section 2–406(b)(2)(i) incorporates the New York approach to abatement of purchase price for nonmaterial diminutions in value.

5. *Allocation of Insurance Proceeds Between Buyer and Seller.* American courts, which have widely followed the English rule of equitable conversion for allocating risk of loss during the executory interval, have not followed the English position on a related question: Who is entitled to the proceeds paid on the seller's insurance policy?

The English rule, formulated in Rayner v. Preston, 18 Ch.Div. 1 (1881), is that the seller is entitled to retain the proceeds free of any claim by the buyer. American courts generally hold that the buyer is entitled to the insurance proceeds, chiefly to avoid giving the seller a windfall (the full purchase price plus the full insurance proceeds). See, for example, Berlier v. George, 94 N.M. 134, 607 P.2d 1152 (1980). Moreover, the proceeds have been held transferrable to the buyer despite a prohibition in the insurance contract against assignment. See, e.g., Smith v. Buege, 182 W.Va. 204, 387 S.E.2d 109 (1989). It would appear to follow under the American approach that if a state adopts the minority rule on risk of loss, and as a consequence allocates that risk to seller rather than to buyer, the seller will be entitled to retain the insurance proceeds. See generally, West Bend Mutual Insurance Co. v. Salemi, 158 Ill.App.3d 241, 110 Ill.Dec. 608, 511 N.E.2d 785 (1978) (allowing seller to proceed against buyer's insurer where buyer agreed to insure for seller's benefit).

The English rule rests on the perception that the insurance policy is strictly a personal contract between the seller and her insurer, and that its benefits do not pass with the land into the buyer's hands. American courts justify their position on three closely connected grounds: that the insurance proceeds are held by the seller in trust for the purchaser; that since, under equitable conversion, the buyer is the equitable owner of the land, he should also be considered the equitable owner of the insurance proceeds which stand in place of the land; and that since insurance is customarily considered to be for the benefit of the property rather than the person insured, the proceeds should go with the land. 3 American Law of Property § 11.31 (A.J. Casner, ed. 1952).

B. STATUTE OF FRAUDS
BALILES v. CITIES SERVICE CO.
Supreme Court of Tennessee, 1979.
578 S.W.2d 621.

COOPER, Justice.

This is an action for specific performance of a contract for the sale of real property or, in the alternative, for damages for its breach. The chancellor decreed specific performance on completion of a condition precedent. The Court of Appeals reversed the chancellor's decree and dismissed the action.

Certiorari was granted to review the determination by the Court of Appeals that the written memorandum of an agreement to sell real estate was not sufficient to comply with the statute of frauds (T.C.A. § 23–201(4)); and that neither the doctrine of part performance nor estoppel was effective to take the transaction out of the statute of frauds.

In July 1974, the respondent Cities Service Company orally agreed to sell one of its employees, Dewey M. Newman, Jr., lots 99 and 100 in the Cherokee Hills Subdivision. It became necessary for Mr. Newman to borrow money from the local bank to cover costs of the construction planned for lots 99 and 100. An official of the bank requested a letter from respondents setting forth its commitment to sell lots 99 and 100 to Mr. Newman. On July 23, 1974, respondent sent the following letter to the bank, addressed to Mr. Newman:

> Cities Service Company has agreed to sell to you lots 99 and 100 in Cherokee Hills for residential purposes.
>
> As soon as residences are well under construction deeds to these lots will be delivered to you.

On receipt of the letter, the bank loaned Mr. Newman $5,000.00. Mr. Newman then began construction of a residence on lot 100. He completed the foundation and the outer walls of the ground-level basement before encountering financial difficulties.

In the summer of 1975, being in financial difficulty and realizing that he had no chance to build a second house, Mr. Newman went to respondent's offices and released lot 99 to respondent. It also appears that he requested a deed to lot 100, but was refused "until the house was in the dry."

On August 25, 1975, Mr. Newman assigned his interest in lots 99 and 100 to petitioner, Billy D. Baliles, for $6,500.00, the approximate value of the labor and materials expended in improving lot 100.

Petitioner wrote respondent on December 14, 1975, informing it that he had acquired Mr. Newman's interest in lot 100. By letter, dated December 16, 1975, respondent took the position that the agreement between it and Mr. Newman was not assignable.

Thereafter petitioner filed a complaint in the Chancery Court of Polk County, Tennessee, seeking specific performance of the agreement between respondent and Mr. Newman or, in the alternative, damages for its breach.

Cities Service Company defended the action on the grounds (1) the written memorandum signed by respondent was not sufficient to comply with the statute of frauds; (2) the agreement was not assignable by Mr. Newman to a non-employee; and (3) that petitioner was not entitled to a deed to lot 100 since the condition precedent of having the residence "well under construction" had not been met.

The chancellor found the memorandum of the agreement for the sale of lots 99 and 100 met the requirements of the statute of frauds. He further found that the assignment by Mr. Newman of his rights in lot 100 under the contract to petitioner was valid and would be enforceable when the residence on lot 100 was "well under construction"—which the chancellor concluded to be when the residence was "under roof." The chancellor then ordered respondent to execute a deed to petitioner for lot 100 when the residence was put "under roof."

The chancellor also found that the assignment by Mr. Newman to petitioner of his rights to lot 99 was ineffectual, as Mr. Newman had returned that lot to defendant before the assignment was executed.

Respondent appealed from that part of the chancellor's decree that affected lot 100. The Court of Appeals reversed the chancellor, holding that the memorandum of the agreement between respondent and Mr. Newman does not comply with the requirements of the statute of frauds. The Court of Appeals further held that part performance would not take the contract in question out of the operation of the statute of frauds, and that plaintiff could not rely upon the doctrine of equitable estoppel under the circumstances of this case. The Court of Appeals also noted that even if the agreement to sell lot 100 was not within the statute of frauds the petitioner was not entitled to a deed to the property because a condition precedent to receiving a deed—that is, to have the residence under roof—had not been met.

The applicable section of the statute of frauds, T.C.A. § 23–201,[a] provides that:

> No action shall be brought: ... (4) upon a contract for the sale of lands ... [u]nless the promise or agreement upon which such action shall be brought or some memorandum or note thereof, shall be in writing, and signed by the party to be charged therewith, or some other person by him thereunto lawfully authorized.

The purpose of the statute of frauds "is to reduce contracts to a certainty, in order to avoid perjury on the one hand and fraud on the other." Price v. Tennessee Products & Chemical Corporation, 53 Tenn. App. 624, 385 S.W.2d 301 (1964). Consequently, to comply with the statute of frauds, a memorandum of an agreement to sell must show, with reasonable certainty, the estate intended to be sold.

> Where the instrument is so drawn that upon its face it refers necessarily to some existing tract of land, and its terms can be applied to that one tract only, parol evidence may be employed to show where the tract so mentioned is located. But, where the description employed is one that must necessarily apply with equal exactness to any one of an indefinite number of tracts, parol evidence is not admissible to show that the parties intended to designate a particular tract by the description. Dobson v. Litton, 45 Tenn. 616. See also Dry Goods Co. v. Hill, 135 Tenn. 60, 185 S.W. 723 (1916).

The memorandum relied on by petitioner as written evidence of the agreement to sell, and which is set out above, does not locate the Cherokee Hills Subdivision by county or state. Neither does it contain any information which would tend to locate the subdivision. Further, the description of the specific property that is the subject of the oral agreement is by lot numbers only. There is no recorded plat to show

---

a. Now codified at Tenn.Code Ann. § 29–2–101.

the location of lot 100 within the subdivision, nor its dimensions or calls.

In Kirshner v. Feigenbaum, 180 Tenn. 476, 176 S.W.2d 806 (1944), it is pointed out that a memorandum of an agreement for the transfer of an interest in real property which fails to designate the county and state where the land is located is insufficient under the statute of frauds, unless the description of the property as set out in the memorandum is otherwise so definite and exclusive that "it does not reasonably appear that the description given would fit equally any other tract, then parol proof is admissible to locate and designate the tract intended."

We think it evident, and we agree with the Court of Appeals, that the description in the memorandum does not describe the tract of land with reasonable certainty, that the description is of no material aid in locating the property that is the subject of the agreement to sell, and consequently does not satisfy the requirements of the statute of frauds.

Petitioner insists that even though the memorandum of the agreement to sell is insufficient to meet the requirements of the statute of frauds, the agreement should be enforced on the basis of part performance, or by the application of the doctrine of estoppel.

The appellate courts of this state consistently have refused to enforce an oral contract for the sale of land on the basis of part performance alone. And, it is now a rule of property in this state that part performance of a parol contract for the sale of land will not take the agreement out of the statute of frauds. The harshness of this rule has been mitigated by the application of the doctrine of equitable estoppel in exceptional cases where to enforce the statute of frauds would make it an instrument of hardship and oppression, verging on actual fraud.

> "Equitable estoppel, in the modern sense, arises from the 'conduct' of the party, using that word in its broadest meaning, as including his spoken or written words, his positive acts, and his silence or negative omission to do any thing. Its foundation is justice and good conscience. Its object is to prevent the unconscientious and inequitable assertion or enforcement of claims or rights which might have existed, or been enforceable by other rules of law, unless prevented by an estoppel; and its practical effect is, from motives of equity and fair dealing, to create and vest opposing rights in the party who obtains the benefit of the estoppel." Evans v. Belmont Land Co., 92 Tenn. 348, 365, 21 S.W. 670, 673–674 (1893).

We think this is such a case. In dealing with Mr. Newman, respondent not only placed him in possession and permitted him to construct improvements on lot 100, but took affirmative action thereafter to aid Mr. Newman to secure a $5,000.00 loan—this latter action being taken with the knowledge that the proceeds of the loan were to be used in the construction of a dwelling on lot 100. In the face of this affirmative action by respondent, to allow it to set up the statute of frauds as bar to enforcement of the agreement to sell lot 100 to Mr. Newman, and thus secure to itself the improvements on lot 100 would be a gross injustice and moral fraud on Mr. Newman.

Petitioner had no direct dealings with respondent relative to lot 100, except to give notice of the assignment executed by Mr. Newman. However, by virtue of the assignment, petitioner acquired all the rights and remedies possessed by Mr. Newman under the agreement to sell, and took the contract subject to the same restrictions, limitations, and defenses as it had in the hands of Mr. Newman. It follows that since it is unconscionable to allow respondent to set up the statute of frauds as a bar to enforcement of the agreement to sell lot 100 to Mr. Newman, it would be unconscionable to permit the defense to be interposed in this action brought by Mr. Newman.

Respondent argues that the agreement to sell lot 100 was not assignable—that it was a special kind of contract entered into only with respondent's employees. We find nothing in the record to indicate that the agreement was not assignable. To the contrary, the representative of respondent who made the agreement testified that there was nothing to prevent an employee from taking a lot, putting up a house, and then selling it to someone who was not an employee.

The Court of Appeals pointed out in its opinion that even if the agreement to sell lot 100 is enforceable, respondent [*sic*] is not now entitled to a deed to the property because a condition precedent to receiving a deed—that is, to have the residence under roof—has not been met. The chancellor also recognized that the condition precedent had not been met by petitioner at the time of trial of the cause. He also noted the practical difficulty, or dilemma, faced by petitioner in expending additional monies on the residence to place it under roof in the face of the insistence of respondent that Mr. Newman's rights in lot 100 were not assignable, and absent a judicial declaration of the efficacy of the agreement between Mr. Newman and respondent. In resolving this dilemma, the chancellor pointed out that the action brought by petitioner "conforms to a certain extent to a declaratory judgment." The chancellor then undertook to declare the rights of the parties in the agreement. He held the agreement to sell was enforceable, the assignment was valid, and that petitioner would be entitled to a deed to lot 100 when he had the residence under roof. We think the chancellor's findings were correct and that his declaration of petitioner's right to a deed to lot 100, when the condition precedent is met, was timely and proper.

The judgment of the Court of Appeals is reversed. The judgment of the chancellor is affirmed. Costs of the cause are adjudged against respondent.

FONES, BROCK, and HARBISON, JJ., and ALLISON B. HUMPHREYS, Special Judge, concur.

NOTES

1. Most American statutes of frauds are closely patterned after the original English Statute of Frauds, 29 Car. II c. 3 (1677), and require both that land sale contracts be in writing and signed by the parties and that deeds conveying an interest in land be in writing and signed by the grantor. Should the writing requirement for contracts be applied less stringently than the writing requirement for deeds? Deeds form links in a parcel's chain of title that must be relied upon to identify the parcel and its owner decades, and even centuries, later, when all witnesses to the transaction have disappeared and a prospective buyer is seeking to determine whether his seller has good title. Sales contracts, by contrast, have short lives—typically 45 or 60 days at most—and are rarely recorded. Once the executory period expires, they are not relied on by anyone for any purpose. Cf. McFadden, Oral Transfers of Land in Illinois, 1988 U.Ill.L.Rev. 667 (arguing for recognition of oral conveyances and maintaining that recording laws could adequately protect third parties).

2. *Signed Writing.* While a formally executed contract of sale meets the requirements of the statute of frauds, other pieces of paper generated during the sales process may also suffice. In Hessenthaler v. Farzin, 388 Pa.Super.37, 564 A.2d 990 (1989), the sellers sent a mailgram accepting a sales contract which had been executed by the purchasers. The court permitted the purchasers to specifically enforce the contract even though there was no signature by the sellers. The court held that no particular form of a signature is required as long as there is reliable indication that the person intended to authenticate the writing. See also George W. Watkins Family v. Messenger, 115 Idaho 386, 766 P.2d 1267 (App.1988), affirmed, 118 Idaho 537, 797 P.2d 1385 (1990) (initials were adequate under the statute).

3. *Adequacy of Description.* *Baliles* lies somewhere between the two polar American views on the adequacy of descriptions in land sale contracts. At one pole, some courts treat contract descriptions far more liberally than deed descriptions, holding that a land sale contract will be enforced if it identifies the land to be conveyed to the exclusion of all other parcels. So long as the description offers some clue or key to identifying the land, parol evidence will be admitted to complete the identification. Thus, in Stachnik v. Winkel, 50 Mich.App. 316, 213 N.W.2d 434 (1973), reversed on other grounds, 394 Mich. 375, 230 N.W.2d 529 (1975), the court held that a contract for "your [seller's] property located in Glen Arbor Twp. Lee Lanau Co. situated on Wheeler Rd.," was sufficiently definite to comply with the statute of frauds. External evidence showed that this was the only property that the sellers owned in Lee Lanau County.

At the other extreme, a few courts insist that the contract description contain all of the detail required for deeds. Martin v. Seigel, 35 Wash.2d 223, 212 P.2d 107 (1949), represents this more stringent, minority position. The Washington Supreme Court there refused specific performance even though the contract identified the parcel by street address, city, county and state, and even though parol evidence further provided the parcel's lot and block numbers. The court subsequently extended the same harsh requirement to real estate brokers, holding that the statute of frauds barred a broker from recovering his commission under a listing agreement that described the property as the "O.H. Faulstich Farm, Route 1, Snohomish, Snohomish County, Wash." Heim v. Faulstich, 70 Wash.2d 688, 424 P.2d 1012 (1967). The court partially recanted its rigid view when it overruled *Heim* in House v. Erwin, 83 Wash.2d 898, 524 P.2d 911 (1974). The holding was, however, expressly limited to descriptions in listing agreements and did not overrule the standard as applied to contracts of sale.

4. *Part Performance.* Was *Baliles* correct to hold that part performance alone will not take an oral contract out of the statute of frauds? Many courts are less exacting. Some hold that the buyer's entry onto the parcel under an oral contract will suffice. Others require possession accompanied by some payment to the seller. Others require possession and the construction of valuable improvements. And still others require possession and proof that removal will cause irreparable injury. See 3 American Law of Property § 11.7 (A.J. Casner ed. 1952); Braunstein, Remedy, Reason, and the Statute of Frauds: A Critical Economic Analysis, 1989 Utah L.Rev. 383 (arguing that exceptions to statute are applied not because they provide satisfactory evidence of an agreement but because adherence to the statute in such cases would sanction economically wasteful behavior).

C. CONTRACT CONDITIONS

The typical land sale contract contains several conditions, some express, others implied, that must be met or waived for the sale to close. Conditions are essentially substitutes for information—information about the home finance market, the condition of title and of the premises and local government regulations. Conditions postpone contract performance to a point when that information can be obtained— through a lender's response to the loan application, a title report, a housing inspection, an environmental audit, and a land use review.

One persistent question is whether the prescribed conditions leave so many terms open that no enforceable contract has been formed. Failure to specify the financing terms, the condition of the premises and the land use restrictions that will be acceptable to the buyer may void the contract for indefiniteness under the applicable statute of frauds. See Anand v. Marple, 167 Ill.App.3d 918, 118 Ill.Dec. 826, 522 N.E.2d 281 (1988) (inadequately completed printed form was not proper contract). And, even if the statute's requirements are met, the conditional contract may be held too indefinite to support a specific performance decree for buyer or seller. Since conditions will characteristically be phrased in general terms, and their fulfillment left to the exclusive control of one of the parties, there is the added question of illusoriness or mutuality of obligation. Generally, the problem is small, for the concept of good faith goes far toward preventing reneging parties from using a financing, title or other condition as an excuse for nonperformance. In such cases, the court will examine the motives of the party relying on the condition. See Greer Properties, Inc. v. LaSalle National Bank, 874 F.2d 457 (7th Cir.1989) (court had to determine whether contract was canceled because of condition permitting seller to terminate if cost of removal of environmental contamination was "economically impracticable" or because seller could now obtain a higher price from another buyer).

The converse problem arises when the conditions have been drafted with excessive detail. A financing clause that specifies the acceptable interest rate to two decimal places and also itemizes points, loan fees, prepayment penalties, term and amortization will inevitably be hard to meet in every respect, giving the buyer considerable opportunity to renege for reasons totally unrelated to financing. Should good faith be required of the parties when the contract condition is overly narrow rather than overly broad? For a thoughtful review of these issues, see Note, Contingency Financing Clauses in Real Estate Sales Contracts in Georgia, 8 Ga.L.Rev. 186 (1973).

1. FINANCING

AIKEN, "SUBJECT TO FINANCING" CLAUSES IN INTERIM CONTRACTS FOR SALE OF REALTY *

43 Marquette Law Review 265–273 (1960).

Certainly there is nothing either new or particularly worrisome in the fact that a high percentage of real estate purchasers, especially over the last decade, and especially in residential transactions, have found it necessary to finance a substantial part of their purchases. What is both new and worrisome, from a legal standpoint, is that this vital provision of the interim contract has ordinarily received such cursory attention from the parties, their brokers, and, occasionally, their lawyers as well. Seldom, if ever, does the clause relating to the purchaser's financing requirements spell out more than a short suggestion of the various considerations involved in modern mortgage financing. Indeed, it is as common to see the simple phrase, "subject to financing", inserted randomly in the contract as it is to find any more definitive provision.

However ineptly the matter is phrased, however, its practical significance is inescapable: unless the intending purchaser can somehow raise a percentage of his purchase price on loan, using the property as security, the purchase and sale envisioned by the contract cannot conceivably be performed. In probably a majority of cases, only the scantiest investigation of the borrowing power of the purchaser has been conducted at the time of interim contract. With somewhat lesser frequency, but still quite commonly, there has been no current appraisal to determine the approximate security-value of the property. And—perhaps most universally of all—a vague set of unfounded preconceptions is the best available indication of the repayment capabilities of the prospective borrower.

What is, in consequence, very commonly unrealized by the parties (if not by the brokers) is that "financing" is a term of broad scope, involving a multitude of complexities. There are, for example, the following minimum considerations:

1.   What amount is sought to be borrowed?

2.   What repayment rate, extending over how long a period of time, is contemplated?

3.   What interest rate, and what initial "service" or "discount" charges will be acceptable?

4.   Is the contemplated loan to be "conventional", or are FHA or VA loan guarantee benefits to be sought?

5.   What special security-protection provisions (tax and insurance reserves, mortgage life insurance, mortgage repayment insurance, ordinary or special acceleration provisions, etc.) are acceptable, and are they to be deemed part of the specified repayment rate?

6.   By whose effort is such loan to be arranged and procured; if by the purchasers (with or without the broker's assistance), what potential sources of the money shall be applied to, and within what span of time?

7.   If a lender should indicate a willingness to make a mortgage loan, assuming that the interim contract specifies no minimum acceptable terms, may the purchaser refuse the offered loan on the ground that its terms are onerous, without violating the agreement (i.e., must the terms be "satisfactory to purchaser," "reasonably satisfactory to purchaser" or merely "reasonable")?

8.   What is the consequence of a prospective lender's withdrawal, after tentative commitment, from his agreement to loan, assuming that neither party to the interim contract foments such withdrawal?

To answer any of these important questions on the basis of an interim contract which merely recites that the transaction is "subject to financing" is to undertake an herculean feat of construction. Whenever it occurs, however, that one of the parties seeks to enforce the contract, and the other takes refuge in the indefinite financing "contingency", the only alternative to judicial construction of the clause is to declare the unenforceability of the sale, frequently in the face of an agreement that is in all other respects unmistakable in its provisions.

Cases may arise under such clauses, it is true, which are entirely too plain for argument. On the one hand, the "subject to financing" clause may spell out with uncommon attention to detail the particular financing requirements envisioned by the parties, specifically declare each element thereof as being "of the essence," and positively state that, unless each such element is satisfied, the agreement shall be null and void. Any litigable question arising under such a clause would necessarily be either a straight question of fact, or would arise under some aspect of the law of waiver or estoppel. On the other hand, regardless of the indefiniteness of the clause itself, it could occur that, after diligent inquiry, the purchaser would find it impossible to obtain any amount of financing from anyone on any terms whatever. In such cases, the only legal problem which can arise with respect to the clause is whether it should be construed to express a contingency at all, or whether it was simply inserted for some incidental purpose, not affecting the primary obligations to buy and sell.

These plain cases, however, are by no means usual. It may be wondered, therefore, why only a comparatively few cases involving the construction and effect of such clauses have reached our appellate courts. The answer is largely a practical one. From the seller's standpoint, his primary aim is ordinarily to convert his property into cash as quickly as possible. Any attempt to enforce the contract, as by declaring the down payment forfeit under the liquidated damage clause, or by suing for damages or for specific performance, would necessarily thwart that primary objective over a protracted period of time. Furthermore, the "demurrage" which may be expected to accumulate over the period of litigation (taxes, insurance, upkeep, lost rents, heating, etc.) is frequently so substantial as to over-shadow completely a small down payment. While such elements of sellers' damages may be recoverable in a proper form of action, the difficulties of collection of such a judgment are usually obvious.

From the buyer's standpoint in any but the plain cases, the trouble and expense of litigation, especially up to the appellate level, will ordinarily not be justified by a nominal amount of "earnest money," which is all the buyer can hope to recover. In close cases, faced with the distinct possibility of sending good money after bad, the buyer will most often be inclined to negotiate rather than to litigate a solution of the dispute.

The ultimate practical decision, however, is most often that of the broker. By the prevailing rule, his commission is earned when the interim contract is executed, regardless of whether the transaction is ever consummated. Whether or not the same rule obtains where the interim contract is itself subject to a contingency is a point that has not yet been clearly determined (though better reason would clearly suggest the negative); but, if the contingency can be successfully argued to have occurred, it seems clear that the commission has been earned. By the usual form of contract, the expenses and commission of the broker are given first claim against the earnest money deposit in the event of forfeiture. The result is that any litigation respecting the proper construction of the "subject to financing" clause will boil down, practically, to a quarrel between broker and buyer.

But practical considerations will ordinarily dissuade the broker from litigating such a question. In the first place, his client, the seller, will be inclined to take a dim view of such proceedings, because they involve the same practical handicaps to the seller's interests as were discussed above. In the second place, the broker is in no position to litigate the issue directly against the buyer. His claim for commission against the down payment is assertable only against the seller, who must, in turn, litigate the question against the buyer. Both of these circumstances will ordinarily be deemed to reflect so seriously upon the broker's business reputation as to deter him from recommending litigation or from claiming commission, if his listing contract remains in force.

The result is that the construction of the "subject to financing" clause is most frequently determined by negotiation rather than by litigation. So long as the real property market continues to enjoy brisk activity, it may be expected that a claimed buyer-default, arising from inability to finance or from different causes, will not be uniformly enforced by litigation. The alternative of prompt and equivalent resale is entirely too promising.

LIUZZA v. PANZER

Court of Appeal of Louisiana, Fourth Circuit, 1976.
333 So.2d 689.

GULOTTA, Judge.

Defendant-buyer appeals from a judgment in the sum of $3,750.00, representing the amount of defendant's deposit made in connection with the purchase of real property.

Plaintiff-seller and defendant-buyer entered into a buy and sell agreement for the sale of real property located in Hammond, Louisiana, at a price of $37,500.00. The agreement, dated April 27, 1973, was a standard real estate form contract and contained the usual provision that the sale was conditioned upon the ability of the purchaser to borrow $30,000.00 on the property at an interest rate not to exceed 9%. The agreement contained the additional provision that:

"Should purchaser or seller be unable to obtain the loan stipulated above within *60* days from acceptance hereof, this contract shall then become null and void and the broker is hereby authorized to return the purchaser's deposit in full. Commitment by lender to make loan subject to approval of title shall constitute obtaining of loan."

Both parties to the agreement were represented by realtors. The deposit was placed with plaintiff-seller's agent.

Following the agreement, defendant-buyer applied to the Pontchatoula Homestead for the $30,000.00 loan. However, the homestead appraised the property at $32,151.20, and would only lend defendant 80% of the appraisal price or approximately $25,000.00. Subsequent to the failure of the homestead to approve the $30,000.00 loan request, defendant, in a letter written to his real estate agent, suggested that the $37,500.00 purchase price be renegotiated and reduced to the sum of $35,000.00. Defendant-buyer's real estate broker, by letter, submitted the offer for renegotiation to the seller, who apparently orally accepted the offer.

The trial judge, in written reasons, concluded the litigants verbally agreed to the reduced purchase price and that defendant made no effort to obtain a loan at the newly agreed figure. Accordingly, the trial judge concluded that defendant breached the purchase agreement.

On appeal, defendant contends the trial judge erred in concluding that a valid modification of the original purchase agreement was entered into. According to defendant, agreements for the purchase and sale of real estate must be in writing. Therefore, defendant contends that since the written offer by the purchaser to renegotiate the sale at a reduced price was not accepted in writing, no valid contract was made for the purchase of the real property at the reduced price. We agree.

Our jurisprudence is well settled that agreements to buy and sell real estate must be in writing to be binding and enforceable. In Torrey v. Simon-Torrey, Inc., 307 So.2d 569 (La.1974), the Louisiana Supreme Court stated that the rule "allowing proof by parol evidence of a subsequent agreement to modify or to revoke a written agreement, is not applicable to a case in which the agreement is one required by law to be in writing". In the instant case, we conclude the written offer to purchase at a reduced price, verbally accepted by the seller, did not constitute a valid agreement to modify the original purchase agreement.

Based on his conclusion that defendant failed to make a good faith effort to obtain financing, the trial judge concluded that defendant breached the purchase agreement.

The agreement states that the contract shall become null and void in the event *the purchaser or seller* is unable to obtain the loan stipulated within 60 days from the date of the acceptance, i.e., April 27, 1973. Defendant's real estate broker testified that defendant made no attempt to arrange a loan at any financial institution other than Pontchatoula Homestead. Defendant also stated that he made no attempts to obtain further financing because he had been advised that lending institutions would not lend in excess of 80% of appraised value.

It is well settled that a provision making a sale of real property contingent upon the purchaser's obtaining a loan imposes a duty upon the purchaser to make a good faith application for the loan. Whether or not a party has acted in good faith depends on the facts and circumstances peculiar to each case.

In Brewster v. Yockey, 153 So.2d 489 (La.App. 4th Cir.1963), our court concluded that a purchaser's single verbal application to one homestead did not constitute a good faith attempt to obtain financing when another homestead was apparently ready, willing and able to make the loan. In the instant case as in *Brewster,* supra, there is evidence that financing was available from other lending agencies.

Mrs. Katie Wainwright, purchaser's real estate broker, testified that had defendant sought to obtain financing from other lending institutions, he could have borrowed the $30,000.00 from other "agencies". Wainwright stated that no other attempts to arrange financing were made because defendant did not care to proceed with the sale. This testimony was supported by Mr. Damien Kinchen, an expert in real estate appraisal who worked with Paul Powell, the listing agent for the seller and who testified that he could obtain the financing from a mortgage company, but was told by Powell that the Panzers had called off the sale.

However, in Katz v. Chatelain, 321 So.2d 802 (La.App.4th Cir.1975), we held that a purchaser's single application to a loan association constituted good faith where an appraisal was made by a central appraisal bureau and that appraisal was used by all of the homesteads in the place where the property was located, i.e., New Orleans. Under the circumstances in the Katz case, since all homesteads used the same appraisal, a denial of a loan by one homestead, based on that appraisal, necessarily would result in a denial of the loan by other homesteads. In the instant case, no evidence exists that Pontchatoula Homestead utilized the Central Appraisal Bureau in arriving at an appraisal figure.

We conclude, under the circumstances, as did the trial judge, that defendant did not make a good faith effort to obtain financing in accordance with the agreement.

Having so concluded, we turn to a determination of the seller's duty to obtain financing under the terms of the agreement. As previously mentioned, the agreement places responsibility on the *seller,* as well as the purchaser, to obtain the loan. However, in the instant case, seller, in oral argument, contends that because defendant repudiated and refused to comply with the terms of the purchase agreement, the seller was relieved of any obligation to attempt to obtain a loan in the stipulated amount, and that under the circumstances, any such attempt to secure financing would have been vain and useless. We agree.

On May 21, 1973, within 30 days of the date of the agreement, the purchaser, in a letter addressed to his real estate agent, advised of the homestead's failure to approve the loan in the sum of $30,000.00, and suggested a reduction of the purchase price to the sum of $35,000.00. This offer was communicated to seller's agent on May 24. According to seller's agent, the $35,000.00 offer was conveyed to the seller and orally accepted. The purchaser's agent testified that on May 31, she was advised by the defendant-purchaser that he would not purchase the property for any price in excess of the appraised sum of $32,151.20. Thereafter, the purchaser's agent, on May 31, 1973, in a letter addressed to seller's agent, enclosed a cancellation agreement. In that letter, purchaser's agent advised seller's agent of defendant's intention not to proceed any further with the sale. Defendant's expressed intention to withdraw from the sale relieved plaintiff of the responsibility of obtaining financing.

When one contracting party announces he will not honor his agreement, the other party is not required to tender performance since to do so would be vain and useless. Therefore, in accordance with the sanctions imposed by the purchase agreement, in the event of purchaser's breach, the seller is entitled to obtain forfeiture of the deposit.

We reject plaintiff's claim for attorneys' fees. No evidence was offered in support of this demand.

Because we find no error on the part of the trial judge when he concluded the purchaser failed to make a good faith effort to obtain a loan in the amount required by the agreement, defendant is not entitled to avail himself of any of the sanctions imposed by the agreement against the seller. It necessarily follows that the purchaser is not entitled to attorneys' fees or damages for inconvenience and mental anguish as claimed by him in a reconventional demand.

Accordingly, the judgment awarding plaintiff $3,750.00, the amount of the deposit, together with interest and costs, is affirmed.

Affirmed.

NOTES

1. *Indefiniteness, Illusoriness, and the Financing Condition.* Judicial treatment of the financing condition exemplifies current attitudes toward contract indefiniteness and illusoriness generally. Increasingly, indefiniteness is being resolved in terms of reasonableness, and illusoriness in terms of good faith. Courts will fill in incomplete financing clauses by looking to the circumstances surrounding the contract, including the prevailing money market conditions, to infer the parties' original intent. See, for example, Hunt v. Shamblin, 179 W.Va. 663, 371 S.E.2d 591 (1988). And, as in *Liuzza*, the contract will be saved from illusoriness by the implied requirement that the buyer diligently seek financing on the terms specified. See also, Grossman v. Melinda Lowell, Attorney at Law, P.A., 703 F.Supp. 282 (S.D.N.Y.1989) (language requiring "best efforts" to secure loan imposed an obligation to make more than a good faith effort).

It is not always easy to keep the two questions, indefiniteness and illusoriness, separate. For example, a financing clause that is detailed in other respects may fail to specify whether a mortgage prepayment penalty will be acceptable to the buyer. If, in shopping for a mortgage, the buyer discovers that all lenders require prepayment penalties, can he get out of the contract on the ground of indefiniteness? On the ground that he fulfilled his good faith obligation by seeking a mortgage on the contract terms? See Fry v. George Elkins Co., 162 Cal.App.2d 256, 327 P.2d 905 (2d Dist.1958). Note that the two grounds are strategically different. Failure of a condition after good faith efforts excuses only the buyer, while indefiniteness allows both buyer and seller to get out of the contract—although a buyer may be able to cure indefiniteness simply by obtaining financing. See, for example, Highlands Plaza, Inc. v. Viking Investment Corp., 2 Wash.App. 192, 467 P.2d 378 (1970).

A well drafted contingency clause should prescribe the timing and type of notice that must be given in order to terminate the contract under the contingency clause. Compare Logalbo v. Plishkin, Rubano & Baum, discussed at page 26 above (strictly construing notice provisions), with Armstrong, Gibbons v. Southridge Investment Assocs., 589 A.2d 836 (R.I.1991) (deviating from the usual rule of closely reading terms of a contingency clause and allowing oral notice to be adequate).

2. *Financing as a Substitute for Other Conditions.* If the financing condition in a land sale contract specifies not only the terms of an acceptable mortgage loan but also the particular institution that is to make the loan, will the buyer be excused if that institution rejects the loan application, but some other institutional lender agrees to make the loan on the terms specified? What if no institutional lender will make the loan, but the seller agrees to finance the transaction herself?

In Kovarik v. Vesely, 3 Wis.2d 573, 89 N.W.2d 279 (1958), the contract price was $11,000, with $4,000 paid on signing and the remainder to be financed through a "$7,000 purchase money mortgage from the Fort Atkinson Savings and Loan Ass'n." One week after unsuccessfully applying to Fort Atkinson Savings & Loan, the buyers were told that the sellers would be willing to take back a purchase money mortgage on the terms and conditions specified in the buyers' application to Fort Atkinson. The buyers declined and brought suit to recover their down payment. Sellers counterclaimed for specific performance.

The court held for the sellers, rejecting buyers' claim that the incomplete financing clause invalidated the contract under the statute of frauds. "We experience no difficulty in determining that the loan application to the Fort Atkinson Savings & Loan Association is a separate writing which is to be construed together with the original contract of the parties, and that together they constitute a sufficient memorandum to comply [with the statute]." The court also upheld the trial court's finding that the "buyers were interested in financing a Seven Thousand Dollar mortgage, and not in any particular loaning agency." It rejected buyers' argument that, because their contract specified Fort Atkinson Savings & Loan, good faith did not require them to accept financing from the seller. 3 Wis.2d at 581, 583, 89 N.W.2d at 284, 285.

Was *Kovarik* correctly decided? Why should a buyer care about the source of his funds? Justice Fairchild, dissenting, offered two possible reasons: "the buyer will feel more confident of his own judgment of the price he is to pay if a lending institution is willing to make a loan" and "the buyer would rather have the matter, in the event of default, in the hands of an established lending institution than in the hands of an individual who might be less able, if not less willing, to adjust matters reasonably." 3 Wis.2d at 583, 89 N.W.2d at 286. For a case reaching a result opposite to *Kovarik*, see Gardner v. Padro, 164 Ill.App.3d 449, 115 Ill.Dec. 445, 517 N.E.2d 1131 (1987).

Is it fair or efficient to let buyers use the financing condition, and the lender's appraisal, to test their own judgment on the worth of the property, giving them an excuse to get out of the contract if financing is refused because the appraisal comes in at less than the contract price? For valuable insights into the appraisal process and its implications for lender liability, see Malloy, Lender Liability for Negligent Real Estate Appraisals, 1984 U.Ill.L.Rev. 53.

Is it fair or efficient to let buyers use the financing condition, and the lender's examination of title, to save the buyer the expense of ordering a title report himself? To allow the financing condition to serve as a substitute for the marketable title condition?

2.   MARKETABLE TITLE

CASELLI v. MESSINA

Supreme Court of New York, Appellate Term, 1990.
148 Misc.2d 671, 567 N.Y.S.2d 972.

Before MONTELEONE, J.P., and PIZZUTO and SANTUCCI, JJ.

Appeal by plaintiffs and cross-appeal by defendants from an order of the Civil Court, Kings County (Diamond, J.) filed on January 11, 1990 which denied the motion by defendants for summary judgment and dismissal of the complaint and which denied the cross motion of the plaintiffs for summary judgment.

Order modified with $10 costs to defendants, motion for summary judgment in favor of the defendants granted and complaint dismissed and, as so modified, order affirmed.

Plaintiffs entered into a contract to purchase the house of the defendants Messina and pursuant to the contract, a downpayment was deposited with the defendant Ajello. The contract provided that it was to be sold subject to "Covenants, restrictions, reservations * * * of record * * * provided same are not violated by present structure or the present use of premises" and the parties added to said clause the phrase "or render title unmarketable." Another clause of the contract provided that "Sellers shall give and purchasers shall accept such title as any New York City title company will be willing to approve and insure in accordance with their standard form of title policy, subject only to the matters provided for in this contract." After receipt of the title report, plaintiffs notified the defendants that the title was unmarketable due to the restrictions and covenants of record and demanded the return of their downpayment. When the demand was refused, this suit was commenced.

The language of this contract, does not call for an unqualified or unlimited title policy. It calls for a standard policy, "subject only to the matters provided for in this contract." This would include that first clause mentioned above in which the property was sold subject to these covenants and restrictions of record *provided that the present structure did not violate them and provided that title was not rendered unmarketable.*

In *Laba v. Carey*, 29 N.Y.2d 302, 307–309, 327 N.Y.S.2d 613, 277 N.E.2d 641, rearg. denied 30 N.Y.2d 694, 332 N.Y.S.2d 1025, 283 N.E.2d 432, the contract of sale contained somewhat similar provisions, covenants and restrictions but did not have the additional phrase "or render title unmarketable." The Court of Appeals noted that the policy issued by the title company would only have to comply with the provisions of the contract of sale and that "The contract before us addressed itself to the existence of easements and [restrictions] * * * of record. The title company, disclosing the existence of a telephone easement and 'Waiver of Legal Grades' restrictive covenant, excluded these items from coverage, except insofar as to say that they had not been violated. In so insuring, it was assuming responsibility for no less than that which respondents had expressly agreed to accept. The exceptions were matters specifically contemplated by the contract ..." The court went on to state:

> "Accordingly, where a purchaser agrees to take title subject to easements and restrictive covenants of record which are not violated, this is the precise kind of title that the seller is obligated to tender and we are not persuaded that, *absent an expression of a contrary intent in the contract*, that obligation is broadened by the existence of the usual 'insurance' clause in a form contract.... A conclusion that the seller would nevertheless be required to furnish title, insurable without exception, would not only render nugatory the 'subject to' clause, but would give every purchaser dissatisfied with his bargain a way of avoiding his contractual responsibilities. Surely, this was not contemplated in the contract before us." (Emphasis added)

In *Laba*, as in the case at bar, neither the easements nor the restrictive covenants were violated by the present use and the contract was *silent* as to any special use intended by the plaintiffs for the property.

The essential issue in this case is whether the mere existence of covenants and restrictions of record renders the title unmarketable. An understanding of what renders title unmarketable can be found in the case of *Regan v. Lanze*, 40 N.Y.2d 475, 481–482, 387 N.Y.S.2d 79, 354 N.E.2d 818, wherein the Court stated:

> "The disposition of this case turns on the marketability of defendants' title. A marketable title has been defined as one that may freely be made the subject of resale (*Trimboli v. Kinkel*, 226 NY 147–152 [123 N.E. 205]; see 62 NY Jur, Vendor and Purchaser, § 48; 3 Warren's Weed New York Real Property, Marketability of Title, § 2.01). It is one which can be readily sold or mortgaged to a

person of reasonable prudence, the test of the marketability of title being whether there is an objection thereto such as would interfere with a sale or with the market value of the property (*Brokaw v. Duffy*, 165 NY 391, 399 [59 N.E. 196]; *Heller v. Cohen*, 154 NY 299, 306 [48 N.E. 527]; *Vought v. Williams*, 120 NY 253, 257 [24 N.E. 195]; Schwartz, Real Estate Manual, p. 581). The law assures to a buyer a title free from reasonable doubt, but not from every doubt [citing authority], and the mere possibility or suspicion of a defect, which according to ordinary experience has no probable basis, does not demonstrate an unmarketable title * * * *.

To be sure, a purchaser is entitled to a marketable title unless the parties stipulate otherwise in the contract (*Laba v. Carey*, 29 NY2d 302, 311 [327 N.Y.S.2d 613, 277 N.E.2d 641]). Except for extraordinary instances in which it is very clear that the purchaser can suffer no harm from a defect or incumbrance, he will not be compelled to take title when there is a defect in the record title which can be cured only by a resort to parol evidence or when there is an apparent incumbrance which can be removed or defeated only by such evidence * * * *."

See also, Voorheesville Rod & Gun Club v. Tompkins County, 158 A.D.2d 789, 551 N.Y.S.2d 382; *Dejong v. Mandelbaum,* 122 A.D.2d 772, 774, 505 N.Y.S.2d 659; *Weiss v. Cord Helmer Realty Corp.,* 140 N.Y.S.2d 95, 98–99; 62 NY Jur, Vendor and Purchaser, § 48).

In applying these rules to the facts of the case at bar, it is readily apparent that the contract was silent as to any special use that plaintiffs may have had in mind for the property. It is also conceded that the present use of the property did not violate said covenants and restrictions of record. It is therefore concluded that no reasonable person, in the absence of contractual provision calling for a special use of the property, would be denied reasonable enjoyment of the property for his "intendea and announced purposes" (*Dejong v. Mandelbaum, supra*). The mere existence of covenants and restrictions of record which did not affect the present use of the property as set forth in the contract between the parties herein provided purchasers with what they had contracted for. Since they were in default under the terms of the contract of sale, they were not entitled to the return of their downpayment.

MONTELEONE, J.P., and SANTUCCI, J., concur.

PIZZUTO, J., dissents in a separate memorandum.

PIZZUTO, Justice, dissents and votes to modify the order of the Court below by granting plaintiffs' motion for summary judgment in the following memorandum.

The majority did not give proper weight to the significance of the fact that added to and made a part of the typed Paragraph 1 of the Rider, which provided that the premises was sold subject to: "(b) covenants, restrictions, reservations, utilities, easements and agreements, of record, insofar as the same may now be in force or effect, provided same are not violated by the present structure or the present use of premises . . .", there was an inked insertion, "*or* render title unmarketable" (emphasis supplied).

Both the NYBTU standard form of contract and the two-page typed rider contained handwritten modifications made at the contract signing, obviously due to the negotiations of the attorneys as to the terms of the contract prior to the execution thereof by the parties.

The issue then becomes whether or not exceptions listed in the report of the Chicago Title Insurance Company concerning a declaration contained in Liber 6150 at Page 569 and Liber 6150 at Page 573 as well as an easement in Liber 6131 at Page 276 and Liber 6104 at Page 65 render title unmarketable. Clearly, the purchasers' attorney modified the aforementioned quoted subject clause by the addition of the words in the disjunctive "*or* render title unmarketable" (emphasis supplied). Those words must be given some meaning in determining under what circumstances, the purchasers were obligated to take title.

The declaration contained in Liber 6150 at Page 573 was a covenant restricting the use of the land, not mentioned anywhere in the contract. The restrictive covenant provided that no building may be erected other than private dwellings, limited the use to two-families, limited the carrying-on of a trade or business at the premises, prescribed minimum setbacks and portions of the land on which no building was to be erected, prohibited the carrying-on of noxious or offensive trades, and prohibited anything being done thereon which may become an annoyance to the neighborhood.

The covenant and restrictions further provided that they shall run with the land and provided that in the event an owner violates or attempts to violate any of the covenants, any other person owning any real estate described in said restrictions may bring an action against the violator seeking an injunction or damages.

These covenants (although not violated by the existing structure or use thereof) prescribed minimum setbacks, restricted the type of building and structure that could be placed on the land and the type of activities that could be carried out on the land. Such restrictions render title unmarketable. (*See, Golden Development Corp. v. Weyant, et al.,* 269 App.Div. 1039, 58 N.Y.S.2d 687 [setback restriction]; *Rosenberg v. Centre Davis Corp.,* 15 A.D.2d 506, 222 N.Y.S.2d 391 [restrictive covenants permitting construction or maintenance of one-family house only].) In *Antin v. O'Shea,* 270 App.Div. 1046, 63 N.Y.S.2d 97, cited in *Rosenberg v. Centre Davis Corp.,* supra, the contract provided in part that the property was sold "subject to covenants and restrictions contained in former recorded deeds affecting said premises, *provided they do not render title unmarketable.*" (Emphasis supplied.) A former deed contained a covenant "that there shall not be erected upon any portion of said premises any building for the sale of intoxicating drinks or garden for the sale of ale or beer." The appellate court held that title was unmarketable and granted the purchaser's motion for summary judgment for foreclosure of its lien and recovery of the down payments and expenses.

In *Laba v. Carey*, 29 N.Y.2d 302, 327 N.Y.S.2d 613, 277 N.E.2d 641, cited and relied upon by the majority, although it contained similar provisions as to title insurance, did not contain similar provisions as to marketability of title.

The pertinent provisions contained in the NYBTU form of contract in the *Laba* case were as follows. It provided that the seller shall give and the purchaser shall accept a title such as any reputable title company would accept and insure. The contract also expressly provided that the sale and conveyance was subject to:

> "4. Covenants, restrictions, utility agreements easements of record if any, now in force, provided same are not now violated.
>
> 5. Any set of facts an accurate survey may show provided same does not render title unmarketable."

The court there held that the purchaser received exactly what he had bargained for in the contract. The purchaser was not entitled to an unconditional title policy without exception since he agreed to take title subject to the covenants, restrictions, utility agreements and easements of record provided that they were not violated, which they were not. There was no additional proviso in the *Laba* case, as there is in this case, to wit: "or render title unmarketable." The only proviso made with reference to marketable title had to do with facts that might be shown on a survey.

The instant case is obviously distinguishable. The purchaser in this case has not been offered that which he had bargained and negotiated for.

In conclusion, to adopt the construction suggested by the majority would do violence to the specific intent of the parties at the time that contract was executed. The majority proposal, that a provision added to the contract is superfluous is contrary to the basic principles of contract law (*see*, 22 NY Jur 2d, Contracts, § 221).

NOTES

1. *What is Marketable Title?* The excerpt from Regan v. Lanze, quoted in Caselli v. Messina, typifies the standard, circular formula for determining whether a seller's title is marketable. One variant of the formula is the rule that a marketable title is one "which at all times and under all circumstances, may be forced upon an unwilling purchaser," Pyrke v. Waddington, 10 Hare 1, 68 Eng.Rep. 813 (Chancery 1852). Another is that a marketable title is one that can be held quietly without fear of litigation to determine its validity. Stack v. Hickey, 151 Wis. 347, 138 N.W. 1011 (1912).

What is the effect on the buyer's marketable title protection of language making the conveyance subject to covenants, restrictions and reservations of record, such as appeared in Laba v. Carey, discussed in *Caselli*? Does such a clause favor the buyer or seller? How did the parties in *Caselli* modify the language and to what effect? As developed in the following notes, the majority opinion in *Caselli* departs from the general rule that holds that the mere existence of a covenant or condition automatically makes title unmarketable. See M. Friedman, Contracts and Conveyances of Real Property 600–615 (5th ed. 1991).

No condition has produced more litigation or confusion than marketable title. The main reason for the confusion is that courts have tried to apply a single formula to a diverse array of questions and have failed to observe important functional distinctions. The principal relevant distinction is between claims of unmarketability based on defects in the record chain of title and those based on encumbrances. Another important distinction is between those encumbrances that will be apparent to a buyer viewing the land and those that will not. It is also important to distinguish between three overlapping concepts—marketable title, insurable title and record title. The notes that follow examine these distinctions.

2. *Chain of Title Defects.* Chain of title defects affect ownership. They may arise from a fraudulent transfer, an irregularity in the conduct of a mortgage foreclosure, tax sale or probate proceeding, or a technical error or omission in a prior conveyance, such as a misspelling in the name of a party, a misdescription of the parcel or the absence of a proper acknowledgement. They may also result from future interests such as possibilities of reverter and rights of entry.

The standard marketability formula of Regan v. Lanze should properly be applied only to chain of title defects. Every state has remedial statutes exclusively aimed at curing chain of title defects and making title freely transferable. Curative acts, statutes of limitations, marketable title acts and recording acts dictate which title defects impair title and which, with the passage of time, have been cured. While these statutes are not specifically concerned with the resolution of contract disputes over marketable title, they do provide an independent and objective basis for determining the sort of title that a seller may be allowed to force upon a buyer and, by implication, the sort of title that the buyer may be allowed to force on some future buyer. A title with a defect that has been cured by passage of the statutory period, or by the occurrence of the statutorily-prescribed events, is not only good in some abstract sense. It is also marketable in the sense that, as a matter of public policy, the legislature has determined that a buyer should, in acquiring this title, feel confident that he can later sell it without fear that it will then be held unmarketable. For an example of the title clearance system at work in the context of a contract dispute over marketable title, see Tesdell v. Hanes, 248 Iowa 742, 82 N.W.2d 119 (1957).

3. *Encumbrances.* Encumbrances reduce the value of land in ways that fall short of breaks in the chain of title. Mainly they take the form of third party claims to money, possession or use affecting the land. Mechanics liens, mortgage liens and judgment liens are typical money claims. Claims of lessees or tenants in common typify possessory encumbrances. And easements, servitudes and party wall agreements are typical encumbrances affecting land use.

No system of independent, objective benchmarks exists for resolving marketable title disputes over encumbrances. Whether, and to what extent, a servitude, right of way easement or encroachment impairs a parcel's value will vary from time to time and from parcel to parcel. As a result, the correct resolution between one buyer and seller may not be the correct resolution as between another two or, more important, as between the present buyer and some future buyer from him. In the context of encumbrances, the standard formula, that a marketable title is one that may freely be made the subject of resale, is simply conclusional.

Properly conceived, the effect of encumbrances on marketability boils down to a single question: who, as between buyer and seller, has best access to the information that will avoid loss? The answer may turn on whether the encumbrance is visible from an inspection of the parcel.

Invisible Encumbrances. Encumbrances imposing use restrictions are completely within the knowledge of the seller at the time she enters into the contract of sale. She presumably knows of the record restrictions existing at the time she purchased, for she should have obtained an abstract of title or title insurance policy at that time. Any subsequent encumbrances would have been the consequence of her own acts.

Buyer is best placed to know about the uses that he plans to make of the property. If the buyer negotiates for the contract to provide that he will take title subject to all restrictions of record except any that prohibit his intended use, the burden should be on seller to provide title free of the specified restrictions or suffer rescission. Probably the same result should follow if there is no specific contract provision on the point, but buyer has told seller of his intended use, or the intended use can easily be inferred from the circumstances—such as buying a residence for residential purposes. Buyer should lose in this context only when he has done nothing to inform the seller of his intended use and his use is unexpected in the circumstances—as, for example, commercial use of a lot in a residential neighborhood.

Visible Encumbrances. Encumbrances in the form of easements or encroachments require a different allocation of responsibility. If an easement or encroachment is visible from a view of the land, rather than just from the paper record, it probably should not excuse buyer performance because it presumably formed an element of the buyer's expectations, and of buyer's and seller's negotiations on price. Courts have as a general rule followed this approach only in the case of public roads running through the property, and have rested their decisions on one of several theories: custom, buyer knowledge, implied waiver, the private benefit to the property afforded by the public road, the road's public importance, and the minimal nature of the interference.

Courts divide, however, on the effect of other physical intrusions, such as private rights of way and irrigation ditches, with the majority leaning toward the position that they are encumbrances excusing performance. Compare Waters v. North Carolina Phosphate Corp., 310 N.C. 438, 312 S.E.2d 428 (1984) (because easement for 100-foot wide right of way, lined with large towers and five power transmission lines, would have materially interfered with buyer's intended use, buyer was excused from performing), with Alcan Aluminum Corp. v. Carlsberg Financial Corp., 689 F.2d 815 (9th Cir.1982) (buyer conclusively presumed to have intended to take property subject to a utility easement where, although easement did not appear in title report, high tension lines were visible from several points on the property).

4. *Access.* Does the lack of access to the property from a public road create an unmarketable title defect or merely affect the value of the property that buyer will receive? Compare Sinks v. Karleskint, 130 Ill.App.3d 527, 85 Ill.Dec. 807, 474 N.E.2d 767 (1985) (distinguishing "merchantability" of title from market value and holding that lack of access does not breach seller's obligation) with Myerberg, Sawyer & Rue, P.A. v. Agee, 51 Md.App. 711, 446 A.2d 69 (1982) (lack of access breached marketability obligation; pending litigation to establish easement by necessity did not adequately free title from doubt). On the question of access, is there unequal availability of information to buyer and seller so that the law should place a burden on seller to address the problem? Or is the availability of access simply a market calculation, such as good property location, that all parties are expected to make and which the law will not normally adjust?

5. *Marketable Title, Record Title and Insurable Title Compared.* Marketable title can be compared to two other forms of title conditions sometimes obtained by buyers as an alternative, or in addition, to marketable title. *Record title* is title, typically in fee simple absolute, that can be proved by reference to the record alone and without resort to collateral proceedings such as quiet title actions brought to establish seller's title by adverse possession. Perfect record title does not necessarily constitute perfect title. A title that, from the record, appears to be perfect may in fact be entirely invalid because of fraud, nondelivery or a wild deed somewhere in the chain of title. *Insurable title* is title that a title insurance company is willing to insure as valid. Insurable title need not be good record title. For example, a title insurer may decide that, because seller's adverse possession appears to be uncontrovertible, it will insure seller's title to the adversely claimed land even though seller has no record title to it. Also, as indicated in Laba v. Carey, insurable title may not be marketable title, for the title policy may except defects or encumbrances that make the title unmarketable.

In Conklin v. Davi, 76 N.J. 468, 388 A.2d 598 (1978), sellers contractually undertook to convey marketable and insurable title but did not expressly undertake to convey good record title. Buyers refused to perform on the ground that the sellers lacked record title because part of their title rested on a claim by adverse possession. The court held that no record title obligation was implied in the agreement and that unless title proved to be uninsurable or unmarketable, buyer would not be entitled to rescind.

Is *Conklin* a good decision? One effect of the decision is to require buyers who have not contracted for record title to keep the funds for their part of the purchase price liquid, and to keep their institutional lender's commitment to finance the remainder of the purchase price alive, throughout the months and possibly years that it will take for litigation to resolve the status of seller's title. As a practical matter it will be virtually impossible for a residential buyer to persuade an institutional lender to extend its financing commitment indefinitely. Commercial buyers may have greater success in obtaining extensions, but at considerable expense.

Obviously, the buyer can protect himself against these consequences if he is aware of the *Conklin* rule *and* if, in the negotiations leading up to the contract of sale, he can get the seller to agree to convey valid title of record on the date of closing. Is it fair or efficient to place this negotiating burden on the buyer? As between seller and buyer who is better placed to acquire information respecting title expeditiously? To resolve adverse possession claims?

3. OTHER PROBLEM AREAS

a. ZONING

DOVER POOL & RACQUET CLUB, INC. v. BROOKING

Supreme Judicial Court of Massachusetts, 1975.
366 Mass. 629, 322 N.E.2d 168.

BRAUCHER, Justice.

On January 31, 1972, the parties entered into a written contract for the sale of real estate in Dover and Medfield. A few days earlier, unknown to them, the planning board of Medfield had published a notice of a public hearing on a proposed amendment to the zoning by-law. The proposed amendment would newly require a special permit for the use of the premises contemplated by both the vendor and the purchaser, and under G.L. c. 40A, § 11, the amendment if adopted would have effect retroactive to the date of publication. The purchaser sought rescission of the contract and return of its deposit. A judge of the Superior Court decreed rescission and return because of a mutual mistake of fact, and we affirm.

The case was referred to a master, whose report was confirmed except for its conclusions. We summarize the master's findings. The

Brookings owned about fifty acres of land, nine acres in Medfield and the rest in Dover, used as a single family residence. The buildings were in Dover, and the only established access was through the Medfield portion. During negotiations with the purchaser (the Club) the Brookings were informed that the Club intended to use the property for a nonprofit tennis and swim club.

Both the Dover and the Medfield zoning by-laws permitted use of the premises as of right for a "club when not conducted for profit and not containing more than five sleeping rooms." The parties discussed the zoning by-law of Dover. The Brookings asked their broker about zoning, and he replied that everything would be all right under the existing Dover and Medfield by-laws. The vice-president of the Club who signed the agreement checked both the Dover and the Medfield zoning by-laws.

The agreement, signed on January 31, 1972, provides for conveyance of "a good and clear record and marketable title thereto, free from encumbrances, except (a) Provisions of existing building and zoning laws ...." The planning board of Medfield on January 27 and February 3, 1972, published notice of a public hearing on February 14, 1972, on proposed amendments to the Medfield zoning by-law, including a requirement of a special permit for use of the Medfield portion of the premises as a "non-profit country, hunting, fishing, tennis or golf club without liquor license." Neither of the parties was aware of the notice, but the Club's board of directors became aware of it about ten days before the agreed closing date of March 1, 1972. The parties met on the closing date, and the Brookings were prepared to deliver a deed, but the Club refused to proceed with the purchase. The proposed zoning amendment was adopted at the Medfield town meeting on March 21, 1972, and approved by the Attorney General in July, 1972.

In general, building and zoning laws in existence at the time a land contract is signed are not treated as encumbrances, and the purchaser has no recourse against the vendor by virtue of restrictions imposed by such laws on the use of the property purchased.

Moreover, changes in such laws after the contract is signed have commonly been held to be part of the risk assumed by the purchaser. In some such cases, however, specific performance at the suit of the vendor has been denied, particularly where both parties knew of the contemplated use later prohibited.

In the present case the agreement itself makes it explicit that "existing building and zoning laws" are not included in the vendor's obligation to convey "free from encumbrances." The Club argues, by contrasting the quoted exception with other exceptions, that the building and zoning laws excepted are those "existing" on the date of the agreement, but we think it is clear that the reference is to laws "existing" on the date of the deed. In other words, the purchaser bore the risk of zoning laws in effect on the date of closing.

We have upheld a decree of rescission of a sale of land by reason of misrepresentations of the zoning situation by the vendors, and in doing so assumed that there would be no liability for bare nondisclosure. In other States rescission has been decreed on the basis of mutual mistake of fact in circumstances like those before us. We have long recognized that land contracts may be rescinded for mutual mistake. But we seem not to have been called on to pass upon a mistake as to zoning.

The Medfield zoning amendment was not an "existing" zoning law at the time of the closing. It was not an encumbrance and it was not within the exception in the agreement. Yet under G.L. c. 40A, § 11,[a] the notice published four days before the agreement was signed had a material impact on the purchaser's intended use of the premises. After the notice was published, the issuance of a building permit or the beginning of work on a building or structure would not protect the purchaser if the steps required for the adoption of the proposed amendment were taken in their usual sequence without unnecessary or unreasonable delay. Meanwhile, no special permit could be issued under the proposed amendment before it was enacted. The agreement provides "that time is of the essence of this agreement," and the record does not indicate any willingness by the vendor to extend the time for closing until after the town meeting which was to act on the proposed amendment. Under Harrison v. Building Inspector of Braintree, 350 Mass. 559, 561, 215 N.E.2d 773 (1966), use of the only established access to the premises might be barred if no special permit were obtained.

Thus at the time the contract was made both parties made the assumption that the zoning by-laws interposed no obstacle to the use of the premises for a nonprofit tennis and swim club. That assumption was mistaken, and we think it was a basic assumption on which the contract was made. It could not yet be said that the purchaser's principal purpose had been frustrated. But a right of vital importance to the purchaser did not exist, and as a result of the mistake enforcement of the contract would be materially more onerous to the purchaser than it would have been had the facts been as the parties believed them to be. The contract was therefore voidable by the purchaser unless it bore the risk of the mistake. The agreement does not provide for that risk, and the case is not one of conscious ignorance or deliberate risk-taking on the purchaser's part. Nor do we think there is any common understanding that purchasers take the risk of the unusual predicament in which the purchaser found itself. We therefore agree with the judge's conclusion that the contract was voidable for mutual mistake of fact.

Decree affirmed with costs of appeal.

---

a. Now codified at Mass.Gen.Laws Ann. ch. 40A, § 6.

b. QUANTITY

HARDIN v. HILL

Supreme Court of Montana, 1967.
149 Mont. 68, 423 P.2d 309.

CASTLES, Justice.

This is an action for rescission of a contract for the sale of a ranch initiated by respondents, hereinafter referred to as Hardin. Rescission was denied, but Hardin obtained a judgment for breach of contract in the amount of $139,450.35, from which the defendants appeal.

The defendants, appellants here, are Arthur D. Hill and Lottie Hill, husband and wife, and their son Glenn D. Hill and his wife Rose Hill, and will be referred to as Hills. The Hills were joint owners of a large cattle ranch lying in Flathead and Lake counties. In 1960 the Hills listed the ranch for sale with various realtors, including Peder Pedersen. Dennis W. Hardin and his wife Joyce S. Hardin, respondents, were residents of Colorado and answered an ad for the ranch placed by Pedersen. After some correspondence between the Hardins and Pedersen, the Hardins came to Montana to inspect the ranch. On October 3, 1960, Pedersen escorted the Hardins to the Hill property to inspect it and enter further negotiations. On the following day the Hardins entered a buy and sell agreement; the final contract was signed on October 5, 1960. The purchase price of $300,000.00 included real estate, two houses, various out-buildings, equipment and machines, and some livestock.

The ranch contained both deeded land and adjacent leased or permitted land owned by four owners, the land, which the parties considered as a lease. The leases were generally for a period of one year and customarily were renewed to the owner of the deeded property. Throughout the period of negotiation, the Hills represented to the Hardins that the ranch contained approximately 5,000 acres of deeded property and 10,000 acres of leased land. The Hills also stated that approximately 11,000 acres of deeded and leased land were under fence; the area so enclosed being the "heart" of the ranch, containing the best grazing land. The Hardins realized that a survey had never been made of the ranch, and that the statements regarding acreage were rough estimates. The alleged source of the representations made by the Hills was a map prepared by the United States Soil Conservation Service which erroneously included a large portion of land within the ranch which in fact was not owned or leased by the Hills. As this map itself indicated, the boundary lines were "used for conservation planning only". Additionally, the testimony indicates that the map was not relied upon, even if seen prior to the contract.

The Hardins entered possession in January of 1961 and continued to raise cattle on the property. In September of 1963 the Hardins discovered a shortage in acreage. A survey revealed a shortage of 279 acres of deeded land and 1,456 of leased. In addition, 2,383 acres were not fenced in as represented. The Hardins attempted to renegotiate the contract and then notified the Hills of their intent to rescind the contract. This action was commenced on December 23, 1963. While rescission was not permitted by the district court, damages for breach of contract were awarded to the Hardins on a rather broad spectrum, as follows: $45,390.00 for the shortage of land within the fence. This amount was deducted from the total purchase price of $300,000.00 for purposes of recomputing the 29 percent down payment used in the contract. The difference between the actual down payment and readjusted down payment was apparently allowed as an element of damages. An additional $24,340.35 was awarded for interest actually paid and interest owing over the life of the contract on the $45,390.00 excess (computed at 4½ percent, the contract rate). The total judgment entered for the shortage of land was $77,566.14. Additional damages were allowed for loss of anticipated profits over the life of the contract in the amount of $61,884.21. This figure was awarded without interest and was payable in annual installments from 1965 to 1972.

Appellants' motion for a new trial was denied; they contend on this appeal that the Hardins were not entitled to any relief and that damages awarded were excessive. There are several interesting issues presented.

Initially we must consider whether the misrepresentations made by the Hills were "fraudulent" by legal definition; and whether the failure of the Hardins to investigate the truth of those assertions would be a bar to relief. Section 13–309, R.C.M.1947,[a] defines constructive fraud to include, "any breach of duty which, without an actually fraudulent intent, gains an advantage to the person in fault, or anyone claiming under him, by misleading another to his prejudice ...." We think that the district court correctly ruled that there was "fraud", but it is evident that the Hills did not intend to deceive anyone and made an honest mistake.

The Hardins relied upon the Hills' statements since they made no attempt to confirm the amount of acreage or obtain an abstract of title prior to entering the contract. We say, parenthetically, that this is astonishing. According to the testimony of Mr. Hardin, a survey monument was discovered in 1963 at the southeast corner of the ranch on the fence line which indicated the true location of the boundary, and which in itself showed that the soil conservation map was in error. The contract described the deeded property by section and lot number from which the deficiency could easily have been computed.

Perhaps the most aggravating aspect of this case is the failure of the buyers to exercise a reasonable degree of circumspection before signing the contract. Certainly this is not the case of a naive or inexperienced party who is led astray by the deliberate manipulations of the seller. Mr. Hardin was an experienced real estate developer and it is clear from the record and evidence that he had every confidence in his ability to consummate the sale to his satisfaction.

a. Now codified at Mont.Code Ann. § 28–2–406.

Goldstein & Korngold Real Est.Trans. 3rd Ed. UCS—4

The only attorney who participated in the sale was Don Olsson, an officer of the Ronan State Bank. He drew up the contract and deed at the request of Pedersen. The bank was the escrow holder of the deed and legal services rendered by Olsson were pursuant to his affiliation with the bank. In any event, the Hardins relied upon their own judgment, based upon their own inspection, and did not seek independent legal advice before entering the agreement.

Montana decisions have held that the defense of *caveat emptor* (let the buyer beware) is available in an action based on false representations. However, these cases apply the rule where the purchaser had actual notice of the true state of affairs prior to entering the contract for sale. Under the facts of this case it is at least arguable that the Hardins knew that the Hills did not have substantial factual support for the statements made concerning the amount of acreage. To allow a defense of *caveat emptor* on this basis involves a degree of conjecture which this court should not entertain, and we do not feel it is necessary to a proper resolution of this dispute to formally rule on the matter of *caveat emptor*. But the relative conduct of the parties in a suit for equitable relief cannot be overlooked. The Hardins at least co-authored the defective transaction before us and should not be heard to deny all responsibility for the consequences.

The Hills urge that this was a sale in gross, as distinct from a sale by the acre, and since the Hardins purchased the ranch as a single unit they would not be entitled to any relief. The evidence clearly shows that the ranch was sold as a single going concern; there was no discussion or agreement on a per acre price. Moreover, the contract described the deeded land by section and lot number and did not indicate the number of deeded acres. The lease land was described as "approximately Ten Thousand (10,000) acres". Taking the language of the contract together with the express intent of the parties to bargain for the ranch as a whole, we feel that the sale was clearly one in gross.

Generally when land is sold in gross, a variation in acreage from what the parties had contemplated is not grounds for rescission or other relief. But this proposition does not apply to a sale in gross induced by material misrepresentations. We therefore hold that the Hardins are entitled to some relief.

It is difficult to understand why the district court refused to grant rescission, yet awarded such extensive damages, even more than under rescission. It is true that the court below was in a better position to determine whether it would be possible to restore the parties to the positions they occupied prior to the contract. We do feel that damages awarded to the Hardins are excessive and cannot be allowed to stand as a final judgment.

. . .

Damages allowable for the missing acreage should be computed from the contract value on a per acre basis, without distinction between deeded and leased land and whether fenced or open. The Hardins testified that they attributed about $210,000 of the total purchase price to the real estate alone, exclusive of buildings, equipment and livestock. Although the Hills placed a somewhat greater value on the improvements, the figure of $210,000 seems fair and reasonable. The value per acre of 15,000 acres calculated at the contract rate would be $14.00. Since the total shortage was 1,735, damages allowable should be $24,-290 (which is 1,735 multiplied by $14).

... A new trial should be granted unless the respondents agree to accept $24,290 plus interest in damages. In the event a new trial is had, we feel that the possibility of allowing rescission should be considered.

The cause is remanded to the district court, with directions to grant a new trial in accordance with this opinion, unless within sixty days after the remittitur is filed with the clerk of that court, the respondents shall file their written consent that the judgment may be reduced to $24,290 plus interest at the rate of 6 percent from the date of the contract.

. . .

JAMES T. HARRISON, C.J., and ADAIR, DOYLE and JOHN C. HARRISON, JJ., concur.

NOTES

1. *Land Use Controls Enacted Before Contract Signing.* In deciding whether to treat compliance with zoning and other public land use controls as a condition to be implied into land sale contracts, courts almost uniformly reject the superficial analogy to private land use controls such as easements, covenants and servitudes. *Dover Pool* accurately states the general rule that ordinances enacted prior to the contract "are not treated as encumbrances, and the purchaser has no recourse against the vendor by virtue of restrictions imposed by such laws on the use of the property purchased." The rule apparently stems from the position that contracts are subject to laws in force at the time of their formation. See Josefowicz v. Porter, 32 N.J.Super. 585, 108 A.2d 865 (App.Div.1954).

Courts have been cautious to rescind for mutual mistake where the adverse land use controls existed at the time the contract was signed. In Rosique v. Windley Cove, Ltd., 542 So.2d 1014 (Fla.App.1989), the contract of sale contemplated that zoning would permit 25 units per acre. Before closing, however, the buyer learned of uncertainties concerning the zoning but nonetheless elected to proceed. The court denied recission of the contract when buyer ultimately learned that only 15 units per acre were permitted. The buyer's predicament in the case seemed to be "one of conscious ignorance or deliberate risk-taking on the purchaser's part," in the words of *Dover Pool.* On the other hand, the court in Britton v. Parkin, 176 Mich.App.395, 438 N.W.2d 919

(1989), ordered the sales contract rescinded since both seller and buyer mistakenly believed that the property was zoned for commercial uses. The court held that a clause making the contract subject to building and use restrictions did not put the risk of zoning on the buyer since seller represented in the listing agreement, advertisements, and drawings that the property was zoned commercial.

Land Use Controls Enacted After Contract Signing. Courts divide on whether land use ordinances enacted *during* the executory period should be treated similarly. *Dover* reflects one view, excusing buyer performance. Other courts hold that the buyer should bear the risk of changes in the law. Some of these courts rest their position on the ground that the situation does not materially differ from cases in which the law was enacted prior to the contract. Others follow the example of equitable conversion, perceiving "no cogent argument for treating losses resulting from zoning changes occurring between the execution of the Agreement of Sale and settlement differently from casualty and other kinds of loss occurring between those periods." DiDonato v. Reliance Standard Life Insurance Co., 433 Pa. 221, 225, 249 A.2d 327, 330 (1969). The court there observed that, as in the casualty context, the parties could have shifted the burden of loss by contract.

Say that, after buyer and seller sign a contract for the sale of a house, the local zoning ordinance is amended. The house would violate the new minimum lot size requirements but for a provision in the ordinance permitting prior nonconforming structures. However, under the ordinance, if the structure is ever destroyed, only a smaller, conforming structure can be built on the parcel. The house is destroyed by fire during the executory period. Who should bear the risk of which loss? Will the answer differ depending on whether equitable conversion or the U.V.P.R.A. applies? Compare Goldfarb v. Dietz, 8 Wash.App. 464, 506 P.2d 1322 (1973).

Land Use Controls Violated Before Contract Signing. Courts also split on the effect of land use control violations existing at the time the contract of sale is signed. One line of authority treats these violations like encumbrances, placing the burden on seller. For example, in Lohmeyer v. Bower, 170 Kan. 442, 227 P.2d 102 (1951), buyers were granted rescission when, after signing the contract, they discovered that the house violated not only deed restrictions but also a local zoning ordinance. Focusing on the ordinance, the court observed that it is not "the existence of protective restrictions, as shown by the record, that constitutes the encumbrances alleged by the appellants; but rather it is the presently existing violation of one of these restrictions that constitutes such encumbrance, in and of itself." For the opposing view, that existing violations do not excuse buyer performance, see Gnash v. Saari, 44 Wash.2d 312, 267 P.2d 674 (1954).

2. *Defective Descriptions.* Hardin v. Hill correctly states the general rules to be applied when the seller owns less, or more, than the land described in the contract. Was the court correct, however, to charac-

terize the sale as "clearly in gross?" Would the use of the phrase "more or less" after the number of acres affect the result? See Marcus v. Bathon, 72 Md.App. 475, 531 A.2d 690 (1987), cert. denied, 313 Md. 612, 547 A.2d 189 (1988). Does an in gross presumption—what you see is what you get—make sense for the farmer or rancher who counts her profits by the number of acres that can be planted or left for grazing, or for the developer who thinks in terms of salable lots or rentable square feet? Or does it make sense only in the residential context, where the buyer's view of the property is sufficient to tell him whether it will suit his needs? The court may have been saying that if precise acreage really meant so much to the Hardins, they should have ordered a survey before going into possession.

Mistaken descriptions occur because it is hard to express the parties' actual expectations and perceptions in terms that coincide with the correct legal description. A homebuyer is in no position to rely on the technically phrased legal description. Rather, he relies on what he sees, visually locating the boundaries by any available physical evidence—hedges, fences, driveways, streets. Although these physical boundaries may not correspond with the property's legal description, devices exist to bridge the gap between legal description and natural expectation. The legal description may refer to monuments such as stone walls or iron pins from which the buyer can approximate the parcel's boundaries. If the area has been mapped and platted, the buyer may be able to identify the parcel with the aid of a lot map. A professionally performed survey offers even more accuracy, locating not only the parcel's boundaries, but also any easements or encroachments that may lie on it.

A contract of sale may also describe the personal property included in the sale of the realty. Generally, a sale of personal property will not be implied as part of the land sale. In Wilkin v. 1st Source Bank, 548 N.E.2d 170 (Ind.App.1990), the personal representative of Olga Mestrovic, the widow of the noted sculptor, Ivan Mestrovic, entered a contract of sale for the decedent's home. After closing, the buyers complained that the premises were left cluttered with personal property. The personal representative and the buyers agreed that the buyers could clean the premises themselves and retain any personal property that they desired rather than having the personal representative hire a cleaning service. The buyers found and claimed eight paintings and one plaster sculpture, all by Ivan Mestrovic. The court found that the parties shared a mutual mistake as to the nature of the property on the premises, not believing it to be works of art but rather "stuff" or "junk." Thus, there was no meeting of the minds and no agreement to sell or dispose of the works.

3. *Is Time of the Essence?* If on the date set for closing seller fails to tender a deed, or buyer fails to tender the purchase price, is the other party discharged from the obligation to perform? The answer will turn on whether the action is in law or in equity. When a legal remedy is sought, performance on the closing date will be considered

essential unless the contract discloses a contrary intent. In actions for an equitable remedy, time is not of the essence unless the contract or surrounding circumstances indicate that it should be. Cf. CDC Nassau Associates v. Fatoullah, 163 A.D.2d 227, 558 N.Y.S.2d 946 (1990), appeal denied, 77 N.Y.2d 802, 566 N.Y.S.2d 587, 567 N.E.2d 981 (1991) (use of phrase "time being of the essence" in connection with exercise of purchase option but not in the immediately following sentence specifying closing date, together with the circumstances, permitted specific performance at a later date). These rules apply not only to closing dates, but also to other deadlines specified in the contract such as the deadline for obtaining a financing commitment. See Kakalik v. Bernardo, 184 Conn. 386, 439 A.2d 1016 (1981).

In Limpus v. Armstrong, 3 Mass.App.Ct. 19, 322 N.E.2d 187 (1975), the contract of sale, dated September 16, called for a closing on or before November 25. After a series of missed telephone calls between buyer and seller, and buyer's failure to perform by November 25, seller on November 29 wrote buyer that the contract was no longer in force and that buyer's $100 deposit was forfeited. Reversing a decision for seller, the court ruled that plaintiff buyer was entitled to specific performance. "The mere fact that the agreement specified a date for closing did not make time of the essence." Further, the court noted, both parties had it within their power to make time of the essence even after they entered into the contract of sale. "Since both the plaintiff and the defendants had failed to perform within the time specified for conveyance, either, by notice to the other upon unreasonable or unnecessary delay by the latter, might have been assigned a reasonable time for the completion of the transaction, thereby making performance within that time of the essence of the contract." 3 Mass.App.Ct. at 24, 322 N.E.2d at 190.

4. *When One Closing is Conditioned on Another.* Conditions are sometimes more complex than timeliness of performance, marketability of title and availability of financing. For example, when the closing of one sale is conditioned on the closing of another, and the second sale is conditioned on yet a third, the conditions can recur like the receding images in multiple mirrors. The results are no less elusive or tantalizing.

In Mann v. Addicott Hills Corp., 238 Va.262, 384 S.E.2d 81 (1989), the sales contract for a home under construction included a clause, inserted at the buyers' request, allowing them to terminate their obligation to perform if they could not find a buyer for their home during the ninety day period after the framing of the new house began. The clause also required the buyers to list their home with a realtor and to provide evidence of the listing within 15 days after the framing started. Although framing began, the purchasers refused to list their home since they believed that the developer could not provide a delivery date for the new house and they did not want to sell their current home and not have a place in which to live. The seller terminated the contract citing the failure to list the current house and executed a contract of sale with another party. The buyers sought specific performance of their contract with the seller claiming a right to unilaterally waive the contingency. The court rejected the claim, finding that the contingency was also "critical" to the seller since its construction loan required it to meet sales quotas and the inability of buyers to sell their home would make closing on the new house less certain. The court concluded that the breach of such a material provision prevented the purchasers from obtaining specific relief.

Was the court's reading of the clause correct? Would a more typical seller have an interest in terminating a contract if the buyer's home is not sold? Should the fact that the house was not completed for ten months after the framing began have been relevant? Could a better clause have been drafted to account for the fact that the house was being constructed?

Complex conditions more frequently arise in commercial transactions, where purchases of land for development purposes must be carefully conditioned on the completion of arrangements for construction and permanent financing and receipt of all the government approvals necessary for the projected development. Sellers, concerned with illusoriness and with the possibility that their land will be tied up for the duration of the government approval process, sometimes insist on an option rather than a contract of sale.

5. *Whose Condition Is It?* It is sometimes unclear whether the parties intended a particular condition to benefit buyer, seller, or both. For example, a financing condition requiring that the mortgage loan be obtained from a specified institutional lender is commonly intended to benefit the buyer, who may be relying on that lender's expertise. In fact, however, the condition may have been included for the benefit of the seller. If the specified institutional lender holds the existing mortgage on the property, the buyer's agreement to assume the obligations of this mortgage may be the only way the seller can avoid the heavy prepayment penalties often charged in the early years of a loan.

The question of who was intended to benefit from a particular condition is obviously important, for only the intended beneficiary can waive the condition. Nonetheless, even well-counselled buyers and sellers often fail to indicate which of them was intended to benefit from the specified conditions. For example, in Loda v. H.K. Sargeant & Associates, Inc., 188 Conn. 69, 448 A.2d 812 (1982), litigation was required to establish that the financing condition was intended to benefit the buyer while the time limit on performance was intended to benefit the seller who did not wish to keep his property tied up by a buyer who had no prospects of obtaining the needed financing.

Contracts will often be imprecise in reflecting the parties' intentions and needs as to who may exercise a condition. Dale Mortgage Bankers Corp. v. 877 Stewart Avenue Associates, 133 A.D.2d 65, 518 N.Y.S.2d 411 (1987), appeal denied, 70 N.Y.2d 612, 523 N.Y.S.2d 496, 518 N.E.2d 7 (1987), held that the buyer could not unilaterally waive a financing condition and proceed on an all cash basis. The court strictly applied the contingency clause which stated that either party could void the sale if the purchaser could not obtain financing. Did the court correctly decide the issue? Was the seller only asserting the cancellation right in order to renegotiate the contract or find a better price? Or was the seller just trying to avoid the delay of waiting until closing to find out that the buyer would not be able to perform?

D. THE CALCULUS OF REMEDIES

A buyer whose seller has breached their land sale contract has four possible remedies. He can obtain a decree of specific performance ordering seller to convey title to him in return for payment of the purchase price. He can obtain damages measured by the difference between the parcel's market value at the date of breach and the contract price, together with any incidental expenses and losses incurred. He can rescind and recover any deposit made. Finally-- although this remedy is not much used—the buyer has a lien (called a "vendee's lien") on seller's legal title, securing the seller's obligation to refund the buyer's deposit in the event the seller breaches. The lien can be foreclosed and the land sold to satisfy this obligation if the seller fails to refund the deposit.

A seller whose buyer has breached also has four remedies, closely paralleling the remedies available to buyer. The seller can obtain a decree of specific performance requiring buyer to pay the purchase price in return for the seller's conveyance of title. The seller can obtain damages measured by the difference between the contract price and the parcel's market value at the date of breach, together with incidental expenses and losses. She can in most jurisdictions rescind and retain any deposits made by the buyer on account. Finally, seller has a lien (called a "vendor's lien") on buyer's equitable title, securing the buyer's obligation to pay the purchase price. If buyer fails to perform, the lien can be foreclosed and the land sold to satisfy the buyer's obligation.

1. SPECIFIC PERFORMANCE

a. BUYER'S RIGHT TO SPECIFIC PERFORMANCE

J. POMEROY, A TREATISE ON THE SPECIFIC PERFORMANCE OF CONTRACTS

(3d ed. 1926).

§ 9. Inadequacy of the damages. Contracts concerning land. ... If money were in all cases a measure of the injury done by the nonfulfillment of a contract, it is evident that an exact equivalent for the wrong might always be rendered by means of damages. But money is an exact equivalent only where by money the loss sustained through the breach can be fully restored. As in a contract for the purchase of merchandise, where there is nothing to impress a peculiar value upon the identical articles, the purchaser can, with the damages which he has recovered, go into the market and buy other goods of exactly the same quality, kind and amount, and so his loss is fully compensated. In many cases, however, the ability of money to purchase an exact equivalent does not exist. One landed estate, though of precisely the same market value as another, may be entirely different in every other circumstance that makes it an object of desire. The vendee in a land contract may recover back the purchase money which he has paid, and with the damages which he thus receives he may purchase another estate of equal market value, but then there may be numerous features and incidents connected with the former tract which induced him to purchase, which made it to him peculiarly desirable, but which were not taken into account in the estimate of his damages, and which cannot be found in any other land which he may buy with the money. It is evident that in this and similar cases there would be a failure of justice unless some other jurisdiction supplemented that of the common law, by compelling the defaulting party to do that which in conscience he is bound to do, namely, actually and specifically to perform his agreement.

MERRITZ v. CIRCELLI

Supreme Court of Pennsylvania, 1949.
361 Pa. 239, 64 A.2d 796.

HORACE STERN, Justice.

At least as early as the seventeenth century the High Court of Chancery in England decreed specific performance of an agreement with an allowance of compensation to the plaintiff because of the defendant's inability fully to carry out his contract; Cleaton v. Gower, Rep. temp. Finch, 164, (Ch. 1674). The practice thus born has become so generally adopted that it is now a commonplace doctrine in equity jurisprudence, it being firmly established that, where it is not in the power of a vendor to make title to all that he has covenanted to convey, the vendee has the right to take what the vendor can give with an allowance out of the purchase money for the deficiency.

The problem presented in the case now before us is whether such relief is available to plaintiff under the particular facts here involved.

Defendants, Michael and Sarah E. Circelli, entered into a written agreement with plaintiff, Harold Merritz, whereby they agreed to sell and convey to him three certain pieces of vacant ground in Philadelphia as described by metes and bounds. The agreement stated that "description of said lots and plot plan of the same is hereto attached and made part of said agreement." The plot plan thus referred to showed that the lots were bounded by Elmwood Avenue, Lindbergh

Boulevard, 57th Street and 58th Street. In the space marked Elmwood Avenue there were printed the words "all improvements" and in the space marked 57th Street and the space marked Lindbergh Boulevard the word "sewer". The purchase price was stated to be $12,500 of which $1,000 was paid at the time the agreement was signed. The premises were to be conveyed "free and clear of all incumbrance and easements", subject to an exception not here relevant.

Before the date fixed for settlement plaintiff learned that the sewers in the beds of 57th Street and Elmwood Avenue could not be connected with any dwellings that might subsequently be erected on the lots in question unless there were first paid to the City of Philadelphia a sewer service charge required by the terms of an ordinance. He also ascertained that, while there was in fact a sewer in the bed of Lindbergh Boulevard, it could never be used by the occupants of such dwellings because it was constructed along the far or remote side of the boulevard and was intended to service only the properties on that side; the cost to these lots of installing an available sewer in Lindbergh Boulevard would be approximately $8,500.

Plaintiff filed a bill in equity praying that defendants be compelled to convey to him the lots as described in the agreement but with an abatement in the purchase price of a sum representing the cost of constructing an available sewer in Lindbergh Boulevard and the sewer service charge which would be imposed when connections were made with the sewers in 57th Street and Elmwood Avenue. The testimony revealed that the allowance thus requested would amount to approximately $9,300. The court below dismissed the bill and plaintiff appeals.

The chancellor found that the word "sewer" on the portion of the plan designated Lindbergh Boulevard indicated that there was a sewer under that avenue "available for use by plaintiff as the purchaser of the lots fronting thereon." He further found that such representation, while untrue, was not made for the fraudulent purpose of misleading plaintiff but innocently and by mistake; this finding was justified because the burden to prove fraud was upon plaintiff but no testimony was offered by him to establish it. The fact, however, that the representation was not made with fraudulent intent does not absolve defendants from liability.

Nor is it a defense that plaintiff might have ascertained the falsity of the representation had he inspected the public records, for he was not required to make such an investigation but could rely on the representation made so as to hold defendants liable in case it proved false in fact.

This brings us to the real question in the case, which is whether, assuming such liability of the vendors to exist, plaintiff is entitled to the remedy which he seeks in the present proceedings. It is not in every instance that specific performance of a contract for the sale of land will be enforced, for an agreement may be perfectly good and binding upon both parties and nevertheless the court may relegate the plaintiff to whatever remedy he may have at law, if, in the exercise of a discretion, not arbitrary or capricious but governed by principles of reason, the chancellor is of opinion that in the particular case before him it would be contrary to equity and justice to decree specific performance.

There are two reasons why the equitable remedy of specific performance with an abatement should not be granted under the circumstances of the present case.

(1) The agreement between the parties did not, of course, involve any contractual obligation on the part of defendants to convey title to the Lindbergh Boulevard sewer nor did it contain any warranty in regard thereto; there was merely a misrepresentation of a fact as to the availability of a sewer which lay under the bed of a public street and not within the lines of the lots which were the subject of the agreement of sale. Only in cases where there is a defect in the vendor's title or a deficiency in the quantity of the land to be conveyed does the doctrine of specific performance with an abatement prevail; where there is merely a claim based upon a representation collateral to the contract the only remedy available to the vendee is rescission or the recovery of damages at law. ...

(2) When the extent to which a good title can be given is relatively small, equity will not assess damages as compensation but will leave the vendee to his remedy at law; it is only when the defect is comparatively incidental and does not involve such a large deduction from the purchase price as practically to constitute a new contract between the parties that equity will grant relief. Thus, where the requested allowance, representing a partial lack of title on the part of the vendors and also the incumbrance of a mortgage on the property, would have exhausted nearly the whole of the purchase money, the chancellor refused, in the early case of Wheatley v. Slade, 4 Sim. 126 (Ch. 1830), to decree specific performance with an abatement.

... In the present case, to compel defendants to convey the lots to plaintiff upon receipt of approximately $3,200 instead of the agreed price of $12,500 would be to enforce a contract so radically different from that which the parties entered into and so beyond their contemplation as to work both a probable hardship and an injustice; under such circumstances it would seem far better to leave plaintiff to whatever remedy may be open to him on the law side of the court. Of course if he were willing to accept a conveyance conditioned upon his paying the entire $12,500 stipulated in the contract he would be entitled to specific performance.

As far as the service charge in connection with the future use of the 57th Street and the Elmwood Avenue sewers is concerned, it has been definitely held that a charge of that nature is not a lien or incumbrance on the title since it will come into existence only if, in the future, dwelling houses or other structures are erected on the premises and connections with the sewer are actually made; until then nothing is payable.

Upon plaintiff's paying the entire purchase price stipulated in the contract a decree of specific performance should be entered by the court below. Otherwise the decree dismissing the bill is affirmed without prejudice to plaintiff's rights at law; the parties to bear their respective costs.

b. SELLER'S RIGHT TO SPECIFIC PERFORMANCE

J. POMEROY, 5 EQUITY JURISPRUDENCE AND EQUITABLE REMEDIES 4875–4877 (1919).

§ 2169. **Specific Performance in Favor of Vendor.**—It is well settled, with scarcely any dissent, that specific performance is granted in favor of a vendor of land as freely as in favor of a vendee, though the relief actually obtained by him is usually only a recovery of money—the purchase price. Three theories have been advanced to explain this rule: (1) It is said that the vendor's remedy in law by damages is inadequate, since the measure of damages is the difference between the agreed price and the market value, whereas the vendor might for particular reasons stand in need of the whole sum agreed to be paid. The objection to this theory is, that it proves too much; since, if the same test were applied generally, damages might be an inadequate remedy in every instance of sale and purchase, of chattels as well as of land. (2) It is said that by the doctrine of equitable conversion the vendee is a trustee of the purchase price for the vendor, and the vendor, in obtaining specific performance, enforces this trust. To this it may be answered, that it proves too little; for the doctrine of equitable conversion is not supposed to extend to contracts for the sale and purchase of chattels or things in action, yet the cases are not infrequent where such contracts have been enforced at the suit of the vendors therein. (3) The rule is more satisfactorily accounted for by reference to the doctrine of mutuality; *viz.,* that where an equitable remedial right in the vendee is recognized, a corresponding remedial right should be admitted in favor of the vendor. This is the usual explanation of the rule, and appears to reconcile most, if not all, of the cases.

TOMBARI v. GRIEPP

Supreme Court of Washington, 1960.
55 Wash.2d 771, 350 P.2d 452.

FINLEY, Judge.

This is an appeal from a judgment on the pleadings in favor of the defendants in an action brought by the plaintiffs specifically to enforce a contract for the sale of realty.

The plaintiffs allege in their complaint that they are husband and wife, and are owners of the realty in question; that a written agreement had been entered into whereby the plaintiff husband agreed to sell and the defendants agreed to buy this realty; that, since the date of the agreement, the plaintiffs have been and are now willing and able to perform said agreement; and that the defendants have at all times refused to perform. The plaintiffs prayed for specific performance of the contract.

The defendants, answering the complaint, admit that they refused to perform the contract. They set up four affirmative defenses and allege: that neither the plaintiff nor the defendant wife had signed the purchase agreement; that the legal description in the agreement was not sufficient; that subsequent to the time the agreement to purchase was entered into, it was determined that the property in question was not suitable for the purposes originally intended by the defendants, and, as a consequence, plaintiffs and defendants orally agreed to substitute other property owned by plaintiffs; and lastly, that the plaintiffs have not performed the contract and are unable to do so. Plaintiffs' demurrer to these affirmative defenses was overruled.

Plaintiffs' reply to defendants' answer admits that plaintiff wife had not signed the purchase agreement; but it further alleges that plaintiff wife was and now is ready, willing and able to consent in writing to said sale. Plaintiffs deny the matter contained in the other three affirmative defenses.

Defendants thereafter filed a motion for judgment on the pleadings on the ground that plaintiffs' complaint and reply raise no material issue and on their face show no cause of action existing for specific performance. The trial judge dismissed plaintiffs' complaint and granted the defendants' motion for judgment on the pleadings. Plaintiffs have appealed.

The trial court based its decision on the fact that appellant wife did not sign the purchase agreement, and that, as a consequence, had the respondents brought this action for specific performance, appellants would have been able to avoid the contract. The trial court relied on Wagner v. Peshastin Lumber Company, 1928, 149 Wash. 328, 270 P. 1032, 1037, wherein this court quoted from Pomeroy's Specific Performance of Contracts (3d ed.), § 165, as follows:

" '. . . if the right to the specific performance of a contract exists at all, it must be mutual; the remedy must be alike attainable by both parties to the agreement.' "

The trial court concluded that the contract must be such that at the time *it is entered into* it is enforcible by either of the parties against the other.

In the present case we cannot agree with the trial court's conclusion respecting the legal significance of the failure of the appellant wife to sign the contract in the first instance. In Leroux v. Knoll, 1947, 28 Wash.2d 964, 184 P.2d 564, which, like the case at bar, was an action for specific performance of a real estate contract, the plaintiff-purchaser did not sign the earnest-money receipt. The court, in granting specific performance, cited Western Timber Co. v. Kalama River Lbr. Co., 42 Wash. 620, 85 P. 338, 340, 6 L.R.A.,N.S., 397, as authority for its decision. In Western Timber Co. v. Kalama River Lbr. Co., supra, the court quoted with approval from 2 Warvelle, Vendors, p. 748:

" 'Equity will not direct a performance of the terms of the agreement of one party when, at the time of such order, the other party is at liberty to reject the obligations of such agreement; yet, as in a case where an agreement which the statute of frauds requires to be in writing has been signed by one of the parties only, or when the contract, by its terms, gives to one party a right to the performance which he does not confer upon the other, upon the filing of a bill for enforcement in equity by the party who was before unbound, he thereby puts himself under the obligation of the contract. The contract then ceases to be unilateral; for by his own act the unbound party makes the contract mutual, and the other party is enabled to enforce it.' "

So, in the instant case, when the appellant wife joined in the action, the contract became mutually binding upon the parties.

Contracts which convey or encumber community realty and which the wife does not sign are not void. They are merely voidable, and it is the wife who has the power of avoidance. She may, as she wishes, either accept or reject the voidable action of her husband. In the case at bar the wife, by joining with her husband in bringing this action for specific performance, has chosen to accept and ratify the voidable action of her husband.

Respondent, however, urges that, even if the absence of appellant wife's signature from the contract is of no significance, in view of her present willingness to perform as evidenced by the fact that she has joined her husband in bringing this action, the contract is still not specifically enforcible for the reason that the appellants have an adequate legal remedy. However, according to the overwhelming weight of authority, a vendor, as well as a vendee, may obtain specific performance of a contract for the sale of land.

. . .

II Restatement of the Law, Contracts, 643, § 360 c., explains the rule as follows:

"c. Before conveyance has been made by the vendor his remedy in damages is not an adequate one. He can not get judgment for the full price, because he still has the land. His damages are usually measured by the contract price less the value of the land retained; but the land is a commodity that has no established market value, and the vendor may not be able to prove what his real harm will be. Even if he can make this proof, the land may not be immediately convertible into money, and he is deprived of the power to make new investments. Prior to getting a judgment, the existence of the contract, even though broken by the vendee, operates as a clog on salability, so that it may not be possible to find a purchaser at any fair price. In addition, the fact that specific performance is available to the vendee is of some weight, because of the rule as to mutuality of remedy (see § 372(2))".

. . .

Respondents' second affirmative defense concerning the sufficiency of the legal description is also without merit. The type of description used in this agreement was held to be legally sufficient in Schmidt v. Powell, 1919, 107 Wash. 53, 180 P. 892.

The third and fourth affirmative defenses raise issues which must be determined on the trial of this action. Appellants urge that evidence of the oral agreement, which is alleged in the third affirmative defense, will not be admissible because of the parol evidence rule. In essence, the respondents, by this defense, have alleged that this contract was mutually rescinded by an oral agreement. In Lamar v. Anderson, 1912, 71 Wash. 314, 128 P. 672, the court said,

"... there can be no question but that the parties to a written contract may by mutual oral agreement abandon it."

For the reasons indicated above, appellants' demurrer to respondents' first and second affirmative defenses should have been sustained. The judgment granting respondents' motion for judgment on the pleadings should be reversed and vacated. It is so ordered.

WEAVER, C.J., and ROSELLINI, FOSTER and HUNTER, JJ., concur.

OTT, Judge.

I dissent for the following reasons:

(1) It is conceded that the contract involved in this proceeding was for the sale of real property owned by appellant husband and wife as community property, and *that the wife did not sign the contract.* A contract to sell real estate is an encumbrance upon the land. By statute, the wife is an indispensable party to the sale, conveyance or encumbrance of community real estate. RCW 26.16.040. Since it is conceded that an indispensable party did not sign the instrument, it is unenforcible and void as a contract of sale.

(2) The majority hold that the contract was voidable at the option of the wife, but that, by joining as a party plaintiff in this action, she thereby ratified the contract. Conceding, *arguendo,* that the wife did ratify by joining in this action, thus giving the instrument efficacy as a contract, it is my opinion that the ratification was not timely.

Prior to ratification by the wife, the purported contract was no more than an offer to buy on the part of the respondents, which created in the appellant wife the power to accept or reject it. An offer can be withdrawn at any time before acceptance. The pleadings disclose that respondents' offer to purchase was withdrawn prior to the commencement of this action. Since the appellant wife's acceptance of the offer (ratification) was admittedly accomplished after the offer to purchase was withdrawn, the acceptance (ratification) was not timely.

Stabbert v. Atlas Imperial Diesel Engine Co., 1951, 39 Wash.2d 789, 238 P.2d 1212, relied upon by the majority, is not in point. In the cited case, the wife had given her husband a power of attorney to act for her "in transactions concerning community real estate." Vested with such authority, the contract signed by the husband only was enforcible from its inception.

(3) The appellants seek specific performance of the contract. This is a request that the court exercise its equity, rather than its law, jurisdiction. It is the law of this state that a court will invoke its equity jurisdiction only when there is no plain, adequate or speedy remedy at law. There are no allegations relative to the inadequacy of the legal remedy in this complaint. It alleges the existence of the contract, the refusal to perform, and

"That the plaintiffs were and have always been and now are ready and willing to perform the said agreement on their part, that the purchase price agreed to be paid for the said real estate by said defendants is a fair and reasonable value thereof, and plaintiff desires that said contract be *specifically performed.*" (Italics mine.)

These allegations, in my opinion, fall far short of affirmatively establishing that the legal remedy of damages is inadequate.

The majority assume that land is ordinarily not readily salable and its market value is difficult of ascertainment; hence, legal damages are inadequate. Such essential facts must be pleaded. They cannot be supplied by the court.

"Since the remedy at law for breach of contract is generally by way of compensatory damages, ordinarily a complainant coming into equity for specific performance must show that a recovery of damages for breach of the contract would not constitute an adequate remedy." 49 Am.Jur. 21, § 12.

Since facts showing the inadequacy of damages are not pleaded, the majority take judicial notice that such are the facts. I am unwilling to take judicial notice that land is not readily salable or that its market value is difficult to ascertain with a reasonable degree of certainty.

Our courts of law do not throw up their hands in despair when faced with the problem of determining the market value of land in condemnation and other proceedings. Why should we find it such an insurmountable task to determine the value of land in an action of this type? If the vendor receives the difference between the market value of the land and the contract price, he has received the benefit of his bargain. What more is he entitled to? I suggest that we reserve equity powers for situations where it is clearly shown by the pleadings that there is no plain, speedy, and adequate remedy at law.

(4) Finally, whether a court will order specific performance of a contract or leave one to his remedy at law *rests within the sound discretion of the trial court.*

The majority do not hold that the trial court abused its discretion. They hold that the appellants can compel the trial court to exercise its extraordinary equity jurisdiction and order the contract specifically performed on the part of the respondents, as a matter of *right.* If it is the desire of the majority to change the law, the cited cases should be specifically overruled. The bench and bar will then know that it is the litigants, and not the courts, who determine whether a case will be tried as one involving the court's equity jurisdiction or its law jurisdiction. I prefer to leave the exercise of discretion in this regard where it has always been—in the trial court.

The trial court, in my opinion, did not abuse its discretion in denying to the appellants the extraordinary equitable remedy sought.

For the reasons stated, the judgment should be affirmed.

MALLERY, J., concurs.

HILL and DONWORTH, Judges.

We concur in the result of the dissent for the third reason given; i.e. no showing that the remedy at law is not adequate.

2. DAMAGES

a. Buyer's Damages

RAISOR v. JACKSON

Court of Appeals of Kentucky, 1949.
311 Ky. 803, 225 S.W.2d 657.

CLAY, Commissioner.

This suit was brought by appellant, the buyer, to recover damages for the seller's breach of a contract to convey real estate. Following the trial Court's instructions, a verdict was returned in appellant's favor for nominal damages of $1. These instructions authorized the jury to award substantial damages (the difference between the contract price and the reasonable market value of the property) only in the event it found appellee acted in bad faith and was guilty of positive or actual fraud. The question before us is whether or not these instructions correctly submitted the applicable law governing the rights of the parties.

On February 14, 1947, the property was sold to appellant at a public auction for $22,252. He complied with the terms of sale by making a down payment of $4,500. A few days later when appellant called on appellee to convey the property, the latter advised he could not do so because his wife, who owned an undivided one-half interest therein, refused to join in the deed. The down payment was returned to appellant, and shortly thereafter appellee and his wife sold the property to another party. On the trial there was evidence the land had a reasonable market value in excess of the sale price.

Appellee clearly breached his contract. He contends, and his contention was upheld by the trial Court in giving the instructions, that if he was acting in good faith and was guilty of no positive or actual fraud, appellant was only entitled to nominal damages. Appellant insists the breach of contract entitled him to recover for the loss of his bargain.

While the question presented is not novel, it is one of broad significance. Research indicates that numberless courts for many years have wrestled with the problem and have reached differing results. In our own jurisdiction we find conflicting decisions. The differences of view are manifest in two cases squarely in point and inconsistent in conclusion. They are: Potts v. Moran's Executors, 236 Ky. 28, 32 S.W.2d 534, and Gober v. Leslie, 307 Ky. 477, 211 S.W.2d 658. The correct decision in this case makes necessary a re-appraisal of the governing principles.

The doctrine that a purchaser of land from a seller unable to make title should only be permitted to recover nominal damages, and not substantial damages for the loss of his bargain, originated in the old English case of Flureau v. Thornhill, (1776) 2 W.Bl. 1078, 96 Eng.Rep. 635. In that case plaintiff purchased a leasehold. When the title was examined, the seller "could not make it out". The buyer sued for damages based on his loss of profit in certain stocks which he had sold to raise the purchase money. In denying the purchaser substantial damages, the Court laid down the rule that "if the title proves bad, and the vendor is (without fraud) incapable of making a good one", the purchaser is not entitled to damages for the "fancied goodness of the bargain". It is difficult to understand how that case, *which simply involved highly speculative damages,* could have been accorded the authoritative position it has enjoyed for the past 173 years.

Subsequent to the Flureau case, the English courts, over a span of almost 100 years, threatened to distinguish it out of existence. In 1874, in Bain v. Fothergill, L.R. 7 H.L. 168, the House of Lords revived it. In that case the defendants agreed to assign plaintiffs a lease. The former were not able to make a good assignment because of their inability to obtain the consent of the landlord, required by the lease. Suit was brought to recover damages for the loss of the buyer's bargain. Drawing heavily on the Flureau case, and disapproving of later cases which had limited the scope of the supposed rule there announced, the majority denied the full relief sought by the plaintiffs. The basis of the decision was that a contract to convey land carries no warranty that the vendor has power to convey, but involves the implied condition, which the buyer is charged with accepting, that the vendor has good title. This is a rather astounding theory which seems contrary to the most fundamental principles of contract law.

Mr. Justice Denman, in a vigorous dissent, accepted the authority of the Flureau case insofar as it related to *an unknown defect in title,* but carefully pointed out that the application of the principle was dependent on *the reason for the seller's inability to convey.* His theory was that a vendor who undertakes to make good title, knowing that he has no title (or knowing that the consent of a third party is necessary), is just as responsible for his failure to perform as anyone else breaking his contract. He quoted from an earlier decision wherein the Court held the original doctrine of the Flureau case should not be extended to those persons who, with knowledge of their present inability, *"take upon themselves to sell in the speculative belief that they will be able to procure an interest and title before they are called upon to execute the conveyance".* In effect this view is that a seller, having positive knowledge he is unable to convey individually, assumes the risk that he will be able to procure the necessary acts of third parties.

Let us now examine the case of Crenshaw v. Williams, 191 Ky. 559, 231 S.W. 45, 48 A.L.R. 5, decided by this Court in 1921. In that case the defendant had agreed to convey a tract of real estate to the plaintiff. Examination of the title indicated the defendant's wife was devised a life estate in the property with remainder to her children. She had two children, one of whom had died and whose interest she had inherited. The other child, with her, joined in the deed plaintiff refused to accept. The wife was of such an age that in the ordinary course of nature she would bear no more children. The imperfection in the title was the possibility that unanticipated, unborn children might have a remainder interest in the property. Under these circumstances it was held that if the vendor acted in good faith and was guilty of no positive or active fraud, the buyer could not recover the difference between the reasonable market value of the land and the price he had agreed to pay for it.

We still think that decision was and is sound. The rule there announced was justified on the ground that the intricate involvement of titles to real estate may often lead the apparent owner into the innocent mistaken belief that his title is good, whereas minute examination by title specialists may disclose some fine but formidable flaw. Under those circumstances the good faith of the seller is a proper factor to consider in balancing the rights of the parties.

We now come to the case of Potts v. Moran's Executors, 236 Ky. 28, 32 S.W.2d 534. In that case the seller was unable to convey to the buyer because his wife, who had a dower interest in the property, refused to sign the deed. It was there decided that in the absence of a showing of bad faith on the part of the seller, the buyer was only entitled to recover nominal damages. The opinion cites with approval the Crenshaw case (191 Ky. 559, 231 S.W. 45, 48 A.L.R. 5) above discussed, but careful examination will demonstrate that the two cases involve quite different circumstances. The opinion goes further, however, and resorts to the reasoning followed in the original English authorities. It is fair to say the decision dropped its anchor squarely on the case of Bain v. Fothergill, L.R. 7 H.L. 158, heretofore considered. Yet it was acknowledged that the rule adopted was in conflict with decisions from the jurisdictions of Alabama, Ohio, Florida, Indiana, Kansas, West Virginia, Virginia and New York.

We are now of the opinion that the Potts case extended the good faith doctrine to a set of circumstances wherein its application has no sound justification. The reasoning in the case is based on a *latent defect* in title, but the rule is applied to a situation involving a *known lack of title*. In the former case there may well be an honest mistake; in the latter such is impossible. It is true a seller may be mistaken concerning his ability to obtain the necessary conveyance from a third party, *but he cannot be mistaken concerning the state of his ownership at the time he executes the contract*. In one case there is a negative failure of title; in the other there is a positive failure of the seller to perform what he has undertaken.

. . .

From what has been said above, it is obvious that the matter of good faith is not material in the type of case we are considering. The seller has simply undertaken to do something which he finds he cannot do. His intentions or motives are without significance. As stated in the case of Doherty v. Dolan, 65 Me. 87, 91, 20 Am.Rep. 677: "The pecuniary damages are the same to the vendee, whether the motive of the vendor in refusing to convey is good or bad. It is a difficult thing to ascertain whether or not a vendor is actuated by good faith in his refusal to convey. There can easily be frauds and deceits about it. The vendor is strongly tempted to avoid his agreement, where there has been a rise in the value of the property. The vendee, by making this contract, may lose other opportunities of making profitable investments. The vendor knows, when he contracts, his ability to convey a title, and the vendee ordinarily does not. The vendor can provide in his contract against such a contingency as an unexpected inability to convey."

In some jurisdictions it has been held that bad faith is *imputable* to the vendor who, knowing his present inability to comply with the contract, undertakes to convey land. Whether we adopt the view that good faith is no defense, or the view that the vendor is ipso facto guilty of bad faith in contracting to do what he knows he is unable to do, the same result follows, i.e., the vendor's inability to convey is no legal excuse for the failure to perform and does not entitle him to special equitable consideration.

The case of Gober v. Leslie, 307 Ky. 477, 211 S.W.2d 658, decided by this Court in 1948, involves facts almost identical with those on this appeal. The opinion does not discuss the authorities herein referred to, but we reached the same conclusion we now consider inescapable: the buyer may recover substantial damages, if he can prove them, without regard to the seller's good faith, if the breach of contract is occasioned by the failure of the seller to obtain a conveyance of his wife's interest in the property.

This is simply a recognition of the principle that where a seller unconditionally agrees to convey real property, knowing he has no title or with knowledge of an outstanding interest therein owned by a third party, he is bound by his undertaking to deliver a good deed to the purchaser; the question of good faith is immaterial if he breaches his agreement; and if the buyer is so damaged, he may recover the difference between the contract price and the reasonable market value of the property at the time the contract was executed. This decision does not impair the rule relating to latent defects in title, applied in the Crenshaw case, but it does overrule, to the extent of any conflict, the holding in the Potts case. This determination requires a reversal of the judgment before us.

Assuming the evidence of the contract and its breach to be the same on a new trial, the instructions should authorize an award of substantial damages, if they are proven, without presenting the issue of appellee's good faith. We do not undertake to pass upon the issue of fraud or collusion on the part of appellant which was raised at the former trial.

For the reasons stated, the judgment is reversed, with directions to grant appellant a new trial and for proceedings consistent herewith.

JACKSON v. RAISOR

Court of Appeals of Kentucky, 1952.
248 S.W.2d 905.

CULLEN, Commissioner.

Raymond Raisor, who was the highest bidder for certain real estate at a voluntary auction sale at which O.N. Jackson (the owner of an undivided one-half interest) had offered the real estate for sale, sued Jackson for damages for "loss of bargain" resulting from his inability to secure title because of the refusal of Jackson's wife (the owner of the other one-half interest) to join in a deed to the real estate. Raisor's petition alleged that the reasonable market value of the real estate at the time of the auction sale was $5,000 more than the price he bid at the sale, and he sought damages for such difference in value. The jury returned a verdict for $2,500, and from the judgment entered on that verdict the defendant Jackson has appealed.

Jackson's contentions are: (1) He was entitled to a peremptory instruction, because (a) the auction sale was a free, fair and voluntary sale and therefore the price obtained at that sale must be found to be the fair market value of the property, and (b) the plaintiff introduced no competent evidence to show that the fair market value of the property exceeded the auction sale price; (2) even if it be conceded that some of the plaintiff's evidence as to value was competent, the remaining evidence was incompetent and its admission was prejudicial error; (3) the court erroneously admitted incompetent and prejudicial evidence as to special damages; (4) the instructions were erroneous; and (5) the verdict is excessive and was the result of passion and prejudice.

We can find no support for the contention that the price obtained at the auction sale is conclusive as to fair market value. It appears to be the general rule that the price received at a free and voluntary auction sale is competent evidence of value. But no court seems to have held that the auction price is conclusive evidence, and we are not sufficiently convinced of the merit of the contention to establish such a precedent. Indicative of reasons why the auction sale price in this case should not be held conclusive evidence of value, are the fact that Mrs. Jackson refused to sign the deed because she thought the price was too low, and the fact that Jackson attempted to prove that the auctioneer through collusion with Raisor cut off the bidding too soon.

Contentions (1), (b), (2) and (5) are closely related, and all involve the basic question of what kind of evidence is admissible to show the market value of real estate. We will consider the question in relation to the various kinds of evidence offered and admitted in this case, which were:

1. The testimony of the plaintiff that on the day of the sale a Mr. Henry offered to buy the real estate from the plaintiff at a $1,000 profit.

2. The testimony of the plaintiff that "I figure I lost at least $5,000 by being messed up."

3. The testimony of Mr. Roy Lewis, a real estate dealer, that approximately one month after the auction sale, he acquired the real estate from Mr. Jackson in a trade, in which he paid Mr. Jackson $12,500 in cash and deeded him a house on Devil's Hollow Hill which, for the purposes of the trade, they valued at $8,000.

4. The testimony of Mr. Lewis that, seven months after the auction sale, he traded the real estate to a Mr. Pennington, for a house in Tanglewood Subdivision and $7,000 "to boot," and that he valued the Tanglewood house at $20,000.

5. Proof that the deed of the real estate from Jackson to Lewis carried Federal Revenue Stamps in the amount of $21.45, indicating a consideration of from $19,000 to $19,500.

The evidence of the offer made by Mr. Henry (No. 1 above) was incompetent.

The plaintiff's statement that he figured he "lost at least $5,000 by being messed up" (No. 2 above) clearly was no evidence as to value.

The question of whether the evidence concerning the two trades (Nos. 3 and 4 above) was competent is one on which we find little authority to serve as a precedent. We do not find that any court has held such evidence to be competent to prove value. To the contrary, in

Hay v. Boggs, 77 Wash. 329, 137 P. 474, the Supreme Court of Washington held that evidence as to the values placed by the parties on properties being exchanged or traded was not competent to prove the value of one of the properties, because the agreed values often may be fictitious or far from the real value.

It seems to be the general rule that "market value" means the highest price obtainable in the open market for *cash*. It is obvious that if evidence of a trade or exchange is to be admitted for the purpose of establishing market value, the value of the property received in trade must be fixed in terms of money in order to have any meaning. Since the cash value of real estate is never capable of absolute determination, but is necessarily an approximation, it may be doubted whether in any case the value of property received in trade, even if proved according to accepted methods, should be received as evidence of the value of the property for which it was traded, because to do so amounts to a pyramiding of approximations. However, it is unnecessary in the case before us to answer that question, because here there was no competent proof as to the market value of the property received in trade, but only testimony as to the value the parties placed on the property for trading purposes. We agree with the Washington Court that this kind of testimony is not competent.

A further reason for rejecting the testimony as to the trade for the house in Tanglewood is that this trade occurred seven months after the auction sale, and there was no proof that the Jackson real estate was in the same condition as at the time of the auction sale. It is conceivable that valuable improvements may have been made upon the real estate during the seven-month period.

The question of whether the amount of the revenue stamps on the Jackson-Lewis deed is admissible to prove market value is again a novel one. A diligent research discloses only one case on the question, in which the Federal District Court for the Southern District of New York said that "the number of revenue stamps would not establish value". Evidence as to the amount of revenue stamps on a deed certainly is of secondary quality, and may approach the character of hearsay evidence. The ultimate fact sought to be proved is the market value of the property; the price at which the property was sold is direct evidence bearing on the question of value; but the revenue stamps merely speak silently of the fact that, if the vendor was an honest taxpayer, the price at which the property was sold did not exceed the amount evidenced by the revenue stamps.

We are of the opinion that evidence of the amount of revenue stamps on a deed is not entitled to substantial weight, and is not sufficient, standing alone, to prove market value, although it might be admissible to corroborate or discredit testimony as to sale price.

We are led to the conclusion that the plaintiff did not establish, by competent evidence of probative value, his right to recover substantial damages for loss of bargain. ...

Upon the two trials already had in this case, the breach of contract by Jackson has been established conclusively. In the event of a third trial, the issues should be limited to the question of damages, under proof in accordance with accepted methods of proving market value, such as the estimates of qualified witnesses, or evidence as to sales of comparable real estate at or about the time as of which the value is to be fixed. If, upon a third trial, the evidence as to market value should be the same as on the second trial, the defendant would be entitled to an instruction limiting his liability to nominal damages.

The judgment is reversed, for proceedings consistent with this opinion.

b.   Seller's Damages

KUHN v. SPATIAL DESIGN, INC.

Superior Court of New Jersey, Appellate Division, 1991.
245 N.J.Super.378, 585 A.2d 967.

Before Judges LONG, R.S. COHEN and STERN.

The opinion of the court was delivered by

R.S. COHEN, J.A.D.

Plaintiffs John and Marlene Kuhn contracted to buy a home from defendant Spatial Design, Inc. The sale was contingent on the Kuhns' obtaining a mortgage to finance the purchase. They applied to Prudential Home Mortgage Company through a mortgage broker, defendant Sterling National Mortgage Company, Inc., with the help of Sterling employees, defendants Ellberger and Wolf. Prudential issued a mortgage commitment but later withdrew it. The Kuhns then sought to void their purchase contract with Spatial Design for failure of the mortgage contingency. When they did not get their deposit back, they started suit. Spatial Design counterclaimed for damages for breach of contract. Judge Patrick J. McGann, Jr., heard the matter and found that the Kuhns had breached. He therefore denied their claim and awarded Spatial Design damages on the counterclaim. We affirm substantially for the reasons expressed in Judge McGann's oral opinion of March 22, 1990, in which he meticulously and thoroughly expressed his findings of fact and conclusions of law. There are two matters, however, on which we feel it would be useful to express our own views.

Judge McGann concluded on compelling evidence that the Kuhns and Sterling's people purposely submitted a mortgage application that presented a materially false picture of the Kuhns' income and assets, because they knew that revealing their true financial situation would not produce the loan they sought. The judge further found that the Kuhns and Sterling were encouraged to submit such an application by Prudential's dependably credulous way of dealing with income and asset information submitted to it.

The Kuhns knew that their application showed that Kuhn was an Air Force colonel, but did not reveal that he had already been approved for retirement; that Mrs. Kuhn had a substantial income from "Plants–R–You," a florist business which existed only in the minds of the Kuhns and Sterling's people; that the fictitious business had assets of $50,000, which did not exist at all; that the $50,000 deposit on the purchase came from savings, when in fact it was borrowed on a second mortgage on the Kuhns' present home, and that the Kuhns had jewelry, antiques, stamps and the like worth $123,000, which Kuhn actually thought would fetch some $47,000.

Kuhn knew that his true current income and assets would not support the mortgage application. He and his wife also knew that Wolf had left some figures blank in the application they signed. Wolf had said they were not going to be "boy scouts" in the matter. Predictably, Sterling's president, Ellberger, who knew what numbers it took to make the application viable, supplied some impressive ones. They showed bank balances of some $240,000 instead of the real $10,000, and total family income of some $218,000 instead of the real $65,000 or even the fictitious $95,000 that earlier appeared. Not surprisingly, Prudential issued a commitment for a $300,000 mortgage for the $515,000 purchase.

All of this was possible because the Kuhns were making a "no documentation" loan application. That meant that Prudential would probably not check to see if the represented facts showing the career Air Force officer's improbably comfortable financial situation were true.[2]

Colonel Kuhn expected the whole business to be ultimately supported by a high-salaried but not-yet-identified private sector job he hoped to find before he retired. The $30,000 in income he thought was going to be attributed to "Plants–R–You" (Ellberger eventually settled on $9400 per month.) was really his Air Force pension. The $65,000 he thought he showed as service income (Ellberger made it $8800 per month.) would be covered by the private sector job he had not yet sought.

When Kuhn put the present home up for sale and looked for a private sector job, he found both the real estate market and the job market unwelcoming. He heard that Spatial Design might have sold the house across the street from their new one for much less than they were paying. He therefore decided to climb down from the shaky limb he was on. He telephoned Prudential and wrote to Sterling, stating that he had decided to retire from the Air Force, and would thus lose some $40,000 in annual income. He inquired innocently if that would affect the mortgage commitment.

2. It is impossible to tell from the evidence if Prudential greeted improbable information in "no documentation" applications with a knowing wink, and counted on ever-rising property values to pick up the slack.

Almost simultaneously, Kuhn wrote to the Air Force to withdraw his approved retirement, thus falsifying the sole expressed basis of his communications with Prudential and Sterling. Prudential withdrew its commitment on the basis of the new information. It had retained the right to withdraw "if any material facts appear that have not previously been revealed by [the applicant]." Kuhn then unsuccessfully tried to cancel the purchase contract on the thesis that the mortgage contingency was not satisfied.

The Kuhns sued Spatial Design, which counterclaimed for the deposit and damages. They then sued Sterling, Wolf and Ellberger for indemnification against the counterclaim. Spatial Design crossclaimed against Sterling, Wolf and Ellberger for fraud, tortious interference, conspiracy and negligence.

After a bench trial, Judge McGann found in favor of Spatial Design and against the Kuhns, and assessed damages at almost $100,000, less the retained deposit of $50,000. He denied the Kuhns' indemnification claim and Spatial Design's damage claim against the mortgage brokers.

Spatial Design has not crossappealed from the denial of its damage claim against the mortgage brokers. We therefore do not comment on it.[5] In all respects material to this appeal, however, Judge McGann's findings and conclusions on the conduct of the parties are supported by compelling evidence. We have considered his conclusions that as wrongdoers the Kuhns are not entitled to indemnification, and that whatever limited knowledge the Kuhns' real estate broker Flo Pulda had about the mortgage application was not attributable to Spatial Design. Those conclusions were factually supported and legally sound.

Now, as to damages. The contract price was $515,000, subject to a real estate commission of 5% or $25,750. The house was eventually sold, free of commission, for $434,000. In the interim, there were carrying charges for taxes and interest. There was no reason suggested by the evidence to doubt the reasonableness either of the time it took to resell the house or the sale price obtained.

Damages arose from two different sources. The first was the decreasing value of the house due to general market conditions. The second was the cost of holding the house until it could be resold. The holding costs are not the subject of this appeal. The Kuhns have two arguments, however, about the loss-of-value damages.

The first argument is that the true measure of a seller's damages for breach of contract by a buyer of real estate is the difference between the contract price and the market value at the time of the breach, less credit for any deposit retained by the seller. ... They point out that if values were steadily declining, as the judge found, they had declined

5. We do note N.J.S.A. 17:11B–14g, which prohibits material misrepresentations, circumventions and concealments by mortgage brokers, and N.J.S.A. 17:11B–17, which makes willful violations third-degree crimes. We do not say whether these statutes create a cause of action, or whether the disappointed seller would have standing to sue.

very little in the few months between contract and breach, and certainly much less than at the time of resale, many months later. Thus, the Kuhns argue, it was error to measure Spatial Design's damages by the difference between the two contract prices.

Neither of the cases cited by the Kuhns involved the assessment of damages resulting from a breach in a falling market. In such circumstances, two basic rules must be consulted. One is that contract damages are designed to put the injured party in as good a position as if performance had been rendered as promised. The other, from *Hadley v. Baxendale*, is that damages should be such as may fairly be considered either arising naturally, *i.e.*, according to the usual course of things, from the breach, or such as may reasonably be supposed to have been in the contemplation of both parties, at the time they contracted, as the probable result of the breach. *Donovan v. Bachstadt*, 91 N.J. 434, 444–445, 453 A.2d 160 (1982).

In the usual course of things, a $515,000 house cannot be resold the instant a contract buyer breaches, and a reasonable time for resale must therefore be allowed. In addition, it is not uncommon for property values to experience a general fall-off after a period of intense run-up. In a falling market, buyers take longer to find, and they buy at reduced prices.

A rule that restricts damages for breach of a contract to buy real estate to the difference between contract price and value at the time of breach (plus expenses) works fairly only in a static market. A damage rule works fairly in a declining market only if it takes account of slowing sales and falling values. In such cases, where the seller puts the property back on the market and resells, the measure is not contract price less value at the time of breach, but rather the resale price, if it is reasonable as to time, method, manner, place and terms. These are matters for the factfinder, who may or may not conclude from the evidence that what actually occurred after breach by way of resale was reasonable and thus provides an accurate measure of damages. Judge McGann found that it did here, on sufficient credible evidence.

We adopt,[6] for these purposes, the essence of the sellers' damage rules provided for sellers of goods in the Uniform Commercial Code, *N.J.S.A.* 12A:2–706 and 708, and adapted for sellers of real estate in §§ 504–507 of the Uniform Land Transactions Act (ULTA), which New Jersey has not adopted. We adopt these rules because they take account of the effect of changing market conditions in sound ways which New Jersey's reported decisions have not yet taken into account.

Where a buyer of real estate wrongfully rejects, repudiates or materially breaches as to a substantial part of the contract, the seller

---

6. The Kuhn contract did not contain a liquidated damage clause, either forfeiting the deposit on the buyer's breach without proof of damages, or limiting liability of the buyer to the amount of the deposit. We do not intend by this opinion to affect the applicability or enforceability of such provisions.

may resell in a manner that is reasonable as to method, manner, time, place and terms. The defaulting buyer must have reasonable notice of the time after which resale will take place. If the resale is a public sale, the defaulting buyer must have notice of the time and place, and may buy. The seller may then recover the amount by which the unpaid contract price and any incidental and consequential damages exceed the resale price, less expenses avoided because of the buyer's breach. See ULTA § 2–504, 13 *U.L.A.* 552 (1977); *N.J.S.A.* 12A:2–706.

A seller's incidental damages include any reasonable out-of-pocket expenses incurred because of the buyer's breach. A seller's consequential damages include any loss the buyer knew or at the time of contracting had reason to know would result from the buyer's breach and which reasonably could not be avoided by the seller. *See* ULTA § 507, 13 *U.L.A.* 555 (1977).

The case may be different where the seller does not put the property back on the market. In such a case, the measure of the seller's damages is the amount by which the unpaid contract price and any incidental and consequential damages exceed the fair market value of the property at the time of breach, less expenses avoided because of the buyer's breach. See ULTA § 2–505(a), 13 *U.L.A.* 553 (1977) (using the value at the time set for conveyance instead of at the time of breach); *see also N.J.S.A.* 12A:2–708(1). Without a resale, value at the time of breach is used, even in a declining market, because the choice of any other time would be so speculative. We need not explore application of the exceptions made by ULTA 2–505(b) and *N.J.S.A.* 12A:2–708(2) for situations in which the difference between contract price and fair market value is inadequate to put the seller in as good a position as performance would have.

. . .

[Judgment affirmed.]

3. RESCISSION

Mutual rescission doubtless represents the most common resolution of land sale contract breaches, at least in the residential setting. By agreeing on rescission, buyer and seller can avoid the expense, delay and uncertainty of litigation and can, through the seller's return of part or all of the buyer's down payment, reach some rough justice between themselves. Mutual rescission creates problems only in retrospect, when one side tries to avoid the asserted rescission, and a court must determine whether rescission has in fact occurred. (*B* writes to *S*, "this whole deal is really a bad idea;" *S* responds, "I guess you could say so".) And, even if a court can piece together an intent to rescind from ambiguous words and conduct, the question remains how the *status quo ante* is to be restored.

Unilateral rescission can take either of two forms. In *equitable rescission,* sometimes called an action *for* a rescission, the disappointed buyer or seller seeks a judicial decree terminating the contract. In *legal rescission,* sometimes called an action *on* a rescission, the buyer or seller simply declares that the other's conduct constitutes grounds for terminating the contract. Legal rescission contains more than the usual hazards of self-help. Pitfalls surround the requirements that the rescission be effected by notice and that the notice be timely. (What constitutes effective notice? At what point does notice become untimely?) There is also the risk that the asserted misconduct does not in fact constitute grounds for termination. A seller wishing to rescind when her buyer fails to perform on the closing date must consider the possibility that time will be held not of the essence. A buyer who wishes to rescind when his seller contracts to sell the land to someone else must consider the possibility that the subsequent buyer will not qualify as a bona fide purchaser who can defeat the original buyer's claims. An added cost of guessing wrong about the effect of the other side's conduct may be a finding that, by seeking to rescind, the rescinding party anticipatorily repudiated the contract.

4. VENDEE'S AND VENDOR'S LIENS

a. VENDEE'S LIEN

NEW YORK LAW REVISION COMMISSION, RECOMMENDATION TO THE LEGISLATURE RELATING TO THE VENDEE'S LIEN ON LAND TO SECURE RESTITUTION OR DAMAGES

Legis. Document No. 65 (1946).

In Elterman v. Hyman, 192 N.Y. 113 (1908), it was held that where the vendor of land was unable to convey the title required by the contract, the vendee was entitled to a lien upon the land to secure his right to reimbursement for the payments made under the contract, but in Davis v. William Rosenzweig Realty Operating Co., 192 N.Y. 128 (1908), a vendee who sued in equity for rescission of the contract because of the fraud of the vendor was denied a lien on the ground that the lien depended upon the contract and that the vendee had rendered the contract void *ab initio* by securing rescission.

In most states a lien is given regardless of the form of action. The rule adopted in the *Davis* case is not only contrary to the weight of authority in other states, but has been widely criticized by courts and writers. The Commission believes that the premise adopted by the majority of the court, that the lien depends upon the continued existence of the contract, is erroneous, for the lien is simply a remedy created by the courts, and has no connection with the contract except that the vendor's failure to perform his contractual obligations furnished the justification for the application of this remedy. Furthermore, the idea that the contract subsists in an action for breach of contract but does not subsist in an action for rescission is questionable, for whatever the relief sought, the vendee does not contemplate performance of the contract. The distinction drawn by the Court of Appeals between a case like Elterman v. Hyman and a case like Davis v. William Rosenzweig Realty Operating Co. has been found difficult to apply by the courts, with resulting confusion.

The rule making the protection given to the vendee depend on the form of the action, rather than the equities of the case, may frequently result in hardship. Particularly at the present time, when many residential properties of moderate value are changing hands, the vendee may well need the security of the lien because of the vendor's inability to make restitution or respond in damages.

The statute proposed by the Commission, while changing the rule in the *Davis* case, is so drawn as not to preclude the granting of a lien in a proper case in actions based upon failure, invalidity or disaffirmance of an agreement, as well as in actions for or based upon rescission.

The Commission therefore recommends the addition of the following new section 112–h to Article 9 of the Civil Practice Act:

§ 112–h. Vendee's lien not to depend upon form of action. When relief is sought in an action or proceeding or by way of defense or counterclaim, by a vendee under an agreement for the sale or exchange of real property, because of the failure, invalidity, disaffirmance or rescission of such agreement, a vendee's lien upon the property shall not be denied merely because the claim for relief is for rescission, or is based upon the rescission, failure, invalidity or disaffirmance of such agreement.

COLE v. HAYNES, 216 Miss. 485, 62 So.2d 779 (1953), ETHRIDGE, J: Appellee argues, however, that even if he has a duty to refund to appellant the amount of the down-payment, still appellant's right is solely in personam; that appellant must therefore sue appellee in the county of appellee's residence; and that appellant therefore cannot bring a suit in equity in Holmes County where the land is located, seeking to impose an equitable lien on the land. However, established principles of justice and law indicate a different conclusion. 55 Am. Jur., Vendor and Purchaser, § 548, states that the general rule is that a purchaser under an executory contract for the sale and purchase of land is entitled to an equitable lien upon the land for the amount which he has paid upon the purchase price, where the vendor is in default or unable to make a good title. Section 549 says this with reference to the nature and basis of the lien:

"The lien of a purchaser of land under an executory contract for the amount which he has paid is to secure to him the repayment of expenditures made in pursuance of the contract. The exact nature of this lien is not clear. The doctrine has been quite generally applied without any discussion as to the nature of the lien, except, perhaps, the statement in general terms that it was an equitable lien, very similar to that of a vendor for unpaid purchase money. It has been said that the basis of the lien is the well-known fundamental rule that in equity what is agreed to be done is regarded as done, so that from the time that a contract is made for the purchase of real estate, the vendor is, in a sense, a trustee for the purchaser, and the purchaser in a sense is the real owner of the land, so that each, under the ordinary equitable rules, has a lien for his protection. The whole practice in equity with reference to such contracts is clearly on the basis that the parties are under equal equitable obligations to each other. It has also been said that all the reasoning by which the vendor's equitable lien for the purchase money after a conveyance is established is applicable in support of the vendee's lien after full or part payment and before conveyance, and that it is difficult to imagine upon what principle a court of equity could enforce the one and deny the other."

b.   VENDOR'S LIEN

GRACE DEVELOPMENT CO., INC. v. HOUSTON

Supreme Court of Minnesota, 1975.
306 Minn. 334, 237 N.W.2d 73.

MacLAUGHLIN, Justice.

This appeal raises the question of whether plaintiff was entitled to file a notice of lis pendens in connection with its action against defendants for certain monies allegedly due to plaintiff pursuant to various contracts for the sale of land and the construction of a house on the land. The district court ordered the notice of lis pendens canceled and expunged from the record. We affirm.

On December 27, 1973, plaintiff commenced an action alleging that on March 5, 1972, plaintiff and defendants had entered into a purchase agreement wherein plaintiff sold to defendants a tract of land upon which plaintiff agreed to build a house. Plaintiff further alleged in his complaint that pursuant to the original purchase agreement, an alleged supplemental agreement dated May 20, 1972, and alleged oral agreements between the parties, defendants had agreed to pay for certain cabinets, a deck, and other costs, but failed to do so. On the same day, plaintiff filed a notice of lis pendens in connection with the suit.

Defendants admitted that they entered into the purchase agreement of March 5, 1972, but denied any other agreements with plaintiff. Under the terms of the purchase agreement, defendants contracted to pay $26,000 for the land and house, and plaintiff promised to deliver a warranty deed upon payment of the purchase price. It is undisputed that plaintiff delivered a warranty deed to defendants conveying the real property in question.

A party may file a notice of lis pendens "[i]n all actions in which the title to, or any interest in or lien upon, real property is involved or affected." Minn.St. 557.02. If the cause of action involves a lien, the lien must exist at the time the action is commenced. "The lien which results merely from an ultimate entry of a judgment provides no basis for the filing of a notice of *lis pendens*." Rehnberg v. Minnesota

Homes, Inc., 236 Minn. 230, 234, 52 N.W.2d 454, 456 (1952). Thus, plaintiff's complaint must involve an existing lien in order to come within the lis pendens statute.

Plaintiff argues that his cause of action involves a common-law vendor's lien. A vendor's lien is an implied equitable lien upon real property for the amount of the unpaid purchase price. It exists independently of any express agreement at the time of the conveyance and without regard to the absence of the grantor's intention to claim it. The basis for the vendor's lien is the broad equitable principle that a person having obtained the estate of another should not be allowed to keep it without paying the purchase price.

The extent of a vendor's lien depends entirely on the amount of the unpaid purchase price. If there is no purchase price owing, then there is no vendor's lien. The fact that a purchaser of real property may owe a vendor money does not by itself establish a vendor's lien. The debt must be solely for the purchase price of real property. Thus, we have held that where realty and personalty are sold at the same time for a gross consideration there is no implied or equitable lien upon the realty unless the court can accurately ascertain the amount of the charge attributable to the purchase of the realty. Shove v. Burkholder Lbr. Co., 154 Minn. 137, 191 N.W. 397 (1923); Peters v. Tunell, 43 Minn. 473, 45 N.W. 867 (1890).

In the instant case, plaintiff does not allege in his complaint that the money owed is for the purchase price of the realty. Indeed, the record indicates that plaintiff's claim is not in fact for the purchase price of the realty but arises from some separate and undisclosed supplemental agreement between the parties. The purchase agreement of March 5, 1972, clearly states that the purchase price for the property is $26,000 and that plaintiff is to convey a warranty deed to defendants upon full payment of the purchase price. The fact that plaintiff subsequently delivered such a deed to defendants raises a strong inference that plaintiff has been paid the full purchase price. Moreover, plaintiff's claim against defendants is not based on any unpaid portion of the lump sum of $26,000 but on specific charges for the construction of cabinets and other items. It is clear that these specific charges, if they are in fact valid, are based upon some separate contract between the parties. Vague references to undisclosed contracts are not sufficient to establish a vendor's lien. In *Peters* we stated (43 Minn. 475, 45 N.W. 868):

"... [A] vendor of real property is not entitled to an implied equitable lien to secure the performance of the consideration when that is of such a nature ... that the court cannot accurately ascertain and define the amount of the charge to be imposed upon the land and enforced out of it."

In the instant case, this court cannot "accurately ascertain and define the amount of the charge to be imposed upon the land" because we do not know the nature or terms of all of the alleged agreements between the parties.

Since plaintiff's complaint does not set forth a claim for the unpaid portion of a fixed and certain purchase price for real property, its cause of action does not involve a vendor's lien and is inadequate to support the filing of a lis pendens. This state does not favor liens against homesteads, and we will not construe vague and unsupported allegations to support such a lien in this case. The trial court's order canceling the notice of lis pendens is therefore affirmed.

Affirmed.

NOTES

1. *Remedial Strategies.* The several remedies available to buyer and seller on breach by the other offer considerable opportunity for strategic maneuvering. The requirement that a party seeking specific performance remain ready to perform puts a burden on the buyer, who must arrange with his lender to keep his loan commitment alive, as well as on the seller, who may have intended to move from the house, using the cash from its sale to buy another. Yet, a seller facing a rapidly falling market, or a buyer facing a rapidly rising one, may prefer specific performance, with all its disadvantages, to the prospect that, in the circumstances, damages will not make her whole. And the rule that specific performance will be denied if the contract involves inadequate consideration or is unconscionable or oppressive to the party against whom it is sought to be enforced does not necessarily promise that the plaintiff will do any better in an action for damages at law where his oppressive conduct may turn the jury against him.

Foreclosure on the vendor's lien may offer an attractive alternative to the seller who is unable to tender the marketable title required for specific performance or whose misconduct would disqualify her from specific performance. See Charles v. Scheibel, 128 Misc. 275, 218 N.Y.S. 545 (N.Y.Sup.Ct.1926). Also, by securing the seller's claim for the contract price, the vendor's lien may give the seller a preferred position over the buyer's general creditors. Two possible disadvantages of foreclosing on the vendor's lien are that, as in mortgage foreclosure, deficiency judgments may be prohibited and statutory redemption periods may be required. For the buyer, the vendee's lien provides security for the return of his deposit but typically will not secure his claim for title examination and survey costs and benefit of bargain damages. See Comment, The Vendee's Lien in New York: Its Development, Application and Status, 37 Alb.L.Rev. 470, 482–485 (1973).

The use, or threatened use, of certain remedies may expose a party to liability. In Askari v. R & R Land Company, 179 Cal.App.3d 1101, 225 Cal.Rptr. 285 (1986), a buyer brought an action against the seller and filed a notice of lis pendens. The seller ultimately prevailed. The court ruled that the seller could recover consequential damages for the period from the beginning of the suit until the dissolution of the lis pendens if the seller could show that during that time it attempted to resell the property but the lis pendens made the title unmarketable. (By the way, is this just another way of addressing the general rule described in *Kuhn* which calculates seller's damages as of the date of breach?) Moreover, the court noted in dictum that while the filing of a lis pendens was privileged and could not be the basis of a slander of title suit, an action for malicious prosecution might be possible. Cf. Piep v. Baron, 133 Misc.2d 248, 506 N.Y.S.2d 838 (Civ.Ct.1986) (no abuse of process found where lis pendens was filed in action by buyer to enforce a contract of sale since the buyer's goal of preventing the sale of the property to another did not show an intent to do harm without excuse or justification nor was the filing a perversion of the process).

The attorney also risks sanctions in these cases. For example, in DeWald v. Isola, 180 Mich.App.129, 446 N.W.2d 620 (1989), appeal after remand, 188 Mich.App. 697, 470 N.W.2d 505 (1991), the attorney who brought an action to enforce a draft sales agreement against a seller was sanctioned for asserting a frivolous claim. The seller had never signed the document and an unauthorized notation on it by the sales agent that seller had agreed to the terms—which seller denied—was inadequate to bind the seller under the statute of frauds. The court reasoned that in light of "basic, longstanding, and unmistakenly evident" reasons in the common and statutory law, and which were brought to the attorney's attention several times, it should have been clear to the attorney that the claim was worthless. 180 Mich.App. at 136, 446 N.W.2d at 623. Would the attorney's behavior in *DeWald* also violate DR 7–102(A)(2) of the Code of Professional Responsibility which states that a lawyer shall not "[k]nowingly advance a claim or defense that is unwarranted under existing law, except that he may advance such claim or defense if it can be supported by good faith argument of an extension, modification, or reversal of existing law?"

2. *Defective Tenders.* The buyer faced with a defective tender from seller should consider the rules on abatement outlined in Merritz v. Circelli and the rules on damages outlined in Raisor v. Jackson. If the defect impairs marketability, the buyer can get rescission and the return of any down payment. If the defect is small, he can obtain specific performance with an abatement of the purchase price to compensate for the defect. If the defect is substantial he may get specific performance but, under *Merritz,* without any abatement. And, under *Raisor* if the defect was known (or, perhaps, should have been known) to the seller, buyer may recover damages.

What sorts of defects will entitle buyer to these remedies? The rule announced in *Merritz,* that specific performance with abatement will be allowed only if the defect is in title or in the quantity of land to be conveyed, is probably a minority position today. Courts now generally permit abatement for other kinds of defects. For a more typical decision, allowing abatement for construction defects, see Billy Williams Builders & Developers, Inc. v. Hillerich, 446 S.W.2d 280 (Ky.1969).

Are the results produced by *Merritz,* and by the *Flureau* rule examined in *Raisor,* consistent with the general assumption today that the seller is best placed to know the state of her own title? Say that the defect is that seller's spouse has not signed the contract. Subsequently, the market value of the property rises and seller enters into a contract with a second buyer. Can the first buyer get specific performance? Damages? Say the market went down, rather than up. Would Tombari v. Griepp give seller and her spouse an action for specific performance against the buyer?

Where the seller has good title but simply sells the property to a third party, buyer may recover seller's profit and does not have to show market value. See, for example, Coppola Enterprises, Inc. v. Alfone, 531 So.2d 334 (Fla.1988) (allowing damages even in absence of bad faith by seller).

3. *The Rule of Flureau v. Thornhill.* The *Flureau* rule has been justified on three grounds. One, probably the original ground for the decision, is to curb the jury's freedom to award unbounded and speculative damages. A second ground, relied on in subsequent cases, is that land records were in such poor shape that it would be unfair to burden the seller with damages unless she in fact knew that her title was bad. Third is the modern ground that marketable title represents a condition, not a covenant, in the contract of sale and that unmarketability gives rise only to rescission and not to damages for breach of warranty.

Approximately fifteen jurisdictions expressly follow the *Flureau* rule. The rule was incorporated in the original Field Civil Code adopted in California, Montana and South Dakota. North Dakota, a Field Code state, amended the *Flureau* rule in its original code in 1895, and Oklahoma, not a Code state, has adopted a statutory formulation of *Flureau.* Doubtless, many other states, even those explicitly rejecting the *Flureau* rule, effectively adopt its result by construing marketable title as a condition rather than as a covenant.

The Maryland Court of Appeals recently addressed the *Flureau* rule in Beard v. S/E Joint Venture, 321 Md. 126, 581 A.2d 1275 (1990). The seller agreed to build and convey a house but did not actually begin to do so. In an action by buyers seeking loss of bargain damages, the court refused to apply *Flureau.* The court reasoned that seller's breach was due not to a failure of title but to its nonperformance of the obligation to build. Moreover, even under *Flureau,* damages should not be barred because seller's failure was not in good faith.

There is a discernible trend away from the rule of Flureau v. Thornhill and toward adoption of an "American" rule. See, for example, Donovan v. Bachstadt, 91 N.J. 434, 441, 453 A.2d 160, 164 (1982): "There is nothing in [our] statute that prevents the Court from adopting the American rule and awarding loss of the benefit of the bargain damages. We are satisfied that the American rule is preferable. The English principle developed because of the uncertainties of title due to the complexity of the rules governing title to land during the eighteenth and nineteenth centuries. At that time the only evidence of title was contained in deeds which were in a phrase attributed to Lord Westbury, 'difficult to read, disgusting to touch, and impossible to understand.' The reason for the English principle that creates an exception to the law governing damages for breaches of executory contracts for the sale of property is no longer valid, and the exception should be eliminated."

4. *Specific Performance.* Rationales abound for the rule making specific performance generally available to land sellers as well as to land buyers. Courts and commentators have enthusiastically shored up the rule with new rationales as the old rationales disintegrated. In addition to the three rationales that Pomeroy cites are another three that you may find more plausible. First, land may possess unique *dis*advantages for the seller, such as exposure to liability for dangerous conditions on the land. Second, a buyer's asserted cause of action may make it impossible for the seller to dispose of the property elsewhere so long as the claim is outstanding. And, third, "in the absence of some objective indicator of the land's market price, such as value established by frequent sales or condemnation proceedings of substantially similar land, it is apparent that the vendor may in fact not have an adequate remedy at law." Comment, 48 Temp.L.Q. 847, 851–852 (1975). See Restatement (Second) of Contracts § 360 Comment e (1979).

Courts have always found occasions to refuse specific performance to buyer or seller. Unfairness, inadequate consideration, unconscionability and overreaching are just a few. But courts have only recently confronted the rule of general availability head on. Centex Homes Corp. v. Boag, 128 N.J.Super. 385, 320 A.2d 194 (Ch.Div.1974), typifies the contemporary challenge. Plaintiff, developer of a high-rise condominium, sought specific performance against defendants who had reneged on their contract for the purchase of a condominium unit. Asserting that "the mutuality of remedy concept has been the prop which has supported equitable jurisdiction to grant specific performance in actions by vendors of real estate," and that "mutuality of remedy is not an appropriate basis for granting or denying specific performance," the court concluded that "the disappearance of the mutuality of remedy doctrine from our law dictates the conclusion that specific performance relief should no longer be automatically available to a vendor of real estate, but should be confined to those special instances where vendor will otherwise suffer an economic injury for which his damage remedy at law will not be adequate, or where other equitable considerations require that relief be granted." 128 N.J.Super. at 390–393, 320 A.2d at 197–198.

The *Centex* court went on to observe that "the subject matter of the real estate transaction—a condominium apartment unit—has no unique quality but is one of hundreds of virtually identical units being offered by a developer for sale to the public." In the circumstances, was the observation gratuitous, or does it imply that, in an action by the buyers against the developer, the court would also have withheld specific performance?   See Suchan v. Rutherford, 90 Idaho 288, 410 P.2d 434 (1966).

5. *Seller's Damages.* The general rule, measuring seller's damages from the date of buyer's breach rather than from the date of resale, has been criticized for failing to account for the difficulties and delay in reselling land.   See Note, Damages: The Illogical Differences in Measuring Breach of Contract Damages When the Contract Involves Land Rather than Goods, 26 Okla.L.Rev. 277 (1973) (suggesting a damage measure analogous to U.C.C. § 2–706).   Despite this criticism, *Kuhn* is an atypical decision, and most courts continue to follow the general rule.   See M. Friedman, Contracts and Conveyances of Real Property 1031–1037 (5th ed.1991).

Is the date of resale measure necessary in light of the other remedies available to the seller, remedies generally not available to sellers of goods at common law or under the U.C.C.?   Supporters of the general rule maintain that the seller who faces a long delay and declining market before resale can be made whole through a decree of specific performance for the contract price.   Possibly, just by reminding the buyer of the disadvantages of specific performance to him, the seller will be able to persuade the buyer to settle on a compromise sufficient to make the seller whole.   It is also argued that quick resale, even in a declining market, will probably make the seller whole, for the resale price is good, and sometimes *prima facie,* evidence of the land's value at the time of breach, particularly if the sale was made at arm's length and shortly after the breach.   See Costello v. Johnson, 265 Minn. 204, 121 N.W.2d 70 (1963).   Consequential damages will also help if the seller can introduce evidence that the land's value at the time of breach was depressed by the dissemination of information about the broken contract.   Further, the seller can collect for maintenance expenses incurred between breach and resale.   See Abrams v. Motter, 3 Cal. App.3d 828, 83 Cal.Rptr. 855 (2d Dist.1970).   Finally, in most cases, seller's retention of the buyer's deposit should suffice to make her whole.

The argument against the present damage measure would appear to be strongest when one or another of these alternative remedies is not available to the seller.   For example, measuring damages from the time of breach rather than resale might very well be unfair to the seller if she is in a jurisdiction that, following *Centex,* would deny her specific performance.   Moreover, consider cases like *Kuhn* where specific performance is available but impracticable.   If a buyer does not close because he lacks the funds to do so, what real effect—and strategic leverage—can a specific performance decree have?   The court will not imprison the buyer for nonpayment of the price.   See Restatement (Second) of Contracts § 360, comment e.   If the court orders the sale of the property, with the buyer to pay the difference between the amount raised and the contract price—i.e., the equivalent of holding the buyer to time of resale damages—the seller will be protected.   See U.L.T.A. § 2–504, comment 1.   If, however, the court instead orders the buyer to either specifically perform or pay damages and the court calculates the damages based on the difference between the contract price and the value at the date of breach, the seller will be left with the loss due to the declining market. See Brett v. Wall, 530 So.2d 797 (Ala.1988) (where trial court ordered buyer either to specifically perform or pay damages equal to the difference between the contract price and value of the property on the date of trial, appellate court reversed and required damages based on date of breach).

6. *Earnest Money.* It is customary on the execution of a land sale contract for buyer to give seller an earnest money deposit securing his performance. The deposit, which commonly ranges from 1% to 10% of the purchase price, may be held by the seller, by the broker or by the escrow agent. The principal question surrounding these deposits is whether the seller may retain the earnest money in the event of the buyer's breach, or must return it in whole or in part.

The rule in most states is that the seller may keep the buyer's deposit even though forfeiture is not expressly prescribed by the contract, and even though the sum exceeds the seller's provable damages. See generally M. Friedman, Contracts and Conveyances of Real Property 1043–1060 (5th ed. 1991). The Restatement of Contracts, which in section 357 adopts a general rule that a defaulting buyer can recover the excess of his deposit over the seller's damages, makes an exception for payments of "earnest money, or if the contract provides that it [buyer's part performance] may be retained and it is not so greatly in excess of the defendant's harm that the provision is rejected as imposing a penalty." Restatement of Contracts § 357(2) (1932). Accord Restatement (Second) of Contracts § 374, Comment c (1979).

In a handful of jurisdictions, the seller can keep only so much of the deposit as is necessary to cover her damages. To avoid unjust enrichment, she must return the rest to the buyer. Yet, even in these states, the seller will as a practical matter probably be allowed to retain the entire deposit, for the buyer's burden of proving that the deposit exceeds seller's damages will not be easy to discharge. For an example of the difficulties encountered in discharging this burden see Zirinsky v. Sheehan, 413 F.2d 481 (8th Cir.1969), cert. denied, 396 U.S. 1059, 90 S.Ct. 754, 24 L.Ed.2d 753 (1970).

7. *Liquidated Damages.* Sellers can by contract forestall claims of unjust enrichment by characterizing the deposit obligation as a liquidated damages provision. This might also serve the buyer's interest since treating the deposit as earnest money leaves the seller free to pursue the full range of remedies while treating it as liquidated damages by definition bars the damages route. See also Colonial at Lynnfield, Inc. v. Sloan, 870 F.2d 761 (1st Cir.1989) (liquidated damages of $200,000 on contract price of $3,375,000 were denied when seller resold property for $251,000 more than buyers agreed to pay since actual damages turned out to be easily ascertainable and liquidated damages were grossly disproportionate to the "loss").

Legislation in Washington permits a contract provision limiting seller's remedy to forfeiture of the deposit as long as the amount forfeited does not exceed 5% of the contract price. The statute requires specific language, typeface, and initialing or signing of the clause by the parties. Wash.Rev. Code Ann. § 64.04.005.

Liquidated damage clauses have their own requirements. To be upheld, the liquidated sum must be proportioned to the contract price and must represent a reasonable forecast of compensation for the harm caused by the breach. Further, the harm caused by the breach must be of the sort that is difficult to estimate accurately. Compare Johnson v. Carman, 572 P.2d 371 (Utah 1977) (to allow seller to retain $34,596.10 paid by buyer, when seller's actual damages were only $25,650.00, would be "grossly excessive and disproportionate to any possible loss") with Vines v. Orchard Hills, Inc., 181 Conn. 501, 435 A.2d 1022 (1980) ("A liquidated damages clause allowing the seller to retain 10 percent [$7,880] of the contract price as earnest money is presumptively a reasonable allocation of the risks associated with default").

III. CLOSING THE CONTRACT

CRAMER, LEGAL ASPECTS OF REPRESENTATION IN PURCHASE AND SALE OF ONE–FAMILY RESIDENCES *

9 Real Property, Probate & Trust Journal 545–546 (1974).

II. STEPS PRIOR TO CLOSING

A. *Assembling "Basic Data."* The attorney should collect the "basic data." The basic data include: where the property is located, the name of the seller and the name of the buyer; in other words, who is taking title, whether it is an individual or joint ownership. He should determine what the sale price is; whether or not there are payments to be made on account; whether or not subsequent payments are to be made prior to the closing; the last date for the closing; are there any special terms to be inserted into the Agreement of Sale; who pays the real estate transfer tax, if any; are there any extras or equipment included; will there be a mortgage or a deed of trust; what is the legal description of the property in metes and bounds; is a survey needed, and if so has one been obtained; what is the record of the last deed; are there any divorce decrees, wills or other previous instruments which may affect the title to the parcel; has title insurance been ordered; and what is the number of the title application, if any.

B. *Financing.* After the attorney has acquired what I called the basic data, then, pending the receipt of the preliminary title report, the attorney should determine if financing has been arranged and, if not, whether he should arrange for financing. He should also determine whether there is to be an assignment of a lease or delivery of immediate possession. He should be sure his client obtains a fire insurance binder.

C. *Examination of Title.* After the title report or title abstract has been received, the attorney should then undertake to send copies of the title report or title abstract to the other interested parties. He should determine whether there are objections on the report that have to be cured prior to the closing. He should then: (a) ascertain that title to the property is vested in the seller; (b) determine the marital status of the parties; and (c) determine whether or not there are any outstanding court proceedings that affect the transaction. The attorney should determine whether or not any objections that remain on the title report are satisfactory to the purchaser and, most importantly, to the mortgagee. He should review any building restrictions or easements and determine how they will affect the purchaser's use of the property.

D. *Taxes and Prior Liens.* The attorney should then obtain the following: a statement from the mortgagee addressed to the title company or to the settlement clerk; the necessary papers to satisfy an existing mortgage, if any; the receipts for taxes, water and sewer rents, if any; the bills for any unpaid taxes computed as of the date of the closing; clearance certificates, if required in the jurisdiction, for water and sewer rents; all receipts for street improvements; if required, inheritance and state tax receipts; letters of indemnity or evidence removing objections from the title company previously insuring the title. He should obtain corporate resolutions if the property is being purchased from a corporation; make sure that the corporate taxes of a corporate seller are paid; and secure a waiver of liens, if new construction or additional construction is involved, as well as a release of liens. In addition, he should determine whether or not the title insurer will insure against mechanics' liens.

E. *Preparing for Closing.* The next step is to prepare for the closing. The attorney should prepare the deed, bond or note, mortgage or deed of trust; determine that the names of the parties are correctly set out on the closing documents. (It would be embarrassing to go to closing and find that the secretary in your office has made a mistake in the typing of the name of one of the parties to the transaction.) The attorney should submit all of his papers, if required by the mortgagee, for prior approval; determine the date and hour of the closing and where it will take place; notify all the parties, including wives if their signatures are needed, of the foregoing information; request the seller to bring receipts, leases or other documents necessary for the closing; advise the buyer to bring the cash or certified check for the amount required to close the transaction; determine that the mortgagee is bringing its check to close, or forwarding its check with a letter of instructions to the closing clerk; and prepare a sample closing statement showing proper credits due buyer and seller.

KUPILLAS, ATTORNEY ETIQUETTE AT RESIDENTIAL REAL ESTATE CLOSINGS

62 New York State Bar Journal No. 4, p. 45 (May 1990).

The closing of a residential real estate transaction is not an adversary proceeding. Despite law school training and experience in other areas of law (most notably litigation) there is no reason to treat the settlement of the purchase of a one or two family dwelling, cooperative apartment or condominium unit, as a cross-examination.

Why then do many attorneys take this hard line adversarial approach? There are several reasons as follows:

1. This is how we are taught. An attorney's job is to look out for the best interests of his client. They only consider their client. Many attorneys translate this into a tough unyielding attitude.

2. In many areas of law it works. This hard-nosed approach can be quite successful in litigation. The reputation of many "bombers" in the field of matrimonial litigation attests to this. The fact is when things have gotten to the litigation stage, being steadfast and visibly tough can mean great gains for your client. The problem in residential real estate areas is that such an attitude can turn a friendly transaction into litigation. Unfortunately to a litigator this seems to be the natural course of events-until the economics of the situation are revealed. In residential real estate cases, clients more often than not are the real losers.

3. Clients like attorneys who are tough. One of the great paradoxes that attorneys face is this: the public's perception of attorneys is terrible and getting worse. People view attorneys as insensitive, money hungry, and unscrupulous. Ironically, this is the very kind of lawyer they want to represent *them.* I believe that one of the reasons attorneys come on this way is because that is what the public wants. Lawyers are not completely at fault for their image and behavior; clients encourage it.

4. Unprepared lawyers can aggravate this situation. The closing of a residential real estate transaction is viewed as routine and easy by many attorneys. This is because the title company and the lender's attorney tend to many of the serious details of insurability of title, accuracy of the legal description, and searches. However, to rely on title companies and bank attorneys will give you a false sense of security. ... It can be very annoying when an attorney shows up at a closing without ever having taken a look at the title report. This can lead to long delays and very short tempers, as the prepared attorney loses patience with his less diligent colleague.

5. Little things get blown out of proportion. Of course, clients can often get extremely upset over "little" things. Missing light fixtures, table and chairs as well as other items of personal property can be the source of much conflict. Why? Because the purchase and sale of residential real estate is to a very large degree, an emotional event. Therefore, seemingly insignificant things can set off these emotions. It is our job as attorneys to diffuse this over-reaction by putting things in perspective. An effective attorney in this area (as in most areas) must be a good psychologist. The ability to deal with people in this area is a far greater asset than legal knowledge.

A. THE FORMALITIES OF TRANSFER
McDONALD v. PLUMB

California Court of Appeal, Second District, 1970.
12 Cal.App.3d 374, 90 Cal.Rptr. 822.

ALLPORT, J.

The record before us discloses without conflict that on February 4, 1960, one Elizabeth Esterline owned certain real property located in

Los Angeles County. On June 22, 1960, unknown to her and without consideration, Stanley Scott Singley caused a deed of said property to be recorded, purporting to convey title to Frank N. Debbas. The grantor's signature was forged. The forged signature was falsely acknowledged by Glen E. Plumb, a notary public bonded as such by United States Fidelity and Guaranty Co. in the penal amount of $5,000. Subsequently the property was deeded, without consideration, by Debbas to Singley and thereafter by Singley to Jack W. and Patricia L. McDonald. The latter transaction was for consideration. Following a nonjury trial judgment was entered quieting title of Esterline to said property against any claims of Singley and the McDonalds and granting judgment in favor of McDonalds and against Singley in the sum of $21,063.51, together with costs in the amount of $254.88. The McDonalds were denied relief against Plumb and United States Fidelity and Guaranty Co., his surety. The litigation was dismissed as to Debbas. The McDonalds have appealed from that portion of the judgment denying them recovery against Plumb and United States Fidelity and Guaranty Co.

It is contended on appeal that the trial court erred as a matter of law in finding that the false acknowledgment of the deed from Esterline to Debbas by Plumb was not the efficient or any other cause of the damage suffered by the McDonalds. We agree with this contention.

The specific finding involved was as follows: "That the false acknowledgment by cross-defendant, Glen E. Plumb, upon the purported deed from Elizabeth Esterline to Frank N. Debbas was not the efficient or any other cause of any damage suffered by cross-complainants or either of them."

Simply stated the trial court found that the false notarial acknowledgment on the forged Esterline deed to Debbas was not the efficient or any other cause of the damage suffered by McDonalds since it was not in fact relied upon in the course of the latters' purchase from Singley and that the McDonalds' damages were solely the proximate result of the fraudulent plans, schemes and acts of Singley against whom they were given judgment.

There appears to be no dispute as to the facts nor as to the sufficiency of evidence to support the judgment. The sole question to be answered is whether or not the trial court erred as a matter of law in finding and concluding that the false notarial acknowledgment was not a proximate cause of the McDonalds' damage.

In order for the McDonalds to prevail in this action they have the burden of establishing first, a duty on the part of defendant Plumb, second, a violation of that duty, third, that such violation was a proximate cause of injury to them, and, fourth, the nature and extent of their damage.

The basis for liability in a case of this type is set forth in Burck v. Buchen, 46 Cal.App.2d 741, at pages 746–747, 116 P.2d 958, as follows: "When taking an acknowledgment, 'the officer should require the acknowledging party to appear in person before him, as he is required to certify that such party "personally appeared." (§ 1189, Civil Code.) If an instrument is acknowledged in violation of this rule, as where it is acknowledged through a telephone, the officer would undoubtedly be liable in damages if it should turn out that it was acknowledged by an imposter.' (1 Cal.Jur. 247.) However, in order 'To render the officer liable for damages, it is, of course, necessary that his act in taking an acknowledgment be the proximate cause of the damage sustained. ... [A]nd, where the right of action is founded on the negligence of the officer, *that the plaintiff be not guilty of contributory negligence*'."

In this case the duty was created by statute. (Civ.Code, § 1185.[1])

Respondent concedes a violation of that duty. The violation creates a liability upon the notary's surety. (Gov.Code, § 8214.[2]) It is undisputed that the McDonalds sustained damage in the sum of $21,063.51.

. . .

... It seems fundamental to us that the requirement of notarial acknowledgment in real estate transactions such as this is calculated to prevent fraud. The failure of the notary in this case to fulfill his duty permitted Singley to defraud the McDonalds. This failure was a basic underlying cause of the loss and, if not the sole proximate cause, at least a proximate cause thereof.

It is argued that other transactions involving this property subsequent to the making of the false acknowledgment broke the chain of causation. We do not agree. We fail to see wherein such can be deemed to have eliminated the false acknowledgment as being at least one of the proximate causes. In Homan v. Wayer, 9 Cal.App. 123 at pp. 127–128, 98 P. 80, at 82, it was said:

"It is apparent, then, that the fact that others have aided in the transaction, and contributed to bringing about the conditions from which the plaintiff's loss arose, does not relieve defendants from liability for the loss of the plaintiff, if the latter relied upon the false certificate when paying out his money. In taking an acknowledgment to a deed a notary's official services are limited. He certifies to the identity of the grantor named in the instrument, but he has no control over the deed to which his certificate is attached. This must be delivered to the grantee by the grantor, or some one on his behalf, in order to become effective. No *official* act of the notary in certifying an acknowledgment to a deed can alone result in injury to anyone. The

---

1. Civil Code, section 1185 reads as follows: "The acknowledgment of an instrument must not be taken, unless the officer taking it knows or has satisfactory evidence, on the oath or affirmation of a credible witness, that the person making such acknowledgment is the individual who is described in and who executed the instrument; or, if executed by a corporation, that the person making such acknowledgment is the president or secretary of such corporation, or other person who executed it on its behalf."

2. Government Code, section 8214 reads as follows: "For the official misconduct or neglect of a notary public, he and the sureties on his official bond are liable to the persons injured thereby for all the damages sustained."

deed cannot become the means of defrauding anyone until used in some transaction entirely outside of the official duties of the notary. For this reason the statutory right of action is not dependent upon a showing that the acts of others have not contributed to the injury, or defeated by a showing that they have so contributed, if it appear that the party defrauded relied upon the notary's false certificate.

"The terms, 'proximate cause,' 'negligence,' and 'contributory negligence,' as used in appellants' presentation of the case, are somewhat misleading here. No official misconduct or neglect of a notary public in taking or certifying the acknowledgment of a deed could ever be the *sole* proximate cause of loss or injury to any person but we cannot for that reason say no recovery can be had for a loss due to a false certificate of acknowledgment under the provisions of section 801 of the Political Code."

Without citation of authority it is urged by Plumb that the issuance of a policy of title insurance at McDonalds' request indicated a lack of reliance upon the original notarial acknowledgment, thus breaking the chain of causation. This contention is answered to the contrary in Inglewood Park Mausoleum Co. v. Ferguson, ... 9 Cal.App.2d 217, 49 P.2d 305. While it is true that McDonalds did not rely directly upon the false acknowledgment in the original deed, direct reliance is not required. On the contrary, indirect reliance is sufficient. In relying upon the record title as of the date of sale, the McDonalds were relying upon the chain of title creating such record title, one link of which was the validity of the deed from Esterline to Debbas. We conclude that the trial court erred in finding and concluding that the false acknowledgment by Plumb was not a proximate cause of the injury to the McDonalds. We find to the contrary.

. . .

That portion of the judgment appealed from is reversed with directions to the trial court to enter judgment on the cross-complaint in favor of Jack W. McDonald and Patricia L. McDonald and against defendant Glen E. Plumb in the sum of $21,063.51, together with costs, and against United States Fidelity and Guaranty Co., a corporation, in accordance with the terms and conditions of the bond.

SCHWEITZER, Acting P.J., and COBEY, J., concur.

NOTES

1. What, if anything, could the McDonalds have done before closing to discover the fraudulent transfer to Debbas? If they had been represented by counsel in the transaction, would their lawyer have discovered the fraud if he or she had followed the standard operating procedure outlined in the excerpt from the Cramer article at page 142? Could their title insurer have discovered it? Plumb's surety? Plumb? Would the McDonalds have been protected by a title insurance policy providing the coverage of the A.L.T.A. Owner's Policy set out in the

Statute, Form, and Problem Supplement? Of all the individuals and institutions involved in residential real estate transactions, did the court impose liability on those best placed to bear it?

The California legislature subsequently amended Civil Code § 1185, relied on in *McDonald,* to relax the proof of identity on which a notary can legally rely. Stats.1982, c. 197 § 1; Stats.1987, c. 307 § 1; Stats. 1988, c. 842 § 1. At the time *McDonald* was decided, the notary had to know the signer personally, or at least had to know the witness who swore to the signer's identity. The 1982 amendment provides that the notary can rely on wallet identification such as a California driver's license. Is this amendment likely to increase opportunities for the type of fraud that occurred in *McDonald?* Would it be better to abolish the acknowledgement formality entirely? See Brussack, Reform of American Conveyancing Formality, 32 Hastings L.J. 561 (1981).

2. A forged deed is inadequate to pass title. Thus, even innocent purchasers like the McDonalds lose title to owners like Esterline, another innocent party. See R. Natelson, Modern Law of the Deeds to Real Property (1992) 391–396. What reasons support this rule? What effect does the rule have on the marketplace? What burdens does it place on buyers?

3. *The Benefits and Costs of Formal Requirements.* Because land is immovable, and because ownership of land is so often separate from possession, interests in land cannot be transferred physically and must instead be transferred through the ritualistic delivery of documents symbolizing the interests. But documents are easily lost, mishandled or counterfeited. Someone bent on fraud need only go to the county recorder's office, find a recorded deed to a vacant piece of land, forge the grantee's name as grantor on a new deed, hoodwink a notary, record the fraudulent deed, and then dispose of the land to an unwitting buyer. See Reuben, Real Estate Title Forgeries Seen Increasing, 100 Los Angeles Daily J., May 11, 1987, p. 5, col. 1 (reporting one title company's experience that forgery claims rose from 3.8% to 12.9% of total claims between 1970 and 1985); Church, Spotting Title Forgeries, 4 Prac. Real Est. Law. 13 (Sept. 1988) (describing fact patterns which give clues to forgeries).

Conveyancers early hoped that strict compliance with formal requirements would reduce the occasions for fraud and produce unassailable chains of title. Legislatures and courts responded by enacting and rigorously enforcing requirements that a deed had to be formally correct and complete and had to clearly and accurately describe the interest being transferred. And, to avoid fraudulent transfers, the deed also had to be properly acknowledged, delivered, accepted and recorded.

One obvious and oft-lamented cost of these formal requirements is that, by invalidating imperfect transfers, the requirements penalize grantors and grantees who retained inept lawyers or no lawyers at all. But formal requirements have another, possibly more substantial cost. By inducing grantees and grantors to reduce their transactions to writing and to have these writings acknowledged and recorded, the American conveyancing system also encourages future grantees to rely on the paper record as perfectly evidencing the current state of title. Unfortunately, as indicated in *McDonald,* even the most perfect-appearing paper record is sometimes flawed.

See generally, Andersen, Conveyancing Reform: A Great Place to Start, 25 Real Prop. Probate & Trust J. 333 (1990).

1. DEED ELEMENTS AND CONSTRUCTION

There is a modern trend to simplify the form and content of real property deeds. Many states have enacted short form deed statutes, prescribing language that eliminates most of the customary redundancies and flourishes. Even so, most deeds contain all of the basic elements that have traditionally been employed since the earliest English deeds.

Deeds typically begin with the *premises* of the deed—the names of grantor and grantee; the words of grant; background facts and purposes; consideration; and the legal description of the parcels conveyed. The next portion of the deed, usually beginning with the phrase, "To have and to hold," is the *habendum,* which describes the interest taken by the grantee, any conditions on the grant and any covenants of title (these covenants are sometimes said to comprise the *warranty clause*). The *execution clause* contains the grantor's signature, her seal, and the date of the deed. (In states that require the deed to be witnessed, the signatures of the witnesses would also appear in the execution clause.) Finally, beneath the grantor's signature is the *acknowledgement,* in which a public officer, typically a notary, attests to the execution.

Although several formalities continue to be required for other aspects of the conveyancing process, most states today require few formalities of a deed. The deed must be written. It must name the grantor and grantee and contain express words of grant. And it must describe the parcel conveyed to the exclusion of all other parcels in the world.

What formalities are *not* required for a deed to be effective? Although it was once commonly required that for a deed to be effective it had to be sealed—stamped with the grantor's mark—most states have since eliminated the requirement. And, even in those states that still impose the requirement, it is easily met through use of the written word, "Seal," or through use of the initials "L.S.," (signifying *locus sigilli,* or "the place of the seal"). And only a few states require acknowledgement for a deed to be effective between the parties. Acknowledgement is, however, required for a deed to be legally recorded. Acknowledgement has traditionally conferred two other benefits. It makes the deed admissible into evidence without further proof of execution, and it creates a presumption that the deed is genuine.

BARRIER v. RANDOLPH

Supreme Court of North Carolina, 1963.
260 N.C. 741, 133 S.E.2d 655.

The hearing below was on plaintiffs' motion for judgment on the pleadings, which consist of the complaint, a copy of the deed attached thereto as Exhibit A and by reference made a part thereof, and the answer.

The facts alleged by plaintiffs and admitted by defendants, summarized except when quoted, are as follows:

The deed of which Exhibit A is a copy, referred to in the opinion as the Randolph-Austin deed, is dated March 24, 1950, and recorded in Book 1432, Page 93, Mecklenburg Registry. By the terms thereof, the present defendants and others conveyed to David Blair Austin and wife, Marian Robinson Austin, a tract of land in Sharon Township, Mecklenburg County, North Carolina, described by metes and bounds, containing 7.51 acres. The granting, habendum and warranty clauses are in terms of a conveyance in fee simple.

After the description, but before the habendum and warranty clauses, this provision is set forth: "And this Deed is made subject to the following conditions, reservations, and restrictions which constitute covenants running with the land and binding upon the parties hereto, their heirs and assigns, to wit": The conditions, reservations and restrictions are then set forth *in extenso* in eleven separate (numbered) paragraphs. They include, *inter alia,* restrictions that the property shall be used only for residential purposes, restrictions as to the size of lots in the event of subdivision, restrictions as to the location, cost and composition of any residence constructed thereon, etc. Too, they include reservations of rights of way for the installation of power and telephone lines.

Thereafter, through mesne conveyances, the 7.51-acre tract was conveyed to plaintiffs herein.

Plaintiffs allege that defendants claim an interest or estate adverse to plaintiffs in the said 7.51-acre tract based on the restrictions and easements set forth in Exhibit A, but that said restrictions and easements purport to limit the estate of plaintiffs "contrary to the granting clause and the habendum and the warranties" in Exhibit A and therefore are invalid and of no effect. Plaintiffs prayed that they be adjudged the owners in fee simple of the said 7.51-acre tract free and clear of any right or claim of defendants on account of the restrictions and easements set forth in Exhibit A.

Defendants denied the legal conclusions alleged by plaintiffs and asserted the restrictive covenants set forth in Exhibit A were and are valid and presently enforceable. Defendants prayed that plaintiffs' action be dismissed and that they recover their costs.

After hearing, the court, by order dated April 25, 1963, denied plaintiffs' motion for judgment on the pleadings. Plaintiffs excepted and appealed.

BOBBITT, Justice.

There has been no adjudication of the rights of the parties. The court did not enter final judgment but simply denied plaintiffs' motion for judgment on the pleadings. It is well established that an appeal does not lie from a denial of a motion for judgment on the pleadings. The proper practice was for plaintiffs to except to the court's denial of their said motion and bring forward this exception in the event of their appeal from an adverse final judgment.

Plaintiffs' appeal must be dismissed as fragmentary and premature. Even so, in the exercise of our discretionary power we deem it appropriate to express an opinion upon one, but only one, of the questions plaintiffs have attempted to raise by their fragmentary and premature appeal.

The one question we consider is that raised by plaintiffs' contention that *all* the "conditions, reservations and restrictions" set forth in the Randolph-Austin deed are repugnant to the granting, habendum and warranty clauses of said deed and therefore are surplusage and void *ab initio*. Plaintiffs base this contention upon Oxendine v. Lewis, 252 N.C. 669, 114 S.E.2d 706, asserting in their brief that "the Oxendine Case is determinative of the controversy herein."

The rule applied in Oxendine v. Lewis, supra, and in decisions cited therein, is stated by Parker, J., as follows: "We have repeatedly held that when the granting clause, the *habendum,* and the warranty in a deed are clear and unambiguous and fully sufficient to pass immediately a fee simple estate to the grantee or grantees, that a paragraph inserted between the description and the *habendum,* in which the grantor seeks to reserve a life estate in himself or another, or to otherwise limit the estate conveyed, will be rejected as repugnant to the estate and interest therein conveyed."

"In the interpretation of a deed, the intention of the grantor or grantors must be gathered from the whole instrument and every part thereof given effect, unless it contains conflicting provisions which are irreconcilable or a provision which is contrary to public policy or runs counter to some rule of law." Lackey v. Hamlet City Board of Education, 258 N.C. 460, 462, 128 S.E.2d 806, 808.

The sufficiency of the Randolph-Austin deed as a conveyance in fee simple of said 7.51-acre tract is not controverted. There is no contention it conveyed a life estate or other estate less than a fee simple.

In express terms, the Randolph-Austin deed provides that it is made subject to the conditions, reservations and restrictions therein set forth and that such conditions, reservations and restrictions constitute covenants. Indeed, the portion of the deed in which these conditions, reservations and restrictions are set forth constitutes the greater part of the entire (including description) deed. The intention of the grantors that such conveyance is made subject to such conditions, reservations and restrictions is manifest. Moreover, "(i)t is a settled principle of law that a grantee who accepts a deed poll containing covenants or conditions to be performed by him as the consideration of the grant, becomes bound for their performance, although he does not execute the deed as a party." Maynard v. Moore, 76 N.C. 158, 165. ...

The foregoing impels us to express the view that Oxendine v. Lewis, supra, does not control decision and that the conditions, reservations and restrictions set forth in the Randolph-Austin deed are not void *ab initio* on the ground they are repugnant to the granting, habendum and warranty clauses of said deed. We express no opinion as to whether these conditions, reservations and restrictions or any of them are void on *other grounds*. Neither do we express any opinion as to whether these conditions, reservations and restrictions, or any of them, are presently enforceable by defendants herein or other persons. These matters are for determination in the first instance in the superior court. Upon further hearing, all factual matters relevant to a proper decision should be brought to the attention of the court.

Appeal dismissed.

NOTE

Courts called on to construe real property deeds typically start from the proposition noted in Barrier v. Randolph that "the intention of the grantor or grantors must be gathered from the whole instrument and every part thereof given effect ...." If, however, the deed contains "conflicting provisions which are irreconcilable," courts will employ one or more standard interpretational canons to resolve the conflict or ambiguity.

For example, if there is an irreconcilable conflict between the granting clause and the habendum, it is generally said that the granting clause will control. And, "so long as they do not conflict, written and printed parts are of equal force; when inconsistent, printed parts must give way to typed or written words, and, between the latter two, written words give a stronger indication of intention than typed words. When contradictory, general words must usually give way to specific words. Where a recital and an operative part of the deed come in conflict, it is the latter which prevails. And it is a general rule, subject to all those just considered, that when two repugnant clauses cannot be reconciled, the earlier of the two will stand. Another rule, not to be applied until all others fail to reconcile a conflict, and only when there is a real ambiguity or uncertainty, is that a deed will be construed most strongly against the grantor, or against the grantee when the instrument was drafted by him." 3 American Law of Property § 12.90 (A.J. Casner ed. 1952). See generally, Herd, Deed Construction and the "Repugnant to the Grant" Doctrine, 21 Tex.Tech.L.Rev. 635 (1990).

It is the rare deed dispute in which some of these canons cannot be asserted on one side, and some on the other. Would these canons help you in giving a title opinion on an ambiguous deed executed thirty or forty years earlier? Consider whether you would feel more or less comfortable with your opinion knowing that, in addition to these canons of construction, a court interpreting the deed will often look to "all the attendant circumstances as to situation of the parties, relationship, object of the conveyance, person who drew the deed, and all surrounding situations which may throw light on the meaning which the parties attached to ambiguous or inconsistent portions of the instruments. And unless forbidden by some rule of law, the courts will follow the construction given a deed by the parties themselves as shown by their subsequent admissions or conduct." 3 American Law of Property § 12.91 (A.J. Casner ed. 1952).

Is it preferable for a court construing a deed to attempt to discern the actual, subjective intent of the original grantor and grantee, or to refuse to look outside the deed's four corners? Which rule will better promote certainty among title examiners and their clients over the long term?

2. DELIVERY AND ESCROW

a. DELIVERY

A deed will not effectively transfer title to an interest in land unless and until it is delivered. Delivery is a term of art, and means something more than physical transfer of the document. In its ideal form, delivery requires both physical transfer and a present intent by the grantor to transfer an interest in the property to the grantee. Often, though, both elements are not clearly present. Physical transfer alone is insufficient. Thus, if the transferor hands a deed to the transferee, delivery will not occur if the requisite intent is missing (e.g., "I am giving you this deed to hold for safekeeping in the event I later decide to give Blackacre to you"). See Jorgensen v. Crow, 466 N.W.2d 120 (N.D.1991) (where transferee picked up deed at closing but grantors lacked intent to transfer, no delivery occurred). If, however, the intent is clear, courts will often find delivery without physical transfer, through devices such as symbolic, constructive or agency delivery (e.g., "I am presently transferring Blackacre to you, but I will hold the deed for you until you reach 18"). Intent is thus pivotal.

Tension exists between this emphasis on intent, provable by parol, and the aim of the conveyancing system to confine all title matters to the paper record. It is no surprise, then, that presumptions have developed bringing delivery rules into line with the reasonable expectations of title searchers. Thus, although physical transfer does not constitute delivery, it is widely held to create a presumption of delivery. Conversely, failure to transfer the deed creates a presumption of nondelivery. Other facts creating a presumption of delivery are recordation of the deed and the deed's acknowledgement.

In order for a deed to be effectively delivered, the grantee must accept the delivery. In most cases, because the grant will benefit the grantee, acceptance will be presumed. However, courts will not presume acceptance if the conveyance might be disadvantageous to the grantee. And, even if the conveyance will be advantageous, courts will allow the presumption of acceptance to be rebutted by evidence that the grantee did not in fact wish to accept title to the land. See Hood v. Hood, 384 A.2d 706 (Me.1978). Recording is not required for delivery. See Graham v. Lyons, 377 Pa.Super. 4, 546 A.2d 1129 (1988), appeal denied, 522 Pa. 576, 559 A.2d 38 (1989).

WIGGILL v. CHENEY

Supreme Court of Utah, 1979.
597 P.2d 1351.

MAUGHAN, Justice:

This case involves the disposition of certain real property located in Weber County, State of Utah. The judgment before us invalidated a Warranty Deed, because of no valid delivery. We affirm. No costs awarded.

The material facts are undisputed. Specifically, on the 25th day of June, 1958, Lillian W. Cheney signed a deed to certain real property located in the city of Ogden, Utah, wherein the defendant, Flora Cheney, was named grantee. Thereafter Lillian Cheney placed this deed in a sealed envelope and deposited it in a safety deposit box in the names of herself and the plaintiff, Francis E. Wiggill. Following the deposition of the deed, Lillian Cheney advised plaintiff his name was on the safety deposit box and instructed plaintiff that upon her death, he was to go to the bank where he would be granted access to the safety deposit box and its contents. Lillian Cheney further instructed, "in that box is an envelope addressed to all those concerned. All you have to do is give them that envelope and that's all." At all times prior to her death, Lillian Cheney was in possession of a key to the safety deposit box and had sole and complete control over it. Plaintiff was never given the key to the safety deposit box.

Following the death of Lillian Cheney, plaintiff, after gaining access to the safety deposit box, delivered the deed contained therein to Flora Cheney, the named grantee.

The sole issue presented here on appeal is whether or not the acts of plaintiff constitute a delivery of the deed such as will render it enforceable as a valid conveyance.

The rule is well settled that a deed, to be operative as a transfer of the ownership of land, or an interest or estate therein, must be delivered. It was equally settled in this and the vast majority of jurisdictions that a valid delivery of a deed requires it pass beyond the control or domain of the grantor. The requisite relinquishment of control or dominion over the deed may be established, notwithstanding the fact the deed is in possession of the grantor at her death, by proof of facts which tend to show delivery had been made with the intention to pass title and to explain the grantor's subsequent possession. However, in order for a delivery effectively to transfer title, the grantor must part with possession of the deed or the right to retain it.

The evidence presented in the present case establishes Lillian Cheney remained in sole possession and control of the deed in question until her death. Because no actual delivery of the deed occurred prior to the death of the grantor, the subsequent manual delivery of the deed by plaintiff to defendant conveyed no title to the property described therein, or any part thereof, or any of its contents.

CROCKETT, C.J., and HALL, WILKINS and STEWART, JJ., concur.

NOTE

Modern escrow practices, considered in the next section, have virtually eliminated delivery as an issue when land is being transferred for consideration. However, delivery remains an issue in donative transfers like the one involved in *Wiggill* and, as a consequence, raises problems for any buyer whose chain of title has a gift as one of its links.

Say that, upon receiving the deed from Francis Wiggill, Flora Cheney recorded it and then conveyed her interest, for value, to a buyer relying on her apparently good record title. How could the buyer have protected himself against the finding that Flora in fact had no title to convey? Obviously, record title and possession in the seller—the traditional indicia of ownership—are insufficient to assure that the seller has anything to convey. Would a standard policy of title insurance offer sufficient protection? A lawyer's opinion on an abstract of title? The local statute of limitations respecting causes of action for recovery of real property?

Compare Agrelius v. Mohesky, 208 Kan. 790, 494 P.2d 1095 (1972). In 1940, the grantors, husband and wife, executed two deeds, one conveying an 80-acre parcel to their son Clair, and one conveying another 80-acre parcel to their son, Kenneth. Neither deed was recorded during the grantors' lifetimes but, in 1944, the grantors placed the deeds in a safe deposit box leased in their names and in Clair's. Sometime later that year, Clair's father told him of the two deeds and, handing the key to the safe deposit box to Clair, said that this would constitute delivery to him. Many years later, after his parent's death, Clair claimed that "delivery of his own deed was effected when his father handed him the key to the safe deposit box, but that the deed to Kenneth was not delivered at that or any other time." 208 Kan. at 798, 494 P.2d at 1102. The Kansas Supreme Court disagreed on the second point, finding support in the evidence for the lower court's ruling that the grantor's actions "constituted an effective constructive delivery of the deeds, and all the circumstances showed a purpose on the part of the grantors that there should be an immediate vesting of title in Clair and Kenneth, enjoyment only being postponed until the death of the grantors." 208 Kan. at 795, 494 P.2d at 1100.

Delivery has even been found absent any physical transfer, symbolic or otherwise. In Grimmett v. Estate of Beasley, 29 Ark.App. 88, 777 S.W.2d 588 (1989), deeds found in the grantor's possession expressly stating that they were effective on grantor's death were valid to convey the properties to grantor's brother. The court noted that when a deed reserves a life estate to the grantor, as in this case, there is no requirement to transfer the instrument beyond grantor's dominion and control. See Case Note, 44 Ark.L.Rev. 219 (1991).

For an excellent analysis of delivery rules and the issues they raise, see A. Dunham, Modern Real Estate Transactions 355–359 (2d ed. 1958). See also, Note, Compressing Testamentary Intent Into Inter Vivos Delivery: What Makes a Conveyance Effective, 64 Wash.L.Rev. 479 (1989).

---

b. ESCROWS

In areas of the country that follow the custom of having a "round the table" closing, the various parties—buyer, seller, lender, title insurer, brokers, etc.—meet together on the closing date to exchange documents and funds. Such a practice does not require the use of an escrow if all goes well. If, however, issues need to be resolved after the closing, someone may act as an escrow to hold the deed or funds until the outstanding performance is rendered.

In other places the practice is for the buyer and seller to close their contract through escrow, an arrangement under which a third party— the escrow holder—holds the deed from seller and the purchase money from buyer and buyer's lender pending fulfillment of the contract conditions. If all conditions are fulfilled, the escrow holder will on the date set for closing deliver and record the deed and mortgage to buyer and lender respectively, deliver the note to the lender, and deliver the purchase money to the seller. (In these areas, the parties do not typically meet together to close the transactions.) If, however, one or more of the contract conditions is not fulfilled, the escrow holder will return the documents and funds to the appropriate parties. This type of escrow arrangement is used both where the contract of sale provides for a short executory period and where the purchase is being made under a long term installment contract.

Since the escrow holder is generally expected to act mechanically, and not to exercise judgment on any point, well-drafted escrow instructions will contain only objectively verifiable conditions. Thus, instead of the judgmental direction to the escrow holder, "You are to close this escrow upon seller's delivery of marketable title," the instructions might read, "You are to close this escrow when there has been deposited into this escrow an irrevocable commitment by the Union Title Insurance Company to issue to Buyer an A.L.T.A. Owner's Policy, Form B–1970 naming buyer as owner in fee simple absolute of the Property described above, and insuring title in fee simple absolute of said property in the amount of $200,000, subject only to a first lien mortgage held by Surety National Bank, in the amount of $160,000, and to taxes for the fiscal year 1985, which are a lien but not delinquent." See generally, Walker & Eshee, The Safeguards and Dilemmas of Escrows, 16 Real Est.L.J. 45 (1987).

HARRIS v. SKYLINE CORP.

Supreme Judicial Court of Massachusetts, 1961.
342 Mass. 444, 173 N.E.2d 644.

WHITTEMORE, J. The hearing of this bill of complaint by way of interpleader proceeded on the premise that when the bill was filed the plaintiff had no obligation in respect of the escrow under which he held the sum of $350 except to make that sum available in court to abide a determination between the defendant Skyline Corporation (Skyline) on the one hand, and the defendants John A. and Mary F. Lundquist, on the other, as to whether the condition of the escrow had been met by Skyline. That premise is untenable on the evidence, all of which is reported, and further proceedings are required.

The evidence establishes the facts stated in this and following paragraphs. The escrow was created on February 27, 1956, in the course of the delivery of a deed and a mortgage, and the payment of the purchase price, cn the sale of real estate in Burlington. Those attending, in addition to the plaintiff, were the treasurer of Skyline (the seller), D. Francis Mahoney; the attorney for Skyline, Mr. John A. McCarty; and the buyers, Mr. and Mrs. Lundquist. The plaintiff, an attorney at law, was present as the representative of the law firm by which he was employed to act for the mortgagee, Lever Cambridge Employees Credit Union (Lever). It developed that necessary grading and landscaping of the lot had not been completed and a check for $350 from Lever to the Lundquists, indorsed to Skyline, being a part of the purchase price, was deposited with the plaintiff. Mr. McCarty required that the determination of whether the work was satisfactorily completed not be left to the Lundquists. The plaintiff then undertook to Mr. McCarty that when the latter produced a compliance certificate issued by the Veterans Administration he would deliver the check to Mr. McCarty. It was express that the proof that the work was done would be the issuance of the certificate. The talk was mostly between the attorneys; "we discussed between us, ... asking questions of our respective parties." The attorneys figured the adjustments. The plaintiff recorded the deed. The inference is required that the plaintiff, although not formally acting as attorney for the Lundquists, looked after their interests and believed that he had seen to it that they understood that they had relinquished their interest in the check unless the escrow condition should not be performed within a reasonable time.

On July 6, 1956, Mr. McCarty wrote the plaintiff that he had the compliance certificate. By this time a partner in the law firm with which the plaintiff remained associated and where he worked (no longer on salary, but, we infer, with an "arrangement") had become counsel for the Lundquists. The plaintiff was informed that the Lundquists contended that the work had not been done and the money was not payable. The plaintiff did not doubt that Mr. McCarty in good faith had obtained what he understood to be a compliance certificate, and, until a stage in the trial, never suggested to Mr. McCarty that there was any question about that. He did notify Mr. McCarty that he would not pay over the money because there was a serious dispute.

The plaintiff filed his bill of complaint on February 14, 1957, alleging that he was merely a stakeholder in respect of a dispute between the Lundquists and Skyline; that as "security" for Skyline's promise to the Lundquists, he was holding the $350 until the work should be done and the certificate issued; that (par. 5) Mr. McCarty had "made demand ... for the payment of said $350, *since he was then in possession of the Veterans Administration Compliance Inspection Report covering the said premises*" (emphasis supplied); that the Lundquists had informed him that the work had not been completed and "he had no right to turn over ... the $350 until" it had been; and that they demanded the money. The bill asked that the plaintiff be authorized to pay the $350 into court and that the defendants be ordered to interplead and litigate the issues between themselves.

In the course of the hearing the plaintiff testified that if a certificate of compliance should be presented to him the condition of the escrow would be fulfilled, and he would turn over the check but for the fact that he had checked the Veterans Administration regulations and looked at the lot and this gave him serious doubt "whether there was a Certificate or if there was any fraud in the issuance of a Compliance Certificate," and he decided, therefore, to hold the check until the court should decide that the Lundquists had had their day in court.

The plaintiff also testified that, although he had gone to the Veterans Administration, all that he found out was "what the requirements of the V.A. were for grading on lots of land." He had "no recollection of being told that ... [the certificate] had been issued" and did not see a copy of it. We infer that he then had no doubt that the certificate had been issued and never made a check. His principal doubt as to whether a certificate had been issued arose in the course of the trial. "Q. Was there any question ...? A. There is now." "Q. You never questioned the fact that a certificate had been issued up to now, did you? A. No."

Later, on examination by the attorney for the Lundquists: "Why did you have these doubts?" A. "You informed me, after checking with the V.A. and summonsing the records here today, that their files don't show one, that one has not been issued." However, he raised no question that Mr. McCarty had information to the contrary and "If I hadn't seen the job, I wouldn't have doubted any more."

Mr. McCarty sought unsuccessfully to have received in evidence what he asserted to be the compliance certificate. The attorney for the Lundquists objected to the absence of due authentication, and we assume the rulings, in the face of objection, were correct.

The paper was shown to the plaintiff and he was asked if that was the compliance inspection report. He answered that he had no way of knowing and that the paper speaks for itself. It developed on the next day that the records which had been in court the day before had not, by error, related to the Lundquists' lot at all, and that the Veterans Administration has regulations in respect of keeping records of compliance inspection, but on objection of the plaintiff as well as the attorney for the Lundquists the unauthenticated copy of the regulations which was in court was not read into the record.

There was testimony justifying the conclusion that the Lundquists were reasonably dissatisfied with what had been done by way of landscaping and grading.

The report of material facts contained findings that the escrow was security for the promise of Skyline to complete the work; the terms of the escrow were that the plaintiff hold the check until the work should be completed and the certificate obtained; the work was never completed; what was done was improper; the evidence did not establish that the certificate was ever issued.

The final decree discharged the plaintiff from liability, and awarded to him $27.90 costs, and to the Lundquists the balance of $322.10.

The findings in respect of the escrow were not justified on the evidence. The plaintiff's testimony was clear that the certificate was to be conclusive; he was corroborated by Mahoney; Mrs. Lundquist testified and was not examined in respect of the escrow terms.

The important circumstance is that the plaintiff's undertaking was an attorney's undertaking to another member of the bar, in reliance upon which the attorney for the seller delivered the deed. The plaintiff, having made an engagement to Mr. McCarty, could not retreat into the position of a mere stakeholder upon notice from the Lundquists that they did not wish the check delivered.

The plaintiff's undertaking to Mr. McCarty imposed upon the plaintiff the duty to examine the tendered certificate, and if he then had doubts of its validity to express them, and give Mr. McCarty an opportunity to dispel them. If he remained uncertain of the validity of the certificate or its controlling force notwithstanding the escrow agreement he should have disclosed the grounds to both parties. The relationship between the plaintiff and the attorney for the Lundquists emphasized the obligation. The bill, in the circumstances, may not be construed to put in issue the validity of the certificate as between the plaintiff and Skyline. Mr. McCarty had reasonable ground, in the form and substance of the escrow undertaking, to construe the somewhat ambiguous allegation of paragraph 5 of the bill ... to be an averment by the plaintiff that Skyline had the certificate. Skyline's answer admitted the allegation; the Lundquists' answer, by the firm with which the plaintiff is associated, averred no knowledge and called upon the plaintiff (not Skyline) for proof.

The disposition of the case must take into account the obligations of the attorneys. Skyline cannot be foreclosed because of its failure at the hearing to prove a validly issued certificate. The Lundquists, on the other hand, may require the plaintiff to be satisfied of the validity and controlling force of the compliance certificate before delivering the check. Skyline cannot be foreclosed of its opportunity to do the work, if more is required (and we intend no suggestion), in the absence of a finding that a reasonable time to do the work had expired. The plaintiff after full disclosure is entitled to the protection of a court decree. The nature of the escrow as an attorney's undertaking having been established at the hearing, as well as the need for further action by the plaintiff, the case could not properly proceed beyond that point pending such action.

The final decree is vacated. Further proceedings are to be stayed for a reasonable time pending such inquiry and investigation by the plaintiff as shall be reasonably necessary to satisfy him whether a valid compliance certificate has issued, and his report thereon to the court and the parties. Amendments of the pleadings are to be allowed as the parties may be advised and the court shall deem appropriate in the light of the report. Such additional relevant evidence shall thereafter be received as any party shall offer. Unless controlled by further evidence, such final decree as may enter in due course shall reflect the construction of the escrow undertaking herein made.

If in the light of the report there remains any issue between the plaintiff and either defendant, or between the defendants, in respect of which the plaintiff's testimony or action will be relevant, we shall expect that the appearances for the respective parties will be such that there will be no possible question of conflicting interest.

The defendant Skyline is to have the costs of this appeal against the plaintiff.

So ordered.

NOTES

1. How could plaintiff in *Harris* have avoided the difficulties that arose during the escrow? How, if at all, could he have better structured the escrow arrangement at the outset? Consider Turbiville v. Hansen, 233 Mont. 487, 761 P.2d 389 (1988), where the escrow holder's

duty under the agreement was, "upon demand," to immediately return the documents to the sellers in the event of a default. The court held that the agreement did not require the escrow agent to determine if the demand for return was justified.

What special responsibilities does a lawyer bear when he or she acts as an escrow agent? Compare *Harris* with In re Lanza and the rules governing representation of clients with potentially conflicting interests, pages 15 to 26 above.

For background on escrow rules see R. Kratovil, Real Estate Law ch. 13 (6th ed. 1974). For an excellent practical overview of closing procedures, see R. Werner, Real Estate Closings (1979).

2. *Escrow Costs.* Practices vary from region to region as to who serves the escrow function—lawyer, broker, lender, title company or independent escrow company. Overall closing costs may vary as a result. The HUD/VA study of closing costs, discussed at page 12, above, compared average title costs in the counties of Denver ($137), King (Seattle) ($291) and Los Angeles ($436) and concluded that one reason for Denver's lower charges was that escrow services there were performed by the lender and the broker, who included their charges in the lender's origination fee and the broker's commission. By contrast, in King and Los Angeles Counties, independent escrow agents performed these services, at fees averaging $135 and $148 respectively.

Escrow agents in King and Los Angeles counties performed tasks well beyond the usual shuffling of papers. According to the HUD/VA study, they also initiated title searches, secured earnest money deposits and balance due statements on existing loans, drew up deeds, computed prepaid items to be paid at closing, arranged financing, recorded instruments, disbursed funds to the seller and the broker, and furnished buyer and seller with statements of charges and disbursements made in the escrow. Dept. of Housing and Urban Development and Veteran's Administration, Mortgage Settlement Costs: Report to Sen. Comm. on Banking, Housing and Urban Affairs, 92nd Cong. 2d Sess. 25–28 (Comm.Print 1972). For an informative breakdown of closing procedures, customs and charges in fifteen geographic areas of the United States, see id. at 443–513.

3. *Regulation.* Several states regulate escrow personnel. Texas supervises escrow officers as part of its general regulation of title insurance companies and requires that escrow officers be licensed and bonded and possess "reasonable experience or instruction in the field of title insurance." Tex.Ins.Code Ann. §§ 9.41, 9.43 (Vernon 1981 & Supp.1991). Other states regulate escrow practices rather than personnel. New Jersey, for example, specifically enjoins real estate brokers from commingling escrowed funds with their own money. N.J.Stat. Ann. 45:15–17(o) (West 1978 & Supp.1991).

California, where independent escrow agents flourish in the southern part of the state, has enacted a law specifically tailored to their activities, regulating both personnel and practices. The law imposes licensing and bonding requirements and controls the details of escrow practice including the proper form of escrow instructions, receipt and disbursement of escrow funds and advertising. Cal.Fin.Code § 17000 et seq.

3. THE DESCRIPTION

To be valid, a deed must adequately describe the property conveyed. The clear trend has been away from punctilio and toward a minimal requirement that the description enable location of the parcel to the exclusion of all others—essentially the standard imposed for land descriptions in contracts. See generally 3 American Law of Property § 12.98. (A.J. Casner ed. 1952).

A deed can employ any one or more of three principal techniques to describe the land conveyed: *metes and bounds,* typically using courses and distances, *reference to government survey,* and *reference to a record-ed instrument,* typically a subdivision map. The lawyer counselling a buyer or seller in a real estate transaction should be familiar with all three techniques to assure not only that the proposed deed description complies with the statute of frauds, but also that it is accurate and that the buyer will get precisely the land he thinks he is getting. The introductory excerpts in this section describe these three land descrip-tion techniques.

C. BROWN, BOUNDARY CONTROL AND LEGAL PRINCIPLES *
9–11, 13–17 (2d ed. 1969).

1.6. WRITTEN PERIMETER DESCRIPTIONS

Land can be described by a sequence of courses, and where the sequence of courses has a direction of travel around a perimeter and has calls for adjoiners, the description is said to be by *metes and bounds. Mete* means to measure or to assign by measure, and *bounds* means the boundary of the land or the limits and extent of a property. Within the generally accepted usage of the term metes and bounds it is not necessary to recite measures of a property as implied by the word metes. A parcel of land can be described without a single measure-ment being given: "Beginning at an oak tree blazed on the north; thence to a large boulder located on the bank of Lake Washington; thence along the lake to ..., etc." Usually metes and bounds descrip-tions are described by successive courses, said courses being fixed by adjoiners, monuments, direction, distance, or all four.

Bounds descriptions are perimeter descriptions, but they do not have a direction of travel: "All of that land bounded on the north by Thelma

Lane; bounded on the south by Rodger River; bounded on the west by the land of Thomas L. Brown; and bounded on the east by the land of Ruth Almstead." The sequence of reciting the bounds is immaterial; the description has no mandatory direction of travel.

Metes descriptions are perimeter descriptions described by measurements, have a direction of travel, and recite no bounds (adjoiners). Often a metes description is included within the common usage of the term metes and bounds. ...

1.9. CALLS IN DESCRIPTIONS

In litigation and in surveying the terms *deed calls* and *running out the calls* are commonly used. According to *Websters International Dictionary* in American land law a call is a "reference to, or statement of, an object, course (meaning direction), distance, or other matter of description in a survey or grant. ..." The calls of a surveyor's field notes are for the objects and measurements noted. A call, as commonly used, can be a phrase in a land description: "thence to a blazed oak tree." This call tells the surveyor to go thence (from the last place mentioned) in a straight line to a blazed oak tree. Other examples of calls are N 10° 15' E, 327.62', along Red River, due north, along the center line of B Street, to the Santa Fe Railroad tracks. ...

1.11. NOMENCLATURE AND UNITS USED IN METES AND BOUNDS DESCRIPTIONS

Deed terms commonly used in metes and bounds conveyances are best understood by examination of Fig. 1.11*a* and by the following explanations.

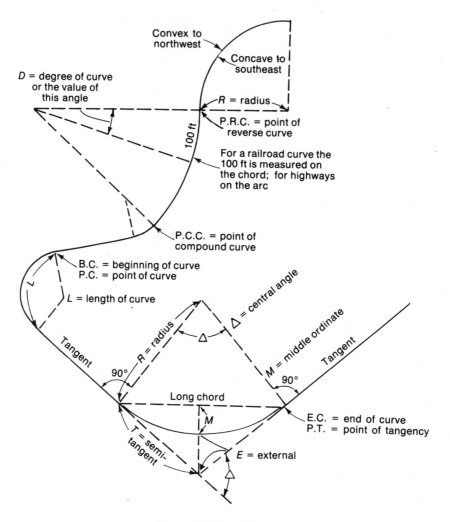

Figure 1.11a Deed terms.

[C982]

DIRECTION OF TRAVEL

True metes and bounds descriptions and many quasi-metes and bounds descriptions have a direction of travel. A bearing may be stated in either of two directions on a map or plat but only one can be used in a written perimeter description. In Fig. 1.11*b*, starting at the point of beginning, the direction of travel is to the southeast, making the first written bearing in the description S 45° 00′ E, not N 45° 00′ W. Because the relationship of one line to another is shown by the plotting of the lines in Fig. 1.11*b*, it is immaterial whether the bearing on the plat is written S 45° 00′ E or N 45° 00′ W.

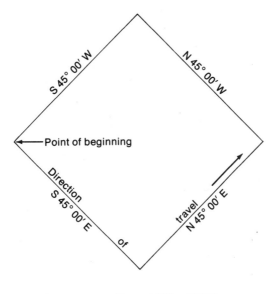

Figure 1.11*b*   [C974]

Monuments

Monuments are classified as either *natural, artificial, record,* or *legal.* Naturally occurring monuments such as rivers, lakes, oceans, bays, sloughs, cliffs, trees, hills, and large boulders are permanent objects found on the land as they were placed by nature and are usually considered controlling over *artificial monuments* (man-made) such as iron stakes, wooden stakes, rock mounds, stones, and wooden fences, but, if the writings clearly indicate a contrary intent, especially where the lines of a survey are called for, the control might be reversed. Some man-made monuments, because of the certainty of location, visibility, stability, and permanence, are considered equal in rank to natural monuments. In this classification would fall sidewalks, street paving, curbs, wells, canals, concrete buildings, and concrete fences.

Record Monuments or Boundaries

These exist because of a reference to them in a deed or legal description; thus, "to Brown's property line" is a call for a record monument (Brown's property). Record monuments may or may not be marked upon the ground by artificial or natural monuments. Where a deed reads "to the side line of the street," the call is for the boundary of a record monument (street) which could be marked by stakes, improvements, fences, or all three, or not marked at all. A call for any record monument is a call for all the monuments, or considerations, that establish the location of the record monument. If a monument is controlling in a legal description, it is often classified as a *legal monument.* "To a stone" is a call for a legal artificial monument; "to Brown's property line" is a call for a legal record monument. The words record monument and legal monument are sometimes used synonymously. Because of the confusion over the various meanings of the term "legal," the words legal monument should be avoided.

Courts may refer to record monuments as natural monuments. The boundaries of a street are marked by man, but the dirt composing the street is naturally occurring, and, in this sense, the street is a natural monument. It is an unfortunate classification. In the order of importance of conflicting elements within deeds, natural monuments are normally considered superior to artificial monuments. A call for a record monument, where no senior right is interfered with, is normally subordinate to a call for an artificial monument. If record monuments are classified as natural monuments, the statement that natural monuments control artificial monuments is not exactly true.

Adjoiners, streets, and parcels of land differ from rivers, lakes, and the like, in that man marks and defines these boundary divisions. Waters and creeks always have visible boundaries, whereas a parcel of land may not be physically marked at all. A deed call for an adjoiner is a call for a monument in the form of a parcel of land that has size, shape, and location, but there is poor foundation for classifying the monument as a natural monument. Since the limits of a parcel of land must be marked by man, why not classify the call for an adjoiner as a call for an artificial monument? Because adjoiners to a conveyance are mainly dependent upon the record for their existence and because they may have invisible lines marking their limits, the classification "record monument" is preferred. The term "natural monument" as used herein is exclusive of record monuments.

PROPERTIES OF MONUMENTS

A good monument should possess the quality of being easily visible, certain of identification, stable in location, permanent in character, and nondependent upon measurement for its location. An artificial monument possesses the qualities of a natural monument to a lesser degree. Thus a stake placed in the ground will rust or rot with time and is less permanent than a naturally occurring large boulder. A stake is easier to move than a boulder and is therefore less stable. The visibility of record monuments is wholly dependent upon the natural or artificial monuments (fences, stakes, cultivation, plantings, and the like) that mark the limits of the record monument.

STRAIGHT LINES

A line in a description is assumed to be the shortest horizontal distance between the points called for unless the contrary is indicated by the writings. To be absolutely correct, a straight line curves with the surface of the earth; but the curvature is so slight that it is not considered in land descriptions. A line to be identified must have a definition of its start, direction, and length. *Free lines* are not terminated by an adjoiner or monument as "beginning at a 2-inch iron pipe; thence N 60° 00' W, 200.00 feet." If the same phrase were reworded "beginning at a 2-inch iron pipe; thence N 60° 00' W, 200.00 feet to a blazed sycamore tree," the terminus of the line is fixed by the tree; the line is not free. Many of the lines described in deeds are dependent upon monuments and are not free lines.

A bearing quoted for a line defines it as a straight line. If a line is defined by monuments, without bearing or distance, the words "in a straight line" or "in a direct line" are sometimes added to emphasize the presumed fact that the line is straight.

DIRECTION

As commonly practiced in this country, direction is defined by either a call for monuments or a bearing; but azimuth, deflection angle, or coordinates may be used. If a deed is written "commencing at a blazed sycamore tree located approximately 100 feet west of Jones' well; thence to a blazed white oak, etc.," the direction is clearly defined. It is very desirable to quote the bearing of the line for plotting purposes, but it is not essential to the legality of the conveyance. Bearings are always read in degrees and minutes (plus seconds if fractions of a minute are involved) from the *north* point or from the *south* point. *Never* from the east or west points. ... The direction of a line is dependent upon [at] which end of the line you are standing; thus on a northwesterly line the direction would be SE if you were at the northerly terminus of a line, whereas it would be NW if you were at the southerly terminus of the same line. On a map it is immaterial which bearing you write, since the drawing shows the relationship of one line to another; but in a written metes and bounds description the exact direction of travel of the line being described must be stated.

CUNNYNGHAM, MAKING LAND SURVEYS AND PREPARING DESCRIPTIONS TO MEET LEGAL REQUIREMENTS *

19 Missouri Law Review 234, 235–238 (1954).

The following [metes and bounds] description of a tract of land in Missouri is copied from a deed written in 1903:

"A tract of land situated in the County of Ste. Genevieve, on the waters of the Establishment Creek, and being part of Survey No. 2088, confirmed to Jean Bte Valle, to-wit—beginning at the Southwest corner of a tract of land sold by the said Felix Valle to Louis Lalumondiere, containing sixty arpents and from thence North 55° West along and with the said Lalumondiere line 35 chains and 60 links, to said Lalumondiere's corner stone and continuing said line to 53 09/100 chains set a Flower stone 18 × 6 × 3 inches for a corner stone from said stone a Post Oak tree 7 inches in diameter bears S. 70° W. 17½ links distant and a Post oak 8 inches in diameter bears S. 27° E. 17 links distant. Thence S. 35° W. 16.14/100 chains intersecting the line sold by said Felix Valle to Charles Carsow, set a corner stone 18 × 6 × 4 inches for a corner stone, and from said stone a Black oak Tree 10 inches in diameter bears S. 55° E. 22 links distant, and a Black oak tree, four inches in diameter bears N. 22° E. 37 links distant, and from thence S. 55° E, with the line of said Carsow 53.00 chains and 9 links to the Establishment Creek, and from thence down said Establishment Creek with the meanders thereof to the place of beginning, containing 103 arpents and 90/100 of an arpent, more or less. Excepting and reserving 1.69/100 acres in the N.W. corner of said tract conveyed to John Kertz in January 1888. Also all that part of U.S. Survey No. 2088 described as follows, begin at most Eastern corner on Establishment Creek, of land belonging to John Kertz at a stone from which a sycamore 14 in. in diameter bears N. 60° W. 60 links distant and a Burr Oak 7 in. in diameter bears N. 8° W. 72 links distance; thence N. 55° W. 11.37/100 chains to a stone for corner; thence S. 18° E. 5.00/100 chains to a point on said Establishment Creek from which a hickory 7 in. in diameter bears N. 10° E. 23 links and an Elm 7 in. in diameter bears N. 60° W. 22 links distant, thence down and with the meanders of said creek to the beginning corner containing one 69/100 acres, more or less."

One of these descriptions might not only become very long, but involve tracking down innumerable descriptions in long chains of title to the ancient sources of many boundary tracts. Yet this is the method used in most of the world, including 19 of the American States (Texas, and the states in, or carved out of the original Thirteen Colonies— Maine, New Hampshire, Vermont, Massachusetts, Rhode Island, Connecticut, New York, Pennsylvania, New Jersey, Delaware, Maryland, Virginia, West Virginia, Kentucky, North Carolina, Tennessee, South Carolina, and Georgia).

Land descriptions in the other 29 states are generally much simpler. Most of the lands in these states were at one time owned by the Federal Government. The disposition of such a vast acreage presented a major problem in identification and description. The fertile imagination and inventive genius of Thomas Jefferson worked out a plan for dividing the public lands into a gigantic checkerboard of uniform square tracts each measuring one mile (80 chains) on its sides, and containing 640 acres. These "sections" are divided into "quarters" of 160 acres each, ½ mile (40 chains) on a side; and may be still further subdivided into "quarter-quarter-sections" (1/16-section) of 40 acres, ¼ mile on each side etc. The boundaries of these sections were to be a series of parallel north-south lines one mile apart, and east-west lines, also one mile apart.

A square of 36 sections constitutes a "township" six miles on each side. The sections in a township are numbered from 1 to 36, starting at the north-east, and proceeding west and then east alternately to the 36th section in the south-east corner. Townships are identified by assigning to each a number which will show how many other townships intervene between the particular township and (1) a certain east-west line on its north or south (called the "*base line*"), and (2) east or west from one of the north-south lines (called the "*principal meridian*"). Under this system it should be possible to describe almost any tract in the 29 states so surveyed, by the simple statement that it is, for example: The (a) north-east one-fourth of the (b) south-east one-fourth of (c) Section 6 in (d) Township 44 north of the Little Rock, Arkansas, Base Line and Range 3 east of the Fifth Principal Meridian, in (e) St. Louis County, (f) State of Missouri, (g) containing 40 acres, more or less. This may be shortened to: A tract of land in St. Louis County, Missouri, being the NE¼, SE¼. Sec. 6, T. 44 N., R. 3 E., containing 40 acres, more or less.

However, in actual practice and for many reasons, sections will not always be found to fit into such a scheme with perfect uniformity. If two lines, drawn exactly one mile apart at the Base Line, are projected due north, they must approach closer together each mile as they proceed north, until they will have merged into a single point at the North Pole.

There are also mechanical and human surveying errors in determining bearings and distances in the east-west, as well as the north-south, lines. We should remember that some of the first surveys were made 150 years ago through almost impenetrable wildernesses, over wild land of little value, perhaps under harassment from hostile Indians, by contract surveyors sometimes interested only in collecting their pay for as little time and effort as possible, using crude instruments and methods (e.g., reputedly measuring distance by counting revolutions of a cartwheel with a rag tied around the rim or by a hemp rope dragged on horse back). Even with the most modern transit, the magnetic needle is not supported to a point toward true north, but toward a "magnetic" north which is continually shifting and changing the magnetic "declination". Local ore deposits, metal objects, and power lines affect the needle. "It (the magnetic compass) is an instrument helpful for finding general directions but not reliable when accuracy is required, nor is it used except for checking purposes in surveys."[4] When using the transit for turning angles from a base line, the finest gradation on the horizontal circle may be one degree, or on the more expensive instruments with vernier attachments, one-half minute.

C. BROWN, BOUNDARY CONTROL AND LEGAL PRINCIPLES *

10–11, 27–29 (2d ed. 1969).

1.8. DESCRIPTIONS BY REFERENCE

The simplest form for writing a land description is by reference to a map or plat as: Lot 1, Block 49 of La Jolla Park, City of San Diego, California. See Fig. 1.8. ...

---

4. Henrie v. Hyer, 92 Utah 530, 70 P.2d 154, 158 (1937).

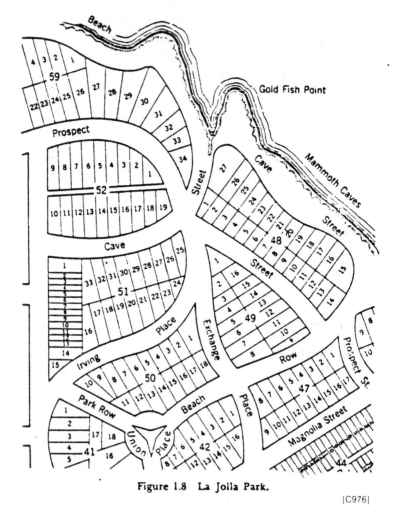

Figure 1.8   La Jolla Park.

[C976]

1.13.   SUBDIVISION DESCRIPTIONS

If a map of parcels of land is filed with a public agency and the parcels thereon are designated by number or letters, the map is commonly referred to as a subdivision map. The precise meaning of the term subdivision varies from state to state, and the meaning within a given state is whatever the law defines it as being within that state. In a number of states the law authorizing preparation of subdivision maps is sometimes called a *platting* act instead of *subdivision* act.

. . .

From the standpoint of the retracement surveyor the important features of a map are the following

1.   What monuments were set or found?

2.   What are the record sizes and locations of the lots and blocks?

From the standpoint of the scrivener, subdivision maps offer the simplest means of describing land since they present the maximum of information and the minimum of words. "Lot 40 of La Mesa Colony, according to Map 346 as filed in the Office of the Recorder, San Diego County, Calif." or "Sec. 16, T15N, R20E, Principal Meridian" or "Lot 2 according to the partition map filed in Superior Court Case 17632" form complete descriptions of land that can be identified from all other parcels of land. The simplicity of the title wording does not mean that a lot and block description of a section of land is easier to survey than is a parcel of land described by a metes and bounds conveyance. Certainty and ease of location are totally unrelated to the length of the deed describing the land.

Most subdivision laws require that, previous to filing a map, survey markers must be established on the land. Many older maps, made before the passage of such laws, were "office maps" made from the record without benefit of survey. ...

Early subdivisions executed by private interests were poorly regulated by law, and any sheet of paper presented as a subdivision map to the land or recorder's office was filed upon payment of the filing fee. Occasionally, maps failed to show street widths, lot sizes, and what was being subdivided. The map of La Jolla Park was compiled with undimensioned lots and undimensioned curved streets laid out with a varying radius french curve (see Fig. 1.8). On old maps the surveyor or engineer rarely made a statement describing what monuments he found or set. How could a later surveyor, ignorant of what markers were originally set, retrace a subdivision? Most modern subdivisions are regulated by rigid laws, which have corrected many of the conditions mentioned. ...

1.14. PARCELS CREATED BY PROTRACTION

Parcels of land or lots drawn upon a subdivision map but not monumented on the ground by an original survey are said to be created by protraction. If a surveyor divides a parcel of land into blocks 200 × 300 feet by setting monuments at each block corner and then draws 12 lots in each block of his map, the lots are said to be protracted. In the sectionalized land system sections are created by prior survey and monumentation; parts of sections are created by protraction (SW¼ of NE¼ of Section 10). The words "protracted lots" or "protracted parcels" imply "created on paper without the benefit of an original survey." If several parcels or lots are protracted on the same map, all are simultaneously created at the moment of approval of the map; no parcel or lot has senior rights over an adjoiner. In New York the date of sale determines prior rights; this is an exception to the general rule.

Tools for Reading Metes, Bounds, Government Survey and Plat Descriptions c

Fig. 1

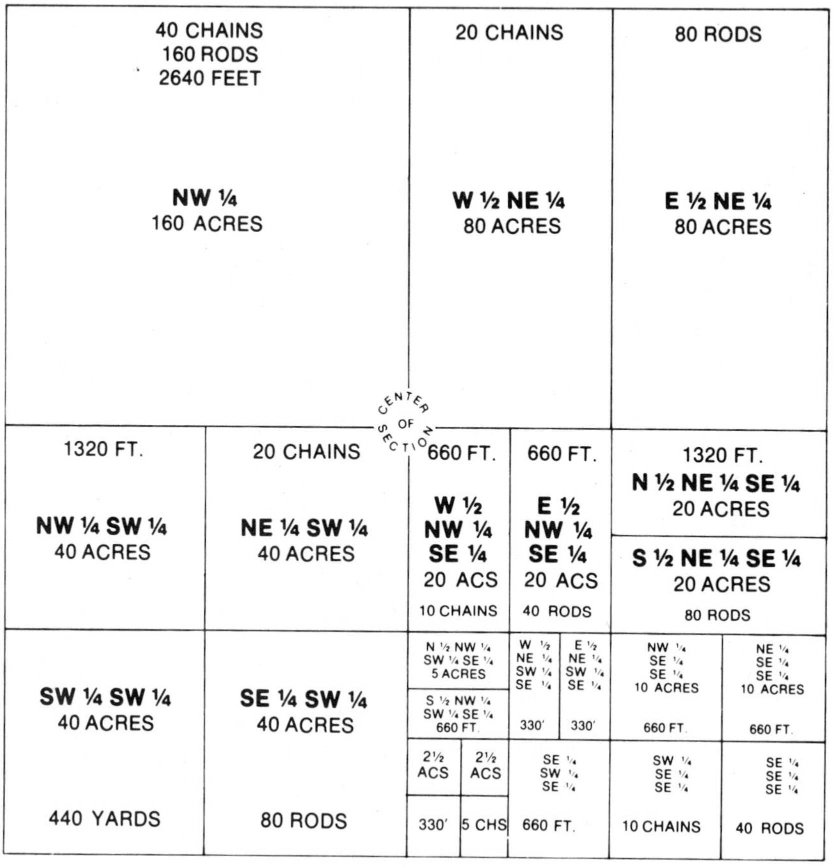

40 CHAINS 160 RODS 2640 FEET	20 CHAINS	80 RODS
NW ¼ 160 ACRES	**W ½ NE ¼** 80 ACRES	**E ½ NE ¼** 80 ACRES

CENTER OF SECTION

1320 FT.	20 CHAINS	660 FT.	660 FT.	1320 FT.
				N ½ NE ¼ SE ¼ 20 ACRES
NW ¼ SW ¼ 40 ACRES	**NE ¼ SW ¼** 40 ACRES	**W ½ NW ¼ SE ¼** 20 ACS	**E ½ NW ¼ SE ¼** 20 ACS	**S ½ NE ¼ SE ¼** 20 ACRES
		10 CHAINS	40 RODS	80 RODS

		N ½ NW ¼ SW ¼ SE ¼ 5 ACRES	W ½ NE ¼ SW ¼ SE ¼	E ½ NE ¼ SW ¼ SE ¼	NW ¼ SE ¼ SE ¼ 10 ACRES	NE ¼ SE ¼ SE ¼ 10 ACRES
SW ¼ SW ¼ 40 ACRES	**SE ¼ SW ¼** 40 ACRES	S ½ NW ¼ SW ¼ SE ¼ 660 FT.	330'	330'	660 FT.	660 FT.
		2½ ACS	2½ ACS	SE ¼ SW ¼ SE ¼	SW ¼ SE ¼ SE ¼	SE ¼ SE ¼ SE ¼
440 YARDS	80 RODS	330'	5 CHS	660 FT.	10 CHAINS	40 RODS

[C975]

c. From "Land Measurements," 37 Title News 30–33 (April 1958). Reprinted with permission of the American Land Title Association.

36	31	32	33	34	35	36	31
1	6	5	4	3	2	1	6
12	7	8	9	10	11	12	7
13	18	17	16	15	14	13	18
24	19	20	21	22	23	24	19
25	30	29	28	27	26	25	30
36	31	32	33	34	35	36	31
1	6	5	4	3	2	1	6

Sectional map of a Township showing adjoining Sections.

Fig. 2.

STANDARD	TSN	PARALLEL		
	T4N			
	T3N			
	T2N			
BASE	TIN	LINE		
R3W	R2W	R1W	R1E	T1S	R2E	R3E	R4E	R5E
	T2S			
	T3S			

Diagram showing division of Tract into Townships.

Fig. 3.

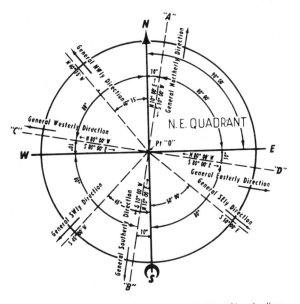

Line direction diagram, showing typical method of describing the direction of lines in preparing legal descriptions of land parcels. Solid heavy lines N-S and E-W are cardinal directions due North-South and East-West. Each Quadrant (NE Quadrant shown) equals 90°00'00" (90 Degrees). One Degree may be written: 60 Minutes; 0°60'00"; 1°; or 1°00'00". 60 Seconds may be written; 0°00'00"* ;1' (one Minute); or 0°01'00". Broken lines A-B and C-D are typical survey lines, showing typical bearings (directions) in each direction.

*[sic]   **Fig. 4.**

[C984]

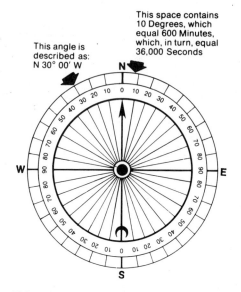

This angle is described as: N 30° 00′ W

This space contains 10 Degrees, which equal 600 Minutes, which, in turn, equal 36,000 Seconds

60 Seconds equal one Minute; 60 Minutes equal one Degree; 360 Degrees equal a complete circle.

Fig. 5

Linear Measure

1 inch =	.0833 ft.
7.92 inches =	1 link
12 inches =	1 foot
1 vara =	33 inches
2¾ feet =	1 vara
3 feet =	1 yard
25 links =	16½ feet
25 links =	1 rod
100 links =	1 chain
16½ feet =	1 rod
5½ yards =	1 rod
4 rods =	100 links
66 feet =	1 chain
80 chains =	1 mile
320 rods =	1 mile
5280 feet =	1 mile
1760 yards =	1 mile

Square Measure

144 sq. in. =	1 sq. foot
9 sq. feet =	1 sq. yard
30¼ sq. yds. =	1 sq. rod
16 sq. rods =	1 sq. chain
1 sq. rod =	272¼ sq. ft.
1 sq. ch. =	4356 sq. ft.
10 sq. chs. =	1 acre
160 sq. rods =	1 acre
4840 sq. yds. =	1 acre
43560 sq. ft. =	1 acre
640 acres =	1 sq. mile
1 section =	1 sq. mile
1 Twp. =	36 sq. miles
1 Twp. =	6 miles sq.

Fig. 6

[C981]

STATEMENT OF ROBERT E. HERNDON, JR., EXECUTIVE DIRECTOR OF THE AMERICAN CONGRESS ON SURVEYING AND MAPPING, HEARINGS BEFORE THE SUBCOMM. ON HOUSING AND URBAN AFFAIRS OF THE COMM. ON BANKING, HOUSING AND URBAN AFFAIRS, U.S. SEN., 93rd CONG. 1ST SESS. PART 2, 1780, 1784, 1786–1787 (1973): ACSM is a professional society comprised of individual members. It is the principal representative organization for land surveyors and cartographers of the United States and provides U.S. representation to international surveying and cartographic organizations. It has 44 affiliated state land surveyor organizations, plus 26 local Sections of ACSM, and these provide the action groups in 45 states. The membership of the affiliated organizations is about 10,000, or more than 20% of the total registered land surveyors in the United States. ... With the transfer of ownership, the purchaser normally wants title to property for which there is clear definition of the location, boundaries, and corners. In 1946, the ACSM developed and issued "Technical Standards for Property Surveys," and these are still in active use today. They require the surveyor to acquire all necessary data, including deeds, maps, certificates of title, centerline and other boundary and easement location data. He must then plan and make the survey with prescribed accuracies. For example, the minimum accuracy for linear measurements must be 1 part in 10,000, and there are comparable requirements for accuracies for angles and for levels. The standard requires "monuments" to mark the property boundaries and a map to record the measurements and locations. The map or plat identifies the licensed surveyor responsible for the work, and normally is made a part of the public record regarding the property.

In 1962, the earlier standards were issued again but in different form. In an effort to establish standard terminology and practices for land title purposes, the ACSM, in conjunction with the American Title Association (nov. American Land Title Association), published "Minimum Standard Detail Requirements for Land Title Surveys." This, too, is still in use. Precise surveys and the resulting plats and documentation are a normal part of the formal records of land ownership.

The general definition of the term "survey" as meaning a close examination or appraisal has application to a second form of services provided by the surveyor. The mortgagee, in offering to loan money for the purchase of a home (or the insurer of the loan or title), wants assurance that the property and structures exist as defined by the legal description of the mortgage, and that there are no encroachments or unusual conditions that might affect the loan or title policy or the mortgagee's liability. If the loan is made at the time of original transfer of property, and the construction of the home, the precise survey performed for land title purposes also meets the needs of the mortgagee, or title or loan insurer. However, if, within a few years, the home is sold again, the needs of the mortgagee, or the insurers of the loan or the title, can probably be met by an *inspection* made by a registered surveyor. This would not be a property or land title survey for the owner, but a professional opinion regarding the property, made by the surveyor who is experienced in measurements and boundaries, and furnished only to the mortgagee or title company. If, by inspection alone, the surveyor is unable to establish the property lines sufficiently to verify location, identify encroachments, etc., the surveyor's report would include a recommendation that a precise survey be made to provide the required degree of assurance.

Recognizing an erroneous and misleading use of the term "surveys," the ACSM, by a formal resolution which was approved and disseminated in 1969, condemned the use of the word "surveys" in connection with such mortgage loan inspections and recommended the use of the term "mortgagee's inspection."

WALTERS v. TUCKER

Supreme Court of Missouri, 1955.
281 S.W.2d 843.

HOLLINGSWORTH, Judge.

This is an action to quiet title to certain real estate situate in the City of Webster Groves, St. Louis County, Missouri. Plaintiff and defendants are the owners of adjoining residential properties fronting northward on Oak Street. Plaintiff's property, known as 450 Oak Street, lies to the west of defendants' property, known as 446 Oak Street. The controversy arises over their division line. Plaintiff contends that her lot is 50 feet in width, east and west. Defendants contend that plaintiff's lot is only approximately 42 feet in width, east and west. The trial court, sitting without a jury, found the issues in favor of defendants and rendered judgment accordingly, from which plaintiff has appealed.

The common source of title is Fred F. Wolf and Rose E. Wolf, husband and wife, who in 1922 acquired the whole of Lot 13 of West Helfenstein Park, as shown by plat thereof recorded in St. Louis County. In 1924, Mr. and Mrs. Wolf conveyed to Charles Arthur Forse and wife the following described portion of said Lot 13:

"The West 50 feet of Lot 13 of West Helfenstein Park, a Subdivision in United States Survey 1953, Twp. 45, Range 8 East, St. Louis County, Missouri, ..."

Plaintiff, through mesne conveyances carrying a description like that above, is the last grantee of and successor in title to the aforesaid portion of Lot 13. Defendants, through mesne conveyances, are the last grantees of and successors in title to the remaining portion of Lot 13.

At the time of the above conveyance in 1924, there was and is now situate on the tract described therein a one-story frame dwelling house (450 Oak Street), which was then and continuously since has been occupied as a dwelling by the successive owners of said tract, or their tenants. In 1925, Mr. and Mrs. Wolf built a 1½-story stucco dwelling house on the portion of Lot 13 retained by them. This house (446 Oak Street) continuously since has been occupied as a dwelling by the successive owners of said portion of Lot 13, or their tenants.

Despite the apparent clarity of the description in plaintiff's deed, extrinsic evidence was heard for the purpose of enabling the trial court to interpret the true meaning of the description set forth therein. At the close of all the evidence the trial court found that the description did not clearly reveal whether the property conveyed "was to be fifty feet along the front line facing Oak Street or fifty feet measured Eastwardly at right angles from the West line of the property ..."; that the "difference in method of ascertaining fifty feet would result in a difference to the parties of a strip the length of the lot and approximately eight feet in width"; that an ambiguity existed which justified the hearing of extrinsic evidence; and that the "West fifty feet should be measured on the front or street line facing Oak Street." The judgment rendered in conformity with the above finding had the effect of fixing the east-west width of plaintiff's tract at about 42 feet.

Plaintiff contends that the description in the deed is clear, definite and unambiguous, both on its face and when applied to the land; that the trial court erred in hearing and considering extrinsic evidence; and that its finding and judgment changes the clearly expressed meaning of the description and describes and substitutes a different tract from that acquired by her under her deed. Defendants do not contend that the description, on its face, is ambiguous, but do contend that when applied to the land it is subject to "dual interpretation"; that under the evidence trial court did not err in finding it contained a latent ambiguity and that parol evidence was admissible to ascertain and determine its true meaning; and that the finding and judgment of the trial court properly construes and adjudges the true meaning of the description set forth in said deed.

Attached hereto is a reduced copy of an unchallenged survey of Lot 13, as made by plaintiff's witness, Robert J. Joyce, surveyor and graduate (1928) in civil engineering at Massachusetts Institute of Technology, for use in this litigation. Inasmuch as the two properties here in question front northward on Oak Street, the plat is made to be viewed from the bottom toward the top, which in this instance is from north to south:

WEST HELFENSTEIN PARK

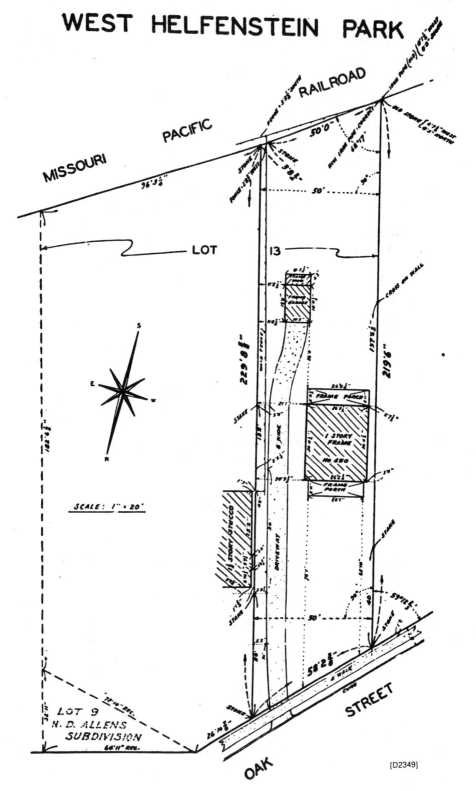

SCALE: 1" = 20'

[D2349]

It is seen that Lot 13 extends generally north and south. It is bounded on the north by Oak Street (except that a small triangular lot from another subdivision cuts off its frontage thereon at the northeast corner). On the south it is bounded by the Missouri Pacific Railroad right of way. Both Oak Street and the railroad right of way extend in a general northeast-southwest direction, but at differing angles.

Joyce testified: The plat was a "survey of the West 50 feet of Lot 13 of West Helfenstein Park". In making the survey the west boundary line of Lot 13 was first established. Lines 50 feet in length (one near the north end and one near the south end of the lot, as shown by the plat) were run eastwardly at right angles to the west line of the lot, and then a line was run parallel to the west line and 50 feet, as above measured, from it, intersecting both the north and south boundaries of the lot. This line, which represented 50 feet in width of Lot 13, made a frontage of 58 feet, 2⅜ inches, on Oak Street, and 53 feet, 8¾ inches, on the railroad right of way. The line, as thus measured, comes within 1 foot, 1¾ inches, of the west front corner of the stucco house (446 Oak Street), within 1 foot, 7 inches, of the west rear corner thereof, and within less than 1 foot of a chimney in the west wall.

The trial court refused to permit the witness to testify, but counsel for plaintiff offered to prove that, if permitted, witness would testify that the methods used by him in making the survey were in accordance with the practices and procedures followed in his profession in determining the boundaries of lots such as was described in the deed. The witness further testified that the method used by him was the only method by which a lot such as that described in the deeds in question could be measured having precisely and uniformly a width of 50 feet; and that a 50 foot strip is a strip with a uniform width of 50 feet.

Defendants also introduced in evidence a plat of Lot 13. It was prepared by Elbring Surveying Company for use in this litigation. August Elbring, a practicing surveyor and engineer for 34 years, testified in behalf of defendants: "In view of the fact that the deed (to the west 50 feet of Lot 13) made reference to the western 50 feet, and in view of the fact that the line which would have been established construing the dimension to be 50 feet at right angles, coming within a foot or so of an existing building (the stucco house), we felt that the line was intended to have been placed using the frontage of 50 feet on Oak Street and thence running the line (southward) parallel to the western line of Lot 13." The line so run, as being the east line of plaintiff's tract, was 8.01 feet west of the northwest corner of the stucco house and 8.32 feet west of its southwest corner. The Elbring plat does not show the actual width of plaintiff's tract as thus measured. But, concededly, there is no point on it where it approximates 50 feet in width; and, while it "fronts" 50 feet on Oak Street, its actual width is between 42 and 43 feet.

Both plats show a concrete driveway 8 feet in width extending from Oak Street to plaintiff's garage in the rear of her home, which, the testimony shows, was built by one of plaintiff's predecessors in title. The east line of plaintiff's tract, as measured by the Joyce (plaintiff's) survey, lies 6 or 7 feet east of the eastern edge of this driveway. Admittedly, the driveway is upon and an appurtenance of plaintiff's property. On the Elbring (defendants') plat, the east line of plaintiff's lot, as measured by Elbring, is shown to coincide with the east side of the driveway at Oak Street and to encroach upon it 1.25 feet for a distance of 30 or more feet as it extends between the houses. Thus, the area in dispute is essentially the area between the east edge of the driveway and the line fixed by the Joyce survey as the eastern line of plaintiff's tract.

Plaintiff adduced testimony to the effect that she and several of her predecessors in title had asserted claim to and had exercised physical dominion and control over all of the 50 feet in width of Lot 13, which included the concrete driveway and 6 or 7 feet to the east thereof. Defendants adduced testimony to the effect that they and their predecessors in title had asserted claim to and had exercised physical dominion and control over all of Lot 13 east of the driveway. The view we take of this case makes it unnecessary to set forth this testimony in detail.

The description under which plaintiff claims title, to wit: "The West 50 feet of Lot 13 ...", is on its face clear and free of ambiguity. It purports to convey a strip of land 50 feet in width off the west side of Lot 13. So clear is the meaning of the above language that defendants do not challenge it and it has been difficult to find any case wherein the meaning of a similar description has been questioned.

The law is clear that when there is no inconsistency on the face of a deed and, on application of the description to the ground, no inconsistency appears, parol evidence is not admissible to show that the parties intended to convey either more or less or different ground from that described. But where there are conflicting calls in a deed, or the description may be made to apply to two or more parcels, and there is nothing in the deed to show which is meant, then parol evidence is admissible to show the true meaning of the words used. "The office of extrinsic evidence as applied to the description of a parcel is to explain the latent ambiguity or to point out the property described on the ground. *Such evidence must not contradict the deed, or make a description of other land than that described in the deed.*" (Emphasis ours.) Thompson on Real Property, Vol. 6 § 3287, p. 468.

No ambiguity or confusion arises when the description here in question is applied to Lot 13. The description, when applied to the ground, fits the land claimed by plaintiff and cannot be made to apply to any other tract. When the deed was made, Lot 13 was vacant land except for the frame dwelling at 450 Oak Street. The stucco house (446 Oak Street) was not built until the following year. Under no conceivable theory can the fact that defendants' predecessors in title (Mr. and Mrs. Wolf) thereafter built the stucco house within a few feet of the east line of the property described in the deed be construed as competent evidence of any ambiguity in the description. Neither could the fact, if it be a fact, that the Wolfs and their successors in title claimed title to and exercised dominion and control over a portion of the tract be construed as creating or revealing an ambiguity in the description.

Whether the above testimony and other testimony in the record constitute evidence of a mistake in the deed we do not here determine. Defendants have not sought reformation, and yet that is what the decree herein rendered undertakes to do. It seems apparent that the trial court considered the testimony and came to the conclusion that the parties to the deed did not intend a conveyance of the "West 50 feet of Lot 13", but rather a tract fronting 50 feet on Oak Street. And, the decree, on the theory of interpreting an ambiguity, undertakes to change (reform) the description so as to describe a lot approximately 42 feet in width instead of a lot 50 feet in width, as originally described. That, we are convinced, the courts cannot do.

The judgment is reversed and the cause remanded for further proceedings not inconsistent with the views expressed.

All concur.

NOTES

1. *Ambiguous Descriptions: Validity of the Deed.* Traditionally, for a deed to be valid the instrument had to describe the parcel conveyed to the exclusion of all other parcels in the world. Contemporary courts have relaxed this requirement somewhat by resorting to parol evidence—oral statements, extrinsic writings, the physical condition of the land and improvements—in order to cure omissions or ambiguities within the deed's four corners.

Colman v. Butkovich, 556 P.2d 503 (Utah 1976), typifies the modern trend. In an action to quiet title, the question arose whether a deed description—"All unplatted land in this Block (29 P.C.) and all land West of this Blk: and Pt. Lot 1: Pt. Lot A"—was sufficient. Upholding the deed, the court observed:

> It is not to be questioned that in order to be valid, a deed must contain a sufficiently definite description to identify the property it conveys .... The problem lies in ascertaining the intent with which it was executed. It should be resolved, if possible, by looking to the terms of the instrument itself and any reasonable inferences to be drawn therefrom; and if there then remains any uncertainty or ambiguity, it can be aided by extrinsic evidence. If from that process the property can be identified with reasonable certainty, the deed is not invalid for uncertainty.

Doubtless the main reason courts are reluctant to invalidate deeds like the one in *Colman* is that the grantor, although she may have been less than clear in describing the parcel conveyed, has been crystal clear in expressing her intention to convey *something* to the grantee; if parol evidence will resolve the ambiguity and make the deed enforceable, it should be admitted.

Which will better serve an efficient conveyancing system: a rule that validates the deed by focusing on buyer's and seller's actual intent, or one that invalidates the deed if that intent has not been expressed clearly in the written instrument? Is the threat of invalidation likely to spur buyers and sellers to draft clear descriptions? For some thoughtful reflections along these lines, see Note, The Use of Extrinsic Evidence to Interpret Real Property Conveyances: A Suggested Limitation, 65 Cal.L.Rev. 897 (1977).

2. *Ambiguous Descriptions: Construction of the Deed.* Parol evidence fades over time and eventually disappears entirely. By contrast, the express language of a deed is indelible and can guide buyer and seller expectations indefinitely. Thus, although the result in *Walters* might seem overly harsh to the immediate buyer who may have relied on parol evidence, it can be justified in terms of the interests of the countless, future buyers and their sellers who will not have access to this parol evidence. Also, the effects on the immediate buyer will frequently be meliorated by adverse possession rules. An owner who invests in mistaken reliance on parol representations will gain title to the land he mistakenly possesses if his possession is not objected to by the true owner for the period prescribed by the statute of limitations.

3. *Canons of Construction.* The main work of courts dealing with deed descriptions is to interpret ambiguous or conflicting language. Professors Cribbet and Johnson have helpfully distilled ten canons of construction from the cases. J. Cribbet & C. Johnson, Principles of the Law of Property 210–212 (3d ed. 1989). Some of these canons can truly help courts to divine the seller's and buyer's original intent. One canon states that in case of a conflict between the various indicators and measures used in a description, "monuments control distances and courses; courses control distances; and quantity is the least reliable guide of all." The canon presumably corresponds with the expectations of buyer and seller: "most monuments would be difficult to mistake so they are probably identified correctly. A course, 'northerly at a 90° angle' is more certain than a distance 'thence 80 ft.,' since most people cannot measure distances with the naked eye." Distance is also subject to the hazards of uneven terrain.

Another helpful canon is that when "a tract of land is bounded by a monument which has width, such as a highway or a stream, the boundary line extends to the center, provided the grantor owns that far." Again, the canon presumably reflects the parties' original expectations—in this case, that the grantee would receive the grantor's entire interest in the parcel. To mark the boundary at the near edge of the highway or stream would mean that if the highway is later abandoned, or the stream diverted, the grantor would have title to the strip between the edge and the center.

Other canons are, as Professors Cribbet and Johnson acknowledge, simply conclusional, explaining rather than predicting results. Among these are, "extrinsic evidence will be allowed to explain a latent ambiguity but a patent ambiguity must be resolved within the four corners of the deed." (What is patent? What is latent?) "Useless or contradictory words may be disregarded as mere surplusage." (What is useless? What is contradictory?) And, "particular descriptions control over general descriptions, although a false particular may be disregarded to give effect to a true general description." (Huh?) See also Note, Operation and Construction of Deeds, 6 St. Mary's L.J. 806 (1975).

4. *Surveyor Malpractice.* Surveyor liability for malpractice has expanded over the past two decades. Breach of contract, the traditional ground of recovery for a faulty survey or description, has recently been joined by the tort of negligent misrepresentation. This tort has no privity requirement and thus can give relief to distant purchasers as well as to the buyer or developer who first contracted with the surveyor. Liability is also being extended by the "discovery" rule under which the statute of limitations for negligent misrepresentation does not begin to run until the misrepresentation has been, or should have been, discovered.

In Rozny v. Marnul, 43 Ill.2d 54, 250 N.E.2d 656 (1969), defendant had prepared an inaccurate survey of plaintiff's house and lot for plaintiff's predecessor in interest, a builder. A legend on the face of the survey stated that the "survey carries our absolute guarantee for accuracy." Plaintiffs sought damages when they discovered that, relying on markers placed in accordance with the faulty survey, they had constructed improvements that encroached on an adjacent lot. Holding for plaintiffs, the Illinois Supreme Court reversed the Appellate Court's decision that the action sounded in contract and was barred for lack of privity. The supreme court chose instead to follow the warranty theory adopted in the Restatement of Torts, Second § 402B (1965). "The Restatement uses the language of misrepresentation to make it clear that the basis of liability is tort and expressly states that the privity of contract requirement is not applicable."

Turning to the extent of defendant's liability, the court acknowledged the specter of unlimited liability, but noted that two facts removed any such danger in the case before it. First, "as might reasonably have been foreseen by defendant who admitted that he knew the plats were customarily used by lending agencies and others, that plat was subsequently relied on to his damage by a third party [plaintiff] in connection with the financing and purchase of the surveyed property." Second, the situation is "not one fraught with such an overwhelming potential liability as to dictate a contrary result, for the class of persons who might foreseeably use this plat is rather narrowly limited, if not exclusively so, to those who deal with the surveyed property as purchasers or lenders. Injury will ordinarily occur only once and to the one person then owning the lot." 250 N.E.2d at 662.

Finally, the court rejected defendant's contention that the five year limitations period began to run when the plat was delivered to the builder who ordered it or, at the latest, from the time the plaintiffs relied on the guarantee. Instead, the court adopted discovery as the starting point for the statute of limitations: "Where the passage of time does little to increase the problems of proof, the ends of justice are served by permitting plaintiff to sue within the statutory period computed from the time at which he knew or should have known of the existence of the right to sue." 250 N.E.2d at 664.

Doctrines limiting surveyor liability are, however, still applied. Some courts will blunt the thrust of liability by limiting the amount of damages that can be awarded. In Allan & Leuthold, Inc. v. Terra Investment Co., 271 Or. 335, 532 P.2d 218 (1975), a surveyor whose errors required a corrective survey was held liable for the costs of the resurvey, but not for additional plumbing costs that did not directly result from the errors. Similarly, in Trump v. Weir, 4 Pa.D. & C.2d 303, 71 Montg.Co.L.R. 327 (1956), even though defendant's survey showed a parcel to be one acre smaller than in fact it was, the seller was denied damages because she sold the land for a flat sum on an "in gross," rather than quantity, basis and offered no evidence that she would have obtained a better price had the full acreage been shown.

5. *Regulation of Surveyors.* Surveying is a closely regulated profession. A state license is generally required of anyone who performs surveying activities within the state. Applicants must meet stiff training requirements to obtain a surveyor's license. They may be required to have completed a four-year undergraduate course of study, with an emphasis on land surveying, and also to have completed two or more years of training in the field. More extensive field experience can in some states substitute for a full college program. An applicant may also be required to successfully complete an examination testing knowledge of basic math and science as well as applied surveying principles.

Once licensed, the surveyor may be required to comply with rigorous professional standards of practice. A surveyor can lose his or her license, or be otherwise disciplined, for committing fraud, failing to meet administratively established requirements such as following the specified forms for maps, plats, plans or designs, or inability to practice in accordance with the standards of the profession. See, for example, Wyo.Stat. § 33–29–101 et seq.; N.Y.Educ.Law § 7200 et seq.; Cal.Bus. & Prof.Code § 8700 et seq.; S.D.Comp.Laws Ann. § 36–18 et seq.

6. *Bibliographic Note.* For background on property description and surveys see, in addition to the works excerpted above, J. Grimes, A Treatise on the Law of Surveying and Boundaries (4th ed. 1976); 1. R. Patton & C. Patton, Land Titles (2d ed. 1957); Keith, Government Land Surveys and Related Problems, 38 Iowa L.Rev. 86 (1952); Boyd & Uelmen, Resurveys and Metes and Bounds Descriptions, 1953 Wis. L.Rev. 657.

B. LIABILITIES THAT SURVIVE THE DEED

Under the doctrine of merger, a deed conveying real property supersedes any conflicting terms in the contract of sale and becomes the sole measure of the parties' rights and liabilities as between themselves and others. This means that even if the contract of sale contains an express or implied covenant that seller will deliver marketable title on closing, buyer's acceptance of the deed will bar buyer from an action against seller if title later proves to be unmarketable—except to the extent that the deed itself contains express warranties of title.

In practice, merger doctrine is not nearly so clear-cut, nor buyer's prospects so bleak. First, merger is a rule of construction, not a rule of law, and when the interests of third parties will not be prejudiced, courts will weigh parol evidence in interpreting the deed. Also, just as the deed may specify obligations not mentioned in the contract, so the contract may effectively provide that it, and not the deed, is to control certain obligations. And, although most courts will not imply title covenants into deeds, many courts today will imply covenants respecting fitness of the premises. See generally, Dunham, Merger by Deed—Was it Ever Automatic?, 10 Ga.L.Rev. 419 (1976).

Merger is characteristically a seller's doctrine, employed to repel buyer claims based on pre-closing undertakings. Can—and should—merger also be used as a *buyer* doctrine to support the claim that post-closing warranties supersede less extensive undertakings made in the contract of sale? Consider the next principal case.

REED v. HASSELL

Superior Court of Delaware, 1975.
340 A.2d 157.

CHRISTIE, Judge.

By contract dated August 16, 1969, the plaintiffs, Thomas J. Reed and Sally Reed, his wife, agreed to purchase from Andrew Hassell (who died before the transaction was completed) and Loretta Hassell, his wife, Lots 82 and 83, Second Addition, Bay View Park, Baltimore Hundred, Sussex County, Delaware.

The printed contract form used by the parties provided that the title was to be "good and merchantable, free of liens and encumbrances except ... publicly recorded easements for public utilities and other easements which may be observed by the inspection of the property."

By deed dated February 4, 1970, Loretta Hassell (the surviving seller and the defendant in this action) conveyed the lots to plaintiffs pursuant to the contract using a special warranty deed as required by the contract.

At the time of the contract and at the time of the conveyance, there was an existing road known as Hassell Avenue which (contrary to the information on the recorded plot plan) seriously encroached upon Lot 82 so as to deprive that lot of about 25 percent of its square footage. This encroachment reduced the lot to a relatively small, inconvenient lot which will be difficult to build upon in view of zoning requirements which include set-back and side line restrictions.

By this suit, plaintiffs seek damages on account of the encroachment. There is no evidence that defendant knew that the road constituted an encroachment at the time of settlement and, of course, the plaintiffs were unaware of the encroachment at the time of settlement.

The evidence indicates that the intention of the seller was to convey building lots essentially as they were shown on the plot plan, and the intention of the buyers was to buy such lots because they were of such size and shape as to be suitable for the construction of houses. Although there was an exception in the contract as to easements observable by inspection of the property, it is clear that the agreement would never have been entered into if it had been known that there was a major encroachment which severely limited the usefulness of the lot. Indeed, the seller made an innocent and unknowing representation to the buyers to the effect that she was able to convey such lots essentially as shown on the plot plan. This the seller was unable to do.

At the time of settlement there was heavy and tall growth on the lots which made it impossible to inspect the boundaries of the land or to measure the lots without costly or time-consuming work to cut down portions of the growth. During the two summers after settlement, the plaintiffs personally cleared the land. In October, 1973, the land had been cleared to the extent that a survey could be conducted and then, for the first time, it was discovered by a professional surveyor that the road was so located as to constitute a major encroachment on Lot 82.

Plaintiffs seek damages based upon alleged "misrepresentation, deceit and fraud" and, by informal amendment of the complaint, they, in the alternative, seek damages on account of an alleged breach of the covenant of warranty contained in the deed.

At the hearing, plaintiffs failed to establish a factual basis for recovery on account of "misrepresentation, deceit and fraud" as such, but it was clearly established that the road constituted a breach of the covenant of special warranty of fee simple title free of encumbrances which the law reads into deeds such as the deed issued by the seller to the buyers in this case.

Thus, the question to be resolved by the Court is whether a major encroachment not known to be an encroachment by either the seller or the buyers at the time of settlement gives rise to an action for damages after such encroachment is discovered by the buyers many months after the deed had been accepted by the buyers. Resolution of this issue, in turn, depends in part upon the effect or lack of effect which is given to the provision in the sales contract which excepted from the title guarantees contained in such contract "easements which may be observed by an inspection of the property."

As to this provision of the contract, plaintiffs claim first of all that the encroachment could not be discovered by inspection because of the heavy and tall growth on the land. Plaintiffs' testimony about the growth is supported by a surveyor who indicated that it would have been necessary to cut a portion of the growth in order to make a survey.

The encroaching road itself was, of course, in plain sight and easily accessible. It appears to constitute the access to the lots. What was not readily accessible were the boundaries of the lots, a survey of which would have shown that the road encroached in Lot 82. Had these boundaries been established by survey, it would have been apparent that the existing road cut across Lot 82 so as to deprive it of about 25 percent of its square footage.

I find that, under the circumstances here present, the encroachment was one which may have been observed by an inspection of the property, but I also find that the parties did not intend that the risk of a major encroachment was to be assumed by the buyers under the contract or the deed here involved. The contract did not specify that the only easements excepted from the title guarantees were those discoverable by any easy-to-conduct amateur inspection free of cost, and it is apparent that a meaningful inspection would involve physical labor and the cost of hiring a surveyor. Plaintiffs' election not to go this expense did not render the inspection impossible; rather, plaintiff assumed the risk of easement encroachments not going to the essence of the contract. The contractual provision provided in legal effect that defendant did not guarantee against existing easements which would be revealed by a survey, but it was also clearly implied in the contract that seller owned and was in a position to convey essentially what was shown on the plot plan as Lot 82.

Plaintiffs also contend that, in any event, the contract "merged" with the deed at time of settlement and, at that time, the contract became void as a separate document. Plaintiffs say the effect of this "merger" is that the seller is now held to the terms of the special warranty of title which the law attaches to a deed and seller is deprived of any benefit from the less exacting terms of the contract pursuant to which the special warranty deed was issued.

We come at last to the real crux of the case: Does a savings clause in the real estate sales contract survive the issuance of a special warranty deed so as to protect the grantor from liability for an encumbrance which was unrecognized by the parties but was in fact in basic derogation of the title the deed purported to convey?

The solution to the problem lies in the application of the merger rule under which the law is generally deemed to provide that a deed makes full execution of a contract of sale and constitutes the overriding contract between the parties as to what the seller conveyed to the buyer thereby rendering ineffective or obsolete any inconsistent terms of the prior contract.

This rule is summarized in 26 C.J.S. Deeds § 91 in the following language:

"Accordingly, although the terms of preliminary agreements may vary from those contained in the deed, the deed alone must be looked to for determination of the rights of the parties, in the absence of fraud or mistake, and the rule as to merger has been held to deny operative effect to prior agreements with respect to set-back restrictions, the amount of land to be conveyed, the nature of the title transferred, freedom from encumbrances, permissible use of the property, and reservation of an easement."

Judge Daniel J. Layton confirmed this rule of law in Delaware in the case of Re v. Magness Construction Co., Del.Super., 117 A.2d 78 (1955) when he wrote the following:

"The authorities are uniform in holding that where a Deed is executed and delivered pursuant to a Contract of Sale of Realty, the latter merges with the former and becomes void."

The C.J.S. article goes on to observe, however, that the merger rule is subject to exceptions and *the intent of the parties is controlling,* the question being one of construction (emphasis added).

The difficulty with the merger rule as applied to the case at bar is that it does not appear to have been developed to resolve the type of problem here posed. The merger rule appears to have been developed to resolve issues raised where a seller of real property undertook certain obligations in a contract of sale and then delivered something less than he promised as, for example, when seller delivered a deed not carrying out all the contract promises or a lot with certain encumbrances or containing a lesser acreage than contracted for. So it is that the annotation as to this type of merger is titled "Deed as superseding or merging provisions of antecedent contract *imposing obligations upon the vendor.*" 38 A.L.R.2d 1310 (emphasis added). The annotation then goes on to show that, although all jurisdictions considering the matter recognize the merger rule, still there are many special situations where the seller is required to comply with promises made in the sales contract even though a deed has been delivered and accepted. The actual use of the merger rule can often be explained as a way of regarding the delivery and acceptance of the deed as a sort of accord and satisfaction.

It could be argued that this large collection of cases and the learned writings about these cases find little direct application here because, in the case before the Court, the sales contract contained an escape clause as to easements for the benefit of the seller. The cited merger cases deal with situations where the purchaser is seeking to get what he originally bargained for but didn't get because the deed he received failed to carry out the express terms of the contract. The case at bar, on the other hand, deals with a case where the seller is seeking to get by with delivering what she claims the purchaser bargained for (i.e., a lot subject to any existing easements which could be discovered by inspection) even though the deed which the seller delivered to the purchaser appears to go beyond the requirements of the sales contract and purports to convey a title clear of such flaws.

Under the merger rule, a deed is often deemed to supersede promises contained in the sales contract and, if the purchaser accepts the deed as compliance with the sales contract, he cannot seek additional rights he formerly had under the contract unless those additional rights survived the acceptance of the deed because they fell within one of the numerous exceptions to the merger rule. Is the converse true? That is, does an unconditional special warranty deed supersede the lesser undertakings or escape clauses contained in the sales contract so that the seller must make good on the warranties of the deed even though the seller was expressly excused from such undertaking in the sales contract?

I think, under the circumstances here present, the merger rule should be applied and the seller should be held to the warranties contained in the deed because the obvious intent of the parties from the very beginning was that the seller would convey and the buyers would receive the two building lots essentially as shown on the plot plan. The exception as to easements contained in the sales contract is found to have been intended to protect the seller against only such easements as do not go to the essence of the bargain and do not seriously limit the usefulness of the lot. The exception surely was not intended to force buyers to accept a lot with such a serious encroachment therein as to render the lot almost useless for the declared purpose which buyers had in mind when they bought.

In short, I find that plaintiffs have established their right to recover damages because defendant failed to convey a good title to Lot 82 to plaintiffs free and clear of all easements except such discoverable easements as did not destroy or severely limit the intended use of the lot. Such major failure and mistake constituted not only a breach of the terms of the sales contract, but more importantly from a technical legal viewpoint, such failure is contrary to the terms of the special warranty deed delivered by defendant to plaintiffs. The merger rule is deemed to apply here because it serves to carry out the basic intent of the parties. The warranties in the deed are deemed to be binding on the seller under the circumstances.

Arguments were not specifically presented under the theory of mutual mistake of fact, but a similar result might have been reached under that theory.

The evidence on damages appears to be somewhat inconclusive since the parties presented their damage evidence under vastly differing theories as to the correct measure of damages.

Further argument and possibly further evidence will be considered before the Court designates the amount of damages.

NOTES

1. *Collateral Promises.* Under an important limit on the merger doctrine, "collateral" promises—those unrelated to title or possession of the property—are not merged into the deed and so survive closing. Courts generally agree that certain promises are collateral, such as seller's promise to build or repair the premises and express and implied promises as to quality of the property. M. Friedman, Contracts and Conveyances of Real Property 887–897 (5th ed. 1991). There are occasional variations on the rule. Compare American National Self Storage, Inc. v. Lopez–Aguiar, 521 So.2d 303 (Fla.App.1988), review denied, 528 So.2d 1182 (Fla.1988) (express warranty that property had water, sewer, and electric service was collateral and survived delivery of the deed) with Toys 'R' Us, Inc. v. Atlanta Economic Development Corporation, 195 Ga.App. 195, 393 S.E.2d 44 (1990), cert. denied (seller's promise in the sales agreement to provide a building pad of certain specifications merged into the deed and was extinguished). How important was the fact that the closing statement in *Toys 'R' Us* expressly stated that all provisions of the sales contract merge into the deed?

2. *The Function of Merger Doctrine.* Merger, though rooted in general contract principles, serves a special function in the context of real property transactions, where the needs of future as well as present buyers and sellers must be served. While the immediate buyer and seller can safely look outside the deed to resolve their mutual intent, a future buyer of the land can rely only on the intent expressed within the four corners of a recorded deed.

Courts today generally recognize the importance of this distinction. They will look outside the deed when only the parties to the immediate transaction will be affected by their decision, but will give the deed conclusive effect when the interests of third parties are implicated. For example, merger will be strictly applied against contract covenants respecting title and freedom from encumbrances, and these covenants will not survive the closing unless restated in the deed. This application of the merger rule enhances efficient conveyancing, for all successors in interest to the original buyer will be able to rely exclusively on recorded instruments to determine whether title covenants have been given whose benefits will run to them. See generally, Berger, Merger By Deed—What Provisions of a Contract for the Sale of Land Survive the Closing? 21 Real Est.L.J. 22 (1992); Note, Merger of Land Contract in Deed, 25 Alb.L.Rev. 122 (1961).

Chappell v. Northern Realty, Inc., 128 Vt. 476, 266 A.2d 453 (1970), typifies the judicial reluctance to apply the merger doctrine where to do so would prejudice the immediate parties without benefitting third parties. Plaintiffs, who had during the executory period discovered defects in the house they had contracted to purchase, nonetheless closed the purchase relying on an oral promise from seller's agent that seller would repair the defects. Some of the promised repairs were not made, and buyer sued. The court held for the buyers. Against the seller's argument that the earlier negotiations merged into the deed, the court ruled that there were in fact "two separate contracts" before it—the deed and the contract to repair the specified defects. "The separate contract to repair does not in any way affect the deed or impair its force or effect. It merely shows a separate undertaking on the part of appellant, not shown by the deed, but collateral to it and independent of it." 266 A.2d at 456.

3. *Fraud.* Merger does not affect seller liability for fraud. Before and after closing, the buyer who meets the strict requirements for proving fraud can obtain rescission and, in some cases, damages. See Ouseley v. Foss, 188 Ga.App. 766, 374 S.E.2d 534 (1988). Liability for fraud is covered at page 198 below.

4. *U.L.T.A.* Section 1–309 of the Uniform Land Transactions Act abolishes the doctrine of merger.

1. FITNESS OF THE PREMISES

Buyers disappointed with the quality of the property which they have purchased have enjoyed some recent, albeit limited, success in attacking the doctrine of caveat emptor. Relief has come under theories of tort (primarily fraud, misrepresentation, and a developing doctrine of nondisclosure) and new notions of implied warranty. Statutes have also come to their aid. Key variables for the courts have been whether the property is residential or commercial and whether it is new or used.

A critical issue of quality is the liability of sellers (and others) for pollutants on the property. Environmental issues are addressed at pages 885–938 below.

a. Liability of Seller

i. Tort

Buyers have found some relief under tort law. Remedies have been extended to buyers of new and used, commercial and residential properties. It is well established that an action lies for misrepresentation, provided that the assertion was untrue, fraudulent or material, and was reasonably relied upon by the buyer. E. Farnsworth, Contracts 249–272 (2d ed.1990). See Crawford v. Williams, 258 Ga. 806, 375 S.E.2d 223 (1989) (false statement that well was located on property might form basis for fraudulent misrepresentation action but there was no reasonable reliance since buyers made no effort to ascertain the boundaries of the parcel). Courts have recognized claims for fraudulent concealment by equating a seller's action in concealing a defect to a false assertion. See, e.g., Stemple v. Dobson, 184 W.Va. 317, 400 S.E.2d 561 (1990) (sellers disguised termite damage by installing new timbers stained to match old wood).

Many courts have imposed liability on sellers who failed to disclose the condition of the property. Consider the following cases. *Thacker*, involving the nondisclosure of major problems with the home's foundations, represents the modern rule. *Stambovsky* is from a jurisdiction that had continued to find no liability for nondisclosure.

THACKER v. TYREE, 171 W.Va. 110, 113, 297 S.E.2d 885, 888 (1982), MILLER, Chief Justice: [W]e conclude that where a vendor is aware of defects or conditions which substantially affect the value or habitability of the property and the existence of which are unknown to the purchaser and would not be disclosed by a reasonably diligent inspection, then the vendor has a duty to disclose the same to the purchaser. His failure to disclose will give rise to a cause of action in favor of the purchaser. As earlier stated, we express no view as to the ultimate outcome but merely hold that the plaintiff's case could not be dismissed as a matter of law on summary judgment based on the doctrine of *caveat emptor.*

STAMBOVSKY v. ACKLEY

Supreme Court, Appellate Division, First Department of New York, 1991.
169 A.D.2d 254, 572 N.Y.S.2d 672.

Before MILONAS, J.P., and ROSS, KASSAL, SMITH and RUBIN, JJ.

RUBIN, Justice.

Plaintiff, to his horror, discovered that the house he had recently contracted to purchase was widely reputed to be possessed by poltergeists, reportedly seen by defendant seller and members of her family on numerous occasions over the last nine years. Plaintiff promptly commenced this action seeking rescission of the contract of sale. Supreme Court reluctantly dismissed the complaint, holding that plaintiff has no remedy at law in this jurisdiction.

The unusual facts of this case, as disclosed by the record, clearly warrant a grant of equitable relief to the buyer who, as a resident of New York City, cannot be expected to have any familiarity with the folklore of the Village of Nyack. Not being a "local," plaintiff could not readily learn that the home he had contracted to purchase is haunted. Whether the source of the spectral apparitions seen by defendant seller are parapsychic or psychogenic, having reported their presence in both a national publication ("Readers' Digest") and the local press (in 1977 and 1982, respectively), defendant is estopped to deny their existence and, as a matter of law, the house is haunted. More to the point, however, no divination is required to conclude that it is defendant's promotional efforts in publicizing her close encounters with these spirits which fostered the home's reputation in the community. In 1989, the house was included in a five-home walking tour of Nyack and described in a November 27th newspaper article as "a riverfront Victorian (with ghost)." The impact of the reputation thus created goes to the very essence of the bargain between the parties, greatly impairing both the value of the property and its potential for resale. The extent of this impairment may be presumed for the purpose of reviewing the disposition of this motion to dismiss the cause of action for rescission (*Harris v. City of New York*, 147 A.D.2d 186, 188–189, 542 N.Y.S.2d 550) and represents merely an issue of fact for resolution at trial.

While I agree with Supreme Court that the real estate broker, as agent for the seller, is under no duty to disclose to a potential buyer the phantasmal reputation of the premises and that, in his pursuit of a legal remedy for fraudulent misrepresentation against the seller, plaintiff hasn't a ghost of a chance, I am nevertheless moved by the spirit of equity to allow the buyer to seek rescission of the contract of sale and recovery of his downpayment. New York law fails to recognize any remedy for damages incurred as a result of the seller's mere silence, applying instead the strict rule of caveat emptor. Therefore, the theoretical basis for granting relief, even under the extraordinary facts of this case, is elusive if not ephemeral.

"Pity me not but lend thy serious hearing to what I shall unfold" (William Shakespeare, Hamlet, Act I, Scene V [Ghost]).

From the perspective of a person in the position of plaintiff herein, a very practical problem arises with respect to the discovery of a paranormal phenomenon: "Who you gonna' call?" as the title song to the movie "Ghostbusters" asks. Applying the strict rule of caveat emptor to a contract involving a house possessed by poltergeists conjures up visions of a psychic or medium routinely accompanying the structural engineer and Terminix man on an inspection of every home subject to a contract of sale. It portends that the prudent attorney will establish an escrow account lest the subject of the transaction come back to haunt him and his client—or pray that his malpractice insurance coverage extends to supernatural disasters. In the interest of avoiding such untenable consequences, the notion that a haunting is a condition which can and should be ascertained upon reasonable inspection of the premises is a hobgoblin which should be exorcised from the body of legal precedent and laid quietly to rest.

It has been suggested by a leading authority that the ancient rule which holds that mere non-disclosure does not constitute actionable misrepresentation "finds proper application in cases where the fact undisclosed is patent, or the plaintiff has equal opportunities for obtaining information which he may be expected to utilize, or the defendant has no reason to think that he is acting under any misapprehension" (Prosser, Law of Torts § 106, at 696 [4th ed., 1971]). However, with respect to transactions in real estate, New York adheres to the doctrine of caveat emptor and imposes no duty upon the vendor to disclose any information concerning the premises (*London v. Courduff*, 141 A.D.2d 803, 529 N.Y.S.2d 874) unless there is a confidential or fiduciary relationship between the parties (*Moser v. Spizzirro*, 31 A.D.2d 537, 295

N.Y.S.2d 188, affd., 25 N.Y.2d 941, 305 N.Y.S.2d 153, 252 N.E.2d 632; *IBM Credit Fin. Corp. v. Mazda Motor Mfg. (USA) Corp.,* 152 A.D.2d 451, 542 N.Y.S.2d 649) or some conduct on the part of the seller which constitutes "active concealment" (*see, 17 East 80th Realty Corp. v. 68th Associates,* 173 A.D.2d 245, 569 N.Y.S.2d 647 [dummy ventilation system constructed by seller]; *Haberman v. Greenspan,* 82 Misc.2d 263, 368 N.Y.S.2d 717 [foundation cracks covered by seller]). Normally, some affirmative misrepresentation (e.g., *Tahini Invs., Ltd. v. Bobrowsky,* 99 A.D.2d 489, 470 N.Y.S.2d 431 [industrial waste on land allegedly used only as farm]); *Jansen v. Kelly,* 11 A.D.2d 587, 200 N.Y.S.2d 561 [land containing valuable minerals allegedly acquired for use as campsite] or partial disclosure (*Junius Constr. Corp. v. Cohen,* 257 N.Y. 393, 178 N.E. 672 [existence of third unopened street concealed]; *Noved Realty Corp. v. A.A.P. Co.,* 250 App.Div. 1, 293 N.Y.S. 336 [escrow agreements securing lien concealed]) is required to impose upon the seller a duty to communicate undisclosed conditions affecting the premises (contra, *Young v. Keith,* 112 A.D.2d 625, 492 N.Y.S.2d 489 [defective water and sewer systems concealed]).

Caveat emptor is not so all-encompassing a doctrine of common law as to render every act of non-disclosure immune from redress, whether legal or equitable. "In regard to the necessity of giving information which has not been asked, the rule differs somewhat at law and in equity, and while the law courts would permit no recovery of *damages* against a vendor, because of mere concealment of facts *under certain circumstances,* yet if the vendee refused to complete the contract because of the concealment of a material fact on the part of the other, equity would refuse to compel him so to do, because equity only compels the specific performance of a contract which is fair and open, and in regard to which all material matters known to each have been communicated to the other" (*Rothmiller v. Stein,* 143 N.Y. 581, 591–592, 38 N.E. 718 [emphasis added]). Even as a principle of law, long before exceptions were embodied in statute law (see, e.g., UCC 2–312, 313, 314, 315; 3–417[2][e]), the doctrine was held inapplicable to contagion among animals, adulteration of food, and insolvency of a maker of a promissory note and of a tenant substituted for another under a lease (*see, Rothmiller v. Stein,* supra, at 592–593, 38 N.E. 718 and cases cited therein). Common law is not moribund. *Ex facto jus oritur* (law arises out of facts). Where fairness and common sense dictate that an exception should be created, the evolution of the law should not be stifled by rigid application of a legal maxim.

The doctrine of caveat emptor requires that a buyer act prudently to assess the fitness and value of his purchase and operates to bar the purchaser who fails to exercise due care from seeking the equitable remedy of rescission (*see, e.g., Rodas v. Manitaras,* 159 A.D.2d 341, 552 N.Y.S.2d 618). For the purposes of the instant motion to dismiss the action pursuant to CPLR 3211(a)(7), plaintiff is entitled to every favorable inference which may reasonably be drawn from the pleadings ... specifically, in this instance, that he met his obligation to conduct an inspection of the premises and a search of available public records with respect to title. It should be apparent, however, that the most meticulous inspection and search would not reveal the presence of poltergeists at the premises or unearth the property's ghoulish reputation in the community. Therefore, there is no sound policy reason to deny plaintiff relief for failing to discover a state of affairs which the most prudent purchaser would not be expected to even contemplate (see, *Da Silva v. Musso*, 53 N.Y.2d 543, 551, 444 N.Y.S.2d 50, 428 N.E.2d 382).

The case law in this jurisdiction dealing with the duty of a vendor of real property to disclose information to the buyer is distinguishable from the matter under review. The most salient distinction is that existing cases invariably deal with the physical condition of the premises (*e.g., London v. Courduff, supra* [use as a landfill]; *Perin v. Mardine Realty Co.*, 5 A.D.2d 685, 168 N.Y.S.2d 647 *affd.* 6 N.Y.2d 920, 190 N.Y.S.2d 995, 161 N.E.2d 210 [sewer line crossing adjoining property without owner's consent]), defects in title (*e.g., Sands v. Kissane*, 282 App.Div. 140, 121 N.Y.S.2d 634 [remainderman]), liens against the property (*e.g., Noved Realty Corp. v. A.A.P. Co., supra*), expenses or income (*e.g., Rodas v. Manitaras, supra* [gross receipts]) and other factors affecting its operation. No case has been brought to this court's attention in which the property value was impaired as the result of the reputation created by information disseminated to the public by the seller (or, for that matter, as a result of possession by poltergeists).

Where a condition which has been created by the seller materially impairs the value of the contract and is peculiarly within the knowledge of the seller or unlikely to be discovered by a prudent purchaser exercising due care with respect to the subject transaction, nondisclosure constitutes a basis for rescission as a matter of equity. Any other outcome places upon the buyer not merely the obligation to exercise care in his purchase but rather to be omniscient with respect to any fact which may affect the bargain. No practical purpose is served by imposing such a burden upon a purchaser. To the contrary, it encourages predatory business practice and offends the principle that equity will suffer no wrong to be without a remedy.

Defendant's contention that the contract of sale, particularly the merger or "as is" clause, bars recovery of the buyer's deposit is unavailing. Even an express disclaimer will not be given effect where the facts are peculiarly within the knowledge of the party invoking it (*Danann Realty Corp. v. Harris*, 5 N.Y.2d 317, 322, 184 N.Y.S.2d 599, 157 N.E.2d 597; *Tahini Invs., Ltd. v. Bobrowsky, supra*). Moreover, a fair reading of the merger clause reveals that it expressly disclaims only representations made with respect to the physical condition of the premises and merely makes general reference to representations concerning "any other matter or things affecting or relating to the aforesaid premises". As broad as this language may be, a reasonable interpretation is that its effect is limited to tangible or physical matters and does not extend to paranormal phenomena. Finally, if the language of the contract is to be construed as broadly as defendant urges to encompass the presence of poltergeists in the house, it cannot be said that she has delivered the premises "vacant" in accordance with her obligation under the provisions of the contract rider.

To the extent New York law may be said to require something more than "mere concealment" to apply even the equitable remedy of rescission, the case of *Junius Construction Corporation v. Cohen,* 257 N.Y.393, 178 N.E. 672, *supra,* while not precisely on point, provides some guidance. In that case, the seller disclosed that an official map indicated two as yet unopened streets which were planned for construction at the edges of the parcel. What was not disclosed was that the same map indicated a third street which, if opened, would divide the plot in half. The court held that, while the seller was under no duty to mention the planned streets at all, having undertaken to disclose two of them, he was obliged to reveal the third (*see also, Rosenschein v. McNally,* 17 A.D.2d 834, 233 N.Y.S.2d 254).

In the case at bar, defendant seller deliberately fostered the public belief that her home was possessed. Having undertaken to inform the public at large, to whom she has no legal relationship, about the supernatural occurrences on her property, she may be said to owe no less a duty to her contract vendee. It has been remarked that the occasional modern cases which permit a seller to take unfair advantage of a buyer's ignorance so long as he is not actively misled are "singularly unappetizing" (Prosser, Law of Torts § 106, at 696 [4th ed. 1971]). Where, as here, the seller not only takes unfair advantage of the buyer's ignorance but has created and perpetuated a condition about which he is unlikely to even inquire, enforcement of the contract (in whole or in part) is offensive to the court's sense of equity. Application of the remedy of rescission, within the bounds of the narrow exception to the doctrine of caveat emptor set forth herein, is entirely appropriate to relieve the unwitting purchaser from the consequences of a most unnatural bargain.

Accordingly, the judgment of the Supreme Court, New York County (Edward H. Lehner, J.), entered April 9, 1990, which dismissed the complaint pursuant to CPLR 3211(a)(7), should be modified, on the law and the facts and in the exercise of discretion, and the first cause of action seeking rescission of the contract reinstated, without costs.

Judgment, Supreme Court, New York County (Edward H. Lehner, J.), entered on April 9, 1990, modified, on the law and the facts and in the exercise of discretion, and the first cause of action seeking rescission of the contract reinstated, without costs.

All concur except MILONAS, J.P. and SMITH, J., who dissent in an opinion by SMITH, J.

SMITH, Justice (dissenting).

I would affirm the dismissal of the complaint by the motion court.

Plaintiff seeks to rescind his contract to purchase defendant Ackley's residential property and recover his down payment. Plaintiff alleges that Ackley and her real estate broker, defendant Ellis Realty, made material misrepresentations of the property in that they failed to disclose that Ackley believed that the house was haunted by poltergeists. Moreover, Ackley shared this belief with her community and the general public through articles published in *Reader's Digest* (1977) and the local newspaper (1982). In November 1989, approximately two months after the parties entered into the contract of sale but subsequent to the scheduled October 2, 1989 closing, the house was included in a five-house walking tour and again described in the local newspaper as being haunted.

Prior to closing, plaintiff learned of this reputation and unsuccessfully sought to rescind the $650,000 contract of sale and obtain return of his $32,500 down payment without resort to litigation. The plaintiff then commenced this action for that relief and alleged that he would not have entered into the contract had he been so advised and that as a result of the alleged poltergeist activity, the market value and resaleability of the property was greatly diminished. Defendant Ackley has counterclaimed for specific performance.

"It is settled law in New York that the seller of real property is under no duty to speak when the parties deal at arm's length. The mere silence of the seller, without some act or conduct which deceived the purchaser, does not amount to a concealment that is actionable as a fraud. ... The buyer has the duty to satisfy himself as to the quality of his bargain pursuant to the doctrine of caveat emptor, which in New York State still applies to real estate transactions." *London v. Courduff,* 141 A.D.2d 803, 804, 529 N.Y.S.2d 874, *app. dism'd.,* 73 N.Y.2d 809, 537 N.Y.S.2d 494, 534 N.E.2d 332.

The parties herein were represented by counsel and dealt at arm's length. This is evidenced by the contract of sale which, inter alia, contained various riders and a specific provision that all prior understandings and agreements between the parties were merged into the contract, that the contract completely expressed their full agreement and that neither had relied upon any statement by anyone else not set forth in the contract. There is no allegation that defendants, by some specific act, other than the failure to speak, deceived the plaintiff. Nevertheless, a cause of action may be sufficiently stated where there is a confidential or fiduciary relationship creating a duty to disclose and there was a failure to disclose a material fact, calculated to induce a false belief. *County of Westchester v. Welton Becket Assoc.,* 102 A.D.2d 34, 50–51, 478 N.Y.S.2d 305, aff'd., 66 N.Y.2d 642, 495 N.Y.S.2d 364, 485 N.E.2d 1029. However, plaintiff herein has not alleged and there is no basis for concluding that a confidential or fiduciary relationship existed between these parties to an arm's length transaction such as to give rise to a duty to disclose. In addition, there is no allegation that defendants thwarted plaintiff's efforts to fulfill his responsibilities fixed by the doctrine of caveat emptor. *See London v. Courduff, supra,* 141 A.D.2d at 804, 529 N.Y.S.2d 874.

Finally, if the doctrine of caveat emptor is to be discarded, it should be for a reason more substantive than a poltergeist. The existence of a poltergeist is no more binding upon the defendants than it is upon this court.

Based upon the foregoing, the motion court properly dismissed the complaint.

NOTES

1. *Theoretical Bases.* Various theories have been offered for imposing an obligation on seller to disclose. First, a key factor in finding liability is the relative access of buyer and seller to pertinent information—what each knew or should have known about the purported defect and what the comparative costs are of discovering the information. As the cases indicate, despite seller's increased duty to disclose, the buyer still has a duty to inquire. The buyer will be presumed to have exercised due diligence in examining the title and premises. Consider what information the buyer in *Stambovsky* could have discovered by reasonable inquiry and what information the seller had available. Is the relative sophistication of the parties relevant? Should a buyer be obligated to use a professional inspector to help discover defects? Should newcomers to the neighborhood be treated differently than long term residents? Should the buyer's inspection be limited to the property under contract?

Others see the disclosure duty as part of a changing moral standard in the marketplace. The court in Ollerman v. O'Rourke Co., 94 Wis.2d 17, 30–34, 288 N.W.2d 95, 101–103 (1980) explained:

> Under the doctrine of caveat emptor no person was required to tell all that he or she knew in a business transaction, for in a free market the diligent should not be deprived of the fruits of superior skill and knowledge lawfully acquired. The business world, and the law reflecting business mores and morals, required the parties to a transaction to use their faculties and exercise ordinary business sense, and not to call on the law to stand *in loco parentis* to protect them in their ordinary dealings with other business people. * * * Over the years society's attitudes toward good faith and fair dealing in business transactions have undergone significant change, and this change has been reflected in the law. * * * The test Dean Keeton derives from the cases to determine when the rule of nondisclosure should be abandoned that is "whenever justice, equity and fair dealing demand it" [quoting Fraud Concealment and Nondisclosure, 15 Tex. L. Rev. 1, 31 (1936)] presents, as one writer states, "a somewhat nebulous standard, praiseworthy as looking toward more stringent business ethics, but possibly difficult of practical application." Case Note, Silence as Fraudulent Concealment Vendor & Purchaser Duty to Disclose, 36 Wash.L.Rev. 202, 204 (1961).

Commentators have examined the effect of disclosure rules on the efficient operation of the marketplace. See Kronman, Mistake, Disclosure, Information, and the Law of Contracts, 7 J.Leg.Stud. 1 (1978) (arguing that there will be a disincentive to obtain information if one must disclose it without compensation, but maintaining that information acquired without much cost should be disclosed); R. Posner, Economic Analysis of Law 97 (3d ed.1986) (noting that a seller does not invest much in discovering defects about his house and so should disclose them, in contrast to a buyer who will be deterred from gathering information about hidden value of the property if he must disclose it). For an excellent discussion of these positions and an added perspective on the issue see Wonnell, The Structure of a General Theory of Nondisclosure, 41 Case W.Res.L.Rev. 329 (1991) (arguing that efficiency gains result from the merger of a resource and information about it, i.e., when a knowing buyer does not disclose, but not when a seller simply severs the resource and information).

On the issue of disclosure in the sale of realty, see Powell, The Seller's Duty to Disclose in Sales of Commercial Property, 28 Am.Bus. L.J. 245 (1990); Comment, Risk Allocation and the Sale of Defective Used Housing in Ohio—Should Silence be Golden, 20 Capital U.L.Rev. 215 (1991).

2. *Extent of Disclosure.* What facts must be disclosed? In *Thacker*, there were "major problems" with the foundation due to water under the footers; after the buyers moved in, the house's walls cracked, part of the basement wall collapsed, and the window sills came loose. *Thacker* limited the disclosure obligation to defects that "substantially affect the value or the habitability of the property." Why limit the rule in this way? Does this reflect a concern that a seller might not remember lesser problems and that all buyers of used housing should reasonably expect some minor defects? Did the court in *Stambovsky* actually think that there were ghosts in the house? If not, why find for buyer?

The facts of Weintraub v. Krobatsch, 64 N.J. 445, 447, 317 A.2d 68, 69 (1974), raise the issues of discoverability and the types of defects that must be disclosed. During the executory period, the buyers entered the unoccupied house at night and when they turned on the lights were "astonished to see roaches literally running in all directions, up the walls, drapes, etc." The court ordered rescission of the contract for seller's failure to disclose. Do you agree?

3. The New York rule described in *Stambovsky* and the case itself deviate from the developing rules in the area (as exemplified by *Thacker*) on both extremes. New York's general refusal to find liability for nondisclosure of physical problems with the property, the court's unwillingness to find a damages remedy, the limitation of relief to rescission, and the opinion's emphasis that relief was appropriate since the problem had been caused by the seller herself, are pro-seller when compared to other jurisdictions. On the other hand, many states have

passed statutes relieving the seller from disclosing that the property
was the scene of a homicide, other felony, or suicide, or that the prior
occupant had AIDS, even though such facts, like a "haunting," arguably would affect the market price of the property. See, e.g., Cal.Civ.
Code § 1710.2 (West Supp.1992) (partially superseding Reed v. King,
145 Cal.App.3d 261, 193 Cal.Rptr. 130 (1983)); Conn.Gen.Stat.Ann.
§ 20–329cc (West Supp.1992); N.M.Ann.Stat. § 47–13–2 (1992); Or.Rev.
Stat. § 93.277 (1991); Tenn.Code Ann. § 66–5–110 (Michie Supp.1992).

On the recovery and calculation of damages, see Wall v. Swilley, 562
So.2d 1252 (Miss.1990) (damages should give the purchaser the benefit
of the bargain).

4. *Buyer's Disclosure Obligation.* In evaluating seller's obligation
to disclose, consider that courts generally hold that a buyer has no duty
to disclose information that she knows concerning the property's value
which the seller does not know. See E. Farnsworth, Contracts 255–256
(2d ed.1990); Restatement (Second) Torts § 551 (stating exceptions).

In Zaschak v. Traverse Corp., 123 Mich.App. 126, 333 N.W.2d 191
(1983), the court found that plaintiffs failed to state a factual basis to
support their assertion that defendant had a duty to disclose certain
information regarding the productivity of their property. The court
stated:

> [P]laintiffs, despite numerous amendments, failed to state a factual
> basis to support the assertion that defendant Robert Faith had a
> duty to disclose certain alleged information regarding the potential
> productivity of plaintiffs' property. ... Plaintiff Robert Zaschak
> testified by deposition that defendant Faith, in response to ques-
> tioning regarding the property, told plaintiffs that he was unaware
> of any oil and gas exploration activity in the area. Because Faith
> possesses a graduate degree in geology and undoubtedly had infor-
> mation regarding oil and gas exploration in the area of plaintiffs'
> land, we have little doubt that Faith could have concealed material
> facts from plaintiff. However, Michigan law dictates that a pro-
> spective purchaser is under no duty to disclose facts or possible
> opportunities within his knowledge which materially affect the
> value of the property. Furman v. Brown, 227 Mich. 629, 199 N.W.
> 703 (1924); Stuart v. Dorow, 216 Mich. 591, 185 N.W. 662 (1921),
> see also Williams v. Spurr, 24 Mich. 335 (1872) (no duty by
> purchaser to disclose the extent and value of iron deposits on the
> property). Michigan courts have not yet recognized a duty on the
> part of a vendee to disclose facts relevant to the value of the real
> estate in question even when specifically asked. We decline to
> promulgate such a duty on the facts of this case. Although
> plaintiffs claim that they would not have sold the mineral rights
> absent Faith's alleged concealment of facts, the record discloses
> that plaintiffs received what was then the accepted value for the
> rights, $200 per acre. Moreover, rather than obtain an indepen-
> dent appraisal of the property's mineral potential, plaintiffs relied

upon [defendant] Francisco, with whom they have previously settled, who assured them that $200 per acre was the going rate for
mineral rights.

Id. at 129–130, 333 N.W.2d at 192–193.

While courts generally agree with *Zaschak* that there is no obligation on buyer to disclose, (see, e.g., Nussbaum v. Weeks, 214 Cal.
App.3d 1589, 263 Cal.Rptr. 360 (1989) (buyer who was general manager
of water district did not disclose to seller that property was subject to a
new water policy which would make it more valuable); Noss v. Abrams,
787 S.W.2d 834 (Mo.App.1990)), some courts do not permit a buyer to
conceal information about which she is directly asked. 3 Amer. Law of
Property 56–59 (A.J.Casner, ed., 1952).

Were defendant's actions in *Zaschak* ethical? What role does access
to information play in the decision? What type of activity does the
court's rule reward and what disincentives would be created with a
contrary rule?

5. *Statutory Provisions.* Some state legislation mandates disclosure by sellers. See, e.g., Cal.Civil Code § 1102 et seq. (Supp. 1991)
(providing specific form of disclosure statement and providing damages
remedy). The Interstate Land Sales Full Disclosure Act, 15 U.S.C.A.
§ 1701 et seq. offers other disclosure requirements. For a comprehensive analysis of the Act, see Malloy, The Interstate Land Sales Full
Disclosure Act: Its Requirements, Consequences, and Implications for
Persons Participating in Real Estate Development, 24 B.C.L.Rev. 1187
(1983).

6. *Effect of "As Is" Clauses.* Real estate contracts often state that
the transfer is made "as is." Most courts find that an "as is" clause
will not bar recovery based on fraud. See, e.g., *Weintraub*, discussed
above in note 2; Stemple v. Dobson, 184 W.Va. 317, 400 S.E.2d 561
(1990) (permitting recovery for undisclosed structural damage due to
termites). This apparently follows the theory that the fraud tainted
the bargaining process concerning the condition of the property so that
there could be no meaningful assent by the buyer to the clause. Some
courts indicate that an "as is" clause which is freely negotiated by a
buyer able to assess its risks may be upheld. See Shapiro v. Hu, 188
Cal.App.3d 324, 233 Cal.Rptr. 470 (1986) (clause relieved sellers from
liability to buyers who were experienced in business); Van Gessel v.
Folds, 210 Ill.App.3d 403, 155 Ill.Dec. 141, 569 N.E.2d 141 (1991). Still
other opinions use an "as is" clause as the basis for following the old
rule that a seller has no disclosure duty in the first place. See, e.g.,
Kaye v. Buehrle, 8 Ohio App.3d 381, 457 N.E.2d 373 (1983).

7. *Other Problem Areas.* Must a seller disclose information that
affects the value of the property but does not relate to the condition of
the land? In McMullen v. Joldersma, 174 Mich.App. 207, 435 N.W.2d
428 (1988) the court found there was no liability for failure to disclose
that a highway project would divert traffic from the store being sold.
However, there were several grounds for the decision—the fact that the

information was of public record, buyers had hired a consultant to investigate and so had relied on him and not the sellers, and the sellers did not have to disclose since the project was still contingent as federal approval and funding had not been obtained. What should the rule be for disclosure of information affecting value in light of the factors discussed above concerning disclosure of physical conditions?

Courts have had particular difficulty striking the fraud balance when the seller has misrepresented the applicable land use control laws. In Gignilliat v. Borg, 131 Ga.App. 182, 205 S.E.2d 479 (1974), the Georgia Court of Appeals refused rescission against a seller who had represented to the buyers that the land was zoned to permit their planned residential development when, in fact, it was zoned to prohibit the development. Noting that the contract of sale was "made subject to zoning ordinances affecting [the land], and thus put the purchaser on notice," the court rested its ruling for seller on the conclusion that he had misrepresented not facts, but law—essentially a nonactionable expression of opinion—and on the assumption that seller is no better placed than buyer to know the law. Judge Pannell, dissenting, expressed what is probably the more widely accepted view today: "If the seller here had stated that a certain ordinance has the legal effect of zoning the property for residential purposes, that might be interpreted as the expression of a legal opinion, but the representation that the property here was zoned, was not as to the legal effect of a certain law or regulation, but as to a fact—this land is zoned residential." 205 S.E.2d at 482. *Gignilliat* is thoughtfully analyzed in Note, 26 Mercer L.Rev. 349 (1974).

ii. Warranty

NOTE, THE HOME OWNERS WARRANTY PROGRAM: AN INITIAL ANALYSIS,* 28 STAN.L.REV. 357, 363–368 (1976): During the first half of this century, *caveat emptor* nullified virtually all purchaser claims of damage to new homes caused by defective workmanship or materials. However, the decided trend of modern decisions is away from this outmoded doctrine. No less than seven theories have been created to aid the new home buyer saddled with a defective unit: tort theories of negligence and strict liability; contract theories of breach of express, implied, and statutory warranties, and breach of the contract of sale; and fraud.

1. TORT LIABILITY.

Negligence. A number of cases have afforded the home purchaser relief for construction defects by holding the builder liable on the general theory of negligence in construction. Others have based the builder's liability on his failure to disclose dangerously defective construction that he knew or should have known about. The builder has also been held responsible for defective construction where the defects were latent.

Strict liability. Traditionally, strict liability has been applied to impose responsibility for personal injury only. Thus, courts have held a new home builder liable where a new dwelling was expected to and did reach a buyer or other user of the dwelling without substantial change in the condition in which it was sold and thereafter caused a human injury. However, at least a few courts have extended this principle to include property damage caused by the defect.

2. CONTRACT LIABILITY.

Actions grounded in breach of warranty have also proved to be a source of judicial relief for the new home buyer. The courts generally have had little difficulty in enforcing oral or written express warranties regarding construction. However, the extraction of a comprehensive express warranty from the builder has until recent years been uncommon except in sales financed by the Federal Housing Administration (FHA) and Veterans' Administration (VA) where blanket warranties have been required since 1954.

In the more frequent instance where no express warranty of the condition, quality, or fitness for habitation of the new dwelling existed, some courts have found an implied warranty similar to the Uniform Commercial Code's implied warranties of merchantability and fitness for a particular purpose.

Further, builders of new houses in Louisiana have been held liable under a state statute providing that the seller of a product warrants it against defects that render the product sold useless or so inconvenient that the buyer would not have purchased it had he known of the defect. In Maryland, express warranties are created by statute if the builder makes any written affirmation or if he is guided by plans, specifications, or a model in building the product. The same state also imposes implied warranties by statute so that new homes must be constructed according to sound engineering standards in a workmanlike manner using nonfaulty materials, and they must be fit for habitation.

Finally, builders have been held liable for defects in dwellings as breaches of specific oral or written covenants in the contract of sale relating to the condition, quality, or fitness of the dwelling. Such liability—similar to that imposed by statute in Maryland—has been imposed by appeal to the common law under covenants to build in a good and workmanlike manner, according to plans and specifications, according to FHA-approved plans and specifications, according to state and local laws, or in conformance with a model house.

3. FRAUD.

In all jurisdictions, intentionally false representations will render a builder liable where the matters misrepresented are material, are relied upon by the purchaser, and result in injury. In some states, a purchaser also has a right of action for innocent misrepresentation and nondisclosure of material defects affecting the value or desirability of real property.

WAWAK v. STEWART

Supreme Court of Arkansas, 1970.
247 Ark. 1093, 449 S.W.2d 922.

GEORGE ROSE SMITH, Justice.

The defendant-appellant Wawak, a house builder, bought a lot in North Little Rock in the course of his business, built a house on it, and sold it to the appellees Stewart for $28,500. The heating and air-conditioning ductwork had been embedded in the ground before the concrete-slab floor was poured above that ductwork. Some months after the Stewarts moved into the house a serious defect manifested itself, in that heavy rains caused water and particles of fill to seep into the ducts and thence through the floor vents into the interior of the house, with consequent damage that need not be described at the moment.

The Stewarts brought this action for damages. The great question in the case, overshadowing all other issues, is whether there is any implied warranty in a contract by which the builder-vendor of a new house sells it to its first purchaser. The trial court sustained the theory of implied warranty and awarded the Stewarts damages of $1,309.

The trial court was right. Twenty years ago one could hardly find any American decision recognizing the existence of an implied warranty in a routine sale of a new dwelling. Both the rapidity and the unanimity with which the courts have recently moved away from the harsh doctrine of caveat emptor in the sale of new houses are amazing, for the law has not traditionally progressed with such speed.

Yet there is nothing really surprising in the modern trend. The contrast between the rules of law applicable to the sale of personal property and those applicable to the sale of real property was so great as to be indefensible. One who bought a chattel as simple as a walking stick or a kitchen mop was entitled to get his money back if the article was not of merchantable quality. But the purchaser of a $50,000 home ordinarily had no remedy even if the foundation proved to be so defective that the structure collapsed into a heap of rubble.

. . .

In the past decade six states have recognized an implied warranty— of inhabitability, sound workmanship, or proper construction—in the sale of new houses by vendors who also built the structures. Carpenter v. Donohoe, 154 Colo. 78, 388 P.2d 399 (1964); Bethlahmy v. Bechtel, 91

Idaho 55, 415 P.2d 698 (1966); Schipper v. Levitt & Sons, 44 N.J. 70, 207 A.2d 314 (1965); Waggoner v. Midwestern Dev. Co., S.D., 154 N.W.2d 803 (1967); Humber v. Morton, Texas, 426 S.W.2d 554, 25 A.L.R.3d 372 (1968); House v. Thornton, Wash., 457 P.2d 199 (1969). The near unanimity of the judges in those cases is noteworthy. Of the 36 justices who made up the six appellate courts, the only dissent noted was that of Justice Griffin in the Texas case, who dissented without opinion.

A few excerpts from those recent opinions will illustrate what seems certain to be the accepted rule of the future. In the *Schipper* case the New Jersey court had this to say:

> The law should be based on current concepts of what is right and just and the judiciary should be alert to the never-ending need for keeping its common law principles abreast of the times. Ancient distinctions which make no sense in today's society and tend to discredit the law should be readily rejected .... We consider that there are no meaningful distinctions between Levitt's [a large-scale builder-seller] mass production and sale of homes and the mass production and sale of automobiles and that the pertinent overriding considerations are the same.
>
> . . .
>
> *Caveat emptor* developed when the buyer and seller were in an equal bargaining position and they could readily be expected to protect themselves in the deed. Buyers of mass produced development homes are not on an equal footing with the builder vendors and are no more able to protect themselves in the deed than are automobile purchasers in a position to protect themselves in the bill of sale. Levitt expresses the fear of "uncertainty and chaos" if responsibility for defective construction is continued after the builder vendor's delivery of the deed and its loss of control of the premises, but we fail to see why this should be anticipated or why it should materialize any more than in the products liability field where there has been no such result.

A similar point of view was expressed in the *House* case by the Washington Supreme Court:

> As between vendor and purchaser, the builder-vendors, even though exercising reasonable care to construct a sound building, had by far the better opportunity to examine the stability of the site and to determine the kind of foundation to install. Although hindsight, it is frequently said, is 20–20 and defendants used reasonable prudence in selecting the site and designing and constructing the building, their position throughout the process of selection, planning and construction was markedly superior to that of their first purchaser-occupant. To borrow an idea from equity, of the innocent parties who suffered, it was the builder-vendor who made the harm possible. If there is a comparative standard of innocence, as well as of culpability, the defendants who built and sold the house were less

innocent and more culpable than the wholly innocent and unsuspecting buyer. Thus, the old rule of caveat emptor has little
relevance to the sale of a brand-new house by a vendor-builder to a
first buyer for purposes of occupancy.

We apprehend it to be the rule that, when a vendor-builder sells
a new house to its first intended occupant, he impliedly warrants
that the foundations supporting it are firm and secure and that the
house is structurally safe for the buyer's intended purpose of living
in it. Current literature on the subject overwhelmingly supports
this idea of an implied warranty of fitness in the sale of new houses.

. . .

To sum up, upon the facts before us in the case at bar we have no
hesitancy in adopting the modern rule by which an implied warranty
may be recognized in the sale of a new house by a seller who was also
the builder. That rule, however, is a departure from our earlier cases;
so, to avoid injustice, we adhere to the doctrine announced in Parish v.
Pitts, [244 Ark. 1239, 429 S.W.2d 45 (1968)] by which the new rule is
made applicable only to the case at hand and to causes of action arising
after this decision becomes final.

There are three subordinate points that require discussion. First
Wawak insists that all warranties, express or implied, were negatived
by this paragraph in the offer-and-acceptance agreement that preceded
the execution of a warranty deed when the sale was consummated:

Buyer certifies that he has inspected the property and he is not
relying upon any warranties, representations or statements of the
Agent or Seller as to age or physical condition of improvements.

Even if we assume that the preliminary contract was not merged in
the warranty deed, we think it plain that the quoted paragraph did not
exclude an implied warranty with respect to the particular defect now
in question, which lay beneath the concrete floor and could not possibly
have been discovered by even the most careful inspection. The quoted
paragraph does not purport to exclude all warranties. It merely states
that the buyer has inspected the property and is not *relying* on any
warranties as to the age or physical condition of the improvements.
Construing the printed contract against the seller, who evidently prepared it, we hold that the clause applies only to defects that might
reasonably have been discovered in the course of an inspection made by
a purchaser of average experience in such matters.

Secondly, the trial court's judgment for $1,309 was composed of the
following items of damage to the house and its furnishings, none of
which the Stewarts had yet paid:

To clean rug	$ 75.00
To paint house (interior)	235.00
To clean furniture	22.00
To replace lamp shades	35.00

To clean duct system	200.00
To replace draperies	300.00
Minor repairs	22.00
Drain tile to correct leakage	420.00
	$1,309.00

Wawak insists that the recovery of the foregoing items is barred by the rule that a plaintiff must use reasonable care to mitigate his damages and that if the damages could have been avoided at reasonable expense then the measure of damages is the amount of such expense.

The pertinent facts are these: The subterranean ductwork radiates from a metal chamber or plenum, which sits under the heating and air-conditioning units. When Wawak and his ductwork subcontractor, Plummer, were first notified by Stewart of the seepage, they siphoned off the water through the plenum. They next installed drain tile and gravel along two sides of the house, but those measures failed to correct the trouble. In the meantime Stewart bought a sump pump at a cost of $12.50. Whenever rains caused seepage in the ductwork Stewart would place his pump in the plenum, about two hours after the water had accumulated, and pump the duct system dry. Under that procedure some of the seepage got into the house and caused most of the damage that we have itemized above.

Soon after the difficulty first arose Wawak and Plummer proposed the installation of an automatic sump pump, which cost $76 or $78. Their plan was to dig out the floor of the plenum so that the automatic pump would be below the level of the ducts. Whenever the water at the site of the pump rose to a depth of three quarters of an inch the pump would start automatically and pump out the water. Thus the water would never rise high enough to overflow the floor vents and damage the interior of the house. Wawak and Plummer do not contend that their plan would have corrected the subterranean defect. From Wawak's testimony: "I figured if we could get the pump in there to pump it out, then we could continue to try to find out where [the water] was coming from. It wasn't our intention to just leave it." Wawak stated that when he offered to put in the automatic pump there was no damage to the house except some staining of the draperies, which were cleaned at Wawak's expense.

Stewart refused to allow the automatic pump to be installed, insisting that he wanted to know where the water was coming from and would accept nothing less. When the proffer of the pump was refused, Wawak and Plummer abandoned their efforts to correct the trouble. Thereafter Stewart used his own pump in the manner that we have described, with attendant damage to the house and its furnishings. A period of two years or more elapsed before this action was finally brought.

In the main Wawak is correct in his argument that the Stewarts should have mitigated their damages by permitting the installation of the automatic pump. On the record made below it is an undisputed fact that such a pump would have avoided practically all the itemized damages that were allowed by the trial court.

The pump, however, would not have corrected the basic defect, nor does Wawak so contend. Stewart testified without contradiction and without objection that a man named Gordon could remedy the defect by installing drain tile along the remaining two sides of the house at a cost of $425. That corrective measure would not have been rendered unnecessary by the installation of the automatic pump; so the Stewarts' duty to mitigate their damages does not involve that item. The amount of the Stewarts' judgment will therefore be reduced to $420— the amount allowed by the trial court for the one item of damage that we find to be recoverable.

Thirdly, Wawak argues that he is entitled to judgment over against the appellee Plummer, who installed the ductwork under a subcontract with Wawak. It cannot be said as a matter of law, however, that Plummer was at fault, because the slab floor above the ducts was poured by another subcontractor. Upon this point the trial court's judgment is sufficiently supported by the proof.

.   .   .

The judgment as modified is affirmed.

HARRIS, C.J., and FOGLEMAN and BYRD, JJ., dissent.

[The opinions of FOGLEMAN, J., dissenting in part, and concurring in part, and BYRD, J., dissenting, are omitted.]

BLAGG v. FRED HUNT CO., INC.

Supreme Court of Arkansas, 1981.
272 Ark. 185, 612 S.W.2d 321.

DUDLEY, Justice.

The appellee, Fred Hunt Company, Inc., a house builder, bought a lot in the Pleasant Valley Addition to Little Rock, built a house on it, and sold it to the Dentons on October 9, 1978. The Dentons sold the house to the American Foundation Life Insurance Company, which on June 29, 1979, sold the house to appellants, J. Ted Blagg and Kathye Blagg. This purchase by appellants was made a few days less than 9 months after the date of the original sale. The appellants filed a two-count complaint alleging that after they purchased the home a strong odor and fumes from formaldehyde became apparent. They traced this defect to the carpet and pad which was installed by appellee. A motion to dismiss was filed by the appellee and the trial court granted the motion on count one of the complaint, the implied warranty count, on the basis of lack of privity. The court denied the motion on count two, which is framed in terms of strict liability.

When considering a motion to dismiss a complaint pursuant to Arkansas Rules of Civil Procedure, Rule 12(b)(6), on the ground that it fails to state a claim on which relief can be granted, the facts alleged in the complaint are treated as true and are viewed in the light most favorable to the party seeking relief.

Count one of the complaint is based upon an implied warranty. The trial judge dismissed this count because the appellants are not in privity with the appellee. This court, in Wawak v. Stewart, 247 Ark. 1093, 449 S.W.2d 922 (1970), abandoned the doctrine of caveat emptor and took the view that a builder-vendor impliedly warranted the home to the first purchaser. The issue of first impression in this case is whether the liability of the builder-vendor should be extended to a second or third purchaser.

Since *Wawak,* the original homebuyer has been able to place reliance on the builder-vendor's implied warranty. This has protected that investment which, in most instances, represents the family's largest single expenditure.

We find no reason that those same basic concepts should not be extended to subsequent purchasers of real estate. This is an area of the law being developed on a case by case basis. Our ruling is based on the complaint before us and involves a home which had a defect that became apparent to the third purchasers, the appellants, within 9 months of the original sale date. Obviously, there is a point in time beyond which the implied warranty will expire and that time should be based on a standard of reasonableness.

We hold that the builder-vendor's implied warranty of fitness for habitation runs not only in favor of the first owner, but extends to subsequent purchasers for a reasonable length of time where there is no substantial change or alteration in the condition of the building from the original sale. This implied warranty is limited to latent defects which are not discoverable by subsequent purchasers upon reasonable inspection and which become manifest only after the purchase. Wyoming adopted this rule in a well reasoned opinion. Moxley v. Laramie Builders, Inc., 600 P.2d 733 (Wyo.1979).

Appellants next contend that even if the implied warranty extends to subsequent purchasers, we should affirm the trial court as there is an express warranty which is exclusive. We do not consider this argument as the complaint does not allege an express warranty, and the sufficiency of the complaint is all that is tested.

We hold that count one of the complaint should not have been dismissed.

Appellee, in its cross-appeal, contends that the trial judge committed error in not dismissing count two of the complaint, the claim for damages under strict liability. We affirm the trial judge's ruling.

Our strict liability statute, Ark.Stat.Ann. § 85-2-318.2 (Supp.1979) is as follows:

Liability of Supplier—Conditions.—A supplier of a product is subject to liability in damages for harm to a person or to property if:

(a) the supplier is engaged in the business of manufacturing, assembling, selling, leasing or otherwise distributing such product;

(b) the product was supplied by him in a defective condition which rendered it unreasonably dangerous; and

(c) the defective condition was a proximate cause of the harm to person or to property. [Acts 1973, No. 111, § 1, p. 331.]

This 1973 act broadens somewhat § 402(A) of the Restatement, Second, Torts (1965)....

Our first issue is whether this strict liability statute encompasses count two of the complaint. It is an oversimplification, but correct, to state that the construction of the word "product" is determinative. To decide the proper construction we have examined the few cases in other jurisdictions and various treatises.

Judge Henry Woods in The Personal Injury Action in Warranty—Has the Arkansas Strict Liability Statute Rendered it Obsolete?, 28 Ark.L.R. 335 (1974), gives a most perceptive preview of the real issue. He notes that we must choose between the persuasive reasoning of two outstanding jurists—Chief Justice Traynor in Seely v. White Motor Company, 63 Cal.2d 9, 403 P.2d 145, 45 Cal.Rptr. 17 (1965), and Justice Francis in Santor v. A & M Karagheusian, Inc., 44 N.J. 52, 207 A.2d 305 (1965). If the Traynor view is adopted, the implied warranty will be very much alive when a purchaser is suing for purely economic loss from a defective product. His view, as stated in *Seely,* supra, is that when economic losses result from commercial transactions, as here, the parties should be relegated to the law of sales:

> Although the rules governing warranties complicated resolution of the problems of personal injuries, there is no reason to conclude that they do not meet the "needs of commercial transactions." The law of warranty "grew as a branch of the law of commercial transactions and was primarily aimed at controlling the commercial aspects of these transactions." ...

> Although the rules of warranty frustrate rational compensation for physical injury, they function well in a commercial setting.

Justice Francis, in *Santor,* supra, prophetically extended the doctrine in a case involving carpeting that developed a defect, a purely economic loss, not a personal injury. In applying the doctrine of strict liability for purely economic loss he said:

> The obligation of the manufacturer thus becomes what in justice it ought to be—an enterprise liability, and one which should not depend on the law of sales....

After lengthy consideration, we choose to adopt the views of Justice Francis. We find no valid reason for holding that strict liability should not apply to property damage in a house sold by a builder-vendor.

Accordingly, in construing the Arkansas strict liability statute, we hold that the word "product" is as applicable to a house as to an automobile.

Reversed and remanded on direct appeal; affirmed on cross-appeal.

NOTES

1. *Incidence of Housing Defects.* A government study, based on a sample of new housing built in 1977 and 1978, revealed that 79% of new housing buyers had at least one complaint about housing quality. Seventy-five percent of the problems were discovered in the first six months of ownership, and ninety-three percent in the first year. According to the study, builders were most ready to correct defects in plumbing, cooling and heating systems, in major appliances and in interior electrical work. They were less willing to correct problems with yard drainage, roofs, foundations and driveways and improperly fitted doors and windows. Seven percent of buyers reported that they consulted a lawyer about the problem and four percent retained lawyers. U.S. Dept. of Housing & Urban Development and Federal Trade Commission, A Survey of Homeowner Experience with New Residential Housing Construction iii-viii, 10–29 (1980).

2. *New Housing.* The implied warranty of fitness represents the main avenue today for buyers of defective new housing to recover from their builder-sellers. With roots in both contract and tort theory, the warranty of fitness has made substantial inroads on *caveat emptor,* giving disappointed buyers an easier and more complete remedy than fraud or negligence. By recent count, forty-two states imply a warranty into new housing sales, variously calling it a warranty of "quality," "habitability," "good workmanship," or "fitness." See Shedd, The Implied Warranty of Habitability: New Implications, New Applications, 8 Real Est.L.J. 291 (1980).

The origin of implied housing warranties can be traced to two English cases decided in the 1930's, Miller v. Cannon Hill Estates, Ltd., 2 K.B. 113, 1 All E.R. 93 (1931), and Perry v. Sharon Development Co., 4 All E.R. 390 (C.A.1937), in which plaintiffs, who had contracted to buy houses under construction, found upon occupying the completed houses that they were defective. The courts could have decided the cases by analogy to either of two black-letter rules of law: the standard rule of *caveat emptor* in sales of completed housing, which would have required a holding for the builders; or the rule entitling landowners to recover for substandard work by builders in their employ, which would have required a holding for the buyers. In both cases, the courts chose the latter rule. "In the first place, the maxim *caveat emptor* cannot apply, since the buyer, insofar as the house is not yet completed, cannot inspect it, either by himself or by his surveyor, and, in the second place, from the point of view of the vendor, the contract is not merely a contract to sell, but also a contract to do building work, and, insofar as it is a contract to do building work, it is only natural and proper that there should be an implied undertaking that the building work should be done properly."   Perry v. Sharon Development Co., 4 All E.R. at 395–396.

The English rule on uncompleted houses was picked up by American courts in the 1950's.   It was only a matter of time before the rule's underlying rationale would be extended to the purchase of a completed house.   The occasion came in Carpenter v. Donohoe, 154 Colo. 78, 388 P.2d 399 (1964), where the buyer complained that a crumbling cellar wall impaired habitability.   Noting that the wall's construction did not comply with the local building code, the court held for the buyer in terms that were to become familiar in the decisions that soon followed: "There is an implied warranty that builder-vendors had complied with the building code of the area in which the structure is located.   Where, as here, a home is the subject of sale, there are implied warranties that the home was built in workmanlike manner and is suitable for habitation."   154 Colo. at 83–84, 388 P.2d at 402.

For a superb analysis of the history and doctrinal implications of seller's liability for housing defects, see Roberts, The Case of the Unwary Home Buyer: The Housing Merchant Did It, 52 Cornell L.Rev. 835 (1967).   For general background see Bearman, Caveat Emptor in Sales of Realty—Recent Assaults Upon the Rule, 14 Vand.L.Rev. 541 (1961); Bixby, Let the Seller Beware: Remedies for the Purchase of a Defective Home, 49 J. of Urb.L. 533 (1971); Haskell, The Case for an Implied Warranty of Quality in Sales of Real Property, 53 Geo.L.J. 633 (1965); McNamara, The Implied Warranty in New-House Construction, 1 Real Est.L.J. 43 (1972); McNamara, The Implied Warranty in New-House Construction Revisited, 3 Real Est.L.J. 136 (1974).   See also Powell & Mallor, The Case for an Implied Warranty of Quality in Sales of Commercial Real Estate, 68 Wash.U.L.Q. 305 (1990).

3.   *Who Is Liable?*   Courts have declined to impose liability under warranty theory on a non-builder seller of a used home.   In Stevens v. Bouchard, 532 A.2d 1028 (Me.1987), the court stated that a builder-vendor of a new home "has ultimate control over the habitability of the premises.   To hold a homeowner who had no part in the construction to the same level of accountability offends considerations of fairness and common sense."

Courts may stretch, however, in defining who is a builder-vendor. In Callander v. Sheridan, 546 N.E.2d 850, 852 (Ind.App.1989), a person, not a professional builder, who acted as his own general contractor for the building of his home was held under warranty as a builder-vendor for defects in the house.   The court noted that he obtained and modified plans, hired and supervised subcontractors, and bought construction materials.   "Apparently [defendant] felt he was qualified to act as a general contractor.   Since he undertook this responsibility he must also accept the attached liability of a builder-vendor to a subsequent buyer."   Do the reasons expressed in *Wawak* for the warranty of habitability apply in this situation?   Compare Oliver v. Superior Court, 211 Cal.App.3d 86, 259 Cal.Rptr. 160 (1989) (holding that a person who built only two homes was not a builder-vendor for the purposes of strict liability recovery for defective housing).

4. *Used Housing.* Most residential sales involve used rather than new housing. Should buyers of used housing be able to recover for latent defects against either the original builder or their immediate seller? Tort actions based on a strict liability theory are usually fruitless because, most commonly, only unrecoverable economic damages are alleged. Warranty actions brought against homebuilders by second and subsequent buyers are usually dismissed for lack of privity. Warranty actions against the immediate seller, with whom the second or subsequent buyer is in privity, are usually dismissed on the ground that the requisite inequality of expertise between buyer and seller is missing.

The barriers to recovery by distant buyers against developers are, however, beginning to break down. Product liability law's requirement that plaintiff demonstrate personal injury was the first barrier to crumble. In Kriegler v. Eichler Homes, Inc., 269 Cal.App.2d 224, 74 Cal.Rptr. 749 (1969), a California Court of Appeal imposed strict liability for defects causing economic injury. Eichler's faulty installation of a radiant heating system in a house that plaintiff had bought from its original buyer eventually caused the system to fail, reducing the value of the house by over $5,000. Holding for plaintiff homeowners, the court noted that "at the time of the installation of the heating system in the Kriegler home," the building industry "had knowledge of methods by which the injury could reasonably have been avoided." A short while later, another California Court of Appeal relied on *Eichler* to impose strict liability for damages to a house and lot caused by the improper compaction of fill and other errors in the developer's preparation of the soil. Avner v. Longridge Estates, 272 Cal.App.2d 607, 77 Cal.Rptr. 633 (1969).

More recently, as indicated in *Blagg*, the privity bar to warranty actions has begun to give way, although some courts still decline to extend the warranty to subsequent purchasers. See, for example, Haygood v. Burl Pounders Realty, Inc., 571 So.2d 1086 (Ala.1990). What reasons are there for *not* extending implied warranty protections to buyers of used housing? Consider some reservations expressed by the Mississippi Supreme Court: "Material and workmanship which may go into a structure are of infinite variety. An original purchaser of land on which a building is situated, for reasons of economy or for any other reason, may be satisfied, and may accept it from the builder in any condition in which it may be.... It would be strange indeed if, when the original purchaser conveyed the property to another, that his vendee could resort to the builder for damages for deficiencies in workmanship or materials which the original purchaser from the builder had accepted. ... Real estate transactions require a written contract or deed, and a purchaser may insist upon having included therein any warranty or guaranty that he may desire as to buildings standing upon it, and, of course, he may refuse to purchase if the prospective vendor will not agree." Oliver v. City Builders, Inc., 303 So.2d 466, 468–469 (Miss.1974).

Representing a developer, would you be comfortable with *Blagg*'s extension of the implied warranty "for a reasonable length of time"? Other courts extending the warranty have been similarly uninstructive about the duration of the builder's exposure. See, for example, Reda-rowicz v. Ohlendorf, 92 Ill.2d 171, 65 Ill.Dec. 411, 441 N.E.2d 324 (1982). Can a developer protect itself against warranty liability to second and successive purchasers by obtaining from its immediate buyer an express disclaimer of any implied warranties? Is indeterminate liability likely to induce developers to build houses that are more durable—and probably more expensive—than their immediate buyers might desire?

See generally, Comment, Builder's Liability to New and Subsequent Purchasers, 20 Sw.U.L.Rev. 219 (1991); Note, Builders' Liability for Latent Defects in Used Homes, 32 Stan.L.Rev. 607 (1980).

5. *Where's the Breach?* Like *Wawak*, most courts that have im-plied a warranty of fitness into sales of new housing have reasoned by analogy to the warranty of fitness implied into sales of personal property. Are there any differences between real and personal proper-ty that make the analogy inapt? That should affect the determination of what kinds of defects will breach the warranty? See generally, Rabin & Grossman, Defective Products or Realty Causing Economic Loss: Toward a Unified Theory of Recovery, 12 Southwestern Univ. L.Rev. 5 (1981).

Justice Fogleman, dissenting in part and concurring in part in *Wawak*, objected to the majority's failure to address the question whether the warranty in fact had been breached. Noting that the implied warranty "does not impose upon the builder an obligation to deliver a perfect house," he concluded that the evidence "simply does not show the breach of any implied warranty." Specifically, he object-ed to the effective ruling of the lower court "that, without any proof or evidence, the house was not constructed in a good workmanlike manner and, without any proof whatever as to the cause of the problem, appellees should recover simply because they bought a new house and subsequently a water situation developed." 247 Ark. at 1101, 449 S.W.2d at 930.

Samuelson v. A.A. Quality Construction, Inc., 230 Mont. 220, 749 P.2d 73 (1988), imposed an unusually strict standard. The court stated that the warranty is "limited to defects which are so substantial as reasonably to preclude the use of the dwelling as a residence," and held that water seepage into the basement affecting a guest bedroom, storage area, recreation area, and crawl space and requiring removal of furniture, carpeting and sheetrock, necessitating the use of floor heat-ers and pumps, and restricting the use of some areas did not violate the standard. The house cost $155,000 and the buyers had to pay more than $11,000 to remedy the problems. Justice Harrison in dissent wrote that the majority "has taken a giant step backwards in protecting the consumer.... Had the basement not been repaired at a cost of over $11,000 by another contractor, about all that it could have been used for would have been a fishery during the periods it leaked. Surely, a homeowner is entitled to more than that." Id. at 223, 749 P.2d at 75.

6. *Disclaimers.* Most courts that imply a warranty of fitness into the sale of new housing will also allow seller and buyer to contract around the implied warranty. Yet there is a general disposition to construe disclaimers and "as is" provisions against builder-sellers. *Wawak* is typical in holding that, strictly construed, the disclaimer clause did not exclude an implied warranty with respect to latent defects— "the clause applies only to defects that might reasonably have been discovered in the course of an inspection made by a purchaser of average experience in such matters."

Indiana, for example, has a statute that permits a builder-vendor to disclaim all warranties. Ind.Code § 34–4–20.5. To do so, however, the builder must give certain express warranties. These include warranties against defects in the structure for ten years, roof materials and workmanship for four years, and electrical, plumbing and heating for two years. Some courts, however, indicate that any attempt to disclaim an implied warranty is void as against public policy. See Buchanan v. Scottsdale Environmental Construction and Development Co., 163 Ariz. 285, 787 P.2d 1081 (App.1989), review denied.

See generally, Abney, Disclaiming the Implied Real Estate Common–Law Warranties, 17 Real Est.L.J. 141 (1988); Powell, Disclaimers of Implied Warranty in the Sale of New Homes, 34 Vill.L.Rev. 1123 (1989); Note, The Implied Warranty of Habitability in the Sale of New Homes: Disclaiming Liability in Illinois, 1987 U.Ill.L.Rev. 649.

7. *The Home Owners Warranty Program.* The Home Owners Warranty (HOW) program was initiated in 1973 by the National Association of Home Builders to provide warranty protection for new owner occupied single-family houses, townhouses, and condominiums. Note, The Home Owners Warranty Program: An Initial Analysis, 28 Stan. L.Rev. 357 (1976). In Home Owner Warranty Corp. v. Elliott, 572 F.Supp. 1059, 1063 (D.Del.1983), the court described the program as it had evolved:

> [The] program has two major components—the Home Warranty and the Risk Retention Insurance policy. A home builder participating in the program issues to the initial purchaser of a home a two year "Home Warranty." For the first year following the sale, the builder warrants to the homeowner that the house will be free of defects due to non-compliance with the "Approved Standards" attached to the warranty. During the second year of occupancy, the warranty continues to cover defects in the plumbing, electrical, heating, and cooling systems due to non-compliance with the "Approved Standards." During this initial, two-year period, the builder also warrants that the house will be free from "Major Structural

Defects," [relating to load-bearing portion of the home, such as beams, foundation, and floors.] ...

Under the HOW program, the builder purchases a "Risk Retention Insurance Policy" from HOW Insurance Company. In return for premium payments which vary depending on the length of time the builder has been in the Program and its claims record, the insurer agrees, in the language of the policy, to insure against loss resulting from: (1) Builder Default under the [two-year] Home Warranty, and (2) "Major Structural Defects" of the home which first occur after expiration of the Home Warranty and before the termination of this Policy. First, if a "Builder Default" occurs under the two-year Home Warranty, the insurer will either "repair, replace or pay to the Purchaser on behalf of the Builder the reasonable cost of such repair or replacement." ... In addition, the policy protects the builder against liability for Major Structural Defects in the home that occur after two years but within ten years of the initial sale. If a Major Structural Defect occurs during this period, HOW Insurance will repair or replace the defect or will pay the homeowner the reasonable costs of the repair, whichever it chooses. The policy ... runs for ten years, regardless of any transfer of the ownership of the home. Claims under the policy are to be pursued by the homeowner with HOW Insurance, not the builder.

HOW Insurance Company was formed by the builders participating in the HOW program after passage of the Product Liability Risk Retention Act, 15 U.S.C.A. § 3901, in 1981. The Act provides for risk retention groups through which manufacturers of products, including homes, can self-insure their products liability risks. See Cobert v. Home Owners Warranty Corp., 239 Va. 460, 391 S.E.2d 263 (1990).

8. *State Statutes.* State warranty legislation ranges from statutes like Maryland's Real Property Code, §§ 10–201 et seq. (1981 & Supp. 1991) and New York's General Business Law § 777 (McKinney Supp. 1991), which follow the general contours of the common law implied warranty, to New Jersey's far more ambitious New Home Warranty and Builders' Registration Act, N.J.Stat.Ann. 46:3B–1 et seq. (1977).

The Maryland statute implies into sales of improved residential real property a warranty that the improvement (defined as a newly constructed private dwelling unit), is habitable, free from faulty materials and constructed according to sound engineering standards in a workmanlike manner. The warranty lasts for one year after closing and excludes any defect that inspection by a reasonably diligent first buyer would have disclosed. The warranty may be waived or modified only through a writing signed by the purchaser that specifically describes the warranty waived and the terms of the new agreement. The statute implies a warranty of fitness for a particular purpose, and also provides that an express warranty is created by a written affirmation of fact or promise, a written description of the improvement, or a sample model that is part of the basis of the bargain. An amendment in 1990 added a two year statute of limitation for claims for structural defects.

The New York statute makes the seller liable for one year for failure to build in a "skillful manner," for two years for defects in major systems (e.g., heat, electrical), and for six years for "material defects" as defined in the statute. See Note, The New York Housing Merchant Warranty Statute: Analysis and Proposals, 75 Corn.L.Rev. 754 (1990). See generally, Grand, Implied and Statutory Warranties in the Sale of Real Estate: The Demise of Caveat Emptor, 15 Real Est.L.J. 44 (1986).

The New Jersey statute directs the Commissioner of the Department of Community Affairs to prescribe home warranties incorporating quality standards for construction materials and methods. The warranty's duration will depend on its subject matter—two years for defects caused by faulty installation of plumbing, electrical, heating and cooling systems, and ten years for major construction defects including damages due to soil subsidence. The builder's liability extends not only to the initial buyer but also to any subsequent buyer whose claim arises during the applicable warranty period. The ceiling on liability is the purchase price of the home in the first good faith sale.

A builder must register with the Department to build houses in New Jersey. One condition of registration is that the builder participate in a warranty security fund, established by the Act, or an approved alternative fund. The fund provides a back-up source of compensation when fund participants have not themselves made good on valid homeowner claims. Before making a claim against the fund, a homeowner must notify the builder of the defects and allow a reasonable time for their repair. Once a claim is made against the fund, it is reviewed through a conciliation or arbitration procedure administered by the Department. If a defect is found, the builder is ordered to correct it and, failing that, the owner is allowed to recover from the fund. While the Act does not preempt private law remedies, it does require the homeowner to elect between statutory and common law relief.

9. *Federal Law.* The Magnuson-Moss Act, 15 U.S.C.A. § 2301 et seq., though primarily concerned with warranties made in connection with the sale of "consumer products," partially covers home sale warranties by defining consumer products to include "any such property intended to be attached to or installed in any real property without regard to whether it is so attached or installed." Congressman Moss gave as examples of housing components covered by the Act, "any separate equipment such as heating and air-conditioning systems which are sold with a new home. However, the definition would not apply to items such as dry wall pipes, or wiring which are not separate items of equipment but are rather integral component parts of a home." 120 Cong.Rec. 31323 (1974). The Act does not apply to any written warranty otherwise governed by federal law, thus apparently exempting the warranties that builders are required to give as a condition to obtaining

FHA, VA or Farmer's Home Administration financing assistance. See generally, Peters, How the Magnuson-Moss Warranty Act Affects the Builder/Seller of New Housing, 5 Real Est.L.J. 338 (1977).

b.   LIABILITY OF LENDERS AND OTHERS

Overview of Lender Liability

"Lender liability" litigation has increased over the past decade. Borrowers, and sometimes junior lenders and lienors, have successfully asserted claims subjecting lenders to damages, reduced lien priority, or the loss of remedies usually available in the event of default, foreclosure, or bankruptcy of the borrower. Courts have employed a broad range of common law theories to hold the lender liable. Among others, these include fraud, breach of fiduciary duty, duress, failure to act in good faith, excessive control of the borrower, intentional infliction of emotional distress, joint venture theory, principal-agent violations, equitable subordination, negligence in loan administration, misrepresentation, and aiding and abetting liability, as well as R.I.C.O (18 U.S.C.A. § 1961 et seq.), federal tax and securities laws, and the Comprehensive Environmental Response, Compensation and Liability Act (see pages 938–95). See Chaitman, The Ten Commandments for Avoiding Lender Liability, 22 U.C.C.L.J. 3 (1989); Ebke and Griffin, Lender Liability to Debtors: Toward a Conceptual Framework, 40 Sw.L.J. 775 (1986); Johnson, Lender Liability Checklist: A Summary of Current Theories and Developments, 59 U.M.K.C.L.Rev. 205 (1991); Lawrence, Lender Control Liability: An Analytical Model Illustrated with Applications to the Relational Theory of Secured Financing, 62 S.Cal.L.Rev. 1387 (1989); E. Mannino, Lender Liability and Banking Litigation (1991); Comment, Stemming the Tide of Lender Liability: Judicial and Legislative Reactions, 67 Denver U.L.Rev. 453 (1990); Comment, What's So Good About Good Faith? The Good Faith Performance Obligation in Commercial Lending, 55 U.Chi.L.Rev. 1335 (1988); Special Project: Lender Liability, 42 Vand.L.Rev. 852 (1989).

The acts for which lenders have been held liable also vary widely. They include improper interference with the borrower's corporate entity (see State National Bank v. Farah Manufacturing Co., 678 S.W.2d 661 (Tex.App.1984)), refusal to lend funds which have been orally promised (see Landes Construction Co. v. Royal Bank of Canada, 833 F.2d 1365 (9th Cir.1987)), failure to obtain credit life insurance for borrower as bank had represented (see Walters v. First National Bank, 69 Ohio St.2d 677, 433 N.E.2d 608 (1982)), lack of adherence to standard policy in denying a loan (see Jacques v. First National Bank, 307 Md. 527, 515 A.2d 756 (1986)), calling a $7 million loan when interest payment was late by only less than one day (see Sahadi v. Continental Illinois National Bank & Trust Co., 706 F.2d 193 (7th Cir.1983)), and failure to give notice before discontinuing funding (see K.M.C. Co. v. Irving Trust, 757 F.2d 752 (6th Cir.1985)).

The only common feature linking the diverse theories of these "lender liability" cases is that they all involve an attempt to make a lender responsible for a claimed harm. The courts have done little to articulate a general theory of lender liability and have focused only on the particular legal doctrine raised in the case. But some larger influences at work, among them, evolving expectations about business practices, articulation of a norm of reasonable lending behavior, a developing notion that a party should not carelessly injure another even though under traditional doctrine there is no duty, and a sense, at least in the early 1980's, that lenders have deep pockets and are able to spread the risk among the class of borrowers.

There is recent evidence that the tide may have turned against lender liability. Some commentators have questioned the doctrine. For a thoughtful critique, see Fischel, The Economics of Lender Liability, 99 Yale L.J. 131 (1989) (maintaining that the doctrine as evolved by the courts is often based on a misunderstanding of basic economic principles). Moreover, various recent cases have severely blunted some of the most important arrows in the lender liability quiver. In Kham & Nate's Shoes No. 2, Inc. v. First Bank of Whiting, 908 F.2d 1351 (7th Cir.1990), the court held that a lender which terminated the borrower's line of credit was not subject to loss of priority by equitable subordination in a bankruptcy proceeding of the borrower. Judge Easterbrook, writing for the unanimous panel, noted that even though the lender knew that its action would be detrimental to the borrower, it did not engage in "inequitable conduct" and use its contractual rights as a lever to get a better deal:

> Firms that have negotiated contracts are entitled to enforce them to the letter, even to the great discomfort of their trading partners, without being mulcted for lack of "good faith." Although courts often refer to the obligation of good faith that exists in every contractual relation [citations omitted], this is not an invitation to the court to decide whether one party ought to have exercised privileges expressly granted in the document. "Good faith" is a compact reference to an implied undertaking not to take opportunistic advantage in a way that could not have been contemplated at the time of drafting, and which therefore was not resolved explicitly by the parties. When the contract is silent, principles of good faith ... fill the gap. They do not block use of terms that actually appear in the contract.

Id. at 1357. See also Penthouse International, Ltd. v. Dominion Federal Savings and Loan Ass'n, 855 F.2d 963 (2d Cir.1988), cert. denied, 490 U.S. 1005, 109 S.Ct. 1639, 104 L.Ed.2d 154 (1989), reproduced at page 718 below); Mitsui Manufacturers Bank v. Superior Court, 212 Cal. App.3d 726, 260 Cal.Rptr. 793 (1989) (finding no special relationship of trust or confidence between the usual lender and borrower which can be the basis of tort liability); Gillman v. Chase Manhattan Bank, N.A., 73 N.Y.2d 1, 537 N.Y.S.2d 787, 534 N.E.2d 824 (1988) (reversing finding that form lending agreement was unconscionable and finding borrower had other choices and an opportunity to consult his attorney); Patterson, A Fable from the Seventh Circuit: Frank Easterbrook on Good Faith, 75 Iowa L.Rev. 503 (1991) (criticizing the *Kham* decision); Note, Breach of Good Faith as an Expansive Basis for Lender Liability Claims: An Idea Whose Time Has Come—and Gone?, 42 Rutgers L.Rev. 177. It is possible that the savings and loan crisis and increasing concerns over the health of some commercial banks and insurance companies played a role in these recent decisions.

This book will examine lender liability claims at various points in the real estate transaction. These include, for example, breach of loan commitments (page 718–752), the lender's responsibility to junior mortgagees and mechanics for loan disbursements (pages 711–714), and environmental liability (pages 938–951), as well as traditional doctrines which cause a mortgagee to lose priority or become liable in the course of a loan, such as alteration of the loan terms affecting a junior lender (page 420) or original mortgagor (page 424).

In evaluating these cases dealing with lender liability consider the following questions. First, what were the expectations of the parties on the issue? What did the agreement provide? Did the lender follow reasonable lender behavior and norms? Were there any obligations created by statute? Second, what policy considerations apply? Does the rule encourage sound lending and borrowing practices and promote efficient capital markets for real estate development? In order to avoid liability, would the lender have to incur additional costs or should the lender already be taking these steps as part of ordinary supervision of loans? Does the rule place the loss on the party able to avoid the loss most cheaply? Finally, what are the institutional ramifications of the decision? If there is an agreement controlling the issue, are there reasons to overturn it because of the nature of the parties, the bargaining process, or unconscionability? Is the rule clear and predictable for the parties before they take action?

RICE v. FIRST FEDERAL SAVINGS AND LOAN ASS'N OF LAKE COUNTY

District Court of Appeal of Florida, Second District, 1968.
207 So.2d 22.

PER CURIAM.

Appellants are appealing a judgment foreclosing a mortgage on a building which they owned. Appellants borrowed $12,000 from appellee and delivered to appellee their promissory note for that amount. As security, they gave appellee a mortgage on the building which was to be constructed partly with the loan proceeds. Appellee deducted from the loan proceeds, as a fee for "inspection and supervision," an amount equal to one per cent thereof. An agent of appellee, in fact, made inspections of the construction site. Soon after the completion of the building, because of certain defects in the construction, its wall began to crack extensively, causing considerable damage.

Appellants defaulted on the payments on their note and appellee sued for foreclosure of the mortgage on the building. Appellants counterclaimed for damages on the theory that appellee had inspected the construction site in a negligent manner so as to breach its contractual duty to appellants to inspect the site for their benefit. They conceded they were in default under the terms of the note and mortgage, and the cause was tried on the sole issue of whether appellee was liable to appellants under the counterclaim. The court below ruled that no contractual duty existed as alleged and ordered foreclosure. The sole question before this court is whether appellee, by undertaking the inspection of the construction site and requiring appellants to pay a fee therefor, impliedly contracted with appellants to make such inspection for their benefit.

The effect to be given to an alleged implied contract is that effect which the parties as fair and reasonable men presumably would have agreed upon if, having in mind the possibility of the situation which has arisen, they had expressly contracted in reference thereto. It would be unreasonable to infer merely from appellee's deduction of an inspection fee a contractual duty to appellants to perform such inspection on their behalf. As the court below aptly stated:

"A lender of construction money has an interest in the progress and quality of the construction of its security proportional to the amount of money invested and would reasonably be expected to inspect the construction and be entitled to additional compensation for its additional costs in making such inspection."

Affirmed.

LILES, C.J., and PIERCE and HOBSON, JJ., concur.

JEMINSON v. MONTGOMERY REAL ESTATE AND CO.

Court of Appeals of Michigan, Division One, 1973.
47 Mich.App. 731, 210 N.W.2d 10, reversed, 396 Mich. 106, 240 N.W.2d 205 (1976).

McGREGOR, Judge.

After the trial court's entry of summary judgment in favor of defendant mortgage corporation for failure of plaintiff to plead a cause of action as to it, plaintiff brings this delayed interlocutory appeal in forma pauperis by leave granted.

Because of the summary judgment aspects of this case, the well-pleaded allegations of the complaint are accepted as true. On July 24, 1970, plaintiff, one of the urban poor, agreed to purchase a home in the inner city of Detroit from defendant real estate company. On September 17, 1970, she signed a mortgage agreement with the defendant mortgage corporation whereby, pursuant to insurance coverage issued by the Federal Housing Administration, it loaned her the purchase price of $11,800.00 in return for which plaintiff executed a mortgage in favor of the mortgage corporation.

Shortly after she moved into her new home, plaintiff realized that defendant real estate company had fraudulently misrepresented the condition and value of the house. She abandoned the house as uninhabitable, whereupon the mortgage was duly foreclosed.

Plaintiff then commenced this suit in circuit court, alleging that, *inter alia,* defendant mortgage corporation was well aware, at the time it entered into the mortgage agreement with her, that her sole means of support was welfare assistance in the form of aid to dependent children, that she was unemployed, possessed of little formal education, and inexperienced in real property or other commercial transactions. Plaintiff further pleaded that defendant mortgage corporation also knew or should have known that the Montgomery Real Estate Company possessed a notorious reputation for using unscrupulous and deceptive practices in the sale of homes, especially older inner-city dwellings sold pursuant to FHA mortgage insurance programs, to inexperienced and unsophisticated buyers. Plaintiff, who is black, further alleges that defendant mortgage company knew that, due to private discriminatory housing practices, she would have fewer opportunities to buy and less bargaining power than white persons similarly situated. She further charges that defendant mortgage corporation is also chargeable with knowledge that the property involved is located in an area where many of the homes are in an advanced state of deterioration. In addition, plaintiff contends that defendant mortgage corporation was or should have been aware that the sales transaction between plaintiff and the real estate company was unfair, fraudulent, or unconscionable; that defendant mortgage corporation should also have known that the real estate company was selling the subject premises to plaintiff at a price more than double the amount paid by the real estate company only a few months previously, and that the agreed sales price was considerably more than the value of the property; that defendant mortgage corporation should have known that the subject dwelling was not in a safe, decent and sanitary condition, was not in conformity with applicable building and health codes, and did not qualify under FHA regulations for financing; that representations made to the plaintiff by the real estate company concerning the condition of the property were materially untrue, and that the mortgage corporation should have known this.

On this appeal, plaintiff seeks reversal of the interlocutory order of the trial court, dismissing plaintiff's suit against defendant mortgage corporation for failure to state a cause of action.

Plaintiff discusses a line of cases from various jurisdictions denying holder in due course status to parties who accepted notes, mortgages, or other commercial paper in bad faith, or where a legal defect appeared on the face of the instrument, such as Matthews v. Aluminum Acceptance Corp., 1 Mich.App. 570, 137 N.W.2d 280 (1965), which involved usurious interest rates and a deceptively procured signature.

Plaintiff's briefs and arguments urge upon this Court as correct and controlling the decision in Connor v. Great Western Savings & Loan Assn., 69 Cal.2d 850, 73 Cal.Rptr. 369, 447 P.2d 609 (1968). In that case, the lender had been intimately involved at every stage of a subdivision construction project, from financing the development to the making of loans to plaintiff purchasers secured by mortgages upon the dwellings. All plans and specifications had been examined and approved by the lender before construction began. Many of the homes proved defective and some of the purchasers brought an action against the developer and the lender seeking rescission and damages. Holding that the lender had been an "active participant" in the enterprise, and because the lender knew or should have known certain facts concerning the developer and the transaction, the Court found that the lender had a duty under the circumstances, which it owed to the individual purchasers, to exercise reasonable care to protect them from damages caused by major structural defects.

"If existing sanctions are inadequate, imposition of a duty at the point of effective financial control of tract building will insure responsible building practices." 69 Cal.2d 868, 73 Cal.Rptr. 378, 447 P.2d 618.

Plaintiff argues that the case at bar is analogous to *Connor*.

The question on appeal is whether the facts as pleaded constitute a cause of action in favor of the plaintiff against the defendant mortgage corporation, not whether those facts can be proved at trial.

It is apparent from the pleadings that the transaction in this matter was not unitary, but binary, in that plaintiff first made and signed a purchase agreement with the real estate company, and several weeks later, in an independent transaction, concluded a mortgage agreement with the mortgage company. These two transactions are distinct and disjoint and, therefore, any fraud or unconscionability attributable to the purchase agreement cannot be ascribed to the subsequent mortgage agreement. The mortgage agreement itself is neither fraudulent nor unconscionable; for good and valuable consideration, defendant mortgage corporation took a mortgage equal in value to the money advanced to the plaintiff.

Connor v. Great Western Savings & Loan Assn., supra, cited by plaintiff, does not support her position. Great Western, the lender, negotiated with two developers with limited experience in tract construction to secure financing for the purchase of 100 acres of land and the construction thereon of 400 tract homes. The arrangement provided that Great Western would first buy the land, and then resell it to the developers at a profit, charging a high interest rate on the loan. A fee was charged for each individual home loan, while if a buyer obtained financing elsewhere, the developers were required to pay Great Western the fees obtained by the other lender. Great Western inspected at least once a week, and maintained the right to halt construction funds during the construction period if the work did not conform to plans and specifications. Great Western negligently failed to discover that the home designs were inadequate for the soil conditions; within two years, numerous foundations cracked. In holding that all buyers and other lenders had a cause of action against Great Western, the California Supreme Court was careful to observe that such liability arose because the lender voluntarily assumed the duty to inspect, and had been involved in the overall transaction to a far greater extent than the usual money lender in such transactions.

The doctrine of "close connectedness", relied upon by plaintiff, is inapplicable to the case at bar. No such close relationship is sufficiently pleaded to bring that doctrine into play.

Even conceding the merits of litigation *pro bono publico,* plaintiff's position in the case at bar is untenable.

The issuance of FHA insurance on the mortgage in the case at bar is central to the overall transaction herein attacked by plaintiff. From a business point of view, once an insurance policy has been issued on a mortgage, the mortgagee has no interest whatsoever in an appraisal of the subject property. Either the mortgage will be paid off by the mortgagor, or the mortgage will be in default. In the latter event, foreclosure will either produce a sales price sufficient to pay off the mortgage, or the mortgagee may simply rely on his insurance, and protect himself from loss that way. Clearly, there is no business reason or well-pleaded allegations by the plaintiff why a mortgagee who is the beneficiary of an FHA mortgage policy should go to the expense and trouble of inspecting the subject premises.

In the instant case, the mortgagee had no real interest in the actual sales transaction. The mortgagee was merely a source of funds, and in the usual course of prudent business practice took a mortgage for the sole purpose of securing its monetary advance to the plaintiff. Given the existence of an FHA insurance policy, the value of the collateral was inconsequential. Existence of the property subject to the mortgage was all that concerned the lender, since that alone, given FHA insurance, was sufficient completely to protect its investment. Plaintiff has pleaded no business reason why the mortgage corporation should have done more than it did.

In the spate of recent cases in which new duties and liabilities have been recognized, or old ones extended, the courts have consistently grounded their decisions on the theory that the person upon whom liability is sought to be imposed is in the best position to spread its losses to those who are benefited by the adverse consequences of their activities.

In the case at bar, the mortgagee is in no position to spread any losses due to fraudulent land sales transactions, nor is the mortgagee in a particularly good position to prevent such losses. Those parties most intimately involved in the sales transaction, the vendor and vendee, respectively, are best able to diminish the number and size of losses due to fraudulent sales. The mortgagee is not a beneficiary of the fraud, if any, which was allegedly perpetrated by the real estate company; all its profits came from the interest it charged on its loan. Any profits realized by the mortgagee because of the underlying fraud are too remote to form a basis for its liability.

Plaintiff has advanced no viable economic theory upon which to impose liability on the mortgage corporation; she must rely on established legal doctrines. But no established legal principle has been cited by plaintiff or discovered by this Court that would warrant finding that defendant mortgage corporation had a duty to protect the plaintiff from the real estate company's cupidity.

Nor do the holder in due course cases add anything to plaintiff's argument. Those cases, applying the so-called "close connectedness" doctrine, differ radically from the case at bar. It may be conceded *arguendo* that, if the mortgage corporation were intimately affiliated with the real estate company, the real estate company's fraud could be chargeable against the mortgage corporation. However, even viewing the complaint in the light most favorable to the plaintiff, there is no allegation that the mortgage corporation acted as a subsidiary of the real estate company, or is the mortgagee of all property sold by the real estate company, or is otherwise somehow viewable as the alter ego of the real estate company.

Of the cases cited by plaintiff, several contain reasoning which serves to defeat plaintiff's assertion that she has a cause of action. For instance, in Financial Credit Corp. v. Williams, 246 Md. 575, 229 A.2d 712 (1967), the Court held that two things are necessary conditions precedent to the imposition of liability: (1) an extraordinary discount, and (2) knowledge, such as an infirmity obvious on the face of the instrument. Matthews v. Aluminum Acceptance Corp., supra. The remaining cases cited by plaintiff involve factual situations in which the mortgagor's title was tainted as against his grantor. Those cases are thus self-distinguishing.

This Court finds that plaintiff does not have a cause of action, because of the relationship between the mortgage corporation and the real estate company, and well-established principles of equity as applied to fraud. Such liability would therefore not be after the fact.

It might be argued that, if the mortgage corporation did not extend a loan to the plaintiff because she was an uneducated black person, buying a house in an allegedly deteriorating neighborhood, it might incur some legal liability under the Federal Housing Administration Act.

Analysis of all the cases cited by both parties, and of additional cases discovered by this Court, discloses that, under the pleadings, no authority supports a cause of action against the Michigan Mortgage Corporation in the case at bar.

Affirmed.

ADAMS, Judge (dissenting).

I dissent.

Judge McGregor states:

"It is apparent from the pleadings that the transaction in this matter was not unitary, but binary, in that plaintiff first made and signed a purchase agreement with the real estate company, and several weeks later, in an independent transaction, concluded a mortgage agreement with the mortgage company."

The final typed-in sentence of the purchase agreement reads as follows: "If purchaser is unable to obtain mortgage, deposit to be refunded less cost of credit report".

Count IV of plaintiff's first amended complaint alleges that defendant Michigan, as part of its normal pre-loan credit check on plaintiff, knew that plaintiff was receiving welfare assistance, was unemployed, had little formal education, and had little, if any, experience in any kind of commercial transactions. Count IV further avers that defendant Michigan knew, as a result of repeated business dealings with defendant Montgomery, that Montgomery was an experienced real estate company with a notorious reputation for using unscrupulous and deceptive practices. Finally said count alleges that defendant Michigan knew, or should have known through its preliminary investigation, the various facts charged to establish fraud by Montgomery, and that since Michigan knew or should have known all of these facts it made itself an integral and necessary part of the fraudulent transaction when it entered into the mortgage loan agreement with plaintiff without warning her of her peril and imminent financial loss. Count V of plaintiff's first amended complaint contains similar allegations and avers that defendant Michigan disregarded its duty to warn plaintiff of her peril or to refrain from taking any action which would increase her danger.

. . .

Judge McGregor states: "It may be conceded *arguendo* that, if the mortgage corporation were intimately affiliated with the real estate company, the real estate company's fraud could be chargeable against the mortgage corporation". Since the purchase agreement is specifically provisioned upon the securing of a mortgage, and in view of the serious allegations raised in plaintiff's complaint, I am unable to conclude, as Judge McGregor does, that the transaction in this case was binary and not unitary and that plaintiff's pleadings failed to state a claim upon which relief could be granted. The appellate courts of this state have repeatedly warned against the improper use of summary proceedings to preclude a party from his day in court.

... I would reverse and remand for further proceedings.

JEMINSON v. MONTGOMERY REAL ESTATE AND CO.

Supreme Court of Michigan, 1976.
396 Mich. 106, 240 N.W.2d 205.

T.G. KAVANAGH, Chief Justice.

For the reasons stated by former Justice Adams in his dissent in this case, 47 Mich.App. 731, 741, 210 N.W.2d 10, 14 (1973), the decision of the Court of Appeals is reversed and the cause remanded for trial.

LEVIN and WILLIAMS, JJ., concur.

LINDEMER and RYAN, JJ., not participating.

COLEMAN and FITZGERALD, Justices.

We would affirm the decision of the Court of Appeals for the reasons set forth in the majority opinion 47 Mich.App. 731, 733–741, 210 N.W.2d 10, 11–14 (1973).

NOTES

1. *Lenders.* What policies should be considered, and what lines drawn, in determining whether and to what extent lenders should be held liable for building defects? In the case of a construction lender, should liability be made to depend on whether the lender in fact undertook an inspection? Charged a separate inspection fee? Did the lender have control of the process that led to the defect? Should a permanent lender's liability turn on whether new or used housing is involved? On whether the mortgage is insured, as in *Jeminson?* On whether the buyer-borrower can show that his contract with the seller contained a subject to financing condition? That, in closing, he was relying on the lender's judgment as to quality and that the lender knew of this reliance?

Actions against lenders have been generally unavailing. Both *Jeminson* and *Connor v. Great Western,* which it cites, are exceptions to the general rule. The judicial trend in and out of California has been to distinguish *Connor* on the ground that Great Western's participation in the development in question involved many non-lending activities. See, for example, Wierzbicki v. Alaska Mutual Savings Bank, 630 P.2d 998 (Alaska 1981); Seymour v. New Hampshire Savings Bank, 131 N.H. 753, 561 A.2d 1053 (1989); Amsterdam Savings Bank FSB v. Marine Midland Bank, N.A., 121 A.D.2d 815, 504 N.Y.S.2d 563, appeal dismissed, 68 N.Y.2d 766, 506 N.Y.S.2d 1040, 498 N.E.2d 151 (1986) (construction lender not liable to permanent lender for defects). The California Legislature subsequently limited *Connor* by amending the Civil Code to provide that

> A lender who makes a loan of money, the proceeds of which are used ... to finance the ... improvement of real or personal property for sale or lease to others, shall not be held liable to third persons for any loss or damage occasioned by any defect in the real or personal property ... unless such loss or damage is a result of an act of the lender outside the scope of the activities of a lender of

money or unless the lender has been a party to misrepresentations with respect to such real or personal property.

Cal.Civ.Code § 3434. Cases interpreting section 3434 offer little insight into the critical issue of what constitutes "the scope of the activities of a lender of money." See generally, Gutierrez, Liability of a Construction Lender Under Civil Code § 3434: An Amorphous Epitaph to Connor v. Great Western Savings & Loan Association, 8 Pac.L.J. 1 (1977).

Cases also reject liability of permanent lenders. See, e.g., Rzepiennik v. U.S. Home Corp., 221 N.J.Super. 230, 534 A.2d 89 (1987) (lender has no duty to inspect for borrower); Stempler v. Frankford Trust Co., 365 Pa.Super. 305, 529 A.2d 521 (1987) (same). Should the result be different if the lender actually learns of a defect and does not disclose it to the borrower?

In some limited circumstances the lender has been held liable for defects in the premises. These include situations where the lender and developer were engaged in a joint venture to develop the property, see Central Bank, N.A. v. Baldwin, 94 Nev. 581, 583 P.2d 1087 (1978), the construction lender took control of the job upon default of borrower and completed the building, see Chotka v. Fidelco Growth Investors, 383 So.2d 1169 (Fla.App.1980), or the construction lender continued to disburse to the builder even though the borrower had complained about defects, see Davis v. Nevada National Bank, 103 Nev. 220, 737 P.2d 503 (1987). A lender who simply takes a deed in lieu of foreclosure and then sells the property will not be liable for construction defects. See Kennedy v. Columbia Lumber & Manufacturing Co., 299 S.C. 335, 384 S.E.2d 730 (1989); see also McKnight v. Board of Directors, 32 Ohio St.3d 6, 512 N.E.2d 316 (1987).

For an excellent analysis of some of these issues see Malloy, Lender Liability for Negligent Real Estate Appraisals, 1984 U.Ill.L.Rev. 53. See generally, Ferguson, Lender's Liability for Construction Defects, 11 Real Est.L.J. 310 (1983); Hiller, Mortgagee Liability for Defective Construction, 108 Banking L.J. 386 (1991); Note, Mortgage Lender Liability to the Purchaser of New or Existing Homes, 1988 U.Ill.L.Rev. 191.

2. *Brokers.* Broker liability for housing defects rests almost exclusively on fraud and typically arises when the seller mentions some material defect to the listing broker who then fails to disclose it to the unsuspecting buyer. See pages 56–66 above.

3. *Architects.* Architect liability to third parties injured as a consequence of negligently prepared plans is a relatively new development. Until the middle 1950's the general rule was that an architect's liability to individuals other than her client evaporated at the moment the client accepted the completed building. There were early exceptions to the rule, for willful negligence and dangerous, latent conditions, but the rule itself did not begin to fall until the 1950's. Architects are now widely held liable for design errors ranging from failure to consider suitability of the underlying soil and specifying an insuffi-

cient foundation, to specifying improper windows, insulation and roofing. For a thorough analysis of architect liability, with proposals for reform, see Comment, Architect Tort Liability in Preparation of Plans and Specifications, 55 Cal.L.Rev. 1361 (1967). See also, Note, Architectural Malpractice: A Contract-Based Approach, 92 Harv.L.Rev. 1075 (1979).

"The American Institute of Architects, along with the National Society of Professional Engineers and the Associated General Contractors, began to push for model legislation which would substantially curtail the limitless duration of liability imposed upon its members. In the span of approximately two years, 1965–67, thirty jurisdictions enacted or amended statutes of limitations specifically for architects, engineers and builders. Though these statutes are not identical in every respect, there is one characteristic common to all. Each of them sets a definite period of years beginning at the time of completion or acceptance of the work, after which no civil actions against the architect, engineer, or builder may be brought." Note, 60 Kentucky L.J. 462, 464–465 (1972).

4. *Government Agencies.* Should the Federal Housing Administration, which insured the homebuyer's mortgage in *Jeminson* and thus had an interest in determining the value of the house as security for the insured loan, have been held liable for not properly inspecting the house and disclosing its condition to the prospective homebuyer? The federal government has generally sought to avoid liability for its participation in home loan and loan insurance programs through express disclaimers and through the doctrine of sovereign immunity.

In Block v. Neal, 460 U.S. 289, 103 S.Ct. 1089, 75 L.Ed.2d 67 (1983), the United States Supreme Court held that the prohibition of the Federal Tort Claims Act against recovery for any "claim arising out of ... misrepresentation" did not bar plaintiff Neal's action for damages against the Farmers Home Administration which, having lent her money for the construction of a prefabricated house, allegedly failed to properly inspect and supervise construction, with the result that the completed house contained fourteen defects. Neal's contract with her builder required that its work "conform to plans approved by FmHA. It also granted FmHA the right to inspect and test all materials and workmanship and reject any that were defective. At the same time, Neal entered into a deed of trust with FmHA and signed a promissory note providing for repayment of the principal sum of $21,170, plus interest of 8% per annum on the unpaid principal." 460 U.S. at 291, 103 S.Ct. at 1091.

In the Court's view, plaintiff's "claim against the Government for negligence by FmHA officials in supervising construction of her house does not 'aris[e] out of ... misrepresentation' within the meaning of 28 U.S.C.A. § 2680(h). The Court of Appeals properly concluded that Neal's claim is not barred by this provision of the Tort Claims Act because Neal does not seek to recover on the basis of misstatements made by FmHA officials. Although FmHA in this case may have undertaken both to supervise construction of Neal's house and to provide Neal information regarding the progress of construction, Neal's action is based solely on the former conduct. Accordingly, the judgment of the Court of Appeals is affirmed." 460 U.S. at 298–299, 103 S.Ct. at 1094–1095.

2.　TITLE

Before paying the purchase price and accepting seller's deed, buyer will want assurance that seller's title is good—that no fraud or formal defect clouds her ownership and that there are no outstanding conditions or encumbrances that might interfere with buyer's ownership or use of the land. Buyer can get this assurance in part by searching seller's record title and updating this search down to the moment of closing. If the search discloses a material defect, the covenant of marketable title in the parties' contract will excuse buyer from performing and entitle him to the return of his deposit. But, if the search discloses no such defect, buyer will, as required by the contract, accept seller's deed and pay the price.

Since some title defects will not be disclosed by a record search, the prudent buyer may want additional assurances that seller's title is good. One form that these assurances commonly take is covenants—promises—incorporated in seller's deed to buyer. Title covenants can be shaped to meet any specific need—that title is good as against a neighbor claiming adverse possession, that a disputed mortgage has been paid off, or that a troublesome relative in fact has no interest in the land. In addition to such custom-crafted covenants are six standard title covenants that have been in common use since at least the seventeenth century in England:

Covenant of Seisin. This covenant is the seller's promise that she owns at least the interest in land that she is purporting to convey to the buyer. (Thus, if seller's deed purports to give buyer complete ownership of Blackacre, but at the time of the conveyance seller had only a twenty-year lease to Blackacre, the covenant would be breached.)

Covenant of the Right to Convey. Here the seller covenants that she has full power to transfer the interest that the deed purports to convey. This covenant substantially overlaps the covenant of seisin, but provides protection in occasional circumstances where the covenant of seisin does not. For example, the fact that X is in adverse possession of Blackacre at the time seller conveys to buyer does not affect seller's ownership of the parcel and, thus, does not breach her covenant of seisin. It would, however, give buyer an action against seller for breach of the covenant of the right to convey.

Covenant Against Encumbrances. This is the seller's promise that no outstanding encumbrances affect ownership or use of the land. Mortgages, leases, unpaid taxes and judgment liens are typical encumbrances affecting ownership. Easements, building restrictions and rights in third parties to remove minerals or other resources from the land are typical encumbrances affecting use.

Covenant of Warranty. This is the single most frequently used covenant in the United States. It obligates the seller to compensate the buyer for any losses when the title conveyed falls short of the title that the deed purports to convey. A covenant of *general warranty* encompasses all defects in title and shortages in the area conveyed, regardless of the reason for the defect or shortage. Covenants of *special warranty* limit the defects covered. They may, for example, cover only those defects that arose while the seller owned the land.

Covenant of Quiet Enjoyment. Under this covenant, the seller promises that the buyer's possession will not be disrupted either by the seller or by anyone with a lawful claim superior to the seller. (The covenant does not, however, protect against intrusions by trespassers.) Courts in the United States generally treat the covenant for quiet enjoyment as equivalent to the covenant of warranty.

Covenant for Further Assurances. Rarely used in the United States, the covenant for further assurances obligates the seller to take such further reasonable steps as are necessary to cure defects in the buyer's title. For example, the seller might be required to obtain the release of an encumbrance or to buy off an adverse possessor. Unlike the covenant of warranty, which gives the buyer damages for the land he has lost, the covenant for further assurances enables the buyer to remain in possession of the land—a particularly valuable right when the land has substantially appreciated in value.

The first three covenants—seisin, right to convey and freedom from encumbrances—are commonly called *present covenants* because they embody representations about the condition of title at the time the deed is delivered to the buyer. As a consequence, these covenants are breached only if the defect they cover exists at the time of delivery, and the statute of limitations for breach begins to run from that time. The second set of three covenants—warranty, quiet enjoyment and further assurances—are called *future covenants* because they protect against interferences with possession occurring at some future time, and obligate the seller to take steps to correct the interference at that time. As a consequence, the statute of limitations for their breach begins to run not from the moment of delivery, but rather from the moment at which the buyer or his successor is first evicted from possession.

Deeds sometimes spell out each of the agreed-upon covenants in detail. Many states, however, have eliminated the need for full explication by providing that a deed's use of a single key word or phrase will automatically incorporate specified covenants in the deed unless the deed expressly excludes them. For example, in Alabama use of the word "grant," "bargain" or "sell" will imply covenants of seisin, freedom from encumbrances created by the grantor, and quiet enjoyment. Ala.Code § 35–4–271 (1975).

BROWN v. LOBER

Supreme Court of Illinois, 1979.
75 Ill.2d 547, 27 Ill.Dec. 780, 389 N.E.2d 1188.

UNDERWOOD, Justice:

Plaintiffs instituted this action in the Montgomery County circuit court based on an alleged breach of the covenant of seisin in their warranty deed. The trial court held that although there had been a breach of the covenant of seisin, the suit was barred by the 10-year statute of limitations in section 16 of the Limitations Act (Ill.Rev.Stat. 1975, ch. 83, par. 17). Plaintiffs' posttrial motion, which was based on an alleged breach of the covenant of quiet enjoyment, was also denied. A divided Fifth District Appellate Court reversed and remanded. We allowed the defendant's petition for leave to appeal.

The parties submitted an agreed statement of facts which sets forth the relevant history of this controversy. Plaintiffs purchased 80 acres of Montgomery County real estate from William and Faith Bost and received a statutory warranty deed containing no exceptions, dated December 21, 1957. Subsequently, plaintiffs took possession of the land and recorded their deed.

On May 8, 1974, plaintiffs granted a coal option to Consolidated Coal Company (Consolidated) for the coal rights on the 80-acre tract for the sum of $6,000. Approximately two years later, however, plaintiffs "discovered" that they, in fact, owned only a one-third interest in the subsurface coal rights. It is a matter of public record that, in 1947, a prior grantor had reserved a two-thirds interest in the mineral rights on the property. Although plaintiffs had their abstract of title examined in 1958 and 1968 for loan purposes, they contend that until May 4, 1976, they believed that they were the sole owners of the surface and subsurface rights on the 80-acre tract. Upon discovering that a prior grantor had reserved a two-thirds interest in the coal rights, plaintiffs and Consolidated renegotiated their agreement to provide for payment of $2,000 in exchange for a one-third interest in the subsurface coal rights. On May 25, 1976, plaintiffs filed this action against the executor of the estate of Faith Bost, seeking damages in the amount of $4,000.

The deed which plaintiffs received from the Bosts was a general statutory form warranty deed meeting the requirements of section 9 of "An Act concerning conveyances" (Ill.Rev.Stat.1957, ch. 30, par. 8). That section provides:

> "Every deed in substance in the above form, when otherwise duly executed, shall be deemed and held a conveyance in fee simple, to the grantee, his heirs or assigns, with covenants on the part of the grantor, (1) that at the time of the making and delivery of such deed he was lawfully seized of an indefeasible estate in fee simple, in and

to the premises therein described, and had good right and full power to convey the same; (2) that the same were then free from all incumbrances; and (3) that he warrants to the grantee, his heirs and assigns, the quiet and peaceable possession of such premises, and will defend the title thereto against all persons who may lawfully claim the same. And such covenants shall be obligatory upon any grantor, his heirs and personal representatives, as fully and with like effect as if written at length in such deed." Ill.Rev.Stat.1957, ch. 30, par. 8.

The effect of this provision is that certain covenants of title are implied in every statutory form warranty deed. Subsection 1 contains the covenant of seisin and the covenant of good right to convey. These covenants, which are considered synonymous assure the grantee that the grantor is, at the time of the conveyance, lawfully seized and has the power to convey an estate of the quality and quantity which he professes to convey.

Subsection 2 represents the covenant against incumbrances. An incumbrance is any right to, or interest in, land which may subsist in a third party to the diminution of the value of the estate, but consistent with the passing of the fee by conveyance.

Subsection 3 sets forth the covenant of quiet enjoyment, which is synonymous with the covenant of warranty in Illinois. By this covenant, "the grantor warrants to the grantee, his heirs and assigns, the possession of the premises and that he will defend the title granted by the terms of the deed against persons who may lawfully claim the same, and that such covenant shall be obligatory upon the grantor, his heirs, personal representatives, and assigns." Biwer v. Martin (1920), 294 Ill. 488, 497, 128 N.E. 518, 522.

Plaintiffs' complaint is premised upon the fact that "William Roy Bost and Faith Post covenanted that they were the owners in fee simple of the above described property at the time of the conveyance to the plaintiffs." While the complaint could be more explicit, it appears that plaintiffs were alleging a cause of action for breach of the covenant of seisin. This court has stated repeatedly that the covenant of seisin is a covenant *in praesenti* and, therefore, if broken at all, is broken at the time of delivery of the deed.

Since the deed was delivered to the plaintiffs on December 21, 1957, any cause of action for breach of the covenant of seisin would have accrued on that date. The trial court held that this cause of action was barred by the statute of limitations. No question is raised as to the applicability of the 10-year statute of limitations (Ill.Rev.Stat.1975, ch. 83, par. 17). We conclude, therefore, that the cause of action for breach of the covenant of seisin was properly determined by the trial court to be barred by the statute of limitations since plaintiffs did not file their complaint until May 25, 1976, nearly 20 years after their alleged cause of action accrued.

In their post-trial motion, plaintiffs set forth as an additional theory of recovery an alleged breach of the covenant of quiet enjoyment. The trial court, without explanation, denied the motion. The appellate court reversed, holding that the cause of action on the covenant of quiet enjoyment was not barred by the statute of limitations. The appellate court theorized that plaintiffs' cause of action did not accrue until 1976, when plaintiffs discovered that they only had a one-third interest in the subsurface coal rights and renegotiated their contract with the coal company for one-third of the previous contract price. The primary issue before us, therefore, is when, if at all, the plaintiffs' cause of action for breach of the covenant of quiet enjoyment is deemed to have accrued.

This court has stated on numerous occasions that, in contrast to the covenant of seisin, the covenant of warranty or quiet enjoyment is prospective in nature and is breached only when there is an actual or constructive eviction of the covenantee by the paramount titleholder.

The cases are also replete with statements to the effect that the mere existence of paramount title in one other than the covenantee is not sufficient to constitute a breach of the covenant of warranty or quiet enjoyment: "[T]here must be a union of acts of disturbance and lawful title, to constitute a breach of the covenant for quiet enjoyment, or warranty ...." (Barry v. Guild (1888), 126 Ill. 439, 446, 18 N.E. 759, 761.) "[T]here is a general concurrence that something more than the mere existence of a paramount title is necessary to constitute a breach of the covenant of warranty." (Scott v. Kirkendall (1878), 88 Ill. 465, 467.) "A mere want of title is no breach of this covenant. There must not only be a want of title, but there must be an ouster under a paramount title." Moore v. Vail (1855), 17 Ill. 185, 189.

The question is whether plaintiffs have alleged facts sufficient to constitute a constructive eviction. They argue that if a covenantee fails in his effort to sell an interest in land because he discovers that he does not own what his warranty deed purported to convey, he has suffered a constructive eviction and is thereby entitled to bring an action against his grantor for breach of the covenant of quiet enjoyment. We think that the decision of this court in Scott v. Kirkendall (1878), 88 Ill. 465, is controlling on this issue and compels us to reject plaintiffs' argument.

In *Scott,* an action was brought for breach of the covenant of warranty by a grantee who discovered that other parties had paramount title to the land in question. The land was vacant and unoccupied at all relevant times. This court, in rejecting the grantee's claim that there was a breach of the covenant of quiet enjoyment, quoted the earlier decision in Moore v. Vail (1855), 17 Ill. 185, 191:

> " 'Until that time, (the taking possession by the owner of the paramount title,) he might peaceably have entered upon and enjoyed the premises, without resistance or molestation, which was all his grantors covenanted he should do. They did not guarantee

to him a perfect title, but the possession and enjoyment of the premises.' "   88 Ill. 465, 468.

Relying on this language in *Moore,* the *Scott* court concluded:

"We do not see but what this fully decides the present case against the appellant.   It holds that the mere existence of a paramount title does not constitute a breach of the covenant.   That is all there is here.   There has been no assertion of the adverse title.   The land has always been vacant.   Appellant could at any time have taken peaceable possession of it.   He has in no way been prevented or hindered from the enjoyment of the possession by any one having a better right.   It was but the possession and enjoyment of the premises which was assured to him, and there has been no distur-bance or interference in that respect.   True, there is a superior title in another, but appellant has never felt 'its pressure upon him.' "   88 Ill. 465, 468–69.

Admittedly, *Scott* dealt with surface rights while the case before us concerns subsurface mineral rights.   We are, nevertheless, convinced that the reasoning employed in *Scott* is applicable to the present case. While plaintiffs went into possession of the surface area, they cannot be said to have possessed the subsurface minerals.   "Possession of the surface does not carry possession of the minerals .... [Citation.]   To possess the mineral estate, one must undertake the actual removal thereof from the ground or do such other act as will apprise the community that such interest is in the exclusive use and enjoyment of the claiming party."   Failoni v. Chicago & North Western Ry. Co. (1964), 30 Ill.2d 258, 262, 195 N.E.2d 619, 622.

Since no one has, as yet, undertaken to remove the coal or otherwise manifested a clear intent to exclusively "possess" the mineral estate, it must be concluded that the subsurface estate is "vacant."   As in *Scott,* plaintiffs "could at any time have taken peaceable possession of it. [They have] in no way been prevented or hindered from the enjoyment of the possession by any one having a better right."   (88 Ill. 465, 468.) Accordingly, until such time as one holding paramount title interferes with plaintiffs' right of possession (*e.g.,* by beginning to mine the coal), there can be no constructive eviction and, therefore, no breach of the covenant of quiet enjoyment.

What plaintiffs are apparently attempting to do on this appeal is to extend the protection afforded by the covenant of quiet enjoyment. However, we decline to expand the historical scope of this covenant to provide a remedy where another of the covenants of title is so clearly applicable.   As this court stated in Scott v. Kirkendall (1878), 88 Ill. 465, 469:

"To sustain the present action would be to confound all distinc-tion between the covenant of warranty and that of seizin, or of right to convey.   They are not equivalent covenants.   An action will lie upon the latter, though there be no disturbance of possession.   A defect of title will suffice.   Not so with the covenant of warranty, or for quiet enjoyment, as has always been held by the prevailing authority."

The covenant of seisin, unquestionably, was breached when the Bosts delivered the deed to plaintiffs, and plaintiffs then had a cause of action. However, despite the fact that it was a matter of public record that there was a reservation of a two-thirds interest in the mineral rights in the earlier deed, plaintiffs failed to bring an action for breach of the covenant of seisin within the 10-year period following delivery of the deed. The likely explanation is that plaintiffs had not secured a title opinion at the time they purchased the property, and the subsequent examiners for the lenders were not concerned with the mineral rights. Plaintiffs' oversight, however, does not justify us in overruling earlier decisions in order to recognize an otherwise premature cause of action. The mere fact that plaintiffs' original contract with Consolidated had to be modified due to their discovery that paramount title to two-thirds of the subsurface minerals belonged to another is not sufficient to constitute the constructive eviction necessary to a breach of the covenant of quiet enjoyment.

Finally, although plaintiffs also have argued in this court that there was a breach of the covenant against incumbrances entitling them to recovery, we decline to address this issue which was argued for the first time on appeal. It is well settled that questions not raised in the trial court will not be considered by this court on appeal.

Accordingly, the judgment of the appellate court is reversed, and the judgment of the circuit court of Montgomery County is affirmed.

Appellate court reversed; circuit court affirmed.

NOTES

1. Was it fair in *Lober* for plaintiffs' action on the covenant of seisin to be barred by the statute of limitations? For plaintiffs' action on the covenant of quiet enjoyment to be dismissed on the ground that the covenant had not yet been breached? What, if anything, could plaintiff have done to precipitate an eviction and hence a breach of the covenant of quiet enjoyment? How would you advise a client caught between one title claim that is not yet ripe and another that is overripe? Can you draft a covenant that would cover the situation that arose in *Lober?*

Should plaintiffs have been barred on the alternative ground that, at the time they accepted delivery they knew or should have known of the outstanding mineral interest? As a general rule, a buyer's actual or constructive knowledge of a title defect or encumbrance will not defeat his action on a covenant that covers the defect or encumbrance. See Jones v. Grow Investment & Mortgage Co., 11 Utah 2d 326, 358 P.2d 909 (1961) ("The very purpose of the covenant is to protect a grantee against defects and to hold that one can be protected only against unknown defects would be to rob the covenant of most of its value. If from the force of the covenant it is desired to eliminate known defects, or to limit the covenant in any way, it is easy to do so.").

2. *Coverage Limitations.* Because deed covenants protect only against defects in title, there can be no action on the warranty on the ground that the configuration of the property does not comply with zoning requirements. See, e.g., Barnett v. Decatur, 261 Ga. 205, 403 S.E.2d 46 (1991). Similarly, title covenants do not warrant the physical quality of the premises. See Casenote, 51 Mont.L.Rev. 205 (1990).

3. *Statutory Short Forms and Presumptions.* Covenants of title may be imposed in a deed absent express covenant language. Under statutes in some jurisdictions, the use of a seemingly innocuous term in a deed implies certain covenants of title. See, for example, Mont. Code Ann. § 70–20–304 ("grant" imports covenant against encumbrances created by grantor). As *Brown v. Lober* indicates, statutes may also authorize short forms of deeds where the use of one phrase may create covenants. See, for example, Ohio Rev. Code § 5302.06 ("general warranty covenants" creates covenants of seisin, right to convey, absence of encumbrances, and general warranty). The attorney must be familiar with local statutes and presumptions in evaluating deeds. For an excellent discussion of this issue, see R. Natelson, Modern Law of Deeds to Real Property 60–62, 332–337 (1992).

IV. ASSURING TITLE

A. THE RECORD SYSTEM

The aim of the record system in America is to protect a buyer of land against the possibility that his seller, or some predecessor in interest to his seller, previously conveyed away all or part of the bundle of rights that the buyer has contracted to buy. The genius of the American recording system is that it operates almost entirely on individual initiative. A buyer who follows the steps prescribed by the system can almost always assure himself of good title.

At early common law, when land was transferred by the ceremony of feoffment with livery of seisin, the possibility of conflicting transfers was small. The required presence of witnesses disciplined landowners from trying to sell the same parcel twice. But, with the growth of documentary transfers after the Statute of Uses, enacted in 1535, and with the proliferation of nonpossessory interests such as covenants, easements and tax and mortgage liens that could simultaneously coexist in a single parcel, it became increasingly probable that a scheming or forgetful grantor would fail to inform her grantee of some prior, adverse transfer. Covenants of title partially protected grantees who obtained less than they bargained for. But breaching covenantors could not always be found and, if found, often lacked the resources to make good on their promises. A rule was needed to determine the rights of competing grantees fairly and efficiently.

The common law had adopted a simple rule for determining who should prevail when grantor A conveyed the same interest in land to two grantees, B and C: *first in time, first in right*. The rule worked fairly and efficiently when the first grantee, B, went into immediate possession of the land. A quick inspection by C before accepting and paying for the deed from A, would disclose that someone other than A was in possession. C's inquiry of B as to why B rather than A was in possession would disclose that B's possession was under a prior deed from A. C could then rescind his contract with A and recover any deposit paid.

But the rule of first in time, first in right was neither efficient nor fair when, as often happened, B did not go into possession. C, seeing either A or no one in possession, would have no reason to inquire into the possibility that someone other than A had title. Nonetheless, C would lose his interest when B later asserted his prior rights.

The first recording acts were passed to resolve this shortcoming. The American acts replaced the common law rule of first in time, first in right with an equally simple, but fairer and more efficient prescription: *first to record, first in right.* By providing a place—typically the county recorder's office—to record instruments transferring real property, and by providing that an instrument of transfer will be valid as against subsequent, competing instruments only if it is recorded, the American record system provided a comparatively cheap and certain method for C not only to determine whether A was conveying good title to him, but also to assure himself that title, once conveyed to him, would not be lost to any subsequent competing grantee.

Specifically, this system enabled C to determine the status of A's title by conducting a record search in the county where the land was situated. Under the system, if prior grantee B was not in possession, C would nonetheless discover the conveyance to B if B had recorded it. The title search would fail to disclose the A–B transfer only if B had not recorded the instrument. But, if B failed to record, his interest would be invalid against C under a first to record, first in right regime—so long as C promptly recorded *his* instrument of transfer. And, by promptly recording, C would gain priority not only over all earlier grantees who failed to record, but against all grantees after him who, by definition, will have recorded later. Subsequent legislation altered some aspects of this early system, and expanded the buyer's duty to look outside the record, but nonetheless retained the paper record as the central feature of title assurance in the United States.

5303 REALTY CORP. v. O & Y EQUITY CORP.

Court of Appeals of New York, 1984.
64 N.Y.2d 313, 486 N.Y.S.2d 877, 476 N.E.2d 276.

OPINION OF THE COURT

COOKE, Chief Judge.

A notice of pendency, commonly known as a "*lis pendens*," can be a potent shield to protect litigants claiming an interest in real property. The powerful impact that this device has on the alienability of property, when conjoined with the facility with which it may be obtained, calls for its narrow application to only those lawsuits directly affecting title to, or the possession, use or enjoyment of, real property. Consequently, a suit to specifically perform a contract for the sale of stock representing a beneficial ownership of real estate will not support the filing of a notice of pendency.

I

This action arises out of plaintiff's unsuccessful attempt to purchase an office building and its land in Manhattan. The fee owner of this property was a limited partnership, defendant 41 Fifth Ave. Associates ("Associates"). Defendants Fruchthandler Brothers Enterprises and Edward J. Minskoff were the limited partners in Associates, owning a 3% interest between them. The remaining 97% was owned by the general partner, defendant 41 Fifth Ave. Realty Corp. ("Realty Corporation"), which, in turn, was wholly owned by defendant O & Y Equity Corp.[1]

After extended negotiations, plaintiff and O & Y Equity reached an agreement to convey the property. Rather than an outright transfer of the title by deed, the transaction was constructed in terms of a sale of stock. This was allegedly done at defendants' request in order to avoid the New York City Real Property Transfer Tax. The contract provided that O & Y Equity would sell its shares in Realty Corporation and would cause the limited partners in Associates to convey their interests as well. The limited partners also signed this contract, agreeing to perform all acts required of them to consummate the transaction.

The contract was a lengthy document running over 40 pages, not including a number of extensive schedules. It expressly specified that Realty Corporation's sole business was owning the general partnership in Associates and that Associates' sole business was owning and operating the office building that plaintiff wished to acquire. The sale of the stock and title to the property were linked throughout the contract, which provided for title warranties and insurance, real estate tax protests, cancellation or adjustment upon taking by condemnation, and representations as to the status of the rents and leases in the building. Article 10 of the contract governed how the building would be operated pending closing. Paragraph 10.03 restricted Associates' power to execute new leases and required O & Y Equity to have an experienced person "expend a reasonable amount of time (i.e., an average of approximately 10 hours per regular work week)" to renew leases or obtain new tenants.

The closing never took place, and plaintiff's $500,000 deposit was paid to defendants out of the escrow account. Plaintiff commenced this suit, alleging that defendants had failed to carry out their obligations under paragraph 10.03, which would cause irreparable injury to plaintiff and make it impossible to close title pursuant to the contract. The complaint further alleged that defendants refused to perform their other obligations. In its prayer for relief, plaintiff requested that defendants be ordered "to specifically perform the Contract specifically to comply with paragraphs 10.03(b) and 10.03(c) thereof and within a reasonable time thereafter, which time is to be set out by the Court to deliver title to the Property to plaintiff or its assignee;" plaintiff also sought an alternative remedy of money damages in the amount of $4,500,000, as well as judgment for $500,000 against defendant Bachner, Tally & Mantell.

Plaintiff filed the complaint and immediately filed a notice of pendency against the property owned by Associates. The notice de-

---

1. The remaining defendant, Bachner, Tally & Mantell, was defendants' counsel who acted as escrow agent and is claimed to have improperly disbursed escrow funds to the other defendants. Unless otherwise specified, the term "defendants" in this opinion will not include Bachner, Tally & Mantell.

scribed the underlying action as one to enforce a contract to sell the fee ownership in the property and to deliver its possession. Defendants moved to cancel the notice. While the motion was pending, plaintiff filed an amended complaint that added allegations of fraudulent conduct by defendants. Supreme Court denied the motion, without considering the effect of the amended complaint, on the ground that the original complaint was sufficient to sustain the notice of pendency. The Appellate Division, First Department, affirmed, with two Justices dissenting.

II

The question presented on this appeal concerns the right to obtain a provisional remedy authorized by the Legislature. Specifically, we are asked to decide whether an action to enforce a contract to sell the ownership interest in a realty-owning entity may be accompanied by a notice of pendency pursuant to CPLR 6501. Because the terms of the statute and its history do not support plaintiff's claimed right to this provisional remedy, this court must reverse the decisions below and order that plaintiff's notice of pendency be canceled.

A

The authority and requirements for securing a valid notice of pendency against real estate are set forth in CPLR article 65. CPLR 6501 provides: "A notice of pendency may be filed in any action in a court of the state or of the United States in which the judgment demanded would affect the title to, or the possession, use or enjoyment of, real property." Once properly indexed, the notice acts as constructive notice to all subsequent purchasers or incumbrancers: "A person whose conveyance or incumbrance is recorded after the filing of the notice is bound by all proceedings taken in the action after such filing to the same extent as if he were a party" (CPLR 6501). It is this special consequence, resulting as a matter of law from the filing of the statutory notice of pendency which is the essence of the remedy afforded by the Legislature.

This, of course, is not a recent innovation. CPLR 6501 can trace its lineage directly back to the Code of Procedure enacted in 1848 (see L.1848, ch. 379, § 111). A still earlier law required a notice of pendency in mortgage foreclosures (see L.1840, ch. 342, §§ 8, 9, as amd. by L.1844, ch. 346, §§ 4, 5). These statutes, however, merely evolved from the common-law doctrine of *lis pendens*.[2]

The doctrine of *lis pendens* is long lived. It was first formally recognized in New York by Chancellor Kent in 1815 (*Murray v. Ballou*, 1 Johns Ch. 566; see 2 Reeves, Real Property, § 750, p. 1045). It can be traced at least to rule 12 of Lord Chancellor Bacon's Ordinances for the Government of the Court of Chancery, adopted in 1618 (see *Murray v.*

---

2. As the reader will have noted, the statutes refer to a "notice of pendency," in contrast to the term "*lis pendens*" used at common law. This distinction will be employed throughout this opinion.

Blatchford, 1 Wend. 583, 594; Bennett, *Lis Pendens*, pp. 57, 437). The doctrine was applied in actions concerning real property before Lord Bacon prescribed its use in chancery (see Bennett, *op. cit.*, at pp. 59, 96), and one commentator ascribed the rule's remote derivation to Roman Law (see *id.*, § 9, pp. 62–63).

The rule itself provided substantially the same protection as the modern statute. The doctrine of *lis pendens*—the pendency of a suit— "was, of itself, notice to the purchaser * * * It is no more than an adoption of the rule in a real action at common law, where, if the defendant aliens after the pendency of the writ, the judgment in the real action will overreach such alienation" (*Murray v. Ballou, supra*, at p. 577.) For the purposes of *lis pendens*, a suit was not begun until the summons was served and the complaint filed.

The purpose of the doctrine was to assure that a court retained its ability to effect justice by preserving its power over the property, regardless of whether a purchaser had any notice of the pending suit. Courts and commentators acknowledged the doctrine's potentially harsh impact on innocent purchasers, but they willingly accepted this as a necessary concomitant to preserving the judicial power (see *Leitch v. Wells, supra*, at pp. 608–609; *Murray v. Ballou, supra*, at pp. 576–577; Bennett, *op. cit.*, §§ 12, 14; 5 Tiffany, Real Property [3d ed.], § 1294, p. 82). Some justification for the doctrine's rugged application was found by reference to the rule of *caveat emptor* (see *Murray v. Ballou, supra*, at p. 577; Bennett, *op. cit.*, § 21, p. 82). The statutes diminished this effect by requiring that a notice of pendency be filed in a central registry.[3]

B

Determining the substantive scope of the notice of pendency, as embodied in CPLR 6501, cannot be divorced from consideration of the relative procedural ease with which it can be imposed throughout the duration of a lawsuit. Basically, a plaintiff can cloud a defendant's title merely by serving a summons and filing a proper complaint and notice of pendency stating the names of the parties, the object of the action, and a description of the property (CPLR 6511, subds. [a], [b]; see *Israelson v. Bradley*, 308 N.Y. 511, 127 N.E.2d 313). Indeed, the notice

3. Notwithstanding the sometimes vehement disavowal of any reliance on the law of notice to explain the rule (see Bennett, *Lis Pendens*, § 17; 5 Tiffany, Real Property [3d ed.], § 1294, p. 82; see, also, *Leitch v. Wells*, 48 N.Y. 585; *Murray v. Ballou*, 1 Johns Ch. 566), a careful review of the decisions reveals a concern that purchasers and incumbrancers should have some opportunity to ascertain whether the transferor had clear title or use of the property at issue. The doctrine presumed that the careful grantee could examine the local court records and thereby learn of the pending suit upon reading the filed complaint, which contained a description adequate to identify the property. This solicitude for the innocent purchaser was unnecessary to protect a court's power to execute its judgments. In formulating this equitable doctrine, the courts clearly were seeking to strike some balance between the interests of the plaintiff, the court, and the transferee (see *Murray v. Blatchford*, 1 Wend. 583, 618). As will be seen (see at pp. 320–321, at pp. 881–882 of 486 N.Y.S.2d, at p. 281 of 476 N.E.2d, *infra*), this emphasis on the statements in the pleadings has not changed over the years.

of pendency may even precede the service of summons (CPLR 6511, subd. [a]; 6512). The notice is valid for three years and it may be extended by court order (CPLR 6513).

Critically, the statutory scheme permits a party to effectively retard the alienability of real property without any prior judicial review. To the extent that a motion to cancel the notice of pendency is available (CPLR 6514), the court's scope of review is circumscribed. One of the important factors in this regard is that the likelihood of success on the merits is irrelevant to determining the validity of the notice of pendency.

Usually, there is little a court may do to provide relief to the property owner. If the procedures prescribed in article 65 have not been followed or if the action has not been commenced or prosecuted in good faith, the notice must be canceled in the first instance and it may be in the second (see *Israelson v. Bradley, supra*; CPLR 6514, subds. [a], [b]). If the notice of pendency is valid, the court may, in its discretion, cancel the notice, but the moving party will generally have to post an undertaking (CPLR 6515).

To counterbalance the ease with which a party may hinder another's right to transfer property, this court has required strict compliance with the statutory procedural requirements (see *Israelson v. Bradley*, 308 N.Y. 511, 127 N.E.2d 313, *supra*). "This is an extraordinary privilege * * * If the terms imposed are not met, the privilege is at an end. Such has been the law of our State, as declared in cases over the years, which did not, however, reach this court." (*Id.*, at p. 516, 127 N.E.2d 313 [citations omitted].)

In entertaining a motion to cancel, the court essentially is limited to reviewing the pleading to ascertain whether the action falls within the scope of CPLR 6501. In conjunction with this concept, the complaint filed with the notice of pendency must be adequate unto itself; a subsequent, amended complaint cannot be used to justify an earlier notice of pendency. This derives from the ancient concern that would-be purchasers obtain adequate notice of the risk to the property's title.

The same considerations that require strict compliance with the procedural prerequisites also mandate a narrow interpretation in reviewing whether an action is one affecting "the title to, or the possession, use or enjoyment of, real property" (CPLR 6501). Thus, a court is not to investigate the underlying transaction in determining whether a complaint comes within the scope of CPLR 6501. Instead, in accordance with historical practice, the court's analysis is to be limited to the pleading's face.

C

The courts have willingly given effect to the statute's broad coverage of actions concerning land. Importantly, however, they have restricted its application by requiring that the relief requested be directly related to the statutory terms (see Aron, N.Y. Real Property Law, p. 205).

Thus, attempts to impose a *lis pendens* against personal property in suits entirely unrelated to real property have been defeated (see *Holbrook v. New Jersey Zinc Co.*, 57 N.Y. 616; *Leitch v. Wells*, 48 N.Y. 585, 612–613, *supra* [Earl, C.]; *American Press Assn. v. Brantingham*, 75 App.Div. 435, 437–438, 78 N.Y.S. 305; but cf. Bennett, *op. cit.*, § 83; Note, 47 Harv.L.Rev. 1023).

The courts have been frequently confronted by attempts to file a notice of pendency in controversies that more or less referred to real property, but which did not necessarily seek to directly affect title to or possession of the land. In the absence of this direct relationship, the remedy was denied. For example, an action brought under a will for an accounting and for a determination of rights to and sale of real property supported filing a notice of pendency (*Kunz v. Bachman*, 61 How.Prac. 519, *supra*). In contrast, a trespass action seeking money damages only did not justify a notice of pendency as the judgment would not affect title to or possession of the realty (*Hailey v. Ano*, 136 N.Y. 569, 575, 32 N.E. 1068).[5] Other decisions carry out this differentiation (compare *Keating v. Hammerstein*, 196 App.Div. 18, 187 N.Y.S. 446, *supra* [accounting for rents and impression of trust on realty; notice of pendency allowed]; and *Small Realty Co. v. Strauss*, 162 App.Div. 658, 147 N.Y.S. 478, *supra* [specific performance of contract to erect specified buildings; notice of pendency allowed], with *Jones v. Armenia Ins. Co.*, 136 App.Div. 453, 121 N.Y.S. 126, *supra* [request for substitution of parties on bond and mortgage, with request for receiver being incidental relief only; no notice allowed]; and *Behrens v. Sturges*, 121 App.Div. 746, 106 N.Y.S. 501 [broker's suit for compensation based on increases in properties' value sought money damages only; no notice allowed]; and *Clark v. McInnis Realty Co.*, 65 Misc. 307, 121 N.Y.S. 683 [purchaser at foreclosure sale not a proper party in suit over ownership of mortgage that did not involve controversy over title to property; no notice allowed]; see, also, 5 Tiffany, *op. cit.*, § 1295; 7A Weinstein–Korn–Miller, N.Y.Civ.Prac., par. 6501.05).

Two other cases demonstrate the niceties of the distinction involved in applying the doctrine. In *Moeller v. Wolkenberg*, 67 App.Div. 487, 73 N.Y.S. 890, the plaintiff sought an injunction to have defendant remove a portion of his building that was encroaching on plaintiff's property and to restrict defendant's further construction that would weaken plaintiff's building. A notice of pendency was deemed proper because the action would limit defendant's use of the property. But a notice of pendency was held inappropriate in another encroachment action when the only relief sought was removal of the offending portions of defendant's building (*McManus v. Weinstein*, 108 App.Div. 301, 95 N.Y.S. 724). *McManus* distinguished *Moeller* on the ground that, in *McManus*, no restriction on the defendant's use of his property was involved (*id.*, at pp. 302–303, 95 N.Y.S. 724).

---

5. Moreover, in a trespass action, alienation of the property would not effectively prevent the court from ultimately awarding the relief requested (*Hailey v. Ano*, 136 N.Y. 569, 575, 32 N.E. 1068), which is the primary purpose of the notice of pendency.

This court has affirmed this strict approach. In *Braunston v. Anchorage Woods*, 10 N.Y.2d 302, 222 N.Y.S.2d 316, 178 N.E.2d 717, plaintiffs brought an action for nuisance for the dumping of surface water on their property. This court held that a notice of pendency was inappropriate in such a suit, which was to recover for a tort rather than to determine a claim of title to property (*id.*, at p. 305, 222 N.Y.S.2d 316, 178 N.E.2d 717). "The usual object of filing a notice of *lis pendens* is to protect some right, title or interest claimed by a plaintiff in the lands of a defendant which might be lost under the recording acts in event of a transfer of the subject property by the defendant to a purchaser for value and without notice of the claim. This is not that kind of situation." (*Id.*, at p. 305, 222 N.Y.S.2d 316, 178 N.E.2d 717.)

III

The "direct relationship" requirement has received its finest application when the action concerns the transfer of a chose in action or other personal property which represents the beneficial ownership of realty. This has most commonly arisen in situations, such as the present, when the transaction was for the sale of stock in a corporation whose sole or primary asset was real estate. Lower courts have placed such suits outside the scope of CPLR 6501 and declined to permit a notice of pendency in those cases. We agree.

As has been shown, the notice of pendency is derived from the *lis pendens*. The common-law rule's potentially harsh effect against innocent purchasers has been alleviated by the statutory filing requirements. Its impact on alienability has also been diminished by authorizing the court to require an undertaking to be posted by the party who files the notice of pendency (CPLR 6515). Nevertheless, many of the concerns over the effect of the *lis pendens* still exist. Consequently, in interpreting the statute, the courts have continued to apply the same, narrow analysis as was invoked at common law. Thus the drastic impact of the notice of pendency authorized by CPLR 6501 requires a strict application of that statute.

In the present action, plaintiff cannot have the advantage of a notice of pendency. Although the prayer for relief seeks a transfer of title, the court must examine the complaint in its entirety. It is apparent from the allegations that the true action is to enforce a contract to sell stock. It is well settled that the property interests of a shareholder and the corporation are distinct. "[T]he corporation in respect of corporate property and rights is entirely distinct from the stockholders who are the ultimate or equitable owners of its assets * * * even complete ownership of capital stock does not operate to transfer the title to corporate property and * * * ownership of capital stock is by no means identical with or equivalent to ownership of corporate property." (*Brock v. Poor*, 216 N.Y. 387, 401, 111 N.E. 229.) To allow plaintiff here to have its notice of pendency would run counter to the *Brock* rule and muddle an otherwise clear concept. Consequently, the notice must be canceled.[7]

Moreover, it is simply improper to use a notice of pendency as a form of attachment (see *Brox v. Riker*, 56 App.Div. 388, 390, 67 N.Y.S. 772, *supra*). But this does not necessarily leave plaintiff, and others similarly situated, with no protective devices whatsoever. The property's conveyance may be blocked by, for example, attachment or injunction. In this way, a party may guard against conduct that will defeat the purpose of a lawsuit, but a court will have an opportunity to review the interference with alienability before it begins to operate.

Other considerations militate against permitting a notice of pendency when the actual subject of the conveyance is stock. It might be easy to justify the notice in the present case where the parties are transferring all of the ownership interest in an entity whose sole business is owning and operating a single office building, but the rule would be far more difficult to apply in other situations. For example, how great an interest must be purchased before a notice of pendency would be permitted? Would 90, 75, or more than 50% be required? Would enough to obtain effective control of the corporation be a sufficiently large interest? Or would any amount, even less than 5%, be adequate? Furthermore, what is to be done if the corporate business is diversified so that its realty ownership is only one facet of its operations? Indeed, the corporate real estate may be only incidental to its primary business (e.g., a manufacturer which owns its factory). To allow a would-be purchaser of stock, particularly of a minority interest, to tie up the corporate real estate merely by filing a complaint and a notice of pendency would be unreasonable.

There is another reason for denying a notice of pendency in cases such as the present. One of this court's paramount goals is to formulate equitable, stable rules by which individuals can reliably order their affairs. The complexity of society requires that exceptions be engrafted to the rules in order to maintain their equity. Exceptions, however, must be reluctantly drawn, lest they proliferate and render the rule meaningless. There is no compelling reason to create an exception to the traditional distinction set forth in *Brock* and, thereby, raise the possibility of future confusion.

7. We have no occasion to consider, as the dissent would invite us to do, whether the special nature of shares in cooperative apartment buildings might require a different result (cf. *Lawlor v. Densmore–Compton Bldg. Co.*, 60 Misc. 555, 112 N.Y.S. 435, affd. no opn. 133 App.Div. 896, 118 N.Y.S. 1120), and, accordingly, that issue is expressly left open. The concerns expressed by the dissent appear to be unfounded. Firstly, nothing in the Insurance Law provisions cited (Insurance Law, § 46, subd. 18; § 432, subd. 2) even suggest that there must be a transfer of title by deed before an interested party can obtain a title insurance policy. Secondly, whether the present transaction, had it been consummated, would have been subject to the Recording Act is not before the court, but it is noted that the very purpose of this type of business deal often is to avoid the transfer of title to realty (which would require compliance with the Recording Act) by instead transferring title to personalty. Lastly, all of the authorities cited by the dissent for the Statute of Frauds question concern cooperative apartments, which, as noted, is not the present situation.

IV

Accordingly, the order of the Appellate Division should be reversed, with costs, and defendants' motion to cancel the notice of pendency should be granted. The question certified is answered in the negative.

JASEN, Judge (dissenting).

I respectfully dissent for the reasons stated in the memorandum opinion of the majority at the Appellate Division (98 A.D.2d 632, 469 N.Y.S.2d 388).

I would only add that, pursuant to CPLR 6501, "[a] notice of pendency may be filed in any action in a court of the state or of the United States in which the judgment demanded would affect the title to, or the possession, use or enjoyment of, real property." It is not disputed that the judgment demanded—specific performance of a contract to compel defendant to transfer full beneficial ownership of 475 Fifth Avenue—would inescapably affect the title to, and the possession, use and enjoyment of a specific parcel of real property. The essence of the instant transaction does not concern recovery of legal tender, securities, or articles of ordinary commerce, but, rather, the conveyance of real property. In recognition of the hybridization of modern applications of corporate law and traditional protections accorded to realty transfers, courts have sought to render such potentially divergent approaches complementary, rather than mutually exclusive. (See, e.g., *Grossfeld v. Beck*, 42 A.D.2d 844, 346 N.Y.S.2d 650 [a *lis pendens* was held applicable in a shareholder's derivative action to impress a constructive trust on certain real property].) Under the plain language of the statute, the instant action for specific performance of what is essentially a contract for the transfer of real property should be subject to the *lis pendens*.

The view of the majority, that a *lis pendens* is inapplicable to a sale of stock representing an interest in real property, constitutes an unwarranted elevation of form over substance, with broad ramifications for the transfer of realty in this State. In an analogous context, the United States Supreme Court has held that the name or label given to a transaction is not dispositive, but, rather, " 'form should be disregarded for substance and emphasis should be on *economic reality*.' " (*United Housing Foundation v. Forman*, 421 U.S. 837, 848, 95 S.Ct. 2051, 2058, 44 L.Ed.2d 621, reh. den. 423 U.S. 884, 96 S.Ct. 157, 46 L.Ed.2d 115, citing *Tcherepnin v. Knight*, 389 U.S. 332, 336, 88 S.Ct. 548, 553, 19 L.Ed.2d 564 [emphasis added].)

By failing to take cognizance of the economic realities involved in this commercial transaction, the majority's view may serve to render inapplicable other devices designed to limit purchaser risks. Inasmuch as the sale of stock representing realty is not a transaction involving real property under the majority's rationale, nor is a sale of shares of stock representing realty considered a transfer of a chattel real (*Matter of State Tax Comm. v. Shor*, 43 N.Y.2d 151, 156, 400 N.Y.S.2d 805, 371 N.E.2d 523), there exists substantial doubt as to whether title insurance companies are empowered to issue title insurance against loss by reason of defective title or encumbrances, upon the transfer of realty by means of a sale of stock. (Insurance Law, § 46, subd. 18; § 432, subd. 2.) There is also question, under the reasoning of the majority, as to whether the transfer of realty by means of a stock transfer would be subject to the protections of the Recording Act. (Real Property Law, § 290; see Note, Legal Characterization of the Individual's Interest in a Cooperative Apartment: Realty or Personalty?, 73 Col.L.Rev. 250, 268–270.) If the transfer of stock intimately intertwined with realty is not to be treated as a real property transfer, nor to be treated as a sale of securities (*United Housing Foundation v. Forman, supra*), the transaction may technically fall outside the scope of the Statute of Frauds (General Obligations Law, § 5–703; Uniform Commercial Code, § 8–319). While the weight of lower court authority suggests that a contract for the purchase of shares of stock representing realty is to be considered a contract for the transfer of real property and, thus, subject to the Statute of Frauds (see, e.g., *Pollard v. Meyer*, 61 A.D.2d 766, 402 N.Y.S.2d 15; *Rosner v. 80 CPW Apts. Corp.*, 73 A.D.2d 39, 424 N.Y.S.2d 723; *Anton Sattler, Inc. v. Cummings*, 103 Misc.2d 4, 425 N.Y.S.2d 476; *Sebel v. Williams*, 88 Misc.2d 411, 388 N.Y.S.2d 494), the majority's position, that traditional protections associated with the transfer of realty are inapplicable to the transfer of realty effected by stock transfer, creates uncertainty in this regard.

Accordingly, I would affirm the order of the Appellate Division denying defendant's motion to vacate the *lis pendens*.

JONES, WACHTLER, MEYER, SIMONS and KAYE, JJ., concur with COOKE, C.J.

JASEN, J., dissents and votes to affirm in a separate opinion.

Order reversed, etc.

NOTES

1. *Off-Record Risks.* Because recording acts have been enacted in every state, and because they so completely dominate the conveyancing system, it is easy to overlook the fact that recording acts only partially displace the common law rule of first in time, first in right. As a result, the common law priorities still govern situations to which the recording acts do not apply.

When will the common law priority, rather than the recording act priority apply? Almost all states today hold that if subsequent purchaser *C* acquired with notice of the prior transfer to *B*, he will not be protected by the recording act and will thus lose out to *B* even though *B* has not recorded. Also, *C* will lose out to adverse possessor *B* even though *C*'s diligently conducted title search would not uncover rights acquired by adverse possession. Nor would it disclose the fact that a deed in the chain of title was forged, undelivered or executed by an incompetent. See Lloyd v. Chicago Title Insurance Co., 576 So.2d 310 (Fla.App.1990) (mortgagee who relied on recorded forged satisfaction of first mortgage is junior to the first mortgage). For a hair-raising catalogue of off-record risks to title, see Straw, Off-Record Risks for Bona Fide Purchasers of Interests in Real Property, 72 Dick.L.Rev. 35 (1967).

Should recording acts be revised to completely preempt the common law priority so that the record is conclusive as to the current state of title? If you were a residential tenant under a short term lease, would you be happy knowing that, under such a regime, your lease could be terminated at any time by a grantee from your landlord unless you had recorded it? Will your answer depend on how easily and cheaply recording can be accomplished?

2. *Unrecordable Instruments.* Another off-record risk arises when the interest that *A* conveyed to *B* is one for which the local recording act does not require recordation. Because recordation is not required, the recording act will not protect the second taker. Thus, *B*, who is first but has not recorded his unrecordable instrument, will prevail over *C*, even though *C* made a title search and recorded promptly. This poses no problem for *C* in states that give an all-encompassing definition to recordable instruments. Arizona, for example, makes any "instrument affecting real property" recordable, Ariz.Rev.Stat.Ann. § 33–411 (1990). Most states, however, specify several exceptions. Some eastern states exempt leases of seven years or less from recording requirements, while western states traditionally except leases of one year or less. Compare Mass.Gen.Laws Ann. c. 183, § 4 (West 1991) with Cal.Civ. Code § 1214 (West 1982 & Supp. 1991).

New York includes within its definition of recordable instruments "every written instrument, by which any estate or interest in real property is created, transferred, mortgaged or assigned, or by which the title to any real property may be affected," but excludes wills, leases for a term of three years or less, executory contracts for the sale of land and instruments containing a power to convey real property as an agent or attorney for the owner of the property. N.Y. Real Prop.Law § 290(3) (McKinney 1989).

3. Why did the plaintiff want to file a notice of lis pendens in *5303 Realty Corp.*? Was it a legitimate use of the lis pendens statute? What did the court see as the purpose behind a notice of lis pendens? What social costs result from a filing? Consider *Braunston*, discussed in *5303 Realty Corp.*, where the court held that no notice of lis pendens could be filed since that suit was essentially a nuisance action. Could the defendants in *Braunston* have counterclaimed for declaration of a prescriptive easement entitling them to divert their surface waters over plaintiff's land and filed a notice of lis pendens against plaintiff's parcel in connection with the counterclaim?

1. TYPES OF STATUTES

JOHNSON, PURPOSE AND SCOPE OF RECORDING STATUTES *

47 Iowa Law Review 231–233 (1962).

The general purpose of the land recording acts is quite clear: it is to provide a public record of transactions affecting title to land. More specific objectives are also readily discernible: (1) to enable interested persons, including public officials such as tax collectors, to ascertain apparent ownership of land; (2) to furnish admissible evidence of title for litigants in a nation where landowners did not adopt the English practice of keeping all former deeds and transferring them with the land; (3) to enable owners of equitable interests to protect such interests by giving notice to subsequent purchasers of the legal title; and (4) to modify the traditional case-law doctrine that purchasers and other transferees, no matter how bona fide, get no better title than the transferor owned. It is no doubt safe to make these generalizations about all of the land recordation statutes in force in the United States, but deeper probing renders generalization hazardous. This is especially true of item four on the above list. The first-in-time rule of priorities is quite logical, but it is of doubtful justice and is utterly incompatible with an economy in which commercial transfers of land occur frequently. But, despite widespread agreement that this doctrine should be changed, the recording acts of the various states and court decisions applying them reflect significant divergence of policy.

A basic policy question is whether emphasis should be upon penalizing those who fail to record or upon protecting those who deserve protection. Conceivably, strict adherence to the penalty approach could lead to requiring recordation as essential to the validity of a deed, even as to the grantor, in addition to the requirements of delivery and writing. On the other hand, it would be consistent with the protection approach to regard unrecorded deeds void only as to those who actually examine the records and who substantially change their positions in reliance thereon. No modern recording act (excluding Torrens acts) goes to either of these extremes. Rather, the impact of both policies—penalty and protection—may be observed in the acts now in force. How these seemingly inconsistent policies have been accommodated is a major question to be considered in this review of the salient features of land recording acts.

I. BASIC TYPES OF STATUTES

Recording acts typically are classified as (1) race, (2) notice, or (3) race-notice. If conveyees are allowed a specified period of time within which to record—a feature which may be added to any of the above types of acts but which is not common today—the statute is also categorized as a "period of grace" act. A recent survey placed the recording acts of only two states, Louisiana and North Carolina, in the race category generally, and those of three other states in that category as to some instruments—mortgages in Arkansas, Ohio, and Pennsylvania (except for purchase money) and oil and gas leases in Ohio. Most states have acts either of the notice or race-notice type, each type having about an equal following.

Of these types, the race statute is most consistent with the penalty principle. The North Carolina act provides: "No conveyance of land ... shall be valid to pass any property, as against lien creditors or purchasers for a valuable consideration ... but from the time of registration thereof ...." [2] Under this act, as construed, an unrecorded conveyance is void even as to a subsequent purchaser who knew of its existence, and a subsequent bona fide purchaser gains no priority over the earlier unrecorded instrument unless he records first. Thus, priority is determined by a race to the records. Of course, an unrecorded conveyance would be valid as to the grantor, his heirs, devisees, donees, and anyone else other than "lien creditors or purchasers for a valuable consideration." The North Carolina act is very similar to the Colonial prototypes. While there are many factors which may have shaped the early acts, it has been asserted that the most significant was a desire to provide a substitute for the publicity afforded by livery of seisin, which had been discarded as a mode of conveyance. In this context there would be a tendency to look upon recording acts as an additional conveyancing formality and to emphasize what was to be required of the grantor rather than what should be the qualifications of those to be protected. Subsequently, probably as a result of experience with actual cases, attention shifted to the latter and to "the view generally accepted in America today that the Recording Acts are an extension of the equitable doctrine of notice." [7]

In some of its applications the race statute seems unfair and out of harmony with the stated objectives of recordation. But instances in which bad faith purchasers are benefited and good faith purchasers are harmed are probably infrequent, and can be almost eliminated by prompt recording. Indeed, the threat of such dire consequences may provide added incentive to prompt recordation. The best argument in favor of the race statute, however, is that it enables the title searcher to rely upon the records without the substantial risk under other types of acts that one will have constructive notice of unrecorded instruments.

A representative "notice" type act is the Iowa statute, which provides: "No instrument affecting real estate is of any validity against subsequent purchasers for a valuable consideration, without notice, unless filed in the office of the recorder of the county in which the same lies, as hereinafter provided." [8] California's act is an example of the "race-notice" type: "Every conveyance of real property ... is void as against any subsequent purchaser or mortgagee of the same property, or any part thereof, in good faith and for a valuable consideration,

---

2. N.C.Gen.Stat. § 47–18 (Supp.1959).   8. Iowa Code § 558.41 (1958).

7. Bordwell, Recording of Instruments Affecting Land, 2 Iowa L.Bull. 51, 52 (1916).

whose conveyance is first duly recorded ...." [9]   Both acts give priority over unrecorded instruments to subsequent purchasers only if they are without notice, and the California act also requires the bona fide purchaser to record first.   The latter is an obvious compromise of the objectives of penalizing nonrecordation and protecting those who are likely to rely upon the records.   By withholding protection from one who has not himself obeyed the statutory mandate to record, the race-notice act may be thought to have the merit of fairness and to encourage recording to a greater extent than would the notice act.   But the seeming fairness of putting beyond the pale of the act both non-recorders is quite superficial, since only one has caused harm.   It is also extremely doubtful that recording is actually stimulated by acts of the race-notice type, since even in a state having a notice type statute failure to record makes those protected by the act vulnerable to subsequent claims.

MATTIS, RECORDING ACTS: ANACHRONISTIC RELIANCE

25 Real Property Probate and Trust Journal 17, 95–96, 98, 99, 100 (1990).

The next step is to determine which type of statute, notice or race-notice, better protects the reliance interest and achieves this fairness goal without unacceptable costs....   The prototypical example is that of an earlier instrument recorded after payment for and delivery of a later instrument, but before the recording of the later instrument. Chronologically: (1) O conveys or mortgages to A. (2) O conveys or mortgages to B, who is without notice. (3) A records before B records. In notice jurisdictions priorities are determined at step (2), and B prevails.   In race-notice jurisdictions priorities are determined at step (3), and A prevails.

Both types of statutes withhold protection from a subsequent taker with notice. Both are fair to A in that regard, unlike the amoral pure race statutes.   B, upon finding A in a vulnerable position, holding an unrecorded interest, cannot wilfully divest A by obtaining a deed or mortgage from O for value and winning a race with A to the court-house. Only the pure notice statute, however, is fair to B, where B has taken her interest without notice of A but then lost the race to the courthouse. Once step (2) has happened, loss to one or the other of A or B is inevitable.   There was never anything that B could have done to avoid it. A could have. To punish the one that did not cause the loss and reward the one who did, on the basis of an event irrelevant to the cause of the loss (step (3)), is unfair.

.   .   .

Efficiency arguments for race-notice might be that by requiring B to record before A to get protection from A : (1) extrinsic evidence about who is the prior and who is the subsequent taker is avoided, and (2)

---

9. Cal.Civ.Code § 1214.

recording is encouraged generally by punishing B for not recording before A.

. . .

To only a limited degree, then, race-notice is more efficient than notice in avoiding extrinsic evidence about which instrument was delivered first in the rare instances when such a controversy might arise. In the great majority of cases the presumption that an instrument was delivered on the date of the instrument is sufficient without extrinsic evidence. The unfairness in the more usual situations when race-notice produces a result different from notice outweighs this small advantage.

. . .

The race-notice methodology for inducing recording is overkill. No person knows at the time of acquiring an interest in Blackacre whether in a future controversy that person will be cast in the role of the prior or the subsequent taker. Relativity is a central tenet of property. To protect B, who has not recorded, from an unrecorded claim of A is not to concede protection to B as against a potential C. If B records after A, she is vulnerable to C because B's out-of-chain recording should not be deemed constructive notice to C. B can now notify potential subsequent takers only by a lawsuit. The peril of B's losing to C is quite sufficient to induce B to get it right the first time by recording in the chain of title, before A. The additional threat of loss to an unknown A is unnecessary.

NOTES

1. Although race statutes and notice statutes rest on sharply divergent conceptual bases, their practical operation is much the same. Whether Blackacre is in a race or a notice jurisdiction, a buyer who is about to acquire the parcel will be well advised to conduct a thorough title search before paying seller and accepting her deed. In a race jurisdiction, only a title search can inform buyer whether there is an outstanding interest adverse to his that has been recorded first. In a notice jurisdiction, a title search will inform buyer of any recorded, adverse interest that will operate to defeat his title under the doctrine of constructive notice. Similarly, once buyer acquires Blackacre, he is well advised, whether in a race or notice jurisdiction, to record his instrument promptly—in a race jurisdiction, in order to win the race to the recorder's office as against any subsequent grantee; in a notice jurisdiction, to give any subsequent grantee constructive notice of his claim.

As a practical matter, race and notice systems differ only in the additional search burden that notice statutes impose on the buyer. Under a race statute, the buyer need do no more than search record title. In a notice jurisdiction, buyer must not only search title, but must also inspect Blackacre for physical evidence of title defects or encumbrances, such as possession by someone other than the seller, putting him on inquiry notice of an adverse claim.

Which system, race or notice, is more efficient? More fair? Do race-notice statutes offer a desirable compromise, or do they only compound the individual defects of race and notice systems?

2. For an additional explanation of the theory and policies of the recording acts, see Schecter, Judicial Lien Creditors Versus Prior Unrecorded Transferees of Real Property: Rethinking the Goals of the Recording System and Their Consequences, 62 S.Cal.L.Rev. 105 (1988) (arguing that a "cost avoidance" rationale explains the system). See also, Berger, An Analysis of the Doctrine that "First in Time is First in Right," 64 Neb.L.Rev. 349 (1985); Mautner, "The Eternal Triangles of the Law:" Toward a Theory of Priorities in Conflicts Involving Remote Parties, 90 Mich.L.Rev. 95 (1991).

2. THE CONDITIONS OF PROTECTION

a. NOTICE

JOHNSON, PURPOSE AND SCOPE OF RECORDING STATUTES *
47 Iowa Law Review 231, 238–243 (1962).

Notice plays two major roles in the recording system. When an instrument is recorded, the record gives constructive notice of its existence and thus may be an important factor in any controversy in which notice is relevant, even in controversies not involving instruments required to be recorded. Even when an instrument is not recorded, notice disqualifies purchasers and creditors from gaining priority and thus, in effect, notice is a substitute for recording. Another way of stating the distinction is to say that in its first role notice aids those who record and in its second role it aids those who do not record.

The policy aspects of these two roles of notice are not identical. To allow notice to substitute for recording at all is debatable, since to do so favors one who was at fault in not recording and tends to weaken the incentive to record. It would seem to follow that notice which disqualifies purchasers and creditors should be narrowly confined. No such consideration is involved in determining what constitutes notice of a recorded instrument. The person who has recorded is not at fault and the only question is whether it would be reasonable, in view particularly of the condition of the records, to expect the party in question to have discovered the recorded instrument. In this situation, there would be no basis for a preference of either a broad or narrow scope of notice. However, the cases do not seem to reflect an awareness of this distinction. Indeed, it is arguable that the scope of notice of recorded interests has been restricted too much and that the scope of notice of unrecorded interests has been unduly expanded.

A. RECORD NOTICE

Although the statutes typically declare that the recording of an instrument shall be notice to "all persons," the courts have generally held that one is given constructive notice only of those recorded instruments which are within his "chain of title." ...

Another example of instruments appearing on the record which are deemed not to be recorded is that where the instrument is not authorized to be on the record, such being true in most states of unacknowledged instruments and instruments of a type not included in the statutory list of recordable instruments. This position has the merit of logic and is probably sound statutory construction, but it is disturbing that purchasers and creditors who could have discovered an instrument by a reasonable search of the records are not deemed to have been given constructive notice. To go further and say that purchasers and creditors may ignore such instruments even if they see them seems unsound, but there is a conflict of authority on this point.

B. NON–RECORD NOTICE

Knowledge of the existence of an unrecorded interest is notice, but notice is broader than knowledge. The most common example is notice of facts which inquiry of the possessor would produce. Implicit here is the policy of protecting only the reasonably cautious, and it is assumed that such persons would not be content with a record search. Granting the soundness of that policy and assumption, the rub is that formulation and application of the required standard of care are likely to be uneven and in some cases too severe.

Thus, there is a conflict as to whether the duty to inquire of the possessor is created by the mere fact of possession or whether it is confined to instances where the fact of possession was known to the purchaser or was discoverable by a reasonable effort. There are also instances of imposition of an unduly severe burden of inquiry. If the purchaser knows, from the record or other sources, that the possessor is a lessee or a tenant in common, the purchaser might reasonably suppose that inquiry would be pointless, nevertheless, in many states he would be charged with notice of additional unrecorded interests of the possessor. According to one view, notice is imparted by such acts as cultivation or erection of improvements by a possessor who does not live on the land, even though such acts point to no one other than the record owner.

But if the purchaser has been abused by the possession-is-notice concept, he has also been spared undeservedly in some instances, particularly where a grantor of a recorded deed remains in possession and claims an unrecorded interest, even though here possession is inconsistent with the record and therefore inquiry-provoking. The unconvincing justification offered for this result is that the "grantor's deed is a conclusive declaration that he has reserved no rights and estops him from setting up any arrangement by which the deed is impaired." [64] This misses the point: the one who has failed to record is always at fault; the relevant question is whether there is notice.

Knowledge of facts unrelated to possession may also raise a duty to inquire, though it appears that, in the absence of such knowledge, a stranger need not investigate the reputation of the title in the community.

Perhaps the most outrageous notice doctrine is that which denies that a purchaser who claims through a quitclaim deed is a bona fide purchaser. In the doctrine's most extreme form, the quitclaim is a bar even though it is remote and inquiry would be unproductive. In this form, the doctrine can hardly be said to be a notice doctrine at all, and justification must be sought in the notion that a quitclaim conveys only what the grantor owns and that a grantor who previously had conveyed his entire interest has nothing left to convey. If this idea is valid, one would expect to encounter it even in states having a race statute, but the Supreme Court of North Carolina has rejected it, saying that it "overlooks the registration statutes," by virtue of which " 'the grantor retains a power to defeat his earlier conveyance.' " [68] Since this power would pass in most states to a donee, devisee, or heir, no reason is apparent why it would not also pass to a quitclaim grantee. If the only effect of the quitclaim is to excite inquiry and charge one with notice of unrecorded interests reasonably discoverable, the question is raised as to what line of inquiry is suggested by the fact that the vendor is reluctant to give more than a quitclaim or that he derives title through a quitclaim. The latter would probably be ignored by the prudent purchaser and the former would, at most, cause a vague suspicion which apparently could not be resolved. It is conceivable, but improbable, that flagrantly suspicious circumstances, though not suggestive of lines of inquiry which would lead to evidence of unrecorded interests, might so strongly indicate lack of title in the grantor that the purchaser would be denied the status of a bona fide purchaser, but the vendor's insistence on giving a quitclaim, standing alone, is hardly such a case. It is generally understood that honest vendors having some confidence in their titles are sometimes unwilling to execute any conveyance other than a quitclaim.

KINCH v. FLUKE

Supreme Court of Pennsylvania, 1933.
311 Pa. 405, 166 A. 905.

KEPHART, Justice.

Kinch and wife, appellants, on September 24, 1923, purchased by written agreement (not recorded) from Robert E. Fluke and James H. O'Rorke, trading as the Home Realty Company, a dwelling house in

---

64. Davis v. Wilson, 237 Iowa 494, 505, 21 N.W.2d 553, 560 (1946).

68. Hayes v. Ricard, 245 N.C. 687, 691–92, 97 S.E.2d 105, 109 (1957).

Altoona, for $6,000. Of this sum $2,261.14 was paid in cash on the execution of the agreement. The balance, $3,738.86, was to be paid in monthly installments of $35 each, with interest on deferred payments. The legal title was in Fluke. On October 8th of the same year, the purchasers entered into open, exclusive, and notorious possession of the premises and occupied it as a dwelling house, residing in it from that time until the present time. Monthly payments were being duly made when, in 1925, Fluke, the vendor, gave a mortgage for $3,000 to the Seaboard Company. It was recorded in January of that year. At the same time, he gave another mortgage for $700 to the Finance Company. It was recorded the same day as the Seaboard mortgage. In December, 1926, Kinch and wife borrowed $4,000 from John C. Peightal and gave a mortgage on the premises as security. With this money, the balance of the purchase money due the vendor was paid. A deed was executed at the same time from Fluke to the appellants. When the purchase price was paid, Kinch and his wife knew nothing of the execution of the two mortgages; neither the Seaboard Company nor the Finance Company made any inquiry as to the condition of Fluke's title by reason of the occupancy of the premises by the appellants.

When appellants desired to borrow the $4,000 above mentioned, they visited an attorney and inquired from him whether he could place the loan. The attorney took up the matter with Peightal. He agreed to make the loan provided he (Peightal) was allowed a commission of $200 for making the loan. When the attorney searched the record for mortgages and other liens, he discovered the two mortgages, but decided the mortgages were not against the land in question, and did not report them to the mortgagees. The loan was made and the commission paid to the attorney, who retained $50 from it and remitted $150 to Peightal.

Appellants, some years later, on discovering the two mortgages as possible liens against their property, brought a bill to remove the cloud on their title imposed by the two mortgages and to obtain a decree of satisfaction as they related to this land. The court below found that the recording of the mortgages to the Seaboard and Finance Companies between the time of the execution of the agreement and the execution of the deed was constructive notice of these liens to Kinch and his wife, the appellants. In addition, the court found that the latter had actual notice of these mortgages through the knowledge their attorney had after searching the record. The court below found that the attorney represented the appellants and the mortgagee. The bill was dismissed, and this appeal followed.

A vendee who purchases land, by entering into open, notorious, and continued possession of it, gives notice, not only of his interest in the land, but that of his vendor. This is true, notwithstanding the fact that the agreement of purchase was not entered of record. Such possession is evidence of title, and, in a certain sense, is a substitute for recording the agreement of purchase, and is sufficient to put a subsequent purchaser or mortgagee on inquiry.

A prospective purchaser is required to make inquiry of those in possession, and, failing to do so, is affected with constructive notice of all that such inquiry would have disclosed. The notice of possession which the law imposes on a subsequent vendee or mortgagee without regard to whether he has actual knowledge or not is of such character that it cannot be controverted. The means of knowledge which possession affords is regarded as the legal equivalent of actual notice.

It is conceded that neither of the mortgagees, the Seaboard or Finance Company, made any inquiry of appellants, who were in possession, as to the nature of their title. The mortgagees, therefore, took subject to the interests under the agreement of sale.

What, then, was the effect of the recording of mortgages on future payments by the vendees, appellants in this case? It has been stated that, where a vendor sells lands by articles of agreement, a subsequent judgment against the vendor binds the legal estate in the vendor, but only to the value of the unpaid purchase money.

As it has been otherwise stated, a judgment against the vendor of land retaining legal title is not so much a lien on the legal title as it is on the unpaid purchase money. These statements of the law are broader than the cases there mentioned will sustain, for they omit any mention of notice to the vendee. The question here involved is whether the recording of a mortgage against the vendor's interest is constructive notice of the lien of that mortgage to vendees in possession under an agreement of sale.

The purpose of recording mortgages or of entering judgment is to give notice of its existence to those who subsequently acquire an interest in or lien upon the property. It is sometimes said "that the record of a deed [or mortgage] is constructive notice to all the world." That, it is evident, is too broad and unqualified an enunciation of the doctrine. Recording is constructive notice only to those who are bound to search for it, subsequent purchasers and mortgagees, and, perhaps, all others who deal with or on the credit of the title, in the line of which the recorded deed (or mortgage) belongs.

The assignment of a mortgage by an instrument duly executed, or the assignment of such mortgage on the margin of the mortgage record, is not such legal notice to the mortgagor as will preclude him from setting up payments made by him to the mortgagee before he has actual notice of the assignment. In order to complete the assignee's right with respect to such an assignment, the law requires actual notice be given to the mortgagor of the assignment. The recording act imposes no duty on the mortgagor to search the record for the purpose of ascertaining whether the mortgagee has assigned the mortgage. To do so would impose too great a burden on the mortgagor. Actual notice must be given to the mortgagor of the assignment.

It has also been held that the docketing of a judgment is not notice of the lien to a purchaser in possession, since, after he has made his contract for the purchase and entered into possession, he is not bound to keep the run of the dockets, and payments subsequently made by him to the vendor pursuant to the contract without actual notice of the judgment are valid as against such liens.

We held in Riddle v. Berg Co., 7 A. 232, 3 Sad. 566, where land was held pursuant to an article of agreement, and before the date of final payment a promissory note was given for the final payment, that it was not the duty of the purchaser, who has given such note in payment of the balance due on the purchase price, to watch the record and, when a judgment is entered, inform the judgment plaintiff of the existence of the note and the possibility of its being negotiated.

If the recording of an assignment of a mortgage, or the docketing of a judgment, is not effective as constructive notice to the vendee of land when payments are to be made by the vendee to the mortgagor or judgment debtor, but actual notice is essential, how then can the rule of law be that the mere recording of a mortgage is effective as constructive notice to the vendee who purchased and was in actual possession of the land before the existence of such mortgage. The mortgagee has ample opportunity to ascertain the state of the possessor's title, the amount of purchase money due the mortgagor, and is given ample opportunity to effectuate his lien by notifying the vendee under articles of his mortgage or judgment. We can readily see where land is sold by articles of agreement, and the purchaser does not go into possession, that his subsequent payment of purchase money to the vendor must be at his peril if judgments or mortgages have been entered in the interim. Such lienholders have no means of information (apart from actual notice) that the mortgagor or judgment debtor has parted with his title. The rule must be otherwise as to the sale of land under articles of agreement where possession is taken thereunder and held openly, continuously, and notoriously. The opportunity is then afforded to the mortgagee of completing his lien by actual notice to the vendee in possession. We, therefore, conclude that the recording of a mortgage or docketing of a judgment is not constructive notice of a lien on land to a vendee then in possession under an agreement of sale. The mortgage operates as an assignment of the balance of the purchase money due, but actual notice is required to make it effective. In other words, the lien of a mortgage or judgment, whether or not recorded or docketed, on the unpaid purchase money due from a vendee of land in possession under an agreement of sale, is not effective so as to require payment of the unpaid purchase money to the mortgagee or holder of the judgment unless actual notice of such mortgage or judgment has been given to the vendee in possession.

If the rule were otherwise in the instant case, before each monthly payment was made, it would be necessary for the purchasers to inquire from the mortgage record whether the vendor had assigned the balance of the purchase money due. This is an unwarranted burden.

. . .

The next question involved is whether appellants received actual notice of the two mortgages against this land given by Fluke, one of appellees, by reason of the search made by the attorney. A careful analysis of this record convinces us that the attorney did not act for both parties; that his employment was by the mortgagee, Peightal, and not by appellants. However, conceding his agency was for both appellants and the mortgagee, it was not for both as to all transactions involved; the attorney was agent for appellants to secure the money; he was agent for the mortgagee to obtain proper security for the money by examining title and preparing the proper documents to evidence the security. Any information the attorney acquired while conducting transactions in behalf of one may not be considered as within his knowledge as agent of the other for different purposes.

. . .

Furthermore, assuming that he was attorney for appellants, they would be affected only with the notice of the record which was fairly within the knowledge of the attorney. Upon examination of the record, we find that the attorney had no knowledge or notice of the existence of these two mortgages as liens on this particular land. He was asked the question, and it was not contradicted:

"Q. You say now that you didn't know of the existence of any lien or incumbrances or mortgages on this Kinch property when you made the examination? A. Yes. That is what I stated to you.

"Q. And you have now just put on the record your statement that you didn't have any knowledge of the mortgage of the Seaboard Insurance Company of $3,000 and the mortgage of the Finance Company of America of $700? A. No. I will explain that this way. I had knowledge of these two mortgages but did not have knowledge of the fact that they were liens of this property.

"Q. Then you were mistaken in the liens on this property? A. I was mistaken in the two descriptions in these two mortgages. That they were not identical with the description in the deed.

"Q. Did you make any effort to determine whether the two descriptions embraced in these two mortgages were the same as the property which was conveyed by Fluke to Kinch? A. I made my examination as I always do. I got the list of the mortgages against the person in the title. And then the description in the mortgage and if I believe they are not liens against the property I check them off. That is what I did here.

"Q. How long after this loan of Peightal's was closed did you find that these two mortgages covered the Kinch property? A. Not until Mr. Robert Hare came up to the office and informed me.

"Q. That was the first information you had? A. Yes. That was the first I had.

"Q. That was how long after the date of the Peightal mortgage? A. I will go the other way. I think that was possibly a year ago, as near as I can recollect.

"Q. Approximately four years after the date of the Peightal mortgage? A. That was about the time. The Peightal mortgage was in 1926."

We do not have before us a copy of the mortgages, and, as a result, are unable to ascertain from an inspection thereof whether Culp's (the attorney's) statement was justified, but the testimony clearly demonstrates that a title searcher would be misled by the description in the mortgage when attempting to trace title from the description in the deed. A principal is not to be affected with knowledge of his agent unless his agent has, or could have had within his duty, the knowledge with which it is sought to affect him; if the agent did not know, then, of course, his principal could not know.

We conclude that the court below was in error in dismissing the bill.

The decree of the court below must be reversed, the bill reinstated, with direction to enter a decree in accordance with the prayer of the bill, costs to be paid by appellee.

SANBORN v. McLEAN

Supreme Court of Michigan, 1925.
233 Mich. 227, 206 N.W. 496.

WEIST, J. Defendant Christina McLean owns the west 35 feet of lot 86 of Green Lawn subdivision, at the northeast corner of Collingwood avenue and Second boulevard, in the city of Detroit, upon which there is a dwelling house, occupied by herself and her husband, defendant John A. McLean. The house fronts Collingwood avenue. At the rear of the lot is an alley. Mrs. McLean derived title from her husband, and, in the course of the opinion, we will speak of both as defendants. Mr. and Mrs. McLean started to erect a gasoline filling station at the rear end of their lot, and they and their contractor, William S. Weir, were enjoined by decree from doing so and bring the issues before us by appeal. Mr. Weir will not be further mentioned in the opinion.

Collingwood avenue is a high grade residence street between Woodward avenue and Hamilton boulevard, with single, double, and apartment houses, and plaintiffs, who are owners of land adjoining and in the vicinity of defendants' land, and who trace title, as do defendants, to the proprietors of the subdivision, claim that the proposed gasoline station will be a nuisance per se, is in violation of the general plan fixed for use of all lots on the street for residence purposes only, as evidenced by restrictions upon 53 of the 91 lots fronting on Collingwood avenue, and that defendants' lot is subject to a reciprocal negative easement barring a use so detrimental to the enjoyment and value of its neighbors. Defendants insist that no restrictions appear in their chain of title and they purchased without notice of any reciprocal negative easement, and deny that a gasoline station is a nuisance per se. We find no occasion to pass upon the question of nuisance, as the case can be decided under the rule of reciprocal negative easement.

This subdivision was planned strictly for residence purposes, except lots fronting Woodward avenue and Hamilton boulevard. The 91 lots on Collingwood avenue were platted in 1891, designed for and each one sold solely for residence purposes, and residences have been erected upon all of the lots. Is defendants' lot subject to a reciprocal negative easement? If the owner of two or more lots, so situated as to bear the relation, sells one with restrictions of benefit to the land retained, the servitude becomes mutual, and, during the period of restraint, the owner of the lot or lots retained can do nothing forbidden to the owner of the lot sold. For want of a better descriptive term this is styled a reciprocal negative easement. It runs with the land sold by virtue of express fastening and abides with the land retained until loosened by expiration of its period of service or by events working its destruction. It is not personal to owners, but operative upon use of the land by any owner having actual or constructive notice thereof. It is an easement passing its benefits and carrying its obligations to all purchasers of land, subject to its affirmative or negative mandates. It originates for mutual benefit and exists with vigor sufficient to work its ends. It must start with a common owner. Reciprocal negative easements are never retroactive; the very nature of their origin forbids. They arise, if at all, out of a benefit accorded land retained, by restrictions upon neighboring land sold by a common owner. Such a scheme of restriction must start with a common owner; it cannot arise and fasten upon one lot by reason of other lot owners conforming to a general plan. If a reciprocal negative easement attached to defendants' lot, it was fastened thereto while in the hands of the common owner of it and neighboring lots by way of sale of other lots with restrictions beneficial at that time to it. This leads to inquiry as to what lots, if any, were sold with restrictions by the common owner before the sale of defendants' lot. While the proofs cover another avenue, we need consider sales only on Collingwood.

December 28, 1892, Robert J. and Joseph R. McLaughlin, who were then evidently owners of the lots on Collingwood avenue, deeded lots 37 to 41 and 58 to 62, inclusive, with the following restrictions:

"No residence shall be erected upon said premises which shall cost less than $2,500, and nothing but residences shall be erected upon said premises. Said residences shall front on Helene (now Collingwood) avenue and be placed no nearer than 20 feet from the front street line."

July 24, 1893, the McLaughlins conveyed lots 17 to 21 and 78 to 82, both inclusive, and lot 98 with the same restrictions. Such restrictions were imposed for the benefit of the lands held by the grantors to carry out the scheme of a residential district, and a restrictive negative easement attached to the lots retained, and title to lot 86 was then in the McLaughlins. Defendants' title, through mesne conveyances, runs back to a deed by the McLaughlins dated September 7, 1893, without restrictions mentioned therein. Subsequent deeds to other lots were executed by the McLaughlins, some with restrictions and some without. Previous to September 7, 1893, a reciprocal negative easement had attached to lot 86 by acts of the owners, as before mentioned, and such easement is still attached and may now be enforced by plaintiffs, provided defendants, at the time of their purchase, had knowledge, actual or constructive, thereof. The plaintiffs run back with their title, as do defendants, to a common owner. This common owner, as before stated, by restrictions upon lots sold, had burdened all the lots retained with reciprocal restrictions. Defendants' lot and plaintiff Sanborn's lot, next thereto, were held by such common owner, burdened with a reciprocal negative easement, and, when later sold to separate parties, remained burdened therewith, and right to demand observance thereof passed to each purchaser with notice of the easement. The restrictions were upon defendants' lot while it was in the hands of the common owners, and abstract of title to defendants' lot showed the common owners, and the record showed deeds of lots in the plat restricted to perfect and carry out the general plan and resulting in a reciprocal negative easement upon defendants' lot and all lots within its scope, and defendants and their predecessors in title were bound by constructive notice under our recording acts. The original plan was repeatedly declared in subsequent sales of lots by restrictions in the deeds, and, while some lots sold were not so restricted, the purchasers thereof, in every instance, observed the general plan and purpose of the restrictions in building residences. For upward of 30 years the united efforts of all persons interested have carried out the common purpose of making and keeping all the lots strictly for residences, and defendants are the first to depart therefrom.

When Mr. McLean purchased on contract in 1910 or 1911, there was a partly built dwelling house on lot 86, which he completed and now occupies. He had an abstract of title which he examined and claims he was told by the grantor that the lot was unrestricted. Considering the character of use made of all the lots open to a view of Mr. McLean when he purchased, we think, he was put thereby to inquiry, beyond asking his grantor, whether there were restrictions. He had an abstract showing the subdivision and that lot 86 had 97 companions. He could not avoid noticing the strictly uniform residence character given the lots by the expensive dwellings thereon, and the least inquiry would have quickly developed the fact that lot 86 was subjected to a reciprocal negative easement, and he could finish his house, and, like the others, enjoy the benefits of the easement. We do not say Mr. McLean should have asked his neighbors about restrictions, but we do say that with the notice he had from a view of the premises on the street, clearly indicating the residences were built and the lots occupied in strict accordance with a general plan, he was put to inquiry, and, had he inquired, he would have found of record the reason for such general conformation, and the benefits thereof serving the owners of lot 86 and the obligations running with such service and available to adjacent lot owners to prevent a departure from the general plan by an owner of lot 86.

While no case appears to be on all fours with the one at bar, the principles we have stated, and the conclusions announced, are supported by Allen v. City of Detroit, 167 Mich. 464.

We notice the decree in the circuit directed that the work done on the building be torn down. If the portion of the building constructed can be utilized for any purpose within the restrictions, it need not be destroyed.

With this modification, the decree in the circuit is affirmed, with costs to plaintiffs.

NOTES

1. *Standard Operating Procedures.* Three forms of notice will operate to defeat subsequent purchasers under notice and race-notice statutes:

(a) *Actual notice* (the notice given by the subsequent purchaser's actual knowledge of the prior transfer);

(b) *Inquiry notice,* sometimes called *implied actual notice* (the notice given by the subsequent purchaser's actual knowledge of facts that, if reasonably inquired into, would produce actual knowledge of the prior transfer);

(c) *Constructive notice,* sometimes called *record notice* (the notice given by the prior transfer's recordation in the public title records so that the subsequent purchaser, conducting a reasonable title search, would obtain actual knowledge of the transfer).

These three forms of notice effectively prescribe the standard operating procedure that a purchaser in notice and race-notice jurisdictions should follow up to the moment of closing: (a) search files, desk drawers and memory for any communications or facts that might have given actual knowledge; (b) inspect the land for physical evidence of an interest held by someone other than the immediate seller; and (c) conduct a title search for documentary evidence of an interest held by someone other than the immediate seller. A purchaser in a race jurisdiction need only conduct a title search to determine whether anyone has beaten him, or any predecessor in title, to the recorder's office. And, in all jurisdictions, standard operating procedure requires the buyer to record his own instrument of transfer immediately after closing.

There is some interplay between actual, inquiry and constructive notice. For example, it is generally held that recordation of an unrecordable instrument, such as an unacknowledged deed, will not give constructive notice of the instrument's contents. See, for example, Metropolitan National Bank v. United States, 901 F.2d 1297 (5th

Cir.1990). But the instrument will give *actual* notice to a title examiner who comes upon the recordation in the course of his or her search. Since, as a practical matter, buyers will almost invariably order title searches before paying their purchase money, they will, in the course of reviewing their examiner's title report, obtain actual notice of recorded, but unrecordable, instruments. Would you ever advise a client *not* to order a title search on the off-chance that he can thus avoid learning of an earlier transaction embodied in a recorded but unrecordable instrument?

2. *Extent of Records Search.* Typically, one must search for documents affecting real property at the office of the recorder of deeds. A title searcher must also check certain other public records, such as probate records, the judgment docket, and tax filings, that disclose interests in the land. Ellingsen v. Franklin County, 117 Wash.2d 24, 810 P.2d 910 (1991), distinguished between those filings in public offices that give constructive notice and those that do not. The county claimed that the owners of land had constructive notice of the county's claim of a roadway over the property as a result of the county's filing of a petition for the establishment of a road in the office of the county engineer in 1908. The court held, however, that although the statute provided that the engineer "shall be an office of record," those filings were only to provide information to the public about locations of roads, bridges, and ditches and were not intended serve as notice of prior interests in land. The court contrasted the language of the engineer statute with the general recording act which indicated that a document filed thereunder "shall be notice to the world." The court explained its unwillingness to broadly construe the engineer statute as providing constructive notice of prior interests in property:

> If it were held that a document is constructive notice of its content because it is designated a public record or because the office in which it is filed is an office of record, the consequences would be disastrous to the stability and certainty heretofore provided by recording with the county auditor and the grantor-grantee index required by RCW 65.04. This prediction of chaos is a natural consequence of reading RCW 42.17 which makes an all-inclusive definition of "public record". RCW 42.17–020(26). Such public record is every writing containing information relating to the conduct of government or the performance of any governmental or proprietary function. ...

> The records which are declared to be public records are those of defined state and local agencies including: (1) every state (a) office, (b) department, (c) division, (d) bureau, (e) board, (f) commission, or (g) other state agency, and (2) every local agency, *i.e.,* every (a) county, (b) city, (c) town, (d) municipal corporation, (e) quasimunicipal corporation, or (f) special purpose district or (g) other local public agency. RCW 42.17.020(1).

Under the County's theory all records of these multiple, scattered public offices would impart constructive notice of everything contained in those records because, like the engineer's office, those are public records in public offices. ... To import constructive notice from every piece of paper or computer file in every government office, from the smallest hamlet to the largest state agency, would wreak havoc with the land title system. As a matter of fact, it would render impossible a meaningful title search.

Id. at 29, 810 P.2d at 913.

3. *Inquiry Notice from Inspection of Land.* One fact that is universally held to put a purchaser on inquiry notice is possession by someone other than his seller. Often in these circumstances the possessor will be a tenant, and the purchaser will thus be placed on notice not only of the tenant's rights under its lease, but of any other rights, such as an option to purchase the property. See Vitale v. Pinto, 118 A.D.2d 774, 500 N.Y.S.2d 283 (1986). Occasionally the possessor will claim ownership of the land through adverse possession or through a prior deed from the present seller or some other owner. See Bump v. Dahl, 26 Wis.2d 607, 133 N.W.2d 295 (1965) (grading, sodding, planting and landscaping of parcel gave subsequent purchaser inquiry notice of prior purchaser's possessory claim).

In some situations, however, physical presence may not give inquiry notice. For example, in Lamb v. Lamb, 569 N.E.2d 992 (Ind.App.1991), a tenant in common entered into a contract to purchase the interests of the other cotenants. Brush cutting by the tenant on the property did not give inquiry notice of his contract to subsequent purchasers since he did not reveal his ownership when asked by the subsequent purchasers and his actions were not so unusual for a cotenant that any further inquiry was required. A statute may also alter the rules. See N.M.Stat.Ann. § 14-9-3 (possession based on an unrecorded executory real estate contract does not give a subsequent purchaser notice or a duty to inquire about the possession).

Nonpossessory interests are more problematic. Will manhole covers suffice to put a purchaser on inquiry notice of an easement for an underlying sewer line? Compare Lake Meredith Development Co. v. City of Fritch, 564 S.W.2d 427 (Tex.Civ.App.1978) (yes) with Fanti v. Welsh, 152 W.Va. 233, 161 S.E.2d 501 (1968) (no). Wolek v. Di Feo, 60 N.J.Super. 324, 159 A.2d 127 (1960), found no inquiry notice, notwithstanding an easement holder's argument that "in the quiet hours of the evening" the purchaser "must have heard the rush of water through the underground pipes." Even public utility easements, offering more clearly visible clues such as power lines and support poles, have been treated differently within the same jurisdiction. Compare Florida Power & Light Co. v. Rader, 306 So.2d 565 (Fla.App.Dist. 4 1975) with McDaniel v. Lawyers' Title Guaranty Fund, 327 So.2d 852 (Fla.App. Dist. 2 1976). For an in depth analysis, see Eichengrun, The Problem of Hidden Easements and the Subsequent Purchaser Without Notice, 40 Okla.L.Rev. 3 (1987).

4. *Inquiry Notice from Inspection of Record.* To what extent will a recorded instrument trigger a duty of further inquiry? The question arises when a recorded instrument has obviously been altered, or phrased in an unusual way, or when a title search reveals only a partial conveyance to the purchaser's grantor or some predecessor in title, and no indication whether, or to whom, the other parts were conveyed. Courts generally hold purchasers to notice of all facts they could have discovered through reasonable inquiry into the discrepancy. See, for example, Mister Donut of America, Inc. v. Kemp, 368 Mass. 220, 330 N.E.2d 810 (1975). See also, Smith v. Arrow Transportation Co., 571 So.2d 1003 (Ala.1990) (claimant's initials following clause in deed naming corporation owned by claimant's husband as grantee did not give constructive notice to subsequent purchaser that claimant had an interest in the property).

The same question arises when an instrument that is disclosed by the title search refers to one that is not disclosed, as when a deed recites that the property is subject to a mortgage and the mortgage is unrecorded. Here, too, courts impose a duty of reasonable inquiry. Many legislatures, however, have acted to relax the duty. Massachusetts, for example, requires that a reference be "definite" in order to put purchasers on notice. An "indefinite reference" is one that recites interests created by unrecorded or improperly recorded documents, ambiguous descriptions of the interest, an indication that the holder of the interest is a "trustee" when the trust is not of record, or any reference that does not disclose where the instrument is recorded. Mass.Gen.Laws Ann. c. 184, § 25 (West 1991). Recitals in Wisconsin must indicate the place of recording or specify "by positive statement" the nature and scope of the outstanding interest and the identity of the holder of the interest. Wis.Stat.Ann. § 706.09(1)(b) (West 1991).

Can you reconcile these rules with the general rule that an instrument, even though it is in the chain of title, will not give constructive notice if it is missing one of the formalities, such as acknowledgement, required of recordable instruments under the recording act?

5. Would the same result have been reached in Kinch v. Fluke if Kinch had been a tenant exercising an option to buy under an unrecorded lease? If Kinch had been a purchaser under a marketing contract and, after paying ten percent down, paid the remainder in a lump sum at closing without a further title search? Was the court correct to conclude that, in searching title, the lawyer was acting only as Peightal's agent? Was it correct to conclude that the attorney's legal judgment on the irrelevance of the two mortgages meant that he "had no knowledge or notice of the existence of these two mortgages as liens on this particular land"?

On the last two questions, compare Farr v. Newman, 14 N.Y.2d 183, 250 N.Y.S.2d 272, 199 N.E.2d 369 (1964), in which plaintiff, who had entered into an unrecorded contract to purchase a parcel for $3,000, sought specific performance against defendant who purchased the parcel for $4,000 before plaintiff's contract was to close, but not before plaintiff informed defendant's attorney of plaintiff's outstanding contract. Holding for plaintiff, the court of appeals noted first that "even if the plaintiff had not affirmatively relied upon the agency of the attorney by giving notice, and the attorney had merely discovered plaintiff's equity in the course of his title investigation, the principal would still be bound by such knowledge. A conflict of interest does not avoid the imputation of knowledge." 199 N.E.2d 373, 14 N.Y.2d 190, 250 N.Y.S.2d 278. The court also ruled that the lawyer's mistaken conclusion as to the contract's unenforceability did not insulate his client from knowledge. Indeed, the mistake defeated any claim of attorney fraud that might have avoided the principal's liability for the agent's conduct.

Farr is in line with the general trend to follow agency rules and impute the lawyer's knowledge to the client. What result should be reached if the attorney, chosen by purchaser from the title insurance company's list of approved attorneys, fails to inform the title company of a defect discovered in the course of the title search? Should the lawyer's knowledge be imputed to the purchaser, with the result that the title company is relieved of liability under the provision in its policy excepting coverage for defects known to the insured at the time the policy was issued? For the startling answer, see Weir v. City Title Ins. Co., 125 N.J.Super. 23, 308 A.2d 357 (1973).

6. What policies would be served, and what policies would be disserved, if states were to drop the inquiry notice bar? The actual notice bar? Representing a buyer, how comfortable would you feel knowing that every tramped-down footpath or half-remembered conversation may later form the basis for a finding of inquiry or actual notice? In terms of fairness or efficiency, what is wrong with a pure race regime?

b.   PURCHASER FOR VALUE

JOHNSON, PURPOSE AND SCOPE OF RECORDING STATUTES *

47 Iowa Law Review 231, 233–237 (1962).

According to one view, the recording acts benefit as purchasers those who have parted with only nominal consideration, but most courts appear to require something more substantial. The latter position is obviously sound if there is to be any real distinction between purchasers and donees.

On the other hand, one who parts with value in reliance upon the record is not necessarily protected. Some courts declare that this is the

---

fate of one who receives notice of the unrecorded instrument after having parted with the consideration but prior to execution of the deed. The thought seems to be that such a person is not a "purchaser." Of course, the equitable doctrine of bona fide purchaser protected only those who acquired a legal title, but the recording acts are much broader and are now generally deemed to protect those who have acquired equitable interests. As a matter of policy, there would seem to be no reason for attaching significance to the execution of the deed. The time when protection is needed is the moment when consideration is given. This problem is most likely to arise when the contract provides for payment of the consideration over a period of years and the execution of a deed at or near the end of that period. It is generally recognized that one who has acquired the legal title but who has paid only a portion of the purchase price before he acquires notice is a pro tanto bona fide purchaser and, as such, entitled at least to a lien and in some cases to the legal title, subject to a lien in the adverse party. The same should be true of a purchaser who has only a contract and there is authority to that effect. Essentially the same problem is raised in a race-notice jurisdiction when notice is received after delivery of the deed but prior to its recordation. The conclusion seems sound that "after having paid the consideration and received a conveyance, the purchaser is qualified to race for priority of record unhampered by any notice that he may thereafter receive." [20]

Other limitations on the protection accorded purchasers by the recording system may be briefly noted. Although a lessee is considered a purchaser, as a practical matter this means very little to the lessee, since he is protected only to the extent of rent paid prior to notice and must vacate the premises at the end of the period for which such rent was paid. This may result in a great hardship when the lessee has made expensive improvements or has otherwise substantially changed his position, as a lessee for a long term may well have done. A mortgagee also comes within the broad category "purchaser," but not when the mortgage is given to secure an antecedent debt, according to the majority view. Not to be overlooked is the omnipresent threat to all groups of recording act beneficiaries that they will be charged with notice of claims which they could not reasonably be expected to discover. This subject will not be explored at this point, but one example may be noted. Consider the burden imposed upon the purchaser who is paying the price in installments by holding that he gets notice of a prior unrecorded deed whenever it is recorded, which means that he must examine the records immediately before paying each installment.

The protection afforded creditors by the recording acts of about half the states is not easy to justify. It is doubtful that more than a few creditors examine the deed records before extending credit. The creditor is more interested in the general financial status of his debtor than he is in the debtor's ownership of particular realty, though, of course,

20. 4 American Law of Property § 17.-11, at 574 (Casner ed. 1952).

the former may be affected by the latter. While apparent land owner-ship is taken into account in the preparation of reports by credit investigation concerns, the deed records are not usually consulted for this purpose and a thorough title search is probably never made. Even if a creditor has relied upon the records in extending credit, he is generally protected only if he acquires a lien by attachment or by judgment without notice, despite an unqualified statutory reference to "creditors." The policy basis for making the acquisition of a lien the crucial event qualifying the creditor for protection is far from clear. It may be reasonable to suppose that an attaching creditor relies upon apparent ownership (though a thorough title search would rarely be made), but this is not likely to be true of the judgment creditor, and in both cases the change of position consists only of the slight expense involved in obtaining the lien. Even the acquisition of a lien may not be sufficient in a race-notice state, it having been held that the creditor must also obtain a recordable instrument, such as a sheriff's deed, and record it prior to the recording of the adverse interests.

In some states, the reliance factor is clearly not in the creditor picture at all. These are states whose courts have held, surprisingly, that the creditor is protected even though he had notice, usually on the basis of an exceedingly doubtful construction of the statutory phrase "void as to creditors and subsequent purchasers for valuable consider-ation without notice." This result might make sense in terms of a policy of penalizing the failure to record by conferring title upon the nearest bystander, but to show greater favor to creditors than to bona fide purchasers, which is exactly the reverse of the relative esteem for these two groups in equity, is indefensible.

In view of the favored position accorded attachment and judgment lien creditors, it is strange that others with claims as good, or better, go unprotected. Consider the mechanics' lien claimant. It has been held that a contractor who erects a house pursuant to a contract with the record owner of the land is denied a mechanics' lien if the record owner had previously conveyed the land to a grantee who failed to record his deed, and who thus reaps a windfall. In states whose recording acts protect purchasers but not creditors, this result has been based upon the ground that a mechanics' lien claimant is not a "purchaser." In one state which protects creditors against unrecorded interests, the question whether a mechanics' lien claimant is a "creditor" was avoid-ed by pointing to the provision of the mechanics' lien statute requiring that the contract be entered into with the "owner" or with his consent, a typical provision in such statutes. Consider also the creditor who seeks security for an existing debt by securing a mortgage, rather than an attachment. As has been observed, he is generally not protected as a "purchaser," but is there any reason why he should be refused protection as a "creditor"? Must the lien be one created by operation of law rather than by agreement? General statements in treatises and judicial opinions containing no hint that a lien other than by attach-ment or judgment will suffice are commonplace. At least one court has held against the mortgagee without considering whether he might be a "creditor." There is authority, however, that he is a "creditor."

GABEL v. DREWRYS LTD., USA, INC.

Supreme Court of Florida, 1953.
68 So.2d 372.

DREW, Justice.

McCaffrey was a beer distributor and became indebted to Drewrys Limited, U.S.A., Inc., for beer in a sum exceeding $20,000. Drewrys received several "rubber" checks from McCaffrey and stopped beer shipments to him. A conference was arranged and as a result McCaffrey gave Drewrys a *demand* note for $10,000 of the debts, secured by a mortgage dated June 30, 1950, on the property involved in this suit. The mortgage was in the usual form and contained a provision for the payment, by the mortgagor, of "costs, charges and expenses ... including reasonable attorney's fees ...." The record discloses that at the same time additional notes, secured by chattel mortgages, were given to make up the balance of the debt.

Concurrently, McCaffrey and Drewrys entered into an agreement which recited the debt due from McCaffrey to Drewrys, the fact that the former did not then have assets to pay it, and that Drewrys had "agreed to accept a note, or notes, payable to its order in the above amount together with certain securities consisting of lien on real and personal property, and to *forbear for the time being any action to enforce the collection of said sum due and owing it* ... said forbearance, however, to be conditioned upon (McCaffrey) making the payments as provided in said notes ..." (Emphasis supplied).

Prior to the time of giving the notes and mortgage, Drewrys had caused the public records to be examined to see that there were no liens against the properties encumbered by the mortgage and found none.

There is some evidence as to the oral statements on forbearance which took place at the time the mortgage was given. Drewrys' attorney testified:

"Q. Now, what period of time did you agree to forbear suit against him? A. *Well, there was no specific date fixed in there.* It was depending on what activity Mr. McCaffrey made in taking care of his obligations and how soon he was able to get this money he was counting on that he said he was going to have. We were going to let him get started with his new operations and capital. *I think within a reasonable time. We had nothing we could lose.* We could have gone ahead into Court and filed an attachment and gotten the advantage through a prior lien through an attachment suit, and he begged almost with tears in his eyes, he begged us to not put him out of business, if we would give him a chance." (Emphasis supplied).

Drewrys' agent testified:

"Q. How much time did you extend to him in not filing suit if he would give you this security? A. *There was no element of time involved in the filing of a suit.* There was no conversation about filing of a suit.

. . .

"Q. You didn't extend any time to him then? A. *There was no extension of time, as you put it, and there was no demand made at the same time.*" (Emphasis added).

The Drewrys mortgage was then promptly recorded although Drewrys did not resume beer shipments to McCaffrey as he said Drewrys had agreed to. McCaffrey became more involved and a few months later appellant Gabel, who held a note from McCaffrey in the principal sum of $2,750, secured by a mortgage on the same real estate as covered by the Drewrys mortgage, said note and mortgage being dated March 14, 1950, but not filed for record, read in the paper that McCaffrey "was in trouble." Whereupon Gabel recorded his mortgage.

Later, Drewrys filed suit to foreclose its mortgage, making Gabel a party. The latter filed a cross-claim to foreclose his mortgage. The learned Circuit Judge, after personally hearing the evidence, entered a final decree holding the Drewrys mortgage to be superior to the Gabel lien and finding:

"2. The consideration for the note executed by the defendant, James McCaffrey and the mortgage executed by the defendants, James McCaffrey and Mary C. McCaffrey, his wife, to the plaintiff *was the forbearance on the part of the plaintiff* to prosecute any legal action against the said defendant, James McCaffrey, for the enforcement of his obligation to the plaintiff at the time of the execution thereof, for an indebtedness in amount of Ten Thousand Dollars ($10,000.00) as represented by said note, as well as an additional indebtedness of approximately Eleven Thousand Dollars ($11,000.00), said note and mortgage being the basis of the plaintiff's complaint.

"3. The plaintiff had no notice of the mortgage held by the defendant, L.A. Gabel, and that the failure of said defendant, L.A. Gabel, to have his mortgage recorded at the time of the execution and recording of the mortgage held by the plaintiff, misled the plaintiff in accepting security for the indebtedness due it, or a portion thereof, in lieu of taking legal action at said time to secure the collection of said indebtedness from the defendant, James McCaffrey, to the plaintiff." (Emphasis added).

Gabel argues that since the agreement to forbear was for no definite time, it amounted to no enforceable right on the part of McCaffrey, hence it was of no benefit to him or detriment to Drewrys, and did not constitute sufficient consideration, and in support cites Strong v. Sheffield, 144 N.Y. 392, 39 N.E. 330. Also cited by appellant were Mitchell v. Harper, 80 Fla. 338, 86 So. 246; Kreiss Potassium Phosphate Co. v. Knight, 98 Fla. 1004, 124 So. 751, regarding consideration to support extension of time for payment. On the other hand, Drewrys says whether the agreement to forbear was for any definite time, or was enforceable by McCaffrey, is immaterial, because in fact there was a forbearance of benefit to the debtor and a detriment to Drewrys. It cites in support of its position, among others, 36 Am.Jur. 795, § 205. Drewrys also cites Sweeney v. Bixler, 69 Ala. 539, where the general rule is well summarized in the following language:

"It has long been settled, both in this court and elsewhere, that the inquiry, whether a mortgagee is a purchaser, depends on the question, whether he parted with anything valuable, surrendered an existing right, incurred a fixed liability, or submitted to a loss or detriment, contemporaneously with the execution of the mortgage, or with the agreement, afterwards performed, to execute the mortgage. If either of these several categories be shown to exist, then the law presumes such act of the mortgagee was done or suffered in consideration of the mortgage executed, or to be executed. In any such case the mortgagee is a purchaser. He is a *bona fide* purchaser, if, at the time he so took the mortgage, he was without notice, actual or constructive, of an older, latent equity in another. What is sufficient notice to put him on inquiry, we do not propose to consider in this case. *On the other hand, if the mortgage be taken to secure a preexisting debt, and no new contemporaneous consideration passes, either of benefit to the mortgagor, or detriment to the mortgagee, then the mortgagee does not thereby become a purchaser.*" (Emphasis supplied).

The authorities cited by Drewrys do not support its contention that it is immaterial whether a definite enforceable time extension is made, if there is forbearance in fact. 36 Am.Jur. 795, § 205, states only that "... if a mortgage is taken for a pre-existing debt, and the creditor *at the time* agrees to extend the time of payment, this additional consideration will entitle the mortgagee to protection as a purchaser for value." (Emphasis supplied). And Jones on Mortgages (8th Ed.), Vol. 1, page 769, states: "... *A definite extension of time for the payment* of an existing debt, by a valid agreement, for any period however short, though it be for a day only, is a valuable consideration, and is sufficient to support a mortgage, or a conveyance, as a purchase for a valuable consideration." (Emphasis supplied).

... The instant after Drewrys accepted the demand note and mortgage, it was in a better position than before because, not only had it the right instantly to sue, but it also reduced a claim to a sum certain and secured a mortgage on the property of the debtor and an additional covenant to pay attorney fees and costs if it should bring action thereon. Instead of "a detriment to the mortgagee" there was a benefit to it. Instead of "a benefit to the mortgagor" there was a detriment to him. In reality, Drewrys' attorney summed it up when he testified it had "nothing to lose."

While we are impressed with the care and caution taken by Drewrys in examining the public records, the facts simply do not place Drewrys in the position of an innocent purchaser for value.

The cause is hereby reversed with directions to enter a final decree in accordance with this opinion.

Reversed.

NOTE

Almost all states today require that, to be protected, a subsequent grantee must have purchased his interest for value. In most states the requirement appears expressly in the recording act. In a few it has been added by judicial gloss. Colorado is apparently alone in not imposing the requirement. See Eastwood v. Shedd, 166 Colo. 136, 442 P.2d 423 (1968); Colo.Rev.Stat.Ann. § 38–35–109 (West 1982 & Supp. 1991). Courts generally agree that although the required value need not approximate the property's market value, it must represent more than merely nominal consideration. See generally, 6A R. Powell, The Law of Real Property ¶ 904(2)(a) (1982).

What interests does the purchaser for value requirement serve? Do the requirement's benefits outweigh the uncertainty about whether someone gave the requisite value? What purposes would be served, and disserved, by exclusive reliance on actual, inquiry and constructive notice? Note that grossly inadequate consideration often signals that the purchaser had some notice of a defect in title. See, for example, Phillips v. Latham, 523 S.W.2d 19 (Tex.Civ.App.1975).

See Schecter, Judicial Lien Creditors Versus Prior Unrecorded Transferees of Real Property: Rethinking the Goals of the Recording System and Their Consequences, 62 S.Cal.L.Rev. 105 (1988).

c.   Circuitous Liens

IN RE DISTRIBUTION OF PROCEEDS FROM SHERIFF'S SALE OF PREMISES 250 BELL ROAD, LOWER MERION TOWNSHIP, MONTGOMERY COUNTY

Superior Court of Pennsylvania, 1975.
236 Pa.Super. 258, 345 A.2d 921.

PRICE, Judge.

This is an appeal by judgment creditors from an order of Judge Richard E. Lowe of the Court of Common Pleas of Montgomery County, sustaining exceptions by appellee-judgment creditor to a sheriff's schedule of distribution. The controversy arises from the following facts.

Appellee, Boenning and Scattergood, Inc. (Boenning) obtained a judgment against John E. Jennings and Helen M. Jennings, his wife, in the amount of $30,500 on April 14, 1966. On July 3, 1970, Boenning initiated execution proceedings against real property owned by Jennings located at 250 Bell Road, Montgomery County. However, this writ of execution was not formally recorded in the judgment index in the Prothonotary's office in Montgomery County. Mr. and Mrs. Jennings moved for a stay order which was issued on July 13, 1970, to abide resolution of the judgment's validity. On July 29, 1972, the stay order was discharged by the lower court and that dismissal was affirmed per curiam by this court in Boenning & Company v. Jennings, 222 Pa.Super. 712, 294 A.2d 739 (1972).

Boenning then attempted to effect a second execution upon the Jennings' property, but again neglected to properly index the writ. Shortly thereafter, Mr. and Mrs. Jennings obtained an injunction from the United States District Court for the Eastern District of Pennsylvania which stayed the proceedings until December of 1973, when the United States Court of Appeals for the Third Circuit reversed the District Court. Boenning, at that time, instituted its third execution and the property was listed for sheriff's sale on February 20, 1974. On the same day the property was also scheduled for sale on the foreclosure of a first mortgage in favor of the Equitable Life Assurance Society. The sum of $85,000 was realized from the sale, and after satisfaction of liens for taxes, costs of execution, and the Equitable mortgage, all of which had undisputed priority, the sum of $66,679.50 was available for distribution. The liens asserted against the remaining funds are as follows:

Debt	Date of Lien	Approx. Amt. of Debt with Interest
1. Boenning Judgment	April, 1966	$48,500
2. Strawbridge and Clothier Judgment	March, 1971	1,650
3. McCoy Mortgage	August, 1971	30,000
4. Margolies Mortgage	December, 1971	17,500
5. Jay Vending Co. Judgment	June 19, 1973	21,000
6. McCoy Judgment	June 20, 1973	1,300
7. O'Hey Judgment	June 20, 1973	21,000

The mortgage and judgment of John H. McCoy were recorded with knowledge of the Boenning judgment. However, the liens of Margolies and Jay Vending Co. against the realty were entered of record more than five years from the entry of the unrevived Boenning judgment of April 14, 1966. Moreover, these lienholders at no time had any knowledge of the Boenning judgment, nor of the execution proceedings relating thereto.

Since Boenning's judgment had not been entered in the judgment index for nearly eight years preceding the date of the sale, the sheriff did not include it in his proposed schedule of distribution. Boenning filed exceptions to the schedule, seeking to maintain its position, claiming its lien had been improperly omitted.

On October 30, 1974, the lower court sustained the exceptions of Boenning and directed that they be accorded priority over all judgment creditors with the exception of Strawbridge and Clothier. We disagree with that result. Boenning's argument that the July 14, 1970, stay order had the effect of relieving it of its duty to revive its judgment is incorrect. Traditionally, an order opening a judgment for the purpose of letting in a defense neither extinguishes nor impairs a lien, and a judge is powerless to amend the lien.

... The present lien law, while not containing language identical to the 1827 lien law, does limit the duration of a lien to five years unless it is revived as provided. A lien is not affected by the opening of a judgment to permit a defense. Whatever effect the litigation involving the stay order had with respect to Boenning's judgment, it did not preclude or excuse Boenning from properly reviving its lien.

As of July 3, 1970, when the writ of execution was issued, Jennings' premises at 250 Bell Road were subject to Boenning's lien. McCoy, who has a lien junior to Boenning's, had full knowledge of the Boenning lien, since McCoy's attorney, Mr. William O'Hey, was also representing Mr. and Mrs. Jennings in their litigation against Boenning. The appellants rely upon the fact that the writ of execution issued on July 3, 1970, was not indexed. However, it is well established that the sole purpose of indexing is to give notice of the lien to subsequent lienors and purchasers. Where there is actual notice, indexing is not necessary. ... Therefore, McCoy and O'Hey, by having actual knowledge of Boenning's lien will take in the same priority as if Boenning had correctly indexed its writ of execution.

Having determined that Boenning's judgment remains superior to those of McCoy and O'Hey, we must align the priorities of all the interested lien creditors. McCoy's mortgage has been shown to be superior to both the Margolies mortgage and the Jay Vending Company judgment. However, it is also clear that Boenning's lien was not revived against Margolies or Jay Vending, neither of which had actual knowledge of the execution proceedings. Therefore, Margolies and Jay Vending have priority over Boenning, and this problem constitutes a circular lien.

Pennsylvania courts have used the temporal priority rule to break the circle and realign the parties: first in time—first in right.

However, the rule of temporal priority has never been applied when the circuity of liens has arisen solely as the result of the neglect of a prior lienholder in failing to properly record or revive his lien.

. . .

Other jurisdictions have been faced with the specific problem we face here—a circuity resulting from the failure of a prior lienholder to record his lien. The courts in Day v. Munson, 14 Ohio St. 488 (1863), and Hoag v. Sayre, 33 N.J.Eq. 552 (1881), faced this dilemma and fashioned clearly reasoned solutions for it.

In Day v. Munson, supra there was a circuitous lien involving three mortgages. The first mortgage lost its lien as against the third by failure to re-file within the statutory period of one year, so that the third mortgage was taken without notice of the first. However, the second mortgage lien was taken with actual notice of the prior mortgage, and had also maintained its priority over the third. As is the situation in the present case, the proceeds of the mortgaged property were insufficient to satisfy all the liens. A similar set of facts occurred in Hoag v. Sayre, supra. Both the *Hoag* court and the *Day* court used the same approach in solving the priorities problem. Both courts marshalled the funds in the following manner: to the third, if it be for as large a sum or a larger sum secured by the first; then the second encumbrance will be paid in full if the property is sufficient, and then the residue to the third, if there is a residue; and then the first lien will come in. Judge Dixon, in his dissent in Hoag v. Sayre, supra, at 562–63, is credited with extending and detailing, in a manner that has subsequently been widely accepted, this position:

"Therefore, if there be three encumbrancers, A, B and C, in the order of time, and A's lien be prior to B's, and B's to C's, but for A's omission to properly register his lien, it is void as to C's, then the fund should be disposed as follows:

1. Deduct from the whole fund the amount of B's lien, and apply the balance to pay C. This gives C just what he would have if A had no existence.

2. Deduct from the whole fund the amount of A's lien, and apply the balance to pay B. This gives B what he is entitled to.

3. The balance remaining after these payments are made to B and C is to be applied to A's lien."

In the present case the judgment creditors shall be identified by the following: Boenning—"A", McCoy—"B", and "C" will represent both Margolies and Jay Vending Co.

We believe a distribution must be made with compliance to the formula previously expressed for the reasons pointed out in *Execution Sales: Lien Divestiture and Distribution of Proceeds in Pennsylvania*, 58 Dick.L.Rev. 244, 265–66 (1954):

"Where A has failed to record, B has recorded with notice, and C has recorded without notice, C alone is in a completely helpless position. A could have prevented the circuity by recording. B could have prevented it by refusing to accept a mortgage unless and until the prior mortgage had been recorded. C, however, cannot protect himself at all if he may not rely on the record. He can do nothing to prevent the circuity. If the only parties involved were A and C, the latter, of course, would be ahead. Shall the intermediation of B be permitted to yield A a windfall merely because B happened to have notice of A's unrecorded mortgage? Since C alone could have done nothing to have prevented the situation from arising, it would seem that he ought to be accorded the protection that reliance on the record was intended to afford. C therefore ought first to be paid that sum which he would have received had the priorities been as they appeared on the record. To hold otherwise would impair the results intended to be achieved by recording acts, and would act as an effective restraint on many security transactions, for no one could safely lend money on the security of real estate if it were already subject to an encumbrance."

An equitable distribution in this case which encourages compliance with the Judgment Lien Law is:

1. Boenning Judgment	$13,470.50
2. Strawbridge and Clothier Judgment (Undisputed)	1,650.00
3. McCoy Mortgage	16,529.50
4. Margolies Mortgage	17,500.00
5. Jay Vending Co.	17,529.50
	$66,679.50

Reversed and remanded to the lower court for a distribution consistent with this opinion.

3.   THE TITLE SEARCH

a.   THE INDICES

NOTE, THE TRACT AND GRANTOR–GRANTEE INDICES,* 47 IOWA L.REV. 481–482 (1962): A practical and convenient means of locating records which an owner of property must rely upon to prove his title and which a prospective purchaser must depend upon when making a title search is an indispensable part of a workable system of recordation. Therefore, it is not surprising to discover that statutory provisions providing for some system of indexing which affords a history of the ownership of land and which discloses instruments or encumbrances affecting title to real property have been enacted in every state. There are currently two types of indices in use: (1) the grantor-grantee index, and (2) the tract index. This should not be interpreted as meaning that a dual system of indexing has always been present in the United States, for under the land owned by the English, French, Mexican, and Spanish governments on the North American Continent, there were no numbered tract systems in existence which could serve as a basis for land description. This was, of course, directly related to the fact that a competent survey had never been made of the land owned by these countries. Under these circumstances, even tax levies had to be against the owners of the land rather than against the land itself. Therefore, it was only logical that when some system of indexing was finally adopted the alphabetical or grantor-grantee system of indexing was selected. Nevertheless, even after the United States Government acquired the land formerly held by foreign countries in what is now the

---

* Copyright 1962 by The University of Iowa (Iowa Law Review).

United States and adequate Government surveys had been undertaken and completed, the grantor-grantee system of indexing was still retained as the basis of land description. However, it was gradually discovered that the grantor-grantee system of indexing was inadequate in many respects. This led several states to enact statutes establishing a tract or numerical system of indexing. Nevertheless, even those states which adopted the tract system of indexing retained the alphabetical system of indexing which they had established at an earlier date.

Under the grantor-grantee or alphabetical index, pages are assigned in the index to each letter of the alphabet. As an instrument is received at the recorder's office, it is first recorded and then indexed under the name of the granting party on the appropriate page of the index. In addition, the county recorder is usually required to make notations on the grantor's page which disclose the name of the other party to the transaction, the book and page of the record where this particular transaction can be found, a description of the property, the date when the instrument was executed, the date when the instrument was filed for recordation, and the nature of the instrument. These same notations are then made as the transaction is indexed under the name of the grantee or the receiving party. After both steps have been completed, the instrument is considered to have been properly indexed.

Under the tract indexing system each parcel of land in a certain area is assigned a separate page in the index and every subsequent transaction affecting this property will be noted thereon. Under the tract system of indexing, a "parcel of land" means any geographical unit of land which has been surveyed and platted, such as sections, blocks, and lots. In addition to describing the property, the tract index also discloses the character of the instrument which affects the title to the property, the date of the execution of the instrument, the date of the filing of the instrument for recordation, and the names of the parties to the transaction. Under this system, therefore, *all* the instruments which affect the title to a particular parcel of realty will be noted on one page of the index. For this reason and innumerable others, the uniform adoption of the tract index has been urged by many legal scholars. However, the reaction of the respective state legislatures to this proposal apparently has not been enthusiastic.

E. BADE, CASES AND MATERIALS ON REAL PROPERTY AND CONVEYANCING

237–238 (1954).

INDICES OF RECORDS

The most widely required forms of indices for real estate records are grantor and grantee indices. In the grantor index, all conveyances are indexed alphabetically and chronologically under the initial letter of the grantor's surname. In the grantee index, a like index is made of conveyances under the initial letter of the grantee's surname. In running these indices the title searcher may begin with a known owner, A, at a stated time. He traces this name in the grantor index from the time A became an owner until he finds A made a conveyance of his title to another—B. The index will give the name of the grantee and other particulars such as the date of the instrument, date of recording, kind of instrument, and place where recorded in extenso. At this point he drops A and turns to B in the grantor index and traces B's name from the *date of the deed* to him (not from the date of recording) until he finds a conveyance of the title from B to C. He repeats this operation for each successive owner in the chain of title. The grantor-index search for each is bounded in time by the date of *acquisition* and the date *of record* of his conveyance out.

Normally, the title search begins with the grantee index. Z, who claims to be the fee owner, is proposing to sell the land to a prospective purchaser. The intending buyer, or his agent, will go to the grantee index and beginning in point of time *presently* where the page is still blank, he will trace back in point of time to see when, if ever, Z became a grantee of the land. If he finds Z's name, the index will tell him the name of Z's grantor, Y, the date of recording, the date of the deed together with the same information contained in the grantor index.

The title searcher now drops his search for Z in the grantee index and turns to Y. He now searches the grantee index to see when Y became a grantee. In point of time, the search for Y as a grantee begins at the date of *the record* of the deed to Z and proceeds backward in time until Y's name is found. In this way the title is traced back link by link. Both indices must be traced to complete the search.

To illustrate the matter for one step or link. When the searcher finds Y was the grantor of Z the searcher will then trace the grantee index to find when Y became a grantee. He will then want to know whether Y at any time since the *date of the deed* (not the date of its record) to him, made any conveyance out. Hence he traces Y in the grantor index from the *date of the deed* to Y down to the point where Y granted all his interest in the land to Z. The search at this point continues to the *date of record* of the deed from Y to Z. This is done because if Z did not record promptly, in notice and notice-race jurisdictions, Y may have made a subsequent conveyance to a bona fide purchaser for value who may have recorded his conveyance first, cutting off Z's rights. In notice jurisdictions, of course, Z's rights could be cut off without a prior recording.

In following this procedure, it will be apparent that if Y made a conveyance of the land before the date of the deed to him and which was recorded before the date of the deed to him, it would not be found. It will be outside the chain of title. So also it will be evident that a serious discrepancy in the name of a person who is a grantor and grantee or a misdescription of the property may break the thread of search.

The other type of index is variously known as a tract index, block index, and numerical index; most commonly as a tract index. Under this type of index a line or column is assigned to conveniently sized tracts. It may be a section, quarter section, platted blocks or lots. Under that land description, every conveyance of any interest in that land is indexed chronologically. For a description of real estate indices see Patton on Titles, sec. 42; Warvelle on Abstracts, 4th Ed. sec. 68. Hence all conveyances affecting the title to that land will appear there. It will appear there no matter who made it, whether he is a stranger to the title or not. Consequently, if a tract index is a required record, purchasers should be, and usually are charged with constructive notice of all conveyances indexed there.

Most abstractors prepare abstracts of title from tract indices. If an abstract so prepared refers to a conveyance outside the chain of title, and is examined by the prospective purchaser or by his agent or attorney, is he put on inquiry even though a tract index is not a required index in the jurisdiction?

NOTES

1. *Indexing Errors.* If a grantee delivers an instrument to the recorder who fails to index it properly, most jurisdictions hold that a subsequent purchaser does not have constructive notice of the instrument. See, e.g., Howard Savings Bank v. Brunson, 244 N.J.Super. 571, 582 A.2d 1305 (1990); but see Frank v. Storer, 308 Md. 194, 517 A.2d 1098 (1986) (following the minority rule, and holding that third parties had constructive notice of an agreement modifying a deed of trust that was not indexed, even though the grantee under the deed of trust actually knew it was not indexed). Is this rule correct? Which party can best prevent the loss from improper indexing? What should standard operating procedure be in such cases? Can the recorder be held liable for incorrect indexing? See Siefkes v. Watertown Title Company, 437 N.W.2d 190 (S.D.1989) (denying negligence action against recorder by title company seeking indemnification for improper indexing).

2. Some form of index is obviously required by the tremendous volume of recorded instruments. According to a 1973 report, approximately 7,000 instruments were recorded each month in Suffolk County, Massachusetts (Boston); about 15,000 documents were recorded each month in Cook County, Illinois (Chicago) and 5,000–6,000 instruments were recorded each *day* in Los Angeles. Basye, A Uniform Land Parcel Identifier—Its Potential for All Our Land Records, 22 Am.U.L.Rev. 251 (1973).

Even the best official indices are incomplete. Many transactions affecting title will be revealed by neither the grantor-grantee index nor the tract index. Thus, a title examiner must consult, among other sources, the indices of wills and administration of decedents' estates in the office of the county surrogate; the index of bankrupts in local federal court; local judgment dockets and dockets of federal tax liens. One problem with these auxiliary indices is that they are designed for purposes other than land title searches. For example, because neither grantor-grantee nor tract indices refer to land transfers by will or intestacy, a title examiner will quickly conclude that if these indices reveal a gap in ownership it is because title to the land at that point passed by devise or descent. But it may take considerable sleuthing to bridge that gap since probate registers are indexed alphabetically by the name of the decedent and not by the name of the estate's recipient—the only name that the examiner knows. See also, State v. Alaska Land Title Ass'n, 667 P.2d 714 (Alaska 1983), cert. denied, 464 U.S. 1040, 104 S.Ct. 704, 79 L.Ed.2d 168 (1984) (publication of federal land orders regarding easements in the Federal Register gives constructive notice to purchasers).

Although tract indices suffer many of the same limitations as grantor-grantee indices, they are clearly superior in terms of depth, speed and accuracy of search. Why, then, have tract indices not been widely adopted across the country? The simple answer is that they have—although not as official public indices, but rather as unofficial private indices maintained in "title plants" by examiners, abstracters and title insurance companies. Recognizing the superiority of tract indices, title examiners long ago began compiling them on their own. Each time an examiner searched title to a parcel, she would place a copy of the search in her files, indexed by reference to the parcel. The next time the examiner was retained to search title to that parcel, she had only to pull the relevant file and update her last search to the present. Title plants represent valuable assets and many, if not most, have been purchased by title insurance companies, enabling them quickly to establish themselves and their services in new locales.

See generally, Cook, Land Law Reform: A Modern Computerized System of Land Records, 38 U.Cin.L.Rev. 385 (1969); Cook, Land Data Systems: The Next Steps, 43 U.Cin.L.Rev. 527 (1974); Jensen, Computerization of Land Records by the Title Industry, 22 Am.U.L.Rev. 393 (1973); McCormack, Torrens and Recording: Land Title Assurance in the Computer Age, 18 Wm. Mitchell L.Rev. 61 (1992).

b. TITLE STANDARDS
L. SIMES & C. TAYLOR, MODEL TITLE STANDARDS
1–5, 14–17 (1960).

THE FUNCTION AND SCOPE OF UNIFORM TITLE STANDARDS

A uniform title standard may be described as a statement officially approved by an organization of lawyers, which declares the answer to a question or the solution for a problem involved in the process of title examination. A brief reference to the task of the title examiner will show why such standards are needed.

I

Perhaps there is no greater delusion current among inexperienced conveyancers than that land titles are either wholly good or wholly bad, and that the determination of the person who has the title is merely a mathematical process of applying unambiguous rules of law to the abstract of the record. Yet the experienced conveyancer knows that the process of determining the marketability of a title is much more like determining whether, under all the facts, a man has a cause of action for negligence, than it is like the calculation of the amount of income tax a person owes on a given date.

No record, or abstract of the record, gives all the facts from which marketability must be determined. Thus, if the grantee in one record-ed deed is Joseph Fremont and the grantor in the next is also Joseph Fremont, it is highly probable that these are one and the same person. But the record does not enable us to know whether it was delivered, whether it was a forgery, or whether the grantor was of sound mind when he executed it. Yet it is patently impossible for the title examin-er to make a factual investigation to determine these things. He must decide, not whether it is absolutely certain that a given person has title, but whether it is reasonable to conclude from the facts which he can be expected to investigate, that this person has title.

As to many fact situations which are constantly recurring, a com-pletely uniform practice of conveyancers is recognized. Thus, all con-veyancers presume that the use of an identical name in one deed as grantee and in the next deed as grantor indicates that these names refer to the same person. All conveyancers presume, in the absence of evidence to the contrary, that a recorded deed has been delivered, that it was not a forgery, and that the grantor had the capacity to execute it. These presumptions may be described as a part of that body of recog-nized procedures known as the practice of conveyancers.

Now while, as to such matters as those already named, the practice of conveyancers is uniform, as to other matters there are notable variations. Thus, such questions as the following may be involved: whether a recorded conveyance should be questioned which does not have a notary's seal, or does not have a statement of the date on which the notary's commission expires; or, if a conveyance is made by a corporation, whether it should be questioned because there is no resolu-tion on record showing the action of the corporation to make the conveyance, or showing whether the people who executed it as officers were in fact such officers at the time. As to these matters some title examiners may reach one conclusion and others the opposite conclu-sion. Uncertainties may also arise as to pure matters of law. Thus, a new probate procedure act may have been passed, and there may be a difference of opinion among members of the bar as to its constitutionality.

If the practice of conveyancers is not uniform, the tendency always is for the standards of the overmeticulous conveyancer to determine the standards of all conveyancers. Lawyer *A* feels that a title should be passed even though there are certain defects in the recorded acknowledgment, and he realizes that the majority of experienced, competent conveyancers would agree with him. But he also knows that Lawyer *B* would refuse to pass the title and would require a quiet title suit. Since Lawyer *A* is aware that his client may some day wish to sell the land to someone who employs Lawyer *B* to pass on the title, he will be inclined to impose the same overmeticulous standard as Lawyer *B*. Like Gresham's law, the result will be that bad title standards drive out good standards.

The remedy for this situation is either uniform title standards or legislation or both. Although Lawyer *A* may not dare to approve a title solely on his individual judgment, the situation is different if his judgment is backed by the official action of a bar association. If the official standards are supported by the great majority of competent, experienced conveyancers, and the prestige of the bar association is high, overmeticulous conveyancers may well follow these standards. Or even if a few do not, the conveyancer who does follow them can justify his position to his client by pointing out that he has followed officially approved standards.

Thus, uniform title standards have great remedial value because they crystallize the practices of conveyancers; and instead of being merely the recognized practices of individuals in a profession, they become also the recognized conclusions of the organized profession itself.

That it is desirable for state bar associations to adopt title standards, for the reasons already stated, has rarely been questioned in recent years. Already such standards are found in twenty-three states and doubtless other states will be added. But it is important, before adopting such standards, and before presenting a set of model standards, to inquire (1) what kind of subject matter is suitable for bar standards, and (2) what limitations exist as to this subject matter. We should also consider the questions: What form should title standards take, and what support from the bar is necessary in order that they accomplish their purpose.

Doubtless there is no hard and fast line which can be drawn to determine the appropriate subject matter of title standards. Nevertheless, a considerable area of agreement can be found in the published writings of those who have discussed this matter. Professor John C. Payne, writing in 1953, suggests the following as to general standards: "Such agreements may extend to: (1) the duration of search; (2) the effect of lapse of time upon defects of record; (3) the presumptions of fact which will ordinarily be indulged in by the examiner; (4) the law applicable to particular situations; and (5) relations between examiners and between examiners and the public" [2] . . . .

An actual survey of all the existing state title standards shows that their subject matter can include almost anything of interest to the conveyancer. Thus they have concerned the conduct of the title examiner, the form of his certificate of title, the form and content of abstracts, the effect of wild deeds, name variances, the application of statutes of limitations and of marketable title acts, tax titles, mechanics' liens, titles derived from decedents, the attitude of the title examiner toward the constitutionality of procedural statutes, and many other subjects.

That there are definite limits to the scope and function of uniform title standards is everywhere recognized. They cannot change or abolish a rule of law. They cannot do away with the requirement of delivery or of a writing for a valid conveyance; they cannot change the length of the statute of limitations, or abolish provisions for the extension of the period of limitations by disabilities. They cannot make a statute constitutional by declaring it so. In short, so far as rules of law are concerned, they can only resolve ambiguities pending their resolution by the highest court of the jurisdiction. So far as facts are concerned, they can determine what risks it is reasonable to expect a client to assume when a title is approved. Even that question of reasonableness is doubtless subject to review by a court. But if the practice of conveyancers is followed by all, the question is not likely to reach a court, and, even if it does, the court will generally follow the title standard.

* * *

STANDARD 2.1

EXAMINING ATTORNEY'S ATTITUDE

THE PURPOSE OF THE EXAMINATION OF TITLE AND OF OBJECTIONS, IF ANY, SHALL BE TO SECURE FOR THE EXAMINER'S CLIENT A TITLE WHICH IS IN FACT MARKETABLE AND WHICH IS SHOWN BY THE RECORD TO BE MARKETABLE, SUBJECT TO NO OTHER ENCUMBRANCES THAN THOSE EXPRESSLY PROVIDED FOR BY THE CLIENT'S CONTRACT. OBJECTIONS AND REQUIREMENTS SHOULD BE MADE ONLY WHEN THE IRREGULARITIES OR DEFECTS REASONABLY CAN BE EXPECTED TO EXPOSE THE PURCHASER OR LENDER TO THE HAZARD OF ADVERSE CLAIMS OR LITIGATION.

Similar Standards: Fla., 00; Idaho, 14; Ill., 1; Iowa, "General Standard"; Kan., 1.1; Minn., "General Statement"; Mo., 2; Mont., 25; N.M., 1; N.D., "General Standard"; S.D., 1.

2. "Increasing Land Marketability L.Rev. 1 at 10 (1953). Through Uniform Title Standards," 39 Va.

Comment: Title Standards are primarily intended to eliminate technical objections which do not impair marketability and some common objections which are based upon misapprehension of the law. The examining attorney, by way of a test, may ask himself after examining the title, what defects and irregularities he has discovered by his examination, and as to each such irregularity or defect, who, if anyone, can take advantage of it as against the purported owner, and to what end.

STANDARD 2.2

PRIOR EXAMINATION

WHEN AN ATTORNEY DISCOVERS A SITUATION WHICH HE BELIEVES RENDERS A TITLE DEFECTIVE AND HE HAS NOTICE THAT THE SAME TITLE HAS BEEN EXAMINED BY ANOTHER ATTORNEY WHO HAS PASSED THE DEFECT, IT IS RECOMMENDED THAT HE COMMUNICATE WITH THE PREVIOUS EXAMINER, EXPLAIN TO HIM THE MATTER OBJECTED TO AND AFFORD OPPORTUNITY FOR DISCUSSION, EXPLANATION AND CORRECTION.

Similar Standards: Colo., 1; Conn., 35; Mont., 1; Ohio, 2.1; Okla., 2; Mo., 1; Wyo., 1.

STANDARD 2.3

REFERENCE TO TITLE STANDARDS IN LAND CONTRACT

AN ATTORNEY DRAWING A REAL ESTATE SALES CONTRACT SHOULD RECOMMEND THAT THE TERMS OF THE CONTRACT PROVIDE THAT MARKETABILITY BE DETERMINED IN ACCORDANCE WITH TITLE STANDARDS THEN IN FORCE AND THAT THE EXISTENCE OF ENCUMBRANCES AND DEFECTS, AND THE EFFECT TO BE GIVEN TO ANY FOUND TO EXIST, BE DETERMINED IN ACCORDANCE WITH SUCH STANDARDS.

Similar Standards: Conn., 67; Mo., 27; Okla., 28.

Comment: An attorney, drawing a real estate sales contract, should recommend the inclusion of the following language or its equivalent in the contract:

It is understood and agreed that the title herein required to be furnished by the seller, or party of the first part herein, shall be marketable and that marketability shall be determined in accordance with the Title Standards of the _____ Bar. It is also agreed that any defect in the title which comes within the scope of any of said Title Standards shall not constitute a valid objection on the part of the buyer provided the seller furnishes the affidavits or other title papers, if any, required in the applicable Standard to cure such defect. ...

STANDARD 3.1

PERIOD OF SEARCH

[In this standard, it is assumed that record titles in the jurisdiction are so long that it is unreasonably burdensome to trace title back to the government, or if land titles do not originate with the United States or with the state, it is impracticable to trace titles back to their origin. Of course, if the Model Marketable Title Act, or similar legislation, were in force, then the length of search, for most purposes, would be determined by such legislation. This standard is not as satisfactory as a marketable title act, since defects in title prior to the period of search as stated in the title standard constitute a risk which a vendee must assume. Whereas, if a marketable title act is in force, defects in title prior to the period of the act are extinguished.]

A RECORD TITLE COVERING A PERIOD OF FIFTY YEARS OR MORE IS MARKETABLE: PROVIDED THAT THE BASIS THEREOF IS A WARRANTY DEED, ONE OR MORE QUITCLAIM DEEDS SUPPORTED BY A REASONABLE RECORD PROOF THAT THEY CONVEY THE FULL TITLE, A PATENT FROM THE UNITED STATES, OR A CONVEYANCE FROM THE STATE, A PROBATE PROCEEDING IN WHICH THE PROPERTY IS REASONABLY IDENTIFIABLE, A WARRANTY MORTGAGE DEED IF SUBSEQUENTLY REGULARLY FORECLOSED, OR ANY OTHER INSTRUMENT WHICH SHOWS OF RECORD REASONABLE PROBABILITY OF TITLE AND POSSESSION THEREUNDER; PROVIDED FURTHER THAT THE PERIOD ACTUALLY SEARCHED DOES NOT REFER TO OR INDICATE PRIOR INSTRUMENTS OR DEFECTS IN TITLE, IN WHICH CASE SUCH PRIOR INSTRUMENTS MAY BE USED IN TURN AS A START, AND THAT THE PERIOD ACTUALLY SEARCHED DISCLOSES INSTRUMENTS WHICH CONFIRM AND CARRY FORWARD THE TITLE SO ESTABLISHED.

Similar Standards: Conn., 1 (60-year period); Mo., 23 (45-year period); N.M., 20 (50-year period); Ohio, 2.2 (65-year period); Utah, 41 (50-year period).

Comment: In applying this standard, it is necessary to trace the record title back to a "root" or "start," which may be, and generally is, more than fifty years back. Any defects in the record title subsequent to the date of recording of the "root" or "start" must be considered by the examiner. Thus, suppose the record shows a warranty deed from A to B in fee simple, recorded in 1880. The next instrument in the chain of record title is a conveyance of flowage rights from B to X, recorded in 1882. The next instrument is a warranty deed from B to C in fee simple, recorded in 1920, in which the flowage rights are not mentioned. In 1959, D, who has contracted to purchase the land from C, employs an attorney to examine the title. The title examiner will have to go back to the deed of 1880 and will have to report that the record title is subject to flowage rights in X, created by the deed of 1882.

NOTE

See Epperson & Sullivan, Title Examination Standards: A Status Report, 4 Probate & Prop. 16 (Sept./Oct. 1990) (1990 survey indicates that twenty states have active title examination standards).

c. Extent of Search: The "Record Chain of Title" Problem

MORSE v. CURTIS

Supreme Judicial Court of Massachusetts, 1885.
140 Mass. 112, 2 N.E. 929.

MORTON, C.J. This is a writ of entry. Both parties derive their title from one Hall. Hall mortgaged the land to the demandant, August 8, 1872. On September 7, 1875, Hall mortgaged the land to one Clark, who had notice of the earlier mortgage. The mortgage to Clark was recorded January 31, 1876. The mortgage to the demandant was recorded September 8, 1876. On October 4, 1881, Clark assigned his mortgage to the tenant, who had no notice of the mortgage to the demandant. The question is, which of these titles has priority? The same question was distinctly raised and adjudicated in the two cases of Connecticut v. Bradish, 14 Mass. 296, and Trull v. Bigelow, 16 Mass. 406. These adjudications establish a rule of property which ought not to be unnoticed, except for the strongest reasons. It is true that in the late case of Flynt v. Arnold, 2 Metc. 614, Chief Justice SHAW expresses his individual opinion against the soundness of these decisions; but in that case the decision of the court was distinctly put upon that ground, and his remarks can be only considered in the light of *dicta,* and not as overruling the earlier adjudications.

Upon careful consideration, the reasons upon which the earlier cases were decided seem to us the more satisfactory because they follow the spirit of our registry laws and the practice of the profession under them. The earliest registry law provides that no conveyance of land shall be good and effectual in law "against any other person or persons but the grantor or grantors, and their heirs only, unless the deed or deeds thereof be acknowledged and recorded in manner aforesaid." St.1783, c. 37, § 4. Under this statute the court, at an early period, held that the recording was designed to take the place of the notorious act of livery of seizin, and that though by the first deed the title passed out of the grantor as against himself, yet he could, if such deed was not recorded, convey a good title to an innocent purchaser who received and recorded his deed. But the court then held that a prior unrecorded deed would be valid against a second purchaser who took his deed with a knowledge of the prior deed, thus ingrafting an exception upon the statute. 3 Mass. 575; Marshall v. Fisk, 6 Mass. 24. This exception was adopted on the ground that it was a fraud in the second grantee to take a deed if he had knowledge of the prior deed. As Chief Justice SHAW forcibly says in Lawrence v. Stratton, 6 Cush. 163, the rule is "put upon the ground that a party with such notice could not take a deed without fraud; the objection was not to the nature of the conveyance, but to the honesty of the taker, and therefore, if the estate had passed through such taker to a *bona fide* purchaser without fraud, the conveyance was held valid." This exception by judicial exposition was afterwards ingrafted upon the statute, and somewhat extended by the legislature. Rev.St. 59, p. 28; Gen.St. c. 59, § 31; Pub.St. c. 120, § 4. It is to be observed that in each of these revisions it is provided that an unrecorded prior deed is not valid against any person except the grantor, his heirs and devisees, "and persons having actual notice of it." The reason why the statutes require actual notice to a second purchaser, in order to defeat his title, is apparent; its purpose is that his title shall not prevail against the prior deed if he has been guilty of a fraud upon the first grantee, and he could not be guilty of such fraud unless he had actual notice of the first deed.

Now, in the case before us, it is found as a fact that the tenant had no actual knowledge of the prior mortgage to the demandant at the time he took his assignment from Clark. But it is contended that he had constructive notice, because the demandant's mortgage was recorded before such assignment. It was held in Connecticut v. Bradish, supra, that such record was evidence of actual notice, but was not of itself enough to show actual notice, and to charge the assignee of the second deed with a fraud upon the holder of the first unrecorded deed. This seems to us to accord with the spirit of our registry laws, and the uniform understanding of and practice under them by the profession. These laws not only provide that deeds must be recorded, but they also prescribe the method in which the records shall be kept and indexes prepared for public inspection and examination. There are indexes of grantors and grantees, so that, in searching a title, the examiner is obliged to run down the list of grantors or run backward through the list of grantees. If he can start with an owner who is known to have a good title, as in the case at bar he could start with Hall, he is obliged to run through the index of grantors until he finds a conveyance by the owner of the land in question. After such conveyance the former owner becomes a stranger to the title, and the examiner must follow down the name of the new owner to see if he has conveyed the land, and so on. It would be a hardship to require an examiner to follow in the index of grantors the name of every person who at any time, through, perhaps, a long chain of title, was the owner of the estate.

We do not think this is the practical construction which lawyers and conveyancers have given to our registry laws. The inconvenience of such a construction would be much greater than would be the inconvenience of requiring a person who has neglected to record his prior deed for a time, to record it, and to bring a bill in equity to set aside the subsequent deed, if it was taken in fraud of his rights. The better rule, and the least likely to create confusion of titles, seems to us to be that if a purchaser, upon examining the registry, finds a conveyance from the owner of the land to his grantor which gives him a perfect record title, complete by what the law at the time it is recorded regards as equivalent to a livery of seizin, he is entitled to rely upon such recorded title, and is not obliged to search the record afterwards made, to see if there has been any prior unrecorded deed of the original owners.

This rule of property, established by the early case of Connecticut v. Bradish, supra, ought not to be departed from unless conclusive reasons therefor can be shown. We are therefore of opinion that in the case at bar the tenant has the better title. Verdict set aside.

SABO v. HORVATH

Supreme Court of Alaska, 1976.
559 P.2d 1038.

BOOCHEVER, Chief Justice.

This appeal arises because Grover C. Lowery conveyed the same five-acre piece of land twice—first to William A. Horvath and Barbara J. Horvath and later to William Sabo and Barbara Sabo. Both conveyances were by separate documents entitled "Quitclaim Deeds." Lowery's interest in the land originates in a patent from the United States Government under 43 U.S.C. § 687a (1970) ("Alaska Homesite Law"). Lowery's conveyance to the Horvaths was prior to the issuance of patent, and his subsequent conveyance to the Sabos was after the issuance of patent. The Horvaths recorded their deed in the Chitna Recording District on January 5, 1970; the Sabos recorded their deed on December 13, 1973. The transfer to the Horvaths, however, predated patent and title, and thus the Horvaths' interest in the land was recorded "outside the chain of title." Mr. Horvath brought suit to quiet title, and the Sabos counterclaimed to quiet their title.

In a memorandum opinion, the superior court ruled that Lowery had an equitable interest capable of transfer at the time of his conveyance to the Horvaths and further said the transfer contemplated more than a "mere quitclaim"—it warranted patent would be transferred. The superior court also held that Horvath had the superior claim to the land because his prior recording had given the Sabos constructive notice for purposes of AS 34.15.290. The Sabos' appeal raises the following issues:

1. Under 43 U.S.C. § 687a (1970), when did Lowery obtain a present equitable interest in land which he could convey?

2. Are the Sabos, as grantees under a quitclaim deed, "subsequent innocent purchaser[s] in good faith"?

3. Is the Horvaths' first recorded interest, which is outside the chain of title, constructive notice to Sabo?

We affirm the trial court's ruling that Lowery had an interest to convey at the time of his conveyance to the Horvaths. We further hold that Sabo may be a "good faith purchaser" even though he takes by quitclaim deed. We reverse the trial court's ruling that Sabo had constructive notice and hold that a deed recorded outside the chain of title is a "wild deed" and does not give constructive notice under the recording laws of Alaska.[2]

The facts may be stated as follows. Grover C. Lowery occupied land in the Chitna Recording District on October 10, 1964 for purposes of obtaining Federal patent. Lowery filed a location notice on February 24, 1965, and made his application to purchase on June 6, 1967 with the Bureau of Land Management (BLM). On March 7, 1968, the BLM field examiner's report was filed which recommended that patent issue to Lowery. On October 7, 1969, a request for survey was made by the United States Government. On January 3, 1970, Lowery issued a document entitled "Quitclaim Deed" to the Horvaths; Horvath recorded the deed on January 5, 1970 in the Chitna Recording District. Horvath testified that when he bought the land from Lowery, he knew patent and title were still in the United States Government, but he did not rerecord his interest after patent had passed to Lowery.

Following the sale to the Horvaths, further action was taken by Lowery and the BLM pertaining to the application for patent and culminating in issuance of the patent on August 10, 1973.

Almost immediately after the patent was issued, Lowery advertised the land for sale in a newspaper. He then executed a second document also entitled "quitclaim" to the Sabos on October 15, 1973. The Sabos duly recorded this document on December 13, 1973.

Luther Moss, a representative of the BLM, testified to procedures followed under the Alaska Homesite Law [43 U.S.C. § 687a (1970)]. After numerous steps, a plat is approved and the claimant notified that he should direct publication of his claim. In this case, Lowery executed his conveyance to the Horvaths after the BLM field report had recommended patent.

The first question this court must consider is whether Lowery had an interest to convey at the time of his transfer to the Horvaths. Lowery's interest was obtained pursuant to patent law 43 U.S.C. § 687a (1970) commonly called the "Alaska Homesite Law". Since Lowery's title to the property was contingent upon the patent ultimately issuing from the United States Government and since Lowery's conveyance to the Horvaths predated issuance of the patent, the question is "at what point in the pre-patent chain of procedures does a person have a sufficient interest in a particular tract of land to convey that land by quitclaim deed." Willis v. City of Valdez, 546 P.2d 570, 575 (Alaska 1976)....

In Willis v. City of Valdez, supra at 578, we held that one who later secured a patent under the Soldiers' Additional Homestead Act had an interest in land which was alienable at the time that he requested a survey. Here, Lowery had complied with numerous requirements

---

2. Because we hold Lowery had a conveyable interest under the Federal statute, we need not decide issues raised by the parties regarding after-acquired property and the related issue of estoppel by deed.

under the Homesite Law including those of occupancy, and the BLM had recommended issuance of the patent. Since 43 U.S.C. § 687a (1970) does not prohibit alienation, we hold that at the time Lowery executed the deed to the Horvaths he had complied with the statute to a sufficient extent so as to have an interest in the land which was capable of conveyance.

Since the Horvaths received a valid interest from Lowery, we must now resolve the conflict between the Horvaths' first recorded interest and the Sabos' later recorded interest.

The Sabos, like the Horvaths, received their interest in the property by a quitclaim deed. They are asserting that their interest supersedes the Horvaths under Alaska's statutory recording system. AS 34.15.290 provides that:

> A conveyance of real property ... is void as against a subsequent innocent purchaser ... for a valuable consideration of the property ... whose conveyance is first duly recorded. An unrecorded instrument is valid ... as against one who has actual notice of it.

Initially, we must decide whether the Sabos, who received their interest by means of a quitclaim deed, can ever be "innocent purchaser[s]" within the meaning of AS 34.15.290. Since a "quitclaim" only transfers the interest of the grantor, the question is whether a "quitclaim" deed itself puts a purchaser on constructive notice. Although the authorities are in conflict over this issue, the clear weight of authority is that a quitclaim grantee can be protected by the recording system, assuming, of course, the grantee purchased for valuable consideration and did not otherwise have actual or constructive knowledge as defined by the recording laws. We choose to follow the majority rule and hold that a quitclaim grantee is not precluded from attaining the status of an "innocent purchaser."

In this case, the Horvaths recorded their interest from Lowery prior to the time the Sabos recorded their interest. Thus, the issue is whether the Sabos are charged with constructive knowledge because of the Horvaths' prior recordation. Horvath is correct in his assertion that in the usual case a prior recorded deed serves as constructive notice pursuant to AS 34.15.290, and thus precludes a subsequent recordation from taking precedence. Here, however, the Sabos argue that because Horvath recorded his deed prior to Lowery having obtained patent, they were not given constructive notice by the recording system. They contend that since Horvaths' recordation was outside the chain of title, the recording should be regarded as a "wild deed".

It is an axiom of hornbook law that a purchaser has notice only of recorded instruments that are within his "chain of title." If a grantor (Lowery) transfers prior to obtaining title, and the grantee (Horvath) records prior to title passing, a second grantee who diligently examines all conveyances under the grantor's name from the date that the grantor had secured title would not discover the prior conveyance. The rule in most jurisdictions which have adopted a grantor-grantee index system of recording is that a "wild deed" does not serve as constructive notice to a subsequent purchaser who duly records.

Alaska's recording system utilizes a "grantor-grantee" index. Had Sabo searched title under both grantor's and grantee's names but limited his search to the chain of title subsequent to patent, he would not be chargeable with discovery of the pre-patent transfer to Horvath.

On one hand, we could require Sabo to check beyond the chain of title to look for pretitle conveyances. While in this particular case the burden may not have been great, as a general rule, requiring title checks beyond the chain of title could add a significant burden as well as uncertainty to real estate purchases. To a certain extent, requiring title searches of records prior to the date a grantor acquired title would thus defeat the purposes of the recording system. The records as to each grantor in the chain of title would theoretically have to be checked back to the later of the grantor's date of birth or the date when records were first retained.

On the other hand, we could require Horvath to rerecord his interest in the land once title passes, that is, after patent had issued to Lowery. As a general rule, rerecording an interest once title passes is less of a burden than requiring property purchasers to check indefinitely beyond the chain of title.

It is unfortunate that in this case due to Lowery's double conveyances, one or the other party to this suit must suffer an undeserved loss. We are cognizant that in this case, the equities are closely balanced between the parties to this appeal. Our decision, however, in addition to resolving the litigants' dispute, must delineate the requirements of Alaska's recording laws.

Because we want to promote simplicity and certainty in title transactions, we choose to follow the majority rule and hold that the Horvaths' deed, recorded outside the chain of title, does not give constructive notice to the Sabos and is not "duly recorded" under the Alaskan Recording Act, AS 34.15.290. Since the Sabos' interest is the first duly recorded interest and was recorded without actual or constructive knowledge of the prior deed, we hold that the Sabos' interest must prevail. The trial court's decision is accordingly.

Reversed.

JOHNSON, PURPOSE AND SCOPE OF RECORDING STATUTES,* 47 IOWA LAW REVIEW 231, 239–240 (1962): While there is disagreement as to the proper application of the "chain of title" concept, it is clear that some limitation of this sort is needed when the only available access to the records is through inadequate official indexes, a situation all too common. But this justification for the "chain of title" limitation largely disappears in a community where easy access to information on the official records is available through unofficial abstracts and where the customary practice is to rely upon the abstracts rather than the official indexes. Unfortunately, this fact seems not to have had an appreciable impact upon shaping the "chain of title" concept.

If recorded instruments outside the "chain of title" do not give constructive notice, does it follow that such instruments are not really recorded and thus are void as to subsequent purchasers and creditors? Statutory language lends no support to this conclusion and the effect of such a construction is to impose the penalty for failure to record upon one who obeyed the statutory mandate. Yet, this position is generally approved. While the "chain of title" concept usually benefits subsequent purchasers and creditors, it is capable of being turned against them with devastating effect. Assuming that the recording of a deed outside the "chain of title" gives no constructive notice, it would seem to follow logically that such a deed need not be recorded. For example, X conveys to A, who does not record, and then X conveys to B, who does not record. If A conveys to C, there is authority that C, although a subsequent-in-time purchaser, is not a subsequent-in-chain purchaser and therefore is not protected against B's unrecorded deed.

NOTES

1. Would and should Morse v. Curtis have been decided differently if demandant had gone into possession of the property? If the Massachusetts legislature had mandated use of an official tract index? If Massachusetts had a race-notice statute? A race statute? The rule of Morse v. Curtis has been rejected in a minority of states. See, for example, Woods v. Garnett, 72 Miss. 78, 16 So. 390 (1894). As a title examiner in one of these minority jurisdictions, is it likely that the cost of your search will be much higher than it would be in a majority jurisdiction? Will your answer depend on whether you have ready access to a private title plant indexing all land transfers in your county by reference to the tract involved?

The court in In re Dlott, 43 B.R. 789, 795 (Bkrtcy.Mass. 1983) questioned the validity of *Morse* in light of modern search techniques:

> The validity of the Morse holding—that one does not have to check the grantor index beyond the period of ownership—might be questioned in view of the fact that its decision was primarily based upon the customary practices of conveyancers in 1886. Today, it is customary to run the grantor's name in the grantor index for a longer period of time than the period of ownership because a lien for real estate taxes arises upon assessment and does not dissolve until three years and nine months after the first of January in the year of assessment, if there has been a conveyance by a recorded instrument during that time. ... Thus, it could arguably be said that a modern conveyancer's title search would disclose the second conveyance by the Trust and thus a bona fide purchaser from the Debtor would be considered to have constructive knowledge of it contents.

2. After the decision in Sabo v. Horvath, would the Horvaths have had an action against Lowery to recover the value they paid for the

land? Note that although the Lowery-Horvath conveyance was by quitclaim deed, the trial court found that "the transfer contemplated more than a 'mere quitclaim'—it warranted patent would be transferred."

3. *Estoppel by Deed.* If Lowery had not subsequently executed a deed to the Sabos, the Horvaths would clearly have prevailed in a quiet title action against Lowery under the venerable doctrine of "estoppel by deed." This doctrine holds that if *A*, not owning Blackacre, purports to convey Blackacre to *B* by warranty deed, then if *A* later acquires title to Blackacre, her title will automatically pass to *B* under the terms of the deed. The rationale for the doctrine is that *A*, by granting under a deed to *B*, is representing that she owns the land and should thus be estopped from later denying the effectiveness of that deed.

What effect will estoppel by deed have on subsequent purchaser *C* who had no notice of the *A* to *B* deed? Although the *Sabo* court expressly sidestepped the issue, other courts have confronted it directly. For example, in Breen v. Morehead, 104 Tex. 254, 136 S.W. 1047 (1911), McKelligon, who had possession of, but not title to, a piece of land, deeded the property to Breen, who promptly recorded. About two years later, McKelligon acquired title to the parcel from the state and subsequently deeded it to Kern who had no knowledge of the earlier transfer to Breen. Other things being equal, the doctrine of estoppel by deed would have given title to Breen. But, of course, other things were not equal, for Kern, a bona fide purchaser for value, had intervened. The Texas Supreme Court held for Kern on the ground that if he were required to look beyond the origin of the title under which he was purchasing, "there could be no limit short of the vendor's life, and such requirement of purchasers would involve land titles in such uncertainty that it would be impracticable to rely on any investigation."

The court concluded: "We believe that the rule stated above that the date when the title originated in McKelligon marked the limit of investigation for previous sales or encumbrances of that tract of land by McKelligon should be applied here. It would be unreasonable to suppose that a man who had just received a title from the state had previously made a transfer of that land. That ordinary care and caution which the subsequent purchaser must exercise would not suggest an investigation for conveyances made before acquisition of title. It follows that the record of Breen's deed in El Paso county gave no notice to the subsequent purchasers from McKelligon who had no actual notice and paid a valuable consideration for the land." 104 Tex. at 258, 136 S.W. at 1049.

A few states reject the rule followed in Breen v. Morehead. See, for example, Tefft v. Munson, 57 N.Y. 97 (1874). After Morse v. Curtis, would you expect Massachusetts to follow or to reject the rule? The surprising answer is that Massachusetts has rejected the rule. See Knight v. Thayer, 125 Mass. 25 (1878). Can you reconcile Knight v. Thayer with Morse v. Curtis?

B. ABSTRACTS, OPINIONS AND TITLE INSURANCE

Using the public records or his own title plant, a title examiner will first search back to a parcel's root of title—when the parcel was last made the subject of an undisputed transfer—and will then search forward, tracing all subsequent transfers up to the present. The examiner will then prepare an abstract of title summarizing every transfer, beginning with the first, and indicating all other matters of record affecting the title. Characteristically, the abstract will conclude with the examiner's certification of the periods and records covered by his search.

Next, a lawyer or title officer will analyze the abstract. She will eliminate cancelled mortgages and expired liens as well as interests barred by the statute of limitations, reducing the abstract to the remaining interests that continue to encumber or otherwise affect title. If this analysis is performed by a lawyer, it will be embodied in a lawyer's opinion on title rendered to the buyer. If a title insurance company performs the analysis, it will state the results in a policy of title insurance that guarantees good title except for specified encumbrances or defects. (The lawyer's opinion will commonly read, "I have examined the abstract of title attached hereto, and from it find that on said date marketable title of record was vested in seller, free from encumbrances or defects, except as follows ...." The title company's guarantee will typically read, "The following estates, interests, defects, objections to title, liens and encumbrances and other matters are excepted from the coverage of this policy ....")

The sources of title services have changed dramatically over the past one hundred years. Originally lawyers conducted the title search, prepared the abstract, and rendered the opinion based on the abstract. Although, in some places, lawyers continue to discharge all these functions, they have in most communities been partially or completely displaced by abstract and title companies. An abstract company may perform the search and compile the abstract while a lawyer selected by the buyer will review and opine on the abstract. Increasingly, though, title insurance companies are serving all of these functions—conducting the search, preparing the abstract and issuing a title policy insuring the accuracy of the search. Lawyers in many communities have responded to these incursions by setting up title insurance companies of their own. "By 1976, over 10,000 lawyers in nineteen states were organized in nine separate bar-related companies, with assets in excess of $18 million." Roussel & Rosenberg, Lawyer-Controlled Title Insurance Companies: Legal Ethics and the Need for Insurance Department Regulation, 48 Fordham L.Rev. 25, 28 (1979). See also, Rooney, Bar Related Title Insurance: The Positive Perspective, 1980 So.Ill.U.L.J. 263.

1. THE ABSTRACT AND THE LAWYER'S OPINION

C. FLICK, 1 ABSTRACT AND TITLE PRACTICE * 116–118, 138–139 (1958): The abstract, as it is finally built up and assembled, contains a synopsis or summary of all instruments which form the chain of title as they appear from the sources referred to in the abstracter's certificate. The abstract should start with a caption, giving a full and correct description of the property, and should in all cases end with the certificate of the abstracter, which gives a list of all records examined and further sets out the period of time covered by the abstract. Each instrument shown in the abstract should be fully abstracted so that the examining attorney may be able to pass upon the title as well as though he had the original record before him. However, a full abstract of a deed does not mean a copy of the instrument. Where the various clauses, covenants and acknowledgments are all in the standard form, it is not necessary to show them. The abstract should be arranged in chronological order and should begin with the first instrument affecting the property in question and the title should then be traced down to the present owner. ...

A map, plat or survey which will aid the examiner in locating the property should be shown. A good map will show railroads, drainage ditches, public highways, creeks and rivers. If a deed describes property by metes and bounds running to or along adjoining lands, a copy of the deeds of the adjoining property should be set forth so that the attorney can locate the property he is examining.

A good abstracter should not confine his showings merely to instruments that describe the real estate under consideration, but should abstract all other showings that might clear up and explain the title to the specific tract he is abstracting. Some of these documents may be difficult for the abstracter to locate, even though recorded, because at the time they were placed on record they did not describe a specific piece of property although they may be very important links in the chain of title. Two examples of this type of document would be an antenuptial or post nuptial agreement or a revocation of a power of attorney filed before the power of attorney was filed. Sometimes the testimony in some other suit will explain heirship. Deeds for other lands will sometimes show parties single or married. ...

The certificate is a cold, hard statement of facts which the abstracter backs with his good name, reputation and resources, and which makes the abstract a formal and acceptable article of usage in real property transactions. In the early days titles were short and uncomplicated and the abstracters made very few errors. Certificates were brief statements that the abstract was a complete and accurate showing of the matters on record and on file in the office of the Register of

---

* Copyright © 1951, 1958 by West Publishing Company.

Deeds and Clerk of the Court and that there were no unpaid taxes or liens against the property as far as the abstracter was able to ascertain from a careful investigation.

The certificate attached to the abstract should describe the land covered; make a clear-cut and plain statement that the abstract of title is a true, correct and complete abstract of all conveyances and other instruments of writing on file or of record in the office of the recorder, or other office or offices where matters relating to titles are to be found. It should also contain a statement that the abstract contains an abstract or sufficient notation of any and all proceedings had in the civil and probate courts of the county affecting the title, and that there are no judgments, mechanics' liens, foreign executions, attachments, suits pending, transcripts of judgment from the United States Circuit or District Courts, or any other such matters which in any way affect the title to said real estate. Finally, there should be a statement relating to the condition of any and all taxes and special assessments that are liens upon said real estate.

The attorney should check to see that the certificate of the abstracter covers all parties in the chain of title for the full statutory period in connection with judgments. Generally all parties in the chain of title for the preceding ten years should be covered but the period may vary from state to state and periods of five and seven years are not uncommon.

WILLIAMS v. POLGAR

Supreme Court of Michigan, 1974.
391 Mich. 6, 215 N.W.2d 149.

WILLIAMS, Justice (To Affirm).

While important, the issue in this case is a relatively narrow one.

Michigan already permits a buyer of property who has relied on a faulty abstract to his detriment to recover from the abstracter, even though there is no clear contractual privity between them, if the abstracter in fact knew the buyer would rely on the abstract.

This case presents the issue whether a faulty abstracter should likewise be liable to a buyer *he should have foreseen would rely* on the abstract as well as to the buyer *he knew would rely* on it. The question boils down to whether there should be liability for *foreseeable* as well as *known* reliance.

This Court has answered that question affirmatively in a related fact situation, and in categorical terms relieved Michigan jurisprudence of the restrictions of "privity." In this opinion, we reaffirm our general decision eliminating privity and specifically apply it to abstracters.

There is a second issue in this case. When does liability accrue and what statute of limitations applies.

I—FACTS

Plaintiffs Williams purchased certain property situated in the City of Warren, Macomb County, from defendants Polgar on a land contract dated August 1, 1959. At the time of purchase, as provided in the land contract, defendants furnished to plaintiffs an abstract of title certified to July 15, 1959 by Abstract and Title Guaranty Company. This abstract was originally issued on February 4, 1926 by the Macomb County Abstract Company and was extended by said company in 1936, 1937, 1943, 1944, 1945, 1946, 1948, 1951, and 1952. Defendant American Title Insurance Company is the successor in interest to Macomb County Abstract Company.

The abstract of title failed to include a deed dated May 1, 1926 which was recorded on May 24, 1926 in Liber 242 of Deeds at page 174 of Macomb County records. This deed conveyed the southerly 60 feet of the property in question to the Macomb County Board of Road Commissioners.

After execution of the land contract on August 1, 1959, plaintiffs learned, allegedly for the first time, of the existence of this omitted deed. As the result thereof, plaintiffs claim they were required to completely remove a building and that certain other damages were incurred.

Plaintiffs filed this action on April 21, 1971. All defendants filed motions for accelerated judgment based on the statute of limitations. The trial court held that plaintiffs' cause of action accrued no later than the execution of the land contract on August 1, 1959. Thus accelerated judgment was granted defendants. Plaintiffs were nonsuited. The Court of Appeals reversed and remanded. 43 Mich.App. 95, 204 N.W.2d 57 (1972). Defendant American Title Insurance Company requested leave to appeal to this Court which was granted on December 12, 1972. 388 Mich. 812 (1972).

II—EFFECT OF ACCELERATED JUDGMENT

Under a motion for accelerated judgment by defendants the facts well pleaded by plaintiffs and the reasonable inferences therefrom must be considered most favorably towards plaintiffs. As the complaint adequately alleges the title company's negligent misrepresentation in the abstract, plaintiffs' reliance thereon and the damage caused thereby as well as the other matters appearing in the above statement of facts, this case presents at this point no dispute as to facts.

Where there is a person negligently injured by another, normally there is recovery therefor. *Ubi injuria, ibi remedium.*

Defendant title company here, however, seeks immunity from liability for the injury it caused plaintiff buyers, pleading two defenses. First, defendant pleads it is immune from suit because it is not in contractual privity with plaintiffs. Second, defendant pleads it is immune from suit because of the statute of limitations. We disagree.

III—DEFENSE OF PRIVITY

A. *Cessante Ratione Legis, Cessat et Ipsa Lex*

The early common law rule restricting liability to those in contractual privity with an abstracter was based on a system where abstracts would only be used by real estate owners.

As time went on the actual usage of abstracts and the class of people relying on them expanded. ...

Responding to the actual change in use of abstracts and the additional classes of persons relying on them, at least six general court-created exceptions have been grafted onto the supposed common law requirement of strict contractual privity. These exceptions include:

(1) abstracter's fraud or collusion,

(2) theory of third-party beneficiary contracts,

(3) theory of foreseeability of use by a third-party,

(4) actual knowledge or notice of third-party,

(5) agent for disclosed or undisclosed principal contracting with an abstracter, and

(6) re-issuance or recertification of an abstract.

Whereas the common law rule limiting abstracter liability provided immunity from all who were injured by a faulty abstract except those in actual contractual privity, of the 35 jurisdictions (outside of Michigan) addressing themselves to this matter only seven retain a rule of strict contractual privity: Arizona, California, Florida, Illinois, Ohio, Texas and Wisconsin. On the other hand, 11 extend liability to known third-parties relying thereon: Alabama, District of Columbia, Hawaii, Idaho, Indiana, Maryland, Missouri, New Jersey, New York, Pennsylvania and Tennessee. Two jurisdictions have allowed recovery by undiscovered principals: Iowa and Washington. Fourteen purport to extend liability by statute to "any person" relying on the abstract: Arkansas, Colorado, Kansas, Minnesota, Montana, Nebraska, Nevada, New Mexico, North Dakota, Oklahoma, Oregon, South Dakota, Utah and Wyoming. And one jurisdiction extends liability to foreseeable relying third-parties by court decision: Louisiana.

B. *Michigan Has Abolished Privity Requirement*

Michigan ended the last century and began this one firmly wed to the rule of contractual privity immunizing abstracters. By the end of the second decade it reluctantly broke away from strict privity in favor of a known third-party beneficiary. Beckovsky v. Burton Abstract & Title Co., 208 Mich. 224, 175 N.W. 235 (1919). Michigan thereby joined a category of 11 other jurisdictions just noted who had opened recovery to parties the abstracter knew would rely on the abstract. In *Beckovsky,* the plaintiff buyer actually accompanied the seller to the office of defendant title company and said he wanted an abstract but the contract in all truth was between the seller and the title company with the seller paying the title company for its work, although in order to avoid the title company's defense of privity, the trial court graciously put that question to the jury.

So *Beckovsky* extends liability to the faulty abstracter who knows a third-party beneficiary will rely on its abstract. The question remains, will liability likewise apply to the faulty abstracter who can reasonably foresee reliance by a third-party.

. . .

C. Privity Conclusion

Michigan's own jurisprudence records the categorical elimination of privity. This Court had previously extended abstracter liability consonant with the historical growth in reliance and use of abstracts and the corresponding changes in the law to known relying third-parties. Confronted now as of first impression with the question of abstracter liability to foreseeable relying third-parties, we have but to apply our own persuasive precedent of categorical elimination of privity to an analogous situation, and we do so.

IV—ABSTRACTER LIABILITY IN TORT FOR NEGLIGENT MISREPRESENTATION

. . .

With respect to the particular type of tort action arising from breach of an abstracter's contractual duty, we hold it to be an action in negligent misrepresentation. Numerous cases and law review articles have debated the precise tort cause of action most appropriate in this context. The theories of fraud, deceit, warranty, and strict liability have all been the subject of extensive discussion with respect to professional misrepresentations of this sort. None of these theories has been found to adequately deal with this particular problem; negligent misrepresentation, on the other hand, precisely fits this situation.

The obvious difficulty with a fraud or deceit action is the requisite element of scienter. The issue we are dealing with in the instant case does not, on the pleadings, involve *intentional* misrepresentation. To supply the element of intent constructively is to do great violence to existing law on the subject of fraud.

. . .

Further, to treat this cause of action as sounding in warranty or strict liability might serve to extend an abstracter's duty beyond the duty anticipated by the original contract. It is important to repeat that the tort cause of action created by an abstracter's nonfeasance or misfeasance stems from the contractual duty originally imposed and does not render an abstracter liable for action beyond such contractually-imposed duty, i.e., to perform in a diligent and reasonably skillful workmanlike manner.

Thus, we adopt the tort action of negligent misrepresentation in this context. It should be noted that this action is premised on negligence in title search; an abstracter is not converted into a title insurer by virtue of our decision today. We repeat that the only liability an abstracter has to an injured third-party is with respect to negligent performance of his or her contractual duty.

. . .

This cause of action arising from breach of the abstracter's contractual duty runs to those persons an abstracter could reasonably foresee as relying on the accuracy of the abstract put into motion. The particular expert-client relationship accruing to a professional contract to certify the condition of the record of title reposes a peculiar trust in an abstracter which runs not only to the original contracting party. There is a clearly foreseeable class of potential injured persons which would obviously include grantees where his or her grantor or any predecessor in title of the grantor has initiated the contract for abstracting services with the abstracter.

V—DEFENSE OF STATUTE OF LIMITATIONS

Defendants below were granted accelerated judgments on the basis of a plea of statute of limitations bar to this action. There is some textbook authority to the effect that the statute of limitations in an abstracter liability action begins to run from the date the abstract was furnished rather than from the time of the discovery of the error.

But the textbook authority referred to is predicated upon an action *in contract* not an action *in tort*. Consider for example, part of the applicable section in American Jurisprudence:

"... the statute of limitations begins to run from the time of the occurrence of the breach of duty ..." 1 Am.Jur.2d 245.

While such a breach of duty creating a cause of action *in a contract action* would date from the actual act of omission or misrepresentation, the cause of action *in a tort action* runs from the date the tort was committed, not the date the actor put his or her force wrongfully into motion.

. . .

VI—CONCLUSION

For the reasons outlined above, we hold that there is a valid tort cause of action in the nature of negligent misrepresentation arising from a contract for an abstracter's services in favor of a non-contracting damaged third-party whose reliance on the abstract could be foreseen. In a tort action of this nature, the statute of limitations begins running from the date the injured party knew or should have known of the existence of the negligent misrepresentation, a date not clearly in evidence in this case. The accelerated judgment granted by the trial court was thus improper.

The judgment of the Court of Appeals is affirmed. This case is remanded to Macomb County Circuit Court for further proceedings not inconsistent with this opinion. Costs to the appellees.

T. M. KAVANAGH, C.J., and T. G. KAVANAGH, and SWAINSON, JJ., concurred with WILLIAMS, J.

. . .

M. S. COLEMAN, J. (dissenting).

Although it characterizes plaintiff's cause of action as "arising from breach of an abstracter's contractual duty", the majority opinion adopts a "tort action of negligent misrepresentation in this context". The effect and purpose of this adoption is to delay the running of the statute of limitations.

I cannot agree with the theory or the result.

I agree with the majority that plaintiff's action is premised on a breach of contractual duty. M.C.L.A. § 600.5807, M.S.A. § 27A.5807 says:

"No person may bring or maintain any action to recover damages or sums due for breach of contract . . . unless, after the claim first accrued to himself or to someone through whom he claims, he commences the action within the periods of time prescribed by this section:

. . .

(8) The period of limitations is 6 years for all other actions to recover damages or sums due for breach of contract."

When did plaintiff's claim accrue? The answer is found in M.C.L.A. § 600.5827, M.S.A. § 27A.5827 which provides, insofar as applicable to these facts,

"[T]he claim accrues at the time the wrong upon which the claim is based was done regardless of the time when damage results."

Plaintiff's claim thus accrued, at the very latest, in 1959, although no specific date was alleged. Suit was not filed until 1971.

. . .

I would reverse the Court of Appeals and affirm the circuit court's grant of accelerated judgment.

NOTES

1. *Abstracter Liability to Third Parties.* Abstracters and lawyers are liable for defects in their work product—abstracters for errors and omissions in compiling the abstract, lawyers for errors in analyzing the abstract and opining on title. Although buyers can pursue both contract and tort theories against the lawyer who represented them, tort theory represents their primary route for recovery against an abstracter with whom they will commonly not be in contractual privity.

Should buyers have a tort action against abstracters? If *Polgar* had gone the other way, is it likely that Michigan buyers would in the future protect themselves against title defects by insisting that their sellers give them warranty deeds? (Note that if a buyer recovers against his seller on a title covenant, the seller can then proceed on a contract theory against the abstracter with whom she will be in privity.) Is there any material difference in the damages a buyer will recover by proceeding against the seller under a covenant theory rather than proceeding against the abstracter under a tort theory? If, as often happens, the property appreciates in value between the time the buyer acquires it and the time he discovers the title defect, which theory—tort or contract—is more likely to make the buyer whole?

For an extensive, state-by-state analysis of abstracters' liability, see Appendix A to the principal case, Williams v. Polgar, 391 Mich. 6, 215 N.W.2d 149 (1974).

2. *Lawyer Liability.* Lawyers who search or analyze title for their clients are held to the traditional negligence standard of reasonable care and skill. Malpractice claims most often involve the failure to note an encumbrance or to determine the property's true owner or proper location. Good faith errors in judgment are excused, and the lawyer is not considered to have guaranteed that title is perfect— unless, of course, he or she specifically makes that guarantee.

While reasonable care will be measured by the skills possessed, and the customs ordinarily followed, by lawyers in the community, custom will not excuse grossly unreliable practices. In Gleason v. Title Guarantee Co., 300 F.2d 813 (5th Cir.1962), a title company sued for damages arising from defendant attorney's erroneous opinion that certain titles were clear when in fact they were encumbered by outstanding mortgages. The attorney had certified to having made a personal examination of the relevant records but had in fact reviewed neither the records nor the abstracts, relying instead on information received by telephone from the abstract company. In response to the attorney's argument that this method of obtaining title information was standard practice in that part of Florida, the court held that an improper custom, no matter how widely practiced, could not reduce the attorney's duty of care. Damages were awarded for the losses suffered by the title company.

3. *Lawyer Disclaimers.* How much liability can a lawyer disclaim? In Owen v. Neely, 471 S.W.2d 705 (Ky.1971), defendant attorney, employed to "do the title work," gave plaintiffs a certificate of clear and merchantable title containing the standard disclaimer that the certificate was "subject to any information that would be revealed by an accurate survey ...." In making the certificate, the attorney had used a description prepared by a surveyor. The lawyer later admitted that he had noticed discrepancies between the deed description and the survey description. In fact, the survey was erroneous, and the house the clients thought they were buying was not situated on the land that they bought. Acknowledging that reservations and disclaimers ex-

pressly set forth in the certificate of title will generally be enforced, the court ruled that if an attorney examining title receives information that would give him or her grounds to suspect a defect, the attorney owes the client a duty of investigation that cannot be disclaimed.

4. *Lawyer Liability to Third Parties.* Will a lawyer, retained by a bank-mortgagee to examine title on its behalf, be liable to the buyer-mortgagor for errors appearing in the lawyer's title report to the bank? In Page v. Frazier, 388 Mass. 55, 445 N.E.2d 148 (1983), the Massachusetts Supreme Judicial Court affirmed a trial court decision rejecting buyers' claim that the lawyer was liable in tort for negligent misrepresentation. (The court also affirmed the trial court's findings that the lawyer was not liable on a contract theory for having breached the terms of an express or implied lawyer-client relationship and that the lawyer was acting as an independent contractor retained by the bank so that his negligence could not be imputed to the bank.)

The court observed that plaintiffs had cited no case in which "a mortgagee's attorney has been held liable to a mortgagor for negligent performance of a real property title examination," and refused to bring the case within the "general common law trend permitting recovery by injured nonclients for the negligent conduct of attorneys:"

> We do not find the plaintiffs' authorities persuasive here, as we deal with the attorney's liability to another where the attorney is also under an independent and potentially conflicting duty to a client.... As the judge noted in the instant case, "It is not only in the matter of items such as prepayment rights, disclosure law, late charge provisions and special mortgage provisions where a conflict of interest could arise if the attorney represented both bank and borrower, but many experienced conveyancers would acknowledge that there is a conflict of interest even with respect to title as there are some title defects which will not make the property unsatisfactory as security but which would concern a buyer."

The court also attached weight to the fact that the buyer had been warned off from relying on the bank's lawyers by strong exculpatory language in the mortgage application: "(1) The responsibility of the attorney for the mortgagee is to protect the interest of the mortgagee, notwithstanding the fact that (a) the mortgagor shall be obligated to pay the legal fees of said attorney, and (b) the mortgagor is billed for such legal services by the mortgagee. (2) The mortgagor may, at his own expense, engage an attorney of his own selection to represent his own interests in the transaction."

What are the implications of Page v. Frazier for situations in which the lawyer expressly undertakes to represent two or more parties with conflicting interests? Compare In re Lanza, page 18, above.

5. *Abstracter Licensing.* Many states, most of them situated west of the Mississippi, have enacted licensing laws governing abstracters and abstracting firms. Among the requirements imposed are maintenance of an adequate set of abstract records and indices, and bonding to

cover liability for errors in compiling the abstract. See, for example, S.D. Codified Laws Ann. § 36–13–15 (1986). Most of the states require abstracting companies to employ at least one licensed abstracter who has successfully completed a state-administered exam.

2. TITLE INSURANCE

D. BURKE, LAW OF TITLE INSURANCE *

2–5, 17–18, 22–23 (1986).

To protect against such defects in real property titles, American abstractors and attorneys, well over 100 years ago, devised the original forms of title insurance. Title insurance is an exclusively American invention. It involves the issuance of an insurance policy promising that if the state of the title is other than as represented on the face of the policy, and if the insured suffers losses as a result of the difference, the insurer will reimburse the insured for that loss and any related legal expenses, up to the face amount of the policy. ...

... The first title insurance company was formed in Pennsylvania as early as 1853 and was known as the "Law Property Assurance and Trust Society." However, it is an 1868 Pennsylvania case holding an abstractor liable for negligence in the course of a title search that many writers have credited with giving impetus to the industry. Some writers add that this is an example of an industry created by the need to protect the insurer rather than the insured—to protect abstractors and lay conveyancers against their own legal liabilities. This is only part of the story, however, because while title insurers have, from the beginning of the industry, performed a title search as the basis for the policy and as a means of preventing claims and losses under the policy, they have also provided insurance against title defects which cannot be ascertained from the records used in the course of a title search, but which may nonetheless be asserted in the future. This latter function is closer to "pure insurance"—protecting the insured against a future event—but the former is a feature which distinguishes title insurance from most other forms of insurance.

A plan for insuring titles and mortgages was published in Pennsylvania in 1871, and three years later that state enacted the first statutes authorizing this type of insurance. The Lawyers' Title Insurance Corporation was formed under this statute in 1876, and by 1887, title insurance companies were established in some of the major urban centers in the eastern United States, including Philadelphia, Washington, D.C., New York City, and Baltimore.

. . .

In the first two or three decades of the twentieth century, title insurance competed with land title registration systems which were then enjoying increased popularity. However, it became clear that title insurance would prevail in this country as title insurers made a national market for their policies between the two World Wars of this century.

The insurers found that their product complemented the growth of a nationwide market for residential mortgages. Third-party commercial lenders of this period became convinced that title insurance was a necessary ancillary service for the financing of residential properties. During the 1920s mortgagees of such property became convinced that title insurance was a help to those of their number who wanted to do a high-volume business in this form of finance. They could use the insurance policy to standardize their own product in order to sell the mortgage at a discount in the then developing national secondary market for such mortgages.

The intervention of the federal government in the housing markets of the 1930s further standardized the formulae for residential mortgage lending by introducing amortization of principal and interest, longer terms and lower interest rates, and, in the process, provided the final impetus that this market for title insurance needed to become nationwide in scope.

As a consequence of these factors, mortgage lenders began to require title insurance as a part of many real estate transactions. In residential transactions, its presence often became routine in many regions and urban areas of the country, and in large commercial transactions title insurance became the norm. By the end of the Second World War, title insurance was the predominant (in number of transactions) form of title assurance in the country.

. . .

By the 1950s there were some 150 title insurance corporations doing business around the country. Most of them offered policies in more than one jurisdiction. By the early 1970s, this number had shrunk through attrition and merger to less than 100. The remaining corporations writing this type of insurance policy are today affiliated with about 15 large insurance holding companies. Indeed, the four largest title insurers today account for more than 50 percent of the market. The largest of these has just under 20 percent of the market. In California, the four largest insurers control over 70 percent of that state's market.

. . .

Title insurance is a one-premium agreement to indemnify a policyholder for losses caused by both on-record and off-record defects found in the title or interest to an insured property in amounts not exceeding the face amount of the policy and which are in existence on the date on which the policy is used.

If the policy-holder does not "own" the property, and so does not have title to it or possession of it, an insurer may nonetheless issue a policy. It will insure the priority of his lien or any other less-than-fee interest in real property. Title insurance thus may be held by both owners of and lenders on real property, and indeed the most common forms of title insurance policies are owner's and lender's policies.

. . .

Title insurance is unlike other types of insurance in at least two significant ways. First, it is not based on the prediction of a future event by an actuary or statistician, as is life or accident insurance. Title insurance is based in large part on the work of an abstractor, one who searches the public records of interests in real property to ascertain if defects already exist. The abstractor searches for pre-existing defects, arising in past transactions, which may be asserted in the future.... [I]f the abstractor's work is accurate and competent, the claims and loss rate for defects in title recorded on those records should be very low indeed, in fact, approaching zero. If any defect is found on the records, it becomes the basis for an exception from coverage written into the policy—and the number of claims based on such defects will still approach zero. Title insurance is issued after the completion of work intended to reduce the number of claims—for a title insurer is in the unique position of being able, through its own work, to eliminate many claims. ...

Second, a title insurance policy is paid for all at once with only one premium and the coverage lasts for as long as the insured has some liability for a title defect, whether as the present owner or possessor, or as a vendor and warrantor of the state of the title upon some later sale.

Title insurance insures not only on-record defects in title, but also covers defects not revealed by an abstractor's search of the public records related to real property. Such defects are known to title insurers as "off-record risks" and not even the most thorough and competent title search will identify them. Included in any listing of off-record risks are:

(1) the misindexing or misfiling of a document by the recorder,

(2) matters pertaining to the identity of the parties to a document,

(3) its delivery to the transferee. ...

LAABS v. CHICAGO TITLE INSURANCE CO.

Supreme Court of Wisconsin, 1976.
72 Wis.2d 503, 241 N.W.2d 434.

CONNOR T. HANSEN, Justice.

This litigation arises from a dispute as to the scope of coverage provided by a policy of title insurance issued by Chicago Title Insurance Company (hereinafter company) to Theodore F. and Selma Laabs (hereinafter insured). Laabs and McKenzies owned adjoining parcels of real estate. The company had issued a policy of title insurance to both property owners. The two properties are described by metes and bounds and it appears the descriptions overlap. The property described in Laabs' deed is located partially in Government Lots four and five. It also appears that the scrivener who prepared the description to the Laabs real estate made no reference to Government Lot five in the description. The result was that the Laabs' deed was not indexed in the tract index under Government Lot five.

The insured commenced a quiet title action against McKenzies and others claiming ownership of the disputed portion. The defendants in that action answered and counterclaimed against the insured. The insured notified the company of the counterclaim, requesting representation in accordance with the terms of the insurance policy. However, the company refused to defend on the ground that the dispute fell within certain exceptions to coverage contained in the policy.

The insured then instituted this action against the company. Trial on this action was held; however, pursuant to stipulation, the trial court postponed determination on the issue of policy coverage until after trial of the quiet title action.

At the conclusion of the quiet title action, the trial court determined that the disputed parcel belonged to the defendants in that action and not the Laabs. Because of this determination, the status of the other defendants is not pertinent to this appeal. It was also determined that the dispute was of such nature as to be within the scope of coverage of the title insurance policy issued by the company. Therefore, judgment was entered against the company for the reasonable value of the disputed property, and for reasonable attorney fees and costs incurred by the insured in the trial of the counterclaim in the quiet title action. The amount of the damages is not an issue on this appeal.

The findings of fact and conclusions of law and the judgment are captioned as in the instant action. The opinion of the trial judge is captioned as in the action to quiet title. All three of these documents are included in the record and address the issue raised in this action.

The company appeals from that portion of the judgment finding it liable to the insured for the value of the disputed parcel of land and for trial-related costs. Following transmittal of the appeal record, the insured moved this court to strike certain portions of the record. Those portions had to do with an action on a policy of title insurance issued by the company to the McKenzies. The insured herein was not a party to that action. The company did not oppose the motion. This court granted the motion, ordering that the trial court's findings of fact and conclusions of law and opinion in that action, as well as the adverse examination of McKenzie in relation to that action, be stricken from the record.

Determination of a single issue will be dispositive of this appeal:

Was the trial court in error in determining that the policy of title insurance issued by the company included within its coverage the loss sustained by the insured? We are of the opinion that the trial court was correct in its determination.

The company contends that several exceptions and conditions contained in the policy should relieve it of liability for payments to the insured.

The policy of title insurance contains the following language in its EXCLUSIONS FROM COVERAGE:

> "The following matters are expressly excluded from the coverage of this policy:"
>
> " . . .

"3. Defects, liens, encumbrances, adverse claims, or other matters . . . (b) not known to the Company *and not shown by the public records but known to the insured claimant either at Date of Policy or at the date such claimant acquired an estate or interest insured* by this policy and not disclosed in writing by the insured claimant to the Company prior to the date such insured claimant became an insured hereunder; . . . ." (Emphasis added.)

The company argues that the dispute and defect were known to the insured prior to the policy date and, therefore, the company is not liable for the loss or for defense costs. The company bases this argument on the decision of the trial court in the action between the McKenzies and the company. There it was apparently found that the company was not liable to the McKenzies in any way because the McKenzies were aware of the dispute with the insured when they applied for their policy. By order of this court, that opinion and the accompanying transcript of McKenzies' adverse examination are no longer part of the record herein and cannot be considered in reaching a determination on this issue. However, as the company observes, other testimony in support of its claim is preserved in the transcript of the quiet title action.

During that trial, the McKenzies' predecessor in title, Mrs. Yunk, testified that she had disputes in 1962 and 1966 with the insured over the parcel of land in question, that a fence had been placed along the disputed boundary line, and that she had torn it down. A neighbor of the parties testified that in 1965 or 1966, he had observed the insured placing a fence along a portion of the disputed parcel and called the Yunks to inform them of the matter. Finally, Mr. McKenzie, who was not called to testify at the trial on policy coverage, testified that approximately two weeks after he purchased his property, he encountered the insured on the disputed parcel at which time he was informed by Mrs. Laabs that he was trespassing, that he had purchased something that belonged to insured and that the amount of land purchased had been misrepresented to him. This was approximately one week prior to the date insured's policy was issued.

With respect to these matters, the insured testified at the trial on policy coverage that she had no knowledge of any dispute with the Yunks, that she had not spoken with the McKenzies prior to the time they began clearing the disputed parcel, and that she applied for the title insurance with a view toward selling the property. She confirmed this testimony at the trial on the quiet title action. She testified further that she and her husband continued to build a fence along the disputed parcel, a portion of which had been begun as far back as 1947 and 1948, and that it had been removed, although she did not know who had removed it. Her brother-in-law, a real estate broker, testified that he had advised her that if she wished to sell the property, she should obtain title insurance. This advice was not given, however, in connection with knowledge of any dispute, but rather because he felt that any prospective purchaser would impose such a requirement.

The company, in its policy, excluded from coverage defects and adverse claims not shown by the public record and not known by the company but known to the insured and not disclosed to the company. If knowledge of such adverse claim or defect could be charged to the insured, this could have provided grounds for avoiding the policy, since the company was not informed thereof. ...

However, the trial court found as fact that the insured had complied with all the requirements of the policy. During the trial of this issue, the court stated:

> "It is my feeling that as to the getting of the policy of title insurance, knowing that there was a dispute there has not been established ...
>
> " ...
>
> "I find that at the time this policy was issued, that the plaintiffs, Selma Laabs and Theodore Laabs did not know of any dispute and did not secure this policy of insurance against a known dispute."

The testimony presented is set forth in unusual detail because there was a great deal of evidence, from various sources, tending to support the company's claim that the insured had knowledge of the existence of a dispute or adverse claim prior to the date of the policy. In addition, the court's statements in connection with its finding, cited supra, were made at the close of the trial on the scope of coverage, prior to the trial at which much of the relevant testimony was given. However, on appeal, review of a trial court's finding of fact is strictly limited. This court has stated on many occasions that the weight of testimony and the credibility of witnesses are matters to be determined by the trial court, and that where more than one reasonable inference can be drawn from the credible evidence, the reviewing court must accept the one drawn by the trier of fact. ...

The trial court in the instant case resolved the conflicting testimony in favor of the insured, determining that the policy was binding on the company in this instance. Although there is testimony which would have supported a contrary finding, there is ample credible evidence to support the determination of the trial court; therefore, the determination is not against the great weight and clear preponderance of the evidence.

Moreover, it is at least arguable that the defect and adverse claim were matters of public record and, for this reason, would not fall within the stated exclusion, even if the insured had been found to have had knowledge of the claim. In resolving the question of title, the trial court pointed out that rightful ownership of the disputed parcel could be shown through tracing its title descent back to a deed conveyance made prior to the time the land was divided into government lots. The policy exclusion applies only to undisclosed defects or adverse claims *which are not matters of public record.* Such limitation is entirely reasonable in view of the nature of title insurance:

> " ... A policy of title insurance means the opinion of the company which issues it, as to the validity of the title, backed by an agreement to make that opinion good, in case it should prove to be mistaken, and loss should result in consequence to the insured...." First Nat. Bank & Trust Co. v. New York Title Ins. Co., supra, p. 710. ...

The company makes three additional arguments in support of its claim that it should not be held liable. These relate to policy exclusions addressed to the interest insured, the loss suffered, and whether insured created the adverse claim or defect.

The company argues that because the insured had never owned the disputed parcel, the policy excluded coverage. This argument is based upon a policy provision contained in paragraph 2 under CONDITIONS AND STIPULATIONS:

> " ... The coverage of this policy shall continue in force as of Date of Policy in favor of an insured so long as such insured retains an estate or interest in the land, ..."

This provision does not exclude the company's liability under the facts of this case. Title insurance policies are subject to the same rules of construction as are generally applicable to contracts of insurance. 13 Couch, Insurance (2d ed.), p. 583, sec. 48.109. The policy is to be read as a whole. D'Angelo v. Cornell Paperboard Products Co. (1973), 59 Wis.2d 46, 51, 207 N.W.2d 846.

The initial insuring clause reads as follows:

"SUBJECT TO THE EXCLUSIONS FROM COVERAGE, THE EXCEPTIONS CONTAINED IN SCHEDULE B AND THE PROVISIONS OF THE CONDITIONS AND STIPULATIONS HEREOF, CHICAGO TITLE INSURANCE COMPANY, a Missouri corporation, herein called the Company, insures, as of Date of Policy shown in Schedule A, against loss or damage, not exceeding the amount of insurance stated in Schedule A, and costs, attorneys' fees and expenses which the Company may become obligated to pay hereunder, sustained or incurred by the insured by reason of:

"1. Title to the estate or interest described in Schedule A being vested otherwise than as stated therein;

" . . ."

That clause connotes coverage for circumstances identical to those herein. The title to the real estate described in the policy has been adjudicated as being vested otherwise than as stated in the policy. Yet the company contends that, for that very reason, the policy stipulation cited, supra, absolves it of liability. However, that stipulation is entitled "Continuation of Insurance after Conveyance of Title." Thus, it was intended to apply only in the event that the title to the real estate described in the policy is conveyed voluntarily by the policyholder.

An insurance policy must be construed with consideration for what a reasonable person in the position of the insured would have understood its words to mean. Luckett v. Cowser (1968), 39 Wis.2d 224, 231, 159 N.W.2d 94. This court stated in Inter–Insurance Ex. v. Westchester Fire Ins. Co. (1964), 25 Wis.2d 100, 106, 130 N.W.2d 185:

"A construction of an insurance policy which entirely neutralizes one provision should not be adopted if the contract is susceptible of another construction which gives effect to all of its provisions and is consistent with the general intent. . . ."

Acceptance of the company's argument would entirely neutralize the general insuring clause and would contravene the intent of the parties as to situations which are to be covered by the policy. The two provisions under consideration are not mutually exclusive. Such a construction of the policy provisions gives the words their ordinary meaning, carries out the reasonable intention of the parties and gives effect to both parts of the insurance agreement. However, even if an ambiguity can be perceived, such ambiguity must be resolved against the company. *Erickson v. Mid–Century Ins. Co.* (1974), 63 Wis.2d 746, 753, 754, 218 N.W.2d 497.

A third ground for reversal relied upon by the company relates to the following policy exclusion:

"The following matters are expressly excluded from the coverage of this policy:

" . . .

"3. Defects, liens, encumbrances, adverse claims, or other matters (a) created, suffered, assumed or agreed to by the insured claimant; . . . ."

The company contends that the insured created the adverse claim by erecting a fence along the boundary and posting the disputed area. This argument appears to be patently erroneous.

Many cases construing the terms contained in the cited exclusion are set forth in 98 A.L.R.2d 527. That annotation indicates that the word "create" as it is used in such exclusion refers to a conscious, deliberate causation or an affirmative act which actually results in the adverse claim or defect. *Hansen v. Western Title Ins. Co.* (1963), 220 Cal.App.2d 531, 33 Cal.Rptr. 668, 98 A.L.R.2d 520; *First Nat. Bank & Trust Co. v. New York Title Ins. Co., supra. See also: Feldman v. Urban Commercial, Inc.* (1965), 87 N.J.Super. 391, 209 A.2d 640, 648. Here, the adverse claim arose from a defect in the insured's title to the disputed property. The insured had no part in affirmatively creating the claim or in the circumstances which gave rise to the defect. The fence was erected and the property posted, not to create an adverse claim but because the insured believed themselves to be owners of the property.

Finally, the company argues that the insured suffered no loss and therefore liability is excluded by the following policy terms:

"The following matters are expressly excluded from the coverage of this policy:

" . . .

"3. Defects, liens, encumbrances, adverse claims, or other matters . . . (c) resulting in no loss or damage to the insured claimant; . . ."

It is the company's position that because the insured never owned the disputed parcel, they suffered no loss by the adjudication of defective title. This argument has been rejected by several courts which have considered it. In *First Nat. Bank & Trust Co. v. New York Title Ins. Co., supra*, p. 711, it was said that:

" . . . The word 'loss' is a relative term. Failure to keep what a man has or thinks he has is a loss. To avoid a possible claim against him; to obviate the need and expense of professional advice, and the uncertainty that sometimes results even after it has been obtained is the very purpose for which the owner seeks insurance. To say that when a defect subsequently develops he has lost nothing and, therefore, can recover nothing, is to misinterpret the intention both of the insured and the insurer. . . ."

See also: Foehrenbach v. German–American Title and Trust Co. (1907), 217 Pa. 331, 66 A. 561. The insured paid for a large parcel of property including the disputed portion, when the defective title was conveyed in 1943. Therefore, having contracted to insure against a title defect, the company cannot now claim that the insured has suffered no loss by reason of the fact that the title to the disputed property was defective.

Judgment affirmed.

NOTES

1. *Title Insurance Today.* Figures compiled by the American Land Title Association show a 1989 industry-wide total operating revenue of

$4107.1 million and a pre-tax loss of $153.8 million, for a pre-tax operating margin of –3.7%. Between 1968 and 1989 there were losses only in 1980 through 1982 and 1988 and 1989. These losses reflect the national slowdown in the real estate industry and an increase in claims paid over recent years. (Title companies also receive income from investments, which is not reflected in the operating figures.) In 1989, the percentage of operating dollars paid for losses and loss adjustment was 9.5% while the percentage paid for operating expenses was 94.3%. The fact that the percentage of operating expenses is higher than those for other types of insurance is due to the nature of title insurance which seeks to eliminate risks through title searches rather than just creating a pool of funds to reimburse inevitable losses. Title searches and examinations, maintaining title plants, and other costs to identify title problems results in high operating expenses. See American Land Title Association, 1990 Fact Book.

Title insurance is available today in all states but one—Iowa, where it is barred by statute, Iowa Code Ann. § 515.48(10) (West 1988). The statute was upheld against constitutional attack in Chicago Title Insurance Co. v. Huff, 256 N.W.2d 17 (Iowa 1977) ("[W]e are in truth here called upon to determine whether the Iowa system for transferring real property titles shall, as a constitutional mandate, be burdened with an additional and costly layer of 'business activity' which our legislature has expressly prohibited.").

2. *Policy Coverage.* Review the form of Owner's Policy reproduced in the *Statute, Form and Problem Supplement* and reconsider the cases that you have read so far, beginning with McDonald v. Plumb at page 144. In each case, what protection, if any, would the injured owner have received under this standard form of title insurance policy?

What protection, if any, does this form of policy provide against a misdescription or surveyor error that results in the insured's house encroaching on a neighbor's parcel? That results in a neighbor's house encroaching on the insured's parcel? What protection does it provide against a subsequent buyer's refusal to perform his purchase contract with the insured because of unmarketable title? Against an undelivered deed in the insured's chain of title? Against a wild deed, appearing outside the insured's chain of title? Compare Ryczkowski v. Chelsea Title & Guaranty Co., 85 Nev. 37, 449 P.2d 261 (1969) (easement, granted by insured's predecessor in title and recorded before predecessor had acquired patent from state, was outside chain of title and thus was excluded from coverage since policy did not insure against loss by reason of easements or claims of easements not shown by public records).

Would the policy protect the buyer in Dover Pool & Racquet Club v. Brooking, at page 99? As governmental regulation of land use has increased, title companies have strengthened policy language that excludes coverage for such laws. See, e.g., Manley v. Cost Control

Marketing & Management, Inc., 400 Pa.Super. 190, 583 A.2d 442 (1990) (excluding coverage for property designated as wetlands).

Would a buyer be barred from recovering under this policy if, knowing that part of the parcel was soon to be condemned, he failed to disclose this fact to the insurer? See L. Smirlock Realty Corp. v. Title Guarantee Co., 52 N.Y.2d 179, 437 N.Y.S.2d 57, 418 N.E.2d 650 (1981) ("We hold that a policy of title insurance will not be rendered void pursuant to a misrepresentation clause absent some showing of intentional concealment on the part of the insured tantamount to fraud. Moreover, because record information of a title defect is available to the title insurer and because the title insurer is presumed to have made itself aware of such information, we hold that an insured under a policy of title insurance such as is involved herein is under no duty to disclose to the insurer a fact which is readily ascertainable by reference to the public records. Thus, even an intentional failure to disclose a matter of public record will not result in a loss of title insurance protection.")

For an excellent treatise on title insurance, see D. Burke, The Law of Title Insurance (1986). On title insurance generally, see A.B.A., Title Insurance: The Lawyer's Expanding Role (1985); Rooney, Title Insurance: A Primer for Attorneys, 14 Real Prop., Probate & Trust J. 608 (1979); Taub, Rights and Remedies Under a Title Policy, 15 Real Prop., Probate & Trust J. 422 (1980).

3. *Municipal Code Violations.* Plaintiff, purchaser of two unimproved lots, sued her title insurer, claiming unmarketability of title on the ground that the City Council had, in violation of a city ordinance, approved a subdivision map on her property without first obtaining a bond from the developer for grading and paving the streets in the subdivision. The city later refused to issue a building permit for her parcels because of the violation. Plaintiff claimed that the ordinance "was a part of her contract of title insurance issued to her by defendant, and that violation by the county recorder of the Subdivision Map Act, constituted a breach of the title policy."

The court held against plaintiff, reasoning that the violation did not "affect the marketability of her *title* to the land but merely impaired the market *value* of the property." The dissenting judge argued that "defendant by insuring the marketability of ... title thereby guaranteed also the title to at least a private easement in the streets. ... Certainly if title is conveyed which shows frontage on a public street, it is defective if there is no public street, or the existence thereof is gravely doubtful, and it has been so held." Hocking v. Title Ins. & Trust Co., 37 Cal.2d 644, 234 P.2d 625 (1951).

Is it relevant that plaintiff might have been able to obtain an endorsement to her policy specifically aimed at the problem that arose?

4. *Title Insurance and Title Warranties Compared.* Many titles are doubly assured, through title warranties given by the seller and title insurance from an institutional insurer. (Title warranties are discussed at page 230, above.) Although title warranties and title insur-

ance overlap at many points, each also offers distinctive protection. A buyer who cannot get his title insurance company to delete an exception from its policy's coverage may turn to his seller and insist that she cover the exception by a deed warranty. Also, there are many defects, including off-record risks, that title insurance may not cover. And the damages recoverable under a title policy are limited to the face amount of the policy; additional damages may be recovered under a warranty deed.

Why would a buyer want title insurance instead of, or in addition to, warranties? Title policies offer a degree of flexibility unattainable through warranties. Endorsements can be obtained to cover off-record risks and to increase the policy's coverage so that it keeps pace with inflation and with the value of improvements put on the premises. The protection of title policies can in certain instances be made to "run" to distant transferees through endorsements insuring assignments. Title companies also offer institutional advantages—basically, an available, solvent and knowledgeable defendant. Probably most important is the fact that title insurance is not issued on a casualty basis. The insurer's title search is aimed at flushing out any possible flaws in title and at reducing the possibility that an insured will someday have to yield his home to a prior claimant and be relegated to the cold comfort of a monetary award.

See generally Freshman, The Warranty Deed: Where and When to Use It, 51 L.A.B.J. 186 (1975); Curtis, Title Assurance in Sales of California Residential Realty: A Critique of Title Insurance and Title Covenants with Suggested Reforms, 7 Pac. L.J. 1 (1976).

5. *Insurer's Liability Outside the Policy.* Like fire, theft and accident insurance, title insurance serves two functions. It spreads casualty losses among many policyholders, and it seeks to reduce the risk that the covered casualty will occur. Title insurance differs from these other forms of insurance by effectively reducing risk to a point at which hardly any casualty element remains. By maintaining a complete and current title plant, conducting careful title searches, and analyzing title meticulously, the company can hope to reduce its risk of loss on title claims to almost zero. This explains why title policies, unlike more typical casualty policies, call for a comparatively modest one-time premium, payable at the time of closing.

Can a buyer who has relied on a title insurer to perform its usual careful search prevail in a tort action against the company when it conducts that search negligently or fails to disclose discovered defects? Although a number of states hold that he can (see, e.g., Dinges v. Lawyers Title Insurance Corp., 106 Ill.App.3d 188, 62 Ill.Dec. 146, 435 N.E.2d 944 (1982)), other courts limit the buyer to the terms of the insurance contract. See, for example, Walker Rogge, Inc. v. Chelsea Title & Guaranty Co., 116 N.J. 517, 562 A.2d 208 (1989); Horn v. Lawyers Title Insurance Corp., 89 N.M. 709, 711, 557 P.2d 206, 208 (1976) ("The rights and duties of the parties are fixed by the contract of title insurance .... Hence, any duty on the part of defendant to search the records must be expressed in or implied from the policy of title insurance .... Defendant clearly had no duty under the policy to search the records, and any search it may have actually undertaken, was undertaken solely for its own protection as indemnitor against losses covered by its policy."). Statutes in some jurisdictions impose a duty on insurers to make a reasonable search (see, e.g., Tenn.Code Ann. § 56–35–129) while others expressly reject liability for negligent search (see, e.g., Cal.Ins.Code § 12340.10–12340.11).

Courts which permit recovery for negligent search and disclosure often do so despite language in the policy limiting recovery for claims, including negligence claims, to the provisions of the policy. See L. Smirlock Realty Corp. v. Title Guarantee Co., 52 N.Y.2d 179, 180, 437 N.Y.S.2d 57, 62, 418 N.E.2d 650, 655 (1981) ("This duty may not be abrogated through a standard policy clause which would, if given the effect urged by the defendant, place the onus of the title company's failure adequately to search the records on the party who secured the insurance protection for that very purpose.").

One commentator notes that courts have resisted a tort duty because it may interfere with contract rights, full disclosure of title defects may frighten purchasers unnecessarily and decrease alienability, and liability may lead to increased costs of title insurance. She argues, however, that such a duty would force insurers to search more carefully, remove the need for a wasteful second search for disclosure purposes, and is in accord with the expectations of the insured. Palomar, Title Insurance Companies' Liability for Failure to Search Title and Disclose Record Title, 20 Creighton L.Rev. 455 (1987).

Why would a buyer prefer tort theory to contract theory in an action against a title insurer? One reason is that if the land has appreciated in value, tort recovery will be more likely to make the buyer whole than will recovery limited to the face amount of the policy. Also, tort theory enables recovery of consequential damages. And, of course, if the buyer relied on his seller's title insurance policy, rather than on a title policy he purchased for himself, the absence of privity will make tort the only available theory of recovery. Compare Williams v. Polgar, page 298 above.

See generally, Note, Title Insurance: The Duty to Search, 71 Yale L.J. 1161 (1962); Note, Does a Title Insurer *Qua* Title Insurer Owe a Duty to Any But Its Insured? 7 Okla. City L.Rev. 293 (1982).

6. *Regulation.* As title insurance companies have grown and expanded into new territories they have inevitably encountered state regulation. Although regulatory patterns vary from state to state, two concerns predominate: the price and quality of insurance, and the insurer's solvency. In Washington, for example, title insurers must file their rates with the state insurance commissioner who "may order the modification of any premium rate or schedule of premium rates found

by him after a hearing to be excessive, or inadequate, or unfairly discriminatory." Wash.Rev.Code Ann. § 48.29.140(3) (West 1984).

Most states require specified reserve funds and capitalization levels to assure the ability of title companies to pay off claims against them. New York, with one of the more extensive and detailed statutes, calls, among other things, for a "loss reserve at least equal to the aggregate estimated amounts due or to become due on account of all such unpaid losses and claims ...." N.Y.Ins.Law § 6405(b) (McKinney 1985). Some states require a cash deposit with the insurance commissioner and prohibit the issuance of any policy exposing the insurer to loss liability for more than fifty percent of its total capital and surplus. See, for example, Hawaii Rev.Stat. § 431:20–112 (1988).

On regulatory issues, see Quiner, Title Insurance and the Title Insurance Industry, 22 Drake L.Rev. 711 (1973).

7. *Antitrust.* One commentator has suggested that title insurance rates in some jurisdictions reflect price fixing and price discrimination as a result of a risk rate benchmark established by a national association and followed by some companies and the use in some states of a rating bureau formed collectively by the title companies to set rates. He proposes the repeal of the federal antitrust exemption for title insurance companies and the end of rating bureaus. Uri, The Title Insurance Industry: A Reexamination, 17 Real Est.L.J. 313 (1989). A later article in the same journal responds, maintaining that there is adequate control over rating bureaus by state regulators to ensure fair and nondiscriminatory prices and arguing that federal intervention would unduly interfere with state decisions. Christie, The Title Insurance Industry: A Reexamination Revisited, 18 Real Est.L.J. 354 (1990).

In Federal Trade Commission v. Ticor Title Insurance Co., ___ U.S. ___, 112 S.Ct. 2169, 119 L.Ed.2d 410 (1992), the F.T.C. challenged the uniform rates for title searches and examinations set by rating bureaus in four states as the product of illegal price fixing. The Court held that the doctrine immunizing state action from antitrust liability prevented the F.T.C. from challenging the practices of the rating bureaus in the two states where the state government actively supervised the bureaus.

8. *Attorneys.* Does an attorney who serves as agent for a title company create an improper conflict of interest when he issues a policy to a client that he is representing in a land purchase? Formal Opinion 331 (1972) of the Committee on Ethics and Professional Responsibility of the ABA states that the attorney may participate in such transactions providing that he obtains consent from both parties after full disclosure of possible conflicts. One commentator maintains, however, that there is an irreconcilable conflict in such situations since the attorney has a pecuniary interest in recommending title insurance and also, as agent of the company, may not strongly represent the buyer's interest to obtain a policy free from as many exceptions and exclusions as possible. See Note, Conflict of Interest: Attorney As Title Insurance Agent, 4 Geo.J.Leg. Ethics 687 (1991). Reconsider *Lanza*, p. 18 above.

Should the attorney be permitted to represent the company and the purchaser after full disclosure? Will disclosure ever be adequate? Will the attorney perhaps be able to get even better coverage for the buyer because of his ties to the company? Is this kind of joint representation more efficient? What if the purchaser has to get a new attorney to review the title policy for fairness?

See Guardian Title Co. v. Bell, 248 Kan.146, 805 P.2d 33 (1991) (upholding as constitutional a Kansas statute prohibiting steering of customers to title companies by persons with an undisclosed financial interest in the company); Kickbacks to Lawyers Rapped, 72 A.B.A.J. 30 (Nov. 1, 1986).

C. INCREASING THE EFFICIENCY OF TITLE ASSURANCE

Paul Basye, a longtime observer of American title assurance methods, identified seven characteristics of an efficient title system: "(1) it should allow the recording of all facts pertinent to ownership and proof of title; (2) it should require that all records affecting land be lodged in a single office rather than in several offices; (3) it should require that the land records be so constituted and organized with indices or other devices as to provide quick access to all instruments and facts affecting the ownership of a particular parcel of land; (4) it should make the record self-proving so that an owner may make prima facie proof of his title by reference to the public records; (5) it should contain all necessary machinery to bar old claims and extinguish old interests and do so in such a way as to make the legal effect of the bar apparent from the record; (6) it should include the means to facilitate the prompt correction of defects and irregularities in conveyancing which give rise to interests which are not real or substantial; and (7) it should define marketability of title in such a way as to make it reasonably simple of determination and within a restricted period of record search and of title examination." P. Basye, Clearing Land Titles 7–8 (2d ed. 1970).

Most states have taken an incremental approach to conveyancing reform, tinkering with the recording acts and introducing modest procedural and substantive innovations such as curative acts, statutes of limitations and marketable title acts. These reforms are considered below. Some states have taken the bolder, generally less successful, step of instituting so-called Torrens systems. Torrens is considered in the second part of this section. And, as indicated in the preceding section, the dramatic institutional reforms wrought by the national title insurance industry are always present in the background, sometimes overshadowing public law reform efforts.

The most recent comprehensive effort at stimulating statutory reform—the Uniform Simplification of Land Transfers Act, approved by the National Conference of Commissioners on Uniform State Laws in 1976 and by the American Bar Association in 1978—follows the modest, incremental tradition. On the Act generally, see Curtis, Simplifying Land Transfers: The Recordation and Marketable Title Provisions of the Uniform Simplification of Land Transfers Act, 62 Or.L.Rev. 363 (1983); Maggs, Land Records of the Uniform Simplification of Land Transfers Act, 1981 So.Ill.U.L.J. 491; Mattis, The Uniform Simplification of Land Transfers Act: Article 2—Conveyancing and Recording, 1981 So.Ill.U.L.J. 511; Bruce, An Overview of the Uniform Land Transactions Act and the Uniform Simplification of Land Transfers Act, 10 Stetson L.Rev. 1 (1980).

-----

1. MARKETABLE TITLE ACTS, STATUTES OF LIMITATIONS AND CURATIVE ACTS

L. SIMES AND C. TAYLOR, IMPROVEMENT OF CONVEYANCING BY LEGISLATION

3–6, 17–19, 37, 41–43 (1960).

MARKETABLE TITLE ACTS

No other remedial legislation which has been enacted or proposed in recent years for the improvement of conveyancing offers as much as the marketable title act. It may be regarded as the keystone in the arch which constitutes the structure of a modernized system of conveyancing.

Without doubt the chief impetus for such legislation has been the increasing length of the record of instruments which must be examined before a land title can be approved. As is well known, the practice still prevails in a very large number of states to trace title back to a grant from the United States or from a state. The period of search thus becomes longer and longer as time goes on; and eventually this practice will have to be abandoned and the period restricted.

There is, of course, nothing new about limiting the period of search to a certain number of years. Obviously, in England, where there is no such thing as tracing land titles back to the government, the practice has long obtained of a vendee requiring title deeds to show a chain of title only for a fixed period of years. In some way this period seems to have been found by using the analogy of the longest period named in statutes of limitations with respect to actions for the recovery of real property. At the present time the period accepted is thirty years, and this practice is embodied in a statute. Similar practices have developed in some of the eastern states, where chains of title may be centuries long and are not traceable to the government.

But these practices of the bar in which titles are traced back only for an agreed period of years are unlike marketable title acts in one important respect. The bar practices leave the risk of loss, by reason of a defect in the title prior to the named period, on the purchaser. But under a marketable title act defects in the title prior to the named period are, by operation of the statute, extinguished.

Sometimes the modern American marketable title act is phrased like a statute of limitations; sometimes it may be analogized to a curative act. But in fact it is neither; and indeed it is definitely unique. Instead of interests being cut off because a claimant failed to sue, as would be the case if a statute of limitations were involved, the claimant's interest is extinguished because he failed to file a notice. In a sense the marketable title act may impose upon an owner a small additional burden, analogous to the burden of recording which was imposed when recording acts were first passed. Thus, before the recording acts, a prior conveyance from an owner of land was unimpeachable. But under recording acts, the grantee in the prior conveyance may lose his if he fails to record. Likewise, under a marketable title act, a claimant under a recorded deed may be required to file a notice in order to protect his title.

The essence of the Model Marketable Title Act which follows is simply this: If a person has a record chain of title for forty years, and no one else has filed a notice of claim to the property during the forty-year period, then all conflicting claims based upon any title transaction prior to the forty-year period are extinguished.

In one sense, the operation of the statute is all inclusive. It cuts off all interests, subject to a few exceptions unlikely to be encountered, which arise from title transactions prior to the forty-year period. It can extinguish ancient mortgages, servitudes, easements, titles by adverse possession, interests which are equitable as well as legal, future as well as present.

Yet in another sense, as a practical matter, the statute will probably cut off nothing at all, because there are no valid outstanding claims. It has been the experience of states with long-term marketable title acts that few if any notices of claim are ever filed, thus indicating that few claims actually exist. Indeed, the very fact that in some states title examination for only a thirty- or forty-year period is commonly accepted, without any legislation so providing, indicates that there are in fact no enforceable claims adverse to the thirty- or forty-year chain of title.

It must not be assumed that the enactment of the Model Marketable Title Act will necessarily usher in an era of forty-year abstracts of title. The very fact that there are exceptions in the statute means that a title examiner will have to look back of the forty-year period to find instruments which may include the exceptions. But a competent title examiner will be able to see at a glance that most of the instruments do not concern the exceptions, and thus his task will be definitely lightened.

An important feature of the operation of the statute, however, is its curative effect. Ancient defects, which do not in fact give rise to substantial claims, but which may be the basis of a refusal to approve a title, are completely wiped out if they appear in the record more than forty years back. Even though the title examiner looks at the entire record from the government down to the present time, he is still greatly aided by the fact that he can ignore ancient defects.

The question may then be asked: If marketable title legislation is all inclusive in its remedial effect, why is any other legislative reform necessary? What else is needed which the marketable title act cannot do? First, the marketable title act of the type here presented must necessarily be based on a long period. Otherwise many claims will be filed; and, unless numerous exceptions are made in the statute, many people will be deprived of substantial interests by the operation of the statute. Yet there are many remedies for defective titles which can and should operate in a much shorter period of time. Curative acts and statutes of limitations are examples.

Furthermore, the Model Act does not extinguish "interests and defects which are inherent in the muniments of which such chain of record title is formed." For example, if, prior to the forty-year period, A conveyed to B a determinable fee simple, thus leaving a possibility of reverter in A, and there have been no further conveyances, A's possibility of reverter is not extinguished by the lapse of forty years. Some other type of legislation is necessary to get rid of it.

One further question may be asked, namely: What advantages does a marketable title act have over an all-inclusive statute of limitations which names an equally long period? First, even though the limitations statute disregards disabilities, there is no rational basis for cutting off future interests before they become possessory, and no such long-term statute has done so. For, by hypothesis the statute of limitations begins to run only when there is a cause of action to recover possession, and the holder of a future interest has no right to possession. Hence, the possibility of future interests being involved would prevent the title examiner from determining that the title was necessarily good at the expiration of the statutory period. Furthermore, a title by adverse possession depends upon facts extrinsic to the record, while a title under a marketable title act depends solely upon the state of the record. Adverse possession for a long period of time is difficult to prove; and, even when proven, there is no satisfactory way to record the fact and thus acquire a good record title, short of a quiet title suit.

. . .

CURATIVE ACTS

A curative act is one which reaches back and corrects an error made in the past. As applied to conveyancing, it provides that certain prior failures to comply with the requirements for the execution or recording of an instrument, or for the transfer of an interest in land, shall be disregarded. Thus, a statute may provide that, after a defectively acknowledged instrument has been on record for two years, it shall be treated for all purposes as if it had been properly acknowledged at the time of its recording.

The permissible scope of curative legislation obviously is limited. Courts have said that one person's property may not be taken away from him and given to another as of a prior date. In general, curative statutes may be said to deal with matters of a formal character and to carry out the intentions of the parties which may otherwise have been frustrated by their failure to comply with formal requirements. Since the legislature could do away with such requirements, and since, quite commonly, the parties could be relieved of the requirements in the particular case by a judicial proceeding, retroactive statutes may be passed relieving the parties of these formal requirements as of a prior time.

In spite of their limitations, curative acts have been in operation since colonial times. They have dealt with a variety of situations, such as the following: absence of a seal; defective acknowledgments; failure to include any acknowledgment; defective conveyances under powers of attorney; defectively executed deeds of corporations; defective records of judicial sales.

The rational basis for the curative act may be stated as follows: Since human nature is fallible, people do make mistakes in executing legal instruments. There is no way to keep mistakes from creeping into the conveyancing process. But after defective instruments have been left standing for a certain period of time, justice is generally secured by providing that the defects are then to be ignored. Thus, the basic intent of the parties will be effectuated. Just where the line is to be drawn between those objectives which can be accomplished by curative acts and those which cannot, will be discussed more fully in connection with the subject of constitutionality of such legislation. Certainly no single formula can be found which will enable us to draw the line. We must, however, recognize that curative legislation has traditionally been approved in certain areas, that it tends to further the intent of the parties, and that it will not be approved to deprive innocent third parties of their property.

If the error to be corrected by curative legislation is of sufficiently long standing, it can equally well be corrected by a marketable title act. The great advantage of having curative acts in addition to a marketable act is that the curative acts become operative, in justice to all concerned, at the expiration of a much shorter period of time than the period of a marketable title act. Hence, curative legislation, when it is used at all to clear land titles, should provide for a relatively short period after which the defect is cured.

A curative statute may take at least three possible forms. First, it may have a continuous and delayed operation, so that it will continue to cure the named defects after a certain period has elapsed. An example has already been given of a statute which continues to cure defective acknowledgments after they have been on record for two years. Second, the statute may name a particular date in the past, and be designed to cure defects in all instruments executed or recorded prior to that date. Thus, a statute might provide that all defectively acknowledged instruments which were recorded prior to January 1, 1954, shall be treated for all purposes, as if properly acknowledged at the time of their recording. The disadvantage of such a form of statute is that, as time passes, the period prior to which instruments are cured becomes longer, and it soon is necessary to enact a new statute naming a later date.

This second form of statute may, however, be desirable when it accompanies a change in legislative policy. Thus, the legislature may have repealed a requirement that instruments of conveyance be sealed. Thereafter, a statute may be enacted curing all unsealed instruments executed prior to the date of the repeal. Thus, the curative provision merely has the effect of making retroactive the statute abolishing the use of seals on instruments of conveyance. The policy in this legislation is not merely to correct the frailty of human nature, but to make retroactive a change of legislative policy.

Or, third, there may be a change in legislative policy with respect to certain formal requirements for conveyancing, and as a part of this legislation, or contemporaneous with it, a curative statute is enacted, immediately effective as to all instruments. Thus, in connection with the abolition of the requirement of a seal for instruments of conveyance, it may be enacted that, from and after the effective date of the act, all instruments of conveyance heretofore executed shall be valid without being sealed. ...

STATUTES OF LIMITATIONS

Essentially, statutes of limitations fix a time beyond which ancient disputes, claims and matters can no longer be brought forth for judicial determination. Simply by withdrawing the privilege to litigate and denying the aid of the courts in asserting claims and interests of ancient origin, they effectuate a number of important public policies. Further, although the application of a rigidly fixed time limitation in a particular case may appear arbitrary, no one doubts that, in general, they tend to promote justice as between parties to controversies. But they also perform other important functions, entirely apart from affecting the course of any actual litigation; and nowhere are such functions more important than in the law of conveyancing. ...

Statutes limiting recovery of real property commonly have three weaknesses as devices to cure defective titles: (1) the time when the period ends is uncertain due to provisions for extension by reason of disabilities and other facts; (2) adverse possession for the statutory period is outside the record and is often difficult to prove; (3) the statutes do not bar future interests. An ideal statute should go as far as possible to obviate these weaknesses.

As to disabilities, the type of statute which merely states an additional period after disabilities have terminated is undesirable. If the disability is insanity, there is no way to determine how long the period may last. It is preferable to name an overall period, which is the maximum regardless of disabilities. Thus, in the model statute the periods are extended by disabilities, but in no case are they extended beyond twenty years from the time the right of recovery first accrued. Furthermore, if the person subject to the disability is under guardianship, it is provided that there is no extension for disability during the period of guardianship. All these provisions as to disabilities are based on precedents in existing legislation, as is indicated in the comment.

The problem of the future interest is not so easily dealt with. The difficulty is that the cause of action which is barred by the statute is based on a right to possession, and the owner of the future interest has no right to possession. It is true, in a few jurisdictions it has been determined by judicial decision that the statute will run before the future interest becomes possessory, principally because the owner of the future interest can bring a suit to remove cloud on title; but this reasoning seems unconvincing and would be unlikely to be approved by most legislatures or courts. What has been done, however, in some existing legislation, is to make the period shorter when counted from the time at which the future interest becomes possessory. Thus, in the Model Act, the period is extended only five years after the future interest becomes possessory. Of course, this still leaves an element of uncertainty in applying the period, since one may not be able to predict when the future interest becomes possessory. But in a case where there is real doubt, title clearance may be aided by a marketable title act or by a statute limiting the duration of possibilities of reverter or rights of entry.

What can be said concerning the enactment of a statute of limitations with a very long period, which at the end of that time cuts off all interests regardless of disabilities or future interests? Such statutes have been enacted in a few jurisdictions, with varying periods up to a maximum of sixty years in one state. Apparently these statutes were designed to function substantially as do marketable title acts, but it would appear that they never have actually done so. The arguments against barring future interests in this way have already been indicated. In interpreting these statutes courts have generally refused to cut off future interests by this means. It is believed that the long-term statute of limitations which applies to all interests is not desirable, and its purpose can best be accomplished by marketable title legislation and by statutes which limit the duration of possibilities of reverter and rights of entry.

It is important, however, to have provisions in the statute naming a short period where there is color of title of record. This results in the clearing of a record title, and does not lead to a title based solely on extrinsic facts. It is here, no doubt, that the statute will have its greatest value for the title man. The Model Act states a period of five years for title by adverse possession with color of title consisting of recorded instruments.

However, we still are faced with the question: How do we prove adverse possession for the statutory period? Various attempts have been made by legislation to avoid the necessity of direct proof of possession. Thus, in some states payment of taxes for the statutory period is made the equivalent of possession for that period. One difficulty with that solution is that payment of taxes is a matter to be determined by tax records and not by title records, and also, tax records may not show who paid the taxes or be available for the requisite period. If it cannot be determined that the person claiming adversely paid the taxes, the payment is of uncertain significance. On the other hand, there is no reason why payment of taxes for the statutory period may not constitute prima facie evidence of adverse possession, and the Model Act so provides. It also provides that present possession together with a recorded instrument of title for the statutory period is prima facie evidence of adverse possession.

MARSHALL v. HOLLYWOOD, INC.

Supreme Court of Florida, 1970.
236 So.2d 114, cert. denied, 400 U.S. 964, 91 S.Ct. 366, 27 L.Ed.2d 384 (1970).

CARLTON, Justice.

We now review an application of the Marketable Record Titles to Real Property Act, Chapter 712, Florida Statutes. The District Court of Appeal, Fourth District, has certified that its decision in this cause, reported at 224 So.2d 743, is one which passes upon a question of great public interest. The District Court held, in effect, that the Act confers marketability to a chain of title arising out of a forged or a wild deed, so long as the strict requirements of the Act are met. We affirm this decision.

The complex facts involved in this case have been presented extensively and with clarity in the opinion of the District Court. We will only briefly summarize these facts. In 1912 Mathew Marshall and Carl Weidling owned a large tract of land in South Florida. In 1913 they organized and incorporated the Atlantic Beach Company. They transferred their property interests in the large tract to the Company, and in return they received two-thirds and one-third, respectively, of the Company's total authorized and issued stock, in direct proportion to their initial ownership interests in the tract. Marshall and Weidling were the sole officers of the Company and they alone participated in its stock.

Mr. Marshall died in December 1923, leaving Louise Marshall as his widow and sole surviving heir. Mrs. Marshall was totally unaware of her husband's interests in the Company, and within a month after his passing, she left the State without ever returning. After her departure, a man named Frank M. Terry, apparently aided and abetted by certain associates, set into motion a clever scheme calculated to defraud the Marshall estate of all interests in the Company and its property.

Although there is some question as to exactly who played what part in this scheme, for purposes of this opinion we shall ascribe all responsibility to Mr. Terry.

Within a few days after Mrs. Marshall's departure, Terry forged her name to an Application for Letters of Administration concerning Mathew Marshall's estate. Letters were subsequently issued by the County Judge, Dade County, to Mrs. Marshall and Terry received them. About this same time, Terry wrote up certain "Minutes of Dissolution of Atlantic Beach Company" and he also prepared a deed conveying all of the Company's property to himself and others residing out of the State, who were alleged in the spurious Minutes to be the remaining stockholders of the Company. Thereafter, these Minutes were purportedly acknowledged, and the deed conveying all of the Company's property was executed by those who were alleged to be the stockholders.

Next, Terry prepared a petition seeking an Order dissolving the Company which was then filed in Circuit Court, Broward County, along with the Minutes of Dissolution. The Court granted the petition since it appeared in order, and a decree dissolving the Company was entered in February 1924. The day before this petition was filed, Terry and the other grantees under the deed from the Company joined in executing a deed conveying the tract to Hollywood Realty Company, a Florida corporation. This deed was recorded in April 1924. In August 1924 Hollywood Realty in turn executed a deed conveying this same property to Homeseekers Realty Company, which was recorded August 22, 1924.

All of the foregoing transactions are alleged by petitioner to have been part of a scheme to defraud the Mathew Marshall estate. The record is silent as to why Carl Weidling, initially owner of a one-third undivided interest in the tract, and subsequently holder of one-third of the Atlantic Beach Company stock, never raised any objections or questions. Mr. Weidling died in 1963; his interests are not represented in this suit. Mrs. Marshall died in 1945 without ever having learned of her husband's interests in the Company. The Company itself was never legally dissolved until September 14, 1936, when it was dissolved by proclamation of the Governor on account of failure to pay capital stock tax.

Homeseekers Realty Company disposed of approximately one-third of the initial Atlantic Beach Company tract through sales before it lost its control over the remainder by forced sheriff's sale in 1929. In that year, the Highway Construction Company of Ohio, Inc., obtained a judgment against Homeseekers and caused the sale at which Highway purchased the remaining unsold two-thirds of the initial tract. A sheriff's deed evidencing the judgment sale was recorded December 30, 1930. Highway Construction Company then conveyed its interests in the tract to respondent Hollywood, Inc., and this deed was recorded on February 21, 1931.

Respondent Hollywood, Inc., still retains title to the two-thirds of the original Atlantic Beach tract which was conveyed to it as a result of the forced sheriff's sale. The other respondents are those numerous persons, or their successors, who derived title to parcels on the one-third portion of the original tract from Homeseekers Realty prior to the 1929 judgment sale. Diagrammed, the chain of title to the property involved in this suit, insofar as it is relevant to the issues involved here, looks like this:

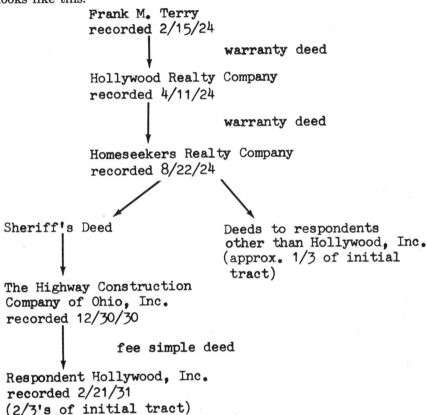

Frank M. Terry
recorded 2/15/24

                warranty deed

Hollywood Realty Company
recorded 4/11/24

                warranty deed

Homeseekers Realty Company
recorded 8/22/24

Sheriff's Deed   Deeds to respondents
other than Hollywood, Inc.
(approx. 1/3 of initial
  tract)

The Highway Construction
Company of Ohio, Inc.
recorded 12/30/30

             fee simple deed

Respondent Hollywood, Inc.
recorded 2/21/31
(2/3's of initial tract)

[C983]

It was not until November 1966, that petitioner, a brother of Mathew Marshall, uncovered Terry's actions. Petitioner obtained appointment as Administrator of the Marshall estate, and subsequently, in his capacity as Administrator, he filed his initial complaint on July 13, 1967. An amended complaint was filed on April 5, 1968. The amended complaint sought a decree establishing the equitable interest of petitioner in the tract initially belonging to the Atlantic Beach Company, confirmation of the ownership of Atlantic Beach stock by petitioner, and also the appointment of a trustee for the Company who could convey legal title to the interest in the original tract to the heirs of Marshall.

Upon respondents' motion, the amended complaint was dismissed by final judgment with prejudice. The order of dismissal stated that petitioner's amended complaint failed to state a cause of action because the estate's claims were barred by operation of the Marketable Record Title Act, Ch. 712, F.S. The dismissal was appealed to the District Court. The issue framed on appeal was whether or not the Act applied to the claim of title asserted in petitioner's amended complaint in a manner which would extinguish the claim.

... The most persuasive argument of petitioner is that the Marketable Record Title Act preserves case law which is inconsistent with dismissal of petitioner's amended complaint. F.S. § 712.07, F.S.A. states:

"Nothing contained in this Act shall be construed to extend the period for the bringing of an action or for the doing of any other act required under any statute of limitations or to affect the operation of any statute governing the effect of the recording or the failure to record any instrument affecting land. This law shall not vitiate any curative act."

Petitioner asserts that by preserving the operation of statutes of limitations, and curative and recording acts, the Legislature intended that the Act must be construed in a manner consistent with these previous enactments and all case law interpreting them. In cases dealing with wild or forged deeds under these various acts, it has consistently been held, according to petitioner, that such deeds are void and of no effect even though they may have been recorded. Therefore petitioner suggests that the Act cannot bar a complaint which demonstrates that the chain of title involved in a cause initiated out of a forgery or a wild deed, even though the forgery or the wild deed came into being more than thirty years before marketability was being determined.

The answer to this argument is simply that the Act in question goes beyond previous enactments and is in a category of its own. We quote with approval the following commentary. Boyer & Shapo, Florida's Marketable Title Act: Prospects and Problems, 18 U.Miami L.Rev. 103, 104:

"The Marketable title concept is simple, although it has fathered many variations in draftsmanship. The idea is to extinguish all claims of a given age (thirty years in the Florida Statute) which conflict with a record chain of title which is at least that old. The act performs this task by combining several features, which generally, are singly labeled as 'statutes of limitations,' 'curative acts,' and 'recording acts.'

"The new act is in fact all of these: It declares a marketable title on a recorded chain of title which is more than thirty years old, and it nullifies all interests which are older than the root of title. This nullification is subject to a group of exceptions—including interests which have been filed for record in a prescribed manner.

"The act is also more: It goes beyond the conventional statute of limitations because it runs against persons under disability. It is broader than the kind of legislation generally described as a curative act, because it actually invalidates interests instead of simply 'curing' formal defects. It also differs from a recording act by requiring a rerecording of outstanding interests in order to preserve them."

. . .

In view of the special nature of this Act and its special purpose, the assertion that its construction and application must be bound by precedents relating to less comprehensive acts does not make good sense and cannot make good law. The clear Legislative intention behind the Act, as expressed in F.S. § 712.10, F.S.A., was to simplify and facilitate land title transactions by allowing persons to rely on a record title as described by F.S. § 712.02, F.S.A., subject only to such limitations as appear in F.S. § 712.03, F.S.A. To accept petitioner's arguments would be to disembowel the Act through a case dealing with a factual situation of a nature precisely contemplated and remedied by the Act itself. This we cannot do.

In summary, although the Atlantic Beach Company/Terry deed initiating the chain of title involved here was forged, this deed formed but one link in the chain coming *before* the effective roots of title in this case as defined by the Act, i.e., transactions with either The Highway Construction Company or the Homeseekers Realty Company as grantors. Claims arising out of transactions, whether based upon forgeries or not, predating the effective roots of title are extinguished by operation of the Act unless claimants can come in under any of the specified exceptions to the Act. In this case, petitioner fails to qualify under any of the exceptions to the Act, and therefore, petitioner's claims are barred.

The certified question involved in this cause was, in effect, whether the Marketable Record Titles to Real Property Act, Ch. 712, F.S., confers marketability to a chain of title arising out of a forged or wild deed, so long as the strict requirements of the Act are met. This question is answered in the affirmative.

The decision of the appellate court here reviewed having properly affirmed the decree of the lower court, the writ heretofore issued in this cause should be and it is hereby discharged.

It is so ordered.

ERVIN, C.J., ROBERTS, DREW, ADKINS and BOYD, JJ., and VANN, Circuit Judge, concur.

2. TITLE REGISTRATION: THE TORRENS SYSTEM
C. FLICK, 1 ABSTRACT AND TITLE PRACTICE *
188–190, 192–194 (2d ed. 1958).

The certificate system is in world-wide use for the purpose of showing ownership of merchant vessels. Every ship is listed in a national registry. A page in the Register is devoted to each ship and on that page there appears its name and description, the name of the owner, and any encumbrances. A duplicate of this page in the form of a certificate is given to the owner and is his evidence of ownership no matter where he may be. It is usually kept on the ship and accordingly is frequently spoken of in literature as the "ship's papers." Any lien or claim against a ship is required to be noted on the original register page so that it is possible for any interested person to tell at a glance exactly the condition of the title. To make a transfer, the owner assigns the certificate which he has and takes it to the registry office whereupon the old certificate is cancelled, the old page is closed, a new page is opened, and a duplicate certificate of the new page is given to the new owner.

In fact the Torrens system grew out of the fact that its originator, Robert R. Torrens, had been connected with the shipping industry for a number of years before he was appointed Registrar General of the Province of South Australia and given charge of registering all instruments affecting the title to real estate in that province. His experience in his former office led him to speculate on the subject of why the title to a tract of land could not be registered with the same simplicity as the title to a ship. He demonstrated that this was entirely possible and the system for which he drafted the law in Australia has proven to be a very efficient method of keeping track of the ownership of real property and of simplifying every transaction concerned with transferring the title or of using that type of property as security.

Torrens Acts have been passed in California, 1897; Colorado, 1903; Illinois, 1895, declared invalid and new act passed in 1897; Massachusetts, 1898; Minnesota, 1901; Mississippi, 1913; New York, 1908; North Carolina, 1913; Ohio, 1896, declared invalid and new act passed in 1913; Oregon, 1901; Washington, 1907; Hawaii, 1903; and the Philippines, 1902.

The only acts of this nature which have been declared unconstitutional were the first acts of Ohio and Illinois. Neither of those provided for a decree of court before there could be registration, and in each state a later act was passed, which did so provide. ...

Upon each voluntary transfer by deed, and upon each involuntary transfer by deed, decree, descent, devise, or otherwise when accompanied by a court order directing it, the registrar cancels the old certificate and its duplicate and enters a new certificate and delivers an owner's duplicate to the new owner—all much the same as in the case of a transfer of corporation stock. It is the registration of a conveyance which is the operative act of transfer to a new owner. Prior to registration, a deed of registered land, like a fulfilled contract for a deed under the recording system, creates merely a right to the title as between the parties and is of no effect as to a bona fide purchaser from the registered owner.

From the foregoing it will be apparent that a report as to ownership may be made, and can only be made, from an examination, direct or indirect, of the original certificate of title on file in the office of the registrar. The certificate will usually be found to be in such definite and certain terms that no construction is required; when this is not the case the principles which govern the construction of deeds also apply to certificates of title. The reliability of an examiner's report will necessarily depend upon the conclusiveness of the certificate of title. This may vary slightly in the different states, but the variation is confined almost entirely to the difference in periods of limitation and periods allowed for appeal, or to reopen, as to a case upon the final order in which a certificate depends. After allowing for these, and for such exceptions as are expressly provided for in the registration statutes, the certificate creates an indefeasible title in the registered owner as against every one else, free from all claims and incumbrances except those noted on the certificate of title. Examination of the certificate alone is all that is necessary to determine ownership of the legal title.

Loss or destruction of duplicates occasionally occurs, and the registration acts all make provision for issuance of a new duplicate. In some states this is only after notice and hearing by the court, in others upon proof of loss and identity to the registrar, but in all states under very careful safeguards. Neither the public nor the owner is subject to any danger of loss from forged deeds so long as the latter safeguards his duplicate with the same care that he keeps any other valuable paper. If he is careless in the matter of to whom he entrusts it, there exists, except for the owner's signature card on file with the registrar, the same danger that exists with unregistered titles—with the loss, however, if not payable from an assurance fund, upon the negligent owner rather than upon an innocent purchaser or mortgagee.

In furtherance of the theory that everything regarding a present title should be ascertainable from the certificate on file in the office of the Registrar of Titles, the statutes provide that no title to registered land in derogation of that of the registered owner may be acquired by prescription or by adverse possession and, in the main, that the time-honored doctrine in most states of constructive notice by reason of occupancy does not prevail. This is the only change in substantive principles, though there are necessarily some changes in purely statutory principles, such as the nonapplicability of the recording act, the inception of judgment liens and other matters.

ECHOLS v. OLSEN

Supreme Court of Illinois, 1976.
63 Ill.2d 270, 347 N.E.2d 720.

WARD, Chief Justice.

What the facts are in this case is not in dispute. Vernal Echols, the petitioner, and her husband Valentine were joint owners of a lot in Chicago that was registered under "An Act concerning land titles" (Ill.Rev.Stat.1973, ch. 30, pars. 45–148) (hereafter cited as the Torrens Act). On September 29, 1966, the circuit court of Cook County entered a decree of divorce in a suit that had been brought by the petitioner. Under the terms of the decree, the petitioner was required to pay her former husband $2,000 and he, in turn, was required to execute a quitclaim deed in her favor surrendering his interest in the lot. The petitioner's attorney recorded the quitclaim deed in the office of the Cook County Recorder of Deeds on October 18, 1966, but he failed at that time to register the deed with the Cook County Registrar of Titles (Registrar).

The Independence Bank of Chicago (the Bank) obtained in 1969 an *ex parte* judgment in the amount of $1,058.67, against Valentine Echols. On January 21, 1971, the Bank had the judgment memorialized on the duplicate Torrens certificate that is maintained in the Registrar's office. As the petitioner had not registered the quitclaim deed, the duplicate certificate had shown Valentine and Vernal Echols as joint owners of the lot. On February 24, 1971, Vernal Echols filed a petition in the circuit court requesting the court to direct the Registrar to remove the Bank's memorial and to issue a new certificate showing title to be in the petitioner alone. Both the Bank and the Registrar were named as respondents.

The Bank moved to dismiss the petition contending that under the Torrens Act a judgment creditor who memorializes his judgment after the judgment debtor has conveyed his interest in property acquires an interest superior to that of a prior transferee who failed to register his deed. On August 4, 1971, the court ordered the Registrar to issue a new certificate of title showing title to be in the petitioner alone but showing that her interest was subject to the Bank's registered judgment.

The petitioner filed a notice of appeal to the appellate court on September 17, 1971, but she served a copy of it only upon the Bank. The petitioner and the Bank briefed and orally argued the case and the court reversed the trial court, holding that the Bank did not acquire an interest in the property since Valentine Echols had conveyed his interest to the petitioner before the judgment was memorialized. 10 Ill.App.3d 752, 755, 295 N.E.2d 319.

On learning of the decision, the Registrar moved the appellate court to dismiss the appeal for failing to provide him with notice of the appeal, or, in the alternative, to have the court withdraw its opinion and to permit him to file a brief and to argue his position, which was the same as the Bank's. The court did not withdraw its opinion but it did allow the Registrar to file a brief. After oral argument on June 4, 1975, by the petitioner and the Registrar, the appellate court on June 9, 1975, announced this order:

"On our own motion we allowed a rehearing. We have again allowed oral argument and considered the briefs that were filed. We find no merit in the request we dismiss the appeal. After thoroughly reviewing the case again, we are of the opinion our original decision was correct and we so hold. It is hereby ordered the rehearing is dismissed."

We granted the Registrar's petition for leave to appeal under our Rule 315.

. . .

We must now consider whether under the Torrens Act, as the Registrar contends, a judgment creditor who has registered his judgment after the judgment debtor has conveyed his interest in the property acquires an interest superior to that of a prior grantee from the debtor who did not register his deed. The principal objective of the Torrens Act is "to provide an independent system of registration, whereby an intending purchaser of land can determine from the register the condition of the title." While generally it has been held that to achieve this all matters affecting title to registered property should be either registered or memorialized so that the Registrar's duplicate certificate will indicate to all interested parties the status of the title, we have held that the provisions of the Act must be construed in light of the established law of property and that the register of title will not always be considered conclusive.

The language of the Torrens Act does not provide any direct answer to the Registrar's contention; nor has the contention been considered in any reported decision in Illinois. The Registrar urges that in order to serve the objective of the Act, that is, to enable an intending purchaser to determine the condition of title from the register we should read into the Act a provision similar to section 30 of "An Act concerning conveyances" (Ill.Rev.Stat.1973, ch. 30, par. 29) (hereafter the Conveyance Act). Section 30 provides that a judgment creditor, as well as a *bona fide* purchaser, who records his judgment in accordance with the provisions of the Conveyance Act acquires rights superior to those of the holder of a prior unrecorded interest. It is only because of this statute that a judgment creditor will prevail over the holder of a prior but unrecorded interest. The plea of the Registrar that we read into the Torrens Act what section 30 of the Conveyance Act provides cannot be allowed. To do so would be an egregious intrusion upon the legislative authority. The Torrens Act was designed by the legislature to protect intending purchasers and has never been considered to extend the preference to judgment creditors. Judgment creditors under section 30 are preferred to holders of prior but unrecorded interests only because of that statute. Section 30 existed prior to the Torrens Act and it is not unreasonable to say that had the legislature intended that judgment creditors receive under the Torrens Act the priority and preference they are given under Section 30 it would have inserted a provision in the Torrens Act similar to section 30.

The Torrens Act provides that in disputes under it, courts should be guided by the provisions of the Act, of course, and by general principles of equity. The holder of an unregistered interest has strong claims to equitable consideration, especially when, as here, the holder of an interest claiming preference (here, the Bank) did not rely upon the absence of a registration. We said in Kostelny v. Peterson, 19 Ill.2d 480, 484, 167 N.E.2d 203, 205 that:

"Whereas at common law a deed took effect upon delivery without regard to recordation, under the Torrens Act it is the registration itself which completes the conveyance of legal title.

"This does not mean, however, that under the registration statute [Ill.Rev.Stat.1973, ch. 30, par. 98] an unfiled deed must be considered as a mere executory contract. Rather, as was pointed out in Klouda v. Pechousek, 414 Ill. 75, 110 N.E.2d 258, and Naiburg v. Hendriksen, 370 Ill. 502, 19 N.E.2d 348, a deed to Torrens property may take effect in equity upon delivery to the grantee so as to immediately pass the equitable title."

Too, it has been held that a judgment creditor's lien extends under section 30 only to the actual interest of the judgment debtor in the property and that this interest will not be extended to allow him to claim property of another in satisfaction of his lien in the absence of a statute specifically giving him this right. It was said in East St. Louis Lumber Co. v. Schnipper, 310 Ill. 150, 156, 141 N.E. 542, 544, that a judgment creditor cannot attach his judgment to a "mere naked legal estate when the entire equitable estate is vested in some third person."

When Valentine Echols quitclaimed his interest to the petitioner in September of 1966, he relinquished all equitable rights in the property. The Bank could not attach its judgment to the legal interest which remained in his name only because the petitioner had not registered the quitclaim deed. The trial court erred in not ordering the Registrar to remove the Bank's memorial.

We do not accept the Registrar's additional argument that since it was the petitioner's neglect that led the Bank to memorialize its judgment, the judgment creditor should prevail as a matter of equity. The force that this argument would have in the case of a *bona fide* purchaser for value who without notice purchased property relying on the state of the registered title of the property or the case of a mortgagee who made a loan because of a similar reliance does not extend to a judgment creditor who has not acted to his prejudice in reliance on the registered state of title.

. . .

For the reasons given the judgment of the appellate court is affirmed.

Judgment affirmed.

KLUCZYNSKI, J., dissenting:

I must respectfully dissent from the majority's opinion.

The issue presented in this appeal is whether a judgment lien, properly memorialized under the Torrens Act, attaches to the legal title of a registered owner after he has executed an unregistered deed of his entire interest to another. The Torrens Act contains a number of provisions relevant to this issue. Section 46 of the Act (Ill.Rev.Stat. 1973, ch. 30, par. 90) provides that the bringing of land under the Act, or any dealings with land registered thereunder, implies an agreement that the land be subject to the terms of the Act, i.e., the holders of title take registered property "subject to all of the rights, privileges and obligations of such registration and the law applicable thereto," and are "presumed to know all of its terms".

Section 54 states that a "deed . . . purporting to convey . . . registered land . . . shall take effect only by way of contract . . . and as authority to the registrar to register the transfer . . ." and that only "on the completion of such registration [does] the land . . . become transferred . . . according to the . . . terms of the deed . . . ." (Ill.Rev. Stat.1973, ch. 30, par. 98.) Accordingly, petitioner's quitclaim deed from her husband was only a contract purporting to convey whatever interest he possessed in the joint tenancy at the time the transfer was completed upon registration. Under the present factual situation, at the time the transfer was completed by registration, the interest of petitioner's husband was already subject to the judgment lien. Since section 45 (Ill.Rev.Stat.1973, ch. 30, par. 89) provides that a lien properly memorialized shall be carried forward until cancelled according to the Act, it necessarily follows that a lien memorialized before land is transferred by registration must be carried forward.

This court has previously held section 54 not determinative in a number of cases, some cited by the majority, on the ground that an unregistered deed is effective to transfer the equitable title. None of these cases, however, involved the rights of a party who duly registered an interest from or through a registered owner as against the rights of another who claimed under a prior unregistered instrument.

. . .

In the present case while petitioner received equitable title at the time of execution of the quitclaim deed from her husband, until she registered her interest, her husband had the power to encumber or transfer, voluntarily or involuntarily, his interest. Until it was registered, petitioner's equitable title was subject to divestment. Had the petitioner's husband voluntarily transferred his registered interest to another who was not a party to fraud, the latter would take the interest free of any claim by the petitioner. The Torrens Act provides no basis for distinguishing in this regard between voluntary or involuntary conveyances, or between those who take by judgment lien, purchase or otherwise. The Act is very explicit:

"Except in case of fraud and except as herein otherwise provided, *no person* taking a transfer of registered land, or *any* estate or interest therein, or of *any charge* upon the same from the registered owner shall be held to inquire into the circumstances under which, or the consideration for which such owner or any previous registered owner was registered, or be affected with notice, actual or constructive, of *any unregistered* trust, lien, *claim,* demand or *interest;* and the knowledge that *any unregistered* trust, lien, *claim,* demand or interest is in existence shall not of itself be imputed as fraud." (Emphasis added.) Ill.Rev.Stat.1973, ch. 30, par. 86.

Section 84 of the Act (Ill.Rev.Stat.1973, ch. 30, par. 121) states that no civil action affecting registered land shall be deemed *lis pendens* or notice to any person unless a certificate of the pendency of such action is filed with the Registrar and memorialized. Since petitioner's divorce action involved her interest in the land and resulted in a decree requiring the execution of a quitclaim deed, it was a suit affecting registered land. Had the action been memorialized according to the provisions of section 84, it would have provided notice to the Bank before it registered its judgment lien.

By virtue of section 30 of the Conveyance Act, a judgment creditor may have priority over the holder of a prior unrecorded interest in the same land. The opinion maintains that "[s]ection 30 existed prior to the Torrens Act and it is not unreasonable to say that had the legislature intended the judgment creditors receive under the Torrens Act the priority and preference they are given under section 30 it would have inserted a provision in the Torrens Act similar to section 30." The defect in this reasoning, however, is that it assumes the Torrens and the recording systems are comparable, while, in fact, the theoretical basis for each system and its practical operations are quite different.

Under the recording system, the legal title and the title of record may be completely different. A party who acquires an interest in land by deed under the recording system may or may not record this instrument. If the interest is not recorded, the party who takes under it faces the risk that a subsequent purchaser entitled to the protection of the recording act may, by virtue of that act, acquire priority. In Illinois, a subsequent purchaser is entitled to the Act's protection if he is a purchaser in good faith, without notice of the prior unrecorded instrument, pays value and records first. The recording of an instrument imparts constructive notice and prevents subsequent purchasers from taking without notice. Under the recording acts of most jurisdictions, judgment creditors are not protected by the acts because they are not considered to be purchasers or are not considered to have paid value within the meaning of those acts. Thus, the necessity of a section 30 is apparent to place judgment creditors at some level of priority.

The Torrens system of registration is an almost completely different system in both theory and practical operation. Under Torrens, the title itself is registered, not merely the evidences thereof. "The Torrens Act differs in many material respects from the usual method of transferring title and the requirement for recording instruments affecting title. In respect to property not registered under the Torrens Act, title is transferred by the delivery of a deed from the owner to the grantee. The recording of such instrument is not necessary to the validity of the transfer." People v. Mortenson, 404 Ill. 107, 111, 88 N.E.2d 35, 38.

The goal of the Torrens system is to make the public record in the Registrar's office and the actual title one and the same.

Unlike the recording system, the Torrens system does not operate by conferring priorities upon those who qualify as protected parties. The latter system operates by making record title in the register and actual title virtually identical, thus enabling anyone to ascertain the true state of the title by only examining the certificate in the register and ordering a tax lien search. Under the Torrens system, questions of good faith (except in cases of fraud), notice, reliance and payment of value are immaterial. (Ill.Rev.Stat.1973, ch. 30, par. 86.) Therefore, it was unnecessary for the legislature to make a special provision for judgment lienors in the Torrens Act similar to section 30 of the Conveyance Act. ...

The opinion attempts to distinguish the present factual situation involving a judgment creditor from one involving a *bona fide* purchaser or a mortgagee. The distinction, it maintains, is that the latter parties would have detrimentally relied upon the state of the registered title, while the judgment creditor has not so relied. This view overlooks the obvious fact that had the judgment creditor not relied upon the condition of the registered title, it would not have memorialized its judgment. As previously stated, the Torrens Act was designed to encourage reliance on the state of the registered title. Between two innocent parties, the judgment creditor and the petitioner herein, the consequences of the petitioner's failure to register her title should be borne by her.

In view of the above-stated considerations, I would affirm the judgment of the circuit court.

UNDERWOOD and CREBS, JJ., join in this dissent.

NOTE

Although as many as twenty-one states at one time authorized the registration of title to real property, the number has since dwindled to ten—Colorado, Georgia, Hawaii, Massachusetts, Minnesota, New York,

North Carolina, Ohio, Virginia, and Washington. See Fiflis, English Registered Conveyancing: A Study in Effective Land Transfer, 59 Nw.U.L.Rev. 468 (1964). And, even in these states, landowners only infrequently register title. According to Fiflis, "In Hawaii, perhaps one-third of all transactions are under the title registration system. In Cook County, Illinois, about 15% of all transactions are in registered land. Except in these states, and Massachusetts, Minnesota and perhaps Ohio, the system is virtually unused." Id. n. 1. The history of state adoption of Torrens is summarized in 6A R. Powell, The Law of Real Property ¶ 908 (1982).

As of January 1, 1992, no additional land can be registered under the Torrens Act. The Act was repealed as of July 1, 2037. Ill.Stat. Ann. ch. 30, ¶ 148.1 et seq. (Smith–Hurd Supp. 1992).

This general rejection of title registration contrasts sharply with the claims for its superiority made in the literature. See for example, Janczyk, An Economic Analysis of the Land Title Systems for Transferring Real Property, 6 J. Legal Stud. 213, 215 (1977) ("The results of this paper indicate that the cost of transferring a title in the Torrens [system] is approximately $100 less than in the recording system, and further, that Cook County could save $76 million by adopting the Torrens system; some other counties could also realize a substantial savings.").

Why has title registration failed to take hold in the United States? Blame is most commonly placed on the title insurance companies: "The chief, major, proximate, and direct cause of the non-use of, or of the public 'disinclination' to use, the Torrens system has been the bitter, multi-form opposition—lobbying against any reform, wounding statutes when enactment is inevitable, conspiring with lending agencies, spreading adverse publicity, and so forth—of title companies and title lawyers." McDougal & Brabner-Smith, Land Title Transfer: A Regression, 48 Yale L.J. 1125, 1147 (1939). Why do title companies oppose title registration? Why should industry opposition alone have succeeded in sinking the concept? What reasons do consumers have to switch from title insurance to title registration, which is initially more costly?

The fight over title registration has produced some of the sharpest scholarly debates in real property law. Compare, for example, R. Powell, Registration of the Title to Land in the State of New York (1938), with McDougal & Brabner-Smith, Land Title Transfer: A Regression, 48 Yale L.J. 1125 (1939). Proposals for the adoption of title registration continue to be made. See, for example, Note, The Torrens System of Title Registration: A New Proposal for Effective Implementation, 29 U.C.L.A.L.Rev. 661 (1982) (also contains footnote references to most of the major literature in the area); Lobel, A Proposal for a Title Registration System for Realty, 11 U.Rich.L.Rev. 471 (1977).

See generally, B. Shick & I. Plotkin, Torrens in the United States (1978); McCormack, Torrens and Recording: Land Title Assurance in the Computer Age, 18 Wm. Mitchell L.Rev. 61 (1992).

V. FINANCING THE PURCHASE

A. THE FORMS, SOURCES AND TERMS OF HOME FINANCE

1. FORMS

B. RUDDEN & H. MOSELEY, AN OUTLINE OF THE LAW OF MORTGAGES

3–6, 8 (1967).

1. THE MORTGAGE AT COMMON LAW

Mortgages of land were made in England long before there was any system of law common to the whole country. There are records of mortgages in Anglo-Saxon days, and at the period immediately after the Conquest when Domesday Book was being compiled. But there was no effective common law over the whole of England until the first half of the 12th century, and it is therefore impossible to state the doctrines of the law concerning mortgages before that time. Even then the practice is obscure, but it is clear that lending money at interest was both a moral wrong and a crime against the usury laws. Even a feudal economy, however, could not flourish without some means of financing development, and so the earliest transactions had to provide both security to the lender and some means of enabling him to obtain a return on his loan in lieu of the forbidden interest. So the lender took a lease of the land, went into possession, and farmed or otherwise managed it, using the profits to pay off the principal—in which case the transaction was called a "live pledge" (in Norman French, *vif gage*). Alternatively, in the harsher type of deal, the lender used the profits of the land for his own gain, leaving the principal advance still owing. This was the "dead pledge" or *mort gage*. The disadvantage of this situation from the point of view of the lender was that, being a mere tenant, he was not, at that time, well protected by the courts. In particular, if he were evicted, his only remedy was damages; so the whole value of the arrangement was lost to him, as he could not be sure of keeping his hands on the land itself. To be absolutely secure he had to be able to show that he was a *freeholder*. Consequently, by the end of the 15th century, most lenders insist that the land be conveyed to them *in fee simple*, in return for the loan. The transaction is still a mortgage, of course, not an out-and-out sale, and so the fee simple is transferred subject to a condition that, if the loan is repaid on the date agreed, the borrower may re-enter the land and claim the fee simple. As a further precaution, and to provide documentary evidence that the borrower has repaid the loan and redeemed the land, the lender covenants that, on repayment, he will reconvey the fee simple.

This gives the lender a great deal of security and, as the usury laws after 1545 allowed interest to be charged (subject to maximum rates), there was not the same need for the lender to go into possession to disguise interest as profits. Consequently, the practice grew of leaving the borrower in possession. In a case in 1620 we find a proviso "that the mortgagee, his heirs and assigns shall not intermeddle with the actual possession of the premises or perception of the rents until default of payment" and after the Restoration this practice became a commonplace.

The lender could afford to leave the borrower in possession since, from the former's point of view, the transaction is simply an investment of money and since he could, if necessary, evict the borrower at once.

Thus the later mortgage at common law consisted of a conveyance of his estate by the borrower (who was, and is, called the mortgagor) to the lender (the mortgagee) as security for the debt or loan owing to or advanced by the latter. The conveyance was a transfer of the fee simple, as a vendor might convey it to a purchaser; but it contained the "proviso for redemption", i.e., a stipulation that, if the mortgagor should repay the debt with a certain rate of interest upon it, *at an agreed date* (usually six months hence) the mortgagee would reconvey the fee simple to the mortgagor.

The common law enforced strictly the proviso for redemption—after all, said the judges, that was what the parties had agreed. Consequently the borrower had one chance *and one only* to redeem his property— on the agreed date. If he did not do so then, at common law, the lender's estate was absolute and could never be redeemed. The transaction was regarded primarily as a bargain between the parties; and, as in the case of any other bargain, the law would enforce it according to its terms. ...

The above is a description of the classical form of the mortgage—a form which it retained until 1925, a form which determines the present appearance of a mortgage deed, and a form which is one long lie. The reason for this is the intervention of equity.

2. THE MORTGAGE IN EQUITY

We have seen that the mortgagor whose date for redemption had passed could not approach the common law courts and ask them to make the lender reconvey the land on receipt of the money. But if the mortgagor petitioned the Court of Chancery he might well succeed. ...

It will be obvious that the mortgage was a fertile field for the growth of the Chancellor's powers. Up to the early 17th century, he would give relief only in special cases as where there was some fraud on the part of the lender, or the borrower's inability to repay on the exact date arose through some accident. After that time, however, Chancery took the view that *all* mortgages were no more than a borrowing upon security, and it became settled that the mortgagor was entitled to redeem at any time, notwithstanding that the date on which he had promised to do so was long past. If the lender refused to allow redemption, Chancery would order him to reconvey the estate. ...

It is most important—even today—to understand this dual nature of the mortgage, which resulted from the fact that the transaction could come before two separate courts. The common law court would do nothing unless the borrower repaid the loan on the agreed date; and, since the lender already had the fee simple conveyed to him by the mortgage, on default in repayment by the mortgagor he was, at common law, the absolute owner. Equity, however, would still intervene, treating the *borrower* as the owner, and confining the mortgagee's rights to those necessary to secure his advance. This affected profoundly the rights of the parties. The practice grew of stipulating in the mortgage deed that the loan should be repaid in six months' time. Usually, of course, both parties expected the loan to be outstanding for a much longer time—after all, it is an investment by the lender. The date was put in, however, so that the mortgagee could, if necessary, call in his loan at any time thereafter; and, as will be shown, he has several remedies to enforce his right to the money. As far as the borrower is concerned, he has two rights to redeem: the *contractual right* on the date specified in the deed, and the *equitable right* to redeem *at any time* thereafter, on paying principal, interest and costs and giving proper notice to the mortgagee.

This equitable right to redeem could be ended by the court itself in an application by the mortgagee—for what the Chancellor had created, he could end. This process of curtailing the equitable right to redeem and so leaving the mortgagee with a fee simple absolute both at law and in equity, is known as *foreclosure.*

TAHOE NATIONAL BANK v. PHILLIPS

Supreme Court of California, 1971.
4 Cal.3d 11, 92 Cal.Rptr. 704, 480 P.2d 320.

TOBRINER, Justice.

Defendant Beulah F. Phillips appeals from a judgment of the El Dorado County Superior Court that holds that an instrument entitled, "Assignment of Rents and Agreement Not to Sell or Encumber Real Property" (hereinafter referred to as "the assignment") was intended to be an equitable mortgage, and decrees its foreclosure.

We conclude that this judgment must be reversed. Plaintiff bank, which occupied the more powerful bargaining position and deliberately chose to use a standardized form providing for the assignment of rents and a covenant against conveyances, cannot be permitted to transform this assignment into a mortgage contrary to the reasonable expectation of its borrower. On examining the terms and purpose of the assignment, we conclude that it is not reasonably susceptible of construction as a mortgage at the instance of the bank, and thus that the trial court erred in invoking extrinsic evidence offered by the bank to prove it to be a mortgage.

Defendant and three co-venturers embarked on a real estate development in the Lake Tahoe area. About April 20, 1965, the venturers not only needed further capital but also owed plaintiff sums due on overdrafts on their accounts. Plaintiff agreed to lend $34,000 to defendant, who transferred the funds to the venture's account. In return, defendant gave plaintiff a single-payment promissory note, payable on demand or on May 20, 1965. At the same time plaintiff executed and delivered to defendant an instrument entitled: "Assignment of Rents and Agreement Not to Sell or Encumber Real Property."[2] This document provided that as security for the loan defendant assigned to plaintiff all rent due from the realty described therein and agreed not to encumber or convey that property. The bank was authorized to record the instrument and did so on May 27, 1965.

The real property described in the document was not the venture's apartment development, but defendant's residence, which she owned one-half in fee and one-half as trustee under the testamentary trust of her deceased husband. This property was unencumbered as of April 20, 1965. On December 6 of that year defendant recorded a declaration of homestead on the property.

Mr. Ross, president of plaintiff bank, testified that the venturers first requested an unsecured loan but that he refused to issue the loan

2. The assignment reads as follows: "ASSIGNMENT OF RENTS AND AGREEMENT NOT TO SELL OR ENCUMBER REAL PROPERTY In consideration and as security for a loan made or purchased by TAHOE NATIONAL BANK (hereinafter called 'Bank') which loan is evidence[d] by a promissory note in favor of Beulah F. Phillips dated April 20, 1965, in the amount of Thirty Four Thousand and 00/100 ($34,000.00), the undersigned, and each of them, (hereinafter sometimes called 'Borrower') hereby covenant and agree with Bank as follows: 1. The real property referred to herein is located in County of El Dorado, State of California, and is described as follows: 'Lot 270, Tahoe Keys Unit No. 1, as said lot is shown on the Official Map of said Tahoe Keys Unit # 1, filed in the office of the County Recorder of the County of El Dorado, State of California, on May 11, 1959, in Map Book C, Map No. 7; 2. Borrower hereby assigns to Bank all moneys due or to become due to Borrower as rental or otherwise for or on account of such real property, reserving unto Borrower the right to collect and retain any such moneys prior to Borrower's default under the terms of the loan described above; 3. Borrower will not create or permit any lien or any encumbrance (other than those presently existing) to exist on said real property and will not transfer, sell, assign or in any manner dispose of said real property or any interest therein without the prior written consent of Bank; 4. Bank is hereby authorized and permitted to cause this instrument to be recorded at such time and in such places as Bank at its option may elect; 5. This agreement is expressly intended for the benefit and protection of Bank and all subsequent holders of the note described above. Borrower warrants and represents that Borrower owns the above-described real property; 6. This agreement shall remain in full force and effect until the loan described above shall have been paid in full or until twenty-one (21) years following the death of the last survivor of the undersigned, whichever first occurs. Dated: April 20, 1965 (s) Beulah F. Phillips"

without security and requested collateral; that defendant then offered her residence as collateral and showed him an FHA appraisal at $34,400. The venturers required the money within two hours, and, for reasons which are not entirely clear,[3] Mr. Ross determined that the bank could not conveniently prepare a trust deed within that time limit; consequently he selected instead a form for an assignment of rents and agreement against conveyances. The document was prepared by his secretary and executed by the parties.

Mr. Ross acknowledged that his bank and other banks make unsecured loans upon agreements by the debtor to maintain unencumbered assets of sufficient value in the county. He denied, however, that his purpose in having defendant sign the document in issue was merely to insure that she would have unencumbered assets reachable by the bank; he maintained that he took the document "knowing it was in actuality a mortgage instrument against that house in lieu of a deed of trust."

Mrs. Phillips testified that she did not intend to sign or believe that she was signing any security interest "like a mortgage or deed of trust." She added that since she owned half her interest as trustee she believed that she lacked authority to execute a mortgage or trust deed on the property.

Plaintiff brought suit against the venture on various notes and overdrafts and, in its fifth cause of action, asked foreclosure of the assignment as an equitable mortgage. The court entered judgment against the venturers, jointly and severally, for $92,386 plus costs, interest, and attorneys' fees. It further found that the assignment was an equitable mortgage securing $34,000 of the debt, and decreed its foreclosure.

Mrs. Phillips alone appealed; her appeal challenges only that portion of the judgment finding the assignment to be an equitable mortgage and ordering foreclosure.

1. *The language of .the assignment is not reasonably susceptible of interpretation as a mortgage at the instance of plaintiff bank.*

We agree with defendant's contention that the assignment cannot reasonably be construed as a mortgage and thus that extrinsic evidence, offered by plaintiff to prove the document a mortgage, is legally irrelevant and cannot support the judgment. We shall examine the purpose and terms of the assignment, and explain that it is a type of

---

3. Defendant's attorney inquired of Mr. Ross: "[W]ouldn't it have been just as easy to prepare a deed of trust on a form as an assignment of rents?" Mr. Ross answered: "No, it would not have been, simply because of the recording from the Tahoe Valley area into Placerville of the deed of trust with an amendment or new title policy showing our position if there had been a proper first deed of trust of record."

This answer of Mr. Ross is inconsistent with his assertion that the assignment was intended to be a mortgage on defendant's property. If the bank requires the protection of a title policy before executing a trust deed, and prompt recording of the trust deed, logically the bank should impose the same conditions on execution of an instrument intended to serve the purpose of a trust deed.

agreement commonly used with unsecured loans, that it contains no words of hypothecation, and that it includes language inconsistent with a mortgage. We shall point out that if, as the bank contends, the word "security" in the assignment renders it ambiguous, the bank bears the responsibility for that ambiguity. Having on hand instruments which unambiguously impose liens on realty, the bank cannot select an ambiguous instrument and then, by extrinsic evidence, give it the effect of the unambiguous form it eschewed.

Assignments similar to the present one are "used by many banks in conjunction with small, nominally unsecured loans such as home improvement loans." (California Real Estate Secured Transactions (Cont. Ed.Bar 1970) § 2.37 (hereinafter cited as "CEB"))[6] They provide the lender with a measure of security unavailable in a totally unsecured loan; the creditor holds an assignment of rents and a contractual guarantee that property in which the debtor has an equity will remain unencumbered and unconveyed, and thus available for levy and execution should the creditor reduce his debt to judgment. Indeed, the plaintiff bank commonly makes loans upon the "security" of a promise by the debtor not to convey or hypothecate property, using for that purpose forms similar to that at issue here.

Thus we are not dealing with homemade security instruments in which the parties labor to produce a mortgage but fall short of the legal requirements and must be rescued by a court of equity. The form used was carefully drafted to produce a security interest with incidents differing from that of a mortgage.[8] ...

We turn now to the language of the assignment. Its title gives no hint of a power of foreclosure. It contains no language of hypothecation, no provisions imposing a lien or creating a mortgage, no discussion of foreclosure. The substance of the document comprises six covenants by the borrower, none of which purport to give the bank a lien on real property. The covenants respecting recordation and duration of the agreement, and persons bound by its terms, are consistent with a mortgage, but they are equally consistent with an instrument designed to afford the bank the security that the borrower retains unencumbered

---

6. A covenant against conveyances and encumbrances is sometimes referred to as a "negative pledge" agreement. ...

8. See CEB, § 2.37. Comment, supra, 12 U.C.L.A.L.Rev. 954, 962, 964, discusses the purpose of assignments such as that employed in the present case: "[L]enders are willing in some instances to advance credit on the basis of a long pay-off period to a person who appears to have property which may be attached or secured in case the debtor becomes in financial difficulty. However, when the property is transferred, the credit picture immediately shifts and the lender wants to be in a position to accelerate maturity at once; he is no long-

er willing to take the risk over the long pay-off period—a risk he would gladly take if the property remained 'locked' with the debtor."

The comment adds: "Even though the Financial Code prohibits savings banks and trust companies from securing their loans by taking second liens, lending institutions have made real estate loans to homeowners using the negative pledge agreement when the property specified in the agreement was already encumbered by a prior mortgage or trust deed on the theory that no security interest was created by the negative pledge agreement."

assets. The third covenant, however, is inconsistent with an instrument creating a lien on real property. It provides in part that "borrower will not create or permit any lien or any encumbrance (other than those presently existing) to exist on said real property ... without the prior written consent of bank." This language apparently assumes that the assignment itself is not an encumbrance; its absolute prohibition on what would be junior encumbrances is inappropriate in a mortgage, and if in fact such a prohibition appeared in a mortgage it might be unlawful as an unreasonable restraint upon alienation. (See Coast Bank v. Minderhout (1964) 61 Cal.2d 311, 317, 38 Cal.Rptr. 505, 392 P.2d 265.) On the other hand, as unsecured creditor the bank would benefit greatly from an assurance that defendant would not encumber her assets.

Plaintiff points out that the assignment specifies that it was given "as security for a loan," and that the word "security" may signify a right of foreclosure. That phrase, however, appears in the preamble which, read as a whole, states that "as security for a loan ... the undersigned ... hereby covenant and agree with Bank as follows." The natural interpretation of this language is that it is the six covenants of the borrower that "secures" that loan; that the word "security" in the preamble does not create additional rights and duties not specified in the covenants.

Plaintiff further contends that the term "security," and the provisions of the assignment describing the real property and permitting recordation, render the assignment ambiguous, thus requiring extrinsic evidence to determine whether it places a lien on defendant's property. If ambiguity there is, that ambiguity may be deliberate. Professor Hetland, referring to assignments similar to that at issue in the present case, states that "the instrument seems to have been designed by a group of lenders to afford the lender the option of being a secured or an unsecured creditor at the time of the debtor's default. ..." (CEB, § 2.38.) Thus, although the assignment primarily serves to protect unsecured loans, it may also be used "to lead a borrower who refuses to give a mortgage into believing he is not doing so" (CEB, § 2.25).

Since the alleged ambiguities appear in a standardized contract, drafted and selected by the bank, which occupies the superior bargaining position, those ambiguities must be interpreted against the bank. ...

In the present case, we conclude that to permit a creditor to choose an allegedly ambiguous form of agreement, and then by extrinsic evidence seek to give it the effect of a different and unambiguous form, would be to disregard totally the rules respecting interpretation of adhesion contracts, and to create an extreme danger of over-reaching on the part of creditors with superior bargaining positions. The bank must bear the responsibility for the creation and use of the assignment it now claims is ambiguous; it is only "poetic justice" (CEB, § 2.38) if such ambiguity is construed in favor of the borrower. Legal alchemy cannot convert an assignment into an equitable mortgage, violating the customer's reasonable expectation and bestowing upon the bank the riches of an hypothecation of title.

We recognize that in Coast Bank v. Minderhout, supra, 61 Cal.2d 311, 38 Cal.Rptr. 505, 392 P.2d 265, we ordered foreclosure as an equitable mortgage of an instrument similar to the assignment in the present case, but we do not consider that case controlling. The agreement in *Coast Bank* contained an acceleration clause and stated that the loan was intended to improve the property described in the agreement—both characteristics indicative of a mortgage and both absent in the present assignment. Of greater significance is the differing context of *Coast Bank* and the present case. In *Coast Bank,* the borrower had breached a covenant prohibiting conveyance of the realty. Such a breach confronts the court with a difficult problem in fashioning a remedy. An award of damages would prove ineffective; "the maximum damages the bank could suffer from breach would be the amount of the debt, the same amount for which it could get a judgment on the note." (CEB, § 2.38.) Specific performance of the covenant against conveyances might create an invalid restraint against alienation. Under these circumstances, enforcement as an equitable mortgage, which permits the property to be conveyed subject to the lien, is the only alternative to invalidation of the instrument.

In the present case defendant has performed all terms of the assignment, with the result that defendant's interest in the realty, over the homestead exemption, is available to satisfy the bank's judgment on the note. If this security is not fully adequate, such is the result of the bank's choice of the governing instrument.

. . .

3. *Conclusion.*

Part 2 of the superior court judgment, the only portion of that judgment from which defendant appeals, held that the assignment was an equitable mortgage and ordered foreclosure. We conclude that this determination is in error; the assignment cannot reasonably be construed as a mortgage at the instance of the party who drafted and selected it.

Part 2 of the judgment against defendant Beulah Phillips is reversed.

WRIGHT, C.J., and McCOMB, PETERS, MOSK and BURKE, JJ., concur.

[The opinion of Sullivan, J., dissenting, is omitted.]

NOTES

1. *Functional Equivalents.* Many thoughtful courts have treated as functional equivalents all devices that are intended to create a security interest in land, regardless of the name chosen for the device.

(Consider the examples described in the following notes). This may reflect an attempt to preserve the special protections of the law of mortgages:

> Mortgage law has long enjoyed a special, almost exalted position in the private law scheme of this country. A mortgage arises out of a private agreement when an owner of real property grants a lender an interest in the property to secure a debt. Once this privately created mortgage comes into existence, however, the private agreement dims in importance, and the mortgagor-mortgagee relationship becomes subject to legal rules that take precedence over the parties' plan. In many of its important elements, the mortgagor-mortgagee relationship is governed by binding laws, by laws that apply anytime a mortgage is created and the parties assume the status positions of mortgagor and mortgagee. Taken as a whole, these status rules aid mortgagors by granting them numerous rights in their dealings with mortgagees.
>
> Courts have developed and applied mortgage law over the years with a distinct goal in mind: to protect mortgagors against sharp dealings by lenders. Courts have been particularly quick to strike down lenders' efforts to develop contractual forms that circumvent the laws governing mortgages. In numerous ways wily lenders have tried to create what might be called a non-mortgage mortgage, an arrangement that gives the lender the security of a mortgage, but deprives the borrower of the protective provisions of mortgage law. Courts, however, have responded vigorously to these attempts, mostly out of sympathy for home-and farm-owners who stand to lose their property. For courts, the substance of a secured transaction is more important than its form. Consequently, courts have long applied mortgage law to any relationship that appeared to be a mortgage in substance.

Freyfogle, Land Trusts and the Decline of Mortgage Law, 1988 U.Ill. L.Rev. 67, 67–68. *

2. *The Mortgage and the Deed of Trust.* The mortgage is probably the most widely used instrument of land finance in America today. The landowner, as mortgagor, gives a mortgage to the lender, as mortgagee, to secure the landowner's obligation to pay a debt, evidenced by a bond or promissory note. Unless the mortgage provides otherwise, the mortgagee can foreclose the mortgagor's equity of redemption only by judicial action and sale. If the mortgage expressly gives the mortgagee a power of sale, and if local statutes do not bar this self help procedure, judicial proceedings are unnecessary and the mortgagee can foreclose simply by public sale after notice to all interested parties.

Lenders in several states prefer the deed of trust to the mortgage with power of sale. Like the mortgage with power of sale, the deed of trust secures an underlying obligation, typically evidenced by a promissory note (although sometimes a bond is used). The deed of trust differs in that, where the mortgage involves two parties, it involves three: the borrower ("trustor") conveys title to the lender's nominee ("trustee") as security for the trustor's performance of its debt obligation to the lender ("beneficiary"). If the trustor defaults, and if the beneficiary so requests, the trustee will arrange a public sale of the land to satisfy the debt.

For the lender, the original advantage of the deed of trust over the mortgage with power of sale was that it permitted the lender to bid at the sale conducted by a nominally independent third party, the trustee. Statutes today have eliminated most of the differences between deeds of trust and mortgages with power of sale, including the lender's ability to bid at the foreclosure sale. See Uniform Land Security Interest Act § 202, comment. The two forms of security are for this reason treated interchangeably in this chapter and in the chapters on commercial finance.

3. *Other Forms of Land Finance.* A financing arrangement arises any time one person provides part or all of the capital needed to support another's activities in return for repayment of the capital, plus consideration, over a period of time. Although mortgages and deeds of trust are the instruments most popularly associated with land finance, other arrangements also qualify. For example, installment land contracts are often used to finance the acquisition of housing or of undeveloped land. The installment land contract is much like a purchase money mortgage, with the buyer making a down payment on the purchase price and the seller financing the rest. Structurally, it is like the marketing contract considered at pages 67 to 141 above. The seller holds title to the land during the entire executory period, until the last payment is made, at which point the contract closes and the seller conveys title to the buyer. The obvious difference is that, while the marketing contract's executory period will rarely exceed the one or two months needed to search title and obtain financing, the installment land contract will run for as long as five, ten or twenty years, the time that it takes the buyer to pay the seller for the property. Installment land contracts are considered at pages 519 to 538.

Leases are also financing arrangements. The leased premises represent the asset lent by the landlord to the tenant; in return, the tenant pays rent for use of the premises. (If, as sometimes happens, the lease gives the tenant an option to buy the premises at the end of the term at a specified price, the lease begins to look much more like an installment land contract or even a purchase money mortgage or deed of trust given by buyer to seller.) Leases may in turn become security for further financing arrangements such as leasehold mortgages. For a fine examination of the efficiency and monitoring benefits of mortgages compared to unsecured debt, see Johnson, Adding Another Piece to the Financing Puzzle: The Role of Real Property Secured Debt, 24 Loyola L.A.L.Rev. 335 (1991).

4. *The Negative Pledge.* A lender may try to use the negative pledge to straddle the otherwise mutually exclusive advantages of secured and unsecured debt. If the defaulting borrower has enough assets to satisfy judgments obtained by the lender and any competing creditors, the lender will prefer to treat the debt as unsecured in order to avoid the debtor-protection provisions that surround mortgage foreclosure. If, however, the borrower has insufficient assets to satisfy its general creditors, the lender will claim to be a real property secured creditor with first claim on the land.

Cases such as *Tahoe* curb this stratagem by preventing lenders from using ambiguous instruments to support claims that the loan was secured by real property. Justice Sullivan, dissenting in *Tahoe,* would have struck the balance differently. In his view, all that need be shown is that the instrument is "reasonably susceptible" to construction as real property security; the trial court's finding that it was susceptible to this interpretation should not have been disturbed.

Say that the parties' positions had been reversed, with the borrower arguing that the loan was secured and the lender that it was not. For whom would the majority have held? For whom would Justice Sullivan have held? For a thoughtful discussion of *Tahoe* and of the negative pledge generally, see Reichman, The Anti-Lien: Another Security Interest in Land, 41 U.Chi.L.Rev. 685 (1974).

5. *The Equitable Mortgage.* At the other extreme from *Tahoe* is the situation in which it is clear that the parties intended to transfer a property interest but it is unclear whether a fee was conveyed, or only a mortgage disguised as a fee. A court will hold a deed absolute to be an equitable mortgage when the evidence suggests that the parties intended a mortgage. The situation often arises when a landowner, faced with tax or mortgage foreclosure, conveys his land to a third party who promises to "straighten things out" and then reconvey the land to the landowner. The situation also sometimes arises when, in an effort to avoid mortgage law's debtor protection provisions, a lender requires its borrower to convey by an absolute deed, the lender promising in a separate agreement to reconvey the land to the borrower if he pays the debt on time.

Courts generally favor debtors in their willingness to pierce the facade of the absolute deed and find an equitable mortgage. Side agreements providing for reconveyance will readily be connected to the deed to support a finding that the deed and agreement formed a single security transaction. Nor is a written agreement essential. Among other facts that will be considered are "declarations of the grantee; the relations subsisting between the parties at the time the deed was executed; the retention by the grantor, subsequent to the execution of the deed, of the possession of the land and the exercise of dominion over it, in making improvements and repairs, paying taxes and the like; the value of the property compared with the consideration actually paid or allowed ...." Winters v. Earl, 52 N.J.Eq. 52, 53, 28 A. 15 (Ch.1893), affirmed mem. 52 N.J.Eq. 588, 33 A. 50 (1894). The Restatement of the Law of Property—Security (Mortgages) § 3.2 (Tent. Draft No. 1 1991) follows this formulation. Although a debt owed by the grantor to the grantee may also be indicative, it is not necessary to a finding that an equitable mortgage has been created. See, for example, Koenig v. Van Reken, 89 Mich.App. 102, 279 N.W.2d 590 (1979).

One problem raised by equitable mortgages is that the putative deed will probably have been recorded. Because a bona fide purchaser from the grantee will generally not be bound to the mortgage characterization, the grantee-lender has good reason to sell or encumber his title as soon as he can, leaving the original grantor with only a personal action against him. Note, too, that the recorded transfer may be used to mislead the *grantor's* creditors into believing that the grantor no longer has an interest in the property against which they can levy.

See generally Cunningham & Tischler, Disguised Real Estate Security Transactions as Mortgages in Substance, 26 Rutgers L.Rev. 1 (1972).

6. *U.L.S.I.A.* The Uniform Land Security Interest Act regulates mortgages and other types of consensual security interests in real estate. The drafters hope that a uniform law among states will further encourage the growth of the secondary market and primary lending by out of state banks and that the Act will simplify and modernize ancient mortgage law. The act defines a "security interest" broadly as "an interest in real estate which secures payment or performance of an obligation." * Leases intended as security to the lessor and retention of title by the seller of land intended as security are included. See § 111(25). On the U.L.S.I.A. generally, see Platt, The Uniform Land Security Interest Act: Vehicle for Reform of Oregon Secured Land Transaction Law, 69 Or.L.Rev. 847 (1990). See page 75 above for the derivation of the U.L.S.I.A. from the Uniform Land Transactions Act.

7. *Title Theory and Lien Theory.* Some states continue to follow the "title theory" of mortgages, clinging to the early common law view that the mortgagee holds title to the land from the moment the mortgage is executed to the time that it is foreclosed or the underlying obligation is paid. Most states, however, now follow the "lien theory," under which the mortgagee has only a lien on the property to secure the mortgagor's performance.

The basic distinction between the two theories lies in the right to possession. In title theory states the mortgagee has the right, rarely exercised, to possess the land from the moment the mortgage is given. In lien theory states it is the mortgagor who has the right to possession, unless and until foreclosure occurs. In a third group of states, following the "intermediate theory," the mortgagor has the right to possession until default on the underlying obligation.

* This and other excerpts from the U.L.S.I.A. are reprinted by permission of the National Conference of Commissioners on Uniform State Laws, 676 N. Clair St., Chicago, IL 60611.

Though much written about, the distinctions between these three theories have little practical consequence. Legislation and judicial decisions in title states have clothed the mortgagor with virtually all the attributes of ownership, although there may still be differences, such as on the question of whether and how a mortgagee may take possession upon the borrower's default. Further, these distinctions may be easily circumvented by private agreement, and the terms struck by lenders and borrowers in title, lien and intermediate states all look very much alike. See generally, G. Nelson, & D. Whitman, Real Estate Finance Law 142–151 (2d ed. 1985).

8. *Bibliographic Note.* For purposes of general reference on land finance, the best single source is G. Nelson & D. Whitman, Real Estate Finance Law (2d ed. 1985), a comprehensive and thoughtful work.

2. SOURCES

The era of modern residential mortgages began as a response to the mortgage defaults and dislocations of the Great Depression. Over the past decade, there have been significant changes in the sources and methods of home financing, both in the primary lending market—those institutions which originate loans—and in the secondary market, where mortgages or mortgage backed securities are traded. These markets are shaped by private economic forces as well as government activity in the form of regulation, sponsorship, and intervention. Moreover, there is a close interdependence of the primary and secondary markets so that changes in the practices of one often will affect the other.

a. PRIMARY LENDING MARKET

i. From the Depression to the S & L Crisis

The principal sources of primary residential mortgages have been savings and loan institutions (S & Ls), mutual savings banks, and commercial banks. Mortgage companies and mortgage brokers also originate loans for sale to investors, either directly to institutions or through the secondary market. Historically, the largest player has been the savings and loan institution, generating approximately one-half of all residential loans. The rise and recent troubles of the industry are described in the following portion of the House Committee Report accompanying the Financial Institutions Reform, Recovery and Enforcement Act of 1989, Pub.L.No. 101–73, 103 Stat. 183 (1989), which was passed to "bail out" the industry.

HOUSE OF REPRESENTATIVES, REPORT OF THE COMMITTEE ON BANKING, FINANCE AND URBAN AFFAIRS, FINANCIAL INSTITUTIONS REFORM, RECOVERY AND ENFORCEMENT ACT OF 1989

H.R. Rep. No. 101–54(i) pp. 87–99 (1989).

INTRODUCTION

Throughout most of its history, the savings and loan industry was dedicated almost entirely to promoting home ownership through home mortgage lending, and as recently as last year, thrift institutions still originated 49% of all 1–4 family mortgages nationwide. However, the rising interest rate environment of the 1970's and early 1980's had a devastating affect on thrifts. Thrifts, locked into long-term, low-yielding, fixed-rate mortgages, experienced enormous operating losses. In response, the Congress and the Reagan Administration agreed to a rapid expansion in the scope of permissible thrift investment powers and a similar expansion in a thrift's ability to compete for funds with other financial services providers. This extensive deregulation, for which many thrifts were unprepared, coupled with a severe economic downturn in the Southwest, left the industry struggling for survival, and has virtually wiped-out its deposit insurance fund, the Federal Savings and Loan Insurance Corporation (FSLIC). ...

ESTABLISHMENT OF THE PRESENT FRAMEWORK: THRIFTS AND THE GREAT DEPRESSION

. . .

The Great Depression spurred the reformation of the thrift industry into a federally-conceived and assisted system to provide citizens with affordable housing funds. It is accurate to say that the present thrift industry structure was born during the Depression.

Due to massive unemployment, the Depression was particularly severe in its impact on housing; over 1,700 thrifts failed during the 1930's because borrowers could no longer service their mortgages. In total, thrift depositors lost roughly $200 million during the Depression. ... [O]n July 22, 1932, President Hoover signed into law the Federal Home Loan Bank Act despite strong opposition from banks and insurance companies complaining that the Act constituted excessive government intervention into the financial services industry. The primary purpose of the Act was to rescue the failing savings and loan industry by channeling cash to thrifts. The legislation authorized the creation of twelve district banks to lend money to thrifts, and established the Federal Home Loan Bank Board (Bank Board) located in Washington, D.C., to oversee the district banks. ...

More help was needed, however. With 40 percent of the nation's $20 billion in home mortgages in default, and foreclosures taking place at a rate of 26,000 per month, Congress recognized the need for additional thrift legislation, and in 1933, the Home Owners' Loan Act (HOLA) was enacted. The HOLA authorized the Bank Board to grant Federal savings and loan association charters and created the Home Owner's Loan Corporation (HOLC) to purchase delinquent loans from lenders and refinance them at terms that allowed the home owner to avoid foreclosure. Over its life, the HOLC refinanced $2.75 billion worth of home mortgages, and invested $300 million in thrift institutions.

In a further attempt to restore public confidence in the nation's financial system, and to continue to assure an adequate supply of funding for home mortgages, the Congress passed the National Housing Act of 1934 (NHA). This Act established the Federal Housing Administration (FHA) and the Federal Savings and Loan Insurance Corporation (FSLIC). FHA insurance was intended to protect mortgage lenders by guaranteeing full repayment of defaulted loans covered by FHA programs. FSLIC insurance was intended to protect small depositors by insuring their time and demand deposits up to $5,000, thus encouraging the public to reinvest their funds in savings and loans.

THE POST–DEPRESSION YEARS

The Post–Depression years saw the thrift industry develop into an important player in the financial services industry. In 1945 the savings and loan industry held 3 percent of the total financial assets in the United States; by 1985 thrifts held 15 percent. During this period the number of FSLIC-insured institutions and their branches increased dramatically while the amount of assets controlled by thrifts grew exponentially.

The Depression and World War II produced a tremendous demand for housing. Although increased savings during the Second World War allowed savings and loans to establish a large deposit base, most of the funds on deposit at thrift institutions were not used to provide mortgages, but instead were used to purchase war bonds or to fund the construction of military housing. The Housing Act of 1949 recognized the national shortage of housing following the War and gave a boost to the thrift industry by making the provision of family housing a national priority.

From 1940–65, the number of FSLIC-insured thrifts more than doubled from 2,277 to 4,508. During that period the assets controlled by FSLIC-insured thrifts jumped from $3 billion to over $124.5 billion. Since 1965, the number of FSLIC-insured institutions has declined to 2,949, but the advent of branching offset this decline.

In 1940 most of the nation's thrifts were single office operations, but by 1960, nearly 3,000 institutions were engaged in branching. During this period the limitation prohibiting thrifts from providing mortgages on property outside a 50 mile radius of the institution's home office was extended to 100 miles. In 1970 thrifts were permitted to lend statewide and by 1983, nationwide except where prohibited. With effective and growing branch networks, deposits in the thrift industry grew to $503 billion by 1980, with 96% of these deposits insured by the FSLIC. During this same period the assets of FSLIC-insured thrifts increased to over $621 billion.

MAJOR CAUSES OF THE THRIFT CRISIS

. . .

The thrift industry and FSLIC are now in perilous financial condition. The causes of this crisis can be traced to a number of factors: poorly timed deregulation; the dismal performance of some thrift managements; inadequate oversight, supervision and regulation by government regulatory agencies and the Reagan Administration; a regional economic collapse; radical deregulation by several large States; and outright fraud and insider abuse. What emerges all too clearly is that when the savings and loan industry was deregulated, the Reagan Administration, the Congress, several State legislatures, the government agencies assigned to supervise and examine these institutions, and the thrifts themselves badly misjudged the extent of the underlying problems.

A DECADE OF MODIFICATION: 1978–1988

The regulatory framework designed by Congress in the 1930's to compartmentalize financial institutions began to experience severe stress during the late 1970's and early 1980's when periods of high interest rates and record levels of inflation rocked the nation's economy. Reacting to these pressures, the Congress and several state legislatures enacted numerous legislative initiatives aimed at securing the thrift industry's place as an important vehicle for promoting our nation's housing goals through the provision of affordable mortgage credit. These changes, summarily recounted in the following paragraphs, had a profound impact on the savings and loan industry.

. . .

The rising interest rate environment of the late 1970's and early 1980's produced conditions ripe for disintermediation, and resulted in large operating losses for most thrifts. In 1979 the Federal Reserve, in order to combat inflation, decided to pursue a different course in its conduct of monetary policy. That policy shift had a truly devastating affect on the thrift industry. With Paul Volcker at the controls, the Federal Reserve switched from a policy of stabilizing interest rates to a policy of controlling the growth of the money supply. This shift caused a dramatic increase in interest rates with an equally dramatic increase in the cost of funds at low-yielding, fixed-rate mortgages. This meant thrifts were paying more to attract funds than they were earning on their mortgage portfolios. This "negative" interest rate mismatch was the beginning of the thrift crisis as we know it.

PHASE–OUT OF REGULATION Q

. . .

The phase-out of Regulation Q culminated a decade long battle to eliminate deposit interest rate controls. Since the 1930's, Regulation Q had placed a ceiling on the rate of interest a financial institution could offer on deposits. As interest rates and inflation gyrated dramatically during the 1970's and 1980's, nonbanking firms such as securities firms and insurance companies began offering money market mutual funds that paid market interest rates to customers. Customers gradually became more sophisticated and realized that as long as the inflation rate was higher than the interest rate they earned on their deposits, they were actually losing money by having major balances in depository institutions. In order to avoid losing money on their deposits, consumers periodically withdrew massive amounts of money from financial institutions, a phenomenon known as disintermediation.

Without loanable funds on hand at banks and savings and loans, the economy experienced credit shortages or "crunches" during periods of disintermediation. The mortgage credit-dependent construction industry experienced several severe downturns and home buyers in turn were harmed by shortages of mortgage funds. These factors persuaded the Congress to enact the Depository Institutions Deregulation and Monetary Control Act of 1980, and with it, the dismantling of deposit rate controls embodied in Regulation Q.

The savings and loan industry, which was subject to Regulation Q limitations starting in 1966, had relied heavily on Regulation Q as a means of attracting depositors. From 1966 until its dismantling, Regulation Q gave thrifts the opportunity to pay savers higher rates than banks on time and savings deposits. This interest rate differential—25 to 50 basis points—provided thrifts with a powerful marketing tool. In repealing Regulation Q, Congress effectively repealed this advantage.

With Regulation Q being phased out, and deposit insurance coverage raised to $100,000, thrifts were able to compete in the marketplace for depositor funds. But competing for funds on even terms with other financial service providers meant paying higher interest rates to customers and dramatically increased the cost of funds for thrifts. Unfortunately, the earnings side of their balance sheets—their permissible investments—contained low-yield, fixed-rate, long-term mortgages. This meant thrifts were paying higher interest rates to attract depositors, but were precluded from making analogous adjustments in their mortgage portfolios. ...

GARN–ST GERMAIN

The Garn–St Germain Depository Institutions Act of 1982, signed into law on October 15, 1982, was considered the most significant piece of thrift legislation since the Great Depression. ... To further stem the tide of disintermediation, Congress allowed thrifts to offer money market deposit accounts, with no interest rate limitations. This action was successful and helped reverse the outflow of funds from thrift institutions for the first time in two years; during the first four months that these accounts were offered, they attracted over $108 billion in deposits.

Garn–St Germain also authorized federally-insured thrifts to commit up to 10% of their assets to commercial or agricultural loans; increased the non-real estate secured loan limit from 20% to 40% of assets; lifted educational loan restrictions making all educational loans permissible; authorized thrifts to invest 100% of their assets in state or municipal securities; permitted investments in time deposits and savings accounts of other thrifts; increased from 20% to 30% the permissible level of assets committed to consumer loans, including inventory and floor-planning loans; authorized thrifts to accept demand deposits from individuals and corporations; and allowed the use of net worth certificates to assist ailing FSLIC- and FDIC-insured institutions.

Altogether, these actions gave thrifts far greater flexibility in deciding how their money could be invested. As history showed, a number of thrift managers did not have the expertise needed to utilize these new powers, and as a whole the industry had great difficulty in exercising its newfound powers in a safe and sound manner. In addition, many states, bowing to the demands of their state-chartered thrifts, and not having to worry about the consequences of deregulation because deposit insurance was "federally-backed", drastically expanded the investment powers of state-chartered thrifts.

STATE–CHARTERED THRIFTS RESPONSIBLE FOR A MAJORITY OF FSLIC LOSSES

In 1980, 51 percent of FSLIC-insured S&L's were still state-chartered and received their powers from their state legislatures. Coinciding with federal efforts to aid ailing thrifts, numerous state legislatures, the most significant being California, Florida, and Texas, passed far reaching provisions to aid their ailing state-chartered institutions. By 1984, more than one third of all states had granted their state-chartered thrifts investment powers beyond those permissible for federally-chartered institutions.

In addition to having greater powers, many state-chartered thrifts found a far less rigorous regulatory and supervisory environment at the state level. For example, the State of California let its thrift examination force drop dramatically during the early 1980's. The State of Texas followed the same pattern. Some of the most abusive and fraudulent activities affecting thrifts occurred in these states.

As long as the federal government was responsible for picking up the tab for a failed state-chartered thrift, there was no great incentive for many state legislatures to deny the sweeping demands for additional investment powers made by the thrift industry. The results were tragic. Seventy percent of all FSLIC expenditures during 1988 went to pay for problems created by high-risk, ill-supervised, state-chartered thrifts in California and Texas. Those same two states absorbed 54 percent of FSLIC expenditures in 1987.

. . .

RAPID GROWTH IN THE INDUSTRY

With little of their own capital at risk, the predominant feeling among many thrift managements was that the easiest way to regain profitability and generate adequate levels of new capital, was to grow rapidly. Factors making this appear as a feasible course of action included rapidly dwindling levels of capital; insurance coverage up to $100,000 on deposits; pent-up mortgage demand from the severe recession; lax supervision; broad new investment powers; few interest rate controls; and the arrival of a robust national economic recovery.

Spurred in part by growing acceptance of broker-originated deposits, FSLIC-insured thrifts attracted net new deposits of $110 billion in 1983, and $111 billion in 1984. In 1984, FSLIC-insured liabilities increased $152.6 billion or 20%. From 1983 through 1986 total thrift liabilities grew a remarkable 65% from $674 billion to $1.1 trillion—with $824 billion insured by FSLIC. However, the Bank Board did not consider rapid growth a "problem" until 1985. ...

POOR MANAGEMENT AND FRAUD AT SAVINGS AND LOANS

The management of a thrift must decide what activities should be undertaken by the thrift, and how much risk should be taken to achieve its goals. These decisions involve consideration of the thrift's financial capacity, current market and customer base, technological developments, and evaluation of general economic and sectoral conditions to name a few ingredients essential for success. The more sophisticated, riskier and complicated decisions become, the easier it is for a wrong choice to affect the safety and soundness of the institution.

Poor thrift management decisions have resulted in failure for hundreds of FSLIC-insured thrifts, and consequently, the insolvency of the FSLIC. While the majority of thrifts are run by adequate and dedicated management, a minority of poorly operated thrifts have impaired the financial condition of the entire thrift industry. The losses were severely compounded by an enormous recession in the Southwest.

Failed institutions have a number of similar traits including inadequate board of director supervision; poor internal controls; poor underwriting and loan administration standards; and a reliance on brokered deposits or other highly volatile sources of funds. These problems are the result of poor management.

. . .

Poor loan underwriting and administration standards have proved particularly detrimental to thrift institutions. Thrift regulators have reported weaknesses related to poor loan documentation and inadequate credit analysis at 92% of failed thrifts. Appraisal deficiencies go hand-in-hand with poor underwriting and administration standards. Federal regulations requiring thrifts to obtain appraisals for loans secured by real estate were violated by 88 percent of failed thrifts. In addition, many appraisals were found to be inaccurate or insufficiently documented.

INSIDER ABUSE AND FRAUD

While the majority of thrifts are run by honest and dedicated management, it is clear that fraud and insider abuse has been a major factor in a significant portion of thrift failures in the 1980's.

Many fraud cases involving FSLIC's largest losses have borne an uncanny resemblance. The general pattern has been a state chartered institution that underwent a change of control during the early 1980's. These institutions participated in rapid growth schemes and adopted risky investment strategies. Poor management techniques and unresponsiveness to regulatory appeals for change are also a hallmark of these institutions; so are high levels of compensation and extravagant expenditures. Regulators estimate that as many as 40% of thrift failures are due to some form of fraud or insider abuse.

The public accounting industry and certified public accountants (CPAs) played a major role in masking the insolvency of many failed thrifts, and often did not report fraud and insider abuse by thrift managements to thrift regulators. ...

INADEQUATE SUPERVISION OF THRIFTS

President Reagan promised the American people he would reduce government regulation because "it was hampering private initiative and impeding the functioning of the market." Throughout the Reagan years, the Treasury Department and the federal bank and thrift regulatory agencies continually pressured Congress to limit government intervention in the financial services industry. In line with this philosophy, the Administration would not support an increase in the number of savings and loan examiners even though the thrift industry was going through its most significant restructuring since the Great Depression. The lack of adequate supervision and examination of thrifts was one of the primary causes of the thrift crisis.

Because of the Administration's lack of support for tough regulation and supervision of high-flying and risk-laden thrifts, the FSLIC was unable to attract an adequate examination force at a critical time. Without adequate supervision, thrifts were free to engage in fraudulent and risky activities, often at the expense of the FSLIC.

Even when the Bank Board realized it needed more examiners, the Administration remained adamantly opposed to any increase in the examination force. In the mid–1980's, the Bank Board, pressured by Congress, finally realized it needed additional regulatory resources to deal with the FSLIC problem. The Bank Board appealed to the Office of Management and Budget (OMB) for additional resources, but was repeatedly ignored. Realizing it needed more examiners to deal with the problems of the thrift industry, the Bank Board finally transferred its examination function to its 12 regional federal home loan banks and out from under the limitations placed on it by the OMB and the Office of Personnel Management (OPM). This maneuver enabled the 12 regional banks to attract more examiners, but came too late; many institutions had already engaged in risky or fraudulent loan and investment activities which would lead to their ultimate failure.

. . .

FINANCIAL CONDITION OF THE THRIFT INDUSTRY

During 1988 thrifts remained the nation's predominant mortgage lender, originating 49% of all residential mortgages in 1988 (up from 46% in 1987) for a dollar volume of $160.7 billion in mortgage loans. Thrifts remained a leading supplier to the secondary mortgage market, selling $271.8 billion in mortgage loans during 1988.

As of December 31, 1988, there were a total of 2,949 FSLIC-insured savings and loans operating nationwide, holding deposits of $971 billion and assets of $1.35 trillion. In total, these institutions lost $12.1 billion in 1988.

Statistics reveal that the present thrift industry crisis is far from systemic (see table below). At the end of 1988, 70 percent of all thrifts were profitable. These thrifts earned over $3.7 billion in 1988 and control well over 70 percent of the industry's assets. There are now approximately 1,225 thrifts with over 6 percent capital based on Generally Accepted Accounting Principles (GAAP). Eighty-one percent of this group was profitable in 1988 earning a combined $2 billion. As a group they had an average GAAP capital-to-assets ratio of nearly 9 percent at year-end 1988, and a respectable average return on assets for the year of .72 percent.

Type of thrift	No. of Thrifts (Dec. 31, 1988)	Total assets (billion dollars)	1988 net income (billion dollars)	Percent profitable
Healthy thrifts (GAAP capital greater than 3 percent)	2,195	923.2	3.7	81
GAAP-insolvent thrifts (GAAP capital less than 0)	364	113.5	(14.8)	12
Troubled thrifts (GAAP capital 0-3 percent)	390	314.8	(1.0)	56
Total FSLIC-insured thrifts	2,949	1,351.5	(12.1)	70

As the table indicates, the healthy savings on loans are more representative of the industry as a whole, but unhealthy thrifts have bankrupted the FSLIC and jeopardized the future of the industry.

ii. Current Status and Future Trends

ROSE & HANEY, THE PLAYERS IN THE PRIMARY MORTGAGE MARKET *

1 Journal of Housing Research 91, 91–93, 96, 98, 99, 105, 107–108, 112 (1990).

The Past Two Decades

During the 1970s and the 1980s, the mortgage markets expanded rapidly, yet they were able to keep pace with the burgeoning growth of the capital markets which had to accommodate continuing federal government deficits and the merger and leveraged buyout booms of the 1980s. The mortgage market growth occurred both in the single-family home loan area and in the broader mortgage markets (see table 1). This growth was in response to the rapid inflation of the 1970s, real estate's widely perceived role as an excellent hedge against that inflation, and the strong economic growth and subsequent overbuilding that occurred during the 1980s.

Table 1. Mortgage Market Growth
year end 1969-year end 1989
(dollars in billions)

	Year				
	1969	1974	1979	1984	1989
Single-family mortgage debt outstanding	$280.2	437.4	861.0	1,336.2	2,331.2
Total mortgage debt outstanding	$438.8	726.4	1,316.3	2,048.8	3,453.9
Total credit market debt outstanding	$1,486.4	2,402.4	4,233.3	7,195.7	12,196.4
Single-family mortgage debt as a percentage of credit market debt	18.9%	18.2	20.3	18.6	19.1
Total mortgage debt as a percentage of credit market debt	29.5%	30.2	31.1	28.5	28.3

Source: *Federal Reserve Bulletin*, selected monthly issues.

During the past two decades, many institutions, led by the traditionally large lender to this market segment—the savings and loan association (S & L)—supplied the demand for single-family mortgage loans. S & Ls have generally provided between 40 and 50 percent of all the single-family home loan money required by borrowers (see table 2). In an ominous note for the S & Ls, however, their market share has declined during each period shown in the table since reaching a high of almost 53 percent in 1975.

. . .

Table 2. Single-family Loan Originations by Type of Lenders
1970–89

	Year				
Lender	1970	1975	1980	1985	1990
Savings and Loan Association					
Originations ($B)	14.8	41.2	61.1	109.3	134.5
Percent of total	41.6%	52.9	45.7	44.3	38.2

Lender	Year				
	1970	1975	1980	1985	1990
Mutual Savings Bank					
Originations ($B)	2.1	4.3	5.4	16.5	23.2
Percent of total	6.0%	5.6	4.1	6.7	6.6
Commercial Bank					
Originations ($B)	7.8	14.5	28.8	51.7	123.2
Percent of total	21.9%	18.5	21.5	20.9	35.0
Mortgage Company					
Originations ($B)	8.9	14.0	29.4	63.3	65.6
Percent of total	25.0%	18.0	22.0	25.6	18.6
Other Lender					
Originations ($B)	1.9	3.9	9.0	6.0	5.6
Percent of total	5.4%	5.0	6.8	2.4	1.6
Total Single-family					
Loan Originations ($B)	35.6	77.9	133.8	246.8	352.0

Source: U.S. Department of Housing and Urban Development, Office of Financial Management, *Survey of mortgage lending activity*, Annual gross flows, selected issues. Note: Some totals do not add due to rounding.

. . .

The 1989 Market Share Shift

Commercial banks, which generally originated between 20 and 22 percent of the single-family home loans during the past two decades, suddenly increased their share of the market to 35.0 percent during 1989. Meanwhile, mortgage companies' market share declined moderately to less than 20 percent during this time. Mutual savings banks continued to originate approximately 6 percent of the loans throughout the period. These market share divergences have profound implications for the primary mortgage markets during the 1990s (see table 2). These divergences were spawned by a number of trends that began during the 1980s and contributed to the major shift in market share during 1989. Many of these trends will continue during the 1990s, along with the establishment of several new ones that we will discuss in the following sections.

Continuing Trends

The trends that began in the 1980s serve as important—even if only partial—determinants of the future direction that the primary mortgage markets will take during the current decade. It is for this reason that we explore many of the trends that will remain significant during the 1990s.

     . . .

Globalization. Another important trend that began in the 1980s was the increasing share of U.S. residential mortgages purchased by foreign investors as U.S. securities firms and federal mortgage agencies made a significant effort to educate foreign investors on the advantages of this financing instrument. Residential mortgage securities have proven to be especially attractive to selected foreign institutional investors in view of their relatively low level of default risk because of government and private loan guarantees and steadily improving liquidity. Moreover, the significant yield margins of most mortgage loans over U.S. government securities of comparable maturity have been especially attractive to foreign-based institutional investors. Recent foreign investment purchases have tended to concentrate upon mortgage-backed securities, particularly those packaged through Fannie Mae and Freddie Mac. Leading foreign dealers in housing-related mortgage instruments include the Industrial Bank of Japan and Nomura Securities, with the latter firm now operating as a primary dealer in Fannie Mae-guaranteed mortgage securities.

. . .

Commercial Bank Involvement. The shift of U.S. banking during the past two decades toward greater relative emphasis upon retail banking and less emphasis on wholesale credit accounts was aided by the spread of interstate banking. Between 1975 and 1989, more than 40 states passed laws allowing out-of-state banking companies to enter their territories. U.S. bankers who had hesitated to invade residential mortgage markets distant from their own traditional market areas now eagerly moved to broaden and diversify their consumer loan portfolios, particularly in those metropolitan and regional markets that appeared to possess excellent prospects for continued economic expansion and in-migration. The passage of tax-reform legislation in 1986 added additional luster to home mortgage credit for banks because the tax-exempt privileges attached to home loans allowed banks to price these loans more profitably compared with non-tax-enhanced consumer credit. Moreover, the spread of home equity credit lines has allowed banks to book somewhat shorter term mortgage loan maturities. The shorter maturity home loans have encouraged greater bank activity in the mortgage market because these credit lines more closely conform to the relatively volatile funding mix banks face compared with traditional long-term lenders in the residential market.

. . .

Thrift Institutions

Minimum Capital Standards. New capital standards at the federal government level now require S & Ls to raise new capital, slow the growth of their assets, or reduce asset-risk exposure by downsizing. The latter two options suggest a retrenchment in home mortgage lending by S & Ls and greater opportunities for commercial banks and mortgage companies to acquire a growing share of new loans.

The new capital requirements for S & Ls are likely to be a particularly difficult feature for the survival of troubled thrifts and for the maintenance of S & Ls' market shares in the primary mortgage market. ...

Many S & Ls will find the new capital requirements of FIRREA too burdensome and financially unattainable. Some of these will convert to commercial banks under the terms specified in FIRREA. Others will alter their organizational structure to become more broadly based financial service companies and surrender the tax benefits of an S & L. Whatever organizational form is ultimately adopted, it seems clear that the S & L industry of the 1990s and beyond will be substantially different in structure than those envisioned in the sweeping federal legislation of the 1930s that sheltered this industry, nurtured its growth in the more stable periods of recent history, and, unfortunately, contributed to the downfall of many thrift institutions in the volatile era of the 1970s and 1980s. Any vacuum left by troubled or failed S & Ls is likely to be filled by aggressively managed commercial banks and bank holding companies whose stronger capital positions and recently enlarged opportunities for full-service interstate banking give them a strategic advantage in the mortgage market of the 1990s.

Mortgage Companies

In contrast to commercial banks, mortgage banking firms face an uncertain future. Changes instituted in the residential finance delivery system by the growth and maturation of the global secondary market as a common funding outlet, by the rolling economic recession of the late 1980s and early 1990s, and by FIRREA's provisions will certainly alter the environmental fabric. These changes must also be coupled with the previously described pressures which offer the greatest rewards to the primary market players that are the most efficient, least cost institutions. Together, they suggest dramatic changes for many residential mortgage companies.

. . .

Mortgage Brokers

Single-family home mortgage brokers, concentrating on the origination of high-quality mortgage loans within a limited marketplace that they know well, will prosper during the 1990s. Taking a share of the origination function market that mortgage bankers and smaller financial intermediaries used to call their own, the mortgage brokers operate with very low overhead. They will frequently use their homes as their places of business; this helps keep their costs low and sets them up as the least cost originator.

. . .

Credit Unions

Credit unions are another depository institution that hold considerable potential as players in the primary mortgage market. They have a substantial base of fairly stable deposits and a user community that is more loyal than the customers of other financial institutions. Moreover, they have been allowed to make 30–year residential mortgage loans since 1978 and have thus had an opportunity to develop substantial expertise. In spite of these advantages, many credit unions have not fully pursued their mortgage market opportunities.

During the past 15 years, most credit unions have continued to concentrate on investments in the consumer installment credit area, primarily loans for automobile purchases. This means they let slip the opportunity to develop an additional area of expertise during the turmoil in the mortgage markets in the 1980s, an opportunity in which traditional borrower-lender relationships were very fluid because of shifting institutional alignments. If credit unions do not develop substantial expertise in one of the primary mortgage market specializations, it is difficult to envision credit unions becoming major players in this marketplace during the 1990s.

b. SECONDARY MARKET AND SECURITIZATION

MALLOY, THE SECONDARY MORTGAGE MARKET— A CATALYST FOR CHANGE IN REAL ESTATE TRANSACTIONS

39 Southwestern Law Journal 991, 992–95, 1001–10 (1986).

I. History of the Secondary Mortgage Market

During the 1930s the economic depression had a devastating impact on real estate finance. The inability of homeowners to meet their payment obligations, under what we would today consider short-term mortgages, led to many foreclosures and to investors losing confidence in the mortgage lending system. In order to restore confidence in this sector of the economy and make home ownership more accessible, the federal government initiated a series of programs to develop both new mortgage instruments and a secondary market for mortgages.

A. Developing the Market

In 1934 Congress created the Federal Housing Administration (FHA) and provided for the development of mortgage insurance programs. FHA-insured loans were developed as a way to insure payment to a lender in the event of a borrower's default on a home mortgage. In 1944 Congress approved a similar program to provide loan guarantees for Veterans Administration (VA) loans. Both the FHA and VA loan programs, as they developed, supported new lending guidelines that led to smaller required downpayments and the acceptability of long-term (twenty to thirty years), fixed-rate mortgages. These programs improved lender confidence in real estate financing and made homeownership more accessible to home buyers.

Congress established the Reconstruction Finance Corporation (RFC) in 1935. One of the RFC's most successful programs involved the buying of FHA-insured and VA-guaranteed mortgages. This activity enhanced the liquidity of FHA and VA loans, made the loans more attractive to loan originators, and thereby assisted the development of mortgage markets.

By 1938 Congress had created the Federal National Mortgage Association (FNMA or Fannie Mae), which joined with the RFC to develop the secondary mortgage market. The RFC, until its dissolution in 1948, concentrated primarily on the purchase of existing or seasoned mortgages on new houses in an effort to stimulate economic activity and new construction. The FNMA, on the other hand, used its buying and selling activities to advance a variety of policy goals. The FNMA supported, for instance, the continued marketability of FHA and VA loans with fixed interest rates. Fannie Mae also acted as a counterbalance to the cyclical effects of general business recessions and the monetary intervention of a more active federal government. The FNMA provided assistance for special housing projects that were unable to generate sufficient private investment, such as low income housing. Finally, Fannie Mae introduced new mortgage arrangements, including longer term financing with little borrower equity required at a time when such arrangements were otherwise untested in the private mortgage market.

In 1968 Congress divided the FNMA into two entities. One entity continued with the same name, but became a federally chartered corporation owned by private shareholders. The second entity, the Government National Mortgage Association (GNMA or Ginnie Mae), was a corporation established within the Department of Housing and Urban Development (HUD). As a result of the split the GNMA became primarily responsible for the government's special assistance and housing support programs. The FNMA, on the other hand, began to concentrate on the secondary mortgage market activities of buying and selling loans for its portfolio, thereby increasing the liquidity and investment opportunities of loan originators.

As the FNMA and GNMA established a ready market for FHA and VA loans, conventional loans, which lenders primarily hold in their own portfolios, continued to be less liquid due to a lack of standard documentation and underwriting guidelines. As various regions of the country began to experience rapid growth and real estate development in the late 1960s, the illiquidity of conventional loans often left local lending institutions without sufficient funds. Although other areas of the country had excess funds, the secondary mortgage market was not yet broad enough to address completely the need for market reallocation of capital assets. Thus, in 1970 Congress created the Federal Home Loan Mortgage Corporation (FHLMC or Freddie Mac) in the Emergency Home Finance Act. The FHLMC, although authorized to purchase FHA and VA loans, focused primarily on conventional mortgages. At the same time, even though the FNMA was given new authority to purchase conventional mortgages, it remained active in FHA and VA loans. Together, the FHLMC and FNMA sought to increase the marketability of all mortgages by developing uniform standards to facilitate the purchase and sale of mortgages in the secondary mortgage market and thereby attract new sources of investment capital to the housing market.

By the 1980s the secondary mortgage market had become so successful and had reached such a level of volume and technological advancement that numerous private entities were entering the market. These private entities provided additional investment services and competed with the three major market entities, the FHLMC, FNMA, and GNMA.

. . .

II. The Operation of the Secondary Mortgage Market

. . .

A. *Major Participants*

The major participants in the secondary mortgage market include the GNMA, FNMA, and the FHLMC. Certain private entities are also heavily involved, but the GNMA, FNMA, and FHLMC remain responsible for most of the activity in the secondary mortgage market.

1. *GNMA.* The GNMA was created by Congress in 1968 and through its secondary mortgage market activities supplies mortgage credit for government housing objectives in that segment of the housing market for which conventional financing is not readily available. The GNMA primarily deals with the purchase of subsidized and unsubsidized single-family and multi-family FHA and VA mortgages. The GNMA also guarantees pass-through mortgage-backed securities that are issued by HUD-approved mortgagees and that represent interest in FHA, VA, and FmHA (Farmers Home Administration) mortgages. The GNMA is a wholly owned government corporation within HUD, and its mortgaged-backed securities carry the full faith and credit of the United States.

2. *FNMA.* Congress created the FNMA in 1938 as a wholly owned government corporation, but in 1968 Fannie Mae became owned by private shareholders. The FNMA purchases single-family and multi-family FHA, VA, and conventional mortgages. The parties from whom the FNMA buys consist primarily of mortgage companies, mutual savings banks, commercial banks, credit unions, savings and loan institutions, and for second mortgages, finance companies. The FNMA issues guaranteed Mortgage–Backed Securities (MBSs), which are backed by loans in its own portfolio as well as by participations in loans that are pooled or packaged through other lenders. Even though FNMA stock is publicly traded, the FNMA is subject to the regulatory authority of the Secretary of HUD, and the U.S. Treasury stands behind FNMA obligations with discretionary authority to purchase up to $2.25 billion of FNMA debt. As a result, the FNMA is considered by the credit markets as having "agency status."

3. *FHLMC.* Congress created the FHLMC in 1970 primarily to provide liquidity for mortgage lenders by developing and maintaining the secondary mortgage market in conventional residential mortgages. The FHLMC buys conventional, FHA, and VA single-family and multi-family loans as well as home improvement loans. Sellers to the

FHLMC consist primarily of savings and loan institutions, but also include mortgage bankers and commercial banks. The FHLMC sells mortgage-backed securities, issues other securities that are debt obligations secured by conventional mortgages, and operates a guarantor program. Because the FHLMC is a corporation whose stock is wholly owned by the twelve Federal Home Loan Banks, the FHLMC is able to elevate its securities to the status of obligations of the United States.

4. *Private Entities.* Several private entities buy, package, and sell mortgages and mortgage-related securities. For the most part, these private entities concentrate on pools of individual mortgages that exceed the statutory limits on loans that the FHLMC and FNMA can purchase. Private entities concentrate their activities in this area because the government relationship attributed to the GNMA, FNMA, and FHLMC allow those entities a better reception in the credit markets for their mortgage-related securities. Private entities thus are hindered more by higher costs than are GNMA, FNMA, and FHLMC in the competition for the same mortgages.

Private mortgage insurance companies (PMICs) are important to the successful market operation of private entities in the secondary mortgage market. PMICs insure the obligations of the underlying conventional mortgages in a fashion similar to the FHA insurance provided in FHA loans. ...

B. Major Offerings

The major offerings in the secondary mortgage market that will be discussed in this Article include: the private sale of whole loans or participations; Ginnie Mae Securities; Mortgage–Backed Securities (MBSs) issued through the FNMA; Participation Certificates (PCs) and Collateralized Mortgage Obligations (CMOs) issued through the FHLMC; Swap programs run by the FNMA and FHLMC; and mortgage-backed bonds. The growth of activity in the secondary market offerings has been dramatic: an estimated sixty-five percent to seventy-five percent of all new loans are presently sold through the market. As the secondary mortgage market matures and expands, mortgage-related securities are becoming more competitive with corporate securities in the investment market.

In considering specific market offerings two concepts must be defined. The first concept is mortgage pooling or packaging. Single home loans are not sold individually into the secondary mortgage market; they must be "pooled" or "packaged." For purposes of this Article, the terms "pooling" and "packaging" refer to the process whereby primary mortgage lenders, also known as originators, group similar loans together to create a sufficient basis for investment. The resulting pool or package of loans is sold to investors or used as the security for the offering of a mortgage-backed security.

The second concept is that of a pass-through security. The sale of a loan participation or of a mortgage-backed security is said to be a pass-through security when the monthly payments of principal and interest on each of the underlying mortgages merely passes from the party servicing the loans, less a fee for servicing, to the investor. With a straight pass-through security, the investors get only their respective share of the funds actually collected on the loans. Thus, if some of the borrowers do not make their monthly payments, the investors receive less for that month.

Pass-through securities can also be fully or partially modified. A fully modified pass-through security involves an arrangement in which the monthly pass-through of principal and interest is fully guaranteed by an entity such as the GNMA, FNMA, or FHLMC. The guarantee means that investors will receive a stated amount each month even if some borrowers fail to make their monthly payments. A partially modified pass-through security generally involves a guarantee by a PMIC to insure against a shortfall in actual collections relative to the expected pass-through amount, usually five or ten percent. This partial guarantee means that the PMIC will make up for any shortfall in actual monthly payments from borrowers up to the predetermined level of five or ten percent. Any shortfall beyond the insured amount represents a reduction in return to the investors.

1. *Private Sales.* Private sales typically consist of the sale of whole loans or loan participations to private investors without using a government agency as an intermediary. The private sale of whole loans is a significant if not major part of the secondary market; in 1982 such sales amounted to approximately $35 billion. In addition to selling whole loans to other investors, loan originators also sell loan participations, which allow investors to purchase a share in the expected return on the mortgage pool. ...

Lenders generally sell their whole loans and participations to insurance companies, pension funds, commercial banks, mutual savings banks, or savings and loan institutions. The sale or participation agreement contains loan and performance requirements and establishes a servicing arrangement. When whole loans are sold the servicing function is frequently transferred as well, but when a loan participation is sold the loan originator almost always continues to service the loans.

. . .

2. *Ginnie Maes.* Ginnie Mae issues three basic types of securities: (1) straight pass-through securities, in which the GNMA guarantees the payment of principal and interest as collected; (2) fully modified pass-through securities, in which the GNMA guarantees the full payment of interest and principal whether or not it is actually collected; and (3) bonds that provide semi-annual interest payments and periodic redemption and are subject to call. ... All of the GNMA guarantees are backed by the full faith and credit of the United States.

. . .

3. *MBSs and PCs.* The FNMA may purchase whole loans or participations on which Mortgage–Backed Securities (MBSs) are issued and offered to investors, or for a fee it may issue MBSs to be returned to the portfolio of the original lender or originator. Likewise, the FHLMC may purchase whole loans or participations on which its Participation Certificates (PCs) are issued, or for a fee it may issue PCs for return to the portfolio of the original lender. PCs and MBSs, whether sold directly to investors by the FNMA or FHLMC or simply returned to the portfolio of the originating lender, each offer purchasers a guarantee providing for a fully modified pass-through security, and each represents an undivided interest in conventional and seasoned FHA and VA mortgages.

. . .

4. *CMOs.* Collateralized Mortgage Obligations (CMOs) are mortgage-backed securities that the FHLMC pioneered. In the first three months of 1984 CMOs constituted approximately one-third of the amount raised by all corporate debt issues. In addition to bringing billions of dollars into the primary mortgage markets, CMOs are given credit for lowering the cost of home mortgages by twenty-five basis points or one-quarter percent between June and December of 1983. Unlike other pass-through securities, the CMO does not provide monthly payments to investors. Instead, the issuing entity makes interest payments at the coupon rate on the outstanding principal balance in the same manner that payments are made on corporate bonds.

The FHLMC designed CMOs to make investments in mortgage-backed securities more manageable and thus more appealing to investors. Mortgagors on the underlying mortgages in a mortgage pool tend to prepay or default on their loans faster as interest rates fall and to repay more slowly as interest rates rise. Consequently, the actual life and yield of an investment in a mortgage-backed security is unpredictable.

Freddie Mac developed the CMO in an attempt to deal with these problems. A single pool of mortgages provides a payment stream that is allocated serially to several classes of securities. Each class has its own yield, and investors can invest in the particular class of their choosing. All investors receive semiannual interest payments in accordance with the coupon rate for their class. Principal payments on the underlying mortgage loans are combined and paid first to the holders of the shortest-maturity bonds. When the first class is fully retired, all of the principal is paid next to the holders of the intermediate-maturity bonds. The longest-maturity bonds do not receive principal until all other classes are retired.

By dividing the pool into these various investment classes, investors can more easily predict payment and yield on their investment. As a result CMOs, have been able to attract investors at lower interest rates than other mortgage-backed securities. The ability to attract investors at lower yields means that the CMO can be offered at a lower cost or rate, and the savings can ultimately be passed on to homebuyers in the form of reduced mortgage rates.

5. *Bonds.* Private issuers in the secondary mortgage market issue two basic types of bonds: (1) mortgage-backed bonds (MBBs); and (2) pay-through bonds. These bonds represent a debt obligation of the issuer that is collateralized by mortgage loans. The holders of the underlying loans for both types of bonds do not sell the loans, but rather pledge them to repay the debt. The loans cannot be used for any other purpose until the holders repay the debt represented by the bonds.

NOTES

1. *The Savings and Loan Crisis.* In reading the Report of the House Committee on Banking, Finance and Urban Affairs, consider whether this is an accurate history, a political document, or both. For a fine telling of the S & L story see Felsenfeld, The Savings and Loan Crisis, 59 Fordham L.Rev. S7 (1991).

Although deregulation of the thrift industry may have contributed to the S & L crisis, it may also have yielded substantial benefits. In an excellent article about the development of a national market for home loans, Professor Michael Schill observed:

> For the next half century, the institutions and regulatory framework that were created after the Great Depression continued largely intact. From the 1930s until the early 1980s the real estate capital market was separate from general capital markets. The typical home mortgage loan during this period was originated by a local savings and loan institution which raised funds from local residents by paying interest on their time deposits. The thrift usually held the loan in its portfolio until it matured, the borrower defaulted, or the borrower prepaid the debt. Interest rates and the supply of credit were sensitive to local economic conditions, as well as national economic trends. Several economists have characterized real estate finance markets during this period as "segmented."

> . . .

> Over the past decade, the segmentation of real estate financial markets has dissolved. Real estate credit markets have been substantially linked to general capital markets as a result of numerous factors including deregulation, the growth of the secondary mortgage market, securitization, and technological advances.

Schill, Uniformity or Diversity: Residential Real Estate Finance Law in the 1990s and the Implications of Changing Financial Markets," 64 S.Cal.L.Rev. 1261, 1264–65 (1991). *

* Reprinted with the permission of the Southern California Law Review.

2. *FIRREA.* FIRREA brought significant changes to the home mortgage industry, affecting the structure and regulation of mortgage lenders. Among other changes, the Act abolished the Federal Home Loan Bank Board, placed supervisory responsibilities over federal and state chartered savings and loans in the Office of Thrift Supervision under the Secretary of the Treasury, created the Federal Housing Finance Board to oversee the twelve regional Federal Home Loan Bank Boards, abolished the FSLIC and made the Federal Deposit Insurance Corporation responsible for insuring savings associations deposits, increased the FDIC's supervisory power, and created the Resolution Trust Corporation to dispose of insolvent S & Ls insured by the FSLIC. FIRREA also limited the type of investments that savings associations can make, generally barring direct equity investment in real estate and limiting the amount of loans secured by nonresidential realty and unsecured construction loans for residential property.

The Act's requirements that the regulatory agencies develop loan to value ratios and appraisal standards will inevitably affect the terms of residential mortgages. See pages 413–414 below. See generally, Loewenthal, McEvoy, Rolls & Wood, The Impact of the Financial Institutions Reform, Recovery, and Enforcement Act of 1989 (FIRREA) on Lending Practices and Procedures of Savings Associations, 26 Real Prop. Probate & Trust J. 577 (1991).

On FIRREA and its effects, see Understanding FIRREA: A Practical Guide to Planning and Compliance (Prentice–Hall, 1989); Adams, Is the Power of the RTC Unlimited?—Federal Preemption of State Banking Law, 18 Fla.St.L.Rev. 995 (1991); Tucker, Meire & Rubinstein, The RTC: A Practical Guide to the Receivership/Conservatorship Process and the Resolution of Failed Thrifts, 25 U.Rich.L.Rev. 1 (1990); Note, Playing with FIRREA, Not Getting Burned: Statutory Overview of the Financial Institutions Reform, Recovery and Enforcement Act of 1989, 59 Fordham L.Rev. S323 (1991); see generally 12 C.F.R. §§ 500–591 for the OTS regulations.

3. *Growth of the Secondary Market.* The growth in the secondary market over recent years has been tremendous, leading to a national home financing system in which loans originated by local lenders are now sold to lenders throughout the country and even internationally. "In the early 1980s less than 5% of all newly originated, conforming conventional fixed rate home mortgage loans were securitized. This proportion has increased to over one-half by 1987." Schill, Uniformity or Diversity: Residential Real Estate Finance Law in the 1990s and the Implications of Changing Financial Markets," 64 S.Cal.L.Rev. 1261, 1272 (1991). "From 1984 through 1988, annual origination of all mortgage securities, including [GNMA, FNMA, and FHLMC] securities, increased by over 300%, totalling $280 billion at the end of 1988. While offerings of [GNMA, FNMA, and FHLMC] pass-through securities have accounted for the bulk of the increase, origination of privately issued mortgage securities ... has grown steadily." Pittman, Economic and Regulatory Developments Affecting Mortgage Related Securities,

64 Notre Dame L.Rev. 497, 538 (1989) (also describing the Secondary Mortgage Market Enhancement Act, Pub. L. No. 98–440, 98 Stat. 1689 (1984), which removed certain impediments to the private secondary mortgage market existing under state and federal securities and investment laws). For an excellent detailed analysis of the past, current, and projected levels of securitization, see Jaffee & Rosen, Mortgage Securitization Trends, 1 J. Housing Research 117 (1990).

For other fine sources describing and analyzing the secondary market, see Browne, The Private Mortgage Insurance Industry, The Thrift Industry and the Secondary Mortgage Market: Their Interrelationships, 12 Akron L.Rev. 631 (1979); Richards, "Gradable and Tradable": The Securitization of Commercial Real Estate Mortgages, 16 Real Est.L.J. 99 (1987); Shenker & Colletta, Asset Securitization: Evolution, Current Issues and New Frontiers, 69 Tex.L.Rev. 1369 (1991).

4. *Federalization of Mortgages.* Mortgage law, like mortgage lending, has traditionally honored state boundaries. Recognizing that local variations in mortgage law and practice could seriously stunt the growth of a truly national mortgage industry, policymakers have taken steps on several fronts to federalize mortgage law and practice, mostly in connection with home loans. First, one of the express purposes of the Uniform Land Security Interest Act is to encourage lending by out of state banks by providing uniform laws. Second, to reduce the cost of individually examining mortgage documents from fifty different jurisdictions, the FHLMC and FNMA have published uniform loan instruments that are now used in about eighty percent of all residential loans. See Lance, Balancing Private and Public Initiatives in the Mortgage–Backed Security Market, 18 Real Prop., Probate & Trust J. 426, 438 (1983). Also, Congress has expressly preempted state laws on usury restrictions on first lien home loans, due on sale clauses, and adjustable rate mortgage instruments for residences, and the Office of Thrift Supervision has issued regulations on loan-value ratio and appraisal standards which supplant local law. See pages 389, 392 and 413–414 below.

Professor Schill argues, however, that federal preemption of state mortgage foreclosure law may not bring great efficiencies and will prevent the states from experimenting with different rules reflecting their economic, cultural, and political diversity. Schill, Uniformity or Diversity: Residential Real Estate Finance Law in the 1990s and the Implications of Changing Financial Markets, 64 S.Cal.L.Rev. 1291 (1991).

5. *Sources of Mortgage Funds.* For additional information see Housing in the Seventies, Report of the Department of Housing and Urban Development, Hearings before the Subcomm. on Housing of the House Comm. on Banking and Currency, Part 3, 93d Cong. 1st Session 2024 (1973) (a comprehensive, though partially dated, review of primary and secondary sources and governmental programs); Fallain & Zorn, The Unbundling of Residential Mortgage Finance, 1 J. Housing Re-

search 63 (1990) (examining the future directions of home mortgages sources and servicing institutions).

3. TERMS

Mortgage terms can be reduced to four variables: interest rate; amortization rate (the rate at which the loan principal is paid off); term; and loan to value ratio (the ratio between the amount of the loan and the value of the property securing it; thus an $80,000 loan on a property appraised at $100,000 has an 8:10 loan to value ratio, sometimes simply called an 80% loan to value ratio). Each variable can be adjusted to meet the particular needs of borrower and lender. For example, a borrower might agree to a shorter loan term—thereby reducing the lender's exposure and risk—in return for a lower interest rate, a slower amortization rate, or a higher loan to value ratio.

The most dramatic shift in the orientation of these four variables occurred as a result of the Depression of the 1930's. The standard pre-Depression mortgage instrument had a short-term (typically 5 years); low loan to value ratio (typically 50%); and little or no amortization (the entire principal was typically payable as a "balloon" at the end of the term). New Deal programs introduced a strikingly different instrument and encouraged its adoption with the lure of FHA insurance. The new instrument had a much longer term (20 to 30 years); a higher loan to value ratio (typically 80%); and complete amortization over the life of the loan. Most instruments of this period were so-called "level payment" mortgages, calling for identical monthly payments covering interest and amortization throughout the loan term. In the loan's early years, most of the level payment goes toward interest and only a small amount toward reduction of principal. But, as principal is reduced, the interest payments on the principal outstanding become smaller and the proportion of the level payment available for reduction in principal becomes consequently larger, resulting in still smaller interest payments and still larger reductions in principal, until the loan is completely paid off.

The long-term fixed rate mortgage, although still widely used, had by the mid-1970's become increasingly unattractive to lenders and borrowers alike. With interest rates constantly rising, lenders were reluctant to commit their capital over a long period at interest rates that they believed would soon fall short of their own cost of capital. Borrowers disliked the higher interest rates, shorter terms, and lower loan to value ratios that lenders began to require in return for their own diminished prospects. This shared dilemma produced a burst of new mortgage instruments that sometimes resembled the instruments used in pre-Depression real estate finance. The principal materials and the first two notes that follow indicate how lenders juggled the four mortgage variables to meet new consumer needs while, at the same time, improving their own loan portfolios.

HOUSING IN THE SEVENTIES, REPORT OF THE DEPARTMENT OF HOUSING AND URBAN DEVELOPMENT

Hearings before the Subcomm. on Housing of the House Comm. on Banking
and Currency, Part 3, 93d Cong. 1st Sess. 2043–2049 (1973).

There are certain advantages to limiting the number of repayment methods available to borrowers and lenders. It is easier for the borrower and lender to become familiar with the terms and implications of each method; transaction costs are reduced due to the limited number of options available; and secondary market operations are facilitated where there are large volumes of a limited number of mortgage types. Uniformity has an important effect upon the marketability of financial instruments, and too many variations of mortgages can impair the development of the secondary mortgage market. On the other hand, limitations on the number of repayment methods limit the flexibility of the borrower and lender in finding a repayment method which suits their special needs. By encouraging the use of fixed interest rate, fully amortizing, level payment mortgages, the Government has significantly limited the choices available to borrowers and lenders.

Government Restrictions on Contracts

The options available to mortgagors and mortgagees are typically restricted by numerous State and Federal laws and regulations which either require or proscribe certain provisions in contracts for mortgage loans. These State and Federal restrictions have been promulgated for various reasons and objectives; however, in the aggregate they reduce the supply and demand for mortgage credit by limiting the options available to both borrowers and lenders.

One of the more obvious restrictions on mortgage contracts is the maximum legal interest rate on the loan as contained in most states' usury laws. State laws also prescribe the conditions and procedures for foreclosures. In addition, the method of repayment is also typically defined or restricted by law or regulation. For example, the fully-amortized mortgage loans made by federally-chartered savings and loan associations cannot have any contractual periodic payment which exceeds the previous period's contractual payment. Therefore, although the Federal Home Loan Bank Board's regulations for federally-chartered savings and loan associations do not require equal monthly payments, they do prohibit any period of increasing contractual periodic payments on fully-amortized mortgage loans. The above restrictions on contracts constitute only a partial list, but they are among the most important restrictions on the options open to borrowers and lenders.

Mortgages Payable in Full at Maturity

Prior to the 1930's, most mortgage loans—like corporate and Treasury bonds—were typically unamortized with all principal being paid at maturity. The term to maturity was usually between 5 and 10 years and borrowers were required to make 50 percent downpayments. A large downpayment was required to reduce the loan-to-value ratio to a level consistent with the nature and risks of this type of mortgage loan.

This arrangement frequently found homeowners without the necessary funds when the loan matured. If the homeowner could not meet the lump-sum payment when the loan was due the alternatives were either refinancing or default. Refinancing was usual and customary but not always available, especially in periods of tight credit.

A variation on the non-amortized loan was the use of sinking funds to accumulate the funds necessary to retire the debt at maturity. A borrower contracted to accumulate funds in a savings account by making periodic deposits so that the balance would equal the debt at maturity. This method closely resembles the fully-amortized mortgage loan with periodic payments; however, it fell into disuse in favor of the direct reduction loan. The direct reduction loan is a long-term, fixed interest rate, equal monthly payment, fully amortized loan. The current regulations of the Federal Home Loan Bank Board specifically instruct federally-chartered savings and loan associations to use the direct reduction method, where the periodic payments are applied directly to the reduction of the loan and not to a sinking fund in the form of a savings account. The use of sinking funds therefore represented the transitional stage between non-amortized and fully-amortized mortgage loans.

The Current Form of the Mortgage Loan....

However, the long term, fixed interest rate, equal monthly payment, fully amortized mortgage loan may not be the best instrument for all housing finance in today's inflationary economy. Most of the problems with this instrument relate to its requirements for a fixed interest rate set at the outset for the full term of the mortgage and equal monthly payments. The alternative mortgage forms to be presented below relax one or both of these requirements in an attempt to produce a more flexible mortgage debt instrument for certain purposes and conditions.

A difficulty with the fixed interest rate requirement is the problem which it creates for thrift institutions when market interest rates rise in response to unanticipated inflation or a general increase in the demand for credit. When market interest rates rise sharply, thrift institutions must raise their deposit rates to retain their depositors' funds. While they must pay higher rates on the entire amount of their borrowed funds, they receive higher rates only on their new loans. Consequently, they become tied to a low-yield portfolio while paying high rates for deposits. If market interest rates rise sharply, the savings and loan industry is threatened with a serious decline in net portfolio yield. If market rates fall sharply, the above sequence is reversed somewhat but limited by the borrower's right to refinance the loan after paying any prepayment penalties which may be required.

The requirement for equal payments may work hardships on certain classes of borrowers. First, the requirements for equal monthly payments is a burden on younger borrowers whose incomes are expected to rise over the life of the loan. This is because the earlier payments take a much larger portion of their disposable income than do later payments. With fixed payment mortgages, young households may have to postpone homeownership until their current income rises by an amount which adequately covers the fixed mortgage payments. As will be shown later in this section, there are alternative mortgage instruments whose repayment schedules better correspond to an individual's expected stream of future income.

A second problem with the fixed interest rate, equal payment requirement is that it creates problems for the borrower when inflation is expected. The lender demands that a premium be built into the interest rate to protect himself against inflation and this raises monthly payments immediately, whereas the borrower's money income is raised by inflation only gradually over the life of the mortgage.

. . .

Alternative Mortgage Forms

Numerous alternative mortgage debt instruments are possible, and a few basic forms are briefly described below. Actually, there are as many possible instruments as there are ways to vary the manner of repayment of principal and interest, and some of these possibilities have already found their way into use. The main point to be made is that there are alternatives available to the mortgage loan instrument currently in general usage, each with its own advantages and disadvantages.

Variable-rate Mortgages

Variable-rate mortgages replace the standard fixed mortgage rate with a flexible rate which is related to prevailing market interest rates. That is, the rate on the mortgage loan changes as market interest rates change. Actually, the variable-rate mortgage may be viewed as a sequence of refinanced short-term loans. In order to avoid the costs of constantly being involved in negotiations, the borrower and lender agree to accept an automatically determined rate tied by some formula to one or more interest rates. As a practical matter the borrower and lender also agree to disregard insignificant changes in market rates, and the rates on variable-rate mortgage loans change only with important changes in market rates of interest.

Variable-rate mortgages assume three forms. One form uses a fixed term to maturity and varies the monthly payments to reflect changes in the mortgage rate. A second form uses equal monthly payments and increases or decreases the term to maturity as interest rates rise or fall, respectively. The third form is a hybrid which varies the payments or the term to maturity, or both simultaneously, to reflect changes in interest rates.

A basic advantage of variable-payment mortgages is that they allow mortgage lenders to keep their deposit rates competitive with market rates and maintain the share of mortgages in the aggregate supply of credit at all times. As a result, borrowers and homebuilders would have a better chance to obtain credit during periods of rising interest rates. In addition, by reducing the risks associated with fixed-rate contracting over long periods of time, a lower average expected cost of borrowing on larger volume may be attained. Both theory and empirical evidence indicate that variable-rate mortgages have a lower average interest rate than fixed-rate mortgages.

A disadvantage of the variable-payment form is that a substantial rise in interest rates could find some borrowers hard-pressed to meet their payments, and this could lead to some increase in default rates. The variable term form does not have this disadvantage.

Variable-rate mortgages are used widely in such developed countries as Britain, France, Germany, Italy, Sweden, Australia, and the Union of South Africa. In addition, experience has shown that both fixed-rate and variable-rate instruments coexist where both are available. ...

Interest-only Mortgages

In one version of the interest only mortgage, the borrower pays only the interest on the outstanding principal during the early years of the loan. Another version entails early payments which do not even cover the full interest costs on the unpaid principal. In either case payments are lower in the initial years and increase when both interest and principal are paid during later years. ...

Mortgage Payments Related to the Borrower's Income

This instrument is a fixed rate, variable monthly payment, fully amortized mortgage which has its monthly payments tied directly to the borrower's income over the period of the loan. This type of loan utilizes a fixed interest rate with variable monthly payments and requires the borrower to commit himself to make monthly payments which are an agreed upon percentage of his monthly income. The term to maturity is varied as the monthly payments vary. ...

**GOEBEL v. FIRST FEDERAL SAVINGS &
LOAN ASSOCIATION OF RACINE**

Supreme Court of Wisconsin, 1978.
83 Wis.2d 668, 266 N.W.2d 352.

CONNOR T. HANSEN, Justice.

The facts in the case are not in dispute. Although First Federal is a federally regulated institution, the resolution of the instant controversy depends on the interpretation of the note and mortgage as a matter of state contract law.

On May 29, 1964, the plaintiffs, as mortgagors, executed a mortgage in favor of First Federal, as mortgagee, in the amount of $17,000, with interest at six percent annually, payable in monthly installments.

The note contained the following interest rate adjustment provision:

"... The interest for each month shall be calculated upon said unpaid balance due as of the last day of the previous month at the rate of 6 per cent per annum or such other rate of interest on unpaid balances as may be fixed by the Association from time to time at its option, provided however, that the Association may not change the rate of interest except at any time after three years from the date hereof, and then upon 4 months or more written notice to the Promissors. Notice shall be deemed received when the same is deposited in the United States mail, postage prepaid, addressed to the Promissors at their last address as it appears on the record of the Association. The Promissors upon receiving notice of such change may repay the entire balance due on this obligation during said 4 months period without penalty. Any change in the rate of interest shall be endorsed on this mortgage note by the Association, stating the effective date of such change, the balance then due, and the new rate."

The plaintiffs do not contest the legality or the conscionableness of such a provision. However, they argue that in the instant case, First Federal is precluded, by other provisions of the mortgage note, from effectuating an interest rate increase either by increasing the term of the note or by increasing the amount of the monthly installments. As completed, the note obligated the plaintiffs to pay to First Federal:

"... the principal sum of Seventeen Thousand and $^{00}/_{100}$— Dollars, ($17,000.00) and such additional sums as may be subsequently advanced hereon to the Promissors and Mortgagors by the ASSOCI-ATION, together with interest as hereinafter provided, until such loan shall have been fully paid; such principal and interest payable in monthly installments of One Hundred Ten___ Dollars ___ Cents, ($110.00) on or before the 10th day of each and every month, commencing January 10, 1965; said principal and interest, including advances, notwithstanding any other provisions in this note or the mortgage given as collateral security, shall be paid in full within 25 years from the date hereof, and in the event of an additional advance hereon over and above the principal sum stated above, such monthly installments shall be adjusted to conform to this provision."

In September, 1973, First Federal notified the plaintiffs that as a result of unfavorable economic conditions, the interest rate on their loan would be increased from six percent to eight percent, effective February 1, 1974. In November, 1973, the plaintiffs were informed that the new rate would be seven percent rather than eight percent and that they could elect to absorb the increased interest expense either by paying an additional $7.49 per month or by extending the term of their loan approximately two years. The plaintiffs did not reply to this letter, and they continued to make monthly payments of $110.

Affidavits submitted in support of the motions for summary judgment allege that First Federal has increased the interest rate of 488 borrowers whose mortgage notes were executed on forms identical to that completed by the plaintiffs, and that 119 of these borrowers have elected to pay larger monthly installments to absorb the increase in interest rates.

This action was commenced by the plaintiffs, as a class action, on behalf of themselves and all others similarly situated. They argue that the terms of their note preclude any alteration by First Federal that would either increase the amount of their monthly payments or extend the term of their loan to accommodate an increased interest rate. The issues presented on appeal are whether the terms of the mortgage note permit First Federal to increase the interest rate by increasing the amount of the monthly installments or by extending the term of the loan [2] and whether the case can proceed as a class action.

Whether First Federal can increase the amount of the plaintiffs' monthly payments so as to absorb a higher interest rate rests, to a significant extent, on the principle of *expressio unius est exclusio alterius.* Under this principle, a specific mention in a contract of one or more matters is considered to exclude other matters of the same nature or class not expressly mentioned, even when all such matters would have been inferred had none been expressed.

The mortgage documents leave no doubt as to the right of the mortgagee to increase monthly payments to accommodate repayment of future advances and the lender's cash expenditures to protect its security interest. With equal clarity, the draftsman could have provided the same express means to accommodate the interest escalation clause. Other mortgage notes introduced in evidence did so by providing that interest could be increased or decreased with a corresponding adjustment in the required monthly payments.

The note specifically states that First Federal may advance additional sums to the borrowers and provides that "... in the event of an additional advance hereon over and above the principal sum stated above, *such monthly installments shall be adjusted to conform to this provision.*" (Emphasis added.) In addition, the note authorizes First Federal to protect its security interest in the mortgaged property by

---

2. A third possible method of implementing an interest rate adjustment clause is referred to as the use of a balloon payment. Under this method, monthly payments would continue to be made in the original amount, but would be applied against principal and interest to reflect the increased rate of interest. Upon expiration of the original term of the loan, a lump-sum balloon payment, in the amount of the then-outstanding principal balance, would be collected. Balloon payments are subject to federal regulation. 12 CFR 541.-14(a), as amended by 37 Fed.Reg. 5118 (1972). However, this method was not used in the instant case, and therefore we do not address it.

paying taxes, purchasing insurance, making repairs or discharging any encumbrance upon the premises, and the note requires the borrowers to repay any such outlays "upon demand" by First Federal. The trial court concluded that First Federal's right to be repaid for such disbursements "upon demand" necessarily embraces a right to forego immediate repayment and instead to increase the borrower's monthly payments to recoup the outlays.

The mortgage note fails to make similar provision for an increase in payments when the interest rate is raised. The trial court interpreted this omission to demonstrate that no such increase was contemplated. This conclusion is supported by the decision of this court in Godfrey v. Crawford, 23 Wis.2d 44, 50, 126 N.W.2d 495, 498 (1964), where this court stated that in some cases such an omission "might well be the decisive factor . . . ."

In Farley v. Salow, 67 Wis.2d 393, 227 N.W.2d 76 (1975), this court relied on the inclusion of an express cut-off date in one contract as a basis for refusing to imply such a cut-off date in a related, contemporaneous contract drafted by the same lawyer. It was observed in *Farley*, supra, that the omission of words from a contract is sometimes instructive. The court quoted from North Gate Corp. v. National Food Stores, 30 Wis.2d 317, 323, 140 N.W.2d 744 (1966), where it was said that:

> ". . . 'We cannot ignore the draftsman's failure to use an obvious term, especially where it is the draftsman who is urging a tenuous interpretation of a term in order to make it applicable to a situation which would clearly have been covered if the obvious term had been chosen.'" *Farley*, supra, 67 Wis.2d at 405, 227 N.W.2d at 83.

This observation reflects the general rule that ambiguous contract language must be construed against the drafter. This rule has particular force where, as here, there is a substantial disparity of bargaining power between the parties, and a standard form is supplied by the party drafting the form.

Applying these principles to the instant case, the trial court properly held that the failure to provide explicitly for an increase in monthly payments to absorb an interest increase demonstrated that no such increase was contemplated by the parties. The trial court stated:

> ". . . The contract does not leave to implication the right of the mortgagee to increase the monthly installment amounts to accomodate [sic] the repayment of future advances, and the lender's outlays to protect the security interest. With a stroke of the pen the draftsman could have provided the same express means for accomodating [sic] an interest rate escalation. Thus, while a court might be willing to imply a right to increase monthly payments in order to effectuate the escalation clause if there were no mention of such a right anywhere in the contract, the express mention of such a right in conjunction with other provisions provides potent evidence that such a right was not intended to be left to implication by the parties."

As the trial court emphasized, the amount of the monthly payments is a consideration of vital importance, and perhaps the single most important consideration, to a potential borrower. It is the factor most directly related to the possibility of default; it is the figure to which a buyer looks to determine whether he can afford to purchase a home and to which the lender looks to determine whether the borrower is capable of repaying the loan. For this reason, a provision empowering the lender to unilaterally increase the amount of the monthly payments, perhaps thereby threatening the borrower with default, will not lightly be inferred, particularly where express provision has been made for such an increase under other circumstances, and where such a provision could easily have been inserted by First Federal. If any increase in this figure was intended to be authorized by the loan contract, such authority should have been expressly stated.

The omission of any reference to increased payments to reflect a higher interest rate precludes the unilateral increase of the amount of the monthly payment.

The second aspect of this issue is whether the mortgage note permits First Federal to effect an increase in the interest rate by extending the term of the loan instead of increasing the amount of the monthly payments.

The mortgage note provides that:

"... principal and interest, including advances, notwithstanding any other provisions in this note or in the mortgage given as collateral security, shall be paid in full within 25 years from the date hereof, ..."

The number "25" inserted in the form by First Federal represents the term necessary to retire the loan at the original interest rate and with monthly payments in the amount specified in the note. The twenty-five year limitation therefore affords no leeway for extension of the loan term to absorb the higher interest rate. The manifest intention that all interest and principal be paid within twenty-five years "notwithstanding any other provisions in this note or the mortgage" is unmistakable, and this court is not at liberty to disregard the plain meaning of the language chosen by the draftsman for First Federal and agreed to by the parties.

First Federal argues, however, that it may elect to waive this requirement on the theory that either party to a contract may waive provisions of the contract included for his benefit.

Such a waiver may not be made, however, where the waiver would deprive the non-waiving party of a benefit under the provision in question. Thus in Godfrey v. Crawford, supra, 23 Wis.2d at 49, 50, 126 N.W.2d at 498, this court permitted a buyer under a land contract to waive a condition with respect to approval of a rezoning proposal when, at the time the waiver was exercised, a waiver would not interfere in any way with the benefits afforded the sellers under the contract and where "the defendant sellers' protection . . . [was not] weakened in the slightest degree" by the decision to permit the waiver. That is not the case here.

First Federal argues that the provision limiting the term of the loan to twenty-five years was included solely for the benefit of First Federal, and that it serves only to permit First Federal to insist that the entire debt be paid within the specified term. First Federal thus argues that it should be able to waive the provision and thereby extend the term of the loan.

However, the fact is that whether the amount of the monthly payment is increased or the term of the loan extended, the mortgagor pays more money and the mortgagee collects more interest than the amount specified in the original note and mortgage. Therefore it cannot be said the provision limiting the term to twenty-five years "notwithstanding any other provisions" is solely for the benefit of First Federal.

Since we have heretofore determined the lender is precluded by the language of the note from increasing the amount of the monthly payments, it follows that the maximum loan term provision is of considerable import to the borrower. When viewed in conjunction with the lender's inability to raise the amount of the monthly payments, this provision may in many cases relieve a borrower of the obligation to pay any additional sum for increased interest.

In such a situation, the provision would operate to the distinct benefit of the borrower. For this reason, the provision is not subject to waiver by First Federal. Therefore, a unilateral extension of the loan term by First Federal would violate the terms of the contract.

First Federal could easily have avoided this result by using a longer loan term than twenty-five years.[3] Precisely this point was made by the author of a Note entitled Adjustable Interest Rates in Home Mortgages: A Reconsideration, in 1975 Wis.L.Rev., 742. After recognizing that an interest rate escalation clause may be implemented by extending the loan term, the author observed that:

> "This could be accomplished without violating contract terms either by including a clause that provided for extension of the maturity date or by originally making the final payment date later than it would be at the initial rate of increase [sic]. Most mortgages have a provision to the effect that 'this mortgage shall be paid in full within ___ years.' The blank could indicate, for example, 30 years, when calculation at the time of the contract would indicate amortization within 20 years." 1975 Wis.L.Rev. at 757, fn. 86.

---

3. Federal regulations require only that conventional mortgage loans made by federal savings and loan associations be re- payable within thirty years. 12 CFR 545.6–1(a) (1977).

Because First Federal failed to include such a provision, it cannot now extend the loan term without violating the provisions of the contract as it was written.

This conclusion rests principally on canons of construction. Such canons are designed to aid in the ascertainment of the intention of the parties, and they would necessarily yield to any contrary intention of the parties, if such an intention could be ascertained from the contract as a whole.

The mortgage note does evince a clear intent that First Federal may impose a higher rate of interest and that the borrowers will have a corresponding duty to pay such interest, consistent with the remaining terms of the note. The accompanying mortgage, which is to be read together with the note, expressly incorporates the terms and conditions of the note "... including duty to ... pay higher interest on notice...." That the plaintiffs signed the note and mortgage does not alone determine the extent of the duty or the conditions and circumstances under which such increased interest may be collected, however. These questions can only be answered with reference to other provisions of the contract.

First Federal relies on the established rule that a contract is to be construed so as to give a reasonable meaning to each provision of the contract, and that courts must avoid a construction which renders portions of a contract meaningless, inexplicable or mere surplusage. First Federal argues that the construction adopted by the trial court renders the interest adjustment clause unenforceable and therefore mere surplusage. A construction which had this result would not only conflict with the rule of construction cited by First Federal, but would also conflict with the manifest intention of the note and the mortgage.

However, it cannot be said that the decision of the trial court has this effect. The interest adjustment clause is not without effect. The interest adjustment clause permits a downward adjustment of the interest rate. If such an interest decrease is implemented, under the contract, First Federal would be able to impose and collect a subsequent interest increase within the twenty-five year term.

More fundamentally, the interest adjustment clause retains its full force with regard to any borrower who prepays his loan. Upon prepayment, the higher rate of interest may be used in calculating the then outstanding principal balance, and in this manner the interest increase may effectively be collected. The trial court observed that many, if not most, mortgages do not reach full term, but rather are paid before maturity.

The instant note specifically includes a "due-on sale" clause by which the full amount of the loan becomes due and payable, at the option of First Federal, whenever the mortgaged premises are sold. Any increased interest charges would thus be recoverable upon sale of the premises. Because there is a substantial likelihood that mortgaged residential property will be sold during the course of a twenty-five year loan term, it cannot be said that the interest adjustment clause is deprived of all effect, or is rendered mere surplusage.

The language in the particular note and real estate mortgage here under consideration precludes First Federal both from increasing the amount of the monthly payments and from extending the term of the loan. ...

Judgment affirmed.

ABRAHAMSON, J., not participating.

NOTES

1. *The "New" Mortgages.* Rising interest rates and housing prices, together with the gradual deregulation of capital markets, have spurred new arrangements for housing finance. Some of the new instruments, such as the renegotiable rate mortgage, were patterned after pre-depression instruments. Some, such as the variable rate mortgage and shared appreciation mortgage, borrowed from contemporary instruments used in commercial land finance. Some, such as the price level adjusted mortgage, drew on arrangements used in other countries. And some of the new instruments, doubtless, were true inventions. Among the more popular or controversial are:

(a) *Adjustable Rate Mortgage* (earlier called the Variable Rate Mortgage, or VRM). In an ARM, the interest rate paid by the borrower varies over the life of the loan according to a designated index of current market rates. Since the conventional wisdom during the 1970's was that interest rates would rise over the long term, ARMs attracted lenders by protecting against inflation; lenders attracted borrowers by offering lower initial interest rates than were available under fixed rate mortgages. Borrowers' concerns that interest increases might outpace increases in their income, thus jeopardizing their ability to make the monthly mortgage payment, were assuaged by legislated limits on the frequency and amount by which interest rates could be increased.

(b) *Price Level Adjusted Mortgage.* Under the PLAM it is the loan principal, not the interest rate, that varies over the term of the mortgage. At the end of each year or other agreed-upon period, the principal outstanding on a PLAM is adjusted up or down according to a prescribed inflation index. For the lender, the attraction of the PLAM is that the loan is repaid in "real" rather than inflated dollars. The attraction to the borrower is that the lender can consequently charge an interest rate that is well below market rates, making debt service more affordable in the loan's earlier years. The risk, of course, is that the borrower's income and ability to meet the debt service will not keep pace with inflation over the life of the loan.

(c) *Renegotiable Rate Mortgage* (also called a "rollover" mortgage). The RRM is a series of renewable short term notes—usually for 3, 4 or 5 years—secured by a long term mortgage—of up to 30 years—with principal fully amortized over the longer term. At the end of each short term loan period, the borrower can choose between paying off the loan or "rolling over" into a new loan. If the borrower rolls over, all terms of the new loan, except interest rate, will be identical to those of the old; the interest rate is negotiable within prescribed limits.

(d) *Graduated Payment Mortgage.* The GPM is a long-term, fixed rate mortgage in which the monthly payment gradually increases over the life of the loan. Although payments in the early years of the loan will be insufficient to amortize the principal, or even to pay all of the interest on the loan, the increased payments in the loan's later years are calculated to make up the difference. The GPM was designed to meet the needs of younger borrowers who cannot initially afford the monthly payments required by a conventional fixed rate mortgage, but who expect their income to increase over time to a point at which they can afford to pay more than the debt service on a standard fixed rate mortgage. A variant of the GPM, called the Graduated Payment Adjustable Mortgage (GPAM), combines the rollover feature of the Renegotiable Rate Mortgage with the GPM's graduated payment schedule.

(e) *Growing Equity Mortgage.* The GEM is a long term, self-amortizing, fixed interest mortgage under which the borrower's monthly payments increase each year by a predetermined amount, typically 4%. The effect of the annual increase in monthly debt service is to amortize the loan more quickly than would a level payment or GPM schedule so that the loan can be completely repaid within as short a period as fifteen years. The GEM has proved attractive to homebuyers who contemplate rises in income over the life of the loan and are willing to trade tax deductible interest payments for the comfort of knowing that their homes will be paid off in a comparatively short time. GEMS are also very attractive to secondary market mortgage purchasers who generally prefer intermediate term—12-15 year—debt to long term—25-30 year—debt.

(f) *Shared Appreciation Mortgage.* A SAM reduces the interest rate to below market levels in return for the lender's right to receive a predetermined portion of the property's increase in value, if any, over the life of the loan. A typical SAM will reduce the interest rate by about ⅓ in exchange for ⅓ of the property's appreciation. SAMs generally have a short—5 to 10 year—term.

(g) *Buy-Downs.* One of the less subtle, but more effective financing techniques is for the seller—typically a developer—to "buy-down" the institutional lender's interest rate for the first three to five years of a long term loan to the homebuyer. In return for the seller's payment of a lump sum to the lender, the lender will reduce the interest charges in the loan's early years to a below market rate. Essentially a marketing device adopted by developers unable to sell their houses because of high interest rates, the buy-down makes housing available to the homebuyer who anticipates rising income and, thus, the ability to pay the undiscounted debt service that will begin to come due at the end of the buy-down period.

(h) *Reverse Annuity Mortgages.* RAMs are aimed at the plight not of young, first-time homebuyers, but rather of older homeowners on fixed incomes who find it difficult to make ends meet in an inflationary economy. Essentially, the RAM is designed to enable these homeowners to draw cash out of the accumulated equity in their homes without selling the house itself. The typical RAM enables the homeowner effectively to use the equity in his home as security for an annuity, giving him monthly payments over his lifetime or some predetermined period. With each monthly payment from the lender, the borrower's debt to the lender, secured by the house, increases. In the usual RAM, the entire debt is to be repaid at the earlier of ten years from the beginning of the loan, or the death of the borrower, with funds to come from the sale of the property or probate of the homeowner's estate.

For a discussion of the factor contributing to consumer choice of fixed rate versus adjustable rate mortgages, see Hendershott, The Composition of Mortgage Originations, 1 J. Housing Research 43 (1990) (forecasting a decline in the use of adjustable mortgages in the 1990's due to declines in house prices and interest rates).

For background and critical evaluation of the new mortgages, see generally, Comment, The New Mortgages: A Functional Legal Analysis, 10 Fla.St.U.L.Rev. 95 (1982); Iezman, Alternative Mortgage Instruments: Their Effect on Residential Financing, 10 Real Est.L.J. 3 (1981); Iezman, The Shared Appreciation Mortgage and the Shared Equity Program: A Comprehensive Examination of Equity Participation, 16 Real Prop., Probate & Trust J. 510 (1981); Walleser, Balancing the Interest: The Changing Complexion of Home Mortgage Financing in America, 31 Drake L.Rev. 1 (1981–82); Friend, Shared Appreciation Mortgages, 34 Hastings L.J. 329 (1982); Kmiec, Shared Appreciation Mortgages: A Step Toward Making Housing a Bad Investment, 10 Real Est.L.J. 302 (1982).

2. *New Mortgages and Common Law Equity of Redemption.* Some features of the new mortgages may conflict with common law rules. Under the traditional equity of redemption doctrine, a mortgagor has a right to redeem the mortgaged property after default and before foreclosure by paying the amount due on the mortgage. Courts have rejected attempts by the mortgagee to "clog" the equity of redemption, such as a provision requiring the mortgagor to deliver a deed to the mortgagee on default. There has been some concern that provisions in alternative mortgages such as a convertible mortgage, that gives the mortgagee an option to buy the property, or mortgages which provide the lender with an "equity kicker" (such as a shared appreciation mortgage) could be found to be an unenforceable clog on the equity of redemption. Commentators have suggested that in order to promote

these desirable alternative mortgage arrangements, no clog should be found as long as the transaction is inherently fair. See Licht, The Clog on the Equity of Redemption and its Effect on Modern Real Estate Finance, 60 St. John's L.Rev. 452 (1986); Preble & Cartwright, Convertible and Shared Appreciation Loans: Unclogging the Equity of Redemption, 20 Real Prop. Probate & Trust J. 821 (1985); Uniform Land Security Interest Act § 211 (no clog on the equity of redemption for equity kickers or for convertible mortgages as long as option to purchase is not triggered by default under the mortgage).

3. *Federal Support for the New Mortgages.* Almost all of the new mortgages violate one or more of the Depression-era regulations that gave shape to the long term, level payment, fixed rate home mortgage. Congress early perceived that existing rules would have to be changed if home finance was to flourish and acted quickly to meet the needs of the new mortgages. For example, the Housing and Urban-Rural Recovery Act of 1983, Pub.L. No. 98–181 Tit. I–V, 97 Stat. 1155 et seq. (1983), lifted the maximum interest rate for most FHA mortgage insurance programs including single family finance programs. The Act also authorized, or updated, FHA insurance programs for GPMs, ARMs and SAMs. Pub.L. No. 98–181, Tit. IV, § 404(a), Nov. 30, 1983, 97 Stat. 1208 repealing 12 U.S.C.A. § 1709–1, Pub.L. No. 98–181, Tit. I–V, Nov. 30, 1983, 97 Stat. 1223–1228, amending 12 U.S.C.A. §§ 1715Z–10, 1715Z–16, 1715Z–17.

Federal agencies have also taken an active role, revising their rules to allow regulated lenders to make these new forms of mortgage loans and also supporting secondary market trading in the new mortgages. For example, the FHA has approved buy-down loans and both FNMA and FHLMC have purchased large quantities of these instruments. By 1982, FNMA's commitment to purchase GEMs "soared 475% since July, to $485 million, and another agency, the Federal Home Loan Mortgage Corp., has agreed to pool an additional $500 million of mortgages for sale to Wall Street." Hill, Growing Equity Home Loans Are Gaining Popularity Because of Quick Repayments, Wall Street Journal, October 6, 1982, at 56. According to another source, by August 1982, FNMA had "purchased more than 85 variations of the ARM, an indication of the extraordinary level of innovation now taking place." Bernstein & Mansfield, Assessing the Alternative Mortgage Instruments, The National Law Journal, (August 9, 1982) p. 29, at 31.

Although state regulators tried to keep pace with federal regulators in updating their controls on home loans, there was often a lag, and consequent inability among state-regulated lenders to compete with federally-regulated lenders in offering the new mortgages. The problem was initially addressed in the Garn-St. Germain Depository Act of 1982, Pub.L. No. 97–320, 96 Stat. 1469 et seq., Title VIII (the "Alternative Mortgage Transaction Parity Act of 1982"), which was amended in 1989 by Pub.L. No. 101–73, Title VII, § 744(c), 103 Stat. 438, and codified at 12 U.S.C.A. § 3801. The statute preempts state regulations of nontraditional mortgages that are more stringent than counterpart federal regulations. Congress declared its purpose "to eliminate the discriminatory impact that those regulations have upon nonfederally chartered housing creditors and provide them with parity with federally chartered institutions by authorizing all housing creditors to make, purchase, and enforce alternative mortgage transactions so long as the transactions are in conformity with the regulations issued by the Federal agencies." 12 U.S.C.A. § 3801. Section 3806, enacted as part of the Competitive Equality Banking Act of 1987, requires that adjustable rate home mortgages include a cap on the interest rate. The Office of Thrift Supervision has issued regulations on adjustments in mortgages of federal savings associations. 12 C.F.R. § 545.33.

The Act gave states the power to expressly reinstate their regulatory programs by statute or referendum at any time prior to October 15, 1985. 12 U.S.C.A. § 3804(a). Maine, Massachusetts, New York, South Carolina, and Wisconsin have done so.

4. Do you agree with the decision in Goebel v. First Federal Savings & Loan? If you had been a borrower under the note in question, would you have expected the interest increments to be reflected in increased monthly debt service, in increased term, or in some other fashion? Or would the instrument's failure to specify the means for effecting the increment suggest to you that the decision lay entirely within the lender's discretion? What effect, if any, did the court give to the provision for increased interest?

As a federal savings and loan association, First Federal was subject to the regulations of the Federal Home Loan Bank Board. (The Federal Institutions Reform, Recovery, and Enforcement Act of 1989 abolished the Board and placed federal savings and loan institutions under the supervision of the Office of Thrift Supervision.) Should the court have tried to interpret the note in light of the Board's requirements for conforming loans?

Might the borrowers in *Goebel* have attacked the increased interest provision on the ground that the instrument provided no benchmark for limiting the interest rate? Compare Constitution Bank & Trust Co. v. Robinson, 179 Conn. 232, 425 A.2d 1268 (1979) (upholding variable interest rate calling for interest at a per annum rate equal to 1.5% over the lender's prime rate. "If the lender may arbitrarily adjust the interest rate without any standard whatsoever, with regard to this borrower alone, then the note is too indefinite as to interest. If however the power to vary the interest rate is limited by the marketplace and requires periodic redetermination, in good faith and in the ordinary course of business, of the price to be charged to *all* of the bank's customers similarly situated, then the note is not too indefinite.")

For a discussion of developments in the "adjustment wars," see Lee, Mancuso, & Walter, Housing Finance: Major Developments in 1990, 46 Bus.Law. 1149, 1171–1177 (1991).

5. *Lender Liability.* Mortgagees have been subject to lender liability claims for various activities in the origination and administration of loans. Reconsider in this regard the note on lender liability on page 218, as well as the *Rice* and *Jemison* cases and related notes on pages 220–227, dealing with mortgagee liability for defects in houses.

Two cases involving the purchase of insurance illustrate some of the key themes in the lender liability area. In Heinert v. Home Federal Savings & Loan Ass'n, 444 N.W.2d 718 (S.D.1989), the mortgagor executed a form presented by the lender at closing which provided that the borrower requested the lender to obtain credit life insurance for the benefit of the borrower and authorized the deduction of a fee each month to pay for it. The lender did not purchase the insurance and the borrower subsequently died, owing some $40,000 on the loan. The court held that a contract to obtain insurance was created by the form, even though there was some ambiguity and the lender never charged the borrower for the insurance. The court found that the lender breached the agreement by failing to do so, making it liable for the amount which would have been paid had the insurance been purchased.

In Beckford v. Empire Mutual Insurance Group, 135 A.D.2d 228, 525 N.Y.S.2d 260 (1988), the borrowers complied with the mortgage provisions requiring the borrowers to obtain casualty insurance on the property, assign the policy to the lender, and make monthly payments to the lender to be escrowed for premiums to become due on the policy. The lender received notice of the policy's cancellation but did not notify the borrowers and the property subsequently was destroyed by fire. The court held that the borrowers had no cause of action against the lender for failure to notify or maintain insurance in the absence of an express agreement to do so.

Were these cases decided correctly? Consider the parties' expectations and whom the insurance was to benefit. Did they think the lender was assuming an obligation to the borrower? Did the lender follow norms of reasonable lending behavior? Will the decisions encourage sound and efficient lending and borrowing practices? Was the borrower simply attempting a search for a deep pocket? Was there anything improper about the bargaining process that required a rearrangement of the deal?

Consider in this regard Hurley v. TCF Banking & Savings, F.A., 414 N.W.2d 584 (Minn.App.1987), where the mortgagors prepaid their mortgage in response to a letter from the lender indicating that they could save 25% of their mortgage payments by prepaying. When the mortgagors had to pay taxes on this savings under Internal Revenue Code § 61 they sued the lender claiming that it failed to disclose the tax ramifications. The appellate court affirmed the trial court's holding that the lender "did not breach a duty to disclose the tax consequences of the transaction, as no duty existed. [Lender] had no way of knowing, or even speculating, what tax consequence, if any, would attach to each of their individual mortgagors who accepted its offer. We see no basic difference between [lender's] solicitation letter and any bank's advertisement to pay, for example, five, six, or seven percent interest to depositors on savings accounts. Banks are not required in their advertising to point out that the depositor will not 'net' the entire amount of interest accrued since interest is subject to taxation." Id. at 587. Compare Small v. South Norwalk Savings Bank, 205 Conn.751, 535 A.2d 1292 (1988) (where lender failed to notify borrower that property was located in flood plain, as required by federal statute, borrower could bring action under state law statutory negligence theory since borrower was within class protected by statute and the injury was of the type the statute was designed to prevent).

6. *Usury.* Usury has always provoked mixed feelings. On one side is the moral precept that interest is bad and excessive interest worse. On the other is the economic precept that high interest may be necessary to attract loans to risky but worthwhile ventures. This conflict between moral and economic command helps to explain usury's troubled history. Dante may have consigned usurers to the Seventh Circle of Hell, but Pope Nicholas III defended them, threatening an English Archbishop with excommunication for trying to renege on a usurious loan from a group of Italian bankers. The Divine Comedy, Inferno: Canto 17; S. Clough & C. Cole, Economic History of Europe 82 (3d ed. 1952).

The American experience with usury laws dates to colonial times. At one time, almost all states prohibited usury in one form or another, with maximum interest rates ranging from six percent to thirty percent. This regulatory pattern changed dramatically in late 1979 when Congress enacted Pub.L. No. 96–161, 93 Stat. 1233–40 (1979), preempting any state statute or constitutional provision that limited interest rates on first lien, residential mortgage loans made after December 28, 1979. After the Act, however, states could enact laws reinstating usury limits. By its terms, the Act was to expire on March 31, 1980.

On March 31, 1980, President Carter signed the Depository Institutions Deregulation and Monetary Control Act of 1980, Pub.L. No. 96–221, now codified at 12 U.S.C.A. § 1735f–7a (1990), perpetuating the provisions of the 1979 Act. The Act's key preemptive provision is section 501(a)(1):

> The provisions of the constitution or the laws of any State expressly limiting the rate or amount of interest, discount points, finance charges, or other charges which may be charged, taken, received, or reserved shall not apply to any loan, mortgage, credit sale, or advance which is—
>
>   (A) secured by a first lien on residential real property, by a first lien on stock in a residential cooperative housing corporation where the loan, mortgage, or advance is used to finance the acquisition of such stock, or by a first lien on a residential manufactured home;
>
>   (B) made after March 31, 1980 ....

Section 501(b)(2) gave states until April 1, 1983 to reinstate usury limits. According to a recent count, fifteen states have elected out of section 501. Uniform Land Security Interest Act, Introductory Comment to Part 4. See generally, Culhane & Kaplinsky, Trends Pertaining to the Usury Laws, 38 Bus.Lawyer 1329 (1983); Ewing & Vickers, Federal Pre-emption of State Usury Laws Affecting Real Estate Financing, 47 Mo.L.Rev. 171, 176 (1982); Randolph, Home Finance in the Shadow World: Unsolved Usury Problems Affecting Adjustable Rate and Wraparound Mortgages in Missouri, 51 U.Mo.K.C.L.Rev. 41 (1982).

State usury limits still govern real estate lending arrangements other than first lien residential loans. Lenders and borrowers employ various strategies to circumvent these limits, and legislatures and courts have strewn the field with pitfalls to trap incautious or overly ambitious lenders. These aspects of usury are considered at pages 689 to 696 below.

7. *Dragnet Clauses.* A mortgage will sometimes provide that it is to serve as security not only for the debt in connection with which it was created, but also as security for any other debt owed by the mortgagor to the mortgagee. These provisions, called dragnet clauses, can come back to haunt the unsuspecting mortgagor. For example, a borrower who obtains a home mortgage loan may, several years later, return to the same lender, this time to finance a vacation trip. If the borrower subsequently defaults on the vacation loan, the dragnet clause will entitle the lender to proceed directly against the security provided by the borrower's home.

Courts divide in their approach to dragnet clauses. Some courts interpret them narrowly, holding, for example, that the mortgage will secure only debts directly related to the property. See Emporia State Bank & Trust Co. v. Mounkes, 214 Kan. 178, 519 P.2d 618 (1974) ("... in the absence of clear, supportive evidence of a contrary intention a mortgage containing a dragnet type clause will not be extended to cover future advances unless the advances are of the same kind and quality or relate to the same transaction or series of transactions as the principal obligation secured or unless the document evidencing the subsequent advance refers to the mortgage as providing security therefor"). See also First Security Bank of Utah v. Shiew, 609 P.2d 952 (Utah 1980).

Other courts interpret these clauses broadly. For example, in State Bank of Albany v. Fioravanti, 51 N.Y.2d 638, 435 N.Y.S.2d 947, 417 N.E.2d 60 (1980), the New York Court of Appeals held that a dragnet clause in a mortgage given by two brothers to secure a $2,500 home loan entitled the lender to proceed against the home to satisfy a deficiency judgment entered against the brothers following foreclosure on another parcel that the bank had financed seven years later. The court attached no weight to the fact that, before foreclosure on the second parcel, the brothers had sold the first parcel to their mother and the full $2,500 loan had been paid off. The three dissenting judges objected that the bank could have drafted language expressly making the dragnet clause survive complete payment of the original mortgage; that the language used by the bank was ambiguous at best; and that the ambiguity should be resolved against the bank since it had drafted the document.

8. *After-Acquired Property Clauses.* After-acquired property clauses, although probably used more frequently in personal property security arrangements, sometimes appear in real property mortgages. Conceptually, they are just the opposite of dragnet clauses. Dragnet clauses use a single property to secure the original debt and all future debts incurred. After-acquired property clauses secure a single debt with the original property and all future property acquired. See generally, R. Kratovil & R. Werner, Modern Mortgage Law and Practice § 8.06 (2d ed. 1981). The Uniform Land Security Interest Act permits after-acquired property clauses except when applied to residential real estate purchased by a "protected party." § 205.

One reason after-acquired property clauses play such a small role in real property security transactions is that the recording acts will shelter the later acquired parcel from the original mortgagee's rights. The original mortgage containing the after-acquired property clause will be completely outside the chain of title searched by purchasers or encumbrancers of the later parcel, whether a grantor-grantee or tract index is used. The original mortgagee may try to protect herself by exacting a covenant that the mortgagor will execute and record a supplemental mortgage in the chain of title of every parcel that he subsequently acquires, bringing the new parcel under the lien of the original mortgage. Breach of the covenant will, however, give the mortgagee only personal rights against the mortgagor.

9. *Uniform Instruments.* The Emergency Home Finance Act of 1970, Pub.L. No. 91–351, Tit. I–VII §§ 201, 305, 84 Stat. 450 (1970), now codified at 12 U.S.C.A. § 1717 (1990), authorized FNMA and FHLMC to establish a secondary market, buying and selling conventional mortgages, principally on single family homes. The two organizations quickly realized that, to function effectively, the secondary market needed a standard form of note and security instrument, and proposed uniform instruments were promulgated in 1972. See generally, Symposium, Uniformity in Mortgage Forms—Nearly, 7 Real Prop.Probate & Trust J. 397 (1972). Currently, FNMA and FHLMC have form documents for both conventional and adjustable loans. There are multistate note forms that are used in all but a few states. In order to reflect the requirements of state law, there are individualized mortgage forms for the various states; still, there are many uniform covenants in the mortgage forms for the different states.

4. EVALUATING THE BORROWER AND THE SECURITY
INSTITUTE OF FINANCIAL EDUCATION, RESIDENTIAL MORTGAGE LENDING *
58, 65–69, 72–74, 76, 87–91, 96–99 (1981).

... The risk to be evaluated in any secured loan represents a combination of three major and potential hazards. First is the security property itself. In a mortgage loan, this is the actual real estate being mortgaged. The value of the property must substantiate the requested loan amount. The property must stand as security for the loan during the first few years of the loan term when the principal due is the greatest—as well as throughout the life of the loan during which the principal is reduced and the property ages. Is the home soundly built and maintained? Is it built of durable materials in a style which will have continuing appeal to buyers? In other words, if the borrower fails to repay the loan and the association forecloses the property, will the association be able to recover enough from the sale of the property to make up for the unpaid balance on the loan plus the costs of foreclosure and sale? Facts needed to evaluate the degree of risk in the security property are examined by an appraiser.

Second, the borrower's ability and willingness to repay the loan must be considered. This includes checking the borrower's income sources, total amount of indebtedness, and loan-paying habits. The processing section of the loan department must complete a thorough credit investigation and analysis. Can the borrower afford this property? Will the borrower continue to have enough income to meet monthly payments, and will he or she make them regularly? What has been the applicant's demonstrated attitude toward the repayment of borrowed money?

Third, the terms of the loan applied for must be reviewed. Is the ratio of the amount of the loan to the appraised value of the property too large? If the borrower applied for a graduated payment mortgage loan, will the borrower's income increase enough to keep up with the increasing monthly payments? The degree of risk involved with the loan terms is analyzed by the loan committee, which may adjust loan terms in light of any undue risk with either the borrower or the security property....

The Equal Credit Opportunity Act (ECOA) passed by Congress in 1975 and amended in 1976 prohibits discrimination in the granting of credit on the basis of sex, marital status, race, color, religion, national origin, age, receipt of public assistance benefits, and/or the borrower's good faith exercise of rights under the Consumer Credit Protection Act. Most of the bases of prohibited discrimination covered by the act are absolute, allowing for no exceptions. However, three important areas requiring further explanation are the special requirements regarding sex, marital status, and age.

* Used, with permission, from Residential Mortgage Lending, © 1981 by the Institute of Financial Education, Chicago, Illinois.

Regarding discrimination on the basis of sex or marital status, ECOA

1. Prohibits questions regarding birth control practices.

2. Imposes rules regarding the evaluation of credit history of accounts on which both spouses are contractually liable.

3. Requires the establishment of separate accounts for both spouses when requested.

4. Imposes rules on the consideration of alimony and child support payments and discounting of spouse's or part-time income.

5. Allows the applicant to use his or her surname at birth or that of the spouse or a combination thereof.

6. Places limitations on the manner and the propriety of inquiry as to marital status.

7. Requires all terms in loan application forms to be neutral as to sex.

8. Requires credit history information to be reported in the names of both spouses when both spouses are contractually liable on the account.

The prohibition relating to age is qualified in recognition of the fact that a person's age is relevant to the ability to repay a loan. Lenders are permitted to consider the applicant's occupation and the amount of time remaining before retirement in an attempt to determine whether the applicant's income (including retirement income) will support the extension of credit under the terms of the prospective loan. The adequacy of the security property may also be considered if the duration of the loan will exceed the life expectancy of the applicant. For example, an elderly applicant might not qualify for a 13 percent, 95 percent loan-to-value, 30-year mortgage because the duration of the loan exceeds the applicant's life expectancy. By contrast, the same applicant might qualify with a larger downpayment and a shorter loan maturity. Finally, the ability of the applicant to enter into a legally binding contract may also be considered. For example, a lender can refuse a loan to a minor.

The Equal Credit Opportunity Act applies to all types of loans including all mortgage and consumer loans offered by savings associations. This law may or may not result in alterations of some previous lending practices. In any case, it involves additional precautions for the loan interviewer who, when talking with applicants, must be careful not to imply unintentionally that the applicant may be discriminated against. ...

The Credit Investigation

In checking an applicant's credit, the association's credit investigator attempts to verify all the data supplied by the applicant. Most associations require that a credit bureau report on all applications for general verification of the data supplied. Many associations also require verification in three special areas: income, assets, and debts. For these three areas, the association's investigator will typically try to verify the data directly. ...

Credit Analysis

When all available facts and reports have been gathered, the risk involved with the loan application is thoroughly analyzed. Assessing risk involves analyzing three major factors: the potential borrower(s), the security property, and the loan terms. Analyzing the credit risk connected with the applicant entails a thorough review of all data supplied on the application form and all data collected in the credit investigation. The risk connected with the security property is analyzed in the appraisal report prepared for the association. If there are any undue risks connected with either the applicant, the property, or the loan terms applied for, these loan terms may be adjusted so that the potential risks are lessened.

This section will examine how the credit risk attributable to the borrower is analyzed. Based in part upon this credit analysis, the loan officer or unit chief will make a recommendation to the loan committee on the disposition of the loan application. In an association using the unit system, the unit chief, aided by his or her team members, will make the recommendation. In an association using the specialist system, the ranking officer of the processing section, guided by advice from the appraiser, the credit investigator, the interviewer, and possibly others, will make the final evaluation. In an association using a one-person system, the loan officer evaluates the information gathered from the appraiser and the credit reporting agency (or his or her own investigation) and makes a recommendation to the loan committee.

The evaluation of the degree of risk connected with an applicant involves analyzing numerous facts and data in the loan application file. In reviewing all of this data, the loan officer or unit chief is attempting to answer two basic questions: (1) Is the borrower *able* to repay this loan? (2) Is the borrower *willing* to repay this loan? To answer these two questions, the loan officer or unit chief focuses on the borrower's income, assets, and liabilities. For this reason, many associations require the added verification in these three areas examined earlier.

The borrower's income obviously is a vital factor in his or her ability to repay a loan. Both the amount and the stability of income must be assessed. The borrower who does not receive enough income to afford the loan would most probably have difficulty repaying the loan. Income is based on earnings from a job and other dependable sources, such as bonds and real estate investments. Income from rental properties may need adjustment, because vacant units cut into the earnings the property would otherwise produce. Some associations count a flat percentage of rental income, such as 70 percent. Money earned from overtime, commissions, and bonuses should be included if these items are typical for the occupation and if, based on foreseeable circumstances, continuation is probable. In addition, total income includes money earned by all applicants including part-time income and income from alimony and child support (if the applicant wished to disclose this).

Over and above the amount of income is the stability factor of income. Perhaps the applicant has enough income presently to afford the loan. However, if it is highly probable that the applicant will have a substantial loss of income in the near future, will he or she still be able to afford the loan then? Seasonal workers, for example, are more vulnerable to periodic layoffs than are professionals and government employees. Also, the applicant's job history must be considered (promotions or demotions, long-time employment or job hopping). Training, technical skills, occupation, past employment history, and length of time to retirement should be taken into account on a case-by-case basis in determining the stability of income.

Here, as in every other aspect of credit analysis, firm rules are few and far between. For instance, frequent job changes may indicate either instability or an honest desire for self-betterment. A self-employed applicant may have far greater opportunities for a steadily rising net income than if he or she were a salaried employee in a large organization. A seasonal worker (perhaps in construction) may budget finances well enough to experience no financial difficulty during slower work periods. Each situation must stand on its own merits.

If the applicant's income results from self-employment in a business enterprise, the firm's financial standing must be checked carefully. How valid and complete are the accounting records? Are assets overstated? Are liabilities understated? Does the business offer a product or service for which there is likely to be a continued demand? In other words, the credit analyst estimates the current soundness of the business and the probability that it will continue to provide the borrower with adequate income in the future.

Once both the amount and stability of income have been established, the officer or unit chief can relate this income to the entire financial picture of the applicant. Frequently, associations use income ratios as guidelines on how much of a loan the applicant can afford. These income ratios may be firm rules put forth in the written underwriting standards, or they may be used more often as guidelines, with exceptions being made on a case-by-case basis. Usually total monthly income versus expected monthly payments (on the loan applied for) is reviewed first. Typically, the expected monthly payments should not exceed 25 to 30 percent of the applicant's total, gross monthly income. In other words, an applicant receiving $2,000 per month (gross) income, could afford a total monthly mortgage payment of $500 to $600. The total of the applicant's monthly payments on all debts (auto, personal, and so on) is then added to the expected monthly mortgage payments. Usually only debts extending from 10 to 12 months or more into the future are considered. Total monthly payments (including the proposed mortgage payment) should not exceed 33 to 36 percent of the total, gross monthly income. Therefore, if the applicant receives $2,000 per month in income, total monthly payments should not exceed $660 to $720.

The above gross monthly income ratios are more frequently used today because of investor requirements in the secondary mortgage market. Other types of income ratios, however, can be used. For example, the ratios can be based upon net monthly income or gross annual income. In past years, one "rule of thumb" used to be that the total purchase price of a home should not exceed two and one-half times the buyer's net annual income. On the other hand, other associations prefer to evaluate the applicant's history of debt payment and ability to accumulate savings. These associations often cite recent surveys that indicate that many borrowers do in fact exceed established income ratios with no undue difficulty in repaying the loans.

In assessing the applicant's ability to repay the loan, the officer or unit chief also reviews overall data concerning assets and debts. With respect to assets alone, the applicant should have enough liquid cash or equity (portions of the downpayment or closing costs may come from the sale of a current home) to be able to close the loan. If the applicant must use virtually all his or her assets to close the transaction, will the applicant have enough funds left over to cover moving expenses or unexpected expenses? If a major portion of the downpayment is coming from the sale of another home, has this other property been sold? If it has been sold, will the closing on this other property occur in time for the applicant to have the funds needed for the proposed closing? The officer or unit chief needs to answer these questions in order to assess whether the applicant can afford the entire transaction. An applicant who is overextended in the purchase of a property may well have difficulty meeting the payments on the new mortgage loan in the very near future.

The officer or unit chief also reviews the applicant's overall debt picture. Total monthly loan payments as they relate to monthly income has already been examined. However, the nature of the debts is also important. The individual who continually supplements his or her income by gradually increasing personal debts may not be realistically living within his or her means. At some point, the "bubble will burst." The individual will not be able to afford any more personal loans and will have to begin to live within his or her income and pay off all the debts. The reverse can also be true. For example, an applicant may have an unusually large amount of loans due to an unexpected emergency. However, if the applicant is paying these loans in a timely manner, he or she could still be an excellent credit risk—despite the large debts. When an applicant appears to have an unusually large amount of debts, the loan officer or unit chief carefully reviews the nature of and reasons for these debts.

In addition to evaluating the applicant's ability to repay the loan, the officer or unit chief also assesses the applicant's willingness to repay the loan. Again, several factors must be considered including whether the applicant has invested his or her own funds in the property. In other words, was the downpayment on the property financed through another source? The borrower who has his or her own money invested in the property has more to lose if the mortgage loan reaches foreclosure status. Furthermore, the borrower who has invested his or her own money in the property will want to protect this investment, just as the association wants to protect its investment in the property.

The applicant's willingness to repay the mortgage loan can also be evaluated by reviewing his or her attitude towards previous credit. Was he or she a slow pay customer or frequently behind in making payments? Did the applicant pay as agreed? Did he or she pay off the debt faster than was required by the terms of the note? If the applicant was a frequent slow pay customer, would the applicant pay the new mortgage loan any differently? Why? These questions must all be answered by the loan officer or unit chief. Delinquent loans that require considerable collection work are very costly to the association. . . .

The Final Determination

The Loan Committee

The loan committee makes the final decision on the disposition of each mortgage application. The loan committee may consist of the entire board of directors, selected members of the board, and/or association officers. In the past, loan decisions were made only by the board. Today, many associations recognize the advantages of establishing a loan committee made up of staff members who have professional mortgage lending knowledge and experience.

Whatever its composition, the loan committee has two major responsibilities. First, only those loans that promise the best possible investments of savers' funds should be approved. Second, the loan approvals must reflect the board's decisions on portfolio mix and other matters. Sound underwriting principles (those factors that determine the risks inherent in various loans and establish suitable terms and conditions for such risks) and the association's lending policies are the guidelines the loan committee uses in fulfilling its board responsibilities.

When members of the loan committee discuss the applications before them for approval, they may call in the appraiser, credit analyst, or loan officer to provide further information or specialized insights. A secretary keeps minutes of each meeting. The loan approvals made by the committee are usually ratified by the board at its next regular meeting. . . .

APPRAISALS . . .

Market Data and Value

One of the principal methods an appraiser may use to estimate value is the market data approach. The appraiser analyzes the sales patterns of recently sold properties that are similar to the property being appraised. In appraisal terminology, these similar properties are called *comparable properties*. The property being appraised is called *the subject property*. The appraiser thoroughly analyzes many features of the comparable properties, such as financing arrangements and physical attributes. A value range for the subject property is indicated by the sales prices of the comparable properties.[2]

At the core of the market data approach to value, indeed to all of the approaches to value, is a basic economic concept referred to as the *principle of substitution*. With respect of the market data approach, this principle is illustrated by the fact that a buyer will pay no more for a property than the price of acquiring an equally desirable, substitute property, assuming there is no undue delay. Thus, within the market data approach, market value bears a strong relationship to the availability of similar properties.

Over time, the appraiser builds a resource file of local real estate transactions for reference when making individual appraisals. Some associations with a large volume of new loans have computerized real estate market data. As a result, the appraiser has almost instantaneously much available information on sales of comparable properties. The key to the success of the market data approach to value is the availability of comparable data. The method can be used with a great deal of success on owner-occupied homes that are typical to an area. Due to a lack of comparable properties in an inactive market or with unique properties, this approach is less valid.

Cost and Value

When considering the value of either an existing or new property, the appraiser frequently finds it useful to estimate the total replacement cost of the subject property. In this second approach, the appraiser estimates the cost of replacing both the land and building. The appraiser uses sales of comparable vacant lots and local construction cost figures. The value of the vacant land is added to the depreciated replacement cost of the building to obtain an indication of value.

Value is controlled by the laws of supply and demand, as are the construction costs of new homes. Rising costs do not necessarily inflate home values indefinitely. At some point, a prospective buyer will balk at the price of a property he or she may want to buy. A safety valve of sorts tells the buyer to "pay no more." The principal of substitution also holds true in the cost approach. A knowledgeable buyer will pay no more for an existing property than the cost of building a similar property. On the other hand, an informed buyer will not accept the cost of building a home if he or she can buy a reasonably similar and existing property for less money. The principal of substitution thus ensures that cost will approach value by assuring that any prospective buyer will weigh the cost of duplicating a structure against his or her conception of the value of owning that particular structure.

2. The sales price of each comparable is its value when the sales transaction meets all of the six conditions contained in the definition of market value.

Income and Value

A third possible way to estimate the value of a property is to consider the income it would produce. Depending upon the type of real estate being appraised, any one of several income approaches may be used. For appraising single-family residences, the most common method is the gross monthly rent multiplier (GMRM) approach.

The basis for value in the GMRM approach is that the worth of a property is related to the rent that the property can be expected to earn. As with the market data approach, an estimate of value is obtained by using comparable properties that were rented at the time of sale. The appraiser estimates the rent that the subject property is expected to earn to arrive at a value indication.

The applicability of the GMRM approach in appraising single-family residences is dependent on the availability of comparable rental properties. As with the other approaches to value, the principal of substitution also holds true in the income approach. A buyer will pay no more for a property than the price of obtaining a similar substitute property, with an equally desirable rental return. With all of the approaches, this principal of substitution is an important ingredient of value. In very slow or inactive markets, when substitute properties may not be selling or may not be available, value indications are very difficult to estimate.

The Appraisal Report

Savings association appraisers virtually always complete a written report form on all appraisals. The sample form in Figure 5–1 is used by many association appraisers. In addition to completing the formal report form, the appraiser typically includes descriptive photographs of the subject property and, often, attaches a sketch of the exterior dimensions of the building.

This report form illustrates the orderly procedure the appraiser should follow when completing an appraisal. After identifying the property, the appraiser collects information on the neighborhood and location and inspects the site and improvements. Finally, the appraiser completes the three approaches to value to arrive at a final estimate of value. ...

Completing The Report

After the appraiser gathers all necessary data on the neighborhood, site, and improvements, the actual analysis begins. Using the three approaches to value—the market data, the cost, and the income—the appraiser reconciles a final estimate of value for the subject property. With the market data approach, the sales pattern of recently sold, comparable properties is analyzed to obtain an indication of value. Using the cost approach, an estimate is made of the current cost of replacing both the site and improvements, taking into consideration depreciation of all kinds. Using the income approach, the appraiser estimates the value of the property based upon its earning power.

FIGURE 5-1: Residential Appraisal Report (Side 1)

NAME OF FINANCIAL INSTITUTION
1234 Street   Your City, State 00000

RESIDENTIAL APPRAISAL REPORT   File No.

Borrower	John J. and Mary M. Smith Census Tract 8046 Map Reference PHC (1)-43
Property Address	309 Oak Street
City	Schaumburg County Cook State Illinois Zip Code 60193
Legal Description	Lot 43, block 2

Sale Price $ 93,900   Date of Sale 6-4-81   Loan Term 30 yrs   Property Rights Appraised ☒ Fee ☐ Leasehold ☐ DeMinimis PUD

Actual Real Estate Taxes $ 1,200 (e) (yr) Loan charges to be paid by seller $ -0-   Other sales concessions -0-

Lender/Client Illinois Federal Savings   Address 2000 Main Street, Schaumburg, Illinois

Occupant J. Jones   Appraiser A. Scott   Instructions to Appraiser ¼ mile west of Rt. #42 and 2 blocks south of Hickory Street

NEIGHBORHOOD

Location	☐ Urban	☒ Suburban	☐ Rural
Built Up	☒ Over 75%	☐ 25% to 75%	☐ Under 25%
Growth Rate ☒ Fully Dev.	☐ Rapid	☐ Steady	☐ Slow
Property Values	☒ Increasing	☐ Stable	☐ Declining
Demand/Supply	☐ Shortage	☒ In Balance	☐ Over Supply
Marketing Time	☒ Under 3 Mos.	☐ 4-6 Mos.	☐ Over 6 Mos.

Present Land Use 90% 1 Family ___% 2-4 Family 10% Apts. ___% Condo ___% Commercial ___% Industrial ___% Vacant ___%

Change in Present Land Use ☒ Not Likely ☐ Likely (*) ☐ Taking Place (*) (*) From ___ To ___

Predominant Occupancy ☒ Owner ☐ Tenant ___% Vacant

Single Family Price Range $ 80,000 to $ 100,000 Predominant Value $ 90,000

Single Family Age 2 yrs to 5 yrs Predominant Age 4 yrs

	Good	Avg.	Fair	Poor
Employment Stability	☐	☒	☐	☐
Convenience to Employment	☐	☒	☐	☐
Convenience to Shopping	☒	☐	☐	☐
Convenience to Schools	☒	☐	☐	☐
Adequacy of Public Transportation	☐	☐	☒	☐
Recreational Facilities	☒	☐	☐	☐
Adequacy of Utilities	☐	☒	☐	☐
Property Compatibility	☒	☐	☐	☐
Protection from Detrimental Conditions	☐	☒	☐	☐
Police and Fire Protection	☐	☒	☐	☐
General Appearance of Properties	☒	☐	☐	☐
Appeal to Market	☒	☐	☐	☐

Note: FHLMC/FNMA do not consider race or the racial composition of the neighborhood to be reliable appraisal factors.

Comments including those factors, favorable or unfavorable, affecting marketability (e.g. public parks, schools, view, noise) Several small parks/ playgrounds within 2-3 blocks of subject. Schools and shopping within walking distance. Large, well-kept, apartment complex 5 blocks west of subject.

SITE

Dimensions 100' x 150' = 1,500 Sq. Ft. or Acres   ☐ Corner Lot

Zoning classification R-3 residential

Highest and best use: ☒ Present use ☐ Other (specify)

	Public	Other (Describe)		OFF SITE IMPROVEMENTS	Topo	Slightly rolling
Elec.	☒		Street Access	☒ Public ☐ Private	Size	1,500 sq. ft.
Gas	☒		Surface	ASPHALT	Shape	Rectangular
Water	☒		Maintenance	☒ Public ☐ Private	View	good
San.Sewer	☒		☒ Storm Sewer ☒ Curb/Gutter	Drainage		good

☐ Underground Elect. & Tel. ☒ Sidewalk ☐ Street Lights   Is the property located in a HUD Identified Special Flood Hazard Area? ☒ No ☐ Yes

Comments (favorable or unfavorable including any apparent adverse easements, encroachments or other adverse conditions) Site typical to area. Well landscaped.

IMPROVEMENTS

☒ Existing ☐ Proposed ☐ Under Constr.   No. Units 1   Type (det, duplex, semi/det, etc.) Detached   Design (rambler, split level, etc.) Ranch   Exterior Walls 80% Brick 20% Alum. Sid.

Yrs. Age: Actual 4 Effective 2 to ___   No. Stories 1

Roof Material Asphalt Shingle   Gutters & Downspouts ☐ None Aluminum   Window (Type): Wood dbl. hung ☐ Storm Sash ☐ Screens ☒ Combination   Insulation ☐ None ☐ Floor ☒ Ceiling ☐ Roof ☒ Walls

☐ Manufactured Housing   50 % Basement ☒ Floor Drain Finished Ceiling ___

Foundation Walls ☐ Outside Entrance ☒ Sump Pump Finished Walls ___

Poured concrete ☒ Concrete Floor 0 % Finished Finished Floor ___

☐ Slab on Grade ☐ Crawl Space Evidence of: ☐ Dampness ☐ Termites ☐ Settlement

Comments

ROOM LIST

Room List	Foyer	Living	Dining	Kitchen	Den	Family Rm.	Rec. Rm.	Bedrooms	No. Baths	Laundry	Other
Basement											
1st Level	X	X	X	X		X		3	2½	X	
2nd Level											

Finished area above grade contains a total of 7 rooms 3 bedrooms 2½ baths. Gross Living Area 2089 sq. ft. Bsmt Area 900 sq. ft.

Kitchen Equipment: ☐ Refrigerator ☒ Range/Oven ☒ Disposal ☒ Dishwasher ☒ Fan/Hood ☐ Compactor ☐ Washer ☐ Dryer

HEAT Type FHA   Fuel GAS   Cond. GOOD   AIR COND. ☒ Central ☐ Other ___ ☒ Adequate ☐ Inadequate

INTERIOR FINISH & EQUIPMENT

Floors	☐ Hardwood ☒ Carpet Over Plywood ☐ ___
Walls	☒ Drywall ☐ Plaster ☐ ___
Trim/Finish	☒ Good ☐ Average ☐ Fair ☐ Poor
Bath Floor	☒ Ceramic ☐ ___
Bath Wainscot	☒ Ceramic ☐ ___

Special Features (including energy efficient items) ___

PROPERTY RATING

	Good	Avg.	Fair	Poor
Quality of Construction (Materials & Finish)	☐	☒	☐	☐
Condition of Improvements	☒	☐	☐	☐
Room sizes and layout	☒	☐	☐	☐
Closets and Storage	☒	☐	☐	☐
Insulation—adequacy	☐	☒	☐	☐
Plumbing—adequacy and condition	☒	☐	☐	☐
Electrical—adequacy and condition	☒	☐	☐	☐
Kitchen Cabinets—adequacy and condition	☐	☒	☐	☐
Compatibility to Neighborhood	☒	☐	☐	☐
Overall Livability	☒	☐	☐	☐
Appeal and Marketability	☒	☐	☐	☐

ATTIC: ☒ Yes ☐ No ☐ Stairway ☐ Drop-stair ☒ Scuttle ☐ Floored

Finished (Describe) ___ ☐ Heated

CAR STORAGE: ☒ Garage ☐ Built-in ☒ Attached ☐ Detached ☐ Car Port

No. Cars 2 ☒ Adequate ☐ Inadequate Condition Good

Yrs. Est. Remaining Economic Life ___ to ___ Explain if less than Loan Term.

FIREPLACES, PATIOS, POOL, FENCES, etc. (describe) Poured concrete patio, 15' x 20'

COMMENTS (including functional or physical inadequacies, repairs needed, modernization, etc.)

FHLMC Form 70 Rev. 7/79   ATTACH DESCRIPTIVE PHOTOGRAPHS OF SUBJECT PROPERTY AND STREET SCENE   FNMA Form 1004 Rev. 7/79

[D3344]

FIGURE 5-1: (continued)

VALUATION SECTION

Purpose of Appraisal is to estimate Market Value as defined in Certification & Statement of Limiting Conditions (FHLMC Form 439/FNMA Form 1004B). If submitted for FNMA, the appraiser must attach (1) sketch or map showing location of subject, street names, distance from nearest intersection, and any detrimental conditions and (2) exterior building sketch of improvements showing dimensions.

Measurements		No. Stories		Sq. Ft.
24'9" x 30'	x	1	=	727.50
20'9" x 53'	x	1	=	1099.75
6'10" x 30' 6"	x	1	=	208.31
2'5" x 22'	x	1	=	53.02
x	x		=	
x	x		=	

Total Gross Living Area (List in Market Data Analysis below) 2088.58

Comment on functional and economic obsolescence: None noted

ESTIMATED REPRODUCTION COST – NEW – OF IMPROVEMENTS:

Dwelling 2089 Sq. Ft. @ $ 36.00	=	$ 75,200
Sq. Ft. @ $	=	
Extras Central air conditioning	=	1,500
1¼ baths	=	1,800
Special Energy Efficient Items	=	
Porches, Patios, etc. Patio, 300sq. ft.	=	300
Garage/Car Port 473 Sq. Ft. @ $ 8.00	=	3,800
Site Improvements (driveway, landscaping, etc.)	=	3,000
Total Estimated Cost New	=	$ 85,600
Less 4% Physical / Functional / Economic Depreciation $ 3,400 $ $	=	$ (-3,400)
Depreciated value of improvements	=	$ 82,200
ESTIMATED LAND VALUE (If leasehold, show only leasehold value)	=	$ 15,000
INDICATED VALUE BY COST APPROACH		$ 97,200

The undersigned has recited three recent sales of properties most similar and proximate to subject and has considered these in the market analysis. The description includes a dollar adjustment, reflecting market reaction to those items of significant variation between the subject and comparable properties. If a significant item in the comparable property is superior to, or more favorable than, the subject property, a minus (-) adjustment is made, thus reducing the indicated value of subject; if a significant item in the comparable is inferior to, or less favorable than, the subject property, a plus (+) adjustment is made, thus increasing the indicated value of the subject.

ITEM	Subject Property	COMPARABLE NO. 1		COMPARABLE NO. 2		COMPARABLE NO. 3	
Address	309 Oak St. Schaumburg	312 Walnut Lane Schaumburg		743 Maple Drive Schaumburg		105 Evergreen Lane Schaumburg	
Proximity to Subj.		1 block		5 blocks		2 blocks	
Sales Price	$ 94,000		$ 97,000		$ 84,400		$ 89,900
Price/Living area	$ 36.00	$ ---		$ ---		$ ---	
Data Source		Comp. File		Comp. File		Comp. File	
Date of Sale and Time Adjustment	DESCRIPTION	DESCRIPTION	Adjustment	DESCRIPTION	Adjustment	DESCRIPTION	Adjustment
	6-4-81	5-81	-0-	4-81	-0-	1-81 (+3%)	+2,700
Location	Good	same	-0-	same	-0-	same	-0-
Site/View	Good						
Design and Appeal	Good						
Quality of Const.	Average						
Age (effect)	2 years						
Condition	Good						
Living Area Room Count and Total	Total / B-rms / Baths 7 / 3 / 2½ 2089 Sq.Ft.	Total / B-rms / Baths 7 / 3 / 2½ 2089 Sq.Ft.	-0-	Total / B-rms / Baths 6 / 3 / 2½ 1864 Sq.Ft.	+8000	Total / B-rms / Baths 7 / 3 / 1½ 2089 Sq.Ft	+1,200
Basement & Bsmt. Finished Rooms	Unfinished Basement	same	-0-	same	-0-	same	-0-
Functional Utility	Good						
Air Conditioning	Central			none	+1,500	none	+1,500
Garage/Car Port	2 car/att.			same	-0-	same	-0-
Porches, Patio, Pools, etc.	Patio					none	+300
Special Energy Efficient Items	None					same	-0-
Other (e.g. fireplaces, kitchen equip., remodeling)	None	fireplace	-2000			fireplace	-2000
Sales or Financing Concessions	Conventional	same	-0-			same	-0-
Net Adj. (Total)		☐ Plus ☒ Minus $2000		☒ Plus ☐ Minus $ 9,500		☒ Plus ☐ Minus $ 3,700	
Indicated Value of Subject			$95,000		$ 93,900		$ 93,600

Comments on Market Data Comp #1 and #3 exact same residence

INDICATED VALUE BY MARKET DATA APPROACH	$ 95,000
INDICATED VALUE BY INCOME APPROACH (If applicable) Economic Market Rent $ 650 /Mo. x Gross Rent Multiplier 146	= $ 94,900

This appraisal is made ☒ "as is" ☐ subject to the repairs, alterations, or conditions listed below ☐ completion per plans and specifications.

Comments and Conditions of Appraisal: _____

Final Reconciliation: More emphasis has been placed on the Market Data Approach as a better indicator of what the typically informed purchaser would pay for the subject.

Construction Warranty ☒ Yes ☐ No   Name of Warranty Program HOW   Warranty Coverage Expires 5-87

This appraisal is based upon the above requirements, the certification, contingent and limiting conditions, and Market Value definition that are stated in ☒ FHLMC Form 439 (Rev. 10/78)/FNMA Form 1004B (Rev. 10/78) filed with client March 15 19 79 ☐ attached.

I ESTIMATE THE MARKET VALUE, AS DEFINED, OF SUBJECT PROPERTY AS OF June 12 19 81 to be $ 95,000

Appraiser(s) Alice B. Scott   Review Appraiser (If applicable) _____ ☐ Did ☐ Did Not Physically Inspect Property

FHLMC Form 70 Rev. 7/79   REVERSE   FNMA Form 1004 Rev 7/79

43570-1 SAF Systems and Forms   [D3345]

Technically, all three approaches to value use forms of market data to support their estimates. In addition to comparable sales, the appraiser also considers land sales, building costs, observed depreciation, and property rentals. All approaches to value are refinements of market facts. And, of course, an appraisal can never be made simply through the use of set formulas. The appraiser's own judgment and experience will play a large role in the process. The appraiser generally uses the three approaches to value as checks against each other, even though his or her informed opinion may be that a single approach gives the most realistic estimate of value. In some cases, the nature of the appraisal will not permit the application of all three approaches. For example, the GMRM (income) approach would be inappropriate when appraising a single-family residence in an area that has virtually no rental properties. Appraisal experts have come to some agreement on what to look for when evaluating properties using each approach. A closer look at the applications of these approaches follows.

Approaches to Value: Market Data

In appraising single-family residences, the market data approach is typically the most applicable and heavily weighted approach to value. Let us recall the objective of the appraisal—to estimate the fair market value of a property. Market value, as defined, is the highest price people are willing to pay for a property in a fair and open market. The market data approach involves analyzing the prices people are actually paying for properties in the market. In this analysis, the sold properties are compared to the subject property with price adjustments being made for any differences. Only in inactive markets or with unique properties does this approach become questionable. In both of these instances, the lack of suitable comparable properties can make this approach difficult to use.

Selecting Comparable Properties. When using this approach, the appraiser must first select appropriate comparable properties. The appraiser considers numerous properties and narrows the selection down to only those that are most similar to the subject property. Ideally, the appraiser chooses comparable properties that have sold recently, are located in the same neighborhood, are the same style of residences (for example, all ranches or all split levels), have similar physical attributes, and were acquired under similar financing arrangements. Obviously, under these ideal conditions, no adjustments would have to be made to the comparables, because they are virtually identical to the subject property. However, appraisal assignments are rarely ever ideal, and adjustments often have to be made. Naturally, the fewer the adjustments, the more reliable the comparable properties are as an indication of value.

Adjusting the Comparable Properties. After selecting suitable comparable properties, the appraiser prepares a comparison chart for the subject property and the comparables (see page 2 of Figure 5–1).

The appraiser uses at least three comparable properties in this chart. The sales price of each comparable property is adjusted to reflect the differences between the comparable and the subject property. The adjusted sales price of each comparable property reflects a reasonable price that the property would have sold for, if it had the same features as the appraised property. For example, assume that a subject property and a comparable property are exactly the same, except that the comparable property has a fireplace (the subject has none). Further assume that the sales price of the comparable property is $80,000 and that the fireplace is worth $2,000. In this case, the comparable property would indicate that the subject is worth $78,000. The value of the fireplace is *subtracted* from the sales price of the comparable, so that the comparable property has identical features to the subject property.

Now, reverse this situation. Assume that the subject property has the fireplace and the comparable has none. Also assume that the comparable property sold for $80,000 and the fireplace is worth $2,000. In this case, the comparable property would indicate that the subject is worth $82,000. The value of the fireplace is *added* to the sales price of the comparable, so that the comparable property has identical features to the subject property.

The appraiser adjusts the sales prices of all of the comparable properties with respect to numerous attributes and considerations. Adjustments are made in dollar figures with respect to time of sale, location, site, physical components, and any other major feature of either the property or the sale. Frequently, a single comparable property will have both added and subtracted adjustments, as shown in the sample appraisal report. After all adjustments have been made, the appraiser reconciles the revised sales prices into an indication of value for the subject property. Reconciling does not mean averaging. Instead, by using reasonable judgment and knowledge, the appraiser estimates a value in this approach by assigning a heavier weight to those properties most similar to the subject property.

Approaches to Value: Cost

The cost approach to value is very frequently completed to provide the appraiser with a useful check to the value indication of the market data approach. In inactive markets or with unique properties, this approach is heavily emphasized, since the market data approach is virtually impossible to complete. In the cost approach, the appraiser must make three separate estimates: site value, replacement cost of the improvements, and accrued depreciation. The reliability of this approach depends upon how accurately the appraiser can measure these variables. An indication of value is obtained by adding the site value to the depreciated replacement cost of the improvements.

Site Valuation. In the cost approach, the appraiser first estimates the value of the subject property's site, exclusive of all buildings. Site is always valued in terms of its highest and best use. The most common approach to estimate site value involves comparing the subject's site to other recently sold, vacant sites. As in the market data approach, the comparable sites' sales prices are adjusted to reflect any differences with the subject site. The appraiser reconciles all of the adjusted sales prices to obtain an estimate of value for the subject site.

Replacement Cost. In arriving at a cost figure for a particular improvement, the appraiser can take one of several possible routes. First, if the building is of a size and style which is still being constructed, the appraiser can determine the volume-builder price of a nearly identical new building, with minor price adjustments for variations.

Second, the appraiser can determine the square- or cubic-foot size of the subject's building and apply local builders' current square- or cubic-foot charges. This is the method used in the sample appraisal report. In the example, special features, such as the added one and one-half baths and central air conditioning, are not included in the square-foot costs.

Third, the appraiser can produce cost figures for the different elements of a home, for example: "Face brick cost X dollars per square foot; plaster walls and ceilings cost X dollars for a room containing X cubic feet," and so on. From this computation of the area or volume of the elements of the subject's improvements, the appraiser determines total cost and adds an additional percentage for the builder's overhead, insurance, and taxes during the construction period. This method is accurate, but normally it is considered too time-consuming when appraising a single-family home.

Fourth, the appraiser can use locally published cost figures for entire buildings or components of buildings. In such situations, the appraiser must be certain that he or she knows exactly what is and is not included in each figure before applying data accurately.

While the appraiser need not be an expert cost estimator, he or she must know the best sources of data on actual building costs. Moreover, the appraiser must constantly analyze these data and file them for future reference.

Depreciation Charges. The last variable the appraiser measures in the cost approach is the sum total of all depreciation charges. Depreciation encompasses functional and economic obsolescence and physical deterioration. Appraisers use many detailed and complex procedures in measuring depreciation. This text will briefly look at some of these procedures.

To estimate depreciation, appraisers typically use one of the following three methods. First, in the *abstraction method*, the appraiser analyzes the sales prices of comparable properties, as an indication of the amount of depreciation the market penalizes each sale. In this procedure, the appraiser computes the difference between each comparable's sale price and its corresponding replacement cost plus site value. This difference reflects the total amount of depreciation and indicates the rate the property has depreciated over time.

The second procedure, called the *age-life method*, would assign a set, annual depreciation rate, for example 2 percent, to the entire structure. In this example, the appraiser assumes that the entire building loses approximately 2 percent of its value each year. For example, a five-year-old building would have lost 10 percent of its value. The annual rate of depreciation that the appraiser selects depends upon the building's condition, functional utility, and external influences.

The third procedure, the *breakdown method*, involves a complex analysis of the amount of depreciation separate components of the building have experienced. For example, a building's foundation and roof would be considered separately. Physical, functional, and economic depreciation are all considered separately. Listing items as either "curable" or "incurable," a feasibility analysis is completed to determine whether a depreciation charge is worthwhile to correct.

Measuring depreciation is a very complex study of a building's condition, design, construction materials, and external influences. Depreciation charges should never be based solely upon a property's age. Many fine older homes have received excellent upkeep and maintenance. Furthermore, regulations flatly prohibit discrimination based upon a property's age. All depreciation charges should be based upon a thorough analysis—inside and out—of each individual building.

Once the appraiser has estimated the three variables, an indication of value in the cost approach is quite simple to obtain. First, all depreciation charges are subtracted from the total replacement cost of the building. Second, site value is then added to the depreciated replacement cost to obtain an indication of value via the cost approach.

Approaches to Value: Income

The third approach an appraiser may use to estimate market value involves considering the income a property can produce. There are several types of income approaches, depending upon the type of real estate being appraised. For example, appraising large apartment buildings and commercial properties involves analyzing their potential income and operating expenditures. After this analysis, different rates and methods of income capitalization are applied. This detailed approach is neither necessary nor appropriate for single-family residences. This is because single-family residences are not developed primarily as sources of rental income. And even if they are rented, they typically cannot justify their existence as a self-sustaining investment.

The most common income approach used in appraising single-family residences is called the gross monthly rent multiplier (GMRM) approach to value. The appropriateness of this approach depends upon whether or not there is a viable rental market for the subject property. In areas where there are quite a few similar properties that are rented, the approach can be used quite successfully. In this situation, the approach provides the appraiser with an indication of value that can be compared to the other two approaches.

In the GMRM approach, the first step involves selecting and analyzing comparable properties that were rented at the time of sale. The comparable properties should be very similar to the subject property. Rarely are adjustments made to the sales prices of the comparables in this approach. The appraiser divides each comparable's sales price by its gross monthly rental to obtain a multiplier. For example, a $70,000 property that rents for $500 per month would have a multiplier of 140. After obtaining multipliers for several comparable properties, the appraiser would select a single multiplier that is appropriate for the subject property.

The second step involves estimating a monthly market rental for the subject property. Again the appraiser reviews other rental properties in the area to make a reasonable judgment as to the rent that the subject property would command.

To obtain an indication of value, the appraiser multiplies the subject property's anticipated monthly rental by the applicable multiplier. The following example illustrates an indication of value by the GMRM approach. After analyzing several comparable properties, an appraiser obtains the following multipliers: 119, 123, 119, 117, 116, and 121. In the appraiser's judgment, the most appropriate multiplier for the subject property is 120. Based upon other rentals in the market, the appraiser then estimates that the subject property would reasonably rent for $450 per month. The indicated value of the subject property in this example would be 120 × $450, or $54,000.

Reconciliation and Certification

If the appraiser could measure the market perfectly, and if every essential fact could be learned about every property, then all three value indicators would yield the same answer. Under such ideal conditions *reconciliation,* the final step in the appraisal process, could be eliminated.

Unfortunately, real estate appraising is not an exact science. It offers few shortcuts. To arrive at a final estimate of value the appraiser must weigh all the factors found in the appraisal search. Exercising sound judgment, the appraiser merges them into the truest possible value picture. In the process, the appraiser may also reconsider the reliability of the data and reexamine each step of the appraisal.

To reconcile does not mean to average the findings of the three value approaches. Rather it means to relate them to each other. It is a weighing operation. If, for example, the appraiser has particular confidence in certain value indicators, considerable weight obviously will be accorded to them. The appraiser should also note whether the estimate of value is subject to repairs or special conditions or whether the estimate of value is made "as is." One final item in the reconciliation of the data is the listing of the date the opinion of value is given;

to speak of market value without relating it to a specific date is meaningless.

On the completion of the appraisal process, the appraiser signs a *certification* .... This attests to three critical activities.

1. The appraiser has inspected the property inside and out.

2. All facts and data have been reported in a true and correct way.

3. The appraiser or his or her colleagues have no undisclosed interests in the property.

This certification conforms to the codes of ethics of various professional appraisal groups.

NOTE: DISCRIMINATION IN LENDING

Discrimination Against Borrowers. As indicated in the principal excerpt, antidiscrimination laws generally forbid lenders from evaluating prospective borrowers on the basis of criteria unrelated to credit-worthiness. The 1968 Civil Rights Act, as amended, prohibits lenders from denying a real estate loan, or discriminating "in the fixing of the amount, interest rate, duration, or other terms or conditions of such loan ... because of the race, color, religion, sex, or national origin of such person...." 42 U.S.C.A. § 3605 (1977). The Equal Credit Opportunity Act of 1974, as amended, prohibits "any creditor to discriminate against any applicant, with respect to any aspect of a credit transaction—(1) on the basis of race, color, religion, national origin, sex or marital status, or age...." and authorizes the Federal Reserve Board to promulgate regulations implementing the Act. 15 U.S.C.A. §§ 1691(a), 1691(b) (1982).

Despite this legislation, data compiled for 1990 by the Federal Financial Institutions Examination Council pursuant to the Home Mortgage Disclosure Act of 1975 and the Financial Institutions Reform, Recovery and Enforcement Act of 1989, indicate that African American and Hispanic applicants were significantly more likely to be denied mortgage loans than white applicants. Even within the same income levels, blacks were about twice as likely to be denied a loan as whites. Canner, Home Mortgage Disclosure Act: Expanded Data on Residential Lending, Federal Reserve Bulletin, Nov. 1991, pp. 859–881. See generally, Symposium, Discrimination in the Housing and Mortgage Markets, 3 Housing Policy Debate 185–745 (1992).

Discrimination Against Neighborhoods. Congress and the state legislatures have been slower to outlaw the more subtle and complex discrimination that can occur when lenders appraise the land being offered as security for a mortgage loan. Many lenders have historically refused to make mortgage loans in blighted or deteriorating urban neighborhoods on the ground that declining property values will impair their mortgage security over the life of the loan. Those lenders that do make mortgage loans in these areas characteristically seek to protect themselves by imposing such onerous terms on the borrower as a shorter than normal term, lower loan to value ratio, or higher interest rates.

"Redlining"—so-called because lenders once marked local maps in red pencil to indicate neighborhoods in which loans were disfavored—poses a classic public policy dilemma. As Professor John Payne has observed, "The conundrum is that of the chicken and the egg: Without private capital, urban redevelopment is difficult to achieve; without urban stability, investment security is difficult to demonstrate. Which should come first?" Payne, Banking Institutions Trim State Efforts to Enforce Anti-Redlining Measures, 9 Real Est. L.J. 357 (1981).

The dilemma is evident in the history of the FHA's policies for insuring mortgages in deteriorating urban areas. In its early years, the FHA acted conservatively, guaranteeing only loans that were "economically sound." Frequently this meant refusing to insure loans in marginal or racially mixed areas. See FHA Underwriting Manual (1938), quoted in U.S. Commission on Civil Rights, Report No. 4, Housing 16–17 (1961). In response to charges that these underwriting policies were contributing to urban decay, Congress relaxed the FHA's stringent appraisal criteria for the most needy situations to a standard that allowed loans in "reasonably viable" areas. 12 U.S.C.A. § 1715n(e). Yet relaxed criteria mean that insured lenders have less incentive to carefully appraise properties in declining areas and to determine whether prospective borrowers are good risks. Compare Jeminson v. Montgomery Real Estate, page 221, above. This in turn can be expected to lead to increased defaults. But, with their losses insured, lenders have little incentive to work problem loans out with their borrowers, even if the cause for default appears only temporary. So long as mortgages are foreclosed and mortgagors dispossessed, abandonment of marginal areas seems likely to continue.

Congress' major response to the redlining problem has been to mandate disclosure of geographic lending patterns. The Home Mortgage Disclosure Act of 1975, 12 U.S.C.A. §§ 2801 et seq., requires federally chartered lenders to publish the geographic distribution of their mortgage loans. The quixotic theory behind the Act was that "once local residents discover the lending policies of institutions located in their communities, they will reward those institutions that are investing in the area by depositing in them and express their dissatisfaction with those that are not by withdrawing from them. As the forces of the marketplace intensify, lenders will become more community minded and mortgage credit will become more plentiful in needy neighborhoods." Note, Attacking the Urban Redlining Problem, 56 B.U.L.Rev. 989, 1007–8 (1976). Several states have adopted similar disclosure statutes for state-chartered institutions. Amendments to the Home Mortgage Disclosure Act, mandated by the Financial Institutions Reform, Recovery, and Enforcement Act, extended the Act's coverage to all mortgage lenders and broadened the disclosure requirements. For a comprehensive analysis of the amendments, see Ulrich, Home Mortgage Disclosure Act Developments, 46 Bus.Law. 1077 (1991).

Direct federal regulation of redlining has been less authoritative. For example, the Fair Housing Act has been applied to prohibit lenders from denying loans to white homebuyers in racially mixed neighborhoods, but only on the limited ground that the refusal was based on the race of the residents in the neighborhood. See, for example, Laufman v. Oakley Building & Loan Co., 408 F.Supp. 489 (S.D.Ohio 1976); Harrison v. Otto G. Heinzeroth Mortgage Co., 430 F.Supp. 893 (N.D.Ohio 1977).

The Fair Housing Act was the subject of comprehensive amendments in 1988. Pub.L. No. 100–430, 102 Stat. 1619 (1989). The new provisions make it unlawful to discriminate on the basis of race, color, religion, sex, handicap, familial status, or national origin in "real estate-related transactions." This revision broadens the scope of the Act to include any loan secured by a dwelling. Before this change, second mortgages used for purposes other than obtaining housing were not covered by the Act. See, e.g., Evans v. First Federal Savings Bank, 669 F.Supp. 915 (N.D.Ind.1987). The 1988 amendments also beefed up enforcement, providing for suits by the attorney general and adjudication by administrative law judges of actions brought by HUD. Recovery is permitted for pain and suffering and humiliation and punitive damages may be awarded. See Dennis, The Fair Housing Act Amendments of 1988: A New Source of Lender Liability, 106 Banking L.J. 405 (1989).

Similarly, the Federal Home Loan Bank Board's regulations are tentative at best. Board Regulation 12 C.F.R. § 528.2 provides that "No savings association may deny a loan or other service, ... or discriminate in fixing the amount ... or other terms or conditions of such loan or other service on the basis of the age or location of the dwelling...." But guidelines appearing in 12 C.F.R. § 571.24(c)(7) add that these restrictions are "intended to prohibit use of unfounded or unsubstantiated assumptions regarding the effect upon loan risk of the age of a dwelling or the physical or economic characteristics of an area. Loan decisions should be based on the present market value of the property offered as security (including consideration of specific improvements to be made by the borrower) and the likelihood that the property will retain an adequate value over the term of the loan. Specific factors which may negatively affect its short range future value (up to 3–5 years) should be clearly documented. Factors which in some cases may cause the market value of a property to decline are recent zoning changes or a significant number of abandoned homes in the immediate vicinity of the property. ... However, arbitrary decisions based on age or location are prohibited, since many older, soundly constructed homes provide housing opportunities which may be precluded by an arbitrary lending policy."

State legislatures have outlawed redlining more authoritatively. See, for example, California Housing Financial Discrimination Act of 1977, Health & Safety Code § 35800 et seq. (West Supp.1992). ("No financial institution shall discriminate in the availability of, or in the provision of, financial assistance for the purpose of purchasing, constructing, rehabilitating, improving, or refinancing housing accommodations due, in whole or in part, to the consideration of conditions, characteristics, or trends in the neighborhood or geographic area surrounding the housing accommodation, unless the financial institution can demonstrate that such consideration in the particular case is required to avoid an unsafe and unsound business practice." Health & Safety Code § 35810).

Do the less rigorous federal regulations preempt application of the more rigorous state statutes to federally-chartered lenders? See Conference of Federal Savings & Loan Associations v. Stein, 604 F.2d 1256 (9th Cir.1979), affirmed per curiam, 445 U.S. 921, 100 S.Ct. 1304, 63 L.Ed.2d 754 (1980) (redlining regulations promulgated by Federal Home Loan Bank Board preempted application of California Housing Financial Discrimination Act to federally-chartered savings and loan associations). For a superb analysis of the preemption issue, see Payne, Banking Institutions Trim State Efforts to Enforce Anti-Redlining Measures, 9 Real Est. L.J. 357 (1981).

See generally, W. Dennis & J.S. Pottinger, Federal Regulation of Banking: Redlining and Community Reinvestment (1980); Note, Redlining, Disinvestment and the Role of the Mutual Savings Banks: A Survey of Solutions, 9 Ford.Urb.L.Rev. 89 (1980); Note, Attacking the Urban Redlining Problem, 56 B.U.L.Rev. 989 (1976); Note, An Analysis of the Effectiveness of the Home Mortgage Disclosure Act of 1975, 28 Case W.Res.L.Rev. 1074 (1978); Comment, Mortgage Discrimination: Eliminating Racial Discrimination in Home Financing Through the Fair Housing Act of 1968, 20 St. Louis U.L.J. 139 (1975). On a closely related problem, see DeWolfe, Squires, & DeWolfe, Civil Rights Implications of Insurance Redlining, 29 DePaul L.Rev. 315 (1980).

NOTES

1. *Appraisals.* Inaccurate, incompetent, and fraudulent appraisals have been cited as one important cause of the crisis in the savings and loan industry. The Financial Institutions Reform, Recovery and Enforcement Act of 1989, 92 Stat. 3694, 12 U.S.C.A. § 3301 et seq., created an appraisal subcommittee made up of the heads of various federal agencies regulating banking institutions. The subcommittee is charged with reviewing state certification requirements for appraisers, monitoring the requirements of federal agencies with respect to appraisers, and reporting annually to Congress on its activities. Pursuant to the statute, the Office of Thrift Supervision promulgated appraisal rules for transactions by institutions regulated by OTS. 12 C.F.R. §§ 564.1–564.8. These regulations require that the appraisal method conform to the Uniform Standards of Professional Appraisal Practice adopted by the Appraisal Standards Board of the Appraisal Foundation. The regulations also require the appraiser to have no financial interest in the property or transaction, be engaged by the institution (rather than the borrower), and be state certified or licensed. The responsibilities of

the management of lending institutions for appraisal review and standards are also set forth.

The basic licensing and certification of appraisers is performed by the states. See, e.g., Conn.Gen.Stat.Ann. ch. 369, § 20–311 et seq.

See Lee, Mancuso, & Walter, Housing Finance: Major Developments in 1990, 46 Bus.Law. 1149, 1157–1171 (1991) (reviewing the OTS regulations); Vickory, Regulating Real Estate Appraisers: The Role of Fraudulent and Incompetent Real Estate Appraisals in the S & L Crisis and the FIRREA Solution, 19 Real Est.L.J. 3 (1990).

2. *Loan–Value Ratios.* OTS has promulgated regulations concerning loan-value ratios. For home loans over 90% of appraised value, the portion that exceeds 80% of value must be insured by a qualified private insurer. 12 C.F.R. § 545.32(d)(2) (covering federally chartered associations), § 563.97 (covering other associations). See also § 545.-33(d).

B. JUNIOR LIENS

GULESERIAN v. FIELDS

Supreme Judicial Court of Massachusetts, 1966.
351 Mass. 238, 218 N.E.2d 397.

CUTTER, Justice.

The plaintiffs (the mortgagors) are the trustees of a Massachusetts real estate trust which owns, subject to the mortgages hereinafter mentioned, land and buildings (the locus) on Garden Street, Cambridge. On September 15, 1960, the mortgagors gave a duly recorded first mortgage covering the locus to Charlestown Savings Bank (the bank) to secure the payment of $750,000 "in fifteen years, with interest thereon, or on any unpaid balance thereof, and on any sums hereafter advanced by the [h]older which lawfully accrued to the mortgage debt, as provided in our * * * note of even date." The note provided that the mortgagors would pay monthly instalments of $6,249.99, consisting of principal and interest at the rate of six per cent per annum.[2]

---

2. The first mortgage authorized the holder of the mortgage to pay taxes and certain other charges and to add the amount so paid to the mortgage debt. The mortgagors, in addition to the statutory mortgage covenants, made various special covenants including one "(7) to remain liable upon the covenants herein and upon the note secured hereby notwithstanding any forbearance, extension or other indulgence given by the [h]older to any future owner of the mortgaged premises or other person, notice of any such forbearance, extension or other indulgence being hereby expressly waived." The mortgage note itself contained a related provision. "All parties * * * personally liable for * * * any * * * indebtedness hereby evidenced agree, by executing or endorsing this note or by entering into * * * any agreement to pay any [such] indebtedness * * * that the * * * holder hereof shall have the right, without notice, to deal in any way at any time with any party or to grant to any party any extensions of time for payment of any of said indebtedness or any other indulgences or forbearances whatsoever without in any way affecting the personal liability of any party hereunder." The first mortgage was upon the statutory condition and contained the statutory power of sale. See G.L. c. 183, §§ 18–21.

On August 1, 1962, the mortgagors gave a second mortgage in statutory form covering the locus to Commander Operating Company (Operating) to secure the payment of $400,000 in twenty years, "as provided in a * * * note of Commander Properties, Inc. * * * of even date" with the second mortgage. The note secured by the second mortgage provided for monthly payments of $1,666.67, on account of principal only, with interest "payable only on any past due installment * * * at the rate of seven per cent * * * per annum."

The mortgagors have sought the consent of Operating, as second mortgagee, to a proposed agreement between the mortgagors and the bank (as first mortgagee) "to extend the terms of payments of principal under * * * [the first mortgage] note in the following manner: The * * * [first] mortgage note provides for the payment of monthly installments of * * * $6,249.99 * * * to be applied first to interest due under * * * [the] note and the balance to principal. The proposed extension agreement * * * would postpone the principal payments included in the twenty-four * * * installments next following * * * the execution of such agreement until October 15, 1975, the stated maturity date of the * * * [first] mortgage note, all of * * * [the] postponed principal payments becoming due in a lump sum on * * * [that] date. Interest at the rate of six per centum * * * per annum, as specified in the note, would continue to be paid monthly on the outstanding principal balance, which by reason of the foregoing arrangement would remain constant during * * * [such] period of twenty-four * * * months."

Operating has refused to consent to this arrangement and has notified the mortgagors that if such an agreement is made with the bank Operating "will demand that * * * [the mortgagors] continue to pay monthly installments according to the present tenor of the first mortgage note, and [will take the position] that failure to make such payments would constitute a default under the terms of the second mortgage." Operating also contends that any such extension agreement will not be binding on it, will constitute a violation of its rights as holder of the second mortgage, and will affect the priorities as between the holders of the first and second mortgages.

The mortgagors by their bill seek a declaration (G.L. c. 231A) "that any lawful extension of the terms of payment of the first mortgage note, made without * * * [Operating's] consent * * * does not constitute a breach by the * * * [mortgagors] of the conditions of the second mortgage." The parties, since the earlier remand of this case have agreed upon a revised case stated. The case for a second time has been reported without decision for the determination of this court by a judge of the Superior Court.

1. The crucial language of each of the mortgages is that of the statutory mortgage condition found in G.L. c. 183, § 20, set out in the margin,[3] so far as relevant. The questions for decision are (a) whether

3. Section 20 provides that a condition may be incorporated by reference in any mortgage, as follows: "Provided, nevertheless, except as otherwise specifically stated

by reason of the proposed extension agreement, the bank, as first mortgagee, will lose in any degree the priority of its security interest in the locus with respect to any part of the secured indebtedness and the interest thereon, and (b) whether the extension agreement, if carried out, will constitute a breach of the second mortgage, entitling Operating, as second mortgagee, to foreclose.

It is important to bear in mind precisely what form of extension is now proposed. There would be no increase in the interest rate payable upon the balance of principal from time to time due upon the first mortgage note. That rate is now fixed at six per cent per annum and is to remain at six per cent. The only change proposed in the terms of the mortgage note is that the monthly payments of principal coming due within the period of twenty-four months following the execution of the extension agreement will be postponed to the maturity date of the first mortgage. There will be no increase, by reason of the extension agreement, in the principal amount due upon the first mortgage at the date of the execution of the extension agreement. Thus the only adverse effects, so far as the second mortgagee is concerned, of the extension agreement will be that the first mortgage debt will not be reduced as rapidly as the parties to the first mortgage and note originally had agreed that it would be (obviously, primarily at least, for the benefit of the first mortgagee), and interest will be paid upon the amount of the postponed principal payments for a longer period than was originally contemplated.

2. The mortgagors and the bank, as between themselves, may extend the time for payment of the first mortgage indebtedness, or any part thereof, by agreement binding on them as parties to the extension. The general rule is that a renewal or extension of an existing senior mortgage and the note (or other obligation) secured thereby, without an increase of the principal or interest payable with respect to the secured indebtedness, will not result in any loss of priority of that senior mortgage over junior encumbrances. The holder of the junior encumbrance is treated as taking his interest "subject to a possible extension of the time of payment" of the debt secured by a senior encumbrance. The holder of the junior encumbrance is regarded as necessarily taking the risk of a postponement (frequently an advantage to a second mortgagee) of the date of payment of the whole or part of the senior

in the mortgage, that if the mortgagor, or his heirs * * * [or personal representatives] shall pay unto the mortgagee or his * * * [personal representatives] the principal and interest secured by the mortgage, and [A] shall perform any obligation secured at the time provided in the note, mortgage or other instrument [B] or any extension thereof, and [C] shall perform the condition of any prior mortgage, and until such payment and performance shall pay when due and payable all taxes, charges and assessments * * * shall keep the buildings on said premises insured against fire * * * [in a manner more fully set out in the statutory condition], and shall not commit or suffer any strip or waste of the mortgaged premises or [D] any breach of any covenant contained in the mortgage or in any prior mortgage, then the mortgage deed, as also the mortgage note or notes, shall be void." The letters in brackets have been inserted for convenient reference to the language immediately following such letters, respectively.

mortgage debt. The rule has been referred to as the "universal rule." Beckman v. Altoona Trust Co., 332 Pa. 545, 550, 2 A.2d 826.

A brief filed by amici curiae places emphasis upon G.L. c. 168, § 36, par. 4 (authorizing savings banks to make certain changes in the amount of periodic payments under mortgages). The existence of this provision has the effect of drawing the attention of junior lienholders to the possibility [6] that the holder of a savings bank mortgage may wish to extend the debt secured by a mortgage of which the savings bank is a holder. The statute, of course, confirms the authority of the bank, within its statutory powers, to make an extension like that now proposed. Apart from the statute, however, the authorities, already cited, show that an extension of the time for payment may be made by a holder of a mortgage without the consent of the holders of junior encumbrances and without loss of priority.[7]

We see no sound basis for any contention that execution of the proposed extension agreement would affect or diminish the priority of the bank's security interest as it existed at the time of the execution of the second mortgage, as against the holder of that mortgage.

3. If the proposed extension agreement in fact should be executed, failure to make any of the postponed twenty-four monthly payments of principal would not constitute a default under the first mortgage. The bank as first mortgagee would not be in a position to foreclose because of any failure of the mortgagors to make such payments on the date originally scheduled. As was said in the Commonwealth Life Ins. Co. case, 234 Ky. 802, 809, 29 S.W.2d 552, 556, "If the party to whom payment is due * * * agrees to a postponement of the date of payment, there is no default in any real sense of the word." By the proposed extension agreement the time for the performance of "the [first mortgage] note * * * or any extension thereof" (see fn. 3, at points [A] and [B]) would be changed, so that there would be no breach of the statutory condition of the second mortgage with respect to payments of principal on the "prior" first mortgage, and also no failure to "perform the condition of" the first mortgage (see fn. 3, at point [C]) or "of any

---

6. Operating was to some extent given warning by this first mortgage of the possibility of an extension. This possibility was indicated by the special covenant (quoted fn. 2) numbered (7) by which the mortgagors were to remain liable notwithstanding any extension granted to a subsequent holder of the equity of redemption in the locus (or any other person), and even if, by transfer of the equity of redemption or otherwise the mortgagors should become essentially sureties. The related provision of the first mortgage note, if examined by Operating, would have given similar warning.

7. The parties have stipulated that, under G.L. c. 168, § 36, par. 4, as amended,

and c. 170, § 24, par. 8, as amended, some savings and coöperative banks "have, as a matter of regular business practice, agreed with owners of equities of redemption to change the amount of the periodic payments of principal and/or [sic] interest or other provisions called for by notes and mortgages held by them. In a majority of such cases this has been done without checking for the existence or seeking the assent of junior lienors on the mortgaged property." This practice we regard as showing only that the statutory authorization of extension agreements by savings and coöperative banks may have met a significant commercial need.

covenant contained in * * * any prior mortgage" (see fn. 3, at point [D]).

Part of the statutory condition found in the second mortgage, viz. that the mortgagors "shall perform the condition of any prior mortgage," of course, would afford Operating (as second mortgagee) opportunity to foreclose the second mortgage in the event of a breach of the first mortgage which would permit foreclosure of that mortgage by the bank as first mortgagee. This part of the second mortgage condition is thus a protection to the second mortgagee against foreclosure of the prior mortgage which would destroy the interests of junior mortgagees and lienholders. Where, however, an extension agreement prevents a breach of the prior mortgage which could give rise to the foreclosure of that prior mortgage, there will be no breach of the junior mortgage which would afford basis for its foreclosure.

Operating, perhaps, could have included in the second mortgage an express condition that the mortgagors must continue, without any extension or postponement, to make the instalment payments of principal on the first mortgage note. If such a provision had been made, postponement of any such payments by the proposed extension agreement would constitute, we assume, a breach of such a special condition of the second mortgage. In the circumstances outlined in the case stated, however, no breach of the statutory second mortgage condition will be caused by the proposed extension agreement.

4. A final decree is to be entered in the Superior Court making a declaration of the rights of the parties in a manner consistent with this opinion.

So ordered.

SPIEGEL, Justice (concurring).

I concur in the result reached by the opinion of the court but not on the basis of its reasoning.

In relation to the existing first mortgage note, the proposed postponement of principal payments for a two year period would cause the unpaid principal balance at any time thereafter to be larger than it would have been had the payments been made as scheduled and commensurately decreases the value of the security to Operating as the junior mortgagee. Thus, in the event of a default by the plaintiffs in their principal payments, Operating would be required to pay more than the amount it would otherwise pay in order to be subrogated to the rights of the bank as first mortgagee.

I agree that the mortgagors and the first mortgagee may make a binding agreement between themselves to alter the terms of the first mortgage. However, it is my belief that the requirement that the mortgagors "perform the condition of any prior mortgage" protects the second mortgagee from such an agreement. Hence, the second mortgagee is able to determine the full effect of the prior mortgage on its security by consulting the terms of the prior mortgage. If the previous mortgage expressly provides for a possible extension of time, the second mortgagee has notice of this and can adjust the terms of its agreement correspondingly.

I observe with special interest the following statement in the brief submitted on behalf of the Massachusetts Conveyancers Association and The Abstract Club as amici curiae: "These amici are satisfied that a sizeable segment of the conveyancing bar have heretofore proceeded upon the assumption that where a mortgagor failed to make payments as and when required by the first mortgage note as it stood at the date of the second mortgage, even with the concurrence of the first mortgagee, the second mortgagee could foreclose. Indulgences granted a mortgagor by the first mortgagee frequently work to the detriment of a second mortgagee,—depreciation on the building continues and may not be matched by reduced amortization payments, balloons sometimes are not paid and invariably affect refinancing. In view of such considerations it is arguable that as a matter of policy protection should be given to the second mortgagee, and the governing board of the Massachusetts Conveyancers Association has subscribed to that policy."

The case of 100 Eighth Ave. Corp. v. Morgenstern, 3 Misc.2d 410, 150 N.Y.S.2d 471, cited by the majority, is distinguishable on its facts. In that case, the second mortgage expressly provided that it was subordinate to the first mortgage "and subordinate to any extensions thereof and to any mortgage or consolidated mortgage which may be placed on the premises in lieu thereof or to any extensions thereof provided in all such events (a) that the interest rate thereof shall not be greater than $4\frac{1}{2}\%$ per annum and provided (b) the amortization shall be no different as presently is payable under the said mortgage."

I note that the Massachusetts Conveyancers Association and The Abstract Club in their brief concluded that "the proposed agreement with the Bank would constitute an extension contemplated by the language of the statutory condition." I do not agree. The statutory condition was enacted in its present form by St.1913, c. 369, at a time when self-amortizing mortgages were rare. I think it is a fair assumption that in 1913 the Legislature did not contemplate that some years in the future the self-amortizing mortgage would become commonplace. I believe that the extension contemplated by the statute was an extension of the date of maturity of the traditional mortgage in which the entire principal amount became due at maturity and not a fundamental change in the form of the mortgage from self-amortizing to traditional.

In the instant case, however, we are confronted with a somewhat unique situation. The mortgage contains a provision that the mortgagors agree "to remain liable upon the covenants herein and upon the note secured hereby notwithstanding *any forbearance, extension or other indulgence* given by the Holder to any future owner of the mortgaged premises or other person" (emphasis supplied). The mortgage also states that payment is to be made "as provided in our certain note of even date." The note provides that "All parties now or hereafter personally liable for the payment of any of the indebtedness hereby evidenced agree, by executing or endorsing this note or by entering into or executing any agreement to pay any indebtedness hereby evidenced, that the owner or holder hereof shall have the right, without notice, * * * to grant to any party *any extensions of time for payment of any of said indebtedness or any other indulgences or forbearances whatsoever* without in any way affecting the personal liability of any party hereunder" (emphasis supplied).

Because it is a condition of the prior mortgage that the time for "payment of *any* of said indebtedness" (emphasis supplied) may be extended, there can be no failure to "perform the condition of any prior mortgage" when payment is made according to the terms of the extension.

NOTES

1. *Rights and Liabilities of Junior Lienors.* Junior lienors wear two hats. With respect to the mortgagor, junior mortgagees are like any other mortgagee. They can proceed against the mortgagor for waste or violation of other obligations imposed by the mortgage. In the event of default, they can proceed against the mortgagor on the debt and, subject to the rights of the senior mortgagee, can proceed by foreclosure against the mortgaged property.

With respect to the senior mortgagee, however, the junior mortgagee shares many of the attributes of the owner-mortgagor. If the mortgagor defaults on the senior mortgage, foreclosure by the senior mortgagee will wipe out the junior mortgagee's interest along with the interest of the mortgagor. And, like the mortgagor, the junior mortgagee can usually protect its interest by taking over the mortgage payments or curing any other defaults on the senior mortgage, by bidding at the foreclosure sale, and by redeeming its interest from the sale.

As a general rule, courts will protect junior mortgagees against loan extensions or negotiated increases in the interest rate or principal amount of senior debt on the theory that these changes increase the probability of default and decrease the cushion of value on which the junior lienor can rely in the event of foreclosure. See Meislin, Extension Agreements and the Rights of Junior Mortgagees, 42 Va.L.Rev. 939–940 (1956) ("Yet, despite these and similar imperatives, first mortgagees blandly extend past due mortgages on New York realty with owners on such new terms as are negotiated between them, but without notice to intervening lienors").

Against this background, do you think Guleserian v. Fields was correctly decided? Was the court wrong to think that postponing principal reduction would not diminish the security available to the junior lienor? Or was the court saying that, since one reason for postponing principal repayment is to decrease the likelihood of borrower default, this fact justified enforcement of the extension against the junior lienor? Should the courts' rules encourage lenders to work out problem loans and not force them to immediately foreclose or exercise other formal remedies?

Were Justice Cutter, who wrote the majority opinion in *Guleserian,* and Justice Spiegel, who wrote the concurring opinion, correct to rely on language in the mortgage instrument, reproduced at footnote 2, under which the mortgagor covenanted "to remain liable upon the covenants herein ... notwithstanding any forebearance, extension or other indulgence given by the holder to any future owner of the mortgaged premises"? As you will see in the next principal case, Zastrow v. Knight, an extension of loan terms granted by the mortgagee to a successor in interest of the original mortgagor will at least partially release the original mortgagor from its obligations to the mortgagee. Should not such an extension, granted by the mortgagee to the original mortgagor similarly discharge the junior mortgagee?

Representing the junior mortgagee in *Guleserian,* how would you have drafted your mortgage to protect against the events that occurred there?

2. *Limitations on Junior Mortgages.* The presence of a junior mortgage may cause the senior lender to lose rights under its mortgage. For example, *Gulesarian* shows how the senior lender may be prevented from adjusting the loan terms in order to maintain flexibility in administering and policing the loan. The senior lender may be subject to increased exposure to liability from a junior lender. See Allee v. Benser, 779 S.W.2d 61 (Tex.1988) (junior lender may assert usury claim arising under first mortgage, although it cannot enforce forfeiture penalty under the Texas statute).

Further, if a second mortgage is foreclosed and the property sold to a new owner, the first mortgagee will have to deal with an owner it did not submit to its screening procedures. This new owner may lack the financial ability to pay the mortgage or, in a commercial context, to manage the property. Also, the senior lender may be concerned that a second mortgage reduces the equity of the borrower in the property— an event which the loan-value ratio of the first mortgage had been designed to protect.

In reaction to this, in some rare cases the first mortgagee may prohibit junior mortgages by requiring payment of the first mortgage if a second mortgage is obtained or by making the placement of the second mortgage a default for which the first mortgagee may foreclose.

The first mortgagee may also receive some protection under its due-on-sale clause which typically requires the mortgage to be paid upon transfer of the property. See pages 431–448 below. In Unifirst Federal Savings & Loan Ass'n v. Tower Loan of Mississippi, Inc., 524 So.2d 290 (Miss.1986), the court held that while the placement of a second mortgage did not trigger the due on sale clause in the first mortgage, the sale of the land pursuant to foreclosure of the second did. The court reasoned that "[w]hile our law should facilitate home equity/second mortgage loans, no reason has been advanced why this should be at the expense of the contractual rights of the first mortgage holder." 524 So.2d at 292.

3. *The Purchase Money Priority.* Purchase money mortgagees have traditionally enjoyed a preferred position, characterized as the "purchase money priority," over prior lienors such as judgment creditors and mortgagees claiming under after-acquired property clauses in mortgages previously executed by the mortgagor. The rationale for the purchase money priority is that these earlier lienors, unlike the purchase money mortgagee, did not rely on the property in question when they extended credit to the mortgagor.

Originally the purchase money priority was given only to sellers who took back a mortgage to finance the buyer's purchase of the property. But, over time, many states extended the purchase money priority to third-party lenders who provided the buyer with part or all of the funds needed to acquire the parcel. Even in these states, however, as between the financing seller and a third party lender providing part of the purchase money, the seller will always receive priority. See generally, G. Nelson & D. Whitman, Real Estate Finance Law §§ 9.1–9.2 (2d ed.1985).

Most often the purchase money priority probably hinders rather than helps the financing seller. For example, it is not unusual for a buyer who has obtained a commitment for 80% purchase money financing from an institutional lender to be strapped for cash and to require financing for another 10% or 15% from the seller. Although the seller would like to make the loan, she realizes that her automatic purchase money priority will result in the institutional lender receiving only a second lien—a position that state and federal regulations will commonly bar an institutional lender from taking. The solution usually employed by the seller and the institutional lender is for the seller expressly to subordinate her lien to the lien of the institutional lender, thus placing the institution in a first lien position and herself in a second lien position. Courts will closely scrutinize subordination agreements for possible overreaching by institutional lenders and will restore the purchase money priority where overreaching or other unfairness to the seller is evident. See pages 753–763 below.

Can you see why—at least in jurisdictions with notice and race-notice recording acts—the parties cannot avoid judicial review, and safely arrange for the institutional lender to obtain the needed priority, simply by recording the institutional lender's mortgage before the seller records hers? Of what is the institutional lender likely to have notice at the time it records?

4. *Developments in Junior Finance.* The market for second mortgages changed dramatically in the 1970's and 1980's. According to a study published in *U.S. Housing Markets,* the ratio of second mortgages to other mortgages was one in twenty at the beginning of the 1970's and two out of five by 1981. "In dollar volume, second mortgages

doubled between 1979 and 1981, while firsts were cut in half." Advance Mortgage Corp., U.S. Housing Markets, Oct. 22, 1982. Homeowners, enjoying dramatic appreciation in the value of their parcels, and discouraged by high interest rates from refinancing their first mortgages, turned to second mortgages to finance enlargement or improvement of their homes. Buyers of used housing encumbered by an assumable first mortgage, carrying an interest rate lower than prevailing interest rates, would leave the first lien loan intact and make up the rest of the purchase price through a second lien loan.

The terms of these new second mortgages also differed from patterns established earlier. The traditional second mortgage, usually designed to help a financially strapped homeowner through a difficult period, rarely had a term exceeding five years and usually called for a balloon payment at the end. The new second mortgage is typically a fifteen-year fully amortized loan. The sources of second lien financing have also changed. According to the *U.S. Housing Markets* study, in 1981 consumer finance companies lent over half ($11.5 billion) of the second mortgage debt, an increase of almost 29% from the preceding year. The bulk of the remaining second-lien loans were divided about evenly, at $2–3 billion each, between second mortgage companies, commercial banks and thrift institutions. The supply of funds to this market doubtless received a substantial boost from the new availability of private mortgage insurance for second lien loans and from the efforts of FNMA, beginning in 1981, to create a secondary market in second-lien loans.

See generally, Randolph, The FNMA/FHLMC Uniform Home Improvement Loan Instruments: A Commentary and Critique, 16 Real Prop., Probate & Trust J. 546 (1981); Randolph, The FNMA/FHLMC Uniform Home Improvement Loan Note: The Secondary Market Meets the Consumer Movement, 60 N.C.L.Rev. 365 (1982).

C. TRANSFERS OF MORTGAGED PROPERTY AND MORTGAGE INTERESTS

1. TRANSFERS BY THE MORTGAGOR

a. Duties of the Transferee

A mortgagee typically has two avenues of relief against a defaulting mortgagor. She may proceed against the mortgagor personally on his promise, embodied in his note or bond, to repay the mortgage debt. And she may proceed against the land securing the promise by foreclosure and sale, using the sale proceeds to satisfy the debt.

Relief becomes a bit more complicated when the mortgagor has transferred the encumbered land. If the transferee has taken *subject to* the mortgage, the mortgagee will have no recourse against the transferee personally but can, as before, obtain relief against the mortgagor personally or against the land through foreclosure. If the mortgagee chooses to proceed against the mortgagor personally, the mortgagor, once having paid the debt, becomes subrogated to the mortgagee's rights against the land and can thus obtain reimbursement from the land itself through foreclosure, sale and satisfaction of the debt out of the sale proceeds.

If, by contrast, the transferee has *assumed* the mortgagor's personal liability for the debt, the mortgagee will be able to obtain relief not only from the mortgagor and from the land, but also from the transferee personally. If the mortgagee elects to proceed against the mortgagor personally, the mortgagor can obtain reimbursement by proceeding both against the transferee on his promise and against the land, which remains the primary security for the debt.

ZASTROW v. KNIGHT

Supreme Court of South Dakota, 1930.
56 S.D. 554, 229 N.W. 925.

CAMPBELL, J.

Plaintiff instituted this action against defendants in July, 1928, to recover a principal balance of $2,500, together with some interest, upon a promissory note executed and delivered by defendants to plaintiff July 29, 1919, bearing interest at 6 per cent. per annum, payable July 29, 1922.

The answer of the defendants admits the execution of the note, plaintiff's ownership thereof, and the balance due thereon, and, by way of defense, alleges substantially as follows:

First. That as a part of the same transaction with the execution of the note and as security for the payment of the note defendants duly executed, acknowledged, and delivered to plaintiff a second mortgage upon certain real estate by defendants then owned.

Second. That very shortly thereafter defendants, with full knowledge and consent of plaintiff, sold and conveyed said mortgaged realty by warranty deed to one Hoy, who assumed and agreed to pay said mortgage.

Third. That Hoy in turn conveyed said realty to another grantee, and Hoy's grantee to another, and so on for several successive conveyances, each of the grantees respectively, by the express terms of the conveyances to them, taking the premises subject to said mortgage, but none of said grantees after Hoy assuming or agreeing to pay the mortgage.

Fourth. That Hoy or his grantees made all interest payments accruing to the maturity of the note, and that, when the note became due, the realty in question was owned by Clear Lake Security Company, a corporation, one of the grantees subsequent to Hoy; the legal title thereto being for the convenience of said corporation in the name of one E.E. Walseth, secretary of the corporation, the title of said corporation being subject to the mortgage aforesaid, but said corporation not having assumed or agreed to pay said mortgage.

Fifth. That on September 1, 1922, the realty being then owned by Clear Lake Security Company as aforesaid, plaintiff, without the knowledge or consent of defendants or any of them, orally agreed with the said corporation and its secretary Walseth as follows, to wit: That the plaintiff would extend the time of payment of the mortgage debt one year, that is, to July 29, 1923, in consideration whereof said corporation would immediately pay to the plaintiff, to apply on the principal of said mortgage debt, the sum of $500, together with interest thereon at 6 per cent. from July 29, 1922, to September 1, 1922, and that said corporation would pay to plaintiff on July 29, 1923, the sum of $2,500, being the remaining principal of the mortgage debt, together with interest thereon from July 29, 1922, to July 29, 1923, at 7 per cent., being 1 per cent. in excess of the amount specified in the note representing the mortgage debt, and that, pursuant to and in execution of said oral agreement, said corporation did pay to the plaintiff on September 1, 1922, the sum of $502.50 on said mortgage debt, being $500 on the principal and $2.50 on the interest.

Sixth. That at the time of making such payment the said E.E. Walseth, acting for himself and for said corporation, made a written memorandum of such payment and extension agreement in duplicate, one copy of which was delivered to and retained by plaintiff; said written memorandum being in the following form:

"No. 6357. Incorporated March, 1892.

"First National Bank, Capital and Surplus, $50,000.00. Clear Lake, South Dakota. J.A. Thronson, President, J.E. Walseth, Vice President, E.E. Walseth, Cashier, C.W. Force, Ass't Cashier, Arnold E. Berg, Ass't Cashier.

"Remittance Letter.

"Clear Lake, So. Dak., Sept. 1, 1922.

"Aug. Zastrow, City.

"Letter No. ———.

"We report collections and remit as follows: ———.

"Our No. 9316

"Your No.

"Name, W.W. Knight et al.

"Principal End 500.00

"Int. or Disc. 2.50

"Collection $502.50

"Int. on 400 7/1 to 9/1

"2500 Bal Extended 1 yr. 7%

"Our Charges: Commission _____.

"Our _____. We Credit your a/c $502.50

"Respectfully yours,

"E.E. Walseth, Cashier.

"Special attention by Bank Attorney if desired."

Seventh. That pursuant to said agreement said corporation and Walseth continued to pay interest on the balance of $2,500 principal of said mortgage debt at the rate of 7 per cent. per annum from July 29, 1922, to July 29, 1926, and made some partial interest payments thereafter computed at the rate of 7 per cent. per annum.

Defendants further alleged "that by reason of the facts aforesaid, defendants are not liable for the payment of said note or any part thereof," and prayed for the dismissal of the action, with costs.

To this answer plaintiff demurred upon the ground that the same did not state facts sufficient to constitute a defense to plaintiff's cause of action, and, the matter coming regularly on for hearing, the learned trial judge duly made and entered his order overruling said demurrer, from which order plaintiff has now appealed.

The rights and liabilities of the first grantee, Hoy, who assumed the mortgage, or of the intervening grantees between Hoy and Clear Lake Security Company (which for convenience will be hereinafter referred to as "the corporation"), are in no manner involved at the present time in this case. So far as the present proceeding is concerned, the rights and liabilities of plaintiff and respondents with reference to each other are exactly what they would have been if respondents, after the execution and delivery of the note and mortgage, had conveyed the premises directly to the corporation with the knowledge of appellant, the corporation taking title in the name of Walseth for convenience, and taking the premises subject to the mortgage, but not assuming or agreeing to pay the same, and thereafter the same transactions had been had between appellant and the corporation as are pleaded in the answer.

Though perhaps comparatively modern in origin, it is nevertheless today an established and universally accepted doctrine of the law of suretyship that a binding agreement between the creditor and the principal debtor, whereby the creditor extends the time for payment or performance, or agrees for a definite period to forbear or postpone the enforcement of his remedy, entirely discharges the surety, whether he is harmed thereby or not. This equitable doctrine is also applied to a number of situations which are not in any strict sense suretyship, but which partake in equitable nature of the suretyship relation. It is the clear weight of authority in this country now that, when a mortgagor conveys mortgaged realty to a grantee, who agrees with the mortgagor to assume and pay the mortgage, a quasi suretyship relation arises between such parties, and as between them the liability of the grantee upon his covenant of assumption is primary and the liability of the mortgagor becomes secondary. The equitable rights between the parties so situated are substantially the same as those between principal and surety, and, if the creditor (mortgagee) receives notice of the existence of such situation, then from that time forward he must observe the equities therefrom arising. If, after knowledge of such situation, the mortgagee, without the consent of the mortgagor, extends time to the assuming grantee, the mortgagor, upon the equitable principle above set out, is entirely discharged.

.   .   .

Respondents maintain that the foregoing doctrine, which is settled as the law of this state as above pointed out, is applicable to the instant case, even though the corporation did not assume and agree to pay the mortgage, but merely took subject to the mortgage. Appellant, on the other hand, contends, first, that there is no valid or binding extension agreement shown by the facts in this case between appellant and the corporation; and, second, that the foregoing doctrine has no application in any event, because the corporation merely took subject to the mortgage without assuming the payment thereof, and is a stranger to the mortgage debt, and an extension agreement between appellant and the corporation, even if valid as between them, would in no manner discharge respondents or affect appellant's rights against respondents on the mortgage debt. . . .

Assuming the validity of the extension agreement between appellant and the corporation, we come now to examine the effect of that agreement upon appellant's rights against respondent on the mortgage note. Respondents maintain that they are completely discharged. Appellant maintains that his rights against respondents upon the note are in no manner affected. We think neither position is entirely correct.

The fundamental reasons for granting an absolute discharge to the surety where the creditor without the consent of the surety extends time to the principal are twofold: First, that the risk of the surety is thereby increased; and, second, that the creditor has thereby limited the surety's right to pay at any time and proceed against the principal by way of subrogation.

It is the duty of the creditor to refrain from doing anything which would impair, delay, or defer the surety's right to pay at any time and proceed immediately against the principal by way of subrogation. When a mortgagor conveys to a grantee, who assumes and agrees to pay the mortgage, such grantee becomes personally liable for the debt. As between themselves, the assuming grantee becomes the principal debtor to the entire extent of the mortgage debt. The original mortgagor may pay the debt at any time when or after it becomes due, and is thereupon entitled by way of subrogation to the rights of the mortgagee to foreclose the mortgage and to proceed personally against the assuming grantee. If the mortgage creditor, with knowledge of that situation, extends time to the assuming grantee, he has impaired these rights of the original mortgagor, who is thereby immediately and completely discharged. Appellant argues that a grantee who takes subject to, but not assuming, the mortgage, does not become personally liable for the mortgage debt. This is undoubtedly true. Appellant therefore argues that, so far as concerns the mortgage debt, the grantee, under such circumstances, is a mere stranger and not a principal, and that an agreement by the creditor with a third person other than the principal for extension of time does not discharge a surety. It is probably true, as a matter of the law of suretyship, that the extension agreement on the part of the creditor which discharges the surety must be an agreement with the principal, or at least an agreement of which the principal has a legal right to avail himself.

Appellant, in urging that the grantee subject to the mortgage is a stranger to the mortgage debt, and therefore that an extension agreement with him does not affect the original mortgagor, overlooks the fact that to the extent of the value of the security such grantee is not a stranger to the transaction. Respondents, on the other hand, in urging that extension to the grantee under such circumstances entirely discharges the original mortgagor, fall equally into error by failing to observe that there is no relation analogous to principal and surety under such circumstances between the original mortgagor and the grantee subject to the mortgage to any other or further extent than the value of the transferred security.

The distinction between the rights and liabilities of a grantee assuming a mortgage and a grantee who merely takes subject to a mortgage without assuming the payment of the mortgage is quite plain. When the grantee assumes the mortgage debt as between the grantee and the mortgagor, not only is the land a primary fund for the payment of the debt, but likewise the personal liability thus assumed by the grantee. On the other hand, when the grantee merely takes subject to the mortgage, while it is true that the grantee assumes no personal liability whatever, nevertheless the security in his hands is liable for the payment of the mortgage debt, which liability as between the grantee and the mortgagor is primary. Therefore, to the extent of the value of such security properly applicable to the mortgage debt, the original mortgagor and the grantee subject to the mortgage stand in a relation one to another, which, while not a true suretyship, is nevertheless equitably analogous thereto and subject to the operation of the same principles. The original mortgagor is entitled to pay the debt at any time and to be immediately subrogated to the right of the mortgagee to foreclose the mortgage, although he has no personal claim against the grantee, and the mortgagee has no personal claim against such grantee to which the mortgagor could be subrogated.

The cases dealing with the effect on the liability of the original mortgagor of an extension given by a mortgagee to a grantee who took subject to, but without assuming, the mortgage have not been entirely unanimous. It has been held that the rights of the mortgagee against the mortgagor are not in any manner affected thereby, as appellant contends in this case. It has also been held that, under such circumstances, the mortgagor is released entirely, as respondents contend in this case.

The weight of authority, however, and we are convinced the sounder reasoning, is in favor of the view we have above indicated that, under such circumstances, the original mortgagor is released to the extent of the value of the security properly applicable to the mortgage debt in the hands of the grantee at the time the extension is granted. To this effect are Murray v. Marshall, 94 N.Y. (49 Sickels) 611. ... Murray v. Marshall, supra, is a leading case upon the question, and in that case the court said in part as follows:

"While, as we have said, no strict and technical relation of principal and surety arose between the mortgagor and his grantee from the conveyance subject to the mortgage, an equity did arise which could not be taken from the mortgagor without his consent, and which bears a very close resemblance to the equitable right of a surety, the terms of whose contract have been modified. We cannot accurately denominate the grantee a principal debtor, since he owes no debt, and is not personally a debtor at all, and yet, since the land is the primary fund for the payment of the debt, and so his property stands specifically liable to the extent of its value in exoneration of the bond, it is not inaccurate to say that as grantee, and in respect to the land, and to the extent of its value, he stands in the relation of a principal debtor, and to the same extent the grantor has the equities of a surety. ... When the mortgagor in this case sold expressly subject to the mortgage, remaining liable upon his bond, he had a right as against his grantee to require that the land should first be exhausted in the payment of the debt. ... When the creditor extended the time of payment by a valid agreement with the grantee, he at once, for the time being, took away the vendor's original right of subrogation. ... But it does not follow that the vendor was thereby wholly discharged. The grantee stood in the quasi relation of principal debtor only in respect to the land as the primary fund, and to the extent of the value of the land. If that value was less than the mortgage debt, as to the balance he owed no duty or obligation whatever, and as to that the mortgagor stood to the end, as he was at the beginning, the sole principal debtor. From any such balance he was not discharged, and as to that no right of his was in any manner disturbed. The measure of his injury was his right of subrogation, and that necessarily was bounded by the value of the land. The extension of time, therefore, operated to discharge him only to the extent of that value. At the moment of the extension his right of subrogation was taken away, and at that moment he was discharged to the extent of the value of the land, since the extension barred his recourse to it, and once discharged he could not again be made liable. . . ."

We are therefore of the opinion that by a valid and binding agreement appellant in the instant case precluded himself from resorting to the mortgage during the period September 1, 1922, to July 29, 1923. Immediately upon the making of that agreement, and by the making of it, appellant knowingly placed respondents, without their consent, where during that period of time they could not, if they desired, pay the mortgage debt and proceed immediately by way of subrogation to foreclose the mortgage. This was an interference by appellant with the rights of respondents which equity will not permit, and by the making of such agreement with the corporation appellant must be held to have discharged the respondents of liability upon the original mortgage debt, not entirely, but to the extent of the value of the land properly applicable to the mortgage debt on September 1, 1922.

The mortgage in question was a second mortgage in its inception. The answer does not allege how much value there was in the land on September 1, 1922, over and above prior incumbrances, if any still existed, properly applicable to the note here sued upon. To the extent of such value, if any, in view of the other allegations of the answer, respondents should stand discharged. The burden is upon respondents, however, to plead and prove such value in order to establish a defense pro tanto. There is nothing in the answer from which it is possible to determine to what extent, if at all, respondents were discharged by the conduct of appellant. The answer therefore fails to state facts sufficient to establish a defense to plaintiff's cause of action, and the order appealed from must be, and it is, reversed.

BROWN, P.J., and POLLEY, SHERWOOD, and BURCH, JJ., concur.

NOTE

The common law locked the mortgagee, mortgagor, and the mortgagor's assuming or nonassuming grantee into a complex triangle of rights and liabilities. These rules were formed in a different era, when personal liability on the mortgage note meant more than it does today, and much thus turned on whether the mortgagor's grantee assumed the mortgage. Anti-deficiency rules, fair value requirements, and other debtor protection provisions wrought by the depression of the 1930's dramatically altered the expectations of mortgagees, mortgagors and grantees respecting their personal rights and liabilities against each other. Changes in the form of home finance, from short term balloon mortgages to long term self-amortizing instruments, reinforced the new expectations.

One result of these changes is that rules like those expounded in *Zastrow* deserve fresh examination. Another result is that the rules just do not have the importance today that they once possessed. As personal liability has diminished, so too have the opportunities for mortgagees to pursue assuming grantees, and for mortgagors to proceed against their grantees.

b. Limitations on the Transferor

NELSON & WHITMAN, CONGRESSIONAL PREEMPTION OF MORTGAGE DUE–ON–SALE LAW: AN ANALYSIS OF THE GARN–ST GERMAIN ACT *

35 Hastings Law Journal, 241, 243–245, 247–254, 257–270, 273–275, 298–299 (1983).

The law of real property usually develops in an evolutionary fashion. Change is often measured in terms of decades and centuries rather than in months and years. Yet economic turmoil can accelerate this process. Just as the Great Depression of the 1930s spurred the enactment of mortgage moratoria and antideficiency legislation, so too has the inflationary economic climate of the 1970s and early 1980s engendered new mortgage law.

The major focus of this latter period has been on the due-on-sale clause, a mortgage provision that affords the mortgagee the right to accelerate the mortgage debt and to foreclose if the mortgaged real estate is transferred without the mortgagee's consent.[2] While the clause is sometimes used to protect mortgagees against transfers that endanger mortgage security or increase the risk of default, its major purpose is to enable mortgagees to recall lower-than-market interest rate loans during periods of rising interest rates. Because its use in this context pits lenders against borrowers and real estate buyers, the clause has become a major economic, political, and legal issue. It has been confronted and evaluated by most state supreme courts, many legislatures, certain federal regulatory agencies, the United States Supreme Court, and ultimately Congress. It has also been the subject of a great deal of scholarly commentary.

Given recent economic conditions, this close scrutiny is hardly surprising. Due to high interest rates and the limited availability of home financing, large numbers of potential home buyers have been excluded from the housing market. For many purchasers, the assumption of an existing lower-than-market interest mortgage has represented one of the few practical financing alternatives. The financial climate has also made it much more difficult for owners to sell. Many sellers have been forced either to reduce significantly the price of their properties to enable buyers to qualify for institutional high-interest

---

* © Copyright 1983 Grant S. Nelson and Dale A. Whitman. An updated and complete version of these materials appears in G. Nelson & D. Whitman, Real Estate Finance Law §§ 5.21–5.26 (4th ed. 1985).

2. A typical due-on-sale clause provides: "If all or any part of the Property or an interest therein is sold or transferred by Borrower without Lender's prior written consent, ... Lender may, at Lender's option, declare all the sums secured by this mortgage to be due and payable." Federal National Mortgage Association/Federal Home Loan Mortgage Corporation Mortgage, Clause 17 (one to four family) [hereinafter cited as FNMA/FHLMC Mortgage].

financing, or to suffer an effective price reduction by financing part of the purchase price themselves at lower-than-market interest rates. Thus, for those sellers with lower-than-market interest rate mortgages on their properties, assumability of the mortgage may be the key to obtaining a higher asking price for the property.

On the other hand, the economic stake of institutional lenders in upholding due-on-sale clauses is also great. During the past several years many institutional lenders, especially savings and loan associations, have experienced severe economic difficulty. Because they hold portfolios that include large numbers of fixed rate, lower-yielding mortgage loans, they have been hard pressed to pay the higher short-term rates demanded by depositors. Many savings and loan associations and similar institutions have failed, and others remain in precarious financial positions. Because the due-on-sale clause provides one means of eliminating lower-interest mortgage loans from institutional portfolios, and does so without resort to expensive federal "bailout" or other subsidy schemes, its enforceability has been deemed important for the economic health of the thrift industry. ...

The Other Types of Mortgage Transfer Restrictions

Due-on-Encumbrance Restrictions

Mortgages may restrict mortgagor transfers by means other than a due-on-sale clause. For example, a mortgage may contain a clause authorizing the mortgagee to accelerate the debt if the mortgagor "further encumbers" the mortgaged real estate. Such language is usually referred to as a "due-on-encumbrance" provision. While due-on-encumbrance language is often included as part of a due-on-sale clause, it is not uncommon for a mortgage to contain a separate due-on-encumbrance clause. Unlike the due-on-sale situation, in which the mortgagee's desire to increase the interest rate predominates, due-on-encumbrance language is utilized mainly to protect against impairment of mortgage security by a debtor who incurs a junior mortgage debt and thus reduces his or her economic stake in the mortgaged real estate. However, the due-on-encumbrance clause probably is used much less frequently than its due-on-sale counterpart.

Increased-Interest-on-Transfer Clauses

Another provision closely related to the due-on-sale clause authorizes the mortgagee to increase or adjust the mortgage interest rate in the event of a transfer by the mortgagor. We refer to this as an "increased-interest-on-transfer" clause. This type of clause fulfills the same economic function as the due-on-sale clause in that it enables the mortgagee to use a transfer by the mortgagor as the basis for increasing the interest yield on the mortgage. However, unlike a due-on-sale clause, it does not confer on the mortgagee an absolute right to accelerate the mortgage debt upon a transfer; hence it gives no direct protection against transfer to an uncreditworthy buyer. Only if the transferee fails to pay the increased mortgage payments will there be grounds for declaration of a default and acceleration of the debt.

Installment Land Contract Prohibitions on Transfer

Transfer restrictions may also appear in installment land contracts, which are probably the most commonly used mortgage substitute. Known in many areas of the country as a "contract for deed" or "long term land contract," the installment land contract performs the same economic function as a purchase-money mortgage: it provides seller financing of all or part of the unpaid real estate purchase price. Vendors often find the installment land contract attractive because of its forfeiture clause—language specifying that "time is of the essence" and that upon vendee default in payment or other contract obligations the vendor has the option to terminate the contract, retake possession of the premises, and retain all prior payments as liquidated damages. However, in many jurisdictions legislatures and courts have placed restrictions on the forfeiture remedy, especially when the vendee has acquired substantial equity in the property. Other jurisdictions have gone so far as to treat the installment land contract as a mortgage, thus affording the vendee the traditional substantive and procedural rights of a mortgagor, including the right to a public sale after a judicial foreclosure proceeding.

Installment land contracts frequently include a provision that prohibits assignment by the vendee without the vendor's permission. Violation of such a provision constitutes a default and might result in vendor termination of the contract and loss of the purchaser's equity. In this respect the provision differs from a due-on-sale clause, under which an unapproved transfer will at most trigger an acceleration of the mortgage debt and, if the accelerated debt is unpaid, a public foreclosure sale of the mortgaged real estate.

Events Triggering Acceleration

A common question is what kind of event will trigger acceleration of a debt under a due-on-sale or other transfer restriction clause. While some early clauses used a "sale" alone as the triggering event, most of the recent forms employ broader language, often modeled after the mortgage form specified for use by lenders who sell mortgages to the Federal National Mortgage Association (FNMA) and the Federal Home Loan Mortgage Corporation (FHLMC). This language refers to a transfer of any part of the property or any interest in it. Under such language, in principle at least, even a short-term lease or a grant of an easement or other limited interest in the land would suffice to trigger the lender's right to accelerate.

Perhaps the most significant question is whether a sale by installment land contract permits acceleration. The answer depends on the exact wording of the clause in question, but under broad language like that of the FNMA/FHLMC clause the courts have nearly uniformly permitted acceleration.

Judicial Responses to Mortgagor Transfer
Restrictions Before the Act

Due-on-Sale Clauses

Due-on-sale clauses have come under judicial attack as unreasonable restraints on alienation. Traditionally, a direct restraint on alienation has been viewed by many courts as invalid per se unless the restraint falls within certain limited exceptions. Under a minority approach, a direct restraint is void unless the policy underlying its purpose outweighs the degree of restraint imposed on the property interest. Indirect restraints, on the other hand, are generally deemed valid if they are reasonable. An indirect restraint is one that arises "when an attempt is made to accomplish some purpose other than the restraint on alienability, but with the incidental result that ... [it] would restrain practical alienability." [40] Thus, a mortgage that provides for forfeiture of the mortgaged real estate to the mortgagee upon an impermissible transfer probably constitutes a direct restraint. To the extent that the mortgagee is able to enforce, through specific performance or injunctive relief, a mortgagor's promise not to convey without the mortgagee's consent, a promissory and presumably direct restraint exists. ...

The vast majority of courts has been unconcerned about classifying the clause into traditional "restraint" categories. No court has held that a due-on-sale clause is per se unlawful as a restraint on alienation. Indeed, some courts have suggested that it is not a restraint on alienation at all. While many courts probably view the clause as an indirect restraint on alienation, all courts recognize that there are circumstances in which enforcement of the clause is reasonable and thus permissible. Some courts, however, are more sympathetic to enforcement than others, and two broad judicial approaches to the clause have emerged.

Under the predominant judicial approach, the clause is deemed per se reasonable unless the borrower can show that the lender engaged in unconscionable conduct. The courts employing this approach have recognized the desirability of protecting the mortgagee from the vagaries of the interest rate market. The mortgagee need not establish that a proposed transfer would impair security; the validity of the due-on-sale clause is not normally judged by the facts of an individual case. Under one variant of this approach, such facts are relevant only to the extent that the mortgagor attempts to meet the burden of proving that enforcement is unconscionable or inequitable in his or her case. An increase in the market interest rate is not usually thought sufficient to meet this burden, and due-on-sale clauses in such jurisdictions are usually enforced.

Under the minority approach, enforcement of due-on-sale clauses must be reasonable in individual cases, necessitating a case-by-case

---

40. L. Simes & A. Smith, The Law of Future Interests § 1112, at 5 (2d ed. 1956).

determination. Under this approach, the mortgagee's desire to increase interest rates is not considered a sufficient reason to justify the clause. The mortgagee has the burden to establish reasonableness, and normally must establish that the transfer would result in security impairment or an increased risk of default. As a practical matter, lenders have rarely sought due-on-sale enforcement in jurisdictions that follow this approach.

Some of the courts that apply the majority approach display a concern that the borrower be fairly warned that the clause can be employed to exact a higher interest rate upon transfer, and insist that language explicitly stating that possibility be included in the documents. There may well be a valid need for such a warning; the FNMA/FHLMC clause, for example, is extraordinarily technical and difficult for a lay reader to follow, and its implication that a higher interest rate may result from a transfer is oblique at best. One court has been even more punctilious, requiring that the clause be inserted in the promissory note and not merely in the mortgage.

As noted above, majority or "automatic enforcement" jurisdictions often state that due-on-sale clauses are unenforceable when the mortgagor can establish that enforcement would be "unconscionable" or "inequitable." While it is difficult to articulate precisely when due-on-sale clauses will be so categorized, it is probable that most courts will be unwilling to enforce the clauses in "non-substantive" or "non-sale" transfers. For example, one court has indicated that enforcement should be denied in situations such as transfers to a spouse who becomes a co-owner, transfers to a spouse incidental to a marriage dissolution proceeding or settlement, and transfers to an inter vivos trust of which the mortgagor is a beneficiary. This principle is recognized in the FNMA/FHLMC form due-on-sale clause, which specifically exempts transfers "by devise, descent or by operation of law upon the death of a joint tenant." ...

State Legislative Regulation of Mortgage Transfer Restrictions Before the Act

Several states have imposed legislative limitations on due-on-sale clauses. While the details of these statutes vary considerably, they commonly prohibit due-on-sale enforcement in residential mortgages unless the mortgagee can establish that a transfer would impair mortgage security. Most of the statutes permit the mortgagee to condition transfer of the property upon payment of a limited "assumption fee" or upon an increase in the mortgage interest rate by a modest amount, usually no more than one percent. Some of the statutes impose similar restrictions on increased-interest-on-transfer provisions. In addition, at least one state, Iowa, confers generous post-foreclosure redemption rights when real estate is foreclosed incident to enforcement of a due-on-sale clause.[77]

77. See Iowa Code Ann. § 535.8(2)(e) (West Supp.1982). While normally an Iowa mortgagor has only a one year post-sale redemption right, id. § 628.3 (West

A few other states legislatively prohibit due-on-sale enforcement in "non-substantive" and certain non-sale transfers. In California, for example, acceleration is prohibited in residential mortgages when there is a transfer to a spouse resulting from the death of the mortgagor, to a spouse who becomes a co-owner, to a spouse incident to a marriage dissolution, or to an inter vivos trust of which the mortgagor is a beneficiary. In addition, some statutes deny enforcement of due-on-encumbrance clauses in a variety of residential housing settings.

Federal Regulation of Due-on-Sale Clauses Before the Act

In 1976 the Federal Home Loan Bank Board (Board), the federal agency that regulates federally-chartered and federally-insured savings and loan associations, became concerned about the increasing controversy over whether federally-chartered associations had the authority to enforce due-on-sale clauses. The Board issued a regulation effective July 31, 1976 (1976 Regulation) which provided that a federal association

> continues to have the power to include ... a provision in its loan instrument whereby the association may, at its option, declare immediately due and payable sums secured by the association's security instrument if all or any part of the real property securing the loan is sold or transferred by the borrower without the association's prior written consent.[81]

Except as provided in paragraph (g) of the regulation, the Board authorized federal associations to exercise the due-on-sale option and provided that all rights and remedies of the association and borrower "shall be exclusively governed by the terms of the loan contract." [82] Paragraph (g) prohibited due-on-sale enforcement in certain "non-substantive" transfers of mortgagor-occupied homes resulting from junior liens, purchase-money security interests in household appliances, transfers by devise, descent, or operation of law upon the death of a joint tenant, and leaseholds for less than three years with no option to purchase. In the preamble to the 1976 Regulation the Board also expressed its intent that the due-on-sale practices of federal associations be governed exclusively by federal law, and emphasized that federal

---

1950), when foreclosure of a mortgage on real property results from the enforcement of a due-on-sale clause, the mortgagor may redeem the real property at any time within three years from the day of sale, id. § 535.8(2)(e) (West Supp.1982). In the meantime, the mortgagor is entitled to possession of the property and for the first thirty months after the sale, the right of redemption is exclusive. Id. The time for redemption by creditors is extended to thirty-three months in any case in which the mortgagor's period for redemption is extended. Id. This statute represents a significant burden on lenders.

This type of redemption should not be confused with "equitable redemption," available in every state, which allows the mortgagor and junior lienors to pay off a mortgage in default at any time until a valid foreclosure sale has occurred.

81. 12 C.F.R. § 545.8–3(f) (1983).

82. Id.

associations "shall not be bound by or subject to any conflicting state law which imposes different ... due-on-sale requirements." [84]

A similar regulation was promulgated in 1978 by the National Credit Union Administration (NCUA) to apply to due-on-sale clauses in federal credit union mortgages. The NCUA regulation went beyond the 1976 Board Regulation by specifically requiring federal credit unions to utilize due-on-sale clauses as well as preempting state restrictions on due-on-sale clause enforcement.

While lower federal courts concluded that the 1976 Board Regulation foreclosed the application of state due-on-sale law to federal associations, a few state courts reached contrary results. Ultimately, this conflict was resolved by the United States Supreme Court in Fidelity First Federal Savings & Loan Association v. de la Cuesta, [89] a case that addressed the effect of the 1976 Regulation on California law. California generally limited due-on-sale enforcement to situations in which impairment of mortgage security was established. In *de la Cuesta,* the Supreme Court held that: 1) the Board intended to preempt state law; 2) the 1976 Regulation in fact conflicted with California law, despite the fact that it merely authorized, and did not require, federal associations to utilize due-on-sale clauses; 3) the Board acted within its statutory authority under section 5(a) of the Home Owner's Loan Act, which authorized the Board to promulgate rules for the operation and regulation of federal associations; and 4) although the 1976 Regulation's merits might be debatable, it was a reasonable, and therefore a valid, exercise of the Board's authority.

The *de la Cuesta* Court did not address the enforceability of due-on-sale clauses included in the mortgage loans made by federal associations before the effective date of the 1976 Board Regulation. The Board had issued an earlier regulation that one federal court held sufficient to preempt contrary state due-on-sale law as to pre-1976 Regulation loans. Also, the 1976 Regulation specified that a federal association *"continues"* to have the power to include due-on-sale clauses in their mortgages. Although this language may have represented bureaucratic timidity in dealing with the retroactivity issue, it can be argued that it signified the Board's view that it had already preempted state law before 1976. The Supreme Court in *de la Cuesta,* however, expressly avoided reaching the retroactivity question. While *de la Cuesta* confirmed the validity of the Board's response to the needs of federally-chartered savings associations with respect to due-on-sale clauses, it did nothing for other types of lenders. Therefore, these lenders sought a uniform national solution: congressional preemption of state laws restricting the enforcement of due-on-sale clauses.

The Garn-St. Germain Depository Institutions Act of 1982

The enactment of section 341 of the Garn-St. Germain Depository

---

84. 41 Fed.Reg. 18,286, 18,287 (1976). **89.** 458 U.S. 141 (1982).

Institutions Act of 1982 (Act) [101] signaled the dawn of a new era for due-on-sale clause enforcement. The Act broadly preempts state laws that restrict the enforcement of due-on-sale clauses, thereby making such clauses generally enforceable.

Yet Congress responded to effective lobbying by the real estate brokerage industry and related interests by softening the impact of the Act in most states that previously restricted due-on-sale enforcement. To accomplish this, Congress created complex exceptions to the preemption based on so-called "window periods," and conferred authority on states with window periods to enact legislation to avoid the impact of the Act on certain mortgage loans. In so doing, Congress created a host of important and difficult interpretation problems. Congress delegated to the Board the authority to issue regulations interpreting the Act, and in April, 1983, the Board issued a final regulation entitled "Preemption of State Due-on-Sale Laws" (Regulation).[106] The following sections of this Article analyze the more important provisions of the Act and Regulation, their scope, and the complex problems of interpretation they have engendered. We consider whether the Regulation reflects congressional intent, and to what extent the Act and Regulation achieve sound public policy goals.

Lenders Covered

The Act covers any "person or government agency making a real property loan." [107] According to the Regulation, the foregoing definition includes,

> without limitation, individuals, Federal associations, state-chartered savings and loan associations, national banks, state-chartered banks and state-chartered mutual savings banks, Federal credit unions, state-chartered credit unions, mortgage banks, insurance companies and finance companies which make real property loans, manufactured-home retailers who extend credit, agencies of the Federal government, [and] any lender approved by the Secretary of Housing and Urban Development for participation in any mortgage insurance program under the National Housing Act.[108]

The Board emphasized that the foregoing list is "intended to be representative and not exclusive." [109] Consequently, every mortgagee, whether a natural person, business entity, or government agency, is covered by the Act. ...

Loans Covered

The Act covers every "loan, mortgage, advance, or credit sale secured by a lien on real property, the stock allocated to a dwelling unit

---

101. 12 U.S.C. § 1701j–3 (1982).

106. 48 Fed.Reg. 21,554 (1983) (to be codified at 12 C.F.R. 591).

107. 12 U.S.C. § 1701j–3(a)(2) (1982). Also included is "any assignee or transferee, in whole or in part, of such a person or agency."

108. 48 Fed.Reg. 21,561 (1983) (to be codified at 12 C.F.R. § 591.2(g)).

109. 48 Fed.Reg. 21,555 (1983) (definitions section of the Regulation).

in a cooperative housing corporation, or a residential manufactured home, whether real or personal property." [116]   Although the Act makes no reference to mortgages on leasehold interests, the Regulation provides that a loan is secured by a lien on real property if it is made on the "security of any instrument ... which makes ... a leasehold or subleasehold ... specific security for payment of the obligation secured by the instrument." [117]   ...

Types of Mortgage Transfer Restrictions Covered

The Act preempts state law only with respect to due-on-sale clauses that "authoriz[e] a lender, at its option, to declare due and payable sums secured by the lender's security instrument if all or any part of the property, or an interest therein, securing the real property loan is sold or transferred without the lender's prior written consent." [125]   The Regulation adopts this statutory definition virtually unchanged.

Presumably the Act is inapplicable to an increased-interest-on-transfer clause because that type of clause confers on the lender only the right to modify or increase the interest rate upon a sale or transfer and not the "option to declare [the debt] due and payable." Consequently, every state is probably free to make increased-interest-on-transfer provisions unenforceable. This result is bizarre, for such clauses have an economic effect similar to that of the due-on-sale clauses. Nevertheless, the practical effect of excluding increased-interest-on-transfer provisions from the scope of the Act is unlikely to be substantial. Mortgagees can simply include due-on-sale language in any mortgages executed after the Act's effective date. As to pre-Act loans, few state courts are likely to exercise their freedom. In states that follow an automatic enforcement approach to the due-on-sale clause, courts are unlikely to restrict enforcement of an increased-interest-on-transfer provision, as it is the less burdensome of the two clauses. Even in states that impose substantial restrictions on due-on-sale clause enforcement, courts that have addressed the issue have been less hostile toward enforcement of increased-interest-on-transfer clauses. Courts in these latter states are thus not likely to take advantage of this "loophole" in the Act's preemptive effect.

One could draft mortgage language that would fall outside the Act's definition of a due-on-sale clause. For example, a provision for *automatic* acceleration upon transfer seems to be outside the definition, which speaks of the lender's "option" to accelerate. Similarly, a clause that merely makes an unapproved transfer by the mortgagor a default, but says nothing about acceleration, may fall outside the Act. However, this argument is weakened if the mortgage or note also contains a standard acceleration-for-default clause that the courts could read together with the no-transfer clause to find the equivalent of a due-on-sale clause. These illustrations should have little practical importance,

---

116. 12 U.S.C. § 1701j–3(a)(3) (1982).

117. 48 Fed.Reg. 21,561 (1983) (to be codified at 12 C.F.R. § 591.2(h)).

125. 12 U.S.C. § 1701j–3(a)(1) (1982).

since in post-Act mortgages well-advised lenders will simply refrain from using such uncommon and idiosyncratic language. An occasional pre-Act document may raise this sort of problem, but the number of documents with such non-standard clauses is small. In any event, only clauses in states that restrict due-on-sale enforcement potentially pose a problem. In overall economic terms, then, the Act's narrow definition of a due-on-sale clause is likely to be of little importance.

Coverage of Installment Land Contracts

While the Act itself does not specifically mention installment land contracts, its preemption does apply to any "loan, mortgage, advance, or credit sale secured by a lien on real property." [131] Does an install-ment contract vendor retain a "lien on real property," as well as legal title? The Regulation answers affirmatively,[132] and is probably correct. While a few courts have had conceptual difficulty with the notion that one can have legal title to land and a lien on it simultaneously, there is substantial authority that the installment land contract vendor retains a "vendor's lien" for the unpaid purchase price. Moreover, courts are increasingly equating installment land contracts with mortgages, and requiring foreclosure as the vendor's primary remedy. In such cases the vendor is surely foreclosing a "lien." Finally, while the analytical underpinnings for their decisions are not always clear, numerous courts routinely afford the vendor the option to foreclose an installment land contract as a mortgage. This practice constitutes a persuasive argu-ment that the contract vendor is also a "lienor."

The conclusion that the Act's preemption applies to installment land contracts does not mean that a violation of a contract prohibition on transfer will necessarily result in a forfeiture of the vendee's interest. When no-transfer provisions are upheld, it is likely that foreclosure of the contract will instead be ordered, and then only after the vendee has been afforded the opportunity to pay off the contract balance. The Act does not appear to change this. Literally, it only validates "due-on-sale" clauses—those that authorize the acceleration of the debt when the real estate is transferred without the lender's consent. A prohibi-tion on transfer that purports to go beyond simple acceleration, and defines the remedies (such as forfeiture) to be imposed on the vendee, is unaffected by the Act and is thus still subject to pre-Act state law. It is highly improbable that a state court would enforce forfeiture, with its harsh consequences, simply because a transfer was made without the vendor's consent. A more likely judicial response would be to permit foreclosure of the contract as a mortgage. Such an approach would not be inconsistent with the policy inherent in the Act.

131. 12 U.S.C. § 1701j–3(a)(3) (1982).

132. 48 Fed.Reg. 21,561 (1983) (to be codified at 12 C.F.R. § 591.2(h)) ("'loan se-cured by a lien on real property' means a loan on the security of any instrument (whether a mortgage, deed of trust, or *land contract*) which makes the interest in real property (whether in fee or on a leasehold or subleasehold) specific security for the payment of the obligation secured by the instrument") (emphasis added).

Time of Transfer

The Act applies to all mortgage *loans,* whether consummated before or after October 15, 1982, the effective date of the Act. However, a *transfer* is covered only if it is made after the Act's effective date. Although the Act itself does not state this, this conclusion is supported by the well-settled rule that a statute has only prospective effect unless Congress evinces a clear intent that it have retroactive effect. Congress indicated no such intent regarding the Act. Note, however, that federally-chartered savings and loan associations have the authority to enforce due-on-sale clauses as to many pre-Act transfers by virtue of the 1976 Regulation upheld in the *de la Cuesta* case. The Act itself recognizes this authority.

The application of the Act can be illustrated as follows. Suppose that on March 1, 1982, MR transferred mortgaged real estate located in State X to Grantee in violation of a due-on-sale clause contained in the mortgage executed in 1980. During early 1983, ME (a state-chartered lender) accelerated the debt and commenced judicial foreclosure proceedings. Because the transfer took place before October 15, 1982, the Act is inapplicable and the State X court is free to apply state law to such pre-Act transfers.

While the Act is inapplicable to pre-Act transfers, it is retroactive in the sense that it governs mortgage loans executed prior to the Act's effective date. Thus, if in the previous example the property had been mortgaged in 1980, but the transfer had taken place on December 20, 1982, the Act would have applied, and the due-on-sale clause would have been enforceable. ...

Transfers in Which Due-on-Sale Enforcement is Prohibited

The Act expressly enumerates several types of transfers that may not be used as the basis for due-on-sale acceleration. The list is similar, but not identical, to the analogous provisions of the FNMA/FHLMC mortgage form and the 1976 FHLBB regulations. It includes:

1) the creation of a lien or other encumbrance subordinate to the lender's security instrument which does not relate to a transfer of rights of occupancy in the property;

2) the creation of a purchase money security interest for household appliances;

3) a transfer by devise, descent, or operation of law on the death of a joint tenant or tenant by the entirety;

4) the granting of a leasehold interest of three years or less not containing an option to purchase;

5) a transfer to a relative resulting from the death of a borrower;

6) a transfer where the spouse or children of the borrower become an owner of the property;

7) a transfer resulting from a decree of a dissolution of marriage, legal separation agreement, or from an incidental property settle-

ment agreement, by which the spouse of the borrower becomes an owner of the property;

8) a transfer into an inter vivos trust in which the borrower is and remains a beneficiary and which does not relate to a transfer of rights of occupancy in the property; or

9) any other transfer or disposition described in regulations prescribed by the Federal Home Loan Bank Board.[152]

When a transfer of one of these types is involved, the Act is preemptive: acceleration under a due-on-sale clause is prohibited even if permitted by state law. Moreover, these prohibitions apply on their face to all types of loan documents.

Most of these transfers fall within the "non-substantive" or "non-sale" category considered earlier, as to which due-on-sale enforcement probably would be impermissible under state law. Not all of these transfers, however, can be so categorized. For example, in item (1) above, the Act prohibits due-on-sale enforcement upon the creation of a junior lien if no transfer of occupancy is involved. Suppose a first mortgage on a shopping center contains a prohibition on further encumbrances without the mortgagee's consent. If the mortgagor borrows money for a non-business purpose and gives the lender a junior mortgage on the center, the Act appears to prohibit acceleration. This is true even if the first mortgagee can establish that the junior lien will increase the risk of mortgagor default or will impair the security of its mortgage. This result may come as an unpleasant surprise to countless mortgage lenders who rely on the due-on-encumbrance concept in a variety of commercial lending contexts. ...

The Exemption for Window Period Loans

As a result of pressure from the real estate brokerage industry and a desire to protect the reasonable expectations of borrowers who believed that they had acquired "assumable" loans for purposes of future resale, Congress provided partial relief from the Act's preemption. Thus, in some states the Act's effect is deferred and state law continues to govern enforcement of certain due-on-sale clauses. This was accomplished through creation of "window periods," which give rise to the postponement of the Act's preemptions. The concept of window periods is complex, and is not clearly defined in the Act or susceptible to easy explanation.

A state may be a window period state if it restricted enforcement of due-on-sale clauses before the Act. The window period in such a state began when the state first restricted enforcement of due-on-sale clauses, and ended when the state ended such restrictions, or upon passage of the Act. Certain loans in a state that had a window period may remain assumable for three years if they would have been assumable under state law prior to the passage of the Act. This three-year deferral

---

152. 12 U.S.C. § 1701j–3(d) (1982).

period began on October 15, 1982, (the effective date of the Act), and will continue until October 15, 1985.[181] Only states that "prohibited the exercise of due-on-sale clauses" [182] before the effective date of the Act qualify for window period treatment and the three year extension. To qualify, a state must have prohibited exercise of the due-on-sale clause by a statute, its constitution, or a decision of its highest court (or if no such decision, a decision by the state's next highest appellate court whose decisions apply statewide).

However, not all loans in states qualifying for window period treatment will remain assumable for this three year period. Only loans that were "made or assumed" between the date of the state's prohibition of enforcement of the due-on-sale clause and October 15, 1982, will be governed by state law and thus remain assumable.[184] The Regulation defines "assumed" to include transfers under which a grantee takes "subject to" the mortgage but does not agree to be personally liable for the mortgage debt.[185]

The window period concept can be best understood through factual examples. Suppose State X enacted a statute on July 1, 1979, limiting due-on-sale enforcement in mortgages on single family dwellings to situations in which the mortgagee can establish impairment of mortgage security. MR purchased his house on September 1, 1980, and simultaneously executed a mortgage on it that contained a due-on-sale clause. If MR sells his house on April 1, 1984, to Grantee, the mortgage will be assumable by Grantee unless the mortgagee can establish that the transfer would impair mortgage security. This would also be true if MR had assumed an existing mortgage on September 1, 1980, rather than obtaining a new loan, since the assumption would have occurred after July 1, 1979, the effective date of the state statute. Finally, the transferees of Grantee, if any, will be able to assume the mortgage so long as the transfer takes place prior to October 15, 1985, and the mortgagee is not able to establish that such a transfer impairs mortgage security.

Although the Board was requested to identify the states that qualify for window period treatment, it declined to do so on the ground that Congress intended window period determinations to be left to "state interpretation and state judicial decision." [187] However, the Board anticipates that its Office of General Counsel will, from time to time, issue advisory opinions with respect to state window period questions. . . .

Special Rules Under the Act for Certain Federally-Chartered Lenders

As noted earlier, federally-chartered savings and loan associations have had the pre-Act power to enforce due-on-sale clauses by virtue of

181. 12 U.S.C. § 1701j–3(c)(1) (1982).
182. Id.
184. Id.

185. 48 Fed.Reg. 21,561 (1983) (to be codified at 12 C.F.R. § 591.2(a)).
187. Id.

the 1976 Bank Board regulation upheld in *de la Cuesta*. The Act, with minor modifications, simply continues that power. Moreover, while prior to the Act some doubt existed as to the enforceability of due-on-sale clauses in pre-1976 regulation mortgage loans, the Act's preemption definitely applies to such clauses, which are now clearly enforceable. Neither the window period concept nor a window period state's ability to "otherwise regulate" window period loans is applicable to such federal associations. Thus, so far as any post-Act transfer is concerned, federal associations are entirely free of state due-on-sale law.

With respect to national banks and federal credit unions, window period loans originated by these lenders are subject to state law until October 15, 1985, unless the Comptroller of the Currency (Comptroller) or the National Credit Union Administration (NCUA) acts prior to that date otherwise to regulate these loans. Thus, the Comptroller or the NCUA has the power to either extend or contract the time period in which these loans are subject to state law. The NCUA acted, effective November 18, 1982, to render immediately enforceable due-on-sale clauses in transfers made on or after that date. In effect, the NCUA's rules preempt state law, regardless of the reasonable expectations of the consumers in states that would otherwise have had assumable window period loans.

The Comptroller's rule, effective December 8, 1983, is similar to the NCUA rule but is more lenient to owners of one to four family homes who obtained or assumed loans during a window period. Until April 15, 1984, such loans can be assumed to the extent allowed by state law, except that the lender may increase the interest rate to a "blended" level that is the average of the original contract rate and the current average contract interest rate on existing homes, as published by the Board. For other types of loans, the full federal preemption is effective immediately.

NOTES

1. *Due on Sale Clauses.* Before Garn-St. Germain was enacted, states took two distinct approaches to due on sale clauses, each embodying longstanding policy preferences that had evolved in contexts outside mortgage law. One group of states invoked the principle of freedom of alienation and put the burden on the lender to demonstrate that circumstances justified enforcement of the clause. Other states invoked the principle of freedom of contract and put the burden on the borrower to demonstrate that enforcement was not justified. For a pre-Garn survey of the different approaches, see A.B.A. Comm. on Real Estate Financing, Enforcement of Due-on-Transfer Clauses, 13 Real Prop., Probate & Trust J. 891 (1978).

States following the freedom of contract approach gave no single rationale or benchmark for requiring the borrower to demonstrate that enforcement of the due on sale clause was unjustified. In Mutual Federal Sav. & Loan Ass'n v. Wisconsin Wire Works, 71 Wis.2d 531, 239

N.W.2d 20 (1976), one of the leading cases endorsing due on sale clauses, the Wisconsin Supreme Court observed that "impairment of security, although an important factor, is not conclusive in the balancing of equities." To the argument that the security was unimpaired because all debt service had been paid and no waste had been committed, the court answered: "[B]asic to the theory of impairment of security is that the lender not only makes a value judgment as to the adequacy of the physical security but also relies upon its evaluation of the business character and reputation of the borrower in determining whether the loan should be made and the rate of interest to be charged. Likewise, if the lender in his evaluation of the business character and reputation of a subsequent obligor believes collection may be more difficult and foreclosure more probable than in the case of the original borrower, even though the physical security may be adequate, the lender may properly rely upon this fact in electing whether to exercise its option in a 'due on sale' clause." 239 N.W.2d at 24.

Other states accepted the rationale that due on sale clauses properly enable lenders to adjust their loan portfolios to rising interest rates. In Malouff v. Midland Federal Sav. & Loan Ass'n, 181 Colo. 294, 509 P.2d 1240 (1973), the Colorado Supreme Court accepted the need to adjust interest rates as an independent justification for enforcement, resting its decision in part on an affidavit, submitted by a vice president of defendant lender, projecting the consequences of a decision for plaintiff: "If lenders were unable to make some form of interest rate adjustments on long-term loans, they would have to make only short-term loans amortized over periods of less than ten years. Original borrowers then would not be able to pay off their home purchases without having to refinance their indebtedness one or more times in the process. Short term loans would also increase monthly payments and make the obtaining of such loans prohibitive to many people." 181 Colo. at 302, 509 P.2d at 1245.

2. *Applications.* After the validation of due on sale clauses by Garn St Germain, various issues remain concerning their interpretation and application. First, when is the clause triggered? Federal regulations promulgated after Garn St Germain state that the exercise of a due on sale clause "shall be exclusively governed by the terms of the loan contract." 12 C.F.R. §§ 591.3, 591.4 (1991). A sale or transfer is defined as "the conveyance of real property of [sic, read or] any right, title or interest therein, whether legal or equitable, whether voluntary or involuntary, by outright sale, deed, installment sale contract, land contract, contract for deed, leasehold interest with a term greater than three years, lease-option contract or any other method of conveyance of real property interests." 12 C.F.R. § 591.2(b) (1991). Under this language, would the execution of an executory contract of sale be a "sale or transfer"? See generally Roszowski, Drafting Around Mortgage Due–On–Sale Clauses: The Dangers of Playing Hide and Seek, 21 Real Prop. Probate & Trust J. 23 (1986).

The mortgage may only give the lender a limited due on sale clause, in an effort by the borrower to pass on a favorable loan to a subsequent buyer. Thus, a lender may only have the right to require that the loan be paid upon transfer of the property if the lender did not give prior written approval to the sale. In Western Life Insurance Company v. McPherson K.M.P., 702 F.Supp. 836 (D.Kan.1988), the mortgage contained such a clause but provided that the lender could not unreasonably withhold consent. The court found that consent was not unreasonably withheld where the mortgagor did not make a formal request for approval and failed to provide any detailed financial information concerning the buyer. If the clause does not have a reasonableness requirement, will the court imply one? Compare Quintana v. First Interstate Bank of Albuquerque, 105 N.M. 784, 737 P.2d 896 (App.1987) (declining to imply a reasonableness standard and permitting absolute discretion) with the Uniform Land Security Interest Act § 108 (imposing an obligation of good faith in every contract or duty governed by the statute).

3. *Prepayment Penalties.* The due on sale clause is not the only device that mortgage lenders employ to protect themselves against interest rate fluctuations. Commonly, a mortgage note will also include a prepayment penalty—often six months' interest—payable in the event the mortgagor seeks to repay the loan before maturity. Typically a mortgagor will seek to prepay when interest rates drop below the rate agreed upon in his mortgage instrument and refinancing becomes attractive.

Absent a specific provision in the note governing prepayment, is the borrower entitled to prepay whenever he wishes? As a general rule he is not. See Trident Center v. Connecticut General Life Insurance Co., 847 F.2d 564 (9th Cir.1988) (permitting extrinsic evidence to construe clause); Clover Square Associates v. Northwestern Mutual Life Insurance Co., 674 F.Supp. 1137 (D.N.J.1987), affirmed, 869 F.2d 588 (3d Cir.1989) (no restraint on alienation). The reason usually given for not presuming a right to pay off the mortgage debt prior to maturity is that lenders typically take mortgage notes as an investment, to be paid off over a specified term.

However, a minority of jurisdictions permit prepayment through various means. Some statutes permit prepayment unless the mortgage instrument provides to the contrary. See, e.g., N.C.Gen.Stats. § 24–2.4 (1991). Cases in a few jurisdictions hold that a right to prepay should be presumed in all cases. See, e.g., Mahoney v. Furches, 503 Pa. 60, 468 A.2d 458, 461 (1983): "Taking cognizance of the general policy in this Commonwealth and elsewhere against restraints on alienation, we find it would be against such policy to presume, simply from the absence of a clause so allowing, that a mortgagor could not pay off his debt and alienate his land as he so desired. Instead, we think it wiser to raise a presumption of a right to prepayment of the note where a mortgage is silent as to that right. This presumption could be rebutted by showing a contrary intent mutually manifested by the parties. Such a presumption would not work a hardship on the mortgagee since, in virtually all instances, he is the drafter of the mortgage note and can thus include within the note a clause stating that the note is not subject to prepayment. This would put the mortgagor on notice that he will in all probability be restrained from selling the land for the duration of the term. If he signs the note containing such a provision, he will then be bound by it even though it may restrain his right to its sale or use." See also Hatcher v. Rose, 329 N.C. 626, 407 S.E.2d 172 (1991) (holding that there was a right to prepay under the common law).

Federal legislation and regulation have preempted the prepayment issue in certain residential situations. For example, a regulation of the Office of Thrift Supervision, governing federal savings banks, bars a penalty in connection with a prepayment of an adjustable rate mortgage on a borrower-occupied home where the prepayment is made within 90 days following a notice of adjustment. 12 C.F.R. § 545.35. Home purchase loans to veterans can be guaranteed under 38 U.S.C. § 3710 only if they are prepayable without penalty. Moreover, the secondary mortgage market has been very influential since the widely used FHLMC and FNMA note forms permit prepayment without penalty.

For excellent discussions of the prepayment issue, see Alexander, Mortgage Prepayment: The Trial of Common Sense, 72 Cornell L. Rev. 288 (1987) (arguing that the presumption against prepayment arose only relatively recently and finding common law support for a prepayment right); Weinberger, Neither an Early Nor a Late Payor Be?— Presuming to Question the Presumption Against Mortgage Prepayment, 35 Wayne L.Rev. 1 (1988).

4. *Prepayment Penalties and Due on Sale Clauses.* Should lenders be allowed to have it both ways—accelerating the loan under a due on sale clause *and* exacting a prepayment penalty from the borrower? While prior to Garn–St. Germain some jurisdictions answered this question in the negative by statute or judicial decision, Federal regulations promulgated by the Office of Thrift Supervision have preempted state rules. Under 12 C.F.R. § 591.6(b)(2), which applies to state and federally chartered banks and other lenders, a prepayment penalty or equivalent fee cannot be imposed upon the exercise of a due on sale clause.

Compare U.L.S.I.A. § 208 which provides that "if a secured creditor demands a rate of interest higher than that specified in the security agreement ... as a condition of approval of a transfer by a protected party of the protected party's interest in residential real estate subject to a security interest, and the higher rate of interest or other consideration is not agreed to, a prepayment penalty may not be charged if the debt is paid in full within 3 months after the failure to agree to a higher rate of interest." See 12 C.F.R. § 591.6(b)(3).

5. *Extension of Window Period.* Arizona, Michigan, Minnesota, and Vermont enacted legislation pursuant to the Garn–St. Germain

Depository Institutions Act, 12 U.S.C.A. § 1701j–3(c)(1)(A), permitting a further extension of the window period, with Michigan, Minnesota, and Utah ultimately granting a permanent extension.

2. TRANSFERS BY THE MORTGAGEE
GIORGI v. PIONEER TITLE INSURANCE CO.

Supreme Court of Nevada, 1969.
85 Nev. 319, 454 P.2d 104.

MOWBRAY, Justice.

Appellant Julio Giorgi, assignee of a promissory note secured by a deed of trust, sued Pioneer Title Insurance Company, trustee named in the deed, for $4,550, representing the principal amount of the note, on the grounds that Pioneer, who held the note in escrow for collection, had wrongfully disbursed the $4,550 to the payee named in the note and reconveyed the real property which was the security for the note.

The facts are not in dispute. On May 28, 1958, William C. Alden and Ula May Alden, his wife, and Mickey E. Keffer and Joyce E. Keffer, his wife, signed a promissory note in the principal sum of $4,550. The note was payable to August Manke and Mabel Manke, his wife, and it was secured by a deed of trust. August died, and Mabel succeeded to his interest in the note. After August's death, but before the note became due, Mabel assigned her interest in the note and deed of trust to Appellant Julio Giorgi. In explaining the absence of the note, Mabel told Julio that the note and deed of trust had been lost. Giorgi caused the assignment to be recorded in Washoe County. Giorgi notified the Aldens and the Keffers of the assignment, but it is agreed that no actual notice of the assignment was ever given to Pioneer, although the assignment recited that Pioneer was the trustee in the deed of trust. At the time the note and deed of trust were executed, the instruments were deposited with Pioneer with instructions to collect and disburse the $4,550 to the payee named in the note and, upon such payment, to reconvey the property covered by the deed of trust. Pioneer did so. When Giorgi attempted to collect the note, he learned that it had been paid and the security for its payment lost by virtue of Pioneer's deed of reconveyance. Giorgi then commenced an action in the district court, in which he named as defendants Pioneer, Mabel Manke, the Aldens and the Keffers. The Aldens and the Keffers were never served. The district judge entered judgment in favor of Giorgi and against Mabel for the full amount of the note, but he refused to hold Pioneer responsible for Giorgi's loss; hence, this appeal.

Appellant concedes that Pioneer did not have actual notice of Mabel's assignment of the note and deed of trust. However, appellant argues as his principal contention on this appeal that when he recorded Mabel's assignment of the note and deed of trust Pioneer received constructive notice of the assignment and became bound by the terms of NRS 106.210.[1]

Respondent contends, however, that the law of negotiable instruments is controlling in this case and that Pioneer, as holder of the negotiable promissory note, was bound to disburse the payment received to the payee named in the note—Mabel Manke. We agree, and we affirm the judgment of the district court.

1. In the case of a payment of a mortgage or deed of trust securing a negotiable instrument, the rule suggested by the great weight of authority is that the rights of the parties thereto, as well as third persons, are governed by rules relating to negotiable paper. Under this law the maker of a negotiable note secured by a mortgage or deed of trust cannot discharge his liability by payment to one not the holder or one not authorized by the holder to receive payment. And a debtor is not justified as against an assignee of the security in making payments to a mortgagee or a beneficiary named in a deed of trust who does not have possession of the instrument.

The general rule has been stated in 4 American Law of Property § 16.117 (A.J. Casner ed. 1952):

" 'Where a negotiable instrument is secured by a mortgage, the latter will not be discharged by payment to the record holder if as a matter of fact the note and mortgage had already been transferred to a bona fide holder for value before maturity, even though no assignment has been recorded.' Such is the general rule by the very definite weight of authority. *This flows from the general rule that in such cases the mortgage follows the rules applicable to the negotiable instrument it secures. Nor will the result be different if the mortgagor asked for the note and was given a plausible but false explanation for its nonproduction. The risk is absolute.*"

2. Appellant contends, however, that in this case the general rule is superseded by our recordation statutes, particularly NRS 106.210, supra, and that when the assignment was recorded Pioneer was given constructive notice of its existence and became bound by its terms. Admittedly, the problem of harmonizing the effect of our recording statutes with the rules of negotiable instruments so as not to interfere with the commercial mobility of the debt is a troublesome one. G. Osborne, Handbook on the Law of Mortgages § 235, at 647, has stated the rule: "The problem of enacting and applying the recording statute is one of trying to satisfy the demands of recordation required by the fact that the subject matter of the mortgage is land and, at the same time, not to interfere with the mobility of the debt or with the

---

1. NRS 106.210 "Recording of assignments of mortgages, beneficial interests in trust deeds; constructive notice.

"1. Any assignment of a mortgage of real property, or of a mortgage of personal property or crops recorded prior to March 27, 1935, and any assignment of the beneficial interest under a deed of trust may be recorded, and from the time any of the same are so filed for record shall operate as constructive notice of the contents thereof to all persons."

functioning of the security aspect of the mortgage which makes it a mere incident of the debt. Since this is so, it is obvious that the rules governing the recording of other conveyances cannot be applied in toto."

3. There is an additional reason for this rule. In this case Pioneer was bound by the escrow instructions which the parties had signed. The instructions directed Pioneer, who held the note for collection, to receive and disburse the $4,550 payment to the payee named in the note. To require any agency—whether a title company, escrow company, bank, or individual—to run a title search before making any disbursements to a payee named in a note held for collection and secured by a deed of trust, or to pay at its peril, would impose an impractical and crushing burden on such agencies.

The judgment of the district court is affirmed.

COLLINS, C.J., ZENOFF and THOMPSON, JJ., and WARTMAN, D.J., concur.

UNITED STATES FINANCE CO. v. JONES

Supreme Court of Alabama, 1969.
285 Ala. 105, 229 So.2d 495.

MERRILL, Justice. This appeal is from a decree setting aside a mortgage given by appellee to one Bell and assigned by him to appellant, United States Finance Company, Inc. Bell does not appeal.

Appellee filed her bill of complaint to quiet title against William E. Bell, d/b/a The Bell Company, and the appellant Finance Company. An answer and cross bill was filed by the appellant which, in substance, stated its claim to the property was that it was the assignee of a mortgage from William E. Bell, which mortgage and assignment was recorded in the Probate Court of Baldwin County, Alabama, and in the cross bill it alleged the execution and assignment of the said mortgage and further that the mortgage was in default and prayed that the mortgage be foreclosed. To the cross bill the appellee filed an answer which, in essence, claimed that the appellant was not a bona fide purchaser for value without notice. This answer was filed on February 7, 1969, and another answer was subsequently filed by the appellee on February 20, 1969, which answer complains that William E. Bell did not do the things to the property which he had agreed to do at the time of the execution of the mortgage. A decree pro confesso was entered by the court against William E. Bell for failure to answer the bill of complaint.

The case was tried on January 24, 1969, and the court entered a final decree granting relief to the appellee-complainant.

The trial court made the following findings of fact:

"1. The allegations in the Complainant's Bill of Complaint are true.

"2. William E. Bell obtained a mortgage on said property by fraudulent means.

"3. The signature of Willie Jones to this mortgage was a forgery; that Willie Jones was dead on the date this mortgage was executed.

"4. The acknowledgment on said mortgage was defective; that it is shown to have been taken in Baldwin County by a Mobile County Notary.

"5. The United States Finance Company had purchased a great number of mortgages from William E. Bell covering land in Baldwin County some of which were defective, and the Court finds that United States Finance Company was not an innocent purchaser for value without notice."

The evidence tended to show that two salesmen from The Bell Company (hereinafter Bell), a Florida contracting company, visited appellee, an uneducated black woman and a widow, one night at her house in Baldwin County. They offered to perform certain repairs on her house. They persuaded appellee to sign a mortgage on her house and land securing a note providing for payments of $30.66 per month for 84 months ($2,575.44). Appellee could only read and write "a little bit." Three days later, Bell sold the note and mortgage to U.S. Finance.

The evidence was undisputed that Bell agreed to work on a back room of appellee's house, put aluminum siding on the outside and put a new roof on the top. It is also undisputed that Bell put tar paper on the sides of the house instead of aluminum, then sprayed it with aluminum paint, and did not adequately perform the work on the back room or roof. It is also undisputed that more harm than good was done to the house by Bell.

The undisputed evidence shows that Bell did not perform as he contracted to do, and did not provide adequate consideration under the contract, note and mortgage. It is also undisputed that the mortgage was executed in Baldwin County. The signature on the mortgage of Willie Jones was an obvious forgery. The acknowledgment of the notary on the mortgage shows that it was taken by Zack Watkins, a Notary Public of Mobile County, in Baldwin County where he had no authority under his affixed seal. He also certified "that Evelyn Jones and Willie Jones whose name is signed to the foregoing conveyance, and who is known to me, acknowledged before me on this day that, being informed of the contents of this conveyance, she executed the same voluntarily on the day the same bears date." He could not possibly have seen Willie Jones that day nor could he have been known to him as a person signing the mortgage.

The note, secured by the mortgage here involved, is not in the record, but is described in the mortgage. When a mortgage securing a note is transferred along with the note, the mortgage follows and is of the same character as the note.

The main question is whether appellant was a holder in due course. The Uniform Commercial Code, Tit. 7A, §§ 1–101 through 10–104, applied to this transaction since it became effective midnight December 31, 1966, and the note was signed on January 23, 1967. Section 3–302(1) provides, in part, that:

"A holder in due course is a holder who takes the instrument

. . .

"(c) without notice that it is overdue or has been dishonored or of any defense against or claim to it on the part of any person."

Section 1–201(25) defines notice as follows:

"A person has 'notice' of a fact when

"(a) he has actual knowledge of it; or

. . .

"(c) from all the facts and circumstances known to him at the time in question he has reason to know that it exists.

"A person 'knows' or has 'knowledge' of a fact when he has actual knowledge of it. . . ."

Appellant's first witness, Bill Patterson, credit manager for appellant when the Jones transaction was handled, testified that appellant purchased the paper from Bell on February 2, 1967 for $1,360.00; that "in order for us to purchase the contract and mortgage from any of these contractors they did have to tell me the work was completed and satisfactory;" that he called appellee on the day the work was completed and she said it was satisfactory, but he did not deny her previous testimony that she told him that it had not rained and was satisfactory but later it leaked when it rained; that he "bought the mortgage, acting on her word."

But he also testified that he examined the mortgage before purchasing it, and the discrepancy as to the signing in Baldwin County before a Mobile County Notary "must have been" on the mortgage when he bought it, and that the assignment of the mortgage bore the date of January 26, 1967, but that he bought it on February 2, 1967. Later in Patterson's cross-examination, the following took place:

"Q. Did you notice the mortgage and certificate of completion is dated the same date?

"A. They are.

"Q. They are the same date?

"A. They are.

"Q. That didn't make you suspicious about buying it?

"A. No sir, that was normal.

"Q. With William E. Bell it is normal?—that is not normal with your transactions with other people?

"A. With other contractors, yes sir."

This testimony smacks of bad faith on the part of appellant. Repairing houses, covering them with siding, re-roofing, and paneling rooms requires the assembling of materials and usually several days' work for the amount of work and the cost on the project here involved. But from the testimony, it seems that appellant gets the mortgage executed, and requires a certificate of completion and satisfaction to be signed at the same time, or at least, on the same day. It apparently wants to guarantee, in writing, its status as a holder in due course whether or not the work is ever completed. Yet, appellant's testimony was that this procedure was "normal" not only with Bell but with other contractors.

There was testimony that the mortgage record in the Probate Office of Baldwin County showed many assignments from Bell to appellant as shown by these questions and answers from a practicing attorney in that county:

"Q. Have you had occasion to run the indexes in the Probate Judge's Office to determine how many mortgages in Baldwin County Mr. William E. Bell has?

"A. Not for that purpose, but I have had occasion to run the record out of William E. Bell to United States Finance Company."

"Q. Would you say there are a multitude of assignments?

"A. Yes sir I would say in the vernacular a myriad."

It taxes credulity to accept the contention that appellant did not have notice of Bell's fraud and manner of dealing with people from his many transactions with appellant.

There is also the matter of the price paid by appellant for the mortgage. It was executed on January 23, 1967, assigned in writing to appellant on January 26, filed for record on February 1, and "purchased" by appellant on February 2, 1967 for $1,360.00, about fifty per cent of the face value of the mortgage.

The mere fact that a note is purchased for an amount less than its face, or that an unusually large discount is accepted, is never of itself sufficient to charge the purchaser with notice of existing equities, unless the consideration is merely nominal. However, inadequacy is always a fact to be considered by the jury as evidence of bad faith, and may, with suspicious circumstances, authorize a finding of bad faith, especially if the consideration is grossly inadequate. Certainly the trial court was entitled to consider the fact of inadequacy along with the other peculiar circumstances of this case.

In Tri-D Acceptance Corporation v. Scruggs, 284 Ala. 153, 223 So.2d 273, we said:

"The indorsee, for value before maturity, of a negotiable promissory note is protected as a holder in due course from the defense of breach of executory warranty unless at the time he acquired the note the condition had then been breached and he had knowledge thereof or was possessed of facts sufficient to impute knowledge, or unless he had knowledge of such facts that his action in taking the instrument amounted to bad faith."

In the instant case, as in Tri-D, we think the trial court was justified from the evidence (all of which we have not delineated) in holding that appellant was not a holder in due course, since it, through its agents, servants or employees had knowledge, or had possession of knowledge of facts sufficient to impute knowledge, at the time appellant purchased the mortgage, of its infirmities, defects, and defenses thereto, and was not a purchaser in good faith.

Affirmed.

LIVINGSTON, C.J., and LAWSON, HARWOOD and MADDOX, JJ., concur.

NOTES

1. Rules governing the rights of mortgage assignees have assumed dramatically increased importance with the growth of secondary markets. United States Finance Co. v. Jones and Giorgi v. Pioneer Title Ins. Co. suggest some of the problems facing purchasers of real estate secured debt. Although both the note and mortgage are transferred, the note is viewed as the controlling document. (An old saw states that "the mortgage follows the note," giving one who has received only the note the right to the security instrument as well.) Thus, Article 3 of the Uniform Commercial Code applies. As a further complication, a new version of Article 3 was promulgated in 1990, introducing some significant changes from the prior version.

2. *Holder in Due Course.* One central issue is whether the assignee of a note qualifies as a holder in due course and thus takes free of certain defenses otherwise available to the payor of the note. To qualify as a holder in due course, the assignee must, among other things, demonstrate that the note is negotiable and was acquired in good faith and for value without notice of defenses to or of certain defects in the note. See U.C.C. § 3–302 (pre–1990 version), §§ 3–302, 3–305 (1990 version). While the assignee in *Jones* was defeated because of the notice requirement, results have differed under the pre–1990 U.C.C. See Universal C.I.T. Credit Corp. v. Ingel, 347 Mass. 119, 196 N.E.2d 847 (1964) (where assignee had received credit report on payee indicating in detail past sharp business practices and complaints to the attorney general, assignee had no reason to know of fraud with respect to the transferred note). A new, "objective" definition of good faith in the 1990 version of section 3–103(a)(4) requires "the observance of reasonable commercial standards of fair dealing." This formulation makes it more likely that an assignee like the one in *Jones* would be found not to be a holder in due course since the inquiry would be whether a reasonably prudent person acting the way the assignee did would have been in good faith. Under a "subjective" test the issue is

whether this particular assignee was in good faith regardless of how sloppy and substandard he may have been in his business practices. J. White & R. Summers, Uniform Commercial Code (3d.ed.1988) § 14–6.

When the Resolution Trust Corporation or the Federal Deposit Insurance Corporation takes over an insolvent lending institution, do they have the status of a holder in due course with respect to notes held by the bank? There has been much confusion in the courts. Some have held that state law controls and that the agency might not have holder in due course status under the facts, while others have found a separate federal common law which gives the agencies the equivalent of holder in due course status. See Federal Deposit Insurance Corp. v. Sather, 488 N.W.2d 260 (Minn.1992); Beach v. Resolution Trust Corp., 821 S.W.2d 241 (Tex.App.1991); 12 U.S.C.A. § 1823(e) (invalidating agreements which reduce the FDIC's interest in bank assets unless agreement complies with certain requirements).

Transactions of the sort involved in *Jones*—at least to the extent they involve household goods rather than real property—may today be more generally immune from holder-in-due course treatment under the FTC Holder-in-Due Course Regulations, 16 C.F.R. § 433.1 et seq. These regulations effectively lift the holder in due course barrier to protect "consumers"—"A natural person who seeks or acquires goods or services for personal, family or household use." However, some recent reports indicate that there has been an increase in home repair fraud where contracts are secured by home equity mortgages and then sold to lenders but the work is never completed by the contractor. See Diesenhouse, Fraud Growing In Lending Push On Home Equity, The New York Times, Oct. 13, 1991, at A–1. See generally, Greenfield & Ross, Limits on a Consumer's Ability to Assert Claims and Defenses under the FTC's Holder in Due Course Rule, 46 Bus.Law. 1135 (1991); Sturley, The Legal Impact of the Federal Trade Commission's Holder in Due Course Notice on a Negotiable Instrument: How Clever Are the Rascals at the FTC? 68 N.C.L.Rev. 953 (1990); J. White & R. Summers, Uniform Commercial Code § 14–8 (3d ed.1988).

3. *Negotiability of Mortgage Notes.* Notes secured by mortgages pose distinctive risks of non-negotiability. If the note contains too detailed a reference to the terms of the mortgage securing it, the note may be non-negotiable because it is no longer an "unconditional promise or order to pay a sum certain in money and no other promise." U.C.C. § 3–104(1)(b) (pre–1990 version); see §§ 3–104(a), 3–106 (1990 version).

Holly Hill Acres, Ltd. v. Charter Bank of Gainesville, 314 So.2d 209 (Fla.Dist.Ct.App.2d Dist.1975), held that the following language incorporated the mortgage into the note, destroying the note's negotiability: "this note with interest is secured by a mortgage on real estate, of even date herewith, made by the maker hereof in favor of the said payee, and shall be construed and enforced according to the laws of the state of Florida. The terms of said mortgage are by this reference made a part hereof." According to the court, "[m]ere reference to a note being secured by a mortgage is a common commercial practice and such reference in itself does not impede the negotiability of the note. There is, however, a significant difference in the note stating that it is 'secured by a mortgage' from one which provides, 'the terms of said mortgage are by this reference made a part hereof.' In the former instance the note merely refers to a separate agreement which does not impede its negotiability, while in the latter instance the note is rendered nonnegotiable." 314 So.2d at 211. Comment 1 to the 1990 text of U.C.C. § 3–106 states that a note indicating that it is "subject to a loan and security agreement dated ..." makes the note nonnegotiable while a statement that "this note is secured by a security interest in collateral described in a security agreement dated ..." does not make the note nonnegotiable since there is no need to look at the security agreement to determine the rights under the note.

Cases have held under the pre–1990 U.C.C. § 3–106, requiring as a condition of negotiability that the holder be able to determine the amount due from the instrument, that adjustable rate notes are not negotiable since they require reference to an external index. See, e.g., Northern Trust Co. v. E.T. Clancy Export Corp., 612 F.Supp. 712 (N.D.Ill.1985); Taylor v. Roeder, 234 Va. 99, 360 S.E.2d 191 (1987); but see Woodhouse, Drake & Carey, Ltd. v. Anderson, 61 Misc.2d 951, 307 N.Y.S.2d 113 (1970) (note providing for "the maximum legal rate" was negotiable). The 1990 version of the U.C.C. permits variable rate notes to be negotiable, provided the other requirements to negotiability are met. §§ 3–104(a), 3–112. What would the effect be on the secondary market if such notes were not negotiable?

4. *U.L.S.I.A.* Section 206 of the Uniform Land Security Interest Act codifies some aspects of existing law. Subsection (a) states that the assignee of a mortgage takes subject to defenses against payment. Subsection (c) states that the mortgagor may continue to pay the original mortgagee until the mortgagor receives notification of the assignment. At the same time, though, Comment 1 indicates that in the case of negotiable instruments Article 3 of the U.C.C. will control.

Section 206 also introduces new rules. Section 206(b) recognizes that under modern servicing arrangements the original mortgagee often continues to service the loan after assignment. The section provides that modifications to the mortgage made by the servicing mortgagee are effective against the assignee. Express clauses in the mortgage waiving mortgagor's defenses against the assignee are generally permitted. § 206(e). However, subsection (d) states that an assignee or holder in due course of a loan to a "protected party" secured by a mortgage on that person's residence is subject to all defenses against the original mortgagee "[n]otwithstanding agreement to the contrary."

5. *Notes, Mortgages and the Recording Acts.* Negotiability and low transaction costs are essential to an efficient national market for mortgage notes. Yet the recording acts require close examination of

the county title records and of the land if the purchaser of the note is to be confident about the quality of title securing the note. These two premises inevitably come into conflict. Title insurance and the growth of national title companies have helped somewhat to resolve the conflict but have not completely removed the obstacles to a fluidly functioning market in real property secured paper.

Consider the following situation. Mortgagee assigns its note and mortgage to A–1 who records the assignment but leaves the instruments in possession of the mortgagee. Mortgagee then assigns the note and mortgage to A–2, delivering the instruments to her. Who will prevail as between A–1 and A–2? One line of decisions holds for A–1, employing the recording act rationale that A–2 is on constructive notice of anything that a title search would have disclosed. See, for example, Murphy v. Barnard, 162 Mass. 72, 38 N.E. 29 (1894). Another line of decisions holds for A–2 on the rationale of negotiability, for which record notice is of no effect. See U.C.C. § 3–304(5) (pre 1990 text); § 3–302(b) (1990 text). There is a third line of decisions that achieves analytical elegance, but little more, by giving A–2 rights on the note, but not against the security, and giving A–1 rights against the security but not on the note. See generally, Note, Transfer of the Mortgagee's Interest in Florida, 14 U.Fla.L.Rev. 98 (1961). As a practical matter, what rights does this third approach give A–1?

In Sixty St. Francis Street, Inc. v. American Savings & Loan Ass'n, 554 So.2d 1003 (Ala.1989), the assignee (American Savings) of a mortgage originally held by First American did not record the assignment. Subsequently the property was conveyed and the grantee's mortgagee satisfied the original mortgage by paying American Savings. Under a statute such as the one in *Giorgi*, was the payment effective to satisfy the mortgage?

6. *Pledges of Real Property Instruments.* When a mortgagee pledges a note and mortgage as security for a loan to *him,* should the subject matter of the pledge be treated as real property or as personal property covered by U.C.C. Article 9? Comment 4 to U.C.C. § 9–102 states: "The owner of Blackacre borrows $10,000 from his neighbor, and secures his note by a mortgage on Blackacre. This Article is not applicable to the creation of the real estate mortgage. Nor is it applicable to a sale of the note by the mortgagee, even though the mortgage continues to secure the note. However, when the mortgagee pledges the note to secure his own obligation to X, this Article applies to the security interest thus created, which is a security interest in an instrument even though the instrument is secured by a real estate mortgage." The cases are in disarray. See generally G. Nelson & D. Whitman, Real Estate Finance Law 367–371 (2d ed.1985).

What if a lessor assigns her lease as security for payment of a note executed by her to Y? What if Y then assigns the lessor's note and lease assignment to Z as security for payment of a note executed by Y

to Z? See generally, Bowmar, Real Estate Interests as Security Under
the UCC: The Scope of Article Nine, 12 U.C.C.L.J. 99 (1979).

D. MORTGAGE DEFAULT

INSTITUTE OF FINANCIAL EDUCATION, RESIDENTIAL MORTGAGE LENDING *

152–155, 157, 160–162 (1981).

Mortgage Loan Delinquencies—Association Perspectives

While an association may make every effort to approve and close
only sound mortgage loans, inevitably a few loans will become delinquent. Delinquencies occur despite association efforts to remind borrowers of their obligations and to urge prompt monthly payments.
Thus, almost as many (if not more) policies and procedures for handling
delinquent loans must be developed as there are for handling current
loans.

The reasons for delinquencies and the collection policies, and procedures to handle these delinquencies, will be examined in this chapter.
Then, the association's last resort to correcting a delinquency—foreclosure—will be reviewed. Finally, the chapter presents an overview to
the management of real estate owned.

Delinquency Rates

By the end of 1979, savings associations as a group held approximately 16 million mortgage loans. The average loan balance was about
$29,800 for a total mortgage loan portfolio of about $476 billion.
Economic conditions in recent years have caused many problems for
American consumers notably high inflation and unemployment rates.
These events disrupt personal income patterns and make it difficult for
many individuals to budget for continuing obligations such as mortgage
payments.

Yet in 1979, only 0.7 percent (112,000) of savings association mortgage loans were delinquent by 60 days or more. However, given the
extensive size of mortgage loan portfolios held by the savings association business (16 million loans), even a small percentage of delinquent
loans can amount to a considerable sum overall. In 1979, for example,
the 112,000 delinquent mortgage loans held at associations translated
into approximately $3.3 billion of delinquent debt.

By contrast, another statistic provides a measure of the success of
collection efforts. In 1979, the rate of foreclosure on all mortgage loans
was 0.108 percent. This is the smallest number of foreclosures in
recent years. Foreclosures during 1972 and 1973 had been especially
high; this can be traced to the impact of HUD's subsidy programs.

These programs led to an epidemic of foreclosures in several large cities across the nation. Since then, foreclosures have decreased due to falling foreclosure rates on federally backed mortgages caused by new HUD forbearance procedures. Thus, although the delinquency rate in 1979 was approximately 0.7 percent on all mortgage loans made by associations, only 15 percent of these delinquencies eventually ended in foreclosure.

Several inferences can be drawn from these data. First, savings association processing and servicing procedures are effective in preventing large numbers of loan delinquencies. Second, the dollar volume involved in even a low delinquency rate is considerable and cannot be underemphasized. Thus, collection efforts must be utilized to reduce risk on as many loans as possible. Third, collection efforts can be very successful in reducing delinquencies and the need for foreclosure.

Slow Loans and Scheduled Items

A strong force behind making collection procedures effective is the Federal Savings and Loan Insurance Corporation (FSLIC). Its regulations stipulate the conditions that constitute a *slow loan* in terms of the number of days the payment is delinquent. Loans less than one year old are slow when they become 60 days delinquent; loans between one and seven years old are slow if payments are 90 days delinquent, and so on. Loans that have been refinanced within the past year, while delinquent, are also considered slow loans.

Additional regulations segregate certain of the association's assets and refer to them as scheduled items. *Scheduled items* include an association's slow loans, real estate owned as a result of foreclosure, and real estate sold on contract or financed by a nonconforming mortgage loan. A *nonconforming mortgage* is one in which term, loan-to-value ratio, or some other aspect of the terms of the loan contract exceeds the maximum specified in FSLIC regulations.

According to FSLIC regulations, an insured savings association must maintain a net worth—which includes the surplus reserves and capital stock of the association—at least equal to the benchmark requirement plus 20 percent of its scheduled items. *Benchmark requirements* equal a specified percentage of the savings dollars held by an association. When scheduled items increase, more funds must be allocated to reserves in order to meet the net worth requirement. As a result, as more earnings are being allocated to reserves, fewer earnings are made available for other purposes such as paying interest on savings accounts or expanding the loan portfolio.

Because of these regulations, association management keeps close watch on delinquency rates, foreclosure rates, and nonconforming mortgages. If slow loans show up among newer loans, the loan-processing supervisor may be asked to determine if the cause is due to internal procedure or external conditions. If a change has been made in the handling of delinquencies shortly before the number of slow loans begins to grow, the new methods may need to be reexamined and possibly revised.

FSLIC regulations also reinforce the conclusion that prompt foreclosure is not necessarily the best solution to a delinquency situation. Unless the savings association can resell the property at once, it remains a scheduled item, and the association must retain 20 percent of the outstanding balance on the property in the required reserves.

Causes Of Loan Delinquencies

Recognizing the causes of delinquencies is the first step in solving many of the financial problems associated with loan delinquencies. With this knowledge at hand, savings associations can help customers avoid problem-causing situations altogether or aid them in resolving those that do arise. The five most common causes of loan delinquencies at savings associations are improper regard for obligations, loss of income, excessive obligations, death or illness, and marital difficulties.

Improper Regard of Obligations

Improper regard for obligations creates the greatest share of loan delinquencies. This attitude has significance for association personnel. It implies that the customer should be educated during the loan application process to the various responsibilities and privileges of a mortgage loan. Loan officers must spend time preparing the customer to become a good borrower. A so-called good borrower retains a positive mental image of the savings association that holds his or her mortgage and realizes the nature and importance of the loan obligation.

Despite the best efforts of an association to encourage borrowers to be responsible, some individuals will always rationalize that the institution holding the mortgage can wait for its money. This type of attitude can be mitigated, however, through good evaluation methods at the loan application stage and firmness at the collection stage.

Loss of Income

Loss of income can present a serious problem to borrowers and often cripples or sets back their ongoing plans. If the association has established a strong contact with the customer before such a difficulty arises, the borrower will probably let the lender know at once about the dilemma. The loan officer and the borrower may then work out a plan to keep the loan from becoming seriously delinquent. Timing is the key in such a situation.

A customer's loss of income can result from circumstances other than job severance. The most likely candidates for wide income fluctuations and subsequent difficulties in meeting financial obligations are the self-employed and commissioned salespeople. They often have no control over swings in the marketplace. Persuading these borrowers to make advance payments when their income is high is a sound way to avoid delinquencies on their mortgages.

Job layoffs are another common cause of income loss. This usually occurs without much warning and continues for an indefinite period of time. Such shortfalls emphasize why building a good line of communication between the borrower and the lender in good times can pave the way to better understanding during bad times. A temporary reduction in principal payments or some other relief can often be worked out to ease the financial tension and ward off a serious delinquency.

Excessive Obligations

Excessive obligations are not synonymous with an improper regard for obligations. A borrower may be sincere about meeting financial commitments, yet may become unwittingly obligated for more payments than he or she can actually make. Associations that offer package-plan financing avert some of this danger by incorporating large household items in the original loan. Even if an association does not provide this kind of lending program, the loan officer is in a unique position, at the time the original loan application is taken, to counsel the borrower about budgeting family income to avoid overextensions.

Careful screening of loan applicants often reveals that the borrower intends to use secondary financing to meet the difference between the sale price of a home and the association's loan. Borrowers who are paying on first and second mortgages are far more likely to encounter financial problems than are those who have a large cash equity in their property. Since applicants ordinarily will not volunteer information about secondary financing, it is up to the loan officer to investigate this contingency so that the loan committee has a true picture of the situation when the loan is considered for approval.

In some instances, heavy obligations can arise after the loan is made. In the current era of high population mobility, a family often moves from one city to another or from one state to another and buys a new home without having first sold the former one. When both parcels of real estate are mortgaged, the borrower may become hard pressed to meet the doubled expenses and is more likely to become delinquent in payments on one or both of the mortgages. Another example of heavy obligation often occurs in a divorce settlement. Depending on the settlement, if divorced persons remarry, these individuals may find themselves legally responsible for maintaining two homes. As a result, the financial obligation of two mortgage commitments can become too burdensome to handle. ...

Collection Policies And Procedures

In the typical association, one person supervises the handling of delinquencies in accord with management's policies. The collection supervisor or manager ascertains that the collection procedure is fully carried out in line with association policy.

The supervisor usually has authority within certain limits to waive penalties, to authorize sending a loan to the attorney at a certain point in its delinquency, and to vary the usual collection procedures to include innovative measures for chronic delinquents. The supervisor may also approve agreements to reinstate delinquent loans within a specified period such as six months. A longer term would require the approval of a higher officer—the collection supervisor's immediate superior—who may be head of the loan department, the executive vice president, or some other high-level officer. Association policy establishes the degree of authority which may be executed by personnel at each level.

To keep collections moving along as efficiently and as rapidly as possible, the collection supervisor assumes responsibility for many day-to-day decisions. For the sake of expediency, the supervisor may delegate some authority to others. At all times, however, the paramount concern of the collection supervisor is to protect the interests of the association and its investments in mortgage loans. ...

Collection Routines ...

The policies and procedures for handling mortgage loans at various stages of delinquency are set by each association. In formulating its delinquency policy, the association pays close attention to state laws governing the conditions that make a loan subject to foreclosure. The following policies are typical of those adopted by savings associations throughout the nation.

• The loan payment is considered *past due* when it is 1 day after the due date.

• The payment is considered *late*, 16 days after the due date, and the customer's credit rating is now in jeopardy.

• The payment is considered *delinquent*, 30 days after the due date.

• After a length of time set by the association's board of directors, the loan is subject to *foreclosure* action.

Collection procedures for delinquent loans will differ from association to association. However, most associations adhere to a few basic principles. In the early stages of delinquency, the least costly and time-consuming procedures (such as notices) are used. However, as a loan becomes more delinquent, more costly and time-consuming procedures (such as field calls) will have to be used. Prompt follow-up on all delinquent loans is essential, as well as the consistent application of collection procedures to all loans. In the following section of this chapter, several commonly used collection procedures are examined. ...

Refinancing the Loan

One widely used method of curing a delinquency is to *refinance* the loan. This simply means making a new loan that is large enough to cover the principal outstanding on the delinquent loan, plus the delinquent amount. Paying up the delinquency with a lump sum from the new loan starts the new loan off on a current basis. Loans refinanced because of delinquency, however, sometimes become delinquent again at a higher rate than other loans. Thus, the association must screen loans selected for refinancing carefully. Generally, the only loans considered are those to borrowers who have defaulted because of circumstances beyond their control. The borrower must also have sufficient equity to make the refinancing economically feasible. Preferably, the monthly payment on the new loan should be no higher than it was on the original one. For this reason, refinancing is very rare during periods of high interest rates, unless an association is willing to refinance at below market rates (perhaps in hardship cases).

Suppose that a borrower, who has a $10,000 loan balance and eight years left to run on the mortgage, becomes several months delinquent because of loss of income due to illness. The delinquency can probably not be made up in a reasonable period of time without causing severe hardship on the borrower. In fact, for the delinquency to be made up, the association will have to carry the loan as a slow loan in its scheduled items category for a long period of time. If, however, it refinances the loan, the slow loan definition will apply for only one year. An alternative would be to make a new loan for $12,000 to cover the remaining loan balance, the delinquent loan amount plus interest, and the costs connected with refinancing (new title search, attorney's fees and other closing costs, recording charges, and very possibly a new appraisal).

If the value of the property warrants it, the association can make the new loan even larger in order to provide additional funds to help cover medical expenses. Loans can always be made against the security of a home for any worthwhile purpose. The association, of course, must ascertain that the payments on the new mortgage loan are within the borrower's budget or that a longer loan term (to reduce the monthly repayment amount) will not exceed the borrower's preretirement income period or normal life expectancy.

Suppose that a borrower, with a 30-year mortgage that is two-years old, goes into delinquency because payments have become too high for his or her current income. A request is then made to refinance the loan. In such a situation, the borrower has built up only a small equity in the property, since monthly payments during the first few years consist largely of interest. Refinancing the loan for 30 years would have little effect in converting burdensome loan payments to manageable proportions. In fact, with delinquent monies and refinancing costs added to the principal balance, the new payments could even exceed the original loan. The association could extend the term of the loan beyond regulatory limits, but a borrower who has difficulty meeting loan payments within the first year or two of loan life has not demonstrated his or her payment credibility, and the association probably would not be willing to carry such a loan on its books as a scheduled item.

Sale of the Property

Sale of a property when the mortgage loan is in default often releases the borrower from responsibility while bringing the loan to current status. When such a sale takes place without the lender's approval, there is no assurance that the loan will be maintained in better condition than before, but ... if an assumption or substitution agreement is entered into, the association has better control. Another advantage of selling the property occurs when the loan is refinanced by an outside lender—a situation in which the current lender is then paid in full.

Other Remedial Steps

A variety of options, other than foreclosure, are available to the savings association in the handling of delinquent mortgage loans. The institution is reluctant in most cases to enter into the lengthy, burdensome, and costly business of foreclosing a loan. Furthermore, property is often badly neglected during the foreclosure period, requiring additional funds to rejuvenate it before it can be sold. For these and other reasons, every effort is made to devise a satisfactory program with the borrower so that he or she can retain the property.

Loans that are being serviced for investors may require the approval of the investor before making any agreement to adjust loan terms in order to eliminate a default. The servicing agreement between the savings association and the investor stipulates the procedures required in handling sold loans and participations.

Salvage Powers

In general, *salvage powers* constitute the association's right and responsibility to do everything possible to avoid loss on a loan. Under its salvage powers, a federal association is permitted to make special agreements with borrowers that go beyond its normal lending powers. A state-chartered association must look to its charter and to state regulations to determine its salvage powers.

A federal association is normally limited to a term of 40 years in making loans on single-family, owner-occupied homes. Suppose, however, that a borrower is permanently disabled in an industrial accident after paying for 5 years on a 40-year loan, the borrower's income is permanently reduced to the level of a disability pension, and it becomes impossible to meet payments on the mortgage loan. Under its salvage powers, the association can extend the term of the loan by 20 years (or any other length of time it deems advisable) in order to bring loan payments in line with the borrower's reduced income, even though the new loan term will be 55 years. Similarly, an association can advance additional funds to a borrower to meet an emergency, even though the advance will bring the total loan to 100 percent or more of the appraised value of the property.

Because mortgage loans which exceed specified regulatory limits must be included in the FSLIC scheduled items category, savings associations must make cautious use of their salvage powers. Nevertheless, there is always the possibility that an individual loan can be rewritten in virtually any form under the privileges inherent in the salvage powers concept. In a subsequent discussion of real estate owned, further reference will be made to salvage powers. ...

Foreclosure

There comes a time when no further options are available to the association, and foreclosure on a delinquent loan is the only recourse. Waiting too long to foreclose can allow the real estate securing the defaulted loan to lose value. When people know they are going to lose their property, they often neglect and occasionally abuse it. It is not unusual for the borrower to abandon the property, leaving it exposed to the elements and vandalism.

Default ordinarily accelerates the due date of the entire mortgage loan. Modern mortgage instruments and promissory notes contain an acceleration clause calling for the payment of the entire debt in the event of default. When a borrower defaults, the mortgagee may try to minimize its losses by accepting from the mortgagor a deed in lieu of foreclosure or by acquiring ownership through foreclosure action under the laws of the state where the property is located. The purpose of either of these acts is to extinguish any equitable rights of the borrower to the property.

NOTES

1. *The Causes of Default.* J. Herzog & J. Earley, Home Mortgage Delinquency and Foreclosure (1970), is an important, statistically-based survey of factors contributing to mortgage default. Applying multiple regression analysis to a national sample of almost thirteen thousand FHA and VA insured mortgages in 1963, the authors found that the most important variables influencing serious loan delinquency were the presence of junior finance and loans made for refinancing purposes. They also found that loan to value ratio was positively related to the probability that a loan was delinquent. Professionals, executives and managers "showed the least delinquency, and self-employed persons and salesmen the most." Among the factors found to have little effect were marital status, the mortgage term, and the ratio between debt service and borrower income ("this ostensibly surprising fact appears to be because both borrowers and lenders watch this ratio very carefully"). (p. xviii.)

2. *Acceleration Clauses.* Mortgage instruments typically contain an acceleration clause making the outstanding loan balance fully payable in the event the mortgagor fails to pay debt service or other financial obligations, such as taxes and insurance premiums, when due, or commits waste or any other act of default. Some acceleration clauses are optional and require the mortgagee's election by notice of acceleration or commencement of an action to foreclose the mortgage. Other clauses provide that the outstanding principal shall automatically become due upon default. If the note does not contain an acceleration clause, the courts will not imply one and the payee can only recover for sums past due. See, e.g., Rosenfeld v. City Paper Company,

527 So.2d 704 (Ala.1988) (rejecting the application of anticipatory breach doctrine); Miller v. Balcanoff, 566 So.2d 1340 (Fla.App.1990).

Should the mortgagee be entitled to declare a default and accelerate the debt if, through an oversight, the mortgagor was one day late in tendering its debt service? Graf v. Hope Building Corp., 254 N.Y. 1, 171 N.E. 884 (1930), the leading case on the question, held that even the smallest, most innocent oversight will not excuse the mortgagor. There "the president of defendant corporation who was the mortgagor was the only person authorized to sign checks in its behalf. Prior to his departure for Europe a clerical assistant computed the interest due on the next installment on the mortgage, but made an error in calculating it. A check for this amount was signed by the president. After his departure the assistant discovered the error, notified the mortgagee of the shortage, assured him of remitting the balance upon the president's return, and forwarded the check as drawn. On the president's return, through forgetfulness of the clerk, he was not informed of the deficiency in the interest payment. At the expiration of 21 days from the interest-payment date, the mortgagee brought an action to foreclose. The mortgagor at once tendered the deficiency, and, the tender being refused, he paid the money into court."

In the view of the majority, "plaintiffs may be ungenerous, but generosity is a voluntary attribute and cannot be enforced even by a chancellor. ... Here there is no penalty, no forfeiture, nothing except a covenant fair on its face to which both parties willingly consented. It is neither oppressive nor unconscionable. In the absence of some act by the mortgagee which a court of equity would be justified in considering unconscionable, he is entitled to the benefit of the covenant. The contract is definite and no reason appears for its reformation by the courts. We are not at liberty to revise while professing to construe." 254 N.Y. at 4, 171 N.E. at 885.

A minority of states follow the position taken by Judge Benjamin Cardozo dissenting in *Graf* and hold that, although these clauses should generally be enforced according to their terms, if the injury suffered by the mortgagee from delay is small, and the injury to be suffered by the mortgagor from acceleration is great, equity should relieve the mortgagor from the consequences of an inadvertent default. See for example, Vonk v. Dunn, 161 Ariz. 24, 775 P.2d 1088 (1989) (acceleration and foreclosure would be "oppressive and unconscionable" and so not permitted where mortgagor's payment check was incorrectly dishonored by bank and tax delinquency was only $66 and not of long duration); Redding v. Gibbs, 203 Neb. 727, 280 N.W.2d 53 (1979) ("In this case it is clear the hardship which would be caused to Cameron ... by allowing Redding to foreclose the mortgage, would be harsh, oppressive, and unconscionable ... [Redding] made no demand for payment before commencing suit, although it is clear payment would have been forthcoming immediately. Although, technically, he may not have been required to demand payment before instituting his foreclosure action, nevertheless his failure to do so in this situation was clearly harsh, oppressive, and unconscionable, and strongly suggests that he wished to take advantage of defendant Cameron's situation. The equities in this case preponderate in favor of the defendants and, in our opinion, justify the action of the trial court in dismissing plaintiff's petition.") See U.L.S.I.A. § 502(a) (requiring written notice and 15 day cure period before acceleration). Even New York courts distinguish inadvertent nonpayment of principal and interest, for which no equitable relief is granted, from inadvertent failure to pay other required sums under the mortgage. See Massachusetts Mutual Life Insurance Co. v. Transgrow Realty Corp., 101 A.D.2d 770, 475 N.Y.S.2d 418 (1984) (failure to pay real estate taxes, on theory that this is only a collateral undertaking under a mortgage).

Like most acceleration clauses currently in use, the acceleration clause in *Graf* had provided for a grace period within which the mortgagor could cure its default; it was the failure to make the payment until one day after expiration of the grace period that precipitated the acceleration. Should courts be less quick to relieve a mortgagor when a grace period contained in the mortgage note, or imposed by statute, provided him with a *locus poenitentiae* for his mistake? Judge Cardozo, dissenting in *Graf,* acknowledged that enforcement of an acceleration clause is less unfair "if there is a period of grace (in this case twenty days) whereby a reasonable leeway is afforded to inadvertence and improvidence. In such circumstances, with one period of grace established by the covenant, only the most appealing equity will justify a court in transcending the allotted period and substituting another." 254 N.Y. at 10, 171 N.E. at 887.

Should the courts find that the lender waived its right to accelerate and foreclose under the note by previously accepting late payments from the borrower? Finding a waiver may be justified if the facts show that the lender's acceptance misled the mortgagor. However, if the courts routinely find a waiver, will lenders be discouraged from negotiating with borrowers in financial difficulty, forcing lenders to accelerate and foreclose on the first default? See generally Kirkham v. Hansen, 583 A.2d 1026 (Me.1990).

Courts have generally barred mortgagees from charging a prepayment penalty when exercising an acceleration clause, unless the borrower intentionally defaulted in an attempt to end the mortgage without having to pay the penalty. See Florida Nat'l Bank of Miami v. Bankatlantic, 589 So.2d 255 (Fla.1991) (where apartment building owner intentionally did not lease units in unsuccessful attempt to make building more marketable to a condominium converter, subsequent default by owner on mortgage due to inadequate cash flow from property was intentional and prepayment penalty could be imposed); U.L.S.I.A. § 502(b), comment 2 (provision barring prepayment penalty with acceleration was made optional because of inherent difficulty in distinguishing between intentional and involuntary default).

For an excellent overview of these issues, see Rosenthal, The Role of Courts of Equity in Preventing Acceleration Predicated Upon a Mortgagor's Inadvertent Default, 22 Syracuse L.Rev. 897 (1971).

3. *Lender Liability.* In Karoutas v. HomeFed Bank, 232 Cal. App.3d 767, 283 Cal.Rptr. 809 (1991), the court found a foreclosing bank liable to the buyers at a deed of trust foreclosure sale for failing to disclose adverse soil conditions which it knew about the property. The court relied on standard disclosure doctrine, rather than on a special relationship between the parties. In Mathews v. Lomas & Nettleton Co., 754 P.2d 791 (Colo.App.1988), the lender failed to credit a payment by the mortgagor. Ultimately, the lender instituted a foreclosure action and the borrowers sold the house before the action was completed. After borrowers sued the lender, a jury awarded damages for outrageous conduct and negligent infliction of emotional distress. The appellate court noted, however, that there was no evidence that the borrowers suffered an unreasonable risk of bodily harm as required in the jurisdiction to recover for negligent infliction of emotional distress. Since the damage award combined recovery for both outrageous conduct and emotional distress, the judgment was reversed.

Consider whether these cases are correctly decided in light of expectations of the parties, reasonable lender behavior and norms, the costs which would be added to land transactions and loans if one or the other party is found liable, and the other considerations discussed at pages 218–220.

4. *Emergency Homeowners Relief Act; Soldiers' and Sailors' Civil Relief Act.* In addition to its more sweeping efforts to bolster and systematize the home finance market, Congress has on occasion sought to protect homeowners from the immediate, crushing effects of mortgage foreclosure. The 1975 Emergency Homeowners Relief Act responded to the "severe recession" that then gripped the nation by creating a "standby authority which will prevent mortgage foreclosure and distress sales of homes resulting from the temporary loss of employment and income through a program of emergency loans and advances and emergency mortgage relief payments to homeowners to defray mortgage expenses." Specifically, the Act authorized the Secretary of HUD to make "emergency mortgage relief loans," "advances of credit," and "emergency mortgage relief payments" to cover debt service and other costs of homeownership to the extent of no more than $250 per month. 12 U.S.C.A. §§ 2701, 2703.

The Soldiers' and Sailors' Civil Relief Act of 1940 operates within a narrower frame. It is aimed at protecting service men and women from the effects of default and foreclosure while they are in the military by tolling statutes of limitations, extending periods of statutory redemption and requiring stays of foreclosure proceedings. 50 App.U.S.C.A. §§ 501, 525, 532 (1990).

5. *Uniformity of Foreclosure Procedures.* The Uniform Land Security Interest Act represents a recent attempt to create uniform foreclosure procedures. Supporters claim that uniform legislation will encourage national lending and will bring efficiency. See generally, Pedowitz, Mortgage Foreclosure Under ULSIA, 27 Wake Forest L.Rev. 495 (1992). Professor Michael Schill argues, however, that the present system of independent state law should be continued because the supposed inefficiencies of the current structure are overstated, the cost of change would be great, and a non-uniform system encourages states to experiment in their foreclosure methods to reflect differences among states' social and economic structures. Schill, Uniformity or Diversity: Residential Real Estate Finance Law in the 1990s and the Implication of Changing Financial Markets, 64 S.Cal.L.Rev. 1261 (1991).

6. *Federal Preemption of State Procedures on Default.* The federal government has generally succeeded in overriding state debtor protection provisions that stand in its way when it seeks to realize on defaulted mortgages that it holds. For example, United States v. View Crest Garden Apartments, Inc., 268 F.2d 380 (9th Cir.1959), cert. denied, 361 U.S. 884, 80 S.Ct. 156, 4 L.Ed.2d 120 (1960), held that federal, not state, law governed the question whether a receiver should be appointed to protect the property and collect rents in a local foreclosure action. "After a default the sole situation presented is one of remedies. ... Now the federal policy to protect the treasury and to promote the security of federal investment which in turn promotes the prime purpose of the Act—to facilitate the building of homes by the use of federal credit—becomes predominant. Local rules limiting the effectiveness of the remedies available to the United States for breach of federal duty cannot be adopted." 268 F.2d at 383.

Federal law has similarly been held to control the availability of statutory redemption and deficiency judgments after foreclosure. United States v. Stadium Apartments, Inc., 425 F.2d 358 (9th Cir.1970), cert. denied sub nom. Lynch v. United States, 400 U.S. 926, 91 S.Ct. 187, 27 L.Ed.2d 185 (1970).

Federal agencies have been less successful in winning enactment of a federal mortgage foreclosure act establishing a nationalized, expedited procedure for foreclosing on mortgages insured, guaranteed or owned by the FHA, VA or Farmer's Home Administration. H.R. 10688, 93 Cong. 1st Sess. tit. iv. (1973); S. 2507, 93d Cong. 1st Sess. tit. iv. (1973). See Hearings on Housing and Community Development Legislation before the Subcommittee on Housing of the House Banking and Currency Committee, 1186–1196, 93d Cong. 1st Sess. (1973). See generally, Pedowitz, Current Developments in Summary Foreclosure, 9 Real Prop., Probate & Trust J. 421 (1974).

1. METHODS OF FORECLOSURE

a. Strict Foreclosure

SKILTON, DEVELOPMENTS IN MORTGAGE LAW AND PRACTICE

17 Temple University Law Quarterly 315, 318–320 (1943).

The type of foreclosure usually employed in England at the end of the seventeenth century was the old "strict foreclosure", whereby the mortgagee, without a sale of the premises, was decreed full owner of the property. Occasionally, where the mortgagor's interests seemed to demand it, a public sale was decreed, and in this case the mortgagee was not privileged to bid. He was, in case the property was sold for an amount less than his claim, entitled to a deficiency judgment. It was not possible, however, for him to acquire the property by strict foreclosure and thereafter claim a deficiency. He could have one but not both; either possession and title to the property, or the proceeds of sale of the property to a third party, and a claim for the balance due. In Ireland, on the other hand, it was general practice to decree public sale of the property in all cases.

The remedy of foreclosure, when imported into the colonies, naturally was subjected to modifications thought to be compatible with domestic needs. As time went on, strict foreclosure was supplanted in practically all states by foreclosure followed by public sale. This change was achieved sometimes simply by court practice, not reenforced by statute; sometimes by statutes permitting courts to order a sale of mortgaged premises in their discretion; and, especially since codes of civil practice became current, frequently by statutory provision making public sale mandatory.

Strict foreclosure has survived today as the usual remedy in only two states: Connecticut and Vermont, where English traditions are especially strong. In these states it is the practice to confer full title upon the mortgagee in this manner in all cases where it does not appear upon appraisement that the property would bring more than the mortgage debt. The mortgagee is entitled to judgment for the balance due, the difference between his claim and the appraised value of the premises.

In a number of additional states, strict foreclosure is available in certain cases where the interests of both parties seem to require it, as where the mortgagor is insolvent, the property insufficient to cover claim and costs, and there is no practical advantage in a deficiency judgment. In other states, statutory provisions, such as the frequent code provisions, "a mortgage shall not be deemed a conveyance", "there shall be but one action upon a debt", etc., have been held to exclude the possibility of strict foreclosure.

NOTE

Strict foreclosure continues to be used in Connecticut and Vermont. Conn.Gen.Stat.Ann. § 49–15; Vt.Stat.Ann. tit. 12, § 4531. Illinois, the one other state allowing strict foreclosure, imposes three requirements aimed at safeguarding the mortgagor and preventing unjust enrichment to the mortgagee: the property's value cannot exceed the debt, a deficiency cannot be recovered, and the mortgagor must be insolvent. See Ill.St.Ann. ch. 110, ¶ 15–1403 (effective in 1987); Great Lakes Mortgage Corp. v. Collymore, 14 Ill.App.3d 68, 302 N.E.2d 248 (1973).

Strict foreclosure is more widely used for two narrower purposes. One use is to cut off the interest of a junior encumbrancer whom the mortgagee mistakenly failed to join in foreclosure proceedings earlier brought against the mortgagor. For example, in Sears, Roebuck & Co. v. Camp, 124 N.J.Eq. 403, 1 A.2d 425 (1938), strict foreclosure was allowed against the assignee of a junior mortgage whose assignment, though recorded, was not disclosed by the mortgagee's title search. It is unclear, though, whether the court was more persuaded by the general utility of strict foreclosure to cut off junior interests or by the "pertinent" facts that "the lands were sold to complainant on its nominal bid of $100, and that it is not suggested another sale would yield more than sufficient to satisfy complainant's mortgage—a vain hope, in view of the long continued depression of the real estate market, consequent upon the general economic crisis." 124 N.J.Eq. at 414, 1 A.2d at 430. See generally, Wietzki v. Wietzki, 231 Neb. 551, 437 N.W.2d 449 (1989) (finding no strict foreclosure by installment sale vendor that would extinguish junior lien on the purchaser's interest in the contract since vendor did not intend to have his lien extinguished when purchaser gave vendor a quitclaim deed after purchaser defaulted).

Second, courts sometimes allow strict foreclosure of equitable mortgages. Thus, in Herrmann v. Churchill, 235 Or. 327, 385 P.2d 190 (1963), the Oregon Supreme Court ruled that because the action sought to construe an absolute deed as a mortgage, and did not seek to foreclose a mortgage, statutory prohibitions against strict foreclosure did not apply. "Every jurisdiction in this country which has passed upon this question, insofar as our research discloses, has held that the statutes as to foreclosure of mortgages are inapplicable in a suit to have a deed absolute declared a mortgage." 385 P.2d at 193. Can you find any fault with Justice O'Connell's dissenting observation that "[the] mortgagor should have the same right to insist on foreclosure by judicial sale whether the mortgage is cast in the usual form or takes the form of an absolute deed"? 385 P.2d at 195.

For excellent discussions of the policy issues raised by strict foreclosure, see Durham, In Defense of Strict Foreclosure: A Legal and Economic Analysis of Mortgage Foreclosure, 36 S.Car.L.Rev. 461 (1985) (arguing that efficiency, equity, and fairness are served by strict foreclosure); Wechsler, Through the Looking Glass: Foreclosure by Sale as De Facto Strict Foreclosure—An Empirical Study of Mortgage Foreclosure and Subsequent Resale, 70 Cornell L.Rev. 850 (1985) (arguing that study shows that foreclosure by sale is the functional equivalent of strict foreclosure since mortgagees often buy the mortgaged property at the sale, resell it a significant profit, and thus eliminate the mortgagor's equity). Tefft, The Myth of Strict Foreclosure, 4 U. Chi.L.Rev. 575

(1937), compares the American and English systems of strict foreclosure.

b. FORECLOSURE BY COURT ACTION AND SALE

SKILTON, DEVELOPMENTS IN MORTGAGE LAW AND PRACTICE, 17 TEMPLE UNIV.L.Q. 315, 319–320 (1943): By 1830, it would seem that strict foreclosure had been superseded in the great majority of states by foreclosure through public sale. In developing the device of public sale, American courts generally made these innovations (1) they permitted the mortgagee to bid in the property himself; (2) they permitted him a claim for the difference between sale price and original claim, thus regarding the sale price as conclusively establishing value. Statutory formulae, developed for the administration of this new process of public sale, accounted, in part, for the growing tendency to treat public sale as finally cutting off the mortgagor's interest, with no succeeding period of redemption—contrary to the English practice in strict foreclosure. These innovations, apparently first appearing in New York cases in the early nineteenth century, represented substantial concessions to the mortgagee: they made his remedies much more potent.

As modified by later statutory developments, equitable foreclosure followed by public sale remains the most popular method of terminating the mortgagor's interest in a majority of American jurisdictions. In spite of the changes introduced to expedite and simplify the procedure, this method continues to be comparatively costly and complicated. The typical equity proceeding involves a preliminary title search to determine all parties in interest; the filing of a *lis pendens,* summons or complaint; service of the process; a time for a hearing, if necessary; the decree or judgment; the delivery to the sheriff of papers authorizing him to sell; notice of sale and service of notice; the actual sale and the issuance of a certificate of sale; and the sheriff's report. The number of steps necessary to consummate foreclosure by court process naturally results in delay, considerable court costs and a fairly large attorney's fee. Foreclosure by court process has, however, been defended as the safest way to determine by *res adjudicata* the rights of the parties.

NATIONAL ACCEPTANCE CO. OF AMERICA v. MARDIGIAN

United States District Court, Eastern District of Michigan, 1966.
259 F.Supp. 612.

FREEMAN, District Judge.

On October 16, 1961, defendant Union Wrecking Company, Inc. (Union) signed an installment negotiable note payable to the order of plaintiff, National Acceptance Company (N.A.C.), in the amount of

$250,000. The last installment was due on April 20, 1964. This note was secured by a mortgage upon certain property in Romulus Township, Wayne County, Michigan (herein referred to as the Romulus property). In addition, Henry and Barbara Mardigian at the same time guaranteed payment of the Union debt, and to secure this guaranty the Mardigians signed another promissory note, also payable to the order of N.A.C., for the sum of $50,000. This second note was itself secured by a mortgage on certain residential property in Dearborn, Michigan (herein designated the Dearborn property). It appears from the complaint that the mortgage on the Dearborn property was recorded on October 16, 1961, and that the mortgage on the Romulus tract was recorded on October 25, 1961.

Union is now bankrupt; and, according to the complaint some $162,000 is still owing to plaintiff—an amount that it now seeks to collect by foreclosing on its mortgages on both the Romulus and the Dearborn properties.

This matter is now before the Court on motions of defendants for partial summary judgment. These motions involve only the Romulus property. They arise largely because of complications attributable to the fact that plaintiff's mortgage on this land, when obtained, was only a second mortgage. More precisely, the instant questions stem from the additional facts that the senior mortgagees, defendants Dombek and wife, had begun foreclosure proceedings in the state court in early June of 1961—at least four months before plaintiff obtained and recorded its mortgage—and that plaintiff never became a party to that foreclosure litigation.

The Dombeks purchased the Romulus property when it was finally sold in September, 1963, at a judicial sale pursuant to a decree entered in their foreclosure suit. Subsequently, the Dombeks sold a portion of the land to defendant M.B.M. Fabricators, Inc. (M.B.M.), which, in turn, mortgaged its interest to defendant National Bank of Wyandotte (Bank). These defendants—the Dombeks, M.B.M., and Bank—have moved this Court for partial summary judgment on the grounds that whatever interest plaintiff may have had in the Romulus property has been cut off by the foreclosure and sale under the Dombek senior mortgage, or, if plaintiff's interest survived, then plaintiff is, nevertheless, barred from foreclosing on it at this time because of laches and estoppel and because plaintiff did not seek to intervene in the Dombek foreclosure proceedings despite notice that such proceedings were in progress.

At the outset it should be observed that unopposed affidavits show conclusively that plaintiff was aware, at least sometime prior to the entry of a decree of foreclosure in favor of the Dombeks in July of 1963, that the Dombeks were in the process of foreclosing on their interest in the Romulus tract. Conversely, these same documents make it apparent that, before the Dombeks purchased at the judicial sale, they had equal notice of plaintiff's second mortgage.

Much of the discussion in the briefs filed in conjunction with the present motions deals with the significance, in light of the Michigan procedural rules in effect at the time of the Dombek foreclosure, of the fact that, after the first foreclosure proceedings had been commenced, the mortgagor, Union, made several additional payments on its obligation to the Dombeks and of the fact that thereafter the Dombeks filed a supplemental bill of foreclosure. Counsel argue whether or not this supplemental bill actually began a new foreclosure proceeding when plaintiff's second mortgage was clearly of record. Doubtless, if the sale to the Dombeks really did take place under a foreclosure commenced when they, as mortgagees, had constructive notice of plaintiff's interest in the Romulus property, many of the difficulties otherwise inherent in the present questions would be absent. Nevertheless, it is not necessary to delve into the fine points of dated Michigan procedure in order to reach the correct result in ruling upon the pending motions.

We begin, rather, with a basic proposition of mortgage law: a junior mortgagee's interest in property, if properly recorded prior to the commencement of proceedings to foreclose a senior encumbrance, is not cut off by the foreclosure unless he is made a party thereto. This rule does not mean, of course, that the junior interest is superior to the senior interest, nor that the unjoined junior interest holder can automatically oust the purchaser at the sale conducted pursuant to a decree of foreclosure entered on behalf of the senior encumbrancer. It means only that the second mortgage is still unforeclosed and that whatever rights were possessed by the junior mortgagee prior to foreclosure of the senior mortgage are still intact. By the same token, the rights of the mortgagor, now held by the purchaser, are still viable as against the unforeclosed junior mortgagee. Thus, the purchaser can redeem the interest held by the junior encumbrancer.

The specific question presented by these motions is whether this fundamental principle is somehow rendered inapplicable by the fact that the junior encumbrance in the present case arose and was recorded a few months after the senior encumbrancers had filed an action to foreclose their mortgage but some two years before the sale pursuant to the foreclosure proceedings took place. It appears that the answer is in the negative.

That this is the conclusion reached, of course, does not necessarily mean that plaintiff is not bound by the foreclosure decree; nor does it appear that plaintiff contends otherwise. It is important to realize exactly what the typical foreclosure decree adjudges and directs. Essentially, such an order shows only that a court has found that a mortgagor is in default on his obligation to the mortgagee and that the mortgagee is entitled to have the mortgaged property sold in partial or total satisfaction of the debt. In entering a decree of foreclosure, a court does not vest title to the property in the mortgagee. Much less does it determine, other than among the parties before it, who does and who does not have certain interests in the property. The court does not guarantee that the eventual purchaser pursuant to its decree is going to get a particular estate, or any estate for that matter, in return for his purchase price. Therefore, the fact that plaintiff may be bound by the Dombek foreclosure decree does not mean that by virtue of that order alone any interests which it might otherwise have had in the property which was the subject of the decree were cut off. For these reasons, unless plaintiff is attacking—and it is not—a determination actually made by the court which conducted the foreclosure proceedings, e.g., the decision that the Dombeks had a right to foreclose their mortgage, cases such as Carpenter v. Carpenter, 136 Mich. 362, 99 N.W. 395 (1904), cited by defendants, are inapposite. . . .

. . . Thus, the real issue boils down to this: did the mere fact that the second mortgage came into existence after the Dombek proceedings had begun deprive its owner of the right to consider the mortgage as viable until he should become a party to a proceeding to foreclose it? It is difficult to understand how ordinarily the simple act of filing a lawsuit can impair the rights of anyone, in particular those of a person who is not even destined to become a party to the litigation.

When property is the subject of a suit, however, the commencement of the action, coupled with the necessary steps creating notice of a *lis pendens,* may have this effect. In Ohio, for example, it appears to be the rule that a junior lien is cut off by completed foreclosure proceedings were the encumbrance arose after a *lis pendens* has been properly noticed. No case in Michigan seems to have dealt with the same problem. It is arguable whether a similar result would be reached in Michigan in light of Union Trust Co. v. C.H. Miles Adams Avenue Corp., 247 Mich. 340, 225 N.W. 594 (1929), a case which will be discussed in greater detail below, and Maximovich v. Wojtowicz, 236 Mich. 643, 211 N.W. 65 (1926).

Speculation upon this issue is unnecessary at the present time, since the record shows nothing to lead the Court to believe that a *lis pendens* was noticed in favor of the Dombeks when plaintiff took its mortgage. Under the law that was in effect in 1961, notice of the foreclosure suit had to have been filed with the Register of Deeds in the county in which the land in litigation was located in order for the bill of complaint to have served as constructive notice of the litigation. Defendants have not indicated that any pertinent document other than the original mortgage on the Romulus property has ever been filed with the Register of Deeds in Wayne County.

Since this motion must be disposed of on the basis that no *lis pendens* was noticed, and since there appears to be no other way by which a plaintiff upon the commencement of a lawsuit can affect the rights of persons without actual knowledge, the only conclusion appropriate to this discussion is that the temporal sequence of the events in this case is no reason for denying to plaintiff the benefit of the general principle of mortgage law referred to previously. In other words, since plaintiff held and properly recorded prior to the Dombek foreclosure sale what must be assumed to have been a valid second mortgage upon the property upon which the Dombeks had the prior encumbrance, and since plaintiff was not a party to the foreclosure action, plaintiff has all the rights under its second mortgage that it would have had if there had never been a foreclosure of the senior mortgage.

Defendants argue that even if plaintiff's right to foreclose on its second mortgage was not cut off under all circumstances by the Dombek foreclosure, it is barred under the facts of this case because plaintiff could have moved to intervene in the Dombek proceedings and could have asserted its interest at that time. However, they have not cited any case from any jurisdiction holding that one in a position similar to that occupied by plaintiff from October, 1961, until the fall of 1963 is obligated to intervene in a foreclosure suit in order to protect his rights. Indeed, such a rule would seem highly anomalous when one considers that the party most likely to gain from such a principle would be the foreclosing senior lienor who, thanks to the junior mortgagee's voluntarily putting his interest on the block, would theoretically be able to realize more at his own foreclosure sale because the property would be sold free of one more encumbrance. In any event, it seems clear on the basis of Union Trust Co. v. C.H. Miles Adams Avenue Corp., supra, that in Michigan not only need the holder of a junior encumbrance which arises after the commencement of a foreclosure suit by a senior mortgagee not intervene in order to protect his interest, but also that he can do so only with the consent of the original plaintiff. In that case, after Union Trust had begun to foreclose its mortgage on a leasehold belonging to the defendant C.H. Miles Corporation, the Netting Company took several judgments against the Corporation and levied upon the leasehold. Netting then moved to intervene in the foreclosure suit. Although the Michigan Supreme Court, affirming the trial court's denial of the motion, observed that Netting desired to intervene principally to attack Union Trust's mortgage rather than to enforce its own lien, the rule announced by the court does not appear to have been tailored to situations where a similar purpose motivates the would-be intervenor. The court said, referring to an opinion of the Minnesota Supreme Court:

"This decision ... is authority for holding ... that a junior incumbrancer, becoming such after the institution of proceedings to foreclose a prior mortgage lien, is not a necessary party defendant, and has no right to intervene in the foreclosure suit."

Although the court mentioned the then controlling statute dealing with intervention, it specifically noted that it was reaching its decision on the basis of judicial policy existing independent of the legislation. Therefore, there is no reason to believe that the principle announced in *Union Trust* has been weakened by changes in the general procedural rules relating to intervention.

Lastly, defendants contend that estoppel and laches still bar plaintiff's right to foreclose, even if he need not have intervened in the Dombek proceedings. The basis of the argument seems to be that there is something inherently inequitable—if not outright unconscionable—about plaintiff's waiting to foreclose on its mortgage until after M.B.M. and Bank, both of which had constructive notice of plaintiff's mortgage, purchased interests in the Romulus property which were accompanied by the benefits of warranties of title given by the Dombeks, who had actual and constructive knowledge of the mortgage. No doubt, a mortgagee can mislead another into believing that he will not enforce his interest and thus be denied by the doctrines of estoppel or laches the right to do so. It is sufficient to say that there is no indication in the record at this time that plaintiff did anything to lead any of the moving parties to act to their prejudice in the belief that plaintiff would not enforce its mortgage.

The motions for summary judgment must be denied. An appropriate order may be submitted.

NOTES

1. Was the result in National Acceptance v. Mardigian correct? At what point should the Dombeks be deemed to have acquired constructive notice of National Acceptance's interest? What were National Acceptance's remedies as an unforeclosed junior lienor?

2. *"Necessary" Parties and "Proper" Parties.* From the mortgagee's viewpoint, the central assumption behind foreclosure is that each mortgagee is entitled to proceed against exactly the interest in land—neither more nor less—that it originally received as security for the loan. A foreclosing first mortgagee is thus able to eliminate all encumbrances, liens, easements, covenants, leases and other interests that attached to the property after its mortgage. Similarly, a junior encumbrancer can wipe out any interests that are junior to its own. But the title transferred on the junior's foreclosure sale will necessarily be subject to any outstanding senior encumbrances, for to enable the junior encumbrancer to terminate the senior encumbrance would effectively give it a greater interest than it originally received as security for its loan.

Procedurally, these concepts are delineated by the division between "necessary" and "proper" parties to the foreclosure proceedings. Because junior lienors stand to lose their interests on foreclosure by a senior lienor, they are "necessary parties" who must be joined if their interests are to be eliminated and a completely effective foreclosure order rendered. In addition to the mortgagor and junior mortgagees, necessary parties include all easement holders, mechanics' lienors and others whose interests first attached after the interest of the foreclosing lienor. The effect of a failure to join junior mortgagees, or others with the right to redeem, is that the redemptive rights they could have exercised at or before the foreclosure sale remain intact. Failure to join easement and covenant holders similarly leaves their nonpossessory interests intact.

Just as senior liens are substantively insulated from junior lien foreclosures, senior lienors are procedurally insulated from the bother of having to join in the junior's foreclosure proceedings. Senior lienors, though not necessary parties, may however be "proper" parties and can be joined without their consent if their presence would aid a full and binding determination on the foreclosure sale. For example, if there is some question about the amount outstanding on the senior debt, or the debt's priority position, the senior lienor may be joinable as a proper party so that the foreclosure decree can settle these issues.

3. *Quality of Title to Purchaser.* It is claimed that judicial foreclosure has the advantage of producing a more stable title for the purchaser because the presence of a judge and the other parties makes it more likely that issues will be raised and disposed of in the action. Moreover, the rule of judicial finality will be applied to limit collateral attacks by a party participating in the court's decision. *National Acceptance* illustrates a key exception to the finality rule in allowing a collateral attack on the foreclosure action by an omitted necessary party. G. Nelson & D. Whitman, Real Estate Finance Law § 7.17 (2d ed.1985).

Was the result in *National Acceptance* fair to M.B.M. and the Bank? *Caveat emptor* generally applies to a purchaser at a foreclosure sale, although there is some disagreement as to whether the doctrine would require the purchaser to accept a deed where the title was not marketable. See G. Nelson & D. Whitman, Real Estate Finance Law § 7.17 (2d ed.1985); CSS Corporation v. Sheriff of Chester County, 352 Pa.Super. 256, 507 A.2d 870 (1986), appeal denied, 514 Pa. 630, 522 A.2d 559 (1987). Which view is correct? Could M.B.M. and the Bank have learned of the defective service, when, and at what cost?

4. *Benefits of Judicial Foreclosure.* Judicial foreclosure, though more costly and time-consuming than nonjudicial foreclosure, continues to be widely used. One reason, described above in note 3, is that the quality of deeds given at judicial foreclosure is believed to be more marketable than deeds given at nonjudicial sales, and capable of attracting a higher bid. Another reason for the wide use of judicial foreclosure is that legislative skepticism about the propriety of nonjudicial foreclosure has in many places curtailed its usefulness, availability, or both.

5. *Attorney Liability.* Cases have held borrowers liable for costs and fines for bringing egregiously frivolous appeals in a foreclosure action. Besides general concerns over such behavior, these cases may well reflect the desire for an efficient, fast, and final foreclosure procedure. For example, in White v. Mid–Continent Investments, Inc., 789 S.W.2d 34, 41 (Mo.App.1990), the court found that the basis of the appeal was that court below erred in not believing mortgagor's testimony rather than the facts contained in evidence which she herself adduced. The court stated: "This appeal utterly lacks merit and constitutes an abuse of process of this court and our system of civil

justice. The plaintiff, a law school graduate of considerable ability, has robbed this court, the trial court and the defendants of precious time and money, asserting baseless claims smacking of fraud."

Attorneys may also be liable. In United States v. Allen L. Wright Development Corporation, 667 F.Supp. 1218 (N.D.Ill.1987), the owner of the mortgagor-corporation and the mortgagor's attorneys were held liable under Rule 11 for the government's costs and attorneys fees in foreclosing a HUD mortgage where the mortgagor's "answer, affirmative defenses, response to the United States' motion for summary judgment and discovery requests were not well grounded in fact or warranted by existing law or even a good faith argument for the extension, modification or reversal of existing law.... Additionally, we find that [mortgagor's] actions and the actions of its attorneys were motivated by an improper purpose, specifically to delay the proceedings as long as possible to garner income tax benefits and to increase the attorneys' fees payable out of the subject of this foreclosure action." Id. at 1221–1222.

c. FORECLOSURE BY POWER OF SALE

SKILTON, DEVELOPMENTS IN MORTGAGE LAW AND PRACTICE

17 Temple University Law Quarterly 315, 323–326 (1943).

Not satisfied with the costly and complicated system of equitable foreclosure obtaining at the end of the eighteenth century, draftsmen representing mortgagees hit upon the idea of inserting in mortgage indentures an express authority to the mortgagee to sell the property without court action, freed of the equity of redemption. The legality of this device was at first questioned in England. In Robert v. Bozan,[42] Lord Eldon objected to the power on the ground that it constituted the mortgagee the trustee of the equity of redemption, and suggested that it would have been more proper had a third party been named as holder of the power. Earlier, an eminent authority on mortgages had remarked that powers of sale were of "too doubtful a complexion to be relied upon as the source of an irredeemable title".[43] It had been said:

> "The objections made to such a power were, that it was another device of the unscrupulous mortgagee to take advantage of the necessities of the mortgagor; that it was susceptible of abuse, as a sale might be forced at an unfavorable time; that it made a mortgagee trustee of the equity of redemption, and that it was in conflict with the jurisdiction of the courts of equity." [44]

42. Chan. (Feb. 1825) M.B. cited in Coventry, 15 Pres.Mort. 150.

43. Powell on Mortgages, quoted in Jones, Power of Sale Mortgages and Trust Deeds (1877) 3 So.L.Rev. 703.

44. Lionberger, Mortgages and Powers of Sale (1888) 16 Cent.L.J. 247, at 248.

Such objections prevented the early use of powers of sale in England, although with the passage of time they gained wide acceptance and approval, and eventually statutory authorization and form.

Powers of sale were recognized as valid in many states at an earlier date than in England. Jones, writing in 1877, stated:

"Fifty years ago power of sale mortgages were not in general use anywhere in this country; and although considerable use was made of them at an earlier time than any corresponding use was made of them in England, they were adopted in the latter country at an earlier time than here, to the exclusion of other forms of security. Within the past half century, however, the use of them has rapidly extended, so that in some states the use of any other form of security is exceptional. The validity of these powers of sale is everywhere recognized, and the use of them, either in mortgages or deeds of trust, is becoming general." [46]

The growing popularity of this device was accompanied by statutes passed in most of the states, establishing conditions of advertisement and sale that had to be met in the valid exercise of the power. These statutes sometimes served to permit the sale out of court of mortgaged premises where no express power of sale was included. There is much statutory material on this point. Illustrative is the case of New York. In 1774 legislation specifically authorized the exercise of such power, thus clearing previous doubts as to its validity. Notice of sale was to be given by publication and posting. In 1844 the statute was amended to prescribe notice by personal service or mail, in addition to the previously stipulated methods. In 1857 it was provided that a copy of the notice should be delivered to the county clerk, and affixed to a book. In 1808 it was provided that the affidavit of the printer should be evidence of publication, posting and notice. In 1838 the mortgagee was permitted to buy the property himself. These and other statutes create a background for the exercise of the power, and their mandatory provisions must be fully complied with if a valid exercise is to be made, regardless of easier requirements in the mortgage.

Although recognized as lawful by the courts in many states, and in some cases reinforced by statutory authority, powers of sale continued to be viewed by courts with jealousy, as an invasion of their sphere. The effect of this judicial jealousy was to impose limiting influences upon the legal development of powers of sale. For example, without statutory authority, the mortgagee was not permitted to buy in the property himself.

Restrictive judicial tendencies were carried to the extent in Virginia and other southern states that a power of sale given personally to the mortgagee was held to be invalid, and the practice developed of naming a third party as trustee to exercise the power. The result is that today

---

46. Jones, Power of Sale Mortgages and Trust Deeds (1877) 3 So.L.Rev. 703, at 707.

in many southern states, and elsewhere, the deed of trust is the popular security device.

The deed of trust is, however, essentially a mortgage and there would seem to be no valid reason for legal distinctions between the two forms. As A.M. Kidd remarked:

"... distinctions are unsound. The trustee under a trust deed is in no sense a fiduciary. He is usually an agent of the lender of the money and in a rational system could well be dispensed with. ... The trustee of a trust deed for security is in reality no more of a fiduciary than the law compels a mortgagee to be." [54]

Unfortunately for simplicity, however, there are many states in which trust deeds and mortgages exist side by side, and somewhat whimsical legal distinctions between them have frequently been made. The exact legal position of each must depend upon the peculiar laws of each state. Such variety, naturally, obstructs a coordinated view of the legal status of the mortgage and related forms.

Powers of sale out of court, either in mortgages or deeds of trust, have developed in popularity until they are in many states the chief method of foreclosure. They achieved such popularity because of the simplicity, speed and cheapness of their execution. There are but two steps necessary: notice and sale. In consequence, costs are light, consisting principally of advertising charges and a small attorney's fee. Whereas the average cost of foreclosure proceeding by judicial process appears to be from $150 to $200, foreclosure by power of sale out of court seems to be about $100 less. Whereas the length of time involved in foreclosure by judicial action is from two to four months, and in some states considerably longer, it usually takes from one to two months to complete foreclosure by power of sale. These periods are, of course, exclusive of the time for redemption, if any exists.

By the time powers of sale received general acceptance, the tide of judicial and legislative interest in the problems of the mortgagee had spent itself. The United States was now beginning to experience a series of land and business depressions which resulted from its emergence as an industrial community. In the business downswings, the pressure of financially distressed classes of the community became too heavy to resist. From the early part of the nineteenth century to the present day, depression legislation has played a large part in shaping the mortgage into a legal cast designedly quite favorable to the interests of the mortgagor.

---

54. Kidd, Trust Deeds and Mortgages in California (1915) 3 Calif.L.Rev. 381, at 383, 384.

ROSENBERG v. SMIDT

Supreme Court of Alaska, 1986.
727 P.2d 778.

Before RABINOWITZ, C.J., and BURKE, MATTHEWS, COMPTON and MOORE, JJ.

OPINION

COMPTON, Justice.

Fred Rosenberg and Rita Rosenberg appeal from a partial summary judgment entered pursuant to Civil Rule 54(b). The judgment divested them of title to a parcel of real property and revested it in Alvin Smidt and Janice Smidt. Since the trial court's decision is based on stipulated facts, the appeal presents only legal issues. The parties dispute whether AS 34.20.070(c) requires a trustee to attempt to discover the current address of a record interest holder before proceeding with a trustee's sale of encumbered real property. The parties also dispute whether AS 34.20.090(c) protects the Rosenbergs as bona fide purchasers without notice of possible defects in the foreclosure sale notifications. We affirm.

I. FACTS AND PROCEEDINGS

In December 1973, Rodney Spendlove and William Johnson [1] sold real property to Alvin Smidt and Janice Smidt (Smidts). At the time of the sale, a first deed of trust executed by Spendlove and Johnson encumbered the property. [2] The Smidts executed a second deed of trust on the property in favor of Spendlove and Johnson, [3] securing the balance of the purchase price, $6,200. Alaska Title Guaranty Company (Alaska Title) was designated trustee on both deeds of trust.

The Smidts made all of the payments due on their note through May 1981. Nevertheless, by early 1980 Spendlove and Johnson had defaulted on the payments due under the note secured by the first deed of trust. At the beneficiaries' request, Alaska Title began nonjudicial foreclosure proceedings in June, 1980.

As required by AS 34.20.070(c), [4] Alaska Title sent copies of the notice of default to the Smidts, Johnson, and Spendlove. Alaska Title

---

1. While both are defendants below, neither are parties to this appeal. Apparently, no final judgment has yet been entered against them.

2. The beneficiaries of this first trust deed are not parties to this dispute.

3. In this trust deed, the Smidts requested Alaska Title to send notices of default (on *that* deed, presumably) to the address listed on the deed. Upon the default in the first trust deed, as requested, Alaska Title did send the notice to the address listed on the second deed.

4. AS 34.20.070(c) provides:

Within 10 days after recording the notice of default, the trustee shall mail a copy of the notice by certified mail to the *last known address* of each of the following persons or their legal representatives (1) the grantor in the trust deed; (2) *the successor in interest to the grantor whose interest appears of record* or of whose interest the trustee or the beneficiary has actual notice, or who is in possession of the property; (3) any other person in possession of or occupying the property; (4) any person having a lien or interest

used the address for the Smidts listed on the 1973 second deed of trust. The Smidts, however, had moved from that address—a mobile home park—in 1975. The certified letters sent to the Smidts were returned to Alaska Title marked "unclaimed." Alaska Title published notice of the sale in an Anchorage newspaper. The Smidts, however, did not get actual notice of the sale.

From the summer of 1975 through the summer of 1980, the Smidts resided and received mail at their home on Old Muldoon Road in Anchorage. Alaska Title could have discovered the Smidts' address by contacting either the Anchorage Municipality Real Property Taxation Department, any of several utility companies, or the State's Department of Motor Vehicles. The Anchorage phone directory listed Alvin Smidt's phone number, but not address. Polk's Greater Anchorage Area Directory listed the Smidt's address in 1979, but not in 1980.

In October 1980, Fred Rosenberg and Rita Rosenberg (Rosenbergs) purchased the property at a public foreclosure sale held by Alaska Title. Although the property was then worth more than $20,000, they bid only $5,626.25. The Smidts, meanwhile, continued making payments to Spendlove and Johnson, ignorant of the sale until April 1981.

The Smidts sued the Rosenbergs, Alaska Title, Spendlove, and Johnson to set aside the sale. The Smidts moved for partial summary judgment. The trial court ruled that "principles of equity" require a trustee to "take reasonable steps to ascertain the current address of the trustor or his assignee." The trial court noted that the mobility of Alaska's youthful population compelled such a duty. It further noted that while professional trustees know of the need to be informed of address changes, the deed of trust here imposed no such requirement on the Smidts. Judgement was entered pursuant to Civil Rule 54(b), and the Rosenbergs appealed.

II. DILIGENT INQUIRY UNDER AS 34.20.070(c).

AS 34.20.070(c) required Alaska Title to mail a notice of Spendlove and Johnson's default to the "last known address" of their assignees, the Smidts. At the time Alaska Title mailed its notice, it had actual knowledge only of the address used by the Smidts seven years earlier. The parties dispute whether Alaska Title should have made some effort to locate the Smidts after it received the returned certified letter marked "unclaimed." Imposition of a due diligence requirement would announce a protection neither required nor precluded by the statute.

No Alaska cases have construed this provision of AS 34.20.070(c). Decisions from other jurisdictions interpreting similar "last known address" clauses provide some insight, but the statutory schemes in

subsequent to the interest of the trustee in the trust deed, where the lien or interest appears of record or where the trustee or the beneficiary has actual notice of the lien or interest. The notice may be delivered personally instead of by mail.

(Emphasis added).

which such clauses occur differ so greatly that no case adequately disposes of this question.[8]

"Last known address" clauses appear most frequently in tax statutes, service of process rules, and trust deed statutes. For instance, Section 6212(b) of the Internal Revenue Code, 26 U.S.C. § 6212(b) (1981), requires the Commissioner of Internal Revenue to mail notice of a tax deficiency to the taxpayer's "last known address." The federal courts require the Commissioner to use reasonable diligence in ascertaining the taxpayer's current address. *See* Annot., 58 A.L.R.Fed. 548, 554–56 (1982). At the same time, the commissioner may rely on "the address appearing on a taxpayer's return as the last known in the absence of clear and concise notification from the taxpayer directing the Commissioner to use a different address." *Alta Sierra Vista, Inc. v. Commissioner*, 62 T.C. 367, 374 (1974), *aff'd mem.*, 538 F.2d 334 (9th Cir.1976).

Thus, while the Internal Revenue Service (IRS) must be diligent to send notices properly, the taxpayer must clearly notify the IRS of any changes. Only when the IRS fails to respond after the taxpayer has communicated changed addresses will the IRS have breached its duty of due diligence. *See, e.g., Crum v. Commissioner*, 635 F.2d 895, 899–900 (D.C.Cir.1980). Absent communication by the taxpayer, the IRS seems under no duty to mail notices to any address other than the one last used by the taxpayer. The tax statutes, however, contemplate at least yearly communications between government and taxpayer.

Substitute service of process rules occasionally allow a party to mail process to defendant's "last known address." *See Shanklin v. Bender*, 283 A.2d 651, 653–54 (D.C.1971) (construing Ill.Rev.Stat. ch. 95 1/2, § 10–301(b) (1967–70)) (service of process on nonresident motor vehicle operator); *Feinstein v. Bergner*, 48 N.Y.2d 234, 422 N.Y.S.2d 356, 397 N.E.2d 1161 (1979) (construing N.Y.Civ.Prac.R. 308(4)) (substitute mail service on defendant's "last known residence" and nail service on "dwelling place' and "usual place of abode"); *Volmer v. Hoel*, 87 Ohio App. 199, 93 N.E.2d 416 (1950) (construing Gen. Code § 6308–2, replaced by Ohio Rev. Code Ann. § 2703.20 (1981)) (service on nonresident motor vehicle operator); *Waddell v. Mamat*, 271 Wis.176, 72 N.W.2d 763, 766 (1955) (construing § 85.05(3) stats., now Wis.Stat.Ann. § 345.-

---

8. The parties do not here dispute the constitutionality of the notice provision. They had disputed below whether due process required better notice than the Smidts received. The trial court originally invalidated the sale on due process grounds. It then reversed its due process ruling and decided instead upon equitable grounds.

The constitutionality of notice of deed of trust sale provisions has been litigated frequently. *See* G. Osborne, G. Nelson & D. Whitman, Real Estate Finance Law §§ 7.23—7.30 (1979) (hereinafter cited as Real Estate Finance Law); *see also* Note,

The Constitutionality of Power of Sale Foreclosure in Alaska, 6 UCLA–Alaska L. Rev. 90 (1976). The trend, however, is to find that nonjudicial sales lack sufficient state action to trigger the federal due process protections. *See Flagg Bros. v. Brooks*, 436 U.S. 149, 98 S.Ct. 1729, 56 L.Ed.2d 185 (1978) (warehouseman's private sale of goods under UCC 7–210 involved no state action); *Garfinkle v. Superior Court*, 21 Cal.3d 268, 146 Cal.Rptr. 208, 578 P.2d 925 (1978) (deed of trust foreclosure sale lacked state action).

09(2) (West 1971)) (nonresident motor vehicle operator); *see also* Ohio Civ.R. 4.4 (1982). *Volmer* appears to require due diligence. 93 N.E.2d at 420. *Shanklin* interpreted Illinois law as requiring reasonable diligence. 283 A.2d at 653. *Waddell* merely paraphrased *Wuchter v. Pizzutti*, 276 U.S. 13, 48 S.Ct. 259, 72 L.Ed. 446 (1928), and stated that "[t]he last known address is that one most likely to give the party to be served notice." 72 N.W.2d at 766.

We recognize that, like cases construing the tax statute, these holdings involve statutory schemes with concerns somewhat different from the deed of trust sale. When service of process is involved, federal due process requires notice reasonably calculated to apprise the parties of the pendency of an action. *See, e.g., Mullane v. Central Hanover Bank & Trust Co.*, 339 U.S. 306, 314, 70 S.Ct. 652, 657, 94 L.Ed. 865, 873 (1950). Moreover, some states require proof of due diligence at attempted personal service *before* allowing substitute service. *See, e.g.,* N.Y.Civ.Prac.R. 308(4) (West 1972). Thus the federal due process concerns raised by tax and process laws require some showing of due diligence. These *federal* due process rights are absent from a deed of trust foreclosure sale. Furthermore, unlike tax and process cases, deed of trust sales involve title to real property. Courts have traditionally favored the free and easy alienability of real property. Deed of trust provisions encourage ready transfer in two ways. By assuring creditors a speedy, inexpensive and uncomplicated remedy in the event of default, deeds of trust allow lenders to loan more cheaply the funds necessary to purchase the property initially. *See* 10 G. Thompson, Commentaries on the Modern Law of Real Property, § 5175 at 204–05 (1957). Thus, deeds of trust encourage debtors to buy by assuring creditors of easy resale. "[W]here it is in common use, power of sale foreclosure has provided an effective foreclosure remedy with a cost in time and money substantially lower than that of its judicial foreclosure counterpart." Real Estate Finance Law, § 7.19 at 477 (footnote omitted).

The Rosenbergs argue that a requirement of due diligence in a provision of notice of default would increase the costs of financing real property transfers. Beyond the administrative costs of searching for absent interested parties, creditors would bear the increased risk of attendant costs of litigation over the trustee's compliance. *See id.* Ultimately, creditors will pass on these costs to future borrowers. Thus, all debtors would be forced to pay the higher costs of protecting those debtors who invest and then move without advising the trustee of their new address. The Rosenbergs, however, do not quantify these increased costs.

Review of the law of other jurisdictions reveals numerous "last known address" statutes governing notice of deed of trust sales.[9] *See,*

---

9. Some states require *no* mailed notice. *See, e.g.,* S.D. Codified Laws § 21–48–6 (1979) (notice by publication alone suffices); Utah Code Ann. § 57–1–25 (Supp.1983) (notice by publication and posting notice on property to be sold, as well as three other

e.g., Cal.Civ.Code § 2924b(2)(a)-(c) (West 1974 & Supp. 1985); D.C. Code Ann. § 45–715(b) (1981) (written notice by certified mail with return receipt requested to the last known address); Idaho Code § 45–1506(2) (1977) (notice by registered or certified mail to last known address); Or.Rev.Stat. § 86.740 (1983) (mail notice by both first class and certified mail with return receipt to the last known address); *compare* Ariz.Rev. Stat.Ann. § 33–809(B)(2) (Supp.1985) (trustee uses address on recorded document unless address missing); Tex.Prop.Code Ann. § 51.002(b)(3) (Vernon 1984) (notice sent to last known address appearing in the records of the holder of the debt); Wash.Rev.Code Ann. § 61.24.040(b) (Supp.1985) (notice sent to address in recorded instrument or otherwise known to trustee). The few reported decisions reveal no holding imposing a due diligence requirement. A recent California decision specifically rejected a due diligence requirement. In *I.E. Associates v. Safeco Title Insurance Co.*, 39 Cal.3d 281, 216 Cal.Rptr. 438, 702 P.2d 596 (1985) the California Supreme Court construed Civil Code 2924b. This statute explicitly defines "last known address" as "the last business or residence actually known by the ... person authorized to record the notice of default." Cal.Civ.Code § 2924b(2)(c). The section also requires the beneficiary to tell the trustee of the last address actually known by the beneficiary. Cal.Civ.Code § 2924b(2)(c). Faced with such strong evidence of a limitation to knowledge "actually" known, the court stated that the section imposed no due diligence requirement upon trustees. 216 Cal.Rptr. at 440, 702 P.2d at 598.

The California statute's explicit definition of "last known address" distinguishes it from AS 34.20.070(c). Further, unlike California, Alaska imposes no duty on the beneficiary of a trust deed to notify the trustee of an actually known last address of an interested party.[11] We therefore decline to follow the reasoning of *I.E., Associates*.

A tension exists between free and easy alienability of real property and notice to persons whose interest in real property is to be affected by governmental o.· private action. Yet it is not so great as to preclude a requirement of due diligence in attempting to get notice to those who will be affected by that action. As this case demonstrates vividly, diligent inquiry by the trustee would readily have provided Smidts' actual address.

On one hand,

public places in the city where property is to be sold).

11. The California court noted that the trustor should learn of the sale through posted notice on the property, *Id.* 216 Cal. Rptr. at 443, 702 P.2d at 601 n. 6, and that only passive investors, uninvolved with daily activity on the property, risk missing notice, *Id.* 216 Cal.Rptr. at 443, 702 P.2d at 601 n. 7.

Like California, Alaska requires both posting and publication before a nonjudi-

cial sale. *See* AS 34.20.080(a)(2), AS 09.35.-140. However, there is little basis for asserting that the only persons not likely to get notice under Alaska's statutory scheme are "passive investors" of undeveloped property who do not list a permanent agent for service of notices upon their original execution of the recorded instruments. Further, it should not make a difference that the affected interest is that of "passive investors."

[w]hile noncompliance with the statutory provisions regarding foreclosure by the power under a mortgage or trust deed is not to be favored, the remedy of setting aside the sale will be applied only in cases which reach unjust extremes.

Semlek v. National Bank of Alaska, 458 P.2d 1003, 1006 (Alaska 1969). On the other, "equity abhors a forfeiture and will seize upon slight circumstances to relieve a party therefrom." *Jameson v. Wurtz,* 396 P.2d 68, 74 (Alaska 1964) (footnote omitted).

We conclude that the last known address is that address most likely to give the affected party notice. The trustee is obligated to exercise due diligence to determine that address. Failure to impose such a requirement would not balance adequately the competing interests involved.

III. DOES AS 34.20.090(c) PROTECT THE ROSENBERGS AS BONA FIDE PURCHASERS?

Under AS 34.20.090(c),[12] recitals in the foreclosure sale deed that the trustee complied with notice provisions become conclusive evidence of compliance in favor of bona fide purchasers (bfp's). The deed the Rosenbergs received stated:

All other requirements of law regarding the mailing, publication and personal delivery of copies of the Notice of Default and all other notices have been complied with, and said Notice of Sale was publicly posted as required by law and published in the Anchorage Times on August 26 and September 2, 9, and 16, 1980.

The parties dispute whether this section barred the Smidts from overturning the sale on the basis of lack of notice. Although the Rosenbergs directed the trial court to this statute, the judgment makes no mention of it.

The Smidts make three arguments to avoid the statute. First, the Smidts claim that the statute does not apply to void sales. They correctly state the general rule that "[t]he doctrine of good faith purchaser for value without notice does not apply to a purchaser at a void foreclosure sale." *Henke v. First Southern Properties, Inc.,* 586 S.W.2d 617, 620 (Tex.Civ.App.1979). They misapply the rule, however, to the sale by Alaska Title. They fail to distinguish "void" from "voidable" sales. *See* Real Estate Finance Law, § 7.20 at 477–78. Only substantial defects such as the lack of a substantive basis to foreclose in the first place will make a sale void. *Id.* at 477 & § 7.21 at 489–90. *Henke* itself illustrates the most common basis for finding a void sale: the absence of default. 586 S.W.2d at 620. Where a defect in a

---

12. AS 34.20.090(c) provides:

A recital of compliance with all requirements of law regarding the mailing or personal delivery of copies of notices of default in the deed executed under a power of sale is prima facie evidence of compliance with the requirements. *The recital is conclusive evidence of compliance with the requirements in favor of a bona fide purchaser or encumbrancer for value and without notice.*

(Emphasis added).

foreclosure sale makes it merely voidable, however, sale to a bfp cuts off the trustor's ability to set aside the sale. *See Swindell v. Overton*, 310 N.C.707, 314 S.E.2d 512, 517 (1984); Real Estate Finance Law, § 7.21 at 489. Here, the alleged defect went not to the trustee's right to proceed with foreclosure but only to "the mechanics of exercising the power." *Id.* at 490. Thus, if the Rosenbergs were bfp's, the Smidts cannot set aside what is not a void, but a voidable, sale. However, as we hereinafter conclude, the Rosenbergs are not bfp's. The sale is therefore voidable.

Second, the Smidts challenge the Rosenberg's status as "bfp's without notice." No case defines this phrase for purposes of AS 34.20.090(c). Cases generally interpret the phrase to apply to one who lacks actual, constructive (*i.e.*, from the land records) or inquiry notice. *See, e.g., Swindell*, 314 S.E.2d at 517; *see also Sabo v. Horvath*, 559 P.2d 1038, 1043 (Alaska 1976). No one here contends that the Rosenbergs had actual or constructive notice of any defects in the notice sent to the Smidts. To bar their status as bfp's, the Smidts must hold the Rosenbergs to inquiry notice of the alleged defects.

This court explained inquiry notice in *Modrok v. Marshall*, 523 P.2d 172 (Alaska 1974).

> It is a settled rule of property that circumstances ... which suggest outstanding equities in third parties, impose a duty upon the purchaser to make a reasonable investigation into the existence of a claim. Given suspicious facts, the status of bona fide purchaser turns upon whether there was a prudent inquiry into their import.

Id. at 174 (footnote omitted). In other words, "the defects are not such that a person attending the sale exercising reasonable care would have been aware of the defect." Real Estate Finance Law, at 478.

The facts stipulated below suggest that the Rosenbergs at most were chargeable with knowledge of the Smidts' status as assignees of Spendlove and Johnson. The facts do not reveal whether anyone else bid at the auction. On one hand, the Rosenbergs could reasonably believe that the Smidts were unable to cure Spendlove and Johnson's default or had made other arrangements with the defaulting debtors. On the other, it is unreasonable to believe that the Smidts would do nothing to protect their interest.

Ultimately, to hold that the interested party's absence from a foreclosure sale imposes a duty upon purchasers to investigate the notice given would gut AS 34.20.090(c). No one would ever be a "bona fide purchaser without [inquiry] notice." By requiring would-be purchasers to "investigate or buy a lawsuit," such a holding would further increase the costs and delays accompanying deed of trust sales.

However, even if the Rosenbergs were not put on inquiry notice by the Smidts' absence from the sale, they may be charged with such notice if the deed contains no more than mere recitals that the trustee has complied with statutory notice requirements.

The Smidts argue that AS 34.20.090(c) contemplates recitals of fact, not conclusions of law. They contend that interpreting "recital" to mean a detailed recitation of the steps taken to notify trustors or their successors will prevent problems such as in this case. A recitation of the "facts" of notice, they argue, would charge the Rosenbergs with inquiry notice of the Smidts' plight and thus prevent the Rosenbergs from becoming bfp's. We agree with each of these points.

Several states have statutory presumptions similar to Alaska's. *See, e.g.,* Cal.Civ.Code § 2924 (West 1974); Or.Rev.Stat. § 86.780 (1983); Utah Code Ann. § 57–1–28(1) (1985). We have found no cases which hold that such statutes either are or are not satisfied by a bare statement that the law was complied with, as distinguished from a factual recitation of the steps which were taken to comply with the law.

According to one commentator on Oregon's statute,

> if the trustee recites in the deed it carried out notice procedures required by the statutes, such recitals provide absolute protection to a bona fide purchaser relying upon them.

Randolph, Jr., *Updating the Oregon Installment Land Contract,* 15 Willamette L.J. 181 at 200 n. 64 (1979). Oregon explicitly lists the required contents of recitals. Or.Rev.State. 86.775 states:

> The trustee's deed to the purchaser at the trustee's sale shall contain, in addition to a description of the property conveyed, a recital of *the facts concerning* the default, *the notice* given, the conduct of the sale and the receipt of the purchase money from the purchaser.

(Emphasis added). Alaska law also specifies that the trustee's "deed shall recite . . . the mailing or delivery of the copies of the notice of default. . . ." [16] though it is less clear than the Oregon statute as to whether the recital should be factual or conclusory.

We are persuaded that what is required is a recital of fact specifying what the trustee has done, not a mere conclusory statement that the trustee has complied with the law. There are several reasons which lead us to this conclusion.

The fact that .080(c) explicitly calls for factual details in the deed recital concerning recording, price, publication, and sale suggests that facts are also called for concerning mailing or delivery.[18] Further,

---

16. AS 34.20.080(c) provides:

The deed shall recite the date and the book and page of the recording of default, and the mailing or delivery of the copies of the notice of default, the true consideration for the conveyance, the time and place of the publication of notice of sale, and the time, place and manner of sale, and refer to the deed of trust by reference to the page, volume and place of record.

18. The principle of statutory construction which is applicable here is that of associated words—words are known by the company they keep. "A widely applied tenet of statutory interpretation is that if 'the legislative intent or general meaning

requiring a factual recital tends to assure that the requirements of law concerning mailing or delivery are complied with. A conclusory statement can be a matter placed in a form, or a programmed deed, and will not require the trustee to review what was actually done. A factual recital does require review in each case. While a factual recital requirement does not protect against fraud in all cases, it does tend to prevent the more common failings of oversight and neglect. A conclusory recital, on the other hand, accomplishes little or nothing.

The dissenting opinion states that the purpose of 34.20.090(c) is to provide extra protection to purchasers at foreclosure sales and to enhance the reliability of their titles. While that is one purpose of the act of which 34.20.090(c) is a part, it is by no means its only purpose. The enactment in question, ch. 116, SLA 1957, added the mailing and delivery requirements now set out in .070(c) (previous law had only required publication, ACLA 1949 § 22–5–2), mandated that the deed recite the mailing or delivery of notice, .080(c), and stated the evidentiary effect of such a recital, .090(c). Thus, the purpose of the act was not only to protect the foreclosure sale purchaser, but to require that effective notice of default and sale be given parties in interest, and to provide a self-effecting method of assuring that such notice is given. Construing the recital requirements in .080(c) and .090(c) to call only for formal conclusions does not accomplish the purpose of assuring mailing or delivery; a construction which holds that a recital of facts is required is consistent with all of the purposes of the statute.

Moreover, the use of the word "recital" suggests that facts rather than conclusions are what the statute calls for. The ordinary meaning of "recital" is a formal statement of relevant facts.

For these reasons we conclude that AS 34.20.080(c) and .090(c) require a recital of facts specifying what the trustee has done regarding mailing or delivery. Since there was no such recital in this case the Rosenbergs were on inquiry notice of a potential voidable defect. They cannot claim bfp status or the protection of .090(c).

AFFIRMED.

MOORE, Justice, with whom RABINOWITZ, Chief Justice, joins, dissenting in part.

I dissent from the majority's conclusion that the Rosenbergs are not Bona Fide Purchasers (BFP). In my view the Rosenbergs' status as BFPs bars the Smidts from overturning the foreclosure sale, and limits their remedy to seeking damages from Spendlove, Johnson and/or the trustee, Alaska Title Guaranty Company. Protecting the Rosenbergs'

---

of a statute is not clear, the meaning of doubtful words may be determined by reference to their association with other associated words and phrases.' " *State, Real Estate Commission v. Johnston,* 682 P.2d 383, 386–87 (Alaska 1984). Thus, since.

080(c) calls for facts concerning other subjects used in a series with mailing or delivery, it is logical to conclude that the statute calls for facts concerning mailing or delivery.

title to the property is compelled by important public policy considerations as well as by the express language of AS 34.20.090(c).

The majority correctly notes that where, as here, a defect in the foreclosure sale makes it merely voidable, the sale to a BFP will completely bar the debtor's ability to set aside the sale. ... This makes perfect sense, as grave consequences would result if the rule were otherwise. For example, if innocent purchasers at foreclosure sales had to face the risk that debtors could easily set aside the sales, then it takes little imagination to realize that participation at foreclosure sales would be significantly and unacceptably chilled. As the court stated in *In re Alsop*, 14 B.R. 982, 987 (Bankr.Alaska 1981), *aff'd* 22 B.R. 1017 (D.Alaska 1982):

> The specter of this uncertainty of title will severely inhibit participation at the foreclosure sale by anyone other than the original creditor, thus depressing bid prices to the general detriment of debtors. [This] would further reduce the willingness of creditors to lend on the security of a deed of trust, to the general detriment of borrowers.

Id. (Citation omitted.)

Furthermore, the innocent purchaser, having absolutely nothing to do with the legal relationship between the trustee and the debtor, should not be forced to bear any loss caused to the debtor by the trustee's failure to diligently protect the debtor's interests.

> As between the mortgagor and the purchaser, the former rather than the latter should suffer the loss, because by granting to the mortgagee the right to sell, the mortgagor put it in the mortgagee's power to work the injury through the execution of that power.

Dugan v. Manchester Federal Savings & Loan Association, 92 N.H. 44, 23 A.2d 873, 876 (1942). Here, where the injury was caused by the trustee's failure to discover the debtor's new address, it should be the debtor, not the innocent purchaser, who should lose title to the property. It is the debtor, not the purchaser, who can most easily notify the trustee of the new address. As between two innocent parties, the loss should fall on the one in the best position to have avoided that loss.

There is no doubt that Alaska follows the universal rule of refusing to set aside a voidable foreclosure sale when title has passed to a BFP. . . .

As the majority opinion illustrates, the Rosenbergs satisfy all of these requirements. They have paid value and are not related to the mortgagee. They had no actual knowledge of the trustee's failure to exercise due diligence in determining the Smidts' new address, and nothing in the recorded instruments put the Rosenbergs on notice of this defect. Finally, the notice defect was not such that attendance at the sale would provide any hint of the defect. As the majority carefully explains, the debtor's absence from the sale does not put the purchaser on inquiry notice nor require him to investigate or buy a lawsuit.

It is therefore clear that the Rosenbergs are BFPs and entitled to possession of the property. How then does the majority justify setting aside the sale? Curiously, the majority takes AS 34.20.090(c), gives it a bizarre interpretation, and uses it to strip the Rosenbergs of their BFP status. Ironically, this statute, like those found in other states, was specifically designed to enhance the reliability of title purchased by a BFP at a foreclosure sale. G. Nelson & D. Whitman, Real Estate Finance Law, § 7.21 at 552; Note, *The Constitutionality of Power of Sale Foreclosure in Alaska*, supra at 112, 116.

. . .

I must also disagree with the majority's decision to engraft onto the statute a requirement of detailed factual statements. The statute nowhere contains this requirement, and it is for the legislature, not this court, to add one if it sees fit to do so. While it is true that to create a conclusive presumption in favor of a BFP, some states require recitals of facts, other states, like Alaska, do not. A third variation does not require recitations at all, but provides that the deed itself creates the conclusive presumption in favor of the BFP. These variations suggest that there is no one way to balance the rights of creditors and BFPs. Our legislature has struck the balance in such a way that the BFP receives protection from the trustee's recitals in the deed. It is not for this court to alter the balance struck by this statutory scheme. The majority is unable to cite any authority that suggests this court can add a detailed factual statement requirement to a statute that obviously lacks one.

. . .

The majority suggests that a trustee will always recite that the law has been complied with, and thus the Rosenbergs' reliance on that recital is hollow. However, this "hollow reliance" is exactly what the statute authorizes. Moreover, since the trustee may be liable to the debtor in damages if wrong, the trustee has ample incentive to avoid issuing incorrect recitals. The BFP is therefore even further justified in relying on the accuracy of those recitals. Finally, even if the trustee had recited factual details, the majority does not explain what the Rosenbergs should have done to protect themselves. The fact that letters are returned unclaimed does not per se establish a notice defect. To discover the defect the potential purchaser would have to mount a costly and time consuming investigation. Language in the majority opinion illustrates the serious shortcomings of such a requirement:

> Ultimately, to ... impose[ ] a duty upon purchasers to investigate the notice given would gut AS 34.20.090(c). No one would ever be a "bona fide purchaser without [inquiry] notice." By requiring would-be purchasers to "investigate or buy a lawsuit," such a

holding would further increase the costs and delays accompanying deed of trust sales.

In conclusion, I dissent from the majority's holding that the Rosenbergs are not BFPs. That decision may have far-reaching effects, possibly clouding the titles of numerous BFPs who have acquired property through foreclosure sales, and chilling the bidding at future sales to the detriment of debtors and creditors alike. I would therefore return title in the property to the Rosenbergs and leave the Smidts free to pursue their remedy in damages against Johnson, Spendlove, and/or the trustee.

NOTES

1. Rosenberg v. Smidt involves two central issues in power of sale foreclosure: fairness of the proceeding and the quality of title that the purchaser receives. Was the case correctly decided on both issues? Did the court correctly resolve issues of statutory construction, policy concerns, and questions about the proper role of the legislature and the courts?

Consider how *Rosenberg* and National Acceptance Co. of America v. Mardigian (page 472) illustrate the advantages and disadvantages of power of sale foreclosure and judicial foreclosure in terms of cost, speed, protection of the mortgagor's and mortgagee's interests, and finality of proceedings.

2. *State Action.* As indicated in the principal case, most courts reject constitutional challenges to power of sale foreclosure on the theory that there is inadequate state action. Compare Mennonite Board of Missions v. Adams, 462 U.S. 791, 103 S.Ct. 2706, 77 L.Ed.2d 180 (1983) (proceeding brought by county to sell mortgaged property for nonpayment of taxes subject to Due Process Clause of Fourteenth Amendment and notice to mortgagee by posting and publication was inadequate). One exception is Turner v. Blackburn, 389 F.Supp. 1250 (W.D.N.C.1975) (finding power of sale foreclosure statute permitting notice by posting and publication unconstitutional as applied). That decision led to changes in the North Carolina statute. See generally, Comment, Real Property—Changes in North Carolina's Foreclosure Law, 54 N.C.L.Rev. 903 (1976).

3. *Trustee Duties.* Judicial ambivalence about private individuals doing what courts probably think they can do better has seriously muddled the standards of conduct applied to nonjudicial sales. The standard nominally applied to trust deed sales is that "a trustee in a deed of trust acts in a fiduciary capacity and he must act with complete integrity, fairness, and impartiality toward both the debtor and the creditor." Spires v. Edgar, 513 S.W.2d 372, 378 (Mo.1974). The standard entirely ignores the reality that trustees typically are nominees of the beneficiary.

Indeed, Spires v. Edgar, although invoking the traditional rule on the trustee's fiduciary duty, reached a refreshingly realistic decision against the trustors' claim that the trustee had acted improperly in failing to inquire into their performance under the note: "We have concluded that in the absence of unusual circumstances known to the trustee, he may, upon receiving a request for foreclosure from the creditor, proceed upon that advice without making any affirmative investigation and without giving any special notice to the debtor. We are not considering here any liabilities or duties of the holder of the note or notes." 513 S.W.2d at 378, 379.

Should a sale be voided if the trustee owns an interest in the debt? If the creditor owns an interest in the trustee? If the trustee buys the land from the successful bidder shortly after the sale? See Smith v. Haley, 314 S.W.2d 909 (Mo.1958), distinguished in Spires v. Edgar. See generally, Dingus, Mortgages—Redemption After Foreclosure Sale in Missouri, 25 Mo.L.Rev. 261 (1960).

4. *Notice.* How can junior lienors and other interested parties be assured that they will receive notice of foreclosure by nonjudicial sale? Although the mortgage or trust deed will typically spell out some of the relevant procedures, local statutes will provide the more comprehensive basis for giving notice.

California's notice procedures for trust deed foreclosures and foreclosures of mortgages with powers of sale are simple and effective. The process begins with a notice of default executed and recorded by the trustee or mortgagee. The trustee or mortgagee will then search title to the property to see if any requests for a copy of a notice of default and sale have been recorded after the trust deed or mortgage and before the notice of default.

The trustee or mortgagee must then mail the notice of default to all who have requested it, as well as to all individuals who fall into any of six statutorily prescribed classes and whose interests can be discovered by a title search. Among those included are any present successors in interest to the mortgagor or trustor, junior beneficiaries or mortgagees and their assignees, lessees and contract vendees. Three months after the notice of default is filed for record, if the default has not been cured, the trustee or mortgagee who wishes to foreclose is required to send a notice of sale, stating the time and place of the sale, to each person entitled to receive a copy of the notice of default. These notices must be sent at least twenty days before the date of sale. Cal.Civ.Code §§ 2924, 2924b.

5. *U.L.S.I.A.* U.L.S.I.A. section 509 permits power of sale foreclosure. The Act discusses both aspects of Rosenberg v. Smidt.

As to the required notification, Section 508 states that notice of foreclosure must be sent to the debtor at the address specified in the mortgage and "[i]f the creditor knows of a different address of the debtor at which notices are more likely to come to the debtor's attention, the notice must also be sent to that address." Under section 112(a) a person "knows" of a fact only when she has "actual knowledge of it."

As to the right of the Rosenbergs to retain the property, section 512 provides that when property is sold either pursuant to judicial fore-closure or a power of sale, "a purchaser for value in good faith acquires the debtor's and creditor's rights in the real estate, free of the security interest under which the sale occurred and any subordinate interest, even though the creditor or person conducting the sale fails to comply with the requirements of this Part on default or of any judicial sale proceeding." Comment 1 states that "[t]his is intended to eliminate the necessity of a rigorous examination to determine whether the fore-closure transaction complies with the statutory requirements in meticu-lous detail."

How would *Rosenberg* have been decided under the U.L.S.I.A? Does the statute satisfactorily resolve the construction and policy issues?

d. Deed in Lieu of Foreclosure

G. OSBORNE, G. NELSON & D. WHITMAN, REAL ESTATE FINANCE LAW *

421–423 (1979).

§ 6.16 Reasons for Use

As we noted earlier, the rule against contemporaneous clogging of the equity of redemption is generally inapplicable to transactions *subsequent* to the original mortgage transaction. Thus most courts, in theory at least, permit the mortgagee to purchase the mortgagor's equity of redemption; however, such transactions are subjected to careful review to ensure that the transaction is free from fraud, is based on an adequate consideration, and that it is, in fact, actually subsequent to the mortgage and not contemporaneous with it.

Relying on the foregoing subsequent transaction exception, a mort-gagee will commonly take a deed from the mortgagor in satisfaction of the mortgage debt. We noted this practice briefly in our preceding sections dealing with merger. The mortgagee engages in this practice, ordinarily, to avoid the further expense of a foreclosure action in which, even though he gets it, a deficiency judgment will often be worthless. The mortgagor on his part is quite frequently glad to give the deed in order to avoid, in states not having anti-deficiency legislation, a possible personal judgment against him which might cause him trouble in the future even though at present it was uncollectable. Also, some mort-gagees are actuated either by a genuine desire to aid the mortgagor, an aversion to the publicity and trouble of a court action against him, or both.

§ 6.17 Potential Pitfalls for the Mortgagee

Whatever its seeming simplicity, the deed in lieu of foreclosure can create substantial problems for the mortgagee and is often, from his perspective, a dangerous device. These problems can entail potential clouds on title and possible difficulties with intervening lienors and other interests. The following materials examine some of these problem areas.

First, we have already noted that courts carefully scrutinize subsequent transactions for evidence of fraud and the adequacy of consideration. There is in this scrutiny the underlying notion that the mortgagor and mortgagee do not share equal bargaining strength. Thus it is possible, "especially if the consideration paid is disproportionately less than the value of the equity or if none is paid where the equity has value, that the whole transaction will be construed as unfair and unconscionable." [87] Moreover, if the deed is not by the mortgagor but by a non-assuming grantee of the mortgagor, a release of the debt, since there was no personal liability, would be no consideration for the conveyance to the mortgagee and subject it to being set aside. Where the transaction is subject to being set aside on such grounds, the mortgagor or his grantee will be permitted to redeem.

Second, there is always the possibility that a court will construe the deed in lieu transaction itself as simply another mortgage transaction. As earlier material has explained, grantor-mortgagors are often successful in establishing by clear and convincing evidence that an absolute deed in favor of a grantee-mortgagee was actually intended as a mortgage. Although a mortgagee will, of course, contest the mortgagor's view of the deed in lieu transaction, mortgagors do occasionally succeed in persuading courts to conceptualize it as a mortgage cast in the form of an absolute deed. If the mortgagor is successful, he will be treated as a mortgagor under two mortgages—under the original mortgage which was not eliminated by the deed in lieu and under the deed in lieu treated as a second mortgage.

Moreover, the possibility exists that because of insolvency of the mortgagor or an actual intent on his part to defraud his creditors the conveyance may be subject to avoidance at the suit of creditors outside of bankruptcy or under the bankruptcy laws should the mortgagor go or be forced into bankruptcy.

Finally, the deed in lieu transaction raises the related problems of the intervening lienor and the merger doctrine. If, subsequent to the original mortgage, the mortgagor has voluntarily or involuntarily created other liens, the deed in lieu to the mortgagee will not operate to cut off such intervening liens. Foreclosure will still be necessary to eliminate such interests. Moreover, to make matters worse, the junior lienor may well utilize the merger doctrine to assert that since, as a result of the deed in lieu, the mortgage and the redemption interest are now held by the first mortgagee, the first mortgage has been destroyed. Thus, the junior lienor will argue that his lien has been promoted in priority. While this merger argument, as we noted earlier, will seldom succeed, it is nevertheless often asserted and, for that reason alone,

---

87. Note, 31 Mo.L.Rev. 312, 314–315 (1966).

worth avoiding. The problems discussed in this paragraph can be avoided only by a thorough title search by the mortgagee prior to taking the deed in lieu to determine whether such intervening interests exist. If such liens or interests are discovered, the only prudent alternative for the mortgagee is to foreclose. However, even if the result of the title search is negative, that result will do nothing to obviate the other problems inherent in the deed in lieu transaction that were considered in earlier paragraphs of this section.

The practice of taking a deed in lieu of foreclosure is probably understandable in states where a judicial proceeding is the only authorized foreclosure method. In such a situation, the problems and risks discussed above may sometimes be outweighed by the costs and delay inherent in judicial foreclosure. However, where valid power of sale foreclosure statutes exist, foreclosure is relatively quick and inexpensive and compelling reasons for such foreclosure alternatives as the deed in lieu simply do not exist.

NOTES

1. *U.L.S.I.A.* U.L.S.I.A. § 507(a) permits deeds in lieu of foreclosure.

2. Deeds in lieu of foreclosure are especially relevant in the negotiation of "work out" arrangements after a default in a commercial real estate transactions. See pages 844–853.

2. STATUTORY REDEMPTION
SKILTON, DEVELOPMENTS IN MORTGAGE LAW AND PRACTICE
17 Temple University Law Quarterly 315, 326–331 (1943).

A statutory period of redemption is to be distinguished from an equity of redemption in that the former is established by the legislature, the latter by adjudication. As we have seen, the tendency has been to view foreclosure as finally terminating or barring the equity of redemption. On the other hand, the statutory period of redemption usually runs after foreclosure sale, being a period of grace which reminds us of a former practice of Chancery courts in allowing at least six months after foreclosure for the mortgagor to redeem. A summary of the growth and spread of this statutory period of redemption, now obtaining in a majority of the states, particularly western and central, may be interesting.

It seems clear that the first redemption periods established by legislatures came as a consequence of early depressions, at a time when the courts had just abandoned their practice of granting the right to redeem after sale. This type of legislation may be traced back to 1820, when the country was sharing in the international economic disturbance following the Napoleonic Wars—in our country evidenced by the collapse of a land boom. The earliest redemptive legislation, however, did not specifically deal with mortgage sales: It referred to execution sales generally, and, as a matter of fact, was construed in two decisions not to include mortgage sales. But it may be viewed as the starting point from which mortgage redemptive legislation sprang.

New York legislation, passed April 12, 1820, provided that on execution sales of land, the sheriff should deliver to the purchaser a certificate, instead of a deed to the land itself: the certificate should recite the terms of the sale. The debtor could redeem within one year of sale. Apparently he kept possession of the property in the meantime. Specific reference was not made to the case of mortgage foreclosure sales. ...

Later legislatures were more specific. When the next depression came along, introduced by the panic of 1836, new redemption legislation was passed in some states; and now mortgage foreclosures are expressly included. From that time to this we may note the general tendency of legislation to give the mortgage debtors the same redemption rights as ordinary contract debtors. The New York Act of 1837 provided for redemption within one year after sale of real estate sold on foreclosure of a mortgage. The Illinois Act of 1841 specifically embraced mortgages. In 1842 Alabama authorized the redemption of mortgaged premises within two years after sale. In 1839 Michigan provided that the Chancellor shall not order the sale of mortgaged premises at a time less than two years and three months from the date of the filing of the bill, sending [sic] the previous law enacted in 1827 which had provided a two year period.

These early redemption statutes came as a result of depression periods, and may be associated with the general collapse of land values, the failure of governmental public land policy, and governmental relief and moratory measures in connection with the sale of public land. Other factors accounted for later developments. The next steps in the development of redemption periods, oddly enough, are associated with the spread of codes of civil practice: the movement for the simplification of civil procedure which began in 1848 with the adoption of the Field Code in New York. This movement, more legalistic than economic in motivation, accounts for the presence of redemption periods in the laws of most of the western states.

What is more natural than that this movement for a simplified and orderly practice, a single code for all civil procedure, embraced by New York after much reflection, should be accepted by the new territories of the west, faced with the problem of forming a government, and with few traditions and customs to guide or restrict them? At the first or second meeting of practically all of the territorial legislatures, the Field Code was adopted, with such changes as seemed to fit the local needs.

The New York version of the Field Code made no general provision for a period of redemption after execution or foreclosure sale. Section 246 merely provided:

"Until otherwise provided by the legislature, the existing provisions of law relating to executions, and their incidents, including the sale and redemption of property, shall apply to the executions prescribed by this chapter." [69]

Section 246 could not be adopted verbatim, there being no preexistent redemption statute in the new territories. Redemption rights must be treated specifically. In 1851, California and Minnesota inserted, among the provisions governing execution sales of real estate, redemption rights of six months and sixty days, respectively.

The California legislation was important for it served as a model. In the important case of Kent v. Laffan,[71] the Supreme Court of California held that the redemption period of six months applied to mortgage sales as well as other execution sales.

The influence of the California example upon neighboring territories and states seems to account for the fact that the period of six months was most frequently used in the nineteenth century in fixing redemption rights. To illustrate the influence of California legislation upon mortgage law in western states, the case of Idaho may be referred to. In 1851 California provided for redemption by the mortgagor within six months of sale, upon payment of 18% interest. In 1864 Idaho adopted the California version of the Field Code practically verbatim, including this provision. The 1872–6 revision of the California code changed the interest payment to 12%. Idaho again followed suit, when it revised its code in 1881.

It is interesting to speculate as to the reason for the selection of the period of six months by the California legislature. Code provisions frequently adopt the best of previous common law and equity practice. It seems that the federal courts had continued the English practice of granting six months after sale within which to redeem, wherever the state laws did not control. Possibly the California legislature in selecting this period was merely codifying the preexistent practice of the federal courts in the territory.

The economic disturbances of the last decade of the nineteenth century contributed to the tendency to enlarge the period of redemption to one year. In 1886, Washington had led the way, changing its six month period to one year. In 1895, Idaho followed suit; Oregon having previously a four month period, changed it to one year; Wyoming, (with no previous period of redemption), established a six month period for the debtor, and another six months thereafter for his creditors. The same year Montana, in adopting a revised code of civil procedure, changed its period from six months to one year. In 1897 California established a one year period. Some years later Nevada did the same.

. . .

69. N.Y.Code Civ.Proc. (1848) § 246.   **71.** 2 Cal. 595 (1852).

On the other hand, when business is on the upswing, there appears to be a tendency to shorten the redemption period, as an incentive to new investment. For example, the Michigan period was reduced by the Act of September 23, 1899, which provided that the court should not order a sale until six months after the filing of the bill, and that thereafter the debtor should have six months within which to redeem. Previously the mortgagor had two years and three months before sale.
. . .

Another tendency to weaken the effect of the redemption period developed in statutory or judicial approval of waiver of redemption rights. If validated by court or legislature, a waiver of a debtor's right to redeem virtually destroys the principle of redemption. It becomes a matter of form to include waiver provisions in all mortgages. For example, recognition of the power to waive debtor's exemption in Pennsylvania has resulted in the general inclusion of waiver clauses in all of the many form contracts used in that state. Courts frequently permit the destruction of a right by waiver by invoking the principle of "freedom of contract". In addition to some instances of judicial approval of waiver clauses in the present field, there is at least one case of legislative permission.

As they existed on the eve of the last depression, the redemption laws of the states were extremely varied. The laws of the states differed in many important respects. There were also gross inconsistencies. In California, for example, there was a redemptive period of twelve months if foreclosure was by court action, but none if foreclosure was by power of sale. Between the states, the laws differed extremely. Differences existed not only with respect to the length of the time of redemption, but also with respect to: (1) whether the redemption period preceded or succeeded the sale; (2) whether the debtor was allowed to retain possession of the mortgaged premises in the interim period; (3) the amount to be paid as the redemptive price. In Indiana, Nebraska, Oklahoma and Wisconsin, the redemptive period preceded the sale. In Washington, Oregon, California, Nevada, Montana, Idaho, Utah, Wyoming, Arizona, Colorado, New Mexico, North Dakota, South Dakota, Kansas, Minnesota, Iowa, Missouri, Arkansas, Illinois, Michigan, Indiana, Kentucky, Tennessee, Alabama, Vermont and Maine it followed sale. The remaining states, in the east and south, had no redemption periods. Nineteen states had redemption periods of one year; five states, of six months; two of nine months; two of two years; one of eighteen months. Nineteen states had no redemption periods. Of those with redemption periods, four allowed the mortgagee to take possession of the premises during the interim period.

MATCHA v. WACHS

Supreme Court of Arizona, 1982.
132 Ariz. 378, 646 P.2d 263.

FELDMAN, Justice.

This declaratory action arose out of a dispute regarding priority between two sets of would-be redemptioners from a mortgage foreclosure sale. The appellees, Michael and Janet Matcha, brought suit against the Maricopa County Sheriff and Wachs and the other appellants (hereinafter referred to as Wachs) seeking a declaratory judgment that they and not Wachs were entitled to redeem the property sold at the foreclosure sale. The trial court found that Wachs had not perfected his right to redeem and entered summary judgment in favor of Matcha. Wachs appealed. On appeal, the court of appeals reversed the judgment of the trial court, finding that Wachs had substantially complied with the requirements of the applicable statutes and therefore was entitled to redeem the property. *See Matcha v. Wachs*, 132 Ariz. 402, 646 P.2d 287 (1981). We granted review in order to decide the issue of whether substantial compliance with the requirements of the redemption statutes (A.R.S. §§ 12–1282–12–1289) is sufficient to perfect a lien creditor's right to redeem. Having concluded that such compliance is sufficient, we approve and modify the decision of the court of appeals, and reverse the judgment of the superior court.

FACTS

Title to the real property which is the subject of this action was originally held by Schulz subject to the following encumbrances, listed in their order of priority:

1. A mortgage to First National Mortgage Association [FNMA];

2. A deed of trust to Wachs in the amount of $628,648.00;

3. A deed of trust in favor of Jerry Lanyon dba Lanyon's Lawn Service;

4. A judgment in favor of the law firm of Beer, Kalyna & Simon, P.C. (the law firm) in the amount of $2,581.35. This judgment was eventually assigned to Matcha.

When Schulz defaulted on his mortgage payments, FNMA foreclosed naming Schulz, Wachs, Lanyon and the law firm as defendants. The sheriff's sale on foreclosure was held on February 9, 1978, and the property was sold to FNMA. Following the foreclosure sale, Schulz as owner/mortgagor had six months within which to redeem the property. *See* A.R.S. § 12–1282(B). If he failed to do so, the junior lienholders, in order of seniority, each had five days to exercise their right to redeem by paying the amount due to the purchaser at the foreclosure sale, *plus* the amount due to those senior lienholders who had previously redeemed the property. *See* A.R.S. § 12–1282(C). The last lienholder to redeem is entitled to the sheriff's deed and thereafter holds title free and clear from the claims of all whose interests have been foreclosed. *See* A.R.S. § 12–1286.

Within the six-month period following the foreclosure sale, Schulz took no steps toward redeeming the property. Wachs, the senior lienholder, filed a timely notice of intent to redeem, specifying the amount of the lien and the order of its priority. He served a copy of the notice of intent to redeem on the sheriff as required by A.R.S. § 12–1284,[1] but failed to serve with it the documents required by A.R.S. § 12–1287,[2] i.e., a certified copy of the record of his lien and an affidavit showing the amount actually due on the lien. The law firm also filed a notice of intent to redeem. It served a copy on the sheriff and also served the sheriff with the documents required by § 12–1287. Thus, within the six-month period, Wachs complied with A.R.S. § 12–1284, but not § 12–1287; the law firm complied with both statutes.

On August 9, 1978, the six months within which the mortgagor/owner could redeem expired. Two days later, Wachs served the sheriff with copies of the documents required by § 12–1287 and tendered a check in the amount of $19,518, which was the amount due the purchaser at the foreclosure sale. Thereafter, Matcha, initially on the law firm's "behalf" and then as its assignee, also made a timely tender of the sum due. He did not, however, tender the additional $628,648 which constituted the amount of the lien held by Wachs. He claimed, rather, that Wachs had failed to comply with A.R.S. § 12–1287 and was not entitled to redeem. After the sheriff's office rejected his tenders, Matcha brought this suit, claiming that by non-compliance with A.R.S. § 12–1287, Wachs had forfeited his right to redeem, thus permitting a junior lienholder to redeem and acquire title without discharging the senior lien.

The question before us, then, is whether Wachs lost his right to redeem because he failed to serve the sheriff with the documents required by A.R.S. § 12–1287 within six months after the foreclosure sale or because, when he finally did serve the necessary documents, he served copies rather than the originals. We answer both questions in the negative.

---

1. A.R.S. § 12–1284 provides:

To entitle a subsequent lienholder [i.e., holder of a lien junior to the one which was foreclosed] to redeem he shall within the applicable period of redemption as provided in § 12–1282, file with the county recorder ... a notice in writing stating that he intends to redeem and specifying his lien and the amount thereof and its order of priority, and shall deliver a copy thereof to the sheriff....

2. A.R.S. § 12–1287 provides:

A. A redeeming creditor shall deliver to the officer or person from whom he seeks to redeem and serve *with his notice to the sheriff*:

1. A copy of the docket of the judgment under which he claims the right to redeem, certified by the clerk of the court ..., or if he redeems a mortgage or other lien, a copy of the record thereof, certified by the recorder.

* * *

3. An affidavit showing the amount actually due on the lien. (Emphasis supplied.)

At the outset, we agree with the trial court's determination that Wachs did not make a timely tender of the documents required by A.R.S. § 12–1287. While that section does not specifically state the time within which the documents must be filed, it does require that they be served "with [the] notice to the sheriff." The word "notice" is used only twice in the redemption statutes; therefore, we conclude that the word "notice" referred to in § 12–1287 can only mean the "notice" specified in § 12–1284. Since under the circumstances of this case the notice required by § 12–1284 must be filed within six months after the foreclosure sale, Wachs' service of the § 12–1287 documents six months and two days after the sale was not timely.

We disagree, however, with the trial court's conclusion that Wachs lost his right to redeem either by failing to file the § 12–1287 documents within six months after the foreclosure sale or by serving the sheriff with copies rather than originals.

In *Western Land & Cattle Co. v. National Bank of Arizona*, 29 Ariz. 51, 58–59, 239 P. 299, 301–02 (1925), this court acknowledged that the statutory right of redemption is a legal right which must be exercised in the manner required by statute, but upheld the right of the creditor to redeem the property despite the fact that in perfecting its right to redeem it had deviated slightly from the statutory requirements. In so holding, the court stated:

> The contention [by the junior lienholder] substantially is that although a redemptioner files his notice in perfect good faith and believing as a matter of law and fact he has correctly stated the amount of his lien and his order of priority, yet, if it afterward appears, at the end of bitterly contested litigation that he may have been in error as to the amount or order of priority, his right of redemption fails entirely. Such a construction of a beneficial statute, meant for the protection of lienholders, would equal in severity the rule required in the interpretation of a penal law. We do not think such was the intent of the legislature. If the lienholder in good faith does the things specified in the statute, the mere fact that it is later determined he was in error as to either amount of lien or order of priority, does not defeat his right of redemption, but merely requires that he pay the correct amount in the order determined by the law, when he finally does redeem.

Thus, in the past, minor deviations from the requirements of the redemption statutes have not resulted in a forfeiture of the right to redeem. It is true that in *Hummel v. Citizen's Building & Loan Ass'n*, 38 Ariz. 54, 59, 296 P. 1014, 1016 (1931), we stated: "[i]f the right given by statute is not exercised strictly according to the terms of the statute, it is lost. ..." However, in *Hummel*, the creditor-redemptioner was more than one year late in filing his notice of intent to redeem. Thus, he hardly attempted compliance with the most important requirement of the redemption statutes. We do not read *Hummel* as authority for the principle that, notwithstanding the lack of prejudice to junior lienholders, any minor deviation from the statutory requirements will result in the forfeiture of the right to redeem.

Whether a statute should be given a strict or equitable interpretation must be decided in accordance with the legislature's intent in enacting that statute. Redemption statutes are remedial in nature and exist for the dual purpose of insuring the property will bring a fair price at a sheriff's sale and that, if the mortgagor does not redeem, his property will be applied to payment of debts in the order of the priority to which his various creditors are entitled. It was not the "intent of the legislature" that the redemption statutes be given the severe application "required in the interpretation of a penal law." *Western Land & Cattle Co. v. National Bank of Arizona*, 29 Ariz. at 58, 239 P. at 302. Accordingly, we hold that in the absence of prejudice to the other parties, substantial compliance with the requirements of §§ 12–1282— 12–1289 will be sufficient to effect a redemption.

It may be argued that the adoption of an equitable rule of substantial compliance which considers the nature and extent of the deviation from the statutory plan, the fulfillment or nonfulfillment of the statutory purpose, and the prejudice or lack of prejudice to junior creditors will result in increased litigation with regard to redemptive rights. This will lead to occasional delay in determining title after foreclosure. However, the establishment of any rule which permits the application of equitable principles invites controversy over what constitutes an equitable result in any particular case. We feel, however, that such a danger, if it be one, is better tolerated than the injustice that can result from the inflexible application of the redemption statutes. As the court stated in *Osborne Hardware Co. v. Colorado Corp.*, 32 Colo.App. 254, 258, 510 P.2d 461, 463 (1973) (quoting *Plute v. Schick*, 101 Colo. 159, 162, 71 P.2d 802, 804 (1937)).

> "The purpose of the redemption law is to help creditors recover their just demands, nothing more. Equity has always prevented the redemption laws from being used as 'an instrument of oppression when substantial justice can be done without enforcing them to the letter.'"

[The] cases support the doctrine that although the right of redemption is a legal right, equitable principles may be utilized to relieve a redeeming lienholder from minor deviations and thus prevent injustice.

We do not hold that every deviation will be acceptable. There are instances where even a minor deviation from the statutory scheme may cause prejudice to the rights of a junior lienholder or other party. In such a situation, equitable principles dictate that the doctrine of substantial compliance will not relieve the redemptioner and that the loss shall fall on the party which caused it. *Salsbery v. Ritter*, 48 Cal.2d 1, 306 P.2d 897 (1957).

Turning to the facts of this case, we find that Wachs substantially complied with the requirements of the redemption statutes by filing his notice of intent to redeem within six months after the foreclosure sale as required by A.R.S. § 12–1284 and by serving copies of the documents required by A.R.S. § 12–1287 on the sheriff two days thereafter. Admittedly, Wachs did not serve the documents required by § 12–1287 within the time specified by statute. The purpose of § 12–1284 is to notify other lienholders who may intend to redeem, thus giving them information which they will need regarding priorities and amounts, in the event they wish to exercise their rights. The other purpose is to give the sheriff the information necessary to determine when he is free to deliver his deed. We agree with the court of appeals that the purpose of the requirement of A.R.S. § 12–1287 that documents be served on the sheriff and the party from whom redemption is to be made is to enable them to verify that the redeeming creditor actually has the lien interest required in order to permit redemption. Here, Wachs provided all parties with the necessary information in a timely manner by complying with § 12–1284. His late attempt to comply with § 12–1287 caused no harm. The sheriff was able to verify his lien and both the law firm and Matcha had all the information they needed. The law firm's original notice of intent to redeem acknowledged the Wachs lien, its priority and its amount. Neither the law firm nor Matcha has ever contested the validity, priority or amount of Wachs' lien, except for the claim of forfeiture by non-compliance with the exact terms of the statute. As the court of appeals stated, to hold that such a minor deviation could work a forfeiture of a valid claim would be to "honor form over substance." It would also allow a junior lienholder to reap a substantial windfall, would produce no benefit—and probably some harm—to Schulz, the original property owner, and would produce a result contrary to the purposes for which the redemption statutes were enacted.

Having made a good faith effort to redeem, having substantially complied with the redemption statutes and no prejudice having resulted to the junior lienholder, Wachs was entitled to redeem. Since Wachs made a tender of the correct amount to the sheriff within the five days allotted to him by A.R.S. § 12–1282(C) after expiration of Schulz' redemption right, Wachs was a redemptioner and Matcha was not entitled to redeem without tendering the amount of Wachs' lien, as required by A.R.S. § 12–1282. Since Matcha did not make such a tender, the trial court erred in ruling against Wachs and in favor of Matcha.

The opinion of the court of appeals is modified, the judgment of the trial court is reversed and the case is remanded with instructions to proceed in accordance with this opinion.

GORDON, V. C. J., and CAMERON, J., concur.

[Dissenting opinion of HAYS, J., joined by Holohan, C.J., omitted]

NOTE

Approximately thirty states allow statutory redemption. Although redemption periods generally run for one year, some states specify different periods for special circumstances. Illinois reduces the period to sixty days if the property is an abandoned residence. Ill.Ann.Stat. Ch. 110, ¶ 12–129(c) (Smith-Hurd 1984). Solicitude towards farmers is evident in Wyoming where the general redemption period is three months but in the case of agricultural land is twelve months. Wyo. Stat. § 1–18–103 (1988). In a few states, the purchaser is allowed to occupy the land during the redemption period but is generally required to credit any rents received against the amount the debtor must pay to redeem. See, for example, N.H.Rev.Stat.Ann. § 529:26 (1974). In nearly half the states that provide for statutory redemption, the debtor is unconditionally allowed to remain in possession. In others he is allowed to stay on only under special conditions such as that the land is a homestead or is used for farming. See, for example, Wash.Rev.Code Ann. § 6.23.110 (West Supp.1991).

A debtor's waiver of the redemption period will usually be subject to judicial scrutiny. Sometimes, though, statutes control. In Kansas, corporations or partnerships are allowed to make agreements reducing or eliminating the redemption period, while individual borrowers can waive only if the land is not used for residential or farm purposes. Kan.Stat.Ann. § 60–2414(a) (1983). In Tennessee, if a deed of trust or mortgage with power of sale is used, anyone can waive under any conditions. Tenn.Code Ann. §§ 66–8–101(3), 66–8–103 (1982).

3. DEFICIENCY JUDGMENTS AND ANTIDEFICIENCY LEGISLATION

BRABNER–SMITH, ECONOMIC ASPECTS OF THE DEFICIENCY JUDGMENT, 20 VIRGINIA LAW REVIEW 719, 722–23 (1934): The reaction of the farmer and the small home owner to the obtaining of a deficiency judgment in the present period of economic distress is of importance in determining our future policy on this subject. The angry demonstration of middle western farmers, in the summer and fall of 1933, against the foreclosure of neighboring farm mortgages, was not so much a protest at exercising the right to foreclose as it was an expression of bitterness against the custom of bidding in for less than the amount of the debt. This class of debtors does not consider complicated price theories or the effect of major economic swings when personal debts are involved. The small property owner recalls that his farm or home cost a certain amount of dollars; that it was valued at an even higher figure when it was mortgaged; that it was mortgaged to a money lender who refused to loan more than one-half or two-thirds of its value; and now, upon default, the agent of this mortgagee is bidding in the property for a fraction of that value.

Moreover, the deficiency includes very heavy costs of foreclosure,— attorneys' fees, court costs, masters' fees, and often fees of a receiver and trustee. The expenses in home and farm foreclosures frequently amount to ten per cent or more of the mortgage debt. The mortgagee had made little effort to keep down these costs. The mortgagor is too despondent or too penniless to engage a lawyer to protect him. When he first appreciates that, legally, he is liable for a deficiency which includes these unusual expenses, he is in a rebellious mood. The result is that a very small proportion, indeed, of deficiency judgments ever prove to be of any value. It is said of one of the largest insurance companies in this country that, of approximately $4,000,000 of deficiency judgments obtained in 1930, it had received in payment less than $5,000. Most of these debtors, when hardpressed for payment of such a debt, resort to bankruptcy. In the past three years of liquidation a great many thousand deficiency judgments have been obtained for a total amount which would be appalling if the figure was anything more than a paper total. Attempts to enforce these judgments as business improves is bound to result in a proportionate number of individual bankruptcies.

CORNELISON v. KORNBLUTH

Supreme Court of California, 1975.
15 Cal.3d 590, 125 Cal.Rptr. 557, 542 P.2d 981.

SULLIVAN, Justice.

In this action for damages for the breach of covenants contained in a deed of trust and for damages for waste, brought by the beneficiary against the trustors and their successors in interest, plaintiff Mary Cornelison appeals from a summary judgment entered in favor of defendant John Kornbluth and against plaintiff. As will appear, we have concluded that upon the record presented, the summary judgment was properly granted and should be affirmed.

On July 15, 1964, plaintiff sold a single-family dwelling in Van Nuys, California, to Maurice and Leona Chanon, taking back a promissory note in the sum of $18,800 secured by a first deed of trust on the property. The deed of trust, recorded on August 21, 1964, contained the following covenants: that the Chanons would pay the real property taxes and assessments against the property; that they would care for and maintain the property; and that if they resold the property, the entire unpaid balance would become immediately due and payable.

On December 10, 1964, the Chanons conveyed the property to defendant by grant deed. On September 6, 1968, defendant sold the property to Richard Larkins. In January 1969 the county health department condemned the house as unfit for human habitation. The Chanons being in default on the promissory note, plaintiff caused the property to be sold at a trustee's sale. Plaintiff purchased the property at the sale for the sum of $21,921.42, that being an amount equal to the balance due on the note plus foreclosure costs.

Plaintiff then brought the instant action for damages, her amended complaint (hereafter "complaint") filed March 24, 1970, setting forth two causes of action, one for breach of contract and one for damages for waste. The first cause of action alleged in substance that defendant "agreed in writing to be bound by and to perform all of the covenants contained in the Note and Deed of Trust theretofore executed by defendants Maurice L. Chanon and Leona Chanon"; and that defendants breached these covenants (a) by selling the property to Larkins, (b) by failing to pay property taxes, (c) by failing to make payments on the note, and (d) by failing to properly care for and maintain the premises.

The second cause of action, after incorporating by reference the material allegations of the first cause of action, alleged in substance that defendant owed a duty to properly and adequately care for the property and that defendant negligently failed to fulfill this duty, thereby causing plaintiff to be damaged in specified particulars and amounts by reason of the loss of improvements to the real property as well as by reason of the loss of its use. On the first cause of action plaintiff prayed for damages in the sum of $18,169.66, and on the second cause of action for damages in the sum of $20,000 plus the reasonable rental of the property, and in addition for $45,000 punitive damages.

Defendant's answer admitted that he purchased the property from the Chanons and sold it to Larkins, but denied all other allegations for lack of information or belief. Defendant then moved for summary judgment. His declaration in support of the motion states in substance that he purchased the subject real property from the Chanons, that at the time of the purchase he knew it was encumbered by the deed of trust in favor of plaintiff as beneficiary, that he never assumed either orally or in writing the indebtedness secured by the deed of trust, and that no such assumption was contained in the deed conveying the property to him. The declaration attaches and incorporates by reference a copy of the grant deed which confirms the last statement.

Defendant also filed in support of the motion the declaration of one of his attorneys stating in substance that plaintiff regained possession of the subject property by purchasing it for $21,921.42 at the foreclosure sale conducted on June 4, 1969, said purchase having been effected "by a full credit bid resulting in the full satisfaction of the remaining indebtedness secured by the deed of trust . . . ." The declaration attaches and incorporates by reference a copy of the "trustee's deed upon sale" which confirmed the statements of the declaration. Plaintiff filed no counteraffidavits. The court granted defendant's motion and entered judgment accordingly. This appeal followed.

Plaintiff contends that the court erred in granting summary judgment because the "complaint is regular on its face and raises issues of fact." . . .

For present purposes, we need be concerned only with the following rule: "Summary judgment is proper only if the affidavits in support of the moving party would be sufficient to sustain a judgment in his favor and his opponent does not by affidavit show such facts as may be deemed by the judge hearing the motion sufficient to present a triable issue." (Stationers Corp. v. Dun & Bradstreet, Inc. (1965) 62 Cal.2d 412, 417, 42 Cal.Rptr. 449, 452, 398 P.2d 785, 788.)

Applying the foregoing rule we are satisfied that defendant's declaration is sufficient to support a summary judgment on the first cause of action for breach of contract. As previously stated, the basic theory of this cause of action is that defendant had a duty to comply with the covenants contained in the deed of trust given plaintiff by the Chanons since the document was recorded and its covenants ran with the land. Plaintiff's legal premise is completely erroneous. Upon the transfer of real property covered by a mortgage or deed of trust as security for an indebtedness, the property remains subject to the secured indebtedness but the grantee is not personally liable for the indebtedness or to perform any of the obligations of the mortgage or trust deed unless his agreement to pay the indebtedness, or some note or memorandum thereof, is in writing and subscribed by him or his agent or his assumption of the indebtedness is specifically provided for in the conveyance. Defendant's declaration states positively that he never assumed either orally or in writing the indebtedness secured by the Chanon deed of trust and that no such assumption was contained in the deed by which the Chanons conveyed the property to him. An examination of a copy of the deed attached to the declaration confirms this. Plaintiff filed no counterdeclaration denying these allegations and as a consequence raised no triable issue of fact. Contrary to plaintiff's contention, a triable issue of fact cannot be raised by the allegations of her complaint. Accordingly, summary judgment on the first cause of action was properly granted.

We now proceed to determine whether defendant's declarations are sufficient to support the summary judgment on the second stated cause of action for waste. On this issue we may outline the positions of the parties as follows: Defendant contends that since, as set forth in his attorney's declaration, plaintiff purchased the property for a full credit bid an action for waste is thereby precluded both by reason of the antideficiency legislation and by reason of the extinguishment of the security interest through a full credit bid at the trustee's sale. Plaintiff on the other hand contends that an action for waste may be maintained independently of the antideficiency provisions of sections 580b and 580d of the Code of Civil Procedure.

In order to resolve this issue it is necessary to first define, and trace the history of an action for waste and secondly to analyze the impact of the antideficiency legislation induced by the depression of the 1930's upon this traditional action.

Section 2929 of the Civil Code provides: *"Waste.* No person whose interest is subject to the lien of a mortgage may do any act which will substantially impair the mortgagee's security." This section, enacted in 1872, codified a portion of the common law action for waste, as developed in England and adopted in earlier California cases. "[W]aste is conduct (including in this word both acts of commission and of omission) on the part of a person in possession of land which is actionable at the behest of, and for protection of the reasonable expectations of, another owner of an interest in the same land.

... Thus, waste is, functionally, a part of the law which keeps in balance the conflicting desires of persons having interests in the same land." (5 Powell on Real Property (1974) § 636, pp. 5–6).

. . .

Over a century ago this court in Robinson v. Russell (1864) 24 Cal. 467, 472–473 ... declared that an action on the case could be maintained by the mortgagee of real property for damages for injuries done to the property which impaired the mortgage security and that action for an injunction would lie to restrain the commission of waste on the premises. It was this cause of action that was codified in 1872 as Civil Code section 2929.

Section 2929 of the Civil Code, though referring only to "the lien of a *mortgage*" (italics added) and to the impairment of "the *mortgagee's* security," (italics added) applies equally to a deed of trust, since a mortgage with power of sale and a deed of trust are treated similarly in California and both are considered as security interests protected from impairment. The statute imposes a duty not to commit waste upon any "person whose interest is subject to the lien." Although a nonassuming grantee of mortgaged property is not personally liable on the debt, his interest in the property is subject to the lien and therefore he is under a duty not to impair the mortgagee's security. Defendant as a nonassuming grantee of the property subject to plaintiff's deed of trust was under a duty not to commit waste.

Defendant contends, however, that assuming arguendo that he was under a duty not to commit waste and that his acts or omissions constituted waste by so materially impairing the value of the property as to render it inadequate security for the mortgage debt, nevertheless plaintiff is not entitled to recover because such recovery for waste would amount to a deficiency judgment proscribed by sections 580b [5] and 580d [6] of the Code of Civil Procedure. In order to resolve this contention it is necessary to briefly summarize the array of legislation

---

5. Section 580b provides in relevant part: "No deficiency judgment shall lie in any event after any sale of real property for failure of the purchaser to complete his contract of sale, or under a deed of trust, or mortgage, given to the vendor to secure payment of the balance of the purchase price of real property, or under a deed of trust, or mortgage, on a dwelling for not more than four families given to a lender to secure repayment of a loan which was in fact used to pay all or part of the purchase price of such dwelling occupied, entirely or in part, by the purchaser."

Hereafter, unless otherwise noted, all section references are to the Code of Civil Procedure.

6. Section 580d provides: "No judgment shall be rendered for any deficiency upon a note secured by a deed of trust or mortgage upon real property hereafter executed in any case in which the real property has been sold by the mortgagee or trustee under power of sale contained in such mortgage or deed of trust."

in the field of secured transactions in real property spawned by the depression of the 1930's.

Prior to 1933, a mortgagee of real property was required to exhaust his security before enforcing the debt or otherwise to waive all right to his security. However, having resorted to the security, whether by judicial sale or private nonjudicial sale, the mortgagee could obtain a deficiency judgment against the mortgagor for the difference between the amount of the indebtedness and the amount realized from the sale. As a consequence during the great depression with its dearth of money and declining property values, a mortgagee was able to purchase the subject real property at the foreclosure sale at a depressed price far below its normal fair market value and thereafter to obtain a double recovery by holding the debtor for a large deficiency. In order to counteract this situation, California in 1933 enacted fair market value limitations applicable to both judicial foreclosure sales (§ 726)[7] and private foreclosure sales (§ 580a)[8] which limited the mortgagee's deficiency judgment after exhaustion of the security to the difference between the fair value of the property at the time of the sale (irrespec-

7. Section 726 provides in part: "In the event that a deficiency is not waived or prohibited and it is decreed that any defendant is personally liable for such debt, then upon application of the plaintiff filed at any time within three months of the date of the foreclosure sale and after a hearing thereon at which the court shall take evidence and at which hearing either party may present evidence as to the fair value of the property or the interest therein sold as of the date of sale, the court shall render a money judgment against such defendant or defendants for the amount by which the amount of the indebtedness with interest and costs of sale and of action exceeds the fair value of the property or interest therein sold as of the date of sale; provided, however, that in no event shall the amount of said judgment, exclusive of interest from the date of sale and of costs exceed the difference between the amount for which the property was sold and the entire amount of the indebtedness secured by said mortgage or deed of trust."

8. Section 580a provides: "Whenever a money judgment is sought for the balance due upon an obligation for the payment of which a deed of trust or mortgage with power of sale upon real property or any interest therein was given as security, following the exercise of the power of sale in such deed of trust or mortgage, the plaintiff shall set forth in his complaint the entire amount of the indebtedness which was secured by said deed of trust or mortgage at the time of sale, the amount for which such real property or interest there-

in was sold and the fair market value thereof at the date of sale and the date of such sale. Upon the application of either party made at least ten days before the time of trial the court shall, and upon its own motion the court at any time may, appoint one of the inheritance tax appraisers provided for by law to appraise the property or the interest therein sold as of the time of sale. Such appraiser shall file his appraisal with the clerk and the same shall be admissible in evidence. ... Before rendering any judgment the court shall find the fair market value of the real property, or interest therein sold, at the time of sale. The court may render judgment for not more than the amount by which the entire amount of the indebtedness due at the time of sale exceeded the fair market value of the real property or interest therein sold at the time of sale with interest thereon from the date of the sale; provided, however, that in no event shall the amount of said judgment, exclusive of interest after the date of sale, exceed the difference between the amount for which the property was sold and the entire amount of the indebtedness secured by said deed of trust or mortgage. Any such action must be brought within three months of the time of sale under such deed of trust or mortgage. No judgment shall be rendered in any such action until the real property or interest therein has first been sold pursuant to the terms of such deed of trust or mortgage, unless such real property or interest therein has become valueless."

tive of the amount actually realized at the sale) and the outstanding debt for which the property was security. Therefore, if, due to the depressed economic conditions, the property serving as security was sold for less than the fair value as determined under section 726 or section 580a, the mortgagee could not recover the amount of that difference in his action for a deficiency judgment.

In certain situations, however, the Legislature deemed even this partial deficiency too oppressive. Accordingly, in 1933 it enacted section 580b which barred deficiency judgments altogether on purchase money mortgages. "Section 580b places the risk of inadequate security on the purchase money mortgagee. A vendor is thus discouraged from overvaluing the security. Precarious land promotion schemes are discouraged, for the security value of the land gives purchasers a clue as to its true market value. If inadequacy of security results, not from overvaluing, but from a decline in property values during a general or local depression, section 580b prevents the aggravation of the downturn that would result if defaulting purchasers were burdened with large personal liability. Section 580b thus serves as a stabilizing factor in land sales." Roseleaf Corp. v. Cheirighino, supra, 59 Cal.2d 35, 42, 27 Cal.Rptr. 873, 877, 378 P.2d 97, 101.

Although both judicial foreclosure sales and private nonjudicial foreclosure sales provided for identical deficiency judgments in nonpurchase money situations subsequent to the 1933 enactment of the fair value limitations, one significant difference remained, namely property sold through judicial foreclosure was subject to the statutory right of redemption (§ 725a), while property sold by private foreclosure sale was not redeemable. By virtue of sections 725a and 701, the judgment debtor, his successor in interest or a junior lienor could redeem the property at any time during one year after the sale, frequently by tendering the sale price. The effect of this right of redemption was to remove any incentive on the part of the mortgagee to enter a low bid at the sale (since the property could be redeemed for that amount) and to encourage the making of a bid approximating the fair market value of the security. However, since real property purchased at a private foreclosure sale was not subject to redemption, the mortgagee by electing this remedy, could gain irredeemable title to the property by a bid substantially below the fair value and still collect a deficiency judgment for the difference between the fair value of the security and the outstanding indebtedness.

In 1940 the Legislature placed the two remedies, judicial foreclosure sale and private nonjudicial foreclosure sale on a parity by enacting section 580d. Section 580d bars "any deficiency judgment" following a private foreclosure sale. "It seems clear that section 580d was enacted to put judicial enforcement on a parity with private enforcement. This result could be accomplished by giving the debtor a right to redeem after a sale under the power. The right to redeem, like proscription of a deficiency judgment, has the effect of making the security satisfy a realistic share of the debt. By choosing instead to bar a deficiency judgment after private sale, the Legislature achieved its purpose without denying the creditor his election of remedies. If the creditor wishes a deficiency judgment, his sale is subject to statutory redemption rights. If he wishes a sale resulting in nonredeemable title, he must forego the right to a deficiency judgment. In either case the debtor is protected." (Roseleaf v. Chierighino, supra, 59 Cal.2d 35, 43–44, 27 Cal.Rptr. 873, 878, 378 P.2d 97, 102.)

In the case at bench, we are now called upon to determine the effect of this antideficiency legislation upon the statutory action for waste. (Civ.Code, § 2929.) It will be recalled that damages in an action for waste are measured by the amount of injury to the security caused by the mortgagor's acts, that is by the substantial harm which "impair[s] the value of the property subject to the lien so as to render it an inadequate security for the mortgage debt." (Robinson v. Russell, supra, 24 Cal. 467, 473.) A deficiency judgment is a personal judgment against the debtor-mortgagor for the difference between the fair market value of the property held as security and the outstanding indebtedness. (§ 726.) It is clear that the two judgments against the mortgagor, one for waste and the other for a deficiency, are closely interrelated and may often reflect identical amounts. If property values in general are declining, a deficiency judgment and a judgment for waste would be identical up to the point at which the harm caused by the mortgagor is equal to or less than the general decline in property values resulting from market conditions. When waste is committed in a depressed market, a deficiency judgment, although reflecting the amount of the waste, will of course exceed it if the decline of property values is greater. However, when waste is committed in a rising market, there will be no deficiency judgment, unless the property was originally overvalued; in this event, there would be no damages for waste unless the impairment due to waste exceeded the general increase in property values.

Mindful of the foregoing, we now proceed to arrive at an assessment of the effect of sections 580b and 580d upon an action for waste. First, we examine the 580b proscription of a deficiency judgment after any foreclosure sale, private or judicial, of property securing a purchase money mortgage. The primary purpose of section 580b is "in the event of a depression in land values, to prevent the aggravation of the downturn that would result if defaulting purchasers lost the land and were burdened with personal liability." (Bargioni v. Hill, 59 Cal.2d 121, 123, 28 Cal.Rptr. 321, 322, 378 P.2d 593, 594.) It is clear that allowing an action for waste following a foreclosure sale of property securing purchase money mortgages may often frustrate this purpose. Damages for waste would burden the defaulting purchaser with both loss of land and personal liability and the acts giving rise to that liability would have been caused in many cases by the economic downturn itself. For example, a purchaser caught in such circumstances may be compelled in the normal course of events to forego the general maintenance and repair of the property in order to keep up his payments on the mortgage debt. If he eventually defaults and loses the property, to hold him subject to additional liability for waste would seem to run counter to the purpose of section 580b and to permit the purchase money lender to obtain what is in effect a deficiency judgment. It is of course true that not all owners of real property subject to a purchase money mortgage commit waste solely or primarily as a result of the economic pressures of a market depression; indeed many are reckless, intentional, and at times even malicious despoilers of property. In these latter circumstances to which we shall refer for convenience as waste committed in bad faith, the purchase money lender should not go remediless since they do not involve the type of risk intended to be borne by him in promoting the objectives of section 580b alluded to above.

Accordingly, we hold that section 580b should apply to bar recovery in actions for waste following foreclosure sale in the first instance but should not so apply in the second instance of "bad faith" waste. We further hold that it is within the province of the trier of fact to determine on a case by case basis to what, if any, extent the impairment of the mortgagee's security has been caused (as in the first instance) by the general decline of real property values and to what, if any, extent (as in the second instance) by the bad faith acts of the mortgagor, such determination, in either instance, being subject to review under the established rule of appellate review.

We now turn to assess the effect upon an action for waste of section 580d which applies to a nonpurchase money mortgage. We are satisfied that a different analysis must be pursued. It will be recalled from our earlier discussion that the Legislature intended to establish parity between judicial foreclosure and private foreclosure by denying a deficiency judgment subsequent to a private sale. Under a judicial foreclosure, the mortgagee is entitled to a deficiency judgment, but must bear the burden of a statutory redemption; under a private sale the mortgagee need not bear the burden of redemption, but cannot recover any deficiency judgment. If following a nonjudicial sale the mortgagee were allowed to obtain a judgment for damages for waste against the mortgagor, he would have the double benefits of an irredeemable title to the property and a personal judgment against the mortgagor for the impairment of the value of the property. This would essentially destroy the parity between judicial foreclosure and private foreclosure in all instances where the waste is actually caused by general economic conditions, since as we have explained, such recovery is in effect a deficiency judgment. If, however, the recovery is limited to waste committed in "bad faith," then the personal judgment would be entirely independent of the problems encompassed by the antideficiency legislation and would not affect the parity of remedies. Accordingly, we hold that in situations arising under section 580d, recovery for waste against the mortgagor following nonjudicial foreclosure sale is barred by the section's proscription against deficiency judgments when the waste actually results from the depressed condition of the general real estate market but not when the waste is caused by the "bad faith" acts of the mortgagor.

. . .

While our foregoing conclusion may expose defendant to liability on the basis of having committed "bad faith" waste, the question need not be resolved. We have further concluded that even assuming that defendant is liable on such basis, nevertheless plaintiff cannot recover since she purchased the subject property at the trustee's sale by making a full credit bid. As stated previously, the measure of damages for waste is the amount of the impairment of the security, that is the amount by which the value of the security is less than the outstanding indebtedness and is thereby rendered inadequate. The point of defendant's argument is that the mortgagee's purchase of the property securing the debt by entering a full credit bid establishes the value of the security as being equal to the outstanding indebtedness and ipso facto the nonexistence of any impairment of the security. As applied to the factual context of the instant case, the argument is that the purchase by plaintiff-vendor-beneficiary of the property covered by the purchase money deed of trust pursuant to a full credit bid made and accepted at the nonjudicial foreclosure sale resulted in a total satisfaction of the secured obligation. We agree.

. . . If the beneficiary or mortgagee at the foreclosure sale enters a bid for the full amount of the obligation owing to him together with the costs and fees due in connection with the sale, he cannot recover damages for waste, since he cannot establish any impairment of security, the lien of the deed of trust or mortgage having been theretofore extinguished by his full credit bid and all his security interest in the property thereby nullified. If, however, he bids less than the full amount of the obligation and thereby acquires the property valued at less than the full amount, his security has been impaired and he may recover damages for waste in an amount not exceeding the difference between the amount of his bid and the full amount of the outstanding indebtedness immediately prior to the foreclosure sale.

Plaintiff complains that it is difficult to calculate precisely the amount of damages recoverable for waste so as to determine the proper amount which the beneficiary or mortgagee should bid at the foreclosure sale; therefore, she urges it is unfair to impose such a burden on the beneficiary or mortgagee. Suffice it to say that no complicated calculations are necessary. The beneficiary or mortgagee need only enter a credit bid in an amount equal to what he assesses the fair market value of the property to be in its condition at the time of the foreclosure sale. If that amount is below the full amount of the outstanding indebtedness and he is successful in acquiring the property at the foreclosure sale, he may then recover any provable damages for waste.

To recapitulate, we conclude that the trial court properly granted summary judgment in favor of defendant and against plaintiff (1) as to the first cause of action for breach of contract since defendant at no time assumed the underlying indebtedness; and (2) as to the second cause of action for waste since, although defendant as a nonassuming grantee could be held liable for waste if proved to have been committed in bad faith, nevertheless plaintiff can establish no impairment of security, having acquired the property at the foreclosure sale by making a full credit bid.

The judgment is affirmed.

WRIGHT, C. J., and McCOMB, TOBRINER, MOSK, CLARK and RICHARDSON, JJ., concur.

NOTES

1. *Cornelison* suggests the variety of approaches available to states that wish to regulate deficiency judgments. In addition to an outright prohibition on deficiency recoveries, a state may limit mortgagor liability by imposing fair value limitations, statutory redemption periods or procedural safeguards on sale. *Cornelison* also suggests the variety of policies that lie behind these rules. One policy is to protect homeowners against the immediate burdens of economic collapse. Another is to spread the risk of dramatic decline in real property values between property owners and secured lenders or, in the case of purchase money mortgages, between land sellers and land buyers. The California scheme discussed in *Cornelison* is unusual only in combining so many rules and policies in a single system.

Should a mortgagor be permitted to waive the protections of the antideficiency statute? Consider the policies behind antideficiency statutes and the policies supporting waivers. See Brunsoman v. Scarlett, 465 N.W.2d 162 (N.D.1991) (waiver not permitted before default but permitted after default as long as waiver is clear, unequivocal, and unambiguous).

For a thoughtful and comprehensive examination of issues in the field generally, see Washburn, The Judicial and Legislative Response to Price Inadequacy in Mortgage Foreclosure Sales, 53 So.Cal.L.Rev. 843 (1980). See also, Schill, An Economic Analysis of Mortgagor Protection Laws, 77 Va.L.Rev. 489 (1991).

2. Should deficiency judgments after judicial and nonjudicial sales be treated differently? In Manoog v. Miele, 350 Mass. 204, 213 N.E.2d 917 (1966), the Massachusetts Supreme Judicial Court considered whether a mortgagee should as a matter of law be barred from recovering a deficiency judgment because of its behavior before and at its nonjudicial sale. Nineteen days before the sale, the mortgagee contracted to sell the land to a third party for $45,000. Contract performance was, of course, conditioned on the mortgagee's success in acquiring the property at sale. At the sale, the mortgagee acquired the property on a bid of $40,000—$5,000 less than the face amount of the

mortgagor's note. After trial, a jury held that the mortgagee was further entitled to $5,488.67 from the mortgagor, the sum of the unpaid balance on the note, interest, taxes and the costs of sale, with credits for rents received by the mortgagee prior to the sale.

Ruling for the mortgagee, the court agreed with the lower court that the question of the mortgagee's good faith in failing to disclose the $45,000 purchase price to the mortgagor before the sale was a question of fact, not law, for the jury to decide. In its view, the lower court had properly instructed the jury that "when, as was the fact here, 'a mortgagee ... is both seller and buyer, his position is one of great delicacy. Yet, when he has done his full duty to the mortgagor in his conduct of the sale under the power, and the bidding begins, in his capacity as bidder a mortgagee may buy as cheaply as he can, and owes no duty to bid the full value of the property as that value may subsequently be determined by a judge or jury.' " 350 Mass. at 206, 213 N.E.2d at 919.

In the circumstances, would a "fair value" requirement have served the mortgagor's interests better than the imposition of a good faith standard on the mortgagee? Is "fair value" intended to reflect the price the market will pay, or the price the community or jury thinks is fair? Consider New York's attempt to finesse the question: "the fair and reasonable market value of the mortgaged premises as of the date such premises were bid in at auction or such nearest earlier date as there shall have been any market value thereof." N.Y.R.P.A.P.L. § 1371 (McKinney 1979).

3. *Waste.* Reconsider the examples that *Cornelison* gave of the types of waste it would not consider actionable. Is it clear that impairment in these cases stems from the "general decline of real property values"? As a practical matter, would the court have done better to rely on the common law distinction between permissive waste, for which apparently the decision would not have allowed recovery, and affirmative waste, for which it would?

Did *Cornelison* establish a rule on the availability of the action for waste generally, or only a rule on remedies? What if, before foreclosure, the mortgagee sought a mandatory injunction requiring the mortgagor to keep the premises in good repair? What if the mortgage required the mortgagor to contribute a fixed monthly sum toward keeping the premises in good repair? How would such a provision differ from one in which the mortgagor waives his immunity from an action for waste? From an express waiver of immunity from a deficiency judgment?

On waste generally, see Leipziger, The Mortgagee's Remedies for Waste, 64 Calif.L.Rev. 1086 (1976).

4. *One-Form-of-Action and One-Action Rules.* Can an undersecured mortgagee circumvent a state's fair value or other antideficiency limitations by proceeding first against the mortgagor personally on the note and then, to the extent the personal judgment is unsatisfied, by

foreclosing on the real property security and applying the sale proceeds to the remainder of the debt? Although the mortgagee would not be allowed a double recovery, the strategy might still seem unfair to those who believe that creditors who seek security for their loans should be obligated to proceed against the security first.

A handful of states require the mortgagee to proceed against the real property securing the debt before obtaining a final judgment in a personal action on the note. Cal.Civ.Proc.Code § 726 (West 1980 & Supp.1992); Idaho Code § 6–101 (1990); Mont.Code Ann. § 71–1–222 (1991); Nev.Rev.Stat. § 40.430 (1987); Utah Code Ann. § 78–37–1 (1987). If the mortgagor fails to raise this rule as a defense on the note, she will suffer a personal judgment. However, she can later prevent the mortgagee from proceeding against the real property on the ground that, by proceeding first on the note, the mortgagee effectively elected that as its exclusive remedy. See Walker v. Community Bank, 10 Cal.3d 729, 111 Cal.Rptr. 897, 518 P.2d 329 (1974).

The rule is sometimes called a "one-form-of-action" rule to connote that a mortgagee seeking enforcement of a real estate secured obligation must bring a foreclosure action, and is sometimes called a "one-action" rule because the mortgagee must proceed against the security and for a deficiency judgment in a single action. Typically, the statutes contemplate that the first stage of the proceeding will involve foreclosure and sale of the property. At the second stage, the court will determine whether any deficiency exists and enter a personal judgment accordingly.

One-action rules create as many pitfalls for lenders as they do safeguards for borrowers. Say that your client, bank, has learned that one of its customers is in default on its credit card obligations to the bank. How would you counsel the bank to proceed if you knew that it had earlier made a loan to the same customer secured by a real property mortgage, and that the mortgage contained a dragnet clause of the sort described at page 394 above? Would you ever advise your lender client to take real property as security for a loan when it is clear at the time of the loan that the security is worth much less than the principal amount of the debt? What might other creditors be doing to the debtor's general assets while the lender is making its way through the required foreclosure proceedings?

For a discussion of sanctions against a lender for violating the one action rule, see Security Pacific National Bank v. Wozab, 51 Cal.3d 991, 275 Cal.Rptr. 201, 800 P.2d 557 (1990); Comment, The Sanction For Violation of California's One–Action Rule, 79 Cal.L.Rev. 1601 (1991).

5. *Other Equitable Relief.* In special circumstances, some courts might go beyond specific statutory protections for mortgagors, such as statutory redemption rights and protection against deficiency judgments, and rely on general equitable principles to set aside a foreclosure sale if the price is so low as to "shock the conscience of the court." See Crown Life Insurance Company v. Candlewood, Ltd., 112

N.M. 633, 818 P.2d 411 (1991) (where price at sale was only 15% to 23% of property's fair market value, court's conscience was "shocked").

6. *U.L.S.I.A.* The Uniform Land Security Interest Act follows majority rules in most instances but takes a few less popular paths as well. Following the majority approach to lender's election of remedies, section 501 allows the lender to proceed against the property and on the note in any order that it chooses, rejecting the "one-action" rule. Section 513 allows no right to redeem after sale, and section 511 provides that if "the debtor is a protected party and the obligation secured is a purchase money security interest, there is no liability for a deficiency notwithstanding any agreement of the protected party." Section 507 gives the secured creditor three remedies after default: the self-help remedy of deed in lieu of foreclosure; judicial sale; and, if the mortgage agreement allows it, foreclosure by nonjudicial sale.

Section 503 departs from the rule on possession applied in lien theory states and adopts the intermediate theory position instead. It provides that, except as to a protected party debtor in possession, a secured creditor can take possession on default and before foreclosure. Behind this departure was the policy decision to reduce the cost of foreclosure. "A provision giving the creditor a right to take possession after default without the intervention of the expensive receivership process is one step in carrying out this policy." Comment 1 to Section 503. See generally, Mixon & Shepard, Antideficiency Relief for Fore-closed Homeowners: ULSIA Section 511(b), 27 Wake Forest L.Rev. 455 (1992).

See Bernhardt, ULSIA's Remedies on Default—Worth the Effort?, 24 Conn.L.Rev. 1001 (1992).

E. FINANCING THROUGH THE LAND SALE CONTRACT

COMMENT, FORFEITURE: THE ANOMALY OF THE LAND SALE CONTRACT

41 Albany Law Review 71, 72–79 (1977).

An elderly couple in Binghamton, unable to obtain a conventional mortgage, bought their home under a land sale contract. Nine years later, experiencing temporary financial problems, they fell a month behind in their payments. As a result, they lost the home and all they had invested in it.

A mother of three, on welfare, could not resist the opportunity to be a homeowner and signed a land contract to purchase a run-down home in Schenectady. After four years of meeting her monthly payments and repairing the heating and plumbing at great expense, she became unable to meet her monthly installments. Consequently, she forfeited not only all the installments made, but the money she had invested in improvements.

A farmer from western New York, having bought his farm eleven years before through a land sale contract, had always been late with his payments during the spring, when his income was its lowest and his expenses the highest. In January he received a notice from his seller that this lateness would no longer be tolerated. This spring the farmer lost the land and eleven years of installments when the seller refused to accept his late payments.

These buyers, and many others like them, saw only an unprecedented opportunity to become landowners. Usually unrepresented, they were ignorant of the many hazards that loomed throughout the life of a land sale contract.

I. INTRODUCTION

The land sale contract is a low equity arrangement for the purchase of real property. Although in years past the land contract has not been a widespread method of purchasing realty in the Northeast, it is presently becoming more common in various sections of New York, either in the form of the traditional land contract or a variant of it, the lease-buy option. Despite its new-found popularity the land contract contains many inherent inequities. Specifically, the laws of New York give land contract purchasers conspicuously little relief; they face upon default the grievous predicament of forfeiting their entire investment. Unlike many other jurisdictions, New York has not adopted legislation equipping the land sale contract with the standard safeguards that surround the mortgage.

The land sale contract, in contrast to a mortgage or trust deed, does not secure a loan or forbear the payment of money. Rather, the land contract is an installment sales contract, providing for periodic payment of the purchase price, often in monthly installments. Unlike mortgagees in New York, the land sale contract seller retains legal title to the realty to secure full and final payment. Although these contracts almost universally grant immediate possession of the property to the purchaser throughout the execution of the contract, possession is not an automatic right of the purchaser, and must be provided for in the contract. The basic attraction of the land contract to the seller is the ease and economy by which the purchaser's interest may be eliminated in the event of his default. Since the purchaser, unlike the mortgagor, has no right of redemption or sale, the seller may avoid the costly and time-consuming foreclosure proceedings mandated under a mortgage. Instead, he simply retains the installments and terminates the purchaser's interest. The seller may receive additional protection through the inclusion of such devices as an acceleration clause and provisions which make the purchaser responsible for paying the taxes, insuring the premises and keeping them in good repair. These factors make the land contract more attractive to the seller than the purchase money mortgage and may explain the present popularity of the land contract among sellers.

Nevertheless, from the perspective of the low-income purchaser the land sale contract is a realistic and often essential mechanism for low-equity land acquisition. It enables low-income families to penetrate the housing market without first accumulating the substantial downpayment which is often impossible for them to amass. The alternative means of financing are rarely available to this economic class of New Yorkers by virtue of the present high requisite mortgage loan to value ratio and the poor credit ratings of the purchasers. Currently, a downpayment of 20–35% of the purchase price is required to obtain a mortgage from a lending institution. Even if a potential buyer were able to save such a sum, the time required to do so would be unrealistically long. The potential buyers of low-income housing are considered high credit risks, thus making it virtually impossible for them to obtain financing from conventional lending institutions. As a result of this credit rating and the frequent location of the property in high risk areas, the Federal Housing Authority has been reluctant to insure mortgages for these low-income buyers. The purchaser's only alternative is to obtain financing with the seller, who is unlikely to grant a purchase money mortgage with little or no downpayment, especially in light of the advantages of a land sale contract. ...

The seller under a land sale contract retains legal title to the property as security against the purchaser's nonperformance during the term of the contract. The extent of the seller's interest and control is attested to by his ability to convey the property to a bona fide third party purchaser, his standing to maintain an action in waste against the purchaser in possession, and his creditors' ability to levy against his interest. In addition, courts have held that the seller has an equitable lien on the property as security against the buyer's nonperformance, regardless of whether that lien is provided for in the contract. To call the vendor's security interest a lien seems a misnomer in view of the fact that he actually retains legal title to the property. It would be more accurate to maintain that the seller may enforce his interest in the property as a lien, rather than to insist that his interest is itself a lien.

Problems also persist in evaluating the purchaser's interest. The commentators universally maintain that a land contract operates as an equitable conversion, making the purchaser the equitable owner of the land while the seller holds the legal title in trust for the purchaser. ...

The purchaser's rights also include an equitable lien on the land for those payments already made, enforceable upon the seller's default only if the purchaser is ready to perform. Usually the lien is limited to the payments made and does not encompass the loss of a bargain, the expenses incurred in examining title or the costs of any improvement made by the purchaser. Since the lien is equitable, it is extinguished if the vendee is in default, regardless of any breach by the seller.

Both the seller's interest—legal title held as security against the purchaser's default—and the purchaser's interest—equitable ownership of the property—are protected and advanced by the various remedies available to each.

SKENDZEL v. MARSHALL

Supreme Court of Indiana, 1973.
261 Ind. 226, 301 N.E.2d 641, cert. denied, 415 U.S. 929,
94 S.Ct. 1421, 39 L.Ed.2d 476.

HUNTER, Justice.

Petitioners seek transfer to this Court as a result of an adverse ruling by the Court of Appeals. Plaintiff-respondents originally brought suit to obtain possession of certain real estate through the enforcement of a forfeiture clause in a land sale contract. Plaintiff-respondents suffered a negative judgment, from which they appealed. The Court of Appeals reversed, holding that the defendant-petitioners had breached the contract and that the plaintiff-respondents had not waived their right to enforce the forfeiture provisions of the contract.

In December of 1958, Mary Burkowski, as vendor, entered into a land sale contract with Charles P. Marshall and Agnes P. Marshall, as vendees. The contract provided for the sale of certain real estate for the sum of $36,000.00, payable as follows:

"$500.00, at the signing, execution and delivery of this contract, the receipt whereof is hereby acknowledged; $500.00 or more on or before the 25th day of December, 1958, and $2500.00 or more on or before the 15th day of January, 1960, and $2500.00 or more on or before the 15th day of January of each and every year thereafter until the balance of the contract has been fully paid, all without interest and all without relief from valuation and appraisement laws and with attorney fees."

The contract also contained a fairly standard section which provided for the treatment of prepayments—but which the Court of Appeals found to be of particular importance. It provided as follows:

"Should Vendees have made prepayments or paid in advance of the payments herein required, said prepayments, if any, shall at any time thereafter be applied in lieu of further principal payments required as herein stated, to the extent of such prepayments only."

The following is the forfeiture/liquidated damages provision of the land sale contract:

"It is further agreed that if any default shall be made in the payment of said purchase price or any of the covenants and/or conditions herein provided, and if any such default shall continue for 30 days, then, after the lapse of said 30 days' period, *all moneys and payments previously paid shall, at the option of the Vendor without notice or demand, be and become forfeited and be taken and retained by the Vendor as liquidated damages* and thereupon this contract shall terminate and be of no further force or effect; provided, however, that nothing herein contained shall be deemed or construed to prevent the Vendor from enforcing specific performance of this agreement in the event of any default on the part of the Vendees in complying, observing and performing any of the conditions, covenants and terms herein contained. ..." (Emphasis added.)

The vendor, Mary Burkowski, died in 1963. The plaintiffs in this action are the assignees (under the vendor's will) of the decedent's interests in the contract. They received their assignment from the executrix of the estate of the vendor on June 27, 1968. One year after this assignment, several of the assignees filed their complaint in this action alleging that the defendants had defaulted through nonpayment.

The schedule of payments made under this contract was shown by the evidence to be as follows:

"Date	Amount Paid	Total of Paid Principal
12/1/1958	$ 500.00	$ 500.00
12/25/1958	500.00	1,000.00
3/26/1959	5,000.00	6,000.00
4/5/1960	2,500.00	8,500.00
5/23/1961	2,500.00	11,000.00
4/6/1962	2,500.00	13,500.00
1/15/1963	2,500.00	16,000.00
6/30/1964	2,500.00	18,500.00
2/15/1965	2,500.00	21,000.00"

No payments have been made since the last one indicated above—$15,000.00 remains to be paid on the original contract price.

In response to the plaintiff's attempt to enforce the forfeiture provision, the defendants raised the affirmative defense of waiver. ...

In essence, the Court of Appeals found that there was no waiver because the vendors were obligated to accept prepayment, and, "the payments made, although irregular in time and amount, were prepayments on the unpaid balance through and including the payment due on January 15, 1965." (289 N.E.2d at 771.) The Court concluded that up to January 15, 1966, "the vendors waived no rights under the contract, because they were obliged to accept prepayment," (Id.) and that, "[t]he vendors could not have insisted on forfeiture prior to January 15, 1966, the date of the first missed payment." (Id.) (We believe the Court of Appeals miscalculated here; the vendors could not have insisted on forfeiture until January 16, 1968.)

If forfeiture is enforced against the defendants, they will forfeit outright the sum of $21,000, or well over one-half the original contract price, as liquidated damages *plus possession.* Forfeitures are generally disfavored by the law. In fact, "... [e]quity abhors forfeitures and beyond any question has jurisdiction, which it will exercise in a proper case to grant relief against their enforcement." 30 C.J.S. Equity § 56

(1965) and cases cited therein. This jurisdiction of equity to intercede is predicated upon the fact that "the loss or injury occasioned by the default must be susceptible of exact compensation." 30 C.J.S., supra.

... "Reasonable" liquidated damage provisions are permitted by the law. However, the issue before this Court, is whether a $21,000 forfeiture is a "reasonable" measure of damages. If the damages are unreasonable, i.e., if they are disproportionate to the loss actually suffered, they must be characterized as penal rather then compensatory. Under the facts of this case, a $21,000 forfeiture is clearly excessive.

... The vendee has acquired a substantial interest in the property, which, if forfeited, would result in substantial injustice.

Under a typical conditional land contract, the vendor retains legal title until the total contract price is paid by the vendee. Payments are generally made in periodic installments. *Legal* title does not vest in the vendee until the contract terms are satisfied, but equitable title vests in the vendee at the time the contract is consummated. When the parties enter into the contract, all incidents of ownership accrue to the vendee. The vendee assumes the risk of loss and is the recipient of all appreciation in value. The vendee, as equitable owner, is responsible for taxes. Stark v. Kreyling (1934), 207 Ind. 128, 188 N.E. 680. The vendee has a sufficient interest in land so that upon sale of that interest, he holds a vendor's lien.

This Court has held, consistent with the above notions of equitable ownership, that a land contract, once consummated constitutes a present sale and purchase. The vendor " 'has, in effect, exchanged his property for the unconditional obligation of the vendee, the performance of which is secured by the retention of the legal title.' " Stark v. Kreyling, supra, 207 Ind. at 135, 188 N.E. at 682. The Court, in effect, views a conditional land contract as a sale with a security interest in the form of legal title reserved by the vendor. Conceptually, therefore, the retention of the title by the vendor is the same as reserving a lien or mortgage. Realistically, vendor-vendee should be viewed as mortgagee-mortgagor. To conceive of the relationship in different terms is to pay homage to form over substance.

The piercing of the transparent distinction between a land contract and a mortgage is not a phenomenon without precedent. In addition to the *Stark* case, supra, there is an abundance of case law from other jurisdictions which lends credence to the position that a land sales contract is in essence a mortgage.

... We believe there to be great wisdom in requiring judicial foreclosure of land contracts pursuant to the mortgage statute. Perhaps the most attractive aspect of judicial foreclosure is the period of redemption, during which time the vendee may redeem his interest, possibly through re-financing.

Forfeiture is closely akin to strict foreclosure—a remedy developed by the English courts which did not contemplate the equity of redemption. American jurisdictions, including Indiana, have, for the most part, rejected strict foreclosure in favor of foreclosure by judicial sale.

... A forfeiture—like a strict foreclosure at common law—is often offensive to our concepts of justice and inimical to the principles of equity. This is not to suggest that a forfeiture is an inappropriate remedy for the breach of all land contracts. In the case of an abandoning, absconding vendee, forfeiture is a logical and equitable remedy. Forfeiture would also be appropriate where the vendee has paid a minimal amount on the contract at the time of default and seeks to retain possession while the vendor is paying taxes, insurance, and other upkeep in order to preserve the premises. Of course, in this latter situation, the vendee will have acquired very little, if any, equity in the property. However, a court of equity must always approach forfeitures with great caution, being forever aware of the possibility of inequitable dispossession of property and exorbitant monetary loss. We are persuaded that forfeiture may only be appropriate under circumstances in which it is found to be consonant with notions of fairness and justice under the law.

In other words, we are holding a conditional land sales contract to be in the nature of a secured transaction, the provisions of which are subject to all proper and just remedies at law and in equity.

Turning our attention to the case at hand, we find that the vendor-assignees were seeking forfeiture, including $21,000 already paid on said contract as liquidated damages and immediate possession. They were, in fact, asking for strict application of the contract terms at law which we believe would have led to unconscionable results requiring the intervention of equity. ...

For all of the foregoing reasons, transfer is granted and the cause is reversed and remanded with instructions to enter a judgment of foreclosure on the vendors' lien, pursuant to Trial Rule 69(C) and the mortgage foreclosure statute as modified by Trial Rule 69(C). Said judgment shall include an order for the payment of the unpaid principal balance due on said contract, together with interest at 8% per annum from the date of judgment. The order may also embrace any and all other proper and equitable relief that the court deems to be just, including the discretion to issue a stay of the judicial sale of the property, all pursuant to the provisions of Trial Rule 69(C). Such order shall be consistent with the principles and holdings developed within this opinion.

Reversed and remanded with instructions.

ARTERBURN, C. J., and DeBRULER and PRENTICE, JJ., concur in this opinion on the merits.

PRENTICE, J., filing an additional statement [which is omitted].

GIVAN, J., dissents.

FINCHER v. MILES HOMES OF MISSOURI, INC.

Supreme Court of Missouri, 1977.
549 S.W.2d 848.

FINCH, Judge.

This is an appeal from a judgment wherein the trial court quieted title in plaintiffs to a tract of land, invalidated a deed of trust thereon on the basis that the purchaser under a contract for a deed has no right to encumber the property, and impressed the tract with an equitable lien in favor of defendant Miles Homes of Missouri, Inc. for $1,883.03 for materials furnished for a house thereon. On appeal to the Missouri court of appeals, Springfield district, that court, contrary to the decision of the trial court, concluded that a purchaser under a contract for a deed has an interest in the property which may be mortgaged. Nevertheless, it affirmed, concluding that terms in this contract of sale prohibited Staceys from mortgaging their interest. Furthermore, said the court, even if rights did accrue thereunder, they were extinguished when the purchaser, having defaulted, surrendered his rights under the contract to seller. Thereafter, we ordered the case transferred to this court and we now decide it as though here on direct appeal. We reverse and remand.

On May 3, 1967, plaintiffs entered into a contract with defendant Lester Stacey and his wife, since deceased, to sell them a tract containing approximately one-half acre. By its terms, plaintiffs were to sell to buyers the tract described therein for $1,200, payable $200 down with the remainder payable in monthly installments of $47.50 each, which included interest. A few days later the same parties executed a second "Contract for Sale of Real Estate" dated May 11, 1967, by which the parcel described therein was to be sold on the same terms as to price and schedule of payments as those in the May 3, 1967 contract, with certain additional restrictions and conditions not spelled out in the prior agreement. This latter contract, according to the evidence, was intended to supersede the prior agreement and constitute the final agreement between the parties. The description in the contract of May 11, 1967, was more detailed and varied somewhat, as later noted, from the earlier description. Neither contract was recorded.

The Staceys also entered into an agreement with Miles Homes dated May 18, 1967, to buy a pre-cut home for erection on the tract purchased by them from plaintiffs. The contract for $6,378 covered materials for the house but no labor. In addition, the contract called for a charge for various loan services of $200. The Staceys paid $2 down, leaving a balance due Miles Homes of $6,576. To evidence that indebtedness, the Staceys executed a note to Miles Homes for $6,576 payable in monthly installments of $52 with the remaining unpaid balance due and payable November 30, 1970. The note was secured by a deed of trust on the tract described in the May 3 contract between Staceys and plaintiffs.

That deed of trust was recorded June 2, 1967. Pursuant to the contract, Miles Homes delivered materials to the site and the Staceys then erected a home thereon.

Staceys made payments to plaintiffs from time to time on the purchase price of the lot. On April 29, 1969, the balance due under the sale contract was $221.70. No further payments were made by Staceys to plaintiffs. Sometime thereafter, Mrs. Stacey died and in December 1971, Mr. Stacey vacated the premises. Plaintiffs meanwhile had visited the house to attempt to collect additional payments from Stacey but to no avail. Finally, plaintiffs notified Stacey that if he did not pay the balance, they would be required to take action. Stacey then informed plaintiffs that he would have to let the property go. On March 1, 1972, at the request of plaintiffs, he signed on the bottom of the May 11, 1967, contract a statement entitled "Release by Buyers" which acknowledged his default and the fact that he had no remaining interest in the property. Stacey then removed his furniture from the house and plaintiffs took possession. They expended certain sums to complete and repair the house in certain respects, and thereafter they rented it for $110 per month.

Meanwhile, Staceys also had made payments to Miles Homes on their note. Total payments thereon amounted to $2,587.24.

In September 1973, plaintiffs instituted this action. Count One of their second amended petition, on which the case was tried, sought to quiet title in plaintiffs. Count Two was in the nature of a declaratory judgment action which sought to have the court declare that the deed of trust given by Staceys to Miles Homes was not a lien on the property. Count Three, pleaded in the alternative, sought a money judgment if plaintiffs were found not to be the owners of the property.

In its answer and counterclaim, Miles Homes admitted that the plaintiffs had legal title to the tract in question, but alleged that equitable title had been vested in the Staceys as a result of the contract to purchase and that the Staceys had a right to execute a deed of trust on that equitable interest. Consequently, alleged Miles Homes, it had an interest in the property by virtue of the note and deed of trust from the Staceys. Miles Homes offered to pay the unpaid balance of the purchase price on the lot plus good faith improvements by plaintiffs and sought, on payment thereof, to receive a deed to the property, or, in the alternative, sought a decree that plaintiffs, while holding the legal title, did so with an obligation to pay Miles Homes the balance due on its note and deed of trust. Finally, Miles Homes pleaded that if its deed of trust was not enforceable, it was entitled to an award of the reasonable value of materials furnished, asserted to be $10,000.

The trial court first quieted title in the plaintiffs. It then held that the deed of trust given by Staceys to Miles Homes was not a valid lien on the real estate. The latter holding was based on conclusions that (1) Staceys had no right to execute a deed of trust on the tract, (2) that the real estate described in the deed of trust was not the same real estate described in the contract of May 11, 1967, and (3) that such interest, if any, as could have been conveyed by Staceys under the deed of trust was extinguished when plaintiffs exercised their rights under the contract of sale to terminate that contract for default thereunder. The trial court went on, however, to hold that Miles Homes was entitled to receive the sum of $3,600, the reasonable value of materials furnished by it and located on the premises, less payments received, leaving a balance of $1,883.03 for which a lien on the property was established.

No complaint is made on appeal concerning the holding of the trial court that fee simple title was vested in plaintiffs. The objections made relate only to the legal conclusions of the trial court that for various reasons the deed of trust given by Staceys to Miles Homes was not a valid lien on the premises.

1. *Did Staceys have a right to execute a deed of trust on property which they had contracted to purchase under a contract for a deed?*

We conclude that they did. In Lewis v. Gray, 356 Mo. 115, 201 S.W.2d 148 (1947), this court held that absent a valid and enforceable restriction to the contrary in a contract for the sale of land, a purchaser's interest therein pursuant to such contract can be mortgaged. In other words, the court recognized that a purchaser with only equitable title to land can execute a note to a third party and give as security for that note a deed of trust on his interest under the terms of that contract.

. . .

2. *Did the Stacey deed of trust contain a description so deficient that it failed to describe the lot sold by plaintiffs to Staceys on which the house was constructed?*

[The court held that the description was not so deficient as to invalidate the deed of trust.]

. . .

3. *Was Miles Homes' lien under its deed of trust from the Staceys eliminated by the termination of Stacey's rights under his purchase contract pursuant to the release he gave to sellers on March 1, 1972?*

This apparently is a question of first impression in Missouri. Necessarily, it requires consideration of all the pertinent facts as they relate to the equities of the situation. We restate them for that purpose.

Finchers in 1967 contracted to sell Staceys a vacant lot for $1200, to be paid in installments. They did not utilize the standard procedure of conveying by deed, taking and recording a deed of trust for the unpaid balance. If they had and Finchers had foreclosed their deed of trust for nonpayment of the note, we would not have the problem which now confronts us. Instead they gave a contract for a deed, to be delivered upon payment of the total purchase price, and did not even record the contract. Staceys paid all of the purchase price except $221.70.

Meanwhile, Staceys had constructed thereon a house containing a living room, kitchen, 3 bedrooms and a bath. Pre-cut material for the house amounting to $6378 was purchased from Miles Homes and a deed of trust was given therefor. Some additional items for the house were purchased by Stacey on open account and Stacey then did the construction work.

On March 1, 1972, Finchers, on the basis of the unpaid balance of $221.70 plus interest thereon of $43.86, a total of $265.56, terminated Stacey's rights in the property by having him so acknowledge on the bottom of the contract of sale. In this suit they have claimed that the surrender of Stacey's rights had the effect of terminating Miles Homes' rights as well.

It is undisputed that prior to the termination by Finchers of Stacey's rights on March 1, 1972, no notice of any kind was given to Miles Homes as to what, if any, balance was due from Stacey to Finchers on the purchase price of the lot, or what, if any, delinquency existed. Neither did Finchers give any notice to Miles Homes of an intention on their part to terminate Stacey's rights and whatever rights Miles Homes had under its recorded deed of trust, even though the evidence of Fincher himself disclosed that he knew almost from the outset about Miles Homes' selling Staceys the materials for a house which Staceys then constructed on this lot.

On April 14, 1972, Fincher wrote Miles Homes as follows: "I am writing in regard to a house plan you sold to Lester Stacy [sic] here. I have made a deal with Stacy [sic] and would like to talk withone [sic] of your representives [sic] and get this worked out if possible.

"Let me know when someone from your company will be in the area."

This letter said nothing about any unpaid balance on the lot or terminating Stacey's interest for default or any idea of foreclosing any rights of Miles Homes. It said nothing to indicate in any way that the balance on Stacey's deed of trust was to be affected or was in jeopardy in any way.

Under such circumstances, should the agreement between Stacey and Finchers terminating Stacey's rights under his purchase contract have the effect of destroying Miles Homes' rights under its deed of trust, in effect giving plaintiffs a windfall of the house? In 59 C.J.S. Mortgages § 184, the following rule is stated:

"A mortgage given by one holding land under an executory contract for its purchase covers his interest, whatever it may be, at the date of the mortgage, giving the mortgagee the right to complete the purchase if his mortgagor refuses to do so; *and the mortgagee cannot be ousted of his rights by a rescission of the contract of sale by the original parties to it.* ..." (Emphasis supplied.)

We agree with the view, expressed in the italicized language, that mere rescission of the original contract of sale by the parties thereto does not oust the mortgagee of his rights under a deed of trust taken from the purchaser in the executory contract of sale. To so permit would open the door to connivance for the purpose of eliminating the rights of an intervening party who might well, as here, have furnished in good faith property or money with which the property was improved and enhanced in value. Accordingly, we hold that the action of Stacey in releasing his interest in the purchase contract on March 1, 1972, did not terminate the rights of Miles Homes under its deed of trust of May 18, 1967.

. . .

In this case, unlike the situation in Kendrick v. Davis [75 Wash.2d 456, 452 P.2d 222 (1969)], vendors knew of the interest of Miles Homes. We hold that they did have an obligation to notify Miles Homes of the delinquency which existed and of their intention to forfeit the contract for that reason. That would have given Miles Homes an opportunity to protect its interest. That notice was not given and, hence, that which has occurred has not had the effect of terminating the rights of Miles Homes under its deed of trust.

Having so concluded, it follows that we must reverse the judgment of the trial court and remand the case in order that the rights of Miles Homes as mortgagee may be declared and enforced. To that end, the court on remand should determine the present unpaid balance on Stacey's note and deed of trust to Miles Homes, taking further testimony for that purpose, if necessary.

When that has been done, Miles Homes is then entitled to have its deed of trust foreclosed and the decree should so provide. From the proceeds of such sale, the costs thereof should be paid, after which proceeds of the sale should be applied in this order: first, the unpaid balance due Finchers on their contract of sale to Staceys; second, reimbursement of Finchers for those sums necessarily and reasonably expended in order to complete or repair the house and put it in shape for rental; third, payment to Miles Homes of the amount due it on Stacey's note and deed of trust; and finally, to Finchers as record title holders as well as successors in interest to the Staceys by reason of their cancellation of their contract to purchase and the surrender of their rights thereunder to Finchers.

We recognize that plaintiffs might prefer to pay the balance on the Miles Homes deed of trust rather than to have the property sold in a foreclosure sale. Accordingly, in fashioning its decree, the trial court may give to plaintiffs the option of paying Miles Homes the balance due them on their note and deed of trust after that balance has been determined. If plaintiffs avail themselves of that opportunity, they would then be entitled to have title quieted in them free and clear of any claim of Miles Homes. However, if plaintiffs do not so elect, the decree should direct that the foreclosure sale be conducted and the proceeds applied as indicated.

By their pleadings in this case, Miles Homes seeks an accounting of the rents and profits from the house while it has been in possession of plaintiffs and it also speaks in its pleadings of receiving a deed to the premises if it pays to plaintiffs the balance due them under the contract of sale, plus sums expended for good faith improvements. There are statements in some of the outstate cases to which we have referred and in 59 C.J.S. Mortgages, which indicate a recognition of such a right. However, we have concluded that Miles Homes is not entitled to receive a deed from plaintiffs by paying the balance on the contract of sale, plus sums expended for improvements. Miles Homes only held a security interest in the property. It held a note secured by a deed of trust. That entitles it to collect the amount which that lien secures, but does not entitle it to more than that. Plaintiffs as title holders and as successors to the rights of Stacey were entitled to the rents and profits and are entitled to the real estate in question, subject to the deed of trust held by Miles Homes.

The judgment is reversed and the cause remanded for further proceedings in accordance with the views expressed in this opinion.

REVERSED AND REMANDED.

SEILER, C. J., and MORGAN, BARDGETT, HENLEY and DON-NELLY, JJ., concur.

WARREN, CALIFORNIA INSTALMENT LAND SALES CONTRACTS: A TIME FOR REFORM *

9 U.C.L.A. Law Review 608, 609–616 (1962).

I. HAZARDS OF PURCHASING UNDER INSTALMENT LAND CONTRACT

A. *Failure of Land Sale Vendor to Pay Lender*

Witness: "Let's put it this way. The ordinary man on the street buys roughly one or two homes in a lifespan. And with the corruption of this law situation it looks to me like when you open up the law book it's nothing but a piece of cheese with holes in it, where, let's say all the rats can keep on crawling through and get no individual any protection."

Thus the layman looks at the California law of land sale contracts. And it is no wonder, for this witness who had kept up his monthly payments on a home purchased on instalment contract learned by reading a newspaper that his house was to be sold on foreclosure. Hundreds of other northern California families had similar experiences in the summer of 1961. Although these parties had made their monthly payments to the party holding legal title to the land they had contracted to buy, these payments were not remitted to the savings and loan associations who held first trust deeds on the land. Proceedings for foreclosure followed. These unhappy events, coming shortly after similar occurrences in southern California, dramatized the plight of the instalment contract buyer as occupying a status of uneasy dependence upon his vendor.

The savings and loan association or other lender financing the development of a subdivision to be marketed by instalment sales contracts deals only with its borrower, the legal title holder. If the land owner fails to appropriate the payments of the contract buyers to the discharge of the loans encumbering the land, the lender may foreclose. The fact that the vendees are not in default in the payments to the land owner is immaterial to the lender. As soon as the owner-vendor goes into default, the lender may file notice of default; it must then send such notice to all persons who have filed a request for such notice. Since the contract vendee normally does not file a request, the lender need not even apprise him of the fact that he may be in imminent danger of losing his home. Commonly the first notice the vendee receives of the vendor's default comes to him by way of panic-spreading rumors, quickly followed by agents with offers to obtain refinancing for the frightened vendee for $100, paid in advance. Unless the default is cured within ninety days after notice of default is filed, the lender may initiate the procedure for the foreclosure sale. The lack of privity between the vendee and vendor's lender is so marked that it is doubtful if the lender need accept money tendered by the vendee to make up defaults of the vendor either before or after notice of default has been filed.

The lender may declare a default immediately upon the vendor's failure to meet his payments; no grace period need be given. Once notice of default is filed, it can be cured only by payment of all sums in default plus the incidental legal expenses, including attorneys' fees. Even if the lender tolerates a period of delay in payments without filing notice of default, a late charge is assessed. In one recent instance, the purchaser of a $13,900 home made his $102 monthly payment on April 11, instead of April 10, when it was due; he thereby incurred a late charge of $2.50. His vendor failed to turn the money over to the lender until May 2; on April 27, the lender, a savings and loan association, filed notice of default. They assessed $3.34 in late charges, and the costs of curing the default ran to $200.49. At various times nine other late charges of $3.34 were assessed due to the landowner's tardiness in accounting to the lender.

B. *Difficulty in Requiring Performance of Vendor*

The legitimate assumption of the instalment contract vendee is that when he has made all of his payments or has obtained refinancing, he will receive a deed from the vendor granting him marketable title. His expectations in this regard are not always fulfilled, at least not without a lawsuit that a tract house buyer is peculiarly incapable of affording.

Since the usual instalment sale does not go through an escrow, and no title policy is issued to the vendee, he has no real assurance that the vendor owns the land he has contracted to sell or that it is not encumbered beyond the contract price at the time of the sale. In 1960 the legislature enacted a requirement that every sales contract of subdivision land must set forth, *inter alia,* the encumbrances outstanding at the date of the sales contract. Though well meant, this statute is based on the questionable premise that if the facts—however technical and incomprehensible—are disclosed to a buyer he can protect himself. It does not prohibit the sale of land not owned by the seller, or encumbered by liens in excess of the contract price; it does not protect the buyer against any encumbrances the seller neglects to list; nor, in fact, does it set out a penalty for the seller who ignores it altogether.

Like any party to an executory contract, the instalment sale vendee faces the possibility that the other party may die, transfer his interest to a minor, be out-of-state, or be in bankruptcy on or before the time of performance. Though the death of an instalment contract vendor does not terminate the contract, the vendee may eventually be faced with having to round up the heirs or legatees of the deceased to compel a conveyance. Some of these parties may be minors, thereby necessitating the appointment of a guardian *ad litem.* A procedure is available to the instalment contract vendee to specifically enforce his contract against an out-of-state vendor if the realty is within California. The vendee must personally serve the nonresident or absent vendor or publish the summons and mail to the vendor a copy of the summons and complaint. Since the vendor is not present to make the conveyance, the court may appoint a receiver to carry the decree into effect.

. . .

C. *Claims of Judgment Creditors*

Though cases abound delineating the rights of the land contract vendor and vendee *inter sese,* there is a surprising dearth of authority regarding the rights of the vendee with respect to third parties who have claims against the vendor. On some important issues one can only reason from general principles and analogies—i.e., guess—to determine what is the vendee's position *vis a vis* third parties.

There are two types of subdivision properties marketed by instalment sale contract: lots with houses and those without, the latter often described as raw land developments. In the case of the improved lots, the purchaser immediately goes into possession by moving into the house, while the raw land purchaser delays going into possession until he is ready to build a house. Some raw land buyers purchase without ever having seen the land and with no immediate intention of building on it. The instalment land contract buyer usually finds that his contract is not in a form suitable for recording. Land sale contracts can be recorded only if acknowledged by the seller; a contract acknowledged only by the buyer is not entitled to recordation and if recorded is insufficient to give constructive notice to third parties. The reluctance of sellers to provide buyers with a recordable contract is attributable to their concern over the effect of a recorded contract as a cloud on the title after default by the buyer.

The California recording act states that every conveyance of real property is void as against subsequent purchasers or mortgagees in good faith and for value "whose conveyance is first duly recorded." The land sale contract has been held to be within the definition of a conveyance of realty. However, possession by the land sale contract vendee—and what possession could be more open and notorious than that of the suburban tract home buyer—gives third parties notice of his rights under the contract. Hence, even though the contract is not recorded, subsequent purchasers or mortgagees of the vendor take subject to the vendee's interest under the contract because his possession precludes them from occupying the position of good faith purchasers. Nor should a judgment creditor of the vendor or the eventual purchaser at a judicial sale of the vendor's interest stand on better footing than these parties. Subsequent purchasers and encumbrancers of the vendor's interest must take this interest with the obligation to convey title to the vendee upon full payment. Since the rights of a trustee in bankruptcy are measured by those of a lien creditor, the possession of the vendee should preserve his interest in bankruptcy proceedings of the vendor.

The more difficult problem is the determination of the rights of the vendee under an unrecorded contract in the raw land development case where the vendee is not in possession of the lot. Judgment creditors enjoy no protection under the recording act, and a vendee under an unrecorded contract should prevail over creditors who attach the vendor's interest even though the vendee was not in possession at the time of attachment. Trustees in bankruptcy, in their status as lien creditors, would similarly be subject to the rights of the vendee. However, a purchaser at a judicial sale does occupy the position of a bona fide purchaser and would take free of the interest of a vendee not in possession under an unrecorded contract if he had no actual notice of the contract.

NOTES

1. *Protecting the Vendee Against Forfeitures.* Courts and legislatures have employed several devices to protect the installment land contract buyer against forfeiture of his accumulated equity. Courts will sometimes protect buyers by minimizing their defaults and finding that they have substantially performed. Another judicial technique is to construe seller nonaction as waiver of any claim based on the buyer's default. Courts may also limit the seller's remedial alternatives to foreclosure of the vendor's lien, or hold that the forfeited sum constitutes an unlawful penalty or improperly liquidated damages.

The most common legislative response to perceived seller overreaching has been to engraft mortgage law's debtor protection provisions onto installment land contracts. For example, some states mandate a grace period during which the buyer can cure his default. See Iowa Code Ann. § 656.4 (Supp.1983). Oklahoma treats installment land contracts as mortgages generally. See Okla.Stat.Ann. tit. 16, § 11A (West 1986); see also U.L.S.I.A. § 102(b). Other state legislatures have taken more innovative approaches. Maryland, for example, entitles an installment buyer who has paid 40% or more of the contract price to receive a deed to the land in return for giving the seller a mortgage for the balance of the contract price owed; the "periodic principal and interest payments required by the mortgage may not exceed the periodic principal and interest payments otherwise required by the land installment contract, except with the consent of the mortgagor." Md. Real Prop. Code Ann., § 10–105 (1981).

2. Skendzel v. Marshall reflects the contemporary trend to incorporate mortgage law's debtor-protection provisions into installment land contracts. Although some language in *Skendzel* suggests an intention to fully incorporate these provisions, the last paragraph of the opinion suggests that the court may only have meant to bar vendor relief through forfeiture. Note, though, that the court's instruction to the lower court to enter a judgment foreclosing the vendor's lien also allowed the lower court order to embrace "any and all other proper and equitable relief that the court deems to be just. ..." Would it have been appropriate for such an order to allow the buyer to redeem from the foreclosure sale within a prescribed period? Does the *Skendzel* court give adequate guidance to lenders as to when forfeiture is permitted or foreclosure required?

Courts will not necessarily apply foreclosure law to all installment sale contracts. In Grombone v. Krekel, 754 P.2d 777 (Colo.App.1988), the court emphasized that a court has discretion to either treat an installment contract as a mortgage or to permit forfeiture. Factors include the amount of the buyer's equity in the property, the length and willfulness of the default, and whether improvements were made and the property maintained. On the facts, the appellate court upheld the trial court's decision not to require foreclosure:

> Here, the trial court found that the defendants defaulted on virtually all of their contract obligations and made no attempt to cure such defaults despite plaintiffs' repeated demands. The record shows that, although defendants were credited with a down payment of approximately $35,000, they actually made only four monthly payments, and then failed to make any further payments. Their total equity was slightly more than 10 percent of the purchase price. The defendants failed to pay taxes, insurance, and sewer and water charges. The record also shows that, during the time defendants were in possession, they made no improvements to the property; instead, they allowed the property to deteriorate to such a degree that all of the tenants moved out.

Id. at 779.

3. Is it good public policy for legislatures to recast installment land contracts and thus limit the forms through which buyers and sellers can structure residential finance? The traditional installment land contract does, to be sure, leave room for an overreaching seller to take advantage of an unsuspecting buyer. But it may also offer buyers and sellers the opportunity to strike a mutually beneficial bargain on terms that would otherwise be unavailable to either. For the seller, the installment land contract may offer a higher sales price than she could otherwise obtain, well-secured by the speedy remedy of forfeiture and enhanced by the favorable income tax treatment that I.R.C. § 453 gives to gain on installment sales. See pages 674–680 below. For the financially strapped buyer, the installment land contract may offer the opportunity to purchase a house with a lower down payment than would be required by institutional mortgage financing and with monthly payments no higher than the rent he would have to pay for equivalent housing. See Freyfogle, Vagueness and the Rule of Law: Reconsidering Installment Land Contract Forfeitures, 1988 Duke L.J. 609, for an excellent analysis of the costs due to vagueness which have resulted from judicial intervention to prevent forfeitures and examining the inadequacy of installment contract remedies.

The installment buyer's bargain is even better in inflationary times and in a rising real estate market. For little money down, the buyer essentially acquires an option, renewable over the term of the contract, to acquire the parcel for a price fixed in terms of values that prevailed at the time the contract was entered into, and with all option payments credited against the purchase price. Rising real property values will also significantly meliorate the risk of forfeiture. Once the parcel's value increases by more than 20%, the buyer can use his equity in the property to refinance the purchase with 80% financing from a third party institutional lender. For example, if the contract price is $30,000 and the buyer has paid the principal balance down $3,000 in the first two years of a ten-year contract, the property need only appreciate about 6% each year over that period (from $30,000 to $33,750) since 80% financing on $33,750 will produce the $27,000 that the temporarily embarrassed buyer needs to pay off the contract and avoid forfeiture.

4. *Protecting Buyer Against Creditors and Successors of Seller.* Under traditional priority rules, the interest of an installment contract buyer will be subordinate to any mortgage or other lien on the parcel previously given by the seller. Although existence of a prior mortgage lien will probably make the seller's title unmarketable, the buyer is in no position to demand marketable title until the date set for closing— which may be five, ten or twenty years hence. See Luette v. Bank of Italy Nat. Trust & Savings Ass'n, 42 F.2d 9 (9th Cir.1930).

Can the buyer protect himself against the risk that seller's default on the prior mortgage will result in foreclosure of the seller's *and* the buyer's interests? Can the buyer protect himself against subsistence of the mortgage right up to the date set for the buyer's closing, leaving title unmarketable even after the buyer has paid virtually all of the purchase price? One solution is for the contract to provide that the buyer will make his monthly payments directly to the prior mortgagee, receiving a credit for these payments against his installment obligations to the seller. Alternatively, seller may agree to convey fee title to the buyer, subject to the mortgage, when the principal outstanding on the contract equals the principal outstanding on the prior mortgage. See generally, Cathey, The Real Estate Installment Sale Contract: Its Drafting, Use, Enforcement, and Consequences, 5 U.Ark. Little Rock L.J. 229, 231–233 (1982).

How can the buyer protect himself against mortgages given by the seller-titleholder *after* the installment land contract has been executed? As indicated in the excerpt from Professor Warren's article, notice-based recording acts will protect the buyer in possession since the subsequent mortgagee will have inquiry notice of the buyer's interest. The buyer out of possession can also protect himself, even if the seller insists that the contract not be acknowledged. The buyer can, for example, record an acknowledged memorandum of the unacknowledged contract, thus putting subsequent lienors on constructive inquiry notice of the contract. Or, the buyer can simply try to record the unacknowledged contract. (Often, recording officers will not insist on acknowledgement of an instrument submitted for recording.) Although this will not give constructive notice to subsequent lienors, it will typically give them actual notice for it is the rare mortgagee who does not perform a title search before closing its loan; this search will give actual notice of a recorded, though legally unrecordable, instrument.

5. *Protecting the Buyer's Creditors.* Most courts today hold that the installment land contract buyer has a mortgageable interest in land, subject of course to the prior interest of the seller. *Fincher* indicates the two problems facing a mortgagee from an installment land contract buyer: putting the seller on notice of the mortgage, thus obligating the seller to inform the mortgagee of any default and possible forfeiture under the contract, and being allowed to step into the shoes of the buyer-mortgagor who has defaulted on the land contract.

Notice. Miles could have protected itself by conducting a title search prior to entering into its financing arrangement with the Staceys. Upon discovering that the Staceys did not have legal title, Miles could have refused the financing or, alternatively, could have asked the Staceys for the name and address of the titleholder—the Finchers—and then given the Finchers notice of its deed of trust. If Fincher had not had actual notice of Miles' interest, should it have been held to inquiry notice from the improvement on the land? Should it have been held to constructive notice from the fact that Miles had recorded its deed of trust? Compare Kendrick v. Davis, 75 Wash.2d 456, 452 P.2d 222, 227–28 (1969) ("Defendants contend that the duty of notice should be on the vendor because he knew that under the terms of the contract the purchaser could have and might have assigned or mortgaged his interest after the execution of the contract and also because prior to his declaration of forfeiture the vendor could have obtained a title search to determine whether anyone might have obtained such interests. We think the obligation is otherwise. The burden is on the mortgagee to notify the vendor of his interest in the contract. No undue burden is thus placed on the mortgagee as he would have actual knowledge both of the identity of the vendor and of the vendor's right to declare a forfeiture of the contract upon the purchaser's default. Conversely, the vendor would not have notice of any mortgage or assignment unless and until he either received notice from the mortgagor or purchaser or made a title search himself.")

Stepping Into the Buyer's Shoes. The court in *Fincher* gave Miles a comparatively limited right—to have its note paid off. Would it have been preferable to view Miles as a second mortgagee, and to give him the right of redemption traditionally given to junior mortgagees? Compare Shindledecker v. Savage, 96 N.M. 42, 627 P.2d 1241, 1243 (1981). ("In such a case the mortgagee cannot have his lien eclipsed by the agreement of the parties to the real estate contract to rescind it. By virtue of his mortgage, the mortgagee obtains the original purchaser's right to purchase the property for the consideration stated in the purchase contract. In other words, the mortgagee assumes the rights of the vendee under the real estate contract.")

6. *Bibliographic Note.* The perceived inequities of installment land contracts have spawned an abundant literature. The following articles, in addition to those excerpted above, are informative: Durham, Ohio Land Contracts Revisited, 14 U.Dayton L.Rev. 451 (1989); Freyfogle, The Installment Land Contract as Lease: Habitability Protections and the Low-Income Purchaser, 62 N.Y.U.L.Rev. 293 (1987); Comment, Remedying the Inequities of Forfeiture in Land Installment Contracts, 64 Iowa L.Rev. 158 (1978); Note, Toward Abolishing Installment Land Sale Contracts, 36 Mont.L.Rev. 110 (1975); Note, Reforming the Vendor's Remedies for Breach of Installment Land Sale Contracts, 47 So.Cal.L.Rev. 191 (1973); Note, Florida Installment Land Contracts: A Time for Reform, 28 U.Fla.L.Rev. 156 (1975).

Nelson & Whitman, The Installment Land Contract—A National Viewpoint, 1977 B.Y.U.L.Rev. 541, offers a well balanced analysis of the interests involved, noting the risks that presently exist for vendors entering into these contracts. See also, Nelson & Whitman, Installment Land Contracts—Revisited, 1985 B.Y.U.L.Rev. 1. The vendor's creditors also encounter risk. See Lynn, Bankruptcy and the Land Sales Contract: The Rights of the Vendee vis-a-vis the Vendor's Bankruptcy Trustee, 5 Tex.Tech.L.Rev. 677 (1974); Lacy, Land Sale Contracts in Bankruptcy, 21 U.C.L.A.L.Rev. 477 (1973); Lacy, Creditors of Land Contract Vendors, 24 Case W.Res.L.Rev. 645 (1973).

VI. FEDERAL INCOME TAX CONSIDERATIONS

D. BRADFORD, BLUEPRINTS FOR BASIC TAX REFORM *
77–81 (2d ed.rev.1984).

OWNER–OCCUPIED HOUSING

Under present law, homeowners are allowed personal deductions for mortgage interest paid and for State and local property taxes assessed against their homes. Furthermore, there is no attempt to attribute to owner-occupiers the income implied by ownership of housing equity. (In the aggregate, this is estimated in the national income and product accounts at $11.1 billion per year, an amount that does not include untaxed increases in housing values.)

Imputed Rental Income

Any dwelling, whether owner-occupied or rented, is an asset that yields a flow of services over its economic lifetime. The value of this service flow for any time period represents a portion of the market rental value of the dwelling. For rental housing, there is a monthly contractual payment (rent) from tenant to landlord for the services of the dwelling. In a market equilibrium, these rental payments must be greater than the maintenance expenses, related taxes, and depreciation, if any. The difference between these continuing costs and the market rental may be referred to as the "net income" generated by the housing unit.

An owner-occupier may be thought of as a landlord who rents to himself. On his books of account will also appear maintenance expenses and taxes, and he will equally experience depreciation in the value of his housing asset. What do not appear are, on the sources side, receipts of rental payment and, on the uses side, net income from the dwelling. Viewed from the sources side, this amount may be regarded as the reward that the owner of the dwelling accepts in-kind, instead of the financial reward he could obtain by renting to someone other than himself. Since a potential owner-occupier faces an array of opportunities for the investment of his funds, including in housing for rental to himself or others, the value of the reward in-kind must be at least the equal of these financial alternatives. Indeed, this fact provides a possible method for approximating the flow of consumption he receives, constituting a portion of the value of his consumption services. Knowing the cost of the asset and its depreciation schedule, one could estimate the reward necessary to induce the owner-occupier to rent to himself.

In practice, to tax this form of imputed income, however desirable it might be from the standpoint of equity or of obtaining neutrality between owning and renting, would severely complicate tax compliance and administration. Because the owner-occupier does not explicitly make a rental payment to himself, the value of the current use of his house is not revealed. Even if market rental were estimated, perhaps as a fixed share of assessed value of the dwelling, the taxpayer would face the difficulties of accounting for annual maintenance and depreciation to determine his net income.

The present tax system does not attempt to tax the imputed income from housing. This is, perhaps, because there would be extreme administrative difficulties in determining it and because there is a general lack of understanding of its nature. The incentive for home ownership that results from including net income from rental housing in the tax base while excluding it for owner-occupied housing also has strong political support, although the result is clearly a distortion from the pattern of consumer housing choices that would otherwise prevail.

Primarily for the sake of simplification, *the model plan continues to exclude from the tax base the portion of housing consumption attributable to owner-occupied dwellings. No imputation of the net income arising from these assets is proposed.*

Deductibility of Homeowners' Property Tax

Present law allows the homeowner to deduct State and local property taxes assessed against the value of his house as well as interest paid on his mortgage. The appropriateness of each of these deductions is considered next, beginning with the property tax.

The model tax would allow no deduction for the local property tax on owner-occupied homes or on other types of property that also have tax-free rental values, e.g., automobiles. This treatment is based on the proposition that deduction of the property tax results in further understatement of income in the tax base, in addition to the exclusion of net rental income. This cannot be justified, as can the exclusion of net income from the dwelling, on grounds of measurement difficulty. Allowing the deduction of property taxes by owner-occupiers results in unnecessary discrimination against tenants of rental housing. Elimination of the deduction would simplify tax administration and compliance and reduce the tax bias in favor of housing investment in general, and owner-occupancy in particular.

Local housing market adjustments normally will insure that changes in property taxes will be reflected in rental values. When the local property tax is increased throughout a market area, the current cost of supplying rental housing increases by the amount of the tax increase. Over time, housing supplies within the area will be reduced (and prices increased) until all current costs are again met and a normal return accrues to owners of equity and suppliers of mortgages. Accordingly, rents eventually must rise dollar-for-dollar with an increase in property tax. (Note that, in an equilibrium market, deductibility of the local tax against Federal income tax would not result in reduced Federal liability for *landlords* because the increase in gross receipts would match the increased deduction.) Tenants will experience an increase in rent and no change in their income tax liability.

Owner-occupiers provide the same service as landlords, and, therefore, must receive the same rental for a dwelling of equal quality. Hence, market rentals for their homes also would rise by the amount of any general property tax increase. If owner-occupiers were allowed to deduct the tax increase from taxable income while not reporting the increased imputed rent, they would enjoy a reduction in income tax that is not available either to tenants or to landlords.

To summarize the effect of the property tax increase, the landlord would have the same net income and no change in income tax; the tenant would have no change in income tax and higher rent; and the owner-occupier would have higher (imputed) rent as a "tenant," but the same net income and a *reduction* in his income tax as a "landlord." He would be favored relative to the renter first by receiving income from assets free of tax, and, in addition, his advantage over the tenant and landlord would *increase* with higher rates of local property tax. This advantage would not be present if the property tax deduction were denied to the owner-occupier. He would be treated as the tenant/landlord that he is—paying higher rent to himself to cover the property tax while his net income and income tax were unchanged.

Deductibility of Mortgage Interest

The mortgage interest deduction for owner-occupiers is often discussed in the same terms as the foregoing property tax argument. There are, however, quite significant differences, and, because of these, the *model tax treatment would continue to allow deductibility of home mortgage interest.*

The effect of this policy may be equated to allowing any taxpayer to enjoy tax-free the value of consumption services directly produced by a house (or other similar asset), regardless of the method he uses to finance the purchase of this asset. The tax-free income allowed is thus the same whether he chooses to purchase the asset out of funds previously accumulated or to obtain a mortgage loan for the purpose.

This position is based on the reasoning that, given the preliminary decision (based on measurement difficulty) not to attempt to tax the net income received from his house by the person who purchases it with previously accumulated or inherited funds, it would be unfair to deny a similar privilege to those who must borrow to finance the purchase.

There is a related reason in favor of allowing the mortgage interest deduction, having to do with the difficulty of tracing the source of funds for purchase of an asset.

Prospective homeowners of little wealth are obliged to offer the house as security to obtain debt financing. By contrast, an individual of greater wealth could simply borrow against some other securities, use the proceeds to purchase housing equity, and take the normal interest deduction. In other words, a mortgage is not the only way to borrow to finance housing, and it is very difficult, if not impossible, to correlate the proceeds of any other loan with the acquisition of a house.

Nevertheless, a case may be made for disallowing the interest deduction for borrowing identifiably for the purpose of financing an owner-occupied home (or other consumer durable). There is no doubt that most people finance home purchases with a mortgage using the home as security. Mortgage interest payments are surely highly correlated with net income produced by the associated housing, and denying the deduction would increase the tax base by an amount equal to a significant fraction of the aggregate net income from owner-occupied dwellings. For those who cannot otherwise finance home purchases, it would end the tax bias against renting. These considerations deserve to be weighed against the view taken here that the efficiency and equity gains from denying the mortgage interest deduction are insufficient to counter-balance the equity losses and the increased administrative complexity of the necessary rules for tracing the sources of funds.

SNOE, MY HOME, MY DEBT: REMODELING THE HOME MORTGAGE INTEREST DEDUCTION

80 Kentucky Law Journal 431, 432–433, 452–453, 457–460, 464, 467–471 (1991–1992).

Congress encourages home ownership by allowing taxpayers to deduct qualified residence interest in calculating taxable income. Generally, Congress allows deductions for business and investment expenses but disallows deductions for personal expenses. Congress gradually has reformed the income tax laws to align interest expenses with the general rule. Thus, instead of allowing a deduction for nearly all interest paid or accrued during the taxable year, as it did in 1954, the Internal Revenue Code currently allows a deduction for most interest paid or incurred in a taxpayer's trade or business or in investment activities and disallows all deductions for personal interest expenses. Despite prohibiting personal interest deductions, Congress specifically allows a deduction for qualified residence interest.

The preferential treatment afforded home mortgage interest partially reflects political reality: the average taxpayer has become accustomed to deducting mortgage interest and likely would be outraged if Congress eliminated the deduction. Although Congress could remove the preferential tax treatment given homeowners, indications are that it will not:

"There is no basic principle in tax law that is more supported by the American people than the principle that you ought to be able to deduct interest on your home from your taxes. We have taken a position that home ownership is something that we want to promote, that that is an objective of our tax policy that is strongly supported, and it is reflected in this bill...." [10]

This attitude underlies the home mortgage interest deduction and other tax preferences for homeowners.

. . .

Congress also uses the tax laws to foster homeownership. Deductibility of qualified residence interest is the most obvious example. Deductibility of property taxes, current deductibility of points, nonrecognition of gain on the sale of a principal residence if a new residence is purchased, complete exclusion of $125,000 from sale of a principal residence after the selling taxpayer reaches age fifty-five, and exemption of sales of principal residence from original issue discount rules further encourage homeownership. Some commentators say Congress' failure to tax the imputed rental value of a residence in the income base is also a tax preference.

In addition, homeowners receive some of the same tax benefits as other investors in property. For example, a homeowner does not recognize as taxable income the annual appreciation in the home's fair market value until the homeowner sells the home. Even then, the rollover provision and exclusion provision for homeowners over age fifty-five delay further or even eliminate any taxable gain. Should recognition be required from the sale of a home, the homeowner would benefit from any capital gains preferences in effect. Homeowners can escape all income tax consequences on value appreciation if they die owning their home because a devisee receives a stepped up basis to the home's fair market value, with no income tax burden to the deceased or the devisee.

Notwithstanding any other tax benefit related to the sale of a principal residence, the current deduction of interest and the deferred taxation, or in many cases tax exemption, of appreciation benefits the homeowner. The homeowner can deduct the mortgage interest currently, saving taxes or receiving refunds, while at the same time not recognizing for tax purposes any value appreciation on the home. If, for example a homeowner buys a home for $100,000, completely on a $100,000 mortgage borrowed at 10% annual interest rate, and the home appreciates $10,000 a year, the homeowner deducts the $10,000 interest annually but does not report as income the home's $10,000 increase in value. A homeowner can invest the taxes saved by the interest deduction and earn money on the investment. In contrast, a person that borrows $100,000 at 10% interest, and puts the money in an account paying 10% interest, saves no taxes because the full $10,000 interest must be reported in income and the interest deduction merely

10. 132 CONG. REC. S7387 (daily ed. June 12, 1986) (statement of Sen. Gramm) (Senator Gramm referred to the Tax Reform Act of 1986, Pub. L. No. 99–514, 100 Stat. 2085 (codified as amended in scattered sections of I.R.C.)).

offsets the interest income. The homeowner that sells his home at a gain, assuming the gain must be recognized, pays a tax only on the gain, with no adjustment for the period of deferral. The interest earned on the tax savings for the years of appreciation results in an economic profit to the homeowner. This ability to profit from the deferral of income, a form of tax arbitrage, is not limited to homeownership. It applies to all assets that may appreciate in value.

. . .

C. The Theories for Denying Home Mortgage Interest Deduction

1. Denial of Home Mortgage Interest Deduction As a Substitute for Imputing Rental Income

Opponents of the home mortgage interest deduction emphasize the homeowner's use of the home as a residence. Their analysis is not based on the personal use in and of itself, but instead on the owner-occupier's rent free use of the home. According to the argument, conceptually the owner-occupier should impute the home's rental value as income. Because imputing rental value into income is administratively impractical, a reasonable substitute would be to deny deductions for all expenses related to the home, including mortgage interest.

The nationwide imputed rental income of owner occupied residences composes a substantial portion of the gross national product (GNP). The Department of Commerce included in the 1987 GNP 317 billion dollars as the annualized rental value of owner occupied housing, which was approximately seven percent of GNP. To place the amount in perspective, the imputed value of owner occupied housing contributed more to the 1987 GNP than did all wholesaling activities and was only ten percent less than the amount of food Americans purchased for off-premises consumption. The sheer magnitude of the value of owner-occupied housing invites taxation. Its inclusion in the GNP calculation seems to indicate possible accurate valuation.

If the homeowner imputed rental income, the homeowner would deduct against that imputed income the same expenses allowable to persons owning rental property. Imputing rental income from home-ownership likely will not occur in the United States. Many countries have taxed the imputed value, but currently governments are moving away from taxing the imputed rent.

As a substitute for taxing imputed rental income, some advocate denying interest deductions. For this theory to prevail, imputed rental income must be income under the tax laws, not just income under economists' definition, and interest must be rationally related to the imputed income, to justify denying the deduction as a substitute for imputing rental income. The current tax framework argues against imputing rental value into the income base. ...

The imputed rent analysis rests on a recognition that a person enjoys owned property. Ownership of that property itself means that owner has more assets and more ability to pay than a person that has no assets but works and spends all earnings on current consumption. Yet, the two may have the same income for tax purposes. Perhaps Congress should incorporate a wealth tax into the income tax, but it has not done so. The federal government has not chosen to do so yet and should not depart from past practice by beginning with the home. As long as Congress excludes imputed income, including imputed rents, from the basic definition of income, no reasonable substitute is needed or proper, including denying interest on the purchase of a home.

If Congress extends the income tax laws to tax imputed rents, it must then determine that denial of mortgage interest would be a reasonable substitute for imputing the income directly. The fascination with interest is that the amount of interest most persons pay in the initial years of ownership approximates the rent the homeowner would pay by renting a similar house. The relationship is not a universal one, however. Over time, homes tend to appreciate in value while interest payments fall due to mortgage reduction. The correlation between interest payments and the rental value of owner-occupied homes is too attenuated and random to form a valid basis for a taxing surrogate.

. . .

D. Horizontal Equity Comparisons

. . .

3. Homeowners and Renters

Renters cannot deduct rent payments. Because interest payments are deductible and normally constitute the largest part of the monthly mortgage payments, commentators have compared the plight of renters to that of homeowners and concluded that the interest deduction favors homeowners. The assertion seems self-evident. A homeowner paying $700–a–month mortgage can deduct the majority of the payment to reduce her tax liability approximately $200 a month, while a renter paying $700 a month rent receives no tax benefit. The inequality is not as graphic as it appears at first blush, however. Homeowners do not deduct all expenses of homeownership. Repairs, maintenance, yard upkeep, water, sewage, pest control, fire insurance, and garbage collection all are nondeductible expenses paid by homeowners. Renters generally do not pay any of these expenses directly. The landlord pays them out of rent proceeds. Homeowners also incur other expenses renters often avoid. For example, most homeowners must purchase draperies, blinds, and appliances, all items many landlords furnish to tenants. Because house occupants usually incur higher gas and electric bills than apartment dwellers, homeowners may spend substantially more on these expenses than their renting counterparts. Of course, the portion of the mortgage payments attributable to principal are nondeductible and homeowners cannot depreciate personal residences for tax purposes. Homeowners also pay property taxes and interest, both of which are deductible. Renters normally avoid paying any property taxes or interest on the rented unit.

Placing dollar amounts on homeowners' nondeductible expenses is difficult. Repair and maintenance costs differ significantly. Under any set of assumptions, however, the homeowner incurs substantial expenses not incurred directly by the renter. The landlord must pay for many of the expenses not paid directly by the tenant, and theoretically sets the rent based to some extent on anticipated expenses. Other expenses, such as higher utility expenses in a home, are not duplicated. Professional management of rental properties, moreover, may provide services and maintenance at a lower cost per unit through more cost efficient procedures than can homeowners. Multi-family units occupy less land per unit, reducing the cost of acquisition and maintenance. Much of a landlord's profits may come from cost efficient operations.

If someone could isolate how much more rent a renter pays than a similarly situated homeowner pays in nondeductible housing costs, Congress might consider allowing some deduction for renters. Allowing a deduction for the full amount of the rent payment would be unjustified, however. A full deduction would give renters a deduction not given to homeowners. To remedy that inequality, Congress then would be obliged to authorize home related expense deductions, including depreciation. One proffered alternative would allow renters to deduct two-thirds of rent payments. It should be less. Even then, special rules would need to address boarding houses, co-renters, and benefits furnished by landlords for the rent charge such as furnishings and maid service. Predictably, persons would spend more on rental housing, possibly reducing the amount spent on other consumer goods, thus reducing the tax base.

. . .

In any case, inequity between renters and homeowners does not support denying the homeowner an interest deduction. Interest should not be the economic equivalent of rent for tax purposes. Interest is the charge for the money to purchase an investment, the home. Denying homeowners an interest deduction would not equalize total housing costs of renters and homeowners. Interest denial would make home purchases more difficult and would encourage more taxpayers to become or remain renters.

McCOMBS, REFINING THE ITEMIZED DEDUCTION FOR HOME PROPERTY TAX PAYMENTS *

44 Vanderbilt Law Review 317, 325–329 (1991).

IV. HOUSING POLICY OVERRIDES ECONOMIC THEORY

David Bradford, a tax reform commentator, has asserted that "[e]limination of the [property tax] deduction would . . . reduce the tax bias in favor of housing investment in general, and owner-occupancy in particular." Despite a theoretical argument that deduction of home property tax should not be allowed in calculating taxable income, one must consider whether other social policies justify an intentional tax bias in favor of owner-occupied housing. The home property tax deduction has been authorized throughout our income tax history. A paucity of legislative history leaves unclear the original reason for this deduction. In recent years, though, a social policy of encouraging home ownership frequently has been identified as the force supporting deduction. The deduction for home mortgage interest shares this motivating social policy.

Numerous social benefits are believed to flow from home ownership. Homeowners move less often than renters. Parents may be induced to take a greater interest in the school system. Voter turnout and other forms of local political involvement increase. Owners maintain their homes better than renters and landlords, thus providing aesthetic benefits to neighbors. Better maintenance of homes also supports local real estate prices, thereby likely increasing motivation of nearby owners to improve and maintain their property and motivation of lenders to finance such activities.

The least articulable social policy favoring home ownership, but certainly the most significant, is that owning one's home is a fundamental part of the "American Dream." Attaining that goal primarily benefits the individual, but a widespread perception that each individual has a good chance of attaining the goal is considered a social benefit. A high rate of home ownership helps persuade those who currently are unable to own that they have a chance to own a home.

All these social benefits seem to be advanced by government programs that make it easier to own a home. Nevertheless, society suffers certain detriments from its decision to maintain owner-occupied housing above a free market level. Equity and debt capital are pulled away from more productive alternate uses, thus lowering the gross national product and raising capital costs to other sectors of the economy. A sector of production that cannot be exported is expanded—partially at the expense of other, exportable production—with negative consequences to our balance of payments. Tax deductions granted to encourage home ownership reduce aggregate taxable income, thereby requiring higher rates to achieve desired revenue, which, in turn, intensifies the distortions and other problems inevitably caused by an income tax. Funds used or revenue foregone to help taxpayers move from a nice rental to a nice owned home might be used more productively to help poorer people move from a squalid rental to a tolerable rental. One might surmise that the desirability of tenants increases with their income. If so, converting middle-class tenants to homeowners decreases the percentage of "good" tenants in the rental market, reduces the general attractiveness of rental housing as an investment or a career, and increases rents for those who remain tenants. Home ownership decreases mobility of labor and increases costs of moving to a new job at a distant location. These negative effects receive very little attention in discussions of a social policy favoring home ownership.

In any event, positive and negative considerations have led Congress to conclude that allowing tax deductions which increase home owner-ship are more important than following a theoretically pure definition of income. It is important to note that such a conclusion might reflect an optimal balancing of policy considerations. This Article proceeds generally as if it does. Certainly, theoretical definitions and free market forces do not always lead to optimal results.

V. SUBSIDY ANALYSIS

Only after the force behind the home property tax deduction has been identified clearly as a social policy of encouraging home ownership can the deduction be analyzed constructively. The analysis will be clearer if the "encouragement" is explicitly acknowledged and ad-dressed as a subsidy. For political reasons, this candid label often is avoided.

Subsidy analysis is neither new nor arcane. The government's goal must be precisely determined and described. A clear statement of what is not intended also may be important. An existing subsidy program then can be subjected to cost-benefit analysis by proposing changes in its terms and estimating the increase or decrease in costs and benefits from these changes. Typically, costs are measured directly in money spent or, as here, in revenue foregone, while benefits must be measured subjectively. Even though a completely objective evaluation cannot be achieved, methodical analysis can clarify the subjective benefits likely to be gained or lost by a proposed change, thereby improving the decision-making process. As Stanley Surrey said twenty years ago, "These methods are being utilized more and more to devise and test direct expenditures, and they should a priori be equally applicable to programs using a tax incentive technique."

The general goal of this subsidy apparently is to increase the rate of home ownership. Qualification of high-income taxpayers for this subsi-dy raises two questions. The first concerns goal definition. Assuming for a moment that this subsidy will increase the rate of home owner-ship among high-income individuals, is such an increase a part of the government's housing policy goal? Should it be?

High-income people financially are able to purchase homes without a subsidy. Those high-income individuals who, in absence of this subsidy, would not purchase a home likely would have based their housing decision on other factors such as a greater satisfaction from alternative consumption expenditures, a greater return on alternative investments, or a desire for mobility. The former factor is one that national housing policy might want to overcome. The latter two would produce benefits to the nation's economy and, therefore, are at odds with a subsidy that operates to convert satisfied, high-income tenants to homeowners.

A second concern about granting the subsidy to high-income taxpayers is based on cost-benefit analysis and consists of two parts. First, continue to assume that the subsidy has its intended effect in this income class. Society's benefits from home ownership decrease as income rises. High-income tenants probably demand and get the same level of home exterior maintenance from their landlords as owners in the same income range obtain for their homes. The neighborhoods where high-income tenants live have sufficient owner and lender support for improvements and repairs. Finally, if we have a national policy favoring a widespread perception that the American Dream is attainable, the homes of most high-income tenants will do their part to encourage middle- and low-income people to persevere.

Society's benefits from encouraging tenants to buy homes decrease with rising income, but society's costs increase. Because this subsidy is delivered through a tax deduction, its value to the taxpayer and its cost to the government increase as the recipient's income and tax rate increase. Congress has placed no limitation on the amount of the deduction. Because high-income people tend to own more expensive and, therefore, more heavily taxed homes, subsidy costs increase with income.

. . .

A subsidy achieves its goal only with those recipients who are at the margin between following or rejecting the subsidized path. Some people inevitably will receive a subsidy as a windfall because they would have taken the preferred action without a subsidy. A recipient's windfall is the government's inefficiency loss, thereby reducing benefit-cost ratio. Although this type of inefficiency cannot be eliminated, a subsidy should be structured to reduce it as much as possible without causing an unacceptable reduction in total benefits.

Because of wealth or income, many taxpayers are unlikely to be at the margin of a decision between renting and owning their homes. Their access to this deduction can be limited or eliminated in several ways. Property tax attributable to home value in excess of a specified amount, perhaps $1 million, could be made nondeductible; a ceiling could be imposed on the deductible amount; or taxpayers with AGI above a specified level could be excluded from the subsidy program.

NOTES

1. *Parity Between Renters and Owners.* The deduction for mortgage interest payments has been the most frequent target of congressional attack. The deduction for real property taxes has proved to be a less popular political target, and the prospects for taxing homeowners

on their imputed rental income are even more distant. The political dangers of challenging the homeowner position may explain why both Senators Buckley and Long so carefully skirted the real issue of their debate: whether it is fair to require landlords, but not homeowners, to pay tax on the value of the income from their property. For excellent discussions of alternative strategies for achieving tax parity between renters and owners, see Hellmuth, Homeowner Preferences, in Comprehensive Income Taxation 163 (J. Pechman, ed., 1977); Note, Federal Income Tax Discrimination Between Homeowners and Renters: A Proposed Solution, 12 Ind.L.Rev. 583 (1979).

Although the 1986 Tax Reform Act eliminated the deduction for personal interest on consumer debt such as charge accounts, it retained the deduction for interest paid on residential real property mortgages. As provided in the 1986 Tax Reform Act and modified in the Revenue Act of 1987, the deduction—for "qualified residence interest"—is, however, limited to interest on debt secured by the taxpayer's principal residence or a second residence, such as a vacation home, and to debt coming within prescribed limits. For example, there can be no interest deduction with respect to an indebtedness in excess of $1 million. In the 1987 legislation, Congress also permitted the deduction of interest on home equity loans, within certain limits. See Internal Revenue Code § 163.

2. Early income tax laws sought to achieve parity between homeowners and renters by allowing renters to deduct rent payments. Act of Mar. 3, 1863, ch. 74, § 11, 12 Stat. 713, 723 (1863). In 1978, the New York Legislature amended section 304 of the Real Property Tax Law to provide that, for purposes of real property taxation, certain residential tenants have an interest in real property and are personally liable for taxes on that interest. Section 926 of the Real Property Tax Law was amended to provide that the "owner of the real property where such a renter is an occupant shall be deemed an agent of the collecting officer of the municipality in which the real property is located for the purposes of collecting the taxes due from each tenant personally liable for taxes." The amendments' original effective date, April 1, 1979, was later postponed to April 1, 1980, pending a ruling from the Internal Revenue Service.

In June, 1979, the Service ruled that the "New York State renters tax paid by renters pursuant to sections 304 and 926–a ... is not a tax on the renter for federal income tax purposes, but rather is part of the renters' rental payments." In the Service's view, the tax did not impose on the renter "any economic burden that did not exist" prior to the amendments. "The lack of an economic burden on the renter is further evidenced by the fact that the owner is not relieved from the obligation of paying all taxes due on the owner's property ... in the event of the renter's nonpayment, section 304 looks to the owner for payment and the taxing authority may enforce payment against the owner's interest in the entire property." Rev.Rul. 79–180, 1979–23 I.R.B. 7.

3. *Is There a Disparity?*   As Professor Snoe indicates, the relative advantages that homeowners enjoy over renters are probably less lopsided than they first appear.   First, it is not clear that landlords pass the full burden of real property taxes on to their tenants.   See generally, Netzer, The Incidence of the Property Tax Revisited, 26 Nat'l. Tax J. 515 (1973); H. Aaron, Who Pays the Property Tax?   A New View (1975).   Second, the federal government provides extensive financial support to low and moderate-income rental housing, and these direct subsidies partially balance the indirect subsidies to homeowners through the tax deductions for interest and taxes.   Third, prior to the 1986 Tax Reform Act the Internal Revenue Code permitted landlords to accelerate the deductions they take for the depreciation of their buildings, and landlords probably passed some of these savings on to their tenants in the form of lowered rent.   Estimates of this reduction to average rentals range between 11% and 17%, depending on the landlord's tax bracket.   See Hellmuth, Homeowner Preferences, in Comprehensive Income Taxation 168 (J. Pechman, ed. 1977).   The 1986 legislation essentially placed all new buildings on a straight line depreciation method, although it permitted existing buildings to continue with accelerated depreciation.   Thus, rental deductions have probably declined.   See pages 637–641 below.

For a Senate debate on the claimed inequities to renters see Congressional Record, Senate, Daily ed. Sept. 23, 1976, S.16483, 16488–16489.

4. *Casualty Losses.*   Internal Revenue Code sections 163, 164, and 165 permit homeowners to take deductions for interest, taxes and casualty losses, respectively.   Section 262 bars deductions for all other costs of upkeep, such as repairs, depreciation, wear and tear and insurance, through its general disallowance of "personal, living or family expenses."

The 1986 Tax Reform Act amended section 165(h)(4) to provide that a taxpayer will not be allowed to deduct a casualty loss for damage to insured property devoted to personal use unless she files a timely insurance claim for the damage.   Although presumably aimed at automobile owners who are reluctant to file insurance claims out of fear that their insurance will be cancelled, or that their rates will increase, the provision will also have an impact on insured homeowners.

Taxpayers sometimes try to obtain deductions for property damage from wear and tear or exposure to the elements by characterizing the damage as a casualty loss, deductible under section 165.   The Commissioner and the courts have, however, generally taken "casualty" to mean only losses that occur suddenly, such as from flood, earthquake or explosion.   As a consequence, taxpayers have had little luck in getting deductions for progressive damage of the sort caused by erosion, corrosion or termite infestation.   Does this definition of casualty mean that the homeowner who promptly identifies, and corrects an invasion of termites, is more likely to get a casualty deduction than the homeowner who takes no action until, after some months, her entire house collapses? See Rosenberg v. Commissioner, 198 F.2d 46 (8th Cir.1952).

5. *Repair or Improvement?* If the taxpayer cannot get her property damage treated as a casualty, she may repair it and try to capitalize the cost of repair by calling the repair an improvement. By adding the cost of the improvement to her basis in the home, she is able to reduce any gain on sale. Courts have, however, taken a hard line here, too. Such expenditures as painting and plastering to keep the property in good, attractive condition will be considered noncapital repairs even though they may prolong the life of the house or otherwise add to its value. Only structural additions, such as a new room or a swimming pool, fall safely within the concept of capital improvements.

Can you find a workable line between the two kinds of expenditure? What differences, if any, are there between keeping a house in good condition, increasing its life, and increasing its value? Would you characterize a new roof as a repair or an improvement? Does the repair-improvement distinction provide an incentive to wasteful—because unnecessary—capital expenditures?

6. *Home Offices; Vacation Homes.* Within stringent limits, a homeowner can treat a portion of her home upkeep and depreciation expenses as deductible business expenses or expenses incurred in connection with the production of income by definitively marking off a part of her house as a home office used by her in her business or as a condition of her employment and deducting the expenses properly allocable to the office. Section 280A, introduced by the 1976 Tax Reform Act, provides rigorous formulae for determining these deductions. The 1986 Tax Reform Act further tightened these restrictions. Where the 1976 Act limited the taxpayer's deduction to gross income from the home business, as reduced by interest and taxes allocable to the part of the house used for the business activities, the 1986 Act further lowered the gross income ceiling by requiring that it be reduced by business expenses, such as accounting and legal expenses, not directly connected to the home office itself. See generally, Mulligan, The Tax Ramification of the Business Use of a Home, 8 Okla. City U.L.Rev. 201 (1983); Eichenbaum, The Office at Home: An Analysis of Section 280A and Recent Tax Court Decisions, 10 J. Real Estate Tax. 63 (1982); Rice, The Controversy with the IRS Over the Rental of Personal Residences, 9 J. Real Estate Tax. 143 (1981–82); Samansky, Deductions for a Former Residence: Don't Leave Home Without Them, 16 Hofstra L.Rev. 615 (1988); Kerr, The Rental of Personal Residences: Implications of Section 280A, 7 J. Real Estate Tax. 139 (1979–80).

The two-home family may under section 280A deduct the expenses of maintaining a vacation home that is sometimes rented out to others.

7. *Gain on Sale of Personal Residence.* The sale of a personal residence is a capital transaction under the Code and gain, if realized, will be treated as capital gain. Although the 1986 Tax Reform Act repealed the preferential capital gains tax rate, the concept of capital

gain remains important under the Act. As noted in the Conference Report, "[t]hese provisions do not change the character of gain as ordinary or capital, or as long- or short-term capital gain." H.R.Rep. No. 841, 99th Cong., 2d Sess. II–105 (1986). The Code offers several techniques for deferring the taxation of gain and one device for partially forgiving taxation altogether.

Under section 1033, a taxpayer may elect deferred taxation of any gain realized from the involuntary conversion of his home through destruction, "theft, seizure, or requisition or condemnation." Within prescribed limits, section 453, discussed at pages 674 to 680, permits gain to be prorated and reported on an installment basis rather than entirely in the year of sale. Section 121 allows taxpayers age 55 or older to exclude up to $125,000 of any gain realized on the sale of their principal residence; they can, however, take advantage of the exclusion only once.

Doubtless, the most widely used deferral technique is section 1034's provision for postponing taxation of gain on the sale of a principal residence if, within two years before or after the sale, the taxpayer acquires another principal residence and the cost of the new home exceeds the adjusted sales price of the old. (Because the basis of the new home will be reduced by the amount of gain untaxed on the sale of the old, taxation of gain is only postponed, not forgiven.) Section 1034's only catch is that it is mandatory, not elective. Thus, the homeowner who wishes to have gain taxed in the year of sale will find this route barred under section 1034 if he purchases another principal residence within two years. See generally, Connealy, Tax Consequences on the Disposition of a Personal Residence, 49 U.M.K.C. L.Rev. 137 (1981); Rice, The Sale of a Personal Residence That Has Been Used for Business, 10 J. Real Estate Tax. 264 (1982–83).

8. *Loss on Sale of Personal Residence.* The taxpayer cannot deduct a loss incurred on the sale of his residence. The reason given for denying a deduction is that, like the costs of upkeep and depreciation, loss is personal to the taxpayer and unrelated to his business or production of income. One way for a homeowner to get at least some loss deduction in a declining market is to rent his home and then sell it, taking a trade or business ordinary loss deduction under I.R.C. § 1231 for the rental period. Consider whether a homeowner could deduct his entire loss through the following strategy: Sell the house on credit to a buyer who, as a poor credit risk, is willing to pay a price considerably above fair market value—say the same price the seller paid for it. If the buyer defaults, the seller will get the property back or see it sold on a foreclosure sale, and will then try to write the loan off as a bad debt. Compare Guffey v. United States, 339 F.2d 759 (9th Cir.1964). See generally, Byrne, Conversion of a Personal Residence to a Business or Investment Use for Tax Purposes, 8 Rut.-Cam. L.J. 393 (1977).

VII. BUILDING ON THE BASICS: CONDOMINIUM AND OTHER COMMUNAL ARRANGEMENTS FOR HOME OWNERSHIP

Condominiums, cooperatives and other forms of communal ownership combine the economic attractions of home ownership with the social and economic attractions of apartment living. They enable occupants to acquire an equity stake, with related tax and finance advantages, in dwellings such as high-rise apartments and townhouses that were traditionally available only as short-term rentals. They make it possible for neighbors to share swimming pools, tennis courts and other recreational facilities that none could afford individually. They also liberate occupants from the homeowner's usual upkeep responsibilities and, at the same time, give them a degree of control over their environment—through the power to hire and fire building managers—that tenants probably never know.

The reasons for the current upsurge in communal ownership are not hard to find. The inflationary spiral of the 1970's and 1980's and rapidly increasing land prices forced many homebuyers to lower their sights from detached single family housing to less costly condominium units offering almost equivalent housing space. At the same time, rental housing for middle and upper income occupants diminished as landlords, faced with increasing labor and utility costs and the prospect of rent control, converted their rental units into condominium arrangements, and as developers invested new housing dollars in condominium rather than rental projects. Changing social patterns have also played a role. Single men and women find the condominium an excellent vehicle for preserving a lifestyle unfettered by home maintenance chores, while offering the advantages of real property tax deductions and appreciation in inflationary times. The no-care aspects of condominium life also attract older individuals. The precise mix of advantages and disadvantages offered by communal ownership will depend on the precise form that the ownership arrangement takes—condominium, cooperative or homeowners' association.

Condominium. Each occupant in a condominium owns his unit in fee simple absolute. His deed will describe the fee as a cube of space bounded by the unit's interior walls, and will also give him an undivided fractional interest, as a tenant in common with all the other unit owners, in the project's common areas—exterior walls, roof, land, hallways, and common facilities such as laundry rooms, tennis courts and swimming pools. Because he has fee title, the unit owner can finance his purchase by giving a mortgage on the unit to secure a purchase money loan from an institutional lender. In addition to his responsibility for the debt service and real property taxes on his own unit, the owner must also pay a periodic maintenance fee to the condominium association to support its upkeep of the common areas. And, because he has fee title, the condominium owner is entitled to all of the federal income tax deductions available to homeowners generally.

The governing document in a condominium is the charter or declaration. In addition to providing a legal description of the project and of the individual units and common areas, the declaration will establish guidelines for the condominium's bylaws. The bylaws, in turn, will outline the procedures to be followed by the condominium owners in selecting a board of managers to supervise the condominium's ongoing activities, in authorizing expenditures for maintenance and reconstruction of common areas and facilities, and in adopting house rules governing day-to-day life in the condominium.

The condominium owners association, created by the condominium charter, is responsible for coordinating the rights and duties of the condominium unit owners and for advancing the condominium's welfare generally. The association's political life centers in a board of directors (or "governing board," "board of managers," or "council of co-owners") elected by the owners to set policy and, in turn, to elect the officers and committees that will execute policy. Many of the association's activities resemble those of municipal government. The association regulates by adopting rules for community behavior and enforcing these rules through court sanctioned fines and injunctions. The association provides services such as utilities, road and park maintenance, garbage pickup and police security, and levies taxes, in the form of assessments, to support these services.

The condominium is proving to be a versatile instrument in other than conventional housing markets. Its easy application to existing multifamily dwellings has made it a particularly attractive vehicle for "sweat equity" and subsidized housing programs aimed at giving the urban poor a stake in their housing. See Teaford, Home Ownership for Low-Income Families: The Condominium, 21 Hastings L.J. 243 (1970); Comment, Condominiums and the 1968 Housing and Urban Development Act: Putting the Poor in Their Place, 43 So.Cal.L.Rev. 309 (1970). Compare Diamond, Rehabilitation of Low-Income Housing Through Cooperative Conversions by Tenants, 25 Am.U.L.Rev. 285 (1976). Condominiums have also been used in structuring medical and other professional office developments.

Although the condominium concept can be traced back at least to medieval times, it did not become popular in the United States until 1961, when Congress amended the National Housing Act to authorize the Federal Housing Administration to insure mortgages on condominiums in states that had statutorily authorized this form of ownership. (Considerable doubt existed whether, without such enabling legislation, an ownership unit described only as a cube dangling in space could be legally conveyed and mortgaged in fee simple.) A model statute promulgated by the FHA the following year was quickly adopted or adapted across the country and, by 1969, every state had enacted a condominium statute. The FHA prototype can be found in FHA, Dept. of Housing & Urban Development, Model Statute for Creation of Apartment Ownership, Form # 3285 (1962). The Uniform Condominium Act, approved by the National Conference of Commissioners on Uniform State Laws in 1977 and amended in 1980, has been adopted in ten jurisdictions. The Uniform Common Interest Ownership Act which governs condominiums, cooperatives, and homeowners associations, was promulgated in 1984 and has been adopted in at least four states. Citations to the state statutes are collected at Appendix B–1 to P. Rohan & M. Reskin, Condominium Law and Practice, vol. 1, part 1 (1992).

Cooperative. Housing cooperatives existed in this country well before condominiums became fashionable, and they continue to occupy an important place in some urban housing markets. In a cooperative, title to the entire project—all of the individual units and all of the common areas—is vested in a single, non-profit cooperative corporation. Unlike the condominium owner, who receives a deed conveying fee title to his unit and an undivided interest in the common areas, each cooperator receives two instruments: a perpetually renewable proprietary lease to her unit, between herself as tenant and the cooperative corporation as landlord, and shares of stock in the cooperative corporation. A single mortgage will encumber the entire project and the cooperative corporation, as mortgagor, will pay the entire debt service as well as all real property taxes. The corporation will meet these and any other obligations from monthly rentals collected from the cooperator-tenants. Cooperators' rights and duties will be set out in the corporate charter, bylaws and proprietary lease. The cooperator who fails to pay rent or to comply with her other leasehold responsibilities faces both summary eviction from the unit and the loss of her stock.

The fact that the cooperative is financed through a blanket encumbrance rather than through mortgages on individual units poses two substantial problems for the cooperator. One is financial interdependence. When a condominium owner defaults, he risks foreclosure and the sale of his unit, but imposes little added burden on his neighbors. By contrast, if a cooperator defaults in her rental obligations, the other tenants must chip in to cover her share of debt service on the blanket encumbrance as well as real property taxes and maintenance expenses. In good times, the burden will be only temporary, for a new tenant can quickly be found to pick up the unit's share of cooperative expenses. In bad times, the results can be disastrous. If the unit cannot be sold, the other tenants must pay the unit charges indefinitely. The increased burden may cause some of these tenants to default, leading to default by still others until the entire house of cards collapses when the cooperative can no longer meet its expenses and so defaults on the blanket obligation.

Financing through a blanket encumbrance will also limit a coopera-tor's ability to liquidate her investment. The cooperator's prospective buyer, unlike the condominium buyer, will find that financing is scarce because statutory restrictions may prohibit institutional lenders from taking second lien mortgages or from treating stock certificates and proprietary leases as real property security. The seller's only alterna-tives will be to finance the sale herself, taking back a note and security interest in the stock and lease, or to hope for a buyer with sufficient cash to cover the seller's original down payment together with the amount of the unit's appreciation during her ownership. Some relief from this dilemma is now available in at least two states, Illinois and New York, which have amended their corporate and banking laws to permit institutional lenders to make real estate loans secured by the cooperator's interest in her unit. Ill.Ann.Stat. ch. 17, § 3121(d) (Smith-Hurd 1981); N.Y. Banking Law §§ 103(5), 235.8–a, 380.2–a (McKinney Supp.1992).

Unlike condominium owners, who have from the beginning enjoyed the tax advantages available to owners of detached homes, cooperators have historically suffered from their status as tenants. A 1928 bill, allowing cooperators to deduct their proportionate share of the interest and real estate taxes paid by the cooperative corporation, passed the House, but was rejected by the Senate, in part on the ground that it would give cooperators preferential treatment over other tenants. H.R. 1, Revenue Bill of 1928, 70th Cong. 1st Sess. §§ 22(b)(9), 23(q), 24(d); S.Rpt. No. 960, 70th Cong. 1st Sess. 20–21 (1928). Congress finally reversed its position in the Revenue Act of 1942, enacting the predeces-sor of I.R.C. § 216 to allow tenant stockholders in "cooperative apart-ment corporations" to deduct the interest and real property tax ex-penses allocable to their units.

Amendments since 1942 have further narrowed the gap between cooperators and condominium owners. The 1954 Act extended pass-through treatment to tenants in all "cooperative housing corporations," not just apartments. The 1962 Revenue Act allowed cooperators to take depreciation deductions to the extent that they used their units in a trade or business or for the production of income. And I.R.C. § 1034(f) now entitles cooperators to the roll-over treatment available to condominium owners and homeowners generally. The 1986 Tax Reform Act amended section 216 to allow corporations, trusts, and other taxpayers besides individuals to be treated as tenant-stockholders and so take deductions. The amendments also permit flexibility in the proportion of deductions allocated to the various tenant-stockholders.

The gap has not been completely closed. Section 216 does not allow cooperators to deduct casualty losses. More important, section 216 expressly conditions the interest and real property tax deductions on compliance with several technical requirements. For an excellent discussion of these and other tax issues affecting the cooperative, see Cowan, Tax Reform on the Home Front: Cooperative Housing Corpora-tions, Condominiums, and Homeowners Associations, 5 J.Real Est.Tax.

101 (1978); Miller, The Co-op Apartment and Qualified Residence Interest, 16 J. Real Est.Tax. 385 (1989).

Although the tax and financing trend has been to treat the cooperator's interest as realty, the fact that corporate stock is involved gives the interest some attributes of personalty. This double aspect has raised no end of consequential issues. In an action by a defaulting buyer to recover his down payment on a contract to buy a cooperative unit, will the Uniform Commercial Code apply, limiting the seller to her actual damages, or will real property principles apply, entitling the seller to retain the entire deposit without proving damages? See Silverman v. Alcoa Plaza Associates, 37 A.D.2d 166, 323 N.Y.S.2d 39 (1971). When a lender forecloses on its security interest in the stock and proprietary lease, what law applies—U.C.C. Article 9, or statutes governing the foreclosure of mortgages on real property? Which is the appropriate place to record transfers of interests in the cooperative unit—the office of the Secretary of State, as personal property, or the County Recorder's office, as real property? Does the sales tax apply or the real property transfer tax? See State Tax Commission v. Shor, 43 N.Y.2d 151, 400 N.Y.S.2d 805, 371 N.E.2d 523 (1977); see generally, Note, Legal Characterization of the Individual's Interest in a Cooperative Apartment: Realty or Personalty? 73 Colum.L.Rev. 250 (1973).

Homeowners Associations and PUDs. The advantages of shared land use have not been lost on owners of detached housing. Subdivision developers, and sometimes existing neighbors, organize homeowner associations to maintain parks and other recreational facilities such as pools, tennis courts and golf courses. Typically, the association will hold the common areas in fee or under a long term lease, and will regularly assess homeowners for their share of common area expenses.

The planned unit development, or PUD, applies the homeowners association concept to particular advantage, since so much space in the PUD is devoted to common facilities. PUDs, a comparatively recent development in land use planning, depart from the grid-like pattern of detached housing that typified zoning's early years and, instead, cluster groups of homes within the parcel being developed, often mixing a number of housing forms in a single development—detached single-family homes, connected townhouse units, duplexes, fourplexes and garden apartments. Instead of individual yards, PUDs offer extensive common areas. The developer may, to obtain subdivision approval, be forced to dedicate some of these common areas to the local government for use by all citizens in the community. But she will usually be able to convey a substantial part of the common recreational areas to an association consisting of all property owners in the PUD. Membership, voting rights and assessments in the PUD association attach automatically upon acquisition of a unit in the PUD. The association typically has the power to promulgate and enforce rules for conduct within the PUD including, for example, the right to review any proposed changes to the exterior of units within the development for their consonance with the PUD's architectural style. See generally, Uniform Planned Community Act, 12 Unif.Laws Ann. 1.

NOTES

1. *Why Communal Arrangements?* Professor Henry Hansmann, in an excellent article, argues that the key reason for the recent surge in condominiums and cooperatives is the large tax subsidy available to owner occupied housing as compared to rental housing. Hansmann, Condominium and Cooperative Housing: Transactional Efficiency, Tax Subsidies, and Tenure Choice, 20 J.Leg.Studs. 25 (1991). Hansmann maintains that despite claimed benefits due to the organizational innovations of communal housing arrangements, condominiums and cooperatives would occupy a smaller share of the market if there were no tax subsidy.

Is the choice to purchase a condominium or cooperative only an economic one? Or do people seek communal arrangements because they offer an environment that the owners believe will maximize their self-fulfillment? See Korngold, Resolving the Flaws of Residential Servitudes and Owners Associations: For Reformation Not Termination, 1990 Wis.L.Rev. 513.

2. *Counselling the Condominium Buyer.* From the perspective of the buyer and her lender, the principal difference between the purchase of a condominium and the purchase of a detached unit lies in the condominium's close legal, financial and physical interconnections. Buyer and lender will want to examine the condominium's declaration, by-laws, house rules and any major management agreements. The buyer will be interested in restrictions on children or pets, her freedom to sell or rent the unit, voting rights in the condominium association and rights against other unit owners, including the right to compel upkeep of the common areas. The lender may insist that there be no restriction on its power to sell or lease the unit in the event that it forecloses or takes a deed in lieu of foreclosure. The lender may also want a commitment from the condominium owners association to give the lender notice of, and the opportunity to cure, any default by the unit owner-mortgagor in paying assessments or performing other obligations.

Lender and buyer will want to see not only that the unit is adequately insured, but also that the association has obtained sufficient liability insurance to immunize the unit owners from devastating tort judgments for accidents occurring in the common areas and sufficient hazard or casualty insurance on the entire structure to pay for repair or reconstruction in the event the structure is partially or substantially damaged.

For a pre-closing checklist to be used in representing condominium purchasers, see Report of Committee on Condominium and Cooperative Ownership of Apartments, Lawyer Counseling Considerations in Representing Condominium Purchasers, 10 Real Prop., Probate & Trust J. 464 (1975).

3. *Taxation of Owner Associations.* Owner associations have an economic life independent of their members. Until enactment of the Tax Reform Act of 1976, associations sought to avoid or reduce their federal income taxes by getting themselves classified as tax exempt entities under I.R.C. § 501(c), initially as "civic leagues" or social welfare organizations under section 501(c)(4). As that avenue was blocked by a series of Revenue Rulings, they sought to be characterized as social clubs, "organized for pleasure, recreation and other nonprofitable purposes" under section 501(c)(7).

The 1976 Tax Reform Act added section 528 to the Code, creating a limited, elective tax exemption specifically for "homeowners associations" and itemizing revenue items that will be treated as exempt income regardless of the purpose to which they are applied. The amendment establishes strict conditions for qualification as a "homeowners association." And the association, even if it qualifies for the exemption, will be taxed on "homeowners association taxable income"—gross income less two items: (1) deductions for expenses incurred in producing gross income and (2) "exempt function income" such as membership fees, dues and assessments received from unit owners.

Section 528 covers homeowner associations and condominium owner associations, but not housing cooperatives. Cooperatives may in fact have received a better deal under the 1976 Reform Act's amendment of section 216(c) to allow cooperatives to take deductions for the depreciation of the entire building, not just the units occupied by non-stockholders. Typically, these depreciation deductions should be sufficient to shelter income not expended in the tax year, putting cooperatives in at least as good a position as condominium and homeowner associations with respect to their unexpended reserve funds.

On the organization and activities of condominium associations generally, see Hyatt & Rhoads, Concepts of Liability in the Development and Administration of Condominium and Home Owners Associations, 12 Wake Forest L.Rev. 915 (1976); Hyatt, Condominiums and Home Owner Associations: Formation and Development, 24 Emory L.J. 977 (1975); Jackson, Why You Should Incorporate a Homeowners Association, 3 Real Est.L.J. 311 (1975). On tax aspects of condominium and homeowner associations, see Cowan, Tax Reform on the Home Front: Cooperative Housing Corporations, Condominiums and Homeowner Associations, 5 J. of Real Est.Tax. 101, 113–141 (1978); Miller, Condominiums and Cooperatives, 15 J. Real Est.Tax. 80 (1987); Note, Taxation of Homeowners Associations Under the Tax Reform Act of 1976, 36 Wash. & Lee L.Rev. 299 (1979).

4. *Timesharing.* Condominium ownership can be divided in time as well as space, giving each of several owners the exclusive right to possess a single unit for a predetermined week or month every year.

Timesharing projects blossomed in the early 1980's, enabling individuals to purchase the right to possess a single unit in a resort townhouse, hotel, motel, campground, or even in a yacht, for increments of one week each year in perpetuity. Under one commonly used technique, *time span ownership,* each participant holds an undivided fee simple interest in the unit as a tenant in common with as many as fifty-one cotenants; a separate agreement between the cotenants identifies the specific week or weeks during the year when each cotenant is entitled to occupy the unit. Another form of timesharing is interval ownership where there is a transfer of different estates for years for different periods to the various owners along with an undivided interest in a remainder in fee simple. A more direct approach is simply to convey a "fee" estate for a specified week or weeks each year in perpetuity. Other timesharing programs employ contracts, rather than real property interests, to give the purchaser a right to periodic use of the real property. See Model Real Estate Time-Share Act § 1–102, comment 4, 7B Unif.Laws Ann. 351; see generally, Comment, Time-Share Condominiums: Property's Fourth Dimension, 32 Me.L.Rev. 181 (1980); Comment, Legal Challenges to Time Sharing Ownership, 45 Mo.L.Rev. 423 (1980).

States moved quickly to regulate timesharing projects. See, for example, Block, Regulation of Timesharing, 60 U.Det.J.Urb.L. 23 (1982). See also Burek, Uniform Real Estate Time-Share Act, 14 Real Prop., Probate & Trust J. 683 (1979); Stone, Federal Trade Commission and Timeshare Resale Companies, 24 Suffolk U.L.Rev. 49 (1990). On tax aspects, see Kinsolving & Caron, Tax Considerations in Time-Share Development, 13 Stetson L.Rev. 25 (1983).

A. MANAGEMENT AND CONTROL

BARCLAY v. DeVEAU

Supreme Court of Massachusetts, 1981.
384 Mass. 676, 429 N.E.2d 323.

LIACOS, Justice.

At issue in this appeal is whether a provision contained in the declaration of a condominium trust that permits the condominium developer to appoint two of the three members of the board of trustees, even though the developer owns only a small percentage of the condominium units, is invalid under G.L. c. 183A, § 10(a). The statute provides: "Each unit owner shall have the same percentage interest in the corporation, trust or unincorporated association provided for in the master deed for the management and regulation of the condominium as his proportionate interest in the common areas and facilities. Such interest shall not be separated from ownership in the unit to which it appertains and shall be deemed conveyed or encumbered with the unit even though such interest is not expressly mentioned or described in the conveyance or other instrument." G.L. c. 183A, § 10(*a*), inserted by St.1963, c. 493, § 1.

In apparent conflict with the statute is § 3.1.3 of the condominium trust which provides that "[u]ntil [the developer] owns less than 12 units, there shall not be more than three Trustees and it shall be entitled to designate two such Trustees."

The plaintiff, trustee of the Vendome Development Trust (development trust), filed a complaint in the Superior Court seeking to enjoin the defendants, who had been selected by the unit owners to replace the plaintiff's appointees, from exercising any power as trustees. The judge entered judgment for the plaintiff. On appeal, the Appeals Court, with one judge dissenting, reversed. We granted the plaintiff's application for further appellate review.

The facts are as follows. In 1975 the Franchi Development Trust, of which Pasquale Franchi is the sole beneficiary, established the Vendome Condominium Trust (condominium trust). The Vendome is Boston's first mixed commercial and residential condominium. After the Franchi Development Trust defaulted on a construction loan with its mortgagee, the Commonwealth Capital Investment Corporation (CCIC), the name of the trust was changed to Vendome Development Trust, the former trustee resigned, and CCIC appointed the plaintiff as trustee to manage the condominium and market the unsold condominium units. The plaintiff, as trustee of the development trust, appointed two trustees to the condominium trust pursuant to § 3.1.3 of the condominium trust.

In late 1977 the trustees of the condominium trust approved a 38% increase in common area charges.[4] At this time all but one of the 110 residential units had been sold. The developer, however, owned twenty-three of the commercial units, twenty of which were under long or short term leases, most with options to purchase. At a special meeting called by the unit owners on May 23, 1978, the unit owners voted, by approximately a 60% majority, to remove the two appointed trustees, expand the board to seven, and appoint as new trustees the five persons who are the defendants in this case.[6] The unit owners purported to act under § 3.3 of the condominium trust, which grants the unit owners the power to remove a trustee by a vote of the owners of 51% of the beneficial interest. By the terms of § 3.3, however, this right is subordinate to the right of the development trust under § 3.1.3 to

---

4. The increase in costs of operating the public areas and common facilities of the building, shared among all unit owners, was caused by increases in insurance premiums, maintenance, repair costs, and payroll. The management fee of $2,000 a month did not increase. The defendants do not contend that the trustees misrepresented the operating costs or otherwise acted fraudulently in this matter.

6. The third member of the existing board, previously elected by the unit owners, was to remain in office. The seventh position on the new board was to be filled by the development trust.

retain the trustees of its choice until fewer than twelve units remain unsold.[7]

The defendants, newly elected as trustees, claim that §§ 3.1.3 and 3.3 of the trust violate G.L. c. 183A, § 10.[8] The defendants argue that § 10(a) requires that a unit owner's percentage ownership interest in the association of unit owners, set up for the management and regulation of the condominium, be the same as his proportionate interest in the common areas and facilities. Although we agree that the unit owners have a proportionate interest in the association, we find nothing in the statute which prohibits the unit owners from entering into valid agreements for management and control of the condominium. The fact that the unit owners are entitled to a certain percentage interest in the association does not necessarily mean that the owners must have the same proportionate interest in management.

General Laws c. 183A, § 10(a), states that "[e]ach unit owner shall have the same percentage interest in the ... trust ... provided for in the master deed for the management and regulation of the condominium as his proportionate interest in the common areas and facilities." The defendants contend that this "interest" must include power to appoint and remove the trustees of the condominium trust and cannot be diluted through a developer control clause such as § 3.1.3. The plaintiff argues that a proportionate interest in the unit owners' association may be a beneficial one that includes, for example, rights in event of casualty losses and the right to make and the obligation to pay for capital improvements without including proportionate management rights.

1. *Legislative History of G.L. c. 183A.* We are mindful of the often-stated principle of statutory construction requiring us first to turn to the statutory language where it is plain and unambiguous for insight into the legislative purpose. But where the language of a provision is unclear, we may look to outside sources for assistance in determining the correct construction of the statute. The crucial language of G.L. c. 183A, § 10(a), is not free of ambiguity. To ascertain what the Legislature intended when it provided in G.L. c. 183A, § 10(a), that unit owners have a proportionate "interest" in the trust set up for the management of the condominium, we turn to the legislative history.

The legislative history of G.L. c. 183A indicates that the Legislature was aware of precisely this issue when it enacted the statute, i.e., whether and by what means the unit owners would be able to control the management association. What is now G.L. c. 183A was first reflected in 1963 House Doc. No. 1708. Under §§ 2(d), 18 & 19 of

---

7. Under the terms of the condominium trust, the trustees may amend the trust with the consent of the holders of 75% of the beneficial interest.

8. Section 2.1 of the condominium trust states that "this trust [is] the organization of the Unit Owners established pursuant to

the provisions of section 10 of said Chapter 183A for the purposes therein set forth." The master deed and the confirmatory master deed of the Vendome Condominium recite that the condominium is governed by and subject to G.L. c. 183A. See G.L. c. 183A, § 2.

House 1708, the condominium would be administered by an unincorporated association whose by-laws were to be recorded as part of the
declaration. This bill went further to structure that association and
particularly referred to voting. Section 2(*k*) defined a majority for
voting purposes as those "apartment owners with fifty-one per cent or
more of the votes in accordance with the percentages assigned in the
declaration to the apartments for voting purposes." Section 19 of
House 1708 required that the by-laws provide for election of a board of
directors for staggered terms from "among the apartment owners."

It was 1963 House Doc. No. 3324 that ultimately became G.L. c.
183A. Although retaining the concept of percentage interests expressed in House 1708 as the vehicle for shared ownership in the
condominium, the provisions of House 1708 dealing with voting rights
and the specific structure of the owners' organization were deleted and
§ 10(*a*) was substituted. Use of a corporate or trust form for the
owners association was approved, rather than the unincorporated form
found in House 1708. The Legislature refrained from including any
specific language as to voting rights in § 10(*a*), which outlines the unit
owners' powers of management, but retained certain limitations on
majority rule by unit owners as set forth in House 1708. The Legislature apparently intended to leave the matter of who shall control the
management of the common areas and facilities of the condominium to
discretionary agreement among the unit owners and the developer. To
infer that "interest" means "voting interest" would be to impose a
structure in the association that the Legislature did not intend to
require.

2. *Validity of § 3.1.3.* Although arguably the concept of a condominium was not unknown to the common law, condominium as a form
of real estate ownership did not flourish until statutory authorization.
The apparent purpose of c. 183A "was to clarify the legal status of the
condominium in light of its peculiar characteristics." Grace v. Brook-
line, 379 Mass. 48, 399 N.E.2d 1038 (1979). Statutes like c. 183A which
imprint the condominium with legislative authorization are essentially
enabling statutes. This statute provides planning flexibility to developers and unit owners. Unless expressly prohibited by clear legislative
mandate, unit owners and developers may validly contract as to the
details of management.

Absent overreaching or fraud by a developer, we find no strong
public policy against interpreting c. 183A, § 10(*a*), to permit the developer and unit owners to agree on the details of administration and
management of the condominium unit. Public policy actually favors
this interpretation. Expert testimony at trial established that developer control clauses similar to § 3.1.3 of the condominium trust are
common in Massachusetts. The developer and its mortgagee risk a
great deal undertaking a condominium and, to protect their large
investment, may need to maintain control of the project for a specific
period of time. See Uniform Condominium Act (1977), 7 Uniform Laws
Annot., § 3–103, Comment 3 (Master ed. 1978) (recognizing practical

necessity of developer control during development phase of condominium project); 1 A. Ferrer & K. Stecher, Law of Condominium § 473, at 314 (1967) (developer desires effective role in project management if unsold units remain). Cf. D. Clurman & E. Hebard, Condominiums and Cooperatives 52 (1970) (unit mortgagees ordinarily impose controls on major management decisions by condominium boards).

The condominium trust in this case contains no express time limit on the developer's control. Under the express terms of the condominium trust the developer may retain control of the unit owners' association as long as twelve units are unsold. The defendants filed requests for rulings of law, one of which stated: "Because no time unit [*sic*] is placed on the power granted to the Vendome Development Trust by Article III, Section 3.1.3, the power, even if valid, will only be enforced for a reasonable period of time." The trial judge allowed this request, and the plaintiff concedes that a limitation of a reasonable period of time is properly placed on such a clause. Consequently, we need not determine whether such a limitation of time is necessarily implicit or will be imposed as a matter of policy on such provisions.

It is arguable, however, that an agreement designed to protect the developers' interests during the development and marketing phase of a condominium implicitly contains limitations of time on such a phase. "What is a reasonable time is a question of law, to be determined in reference to the nature of the contract and the probable intention of the parties as indicated by it." Warren v. Ball, 341 Mass. 350, 353, 170 N.E.2d 341 (1960), quoting from Campbell v. Whoriskey, 170 Mass. 63, 67, 48 N.E. 1070 (1898). A reasonable period of time is the period necessary to carry out the supposed intention of the parties, i.e., protect the developer while it is at risk. Such a view would be consistent with the basic concept of condominium, i.e., that unit owners will be afforded a proportionate voice in the management of the common areas and facilities.

We note that the judge treated the "marketing phase" of a condominium project as a reasonable period of time in which the developer may maintain control of the unit owners' association. The marketing phase of the condominium is that time during which the developer actively engages in selling the condominium units.[16] Notwithstanding this good faith effort, however, a point in time may be reached where, despite the presence of unsold units, the developer must relinquish control.[17]

---

16. Indicia of the "marketing phase" may include incomplete construction, retention of real estate brokers, advertisement in trade journals and local newspapers, and maintenance of a sales office. This list is neither exhaustive nor exclusive.

17. Although the Legislature has not adopted those portions of the Uniform Condominium Act dealing with developer control of a condominium association, § 3–103(d)–(e) of the Act may present useful guidelines to a trial judge in determining the reasonableness of developer control in terms of time, percentage interest owned, and marketing efforts. The relevant portions are as follows: "(d) Subject to subsection (e), the declaration may provide for a period of declarant control of the associa-

The record before us does not clearly indicate what criteria the judge considered in determining that the Vendome Condominium was still in the marketing phase, nor does it reveal whether he considered the question of reasonable time apart from marketing efforts. In the amended findings and judgment, the judge stated that "[t]he primary aim of the Vendome Development Trust under Franchi's and the mortgage[e]'s direction, has been to sell the units and since twenty-three (23) commercial units were unsold, the Vendome Condominium was still in the marketing phase." As stated earlier, however, the inquiry is not whether a particular number of units remain unsold, but whether the developer is actively engaged in a bona fide effort to sell the units, and whether, in any event, the circumstances, considered as a whole, require a conclusion that control must pass to the unit owners.

3. *Conclusion.* We set aside the judgment and remand the case to the Superior Court for further proceedings consistent with this opinion.

So ordered.

DUTCHER v. OWENS

Supreme Court of Texas, 1983.
647 S.W.2d 948.

RAY, Justice.

This is a case of first impression concerning the allocation of liability among condominium co-owners for tort claims arising out of the ownership, use and maintenance of "common elements." The defendant was found to be vicariously liable for the homeowners' association's negligence. The trial court ordered that the plaintiffs recover from the defendant an amount based upon the defendant's proportionate ownership in the condominium project. The court of appeals reversed in part the judgment of the trial court, holding "that

---

tion, during which period a declarant, or persons designated by him, may appoint and remove the officers and members of the executive board. Regardless of the period provided in the declaration, a period of declarant control terminates no later than the earlier of: (i) [60] days after conveyance of [75] percent of the units which may be created to unit owners other than a declarant; (ii) [2] years after all declarants have ceased to offer units for sale in the ordinary course of business; or (iii) [2] years after any development right to add new units was last exercised. A declarant may voluntarily surrender the right to appoint and remove officers and members of the executive board before termination of that period, but in that event he may require, for the duration of the period of declarant control, that specified actions of the association or executive board, as described in a recorded instrument executed by the declarant, be approved by the declarant before they become effective.

"(e) Not later than [60] days after conveyance of [25] percent of the units which may be created to unit owners other than a declarant, at least one member and not less than [25] percent of the members of the executive board must be elected by unit owners other than the declarant. Not later than [60] days after conveyance of [50] percent of the units which may be created to unit owners other than the declarant, not less than [33⅓] percent of the members of the executive board must be elected by unit owners other than the declarant." Uniform Condominium Act (1980), 7 Uniform Laws Annot., § 3–103(d)–(e) (Master ed. supp. 1981).

each unit owner, as a tenant in common with all other unit owners in the common elements, is jointly and severally liable for damage claims arising in the common elements." 635 S.W.2d 208, 211. We reverse the judgment of the court of appeals and affirm the trial court's judgment.

J.A. Dutcher, a resident of San Diego, California, owned a condominium apartment in the Eastridge Terrace Condominiums, located in Dallas County, which he leased to Ted and Christine Owens. Ownership of the apartment includes a 1.572% *pro rata* undivided ownership in the common elements of the project. The Owenses suffered substantial property loss in a fire which began in an external light fixture in a common area.

The Owenses filed suit in Tarrant County against Dutcher, the Eastridge Terrace Condominium Association, Joe Hill Electric Company, IHS–8 Ltd. (the developer) and a class of co-owners of condominiums in Eastridge Terrace represented by the officers of the homeowners' association. All defendants with the exception of Dutcher obtained a change of venue to Dallas County. The case was tried before a jury, which found the following:

(1) The fire was proximately caused by the lack of an insulating box behind the light fixture in the exterior wall air space;

(2) The homeowners' association knew of this defect;

(3) The homeowners' association alone was negligent in failing to install an insulating box with knowledge of the defect; and

(4) The negligence of homeowners' association resulted in damage to the Owens' property in the amount of $69,150.00.

The trial court rendered judgment against Dutcher on the jury's verdict in the amount of $1,087.04. The award represents the amount of damages multiplied by Dutcher's 1.572% *pro rata* undivided ownership in the common elements of the Eastridge Terrace Condominium project.

By an agreed statement of facts filed with the court of appeals, the parties stipulated that the sole issue for determination on appeal was whether a condominium co-owner is jointly and severally liable or is liable only for a *pro rata* portion of the damages.

In enacting the Texas Condominium Act (the Act), Tex.Rev.Civ.Stat. Ann. art. 1301a, the Texas Legislature intended to create "a new method of property ownership." 1963 Tex.Gen.Laws, Ch. 191, § 26 at 512. A condominium is an estate in real property consisting of an undivided interest in a portion of a parcel of real property together with a separate fee simple interest in another portion of the same parcel. In essence, condominium ownership is the merger of two estates in land into one: the fee simple ownership of an apartment or unit in a condominium project and a tenancy in common with other co-owners in the common elements.

"General common elements" consist of, *inter alia,* the land upon which the building stands, the "foundations, bearing walls and columns, roofs, halls, lobbies, stairways, and entrances and exits or communication ways; ... [a]ll other elements of the building desirable or rationally of common use or necessary to the existence, upkeep and safety of the condominium regime, and any other elements described in the declaration ...." Tex.Rev.Civ.Stat.Ann. art. 1301a, § 2(*l*), subsections (1), (2) & (7). An individual apartment cannot be conveyed separately from the undivided interest in the common elements and *vice versa.* Id. § 9.

A condominium regime must be established according to the Act. The declaration must be filed with the county clerk, who must record the instrument in the Condominium Records. Once the declarant has complied with the provisions of the Act, each apartment in the project is treated as an interest in real property. Id. §§ 3, 4, & 7. Administration of the regime is established by the Act. Id. §§ 13, 14 & 15.

The condominium association or council is a legislatively created unincorporated association of co-owners having as their common purpose a convenient method of ownership of real property in a statutorily created method of ownership which combines both the concepts of separateness of tenure and commonality of ownership. The California Supreme Court has concluded that "the concept of separateness in the condominium project carries over to any management body or association formed to handle the common affairs of the project, and that both the condominium project and the condominium association must be considered separate legal entities from its unit owners and association members." White v. Cox, 95 Cal.Rptr. at 262.

Given the uniqueness of the type of ownership involved in condominiums, the onus of liability for injuries arising from the management of condominium projects should reflect the degree of control exercised by the defendants. We agree with the California court's conclusion that to rule that a condominium co-owner had any effective control over the operation of the common areas would be to sacrifice "reality to theoretical formalism," for in fact a co-owner has no more control over operations than he would have as a stockholder in a corporation which owned and operated the project. White v. Cox, 95 Cal.Rptr. at 263. This does not limit the plaintiff's right of action. The efficiency found in a suit directed at the homeowner's association and its board of directors representing the various individual homeowners, as well as any co-owner causally or directly responsible for the injuries sustained, benefits both sides of the docket as well as the judicial system as a whole.

Such a result is not inconsistent with the legislative intent. While the Act creates a new form of real property ownership, it does not address the issue of the allocation of tort liability among co-owners. Nevertheless, we are guided in our decision by the other provisions in the Act which appear *in pari materia,* and which proportionately allocate various financial responsibilities. For example, the Act provides for *pro rata* contributions by co-owners toward expenses of administration and maintenance, insurance, taxes and assessments. *Pro rata* provisions also exist for the application of insurance proceeds. ...

The theories of vicarious and joint and several liability are judicially created vehicles for enforcing remedies for wrongs committed. Justified on public policy grounds, they represent a deliberate allocation of risk.

Texas follows the rule that statutes in derogation of the common law are not to be strictly construed. Tex.Rev.Civ.Stat.Ann. art. 10, § 8. Nevertheless, it is recognized that if a statute creates a liability unknown to the common law, or deprives a person of a common law right, the statute will be strictly construed in the sense that it will not be extended beyond its plain meaning or applied to cases not clearly within its purview. Since the Act is silent as to tort liability, we are dealing with rights and liabilities which are not creatures of statute but with the common law, which is our special domain. Hence, the rule we have reached is not a usurpation of the legislative prerogative. To the contrary, it is one reached in the public interest.

We hold, therefore, that because of the limited control afforded a unit owner by the statutory condominium regime, the creation of the regime effects a reallocation of tort liability. The liability of a condominium co-owner is limited to his *pro rata* interest in the regime as a whole, where such liability arises from those areas held in tenancy-in-common. The judgment of the court of appeals is reversed and the judgment of the trial court is affirmed.

NOTES

1. *Condominium Statutes.* State condominium statutes, such as the one construed in Barclay v. DeVeau, prescribe the ground rules for condominium organization and management. They specify the instruments needed ⅃o create the condominium and to govern the unit owners, the structure, jurisdiction and powers of the management association and its board of managers, and the voting requirements for changing these instruments or institutions. The statutes also impose substantive rules. For example, because of the central importance of the common areas, in which all unit owners have an undivided interest, most statutes provide that they cannot be partitioned.

The first generation of condominium statutes in the United States was patterned after the FHA's prototype statute, Federal Housing Administration, Department of Housing and Urban Development, Model Statute for Creation of Apartment Ownership, Form # 3285 (1962). These statutes soon revealed their shortcomings. Developers objected to the statutes on the ground that they had been framed with high-rise apartment buildings in mind and thus ignored problems posed by low-rise lateral developments and by the frequent need to develop condominiums in stages rather than all at once. Consumers objected that the early statutes did not control such prevalent developer abuses as obtaining overly generous management contracts from captive management associations.

The second generation of condominium statutes, typified by the National Conference of Commissioners' 1977 Uniform Condominium Act, responded to these developer and consumer objections. The Act was extensively amended in 1980. The Act provides for a "flexible condominium," where land may be added or withdrawn from the project by the developer. In addition to addressing creation, termination, and operation of the condominium, various consumer protection provisions are included. These include limitations on "sweetheart" contracts and leases entered into by the developer, disclosure requirements, a right in the buyer to cancel a sales contract in certain circumstances, and developer's warranties of quality concerning the units and common areas.

For background on the two generations of condominium legislation, see Schreiber, The Lateral Housing Development: Condominium or Home Owners Association? 117 Pa.L.Rev. 1104 (1969); Rohan, The "Model Condominium Code"—A Blueprint for Modernizing Condominium Legislation, 78 Colum.L.Rev. 587 (1978); Judy & Wittie, Uniform Condominium Act: Selected Key Issues, 13 Real Prop., Probate & Trust J. 437 (1978); Note, Recent Innovations in State Condominium Legislation, 48 St. John's L.Rev. 994 (1974); Thomas, The New Uniform Condominium Act, 64 A.B.A.J. 1370 (1978).

In 1980, the National Conference of Commissioners adopted a Uniform Planned Community Act for homeowner associations. In 1981 the Conference adopted a Model Real Estate Cooperative Act and, one year later, a Uniform Common Interest Ownership Act embracing all three forms of communal ownership—condominium, cooperative and homeowners' association. These acts were all modeled on the Uniform Condominium Act. See generally, Geis, Beyond the Condominium: The Uniform Common-Interest Ownership Act. 17 Real Prop., Probate & Trust J. 757 (1982).

2. *Regulation.* Condominium acts represent just one set of regulatory hurdles that condominium developers regularly face. In addition to the usual approvals for subdivision maps, architectural review and zoning or rezoning, federal and state securities laws may apply, and if the condominium is being created through the conversion of an existing multiple family dwelling, the developer may have to cope with local laws and moratoria governing condominium conversions. See generally, Feldman, Regulating Condominium Conversions: The Constitutionality of Tenant Approval Provisions, 21 Urb.Law. 85 (1989); Comment, Cooperative and Condominium Conversions in New York: The Tenant in Occupancy, 31 N.Y.L.Sch.L.Rev. 763 (1986); Comment, The Condominium Conversion Problem: Causes and Solutions, 1980 Duke L.J. 306; Comment, The Legality and Practicality of Condominium Conversion Moratoriums, 34 U. Miami L.Rev. 1199 (1980); Note, The Validity

of Ordinances Limiting Condominium Conversion, 78 Mich.L.Rev. 124 (1979).

On securities law aspects of condominiums, see Hocking v. Dubois, 885 F.2d 1449 (9th Cir.1989), cert. denied, 494 U.S. 1078, 110 S.Ct. 1805, 108 L.Ed.2d 936 (1990) (finding that the resale of a condominium along with a rental pool contract was an investment contract, making the broker packaging the transaction subject to federal securities law); Rosenbaum, The Resort Condominium and the Federal Securities Laws—A Case Study in Governmental Inflexibility, 60 Va.L.Rev. 785 (1974); Clurman, Condominiums as Securities: A Current Look, 19 N.Y.L.F. 457 (1974); Dickey & Thorpe, Federal Security Regulation of Condominium Offerings, 19 N.Y.L.F. 473 (1974); Comment, U.H.F. v. Forman: The Relationship Between Cooperative Housing Shares and the Federal Securities Law, 61 Iowa L.Rev. 920 (1976). On the regulatory maze generally, see Geis, Representing the Condominium Developer: Tending the Paper Jungle, 10 Real Prop., Probate & Trust J. 471 (1975); Note, Condominium Regulation: Beyond Disclosure, 123 U.Pa. L.Rev. 639 (1975); Levine, Registering a Condominium Offering in New York, 19 N.Y.L.F. 493 (1974).

3. *Tort Liability of Condominium Unit Owners.* Each owner of a condominium unit will also own a fractional interest in the project's common areas as a tenant in common. The traditional rule, that tenants in common are jointly and severally liable for torts committed on the common property, poses an unacceptable, because virtually unlimited, risk of liability to individual owners.

One solution, followed in many if not most condominiums, is for the owners association to insure against liability with a blanket policy from a reputable insurer. Another solution, reached in Dutcher v. Owens, is for courts to alter the common law rule on liability of tenants in common. Yet another solution is for the state condominium statute to require tort victims to sue the condominium association rather than individual unit owners, and to limit owner liability in any event to a share of the judgment proportioned to the unit owner's interest in the condominium project. For an excellent discussion of these issues, see Freyfogle, A Comprehensive Theory of Condominium Tort Liability, 39 U.Fla.L.Rev. 877 (1988); see generally P. Rohan & M. Reskin, 1 Condominium Law and Practice Ch. 10A (1991).

B. RESTRAINTS ON ALIENATION

JONES v. O'CONNELL

Supreme Court of Connecticut, 1983.
189 Conn. 648, 458 A.2d 355.

PETERS, Associate Justice.

This case concerns the right of owners of a cooperative apartment building to impose restraints on the right to alienate one of the cooperative apartments. The plaintiffs, Conrad Jones and Florence McNulty, who had entered into a contract of sale for a cooperative apartment, brought suit against the defendants, Walter F. O'Connell, Pauline F. O'Connell, Margaret Cavanaugh, Christopher H. Smith and Harbor House, Inc., to enjoin the defendants' disapproval of the contemplated sale. The plaintiffs also sought monetary damages from the individual defendants for their tortious interference with the plaintiffs' contract. After a trial to the court, judgment was rendered for the defendants and the plaintiffs have appealed.

The underlying facts are undisputed. In 1975, the defendant Walter F. O'Connell transferred property at 252–58 Main Street, Southport, to a newly formed Connecticut corporation, the defendant Harbor House, Inc., so that Harbor House might hold the property as a cooperative residential apartment house. The defendant Christopher H. Smith, an attorney, prepared the appropriate documentation, consisting of a memorandum of offering for the stock, proprietary leases for the individual apartments, and by-laws for the corporation. From the time of the first meeting of the corporation, the Harbor House directors have been the individually named defendants, Walter and Pauline O'Connell, Christopher Smith, and Margaret Cavanaugh.

In 1979, just before the present controversy arose, the leasehold interests in Harbor House, manifested by ownership of stock and assignments of proprietary leases, were distributed among the defendants and the plaintiffs as follows: The plaintiff Florence McNulty owned 11.2 percent of the stock and was the lessee of apartment 1A. The plaintiff Conrad Jones owned 25.5 percent of the stock and was the lessee of apartment 2. The defendant Margaret Cavanaugh owned 25.5 percent of the stock and was the lessee of apartment 3. The defendant Walter O'Connell owned 37.8 percent of the stock and was the lessee of apartments 1B, 1C and 4.

On November 5, 1979, the plaintiffs entered into a written contract for Florence McNulty to sell her stock in Harbor House and to assign her proprietary lease in apartment 1A to Conrad Jones. This contract of sale was expressly made "subject to the approval of the directors or shareholders of the Corporation as provided in the Lease or the corporate by-laws." Had the transfer to Jones been approved, he would have become the owner of 36.7 percent of the Harbor House stock and the lessee of two apartments, one underneath the other. Jones was interested in acquiring additional living space for his family because in 1979, one year after his acquisition of apartment 2, he had remarried and become the stepfather of two daughters, aged 9 and 13.

Any lessee's right to sell shares and to assign a proprietary lease in Harbor House is expressly made conditional upon the consent of the Harbor House board of directors, or of at least 65 percent of the corporation's outstanding shares, by virtue of separate and somewhat inconsistent provisions in the Harbor House documentation. Under the memorandum of offering, assignments are to be approved only for persons of suitable "character and financial responsibility." Under the proprietary lease, however, consent to assignments can be granted or withheld "for any reason or for no reason." The corporate by-laws are silent as to what may constitute an adequate basis for withholding consent to an assignment.

The plaintiffs were unable to procure the requisite consent for their contemplated transfer. First the board of directors and later the stockholders of Harbor House refused to approve their contract of sale. Subsequent to this disapproval, Walter O'Connell and Margaret Cavanaugh offered to purchase the stock and the lease of apartment 1A from Florence McNulty, an offer she refused because of her commitment to Conrad Jones. The present litigation then ensued.

In the trial court, after an exhaustive examination of the plaintiffs' claims, judgment was rendered for the defendants. The court found that the defendants had acted reasonably and in good faith, and that the plaintiffs had failed to prove their various claims of wrongful interference with their contract. Each of these conclusions is challenged on this appeal. We find no error.

I

The plaintiffs' principal claim of error asserts that the evidence presented at trial fails to support the trial court's conclusion and finding that the defendants acted reasonably in disapproving the transfer of the stock and the leasehold interest appurtenant to apartment 1A. Before we reach that issue, however, we must first determine the standard by which the propriety of the defendants' withholding of their consent is to be measured.

Although this court has not previously confronted the question of restraints on alienation of property interests in cooperative residential apartments, we have addressed the legality of such restraints on alienation in related contexts. On the one hand, in cases involving the construction of wills involving the devise of both real and personal property, we have noted that "[t]he law does not favor restraints on alienation and will not recognize them unless they are stated 'in unequivocal terms'; Williams v. Robinson, 16 Conn. 517, 523 [1844]", and that "[i]t is the policy of the law not to uphold restrictions upon the free and unrestricted alienation of property unless they serve a legal and useful purpose." Peiter v. Degenring, 136 Conn. 331, 336, 71 A.2d 87 (1949). On the other hand, in a case involving a lease provision requiring that a lessor consent in writing to the assignment of a commercial lease, we have cited with approval the majority rule that "the lessor may refuse consent and his reason is immaterial." Robinson v. Weitz, 171 Conn. 545, 549, 370 A.2d 1066 (1976), relying on Segre v. Ring, 103 N.H. 278, 279, 170 A.2d 265 (1961).

An assessment of how to apply these competing principles to restraints on the alienation of cooperative apartments must take account of the reality that cooperative ownership is in many ways sui generis, a legal hybrid. For some purposes, the "owner" of such an apartment has legal title and an interest in real property, while for other purposes his rights as a tenant of the corporation and a holder of its stock more closely resemble an interest in personal property.

As did the trial court, we deem it appropriate to take a middle road in enforcing provisions that impose conditions upon the transfer of the hybrid cooperative apartment. Provisions conditioning transfers upon the consent of the cooperative corporation are neither automatically void nor automatically valid. If the provisions are stated unequivocally, and serve a legal and useful function, i.e., the reasonable protection of the financial and social integrity of the cooperative as a whole, they are not barred by our policy disfavoring restraints on alienation. Such provisions are permissible, however, only insofar as they are limited to the purpose for which they are designed. Unlimited consent clauses, permitting disapproval of transfers for any reason whatsoever, or for no reason, constitute illegal restraints because they fail sufficiently to recognize the legitimate interest of the holder of a leasehold to enjoy reasonable access to a resale market. These distinctions are consistent with the holdings of the majority of courts in other jurisdictions that have addressed this issue.

Applying these principles to the provisions of the Harbor House documentation, we agree, for two reasons, with the trial court's conclusion invalidating the clause in the proprietary lease purporting to permit consent to an assignment of the lease to be granted or withheld "for any reason or for no reason." As a matter of interpretation, that clause is not unequivocal, because it must be read conjointly with the memorandum of offering which limits the authority to disapprove assignments to cases in which the transferee is a person of unsuitable "character and financial responsibility." Given our reluctance to enforce restraints on alienation, the limited clause in the memorandum of offering must prevail over the unqualified consent clause in the proprietary lease. As a matter of public policy, furthermore, we hold, as do the authorities cited above, that only consent clauses reasonably tailored to the protection of the legitimate interests of the cooperative serve the kind of "legal and useful purpose" which protects them from avoidance as illegal restraints on alienation.

We must turn then to the plaintiffs' assertion that the trial court, on the evidence before it, erred in determining that the defendants acted reasonably, in light of the interests of the cooperative as a whole, in refusing consent to the transfer of apartment 1A. Although the defendants, at the time of their vote as directors and as stockholders, had specified no reasons for their withholding of consent, they did provide the court at trial with the propositions upon which they had relied. No special issue has been raised on this appeal that the delay in notifying the plaintiffs of the reasons for the denial of consent materially prejudiced the plaintiffs.

The trial court's memorandum of decision sets forth the reasons given by the defendants for withholding consent to the contemplated transfer. These reasons have nothing to do with the financial responsibility of Jones, which is conceded. Instead, they focus on Jones' tenancy of apartment 2 and upon functional consequences of a combined tenancy for apartments 2 and 1A. The defendants claimed that Jones was responsible for a recurrently unlocked front hall entrance door, that Jones had misled the defendants about his intended use of apartment 2, that Jones had behaved abrasively at a corporation meeting considering the Harbor House budget, that Jones and his guests had misused the cooperative parking lot, and that Jones' stepdaughters were noisy. The trial court found some of these reasons unproven, and the others of minor significance. The defendants also maintained that the character of the building would be destroyed by having one family occupy apartments on the first and second floors connected for purposes of access only by the common stairway for the building as a whole. This ordinary everyday use of the two apartments would make the stairway a part of the two affected apartments in such a way as to interfere with its common use by the other tenants, who had an interest in the preservation of the building as a cooperative with six separate apartments. Relying principally on this structural reason, the trial court concluded that the defendants "had reasons to deny consent which were based on character, and the purposes and interests of their co-operative."

The plaintiffs argue that this structural reason is insufficient in light of the Harbor House by-laws that specifically authorize the board of directors to permit an owner of one or more apartments "to combine all or any portions of any such apartments into one or any desired number of apartments; and ... to incorporate other space in the building not covered by any proprietary lease, into one or more apartments covered by a proprietary lease...." The by-laws do not, however, require combinations of apartments to be approved, particularly where impairment of common access would be likely to result from the combination. The trial court did not err in finding that the structural problem, arguably aggravated by the irritations associated with Jones' occupation of apartment 2, furnished a basis for denying consent that was reasonably rooted in the purposes and interests of the cooperative apartment living and that reasonably served to protect the financial and social integrity of the cooperative as a whole.

II

The determination that the defendants acted reasonably in the furtherance of reasonable cooperative purposes when they withheld their consent to the transfer of apartment 1A deprives the plaintiffs' other claims of error of their necessary factual underpinnings. ...

There is no error.

In this opinion the other Judges concurred.

NOTE

Would Jones v. O'Connell have been decided differently if a condominium rather than a cooperative had been involved? Courts applying the common law rule against restraints on alienation have generally been more willing to accept restraints on the sale of a cooperator's stock and proprietary lease than to accept restraints on the sale of a condominium owner's fee interest. In part this different treatment stems from the technical distinction between leaseholds, which can lawfully be subjected to restraints on alienation, and fee estates, which cannot. And in part the difference stems from judicial recognition that cooperators are financially more interdependent than condominium owners and thus have more legitimate reasons to screen prospective members who will, once accepted, share the communal mortgage and real property tax burdens. See, for example, Weisner v. 791 Park Avenue Corp., 6 N.Y.2d 426, 434, 190 N.Y.S.2d 70, 74, 160 N.E.2d 720, 724 (1959) ("there is no reason why the owners of the co-operative apartment house could not decide for themselves with whom they wish to share their elevators, their common halls and facilities, their stockholders' meetings, their management problems and responsibilities and their homes"). See generally, Note, *Weisner* Revisited: A Reappraisal of a Co-op's Power to Arbitrarily Prohibit the Transfer of Its Shares, 14 Fordham Urb.L.J. 477 (1986).

Whether in the cooperative or condominium setting, courts have been more disposed to honor rights of first refusal—under which the governing board can match any offer received by a unit owner—than to honor outright prohibitions on resale without board approval. The right of first refusal, also called a "preemptive option," can either be at a fixed, predetermined price or at a price that matches the best bona fide offer received by the unit seller; the latter type is usually considered less offensive than the former. See Browder, Restraints on the Alienation of Condominium Units (The Right of First Refusal), 1970 U.Ill.L.Forum 231, 240–243; DiLorenzo, Restraints on Alienation in a Condominium Context: An Evaluation and Theory for Decision Making, 24 Real Prop. Probate & Trust J. 403 (1989).

C. RESTRICTIONS ON OCCUPANCY AND USE

LEVANDUSKY v. ONE FIFTH AVENUE APARTMENT CORP.

Court of Appeals of New York, 1990.
75 N.Y.2d 530, 554 N.Y.S.2d 807, 553 N.E.2d 1317.

KAYE, Judge.

This appeal by a residential cooperative corporation concerning apartment renovations by one of its proprietary lessees, factually centers on a two-inch steam riser and three air conditioners, but fundamentally presents the legal question of what standard of review should apply when a board of directors of a cooperative corporation seeks to enforce a matter of building policy against a tenant-shareholder. We conclude that the business judgment rule furnishes the correct standard of review.

In the main, the parties agree that the operative events transpired as follows. In 1987, respondent (Ronald Levandusky) decided to enlarge the kitchen area of his apartment at One Fifth Avenue in New York City. According to Levandusky, some time after reaching that decision, and while he was president of the cooperative's board of directors, he told Elliot Glass, the architect retained by the corporation, that he intended to realign or "jog" a steam riser in the kitchen area, and Glass orally approved the alteration. According to Glass, however, the conversation was a general one; Levandusky never specifically told him that he intended to move any particular pipe, and Glass never gave him approval to do so. In any event, Levandusky's proprietary lease provided that no "alteration of or addition to the water, gas or steam risers or pipes" could be made without appellant's prior written consent.

Levandusky had his architect prepare plans for the renovation, which were approved by Glass and submitted for approval to the board of directors. Although the plans show details of a number of other proposed structural modifications, including changes in plumbing risers, no change in the steam riser is shown or discussed anywhere in the plans.

The board approved Levandusky's plans at a meeting held March 14, 1988, and the next day he executed an "Alteration Agreement" with appellant, which incorporated "Renovation Guidelines" that had originally been drafted, in large part, by Levandusky himself. These guidelines, like the proprietary lease, specified that advance written approval was required for any renovation affecting the building's heating system. Board consideration of the plans—appropriately detailed to indicate all structural changes—was to follow their submission to the corporation's architect, and the board reserved the power to disapprove any plans, even those that had received the architect's approval.

In late spring 1988, the building's managing agent learned from Levandusky that he intended to move the steam riser in his apartment, and so informed the board. Both Levandusky and the board contacted John Flynn, an engineer who had served as consulting agent for the board. In a letter and in a subsequent presentation at a June 13 board meeting, Flynn opined that relocating steam risers was technically feasible and, if carefully done, would not necessarily cause any problem. However, he also advised that any change in an established old piping system risked causing difficulties ("gremlins"). In Flynn's view, such alterations were to be avoided whenever possible.

At the June 13 meeting, which Levandusky attended, the board enacted a resolution to "reaffirm the policy—no relocation of risers." At a June 23 meeting, the board voted to deny Levandusky a variance to move his riser, and to modify its previous approval of his renovation plans, conditioning approval upon an acceptable redesign of the kitchen area.

Levandusky nonetheless hired a contractor, who severed and jogged the kitchen steam riser. In August 1988, when the board learned of this, it issued a "stop work" order, pursuant to the "Renovation Guidelines." Levandusky then commenced this article 78 proceeding, seeking to have the stop work order set aside. The corporation cross-petitioned for an order compelling Levandusky to return the riser to its original position. The board also sought an order compelling him to remove certain air-conditioning units he had installed, which allegedly were not in conformity with the requirements of the Landmarks Preservation Commission.

Supreme Court initially granted Levandusky's petition, and annulled the stop work order, on the ground that there was no evidence that the jogged pipe had caused any damage, but on the contrary, the building engineer had inspected it and believed it would likely not have any adverse effect. Therefore, balancing the hardship to Levandusky in redoing the already completed renovations against the harm to the building, the court determined that the board's decision to stop the renovations was arbitrary and capricious, and should be annulled. Both counterclaims were dismissed, the court ruling that the corporation had no standing to complain of violations of the Landmarks Preservation Law, particularly as the building had not been cited for any violation.

On reargument, however, Supreme Court withdrew its decision, dismissed Levandusky's petition, and ordered him to restore the riser to its original position and submit redrawn plans to the board, on the ground that the court was precluded by the business judgment rule from reviewing the board's determination. The court adhered to its original ruling with respect to the branch of the cross motion concerning the air conditioners, notwithstanding that the Landmarks Preservation Commission had in the interim cited them as violations.

On Levandusky's appeal, the Appellate Division, 150 A.D.2d 167, 540 N.Y.S.2d 440 modified the judgment. The court was unanimous in affirming the Supreme Court's disposition of the air conditioner claim, but divided concerning the stop work order. A majority of the court agreed with Supreme Court's original decision, while two Justices dissented on the ground that the board's action was within the scope of its business judgment and hence not subject to judicial review. Concluding that the business judgment rule applies to the decisions of cooperative governing associations enforcing building policy, and that the action taken by the board in this case falls within the purview of the rule, we now modify the order of the Appellate Division.

At the outset, we agree with the Appellate Division that the corporation's cross claim concerning Levandusky's three air conditioning units was properly dismissed, as the appropriate forum for resolution of the complaint at this stage is an administrative review proceeding. That brings us to the issue that divided the Appellate Division: the standard to be applied in judicial review of this challenge to a decision of the board of directors of a residential cooperative corporation.

As cooperative and condominium home ownership has grown increasingly popular, courts confronting disputes between tenant-owners and governing boards have fashioned a variety of rules for adjudicating such claims (*see generally*, Goldberg, *Community Association Use Restrictions: Applying the Business Judgment Doctrine*, 64 Chi–Kent L.Rev. 653 [1988] [hereinafter Goldberg, *Community Association Use Restrictions*]; Note, *Judicial Review of Condominium Rulemaking*, 94 Harv.L.Rev. 647 [1981]). In the process, several salient characteristics of the governing board homeowner relationship have been identified as relevant to the judicial inquiry.

As courts and commentators have noted, the cooperative or condominium association is a quasi-government—"a little democratic sub society of necessity" (*Hidden Harbour Estates v. Norman*, 309 So.2d 180, 182 [Fla.Dist.Ct.App.]). The proprietary lessees or condominium owners consent to be governed, in certain respects, by the decisions of a board. Like a municipal government, such governing boards are responsible for running the day-to-day affairs of the cooperative and to that end, often have broad powers in areas that range from financial decisionmaking to promulgating regulations regarding pets and parking spaces (*see generally*, Note, *Promulgation and Enforcement of House Rules*, 48 St. John's L.Rev. 1132 [1974]). Authority to approve or disapprove structural alterations, as in this case, is commonly given to the governing board. (*See*, Siegler, *Apartment Alterations*, N.Y.L.J., May 4, 1988, at 1, col. 1.)

Through the exercise of this authority, to which would-be apartment owners must generally acquiesce, a governing board may significantly restrict the bundle of rights a property owner normally enjoys. Moreover, as with any authority to govern, the broad powers of a cooperative board hold potential for abuse through arbitrary and malicious decisionmaking, favoritism, discrimination and the like.

On the other hand, agreement to submit to the decisionmaking authority of a cooperative board is voluntary in a sense that submission to government authority is not; there is always the freedom not to purchase the apartment. The stability offered by community control, through a board, has its own economic and social benefits, and purchase of a cooperative apartment represents a voluntary choice to cede certain of the privileges of single ownership to a governing body, often made up of fellow tenants who volunteer their time, without compensation. The board, in return, takes on the burden of managing the property for the benefit of the proprietary lessees. As one court observed: "Every man may justly consider his home his castle and himself as the king thereof; nonetheless his sovereign fiat to use his property as he pleases must yield, at least in degree, where ownership is in common or cooperation with others. The benefits of condominium living and ownership demand no less." (*Sterling Vil. Condominium v. Breitenbach*, 251 So.2d 685, 688, n. 6 [Fla.Dist.Ct.App.].)

It is apparent, then, that a standard for judicial review of the actions of a cooperative or condominium governing board must be sensitive to a variety of concerns—sometimes competing concerns. Even when the governing board acts within the scope of its authority, some check on its potential powers to regulate residents' conduct, lifestyle and property rights is necessary to protect individual residents from abusive exercise, notwithstanding that the residents have, to an extent, consented to be regulated and even selected their representatives (*see*, Note, *The Rule of Law in Residential Associations*, 99 Harv.L.Rev. 472 [1985]). At the same time, the chosen standard of review should not undermine the purposes for which the residential community and its governing structure were formed: protection of the interest of the entire community of residents in an environment managed by the board for the common benefit.

We conclude that these goals are best served by a standard of review that is analogous to the business judgment rule applied by courts to determine challenges to decisions made by corporate directors (*see*, *Auerbach v. Bennett*, 47 N.Y.2d 619, 629, 419 N.Y.S.2d 920, 393 N.E.2d 994). A number of courts in this and other states have applied such a standard in reviewing the decisions of cooperative and condominium boards (*see, e.g.*, *Kirsch v. Holiday Summer Homes*, 143 A.D.2d 811, 533 N.Y.S.2d 144; *Schoninger v. Yardarm Beach Homeowners' Assn.*, 134 A.D.2d 1, 523 N.Y.S.2d 523; *Van Camp v. Sherman*, 132 A.D.2d 453, 517 N.Y.S.2d 152; *Papalexiou v. Tower W. Condominium*, 167 N.J.Super. 516, 401 A.2d 280; *Schwarzmann v. Association of Apt. Owners*, 33 Wash.App. 397, 655 P.2d 1177; *Rywalt v. Writer Corp.*, 34 Colo.App. 334, 526 P.2d 316). We agree with those courts that such a test best balances the individual and collective interests at stake.

Developed ir the context of commercial enterprises, the business judgment rule prohibits judicial inquiry into actions of corporate directors "taken in good faith and in the exercise of honest judgment in the lawful and legitimate furtherance of corporate purposes." (*Auerbach v. Bennett*, 47 N.Y.2d 619, 629, 419 N.Y.S.2d 920, 393 N.E.2d 994, *supra*.) So long as the corporation's directors have not breached their fiduciary obligation to the corporation, "the exercise of [their powers] for the common and general interests of the corporation may not be questioned, although the results show that what they did was unwise or inexpedient." (*Pollitz v. Wabash R.R. Co.*, 207 N.Y. 113, 124, 100 N.E. 721.)

Application of a similar doctrine is appropriate because a cooperative corporation is—in fact and function—a corporation, acting through the management of its board of directors, and subject to the Business Corporation Law. There is no cause to create a special new category in law for corporate actions by coop boards.

We emphasize that reference to the business judgment rule is for the purpose of analogy only. Clearly, in light of the doctrine's origins in the quite different world of commerce, the fiduciary principles identified in the existing case law—primarily emphasizing avoidance of self-dealing and financial self-aggrandizement—will of necessity be adapted over time in order to apply to directors of not-for-profit home-owners' cooperative corporations (*see*, Goldberg, *Community Association Use Restrictions, op. cit.*, at 677–683). For present purposes, we need not, nor should we determine the entire range of the fiduciary obligations of a cooperative board, other than to note that the board owes its duty of loyalty to the cooperative—that is, it must act for the benefit of the residents collectively. So long as the board acts for the purposes of the cooperative, within the scope of its authority and in good faith, courts will not substitute their judgment for the board's. Stated somewhat differently, unless a resident challenging the board's action is able to demonstrate a breach of this duty, judicial review is not available.

In reaching this conclusion, we reject the test seemingly applied by the Appellate Division majority and explicitly applied by Supreme Court in its initial decision. That inquiry was directed at the *reasonableness* of the board's decision; having itself found that relocation of the riser posed no "dangerous aspect" to the building, the Appellate Division concluded that the renovation should remain. Like the business judgment rule, this reasonableness standard—originating in the quite different world of governmental agency decisionmaking—has found favor with courts reviewing board decisions (*see, e.g., Amoruso v. Board of Managers*, 38 A.D.2d 845, 330 N.Y.S.2d 107; *Lenox Manor v. Gianni*, 120 Misc.2d 202, 465 N.Y.S.2d 809; *see*, Note, *Judicial Review of Condominium Rulemaking, op. cit.*, at 659–661 [discussing cases from other jurisdictions]).

As applied in condominium and cooperative cases, review of a board's decision under a reasonableness standard has much in common with the rule we adopt today. A primary focus of the inquiry is whether board action is in furtherance of a legitimate purpose of the cooperative or condominium, in which case it will generally be upheld. The difference between the reasonableness test and the rule we adopt is twofold. First—unlike the business judgment rule, which places on the owner seeking review the burden to demonstrate a breach of the board's fiduciary duty—reasonableness review requires the board to demonstrate that its decision was reasonable. Second, although in practice a certain amount of deference appears to be accorded to board decisions, reasonableness review permits—indeed, in theory requires—the court itself to evaluate the merits or wisdom of the board's decision (*see, e.g., Hidden Harbour Estates v. Basso*, 393 So.2d 637, 640 [Fla.Dist. Ct.App.]), just as the Appellate Division did in the present case.

The more limited judicial review embodied in the business judgment rule is preferable. In the context of the decisions of a for-profit corporation, "courts are ill equipped and infrequently called on to evaluate what are and must be essentially business judgments * * * by definition the responsibility for business judgments must rest with the corporate directors; their individual capabilities and experience peculiarly qualify them for the discharge of that responsibility." (*Auerbach v. Bennett,* 47 N.Y.2d, *supra,* at 630–631, 419 N.Y.S.2d 920, 393 N.E.2d 994). Even if decisions of a cooperative board do not generally involve expertise beyond the usual ken of the judiciary, at the least board members will possess experience of the peculiar needs of their building and its residents not shared by the court.

Several related concerns persuade us that such a rule should apply here. As this case exemplifies, board decisions concerning what residents may or may not do with their living space may be highly charged and emotional. A cooperative or condominium is by nature a myriad of often competing views regarding personal living space, and decisions taken to benefit the collective interest may be unpalatable to one resident or another, creating the prospect that board decisions will be subjected to undue court involvement and judicial second-guessing. Allowing an owner who is simply dissatisfied with particular board action a second opportunity to reopen the matter completely before a court, which—generally without knowing the property—may or may not agree with the reasonableness of the board's determination, threatens the stability of the common living arrangement.

Moreover, the prospect that each board decision may be subjected to full judicial review hampers the effectiveness of the board's managing authority. The business judgment rule protects the board's business decisions and managerial authority from indiscriminate attack. At the same time, it permits review of improper decisions, as when the challenger demonstrates that the board's action has no legitimate relationship to the welfare of the cooperative, deliberately singles out individuals for harmful treatment, is taken without notice or consideration of the relevant facts, or is beyond the scope of the board's authority.

Levandusky failed to meet this burden, and Supreme Court properly dismissed his petition. His argument that having once granted its approval, the board was powerless to rescind its decision after he had spent considerable sums on the renovations is without merit. There is no dispute that Levandusky failed to comply with the provisions of the "Alteration Agreement" or "Renovation Guidelines" designed to give the board explicit written notice before it approved a change in the building's heating system. Once made aware of Levandusky's intent, the board promptly consulted its engineer, and notified Levandusky that it would not depart from a policy of refusing to permit the movement of pipes. That he then went ahead and moved the pipe hardly allows him to claim reliance on the board's initial approval of his plans. Indeed, recognition of such an argument would frustrate any systematic effort to enforce uniform policies.

Levandusky's additional allegations that the board's decision was motivated by the personal animosity of another board member toward him, and that the board had in fact permitted other residents to jog their steam risers, are wholly conclusory. The board submitted evidence—unrefuted by Levandusky—that it was acting pursuant to the advice of its engineer, and that it had not previously approved such jogging. Finally, the fact that allowing Levandusky an exception to the policy might not have resulted in harm to the building does not require that the exception be allowed. Under the rule we articulate today, we decline to review the merits of the board's determination that it was preferable to adhere to a uniform policy regarding the building's piping system.

Turning to the concurrence, it is apparent that in many respects we are in agreement concerning the appropriate standard of judicial review of cooperative board decisions; it is more a matter of label that divides us. For these additional reasons, we believe our choice is the better one.

For the guidance of the courts and all other interested parties, obviously a single standard for judicial review of the propriety of board action is desirable, irrespective of the happenstance of the form of the lawsuit challenging that action. Unlike challenges to administrative agency decisions, which take the form of article 78 proceedings, challenges to the propriety of corporate board action have been lodged as derivative suits, injunction actions, and all manner of civil suits, including article 78 proceedings. While the nomenclature will vary with the form of suit, we see no purpose in allowing the form of the action to dictate the substance of the standard by which the legitimacy of corporate action is to be measured.

By the same token, unnecessary confusion is generated by prescribing different standards for different categories of issues that come before cooperative boards—for example, a standard of business judgment for choices between competing economic options, but rationality for the administration of corporate bylaws and rules governing shareholder-tenant rights. There is no need for two rules when one will do, particularly since corporate action often partakes of each category of issues. Indeed, even the decision here might be portrayed as the administration of corporate bylaws and rules governing shareholder-tenant rights, or more broadly as a policy choice based on the economic consequences of tampering with the building's piping system.

Finally, we reiterate that "business judgment" appears to strike the best balance. It establishes that board action undertaken in furtherance of a legitimate corporate purpose will generally not be pronounced "arbitrary and capricious or an abuse of discretion" (CPLR 7803[3]) in article 78 proceedings, or otherwise unlawful in other types of litigation. It is preferable to a standard that requires Judges, rather than directors, to decide what action is "reasonable" for the cooperative. It avoids drawing sometimes elusive semantical distinctions between what is "reasonable" and what is "rational" (the concurrence rejects the former but embraces the latter as the appropriate test). And it better protects tenant-shareholders against bad faith and self-dealing than a test that insulates board decisions "if there is a rational basis to explain them" or if "an articulable and rational basis for the board's decision exists." The mere presence of an engineer's report, for example— "certainly a rational explanation for the board's decision"—should not end all inquiry, foreclosing review of nonconclusory assertions of malevolent conduct; under the business judgment test, it would not.

Accordingly, the order of the Appellate Division should be modified, with costs to appellant, by reinstating Supreme Court's judgment to the extent it granted appellant's cross motions regarding the steam riser and severed and set down for assessment the issue of damages and, as so modified, affirmed.

[WACHTLER, C.J., and SIMONS, ALEXANDER, HANCOCK and BEL-LACOSA, JJ., concur with KAYE, J.; TITONE, J., concurs in a separate opinion which is omitted.]

NOTES

1. *Regulation of Use.* Every social benefit of communal life can be measured in the increments of freedom lost to individual unit owners. The happy prospect of tight regulation to exclude undesirables quickly turns sour when an owner tries to sell her unit to someone the board considers undesirable. The virtues of architectural harmony will not be so evident to the owner whose preference for fuchsia colonial-style shutters put him in an outvoted minority of one. The condominium, cooperative or homeowners association is more than just a community. It is, as *Levandusky* suggests, a community that regulates the life, liberty and welfare of its members with an intensity unmatched in public government.

These perennial frustrations of communal life are doubtless aggravated by the fact that the ties that bind project owners are economic as well as social and political. All owners are required to pay a periodic assessment for maintenance, repairs and improvements. When the assessment is for existing common areas and facilities, the gripes will be relatively few. Objections will, however, be far more frequent and substantial when the board levies an assessment for construction of an improvement, such as a tennis court or swimming pool, that some members will never use, or refuses to levy an assessment to repair casualty damage that offends the handful of residents who live near the damaged area, but not residents in other parts of the project. See Natelson, Consent, Coercion, and "Reasonableness" in Private Law: The Special Case of the Property Owners Association, 51 Ohio St.L.J. 41 (1990).

2. *Regulation of Occupancy.* Condominiums, cooperatives, and homeowners associations often attempted to bar children from the premises, especially in projects designed for senior citizens or young

adults. A family with children would be barred from buying into the project; a family having a child while living in a unit would be forced to move.

Although there were some exceptions, courts generally upheld such provisions, emphasizing the importance of contract reliance. Those striking such restrictions relied on state statutory grounds and a policy favoring housing for children. See Korngold, Single Family Use Covenants: For Achieving A Balance Between Traditional Family Life and Individual Autonomy, 22 U.C.Davis L.Rev. 951 (1989).

This issue was largely preempted by the Fair Housing Amendments Act of 1988, Pub.L. No. 100–430, 102 Stat. 1619, which bars discrimination in the sale or rental of dwellings on the basis of "familial status." The legislative history indicates that the measure was to end barriers to housing for children. At the same time, the statute specifically did not bar discrimination against families with children in "housing for older persons," thus leaving open the possibility of bona fide senior citizen communities.

3. *Private Government.* Condominiums, cooperatives and homeowners associations are in effect small, private communities and are in many respects governed and taxed—through assessments—much like more traditional communities such as villages and cities. These similarities raise the obvious question whether rulemaking by condominium and cooperative boards or homeowners associations should, like land use decisions made by local governments, be subjected to judicial review. Many courts have answered in the affirmative, and have tested board decisions against the same standards they apply to local governments' exercise of the police power: Is the rule reasonably related to its stated purposes? Are the stated purposes related to the community's health, safety, welfare and morals? Was the rule's enactment procedurally correct? Does it interfere with a vested right or expectation? Probably because the private community is smaller and more clearly consensual than the usual municipal community, the answers that courts have given are more dramatically slanted in favor of community power over individual choice. See Alexander, Freedom, Coercion, and the Law of Servitudes, 73 Cornell L.Rev. 883 (1988); Ellickson, Cities and Homeowners Associations, 130 U.Pa.L.Rev. 1519 (1982); Epstein, Covenants and Constitutions, 73 Cornell L.Rev. 906 (1988); Korngold, Resolving the Flaws of Residential Servitudes and Owners Associations: For Reformation Not Termination, 1990 Wis. L.Rev. 513; Reichman, Private Residential Governments: An Introductory Survey, 43 U.Chi.L.Rev. 253 (1976); Winokur, The Mixed Blessings of Promissory Servitudes: Toward Optimizing Economic Utility, Individual Liberty, and Personal Identity, 1989 Wis.L.Rev. 1; Note, Judicial Review of Condominium Rulemaking, 94 Harv.L.Rev. 647 (1981); Comment, Community Association Use Restrictions: Applying the Business Judgment Doctrine, 64 Chi.–Kent L.Rev. 653 (1988).

Part Two

ELEMENTS OF THE COMMERCIAL
REAL ESTATE TRANSACTION

The basic elements of commercial real estate transactions are the same as the basic elements of single-family residential transactions. Brokers will be engaged and lawyers retained to bring seller, buyer and lender together and to structure and document the transaction. An executory instrument, typically a contract, will be used to bind the parties while buyer and lender make the necessary inquiries into title and into the parcel's suitability for the buyer's and lender's investment purposes. An escrow or some similar closing mechanism will be employed to assure that delivery and other conveyancing formalities are met. Finance will play a large role, and federal tax benefits may offer substantial inducements to the transaction.

The chief consequential distinction between commercial and residential land transactions is scale. Because commercial transactions usually have much greater value than residential transactions, they can support a greater number of professional participants engaged in an array of more particularized tasks. For example, instead of relying on the seller's broker, or that broker's subagent, the commercial buyer may engage and pay his own real estate broker to seek out properties for him. Instead of the parties relying on one or possibly two lawyers to oversee all aspects of the transaction, the commercial buyer, seller and lender will each retain at least one lawyer to represent their respective interests. The economics of large commercial transactions also make it possible, and desirable, for these lawyers to custom-tailor some aspects of the transaction and its documentation to the special needs of their clients and the attributes of the parcel.

The buyer's and seller's lawyers will sometimes document the parties' executory period obligations with the same one- or two-page form of deposit receipt or contract of sale that is used in residential transactions. Yet the magnitude of the parties' risk and potential rewards, and the number of conditions involved, will usually dictate a lengthier, more detailed document. For example, in place of the three-page contract of sale used in New York residential transactions, parties to a commercial purchase in New York may use a form of "Contract of Sale for Office, Commercial or Multifamily Residence" that runs to over twice the length and includes sections on seller warranties, covenants and responsibility for violations, in addition to the standard provisions on marketable title and payment of the purchase price. See Holtzschue, Contract of Sale for Office, Commercial and Multi-Family Residential Premises—A Commentary, 17 Real Prop.Probate & Trust J. 382

(1982). In some situations, the difficulty of striking a balance between an agreement that will incorporate all contingencies that concern the buyer, and one that will not be so open-ended that it will be considered illusory, may persuade the parties to use a purchase option instead.

Title insurance, used in some but not all residential transactions, is today the norm in large commercial transactions. The principal reason is that the major institutional lenders, principally life insurance companies, that finance these transactions insist that title to their security be insured by large well-established institutions possessing sufficient trained personnel to assist in their negotiations, and sufficient resources to pay off on any title claims. Similarly, surveys, which are only sporadically used in residential transactions, are commonly insisted on in commercial transactions, particularly when encroachments or easements may interfere with the buyer's proposed development. Escrow instructions, which commonly run to one or two pages in residential transactions, may in commercial transactions grow to twenty pages or more to meet the needs of the many documents, parties, interests, and federal income tax requirements that may be involved. See generally, Kuklin, Commercial Title Insurance and the Lawyer's Responsibility, 15 Real Prop., Probate & Trust J. 557 (1980); J. Pedowitz (ed.), Title Insurance: The Lawyer's Expanding Role (1985).

Finance plays an even larger role in commercial real estate transactions than it does in residential transactions. The basic finance instruments—mortgage, trust deed, installment land contract—may be the same, but the purposes to which they are put will differ, their provisions will be more detailed, and they will more frequently be used in connection with other financing devices. Leases represent a popular alternative or complement to mortgage and trust deed finance and can themselves become security for a mortgage or deed of trust. Federal income tax considerations, always an inducement to home purchase, sometimes become the sole justification for a commercial real estate transaction.

Bibliographic Note. For a thoughtful, well-detailed introduction to commercial real estate transactions, see R. Lifton, Practical Real Estate in the '80s: Legal, Tax and Business Strategies (2d ed. 1983). Several newsletters report current developments in real estate law and practice. Among the more informative and comprehensive are: The Mortgage and Real Estate Executives Report; Real Estate Syndication Alert; and the Commercial Lease Law Insider.

W. ZECKENDORF, ZECKENDORF * 144–148 (1970).

Standing out in the sun, in my bare feet and shorts I thought enviously about how an investment banker acquiring a ten-million-dollar industrial corporation has a much easier time of it than a real-estate man buying a ten-million-dollar building. The investment banker can divide and sell the ownership and rights in a corporation in a great many ways, a piece at a time. For instance, he can sell first-mortgage bonds to an insurance company, at the prime rate of interest. He could also offer debentures, which, though they take a second position to the bonds, offer a higher rate of interest in compensation. For investors interested in a speculative fillip (in case the company does very well), there are convertible debentures that can be turned into common stock. He can issue preferred shares (convertible or straight), which tend to be especially attractive to corporate investors, because preferred dividends passing from one corporation to another are taxed only seven percent. Finally, there is the common stock, the basic equity of a corporation, but the availability of capital does not stop there; there are also bank loans, accounts receivable (which may be financed with a factor), warrants to buy stock, and various other ways to draw investment capital into a corporation. In fact, investment bankers have over the generations invented as many ways of catering to investors as there are investors with particular personal needs, whims, or tax requirements.

While hauling in an empty line from the Hawaiian seaside, it occurred to me that if an investment banker did not have all these ways to reach various kinds of investors, he would be in just as difficult a position as I was with 1 Park Avenue. If he had to sell a corporation in toto, to one buyer, an investment banker would not get nearly as much money as he did by dividing it up for special customers ... the lucky devil.

This kind of thinking was not really getting me anywhere; I pulled back with my rod and cast way out into the water again. Then an idea came to me: "Why can't we break the property up, just the way an investment banker does? "

With a corporate financial structure as my model, I began mentally to divide up 1 Park Avenue to see how and at what price the building might appeal to various kinds of investors. As the pieces and the arithmetic began to dovetail, I forgot my fishing or even where I was until I suddenly realized I was standing on a Hawaiian beach, in water up to my ankles, with a useless rod and reel in my hands. I went into the house, and in the course of two hours on the telephone I began to make the first application of what was to become known in the trade as the Hawaiian Technique.

In practice, because it involves a long chain of interconnected events and multiple side branches, the Hawaiian Technique can become as complex as some of the long molecule chains chemists work with and link together to concoct new products. In essence, however, like most good ideas, it is simple. I determined how it could work, in the case of

1 Park Avenue, which earned one million dollars in rentals a year and had a ten-million-dollar price tag on it.

Though most homeowners don't think of it this way, a major urban property breaks naturally into two parts—the land, and a lease which gives you a right to the use of the land. A building usually comes with this lease, but as the basic leaseholder and building owner you can alter, tear down, or rebuild on your site in any way you want—as long as you pay your ground rent for the land.

Now, considering only the land, I determined that $250,000 of the total million-dollar income of the property should go to the ground rent. This ground rent, since it must be paid before any other expenses, is the safest of all possible incomes to the property. Capitalized at the rate of five percent, therefore, the ground should be worth five million dollars. I could try to find a buyer directly at this price, or I might do something else: since ground income is so sure, a mortgage on the ground (which would have first call on the already ultrasafe ground rent) would be even more secure. I should have little trouble finding an insurance company or pension fund willing to take a four-percent return for such a safe risk and could therefore sell them a mortgage on the ground for three million dollars which would eat up $120,000 of the land's total income. The remaining $130,000 of income capitalized at the rate of 6½ percent would be worth two million, and for this sum I would sell the land to an institutional or individual investor.

The land mortgagor and land owner would be our equivalent of a corporation's bond and debenture holders, and at this point, having first mortgaged and then sold off our land, we would have five million dollars, plus a building and, of course, a basic lease giving us undisturbed use of the property.

The earnings on this property, after payment of ground rent, would be one million dollars, minus $250,000, or $750,000. The job now was to properly fraction and sell this leasehold and its income so as to attract particular buyers. What I did, basically, was to create two leases, an inner (or sandwich) lease, and outer (or operating) lease. Whoever purchased the operating lease would, in effect, be the manager of the building. He would solicit tenants and collect rents. He would get one million dollars in income, pay $750,000 in rent, and keep $250,000 for himself. The holder of the inner lease would, in effect, be the owner of the building. He would get $750,000 in rent, pay $250,000 to the owner of the land, and keep $500,000 for himself.

Before selling the inner lease and its $500,000 income, however, I could readily mortgage it with a leasehold first mortgage of 6½ percent for four million dollars. The mortgage payments on this would come to $270,000 per year plus two percent or $80,000 per year for amortization. This would leave $500,000 minus $350,000, or $150,000, to the building owner. Capitalizing this $150,000 at an attractive six percent, I would readily find a buyer for 2.5 million dollars. Thus the inner lease would bring me four million dollars when mortgaged, plus 2.5 million when sold.

As for the operating lease, with its $250,000 income, we could, at a seven-percent return to investors, get a price of almost 3.6 million dollars. If we provided the financing, by taking back a mortgage, it might be even higher, but holding things as is (in this simplified case), it turns out we have arranged to: (1) sell and mortgage the land (for five million dollars), (2) sell and mortgage the inner lease (for 6.5 million dollars), and (3) sell an operating lease (for 3.6 million dollars). All for a grand total of 15.1 million dollars on a purchase price to us of ten million.

In this profitably fractioned property, the holder of the operating (or outer) lease, who acted as manager of the building, in that his costs were fixed (at $750,000), was in a position not unlike that of a common stockholder. He was relatively secure against inflation, and if he could increase sales or rentals, his income would rise phenomenally; a ten-percent rise in rentals, for instance, would give him a forty-percent rise in income.

The building owner, or innerlease holder, would be in a cash position much like that of a preferred stockholder, with fixed income but with tax advantages even better than those available to corporations that pay only seven percent of their preferred dividends. This, because the building owner can write off the annual depreciation of the building against his cash income from the structure. What with the accelerated depreciation, such investors would be able to pocket their $230,000 income with no tax—and to garner extra tax credits against other income—until such time, of course, as yearly depreciation on the building began to equal amortization payments. At this point the individual owner would likely want to sell his interest in the building (paying only twenty-five percent in capital gains if he sold at a profit), to wind up with an excellent net return.

These, as with a great many other tax possibilities that we realized for investors, were perfectly legal and well within the concepts and spirit of the law as it existed then. They also led to much new legislation, however, because the Internal Revenue Service, upset about the amount of money they were not getting, instituted new rulings to plug the new holes we had discovered.

The example of property-fractioning I have given above is a simplified one. In an actual case there might be quite a number of individual variations and many more investors. For instance, in an inner (or sandwich) lease, aside from the first mortgage we might create a two-million-dollar second mortgage, this second mortgage to pay interest but no amortization, till the first mortgage had been paid off. Or we might create a dormant mortgage which did not pay anything for twenty-five years. Only after the first mortgage was paid would this dormant mortgage take over, but then, as a first mortgage, it would acquire full value. One might be able to sell such a mortgage for, say,

$750,000 to a man who wants to give it to his children twenty-five years hence.

Similarly, the operating (or outer) lease, instead of being sold outright, might be mortgaged, broken into subleases or subsubleases, hedged against various possibilities, and sold to as many as ten or twelve different investors.

The Hawaiian Technique was so flexible that it became a very powerful tool which often could make two plus two equal to four plus one plus two plus more. I was not the first one to package real-estate deals for particular customers or to use a sale-and-leaseback technique (I, for one, had been doing just such things since the 1930's), but this was the first time anyone consciously and deliberately fractioned a great property off beforehand in order to tap many markets at once. We used the technique with 1407 Broadway, with West Thirty-fourth Street, with the Graybar Building, and with just about every other one of our major properties. The Hawaiian Technique, because it permitted us to anticipate and make early use of the future earnings of our properties, became the principal tool of Webb & Knapp expansion. And, as the technique spread and was adapted by others, it brought a new liquidity and flexibility to real-estate financing in general.

I. FEDERAL INCOME TAX CONSIDERATIONS

A. TAX PLANNING: HOW PROPERTY IS HELD

At one time, two facts dominated federal income tax planning for real estate investments. First, it was worth more to the taxpayer to have a dollar on one day than to have the same dollar the next day. Second, it was less costly to the taxpayer to be taxed on income at the lower capital gains rates than at the higher ordinary income rates. Guided by these two facts, taxpayers would commonly try to take as many deductions as possible, as early as possible. They would try to defer income taxation for as long as possible and, when income had to be taxed, they would try to have it taxed at capital gains rates. If losses were incurred, the taxpayer would usually want to have the loss deducted early and as an offset to ordinary income rather than as a capital loss.

The 1986 Tax Reform Act, which for most purposes went into effect on January 1, 1987, altered the second fact but not the first. Under prior law, a 60% deduction for net long term capital gains gave individual taxpayers in the highest, 50%, tax bracket an effective capital gains tax rate of 20%. With the 1986 Act's repeal of the capital gains deduction, capital gains are now taxed at the taxpayer's ordinary income rate. The 1986 Act partially offsets the loss of this tax benefit with a new ordinary income tax rate structure prescribing a top marginal rate for ordinary income of 28% or, for individuals with taxable income above specified levels, 33% in certain cases. It was not long, however, before the distinction between ordinary income and capital gains was revived, albeit to a small degree. The Revenue Reconciliation Act of 1990 set the maximum tax rate for capital gains at 28% and the highest rate for taxation of ordinary income is 31%. The Act thus restored a slight preference for capital gains in situations where the taxpayer's ordinary income would be taxed at 31%. 26 U.S.C.A. § 1(j) (West Supp.1992). Moreover, after the 1986 legislation, the concept of capital losses is still important as is the netting of capital gains against capital losses. See Internal Revenue Code § 1212.

The Internal Revenue Code divides commercial real property into three classes: property held for investment or production of income; property used in trade or business; and property held primarily for sale to customers in the ordinary course of trade or business. To each class of property the Code attaches a set of specific attributes for taking deductions and for recognizing gains and losses. While the Code's approach substantially limits the taxpayer's ability to jockey for the best tax position, it does leave room for creative tax planning and for structuring investments to fit into the most advantageous class.

Property held for investment or production of income. Property held for investment or production of income qualifies as a capital asset under section 1221, and all gains or losses realized on its sale or exchange are treated as capital gains or losses. Under section 212, which allows deductions for "the management, conservation, or maintenance of property held for the production of income," the property owner can deduct the expenses of real property taxes, interest, maintenance and repairs. Under section 167, the taxpayer can also take a deduction for the depreciation of improvements situated on the land. Compliance with section 1031's criteria for tax-free exchanges will postpone recognition of gain or loss on transfer of the property.

Property used in the taxpayer's trade or business. Section 1221 expressly excludes a taxpayer's "real property used in his trade or business" from its definition of capital asset. While capital asset treatment is thus lost to this class of real estate investment, section 1231 treats gain on the disposition of trade or business property as capital gain, while it treats loss as ordinary loss which can be offset against ordinary income. Section 1231 property is entitled to all of the expense deductions, including the depreciation deduction, allowed to section 1221 property, and similarly qualifies for deferred recognition of gain and loss under section 1031.

Property held primarily for sale to customers in the ordinary course of trade or business. Section 1221 excludes from its definition of capital asset, and section 1231 excludes from its definition of trade or business property, "property held by the taxpayer primarily for sale to customers in the ordinary course of his trade or business." Gains or losses on sales or exchanges of property in this class are treated as ordinary income and ordinary loss rather than as capital gains and losses. While most expenses incurred in connection with holding this property—interest, taxes, maintenance expenses, casualty losses—are deductible, depreciation is not. Property in this class does not qualify for deferred recognition of gain or loss under section 1031. The 1986 Tax Reform Act repealed the capital gains deduction, taxing all gain at ordinary income rates, and curtailed the tax benefits of the depreciation deduction. The 1986 Act has thus reduced some of the comparative disadvantages of classification as property held primarily for sale to customers in the ordinary course of trade or business.

Bibliographic Note. In addition to the standard tax treatises and textbooks, you may find the following sources helpful: A. Arnold, Real Estate Investments After the Tax Reform Act of 1986 (1987); P. Anderson, Tax Planning of Real Estate (7th ed. 1977); P. Anderson, Tax Factors in Real Estate Operations (6th ed. 1980); G. Robinson, Federal Income Taxation of Real Estate (1988); I. Faggen, et al., Federal Taxes Affecting Real Estate (6th ed. 1990); M. Levine, Real Estate Transactions: Tax Planning and Consequences (1991); S. Guerin, Taxation of

Real Estate Transactions (2d ed. 1988). The Journal of Real Estate Taxation, published quarterly, is an excellent source of articles on currently important tax topics.

MALAT v. RIDDELL

Supreme Court of the United States, 1966.
383 U.S. 569, 86 S.Ct. 1030, 16 L.Ed.2d 102.

PER CURIAM.

Petitioner was a participant in a joint venture which acquired a 45-acre parcel of land, the intended use for which is somewhat in dispute. Petitioner contends that the venturers' intention was to develop and operate an apartment project on the land; the respondent's position is that there was a "dual purpose" of developing the property for rental purposes or selling, whichever proved to be the more profitable. In any event, difficulties in obtaining the necessary financing were encountered and the interior lots of the tract were subdivided and sold. The profit from those sales was reported and taxed as ordinary income.

The joint venturers continued to explore the possibility of commercially developing the remaining exterior parcels. Additional frustrations in the form of zoning restrictions were encountered. These difficulties persuaded petitioner and another of the joint venturers of the desirability of terminating the venture; accordingly, they sold out their interests in the remaining property. Petitioner contends that he is entitled to treat the profits from this last sale as capital gains; the respondent takes the position that this was "property held by the taxpayer primarily for sale to customers in the ordinary course of his trade or business," and thus subject to taxation as ordinary income.

The District Court made the following finding:

"The members of [the joint venture] as of the date the 44.901 acres were acquired, intended either to sell the property or develop it for rental, depending upon which course appeared to be most profitable. The venturers realized that they had made a good purchase price-wise and, if they were unable to obtain acceptable construction financing or rezoning ... which would be prerequisite to commercial development, they would sell the property in bulk so they wouldn't get hurt. The purpose of either selling or developing the property continued during the period in which [the joint venture] held the property."

The District Court ruled that petitioner had failed to establish that the property was not held *primarily* for sale to customers in the ordinary course of business, and thus rejected petitioner's claim to capital gain treatment for the profits derived from the property's resale. The Court of Appeals affirmed, 347 F.2d 23. We granted certiorari (382 U.S. 900) to resolve a conflict among the courts of appeals with regard to the meaning of the term "primarily" as it is used in § 1221(1) of the Internal Revenue Code of 1954.

The statute denies capital gain treatment to profits reaped from the sale of "property held by the taxpayer *primarily* for sale to customers in the ordinary course of his trade or business." (Emphasis added.) The respondent urges upon us a construction of "primarily" as meaning that a purpose may be "primary" if it is a "substantial" one.

As we have often said, "the words of statutes—including revenue acts—should be interpreted where possible in their ordinary, everyday senses." Crane v. Commissioner, 331 U.S. 1, 6. Departure from a literal reading of statutory language may, on occasion, be indicated by relevant internal evidence of the statute itself and necessary in order to effect the legislative purpose. But this is not such an occasion. The purpose of the statutory provision with which we deal is to differentiate between the "profits and losses arising from the everyday operation of a business" on the one hand (Corn Products Co. v. Commissioner, 350 U.S. 46, 52) and "the realization of appreciation in value accrued over a substantial period of time" on the other. (Commissioner v. Gillette Motor Co., 364 U.S. 130, 134.) A literal reading of the statute is consistent with this legislative purpose. We hold that, as used in § 1221(1), "primarily" means "of first importance" or "principally."

Since the courts below applied an incorrect legal standard, we do not consider whether the result would be supportable on the facts of this case had the correct one been applied. We believe, moreover, that the appropriate disposition is to remand the case to the District Court for fresh fact-findings, addressed to the statute as we have now construed it.

Vacated and remanded.

Mr. Justice BLACK would affirm the judgments of the District Court and the Court of Appeals.

Mr. Justice WHITE took no part in the decision of this case.

BIEDENHARN REALTY CO., INC. v. UNITED STATES

United States Court of Appeals, Fifth Circuit, 1976.
526 F.2d 409, cert. denied, 429 U.S. 819, 97 S.Ct. 64, 50 L.Ed.2d 79.

GOLDBERG, Circuit Judge:

The taxpayer-plaintiff, Biedenharn Realty Company, Inc. [Biedenharn], filed suit against the United States in May, 1971, claiming a refund for the tax years 1964, 1965, and 1966. In its original tax returns for the three years, Biedenharn listed profits of $254,409.47 from the sale of 38 residential lots. Taxpayer divided this gain, attributing 60% to ordinary income and 40% to capital gains. Later, having determined that the profits from these sales were entirely ordinary income, the Internal Revenue Service assessed and collected additional taxes and interest. In its present action, plaintiff asserts that the whole real estate profit represents gain from the sale of capital assets and consequently that the Government is indebted to taxpayer for $32,006.86 in overpaid taxes. Reviewing the facts of this case in the light of our previous holdings and the directions set forth in this opinion, we reject plaintiff's claim and in so doing reverse the opinion of the District Court.

I.

Because of the confusing state of the record in this controversy and the resulting inconsistencies among the facts as stipulated by the parties, as found by the District Court, and as stated in the panel opinion, we believe it useful to set out in plentiful detail the case's background and circumstances as best they can be ascertained.

A. *The Realty Company.* Joseph Biedenharn organized the Biedenharn Realty Company in 1923 as a vehicle for holding and managing the Biedenharn family's numerous investments. The original stockholders were all family members. The investment company controls, among other interests, valuable commercial properties, a substantial stock portfolio, a motel, warehouses, a shopping center, residential real property, and farm property.

B. *Taxpayer's Real Property Sales—The Hardtimes Plantation.* Taxpayer's suit most directly involves its ownership and sale of lots from the 973 acre tract located near Monroe, Louisiana, known as the Hardtimes Plantation. The plaintiff purchased the estate in 1935 for $50,000.00. B.W. Biedenharn, the Realty Company's president, testified that taxpayer acquired Hardtimes as a "good buy" for the purpose of farming and as a future investment. The plaintiff farmed the land for several years. Thereafter, Biedenharn rented part of the acreage to a farmer who Mr. Biedenharn suggested may presently be engaged in farming operations.

1. *The Three Basic Subdivisions.* Between 1939 and 1966, taxpayer carved three basic subdivisions from Hardtimes—Biedenharn Estates, Bayou DeSiard Country Club Addition, and Oak Park Addition—covering approximately 185 acres. During these years, Biedenharn sold 208 subdivided Hardtimes lots in 158 sales, making a profit in excess of $800,000.00. These three basic subdivisions are the source of the contested 37 sales of 38 lots. Their development and disposition are more fully discussed below.

a) Biedenharn Estates Unit 1, including 41.9 acres, was platted in 1938. Between 1939 and 1956, taxpayer apparently sold 21 lots in 9 sales. Unit 2, containing 8.91 acres, was sold in 9 transactions between 1960 and 1965 and involved 10 lots.

b) Bayou DeSiard Country Club Addition, covering 61 acres, was subdivided in 1951, with remaining lots resubdivided in 1964. Approximately 73 lots were purchased in 64 sales from 1951 to 1966.

c) Oak Park Units 1 and 2 encompassed 75 acres. After subdivision in 1955 and resubdivision in 1960, plaintiff sold approximately 104 lots in 76 sales.

2. *Additional Hardtimes Sales.* Plaintiff lists at least 12 additional Hardtimes sales other than lots vended from the three basic subdivisions. The earliest of these dispositions occurred in November, 1935, thirteen days after the Plantation's purchase. Ultimately totaling approximately 275 acres, most, but not all, of these sales involved large parcels of nonsubdivided land.

C. *Taxpayer's Real Property Activity: Non-Hardtimes Sales.* The 208 lots marketed from the three Hardtimes subdivisions represent only part of Biedenharn's total real property sales activities. Although the record does not in every instance permit exactitude, plaintiff's own submissions make clear that the Biedenharn Realty Company effectuated numerous non-Hardtimes retail real estate transactions. From the Company's formation in 1923 through 1966, the last year for which taxes are contested, taxpayer sold 934 lots. Of this total, plaintiff disposed of 249 lots before 1935 when it acquired Hardtimes. Thus, in the years 1935 to 1966, taxpayer sold 477 lots apart from its efforts with respect to the basic Hardtimes subdivisions. Biedenharn's year by year sales breakdown is attached as Appendix I of this opinion. That chart shows real estate sales in all but two years, 1932 and 1970, since the Realty Company's 1923 inception.

Unfortunately, the record does not unambiguously reveal the number of *sales* as opposed to the number of *lots* involved in these dispositions. Although some doubt exists as to the actual *sales* totals, even the most conservative reading of the figures convinces us of the frequency and abundance of the non-Hardtimes sales. For example, from 1925 to 1958, Biedenharn consummated from its subdivided Owens tract a minimum of 125, but perhaps upwards of 300, sales (338 lots). Eighteen sales accounted for 20 lots sold between 1923 and 1958 from Biedenharn's Cornwall property. Taxpayer's disposition from 1927 to 1960 of its Corey and Cabeen property resulted in at least 50 sales. Plaintiff made 14 sales from its Thomas Street lots between 1937 and 1955. Moreover, Biedenharn has sold over 20 other properties, a few of them piecemeal, since 1923.

Each of these parcels has its own history. Joseph Biedenharn transferred much of the land to the Realty Company in 1923. The company acquired other property through purchases and various forms of foreclosure. Before sale, Biedenharn held some tracts for commercial or residential rental. Taxpayer originally had slated the Owens acreage for transfer in bulk to the Owens-Illinois Company. Also, the length of time between acquisition and disposition differed significantly among pieces of realty. However, these variations in the background of each plot and the length of time and original purpose for which each was obtained do not alter the fact that the Biedenharn Realty Company regularly sold substantial amounts of subdivided and improved real property, and further, that these sales were not confined to the basic Hardtimes subdivisions.

D. *Real Property Improvements.* Before selling the Hardtimes lots, Biedenharn improved the land, adding in most instances, streets, drainage, water, sewerage, and electricity. The total cost of bettering the Plantation acreage exceeded $200,000 and included $9,519.17 for Biedenharn Estates Unit 2, $56,879.12 for Bayou DeSiard Country Club Addition, and $141,579.25 for the Oak Park Addition.

E. *Sale of the Hardtimes Subdivisions.* Bernard Biedenharn testified that at the time of the Hardtimes purchase, no one foresaw that the land would be sold as residential property in the future. Accordingly, the District Court found, and we do not disagree, that Biedenharn bought Hardtimes for investment. Later, as the City of Monroe expanded northward, the Plantation became valuable residential property. The Realty Company staked off the Bayou DeSiard subdivision so that prospective purchasers could see what the lots "looked like." As demand increased, taxpayer opened the Oak Park and Biedenharn Estates Unit 2 subdivisions and resubdivided the Bayou DeSiard section. Taxpayer handled all Biedenharn Estates and Bayou DeSiard sales. Independent realtors disposed of many of the Oak Park lots. Mr. Herbert Rosenhein, a local broker, sold Oak Park Unit 1 lots. Gilbert Faulk, a real estate agent, sold from Oak Park Unit 2. Of the 37 sales consummated between 1964 and 1966, Henry Biedenharn handled at least nine transactions (Biedenharn Estates (2) and Bayou DeSiard (7)) while "independent realtors" effected some, if not all, of the other 28 transactions (Oak Park Unit 2). Taxpayer delegated significant responsibilities to these brokers. In its dealings with Faulk, Biedenharn set the prices, general credit terms, and signed the deeds. Details, including specific credit decisions and advertising, devolved to Faulk, who utilized on-site signs and newspapers to publicize the lots.

In contrast to these broker induced dispositions, plaintiff's nonbrokered sales resulted after unsolicited individuals approached Realty Company employees with inquiries about prospective purchases. At no time did the plaintiff hire its own real estate salesmen or engage in formal advertising. Apparently, the lands' prime location and plaintiff's subdivision activities constituted sufficient notice to interested persons of the availability of Hardtimes lots. Henry Biedenharn testified:

> "[O]nce we started improving and putting roads and streets in people would call us up and ask you about buying a lot and we would sell a lot if they wanted it."

The Realty Company does not maintain a separate place of business but instead offices at the Biedenharn family's Ouachita Coca-Cola bottling plant. A telephone, listed in plaintiff's name, rings at the Coca-Cola building. Biedenharn has four employees: a camp caretaker, a tenant farmer, a bookkeeper and a manager. The manager, Henry Biedenharn, Jr., devotes approximately 10% of his time to the Realty Company, mostly collecting rents and overseeing the maintenance of various properties. The bookkeeper also works only part-time for plaintiff.

Having set out these facts, we now discuss the relevant legal standard for resolving this controversy.

II.

The determination of gain as capital or ordinary is controlled by the language of the Internal Revenue Code. The Code defines capital asset, the profitable sale or exchange of which generally results in capital gains, as "property held by the taxpayer." 26 U.S.C.A. § 1221. Many exceptions limit the enormous breadth of this congressional description and consequently remove large numbers of transactions from the privileged realm of capital gains. In this case, we confront the question whether or not Biedenharn's real estate sales should be taxed at ordinary rates because they fall within the exception covering "property held by the taxpayer primarily for sale to customers in the ordinary course of his trade or business." 26 U.S.C.A. § 1221(1).

The problem we struggle with here is not novel. We have become accustomed to the frequency with which taxpayers litigate this troublesome question. Chief Judge Brown appropriately described the real estate capital gains-ordinary income issue as "old, familiar, recurring, vexing and ofttimes elusive." Thompson v. Commissioner of Internal Revenue, 5 Cir.1963, 322 F.2d 122, 123. The difficulty in large part stems from ad-hoc application of the numerous permissible criteria set forth in our multitudinous prior opinions. Over the past 40 years, this case by case approach with its concentration on the facts of each suit has resulted in a collection of decisions not always reconcilable. Recognizing the situation, we have warned that efforts to distinguish and thereby make consistent the Court's previous holdings must necessarily be "foreboding and unrewarding." *Thompson,* supra at 127. Litigants are cautioned that "each case must be decided on its own peculiar facts. ... Specific factors, or combinations of them are not necessarily controlling." *Thompson,* supra at 127. Nor are these factors the equivalent of the philosopher's stone, separating "sellers garlanded with capital gains from those beflowered in the garden of ordinary income." United States v. Winthrop, 5 Cir.1969, 417 F.2d 905, 911.

Assuredly, we would much prefer one or two clearly defined, easily employed tests which lead to predictable, perhaps automatic, conclusions. However, the nature of the congressional "capital asset" definition and the myriad situations to which we must apply that standard make impossible any easy escape from the task before us. No one set of criteria is applicable to all economic structures. Moreover, within a collection of tests, individual factors have varying weights and magnitudes, depending on the facts of the case. The relationship among the factors and their mutual interaction is altered as each criterion increases or diminishes in strength, sometimes changing the controversy's outcome. As such, there can be no mathematical formula capable of finding the X of capital gains or ordinary income in this complicated field.

Yet our inability to proffer a panaceatic guide to the perplexed with respect to this subject does not preclude our setting forth some general, albeit inexact, guidelines for the resolution of many of the § 1221(1) cases we confront. This opinion does not purport to reconcile all past precedents or assure conflict-free future decisions. Nor do we hereby obviate the need for ad-hoc adjustments when confronted with close cases and changing factual circumstances. Instead, with the hope of clarifying a few of the area's mysteries, we more precisely define and suggest points of emphasis for the major *Winthrop* delineated factors [22] as they appear in the instant controversy. In so doing, we devote particular attention to the Court's recent opinions in order that our analysis will reflect, insofar as possible, the Circuit's present trends.

III.

We begin our task by evaluating in the light of *Biedenharn's* facts the main *Winthrop* factors—substantiality and frequency of sales, improvements, solicitation and advertising efforts, and brokers' activities—as well as a few miscellaneous contentions. A separate section follows discussing the keenly contested role of prior investment intent. Finally, we consider the significance of the Supreme Court's decision in Malat v. Riddell.

A. *Frequency and Substantiality of Sales*

Scrutinizing closely the record and briefs, we find that plaintiff's real property sales activities compel an ordinary income conclusion. In arriving at this result, we examine first the most important of *Winthrop's* factors—the frequency and substantiality of taxpayer's sales. Although frequency and substantiality of sales are not usually conclusive, they occupy the preeminent ground in our analysis. The recent trend of Fifth Circuit decisions indicates that when dispositions of subdivided property extend over a long period of time and are especially numerous, the likelihood of capital gains is very slight indeed. Conversely, when sales are few and isolated, the taxpayer's claim to capital gain is accorded greater deference.

On the present facts, taxpayer could not claim "isolated" sales or a passive and gradual liquidation. Although only three years and 37 sales (38 lots) are in controversy here, taxpayer's pre-1964 sales from the Hardtimes acreage as well as similar dispositions from other properties are probative of the existence of sales "in the ordinary course of his trade or business." As Appendix I indicates, Biedenharn

---

22. In United States v. Winthrop, 5 Cir. 1969, 417 F.2d 905, 910, the Court enumerated the following factors:

(1) the nature and purpose of the acquisition of the property and the duration of the ownership; (2) the extent and nature of the taxpayer's efforts to sell the property; (3) the number, extent, continuity and substantiality of the sales; (4) the extent of subdividing, developing, and advertising to increase sales; (5) the use of a business office for the sale of the property; (6) the character and degree of supervision or control exercised by the taxpayer over any representative selling the property; and (7) the time and effort the taxpayer habitually devoted to the sales.

The numbering indicates no hierarchy of importance.

sold property, usually a substantial number of lots, in every year, save one, from 1923 to 1966. Biedenharn's long and steady history of improved lot sales at least equals that encountered in Thompson v. Commissioner of Internal Revenue, 5 Cir.1963, 322 F.2d 122, where also we noted the full history of real estate activity. Supra at 124–25. There taxpayer lost on a finding that he had sold 376½ lots over a 15 year span—this notwithstanding that overall the other sales indicia were more in taxpayer's favor than in the present case. Moreover, the contested tax years in that suit involved only ten sales (28 lots); yet we labeled that activity "substantial." Supra at 125.

The frequency and substantiality of Biedenharn's sales go not only to its holding purpose and the existence of a trade or business but also support our finding of the ordinariness with which the Realty Company disposed of its lots. These sales easily meet the criteria of normalcy set forth in *Winthrop,* supra at 912.

Furthermore, in contrast with Goldberg v. Commissioner of Internal Revenue, 5 Cir.1955, 223 F.2d 709, 713, where taxpayer did not reinvest his sales proceeds, one could fairly infer that the income accruing to the Biedenharn Realty Company from its pre-1935 sales helped support the purchase of the Hardtimes Plantation. Even if taxpayer made no significant acquisitions after Hardtimes, the "purpose, system, and continuity" of Biedenharn's efforts easily constitute a business.

    . . .

Citing previous Fifth Circuit decisions including Goldberg v. Commissioner of Internal Revenue, 5 Cir.1955, 223 F.2d 709, 713, and Ross v. Commissioner of Internal Revenue, 5 Cir.1955, 227 F.2d 265, 268, the District Court sought to overcome this evidence of dealer-like real estate activities and property "primarily held for sale" by clinging to the notion that the taxpayer was merely liquidating a prior investment. We discuss later the role of former investment status and the possibility of taxpayer relief under that concept. Otherwise, the question of liquidation of an investment is simply the opposite side of the inquiry as to whether or not one is holding property primarily for sale in the ordinary course of his business. In other words, a taxpayer's claim that he is liquidating a prior investment does not really present a separate theory but rather restates the main question currently under scrutiny. To the extent the opinions cited by the District Court might create a specially protected "liquidation" niche, we believe that the present case, with taxpayer's energetic subdivision activities and consummation of numerous retail property dispositions, is governed by our more recent decision in Thompson v. Commissioner of Internal Revenue, supra at 127–28. There, the Court observed:

The liquidation, if it really is that, may therefore be carried out with business efficiency. Smith v. Commissioner of Internal Revenue, 5 Cir.1956, 232 F.2d 142, 145. But what was once an investment, or what may start out as a liquidation of an investment, may become something else. The Tax Court was eminently justified in concluding that this took place here. It was a regular part of the trade or business of Taxpayer to sell these lots to any and all comers who would meet his price. From 1944 on when the sales commenced, there is no evidence that he thereafter held the lots for any purpose other than the sale to prospective purchasers. It is true that he testified in conclusory terms that he was trying to "liquidate" but on objective standards the Tax Court could equate held solely with "held primarily." And, of course, there can be no question at all that purchasers of these lots were "customers" and that whether we call Taxpayer a "dealer" or a "trader", a real estate man or otherwise, the continuous sales of these lots down to the point of exhaustion was a regular and ordinary (and profitable) part of his business activity.

B. *Improvements*

Although we place greatest emphasis on the frequency and substantiality of sales over an extended time period, our decision in this instance is aided by the presence of taxpayer activity—particularly improvements—in the other *Winthrop* areas. Biedenharn vigorously improved its subdivisions, generally adding streets, drainage, sewerage, and utilities. These alterations are comparable to those in *Winthrop*, supra at 906, except that in the latter case taxpayer built five houses. We do not think that the construction of five houses in the context of *Winthrop's* 456 lot sales significantly distinguishes that taxpayer from Biedenharn.

C. *Solicitation and Advertising Efforts*

Substantial, frequent sales and improvements such as we have encountered in this case will usually conclude the capital gains issue against taxpayer. Thus, on the basis of our analysis to this point, we would have little hesitation in finding that taxpayer held "primarily for sale" in the "ordinary course of [his] trade or business." "[T]he flexing of commercial muscles with frequency and continuity, design and effect" of which *Winthrop* spoke, supra at 911, is here a reality. This reality is further buttressed by Biedenharn's sales efforts, including those carried on through brokers. Minimizing the importance of its own sales activities, taxpayer points repeatedly to its steady avoidance of advertising or other solicitation of customers. Plaintiff directs our attention to stipulations detailing the population growth of Monroe and testimony outlining the economic forces which made Hardtimes Plantation attractive residential property and presumably eliminated the need for sales exertions. We have no quarrel with plaintiff's description of this familiar process of suburban expansion, but we cannot accept the legal inferences which taxpayer would have us draw.

The Circuit's recent decisions in *Thompson*, supra at 124–26, and *Winthrop*, supra at 912, implicitly recognize that even one inarguably in the real estate business need not engage in promotional exertions in the face of a favorable market. As such, we do not always require a showing of active solicitation where "business ... [is] good, indeed brisk," *Thompson,* supra at 124, and where other *Winthrop* factors make obvious taxpayer's ordinary trade or business status. Plainly, this represents a sensible approach. In cases such as *Biedenharn,* the sale of a few lots and the construction of the first homes, albeit not, as in *Winthrop,* by the taxpayer, as well as the building of roads, addition of utilities, and staking off of the other subdivided parcels constitute a highly visible form of advertising. Prospective home buyers drive by the advantageously located property, see the development activities, and are as surely put on notice of the availability of lots as if the owner had erected large signs announcing "residential property for sale." We do not by this evaluation automatically neutralize advertising or solicitation as a factor in our analysis. This form of inherent notice is not present in all land sales, especially where the property is not so valuably located, is not subdivided into small lots, and is not improved. Moreover, inherent notice represents only one band of the solicitation spectrum. Media utilization and personal initiatives remain material components of this criterion. When present, they call for greater Government oriented emphasis on *Winthrop's* solicitation factor.

D. *Brokerage Activities*

In evaluating Biedenharn's solicitation activities, we need not confine ourselves to the *Thompson-Winthrop* theory of brisk sales without organizational efforts. Unlike in *Thompson* and *Winthrop* where no one undertook overt solicitation efforts, the Realty Company hired brokers who, using media and on site advertising, worked vigorously on taxpayer's behalf. We do not believe that the employment of brokers should shield plaintiff from ordinary income treatment. Their activities should at least in discounted form be attributed to Biedenharn. To the contrary, taxpayer argues that "one who is not already in the trade or business of selling real estate does not enter such business when he employs a broker who acts as an independent contractor. Fahs v. Crawford, 161 F.2d 315 (5 Cir.1947); Smith v. Dunn, 224 F.2d 353 (5 Cir.1955)." Without presently entangling ourselves in a dispute as to the differences between an agent and an independent contractor, we find the cases cited distinguishable from the instant circumstances. In both *Fahs* and *Smith,* the taxpayer turned the entire property over to brokers, who, having been granted total responsibility, made all decisions including the setting of sales prices. In comparison, Biedenharn determined original prices and general credit policy. Moreover, the Realty Company did not make all the sales in question through brokers as did taxpayers in *Fahs* and *Smith.* Biedenharn sold the Bayou DeSiard and Biedenharn Estates lots and may well have sold some of the Oak Park land. In other words, unlike *Fahs* and *Smith,* Biedenharn's brokers did not so completely take charge of the whole of the Hardtimes sales as to permit the Realty Company to wall itself off legally from their activities.

E. *Additional Taxpayer Contentions*

Plaintiff presents a number of other contentions and supporting facts for our consideration. Although we set out these arguments and briefly discuss them, their impact, in the face of those factors examined above, must be minimal. Taxpayer emphasizes that its profits from real estate sales averaged only 11.1% in each of the years in controversy, compared to 52.4% in *Winthrop*. Whatever the percentage, plaintiff would be hard pressed to deny the substantiality of its Hardtimes sales in absolute terms (the subdivided lots alone brought in over one million dollars) or, most importantly, to assert that its real estate business was too insignificant to constitute a separate trade or business.

The relatively modest income share represented by Biedenharn's real property dispositions stems not from a failure to engage in real estate sales activities but rather from the comparatively large profit attributable to the Company's 1965 ($649,231.34) and 1966 ($688,840.82) stock sales. The fact of Biedenharn's holding, managing, and selling stock is not inconsistent with the existence of a separate realty business. If in the face of taxpayer's numerous real estate dealings this Court held otherwise, we would be sanctioning special treatment for those individuals and companies arranging their business activities so that the income accruing to real estate sales represents only a small fraction of the taxpaying entity's total gains.

Similarly, taxpayer observes that Biedenharn's manager devoted only 10% of his time to real estate dealings and then mostly to the company's rental properties. This fact does not negate the existence of sales activities. Taxpayer had a telephone listing, a shared business office, and a few part-time employees. Because, as discussed before, a strong seller's market existed, Biedenharn's sales required less than the usual solicitation efforts and therefore less than the usual time. Moreover, plaintiff, unlike taxpayers in *Winthrop*, supra, and *Thompson*, supra, hired brokers to handle many aspects of the Hardtimes transactions—thus further reducing the activity and time required of Biedenharn's employees.

Finally, taxpayer argues that it is entitled to capital gains since its enormous profits (74% to 97%) demonstrate a return based principally on capital appreciation and not on taxpayer's "merchandising" efforts. We decline the opportunity to allocate plaintiff's gain between long-term market appreciation and improvement related activities. Even if we undertook such an analysis and found the former element predominant, we would on the authority of *Winthrop*, supra at 907–908, reject plaintiff's contention which, in effect, is merely taxpayer's version of the Government's unsuccessful argument in that case.

IV.

The District Court found that "[t]axpayer is merely liquidating over a long period of time a substantial investment in the most advantageous method possible." 356 F.Supp. at 1336. In this view, the original investment intent is crucial, for it preserves the capital gains character of the transaction even in the face of normal real estate sales activities.

. . .

We reject the Government's sweeping contention that prior investment intent is always irrelevant. There will be instances where an initial investment purpose endures in controlling fashion notwithstanding continuing sales activity. We doubt that this aperture, where an active subdivider and improver receives capital gains, is very wide; yet we believe it exists. We would most generally find such an opening where the change from investment holding to sales activity results from unanticipated, externally induced factors which make impossible the continued pre-existing use of the realty. *Barrios Estate,* supra, is such a case. There the taxpayer farmed the land until drainage problems created by the newly completed intercoastal canal rendered the property agriculturally unfit. The Court found that taxpayer was "dispossessed of the farming operation through no act of her own." Supra at 518. Similarly, Acts of God, condemnation of part of one's property, new and unfavorable zoning regulations, or other events forcing alteration of taxpayer's plans create situations making possible subdivision and improvement as a part of a capital gains disposition.

. . .

Clearly, under the facts in this case, the distinction just elaborated undermines Biedenharn's reliance on original investment purpose. Taxpayer's change of purpose was entirely voluntary and therefore does not fall within the protected area. Moreover, taxpayer's original investment intent, *even if* considered a factor sharply supporting capital gains treatment, is so overwhelmed by the other *Winthrop* factors discussed supra, that that element can have no decisive effect. However wide the capital gains passageway through which a subdivider with former investment intent could squeeze, the Biedenharn Realty Company will never fit.

V.

The District Court, citing Malat v. Riddell, 1966, 383 U.S. 569, 86 S.Ct. 1030, 16 L.Ed.2d 102, stated that "the lots were not held . . . primarily for sale as that phrase was interpreted . . . in *Malat* . . . ." 356 F.Supp. at 1335. Finding that Biedenharn's primary purpose became holding for sale and consequently that *Malat* in no way alters our analysis here, we disagree with the District Court's conclusion. *Malat* was a brief per curiam in which the Supreme Court decided only that as used in Internal Revenue Code § 1221(1) the word "primarily" means "principally," "of first importance." The Supreme Court, remanding the case, did not analyze the facts or resolve the controversy which involved a real estate dealer who had purchased land and held it at the time of sale with the dual intention of developing it as rental property or selling it, depending on whichever proved to be the more profitable. In contrast, having substantially abandoned its investment and farming intent, Biedenharn was cloaked primarily in the garb of sales purpose when it disposed of the 38 lots here in controversy. With this change, the Realty Company lost the opportunity of coming within any dual purpose analysis.

We do not hereby condemn to ordinary income a taxpayer merely because, as is usually true, his principal intent at the exact moment of disposition is sales. Rather, we refuse capital gains treatment in those instances where over time there has been such a thoroughgoing change of purpose, as to make untenable a claim either of twin intent or continued primacy of investment purpose.

VI.

Having surveyed the Hardtimes terrain, we find no escape from ordinary income. The frequency and substantiality of sales over an extended time, the significant improvement of the basic subdivisions, the acquisition of additional properties, the use of brokers, and other less important factors persuasively combine to doom taxpayer's cause. Applying *Winthrop's* criteria, this case clearly falls within the ordinary income category delineated in that decision. In so concluding, we note that *Winthrop* does not represent the most extreme application of the overriding principle that "the definition of a capital asset must be narrowly applied and its exclusions interpreted broadly." Corn Products Refining Co. v. Commissioner of Internal Revenue, 1955, 350 U.S. 46, 52, 76 S.Ct. 20, 24, 100 L.Ed. 29, 35. ... The opinion of the District Court is reversed.

APPENDIX I

(Plaintiff's Answers to Interrogatory 26)

YEAR	GROSS SALES	NUMBER LOTS	YEAR	GROSS SALES	NUMBER LOTS
1923	1,900.00	4	1948	23,850.00	22
1924	1,050.00	2	1949	8,830.00	26
1925	7,442.38	18	1950	9,370.00	19
1926	11,184.00	29	1951	55,222.99	16
1927	9,619.25	52	1952	38,134.29	16
1928	49,390.55	37	1953	123,007.22	17
1929	35,810.25	55	1954	235,396.04	10
1930	8,473.00	24	1955	76,805.00	20
1931	5,930.00	18	1956	100,593.25	61
1932	none	none	1957	133,448.10	36
1933	520.00	2	1958	110,369.00	27
1934	5,970.00	8	1959	44,400.00	12
1935	2,639.00	7	1960	130,610.19	21
1936	2,264.00	3	1961	48,729.60	25
1937	14,071.00	8	1962	6,720.00	1
1938	1,009.00	3	1963	7,475.00	1
1939	5,558.00	10	1964	77,650.00	10
1940	3,252.00	4	1965	75,759.00	10
1941	2,490.00	3	1966	155,950.00	20
1942	6,714.00	9	1967	75,380.00	9
1943	6,250.00	12	1968	89,447.50	10
1944	9,250.00	38	1969	31,010.00	3
1945	15,495.00	20	1970	none	none
1946	12,732.58	29	1971	130,000.00	139
1947	38,310.00	169			

[The opinion of RONEY, J., specially concurring, is omitted.]

GEE, Circuit Judge, with whom BELL, COLEMAN, AINSWORTH and DYER, Circuit Judges, join, dissenting.

Viewing as incorrect the en banc majority's restatement of facts and law, I must respectfully dissent. I would adhere to the panel opinion, reported at 509 F.2d 171, which attempted to apply existing, controlling precedent in our circuit to the facts of this very close case as they were found by the district court. To obtain a different result, the majority has found it necessary to revise the law and refind the facts in important respects, as though the obtaining of capital gains treatment by this taxpayer in the three years in question were a catastrophe to be avoided at all costs.

First, in setting out the facts of this case, the majority summarily discounts a critical trial court factfinding without ruling it clearly erroneous. The majority rejects the district court's finding that taxpayer "is still farming a large part of the land," 356 F.Supp. at 1336, refinding the facts as being that taxpayer's tenant farmer "may" presently be farming the land, supra at 411, and that neither plaintiff nor the lower court claimed any dual purpose, id. at 423 n. 43. But the record affirmatively shows that the land has been and continues to be farmed, and the lower court specifically found multi-purpose use of the land.

Second, although insisting at one point that it only "resummarizes" the relevant case law, id. at 415 n. 23, the majority revises the old test by placing pre-eminent emphasis on sales activity and improvements, effectively eliminating the other factors enunciated in United States v. Winthrop, 417 F.2d 905 (5th Cir.1969). ...

To explain its emphasis on improvements, the majority stresses the similarity between taxpayer's improvements and those present in *Winthrop*. Supra at 417. But this comparison, too, is mistaken. The *Winthrop* court emphasized that property does not cease to be a capital asset merely because its increase in value was due in part to the taxpayer's efforts in making improvements, 417 F.2d at 907–09, quoting the same portion of Barrios' Estate v. Commissioner of Internal Revenue, 265 F.2d 517 (5th Cir.1959), that the panel in this case cited:

"The idea of selling a large tract of land in lots embraces necessarily the construction of streets for access to them, the provision of drainage and the furnishing of access to such a necessity as water. It is hardly conceivable that taxpayer could have sold a lot without doing these things."

Id. at 520, quoted with approval in Winthrop, 417 F.2d at 909, and Biedenharn, 509 F.2d at 174 (panel opinion). ...

NOTES

1. *Legislative History.* The phrase, "held by the taxpayer primarily for sale to customers in the ordinary course of his trade or business" did not appear in section 1221's original formulation, enacted in 1921, which withheld capital asset treatment from "stock in trade of a taxpayer or property of a kind which would properly be included in the inventory of the taxpayer if on hand at the close of the taxable year." Revenue Act of 1921, ch. 136, § 206(a)(6), 42 Stat. 233. Following standard accounting practice, which would not treat real property as inventory, the Commissioner took the position that real property could never be "stock in trade." In an effort to plug this gap, Congress in 1924 amended the exclusion to add "or property held by the taxpayer primarily for sale in the course of his trade or business." Revenue Act of 1924, ch. 234, § 208(a)(8), 43 Stat. 263. The words, "to customers" and "ordinary," were added in 1934 to make clear that stockbrokers trading on their own account were not in the trade or business of selling stocks. H.R.Rep. No. 1385, 73rd Cong.2d Sess. 22 (1934).

2. The concept of property held "primarily for sale to customers" was originally designed for personal property inventory and does not easily fit real property subject matter. Land, even when it is acquired

with marketing in mind, will characteristically be held for longer than typical stock in trade. As a consequence, changes in value are likely to be the result of general market changes as well as of specific marketing efforts. The problem, still unresolved, is to devise an approach to real property that will properly account for both these sources of change in value.

The investor-dealer conundrum has spawned an extensive literature. Among the better analyses are Brown, Individual Investment in Real Estate: Capital Gains Versus Ordinary Income, 34 Ann.N.Y.U.Tax L.Inst. 189 (1976); Sills, The "Dealer-Investor" Problem: Observations, Analysis, and Suggestions for Future Development, 2 J.Real Est.Tax. 51 (1975); Weiner, Real Property: For Connoisseurs of the Preposterous— When Is It a Capital Asset? 24 Clev.St.L.Rev. 573 (1975); Bernstein, "Primarily for Sale": A Semantic Snare, 20 Stan.L.Rev. 1093 (1968); Olson, Toward a Neutral Definition of "Trade or Business" in the Internal Revenue Code, 54 U.Cin.L.Rev. 1199 (1986); Comment, Trade or Business for the Full-Time, Active Investor: A Call For A Qualitative Standard, 29 Santa Clara L.Rev. 209 (1989).

3. *Malat* represents one phase in the struggle to bring meaning to section 1221 as applied to real property, and *Biedenharn* represents another. *Malat* was the easier of the two because the taxpayer's two purposes, investment and marketing, existed side by side, allowing the Court to say that "primarily" simply meant that one purpose predominated over the other. *Biedenharn* was harder because there the two purposes occurred consecutively—first investment, then marketing. Focussing on the purpose that was formed last, the court chose not to apply the "liquidation test," that had earlier flourished in the Fifth Circuit. Under that test, capital gains treatment was allowed if the property was acquired for an investment purpose, and if the taxpayer's marketing efforts in disposing of it involved no more than was reasonably necessary for the liquidation of a capital asset. See, for example, Goldberg v. Commissioner, 223 F.2d 709 (5th Cir.1955). Should one purpose be counted to the exclusion of another? Should weight be given to the chronological order in which the motives are formed?

Biedenharn's chronological approach, discounting the taxpayer's earlier motive and focussing only on his final one, has been applied symmetrically. A series of Tax Court decisions allowed capital asset treatment in circumstances in which the taxpayer acquired the property for sale to customers in the ordinary course of business as a subdivision development and subsequently changed his purpose, disposing of the land as a single, unimproved unit. See, for example, Maddux Constr. Co. v. Comm'r, 54 T.C. 1278 (1970); Estate of Walter K. Dean v. Comm'r, 34 T.C.M. 631 (1975).

4. Judge Goldberg recast the *Biedenharn* analysis four years later in Suburban Realty Co. v. United States, 615 F.2d 171 (5th Cir.), cert. denied, 449 U.S. 920, 101 S.Ct. 318, 66 L.Ed.2d 147 (1980), an action filed by the taxpayer for a tax refund. The question there, "put into

the *Biedenharn* framework," was, "when a taxpayer engages in frequent and substantial sales over a period of years, but undertakes no development activity with respect to parts of a parcel of land, and engages in no solicitation or advertising efforts or brokerage activities, under what circumstances is income derived from sales of undeveloped parts of the parcel ordinary income?"   615 F.2d at 176.   Judge Goldberg recognized that taxpayer "Suburban's case is at once more favorable to the taxpayer than Biedenharn's and less so.   It is more favorable because, *with respect to the particular parcels of land here at issue*, it is undisputed that Suburban undertook no development or subdivision activity.   It is less favorable because Biedenharn was continually engaged in business activities other than real estate sales, whereas Suburban was for many years doing little else."   615 F.2d at 177 (Emphasis in original).

Judge Goldberg recognized, too, that if the court followed "the *Biedenharn* framework alone, we would be left with yet another essentially *ad hoc* decision to be made."   He turned instead to the plain language of section 1221 and concluded that "the principal inquiries demanded by the statute are:

1) was taxpayer engaged in a trade or business, and, if so, what business?

2) was taxpayer holding the property primarily for sale in that business?

3) were the sales contemplated by taxpayer 'ordinary' in the course of that business?"

Judge Goldberg indicated no disagreement "with anything decided by the recent Fifth Circuit decisions.   *Biedenharn* guides our decision-making process.   But after the relevant three independent statutory inquiries are pried apart, it becomes apparent that the central dispute in *Biedenharn* was a narrow one: was Biedenharn Realty Company holding the land in dispute 'primarily for sale?'   The majority, applying the *Winthrop* factors, decided this question in the affirmative.   The dissent, emphasizing the continuing farming activities being conducted by Biedenharn, see *Biedenharn*, 526 F.2d at 425, n. 5, 426 (dissenting opinion), disagreed as to this conclusion."   615 F.2d at 178.

Judge Goldberg then applied this three-part analysis to the facts before the court.   First, the court concluded that Suburban was engaged in the real estate business.   ("It is clear to us that Suburban engaged in a sufficient quantity of activity to be in the business of selling real estate.   Suburban's sales were continuous and substantial.")   Second, the court traced Suburban's primary holding purpose over the entire course of its ownership of the property and concluded that for most, if not all, of the holding period, "Suburban's primary holding purpose was 'for sale'."   Third, the court found that these sales were "ordinary" in the course of Suburban's business, relying for this conclusion on an observation made in *Winthrop*:

The concept of normalcy requires for its application a chronology and a history to determine if the sales of lots to customers were the usual or a departure from the norm. History and chronology here combine to demonstrate that [taxpayer] did not sell his lots as an abnormal or unexpected event. [Taxpayer] began selling shortly after he acquired the land; he never used the land for any other purpose; and he continued this course of conduct over a number of years. Thus, the sales were . . . ordinary.

615 F.2d at 185–186. The court thus affirmed the decision of the district court dismissing Suburban's complaint and holding that gain on the sales in issue was taxable as ordinary income rather than as capital gain.

In Major Realty Corp. and Subsidiaries v. Commissioner of Internal Revenue, 749 F.2d 1483, 1488 (11th Cir.1985), the court noted that "[t]he most important factor [in determining whether realty sales are to customers in the ordinary course of business] is the frequency and substantiality of the taxpayer's sales." The court upheld the lower court's finding that the sale of the parcel in question was in the ordinary course of business. It relied on the fact that the taxpayer had sold 16% of the total value of the larger tract of which this parcel was a part over the prior two years, as well as on the substantial road, utility, and sewer improvements made by the taxpayer.

5. *Section 1237's Safe Harbor.* Section 1237, added to the Internal Revenue Code in 1954, was intended to provide subdividers with a safe harbor, offering capital asset treatment within narrowly prescribed limits. Among the conditions are that the taxpayer must have held the qualifying property for five years, must not have held it as inventory, and must not have made any substantial improvements that substantially enhanced the value of the lots sold.

Section 1237 has by all estimates been a dismal failure. Its terms have proved to be as fuzzy as those of section 1221, leaving developers largely in the dark as to the meaning of "substantial improvements," and "substantially enhanced." While regulations adopted under section 1237 offer some guidance, courts have felt free to ignore them, substituting their own notions of "substantial" for those of the Commissioner. See, for example, Kelley v. Commissioner, 281 F.2d 527 (9th Cir.1960). Also, the section does not permit full capital asset treatment and its requirements are so stringent that compliance would probably qualify the developer as an investor under section 1221, with full capital asset treatment, in any event. See generally, Chandler, The Failure of Section 1237 in Dealing with Sales of Subdivided Realty, 60 Minn.L.Rev. 275 (1976); Martin, Real Estate Taxation: Gaining Investor Status on Real Property Sales—Section 1237, 12 Real Estate Rev. 14 (Spring 1982).

6. Many apartment house owners, faced with the prospect of declining rental profits, have converted their properties to condominiums. Although some acted as dealers, promoting the conversion and selling

units one by one, others, in the years before the 1986 Tax Reform Act repealed the capital gains deduction, employed a variety of strategies in an attempt to get capital gains treatment for their profits. For an evaluation of some of these strategies, see Guerin, Condominium Conversions: An Analysis of Alternative Routes to Capital Gain Treatment, 1 Tax Law J. 1 (Winter 1982); Limberg, *Bradshaw* Provides Support and Guidelines for Capital Gains in Condominium Conversions, 11. Real Estate Tax. 328 (Summer, 1984).

7. *"Production of Income" or "Use in Trade or Business"?* Real property held for rental, rather than for investment or sale, raises classification problems of its own. Is the property held for the production of income, and thus within section 1221? Or is it held "for use in the trade or business," within section 1231? Although the distinction is narrow, its consequences are significant. Losses on the sale or exchange of property held for the production of income are capital losses, while those on the disposition of property used in trade or business are treated as ordinary losses. Characterization as section 1221 or 1231 property will also determine the availability and extent of loss carryovers under sections 1212 and 172.

In making the distinction, courts have generally used a definition of "trade or business" that the Supreme Court took from Bouvier's Law Dictionary and employed in a very different context: "that which occupies the time, attention, and labor of men for the purpose of a livelihood or profit." Flint v. Stone Tracy Co., 220 U.S. 107, 171, 31 S.Ct. 342, 55 L.Ed. 389 (1911). Under this formula, the ownership of several rental properties, with its consequent demands on the taxpayer's attention, has been held to constitute a trade or business. See Pinchot v. Commissioner, 113 F.2d 718 (2d Cir.1940). So has ownership of a single block of rental property, at least where its management involved a "necessarily regular and continuous activity." Gilford v. Commissioner, 201 F.2d 735, 736 (2d Cir.1953). See generally, Cottle v. Commissioner cf Internal Revenue, 89 T.C. 467 (1987) (where taxpayer purchased three apartment units to rehabilitate and lease but subsequently sold them due to changed conditions in the apartment complex, taxpayer entitled to capital gain treatment since he did not hold the units primarily for sale to customers but rather intended to use them for a new trade or business of renting apartments).

B. DEDUCTIONS: LEVERAGE, DEPRECIATION AND TAX SHELTER

The following materials describe the rise and fall of a system of real estate depreciation deductions and leveraging that permitted the sheltering of not only the taxpayer's income generated from the property itself but also income from other activities. This section first describes the golden age of real estate tax shelters and how they were structured. It then traces the various interim reforms of the system. The section concludes with the ultimate reform of—or requiem for?—tax shelters in the 1986 Tax Reform Act.

1. THE GOLDEN AGE OF TAX SHELTERS

RABINOWITZ, REAL ESTATE AND THE FEDERAL INCOME TAX: THE STATUS OF THE LAW TODAY

32d Annual N.Y.U. Tax Institute 1593, 1594–1598 (1974).

The ability to write off investment cost at a rapid rate has been a keystone of tax policy to encourage investment in general. In the case of real estate the significance of this incentive is greatly magnified by two factors: (1) The availability of institutional debt (mortgage) financing for purchase or development of realty—i.e., leveraged financing, and (2) recognition of that mortgage financing as part of an investor's depreciable basis in the property—i.e., "leveraged" depreciation.

The investor's tax basis in acquired property normally is his cost, which includes not only his own investment but any debt incurred to purchase or improve the property.[2] The Supreme Court has held that basis includes debt on which the investor has no personal liability.[3] Because institutional mortgage financing commonly furnishes from 75 percent to 95 percent of the funds necessary to acquire and develop real property, the tax basis of the property is ordinarily several times the amount of the investor's cash investment. Such mortgage financing is generally for a term of 25 to 30 years and, in the case of subsidized housing, can extend to 40 or even 50 years. Financing terms are frequently on a self-liquidating basis, although some loans provide for payment of an unamortized "balloon" at maturity. As a result, in the initial years of the investment, most of debt service is applied to the payment of deductible interest. During this period, the annual allowance for depreciation, which is calculated on the investor's basis in the property, may be quite large. Because depreciation is a deduction which may be offset against the income generated by the property, the excess of depreciation over mortgage amortization, in effect, "shelters" income from taxation generated by the property. Further, to the extent that the annual depreciation deduction exceeds the annual taxable income of the property, the property will produce a loss for tax purposes which may be used to offset or shelter the taxpayer's other income.

For example, assume that a taxpayer can obtain 90 percent financing for a $10,000,000 project, of which $1,000,000 represents the cost of land and $9,000,000 represents the cost of the building. The project has a useful life, for tax purposes, of 25 years. If the loan carries a 9 percent interest rate with a 10 percent constant payment, the first

---

2. This includes not only funds borrowed by the investor, but any debt to which the property is subject at the time of acquisition.

3. Crane v. Comm'r, 331 U.S. 1 (1947).

year's debt service will be $900,000, of which $810,000 represents deductible interest and $90,000 represents amortization of principal. Further, assuming that the property, after debt service, generates $200,000 of income, and that the taxpayer is using the straight-line method of depreciation, the taxpayer will be considered to have received $290,000 of taxable income, against which he may deduct $360,-000 of depreciation. For tax purposes, he has a net loss of $70,000 with respect to the property, which he may use as a deduction against his other income.

The Government itself has encouraged real estate investment through the use of tax incentives. Government-subsidized loans often permit an investor to borrow amounts in excess of those otherwise available from private lenders. This significantly increases the ratio of depreciation deductions to the taxpayer's cash investment. As these loans have longer maturities than private financing, the amortization portion of the investor's debt service is decreased. As a result, a larger percentage of the funds utilized to service the debt constitutes deductible interest. The combination of greater leverage and longer maturities increases the tax loss available to the investor from the property. This is particularly true of projects to rehabilitate or build low-income rental housing, where the investor must agree to a maximum return on his investment as a condition of obtaining the loan. Often such a project has only minimal economic value as an investment. For a high bracket taxpayer, the principal value of a project qualifying for a Government-subsidized loan is in its tax benefits.

Another method of financing investment has been the ability of investors to separate the ownership of the land underlying a building from the ownership of the building itself. Institutional investors, such as real estate investment trusts, are willing to purchase a fee interest in the land, leasing it to the building owner for a term exceeding the useful life of the building, as determined for tax purposes. This permits the investor to further leverage his investment by financing the entire cost of the land. More significantly, it further enables him to depreciate 100 percent of his investment which is entirely in the depreciable building. Because the investor, in using this technique, subordinates his interest to both the usual mortgage financing and the interest of the ground lessor, the land sale-leaseback increases his financial risk with respect to the investment. The substantial tax benefits provide a major offset against this risk.

To illustrate: Assume an office building will cost $7,950,000 to build and the land underlying the building is worth $1,600,000. If the land is sold for its value in a sale-leaseback transaction in which the land is subordinated to the mortgage, the investor will be able to obtain a mortgage of $7,200,000 to build and carry the building because the value of the land will be taken into account in determining the amount of the mortgage. In this way, the investor will be required to put up only $750,000 of equity of the $7,950,000 total investment in the building. Assuming that the building has a 30-year useful life and it is depreciated on the 150 percent declining balance method, the investor will obtain more than $402,400 annually in depreciation deductions on his $750,000 investment.

NOTES

1. *Computing the Depreciation Deduction.* The depreciation deduction is probably the single greatest boon—some would say boondoggle—available to owners of income or business property. Unlike the deductions for interest, real property taxes and maintenance, each of which reflects an equivalent cash outlay by the taxpayer, section 167's depreciation provisions enable taxpayers to take deductions without any matching cash outlay. So long as depreciation deductions (tax deductions without corresponding cash expenditures) exceed amortization of any debt on the property (cash expenditures without corresponding tax deductions), the investment will provide a "tax shelter" for the taxpayer's income.

The taxpayer's first step in computing the depreciation deduction is to determine the basis of her investment by aggregating the cost of the land and improvements, including the amount of any debt secured by the property, and transaction costs such as broker's commissions, title insurance premiums and fees for survey, legal, appraisal and escrow services. The next step is to identify that part of the investment's basis that is allocable to depreciable assets. (Say that the taxpayer's overall cost is $650,000, with $200,000 of that allocable to the land, which is not depreciable, and $450,000 to the improvements, which are depreciable.) Next, she must assign a useful life to the improvements (say 20 years) and a salvage value for the improvements at the end of the useful life (say $50,000). By subtracting salvage value from total improvement value ($450,000 minus $50,000) she arrives at the depreciable basis that she can write off over the period of the asset's useful life. (Thus in the example given the taxpayer can take depreciation deductions totaling $400,000 over 20 years.)

The taxpayer's next step is to choose a depreciation method—straight line or declining balance. The choice can have a significant impact on the extent and timing of tax shelter. The straight line method of depreciation prorates the improvement's depreciable basis equally over its useful life. (In the example given, this would mean $400,000 divided by a 20-year useful life, or a $20,000 depreciation deduction each year.)

Under the declining balance method, a constant rate (a predetermined multiple of the straight line rate) is applied each year to a decreasing depreciable basis consisting of the original depreciable basis, diminished each year by the total amount of depreciation taken in the preceding years. While salvage value is for these purposes included in depreciable basis, the improvement cannot be depreciated below its salvage value. (In the example given, the straight line rate is $20,000/$400,000 or 5%. Thus under the "double declining balance" method, twice that rate, or 10% is applied to $450,000 to determine the first year's depreciation, or $45,000. In the second year, depreciation is [$450,000 minus $45,000] × 10% or $40,500; in the third year it is [$405,000 minus $40,500] × 10% or $36,450.) Use of the 175% declining balance method entails only a change in the number by which the straight line rate is multiplied from 2 to 1.75.

A comparative chart will give you some idea of the advantages and disadvantages of each method to the taxpayer and to the Treasury. The figures are based on the example already used—a $450,000 improvement with a salvage value of $50,000 and a useful life of 20 years.

| | STRAIGHT LINE | | DOUBLE DECLINING BALANCE | |
YEAR	ANNUAL DEDUCTION	TOTAL COST RECOVERED	ANNUAL DEDUCTION	TOTAL COST RECOVERED
1	$20,000	$20,000	$45,000	$45,000
2	20,000	40,000	40,500	85,500
3	20,000	60,000	36,450	121,950
4	20,000	80,000	32,805	154,755
5	20,000	100,000	29,525	184,280
6	20,000	120,000	26,572	210,852
7	20,000	140,000	23,915	234,767
8	20,000	160,000	21,523	256,290
9	20,000	180,000	19,371	275,661
10	20,000	200,000	17,434	293,095
11	20,000	220,000	15,691	308,786
12	20,000	240,000	14,121	322,907
13	20,000	260,000	12,709	335,616
14	20,000	280,000	11,438	347,054
15	20,000	300,000	10,295	357,349
16	20,000	320,000	9,265	366,614
17	20,000	340,000	8,339	374,953
18	20,000	360,000	7,505	382,458
19	20,000	380,000	6,754	389,212
20	20,000	400,000	6,079	395,291

Straight line, though it is the most conservative method of depreciation, in fact accelerates the taxpayer's true depreciation. Mainly, this is because useful life is not measured objectively, by reference to physical wear and tear and market value, but rather by reference to the asset's particular utility to the taxpayer's business or investment interests. Even apart from general increases in real estate values during the asset's holding period, a fully depreciated asset will probably have a market value well over its salvage value.

Because depreciation deductions are subtracted from the property's basis, they will be partially offset by an increase in the gain realized when the taxpayer disposes of the property. (In the example above, the taxpayer, having taken a total of $60,000 in depreciation deductions [$20,000 + $20,000 + $20,000] over three years, must reduce her basis by that amount, leaving a basis of $590,000 [$650,000 − $60,000]. If the taxpayer sold the property at the end of the third year for no more than the $650,000 she paid for it, she would have to pay tax on a capital gain of $60,000—the difference between amount realized, $650,000, and adjusted basis, or $590,000.) Before the 1986 Tax Reform Act's repeal of the preferential capital gains rate, the depreciation deduction's main advantage to the taxpayer was that it gave her the economic benefit of present deductions against ordinary income while requiring only that she pay for this benefit by recognizing future gains taxed at the more favorable capital gains rate.

On the depreciation deduction generally, see Tucker, Real Estate Depreciation: A Fresh Examination of the Basic Rules, 6 J. Real Est.Tax. 101 (1979); McKee, The Real Estate Tax Shelter: A Computerized Exposè, 57 Va.L.Rev. 521 (1971); Calkins & Updegraft, Tax Shelters, 26 Tax Law. 493 (1973). The justification for accelerated depreciation deductions is the subject of a lively debate in Kahn, Accelerated Depreciation—Tax Expenditure or Proper Allowance for Measuring Net Income? 78 Mich.L.Rev. 1 (1979); Blum, Accelerated Depreciation: A Proper Allowance for Measuring Net Income?!!, 78 Mich.L.Rev. 1172 (1980); Kahn, Accelerated Depreciation Revisited—A Reply to Professor Blum, 78 Mich.L.Rev. 1185 (1980).

2. *Leveraged Depreciation.* Depreciation tax shelters are most advantageous to taxpayers who finance their acquisition of the depreciable property. Because the amount of mortgage financing will be included in the taxpayer's depreciable basis, it represents a tax-free means to inflate the depreciation deduction—a phenomenon called "leveraged depreciation." Thus, the taxpayer in note 1, above, may have financed her purchase of the $650,000 parcel with a $600,000 mortgage loan, putting up only $50,000 of her own cash. As a result, for a total investment of $50,000, the taxpayer using the straight line method is able to write off $20,000 in depreciation deductions each year for 20 years; if she is in the 50% bracket, this means an extra $10,000 cash in her pocket every year for 20 years. Use of the double declining balance method will enable the taxpayer to write off $45,000—almost her complete investment—in the first year.

The taxpayer need not be personally obligated on the debt encumbering her property for the debt to be included in her basis. Crane v. Commissioner, 331 U.S. 1, 67 S.Ct. 1047, 91 L.Ed. 1301 (1947). This rule, which is particularly congenial to the real estate market where so much financing is nonrecourse, may lead to abuses. Consider the following example: Taxpayer acquires an office building and underlying land with an aggregate market value of $2,500,000 ($500,000 allocable to land, $2,000,000 allocable to the improvement). She buys the land for $1,000,000, giving seller a 10-year, interest-only purchase money mortgage, at 5% interest, with a $1,000,000, balloon at the end. She acquires the building in fee for $5,000,000, giving the seller a purchase money mortgage for that amount. The mortgage is for ten years, is nonrecourse, interest only, with an interest rate of 5% and a $5,000,000 balloon payment of principal at the end of ten years. The taxpayer's net income from the property is $300,000, just enough to cover her mortgage payments. Because these payments are fully deductible, this aspect of the transaction is a wash. If the building has a twenty-five year useful life and no salvage value, the taxpayer, using straight line depreciation, will have an annual depreciation deduction available for setoff against other income of $200,000 ($5,000,000/25). This is two and one-half times the deduction she would have had if she had given a mortgage not for $5,000,000, but for the building's market value of $2,000,000. Presumably the taxpayer will default and abandon the property just as the mortgage principal becomes due, leaving the seller with his security, worth $2,500,000 (assuming no change in market value) and, for having participated in the charade, receipt over the ten years of an above-market return on his mortgage notes. Compare Manuel D. Mayerson, 47 T.C. 340 (1966).

Will such an abuse be tolerated? In *Crane* the Supreme Court expressly noted that "if the value of the property is less than the amount of the mortgage, a mortgagor who is not personally liable cannot realize a benefit equal to the mortgage. Consequently, a different problem might be encountered where a mortgagor abandoned the property or transferred it subject to the mortgage without receiving boot. That is not this case." 331 U.S. at 14 n. 37, 67 S.Ct. at 1054 n. 37. How should such a mortgage debt be accounted for? Is it really debt? These questions are considered, respectively, in the next two cases. The 1986 Tax Reform Act took a different route to preventing this abuse by partially subjecting real property investments to the Internal Revenue Code's "at risk" provisions. See p. 640, below.

COMMISSIONER OF INTERNAL REVENUE v. TUFTS

Supreme Court of the United States, 1983.
461 U.S. 300, 103 S.Ct. 1826, 75 L.Ed.2d 863.

Justice BLACKMUN delivered the opinion of the Court.

Over 35 years ago, in Crane v. Commissioner, 331 U.S. 1, 67 S.Ct. 1947, 91 L.Ed. 1301 (1947), this Court ruled that a taxpayer, who sold property encumbered by a nonrecourse mortgage (the amount of the mortgage being less than the property's value), must include the unpaid balance of the mortgage in the computation of the amount the taxpayer realized on the sale. The case now before us presents the question whether the same rule applies when the unpaid amount of the nonrecourse mortgage exceeds the fair market value of the property sold.

I

On August 1, 1970, respondent Clark Pelt, a builder, and his wholly owned corporation, respondent Clark, Inc., formed a general partnership. The purpose of the partnership was to construct a 120-unit apartment complex in Duncanville, Tex., a Dallas suburb. Neither Pelt nor Clark, Inc., made any capital contribution to the partnership. Six days later, the partnership entered into a mortgage loan agreement with the Farm & Home Savings Association (F & H). Under the agreement, F & H was committed for a $1,851,500 loan for the complex. In return, the partnership executed a note and a deed of trust in favor of F & H. The partnership obtained the loan on a nonrecourse basis: neither the partnership nor its partners assumed any personal liability for repayment of the loan. Pelt later admitted four friends and relatives, respondents Tufts, Steger, Stephens, and Austin, as general partners. None of them contributed capital upon entering the partnership.

The construction of the complex was completed in August 1971. During 1971, each partner made small capital contributions to the partnership; in 1972, however, only Pelt made a contribution. The total of the partners' capital contributions was $44,212. In each tax year, all partners claimed as income tax deductions their allocable shares of ordinary losses and depreciation. The deductions taken by the partners in 1971 and 1972 totalled $439,972. Due to these contributions and deductions, the partnership's adjusted basis in the property in August 1972 was $1,455,740.

In 1971 and 1972, major employers in the Duncanville area laid off significant numbers of workers. As a result, the partnership's rental income was less than expected, and it was unable to make the payments due on the mortgage. Each partner, on August 28, 1972, sold his partnership interest to an unrelated third party, Fred Bayles. As consideration, Bayles agreed to reimburse each partner's sale expenses up to $250; he also assumed the nonrecourse mortgage.

On the date of transfer, the fair market value of the property did not exceed $1,400,000. Each partner reported the sale on his federal income tax return and indicated that a partnership loss of $55,740 had been sustained.[1] The Commissioner of Internal Revenue, on audit, determined that the sale resulted in a partnership capital gain of approximately $400,000. His theory was that the partnership had realized the full amount of the nonrecourse obligation.[2]

Relying on Millar v. Commissioner, 577 F.2d 212, 215 (CA3), cert. denied, 439 U.S. 1046, 99 S.Ct. 721, 58 L.Ed.2d 704 (1978), the United States Tax Court, in an unreviewed decision, upheld the asserted deficiencies. 70 T.C. 756 (1978). The United States Court of Appeals for the Fifth Circuit reversed. 651 F.2d 1058 (1981). That court expressly disagreed with the *Millar* analysis, and, in limiting Crane v.

1. The loss was the difference between the adjusted basis, $1,455,740 and the fair market value of the property, $1,400,000. On their individual tax returns, the partners did not claim deductions for their respective shares of this loss. In their petitions to the Tax Court, however, the partners did claim the loss.

2. The Commissioner determined the partnership's gain on the sale by subtracting the adjusted basis, $1,455,740, from the liability assumed by Bayles, $1,851,500. Of the resulting figure, $395,760, the Commissioner treated $348,661 as capital gain, pursuant to § 741 of the Internal Revenue Code of 1954, 26 U.S.C. § 741, and $47,099 as ordinary gain under the recapture provisions of § 1250 of the Code. The application of § 1250 in determining the character of the gain is not at issue here.

Commissioner, supra, to its facts, questioned the theoretical underpinnings of the *Crane* decision. We granted certiorari to resolve the conflict. 456 U.S. 960, 102 S.Ct. 2034, 72 L.Ed.2d 483 (1982).

II

Section 752(d) of the Internal Revenue Code of 1954, 26 U.S.C. § 752(d), specifically provides that liabilities incurred in the sale or exchange of a partnership interest are to "be treated in the same manner as liabilities in connection with the sale or exchange of property not associated with partnerships." Section 1001 governs the determination of gains and losses on the disposition of property. Under § 1001(a), the gain or loss from a sale or other disposition of property is defined as the difference between "the amount realized" on the disposition and the property's adjusted basis. Subsection (b) of § 1001 defines "amount realized": "The amount realized from the sale or other disposition of property shall be the sum of any money received plus the fair market value of the property (other than money) received." At issue is the application of the latter provision to the disposition of property encumbered by a nonrecourse mortgage of an amount in excess of the property's fair market value.

A

In Crane v. Commissioner, supra, this Court took the first and controlling step toward the resolution of this issue. Beulah B. Crane was the sole beneficiary under the will of her deceased husband. At his death in January 1932, he owned an apartment building that was then mortgaged for an amount which proved to be equal to its fair market value, as determined for federal estate tax purposes. The widow, of course, was not personally liable on the mortgage. She operated the building for nearly seven years, hoping to turn it into a profitable venture; during that period, she claimed income tax deductions for depreciation, property taxes, interest, and operating expenses, but did not make payments upon the mortgage principal. In computing her basis for the depreciation deductions, she included the full amount of the mortgage debt. In November 1938, with her hopes unfulfilled and the mortgagee threatening foreclosure, Mrs. Crane sold the building. The purchaser took the property subject to the mortgage and paid Crane $3,000; of that amount, $500 went for the expenses of the sale.

Crane reported a gain of $2,500 on the transaction. She reasoned that her basis in the property was zero (despite her earlier depreciation deductions based on including the amount of the mortgage) and that the amount she realized from the sale was simply the cash she received. The Commissioner disputed this claim. He asserted that Crane's basis in the property, under § 113(a)(5) of the Revenue Act of 1938, 52 Stat. 490 (the current version is § 1014 of the 1954 Code, as amended, 26 U.S.C. § 1014 (1976 ed. and Supp. V)), was the property's fair market value at the time of her husband's death, adjusted for depreciation in the interim, and that the amount realized was the net cash received plus the amount of the outstanding mortgage assumed by the purchaser.

In upholding the Commissioner's interpretation of § 113(a)(5) of the 1938 Act,[3] the Court observed that to regard merely the taxpayer's equity in the property as her basis would lead to depreciation deductions less than the actual physical deterioration of the property, and would require the basis to be recomputed with each payment on the mortgage. The Court rejected Crane's claim that any loss due to depreciation belonged to the mortgagee. The effect of the Court's ruling was that the taxpayer's basis was the value of the property undiminished by the mortgage.

The Court next proceeded to determine the amount realized under § 111(b) of the 1938 Act, 52 Stat. 484 (the current version is § 1001(b) of the 1954 Code, 26 U.S.C. § 1001(b)). In order to avoid the "absurdity," see 331 U.S., at 13, 67 S.Ct., at 1054, of Crane's realizing only $2,500 on the sale of property worth over a quarter of a million dollars, the Court treated the amount realized as it had treated basis, that is, by including the outstanding value of the mortgage. To do otherwise would have permitted Crane to recognize a tax loss unconnected with any actual economic loss. The Court refused to construe one section of the Revenue Act so as "to frustrate the Act as a whole." Ibid.

Crane, however, insisted that the nonrecourse nature of the mortgage required different treatment. The Court, for two reasons, disagreed. First, excluding the nonrecourse debt from the amount realized would result in the same absurdity and frustration of the Code. Second, the Court concluded that Crane obtained an economic benefit from the purchaser's assumption of the mortgage identical to the benefit conferred by the cancellation of personal debt. Because the value of the property in that case exceeded the amount of the mortgage, it was in Crane's economic interest to treat the mortgage as a personal obligation; only by so doing could she realize upon sale the appreciation in her equity represented by the $2,500 boot. The purchaser's assumption of the liability thus resulted in a taxable economic benefit to her, just as if she had been given, in addition to the boot, a sum of cash sufficient to satisfy the mortgage.[4]

---

3. Section 113(a)(5) defined the basis of "property ... acquired by ... devise ... or by the decedent's estate from the decedent" as "the fair market value of such property at the time of such acquisition." The Court interpreted the term "property" to refer to the physical land and buildings owned by Crane or the aggregate of her rights to control and dispose of them. 331 U.S., at 6, 67 S.Ct., at 1050.

4. Crane also argued that even if the statute required the inclusion of the amount of the nonrecourse debt, that amount was not Sixteenth Amendment income because the overall transaction had

been "by all dictates of common sense ... a ruinous disaster." Brief for Petitioner in Crane v. Commissioner, O.T.1946, No. 68, p. 51. The Court noted, however, that Crane had been entitled to and actually took depreciation deductions for nearly seven years. To allow her to exclude sums on which those deductions were based from the calculation of her taxable gain would permit her "a double deduction ... on the same loss of assets." The Sixteenth Amendment, it was said, did not require that result. 331 U.S., at 15–16, 67 S.Ct., at 1055.

In a footnote, pertinent to the present case, the Court observed:

"Obviously, if the value of the property is less than the amount of the mortgage, a mortgagor who is not personally liable cannot realize a benefit equal to the mortgage. Consequently, a different problem might be encountered where a mortgagor abandoned the property or transferred it subject to the mortgage without receiving boot. That is not this case." Id., at 14, n. 37, 67 S.Ct., at 1054–55, n. 37.

B

This case presents that unresolved issue. We are disinclined to overrule *Crane,* and we conclude that the same rule applies when the unpaid amount of the nonrecourse mortgage exceeds the value of the property transferred. *Crane* ultimately does not rest on its limited theory of economic benefit; instead, we read *Crane* to have approved the Commissioner's decision to treat a nonrecourse mortgage in this context as a true loan. This approval underlies *Crane's* holding that the amount of the nonrecourse liability is to be included in calculating both the basis and the amount realized on disposition. That the amount of the loan exceeds the fair market value of the property thus becomes irrelevant.

When a taxpayer receives a loan, he incurs an obligation to repay that loan at some future date. Because of this obligation, the loan proceeds do not qualify as income to the taxpayer. When he fulfills the obligation, the repayment of the loan likewise has no effect on his tax liability.

Another consequence to the taxpayer from this obligation occurs when the taxpayer applies the loan proceeds to the purchase price of property used to secure the loan. Because of the obligation to repay, the taxpayer is entitled to include the amount of the loan in computing his basis in the property; the loan, under § 1012, is part of the taxpayer's cost of the property. Although a different approach might have been taken with respect to a nonrecourse mortgage loan [5], the Commissioner has chosen to accord it the same treatment he gives to a recourse mortgage loan. The Court approved that choice in *Crane,* and

---

5. The Commissioner might have adopted the theory, implicit in Crane's contentions, that a nonrecourse mortgage is not true debt, but, instead, is a form of joint investment by the mortgagor and the mortgagee. On this approach, nonrecourse debt would be considered a contingent liability, under which the mortgagor's payments on the debt gradually increase his interest in the property while decreasing that of the mortgagee. Because the taxpayer's investment in the property would not include the nonrecourse debt, the taxpayer would not be permitted to include that debt in basis.

We express no view as to whether such an approach would be consistent with the statutory structure and, if so, and Crane were not on the books, whether that approach would be preferred over Crane's analysis. We note only that the Crane Court's resolution of the basis issue presumed that when property is purchased with proceeds from a nonrecourse mortgage, the purchaser becomes the sole owner of the property. Under the Crane approach, the mortgagee is entitled to no portion of the basis. The nonrecourse mortgage is part of the mortgagor's investment in the property, and does not constitute a coinvestment by the mortgagee.

the respondents do not challenge it here. The choice and its resultant benefits to the taxpayer are predicated on the assumption that the mortgage will be repaid in full.

When encumbered property is sold or otherwise disposed of and the purchaser assumes the mortgage, the associated extinguishment of the mortgagor's obligation to repay is accounted for in the computation of the amount realized. Because no difference between recourse and nonrecourse obligations is recognized in calculating basis,[7] *Crane* teaches that the Commissioner may ignore the nonrecourse nature of the obligation in determining the amount realized upon disposition of the encumbered property. He thus may include in the amount realized the amount of the nonrecourse mortgage assumed by the purchaser. The rationale for this treatment is that the original inclusion of the amount of the mortgage in basis rested on the assumption that the mortgagor incurred an obligation to repay. Moreover, this treatment balances the fact that the mortgagor originally received the proceeds of the nonrecourse loan tax-free on the same assumption. Unless the outstanding amount of the mortgage is deemed to be realized, the mortgagor effectively will have received untaxed income at the time the loan was extended and will have received an unwarranted increase in the basis of his property.[8] The Commissioner's interpretation of § 1001(b) in this fashion cannot be said to be unreasonable.

C

The Commissioner in fact has applied this rule even when the fair market value of the property falls below the amount of the nonrecourse obligation. Treas.Reg. § 1.1001–2(b), 26 CFR § 1.1001–2(b) (1982); Rev. Rul. 76–111, 1976–1 Cum.Bull. 214. Because the theory on which the rule is based applies equally in this situation, we have no reason, after *Crane*, to question this treatment.[11]

7. The Commissioner's choice in *Crane* "laid the foundation stone of most tax shelters," Bittker, Tax Shelters, Nonrecourse Debt, and the *Crane* Case, 33 Tax.L.Rev. 277, 283 (1978), by permitting taxpayers who bear no risk to take deductions on depreciable property. Congress recently has acted to curb this avoidance device by forbidding a taxpayer to take depreciation deductions in excess of amounts he has at risk in the investment. Pub.L. 94–455, § 204(a), 90 Stat. 1531 (1976), 26 U.S.C. § 465; Pub.L. 95–600, §§ 201–204, 92 Stat. 2814–2817 (1978), 26 U.S.C. § 465(a) (1976 ed., Supp. V). Real estate investments, however, are exempt from this prohibition. § 465(c)(3)(D) (1976 ed., Supp. V). Although this congressional action may foreshadow a day when nonrecourse and recourse debts will be treated differently, neither Congress nor the Commissioner has sought to alter *Crane's* rule of including nonrecourse liability in both basis and the amount realized.

8. Although the *Crane* rule has some affinity with the tax benefit rule, see Bittker, supra, at 282; Del Cotto, Sales and Other Dispositions of Property Under Section 1001: The Taxable Event, Amount Realized and Related Problems of Basis, 26 Buffalo L.Rev. 219, 323–324 (1977), the analysis we adopt is different. Our analysis applies even in the situation in which no deductions are taken. It focuses on the obligation to repay and its subsequent extinguishment, not on the taking and recovery of deductions. See generally Note, 82 Colum.L.Rev., at 1526–1529.

11. Professor Wayne G. Barnett, as *amicus* in the present case, argues that the liability and property portions of the transaction should be accounted for separately. Under his view, there was a transfer of the property for $1.4 million, and there was a

Respondents received a mortgage loan with the concomitant obligation to repay by the year 2012. The only difference between that mortgage and one on which the borrower is personally liable is that the mortgagee's remedy is limited to foreclosing on the securing property. This difference does not alter the nature of the obligation; its only effect is to shift from the borrower to the lender any potential loss caused by devaluation of the property.[12] If the fair market value of the property falls below the amount of the outstanding obligation, the mortgagee's ability to protect its interests is impaired, for the mortgagor is free to abandon the property to the mortgagee and be relieved of his obligation.

This, however, does not erase the fact that the mortgagor received the loan proceeds tax-free and included them in his basis on the understanding that he had an obligation to repay the full amount. When the obligation is canceled, the mortgagor is relieved of his responsibility to repay the sum he originally received and thus realizes

cancellation of the $1.85 million obligation for a payment of $1.4 million. The former resulted in a capital loss of $50,000, and the latter in the realization of $450,000 of ordinary income. Taxation of the ordinary income might be deferred under § 108 by a reduction of respondents' bases in their partnership interests.

Although this indeed could be a justifiable mode of analysis, it has not been adopted by the Commissioner. Nor is there anything to indicate that the Code requires the Commissioner to adopt it. We note that Professor Barnett's approach does assume that recourse and nonrecourse debt may be treated identically.

The Commissioner also has chosen not to characterize the transaction as cancellation of indebtedness. We are not presented with and do not decide the contours of the cancellation-of-indebtedness doctrine. We note only that our approach does not fall within certain prior interpretations of that doctrine. In one view, the doctrine rests on the same initial premise as our analysis here—an obligation to repay—but the doctrine relies on a freeing-of-assets theory to attribute ordinary income to the debtor upon cancellation. According to that view, when nonrecourse debt is forgiven, the debtor's basis in the securing property is reduced by the amount of debt canceled, and realization of income is deferred until the sale of the property. Because that interpretation attributes income only when assets are freed, however, an insolvent debtor realizes income just to the extent his assets exceed his liabilities after the cancellation. Similarly, if the nonrecourse indebtedness exceeds the value of

the securing property, the taxpayer never realizes the full amount of the obligation canceled because the tax law has not recognized negative basis.

Although the economic benefit prong of *Crane* also relies on a freeing-of-assets theory, that theory is irrelevant to our broader approach. In the context of a sale or disposition of property under § 1001, the extinguishment of the obligation to repay is not ordinary income; instead, the amount of the canceled debt is included in the amount realized, and enters into the computation of gain or loss on the disposition of property. According to *Crane,* this treatment is no different when the obligation is nonrecourse: the basis is not reduced as in the cancellation-of-indebtedness context, and the full value of the outstanding liability is included in the amount realized. Thus, the problem of negative basis is avoided.

12. In his opinion for the Court of Appeals in *Crane,* Judge Learned Hand observed:

"[The mortgagor] has all the income from the property; he manages it; he may sell it; any increase in its value goes to him; any decrease falls on him, until the value goes below the amount of the lien .... When therefore upon a sale the mortgagor makes an allowance to the vendee of the amount of the lien, he secures a release from a charge upon his property quite as though the vendee had paid him the full price on condition that before he took title the lien should be cleared ...." 153 F.2d 504, 506 (CA2 1945).

value to that extent within the meaning of § 1001(b). From the mortgagor's point of view, when his obligation is assumed by a third party who purchases the encumbered property, it is as if the mortgagor first had been paid with cash borrowed by the third party from the mortgagee on a nonrecourse basis, and then had used the cash to satisfy his obligation to the mortgagee.

Moreover, this approach avoids the absurdity the Court recognized in *Crane*. Because of the remedy accompanying the mortgage in the nonrecourse situation, the depreciation in the fair market value of the property is relevant economically only to the mortgagee, who by lending on a nonrecourse basis remains at risk. To permit the taxpayer to limit his realization to the fair market value of the property would be to recognize a tax loss for which he has suffered no corresponding economic loss.[13] Such a result would be to construe "one section of the Act ... so as ... to defeat the intention of another or to frustrate the Act as a whole." 331 U.S., at 13, 67 S.Ct., at 1054.

In the specific circumstances of *Crane*, the economic benefit theory did support the Commissioner's treatment of the nonrecourse mortgage as a personal obligation. The footnote in *Crane* acknowledged the limitations of that theory when applied to a different set of facts. *Crane* also stands for the broader proposition, however, that a nonrecourse loan should be treated as a true loan. We therefore hold that a taxpayer must account for the proceeds of obligations he has received tax-free and included in basis. Nothing in either § 1001(b) or in the Court's prior decisions requires the Commissioner to permit a taxpayer to treat a sale of encumbered property asymmetrically, by including the proceeds of the nonrecourse obligation in basis but not accounting for the proceeds upon transfer of the encumbered property. ...

IV

When a taxpayer sells or disposes of property encumbered by a nonrecourse obligation, the Commissioner properly requires him to include among the assets realized the outstanding amount of the obligation. The fair market value of the property is irrelevant to this calculation. We find this interpretation to be consistent with Crane v. Commissioner, 331 U.S. 1, 67 S.Ct. 1047, 91 L.Ed. 1301 (1947), and to implement the statutory mandate in a reasonable manner.

The judgment of the Court of Appeals is therefore reversed.

---

13. In the present case, the Government bore the ultimate loss. The nonrecourse mortgage was extended to respondents only after the planned complex was endorsed for mortgage insurance under § 221(b) and (d)(4) of the National Housing Act, 12 U.S.C. § 1715*l*(b) and (d)(4) (1976 ed. and Supp. V). After acquiring the complex from respondents, Bayles operated it for a few years, but was unable to make it profitable. In 1974, F & H foreclosed, and the Department of Housing and Urban Development paid off the lender to obtain title. In 1976, the Department sold the complex to another developer for $1,502,000. The sale was financed by the Department's taking back a note for $1,314,800 and a nonrecourse mortgage. To fail to recognize the value of the nonrecourse loan in the amount realized, therefore, would permit respondents to compound the Government's loss by claiming the tax benefits of that loss for themselves.

It is so ordered.

Justice O'CONNOR, concurring.

I concur in the opinion of the Court, accepting the view of the Commissioner. I do not, however, endorse the Commissioner's view. Indeed, were we writing on a slate clean except for the *Crane* decision, I would take quite a different approach—that urged upon us by Professor Barnett as *amicus*.

Crane established that a taxpayer could treat property as entirely his own, in spite of the "coinvestment" provided by his mortgagee in the form of a nonrecourse loan. That is, the full basis of the property, with all its tax consequences, belongs to the mortgagor. That rule alone, though, does not in any way tie nonrecourse debt to the cost of property or to the proceeds upon disposition. I see no reason to treat the purchase, ownership, and eventual disposition of property differently because the taxpayer also takes out a mortgage, an independent transaction. In this case, the taxpayer purchased property, using nonrecourse financing, and sold it after it declined in value to a buyer who assumed the mortgage. There is no economic difference between the events in this case and a case in which the taxpayer buys property with cash; later obtains a nonrecourse loan by pledging the property as security; still later, using cash on hand, buys off the mortgage for the market value of the devalued property; and finally sells the property to a third party for its market value.

The logical way to treat both this case and the hypothesized case is to separate the two aspects of these events and to consider, first, the ownership and sale of the property, and, second, the arrangement and retirement of the loan. Under *Crane*, the fair market value of the property on the date of acquisition—the purchase price—represents the taxpayer's basis in the property, and the fair market value on the date of disposition represents the proceeds on sale. The benefit received by the taxpayer in return for the property is the cancellation of a mortgage that is worth no more than the fair market value of the property, for that is all the mortgagee can expect to collect on the mortgage. His gain or loss on the disposition of the property equals the difference between the proceeds and the cost of acquisition. Thus, the taxation of the transaction *in property* reflects the economic fate of the *property*. If the property has declined in value, as was the case here, the taxpayer recognizes a loss on the disposition of the property. The new purchaser then takes as his basis the fair market value as of the date of the sale.

In the separate borrowing transaction, the taxpayer acquires cash from the mortgagee. He need not recognize income at that time, of course, because he also incurs an obligation to repay the money. Later, though, when he is able to satisfy the debt by surrendering property that is worth less than the face amount of the debt, we have a classic situation of cancellation of indebtedness, requiring the taxpayer to recognize income in the amount of the difference between the proceeds of the loan and the amount for which he is able to satisfy his creditor.

26 U.S.C. § 61(a)(12). The taxation of the financing transaction then reflects the economic fate of the loan.

The reason that separation of the two aspects of the events in this case is important is, of course, that the Code treats different sorts of income differently. A gain on the sale of the property may qualify for capital gains treatment while the cancellation of indebtedness is ordinary income, but income that the taxpayer may be able to defer. Not only does Professor Barnett's theory permit us to accord appropriate treatment to each of the two types of income or loss present in these sorts of transactions, it also restores continuity to the system by making the taxpayer-seller's proceeds on the disposition of property equal to the purchaser's basis in the property. Further, and most important, it allows us to tax the events in this case in the same way that we tax the economically identical hypothesized transaction.

Persuaded though I am by the logical coherence and internal consistency of this approach, I agree with the Court's decision not to adopt it judicially. We do not write on a slate marked only by *Crane*. The Commissioner's longstanding position, Rev.Rul. 76–111, 1976–1 C.B. 214, is now reflected in the regulations. Treas.Reg. § 1.1001–2, 26 CFR § 1.1001–2 (1982). In the light of the numerous cases in the lower courts including the amount of the unrepaid proceeds of the mortgage in the proceeds on sale or disposition, it is difficult to conclude that the Commissioner's interpretation of the statute exceeds the bounds of his discretion. As the Court's opinion demonstrates, his interpretation is defensible. One can reasonably read § 1001(b)'s reference to "the amount realized *from* the sale or other disposition of property" (emphasis added) to permit the Commissioner to collapse the two aspects of the transaction. As long as his view is a reasonable reading of § 1001(b), we should defer to the regulations promulgated by the agency charged with interpretation of the statute. Accordingly, I concur.

ESTATE OF FRANKLIN v. COMMISSIONER OF INTERNAL REVENUE

United States Court of Appeals, Ninth Circuit, 1976.
544 F.2d 1045.

SNEED, Circuit Judge:

This case involves another effort on the part of the Commissioner to curb the use of real estate tax shelters.[1] In this instance he seeks to

---

1. An early skirmish in this particular effort appears in Manuel D. Mayerson, 47 T.C. 340 (1966), which the Commissioner lost. The Commissioner attacked the substance of a nonrecourse sale, but based his attack on the nonrecourse and long-term nature of the purchase money note, without focusing on whether the sale was made at an unrealistically high price. In his acquiescence to *Mayerson*, 1969–2 Cum. Bull. xxiv, the Commissioner recognized that the fundamental issue in these cases generally will be whether the property has been "acquired" at an artificially high price, having little relation to its fair market value. "The Service emphasizes that its acquiescence in *Mayerson* is based on the particular facts in the case and will not

disallow deductions for the taxpayers' distributive share of losses reported by a limited partnership with respect to its acquisition of a motel and related property. These "losses" have their origin in deductions for depreciation and interest claimed with respect to the motel and related property. These deductions were disallowed by the Commissioner on the ground either that the acquisition was a sham or that the entire acquisition transaction was in substance the purchase by the partnership of an option to acquire the motel and related property on January 15, 1979. The Tax Court held that the transaction constituted an option exercisable in 1979 and disallowed the taxpayers' deductions. Estate of Charles T. Franklin, 64 T.C. 752 (1975). We affirm this disallowance although our approach differs somewhat from that of the Tax Court.

The interest and depreciation deductions were taken by Twenty-Fourth Property Associates (hereinafter referred to as Associates), a California limited partnership of which Charles T. Franklin and seven other doctors were the limited partners. The deductions flowed from the purported "purchase" by Associates of the Thunderbird Inn, an Arizona motel, from Wayne L. Romney and Joan E. Romney (hereinafter referred to as the Romneys) on November 15, 1968.

Under a document entitled "Sales Agreement," the Romneys agreed to "sell" the Thunderbird Inn to Associates for $1,224,000. The property would be paid for over a period of ten years, with interest on any unpaid balance of seven and one-half percent per annum. "Prepaid interest" in the amount of $75,000 was payable immediately; monthly principal and interest installments of $9,045.36 would be paid for approximately the first ten years, with Associates required to make a balloon payment at the end of the ten years of the difference between the remaining purchase price, forecast as $975,000, and any mortgages then outstanding against the property.

The purchase obligation of Associates to the Romneys was nonrecourse; the Romneys' only remedy in the event of default would be forfeiture of the partnership's interest. The sales agreement was recorded in the local county. A warranty deed was placed in an escrow account, along with a quitclaim deed from Associates to the Romneys, both documents to be delivered either to Associates upon full payment of the purchase price, or to the Romneys upon default.

The sale was combined with a leaseback of the property by Associates to the Romneys; Associates therefore never took physical possession. The lease payments were designed to approximate closely the principal and interest payments with the consequence that with the exception of the $75,000 prepaid interest payment no cash would cross between Associates and Romneys until the balloon payment. The lease

be relied upon in the disposition of other cases except where it is clear that the property has been acquired at its fair market value in an arm's length transaction creating a bona fide purchase and a bona fide debt obligation." Rev.Rul. 69–77, 1969–1 Cum.Bull. 59.

was on a net basis; thus, the Romneys were responsible for all of the typical expenses of owning the motel property including all utility costs, taxes, assessments, rents, charges, and levies of "every name, nature and kind whatsoever." The Romneys also were to continue to be responsible for the first and second mortgages until the final purchase installment was made; the Romneys could, and indeed did, place additional mortgages on the property without the permission of Associates. Finally, the Romneys were allowed to propose new capital improvements which Associates would be required to either build themselves or allow the Romneys to construct with compensating modifications in rent or purchase price.

In holding that the transaction between Associates and the Romneys more nearly resembled an option than a sale, the Tax Court emphasized that Associates had the power at the end of ten years to walk away from the transaction and merely lose its $75,000 "prepaid interest payment." It also pointed out that a *deed* was never recorded and that the "benefits and burdens of ownership" appeared to remain with the Romneys. Thus, the sale was combined with a leaseback in which no cash would pass; the Romneys remained responsible under the mortgages, which they could increase; and the Romneys could make capital improvements.[2] The Tax Court further justified its "option" characterization by reference to the nonrecourse nature of the purchase money debt and the nice balance between the rental and purchase money payments.

Our emphasis is different from that of the Tax Court. We believe the characteristics set out above can exist in a situation in which the sale imposes upon the purchaser a genuine indebtedness within the meaning of section 167(a), Internal Revenue Code of 1954, which will support both interest and depreciation deductions. They substantially so existed in Hudspeth v. Commissioner, 509 F.2d 1224 (9th Cir.1975) in which parents entered into sale-leaseback transactions with their children. The children paid for the property by executing nonnegotiable notes and mortgages equal to the fair market value of the property; state law proscribed deficiency judgments in case of default, limiting the parents' remedy to foreclosure of the property. The children had no funds with which to make mortgage payments; instead, the payments were offset in part by the rental payments, with the difference met by gifts from the parents to their children. Despite these characteristics this court held that there was a bona fide indebtedness on which the children, to the extent of the rental payments, could base interest deductions. See also American Realty Trust v. United States, 498 F.2d 1194 (4th Cir.1974); Manuel D. Mayerson, 47 T.C. 340 (1966).

In none of these cases, however, did the taxpayer fail to demonstrate that the purchase price was at least approximately equivalent to the fair market value of the property. Just such a failure occurred here.

---

2. There was evidence that not all of the benefits and burdens of ownership remained with the Romneys. Thus, for example, the leaseback agreement appears to provide that any condemnation award will go to Associates. Exhibit 6-F, at p. 5.

The Tax Court explicitly found that on the basis of the facts before it the value of the property could not be estimated. 64 T.C. at 767–768.[4] In our view this defect in the taxpayers' proof is fatal.

Reason supports our perception. An acquisition such as that of Associates if at a price approximately equal to the fair market value of the property under ordinary circumstances would rather quickly yield an equity in the property which the purchaser could not prudently abandon. This is the stuff of substance. It meshes with the form of the transaction and constitutes a sale.

No such meshing occurs when the purchase price exceeds a demonstrably reasonable estimate of the fair market value. Payments on the principal of the purchase price yield no equity so long as the unpaid balance of the purchase price exceeds the then existing fair market value. Under these circumstances the purchaser by abandoning the transaction can lose no more than a mere chance to acquire an equity in the future should the value of the acquired property increase. While this chance undoubtedly influenced the Tax Court's determination that the transaction before us constitutes an option, we need only point out that its existence fails to supply the substance necessary to justify treating the transaction as a sale *ab initio*. It is not necessary to the disposition of this case to decide the tax consequences of a transaction such as that before us if in a subsequent year the fair market value of

---

4. The Tax Court found that appellants had "not shown that the purported sales price of $1,224,000 (or any other price) had any relationship to the actual market value of the motel property ...." 64 T.C. at 767.

Petitioners spent a substantial amount of time at trial attempting to establish that, whatever the actual market value of the property, Associates acted in the good faith *belief* that the market value of the property approximated the selling price. However, this evidence only goes to the issue of sham and does not supply substance to this transaction. "Save in those instances where the statute itself turns on intent, a matter so real as taxation must depend on objective realities, not on the varying subjective beliefs of individual taxpayers." Lynch v. Commissioner, 273 F.2d 867, 872 (2d Cir.1959).

In oral argument it was suggested by the appellants that neither the Tax Court nor they recognized the importance of fair market value during the presentation of evidence and that this hampered the full and open development of this issue. However, upon an examination of the record, we are satisfied that the taxpayers recognized the importance of presenting objective evidence of the fair market value and were awarded ample opportunity to present their proof; appellants merely failed to

present clear and admissible evidence that fair market value did indeed approximate the purchase price. Such evidence of fair market value as was relied upon by the appellants, *viz.* two appraisals, one completed in 1968 and a second in 1971, even if fully admissible as evidence of the truth of the estimates of value appearing therein, does not require us to set aside the Tax Court's finding. As the Tax Court found, the 1968 appraisal was "error-filled, sketchy" and "obviously suspect." 64 T.C. at 767 n. 13. The 1971 appraisal had little relevancy as to 1968 values. On the other side, there existed cogent evidence indicating that the fair market value was substantially less than the purchase price. This evidence included (i) the Romneys' purchase of the stock of two corporations, one of which wholly-owned the motel, for approximately $800,000 in the year preceding the "sale" to Associates ($660,000 of which was allocable to the sale property, according to Mr. Romney's estimate), and (ii) insurance policies on the property from 1967 through 1974 of only $583,200, $700,000, and $614,000. 64 T.C. at 767–768.

Given that it was the appellants' burden to present evidence showing that the purchase price did not exceed the fair market value and that he had a fair opportunity to do so, we see no reason to remand this case for further proceedings.

the property increases to an extent that permits the purchaser to acquire an equity.[5]

Authority also supports our perception. It is fundamental that "depreciation is not predicated upon ownership of property *but rather upon an investment in property.* Gladding Dry Goods Co., 2 BTA 336 (1925)." *Mayerson,* supra at 350 (italics added). No such investment exists when payments of the purchase price in accordance with the design of the parties yield no equity to the purchaser. In the transaction before us and during the taxable years in question the purchase price payments by Associates have not been shown to constitute an *investment in the property.* Depreciation was properly disallowed. Only the Romneys had an investment in the property.

Authority also supports disallowance of the interest deductions. This is said even though it has long been recognized that the absence of personal liability for the purchase money debt secured by a mortgage on the acquired property does not deprive the debt of its character as a bona fide debt obligation able to support an interest deduction. *Mayerson,* supra at 352. However, this is no longer true when it appears that the debt has economic significance only if the property substantially appreciates in value prior to the date at which a very large portion of the purchase price is to be discharged. Under these circumstances the purchaser has not secured "the use or forbearance of money." Nor has the seller advanced money or forborne its use. Prior to the date at which the balloon payment on the purchase price is required, and assuming no substantial increase in the fair market value of the property, the absence of personal liability on the debt reduces the transaction in economic terms to a mere chance that a genuine debt obligation may arise. This is not enough to justify an interest deduction. To justify the deduction the debt must exist; potential existence will not do. For debt to exist, the purchaser, in the absence of personal liability, must confront a situation in which it is presently reasonable from an economic point of view for him to make a capital investment in the amount of the unpaid purchase price. Associates, during the taxable years in question, confronted no such situation. Compare Crane v. Commissioner, 331 U.S. 1, 11–12, 67 S.Ct. 1047, 91 L.Ed. 1301 (1947).

Our focus on the relationship of the fair market value of the property to the unpaid purchase price should not be read as premised upon the belief that a sale is not a sale if the purchaser pays too much. Bad bargains from the buyer's point of view—as well as sensible bargains from buyer's, but exceptionally good from the seller's point of view—do not thereby cease to be sales. We intend our holding and explanation thereof to be understood as limited to transactions substantially similar to that now before us.

---

5. These consequences would include a determination of the proper basis of the acquired property at the date the incre- ments to the purchaser's equity commenced.

Affirmed.

NOTE

Does *Tufts* discredit *Franklin?* Recall that, in rejecting the economic benefit theory, Justice Blackmun read *Crane* "to have approved the Commissioner's decision to treat a nonrecourse mortgage in this context as a true loan. This approval underlies *Crane's* holding that the amount of the nonrecourse liability is to be included in calculating both the basis and the amount realized on disposition. That the amount of the loan exceeds the fair market value of the property thus becomes irrelevant." Can this *dictum* be limited, and can cases like *Franklin* be distinguished, on the ground that a nonrecourse mortgage given to support an artificially inflated purchase price is not debt at all, and thus is not properly includible in basis for purposes of depreciation *or* amount realized on sale or exchange? Reconsider *Tufts'* footnote 5 which, in its suggestiveness, may rival *Crane's* footnote 37.

Is it practicable to rest the operative distinction on whether, at the time of the taxpayer's purchase, the mortgage exceeded the property's fair market value? Is it relevant to rest the distinction on whether the debt is recourse or nonrecourse? Would it be preferable to distinguish instead between seller-financed transactions and transactions financed by third parties who, unlike the seller, have no incentive to agree on an artificially inflated purchase price?

See Jensen, The Unanswered Question in *Tufts*: What Was the Purchaser's Basis?, 10 Va.Tax Rev. 455 (1991); Coven, Limiting Losses Attributable to Nonrecourse Debt: A Defense of the Traditional System Against the At-Risk Concept, 74 Cal.L.Rev. 41 (1986); Rohrbach, Disposition of Properties Secured by Recourse and Nonrecourse Debt, 41 Baylor L.Rev. 231 (1989); Avent & Grimes, Inflated Purchase Money Indebtedness in Real Estate and Other Investments, 11 J.Real Estate Tax. 99 (Winter 1984); Weinstein, *Tufts v. Comm'r.*—Good-Bye, Footnote 37; Hello, Footnote 5, 12 Real Est.L.J. 261 (1983). For an excellent analysis of *Tufts* in the context of legislative, administrative and judicial attacks on tax shelter generally, see Note, Nonrecourse Liabilities as Tax Shelter Devices After *Tufts:* Elimination of Fair Market Value and Contingent Liability Defenses, 35 U.Fla.L.Rev. 904 (1983).

2. INTERIM REFORMS OF TAX SHELTERS

WEIDNER, REALTY SHELTERS: NONRECOURSE FINANCING, TAX REFORM, AND PROFIT PURPOSE *

32 Southwestern Law Journal 711, 728–734 (1978).

V. THE PATH OF TAX REFORM

Prior to the Tax Reform Act of 1976, the primary focus of tax reform in the real estate area was on the depreciation deduction and the use of accelerated methods of computing depreciation. Owners of property used in a trade or business or held for the production of income are allowed annual depreciation deductions for the exhaustion, wear and tear of such property.[66] The straight line method of computing depreciation allocates equal deductions over each year of the estimated useful life of the property. Accelerated depreciation methods, however, allow the taxpayer much greater depreciation deductions in the earlier years of the property's useful life, and smaller deductions in later years. The use of accelerated depreciation deductions to shelter income from other sources was felt to be particularly offensive because the accelerated depreciation claimed often grossly exceeded the actual deterioration, if any, that had taken place.

Prior to the Revenue Act of 1964, a taxpayer "paid the piper" for the depreciation deductions taken only insofar as those deductions were subtracted from his basis in the property. Because gain on the sale of property is calculated as sale price less adjusted basis, the amount of gain is increased by the amount of the depreciation deductions taken. This, however, does not negate the benefit obtained by using the depreciation deduction to shelter ordinary income from other sources, because the gain is postponed until sale and is generally taxed at favorable capital gains rates. Thus, both tax deferral and tax conversion are achieved.

An example of the classic pre-1964 Act shelter illustrates the point. Assume that a taxpayer in the sixty percent bracket reported a depreciation deduction of $10,000. This resulted in a tax savings of $6,000 in the year of the deduction. The amount of the depreciation deduction that had been taken was subtracted from his basis in the property. Thus, when he sold the property, the gain he recognized was $10,000 greater than it would have been had there been no depreciation deduction taken. This gain, however, received capital gains treatment. In a year in which the maximum tax on capital gains was twenty-five percent, the tax bill on the additional $10,000 gain was only $2,500. Thus, taxpayer, in effect, "bought" a $6,000 tax saving in the year in which he took his depreciation deduction, for only $2,500, which he did not have to pay until the sale of the property. The 1964 Act was the first legislation to require that part or all of the gain on the sale of property that had been depreciated at an accelerated rate be "recaptured," that is, taxed as ordinary income. It was not until the 1976 Act

---

66. I.R.C. § 167(a). There are two basic types of depreciable property, § 1245 property and § 1250 property. Section 1245 property is depreciable tangible personal property and includes elevators and escalators. Id. § 1245(a)(3). Section 1250 property is depreciable real property, that is, buildings and their structural components, but not elevators and escalators. Id. § 1250(c). The distinction is important because each is subject to its own rules concerning the availability of accelerated depreciation methods and depreciation recapture.

that Congress specifically focused on the inclusion of nonrecourse liabilities in depreciable basis.

A.   The Tax Reform Act of 1969

The Tax Reform Act of 1969 was a continuation of the confinement of real estate tax shelters that began with the initial recapture provision in the 1964 Act.   The basic thrust of the 1969 Act with regard to real estate tax shelters was threefold: (1) restrict the use of accelerated depreciation methods that permit taxpayers to take larger depreciation deductions in the earlier years of the property's useful life rather than spread them evenly over the useful life; (2) strengthen the 1964 Act provisions that treat some of the gain on sale as ordinary income when accelerated methods of computing depreciation have been used; and (3) include accelerated depreciation and one half of net capital gains in with certain other items of "preference" subject to a new ten percent tax.

Limitation on the Availability of Accelerated Depreciation Methods. The general rule of the 1969 Act with respect to depreciation of real property [70] is that *new* property may be depreciated only by the 150% declining balance or straight line methods, and *used* property may be depreciated only by the straight line method.   The most important exceptions to this general rule apply to residential rental property and to rehabilitation expenditures on low income rental housing.   Urban riots had left legislators more susceptible to incentives to develop and refurbish rental housing.   With respect to new residential rental properties, all accelerated depreciation methods previously available remained available.   Therefore, *new* residential rental properties may still be depreciated according to the very rapid 200% declining balance or sum-of-the-years-digits methods.   With respect to *used* residential rental property, only the straight line method is preserved, unless the property has a useful life of twenty years or more, in which case the 125% declining balance method is still available.   With respect to certain rehabilitation expenditures on low income rental housing, the taxpayer may elect to depreciate such expenditures by the straight line method over a sixty-month period.   Under prior law, such expenditures had to be capitalized and depreciated over the entire remaining useful life of the property.

Recapture of Ordinary Income.   The 1969 Act strengthened the "recapture" provisions applied to real estate by the 1964 Act.   The recapture rules reduce the tax shelter benefits of accelerated depreciation by treating some of the gain on the sale of property that has been depreciated at an accelerated rate as ordinary income.   The amount of depreciation "recaptured" is determined by applying the appropriate "applicable percentage" to the amount of depreciation that has been

---

70. The 1969 Act did not place any limitations on the use of accelerated methods to depreciate new personal property, which can be depreciated even by use of the very rapid double declining balance or sum-of-the-years-digits methods.   Treas.Reg. § 1.167(b)–0(b) (1960).

taken in *excess* of the amount that would have been taken under the straight line method.[76] Separate rules are provided for determining the applicable percentages to be applied to pre-1970 and post-1969 "excess" depreciation. The applicable percentage imposed by the 1969 Act on pre-1970 excess depreciation is 100% less one percent for each month the property is held beyond twenty months. Thus, if the property is held for more than ten years, none of the pre-1970 excess depreciation will be recaptured.

Generally, the applicable percentage on post-1969 excess depreciation of real property is 100%. That is, all of the excess depreciation will be recaptured, regardless of the length of time the property is held. The 1969 Act, however, applied more lenient recapture provisions to residential rental properties. With respect to such property, the applicable percentage was 100% less one percent for each month the property was held beyond 100 months. Thus, if a residential rental property were held for more than sixteen years and eight months there was no recapture. With respect to property financed under the National Housing Act or similar programs and subject to certain limitations on the rate of return and profit, the applicable percentage was the same as it would be for pre-1970 excess depreciation, such that there is no recapture if the property is held for more than ten years.

The Tax on Preferences. The 1969 Act imposed a new tax on items of "tax preference," certain deductions not used by most taxpayers, but used to great advantage by others. The tax was ten percent of the excess of the year's preferences over the sum of $30,000 plus the taxpayer's regular federal tax. "Excess depreciation," the depreciation taken in excess of the amount of depreciation allowable under the straight line method, was made an item of tax preference subject to this tax. Consequently, although excess depreciation is not recaptured until the property is sold, it is taxed as a preference item each year accelerated depreciation is taken. Further, the minimum tax also applies not only to the accelerated depreciation as it is taken each year, it also applies in the year of sale to one-half of the net capital gain for the year.

B.   The Tax Reform Act of 1976

From a real estate point of view, the 1976 Act may be more significant for what the Congress chose not to do to real estate, rather than for what it actually did. It chose, for example, not to subject real estate to the "at risk" limitation it applied to other tax shelters. Nevertheless, the 1976 Act did include several significant changes that restrict real estate tax shelters.

Strengthened Recapture Provisions. The 1976 Act left intact the 1969 Act rules that limit the availability of accelerated depreciation methods. The 1976 Act, however, provides for greater depreciation

---

76. In contrast, in the case of depreciable *personal* property, *all* depreciation is recaptured, to the extent of gain, at ordinary income rates. Id. § 1245(a)(1).

recapture than did the 1969 Act. There is no change with respect to commercial properties; as under the 1969 Act, all excess depreciation will be recaptured. The 1976 Act, however, extends this rule of 100% recapture to all residential rental housing other than assisted housing. Congress learned that the preferred treatment it had given broadly to *all* residential rental housing would not necessarily result in the reconstruction of the inner cities or, indeed, in the construction of much low-income housing anywhere. Thus, the incentive was confined more narrowly to government assisted low and moderate income housing projects. In the case of assisted housing, the amount of excess depreciation subject to recapture is 100% less 1% for each month the property is held after its first eight years and four months in service.

Capitalization of Construction Period Items. The 1976 Act contains several provisions to prevent the real estate industry from currently deducting items of a capital nature. The most significant of these provisions is the completely new section 189. Prior to the 1976 Act, interest and taxes incurred during the construction period were deducted immediately rather than capitalized and written off over the life of the improvement. When fully phased in, section 189 will require construction period interest and taxes to be capitalized and written off on a straight line basis over a ten-year period. The section applies to individuals, Subchapter S corporations, and personal holding companies. The first write-off year is that in which the expenses are paid or accrued, depending on the taxpayer's method of accounting; the second write-off year is the first year in which the property is placed in service; and each year thereafter is a write-off year until expiration. Intervening construction period years are skipped; thus, the ten-year amortization period may not be consecutive. ...

The Minimum Tax on Preferences. The minimum tax on preferences introduced by the 1969 Act proved to be an insignificant revenue raiser. In response, the 1976 Act included a general tightening of the minimum tax on preferences. The rate was increased from ten to fifteen percent and the exemption for tax preferences was reduced from $30,000 plus regular taxes paid, to the greater of $10,000 or one-half of regular taxes paid in the case of individuals. These changes in the minimum tax rules also affected the maximum tax rules on earned income because tax preference income reduces the amount that would otherwise qualify as earned income eligible for the fifty percent maximum rate.

Prepaid Interest. The Code contains a broadly worded interest deduction, which provides: "There shall be allowed as a deduction all interest paid or accrued within the taxable year on indebtedness." In 1945, the Service ruled that it was permissible for taxpayers who computed their income using a cash method of accounting to deduct up to five years of prepaid interest in the year of payment. Consequently, prepayments of interest in real estate transactions became as common as mortgages. In 1968, the Service revoked the earlier ruling "[i]n view of certain abuses." It relied on its statutory authority to require a taxpayer to use a different method of accounting if the method he chooses for himself "does not clearly reflect income," and ruled that the prepayment of more than one year's interest by a cash method taxpayer "will be considered as materially distorting income." Hence, the taxpayer making such a payment is required to report it on an accrual method of accounting, and postpone deduction until the year to which the interest is chargeable. The Ruling further declared that any prepayment for one year or less will be considered on a case-by-case basis to determine whether a material distortion of income has resulted. The 1968 Ruling's dramatic change of position was controversial, particularly because of its automatic disqualification of all prepayments for more than a twelve-month period.

The 1976 Act put to rest any controversy about the 1968 Ruling by introducing section 461(g), which eliminated deductions for prepaid interest. The legislative history of the section makes clear that the material distortion of income principle is no longer to control the reporting of interest deductions; cash method taxpayers must simply report interest payments as would an accrual method taxpayer. The legislative history also makes clear that previous law continues to control the definition of interest. Thus, the Service may continue to argue that payments denominated "interest" constitute something other than interest, such as a deposit, a portion of principal, or a payment for an option. The Service can be expected to be particularly aggressive with respect to claims of "interest" deductions in wraparound mortgage situations.

3. REQUIEM FOR THE TAX SHELTER?

a. Legislative Developments, 1976–1986

As indicated in the excerpt from Professor Weidner's article, virtually every tax revision measure in recent years has tinkered with the depreciation tax shelter. These measures have usually adjusted one or more of the depreciation tax shelter's four principal aspects: length of the allowable cost recovery period; permitted rate of depreciation; recapture of excess depreciation; and the use of tax shelter to completely avoid tax liability.

Cost Recovery Period. After a series of reforms curtailing the availability and benefits of accelerated depreciation, The Economic Recovery Tax Act of 1981 (ERTA), Pub.L. No. 97–34, 95 Stat. 172, dramatically increased the available depreciation deductions by introducing an accelerated cost recovery system (ACRS) applicable to property placed in service on or after January 1, 1981. Under ERTA, ACRS allowed real property improvements to be depreciated over a 15-year period (as compared with useful lives ranging generally between 40 and 60 years under previous I.R.S. guidelines). ERTA also allowed taxpayers to elect a 35- or 45-year recovery instead. The 1984 Tax Reform

Act, Pub.L. No. 98–369, 98 Stat. 494–1210, reduced the depreciation tax benefit by increasing the allowable cost recovery period from fifteen years to eighteen years for most properties. The 1984 Act did, however, allow low-income housing, as defined in I.R.C. § 1250(a)(1)(B), to be depreciated over the fifteen-year period.

Depreciation Method. ERTA allowed the taxpayer to choose between straight line and accelerated methods of depreciation. While straight line could be used in connection with the 15-, 35- or 45-year recovery period, the accelerated depreciation method could be used only in connection with the fifteen-year recovery period (which is like saying to a child, if you choose to have the chocolate cake, you can only have it with ice cream on top). Further, ERTA required the taxpayer who opts for accelerated depreciation to calculate depreciation on the basis of tables that approximate 175 percent declining balance or, if the real property is a qualifying subsidized housing project, that approximate double declining balance. ERTA eliminated the depreciation methods discussed in Professor Weidner's article—125 percent declining balance, 150 percent declining balance, and sum-of-the-years-digits. It also ended the distinction between new and used property and, except with respect to depreciation recapture, the distinction between residential and nonresidential property.

Recapture. The taxpayer who employed an accelerated depreciation method would see part or all of his depreciation deductions recaptured at the time of disposition and taxed at ordinary income rates. Under ERTA, the extent of recapture turned on whether the property was residential or nonresidential real estate. If it was residential real estate, such as an apartment building, only depreciation deductions taken in excess of the amount that would have been taken under the straight line method would be recaptured and taxed as ordinary income. By contrast, if the property was nonresidential real estate such as a factory or warehouse, gain on disposition would be treated as ordinary income to the extent of *all* depreciation taken, and not just depreciation in excess of the amount that would have been taken under the straight line method.

Alternative Minimum Tax. The minimum tax on preferences, introduced by the 1969 Act and expanded by the 1976 Act, was further expanded by the Tax Equity and Fiscal Responsibility Act of 1982, Pub.L. No. 97–248, 96 Stat. 324, for tax years beginning in 1983. In an effort to assure that everyone paid some tax, TEFRA required the taxpayer to compute his regular tax liability and his alternative minimum tax liability, and then to pay whichever is greater. Essentially, computation of the alternative minimum tax required the taxpayer to add back to adjusted gross income any items of tax preference and, after subtracting permitted deductions and a uniform exemption, to pay a flat 20% tax on this figure. For real estate investors, the important tax preference items were accelerated depreciation on real property improvements and the portion of long-term capital gains otherwise exempt from tax—60% of the gain realized.

See generally, Solomon, Choosing Between Accelerated and Straight-Line Cost Recovery for Commercial Real Estate Under ACRS, 10 J.Real Estate Tax 18 (1982–83); Brueggeman, Fisher & Stern, Choosing the Optimal Depreciation Method Under 1981 Tax Legislation, 11 Real Estate Rev. 32 (Winter 1982); Goodman & Tremlett, The Tax Reform Act of 1984: How It Affects Real Property, 7 Real Prop. L.Rptr. 131 (1984).

b.   The 1986 Tax Reform Act

The 1986 Tax Reform Act, which for most purposes went into effect on January 1, 1987, dramatically reduced the scope of real estate tax shelter. In part the Act achieved this reduction by further adjusting the allowable period over which a property may be depreciated, the method for computing depreciation, and the alternative minimum tax. The Act also reduced real estate tax shelter by reforms aimed at the very nature of the taxpayer's real estate investment. The Act's repeal of the preferential capital gains rate further reduced the attraction of real estate tax shelters by depriving the taxpayer of the economic benefits of taking present deductions against ordinary income and paying for these deductions with a tax on future gains at the more favorable capital gains rate.

Passive Loss Limitation. For high bracket taxpayers, one of the principal attractions of real estate tax shelters was the ability to set off losses from the investment (often paper losses) against income from other sources. The 1986 Tax Reform Act substantially limits tax shelters for individuals, estates, trusts and personal service corporations by adding new Code Section 469 which allows losses from "passive activities" to be set off only against income from other "passive activities," and not against the taxpayer's other income, such as salary, interest, dividends and active business income. Unused passive losses can be carried forward and set off against passive income in subsequent tax years. If passive losses remain at the time of the property's disposition they can then be set off against the gain, if any, from the disposition.

Section 469(c)(1) defines passive activity as "any activity (A) which involves the conduct of any trade or business, and (B) in which the taxpayer does not materially participate." Section 469(h) provides that a taxpayer is "materially participating" only if he "is involved in the operations of the activity on a basis which is—(A) regular, (B) continuous, and (C) substantial."

Section 469 includes rental activities within its definition of passive activities even if the taxpayer materially participates in the rental activity. But the Act allows taxpayers who "actively" participate in rental real estate activity, and whose adjusted gross income is less than $100,000, to deduct up to $25,000 of losses from the rental activity against other non-passive income. According to the Senate Finance

Committee Report, "active participation" implies a lower standard of involvement than "material participation" and can be satisfied without regular, continuous and substantial involvement in operations. S.Rep. No. 313, 99th Cong., 2d Sess. 719–721 (1986). An individual will not, however, be treated as actively participating in any activity if she and her spouse together own an interest of less than 10%. For taxpayers whose adjusted gross income exceeds $100,000, the $25,000 maximum allowable deduction will be reduced by half the income excess over $100,000, thus eliminating the allowable deduction when the taxpayer's adjusted gross income reaches $150,000.

The Conference Report, H.R. Rep. No. 841, 99th Cong., 2d Sess. II–139 (1986), makes clear that "the passive loss rule applies to all deductions that are from passive activities, including deductions allowed under sections 162, 163, 164, and 165. For example, deductions for State and local property taxes incurred with respect to passive activities are subject to limitation under the passive loss rule whether such deductions are claimed above-the-line or as itemized deductions under section 164." Also, "interest deductions attributable to passive activities are treated as passive activity deductions, but are not treated as investment interest. Thus, such interest deductions are subject to limitation under the passive loss rule, and not under the investment interest limitation," which limits the deduction for investment interest to the amount of net investment income.

At Risk Limitation. Before passage of the 1986 Act, real property owners enjoyed a unique benefit—the ability to include nonrecourse financing in an investment's basis for the purpose of writing off losses such as those attributable to depreciation. This result obtained whether the nonrecourse financing came from a third party or from the seller of the investment property. The 1986 Act partially eliminated this benefit by striking I.R.C. § 465(c)(3)(D), which had excluded real property from the at risk rules, and amending section 465(b) to provide that "in the case of an activity of holding real property, a taxpayer shall be considered at risk with respect to the taxpayer's share of any qualified nonrecourse financing which is secured by real property used in such activity."

Section 465(b)(6)(B) effectively defines "qualified nonrecourse financing" to include nonconvertible debt to an independent third party lender regularly engaged in the business of lending money or to a governmental agency. A loan will not lose its status as "qualified nonrecourse financing" if it is from a related party, so long as the loan's terms are commercially reasonable and substantially conform to the terms of loans made to unrelated parties. Thus, a real estate investor who obtains nonrecourse purchase money financing from his seller, or whose loan otherwise fails to qualify as qualified nonrecourse financing, will be able to write off losses on his investment only to the extent of the amount he has at risk—his invested cash plus debt on which he is personally liable.

Depreciation. The 1986 Act substantially reduces the tax benefits available from depreciable real property by lengthening the period over which the property must be depreciated and by limiting the taxpayer to the straight line method of computing depreciation. Where prior law generally allowed the taxpayer to recover the cost of real property over an eighteen year period using statutory tables approximating the 175 per cent declining balance method, the 1986 Act requires that, for property placed in service after December 31, 1986, investments in residential real property cannot be written off over less than 27.5 years and investments in commercial real property cannot be written off over less than 31.5 years, both computed on the basis of the straight line method.

Alternative Minimum Tax. The 1986 Tax Reform Act increased the alternative minimum tax rate for individuals from 20% to 21%, beginning in 1987, and also increased the number of tax preference items subject to the alternative minimum tax. Among the new items of tax preference related to real estate investments are net losses from passive investments such as limited partnership interests and rental activities and gains deferred through use of the installment method of accounting. See generally Lispey & Witners, Applying the New Alternative Minimum Tax to Real Estate, 15 J. Real Est.Tax. 124 (1988).

For an excellent examination of the various aspects of the 1986 Tax Reform Act, see Gibson, The Impact of the Tax Reform Act of 1986 on Tax Shelters, 11 The Rev. of Taxation of Individuals 323 (1987). For a fine comparison of pre and post 1986 law, see M. Levine, Real Estate Transactions, Tax Planning and Consequences 65–85 (1991).

In the following excerpt, Professor Edward Zelenak questions whether the 1986 Act was the best solution to the tax shelter problem.

ZELENAK, WHEN GOOD PREFERENCES GO BAD: A CRITICAL ANALYSIS OF THE ANTI–TAX SHELTER PROVISIONS OF THE TAX REFORM ACT OF 1986 *

67 Texas Law Review 499, 513–515, 518–522, 524–529 (1989).

II. When Good Preferences Go Bad

A. *Common Antishelter Arguments*

Congress (in the legislative history of the 1986 Act) and commentators have advanced a number of arguments supporting the policy of retaining tax preferences while preventing the use of those preferences in tax shelters. None adequately supports such a policy.

1. *The Problem of Nonprofitable Investments.* —A frequently advanced argument for curbing the deductibility of tax shelter losses is

* Published originally in 67 *Texas Law Review* 499, 513–15, 518–22, 524–29 (1989).

that the deductibility of such losses encourages taxpayers to make investments that would be losing propositions but for the tax savings they generate, and that such investments harm the economy. This argument takes two different forms. One aspect holds that because returns on preferred assets will generally be lower than the taxable interest rate, borrowing to invest in a preferred asset will ordinarily yield a net loss, tax savings aside. The other aspect provides that in periods of high inflation, tax shelter investors may actually find it profitable to invest in preferred assets that yield a negative return (a return that is lower than the rate of inflation). This section examines both forms of the argument.

(a) The lower return on preferred assets. —The Senate Finance Committee report on the 1986 Act makes the argument in its first form:

> The availability of tax benefits to shelter positive sources of income ... has harmed the economy generally, by providing a non-economic return on capital for certain investments. This has encouraged a flow of capital away from activities that may provide a higher pre-tax economic return, thus retarding the growth of the sectors of the economy with the greatest potential for expansion.[1]

To illustrate this argument, consider a simple example. A taxpayer borrows $100 at 8% and invests it in an asset yielding a tax-free 6% annual return (with Congress intending the nontaxability of the return to be an incentive preference). Tax consequences aside, this investment results in a $2 economic loss. But the investment generates an $8 tax loss (zero taxable income less $8 in interest expense), which will save a 50% bracket taxpayer $4 in taxes. The $4 tax savings turns a $2 pre-tax economic loss into a $2 after-tax economic gain, and it thus makes profitable what would otherwise be a losing investment. The artificial tax loss thus may have encouraged a tax payer to invest in an asset yielding a $6 annual return, at an annual interest cost of $8. It is arguably bad policy for the tax laws to encourage such investments, and section 469, if it applies, would remove the encouragement by denying the investor the $8 loss deduction.

A second example, however, calls into question the logic of the congressional approach. Suppose the same taxpayer has invested $100 cash in a certificate of deposit (CD) earning $8 of annual interest. If the interest is taxed at a 50% rate, the after-tax return is $4. Aside from tax consequences, it would not make sense for the tax-payer to withdraw his $100 from the CD and use it to buy the tax-favored asset for $100. The asset yields only a $6 annual return, and the certificate of deposit yields an $8 annual return. Just as it would not make sense (apart from tax consequences) to borrow from someone else at 8% to make an investment yielding a 6% return, it would not make sense

---

1. [Senate Comm. on Finance, Report   313, 99th Cong., 2d Sess. 716 (1986).]
on Tax Reform Act of 1986, S. Rep. No.

(apart from tax consequences) to borrow, in effect, from oneself at 8% to make an investment yielding a 6% return.

But now consider the tax consequences. While the economic income from the preferred asset is $6, the tax preference sets the taxable income at zero. Thus, the taxpayers after-tax return from the asset is $6—the same amount as the pre-tax return. Even though the pre-tax income from the asset ($6) is $2 less than the pre-tax income from the CD ($8), the after tax income from the asset ($6) is $2 more than the after-tax income from the CD ($4). Just as in the first example, the tax preference for the income from the asset in the second example causes a taxpayer to make an investment that he otherwise would not make. The tax system distorts the economy in the second example just as much as in the first; both illustrate tax-motivated investments in a relatively non-productive asset. If the distortion of the economy in the first example calls for a legislative cure, the distortion in the second example—which is just as bad—should call for similar legislative action. Section 469 would not apply in the second example, however, because the preference shelters only income from the investment, not unrelated income.

The very purpose of an incentive preference is to encourage taxpayers to make investments that they would not make except for the preference. The existence of a preference signifies that by reducing the tax on income from a tax-favored asset, Congress has decided to encourage additional investment in that asset. Simply put, a preference that influences the investments of taxpayers is working exactly as it should. A preference is supposed to distort the economy, whether the taxpayer invests in the tax-preferred asset with his own money or with borrowed money. Thus, the Finance Committees complaint against tax shelters—that they cause capital to flow into tax-favored assets—is a complaint that preferences in shelters are doing what they are supposed to do. One can coherently oppose preferences generally because of the distortions they produce. One can also coherently favor some preferences, on the grounds that they cause a desirable shift in the allocation of resources. But one cannot coherently condemn the economic distortions caused by preferences in debt-financed tax shelters and at the same time approve of the distortions caused by preferences in equity-financed investments. If there is a valid justification for attacking shelters without attempting to eliminate preferences generally, it must be something other than concern about economic distortion.

. . .

2. *The Netting Theory.* —Calvin Johnson has argued that in theory, interest expense should be deductible only when it is a cost of generating fully taxed income, not when it is a cost of generating tax-exempt income.[2] Johnson explains that because the income tax is a tax on net income (profit) rather than on gross receipts, all costs (including

2. [Johnson, *Is An Interest Deduction Inevitable?*, 6 Va. Tax Rev. 123 (1986).]

interest costs) of generating taxable income must be deducted in order to determine net income to be taxed. He contends, however, that the "process of netting does not require that we allow an ordinary deduction for a given cost if the gross receipts to which it is related are not fully taxed."[3] The allowance of a deduction for costs related to tax-favored income "would strip apart or mismatch revenue and expense, would 'unnet' rather than net, and would describe the transaction inaccurately."[4] Regarding tax shelter interest—interest expense incurred to generate tax-preferred or tax-exempt income—Johnson states:

> Interest is like any other cost. It is netted against the item of which it is a cost and draws its appropriate tax treatment from that netting process. If the interest is a cost of tax-exempt income, it should reduce the net tax-exempt income and thus should not be deductible.[5]

Johnson's position assumes that the goal of the tax system should be for taxable income to reflect economic income as accurately as possible. Thus, interest should be deductible when the related income is fully taxed, because that deduction will accurately reflect economic income. But the deduction of interest when the related income is not taxed will usually cause taxable income to diverge further from economic income than would disallowance of the interest deduction; therefore, the interest deduction should be disallowed in such cases.

The weakness in this analysis is its assumption that the tax structure should incorporate a reasonably accurate reflection of economic income. When Congress enacts an incentive preference, it uses the tax system to achieve some nontax purpose by providing that taxable income need not accurately reflect the economic from the preferred asset. In the case of equity investments in preferred assets, Congress's desire to further the purposes of the preferences subjugates any perceived need to measure economic income accurately. The netting argument fails to explain why the goal of the tax system should shift to an accurate measurement of economic income when the investment in the preferred asset happens to be debt-financed. Nor does it explain why a mismeasurement of income that Congress considers good when it arises from an equity-financed investment in preferred asset is bad when it stems from a debt-financed investment in the same asset.

3. Keeping Nonincentive Preferences Within Bounds. —In a recent article, Cecily Rock and Daniel Shaviro defended the passive loss rules as a means of improving the measurement of net income for tax purposes.[6] Their analysis justifies section 469 primarily as a means of preventing shelters based on nonincentive preferences from interfering with the accurate measurement of unrelated income—especially income from personal services.

---

3. *Id.*
4. *Id.* at 128.
5. *Id.*

6. See Rock & Shaviro, Passive Losses and the Improvement of Net Income Measurement, Va. Tax Rev. 1, 252–27 (1987).

To illustrate the argument, consider the case of an equity investment in an asset that produces income in the form of unrealized appreciation (in the nontaxation of which is the classic example of a nonincentive preference). The effect of the nonincentive preference is merely the avoidance or deferral of tax on the income from the investment. Now imagine a debt-financed investment in that asset, in which the interest expense equals the unrealized appreciation in the asset. Although the taxpayer has no net economic (pre-tax) gain or loss from the investment, the taxpayer will have a substantial tax loss if the interest is deductible while the unrealized appreciation is not taxable. The taxpayer could use this artificial tax loss to shelter unrelated income—especially income from services—from taxation.

Of course, the amount by which taxable income understates economic income is the same in either case: the amount of the unrealized appreciation (or other nonincentive preference). Rock and Shaviro suggest, however, that the use of a nonincentive preference to shelter unrelated income may be objectionable in a way that the use of the preference to shelter income from the preferred asset is not. Their argument posits that the tax system can measure some kinds of income with reasonable accuracy—primarily income from services, but also some kinds of capital income, such as interest and dividends—but has difficulty gauging other kinds of income—especially that undermeasured by nonincentive preferences, such as unrealized appreciation. According to Rock and Shaviro, the system should not allow its problems in measuring these latter types of income to spill over into its assessment of those kinds of income that it can accurately measure. It is one thing to accept the nontaxation of unrealized appreciation as an administrative necessity or as an unavoidable evil, when the result is simply the nontaxation of the unrealized appreciation itself; it is quite another to permit the nontaxation of unrealized appreciation to infect the accurate measurement of income from services through the use of tax shelters. Rock and Shaviro thus conclude that the passive loss rules are justified as a means of keeping nonincentive preferences within bounds.

The idea of prohibiting the use of nonincentive preferences in tax shelters has considerable appeal. If one accepts nonincentive preferences only as administrative necessities, it may make sense to limit their scope to the extent administratively feasible. The difficulty with the Rock–Shaviro position lies not in its logic but in its failure to explain the actual structure of section 469. The passive loss rules do not apply only to nonincentive preferences, as the Rock–Shaviro argument would suggest; section 469 applies to all passive losses, whether attributable to nonincentive or incentive preferences. Many—perhaps most—tax shelters traditionally have been based on incentive preferences, such as ACRS, preferences for research and development, and preferences for development and exploitation of natural resources. The Rock–Shaviro analysis offers no explanation of why section 469 should apply to passive losses attributable to incentive preferences. In the case of an incentive preference, Congress has made a policy decision to measure economic income inaccurately for tax purposes, in order to further some nontax goal. Preventing the use of an incentive preference in a shelter would seem inconsistent with this nontax goal.

. . .

The implementation of a distinction between incentive and nonincentive preferences seems crucial to any loss limitation provision based on the Rock–Shaviro analysis. The absence of such a distinction in section 469 undercuts the ability of the Rock–Shaviro analysis to justify the 1986 Act's passive loss rules.

   4. *The Problem of Abusive Shelters.* —Even if one accepts in theory the case for permitting the use of preferences in tax shelters, one might favor antishelter legislation as a way of controlling "abusive" shelters. Like a "legitimate" shelter, an abusive shelter generates artificial tax losses to shelter unrelated income. The difference between the two is that a taxpayer can properly deduct the artificial losses from the legitimate shelter but not those from the abusive shelter. Abusive shelters may be based on misrepresentations of fact, misinterpretations (often intentional) of law, or both. Unlike a legitimate shelter, which furthers the congressional goals of the preference on which the shelter is based, an abusive shelter serves no public purpose. It simply erodes the tax base and lessens taxpayers' confidence in the integrity of the system.

   One might attempt to justify section 469 as a rather drastic way of ending the problem of abusive shelters. Abusive shelters have depended on their superficial similarity to legitimate shelters in order to escape detection by the Internal Revenue Service (IRS). If, because of section 469, previously legitimate shelters are no longer viable, abusive shelters can no longer be disguised as legitimate shelters. Although this approach certainly solves the problem of abusive shelters, it may be overly broad in its elimination of nonabusive shelters. If nonabusive shelters are consistent with good tax policy, their elimination as a means of controlling abusive shelters should be a last resort—that is, only if there are no other effective means of controlling abusive shelters.

   In fact, Congress and the IRS have taken numerous steps in recent years to control abusive shelters without eliminating nonabusive shelters. Investors in and promoters of abusive shelters formerly relied on the audit lottery for the success of their shelters. They knew that it was unlikely that the IRS would detect an abusive shelter, and that even if it did, there was little risk of the imposition of any civil or criminal penalties. Legislation requiring tax shelter promoters to register their shelters with the IRS has reduced the chances that an abusive shelter will escape detection. Each registered shelter is given a tax shelter identification number, and an investor in the shelter must include that number on his return. Thus, the IRS now receives notice of the existence of shelters that it may wish to investigate and is aware of the identity of the investors in those shelters. If the IRS detects an abusive shelter, the investor may be subject to one or more of the tax shelter penalty provisions added to the Code in this decade. These congressional efforts have increased not only the likelihood that the IRS will detect an abusive shelter but also the adverse consequences if it does. The legislation should thus deter many taxpayers from investing in abusive shelters.

It appeared that Congress and the IRS were well on the way to winning the war on abusive shelters, even without the 1986 addition of section 469. Moreover, much of the anti-abusive shelter arsenal was new—some of the most important weapons were added as recently as 1984—and enough time may not have passed for their full effect to be felt. Congress may not have already won the battle against abusive shelters at the time of section 469's enactment, but it was far too early to say that the existing weapons against abusive shelters had been fully tried and that they had failed. At the very least, a longer test period was needed. Because there was good reason to think that the tax system could have eliminated abusive shelters without taking the drastic step of eliminating nonabusive ones, it is difficult to accept section 469 as a means of controlling abusive shelters.

Moreover, control of abusive shelters is strikingly absent from the Senate Finance Committee report's explanation of the reasons for the enactment of section 469. The report addresses only difficulties caused by shelters that were legitimate under prior law; it does not discuss problems caused by abusive shelters. If the tax system did not need section 469 to control abusive shelters, and if Congress did not even offer that explanation for section 469, we must seek out its justification and purpose elsewhere. Supporters of section 469 must justify the elimination of previously legitimate shelters as an end in itself, not merely as a means of eliminating abusive shelters.

5. *Shelters, Appearances, Taxpayer Morale, and Compliance.* —A major problem with shelters is that they give many taxpayers the impression that the income tax is fundamentally unfair. A taxpayers without shelters pays a substantial tax on his earned income. He hears of other taxpayers, many of whom have much more earned income, who pay little or no tax because of their use of tax shelters. As a result, he loses faith in the tax system's fairness and so loses respect for the system. He begins to cheat on his income tax by failing to report income or by claiming unjustified deductions. In this way, shelters undermine the voluntary compliance on which the income tax system depends. Even if a taxpayer who is demoralized by shelters does not turn to cheating, he will at least cease to give the income tax system his political support. This erosion of political support also threatens the income tax structure.

One can argue that these problems of appearances, taxpayer morale, and compliance are unique to tax shelters and thus provide a reason for attacking tax shelters without eliminating the availability of preferences outside of shelters. The argument goes as follows. A preference used to shelter earned income is highly visible and creates taxpayer morale problems, and thus must be curbed. When a taxpayer uses a preference merely to shelter income from the investment to which it relates, however, the general public does not care or even notice, and therefore the preference need not be eliminated.

Is this difference in appearances alone a sufficient justification for restricting the use of preferences in shelters without limiting the use of preferences outside of shelters? At a very pragmatic level, the answer might well be yes. Preferences that shelter earned income undoubtedly create appearance problems far exceeding any caused by preferences that merely shelter income from the property to which they relate.

Nevertheless, appearances alone provide an unsatisfactory rationale for distinguishing preferences in tax shelters from other preferences. If differences in public perception are the only good reason for treating shelter preferences differently from others, one of two things must be true. One possibility is that the average taxpayer would be just as outraged about the use of preferences outside of tax shelters as about their use in shelters if he understood that the two types of preferences understate economic income in essentially the same way. If so, attacking only the preferences of which the average taxpayer is aware and which he opposes, and leaving intact those preferences of which he is unaware, seems to be taking advantage of the ignorance of the average taxpayer. The other possibility is that the average taxpayer accepts the idea of nonshelter preferences and that he would also accept the use of shelter preferences if he understood that the same arguments support both. In that case, Congress should not legislate to limit shelters, but should educate the public as to why it should support shelters if it supports preferences.

Either way, the basic point is the same: if the only reason for a tax law that distinguishes between preferences used in shelters and preferences used outside of shelters is that the public irrationally distinguishes between the two, that is not a very good reason. Congress should educate the public as to why its attitude is irrational, rather than enact legislation because of that irrationality. If education failed to convince the public that its attitude was irrational, Congress might then need to respond to that attitude with legislation. But unless and until education has been tried and has failed, public perception alone seems an inadequate reason for distinguishing between preferences used in shelters and the same preferences used outside of shelters.

6. *Summary.* —None of the five antishelter arguments examined provides persuasive support for the Act's policy of permitting the use of preferences outside of shelters while prohibiting the use of preferences in shelters. Some of the arguments, however, do identify problems caused by certain kinds of shelters. Congress could better deal with these problems by drafting more narrowly focused legislation. The

criticism that the ability to use preferences in shelters encourages nonprofitable investments is really nothing more than an observation that the preference is fulfilling its purpose of encouraging investment in the preferred asset. The use of preferences outside of shelters similarly affects the allocation of resources; thus, this criticism fails to explain why the tax laws should distinguish between shelter and nonshelter preferences. If the use of tax shelters during high inflation causes special problems, the solution is to inflation-proof the tax laws, not to prohibit sheltering. The netting argument against shelters is based on the assumption that the goal of the tax system is to measure economic income accurately—an assumption that is not valid in the case of incentive preferences. It may be reasonable to attempt to prevent the use of nonincentive preferences in shelters, but the provisions of the 1986 Act—which apply equally to shelters based on incentive and nonincentive preferences—are far broader than necessary to accomplish that limited purpose. Congress and the IRS were bringing abusive shelters under control without the draconian measures of the 1986 Act. The use of preferences in shelters may cause problems of appearances, taxpayer morale, and compliance that are not caused by the use of preferences outside of shelters. If, however, this is the only objection to shelters—if, in other words, the public is wrong in thinking that there is an important difference between the use of shelter and nonshelter preferences—it would be better to attempt to correct the public's misperception than to legislate on the basis of it.

NOTES

1. In a reply to Professor Zelenak, Professor Calvin H. Johnson defended the antishelter restrictions of the 1986 Act. Johnson, Why Have Anti–Tax Legislation? A Response to Professor Zelenak, 67 Tex.L.Rev. 591, 625 (1989).* Professor Johnson concluded:

> It would, of course, be wonderful to have a perfect income tax system in which debt posed no difficulties, and it would also be wonderful to cut back on tax preferences to equalize the implicit tax and the maximum statutory rates. But those goals may have to await another [millennium]. In the meantime, despite the theoretical criticism levied by commentators such as Professor Zelenak, we will need some kinds of antishelter overrides to screen out artificial tax losses that arise under normal tax rules. The passive loss limitations have been successful beyond any reasonable expectation. "Tax shelters" of a certain sort have disappeared, and the "tax shelter crisis" has ended. Prior to 1986, one could either pay tax or buy an indulgence by purchasing a partnership interest in a year-end syndication. Every year the syndications sold their deductions and credits to ever-lower-bracket taxpayers. Some of the shelters might have been "abusive" shelters that the IRS could

* Published originally in 67 *Texas Law Review* 591, 625 (1989). Copyright 1989 by the Texas Law Review Association. Reprinted by permission.

have beaten in court, but some of them might have been "nonabusive" shelters that could have survived in a court of law—though not necessarily in a higher court of good tax policy. But the syndications emanated from an open and flagrant market for tax deductions, like a red-light district a block from city hall. The tax deduction syndications have now ended. Whether based in good theory or bad, the passive loss limitations have made it impossible to sell naked tax deductions. We may have to be satisfied with such miracles as we can get.

Professor Zelenak, however, had another word in the debate. Zelenak, Do Anti–Tax Shelter Rules Make Sense? A Reply to Professor Johnson, 68 Tex.L.Rev. 491 (1989).

2. For discussions of the policy and mechanics of the passive loss provisions of Internal Revenue Code section 469, see Bankman, Case Against Passive Investments: A Critical Appraisal of the Passive Loss Restrictions, 42 Stan.L.Rev. 15 (1989); Peroni, Policy Critique of Section 469 Passive Loss Rules, 62 S.Cal.L.Rev. 1 (1988); Rodgers, Material Participation Under the Passive Activity Loss Provisions, 39 U.Fla. L.Rev 1083 (1987).

C. DISPOSITION: DEFERRING THE RECOGNITION OF GAIN (AND LOSS)

1. TAX–FREE EXCHANGES

FISCHER, TAX FREE EXCHANGES OF REAL PROPERTY

UNDER SECTION 1031 OF THE INTERNAL REVENUE

CODE OF 1954 *

78 Dickinson Law Review 617–619; 623; 633–634; 637–641 (1974).

Section 1002 of the Internal Revenue Code of 1954 provides, "Except as otherwise provided in this subtitle, on the sale or exchange of property the entire amount of gain or loss, determined under section 1001, shall be recognized." Section 1001(a) of the Code provides that the gain or loss to be recognized is the difference between the amount realized on the disposition of the property and the adjusted basis of the property at the time of the disposition. The amount realized is defined in section 1001(b) as the sum of any money received plus the fair market value of property other than money received. Section 1031 is one of the several exceptions to these rules.

In an exchange to which section 1031(a) is applicable, recognition of gain or loss is deferred until the property is transferred in a subsequent taxable exchange. The property acquired assumes the basis of the property transferred. The purpose of the provision is to save a taxpayer from immediate recognition of gain and to intermit the claim of a loss in exchange transactions where a gain or loss may have occurred in a bookkeeping or accounting sense but in a practical and economic sense the gain or loss was a mere paper transaction.

The taxpayer with substantial real estate assets may find the section 1031 exception to the general rule a useful tax-planning procedure or a frustrating trap. In many instances a section 1031 exchange may be the only practical method of extracting a taxpayer's investment from an asset that is no longer a useful or desirable part of his investment portfolio. Real estate is typically an investment that is held for long periods of time and has an enormous propensity to appreciate in value. In some instances, because of the fortunes of location and community development, the appreciation in value is rapid and substantial. While the owner is pleased with his increased fortune, he may find himself in a classic real estate lock-in situation. His basis may be so low, relative to the market value of his property, that a taxable sale may not be practical.

Even if the tax burden were not the controlling consideration, an exchange under section 1031 may be useful. Thus, taxpayers who wish merely to change the form of their real estate investment, rather than to liquidate their holdings, should certainly consider a tax-free exchange under section 1031. This group of taxpayers would include both individuals near retirement who want to change from passive investments to property that will provide an income after retirement and high income taxpayers who seek to change their investments from income producing to passive. Income considerations aside, a taxpayer simply may want to relocate. A farmer may find urbanization crowding his farm operation or increasing his real estate taxes to an impractical level, or a taxpayer may want to move from one part of the country to another or even to a foreign country. In all of these situations, an exchange under section 1031 may permit the taxpayer to accomplish his objectives without a needless tax erosion of his investment.

While section 1031 can frequently be used to advantage, its application to a transfer is not always advantageous or desirable. In some instances, it may be appropriate to effect a taxable transaction. Thus a taxpayer may wish to sell real estate in a taxable transaction in order to take advantage of a loss for tax purposes. Another often encountered example is the taxpayer who seeks a taxable transaction in order to increase his depreciable basis in newly acquired property. If either of these results are desirable, qualification of the transaction under section 1031 should be avoided. If the transaction qualifies as a section 1031 exchange, the recognition of loss will not be allowed and the basis of the transferred property will be carried over to the newly acquired property. Basis will only be increased if taxable, non-qualifying property is included in the exchange.

The trap for the unwary in these situations is that the application of section 1031 to a transaction is not elective. If the transaction meets the requirements of section 1031, the nonrecognition rules will be applicable. The intent of the parties or the labels they have given the arrangement will not serve to avoid the nonrecognition result. ...

A. NONRECOGNITION OF GAIN OR LOSS FROM EXCHANGES SOLELY IN KIND: SECTION 1031(a)

1. Definition of Property for Purposes of Section 1031(a)

The nonrecognition provisions of section 1031(a) are applicable only to certain types of property which are exchanged under certain conditions. Although neither the Code nor the Regulations offer a precise definition of property that will qualify for a section 1031 exchange, they do offer a broad description of the classes of property that will and will not qualify.

The property must be property held by the taxpayer for productive use in a trade or business or for investment. Non-business property such as a personal residence, or an automobile used solely for personal purposes will not qualify. Whether property is being held for productive use in a trade or business or for investment is a question of fact, to be determined by the actual use of the property *at the time of the exchange*. The test is applied to each party to the exchange separately. It is possible for any particular transaction to be a qualified exchange for one of the parties and at the same time a wholly taxable event for the other. In addition, the section specifically excludes from coverage stock in trade, property held primarily for sale, stocks, bonds, notes, choses in action, certificates of trust or beneficial interest, or other securities or evidences of indebtedness or interest. ...

7. Like-Kind Property

In addition to the requirement that qualified property be transferred in a qualified exchange, section 1031(a) will apply only if the properties exchanged are of like-kind. The Regulations provide:

"[T]he words 'like kind' have reference to the nature or character of the property and not to its grade or quality. One kind or class of property may not, under that section, be exchanged for property of a different kind or class. The fact that any real estate involved is improved or unimproved is not material, for that fact relates only to the grade or quality of the property and not to its kind or class. ..."[70]

"No gain or loss is recognized if ... (2) a taxpayer who is not a dealer in real estate exchanges city real estate for a ranch or farm, or exchanges a leasehold of a fee with 30 years or more to run for real estate, or exchanges improved real estate for unimproved real estate ...."[71]

---

70. Treas.Reg. § 1.1031(a)–1(b), T.D. 6935, 1967–2 C.B. 272.

71. Treas.Reg. § 1.1031(a)–1(c)(2), T.D. 6935, 1967–2 C.B. 272.

The application of the "like kind" requirement to real estate exchanges is extremely broad. It refers to the broad classes of property such as real or personal but not to distinctions between tracts of real property even where there are substantial dissimilarities in location, physical attributes or possibilities for productive utilization. The exchange of real estate held for investment with real estate held for productive use in a trade or business may be a "like kind" exchange if the transaction is otherwise qualified. To determine whether real estate exchanges qualify as "like kind" exchanges, reference must be made to the nature of the rights or interests in the real estate which are exchanged. The rights in the respective grantees to the property exchanged must be of the same general character or substantial equality. ...

Regulations section 1.1031(a)–1(c)(2) provides that an exchange of a leasehold of thirty years or more for a fee interest will be an exchange to which section 1031(a) will be applicable. While the Service has followed this rule, no court has yet been required to rule directly on the validity of the Regulation. In practically every case coming before the courts, the transfer of the leasehold interest has been contemporaneous with a sale of the same property. In those instances, the courts have concerned themselves with the validity of the sale. Accordingly, the current status of the Regulation as applied to leases greater than thirty years is unclear.

8. *Property Received to be Held for Productive Use in a Trade or Business or Investment*

The final requirement for a qualified exchange is that the property received must be held either for investment or for productive use in a trade or business. Consequently, section 1031 will not be applicable to an exchange if the property exchanged is acquired for resale. Property acquired in an otherwise qualified exchange was held not qualified where it was previously committed to resale. In Ethel Black,[91] the taxpayer exchanged desert land for a house which she repaired and sold. The court held that the transaction was not entitled to nonrecognition treatment because the property was held primarily for sale.

The requirement here is essentially the same as discussed above with reference to qualifying property for exchange. The significant point is that the requirement is a condition subsequent that may cause an otherwise qualified exchange to be disqualified some point in time after the exchange has been effected. How long property must be held is not clear. It would seem sufficient if the original intent of the taxpayer was to hold it for a qualifying purpose. However, intent is difficult to prove and a sale too soon after the exchange may be considered indicative of the taxpayer's intent at the time of the exchange. Such a presumption may be overcome if the taxpayer is able

---

91. 35 T.C. 90 (1960).

to show a significant change in circumstances which make a sale appropriate.

B. GAIN FROM EXCHANGES NOT SOLELY IN KIND

1. Transfer of Unqualified Property

The nonrecognition provisions of section 1031 are applicable only to exchanges of the certain qualified property described in section 1031(a) of the Code. The Regulations provide:

> "A transfer of property meeting the requirements of section 1031(a) may be within the provisions of section 1031(a) even though the taxpayer transfers in addition property not meeting the requirements of section 1031(a) or money. However, the nonrecognition treatment provided by section 1031(a) does not apply to the property transferred which does not meet the requirements of section 1031(a)." [93]

Consequently, if a taxpayer transfers qualified plus unqualified property in exchange for qualified property, he must recognize any gain or loss realized on the transfer of the unqualified property. Recognition will be pursuant to the general provisions of sections 1001 and 1002 of the Code. For this purpose, the taxpayer is deemed to have received in exchange for the unqualified property an amount equal to its fair market value on the date of the exchange. However, no gain or loss is recognized if a taxpayer transfers qualified property together with cash in exchange for qualified property. Nor will the transfer of qualified property together with unqualified property disqualify the exchange with respect to the qualified property.

The application of these principles as they relate to recognition of a loss is well illustrated by an example contained in the Regulations:

> "A exchanges real estate held for investment plus stock for real estate to be held for investment. The real estate transferred has an adjusted basis of $10,000 and a fair market value of $11,000. The stock transferred has an adjusted basis of $4,000 and a fair market value of $2,000. The real estate acquired has a fair market value of $13,000. A is deemed to have received a $2,000 portion of the acquired real estate in exchange for the stock, since $2,000 is the fair market value of the stock at the time of the exchange. A $2,000 loss is recognized under section 1002 on the exchange of the stock for real estate. No gain or loss is recognized on the exchange of the real estate since the property received is of the type permitted to be received without recognition of gain or loss. ..." [97]

These principles are equally applicable to recognition of gain. It should also be noted that whether a particular property is qualified or not depends on the nature of each exchange. Otherwise qualified real estate will not be qualified property if it is part of an exchange of

---

93. Treas.Reg. § 1.1031(a)–1(a), T.D. 6935, 1967–2 C.B. 272.

97. Treas.Reg. § 1.1031(d)–1(e), T.D. 6935, 1967–2 C.B. 272.

personal property. There must be an exchange of like-kind property or an exchange, or part of it, will not be qualified regardless of the type of property involved.

2. *Receipt of Unqualified Property*

Contrary to the transfer of unqualified property, the Code and Regulations under section 1031(b) make very specific provisions for the receipt of unqualified property in an otherwise qualified exchange. If a taxpayer receives, in a section 1031 exchange, other property or money in addition to property permitted to be received without recognition of gain or loss, any gain realized must be recognized but only in an amount not in excess of the fair market value of the other property and/or the sum of money received. For purposes of section 1031(b), "other property or money" includes liabilities transferred, property not eligible for nonrecognition treatment under section 1031(a), and property which, though eligible by definition, is not of like-kind to the other property involved in the exchange.

a. *Receipt of Money*

The receipt of cash in partial consideration for the exchange of property is tantamount to a partial sale of the property and will cause the recognition of any gain accordingly. If the taxpayer *realizes* gain on a section 1031 exchange, he will *recognize* his gain to the extent of the cash received. It has been held that where cash is advanced by the transferor to enable the transferee to pay off a mortgage on the property he is exchanging, the transferee has not realized a gain but rather merely changed creditors. However, if there is no requirement that the money be used to pay off the mortgage, the receipt of the cash will be treated as taxable gain.

It is important to note the two limitations on recognition, i.e., the lesser of the gain realized or the cash received. An example from section 1.1031(b)-1 of the Regulations illustrates the principle well:

"A, who is not a dealer in real estate, in 1954 exchanges real estate held for investment, which he purchased in 1940 for $5,000, for other real estate (to be held for productive use in a trade or business) which has a fair market value of $6,000, and $2,000 in cash. The gain from the transaction is $3,000, but is recognized only to the extent of the cash received of $2,000."

Recognition of the remaining gain is deferred under the general provisions of section 1031(a).

The cash giving rise to the recognition of gain is the net cash received. Thus, in Revenue Ruling 72-456, a taxpayer was allowed to deduct brokerage commissions from the cash he received and recognized gain only on the net. In Gabe P. Allen,[103] the "expenses incurred in connection with the sale" were permitted to reduce the cash realized from $62,500 to $24,358.26.

---

103. 10 T.C. 413 (1948).

b. *Liabilities*

Regulations section 1.1031(b)–1(c) provides that:

"Consideration received in the form of an assumption of liabilities (or a transfer subject to a liability) is to be treated as 'other property or money' for the purposes of section 1031(b) . . . ."

The Code contains no such specific reference and the language first appeared in the Regulations in 1956. However, the proposition found support in the courts and administrative rulings for many years prior to the 1954 Revenue Act.

Under this provision, when the taxpayer transfers mortgaged property in an exchange and receives unencumbered property, the amount of the mortgage is treated as money received by the taxpayer. This result is the same whether or not the mortgage is assumed by the transferee. In Allen,[108] the taxpayer transferred mortgaged real estate for unencumbered properties plus cash. The transferee took the property subject to the mortgage but did not assume it. The Tax Court held that it was a well established proposition of law that the mortgage indebtedness constituted "other property or money" whether or not the transferee assumed it.

STARKER v. UNITED STATES

United States Court of Appeals, Ninth Circuit, 1979.
602 F.2d 1341.

GOODWIN, Circuit Judge:

T.J. Starker appeals from the dismissal, on stipulated facts, of his tax refund action. We affirm in part and reverse in part.

I. FACTS

On April 1, 1967, T.J. Starker and his son and daughter-in-law, Bruce and Elizabeth Starker, entered into a "land exchange agreement" with Crown Zellerbach Corporation (Crown). The agreement provided that the three Starkers would convey to Crown all their interests in 1,843 acres of timberland in Columbia County, Oregon. In consideration for this transfer, Crown agreed to acquire and deed over to the Starkers other real property in Washington and Oregon. Crown agreed to provide the Starkers suitable real property within five years or pay any outstanding balance in cash. As part of the contract, Crown agreed to add to the Starkers' credit each year a "growth factor", equal to six per cent of the outstanding balance.

On May 31, 1967, the Starkers deeded their timberland to Crown. Crown entered "exchange value credits" in its books: for T.J. Starker's interest, a credit of $1,502,500; and for Bruce and Elizabeth's interest, a credit of $73,000.

---

108. Gabe P. Allen, 10 T.C. 413 (1948).

Within four months, Bruce and Elizabeth found three suitable parcels, and Crown purchased and conveyed them pursuant to the contract. No "growth factor" was added because a year had not expired, and no cash was transferred to Bruce and Elizabeth because the agreed value of the property they received was $73,000, the same as their credit.

Closing the transaction with T.J. Starker, whose credit balance was larger, took longer. Beginning in July 1967 and continuing through May 1969, Crown purchased 12 parcels selected by T.J. Starker. Of these 12, Crown purchased 9 from third parties, and then conveyed them to T.J. Starker. Two more of the 12 (the Timian and Bi-Mart properties) were transferred to Crown by third parties, and then conveyed by Crown at T.J. Starker's direction to his daughter, Jean Roth. The twelfth parcel (the Booth property) involved a third party's contract to purchase. Crown purchased that contract right and reassigned it to T.J. Starker.

The first of the transfers from Crown to T.J. Starker or his daughter was on September 5, 1967; the twelfth and last was on May 21, 1969. By 1969, T.J. Starker's credit balance had increased from $1,502,500 to $1,577,387.91, by means of the 6 per cent "growth factor". The land transferred by Crown to T.J. Starker and Roth was valued by the parties at exactly $1,577,387.91. Therefore, no cash was paid to T.J. Starker, and his balance was reduced to zero.

In their income tax returns for 1967, the three Starkers all reported no gain on the transactions, although their bases in the properties they relinquished were smaller than the market value of the properties they received. They claimed that the transactions were entitled to nonrecognition treatment under section 1031 of the Internal Revenue Code (I.R.C. § 1031), which provides in part:

"(a) Nonrecognition of gain or loss from exchanges solely in kind.

No gain or loss shall be recognized if property held for productive use in trade or business or for investment (not including stock in trade or other property held primarily for sale, nor stocks, bonds, notes, choses in action, certificates of trust or beneficial interest, or other securities or evidences of indebtedness or interest) is exchanged solely for property of a like kind to be held either for productive use in trade or business or for investment."

The Internal Revenue Service disagreed, and assessed deficiencies of $35,248.41 against Bruce and Elizabeth Starker and $300,930.31 plus interest against T.J. Starker. The Starkers paid the deficiencies, filed claims for refunds, and when those claims were denied, filed two actions for refunds in the United States District Court in Oregon.

In the first of the two cases, Bruce Starker v. United States (Starker I), 75–1 U.S. Tax Cas. (CCH) ¶ 8443 (D.Or.1975), the trial court held that this court's decision in Alderson v. Commissioner, 317 F.2d 790 (9th Cir.1963), compelled a decision for the taxpayers. Bruce and Elizabeth

Starker recovered the claimed refund. The government appealed, but voluntarily dismissed the appeal, and the judgment for Bruce and Elizabeth Starker became final.

The government, however, did not capitulate in T.J. Starker v. United States (Starker II), the present case. The government continued to assert that T.J. Starker was not entitled to section 1031 nonrecognition. According to the government, T.J. Starker was liable not only for a tax on his capital gain, but also for a tax on the 6 per cent "growth factor" as ordinary income (interest or its equivalent).

The same trial judge who heard *Starker I* also heard *Starker II*. Recognizing that "many of the transfers here are identical to those in *Starker I*", the court rejected T.J. Starker's collateral-estoppel argument and found for the government. The judge said:

"I have reconsidered my opinion in *Starker I*. I now conclude that I was mistaken in my holding as well in my earlier reading of *Alderson*. Even if *Alderson* can be interpreted as contended by plaintiff, I think that to do so would be improper. It would merely sanction a tax avoidance scheme and not carry out the purposes of § 1031." T.J. Starker v. United States, 432 F.Supp. 864, 868, 77–2 U.S. Tax Cas. (CCH) ¶ 9512 (D.Or.1977).

Judgment was entered for the government on both the nonrecognition and ordinary income (interest) issues, and this appeal followed.

T.J. Starker asserts that the district court erred in holding that: (a) his real estate transactions did not qualify for nonrecognition under I.R.C. § 1031; (b) the government was not collaterally estopped from litigating that issue; and (c) the transactions caused him to have ordinary income for interest, in addition to a capital gain.

II. COLLATERAL ESTOPPEL

T.J. Starker argues that the decision in Bruce Starker v. United States collaterally estops the government from litigating the application of section 1031 to his transactions with Crown. The government urges this court to affirm the trial court on this point, claiming that the two cases presented different legal questions, facts and parties.

. . .

The government, having lost its case against this taxpayer's son based on the same contract to transfer the same family lands, decided not to pursue an appeal in that case, but instead to pursue this taxpayer. Although T.J. Starker's transactions involving three of the parcels differed in a relevant way from those of his son, the legal issues and facts surrounding the other nine are so similar that collateral estoppel applies. Except as to the Bi-Mart, Timian, and Booth properties, the government should have been held collaterally estopped by *Starker I* from relitigation of the applicability of I.R.C. § 1031 in *Starker II*.

III.   TIMIAN, BI–MART, AND BOOTH PROPERTIES

As to Timian, Bi-Mart, and Booth properties, the facts of *Starker I* are so different from those of this case that the entire issue of the applicability of section 1031 to them was properly before the district court in *Starker II.* The court therefore correctly went to the merits of the litigants' arguments as they pertained to these parcels. We now turn to those arguments.

As with the other nine parcels T.J. Starker received, none of these three properties was deeded to him at or near the time he deeded his timberland to Crown. T.J. Starker admits that he received no interest in these properties until a substantial time after he conveyed away title to his property. Thus, the question whether section 1031 requires simultaneity of deed transfers is presented as to all three. In addition, each of these parcels presents its own peculiar issues because of the differing circumstances surrounding their transfers.

A.   *Timian and Bi-Mart Properties.*

The Timian property is a residence. Legal title to it was conveyed by Crown at T.J. Starker's request to his daughter, Jean Roth, in 1967. T.J. Starker lives in this residence, and pays rent on it to his daughter. The United States argues that since T.J. Starker never held legal title to this property, he cannot be said to have exchanged his timberland for it. Furthermore, the government contends, because the property became the taxpayer's personal residence, it is neither property "held for investment" nor of a like kind with such property under the meaning of the Code. On the other hand, the taxpayer argues that there was, in economic reality, a transfer of title to him, followed by a gift by him to his daughter.

The Bi-Mart property, a commercial building, was conveyed by Crown to Roth in 1968. The government raises the same issue with regard to the Bi-Mart property: since T.J. Starker never had title, he did not effect an exchange. T.J. Starker points out, however, that he expended substantial time and money in improving and maintaining the structure in the three months prior to the conveyance of the property to his daughter, and he emphasizes that he controlled and commanded its transfer to her.

We begin our analysis of the proper treatment of the receipt of these two properties with a consideration of the Timian residence. T.J. Starker asserts that the question whether such property can be held "for investment" is unsettled. We disagree. It has long been the rule that use of property solely as a personal residence is antithetical to its being held for investment. Losses on the sale or exchange of such property cannot be deducted for this reason, despite the general rule that losses from transactions involving trade or investment properties are deductible. A similar rule must obtain in construing the term "held for investment" in section 1031. Thus, nonrecognition treatment cannot be given to the receipt of the Timian parcel.

Moreover, T.J. Starker cannot be said to have received the Timian or Bi-Mart properties in exchange for his interest in the Columbia County timberland because title to the Timian and Bi-Mart properties was transferred by Crown directly to someone else, his daughter. Under an analogous nonrecognition provision, section 1034 of the Code, the key to receiving nonrecognition treatment is maintaining continuity of title. Under section 1034, if title shifts from the taxpayer to someone other than the taxpayer's spouse, nonrecognition is denied. Marcello v. Commissioner, 380 F.2d 499 (5th Cir.1967); Boesel v. Commissioner, [65 T.C. 378 (1975)], we find similar reasoning compelling here. Although in some cases a father and his daughter may be seen as having an identity of economic interests, that unity is not sufficient to make transfer of title to one the same as transfer of title to the other. T.J. Starker has not shown that he has any legally cognizable interest in the Timian or Bi-Mart properties that would entitle him to prevent Jean Roth from exercising full ownership rights. In case of a disagreement about the use or enjoyment of these properties, her wishes, not his, would prevail. In these circumstances, T.J. Starker cannot be said to have "exchanged" properties under section 1031, because he never received any property ownership himself.

B. *Booth Property.*

The Booth property is a commercial parcel, title to which has never been conveyed to T.J. Starker. The transfer of this property to him was achieved in 1968 by Crown's acquiring third parties' contract right to purchase the property, and then reassigning the right to T.J. Starker. In addition to emphasizing the lack of simultaneity in the transfers, the government points here to the total lack of deed transfer.

An examination of the record reveals that legal title had not passed by deed to T.J. Starker by the time of the trial. He continued to hold the third-party purchasers' rights under a 1965 sales agreement on the Booth land. That agreement notes that one of the original transferors holds a life interest in the property, and that legal title shall not pass until that life interest expires. In the meantime, the purchasers are entitled to possession, but they are subject to certain restrictions. For example, they are prohibited from removing improvements and are required to keep buildings and fences in good repair. Under the agreement, a substantial portion of the purchase price must be invested, with a fixed return to be paid to the purchaser of the life interest. Should any of these conditions fail, the agreement provides, the sellers may elect, *inter alia*, to void the contract.

Despite these contingencies, we believe that what T.J. Starker received in 1968 was the equivalent of a fee interest for purposes of section 1031. Under Treas.Regs. § 1.1031(a)–1(c), a leasehold interest of 30 years or more is the equivalent of a fee interest for purposes of determining whether the properties exchanged are of a like kind. Under the assigned purchase rights, Starker had at least the rights of a long-term lessee, plus an equitable fee subject to conditions precedent.

If the seller's life interest lasted longer than 30 years, the leasehold interest would be the equivalent of a fee; the fact that the leasehold might ripen into a fee at some earlier point should not alter this result. Thus, we hold that what T.J. Starker received in 1968 was the equivalent of a fee.

This does not solve the riddle of the proper treatment of the Booth parcel, however. Since the taxpayer did not receive the fee equivalent at the same time that he gave up his interest in the timberland, the same issue is presented as with the nine parcels on which the government was estopped, namely, whether simultaneity of transfer is required for nonrecognition treatment under section 1031.

The government's argument that simultaneity is required begins with Treas.Reg. § 1.1002–1(b). That regulation provides that all exceptions to the general rule that gains and losses are recognized must be construed narrowly:

"'* * * Nonrecognition is accorded by the Code only if the exchange is one which satisfies both (1) the specific description in the Code of an excepted exchange, and (2) the underlying purpose for which such exchange is excepted from the general rule."

There are two problems, however, with applying this regulation to section 1031.

First, the "underlying purpose" of section 1031 is not entirely clear. The legislative history reveals that the provision was designed to avoid the imposition of a tax on those who do not "cash in" on their investments in trade or business property. Congress appeared to be concerned that taxpayers would not have the cash to pay a tax on the capital gain if the exchange triggered recognition. This does not explain the precise limits of section 1031, however; if those taxpayers sell their property for cash and reinvest that cash in like-kind property, they cannot enjoy the section's benefits, even if the reinvestment takes place just a few days after the sale. Thus, some taxpayers with liquidity problems resulting from a replacement of their business property are not covered by the section. The liquidity rationale must therefore be limited.

Another apparent consideration of the drafters of the section was the difficulty of valuing property exchanged for the purpose of measuring gain or loss. Section 1031(a) permits the taxpayer to transfer the basis of the property he or she gives up to the property he or she receives, thus deferring the valuation problem, as well as the tax, until the property received is sold or otherwise disposed of in a transaction in which gain or loss is recognized.

But this valuation rationale also has its limits. So long as a single dollar in cash or other non-like-kind property ("boot") is received by the taxpayer along with like-kind property, valuation of both properties in the exchange becomes necessary. In that case, the taxpayer is liable for the gain realized, with the maximum liability being on the amount of cash or other "boot" received, under I.R.C. § 1031(b). To compute the gain realized, one must place a value on the like-kind property received. Moreover, the nonrecognition provision applies only to like-kind exchanges, and not to other exchanges in which valuation is just as difficult. Therefore, valuation problems cannot be seen as the controlling consideration in the enactment of section 1031.

In addition to the elusive purpose of the section, there is a second sound reason to question the applicability of Treas.Regs. § 1.1002–1: the long line of cases liberally construing section 1031. If the regulation purports to read into section 1031 a complex web of formal and substantive requirements, precedent indicates decisively that the regulation has been rejected. We therefore analyze the Booth transaction with the courts' permissive attitude toward section 1031 in mind.

Two features of the Booth deal make it most likely to trigger recognition of gain: the likelihood that the taxpayer would receive cash instead of real estate, and the time gap in the transfers of the equivalents of fee title.

In assessing whether the possibility that T.J. Starker might receive cash makes section 1031 inapplicable, an important case is Alderson v. Commissioner, 317 F.2d 790 (9th Cir.1963). There, this court held that a "three corner" exchange qualified for nonrecognition treatment. The taxpayer and Alloy entered into an agreement for the simple cash sale of the taxpayer's property, but later amended the agreement to provide that Alloy would purchase another parcel to effect a swap with the taxpayer. This amendment did not totally eradicate the possibility that the cash transaction would take place; it provided, in the words of the court, that "if the exchange was not effected by September 11, 1957, the original escrow re the purchase for cash would be carried out." 317 F.2d at 791. The exchange was effected when reciprocal deeds were recorded. Said the court:

> "True, the intermediate acts of the parties could have hewn closer to and have more precisely depicted the ultimate desired result, but what actually occurred on September 3 or 4, 1957, was an exchange of deeds between the petitioners and Alloy which effected an exchange of the Buena Park property for the Salinas property." Alderson v. Commissioner, 317 F.2d at 793.

The court stressed that, although at the time the contract was amended there was a possibility that a cash sale would take place, there was from the outset no intention on the part of the taxpayer to sell his property for cash if it could be exchanged for other property of a like kind. Thus, *Alderson* followed Mercantile Trust Co. of Baltimore v. Commissioner, 32 B.T.A. 82 (1935), a case in which the taxpayer could have required the other party to the exchange to pay cash if that other party was unable to purchase an identified parcel that the taxpayer desired. In *Mercantile Trust*, the taxpayer succeeded in getting nonrecognition treatment by virtue of its intention to get other property, rather than cash, if possible.

Coastal Terminals, Inc. v. United States, 320 F.2d 333 (4th Cir.1963), held similarly. There, a "three corner" exchange was effected, with both the taxpayer and the other party to the exchange maintaining until the closing the option to cancel the exchange and bring about a cash sale instead. Citing *Alderson* with approval, the court noted that the taxpayer intended to sell the property for cash only if it was unable to locate a suitable piece of property to take in exchange. Because an exchange took place, nonrecognition treatment was granted. ...

Thus, the mere possibility at the time of agreement that a cash sale might occur does not prevent the application of section 1031. Even in cases such as *Coastal Terminals,* where the taxpayers had the contract right to opt for cash rather than property, a preference by the taxpayers for like-kind property rather than cash has guaranteed nonrecognition despite the possibility of a cash transaction.

In this case, the taxpayer claims he intended from the very outset of the transaction to get nothing but like-kind property, and no evidence to the contrary appears on the record. Moreover, the taxpayer never handled any cash in the course of the transactions. Hence, the *Alderson* line of cases would seem to control.

The government contends, however, that *Alderson* and other precedents of its type are distinguishable. It points out that in those cases, there may have been a possibility of a receipt of cash at the time of the exchange *agreement,* but there was no possibility of receiving cash at the time the taxpayer *transferred* the property pursuant to the agreement. This difference in timing, says the commissioner, renders the *Alderson* line of cases inapplicable.

At least one appellate decision indicates, however, that title may not have to be exchanged simultaneously in order for section 1031 to apply. In Redwing Carriers, Inc. v. Tomlinson, 399 F.2d 652 (5th Cir.1968), the government argued successfully that mutual transfers of trucks that occurred "at or about" the same time were in fact an "exchange" under section 1031. In *Redwing Carriers,* the taxpayer was attempting to deduct a loss in the purchase of new trucks to replace old trucks; the government disallowed recognition of the loss on the ground that section 1031(c) applied. To keep its replacement transaction outside the scope of the section, a parent corporation transferred its old trucks to a subsidiary, bought new trucks for cash, and had the subsidiary sell the old trucks to the manufacturer for cash. The court viewed the transactions as a whole, and disallowed the loss under section 1031. Some lack of simultaneity was apparently "tolerated" by the commissioner and the court. As the court explained, the transfers to the subsidiary by the parent and to the parent by the manufacturer took place "at or about" the same time. 399 F.2d at 655. Nonetheless, the government urges this court to distinguish *Redwing Carriers,* and *Alderson* and its kin, on the ground that the transfers of title in T.J. Starker's case were separated by a "substantial" period of time. We decline to draw this line.

The government also argues that the contract right to receive property or cash was not "like" title to property, because it was like cash. It asks us to impose a "cash equivalency" test to determine whether section 1031 applies. One flaw in this argument is that title to land is no more or less equivalent to cash than a contract right to buy land. The central concept of section 1031 is that an exchange of business or investment assets does not trigger recognition of gain or loss, because the taxpayer in entering into such a transaction does not "cash in" or "close out" his or her investment. To impose a tax on the event of a deed transfer upon a signing of an exchange agreement could bring about the very result section 1031 was designed to prevent: "the inequity * * * of forcing a taxpayer to recognize a paper gain which was still tied up in a continuing investment of the same sort." Jordan Marsh Co. v. Commissioner, 269 F.2d 453, 456 (2d Cir.1959).

Against this background, the government offers the explanation that a contract right to land is a "chose in action", and thus personal property instead of real property. This is true, but the short answer to this statement is that title to real property, like a contract right to purchase real property, is nothing more than a bundle of potential causes of action: for trespass, to quiet title, for interference with quiet enjoyment, and so on. The bundle of rights associated with ownership is obviously not excluded from section 1031; a contractual right to assume the rights of ownership should not, we believe, be treated as any different than the ownership rights themselves. Even if the contract right includes the possibility of the taxpayer receiving something other than ownership of like-kind property, we hold that it is still of a like kind with ownership for tax purposes when the taxpayer prefers property to cash before and throughout the executory period, and only like-kind property is ultimately received.

The metaphysical discussion in the briefs and authorities about whether the "steps" of the transactions should be "collapsed", and the truism that "substance" should prevail over "form", are not helpful to the resolution of this case. At best, these words describe results, not reasons. A proper decision can be reached only by considering the purposes of the statute and analyzing its application to particular facts under existing precedent. Here, the statute's purposes are somewhat cloudy, and the precedents are not easy to reconcile. But the weight of authority leans in T.J. Starker's favor, and we conclude that the district court was right in *Starker I,* and wrong in *Starker II.* Thus, on the merits, the transfer of the timberland to Crown triggered a like-kind exchange with respect to the Booth property.

IV. SIX PER CENT "GROWTH FACTOR"

The next issue presented is whether the 6 per cent "growth factor" received by T.J. Starker was properly treated as capital gain or as ordinary income. The government successfully argued below that this amount should be treated as ordinary income because it was disguised interest. The taxpayer, on the other hand, contends that the 6 per cent "growth" provision merely compensated him for timber growth on the Columbia County property he conveyed to Crown.

The taxpayer's argument is not without some biological merit, but he was entitled to the 6 per cent regardless of the actual fate of the timber on the property. He retained no ownership rights in the timber, and bore no risk of loss, after he conveyed title to Crown. We agree with the government that the taxpayer is essentially arguing "that he conveyed $1,502,500 to a stranger for an indefinite period of time [up to five years] without any interest." The 6 per cent "growth factor" was "compensation for the use or forbearance of money," that is, for the use of the unpaid amounts owed to Starker by Crown. Therefore, it was disguised interest.

V.   TIMING OF INCLUSION

Our final task, having characterized the proper nature of T.J. Starker's receipts, is to decide in which years they are includable in income. The Timian and Bi-Mart properties do not qualify for nonrecognition treatment, while the other 10 properties received do qualify. In this situation, we believe the proper result is to treat T.J. Starker's rights in his contract with Crown, insofar as they resulted in the receipt of the Timian and Bi-Mart properties, as "boot", received in 1967 when the contract was made. We hold that section 1031(b) requires T.J. Starker to recognize his gain on the transaction with Crown in 1967, to the extent of the fair market values of the Timian and Bi-Mart properties as of the dates on which title to those properties passed to his appointee.

We realize that this decision leaves the treatment of an alleged exchange open until the eventual receipt of consideration by the taxpayer. Some administrative difficulties may surface as a result. Our role, however, is not necessarily to facilitate administration. It is to divine the meaning of the statute in a manner as consistent as possible with the intent of Congress and the prior holdings of the courts. If our holding today adds a degree of uncertainty to this area, Congress can clarify its meaning.

As to the disguised interest, the district court erred in holding T.J. Starker liable for ordinary income in 1967. As a taxpayer reporting on the cash method, T.J. Starker was not liable for taxes on interest income until that interest was received. Although receipt may be actual or constructive, Crown's liability for the "growth factor" did not commence until after 1967 had expired. Had suitable properties been found for T.J. Starker in 1967 (as was the case with Bruce and Elizabeth), Crown would have owed T.J. Starker no "growth factor" at all. Therefore, the government should not have assessed an ordinary income tax on the "growth factor" in 1967. The proper years of inclusion would have been those in which the taxpayer received the interest. To the extent T.J. Starker paid the ordinary tax for 1967, he was entitled to his refund.

VI. CONCLUSION

We affirm the judgment of the district court in part, and reverse it in part. We remand for a modified judgment consistent with this opinion.

Vacated and remanded.

BIGGS v. COMMISSIONER OF INTERNAL REVENUE

United States Court of Appeals, Fifth Circuit, 1980.
632 F.2d 1171.

HENDERSON, Circuit Judge:

The Commissioner of Internal Revenue appeals from the decision of the United States Tax Court holding that a transfer of real property effected by the taxpayer, Franklin B. Biggs, constituted an exchange within the meaning of § 1031 of the Internal Revenue Code of 1954. We affirm.

The numerous transactions which form the subject of this suit are somewhat confusing and each detail is of potential significance. Thus, it will be necessary to recount with particularity the facts as found by the Tax Court.

Biggs owned two parcels of land located in St. Martin's Neck, Worcester County, Maryland (hereinafter referred to as the "Maryland property"). Sometime before October 23, 1968, Biggs listed this property for sale with a realtor. The realtor advised Biggs that he had a client, Shepard G. Powell, who was interested in purchasing the property.

Biggs and Powell met on October 23, 1968 to discuss Powell's possible acquisition of the Maryland property. Biggs insisted from the outset that he receive real property of like kind as part of the consideration for the transfer. Both men understood that Biggs would locate the property he wished to receive in exchange, and Powell agreed to cooperate in the exchange arrangements to the extent that his own interests were not impaired.

On October 25, 1968, Biggs and Powell signed a memorandum of intent which provided, in pertinent part, the following:

I. PURCHASE PRICE: $900,000 *NET* to SELLERS.

* * *

    c. $25,000.00 down payment at signing of contract, * * *
    d. $75,000.00 additional payment at time of settlement, which shall be within ninety (90) days after contract signing, making total cash payments of $100,000.00.

II. MORTGAGE:

    a.   Balance of $800,000.00 secured by a first mortgage on Real Estate to SELLERS at a 4% interest rate; 10 year term.

* * *

The memorandum contained no mention of the contemplated exchange of properties. Upon learning of this omission, Biggs' attorney, W. Edgar Porter, told Powell that the memorandum of intent did not comport with his understanding of the proposed transaction. Powell agreed to have his attorney meet with Porter to work out the terms of a written exchange agreement.

Biggs began his search for suitable exchange property by advising John Thatcher, a Maryland real estate broker, of the desired specifications. Subsequently, Biggs was contacted by another realtor, John A. Davis, who had in his inventory four parcels of land located in Accomack County, Virginia, collectively known as Myrtle Grove Farm (hereinafter referred to as "the Virginia property"). Biggs inspected the property, found it suitable, and instructed Davis to draft contracts of sale.

As initially drawn, the contracts named Biggs as the buyer of the Virginia property. However, at Porter's suggestion, they were modified to describe the purchaser as "Franklin B. Biggs (acting as agent for syndicate)." The contracts were executed on October 29th and 30th, 1968, and contained the following terms:

Paid on execution of contract	$ 13,900.00
Balance due at settlement	115,655.14
Indebtedness created or assumed	142,544.86
Total—Gross Sales Price	$272,100.00

Upon signing the contracts, Biggs paid $13,900.00 to the sellers of the Virginia property.

Because Powell was either unable or unwilling to take title to the Virginia property, Biggs arranged for the title to be transferred to Shore Title Company, Inc. (hereinafter referred to as "Shore"), a Maryland corporation owned and controlled by Porter and certain members of his family. However, it was not until December 26, 1968 that the purchase was authorized by Shore's board of directors. On January 9, 1969, prior to the transfer to Shore, Biggs and Shore entered into the following agreement with respect to the Virginia property:

1. At any time hereafter that either party hereto requests the other party to do so, Shore Title Co., Inc. will and hereby agrees to convey unto the said Franklin B. Biggs, or his nominee, all of the above mentioned property, for exactly the same price said Shore Title Co., Inc. has paid for it, plus any and all costs, expenses, advances or payments which Shore Title Co., Inc. has paid or will be bound in the future to pay, over and above said purchase price to Shore Title Co., Inc., in order for Shore Title Co., Inc., to acquire or hold title to said property; and it [is] further agreed that at that time, i.e.,—when Shore Title Co., Inc. conveys said property under this paragraph and its provisions, the said Franklin B. Biggs, or his nominee will simultaneously release or cause Shore Title Co., Inc. to

be released from any and all obligations which the latter has created, assumed or become bound upon in its acquisition and holding of title to said property.

2.   All costs for acquiring or holding title to said property by both the said Shore Title Co., Inc. and Franklin B. Biggs, or his nominee shall be paid by the said Franklin B. Biggs, or his nominee at the time of transfer of title under paragraph numbered 1 hereof.

On or about the same date, the contracts for the sale of the Virginia property were closed.   Warranty deeds evidencing legal title were delivered to Shore by the sellers.   Biggs advanced to Shore the $115,-655.14 due at settlement and, by a bond secured by a deed of trust on the property, Shore agreed to repay Biggs.   Shore also assumed liabilities totalling $142,544.86 which were secured by deeds of trust in favor of the sellers and another mortgagee.   Biggs paid Thatcher's finder's fee and all of the closing costs.

On February 26, 1969, Shore and Powell signed an agreement for the sale by Shore of the Virginia property to Powell or his assigns. Payment of the purchase price was arranged as follows:

Upon execution of the agreement	$ 100.00

Vendee assumed and covenanted to pay the following promissory notes, all secured by deeds of trust on Virginia property:

To Shore Savings & Loan Association	$ 58,469.86
To those from whom Shore acquired the Virginia property	84,075.00
To Franklin B. Biggs	115,655.14
Balance due at settlement	13,900.00
Total purchase price	272,200.00

The next day, February 27, 1969, Biggs and Powell executed a contract which provided that Biggs would sell the Maryland property to Powell or his assigns upon the following terms:

Cash, upon execution	$ 25,000.00
Cash, at settlement	75,000.00
First mortgage note receivable from Mr. Powell	800,000.00
Total	$900,000.00

The contract further stated:

Sellers and Purchaser acknowledge the existence of a Contract of Sale dated February 26th, 1969, between Shore Title Co., Inc., Vendor-Seller, and Shepard G. Powell or Assigns, Vendee-Purchaser, copy of which is attached hereto and made a part hereof, whereby that Vendor has contracted to sell and that Vendee has agreed to buy from that Vendor at and for the purchase price of Two Hundred Seventy Two Thousand Two Hundred Dollars ($272,200.00)

* * * [the Virginia property]. As a further consideration for the making of this Contract of Sale * * * for the sale and purchase * * * of * * * [the Maryland property] the said Shepard G. Powell or Assigns, for the sum of One Hundred Dollars ($100.00) in cash, in hand paid, receipt whereof is hereby acknowledged, does hereby bargain, sell, set over and transfer unto said Franklin B. Biggs all of the right, title and interest of the said Shepard G. Powell or Assigns in and to said Virginia property and said Contract of Sale relating thereto, upon condition that the said Franklin B. Biggs assumes and covenants to pay (which he hereby does) all of the obligations assumed by the said Shepard G. Powell under the aforesaid Contract of Sale between him and Shore Title Co., Inc.; and said Franklin B. Biggs hereby agrees to hold Shepard G. Powell or Assigns harmless from any liability under any and all of said obligations on said Virginia property, and the said Shepard G. Powell and said Franklin B. Biggs do hereby jointly and separately agree to execute and deliver any and all necessary papers to effect delivery of title to said Virginia property to said Franklin B. Biggs and to relieve said Shepard G. Powell from any and all obligations assumed by him thereon.

On the same date, Powell and his wife assigned their contractual right to acquire the Maryland property to Samuel Lessans and Maurice Lessans. The Lessanses, in turn, sold and assigned their rights to acquire the Maryland property to Ocean View Corporation (hereinafter referred to as "Ocean View") a Maryland corporation, for $1,300,000.00 by an agreement dated May 22, 1969. The purchase price was comprised of $150,000.00 to be paid into escrow at the time the contract was signed, an $800,000.00 note executed by Ocean View in favor of Biggs at the time of settlement, a $250,000.00 note from Ocean View to the Lessanses, and a $100,000.00 note from Ocean View to the real estate agents at closing.

Ocean View was incorporated on May 21, 1969. At the first meeting of its board of directors, the corporation was authorized to acquire the Maryland property and, also, to quit-claim any interest it might have in the Virginia property. It is undisputed, though, that neither the Lessanses nor Ocean View had any interest whatsoever in that property.

On May 24, 1969, Shore executed a deed conveying all of its right, title and interest in the Virginia property to Biggs. Powell and his wife, the Lessanses and Ocean View all joined in executing the deed as grantors, despite their apparent lack of any cognizable interest in the property. This instrument provided that:

> [T]he said Shore Title Co., Inc., a Maryland corporation, executes this deed to the Grantee herein for the purpose of conveying the * * * Virginia property hereinafter described by good and marketable title, subject to the assumption by the Grantee herein of the obligations hereinafter referred to, and all of the other Grantors

herein join in the execution of this deed for the purpose of releasing and quit-claiming any interest in and to the property described herein and for the purpose of thereby requesting Shore Title Co., Inc. to convey said property to the Grantee herein in the manner herein set out ....

By the same deed, Biggs agreed to assume and pay the notes in favor of the mortgagee and the owners from whom Shore had acquired the Virginia property, in the total sum of $142,544.86. On May 29, 1969, Biggs executed a deed of release in favor of Shore indicating payment in full of the $115,655.14 bond.

On May 26, 1969, Biggs and his wife, Powell and his wife and the Lessanses sold the Maryland property to Ocean View. Contemporaneously, Ocean View executed a mortgage in the face amount of $800,-000.00 in favor of Biggs. Also on this date, all of the contracts were closed. Ocean View received the deed to the Maryland property and Biggs accepted title to the Virginia property.

Biggs reported his gain from the sale of the Maryland property on his 1969 federal income tax return as follows: [1]

Selling price of Maryland property	$900,000.00	100.00%
Exchange-Virginia property	298,380.75[a]	33.15%
Boot	$601,619.25	66.85%
Selling price Maryland property	$900,000.00	
Basis-date of exchange	186,312.80	
Gain	$713,687.20	
Not recognized-exchange (Sec. 1031 I.R.C.) 33.15%	236,587.31	
Taxable gain	$477,099.89	53.011%

[a] Such figure included finders' fees and legal costs incident to the acquisition of the Virginia property.

Biggs elected to report the transaction under the installment sales provision of § 453 of the Code. The Commissioner issued a notice of deficiency based upon his determination that there was no exchange of like-kind properties within the meaning of § 1031. The Tax Court disagreed, and ruled in favor of Biggs.[2]

Section 1031 provides, in pertinent part, that the gain realized on the exchange of like-kind property held for productive use or investment shall be recognized only to the extent that "boot" or cash is received as additional consideration. The Commissioner does not deny that Biggs fully intended to carry out an exchange that would pass muster under § 1031. It was undoubtedly for this purpose that Biggs insisted from the beginning of his negotiations with Powell that he receive property of like kind as part of the consideration for the

1. Biggs admits that, even if the transaction qualifies as a § 1031 exchange, he used an incorrect method to calculate the gain to be recognized.

2. The Tax Court opinion is reported at 69 T.C. 905 (1978).

transfer of the Maryland property. However, as this court made clear in Carlton v. United States, 385 F.2d 238 (5th Cir.1967), the mere intent to effect a § 1031 exchange is not dispositive. Indeed, the Commissioner's primary contention is that, under the authority of our holding in *Carlton,* Biggs failed to accomplish an exchange because the purchaser, Powell, never held title to the Virginia property.

The facts on which *Carlton* was decided parallel those which we now consider in several respects. Carlton, the taxpayer, wished to trade a tract of ranch land for other property of a similar character in order to obtain the tax benefits afforded by § 1031. This intent was made explicit in the negotiations and resulting option contract entered into by Carlton and General, a corporation which desired to purchase the ranch property. Carlton proceeded to locate two parcels of suitable exchange property, negotiate for the acquisition of this property, and pay a deposit on each parcel. General executed the actual agreements of sale and then assigned its contract rights to purchase the exchange property to the taxpayer. However, the crucial factor which distinguishes *Carlton* from the instant case is that General actually paid cash for the ranch property which Carlton then used two days later to purchase the exchange property. A panel of this court held that the receipt of cash transformed the intended exchange into a sale:

> [W]hile elaborate plans were laid to exchange property, the substance of the transaction was that the appellants received cash for the deed to their ranch property and not another parcel of land. The very essence of an exchange is the transfer of property between owners, while the mark of a sale is the receipt of cash for the property.

385 F.2d at 242 (footnote and citations omitted).

Although the payment and receipt of cash was the determinative factor, the court went on to cite additional reasons to support its holding of a sale, rather than an exchange:

> Further, General was never in a position to exchange properties with the appellants because it never acquired the legal title to either the Lyons or the Fernandez property. Indeed, General was not personally obligated on either the notes or mortgages involved in these transactions. Thus it never had any property of like kind to exchange. Finally, it cannot be said that General paid for the Lyons and Fernandez properties and merely had the properties deeded directly to the appellants. The money received from General by the appellants for the ranch property was not earmarked by General to be used in purchasing the Lyons or Fernandez properties. It was unrestricted and could be used by the appellants as they pleased.

385 F.2d at 242–243. The Commissioner maintains that this language in *Carlton* establishes as an absolute prerequisite to a § 1031 exchange that the purchaser have title to the exchange property. We do not agree with this interpretation. The *Carlton* decision was based on the

aggregate circumstances discussed therein and, as we have noted, the most significant of these was the receipt of cash by the taxpayer. In the present case, the transfer of the Maryland property and the receipt of the Virginia property occurred simultaneously, and the cash paid to Biggs at the closing constituted "boot." Also in contrast to the facts found in *Carlton*, Powell, as contract purchaser, did "assume [] and covenant [] to pay ... promissory notes, all secured by deeds of trust on the Virginia property," plus the balance due at settlement. We cannot ignore the legal obligations and risks inherent in this contractual language, even though Powell was subject to such risks only for a short period of time. Also, the unrestricted use of funds which was a problem in *Carlton* is of no concern here because Biggs received cash only upon the closing of all transactions.

Thus, we are left with the sole consideration that Powell never acquired legal title to the Virginia property. Yet, if we were to decide, as the Commissioner urges, that this factor alone precludes a § 1031 exchange, we would contravene the earlier precedent established by this court in W.D. Haden Co. v. C.I.R., 165 F.2d 588 (5th Cir.1948). *Haden* also involved a multi-party exchange in which the purchaser, Goodwin, never held title to the exchange property. However, since Goodwin had contracted to purchase the property, the court held that the taxpayer had effected a like-kind exchange, stating that the purchaser "could bind himself to exchange property he did not own but could acquire." 165 F.2d at 590.

Our resolution of the title issue is also tangentially supported by language contained in the Ninth Circuit's recent opinion in Starker v. United States, 602 F.2d 1341 (9th Cir.1979).

> ... title to real property, like a contract right to purchase real property, is nothing more than a bundle of potential causes of action: for trespass, to quiet title, for interference with quiet enjoyment, and so on. The bundle of rights associated with ownership is obviously not excluded from section 1031; a contractual right to assume the rights of ownership should not, we believe, be treated as any different than the ownership rights themselves. Even if the contract right includes the possibility of the taxpayer receiving something other than ownership of like-kind property, we hold that it is still of a like kind with ownership for tax purposes when the taxpayer prefers property to cash before and throughout the executory period, and only like-kind property is ultimately received.

602 F.2d at 1355. Of course, we need not, and do not, express either acceptance or disapproval of the ultimate holding in *Starker*. However, the Ninth Circuit's discussion of the title versus right-to-purchase problem is, we believe, consistent with our own analysis.

We must also reject the Commissioner's assertions that the Tax Court applied the so-called "step-transaction doctrine" incorrectly, and that the transactions which occurred here were in substance a sale for cash of the Maryland property and an unrelated purchase of the Virginia property. The step-transaction doctrine was articulated in Redwing Carriers, Inc. v. Tomlinson, 399 F.2d 652 (5th Cir.1968):

> [A]n integrated transaction may not be separated into its components for the purposes of taxation by either the Internal Revenue Service or the taxpayer. In Kanawha Gas and Utilities Co. v. Commissioner, 5 Cir.1954, 214 F.2d 685, 691, our Court through Judge Rives said:

> 'In determining the incidence of taxation, we must look through form and search out the substance of a transaction.... [cases cited] This basic concept of tax law is particularly pertinent to cases involving a series of transactions designed and executed as parts of a unitary plan to achieve an intended result. Such plans will be viewed as a whole regardless of whether the effect of so doing is imposition of or relief from taxation. The series of closely related steps in such a plan are merely the means by which to carry out the plan and will not be separated.'

399 F.2d at 658. The Tax Court found that the many transactions leading to the ultimate transfers of the Maryland and Virginia properties were part of a single, integrated plan, the substantive result of which was a like-kind exchange. This finding is amply supported by the evidence. Biggs insisted at all times that he receive like-kind property as part of the consideration for the transfer of the Maryland property. Powell agreed to this arrangement and assured Biggs of his cooperation. Biggs was careful not to contract for the sale of the Maryland property until Powell had obtained an interest in the Virginia land. When he and Powell did enter into an agreement of sale on February 26, 1969, the exchange was made an express condition of the contract. Biggs also avoided the step which was fatal to the taxpayer's intended exchange in *Carlton;* i.e., he did not receive any cash prior to the simultaneous closings of the properties on May 26, 1969. Under these circumstances, the Tax Court correctly determined that all transactions were interdependent and that they culminated in an exchange rather than a sale and separate purchase.

Finally, we examine the Commissioner's claim that Shore was serving as an agent for Biggs throughout the transactions, and that the accomplishment of the intended exchange was thereby precluded.[4] Admittedly, the exchange would have been meaningless if Shore, acting as Biggs' agent, acquired title to the Virginia property and then executed the deed conveying title to Biggs. For, in essence, Biggs would have merely effected an exchange with himself. However, while the Tax Court refused to find, in contrast to its decision in *Coupe,* that Shore acted as an agent for the purchaser, Powell, it also specifically

---

4. In advancing this argument, the Commissioner does not seem to focus on Shore's purported status as Biggs' agent, but rather on the fact that Shore was not Powell's agent for purposes of accepting title to the Virginia property. However, our disposition of the title question renders the absence of a principal-agent relationship between Powell and Shore irrelevant.

determined that Shore was not an agent of Biggs. Rather, Shore accepted title to the Virginia property, albeit at Biggs' request, merely in order to facilitate the exchange. We believe that this is an accurate characterization of Shore's role in the transactions. Consequently, we reject the Commissioner's agency notion also.

Undoubtedly, the exchange of the Maryland and Virginia properties could have been more artfully accomplished and with a greater economy of steps. However, we must conclude on the facts before us that the taxpayer ultimately achieved the intended result. Accordingly, the decision of the Tax Court is

AFFIRMED.

2. TAXES ON THE INSTALLMENT PLAN

THEOPHILOS, THE INSTALLMENT SALES REVISION ACT OF 1980 AND ITS IMPACT ON REAL PROPERTY TRANSACTIONS *

4 Real Property Law Reporter 1–5 (1981).

Most attorneys familiar with real property tax planning have at one time or another utilized the installment method of reporting income under IRC § 453. Simply stated, the basic purpose of the installment sale provisions of the Internal Revenue Code is to allow income from the sale of real property under an installment note to be reported in the year each installment is received, thus deferring gain, and the taxes due on such gain, to future tax years. Furthermore, gain on each installment payment is recognized in the same proportion as the gross profit from the sale bears to the "total contract price" (specifically defined in Reg. § 1.453–4(c)). For example, if 50 percent of the total contract price represents "gross profit," then 50 percent of the installment payments received in each subsequent tax year is recognized as "gain" in that year.

Unfortunately for taxpayers, a number of technical requirements and limitations were either expressly set forth in IRC § 453 or read into it by the IRS or the courts. Moreover, failure to comply precisely with these rules resulted in the immediate recognition of *all* gain in the year of sale. However, Congress recently enacted the Installment Sales Revision Act of 1980, which modifies or eliminates some of the basic requirements and limitations of IRC § 453, while leaving unchanged its basic purpose. In taking this action, Congress removed much of the threat of recognition of all gain on the taxpayer's failure to comply with the previously existing requirements and limitations. Also, Congress provided additional vehicles for more precise real property tax planning.

This article first reviews briefly the requirements and limitations which existed under IRC § 453 before adoption of the Act. It then examines the newly revised § 453, emphasizing the changes from previous law. However, the article is not intended as a comprehensive outline of the new statute, but a summary of the new installment sale provisions relevant to real property practitioners and their impact on real property transactions.

IRC § 453 Before the Act

With respect to dispositions of real property made before the Act's effective dates, practitioners were faced with a number of requirements and limitations which had to be satisfied for a sale to qualify as an installment sale under § 453. These requirements and limitations included the following:

1. **Thirty Percent Rule:** No more than 30 percent of the total selling price could be received by the taxpayer in the year of the sale. Often, this created confusion for sellers because the IRS would calculate the 30 percent by adding to any down payment received such items as other installment payments received in the same tax year as the down payment, interest imputed under IRC § 483, and the amount by which existing encumbrances on the property exceeded the seller's adjusted basis. Consequently, attorneys generally counseled clients to accept no more than 29 percent of the sales price as a down payment so as to provide a 1 percent cushion against inadvertently triggering recognition of all gain.

2. **Two-Payment Rule:** At least two installment payments were required to be made, each in different tax years. In a real property context, this was evidenced generally by a down payment in the year of sale (not exceeding 30 percent) and at least one additional payment in a subsequent tax year.

3. **Installment Election:** The taxpayer had to elect affirmatively the installment method of reporting gain.

4. **Fixed and Determinable Sale Price:** The sales price of the real property must have been fixed and determinable. In other words, if the ultimate sales price of the property was subject to a contingency, the installment method of reporting income was not available.

5. **Third-Party Guaranty:** The IRS has taken the position in the past that a third-party guaranty (including a standby letter of credit) used as security for a deferred payment should be treated as a payment received on the installment obligation. Thus, if a taxpayer required an installment obligation to be secured by a device such as a standby letter of credit, the IRS insisted on characterizing the payment as received in the year of sale.

6. **Receipt of Like Kind Property:** In the past, a sale of real property may have qualified as both: (a) a tax-deferred exchange under IRC § 1031 with respect to any "like kind" property received; and (b) an installment sale under IRC § 453 with respect to any cash or other

property received. However, the like kind property would be valued by the IRS and treated as a payment received for purposes of computing both the total sales price and the gain to be recognized under the installment portion of the transaction. Accordingly, gain on each installment payment would be recognized in the same proportion as the gross profit bears to the total contract price (which would *include* the value of any like kind property received under IRC § 1031).

The Act

The Installment Sales Revision Act of 1980 greatly simplifies and improves IRC § 453. As previously noted, the Act makes a number of specific changes, while preserving the basic thrust of the law. Thus, income from the sale of real property is still reported in the tax year in which payment is received, effectively deferring gain to the future. As outlined in the ensuing discussion, the Act provides practitioners with greater flexibility and opportunity for creative tax planning.

The Act also reorganized the coverage of IRC § 453. Before its amendment, § 453 lumped together rules for installment method reporting for dealers in personal property and sales of real property and nondealer personal property, as well as special installment obligation disposition rules. The Act structurally revised § 453 by shifting to new IRC § 453A the rules for personal property dealer transactions and by shifting to new IRC § 453B the installment obligation disposition rules. Thus, new IRC § 453 covers only nondealer transactions in real and personal property.

Regulations applicable to new IRC § 453 have not yet been promulgated. However, much of the rationale behind the specific changes implemented by the Act is set forth in the September 28, 1980, Senate Finance Committee Report on the Installment Sales Revision Act of 1980, Pub.L. 96–471. Consequently, in the absence of regulations, the Senate Finance Committee Report is an invaluable source of guidance and should be reviewed carefully by counsel.

The substantive changes implemented by the Act and their impact on real property transactions may be summarized as follows:

1. No Maximum Down Payment: The Act eliminates entirely the previously existing requirement which limited down payments to 30 percent or less of the sales price. Counsel no longer need be concerned with inadvertently exceeding the 30 percent limitation and triggering recognition of all gain in the year of sale. Hence, a seller of real property can now conduct tax planning with a much higher degree of precision. For example, a seller may prefer to recognize one half of his gain in the year of sale, deferring the balance only until the next tax year. Previously, this was impossible.

2. One-Payment Rule: The Act amended IRC § 453 to eliminate the two-payment rule. New IRC § 453(b)(1) defines an installment sale as a "disposition of property where at least 1 payment is to be received after the close of the taxable year in which the disposition occurs."

Again, this change provides an opportunity for greater flexibility and more precise tax planning. In the past, a seller who desired to defer the entire gain only until the next tax year was forced to accept at least a token down payment in the year of sale. This is no longer the case. As discussed below, this complete deferral of gain is capable of even further refinement.

3. No Election Required: As amended by the Act, IRC § 453(a) eliminates the need for a taxpayer to "elect" affirmatively the installment method of reporting gain. Thus, installment reporting automatically applies to a sale unless the taxpayer specifically elects not to have the provision apply. However, the "election out" cannot be changed once made, unless the IRS consents to its revocation.

4. Contingent Sales Price: Installment sale reporting is now available for a sale of real property even when the selling price is not fixed or is otherwise subject to a contingency. To illustrate, a seller of an apartment building can now fix the sales price as a multiple of gross rents collected at the end of the year following sale of the building, while recognizing gain on the installment method. Although regulations have not yet been promulgated, the Senate Finance Committee Report states that it is intended that income from the sale would be reported on a pro rata basis with respect to each installment payment using the maximum selling price, determined, if possible, from the "four corners" of the contract. If the maximum selling price is not achieved as a result of the contingency, the taxpayer's income would at that time be recomputed. In fact, the Senate Finance Committee Report notes that, if the taxpayer has reported more income from installment payments received in previous taxable years than the total recomputed income, the taxpayer should be able to deduct the excess in the adjustment year as a loss. Inclusion of sales for a contingent price within the installment reporting provisions carries with it Congress' intent to limit reporting under the "cost-recovery" method sanctioned in Burnet v. Logan (1931) 283 US 404, to those "rare and extraordinary cases" in which the fair market value of the buyer's obligation cannot reasonably be ascertained.

5. Third-Party Guaranty: A third-party guaranty used as security for an installment payment is no longer considered a payment actually received on the installment obligation, provided, however, that it is not otherwise marketable or transferable before default by the obligor under the installment obligation. For example, a seller of real property may prefer to defer *all* gain to subsequent tax years. To accomplish this, the property in question would be sold under an installment note secured by the property, with no down payment. Although such a complete deferral was feasible under prior law, it would result in a loan-to-value ratio of 100 percent, certainly not a conservative position for the lender/seller. However, under the new IRC § 453, the installment payments representing the first 10 or 20 percent of the loan could be secured by a nonassignable standby letter of credit issued to the seller for the account of the buyer. This has the practical effect of reducing the loan-to-value ratio for the seller to a more reasonable and conservative 80 or 90 percent.

This device is particularly useful for year-end sales of real property where the seller traditionally prefers to close after the first of the year, so as to defer gain on what otherwise would have been a down payment, while the buyer wants to close and take possession before year end. Using a nonassignable standby letter of credit, there is no reason both parties cannot be satisfied. The seller can accept a short-term promissory note for what would otherwise be the down payment, secured by a nonassignable standby letter of credit instead of a deed of trust.

6. Receipt of Like Kind Property: Under the new IRC § 453, a sale of real property may still qualify as both a tax-deferred exchange and an installment sale, but with one significant difference. Specifically, the like kind property is no longer valued or treated as a payment for the purpose of calculating the total sales price and the gain recognized on the installment portion of the transaction. Consequently, gain on each installment payment is recognized in the same proportion as the total gross profit from the sale bears to the total contract price (*not* including any like kind property).

Summarized below is an example outlined in the Senate Finance Committee Report which illustrates the difference between former IRC § 453 and the new IRC § 453. In this example, it is assumed that a taxpayer exchanges property with a basis of $400,000 for like kind property valued at $200,000 and an installment note for $800,000, with $100,000 payable under the note in the tax year of sale and the balance payable in the next tax year.

	Old § 453 (like kind property taken into account)	New § 453 (like kind property not taken into account)
Contract price	$1,000,000	$800,000
Gross profit	600,000	600,000
Gross profit ratio (%)	60%	75%
Gain to be reported for		
1. Taxable year of sale:		
(a) 60% of $300,000 (*i.e.*, payments "received" of $100,000 cash and $200,000 of like kind property)	180,000	
(b) 75% of $100,000 (*i.e.*, cash payments)		75,000
2. Succeeding taxable years:		
(a) 60% of $700,000 (cash received)	420,000	
(b) 75% of $700,000 (cash received)		525,000
Total gain recognized	$600,000	$600,000

In short, although the total gain recognized is the same, under the new IRC § 453 more gain is deferred to succeeding tax years.

Conclusion

Simply stated, the Act has the following impact on IRC § 453:

1. It eliminates in its entirety the 30 percent rule;

2. It eliminates the two-payment rule, replacing it with a requirement that at least one installment payment be made in a succeeding tax year;

3. It eliminates the need to elect the installment method of reporting income;

4. It eliminates the prohibition against contingent sales prices;

5. It relaxes the prohibition against third-party guaranties; and

6. It revises the method by which gain is computed when like kind property is received.

Although the effective date varies depending on the specific provision, none is later than October 20, 1980. Thus, any disposition of property occurring subsequent to that date should be governed by the Act. Furthermore, elimination of the 30 percent and two-payment rules is effective for taxpayers whose taxable years end after October 20, 1980.

NOTES

1. *Tax Free Exchanges.* The 1984 Tax Reform Act curtailed some tax benefits of real estate transactions. It curbed *Starker*-type exchanges by amending section 1031(a) to impose a 45-day deadline on identifying the exchange property and a 180-day deadline on the taxpayer's actual receipt of the exchange property. Property identified or received past these deadlines will no longer qualify as "like-kind" property. By repealing the preferential tax rate on capital gains, the 1986 Tax Reform Act created a new incentive for taxpayers to defer tax on gains by engaging in tax free exchanges. The Omnibus Budget Reconciliation Act of 1989 added subsection (f), setting special rules for exchanges between related persons, and subsection (h), providing that real property outside of the United States and real property within the United States are not property of a like kind.

2. *Installment Sales.* The 1986 Tax Reform Act substantially limits the tax benefits of reporting gain through the installment method in situations where property is sold for more than $150,000 and where the seller has other debt obligations. Through a complex formula, the Act effectively requires the seller to treat part of her outstanding debt obligations as constructive payments made by the buyer in addition to any payments made by the buyer, resulting in the recognition of more gain in any year than would previously be the case. The change was aimed at the practice of some installment sellers to obtain cash approximating the full purchase price in the first year of the

installment sale by borrowing funds on the security of the installment sale note.

The Revenue Act of 1987 generally repealed the provision for use of the installment method by dealers in real property for dispositions occurring after December 31, 1987 and altered the 1986 amendments in other respects.

See generally Miller, Coexisting with the 1986 Code's "Proportionate Disallowance" of the Installment Method, 15 J. Real Est.Tax. 115 (1988); Robinson, Installment Reporting for Real Estate: Complexification After the Tax Reform Act of 1986, 14 J. Real Est.Tax. 264 (1987).

3. *Bibliographic Note.* See generally, S. Guerin, Taxation of Real Estate Dispositions (1984). On section 1031 generally, see Kornhauser, Section 1031: We Don't Need Another Hero, 60 S.Cal.L.Rev. 397 (1988); Dentino, Recapture on the Exchange of Real Property After ERTA, 11 J.Real Estate Tax. 254 (Spring 1984); Solomon, The Section 1031 Exchange of Real Estate—Has ACRS Decreased its Attractiveness? 10 J.Real Estate Tax. 346 (1982–1983); Van Dorn, Planning Tax-Free Like-Kind Exchanges of Real Estate, 5 J.Real Estate Tax. 293 (1977–78); Righter, The Real Estate Exchange: A Flexible Financing Tool, 1 J.Real Estate Tax. 62 (1973); Winokur, Real Estate Exchanges: The Three Corner Deal, 28 N.Y.U.Inst. on Fed.Tax. 127 (1970).

On section 453 generally, see Allison & Latham, The Installment Sales Revision Act of 1980—Important Changes for Practitioners, 10 Stetson L.Rev. 453 (1981); Kurn & Nutter, The Installment Sales Revision Act of 1980: In the Name of Simplification Has a Measure of Complexity Been Added? 8 J.Real Estate Tax. 195 (1980–81); Heinkel, The Impact of the Installment Sales Revision Act of 1980 on *Starker*-Type Exchanges, 10 J.Real Estate Tax. 3 (1982–83).

II. COMMERCIAL LAND FINANCE

The contemporary market for commercial real estate finance differs dramatically from the market that existed thirty, twenty, and even ten years ago. The long term, fixed rate mortgage, once the standard financing instrument, has fallen victim to concerns for continuing inflation and has been substantially displaced by a variety of more flexible instruments. Usury ceilings, tied to obsolete interest rates, have forced lenders to restructure their loan terms and lending policies. Less development funds have been available in the 1990's as a result of the savings and loan crisis and weakness in some commercial banks, greater caution by remaining lenders, and an increase in standards and activity by bank regulators. These changes, together with changes in the federal income tax law and the partial deregulation of institutional lending activity, have also produced significant shifts in the sources of commercial land finance. Life insurance companies, once the primary source of commercial real estate finance, have been joined in the marketplace by other institutional lenders and by new aggregations of individual investors. Although the sources and terms of commercial real estate finance will doubtless continue to change, it is possible to trace some fundamental patterns.

Terms. The most common lender strategy in fighting inflation has been to agree only to short term notes or notes renewable at specified intervals, with the renewal rate adjusted up or down according to some measure of inflation such as the consumer price index. Alternatively, the lender may agree to a long term loan, but only if the interest rate is allowed to float according to an inflation index, or if the note contains a call provision entitling the lender to call in the note for complete repayment at a specified intervals before the loan has been fully amortized.

Another lender strategy has been to participate in the income from the mortgaged property. Lender and borrower might, for example, agree on a fixed, below market interest rate augmented by a specified percentage of the property's rental income and a further percentage of the property's appreciation in value at the time the mortgage is discharged. Or the parties may agree on a convertible mortgage—a fixed rate loan that entitles the lender at a specified point to convert the unamortized portion of the loan (say, 70% of the property's initial value) into an equity interest (again 70%) in the property. Frequently, a convertible mortgage will give the lender the right to buy out the mortgagor's remaining equity interest (here 30%) at a predetermined price or at a price calculated on the basis of a predetermined formula.

681

Sources. Insurance companies are today investing less of their own funds in real estate debt and are using their real estate expertise to place loans for other, comparatively inexperienced capital sources. One such source, pension funds, have emerged as a potentially significant factor in the industry. Also, as mortgage terms have become shorter and interest rates have become more readily adjustable, commercial banks have shown a new willingness to enter the commercial real estate loan market, as have the real estate credit subsidiaries of large industrial corporations. Foreign investment in U.S. real estate has also increased, and has proved to be a particularly volatile issue. See R. Barak, Foreign Investment in U.S. Real Estate (1981); Pedersen & Sharp, Real Estate Investments by Foreign Persons After the Foreign Investment in Real Property Tax Act of 1980, 11 Real Est.L.J. 47 (1982); Feingold & Alpert, Observations on the Foreign Investment in Real Property Tax Act of 1980, 1 Va.Tax Rev. 105 (1981); Wood, Proposed Barriers to Foreign Investment in U.S. Real Estate, 4 Probate & Prop. 12 (Jan.-Feb.1990); Hardy & Ullman, Alternative Forms of U.S. Real Estate Investment By Foreign Institutions, 20 Tax Mgmt.Int'l J. 244 (1991). For an excellent overview and comprehensive bibliography, see A.B.A. Comm. on Foreign Investment in U.S. Real Estate, Foreign Investment in U.S. Real Estate: Federal and State Laws Affecting the Foreign Investor—An Update, 16 Real Prop., Probate & Trust J. 465 (1981).

Three arrangements for assembling real estate debt and equity enjoyed varying popularity between the 1960's and the early 1980's: the limited partnership, the real estate investment trust and the joint venture. Prior to the 1986 Tax Reform Act, the limited partnership enabled individual, high bracket investors to capture the tax advantages of owning improved, depreciable property. As a result, many limited partnerships were created for the main, or even sole, purpose of obtaining tax benefits. As discussed at pages 637–650 above, these tax advantages have largely disappeared. Real estate limited partnerships are still important investment vehicles, however, when the project is economically sound, producing cash flow and appreciation. The 1986 Tax Reform Act also authorized a new investment vehicle—real estate mortgage investment conduits (REMICs)—to acquire and hold both commercial and residential mortgage loans and to issue securities embodying interests in these loans on the secondary mortgage market.

The real estate investment trust, like the limited partnership, enables the individual investor-shareholder to share in the investment advantages of real estate. One difference is that, unlike the limited partnership, which typically owns a single property, the REIT operates much like a mutual fund, holding a pool of real property assets. The REIT also offers some, but not all, of the limited partnership's tax advantages. So long as the REIT qualifies under the applicable Internal Revenue Code requirements respecting organization, operation, assets, income and dividend distribution, it can—like a partnership and unlike a corporation—pass its income and capital gains directly through to its investors, without any tax liability at the entity level of the REIT. See I.R.C. §§ 856–860. After a burst of great popularity in the 1960's, REITs plunged in value during the 1970's. By the early 1980's, however, some observers saw a resurgence. See Wayne, The Return of the REITs, N.Y. Times, Dec. 5, 1982, § 3, at 1, col. 1; Mai & Greenfield, The New Uses of Real Estate Investment Trusts, 32 Prac. Law. 27 (Mar.1986). On the reasons for the collapse of the REIT market, see Taylor, The Financial Collapse of the REIT Industry: An Analysis and Proposed Regulatory Framework, 9 Tex. Tech L.Rev. 451 (1978). On the tax aspects of REITs, see Halpern, Real Estate Investment Trusts and the Tax Reform Act of 1976, 31 Tax Lawyer 329 (1977).

Institutional lenders seeking an equity position in real estate will sometimes form a joint venture with a developer or other entrepreneur to build and operate the project. The lender ("money partner") provides the cash, or sometimes the land, needed for the project, and the developer ("operating partner") provides services and expertise. In return for their contributions, each co-venturer shares in the ownership, income and losses from the project in predetermined shares. Although joint ventures are most commonly structured as general partnerships between the co-venturers, they may also take the form of a limited partnership, corporation, REIT or tenancy in common.

A. MORTGAGES

1. TERMS

SMITH & LUBELL, THE PROMISSORY NOTE: FORGOTTEN DOCUMENT *

8 Real Estate Review 15–17 (Spring 1978).

The completion of a modern mortgage loan transaction requires an imposing number of documents. At the closing of complex financing transactions, such as high-credit lease loans, attorneys make use of extensive checklists that enumerate, among other documents, note purchase agreements, leases, assignments of leases, promissory notes, mortgages, financing statements, various types of certifications, and detailed legal opinions. Many of the instruments are lengthy, and copies of the entire package of documents are often bound into volumes which, in size and weight, rival *Webster's New Third International Dictionary*.

When the financing of office buildings, shopping centers, and industrial facilities is arranged, many of the instruments, particularly the mortgage and leases, are the subjects of protracted negotiations. However, one of the most significant instruments is also one of the briefest and is often an almost forgotten document. It is the promissory note.

WHAT IS THE PROMISSORY NOTE?

The promissory note and the mortgage (or deed of trust) are the two essential documents of a real estate loan. The note is the evidence of the indebtedness and the promise to repay the loan, while the mortgage is the pledge of specific realty as security for the debt. The principal attributes of a valid note are the following:

- The note must be in writing.

- The borrower and lender must have contractual ability to act. (They must be under no legal incapacity, such as minority or insanity.)

- The borrower must promise to pay a specific sum of money.

- The terms of payment must be stated, e.g., the note normally is payable in periodic installments for a specified number of years.

- The rights of the parties in the event of a default must be specified.

- The note must be properly executed by the borrower. However, a note is not recorded and accordingly is not acknowledged before a notary public.

- There must be voluntary delivery by the borrower and acceptance by the lender.

Since the note is evidence of a debt and is a negotiable instrument, only one copy of it should be signed by the borrower. Were several copies to be signed, there would be evidence of multiple debts from the several negotiable instruments that would be created.

When a recorded instrument such as a mortgage is lost, evidence of the document is readily available in the office of recordation. However, the loss of an unrecorded promissory note may give rise to all sorts of problems. For example, assume that Bill Borrower obtained a mortgage loan in 1965. In 1970, he sold the property subject to the mortgage to Investment Inc. A default in payment by Investment Inc. occurs in 1978. The lender, Frantic Mortgage Corp., cannot find the note. Neither the attorneys who prepared the original promissory note nor others with knowledge of its terms are available. No copies or drafts are to be found. Since the note was nowhere recorded it is difficult to establish what remedies are available to Frantic. Thus, it is easy to see why lenders must conscientiously guard the possession of original promissory notes.

TERMS OF PAYMENT

Developers and investors in income-producing property are primarily interested in the following aspects of a mortgage loan:

- The amount of the loan.
- The interest rate.
- The term to maturity.
- The repayment provisions.
- The prepayment provisions.

All this information is included in the promissory note.

The following paragraph in a note evidencing a self-amortizing loan is typical. The loan was closed on January 20, 1978, in the amount of $3,200,000 for a term of twenty-eight years, at an interest rate of $9\frac{1}{4}$ percent.

"This note shall be paid as follows: On February 1, 1978 accrued interest only shall be paid. Thereafter, Maker shall pay equal monthly installments of Twenty-Six Thousand Four Hundred Five and No/100 Dollars ($26,405) commencing March 1, 1978 and continuing on the first day of each and every month thereafter until January 1, 2006, whereupon the balance of said principal sum and interest then remaining shall be paid. Each of said installments when paid shall be applied by the holder hereof to the payment of interest and the balance in reduction of principal."

When mortgage money is scarce, institutional lenders frequently seek an equity participation (a "kicker") in addition to the prevailing rate of interest. This feature of the loan is reflected by a provision in the note requiring the payment of a percentage of gross or net income of the property to the lender as additional interest.

PREPAYMENT PROVISIONS

Lenders usually seek to restrict prepayment of loans. Lenders want assurance that their money is invested for the full term of the loan, and that they will not unexpectedly have to seek other investment opportunities. On the other hand, borrowers prefer to be in a position to refinance so that they can take advantage of lower interest rates or the possibility of increasing the size of the loan if the value of the property appreciates.

It is therefore customary for lenders to charge a premium for the privilege of prepayment. The amount of the premium is usually expressed as a percentage of the outstanding balance of the loan. This percentage declines as the loan matures. Prepayment privileges in residential loans and in FHA or VA mortgages are governed by statute. Prepayment terms in all other real estate loans vary from lender to lender and are determined by market conditions.

A typical paragraph concerning the prepayment privilege follows. The specific terms have been omitted.

"No privilege is reserved to prepay during the first ___ loan years. Beginning with the ___ loan year and on ___ days' written notice, privilege is reserved to pay the loan in full on any interest date, on payment of a prepayment charge of ___ percent, if the loan is paid in full during the ___ loan year, such prepayment charge to decline by ___ percent per year thereafter. The prepayment charges are to be computed on the unpaid principal balance at the time of such prepayment. It is understood that the loan year stated herein commences on the expiration of ___ years from the date of the first payment of principal and interest."

In high-credit loan transactions, the borrower may negotiate a more favorable privilege. Since credit loans are based primarily on the financial strength of the borrower rather than on the value of real property, the prepayment terms are sometimes related directly to the economic serviceability of the property. The prepayment provision in such a loan may permit prepayment much sooner than is typical in other types of mortgage loans.

"If the premises shall have become uneconomical for Maker's continued use and occupancy in Maker's business, and if Maker's Board of Directors has determined to discontinue the use of the premises in Maker's business, or if Maker has already discontinued such use, then Maker may give notice to Payee, on or after the ___ loan year, of Maker's intention to prepay the note."

Of course, a premium will still be required in the event of prepayment.

Ordinarily, when prepayment occurs, the entire balance of the loan is prepaid. While there may be circumstances when it is advantageous to a borrower to prepay only a portion of the loan, this right to prepay is not customary.

SPECIAL SAFEGUARDS

The large number of loan defaults during the mid-70s has encouraged conservatism in current lending practices. The twenty-five-year and thirty-year mortgages of the 1960s did not anticipate soaring fuel prices, continuing inflation, overbuilding, or changing demographic patterns. Institutional lenders today seek a hedge against unpredictable conditions that may render a loan less attractive in the future. The following safeguards now frequently are found in the promissory note:

Due-on-Sale Provision. A due-on-sale provision assures the lender that in the event of a sale of the property, he can declare the loan due and payable. This means that the lender can prohibit the sale of the property to an entity which may not be as sound as the original borrower or which, in the lender's opinion, does not possess the requisite managerial ability. There are limitations on the enforceability of due-on-sale provisions in some states.

Prohibition Against Junior Financing. Such a prohibition seeks to prevent overfinancing. The relative ease with which property owners could obtain secondary financing during the zenith of real estate investment trust lending in the period from 1970 to 1973 overburdened many properties with debt and led to defaults.

Option to Call. Lenders may insist on an option to call the loan if they have doubts about the stability of a property's income over the term of a loan. Lenders tend to worry about properties in which tenant leases are for short terms or which are located in areas with changing rental markets. In such situations, the lender may provide in the promissory note that it has the option at a specific time during the term to call the loan upon six months prior written notice to the borrower. For example, a twenty-five-year loan may include an option to call during the fifteenth year.

Option to Recast. An option to recast, like an option to call, hedges against future uncertainty. For example, the note for a thirty-year mortgage loan on a small medical office building with five-and ten-year occupancy leases might provide as follows:

> "During the twelfth (12th) loan year, the Mortgagee upon six (6) months notice, will have the option to require an increase of monthly payments to amortize the loan in twenty-five (25) years from the date of closing rather than thirty (30) years. In the event this option is exercised, the Mortgagor shall have the right to prepay the loan in full without a prepayment charge within six (6) months after notice of the exercise of the option is given by the Mortgagee."

DEFAULT PROVISIONS

If installments are not paid when due or before the expiration of a reasonable grace period specified in the note, the lender may elect to accelerate payment and require payment of the entire balance of principal together with accrued interest. This option to accelerate payment may also be exercised if other promises in the note are breached by the borrower. If the accelerated payment is not made, an obvious remedy is to foreclose in accordance with the terms of the mortgage securing the note and pursuant to the laws of the state in which the property is located.

The note may provide, alternatively, for the payment of a "late charge" or additional interest as liquidated damages for the additional expense and loss resulting from the delinquency. Following is an example of a late charge provision.

> "Should Maker fail to make due and punctual payment of any money which Maker is required to pay hereunder within ten (10) days after the date on which the same shall become due and payable, such sum as shall be overdue shall bear interest from and after the due date thereof until paid at the rate of ___ percent (___%) per annum."

The penalty rate usually will exceed the face rate of the mortgage.

In order to avoid deliberate default by a borrower who wants the debt accelerated so that he may pay off the loan and thus not pay a prepayment charge, the lender includes the following provision in the note:

> "Maker agrees that if an event of default occurs under this note, or under the mortgage or any other instruments securing the indebtedness evidenced hereby, and the maturity date is therefore accelerated, then a tender of payment by Maker, or by anyone on behalf of the Maker, of the amount necessary to satisfy all sums due hereunder made at any time prior to judicial sale of the mortgaged property or a redemption after foreclosure, shall constitute an evasion of the payment terms hereof and shall be deemed to be a voluntary prepayment hereunder, and any such payment, to the extent permitted by law, will therefore include the fee required under the prepayment privilege."

PERSONAL LIABILITY

Currently, the majority of loans on income-producing property are nonrecourse loans. This means that the maker of the note has no personal liability. Appropriate exculpatory language is inserted in the note. The following is an example of an exculpatory provision:

> "Maker shall have no personal liability under this Note, the Mortgage, or any other instrument given as security for the payment of this Note; the sole remedy of the holder of this Note in the event of any default shall be to proceed against the property described in the said Mortgage, the rents, issues, and profits therefrom and any further security as may have been given to secure the payment hereof; provided, however, that nothing contained herein shall limit or be construed to limit or impair the enforcement against such property and the rents, issues, and profits therefrom of the rights and remedies of the Holder hereof under this Note, the said Mortgage, and any other security investment given to secure the payment hereof."

The exculpatory provision is one of the few provisions in the note which is subject to negotiation among attorneys. The concern for avoidance of personal liability and the tax consequences associated with the nonrecourse aspect of a loan focus attention on the language of exculpation. A properly drafted provision assures the borrower that he has no personal liability for the obligations of the note, but does not impair the remedies of the lender seeking enforcement in the event of a default.

CONCLUSION

Although the documentation for a mortgage loan transaction has become complex, the promissory note remains a relatively simple instrument. The note is one of the key documents of the transaction, but it often receives insufficient attention. It merits careful scrutiny because it incorporates the basic terms of the loan transaction.

a. Usury

McELROY v. GRISHAM

Supreme Court of Arkansas, 1991.
306 Ark. 4, 810 S.W.2d 933.

HOLT, Chief Justice.

The appellant/cross-appellee, Ernest McElroy, initially filed suit in the Boone County Chancery Court requesting equitable relief in the cancellation of a warranty deed, option contract, and deed for sale, as well as the quieting of title to the real estate in question.   These requests were predicated, in part, on Mr. McElroy's allegations that the deed and contracts between him and the appellees/cross-appellants, C.C. Grisham, Bill Doshier, and H.K. [*sic*] McCaleb, individually and doing business as BBS Company, constituted a usurious scheme to loan money.

The chancellor found that the transaction was a usurious loan and that the deed from the appellant to the appellees "was in fact a mortgage" and issued his orders accordingly.

. . .

We agree with the chancellor's findings that the transaction was usurious but reverse and remand as to his calculation of interest paid and the award of a penalty.   We affirm the trial court as to the appellees' cross-appeal.

Mr. McElroy is engaged in the residential home construction business.   In 1984 and 1985, he acquired a total of 104 acres of property for which he paid $238,357.   In addition, Mr. McElroy claims to have invested approximately $19,200 preparing the land for residential development.

By early 1987, Mr. McElroy was experiencing financial difficulties and contacted Mr. C.C. Grisham for help.   He claims to have requested an initial loan of $100,000 from Mr. Grisham.   This proposal was rejected, but, after lengthy negotiations, the parties agreed that Mr. McElroy would deed the property to Mr. Grisham and his partner, Mr. H.D. McCaleb, in exchange for $80,000.   In addition, Mr. McElroy was to receive a contract for deed allowing him to repurchase the property for $120,000, of which $40,000 was to be paid in one year and the balance of $80,000 at the end of two years.

Mr. Grisham referred Mr. McElroy to Mr. Bill Doshier, an attorney, to complete the necessary legal work.   Mr. Doshier was subsequently brought into the transaction as an equal partner with Mr. Grisham and Mr. McCaleb, which partnership was named BBS Company.   At Mr. Doshier's suggestion, the contract for deed was changed to an option contract and, on February 13, 1987, the parties executed a warranty deed, in which Mr. McElroy conveyed the property to the appellees, and an option contract, wherein Mr. McElroy was given one year to exercise his option to repurchase the property; $40,000 to be paid at the time of purchase and $80,000 to be paid within a total of two years, interest free. The appellees disbursed $80,000 to Mr. McElroy through an abstract and title company and required Mr. McElroy to obtain release of over $120,000 in liens against the property.

Mr. McElroy claims that in February, 1988, before the expiration of the option contract, he approached the partnership about exercising his option. This is disputed by the appellees who claim that Mr. McElroy allowed the option contract to expire. In either event, the parties disregarded the option contract and executed a contract for deed on March 1, 1988, in which Mr. McElroy agreed to pay $125,000 for repurchase of the property (less three lots to be retained by the "sellers"). This price was $5,000 more than the "option price". Mr. McElroy was to pay $16,000 at closing and the balance of $109,000 in installments, at an annual rate of 10%, which was evidenced by a promissory note. The parties have stipulated that during the term of this agreement, Mr. McElroy made payments to the appellees totalling $45,195.

In April, 1989, Mr. McElroy was informed by the appellees that he still owed over $86,000 on the debt. He filed suit in the Boone County Chancery Court shortly thereafter.

Following trial, the chancellor entered two opinion letters in which he held that "the underlying and real purpose of this transaction was a loan to plaintiff in the amount of $80,000, and that since it was a loan, under its terms, it exceeded the lawful rate of interest." The court found that Mr. McElroy had repaid $45,195, of which $10,866 was interest, leaving $34,329 paid on the principal and $45,671 owing. This amount was offset by a penalty of $16,300, assessed against the appellees, which resulted in a final judgment of $29,371 in favor of the appellees. Mr. McElroy was ordered to pay the debt within 30 days of judgment or face foreclosure.

Since all of the issues before us hinge on the central question of whether there was, in fact, a usurious loan, we address the appellees' arguments on cross-appeal, first.

I. USURIOUS LOAN

Initially, we note that while we review chancery cases *de novo*, we recognize the superior position of the chancellor to weigh issues of credibility and therefore we do not reverse unless the chancellor's findings are clearly erroneous. *Taylor's Marine, Inc. v. Waco Mfg.*, 302 Ark. 521, 792 S.W.2d 286 (1990).

In denying that the transactions amounted to a usurious loan, the appellees first contend that the documents were not usurious on their face. While it is true that, taken alone, the original warranty deed and option contract appear to be documents concerning only the sale of land, and no mention of a loan or obligation on the part of Mr. McElroy to repay the appellees is recited, these transactions call to mind an oft quoted maxim: "The law shells the covering and extracts the kernel. Names amount to nothing when they fail to designate the facts." *Sparks v. Robinson*, 66 Ark. 460, 51 S.W. 460 (1899). In *Sparks*, we upheld the trial court's conclusion that an absolute bill of sale of a sewing machine, coupled with an absolute right of redemption, amounted to nothing more than a mortgage with a usurious rate of interest.

Here, the chancellor found that the purported sale and option to repurchase were nothing more than a cloaking device to hide the true transaction—a loan in the amount of $80,000 to be repaid in two years, with interest totalling $40,000. Such a transaction has been historically recognized as one of several simple devices to evade Arkansas usury laws. *See* G. Collins and V. Ham, *The Usury Law of Arkansas: A Study in Evasion*, 8 Ark.L.Rev. 399 (1954).

The burden is upon the one asserting usury to show the transaction is usurious, and usury will not be presumed, imputed, or inferred where an opposite result can be fairly reached. *Winkle v. Grand Nat'l Bank*, 267 Ark. 123, 601 S.W.2d 559 (1980). The test, however, is not whether the "lender" intended to violate the usury laws, but whether the lender knowingly entered into a usurious contract intending to profit by the methods employed. *See Id.*; *Davidson v. Commercial Credit Equip. Corp.*, 255 Ark. 127, 499 S.W.2d 68 (1973). Furthermore, it is unnecessary that both parties intend that an unlawful rate of interest be charged; if the lender alone charges or receives more than is lawful the contract is void. *Superior Improvement Co. v. Mastic Corp.*, 270 Ark. 471, 604 S.W.2d 950 (1980) (decision under prior law).

The chancellor was faced with conflicting testimony throughout the trial in this case. He obviously found Mr. McElroy's version of the events to be the more credible and, deferring to his advantage in observing the witnesses' demeanor and in considering the evidence presented in the record, we cannot conclude that his decision was clearly erroneous.

Mr. McElroy testified that prior to contacting the appellees, he had approached a number of banks and individuals for a loan and had been rejected. He testified that he was in dire financial trouble and that the appellees were aware of his situation.

Mr. McElroy contacted Mr. Grisham and initially requested a loan of $100,000. This request was rejected but, after further discussions, Mr. Grisham agreed to a loan of $80,000, of which $40,000 was to be repaid in one year and another $80,000 within the following year. This agreement later developed into a warranty deed combined with an option to purchase. Mr. McElroy admitted it was he who proposed the terms finally agreed upon, and we have said that a debtor may be estopped from asserting the defense of usury when the debtor created the infirmity in the contract in order to take advantage of the creditor. *Ford Motor Credit Co. v. Hutcherson*, 277 Ark. 102, 640 S.W.2d 96

(1982). Such was not the case here. Mr. McElroy stated that he was in financial straits and testified repeatedly that it was never his intention to relinquish his land, but simply to arrange a loan for temporary financial relief. Clearly, it was the appellees, not Mr. McElroy, who received an unfair advantage.

Furthermore, there was testimony from Mr. McElroy's expert witness that the land was valued at $227,200, and, in fact, Mr. McElroy stated that he paid approximately $238,357 for it. This evidence reflects a gross disparity between what Mr. McElroy paid for it, and the appellees' purchase price of $80,000.

There was also disagreement in the record as to the execution of the contract for sale. The appellees maintain that Mr. McElroy simply failed to exercise his option in time and that a lawful contract for deed was then executed after the allegedly usurious transaction was obsolete. Again, the trial court gave credence to Mr. McElroy's testimony that he began discussing the exercise of his option before the February 13, 1988, expiration date. The parties discussed Mr. McElroy selling a condominium to the appellees for $45,000, which could be rolled over to the option contract, but this plan was not carried out. When it became apparent that Mr. McElroy would be unable to make the $40,000 payment, as required by the option contract, the parties renegotiated and executed the contract for deed with new terms of payment. Although the document was signed on March 1, 1988, Mr. McElroy claims that its terms were decided prior to the expiration of the option contract and introduced into evidence a typewritten memo setting out such terms, which he claims to have signed on February 13, 1988.

In deciding whether a certain transaction is usurious, all attendant circumstances must be taken into consideration. *Sammons–Pennington Co. v. Norton*, 241 Ark. 341, 408 S.W.2d 487 (1966). Mr. McElroy's obvious financial troubles, his expressed intent to keep the land, the substantial disparity between what Mr. McElroy paid for the property and the appellees' purchase price, and the appellees' immediate renegotiation of a contract for deed when it became apparent Mr. McElroy could not "exercise his option," all point to the conclusion that none of the parties intended for the property to come into the hands of the appellees any more than was necessary to secure the loan and for the appellees to make a profit from such loan.

Similar transactions have previously been scrutinized by this court and all were deemed usurious. *See Tillar v. Cleveland*, 47 Ark. 287, 1 S.W. 516 (1886); *Sparks v. Robinson*, 66 Ark. 460, 51 S.W. 460 (1899); *Banks v. Walters*, 95 Ark. 501, 130 S.W. 519 (1910); *Ringer v. Virgin Timber Co.*, 213 F. 1001 (E.D.Ark.1914); *Sleeper v. Sweetser*, 247 Ark. 477, 446 S.W.2d 228 (1969). We have no trouble in reaching the same conclusion and uphold the chancellor's finding that all of the transactions constituted one scheme to loan money at a usurious rate of interest.

. . .

III.   INTEREST PAYMENT

Mr. McElroy first contends that the trial court erred in determining the amount of interest he paid on the loan. Ark. Const. art. 19, § 13(a) provides that the maximum rate of interest shall not exceed 5% per annum above the applicable Federal Reserve Discount Rate. This was established at trial to be 10.5%. Art. 19, § 13 further provides that all contracts having a rate of interest in excess of the maximum lawful rate will be void as to the unpaid interest.

. . .

Since the usurious transaction began with the original loan of $80,000 to be repaid at $120,000, the amount of interest paid must be calculated on the basis of that initial transaction, rather than the second contract for deed.

At trial, Mr. Danny Criner, President of Newton County Bank, testified that an $80,000 loan, repaid at $40,000 in one year and $80,000 the following year, would result in an annual interest rate of 30 to 35%. No further testimony or calculations were offered to explain these figures. Mr. McElroy's computations place the illegal rate at approximately 25%.

Because of these discrepancies, we remand the case so that the correct annual interest rate of the original transaction can be calculated.

. . .

IV.   PENALTY

Mr. McElroy next argues that the chancellor erred in refusing to award twice the amount of interest paid. We agree.

Art. 19, § 13(a)(ii) provides:

All such contracts having a rate of interest in excess of the maximum lawful rate shall be void as to the unpaid interest. *A person who has paid interest in excess of the maximum lawful rate may recover, within the time provided by law, twice the amount of interest paid.* It is unlawful for any person to knowingly charge a rate of interest in excess of the maximum lawful rate in effect at the time of the contract, and any person who does so shall be subject to such punishment as may be provided by law. (Emphasis added).

The trial court interpreted the above language to be discretionary and awarded only $16,300 as penalty, based on an interest calculation of $10,866. Whether this specific provision is mandatory or discretionary has not been decided by this court, although we have upheld awards for twice the amount of interest paid. *See Taylor's Marine v. Waco Mfg.,* *supra.*

In *Taggart & Taggart Seed Co., Inc. v. City of Augusta*, 278 Ark. 570, 647 S.W.2d 458 (1983), however, we reaffirmed our principle that those things which are of the essence of the thing to be done are mandatory, while those not of the essence of the thing to be done are directory only. 278 Ark. at 574, 647 S.W.2d at 459 (1983) (citing *Edwards v. Hall*, 30 Ark. 31 (1875)). Art. 19, § 13, as we interpret it, is penal in nature. This is evidenced by the language following the provision for recovery of interest. The purpose of the article was obviously to discourage usurious contracts, and to allow the trial courts to dispense with the penalty at their discretion would be to defeat this purpose.

Furthermore, we reminded, in *Arkansas State Racing Comm'n v. Southland Racing Corp.*, 226 Ark. 995, 295 S.W.2d 617 (1956) that "[i]t is of course a familiar rule of statutory construction that 'may' is to be construed as 'shall' when the context of the statute so requires." Constitutional provisions are construed in the same manner as statutes. *See Shepherd v. City of Little Rock*, 183 Ark. 244, 35 S.W.2d 361 (1931); *McDonald v. Bowen*, 250 Ark. 1049, 468 S.W.2d 765 (1971).

We hold that the language in Art. 19, § 13 is mandatory, and further remand with directions to award Mr. McElroy twice the amount of the interest to be calculated in accordance with our previous instructions.

. . .

The decision of the trial court is affirmed in part and reversed and remanded in part, with instructions not inconsistent with this opinion.

NOTES

1. *Elements of Usury.* There is some ambivalence about restrictions on usury. On the one hand, usury laws may limit the market choices of parties, prevent a willing borrower from obtaining a needed loan, and permit a debtor to evade his obligation. See generally, DCM Partners v. Smith, 228 Cal.App.3d 729, 278 Cal.Rptr. 778 (1991) (refusing to extend usury statute to modification of purchase money note since legislature excepted sales on credit from the statutory protection). On the other hand, usury laws protect borrowers from overreaching lenders, especially in a modern era of concentrated capital. For example, the *McElroy* court favored borrower protection in its construction of the penalty aspect of the statute. See also, Carboni v. Arrospide, 2 Cal.App.4th 76, 2 Cal.Rptr.2d 845 (1991) (real estate loan providing for 200% annual interest rate was not subject to usury statute which specifically excepted loans by real estate brokers, but court refused to enforce the interest rate on theory of unconscionability and substituted rate of 24%). See pages 392–393 above describing federal preemption of usury laws.

Four elements must coincide for a loan to be held usurious: (1) an agreement to lend money; (2) interest in excess of that allowed by statute; (3) an absolute, not contingent, obligation to repay the principal; and (4) an intention to violate the usury laws. One way for borrower and lender to avoid usury is to structure their loan so that one of these four elements is missing. As indicated in *McElroy*, the fourth, intent element, can readily be found and the third element—an absolute obligation to repay—is difficult to avoid without defeating the parties' business objectives. It is the other two elements that have produced the most ingenious and effective efforts at usury avoidance. Parties circumvent the second element by characterizing the excessive payments as something other than interest, and circumvent the first by casting the transaction as something other than a loan.

Among the more common efforts at usury avoidance, in addition to the sale and repurchase technique considered in *McElroy,* are discounts from the face value of the note; prepayment penalties; brokerage or placement fees; late fees; inspection fees; standby or commitment fees if the lender is funding a permanent loan; requirements that the borrower deposit part of the loan proceeds in an interest-free account with the lender; sale-leaseback arrangements; and equity "kickers" such as a percentage of the borrower's gross or net income earned from the security.

Judicial acceptance of these ploys is hard to predict, creating difficulties for the lawyer who is asked to give an opinion letter stating that a particular transaction is free from any taint of usury. Would you, for example, have given such a letter in connection with the transaction in *McElroy*? Did it matter that McElroy was not initially bound to repurchase the land as he executed an option, not a contract of sale, so that appellees having made a good deal might have ended up owning the land? In light of the decision, how would you have restructured the financing to achieve the same economic result without violating the usury rules? Would it have helped to give the lender a share of the borrower's profits from residences to be constructed on the land, even if the share might have pushed the lender's total return above the usury level? What test does the court use to distinguish between a sale and a loan? One court stated that "in a loan the lender does not share in the profits of the enterprise, nor does he run any risk of loss of his capital other than that of the insolvency of the borrower attendant upon all loans." Golden State Lanes v. Fox, 232 Cal.App.2d 135, 139, 42 Cal. Rptr. 568, 570 (1965). Does this mean that an "equity kicker" would have saved the transaction?

On usury in land finance generally, see Shanks, Practical Problems in the Application of Archaic Usury Statutes, 53 Va.L.Rev. 327 (1967); Podell, The Application of Usury Laws to Modern Real Estate Transactions, 1 Real Est.L.J. 136 (1972); Hershman, Usury and "New Look" in Real Estate Financing, 4 Real Prop.Probate & Trust J. 315 (1969); Rabin & Brownlie, Usury Law in California: A Guide Through the Maze, 20 U.C. Davis L.Rev. 397 (1987).

2. *Corporate Borrower Exemption.* The most common statutory exemption from usury rules is for corporate borrowers. Hershman,

Usury and "New Look" in Real Estate Financing, 4 Real Prop., Probate & Trust J. 315, 325 (1969). The central question in administering the corporate exemption, and in structuring transactions to comply with its requirements, concerns the extent to which, to qualify, a corporation must have a life and business purpose independent of usury avoidance. New York and several other states take the view that any corporation, even one formed exclusively for the purpose of avoiding usury limitations, qualifies for the corporate exemption. See, for example, Werger v. Haines Corp., 302 N.Y. 930, 100 N.E.2d 189 (1951); Galloway v. The Travelers Insurance Co., 515 So.2d 678 (Miss.1987). New Jersey and other states take a more jaundiced view, denying the exemption if the loan was only nominally made to a corporation and in fact was made to the corporation's principal. See, for example, Gelber v. Kugel's Tavern, 10 N.J. 191, 89 A.2d 654 (1952). The New Jersey approach creates particular difficulties for the lawyer who wants to form a corporation that is at once substantial enough to withstand attack as a usury sham and, at the same time, is insubstantial enough to avoid federal income taxation at the entity level.

See generally, Weinstein, Can a Nominee Corporation Be Ignored for Tax Purposes? An Issue Headed for Supreme Court Review, 13 Real Est.L.J. 159 (1984); Payne, Playing a Shell Game With Usury Statutes, 10 Real Est.L.J. 337 (1982).

3. *Time-Price Doctrine.* When it is the seller who finances the buyer's purchase, the parties can avoid usury by increasing the sales price, and consequently the loan principal, so that a nominally lawful interest rate will in fact produce a greater than lawful return. Courts have generally accepted this technique, refusing under the time-price doctrine to examine the difference between cash and credit prices to determine whether the credit price embodies a usurious interest rate. In Mandelino v. Fribourg, 23 N.Y.2d 145, 295 N.Y.S.2d 654, 242 N.E.2d 823 (1968), the New York Court of Appeals carried this approach one step further, sustaining a purchase money interest rate that *expressly* exceeded the lawful rate. The court's reasoning: a purchase money mortgage is simply not a loan within the terms of the usury statute. See generally, Comment, Application of the Time-Price Doctrine in Credit Sales of Real Property, 40 Baylor L.Rev. 573 (1988).

4. *"Governing Law" Clauses.* Since permitted interest rates vary from state to state, and since states differ in their prescribed exemptions from usury limits, lender and borrower can try to avoid local usury restrictions by agreeing to a "governing law" clause that rests the debt instrument's interpretation and validity on the law of some more favorable state. Whether a court will honor this designation of applicable law of course depends on how seriously the foreign usury rule offends the public policy of the state whose judicial system is being asked to enforce the debt.

b.　The Wrap-Around Mortgage

COMMENT, THE WRAP–AROUND MORTGAGE: A CRITICAL IN-QUIRY,* 21 U.C.L.A. Law Review 1529–31 (1974): In recent years there has been a resurgence in the use of a real estate financing device born in the 1930's and known as the wrap-around mortgage. The renewed use of the wrap-around mortgage has been prompted by the relatively high rates of interest on real property loans which presently prevail and by the correspondingly tight money market. The device has been hailed as a "substitute for money," and indeed, it has been utilized in just that manner to overcome and even to take advantage of tight money and the high cost of borrowing.

The wrap-around mortgage has also been called a "hold-harmless deed of trust," an "all-inclusive deed of trust," and an "over-riding deed of trust." But all these terms refer to the same type of instrument: a second mortgage securing a promissory note, the face amount of which is the sum of the existing first mortgage liability plus the cash or equity advanced by the lender. The wrap-around borrower must make payments on the first mortgage debt to the wrap-around lender, who, as required by the wrap-around mortgage agreement, must in turn make payments on the first mortgage debt to the third party, the first mortgagee. If the wrap-around mortgagee should fail to perform his obligation to pay off the first mortgage, the wrap-around agreement normally gives the non-defaulting mortgagor the right to pay the interest and principal owing on the first mortgage, reducing his wrap-around obligation pro tanto.

Although the wrap-around mortgage can be used in a variety of transactions, this Comment will discuss only the "purchase money" wrap-around mortgage. Other variations of the wrap-around mortgage—the "third party purchase money"[7] and the "refinancing"[8]

---

* Reprinted by permission from U.C.L.A. Law Review, Volume 21 (1974) Copyright © 1974 by the Regents of the University of California, which is the sole source of such permission.

7. A third party purchase money wrap-around mortgage may best be illustrated by an example. Assume that S wishes to sell Blackacre which is subject to a first mortgage lien of $30,000 bearing interest at 6 percent per annum. The purchase price is $60,000. S wants cash for his equity, but B cannot come up with more than $10,000. So a third party lender pays $20,000 to S. The lender then agrees to pay off the existing first mortgage so long as B makes payments on a $50,000 wrap-around note B has executed in the lender's favor. The wrap-around note bears interest at 8 percent per annum.

8. The refinancing wrap-around mortgage does not involve a sale but a refinancing. For example: A borrower owns real estate worth $150,000, but subject to a first mortgage of $75,000 at 6 percent. Borrower seeks to obtain funds by mortgaging $45,000 worth of his "equity." Lender offers to advance cash in the amount of $45,000, but asks for a wrap-around mortgage and note for $120,000 at 8½ percent interest, and in turn promises (as in all wrap-around transactions) to pay off the first mortgage ($75,000) as it falls due. One writer has made the following remarks with respect to both the third party purchase money and the refinancing wrap-around:

　In some documents the exuberance of the parties has produced language tantamount to an assumption of the first

types—will not be dealt with here. The purchase money wrap-around mortgage is one which is taken back by a seller of land in return for his conveyance; for example: Seller conveys his property to Buyer for $150,000 subject to a first mortgage lien of $75,000 at 6 percent interest per annum. Buyer gives Seller $30,000 in cash and a promissory note for $120,000 which is secured by a second mortgage on the property. This note bears interest at 9 percent per annum. Since the $120,000 promissory note "includes" the unpaid loan of $75,000 secured by the first mortgage, the purchase money note and mortgage are said to be "wrapped around" the first mortgage.

GALOWITZ, HOW TO USE WRAPAROUND FINANCING *

5 Real Estate Law Journal 107, 112–113, 118–119 (1976).

OBTAINING NEW PROCEEDS IN A REFINANCING

Most wraparound mortgages are probably made in order to refinance an existing indebtedness, for the purpose of obtaining additional proceeds without disturbing the existing mortgage financing. There are at least four distinct reasons for doing this.

Where an existing mortgage is not prepayable, or the penalty for prepayment is burdensome, a wraparound mortgage used in a refinancing leaves the existing mortgage undisturbed. Thus, no penalty is incurred.

The wraparound is also commonly used for refinancing when the existing mortgage is at terms so favorable as to make a prepayment uneconomic. The existing mortgage may be favorable in rate of interest or in its low rate of amortization.

The most frequent use of the wraparound mortgage has been to reduce the cost of secondary financing, which commands a high rate because of the higher risk. True, the risk entailed in a wraparound mortgage is at least as great and perhaps greater than the risk involved in an ordinary second mortgage situation. A second mortgage lender's security is based upon either the ability of a property to bring a price at a distress sale equal to the underlying mortgage plus the second mortgage, or the willingness of the second mortgage lender to acquire the fee at the cost of the balance of the first mortgage. The ordinary secondary mortgage lender is never obligated to pay either principal or

mortgage by the WA lender. The legal effect of assumption, however, is almost always dispelled by conditioning this obligation upon *actual* receipt of the debt service on the WA mortgage. If the WA lender does not receive the debt service on the WA mortgage, there is no obligation to remit the debt service on the first mortgage. Failure to pay debt service on a WA mortgage, of course, constitutes a default under that mortgage.

Gunning, The Wrap-Around Mortgage . . . Friend or U.F.O.?, 2 Real Estate Rev., Summer 1972, at 37.

* Reprinted by permission from Real Estate Law Journal, Volume 5, Number 2, Fall 1976, Copyright © 1976 Warren, Gorham and Lamont, Inc., 210 South Street, Boston, Massachusetts. All Rights Reserved.

debt service on the first mortgage. The wraparound mortgagee, on the other hand, must pay the debt service on the first mortgage (and may have this burden even if the debt service on the wraparound mortgage is not paid, because of lien priority considerations described below). Thus, in a distress situation the wraparound mortgagee may not only be exposed holding a debt on a property of questionable value but may also be increasing its exposure by an obligation to pay principal and interest on the underlying mortgage.

The compensation to the wraparound mortgagee for its risks is, of course, added interest. But the borrower, too, gets a bonus.

Consider, for example, a borrower with a low interest rate mortgage who requires an additional advance. The borrower may obtain the secondary financing at the high interest rate available for an ordinary second mortgage or, alternatively, seek a wraparound mortgage which will reduce his overall interest cost. The first mortgage at its below-market-rate interest offers a bonus to the wraparound mortgagee; i.e., the wraparound mortgagee retains the differential between the bargain interest rate of the existing mortgage and the wraparound interest rate. The differential is usable to reduce the wraparound mortgage rate and still produce a sufficient yield to the second mortgage lender to compensate it for the risks.

Finally, a wraparound may also be useful where mortgagee lending limits—whether statutory, regulatory, or self-imposed—limit the ability to obtain proceeds.

In a refinancing where the first mortgagee is limited to an amount less than the property's mortgage value—say, where an institutional lender is limited to a percentage of appraised value and, because of a low foreclosure sales value due to a special use, the appraisal produces a mortgage value less than the cash flow would support—a wraparound may increase the proceeds. ...

INCREASING EFFECTIVE YIELD

Earning interest on funds not advanced must be the secret dream of all lenders. With the wraparound mortgage, the lender not only earns on unadvanced funds but has a spread in interest on advanced funds and additionally builds an equity.

For example, assume an owner has $100,000 original principal balance mortgage at a $4\frac{1}{2}$ percent interest rate amortized over twenty-five years. His debt service is $555.83 per month. At the tenth year the balance is approximately $72,600. If a new loan is made to provide new proceeds equal to the amortized portion of the loan, approximately $27,400, the constant payment rate can be up to $6\frac{2}{3}$ percent and not increase the debt service. ($100,000 × .0667, divided by 12 = $555.83 per month).

Assuming that a new loan interest rate is $8\frac{1}{2}$ percent, the debt service would have to be $985 per month to amortize the new $100,000 total balance over the remaining fifteen years. If the lender advances the sum of $27,400, receiving each month $985 and paying out of such sum $556, it would net $429 per month or an effective yield of 19 percent.

BUILDING EQUITY

In the preceding example, the debt service was increased with the increased interest rate. If the debt service rate was unchanged and the wraparound mortgage made on an interest-only basis (which would mean a 6⅔ percent rate), the annual effective yield during its term would be zero; the lender would receive $556 monthly and pay out an equal sum to the holder of the underlying mortgage. The effect, however, is that when the underlying mortgage has been fully amortized in fifteen years, the balance of the wraparound mortgage is still $100,000. Thus, the $27,400 has increased by a $72,600 buildup over a period of fifteen years. Economically, this is an 18 percent per year return, with the cash proceeds deferred for fifteen years. Clearly, the lender's tax posture must be carefully examined since all of the money it receives in payment of debt service constitutes income, while its offsetting payments are only partially deductible. Ordinarily, therefore, the structure is most suited to a lender whose income is not taxable or to one with sufficient offsetting losses.

NOTES

1. *Usury.* Can the wrap-around mortgage be employed to avoid usury restrictions? In the second example given in the Galowitz article, the lender is nominally making a $100,000 loan at 6⅔% interest but is effectively receiving 18% interest annually, a rate well in excess of most state usury limits. The question is whether a court will choose form (6⅔% on $100,000) over substance (18% on $27,400). What little law there is on the question suggests that courts will in these circumstances pierce the loan's formal structure and declare it usurious, unless of course the loan qualifies under some specific exception such as the corporate borrower exemption. See, for example, Mindlin v. Davis, 74 So.2d 789 (Fla.1954). In any event, the device is probably not sufficiently foolproof to attract the more conservative institutional lenders. See Note, Wrap-Around Financing: A Technique for Skirting the Usury Laws? 1972 Duke L.J. 785. See also Kraus, Tax Advantages of Wraparound Financing, 11 Real Est.Rev. 11 (Spring 1981).

2. *Foreclosure.* When a wraparound mortgage is foreclosed, is the amount of the indebtedness, for the purpose of calculating a deficiency or surplus at foreclosure sale, the total outstanding balance due on the wraparound note, which includes the amount due on the initial note as well as funds advanced by the wraparound mortgagee? Or is it only the amount of new debt provided by the wraparound mortgagee? In Summers v. Consolidated Capital Special Trust, 783 S.W.2d 580 (Tex. 1989), the Supreme Court of Texas held that the outstanding balance

method should be used, reversing the court of appeals which had used the "true debt" approach. The amount of the foreclosure bid ($2.75 million) was thus credited to the total outstanding balance on the wraparound note ($6.207 million), leaving the mortgagor with a deficiency. If the true debt method had been used there would have been a surplus of approximately $500,000.

Was the court's decision correct? Would the true debt method allow the mortgagor to evade its contractual liability under the wraparound note for the initial debt plus the new funds? Did the court's decision give the wraparound mortgagee a windfall by retaining the property and obtaining a deficiency judgment for the outstanding balance of the debt. See Note, Unwrapping the Wraparound Mortgage Foreclosure Process, 47 Wash. & Lee L.Rev. 1025 (1990); St. Claire, Wraparound Mortgage Problems in Nonjudicial Foreclosure, 20 Real Est.L.J. 221 (1992).

2. CONSTRUCTION FINANCE

The lender who is asked to make a construction loan has a riskier, more complicated task than the lender who is asked to lend money on already improved land. The task is riskier because the construction lender must base its appraisal on pieces of paper—project plans, specifications and income projections—and has no assurance that strikes, increased construction costs or natural disasters will not make the project more expensive than originally contemplated. Nor will the lender have any assurance that, once the project is completed, the right number and mix of tenants will sign leases and pay sufficient rents for the borrower to pay off the loan. The construction lender's task is complicated by the need to devise and enforce safeguards against these construction and investment risks and also, if the lender is a regulated institution, by the need to maintain a first lien position over the common law and statutory priorities that attach to the interests of financing sellers and unpaid mechanics, materialmen and fixture suppliers.

The lending industry traditionally has resolved this increased risk and complexity by dividing development finance between a *construction lender*—usually a commercial bank primarily interested in making short term, floating rate loans—and a *permanent lender*—usually an insurance company primarily interested in a long term loan, possibly with an equity participation feature. The construction lender will advance the needed construction funds in stages over the course of construction, with its loan secured by a first lien mortgage on the property. The permanent lender will "take out" the construction mortgage upon the completion of construction by replacing the construction mortgage with a long term mortgage. Although two separate sets of instruments—construction note and mortgage and permanent note and mortgage—may be used, the terms of the permanent loan are often embodied in the construction note and mortgage so that, when construction is completed, the original note will pass from construction lender to permanent lender with no need for execution of a new note by a possibly recalcitrant borrower.

Construction lending is labor-intensive and construction loan departments are usually well-staffed with loan administrators, architects, engineers and inspectors to monitor loan disbursements at every stage of a construction project. Permanent lending, by contrast, is essentially capital intensive. It requires the permanent lender to evaluate the proposed project only at the time the developer applies for the permanent loan commitment and later, when the time comes to take out the construction loan, to determine that construction has been completed according to the terms and specifications of its commitment letter.

Construction lenders will usually structure and administer their disbursement programs carefully to protect against the possibility that funds disbursed for construction purposes will be diverted to other purposes and that, as a result, the permanent lender will refuse to take out the construction loan on the ground that the project was not completed in accordance with specifications, or that its first lien position is impaired by the prior lien of an unpaid mechanic, materialman or purchase money lender. But disbursement control programs occasionally break down, and even the best-run programs offer no protection against the widespread judicial solicitude for mechanics, materialmen and purchase money mortgagees, nor against permanent lenders who decide, for good reason or bad, simply not to honor their takeout commitments. The cases and materials in this section indicate the sources of some of these problems and the legal strategies that construction lenders—as well as borrowers, permanent lenders, sellers, mechanics, materialmen and fixture suppliers—have employed to resolve them.

Bibliographic Note. Two excellent introductions to the field are Livingston, Current Business Approaches—Commercial Construction Lending, 13 Real Prop., Probate & Trust J. 791 (1978); Walsh, A Practical Guide to Mortgage Loan Commitments, 8 Real Est.L.J. 195 (1980). For an analysis of the legal relationships among the parties to these arrangements, see Korngold, Construction Loan Advances and the Subordinated Purchase Money Mortgagee: An Appraisal, A Suggested Approach and the ULTA Perspective, 50 Fordham L.Rev. 313 (1981).

a.   THE CONSTRUCTION LOAN

HALL, HOW TO BUILD LENDER PROTECTION INTO CONSTRUCTION LOAN AGREEMENTS *

6 Real Estate Law Journal 21, 22–24, 26, 28–30 (1977).

In simple real estate loans the value of the security, the mortgaged property, may be fairly accurately estimated before making the loan.

For a construction loan the value of the security depends on both successful completion of construction and realization of the projected economic value of the completed project. The lender, being greatly dependent upon successful completion, must be protected from difficulties arising during construction, such as unsatisfactory work, slow progress, violation of building codes, failure to administer subcontracts properly, and misuse of funds advanced.

Although foreclosure on a mortgage lien, the classical lender's safeguard, offers some protection, foreclosure is always an expensive and time-consuming process. If construction is halted, as usual during foreclosure, weather damage, vandalism, and the expense of recontracting and restarting the job are likely to impose heavy penalties.

Breach of contract suits are useless if there are insufficient resources to make such a suit worthwhile. It is, in any case, far better to detect difficulties and proceed toward some solution before damages are large and collection increasingly remote.

A bond on the contractor offers some *in extremis* protection, but a bond requires careful preparation, with full coverage coming at a relatively high cost. Bonding companies pay off carefully, almost always slowly, and frequently only after a legal determination of their liability with all the delays that such a process may require. Bonds are like life insurance, good if the project dies. They don't substitute for first aid before the project dies. Collecting under bond always means some loss for the lender or the owner. Bonding companies employ attorneys to make sure their payments aren't a bonanza for an owner or for a lending institution. The delays inherent in completing on a bond payment can be fatal to a closely calculated project. Many owners and many lending institutions are not thoroughly familiar with the many variations and changes that are available in writing a bond for a contractor. Too often the words "he's bondable" end consideration of the subject. Contractor bonds should be very carefully considered and not placed in the construction loan agreement automatically. In many cases, bonds are not the best instrument for protection of the lender. If the contractor is expanding outside his previous area of performance, a bond may be either very expensive or not available. On the other hand, a well-financed long-established contractor will have no trouble getting a bond because he really doesn't need a bond—his assets are sufficient to guarantee his performance.

Many lenders, while expert in the financial field, have only incidental and superficial knowledge of the details of construction administration. They frequently fail to identify the design architect as being employed by the developer or owner and, all too often, charge him with protecting their interests as well. This creates problems.

To represent the lending source, there should be an individual who in the construction practice is called the "draw inspector." He supervises payments by the lender, ensuring that the work claimed is actually completed, that the work is of good quality and complies with code requirements, and that the money advanced is actually applied to paying subcontractors and suppliers. In general, he serves as the agent of the lender, representing the interests of the lender with the developer, the contractor, and the design architect and associated engineers. The draw inspector's duties, responsibilities, and rights must be identified and specified in the construction loan agreement.

COMMON CAUSES OF DEFAULT

Projects may fail during the construction in several ways, causing losses to the financing institution. The schedule of costs submitted during the loan negotiation may be found to be inadequate. The loan amount is insufficient and the developer does not have additional funds to cover the shortage. Frequently, sufficient funds are allotted, but advances to the developer are diverted to another use, rather than used to pay the bills, so that there is no money left to finish the project. This condition may be encouraged if advances made from the construction loan are greater than justified by the work done. The developer or contractor converts the extra funds to its own purposes in such a way as to prevent ready recovery.

Defective work may present such serious difficulties that completion of the project becomes uneconomic. This rarely occurs suddenly, but happens over a period of months on projects where the lender is either not represented or inadequately represented on periodic inspections. The cost of corrective measures may leave insufficient funds for completion.

There may be delays so serious as to increase costs of construction beyond hope for completing at a reasonable price. Slow work is expensive since many costs such as overhead, interest, security, and so on continue irrespective of work progress. Slow progress also invites vandalism, theft, and poor-quality work.

Inadequate technical evaluation of plans may result in considerable work to be done in a situation where satisfactory completion of the project is very doubtful, because of site problems, lack of utility services, intrusion on zoning requirements, failure to meet building code requirements, or difficulties with access.

The most usual problem is excessive advances of the construction loan made in response to unjustified claims by the developer (who may also be the contractor). These advances are diverted by the developer to other projects, usually in a desperate attempt to shore up those projects to make enough to cover losses. ...

PROTECTIVE MEASURES IN THE LOAN AGREEMENT

The Draw Inspector

Probably the most important provision in the construction loan agreement concerns the identification, the duties, and the rights of the draw inspector representing the lender. He should be a registered professional engineer, properly licensed to practice engineering. Although he may be an employee of the lending institution, it is usually preferable, for the same reasons that independent law firms are preferable to in-house lawyers in delicate negotiations, that he be an independent consulting engineer, specializing in draw inspections. Independent professionals are more likely to provide unbiased advice and to proceed professionally without regard to internal attitudes in the client firm. Generally, there is, in addition, a cost saving, since only actual time spent is charged.

The primary duty of the draw inspector is to visit the building site periodically, usually once each month, and determine the value of the work satisfactorily completed. This determination will enable an evaluation of the contractor's claim for payment, which may be submitted directly to the lending agency or go through the owner. The payment approved by the lender should be no greater than the value of work in place, as appraised by the draw inspector. It will usually be less, if the construction loan agreement fully protects the lender.

In order for the draw inspector to perform this duty efficiently, he should be permitted access to the contractor's books on the project. This is a ticklish point with some contractors but a useful and sometimes essential procedure that can quickly lay to rest questions of costs and payment that would otherwise cause claims and counterclaims. He must have copies of all contracts and subcontracts. He must, of course, have prints of the plans, the specifications, and copies of all change orders. Generally, he should get a copy of all correspondence relating to the construction work.

It is best, of course, if the draw inspector's duties and rights are set forth clearly in both the construction loan agreement and the construction contract. It is essential, in any case, that all interested parties understand that the draw inspector has power to withhold funds claimed but not justified by satisfactory work completed, and that the specified sources of information are to be fully available to him.

. . .

Retainage

One widely accepted safeguard for the lender is the device of retainage, which provides for a percentage—usually 10 percent, but sometimes 5 percent—of the estimated cost of work in place to be withheld. Retainage provides a necessary cushion for uncertainties in estimating the value of work completed and in providing for unexpected deficiencies. Problems arise when an inept draw inspector permits the common practice of letting the contractor or his subcontractors inflate claims to cover all costs and profit after retainage is deducted. Such tactics weaken the lender's position. They can be prevented by a professional analysis of the cost breakdown and by careful and skilled work by the draw inspector. It is obvious that a design architect is far less likely to ferret out and question a practice of this sort than a draw inspector, who is accustomed to the work and is answerable to the lending agency.

Lien Waivers

Lien waivers deserve special consideration in the construction loan agreement. Rarely do these agreements specify the form of lien waivers, and the lien waivers submitted do not always protect the lender. Lien waivers are frequently viewed primarily as a protection for the owner/developer while, in truth, for most construction loans they are a necessary protection for the lender, whose risk is often greater. Sometimes lien waivers end up as multipage forms that are difficult to process, impossible to file, and confusing to all. The lien waiver must be as short as legally permissible and always include a description of the work done for the current claim, the total amount paid to the recipient to date, the amount now claimed, the amount of retainage, and a release for all work done and payments made to the date of the lien waiver. Thus, each lien waiver will serve for all work done previously, providing a dollar amount of all payments made, so that a bookkeeping justification of all lien waivers received is not needed and a complete picture is available with the current lien waiver.

The description of the work and any claim for stored material is important should any question arise of just what the lien waiver covers, as frequently happens. In case of default before the project is completed, lien waivers, properly prepared, will provide an exact measure of the work actually accomplished by each subcontractor and the amount paid for this work. This greatly facilitates negotiations to reimburse the subcontractors (if this course is selected) and to finish the job. If a subcontractor performs poorly, lien waivers detailing the work claimed to be done and its cost provide a firm basis for invoking contract provisions to remedy the unsatisfactory performance. The ownership of stored material may be an issue if the subcontractor leaves the job; this can be rapidly adjudicated if each lien waiver details the stored material on hand at the time of the claim for payment.

Lien waivers, if made out in a complete manner, can serve to facilitate solution to many construction problems, in addition to serving their ostensible purpose of freeing the property from the threat of mechanics' liens.

The draw inspector should be expected to verify the lien waivers directly with responsible representatives of each subcontractor and supplier. Subcontractors will sometimes sign lien waivers for more money than actually received. At other times, lien waivers will not be executed by responsible people and this might present a difficult problem later. Outright forgery is rare, but always a threat. A notarized lien waiver is not a guarantee that the lien provides proper coverage.

FIRST NAT. BANK OF CONWAY v. CONWAY
SHEET METAL CO., INC.

Supreme Court of Arkansas, 1968.
244 Ark. 963, 428 S.W.2d 293.

HARRIS, Chief Justice.

T. & C. Construction Company was the owner of Lot 8, Heritage Subdivision, in Conway. This lot, along with others, was subject to a mortgage held by Capitol Savings and Loan Association, such instrument providing that any lot which was subject to the mortgage would be released by payment of $2,000.00 toward retirement of the debt. Lot 8 was sold by T. & C. Construction Company on January 31, 1966, to John W. Fent and wife, the consideration being $2,900.00. First National Bank of Conway, appellant herein, loaned the amount of the purchase price to the Fents, this indebtedness being evidenced by a note for that amount, signed by Fent and his wife, and by the president of T. & C., George Shaw, Jr. Two thousand dollars of this loan was paid at that time to release the lot from the Capitol Savings and Loan Association mortgage, and the $900.00 was paid to T. & C. by deposit to its account. The bank officer who handled the transaction knew the specific purpose for which the $2,900.00 would be used.

On February 2, 1966, the Fents executed a mortgage to the bank on Lot 8, which recited an obligation on the bank's part to lend $12,900.00 to be used solely in the construction of a residence on this lot, funds to be advanced from time to time as the work progressed. The bank recorded the mortgage, and did, over a period of time, advance $10,-000.00, which the Fents used to pay the general contractor. Thereafter, the Fents encountered financial difficulties, and Conway Sheet Metal Company, Inc., appellee herein, and other sub-contractors, filed suits to foreclose materialmen's and laborers' liens, and the bank sought to foreclose its mortgage. On trial, the court found the bank's mortgage to be a valid construction mortgage upon the property in question, prior and superior to all asserted liens. A few months later, following our decision in the case of Planters Lumber Company, Inc. v. Wilson Company, Inc., 241 Ark. 1005, 1100, 413 S.W.2d 55, appellee filed a motion to vacate the judgment, and on March 24, 1967, still within term time, the Chancery Court set aside and vacated the order of distribution which it had earlier entered, insofar as it pertained to the relative priority of appellee's claim. The cause was thereafter submitted upon the stipulation of the parties, and the court, on May 19, entered a new decree in which it held, as follows:

First, that all costs should be paid; second, that First National Bank should be paid the sum of $13,666.98, representing the $10,000.00 actually advanced for construction purposes, the $2,000.00 advanced in discharging Lot 8 from the mortgage in favor of Capitol Savings and Loan, and $1,666.98, representing interest, costs, and attorney fees provided for in the note and mortgage held by the bank. Third, the court held that appellee should be paid the sum of $1,133.49, it having established its right to a lien upon the property in the amount of $1,472.06.

"... Said lien claimant is entitled to share pro rata in any sums remaining in the hands of said commissioner after payment of the two aforementioned prior claims upon said funds, pro rata and to the same extent as if all other lien claimants remained parties to this action, in which event Conway Sheet Metal Company, Inc., would be entitled to receive a total of 77% of its aggregate lien claim of $1,472.06."

Finally, the decree directed that, since other lien claimants had not moved to set aside the original decree, any balance of funds remaining would be paid to the bank to apply on the indebtedness owed it by the Fents and George Shaw, Jr. From the decree so entered, the bank brings this appeal. Appellee cross-appeals from that part of the decree which awards the bank a first lien upon the property involved for any amount above the $10,000.00 actually advanced for construction purposes, plus interest, costs, and attorney fees therein.

The priority given the bank on the $10,000.00 advanced by the bank for construction is not questioned, the mortgage having been recorded before construction was begun, the bank being obligated to advance that amount, and admittedly having done so. Therefore, the only items involved in this litigation are the $2,000.00 advanced for release of the lot, and the $900.00 which was used to pay the balance due the seller of the lot. Appellant asserts that it is entitled to the entire $2,900.00, and appellee asserts that it is entitled not only to priority over the $900.00, but also to priority over the $2,000.00.

The question then is, "Can a construction money mortgagee, who is obligated under the mortgage to advance a certain sum of money solely for construction purposes, divert a part of the funds to some other purpose, and still claim (as to the funds diverted) the protection that would be afforded had the entire amount been used for construction?" Appellant relies, in large measure, upon Ashdown Hardware Company v. Hughes, 223 Ark. 541, 267 S.W.2d 294, and argues that the controlling circumstance is the purpose for which the money was borrowed.

Hughes is easily distinguishable from the case at hand in that there, the portion of the money which was to be used to retire an already existing mortgage was given particular mention in the new mortgage, same providing that the grantors were justly indebted to the lender of the money in the amount of $4,500.00; the instrument further recited, "And this mortgage likewise secures an additional advance to be made by the mortgagee in the total sum of Five Thousand, Five Hundred dollars ...." This last amount was to be used for the construction of tourist cabins. In the instant case, according to the mortgage given, the entire $12,900.00 is "to be used solely for and in the construction of a residence upon the lands hereinabove described, and Grantee has agreed to make said loan for such purposes, and Grantors are justly indebted to Grantee for advances made or to be made hereafter by Grantee to Grantors from time to time for such purposes, aggregating the principal sum aforesaid .... Grantee agrees that the acceptance and recordation of this mortgage binds Grantee, its successors and assigns, absolutely and unconditionally to make said loan in advances. Such advances will be made as requested by Grantors as such work progresses."

The distinction is at once apparent, for in *Hughes,* materialmen and laborers could quickly ascertain that, though the entire amount loaned by the mortgagee was $10,000.00, only $5,500.00 was to be used for construction.

In Planters Lumber Company, Inc. v. Wilson Company, Inc., supra, we held that where a lender withheld certain sums from the amount of construction funds stated in the mortgage, *inter alia,* the cost of the lots, he could not claim priority in those amounts withheld. Appellant endeavors to distinguish the case before us from *Wilson* by pointing out that there, The Wilson Company owned the lots, and did not advance any money for the payment of same, nonetheless holding out the price of the lots, while here, the bank actually did advance the $2,900.00, which was used for the purchase of Lot 8. It may be, from the standpoint of equity, that appellant, in the present case, is in a better position than Wilson—but the principle which is controlling is exactly the same. Actually, *Wilson,* to some extent, modified earlier holdings in that the following principle is announced: Where a construction money mortgage recites that a certain amount of money will be advanced for construction—it must be used for that explicit purpose if the mortgagee is to have priority over lien holders. Certainly, this is only fair. A materialman or laborer, who plans to furnish materials, or labor, on a particular job is entitled to know how much money the lender is bound absolutely and unconditionally to advance as work progresses. As stated in *Wilson:*

"With this information gleaned from the record, an alert material-man might desire to make another financial check as the work progresses; namely, to check with the disbursing agent to get the total expended for construction."

It might also be mentioned that the purpose clauses in *Wilson* and the present case are practically identical. Appellant asserts that a decision adverse to their side of the case "cannot help but result in great harm to the building industry and the well-being of the state, as the impact of this decision will be felt for many years to come. That is the primary reason for this appeal." We are unable to agree with this statement, for there is more than one way that the bank can give itself absolute protection. One has already been mentioned in this opinion, in referring to the *Hughes* case. We see no great difficulty in having the mortgage recite that a portion of the money (giving the amount) has, or will be, used to pay off an existing indebtedness. Complete protection for the full amount (advance for retirement of indebtedness and construction advances) is thus afforded.

In accordance with what has been said, it follows that the court erred in giving the bank priority on any amounts advanced in excess of the $10,000.00 used for construction. The decree is therefore affirmed on direct appeal (involving the $900.00), and is reversed on cross-appeal (as to the $2,000.00), and the cause is remanded with directions to enter a decree not inconsistent with this opinion. It is so ordered.

DISSENTING OPINION

FOGLEMAN, Justice.

. . .

While the deed in this case was dated January 31, 1966, it was not delivered until February 2, 1966, the date of the construction money mortgage and the date of the advance of $2,900.00. Two thousand dollars of this was by check for the purpose of paying off a first lien on the property held by Capitol Savings & Loan Association. The balance of the purchase money due T. & C. Construction was paid by depositing $900.00 to its account. This advance of $2,900.00 was evidenced by a note dated February 2, 1966. The advance thus came after the loan was made.

It must be remembered that the statutes we are considering are designed to protect a lien of mechanics or materialmen and that the purpose is not to assure them of a source of funds for payment.

If appellant had not advanced the money to pay for the lot, the liens of the materialmen and mechanics would have been subject to these prior liens of $2,900.00 insofar as the land is concerned. Ark.Stat.Ann. § 51–605 (1947) only gives priority over existing encumbrances on the building erected. By the court's decision, the position of these lienors has been improved at the expense of appellant. Their liens are now upon both land and building, subject only to the lien for $10,000.00 advanced for construction. If the bank had advanced the entire $12,-900.00 to the borrower without the purchase price having been paid, the mechanics' and materialmen's liens would be subject to the $12,-900.00 plus the original debt on the property insofar as the lot is concerned and to $12,900.00 on the building. Or if the bank had advanced the $12,900.00 to the borrower and he had paid for the lots without the bank's knowing he intended to do so, the mechanics' and materialmen's liens would still have been subject to the $12,900.00 on the lot and building. The bank was not acting for its own benefit by withholding funds as was the case in Planters Lumber Company v. Wilson, supra.

. . .

I would reverse on direct appeal and affirm on cross-appeal.

NOTE: OBLIGATORY AND OPTIONAL ADVANCES

Construction mortgagees will typically agree to advance loan proceeds only in predetermined installments as construction progresses. As a result, the complete proceeds of the construction loan will not be paid out until construction is virtually completed. Nonetheless, the mortgage that the borrower executes and the lender records before construction begins, and before the first installment is paid out, will secure the total amount of all future advances.

The traditional rule on mortgages securing future advances is that, if the advances are obligatory, they will enjoy the priority that attached to the mortgage when it was first recorded. This rule underlies the observation in *Conway Sheet Metal* that the "priority given the bank on the $10,000 advanced by the bank for construction is not questioned, the mortgage having been recorded before construction, the bank being obligated to advance that amount, and admittedly having done so." By contrast, if the advances are optional or voluntary they will enjoy the mortgage's initial priority only if the mortgagee, when making the advance, had no notice of the intervening junior lien.

The obligatory/optional advance rule has classically been justified as an attempt to protect borrowers rather than junior lenders or lienors. The rule supposedly protects a property owner who has a mortgage to secure future advances on her property but no contractual ability to compel the lender to disburse funds. It would be difficult for such an owner to obtain a junior mortgage if the senior lender could subsequently make advances and take priority over the junior lender. The owner is thus left in a difficult position, unable to extract her equity from the property.

Although this classic explanation for the rule focuses on the borrower, note how the court in *Conway Sheet Metal* applies the theory to achieve a far different policy goal—protection of mechanics. Courts have also used the doctrine to assist subordinated purchase money mortgagees who, as discussed at pages 753–763, may have been misled by developers. See, e.g., Housing Mortgage Co. v. Allied Construction Inc., 374 Pa. 312, 97 A.2d 802 (1953). More specifically, the obligatory/optional advance rule has been used by some courts to rearrange priorities and achieve a fair result in cases where a senior lender makes advances in an unreasonable manner and so injures the security of a junior mortgagee or mechanic.

While the outcomes in these cases may be correct, the obligatory/optional rule is too rough and arcane to be an effective response. Some courts address unreasonable lender behavior in a more straightforward manner, by imposing a duty of good faith and fair dealing on construction lenders in their disbursement activities. See, e.g., Crum v. AVCO Financial Services, 552 N.E.2d 823 (Ind.App.1990); Peoples Bank & Trust Co. and Bank of Mississippi v. L & T Developers, Inc., 434 So.2d 699 (Miss.1983), judgment corrected, 437 So.2d 7 (1983), discussed at p. 775–776 below. Other courts, however, reject an implied duty to monitor advances for the benefit of borrower or other lienors. See Thormahlen v. Citizens Savings and Loan, 73 Or.App. 230, 698 P.2d 512 (1985), review denied, 299 Or. 443, 702 P.2d 1111 (1985).

The intricacies of the doctrine, the confused policy bases, and concerns about loss of priority by construction lenders and other open end mortgagees, such as home equity lenders, has led to increased doubts about the viability of the obligatory/optional advance doctrine. As discussed below, the obligatory/optional advance rule has been rejected in numerous jurisdictions over recent years.

On the theory of the obligatory/optional rule and reasonable lender behavior, see Korngold, Construction Loan Advances and the Subordinated Purchase Money Mortgagee: An Appraisal, a Suggested Approach, and the ULTA Perspective, 50 Fordham L.Rev. 313 (1981).

Notice. The majority rule subordinates the lien of the mortgagee's subsequent optional advances only to the extent that the mortgagee had actual notice of the intervening lien before making the advance. To be safe in these jurisdictions, the intervening lienor must search the record, identify any prior mortgagees and give these mortgagees actual notice of its lien. The minority rule requires only constructive notice to the mortgagee. In these jurisdictions, the mortgagee must search title before making each advance at the risk of losing the advance's priority to the recorded lien. See J.I. Kislak Mortgage Corp. v. William Matthews Builder, Inc., 287 A.2d 686 (Del.Super.1972), affirmed, 303 A.2d 648 (Del.1973) (the fact that the lender's site inspector saw the subcontractor working on the premises was notice to the lender of an inchoate mechanic's lien).

Which rule better allocates the burden of search? If the intervening lienor is going to search anyway, and if the mortgagee's address can easily be found in the record, the majority rule would appear to make more sense. But consider who mortgagees and intervening lienors typically are. How likely, and desirable, is it for mechanics and materialmen to perform a title search before committing their labor or goods to a project? How burdensome is it for the mortgagee to order an update of its original title report? Is it a desirable check against developer misbehavior to give construction lenders another incentive to search title before disbursing additional funds? Reconsider *Kinch v. Fluke,* p. 256 above.

Optional or Obligatory Advance? What criteria should govern the determination whether an advance is obligatory or optional? In the context of construction loans, a program of future advances enables the construction lender to hold back loan proceeds at each stage of construction until it has determined that work is progressing adequately. An obligatory commitment would not serve this purpose. Yet, an absolutely discretionary commitment could defeat the desired priority as all advances could be deemed to be voluntary. Construction lenders usually look for solutions somewhere in the middle, conditioning disbursements on the project's compliance with specified, objective criteria.

Unfortunately, courts have provided no consistent or principled rules for determining whether clauses in this middle ground are optional or obligatory. See e.g., Housing Mortgage Co. v. Allied Construction, Inc., 374 Pa. 312, 97 A.2d 802 (1953) (stating that an obligatory advance is found when the mortgagee is "under a binding obligation" or "contractually obligated" to make the advance).

In Briarwood Towers 85th Co. v. Guterman, 136 A.D.2d 456, 523 N.Y.S.2d 98 (1988), a lender was obligated to make advances if the borrower complied with certain conditions in the building loan agreement, including a promise to obtain a title insurance policy insuring the lender's mortgage as a valid first lien. When the lender received a notice from a party claiming that it had a prior mortgage on the property, the lender notified the title company. The title company informed the lender that no additional title exceptions would be raised and advised the lender that it could proceed with funding. The court reversed the trial court which had found that these events made the advance voluntary, holding that the condition to funding, i.e., title company insurance of a first lien, had been met. The court noted that the binding force of the lender's obligation was not vitiated, quoting from an earlier opinion: "where the obligation to advance exists, or where the right to decline upon facts *dehors* the instrument, and which may be the subject of dispute or contention, the holder of the first security is warranted in making the advances in reliance upon his mortgage." Id. at 459, 523 N.Y.S.2d 101 (quoting Hyman v. Hauff, 138 N.Y. 48, 55, 33 N.E. 735, 737 (1893)).

Despite the court's holding that the advance was "obligatory", if the action had been by the borrower to compel the lender to fund, would the court have actually found the senior lender obligated to make advances in light of information that there was a mortgage prior to the lender's? Does the court's holding reflect a belief that the lender was acting reasonably under the circumstances and that it did not want the obligatory/optional advance rule to punish that behavior?

What are the implications of this muddle for title insurers deciding whether to insure the first lien status of mortgages calling for future advances? See generally, Jones & Mesall, Mechanic's Lien Title Insurance Coverage for Construction Projects: Lenders and Insurers Beware, 16 Real Est.L.J. 291 (1988).

Advances to Preserve Collateral. Should it make a difference if a mortgagee, committed only to optional advances, finds it necessary to advance funds in order to cover unpaid real property taxes, insurance premiums, the cost of maintenance and repair, or otherwise to preserve its collateral? Some writers take the view that these advances are "obligatory in the sense that they are necessary to protect previous loans and advances made by the mortgagee," and thus should be given the priority enjoyed by obligatory advances. Note, Mortgages—Advance Money Provisions—Effect on Preferences and Recording Acts, 29 N.Y.U.L.Rev. 733, 738 (1954). Legislatures have been quick to adopt the analogy, Cal.Civ.Code § 3136; Md.Real Prop.Code Ann. § 7–102; and Me.Rev.Stat.Ann. tit. 9–B § 436 represent three distinctive steps in this direction. See generally, Skipworth, Should Construction Lenders Lose Out on Voluntary Advances if a Loan Turns Sour? 5 Real Est.L.J. 221 (1977); Comment, Mortgages to Secure Future Advances: Problems of Priority and the Doctrine of Economic Necessity, 46 Miss.L.J. 433 (1975).

Rejection of Obligatory/Optional Advance Rule. There have been various statutory responses to the dissatisfaction with the obligatory/optional distinction. Some states have attempted to fix specific problems inherent in the doctrine. See, e.g., Uniform Land Security Interests Act § 111(19) (addressing the definitional difficulties by defining an advance as "obligatory"—or "pursuant to commitment"—"if the obligor has bound itself to make it, whether or not a default or other event not within its control has relieved or may relieve it from its obligation"); 42 Pa.Cons.Stat.Ann. § 8143(a) (1991) (requiring written notice by junior encumbrancer in order for a senior lender to lose priority for voluntary advances). Other states simply reject the obligatory/optional rule and give all future advances priority as of the filing of the original mortgage. See, e.g., Md. Real Prop. Code Ann. § 7–102 (1991). Yet other states have adopted "cut-off notice" provisions which permit the mortgagor to issue a notice which freezes advances having priority under the open end mortgage at their current amount. The mortgagor can then obtain a second mortgage more readily, as the junior lienor will not face loss of priority to the senior mortgagee. See, e.g., Fla.Stat.Ann. § 697.04(b).

See Rest. Law Prop.—Security (Mortgages) §§ 2.1–2.4 (Tent. Draft No. 1, 1991); G. Nelson & D. Whitman, Real Estate Finance Law § 12.7 (2d ed.1985).

b. The Permanent Loan

DAVIS, THE PERMANENT LENDER'S ROLE IN THE CONSTRUCTION PROCESS *

3 Real Estate Review 70–75 (No. 1, 1973).

Lurking in the background in any discussion of construction lending is the specter of the *permanent lender.* Writing as one who represents a permanent lender, my own inclination is to state that the permanent lender is the key man in any new real estate venture. At the very least, certainly, the permanent lender is a vital factor in a new real estate venture. It is his money that is relied upon to finance the project even though it will not be disbursed until after completion of construction. Without a permanent commitment most construction lenders will not make a construction loan.

Nevertheless, once the permanent commitment is issued, the other parties feel free to criticize the permanent lender for seeking various rights to approve, for refusing to waive commitment requirements, and for declining to take a backseat during construction. The construction lender and the borrower would like to have the permanent lender bound to make the loan, with neither of them so bound until the time of permanent closing. To a permanent lender this is unthinkable. Certain facts such as building size, number of units, estimated income, and so forth, have been represented to him. He has underwritten the deal and agreed to make a certain kind of loan based on those representations. He has set forth requirements in his commitment to be satisfied prior to closing which will ensure that the project has been completed in compliance with those representations. Such requirements and conditions have been agreed to by the borrower in accepting and executing the commitment. The permanent lender should not be expected, or be asked, to waive such requirements. He must see to their fulfillment, and he is therefore entitled to be in the picture from the start. This article will be concerned with the permanent lender's interest in construction, with the relationship between construction lender and permanent lender in accomplishing their respective goals, and with the potential problem areas in their relationship.

PERMANENT LENDER'S INTEREST IN CONSTRUCTION OF THE PROJECT

Why should the permanent lender be interested in construction matters? He concerns himself with construction primarily because he wishes to be sure that the building to be constructed is the one on which he has committed himself to make a loan. It too often occurs that the final structure is not the one envisioned by the permanent lender at the time of making the commitment.

Second, he is concerned with construction because he will have a security interest in the building for as long as he holds the mortgage, which may be for twenty to thirty years (and in this age of "kickers," he may have an immediate equity interest as well). If the building is improperly constructed, the permanent lender's security can be severely impaired since in most instances, he looks first to the improvements and to the income therefrom for security, and only to a lesser extent, to the borrower. Needless to say a potential owner is interested in the building he may someday own.

INSURING PROPER CONSTRUCTION OF THE BUILDING

What can the permanent lender do to insure proper construction of a project and so protect his interests?

Plans and Specifications

The permanent lender's most potent right is to examine the plans and specifications in advance and insist that the building be put up in compliance with them. The plans and specifications should be in great detail, setting forth site plans, floor plans, elevations and wall sections, special construction details, footings and foundations, structural framing, and mechanicals (plumbing, electrical, heating, ventilating, and air conditioning). They should be examined by a professional architect or engineer fully familiar with construction in the particular locale involved. The permanent lender must insist that construction be strictly in accordance with these plans and specs. His appraisal being based on them, any variation destroys the underwriting basis.

RELATIONSHIP BETWEEN CONSTRUCTION LENDER AND PERMANENT LENDER

Having discussed the relevance of construction matters to the permanent lender, let us now consider the relationship between the construction lender and the permanent lender. Basically, their interests are substantially similar:

To have the building completed as provided for in their commitments and in accordance with the approved plans and specifications. (It is a good idea to have the two lenders use the same engineer or architect; this will reduce the likelihood of disputes over the adequacy of the plans.)

To have their funds invested pursuant to their commitments.

To have the construction loan paid upon completion of construction.

To have the permanent lender then hold the loan with the long-term security he contemplated when making his commitment.

Notwithstanding these basic objectives, differences between the two lenders may occur. The construction lender's overwhelming desire for completion and repayment may lead him, for purposes of expediency, to approve changes in plans which are unacceptable to the permanent lender. The construction lender also would at all times like to have the permanent lender bound to close his loans. He would like to have an agreement enforceable against the permanent lender subject to a minimum of conditions, but not necessarily enforceable against himself unless he so agrees.

Very often, for example, the borrower is a depositor in the institution making the construction loan and so is in a position to exert sufficient pressure on the construction lender during a period of declining interest rates to convince him not to sell the loan to the permanent lender. To minimize this possibility, the permanent lender wants an agreement enforceable against *all* parties, including the borrower and the construction lender; in exchange, he is willing to be bound himself provided there is compliance with the condition of his commitment.

How are these objectives met and differences resolved to the satisfaction of both lenders?

Buy-Sell Agreement

In most cases, a condition of the permanent lender's commitment is the execution of a buy-sell agreement prior to the start of construction. This three-party agreement, among permanent lender, construction lender, and borrower, has the purpose of insuring that the permanent lender will buy the loan from the construction lender and that the construction lender will sell the loan to nobody else. Recent litigation by a permanent lender arising from a construction lender's refusal to comply with the terms of a buy-sell agreement resulted in a lower court decision that the agreement was binding and a judgment that the construction lender pay damages for failure to convey the loan to the permanent lender in compliance with the agreement.

. . .

The pertinent provisions of the buy-sell agreement are usually the following:

The consent of the permanent lender to the assignment by the borrower to the construction lender of the proceeds to be forthcoming under the permanent commitment;

The agreement of the construction lender to sell the loan to no one except the permanent lender and to refuse to accept prepayment;

The agreement of the permanent lender to buy the loan at par, subject to compliance with the commitment;

The remedies in the event of the borrower's default under the building loan agreement or under the permanent commitment; and

The agreement of the borrower to comply with the permanent commitment and to amend the mortgage documents if the permanent lender requests it, and the agreement of the construction lender to obtain such amendments from the borrower. ...

TRANSITION FROM CONSTRUCTION
LOAN TO PERMANENT LOAN

In most transactions involving permanent financing, the transition from the construction loan stage to the permanent loan stage goes smoothly. The permanent lender wants a mortgage on the building he contemplated; the construction lender wants to be paid off. But there are areas of friction and potential conflict that must be ironed out.

Advance Approval of Some Items

During the early stages of discussion, before he closes his construction loan, the construction lender will want approvals from the permanent lender on as many closing conditions of the permanent commitment as possible. He will ask for approval of title, survey, leases, appraisal, plans and specifications, and the operating agreement.

The permanent lender can review the state of title at this early date and set forth those exceptions or areas which disturb him. At the time of the construction loan closing, however, he can neither know nor approve the state of title for purposes of the permanent closing. Any approvals he gives, therefore, must reserve his right to reexamine title for the permanent closing.

The permanent lender can also approve the survey at this stage, okaying the location of the premises and its relation to roads, intersections, and so forth. But he must reserve the right to see a final survey showing the improvements as built to determine if they accord with the commitment he contemplated. To avoid confusion, any approvals the permanent lender gives to plans and specifications should be by detailed plan number, date, and revision number.

The permanent lender may approve leases and any operating agreements if they are in existence at the time of the construction loan closing, but this is unlikely.

The items which the permanent lender cannot approve in advance can cause great concern to a construction lender. But by the nature of things, certain matters are not in existence at the time of the construction loan closing; and so the risk of the permanent lender not giving final approval to them must remain with the construction lender. Such items include the final survey, an independent engineer's report, any estoppel certificates that the permanent lender may want from tenants and from adjoining department stores (in the case of a shopping center), the final title search, and executed leases.

PENTHOUSE INTERNATIONAL, LTD. v. DOMINION FEDERAL SAVINGS AND LOAN ASSOCIATION

United States Court of Appeals, Second Circuit, 1989.
855 F.2d 963, cert. denied, 490 U.S. 1005, 109 S.Ct. 1639, 104 L.Ed.2d 154.

Before MESKILL and ALTIMARI, Circuit Judges, and MISHLER, District Judge.

ALTIMARI, Circuit Judge:

Defendants-appellants Dominion Federal Savings & Loan Association ("Dominion") and Melrod, Redman & Gartlan, P.C. ("Melrod" or the "Melrod firm") appeal from judgments entered in favor of plaintiffs-appellees Penthouse International, Ltd. and its wholly-owned subsidiary, Boardwalk Properties, Inc. (hereafter referred to as "Penthouse"), and third-party defendant-appellee Queen City Savings & Loan Association ("Queen City"). After a three-week bench trial in the United States District Court for the Southern District of New York (Judge Kevin T. Duffy), the district court held that Dominion committed an anticipatory breach of its agreement to participate in a $97 million loan transaction. The district court awarded Penthouse approximately $128.7 million and awarded Queen City nearly $7.7 million (plus interest and costs) for the damages caused by Dominion's anticipatory breach. In addition, the court dismissed with prejudice Dominion's cross-claim against Queen City. After the court issued its opinion, it ordered that the Melrod firm be held jointly and severally liable for the Penthouse judgment, not on breach of contract grounds, but for fraud.

Dominion and the Melrod firm present several arguments on appeal. Dominion's principal contention is that the district court erred when it found that Penthouse carried its burden of demonstrating the existence of an anticipatory breach and that, in absence of the breach, Penthouse had the ability to perform its contractual obligations before the loan commitment expired. The Melrod firm argues that there is no basis in law or fact for holding it liable for the Penthouse judgment.

For the reasons that follow, we reverse in part, affirm in part and remand.

FACTS and BACKGROUND

Sometime after gambling was legalized in Atlantic City, New Jersey, Penthouse's President, Robert Guccione, conceived the idea of opening a Penthouse Hotel and Casino along Atlantic City's famed Boardwalk. To implement this idea, Guccione set about to locate prospective financiers and potential partners to assist in underwriting the construction project. Boardwalk Properties, Inc. was formed as a wholly-owned subsidiary of Penthouse for the purpose of handling Penthouse's affairs in connection with the hotel and casino project.

Initially unsuccessful in its efforts to obtain outside financing, Penthouse used its own resources to commence the project. Penthouse proceeded to assemble five contiguous plots of land along Missouri Avenue adjacent to the Boardwalk. Three of these parcels Penthouse held in fee simple and the other two were obtained through leasehold estates. The first leased property, on which was located a Holiday Inn Hotel, was obtained from the Boardwalk and Missouri Corporation, an entity controlled by New York real estate financier Harry Helmsley (the "Helmsley lease"). The second leasehold estate, which was then occupied by a Four Seasons Hotel, was obtained from Albert and Robert Rothenburg (the "Rothenburg lease").

Penthouse's construction plans included the use of the existing tower structure from the Holiday Inn, the rebuilding of the structure from the Four Seasons into a second tower and the construction of a seven-story building between the two towers. In these structures, Penthouse planned to house its casino, a 515 room hotel, a health club and other facilities. By June 1983, Penthouse had invested between $65 and $75 million into construction of the hotel and casino which was approximately 40 to 50 percent complete.

Although Guccione believed that the entire project could be financed with Penthouse's own funds when construction commenced, as time passed and costs escalated, it became apparent that it would be necessary to obtain outside financing. Penthouse then sought financing unsuccessfully from various sources. In or about April 1983, Penthouse retained Jefferson National Mortgage, a mortgage broker, to locate prospective lending institutions interested in providing Penthouse with construction and permanent financing for the hotel and casino project. As a result of Jefferson National's efforts, Queen City extended to Penthouse in June 1983 a $97 million loan commitment.

On June 20, 1983, Queen City issued to Penthouse (through Boardwalk Properties, Inc.) a commitment to lend Penthouse $97 million for construction and permanent financing in connection with the Penthouse Hotel and Casino project (the "Queen City loan commitment" or the "loan commitment"). The Queen City loan commitment was accepted by Penthouse on June 29, 1983. In the loan commitment, Queen City advised Penthouse that "your request for construction/permanent financing ... with Queen City Savings and Loan Association ... has been approved subject to the following terms and conditions [.]" The term of the loan was ten years with a construction phase in effect during either the first 24 months or until Penthouse received a certificate of occupancy from Atlantic City and permission to operate the casino. The interest rate was fixed at 14 7/8 % for years one through five and 15 3/8 % for years six through ten.

To secure the loan, pursuant to paragraph 6 of the loan commitment, Penthouse was required to deliver to Queen City a mortgage on the hotel and casino and the underlying properties. Thus, Penthouse was required to deliver a note secured by a "valid first mortgage lien on all real estate owned by [b]orrower covering the project site" and all improvements thereon and was required to provide a "valid first leasehold interest" in the Rothenburg and Helmsley leases and "a first mortgage covering the improvements thereon." Penthouse also was required to provide assignments of its interest in the leasehold estates to be effective in the event of Penthouse's default. Paragraph 6 required Penthouse to certify at closing that there were "no violations" of the Helmsley or Rothenburg leases.

Paragraph 14 of the loan commitment required Penthouse to represent and warrant 1) that there was no pending litigation that would affect title to the properties, the validity of the mortgage liens, the validity and non-violations of the leases, etc., 2) that the final plans and specifications for construction would satisfy and conform with local, state and federal regulations, and 3) that all necessary utilities (i.e., water, electricity, sewer, telephone service and gas) were available to the full needs of the property and that "valid and enforceable agreements to supply such services have been entered into[.]"

Under the heading of "Commitment Expiration Date," paragraph 15 provided that the commitment would

> expire one hundred twenty (120) days after the date hereof (the "Commitment Expiration Date") unless mutually extended in writing by Lender, and upon such expiration Lender shall have no

further obligation to Borrower, except as set forth in item 19 of the attached Conditions.

Paragraph 16 of the commitment, which was headed by the term "Closing", stipulated that the "[c]losing of the Loan ("Closing") shall be held ... on or before the Commitment Expiration Date[.]"

Paragraph 17 of the loan commitment provided that an additional twenty enumerated "Conditions Prior to Closing" ("preclosing conditions") contained in a document attached to the commitment were incorporated as part of the commitment. Paragraph 17 also stipulated that "[l]ender's obligation to close the Loan [was] contingent upon the satisfaction of each of said conditions."

In relevant part, the preclosing conditions provided:

* * *

5. TITLE INSURANCE: There shall be furnished to Lender, at least 15 days prior to Closing, a current preliminary title insurance binder, issued by a title company initially approved by Lender. At Closing, a standard ALTA title policy shall be issued by such company insuring Lender's interest or lien in or on the Property subject only to such title objections as Lender shall approve. Such title insurance policy shall affirmatively insure the priority of the lien of the Mortgage. The title company insuring Lender's lien shall obtain re- insurance in such amounts and with such companies, as Lender may require.

* * *

10. UTILITIES: The Lender shall be furnished with copies of all agreements for providing the utility services required for the operation of the Property, including without limitation thereto, agreements pertaining to water, sewer, and electricity and/or original current letters from the suppliers of such utilities stating that the utilities are available and are offered in sufficient quantities for the project.

11. PLANS AND SPECIFICATIONS: The written approval of all plans and specifications for the Improvements to be erected must be obtained from Lender. No change of any substance shall be made in the final plans and specifications without the prior written approval of Lender and all governmental authorities having jurisdiction.

12. CERTIFICATION BY ARCHITECT AND CONSTRUCTION MANAGER: Borrower shall deliver to Lender at Closing a certification by Borrower's architect and construction manager containing (i) a detailed listing of the then-current plans and specifications for the Improvements; (ii) a statement that said plans and specifications are complete documents for the construction of the Improvements and contain all details requisite for the completion, occupancy and operation thereof; and, (iii) a statement that said plans and specifications are

in full compliance with all local, state and federal (if any) rules, ordinances and regulations governing or applying to the construction of the Improvements.

* * *

16. CONSTRUCTION—CONTRACTS: Borrower shall submit, for Lender's approval, Borrower's contract with its architect, construction project manager and all major trade contractors. Lender may at its option require assignment of the aforesaid contracts or any of them.

* * *

19. PARTICIPATION: Lender's obligation to complete the Closing is also contingent upon execution of a participation agreement between Lender and other lenders pursuant to which said other lenders will participate in making the Loan (through the Lender as "lead institution") at least to the extent of $90,000,000.00 on terms and conditions satisfactory to the Lender. Borrower acknowledges that it is Borrower's sole responsibility (either directly or through mortgage brokerage companies) to obtain such participants who are satisfactory to Lender, it being understood that Lender shall have no obligation to obtain such participants. In the event the aforesaid $90,000,000.00 participation agreements are not obtained, then Lender shall refund to Borrower the origination fees it received pursuant to Item 8 of the Commitment.

* * *

The preclosing conditions also established that New Jersey law would govern the terms of the loan commitment and stipulated that Queen City's attorneys would have the final decision on whether the various preclosing conditions had been satisfied. Nowhere, however, did the commitment or the preclosing conditions provide that Queen City was authorized by the participating lending institutions to waive Penthouse's compliance with any of the terms of the commitment.

Once the loan commitment was in place, pursuant to preclosing condition 19, Queen City and Penthouse began searching for financial institutions interested in participating in a syndicate of lenders to underwrite the loan. Lending institutions that decided to participate in the syndicate (the "participants") would enter into a "Loan Participation Sale and Trust Agreement" (the "participation agreement"). Under the commitment, Queen City was designated to serve as the lead lending institution (the "lead lender") for the syndicate. Under the participation agreement, the participants would purchase from Queen City "undivided participating ownership" interests in the mortgage loan. Pursuant to the participation agreement, Queen City assumed various administrative responsibilities for servicing the loan. The agreement stipulated, however, that Queen City was to act, not as an agent, but as an "independent contractor" for the participants and would serve "as a trustee with fiduciary duties" in connection with protecting the rights of the participating lenders. In addition, the participation agreement contained an integration clause, provided that it could not be modified except by written agreement and established New Jersey law as the governing law.

By the fall of 1983, twelve financial institutions, including Queen City, had agreed to participate in the financing syndicate and had committed to provide a total of $62 million for the project. In mid-November 1983, Dominion expressed interest in providing Penthouse with financing and on November 14th offered directly to Penthouse a commitment to provide $40 million in financing for the project. Although Dominion's offer was never accepted, it did lead to Dominion's decision on November 21, 1983 to participate in the $97 million loan syndicate.

On November 21, 1983, a meeting was held at Penthouse's offices in New York City. In attendance at the meeting were representatives of Penthouse, including its Chief Operating Officer and General Counsel, David J. Myerson, and Penthouse's outside counsel for the loan transaction, Jay Newman; representatives of Queen City, including its Senior Vice President, John E. Beahan, and Queen City's attorney, John J. Lipari; and representatives of Dominion, including its Executive Vice President, David A. Neal, and its outside counsel, William J. Dorn. At this meeting, Dominion agreed to participate in the loan syndicate to the extent of $35 million. Dominion's agreement to participate in the loan was embodied in three documents: two letter agreements exchanged between Queen City and Dominion and a third document which was a letter from Penthouse to Dominion. In substance, Dominion "accepted" all of the terms and conditions of both the loan commitment and the participation agreement except that the participation agreement was amended to include Dominion as "co-lead seller" for the syndicate. In addition, the loan commitment was modified at the meeting in a side agreement between Penthouse and Queen City to include as a preclosing condition that "arrangements, reasonably satisfactory to [Queen City], shall have been made with the staff o[f] the Casino Control Commission to permit the opening of the casino and hotel, upon completion of construction, utilizing a trustee or fiduciary in the event the license to [Penthouse] . . . or any of its principals has not been granted."

Although it does not appear that Dominion entered into any written agreement with Penthouse directly, Penthouse did deliver to Dominion a letter indicating that it agreed to pay Dominion certain fees "[i]n consideration" for Dominion's agreement to participate "as a Co-Seller" for the syndicate. Penthouse also gave Dominion a check for $175,000 for fees it agreed to pay.

Also on November 21st, Penthouse and Queen City mutually agreed to extend the Commitment Expiration Date to December 1, 1983. This written extension was prompted by Lipari's observation that the 120–

day condition of the commitment had expired and his belief that, in order to have a "valid commitment," it was necessary for Queen City and Penthouse to mutually extend the expiration date. In addition, Lipari discussed the timing of the loan closing with Newman and Dorn, and then, in a letter also dated November 21st, Lipari and Newman agreed that "we shall close th[e] loan no earlier than February 1, 1984 or later than March 1, 1984."

Once the loan commitment syndicate was complete, Penthouse and Queen City directed their efforts to closing the transaction. Toward that goal, Lipari and Newman maintained regular contact and Lipari held a series of "status meetings" during which representatives of Penthouse and Queen City reviewed the steps taken in connection with Penthouse's satisfaction of the preclosing conditions. During these status meetings, Penthouse sought alternate arrangements for satisfying some of the preclosing conditions. For example, although preclosing condition 10 required Penthouse to deliver copies of all agreements for providing utility services required for the operation of the hotel and casino and/or original, current letters indicating that the utilities would be available in sufficient quantities for the project, Penthouse sought to proceed without having fully satisfied this condition. Penthouse did not have agreements with some utility companies to provide certain essential services and it did not have written assurances that those services were available to meet the demands of the proposed hotel and casino. Similarly, Penthouse sought to proceed to closing without having fully complied with preclosing conditions 11, 12 and 16.

Penthouse's position in this regard was that, since the construction project was 40 to 50 percent complete, many of the requirements of the preclosing conditions could be satisfied through substitute arrangements. Thus, instead of providing an architect's and construction manager's certificate, as required by preclosing condition 12, Penthouse offered to provide a certificate from its project engineer and to allow Queen City's architect to examine the project. This substitute performance was necessary because, at that time, Penthouse had not retained an architect. In place of providing Queen City with copies of final plans and specifications for the project, as required by the preclosing conditions, Penthouse sought to provide Queen City with its original plans and specifications for the project, even though they were out of date due to changes in the applicable building codes and despite the fact that Penthouse had no final plans for the electrical or mechanical work on the project. Notwithstanding the modifications Penthouse sought, Lipari was satisfied that the transaction could close in light of Penthouse's proffered substitute performance. It does not appear, however, that Lipari sought Dominion's or the other participants' consent to a waiver of Penthouse's full compliance with any preclosing conditions.

After the second status meeting, Queen City sent Dominion and the other participants a letter stating in essence that substantial progress had been made toward satisfying the preclosing conditions and announcing that a "preclosing meeting" would occur sometime between February 1 and 8, 1984. It was later determined that the "preclosing meeting" would occur on February 9, 1984 at Penthouse's New York offices.

Once Dominion agreed to participate in the loan syndicate, it proceeded to attempt to sell in the secondary market sub-participation interests of its $35 million interest in the loan syndicate. Dominion's decision to sub-participate out its interest in the loan was motivated in part by the fact that its legal lending limit was $18.5 million. Thus, Dominion could not lend to a single borrower more than that amount. By letter agreement dated December 2, 1983, Dominion sold to Community Savings & Loan Association ("Community") a $17.5 million interest in its original $35 million participation interest. At that time, Community had not completed its underwriting analysis of the loan, and proceeded with this analysis in December 1983 and continued on through February 1984. In early-February 1984, however, Community started to show some reticence with proceeding in the transaction.

As Penthouse and Queen City prepared for the "preclosing meeting" set for February 9, 1984, Newman received a letter from Commonwealth Land Title Insurance Company regarding Penthouse's ability to furnish the mortgage security required by the loan commitment. This letter indicated that there were several objections to title on the Helmsley lease. That parcel was subject to two mortgages, the McShane mortgage and the Chase mortgage, which needed to be discharged or subordinated before Penthouse could furnish the required security. Unless the McShane and Chase mortgages were discharged or subordinated, if foreclosed upon, they potentially could wipe out the Helmsley lease and any security interest in that lease. The letter also raised title objections to the Rothenburg lease and pointed out that there was a declaration of encumbrances in connection with the parcels held in fee simple which had to be removed or modified. In addition to the title problems, it also appears that the Helmsley lease had to be modified before closing. Unless the lease was modified, the closing of the loan would violate its terms. The commitment required, however, that Penthouse certify, at closing, that there were "no violations" of that lease.

To resolve the various title problems and the problems with the terms of the lease, Newman knew that he would have to negotiate a discharge or subordination of the McShane and Chase mortgages, negotiate with Helmsley to obtain amendments to the lease and obtain a subordination of encumbrances in connection with the Helmsley leased property. Although Penthouse had made some initial contacts with Helmsley's representatives by February 9th, no agreement resolving these problems had been reached, nor had actual negotiations with Helmsley's representatives commenced. It is also unclear whether the holders of the Chase and McShane mortgages were willing to discharge or subordinate their liens because they apparently had not been contacted by February 9th.

On February 9, 1984, representatives of the parties to the loan transaction and the participants met at Penthouse's offices in New York City for the preclosing meeting. Among several others, Lipari was present to represent Queen City and Newman was there representing Penthouse. Penthouse's Myerson made sporadic appearances throughout the meeting. Dominion was represented by Philip Gorelick of the Melrod firm who had been brought into the deal on February 8th. At the meeting, after Penthouse made a presentation of a scale model of the planned hotel and casino, Lipari handed out some press clippings, copies of status reports and copies of draft loan closing documents. He then reviewed each of the preclosing conditions and described the progress made toward their satisfaction. Among the draft closing documents Lipari circulated was a standard, preprinted, six-page "Blumberg" form for a "plain language" mortgage and a standard, six-page, preprinted form for a "security agreement" for the furniture and fixtures. At the top of the Blumberg form appeared the admonition: "Consult your lawyer before signing this mortgage—it has important legal consequences." The draft mortgage included a rider requiring that Penthouse satisfy each of the preclosing conditions. Nowhere in the draft closing documents was there a provision allowing for preclosing conditions to be waived or modified.

After sitting through the meeting and reviewing the documents prepared by Lipari, Gorelick presented a list of items he wanted to review prior to deciding whether Dominion could proceed. He also indicated his belief that the loan transaction was not in a position to close, explaining that, in light of the unresolved title problems, problems with the leases, the unfulfilled status of some of the preclosing conditions and the inadequacy of the draft loan documents, he could not advise his client to proceed.

Gorelick gave the strong impression that the entire deal had to be overhauled. In giving this impression, Gorelick was less than tactful. He was particularly vehement about the inadequacy of the documents prepared by Lipari, which he described as "idiotic." To satisfy Gorelick's concerns, Queen City and Penthouse agreed to allow Gorelick and his firm to prepare appropriate closing documents and to review condition compliance in order to bring the deal to a close. Penthouse also agreed to pay the Melrod firm's fees while it focused its resources on the loan transaction.

After Penthouse and Queen City gave Gorelick and the Melrod firm responsibility for moving the deal toward closing, Gorelick immediately sought documents and information from Penthouse concerning all aspects of the transaction. Gorelick then drafted checklists of the documents and information he felt was necessary to review and communicated these checklists to Newman. Gorelick's checklists were very broad in scope and covered all facets of the hotel and casino project. Gorelick's initial requests for information regarding the transaction were communicated on February 9th, but were followed up by several additional requests later that month. Newman responded at length to these requests in letters dated February 29th and March 1st 1984.

Responsive to the problems with the Helmsley lease, Melrod lawyers prepared a list of proposed amendments to the Helmsley lease that they believed were necessary before closing. Gorelick insisted that Penthouse seek the proposed amendments from Helmsley and described each amendment as being "required." When, however, the proposed amendments were sent to Penthouse, they were accompanied by a cover letter from Gorelick's partner, Louis Trotter, that indicated that the proposed amendments reflected "a nearly final version of what the lender will be looking for and [would] certainly provide you with a jumping off point for your discussions with Helmsley."

To respond to an inquiry concerning the status of alternate licensing arrangements, which was required as a preclosing condition, Penthouse's attorney, Arthur S. Goldstein, sent the Melrod firm two letters. These letters addressed the status of Penthouse's license application and set forth the results of Goldstein's inquiries with the staff of the New Jersey Casino Control Commission ("CCC"). In the first letter, after providing an overview of the New Jersey Casino Control Act (the "act") and explaining in detail the license application process, Goldstein discussed the status of Penthouse's application. He stated that Penthouse had commenced the application process but that, at its request, the process had been suspended in September 1982 pending the outcome of Penthouse's efforts to obtain financing. As of February 1984, the application process had not been reactivated. Goldstein also explained that the financial institutions participating in the loan transaction would have to "qualify" under the act. Goldstein's prognosis as to the timing of licensing was that the whole process might be accomplished within a year.

More directly responsive to the status of the preclosing condition was Goldstein's second letter. The preclosing condition required that "reasonably satisfactory" arrangements be made with the staff of the CCC to permit the opening of the casino in the event that Penthouse did not obtain a license. In the second letter, Goldstein stated that he had discussed the matter with staff members at the CCC, but he explained that they had no authority to make binding decisions and that it would be necessary for Penthouse to submit a formal proposal. Nevertheless, based upon his informal discussions with the CCC staff, Goldstein opined that if Penthouse became unlicenseable, it would be necessary for it to completely divest itself of any "beneficial interest" in the casino. He suggested that this could be accomplished by using a trustee who would buy out Penthouse's interest in the casino. He also stated that this transaction would have to be structured in such a manner to insure that Penthouse would have no recourse against the casino in the event of default. After Goldstein set forth additional details of the proposed trusteeship and the buy-out transaction, he concluded by stating that his comments only reflected a "rough outline of what I believe to be a proposal that might be acceptable to the Commission."

In addition to the document and information exchanges, Gorelick and representatives of Dominion engaged in a series of meetings with Myerson and, subsequently, Guccione. At one meeting held on February 29, 1984, Myerson met with Gorelick and other Melrod attorneys to discuss the progress toward closing. Gorelick indicated that he was still in the process of revising his closing checklists and that until he had finished that analysis there has not much to discuss. At that meeting or shortly thereafter, Gorelick reminded Myerson that, since the loan commitment would expire on March 1, 1984, Myerson should submit a request for an extension of the commitment expiration date. Myerson refused, however, to make such a request. Myerson believed that the loan commitment could not expire unless and until Penthouse was presented with the closing documents.

Later in the day on February 29th, Myerson went to Dominion's offices in McLean, Virginia where he met with Dominion's President, David Neal, and a representative of Community, William J. Wienke, Jr. Neal explained that Wienke was present at the meeting because Community was a participant in the loan. During the course of the meeting, the parties discussed various aspects of the project. At the conclusion, however, Wienke expressed his concern about the delays in closing and told Myerson that he needed more information about the loan. Wienke then presented Myerson with a list of thirty-five items concerning the transaction and explained that "this is the kind of stuff that I need." Myerson said that he would review the matters raised in Wienke's list.

Also on February 29th, Gorelick, Wienke and Neal engaged in a telephone conference call to discuss the transaction. During this telephone conference, Wienke explained that he was "getting a bad feeling" about the transaction and inquired whether the commitment should be terminated due to Penthouse's failure to satisfy the preclosing conditions by the March 1st date. Gorelick advised against this and Wienke acquiesced.

In addition to Gorelick's work on the transaction, representatives of Dominion were sending information requests and other items to Penthouse directly. For example, on March 1, 1984, Dominion's Vice-President, James Winston Bray, sent Myerson a letter recapping the "areas of concern" which he felt "need[ed] particular attention." Bray stated that one matter he thought needed addressing—"to make the proposed financing for the project marketable"—was the existence of "[a] satisfactory management agreement, prior to loan closing, for the operation of the proposed hotel." Nevertheless, he prefaced his comments by stating that his concerns were not intended "to replace or diminish" the various other aspects of the loan transaction.

On March 6, 1984, Myerson met with Guccione and Dominion's Chairman of the Board, William L. Walde, at Guccione's home. Although Walde expressed Dominion's continued interest in financing the project, he raised concerns regarding Queen City's ability to serve as the lead lender for the transaction. Walde described Queen City as a small and inconsequential savings and loan and suggested that it was ill-equipped to handle a transaction of this size. Guccione said that he would speak to Queen City about Walde's concerns, but he also stated that he thought it would be unfair to remove Queen City from the lead position.

On March 14, 1984, Guccione flew to Washington, D.C. to meet with Walde. At that meeting, Guccione told Walde that Queen City would not relinquish its lead position, but he offered to compensate Dominion for the fees that it otherwise would have earned had it been the lead lending institution. Also at this meeting, Walde informed Guccione that he wanted to appoint a construction company, Sigal, to perform a long in-depth reevaluation of the structure, the steel and all the parts thereon. Guccione explained that he thought that this was unnecessary. Walde also requested that Penthouse designate a specific individual at Penthouse whose sole responsibility would be to address matters of concern raised by Dominion in connection with the loan transaction.

On March 15, 1984, Walde followed up the meeting with Guccione by sending him a letter summarizing the issues discussed which Guccione had agreed "to look into." One of the items for review was that "[t]he hotel manager [was] to submit to lender a hotel management program." On March 22, 1984, Dominion's Neal sent a letter to Guccione recommending that Penthouse engage Sigal to formulate a construction cost evaluation. Neal concluded the letter by stating that he felt that "this project has been allowed to drift without direction entirely too long. I sincerely hope that you will implement our recommendations ... at the earliest possible time, the decision is, of course, entirely yours." Not long after the March 22nd letter, Penthouse broke off communications with Dominion and the Melrod firm and refused to respond to their telephone calls.

Beginning on March 20, 1984, the loan participation syndicate began to unravel. First, on March 20th, Community sent a letter to Dominion stating that it had "elected not to extend its offer to participate" in the loan. Then, on March 28, 1984, another participant, Shadow Lawn Savings & Loan Association, wrote to Queen City and indicated that in view of the fact that the loan commitment "has now expired" and because interest rates had changed, it had to meet with Queen City before it would "reconsider an extension" of its participation interest. In May and June 1984, several other participants sent notices to Queen City indicating their belief that the loan commitment had expired and that they were relieved of their participation commitments. Subsequently, after it was unsuccessful in obtaining alternate financing, Penthouse filed the instant action in June 1984.

PROCEEDINGS IN THE DISTRICT COURT AND ITS DECISION

A brief review of the district court's docket sheet reveals that the instant litigation was hard fought with several discovery battles and other disagreements. The case proceeded to a bench trial on May 11, 1987 before Judge Duffy and concluded on June 1, 1987. A number of witnesses appeared for both sides and the record was supplemented by affidavits of witnesses who did not appear at trial.

Important to Dominion's defense to the anticipatory breach claim was its insistence that Penthouse was not in any position to close the loan by March 1st because it could not have satisfied various terms and preclosing conditions of the commitment by that time. To address this point, Dominion presented the testimony of an expert in real estate construction and permanent financing transactions, John C. Nelson, who was a partner in the New York City law firm of Milbank, Tweed, Hadley & McCloy. After setting forth the factual predicate upon which he based his opinion, Nelson opined that, in light of the various title problems (which were supported by the objections to title asserted by Commonwealth), the lack of agreements with certain utility companies, the absence of final plans and specifications, no final project budget, the lack of contracts with an architect, a major construction contractor and major trade contractors, and no agreement concerning casino licensing, the transaction was in no position to close any time from 60 days to six months from the February 9th preclosing meeting. When Nelson presented his opinion at trial, however, the district court asked him how long it would take to close the transaction if all of the preclosing conditions he had taken into account when formulating his opinion (i.e., final plans and specifications, project budgets, trade contracts, etc.) had been waived. Nelson replied that the deal could close as soon as the papers were drawn up. He qualified his response, however, by insisting that a prudent lender would not waive the various conditions which the hypothetical question assumed were waived.

Also important to Dominion's case was the testimony of Melrod partner, Philip Gorelick. Because of his extensive involvement in the transaction, he was in the best position to present Dominion's perspective concerning the deal. The district court was not, however, receptive to Gorelick's testimony. After Gorelick had concluded his testimony on direct examination and began responding to questions on cross-examination, Judge Duffy called a morning recess. As the Judge was leaving the courtroom, he requested that the Melrod firm's attorney, Robert L. Tofel, join him in the robing room. When Tofel met Judge Duffy in the robing room, the judge handed him a copy of Volume 377 of the Federal Supplement and requested that Tofel read the first line in *United States v. Tramunti*, 377 F.Supp. 1 (S.D.N.Y.1974) (Duffy, J.). That line reads: "John Spurdis is a liar." After reading the sentence to himself, Tofel looked at the judge. Saying nothing, Judge Duffy simply shrugged expressively. Tofel then said in essence that Judge Duffy had misread Gorelick. Tofel explained that Gorelick may have been obnoxious or aggressive but that he was not a liar. Again, Judge Duffy did not respond and simply shrugged.

On July 29, 1987, the district court filed its reported decision in which it held in favor of Penthouse and Queen City and against

Dominion. *See* 665 F.Supp. 301 (S.D.N.Y.1987). The district court held that Dominion's conduct during February and March 1984 constituted an anticipatory breach of the loan commitment. The district court began its analysis by reasoning that a party to a contract commits an anticipatory breach when it "indicates its refusal to perform unless entirely new or different conditions are first met[.]" *Id.* at 310 (citations omitted). The district court then found that Dominion's conduct on at least four occasions gave rise to an anticipatory breach. Specifically, the court found that 1) Gorelick's demand that Penthouse obtain amendments to the Helmsley lease, 2) Dominion's insistence that a hotel management agreement be entered into prior to closing, 3) Dominion's insistence that Penthouse hire Sigal to perform a construction cost evaluation, and 4) Dominion's insistence that it replace Queen City as lead lender, taken together, "amounted to an unambiguous refusal to close by Dominion", *id.* at 311, and thus constituted an anticipatory breach.

In response to Dominion's argument that Penthouse was not in a position to satisfy the preclosing conditions before March 1st, the district court found that, by the February 9th preclosing meeting, "all of the conditions precedent had been met, waived, or were in a position to have been met by the date set for closing the loan." *Id.* at 310. The district court specifically found 1) that the title and lease problems were "minor" and could be worked out during the "ongoing" discussions with Helmsley, 2) that Queen City had waived Penthouse's full compliance with preclosing conditions 10, 11, 12, and 16; 3) that Penthouse had satisfied preclosing condition 13, and 4) that arrangements with the Casino Control Commission were "easily within reach." *See id.* at 304–05, 310. The court failed to make factual findings or legal conclusions establishing Queen City's authority to waive any preclosing conditions on behalf of Dominion.

The district court explored Dominion's motive for committing the anticipatory breach and found that "[b]ecause of Community's withdrawal on February 29, ... Dominion either had to stall the closing until the loan expired and then withdraw from its commitment, or breach its agreement." *Id.* at 310. According to the district court, Gorelick was employed to serve as "Dominion's hatchet man intent on destroying the deal," *id.* at 308, that "Dominion hired Gorelick to bully and intimidate the plaintiffs into delaying the loan until Community could be replaced or[,] failing that, to delay until the Commitment expired and Dominion was released from its obligation." *Id.* at 307.

The district court also carried forward its earlier, private attack on Gorelick's veracity. In its decision, the district court found that Gorelick committed "outrageous perjury" during trial. *Id.* at 306–07. Making reference to Gorelick's trial testimony, the district court stated

> [t]he decision as to the credibility of witnesses is properly left to the trial judge or to the jury because as finders of fact they are in a position to view the demeanor of the witnesses.

Gorelick took the stand and attempted brazenly to lie to the court. During cross-examination, the crucible of truth, Gorelick continuously shifted uneasily in the chair, sweated like a trapped liar, and the glaze that came over his shifty eyes gave proof to his continuing perjury. His total lack of veracity was shown not only by his demeanor but by the shady practices he seemingly reveled in. He charged needless and exorbitant fees, Joint Exh. 41, for work that was intentionally unproductive. While representing the bank he demanded a $150,000 "bonus" from the borrower if the loan closed, an arrangement Gorelick never disclosed to his bank-client.

Id. at 306 n. 1. Thus, the court made a specific factual finding that Gorelick committed perjury during his trial testimony.

After reaching its decision on the liability issue, the district court considered the damage question. The court first determined that Penthouse was entitled to various out-of-pocket and "carrying" expenses. Then, the court turned to the question of whether Penthouse was entitled to recover the profits it would have made had the construction been completed and the hotel and casino become operational. Applying the rationale of *Perma Research & Development v. Singer Co.,* 542 F.2d 111 (2d Cir.1976), the court determined that Penthouse's lost future profits over a ten-year period could be properly awarded. Accordingly, the district court held that Penthouse was entitled to recover damages in the amount of $129,904,455, $112,083,583 of which was for the lost future profits.

Also in its decision, the district court concluded that Queen City should prevail on its counterclaim in the third-party action: "Having held that Dominion breached its agreement, I must also find it liable to Queen City for that breach." 665 F.Supp. at 312. In addition, the court concluded that Dominion should lose on its third-party claim against Queen City because "[t]here [was] a total failure of proof that Queen City breached any duty owed to Dominion." *Id.*

After the court issued its opinion, Penthouse submitted its proposed judgment to the district court. In the proposed judgment, Penthouse did not name the Melrod firm as a judgment-debtor for the lost profits award. To correct what it perceived as a discrepancy, the district court *sua sponte* conformed the pleadings to the proof and held that the Melrod firm was jointly and severally liable for the entire Penthouse judgment. The court explained that the Melrod firm was liable for the Penthouse judgment because its conduct amounted to active fraud. The district court did not, however, make any factual findings concerning what acts or omissions allegedly perpetrated by the Melrod firm gave rise to the court's conclusion that it committed fraud. Nor did the court explain how a judgment for lost profits which resulted from an alleged anticipatory breach of a loan commitment could also serve as the basis for a fraud judgment.

After amending its original decision, the district court entered final judgment on October 2, 1987 and awarded Penthouse $128,682,830.80, held Dominion and the Melrod firm jointly and severally liable for that judgment, awarded Queen City $7,652,352.91 plus interest and dismissed Dominion's claim against Queen City with prejudice. Subsequently, in a memorandum and order dated December 2, 1987, the district court denied the defendants' motion for a new trial. 678 F.Supp. 61.

DISCUSSION

Dominion and the Melrod firm raise several arguments on this appeal. Dominion contends that the district court erred in concluding that its conduct amounted to an anticipatory breach of the loan commitment and that the court erred in concluding that Penthouse was ready, willing and able to perform its obligations under the loan commitment. Dominion also argues that the district court applied an incorrect legal standard when it awarded Penthouse damages for its lost future profits and that the court erred when it dismissed its claim against Queen City. The Melrod firm challenges the judgment entered against it on fraud grounds, arguing, inter alia, that because such a finding was not supported in law or fact, the district court erred in sua sponte holding Melrod jointly and severally liable for the Penthouse judgment.

For the reasons that follow, we reverse the judgments entered in favor of Penthouse and Queen City, affirm the dismissal of Dominion's cross-claim and remand with instructions that judgment be entered in favor of Dominion and the Melrod firm.

I. DOMINION'S APPEAL OF PENTHOUSE JUDGMENT

A. *Preliminary matters.*

At the outset, Dominion argues that the loan commitment expired by its own terms on March 1, 1984 and contends that, after that date, Dominion, Queen City and the other participating lenders were under "no further obligation" to proceed with the mortgage financing. Dominion therefore suggests that the March 1st date has crucial significance in part because it would constitute the date on or before which the parties would have been required to perform and/or satisfy their obligations under the loan commitment.

At the November 21st meeting, the parties understood that the commitment had expired by its own terms. A written extension of the expiration date was therefore necessary to have a "valid" commitment as of the date Dominion agreed to participate. The parties then mutually extended the expiration date to December 1, 1983, but they simultaneously agreed that the "closing date" for the loan would occur "no earlier than February 1, 1984 or later than March 1, 1984." Aside from these agreements, the parties entered into no other arrangements with respect to further extensions of the expiration date or the closing date.

"An agreement must be construed in the context of the circumstances under which it was entered into and it must be accorded a rational meaning in keeping with the express general purpose." *Tessmar v. Grosner*, 23 N.J. 193, 128 A.2d 467, 471 (1957) (citations omitted). While courts must accord an agreement "the most fair and reasonable construction, imputing the least hardship on either of the contracting parties ... so that neither will have an unfair or unreasonable advantage over the other[,]" *id.* (citations omitted), "[w]here no ambiguity exists in a contract it is the duty of the court, as a matter of law, to interpret the same ... [and] where the parties have said, by very plain words, what they meant, the court has no duty to perform other than to carry their meaning into effect." *Korb v. Spray Beach Hotel Co.*, 24 N.J.Super. 151, 93 A.2d 578, 580 (1952) (per curiam) (citations omitted). In the guise of construing the terms of an agreement, "court[s] will not make a different or better contract than the parties themselves have seen fit to enter into [.]" *In the Matter of the Community Medical Center*, 623 F.2d 864, 866 (3d Cir.1980) (citing *Washington Construction Co. v. Spinella*, 8 N.J. 212, 217–18, 84 A.2d 617, 619 (1951)).

The loan commitment provisions concerning the expiration date and closing date are unambiguous. The loan commitment expired by its own terms 120 days after it was issued on June 20, 1983 unless the parties mutually extended it in writing. After the expiration date passed, the commitment clearly provided that the lender would be under "no further obligation" to fund the loan. It also provided that the closing had to occur on or before the expiration date. The parties' conduct in connection with the written extension to December 1st clearly reflected their belief that the expiration clause was self-executing and that the loan commitment could expire by its own terms.

What we must resolve is whether, when the parties agreed to close the loan "no later than March 1, 1984", they intended on extending the expiration date to March 1st. We believe they did. Reading the expiration date clause together with the clause regarding the closing date leads us to conclude that the parties must have intended to extend the expiration date when they agreed that the closing would occur no later than March 1st. Any other construction of these documents would leave the parties agreeing to close the loan after the commitment had expired which would make no sense.

Some participants clearly believed that when Penthouse and Queen City agreed that the closing date would be "no later than" March 1st, this had the effect of extending the expiration date to that date. Thus, when Community, Shadow Lawn and other participants withdrew their commitments, they all based their decisions upon the fact that the commitment expired on March 1st. In addition, Gorelick and Wienke both believed that the loan commitment expired on that date. Indeed, Gorelick brought the problem of the March 1st expiration to Myerson's attention when he suggested that Myerson obtain an extension of the expiration date. Finally, and most importantly, even Penthouse has acknowledged, albeit indirectly, that the commitment was in effect only until March 1, 1984. Thus, in paragraph 7 of Penthouse's complaint, it alleged as a fact that "[t]he loan commitment was scheduled, by its terms, to remain in effect for 120 days after issuance, and was subsequently extended to March 1, 1984." A necessary inference from this allegation is that Penthouse did not believe that the commitment was extended past March 1st.

The district court did not specifically find that the parties extended the expiration date to March 1st, but it did find that the parties had set March 1st as the closing date. Thus, when the district court was reviewing Penthouse's ability to resolve the title problems, it found "that the entire matter could have been resolved in time to close the deal before March 1, 1984." 665 F.Supp. at 305. Although the district court could have been more deliberate by specifically holding that March 1st was the closing date, we are satisfied that it found that March 1st was the date set for closing.

In view of the above, we conclude that not only was March 1st the closing date, but also that the commitment expired on that date. We acknowledge that the parties' conduct in continuing to negotiate after March 1st may be consistent with an implied extension of the expiration date. We observe, however, that Penthouse and Queen City had allowed the commitment to expire by its own terms once before. Thus, we do not believe that our conclusion here is at odds with the parties' expectations. In holding that the commitment expired on March 1st, we simply construe the terms of relatively unambiguous documents. The parties bargained for a loan commitment that remained open only for a stated duration and we are not at liberty to construe that agreement in a manner inconsistent with its clear language.

B. *Existence of an anticipatory breach.*

We now turn to the district court's factual findings and legal conclusions concerning the existence of an anticipatory breach. The district court determined that "Dominion's representatives' conduct and statements amounted to a clear refusal to proceed to closing unless conditions beyond those required by the Loan Commitment were first met." 665 F.Supp. at 310. As examples of Dominion's "clear refusal to proceed," the district court relied on 1) Gorelick's insistence on the proposed amendments to the Helmsley Lease, 2) Dominion's alleged insistence that a hotel management agreement be in place prior to closing, 3) Dominion's alleged requirement that Penthouse hire Sigal, and 4) Dominion's alleged demand that it replace Queen City as lead lender. Pointing out that three of the four examples the district court took into account when it found that an anticipatory breach occurred all took place after March 1st, Dominion argues that the district court erred as a matter of law by considering Dominion's post-March 1st conduct. In addition, Dominion contends that, when only its pre-March 1st conduct is taken into account, it is clear that it did not by word or conduct commit an anticipatory breach. We agree.

"Ordinarily no action for damages or for restitution can be maintained until the time for performance has come and there has been an actual failure to perform." *Miller & Sons Bakery Co. v. Selikowitz*, 8 N.J.Super. 118, 73 A.2d 607, 609 (1950). Nevertheless, "where ... one party [to a contract] either disables himself from performing, or prevents the other from performing, or repudiates in advance his obligations under the contract, and refuses to be longer bound thereby, communicating such repudiation to the other party," the nonbreaching party "is not only excused from further performance ..., but may at his option treat the contract as terminated for all purposes of performance, and maintain an action at once for damages occasioned by such repudiation, without awaiting the time fixed by the contract for performance by the defendant." *Dun & Bradstreet, Inc. v. Wilsonite Products Co.*, 130 N.J.L. 24, 31 A.2d 45, 47 (1943) (quoting *O'Neill v. Supreme Council American Legion of Honor*, 70 N.J.L. 410, 412, 57 A. 463, 464 (1904)).

"An anticipatory breach is a definite and unconditional declaration by a party to an executory contract—through word or conduct—that he will not or cannot render the agreed upon performance." *Ross Systems v. Linden Dari–Delite, Inc.*, 35 N.J. 329, 173 A.2d 258, 264 (1961) (citations omitted). Likewise, "[i]f one party to a contract, either wilfully or by mistake, demands of the other a performance to which he has no right under the contract and states definitely that, unless his demand is complied with, he will not render his promised performance, an anticipatory breach has been committed." 4 A. Corbin, Corbin on Contracts § 973, p. 910 (1951).

The term anticipatory breach is self-defining as one which occurs before the time of performance and while the contract is in existence. As we concluded above, March 1st was the closing date and the expiration date for this loan transaction. Thus, we are compelled to agree with Dominion's argument that the district court erred as a matter of law when it took into account Dominion's post-March 1st conduct when determining the existence of an anticipatory breach. Only Dominion's conduct before March 1st is relevant to the determination of whether an anticipatory breach has occurred, and taking only that conduct into account, we conclude that the district court clearly erred when it found that Dominion committed an anticipatory breach.

New Jersey adheres to the view that an anticipatory breach occurs only if there is a *"clear and unequivocal declaration"* that "the agreed upon performance would not be forthcoming." *Seitz v. Mark–O–Lite Sign Contractors, Inc.*, 210 N.J.Super. 646, 510 A.2d 319, 324 (1986) (emphasis added); *see Ross Systems Inc.*, 35 N.J. 329, 173 A.2d at 264; *Miller & Sons Bakery Co.*, 8 N.J.Super. 118, 73 A.2d at 609; *see generally* 4 A. Corbin, Corbin on Contracts § 973 (1951). "Doubtful and indefinite statements that performance may or may not take place and statements that, under certain circumstances that in fact do not yet exist, the performance will not take place," will not give rise to a claim for anticipatory breach. 4 A. Corbin, Corbin on Contracts § 973, p. 905 (1951) (footnote omitted).

In recounting the evidence concerning Gorelick's conduct at the February 9, 1984 preclosing meeting, the district court found that "[t]he overwhelming evidence shows that Gorelick's demands were equal to a demand that the deal be completely done over[.]" 665 F.Supp. at 307. Subsequently, the court found that "[t]hroughout February *and March*, Dominion, through the Melrod firm, continued to make requests for more information which Newman described as 'never ending.' ... Dominion further demanded numerous changes in the way the entire deal was to be structured, the parties involved, and other changes not required by the Loan Commitment." *Id.* at 309. When, however, the court sought to provide specific examples of the "changes not required" by the commitment, the only one that occurred before March 1st was Gorelick's demands concerning amendments to the Helmsley lease. The evidence established that Gorelick did in fact insist that the proposed amendments were "required." Thus, the issue we confront is whether Gorelick's insistence on the proposed amendments represented a demand for performance for which Dominion had no right and whether his insistence amounted to a "definite and unequivocal refusal" by Dominion to fulfill its obligations under the agreement unless this condition was met.

It is undisputed that, unless amended, the Helmsley lease would have been violated by the closing of the Queen City deal. Because the loan commitment required that there be "no violations" of that lease at closing, it is clear that some amendments were necessary to satisfy the terms of the loan commitment. To this end, the Melrod lawyers submitted a list of proposed amendments to Penthouse. Even though Gorelick insisted that each proposed amendment was required, when the proposed amendments were sent to Penthouse, Dominion's position was equivocal. Trotter's cover letter indicated that the amendments represented what Dominion would be "looking for" and would provide Penthouse "with a jumping off point" for its negotiations with Helmsley. Thus, Gorelick's statements that the proposed amendments were required clearly were qualified by the statements made in Trotter's cover letter.

In addition, we observe that the list of proposed amendments was just that—a proposal. With the proposed amendments, it was contemplated that Penthouse would then engage in negotiations with Helmsley. As indicated in Trotter's letter, the proposed amendments constituted a starting point for the negotiations with Helmsley, but they did not represent Dominion's "final" position. Viewed in this light, we are persuaded that the district court clearly erred when it found that Gorelick's insistence on the proposed amendments gave rise to an anticipatory breach. New Jersey consistently requires that the breaching party in these cases make a "clear and unequivocal declaration" that performance would not be forthcoming and Gorelick's conduct in this regard falls short.

Nevertheless, we are left with the court's general finding that Dominion refused to perform unless the entire deal was restructured. As pointed out above, most of the specific instances of conduct cited by the court occurred after March 1st and thus are not relevant to our inquiry. We do confront, however, the district court's finding that Gorelick demanded at the February 9th meeting that everything in connection with the deal be "completely done over." We observe that Gorelick was so adamant in this regard that the parties allowed him to assume responsibility for drafting the closing documents and reviewing condition compliance. Thus, it is arguable that his demands at the February 9th meeting were sufficiently clear and unequivocal to give rise to an anticipatory breach if his refusal to proceed was unjustified.

When Gorelick attended the February 9th meeting, he only recently had been brought into the deal. He was there to represent his client's interests in connection with its agreement to participate in a $97 million construction and permanent financing transaction, of which more than a third was to be funded by his client. At the time of the preclosing meeting, the parties contemplated closing the transaction within a few weeks—by March 1st at the latest. At the meeting or shortly before, Gorelick discovered that there were significant problems affecting title and problems with the Helmsley lease and yet there were no active negotiations to resolve those problems. Gorelick also learned that Queen City intended on closing the transaction without insisting that Penthouse comply fully with all of the preclosing conditions. In addition, he received draft loan documentation which, in his judgment, was amateurish and substandard for a transaction of this magnitude.

While we do not pass upon the reasonableness of each of Gorelick's objections, we note that Nelson's expert testimony fully supported Gorelick's position that the transaction was not in a position to close any time in the near future. We also note that although the district court found that some of Gorelick's objections were unreasonable, it did not find that most of his concerns were unfounded. Gorelick attended the preclosing meeting in order to ensure that the interests of his client were protected. In so doing, he insightfully observed serious problems with the transaction and promptly raised his objections. Gorelick's insistence on marketable title in the face of the objections reported by the title company all by itself would justify his position that the deal was in no position to close and thus cannot, as a matter of law, constitute an anticipatory breach. Coupling the title and lease problems with Penthouse's failure to establish that it was in a position to fully satisfy all of the preclosing conditions, we conclude that Gorelick properly refused to proceed unless his concerns were addressed. We therefore conclude that the district court clearly erred when it found that Dominion committed an anticipatory breach of its agreement to participate. Accordingly, we reverse the judgment entered against Dominion.

C. *Plaintiffs' ability to perform.*

As part of this damages action for an alleged anticipatory breach, Penthouse bore the burden of establishing its willingness and ability to perform all of the obligations under the agreement. As Professor Corbin has explained,

> *[i]n an action for breach by an unconditional repudiation it is still a condition precedent to the plaintiff's right to judgment for damages that he should have the ability to perform all such conditions. If he could not or would not have performed the substantial equivalent for which the defendant's performance was agreed to be exchanged, he is given no remedy in damages for the defendant's non-performance or repudiation. Of course, the willingness and ability that remains a condition precedent in spite of the defendant's repudiation, is willingness and ability to perform if there had been no repudiation.*

4 A. Corbin, Corbin on Contracts § 978, pp. 924–25 (1951) (emphasis added) (footnote omitted). New Jersey follows this general rule. *See Bertrand v. Jones*, 58 N.J.Super. 273, 156 A.2d 161, 168 (App.Div.1959) (following Corbin), *certif. denied*, 31 N.J. 553, 158 A.2d 452 (1960); *cf. Caporale v. Rubine*, 92 N.J.L. 463, 105 A. 226, 227 (1918) (in breach of contract action for damages, plaintiff has the burden of establishing "that he was able and ready to perform his part of the undertaking"); *accord Korb*, 24 N.J.Super. 151, 93 A.2d at 581 (in an action for specific performance, plaintiff must establish that he is "ready, desirous, prompt and eager to perform the contract on his part").

That the plaintiff must establish its readiness and ability to perform does not mean that it is required to tender performance. After the occurrence of an anticipatory breach, "[i]t is no longer necessary for the plaintiff to perform or tender performance." 4 A. Corbin, Corbin on Contracts § 977, p. 920 (1951) (footnote omitted); *see Dun & Bradstreet*, 130 N.J.L. 24, 31 A.2d at 47. This is so because "[t]he defendant's wrongful repudiation justifies the plaintiff in taking him at his word and at once taking steps that may make subsequent performance impossible." 4 A. Corbin, Corbin on Contracts § 978, p. 925 (1951). Nevertheless, the plaintiff must demonstrate that it had the willingness and ability to perform "before the repudiation and that the plaintiff would have rendered the agreed performance if the defendant had not repudiated." *Id.*

In the instant case, the district court found that "at the time of the preclosing meeting, all of the conditions precedent had been met, waived, or were in a position to have been met by the date set for closing the loan." 665 F.Supp. at 310. Thus, it found that Penthouse was ready, willing and able to proceed by the time of the alleged anticipatory breach. In challenging this conclusion, Dominion argues that Penthouse had not met and could not have met its obligations to convey valid mortgages and to satisfy certain of the preclosing conditions and that the district court's findings in this regard are clearly erroneous. Dominion also argues that the district court erred in concluding that certain conditions had been waived, contending that Queen City had no authority to waive preclosing conditions. Dominion concludes that, when properly viewed, the evidence demonstrates that Penthouse was in no position to satisfy the preclosing conditions on or before March 1st and thus failed to establish that it was ready, willing and able to proceed. We agree.

Despite the fact that Penthouse and Queen City never argued at trial that any of the preclosing conditions had been waived, the district court determined that Penthouse's full compliance with preclosing conditions 10, 11, 12 and 16 had been waived as a result of Lipari's meetings with Penthouse during the January 1984 status conferences. The district court's waiver finding was integral to its determination that Penthouse was ready, willing and able to perform by the closing date because, in the absence of a waiver, it is clear that those material preclosing conditions were not and could not have been satisfied by March 1st. Penthouse offered at trial no evidence to contradict Nelson's opinion that it would have taken at least 60 days, and more than likely 6 months, from February 9, 1984 for Penthouse to comply with all of the preclosing conditions. Nelson's prognosis changed only after the district court inquired as to how long it would have taken to close if the unsatisfied preclosing conditions had been waived. Although he bristled at the suggestion that those preclosing conditions would ever be waived by a prudent lender—let alone an institutional lender—he testified that, assuming a waiver, the loan could have been closed as soon as the papers were drawn up. In the face of this testimony, we must squarely decide the propriety of the district court's waiver finding. This inquiry requires, in turn, that we examine whether Queen City had the authority in the first instance to waive Penthouse's compliance with preclosing conditions. We conclude that it did not.

Before we inquire into Queen City's authority to waive compliance with preclosing conditions, we must examine the nature of Dominion's agreement to participate. On November 21st, Dominion entered into an agreement with Queen City whereby it agreed to participate in the lending syndicate to the extent of $35 million. That agreement was embodied in several documents which, in turn, incorporated the terms and conditions of *both* the Queen City loan commitment and the participation agreement. When construing Dominion's agreement, we read these documents "together as one instrument, and the recitals in one may be explained or limited by reference to the other." *Schlein v. Gairoard*, 127 N.J.L. 358, 22 A.2d 539, 540–41 (1941); *see Schlossman's, Inc. v. Radcliffe*, 3 N.J. 430, 70 A.2d 493, 495 (1950). Applying this rule, we therefore look to the terms of both the loan commitment and the participation agreement when examining whether Queen City had the authority to effect a waiver of preclosing conditions.

The loan commitment provided that "[a]ll title questions and all other legal matters relating to or arising out of the Loan shall be subject in all respects to the approval of the Lender's counsel ... and the decision of the Lender's counsel as to whether all conditions of the commitment have been met shall be final." The commitment also provided, however, that "[l]ender's obligation to close the loan is contingent upon the satisfaction of each of [the preclosing] conditions." Reading these two provisions together, we conclude that, although Queen City had the final word on whether the preclosing conditions had been satisfied, Penthouse nevertheless was required to satisfy each of the preclosing conditions. Thus, Queen City was granted essentially administrative authority to oversee the manner in which the preclosing conditions were satisfied, but it was not empowered to waive Penthouse's compliance with the preclosing conditions.

The participation agreement further limited Queen City's authority in connection with the administration of the loan transaction. It expressly provided that its terms could not be modified except by an agreement in writing. Thus, Queen City was not empowered to modify the terms or conditions of the participation agreement without obtaining the participants' prior approval. In addition, when the participants entered into the agreement with Queen City, they only authorized Queen City to act on their behalf in the capacity of an independent contractor; Queen City was not authorized to act as their agent. To this end, Queen City was given discretionary power as to the means and manner of contractual performance, *see, e.g., Errickson v. F.W. Schwiers, Jr. Co.*, 108 N.J.L. 481, 158 A. 482, 483 (1932), but was not empowered to make material changes that rendered the participants less secure. Even if we were to conclude that Queen City was authorized to act as agent for the participants, it would not have been empowered to waive or alter material terms "or otherwise to diminish or discharge the obligation of the third person[.]" *See* Restatement (Second) of Agency § 51 comment C (2d ed. 1979).

In view of the above, it is clear that Queen City was not authorized expressly or inferentially in the commitment or the participation agreement to modify the terms of the commitment by waiving Penthouse's full compliance with preclosing conditions. In addition, when Dominion was first informed concerning the full extent of Penthouse's proposed substitute performance for preclosing conditions 10, 11, 12 and 16, Gorelick objected. Then, after the Melrod firm was given responsibility for reviewing condition compliance and Gorelick transmitted his various checklists, it was made clear that Dominion expected that Penthouse would comply with the terms of each preclosing condition. Thus, there could be no implied waiver of these conditions here, either. We therefore conclude that the district court erred when it found that Queen City waived Penthouse's full compliance with preclosing conditions 10, 11, 12 and 16. Because Queen City could not waive these conditions in the first place, it could not accept Penthouse's substitute performance without first obtaining the participants' approval.

Sound national banking policies support the conclusion we reach here. As *amicus curiae* Federal Home Loan Bank Board points out:

the proposition ... that a lead lender may, without consulting participating lenders, waive or modify significant conditions of a loan to the detriment of participants, seriously undermines the Bank Board's supervisory policies concerning safe and sound underwriting of participation purchases and is completely at odds with the Bank Board's policy that loan participants must satisfy themselves that the participation is a loan that the participating association would make itself.

If a lead lender has this authority ..., the Bank Board's supervisory control regarding underwriting of participation purchases is rendered more difficult or impossible and the FSLIC fund is exposed to inordinate risk. A savings and loan association's independently and prudently underwritten participation in a loan could be changed into an entirely reckless act if fundamental terms and conditions of the loan are altered prior to closing by the lead lender on its own initiative and without consulting the participant. This would make it very difficult, if not impossible, for a participant to assure prudent underwriting or participations. While we do not necessarily find that these policy considerations by [themselves] are binding if the parties had agreed otherwise, they certainly militate against the district court's unsubstantiated and erroneous finding that Queen City had the authority to waive various essential preclosing conditions.

As a separate matter, Dominion contends that the district court's other findings that bore upon Penthouse's ability to perform were erroneous. The district court found that the outstanding title and lease problems were "minor," 665 F.Supp. at 310, and that "the entire matter could have been resolved in time to close the deal before March 1, 1984." *Id.* at 305. The district court also held that, although licensing discussions with the Casino Control Commission "were to resume after the closing, ... it appeared an arrangement with the Commission was easily within reach." *Id.* Dominion argues that, notwithstanding the court's characterization, the title and lease problems were not minor and that there was no evidence to support the court's conclusion that those matters could have been resolved by March 1st. With regard to its finding concerning the licensing arrangements, Dominion contends that it supports the view that Penthouse could not have satisfied this preclosing condition before closing and that the court's characterization that these arrangements were "easily within reach" is belied by the evidence. We agree with both of Dominion's contentions.

Turning to the court's findings concerning the title and lease problems, we are compelled to conclude that the district court clearly erred when it characterized these matter's as being "minor." Unless these problems were resolved, they absolutely would have prevented Penthouse from delivering the title required in the commitment. Likewise, unless the Helmsley lease was modified, Penthouse could not certify that there were "no violations" of that lease. Thus, in view of the gravity of these problems, Penthouse knew that they had to be resolved by the closing date. We therefore cannot conclude that they were "minor."

In addition, the district court's characterization of the title and lease problems as "minor" presupposed that several contingencies could and would occur to resolve them before closing. As Nelson described the situation, since Helmsley was a sophisticated participant in real estate transactions, there probably would be no insurmountable barriers to reaching an accord with him to address the title and lease problems, "but it would take time and probably money." Thus, the court may have believed that the problems were minor because they could have been resolved in time and with money. To reach an agreement resolving these problems, however, it was incumbent upon Penthouse to commence negotiations. Thus, the district court's conclusion that these matters were minor and resolvable by March 1st rested on the assumption that negotiations with Helmsley were "ongoing" and would be concluded favorably before March 1st. This assumption was erroneous.

Both Myerson and Newman testified that actual negotiations with Helmsley had not occurred by February 9th. Although Newman had made indirect contact with Helmsley's attorney, no formal proposals had been submitted and no negotiations had begun. This uncontradicted evidence leads us to conclude that the district court clearly erred when it found that negotiations with Helmsley were "ongoing." Negotiations cannot be characterized as "ongoing" when they have not even begun. The absence of ongoing negotiations undermines the district court's finding that the title and lease problems could have been resolved before March 1st, and no evidence in the record indicates that negotiations would have commenced by March 1st, let alone be concluded by that date, to resolve the problems with the lease and title.

In addition, Penthouse failed to establish that it was working toward clearing up the problems posed by the McShane and Chase mortgages. Those mortgages had to be subordinated in order for Penthouse to provide the security required by the commitment and Penthouse apparently had not even made contact with the holders of those mortgages. This fact plus the problems surrounding the Helmsley lease lead us to conclude that the district court's factual finding that these problems could have been resolved by March 1st is clearly erroneous.

With regard to the court's finding concerning the status of the alternate licensing arrangements condition, we note that the district court overlooked the fact that this was a *preclosing* condition. Because the court found that those arrangements could have been made *after* closing, it is clear that Penthouse did not carry its burden to demonstrate its ability to perform this condition *before* closing. In addition, we observe that record evidence does not support the district court's finding that these arrangements were "easily within reach." Goldstein's letter clearly indicated the tentative nature of his proposal. He described it as a "rough outline" of what he thought "might be acceptable" to the CCC. From Goldstein's letter, it is clear that no arrangements had actually been made. Presumably, Penthouse and the lenders were going to have to draft agreements for the alternate licensing arrangements. This would take time. Therefore, due to the tentative status of the proposed alternate arrangements and the absence of an actual agreement, we are convinced that the district court also erred in this regard.

In view of the foregoing, we conclude that Penthouse failed to carry its burden at trial to demonstrate that it was ready, willing and able to perform its contractual obligations at any time before March 1st. Thus, even if we were to agree that Dominion had refused to perform, we would nevertheless be compelled to conclude that it could not recover damages. We could conclude that Penthouse's failure to demonstrate that it could deliver marketable title by March 1st would be a complete answer to a charge of anticipatory breach. When, however, the title and lease problems are combined with Penthouse's inability to perform the various preclosing conditions, we are left with the firm belief that it should not be entitled to recover on its complaint for an anticipatory breach. Accordingly, the judgment in favor of Penthouse is reversed.

D. *Damages.*

Having found that Penthouse failed to establish the essential elements of its anticipatory breach claim, we need not address the merits of the district court's award of lost future profits. Nevertheless, we are compelled to point out that the case upon which the district court relied when holding that the lost profits were recoverable may not be good law. In reaching its decision on the damages issue, the court relied on our decision in *Perma Research and Development v. Singer Co.*, 542 F.2d 111 (2d Cir.1976), a diversity action involving questions of New York law. Since our decision in *Perma Research*, however, New York's highest court has considered the damages issue decided in *Perma Research* and has flatly rejected the rationale of that decision. *See Kenford Co. v. Erie County*, 67 N.Y.2d 257, 502 N.Y.S.2d 131, 493 N.E.2d 234 (1986) (per curiam). In view of the New York Court of Appeal's decision in *Kenford*, the rationale of our decision on the damages issue in *Perma Research* is seriously in doubt and we conclude that the district court's reliance on that case was misplaced.

II. DOMINION'S APPEAL OF QUEEN CITY JUDGMENT

A. *Anticipatory breach claim.*

After it concluded that Dominion was liable to Penthouse for Dominion's alleged anticipatory breach, the district court addressed Queen City's claim, stating:

> Queen City counterclaims against Dominion for breach of its obligations to Queen City. As a direct result of Dominion's failure to close the loan, Queen City claims to have suffered a loss of profits it otherwise would have earned. In one of the documents signed

November 21, 1983 Dominion accepted the Queen City commitment ..., and thus, Dominion's breach gives rise to claims by all parties to which it was contractually obligated. Having held that Dominion breached its agreement, I must also find it liable to Queen City for that breach.

665 F.Supp. at 312. Thus, when the district court held in favor of Queen City on the counterclaim, the court based its decision solely upon its earlier conclusion that Dominion committed an anticipatory breach. In view of our determination that the court erred in concluding that Dominion committed an anticipatory breach and that Penthouse was ready, willing and able to proceed by March 1st, we reverse the judgment entered in favor of Queen City. Because Dominion's conduct did not amount to an anticipatory breach, it is not liable to Queen City on the counterclaim. Likewise, because Penthouse did not establish that it could have satisfied the preclosing conditions before March 1st, Queen City is also precluded from recovery against Dominion.

B. *Dismissal of Dominion's cross-claim.*

Dominion contends that the district court erred when it dismissed with prejudice its third-party claim against Queen City. Dominion predicated its theory of Queen City's liability on the argument that, if Queen City did in fact waive four preclosing conditions, in so doing it breached its fiduciary duties owed to Dominion and the other participants. Because, however, we conclude that no waiver occurred— because Queen City had no authority to waive conditions—it follows that Queen City is not liable for any purported waiver. Accordingly, we affirm the district court's dismissal of this claim.

III. THE MELROD FIRM'S APPEAL
OF PENTHOUSE JUDGMENT

A. *Background.*

Nowhere in the district court's reported opinion did it find that Dominion or the Melrod firm committed fraud. The entire decision was devoted to a discussion of Dominion's alleged anticipatory breach and the damages resulting therefrom. There was no suggestion that Gorelick and the Melrod firm were to be held liable for the Penthouse judgment. In addition, while the district court made findings concerning Dominion's alleged undisclosed intent and Gorelick's purported role as "hatchet man," we observe that the court found no fraud or misrepresentation concerning the November 21st agreement and made no other specific findings with regard to subsequent events or statements suggesting that fraud was committed. Indeed, although Penthouse specifically sought in the pretrial order a finding that its agreement to pay the Melrod firm's fees was void and unenforceable (a claim that was part of the fraud count in its complaint), the district court never made such a finding.

After the district court issued its reported decision, the parties submitted proposed judgments. Penthouse's proposed judgment form requested from the Melrod firm approximately $1.7 million, not the $128.7 million amount of its anticipatory breach judgment. In contrast, in addition to submitting its proposed judgment, the Melrod firm submitted a letter to the court in which it argued that it had been exonerated and should be free of liability. In response to these two conflicting proposed judgments, the district court filed an order dated September 30, 1987, in which it held the Melrod firm jointly and severally liable for the $128.7 million Penthouse judgment. Explaining its rationale for this decision, the district court stated:

> It is urged that the law partnership was merely an agent for a disclosed principal and as such could not be liable for any wrongdoing. This argument ignores two items: first, the firm did not disclose the true nature of the agency which it undertook; and, the actions of the firm through its partner constituted active fraud. The analogy that comes to mind when considering the law firm's argument is that of a hoodlum enforcer for a loan shark claiming innocence as the agent of a disclosed principal. In this case the Melrod firm did not disclose the true nature of its agency, i.e., to scuttle the deal and cause damage to the plaintiffs and others. Certainly no one can imagine Philip Gorelick coming to the pre-closing meeting to tell everyone that he had been delegated to subvert the deal.

> For some unexplained reason the various judgments submitted do not name the Melrod firm as a judgment debtor for the lost profits. This may be occasioned because of a defect in the pleadings at the start of the trial. As part of the pro forma disposition of the "usual motions" made at the end of the case, I granted the "usual" motion to conform the pleadings to the proof. Thus it is appropriate and just for the Melrod firm to stand as a joint and several debtor for the profits lost by the Penthouse plaintiffs.

Notwithstanding the district court's assertions, no motions—"usual" or otherwise—to conform the pleadings to the proof appear in the record.

Thereafter, the Melrod firm filed a motion for a new trial in which it argued *inter alia* that the robing room incident, the court's bias against Gorelick and its *sua sponte* order holding the Melrod firm jointly and severally liable on a fraud theory all constituted reversible error and merited a new trial. In an order dated December 2, 1987, the district court denied the Melrod firm's motion. In that order, the court first concluded that it had not prejudged the case against the Melrod firm and had treated Gorelick appropriately, and then, turning to its *sua sponte* order, the court stated:

> [t]he last item raised in this motion for a new trial is a claim by the Melrod law firm that it was denied a fair trial because after the trial was finished I deemed the pleadings amended to make them responsible for all of the damages rather than the approximately

$3 million for which they originally thought that they were potentially liable. Like the others, this claim also lacks substance. Somehow the Melrod firm claims that they were unprepared to defend against such a large claim. This ignores the fact that both Melrod and Dominion had but one counsel and he was totally prepared. Loss of the case by defense counsel cannot be attributed to anything other than the fact that the defendants were wholly responsible for the injury which they caused by illegal means. No counsel could change the facts. The one trial counsel for the two parties was as prepared as anyone could have been. Melrod's claim apparently, however, is not that they were unprepared to meet the allegations of the complaint as amended, but rather that they are now unprepared to pay the sum of money for which they have been held liable. Clearly this is not grounds for a new trial.

B. *The Melrod firm's claims.*

The Melrod firm presents a multitude of arguments in favor of reversal of this judgment. The firm argues that the trial itself was rendered unfair by the district court's premature assessment of Gorelick's credibility (as demonstrated by the robing room incident) and the court's excessive intervention during trial. The Melrod firm also contends that the court's perjury finding, by itself, was both legally and factually erroneous. Finally, the Melrod firm contends that the court's actions in holding it jointly and severally liable sua sponte violated the Federal Rules of Civil Procedure as well as due process.

The Melrod firm is not alone in challenging the fraud judgment. Dominion, joined by the Melrod firm, contends that, on the merits, the $128.7 million judgment cannot be sustained under a fraud theory.

C. *Non-existence of fraud.*

Penthouse's fraud cause of action was set forth in Count III of its complaint. In that count, after realleging the facts surrounding the alleged anticipatory breach, Penthouse alleged the following: 1) On February 10, 1984, Dominion through the Melrod firm represented to Penthouse that Dominion was prepared to proceed with the loan closing according to the terms of the loan commitment, 2) the February 10, 1984 representation was false because Dominion did not intend to proceed with the loan unless Penthouse would agree to numerous additional conditions and terms that were not contained in the commitment, 3) in reliance on that representation, Penthouse entered into an agreement on February 10, 1984 to pay Dominion's costs and legal fees, and 4) Penthouse suffered damages in excess of $1 million in addition to the nearly $32,000 paid for Dominion's legal fees. Thus, Penthouse's fraud theory was that, on February 10, 1984, the Melrod firm falsely represented to Penthouse that Dominion would proceed with its agreement to participate according to the terms of the loan commitment at a time when it in fact did not intend to proceed. In other words, Penthouse alleged that by February 10th Dominion no longer intended to fulfill its agreement to participate unless the commitment was restructured. Accordingly, Penthouse's position was that when Gorelick made statements on February 9–10, 1984 to the effect that Dominion intended to proceed, he committed a fraud for which his firm was liable.

The district court did not make factual findings in connection with Penthouse's fraud claim. Instead, it made its decision to hold the Melrod firm jointly and severally liable *sua sponte* and stated that the firm's actions constituted "active fraud." Thus, the court failed to make specific findings on each element of the fraud cause of action, i.e., that the Melrod firm—through Gorelick—knowingly made a false representation of present or past material fact with the intent to cause actual reliance and that Penthouse in fact relied on the misrepresentation to its detriment. The district court did, however, find that Gorelick attended the February 9th meeting for the sole purpose of sabotaging the deal and that Dominion did not intend on fulfilling its commitment at that time. Thus, if we assume that, on February 10th, Gorelick made the representations Penthouse claims, then, arguably, he would have made a false representation of Dominion's present intent which could give rise to a claim for fraud. At the bottom of the fraud claim, then, is the district court's determination that, by February 9th, Dominion did not intend on fulfilling its contractual obligation and that it had hired Gorelick to break up the deal. Dominion contends that this finding is clearly erroneous. We agree.

In its opinion, the district court labored to develop a factual basis supporting its conclusion that Gorelick was called in by Dominion to "sabotage" the transaction. To find that by February 9th Dominion had decided to breach its commitment, the court relied on no testimonial evidence. Rather, the district court turned to a document offered in evidence and observed that "on its Commitment Participation Report for February, Dominion dropped Penthouse as a listed borrower." 665 F.Supp. at 306. The court then concluded that this was "almost conclusive proof that Dominion's officers had decided to breach its commitment by that time." *Id.* The district court did not recognize, however, that that report was not prepared in early-February, but was dated February 29th. Nor did the court take into account Dominion's Secondary Market Department's weekly list of loan commitments—also put into evidence—which indicated that Dominion carried the Penthouse participation on that list for every week through early-April 1984.

In addition to the unexplained omission of the Penthouse loan from Dominion's monthly report, the district court relied on Community's allegedly tenuous status when it found that Dominion intended to breach its commitment. The district court found that, by early-February, "Dominion should have been aware of Community's tenuous status as a loan participant." 665 F.Supp. at 306. Later, the court determined that, "[b]ecause of Community's withdrawal on February 29, Dominion was in the awkward position of having committed itself to lend more than the amount it was legally permitted to lend.... Thus, Dominion either had to stall the closing until the loan expired and then withdraw from its commitment, or breach its commitment." *Id.* at 310.

The district court's factual findings belie its conclusion that Dominion intended not to proceed on February 9th. According to the court's reasoning, Dominion was not in this "awkward position" until late-February—when it allegedly dropped the Penthouse loan off the monthly report and purportedly received Community's withdrawal. Thus, even if we were to accept the court's findings regarding Community's withdrawal and the inferences to be drawn from the omission on the report, we would be compelled to conclude that the court clearly erred when it determined that this evidence established that Dominion intended not to proceed on February 9th.

Nevertheless, we also reject the court's finding regarding the timing of Community's withdrawal. Although Wienke had expressed his reservations about the transaction to Dominion and Queen City on February 8th and then to Gorelick and Myerson in late February, there is no evidence of Community's withdrawal prior to its March 20th letter. Thus, we conclude that the court clearly erred in this regard also.

Aside from the district court's erroneous factual findings, there is no other evidence establishing that Dominion intended not to proceed and there is abundant evidence to indicate just the opposite. Even after the commitment expired, Dominion indicated its continued interest in the transaction and maintained steady contact with Penthouse. And, it was Penthouse, not Dominion, who cut off communications. Thus, we conclude that there is no basis to conclude that Gorelick or Dominion harbored a secret intent not to proceed on February 9–10 or otherwise. It therefore follows that, even assuming that Gorelick made a representation to Penthouse of Dominion's intent to proceed on February 10th, that representation of fact cannot give rise to a claim for fraud. Accordingly, the judgment entered against the Melrod firm is reversed.

Having concluded that Penthouse does not prevail on the merits of the fraud claim, it is unnecessary to pass on the several other arguments raised on this appeal. Nevertheless, we are quite concerned by the district court's conduct during the robing room incident as well as by its perjury finding. Suffice it to say that we believe that *ex parte* communications between the district court and only one of the litigants are rarely, if ever, looked upon with favor, even if intended to impart advice to a fellow member of the profession. With regard to the perjury finding, we are somewhat surprised by its presence in the court's decision. If the court viewed Gorelick's testimony as incredible, that is its prerogative as the trier of fact in a non-jury case, but unless perjury is at issue in a case, such a finding is not necessary once the trier of fact finds the witnesses' testimony incredible. The perjury finding here, however, was not only unnecessary but also was erroneous since it was not based upon clear and convincing proof. *See Barr Rubber Products Co. v. Sun Rubber Co.*, 425 F.2d 1114, 1120 (2d Cir.), *cert. denied,* 400 U.S. 878, 91 S.Ct. 118, 27 L.Ed.2d 115 (1970). Accordingly, we specifically reverse that finding.

CONCLUSION

In view of the foregoing, we reverse the judgments entered against Dominion and the Melrod firm in favor of Penthouse and against Dominion in favor of Queen City, affirm the dismissal of Dominion's cross-claim, and remand to the district court for the purpose of entering judgment in favor of Dominion and the Melrod firm and against Penthouse and Queen City dismissing the complaint and the related cross-action.

NOTES

1. *Penthouse International* raises several issues related to commercial real estate lending. The substantive issue—enforceability of a loan commitment—arises when the permanent lender refuses to fund. This refusal may be due to legitimate concerns about the borrower's compliance with the commitment, but may also be fueled by an increase in prevailing interest rates since the commitment was issued. The borrower usually seeks to enforce the permanent loan commitment because its terms are superior to those currently available, because the borrower has timing concerns even if other comparable funds can be obtained, or because the construction mortgage is due or requires a prohibitive rate of interest.

Courts have specifically enforced mortgage commitments against hesitant lenders on the theory that money damages are inadequate because of the unavailability of other funding or the time required to obtain a substitute loan. See, e.g., Selective Builders, Inc. v. Hudson City Savings Bank, 137 N.J.Super. 500, 349 A.2d 564 (Chan.1975). In contrast, where lenders bring actions based on the failure of the borrower to close under a loan commitment, courts have generally denied specific performance on the theory that the lender's damages can be estimated with reasonable precision based on the difference between the commitment's interest rate and the current interest rate. See, e.g., City Centre One Associates v. Teachers Insurance and Annuity Association of America, 656 F.Supp. 658 (D.Utah 1987).

In many cases there are three interested parties when the permanent lender balks at funding—the borrower, the permanent lender, and the construction lender. *Penthouse International* involved a situation where the lender refusing to fund was committed to provide both construction and permanent financing. In transactions where there are separate construction and permanent lenders, both want to assure that the loan will pass without a hitch from one to the other upon completion of construction. While specific performance and damages are generally available to the construction or permanent lender whose counterpart has reneged, what both sides really want is an agreement that will be virtually self-executing. The buy-sell agreement, sometimes called a "tri-party agreement," aims to serve this purpose. Two attorneys for a leading permanent lender offer the following provision as expressing the essence of the buy-sell agreement:

> The Temporary Lender agrees to sell to the Permanent Lender, and subject to compliance by the Borrower with all of the terms and conditions of the Permanent Loan and of this agreement, the Permanent Lender agrees to purchase from the Temporary Lender, the Building Loan Note and the Building Loan Mortgage. The Permanent Lender agrees to pay to the Temporary Lender for the Building Loan Note and the Building Loan Mortgage the aggregate of the Temporary Lender's principal advances under the Building Loan Agreement, in no event, however to exceed the amount of the Permanent Loan Commitment, and the Temporary Lender will assign the Building Loan Note and the Building Loan Mortgage to the Permanent Lender.

Smith & Lubell, The Buy-Sell Agreement, 9 Real Est.Rev. 13 (Spring 1979).*

Buy-sell agreements can run to great length. According to Smith and Lubell, "The permanent loan commitment contains several conditions that must be fulfilled before the permanent lender actually makes the loan. The construction lender wants the permanent lender to approve as many of those conditions as possible even before the construction lender makes its loan. Such approvals are incorporated into the buy-sell agreement and they frequently are the cause of extensive negotiation between the two lenders."

The article by Davis, excerpted at page 714 above, lists several of the approvals to be included in the buy-sell agreement. Smith and Lubell add some others:

> The form of the promissory note and mortgage. The form of other documents evidencing the security for the loan such as assignments of rents and financing statements under the Uniform Commercial Code.

> The survey. Although the survey presented prior to completion of construction can only show perimeter boundaries and existing easements, the permanent lender may approve the perimeter survey and reserve approvals of easements until completion of the improvement.

> Plans and specifications for the improvements. (The permanent loan commitment requires that the permanent lender must approve material changes from the original plans and specifications. Problems arise because it is extremely difficult to define a "material" change. Any series of minor changes may be tantamount to a material change.)

The evidence of ownership of property as reflected in a title policy. If the developer owns a leasehold estate, approval of the ground lease is required.

Major tenant leases and standard lease forms. The form of proof of completion of the improvements acceptable to the permanent lender, such as the certificate of occupancy and architectural certification.

The form of various opinions required by the permanent lender with respect to compliance with environmental and zoning requirements.

See also, Smith & Lubell, The Permanent Mortgage Loan Commitment, 4 Real Est.Rev. 7 (Winter 1975).

On the enforceability of permanent loan commitments generally, see Draper, The Broken Commitment: A Modern View of the Mortgage Lender's Remedy, 59 Cornell L.Rev. 418 (1974); Draper, Tight Money and Possible Substantive Defenses to Enforcement of Future Mortgage Commitments, 50 Notre Dame Law. 603 (1975); Mehr & Kilgore, Enforcement of the Real Estate Loan Commitment: Improvement of the Borrower's Remedies, 24 Wayne L.Rev. 1011 (1978).

2. *Participations.* As indicated in *Penthouse International*, lenders sometimes do not wish to fund the entire loan due to regulatory limitations or investment practices. The lender thus might recruit other lenders to participate in the loan by lending a portion of the total funds. The initial lender serves as the "lead lender" with the others having participation interests. As demonstrated in *Penthouse International*, the participants are concerned that the loan is sound even though the lead lender is directly responsible for servicing the loan and remitting payments to the participants. Moreover, there is a danger for the participants if the lead lender becomes financially unstable or insolvent. See generally, Comment, Lead Lender Failure and the Pitfalls for the Unwitting Participant, 42 Southwestern L.J. 1071 (1989).

3. *Lender Liability. Penthouse International* was hailed by lenders as reversing the trend of lender liability, discussed on pages 218–220. In what way does the court limit the lender's obligation? The court also appeared to support the lender's position on the basis that it followed reasonable lending behavior in its actions. While a reasonable lending standard was helpful to the bank in this case, could that standard be used as a sword against a lender that failed to follow usual lending practices?

4. *The Role of the Attorney.* What do you think of the behavior and professionalism of the attorneys for Queen City and Dominion as described in *Penthouse International*? Did the attorneys properly balance their responsibility to protect their clients from loss and their obligation to serve their clients' interests by facilitating the closing of the transaction?

c.   SUBORDINATED PURCHASE MONEY FINANCING

MIDDLEBROOK–ANDERSON CO. v. SOUTHWEST SAV. & LOAN ASS'N

California Court of Appeal, Fourth District, 1971.
18 Cal.App.3d 1023, 96 Cal.Rptr. 338.

GABBERT, Associate Justice.

The plaintiffs appeal from a judgment of dismissal entered after defendants' general and special demurrers were sustained without leave to amend in this complicated land development action.   Plaintiffs are two California corporations, doing business as Middlebrook-Anderson Co., a partnership, hereinafter referred to as "seller".

The seller owned real property consisting of 28 lots in Orange County.   It entered into a land sale contract with certain developers, hereinafter referred to as "buyers", who are not before us in this action. An escrow at a bank was opened between seller and the buyers; the instructions specified the sale price to be $365,000, which was to be partially paid by a purchase money deed of trust in the amount of $169,500.   This deed was to be second and junior to a construction loan to be obtained at some later time by the buyers.

During a period of several months buyers negotiated for a construction loan from defendant Southwest Savings and Loan Association, hereinafter referred to as "lender".   Defendant Western Escrow Company was the escrow agent for the buyers and the lender.   The buyers represented to the seller that the bank escrow would have to be revised to provide for a purchase money deed of trust in favor of seller in the sum of $69,500 and to allow the lender to obtain priority over seller's deed of trust by priority of recording.   The bank escrow between seller and buyers was amended accordingly.

After these terms were agreed to by the seller and the buyers, the construction loan was consummated.   Western Escrow prepared 28 deeds of trust in favor of lender, with Western named as trustee, each in the amount of $52,300.   A deed of trust in favor of seller in the amount of $69,500, expressly stating it was junior to the lender's deeds of trust, was also prepared.   These 29 trust deeds were recorded on April 22, 1966.   Three days later, to repair the distortion caused by the $100,000 reduction in the apparent size of the purchase money loan, the $69,500 deed was reconveyed and 28 new ones prepared and recorded, each in the amount of $6,053.

The third amended complaint alleges the lender disbursed $1,464,-400 into a construction loan account, and allowed the buyers to use $300,000 of this for purposes other than for construction improvements. When the loan funds ran out in November 1966, the buyers abandoned the unfinished apartment houses on the property.   In the same month, Western Escrow gave notice of default and election to sell under lender's trust deeds. Seller tendered payment of the due principal, interest, and late charges to cure the default, but Western and lender demanded in excess of $50,000, in addition, to repay lender for sums it claimed it had expended for repairs caused by vandalism on the property and completion of the construction. Lender purchased the property at a series of foreclosure sales in April and May 1967, remained in possession and collected rents for a period of time, and then sold the properties to members of the public not parties to this action.

This litigation was commenced by a complaint filed before the foreclosure sales were complete. After plaintiffs' third amended complaint, attempting to state seven different causes of action against Southwest Savings and Loan and Western Escrow was filed, the trial court sustained defendant's general demurrers to the complaint on grounds of failure to state a cause of action, and 44 special demurrers on grounds of uncertainty.

Plaintiffs' causes of action are based essentially on the failure of lender to limit the use of the loan funds to construction purposes. The theories of recovery and remedies sought in the respective numbered causes of action are:

(1) a restoration of the priority of seller's trust deeds;

(2) damages for rendering seller's trust deeds valueless by foreclosure on lender's first trust deeds;

(3) either restoration of priority or money damages based on lender's knowingly permitting the use of $300,000 for nonconstruction purposes;

(4) either restoration of priority or damages based on seller's status as a third party beneficiary of the construction loan contract between lender and the buyers;

(5) setting aside the trustee's foreclosure sale of the property, or damages, based on lender's and Western Escrow's refusal to accept seller's tender of principal, interest and late charges to cure the default on the construction loan;

(6) an accounting of funds received by lender from the property after the foreclosure sales, both as rents and proceeds of re-sales, and application of such funds to repayment of the construction loan, plus reasonable rental value of the property for the period lender was in possession;

(7) (labeled "tenth" because the seventh, eighth, and ninth causes of action named only the buyers) punitive damages based on alleged malice involved in every act of the defendants.

The pleadings allege an original contract existed between the seller and buyers; the escrow at the bank was solely between seller and buyers; the sellers were to receive a purchase money trust deed which would be junior to a construction loan that was to be negotiated.

Thereafter negotiations with the lender by the buyers resulted in a commitment by the lender to the buyers on the condition, as represented by the buyers to the seller, that the lender would make a construction loan and would require documents to show the buyers had made a greater cash investment in the property than originally contemplated and would require subordination of seller's trust deed by priority of recording rather than through a formal subordination agreement.

The complaint further alleges the buyers represented to the seller the funds received from the lender would be used exclusively for construction of improvements on the property and, based on these representations, the seller agreed to the terms. The buyers then entered into the escrow with Western Escrow which, acting as agent for the buyers and the lender, received a copy of the escrow instructions between the seller and buyers.

The seller alleges the lender had knowledge of the second trust deeds taken by the seller and had a duty to inquire of the seller as to the terms and conditions under which the seller agreed to accept a junior lien. The complaint further alleges the lender voluntarily undertook to control disbursements from the construction loan fund and that the seller did not attempt to follow the progress of the construction or status of disbursements because it relied on such control by the lender, who knew and intended that seller so rely.

The seller continues that the lender owed a duty to seller because of lender's conduct which induced the seller to "subordinate" its lien, because of lender's voluntary assumption of control of disbursements and because of the lender's knowledge of the security interest of the seller and knowledge that the seller would subordinate its lien on condition the loan funds were to be used only for construction improvements. Seller alleges the lender disbursed $300,000 in funds which were not for construction purposes, in wanton, reckless disregard of the security interest of seller.

The complaint also alleges that by reason of these improper disbursements the construction of the project was not completed and the market value of the property did not increase through the construction of improvements to a sufficient extent to support the security interests of both seller and lender. The value of seller's security interest in the property was thus diminished to the extent of the alleged wrongful disbursements. The seller finally contends that at the time of the commencement of the case the unpaid balance on the trust deeds in favor of sellers was in the sum of $141,250.23, plus interest.

All of plaintiffs' causes of action depend upon a conclusion that seller's agreement to take a second trust deed constituted a subordination agreement or an agreement in the nature of a subordination agreement. Lender, on the other hand, claims seller got what it bargained for—a second trust deed—and thus had no prior lien to subordinate. Lender would thus conclude no priority existed which could be restored, the seller could not state any cause of action, and the trial court correctly sustained the demurrers.

As we state below, we conclude that the duties owed by a lender to a seller under a formal subordination agreement do not differ from the duties owed by a lender to a seller when the lender obtains priority over the seller under an agreement by the seller to record after the lender. We thus conclude that, in part, the complaint is sufficient to withstand defendants' general demurrers.

Subordination is, strictly speaking, a status, not an agreement or form of litigation. It refers to the establishment of priority between different existing encumbrances on the same parcel of property, by some means other than the basic priority involved in the concept of "first in time, first in priority", or the automatic priority accorded purchase money liens.

By statute, a purchase money deed of trust is prior to other liens on real property. (Civil Code, § 2898.) But banks and savings and loan institutions may not lend money on the security of real property unless they hold first liens. (Fin.Code, §§ 1413 subd. (d), 7102 subd. (a), 1560.) The two common methods of arranging for the commercial lender to hold the first lien include: (1) an express subordination agreement in which the seller agrees to make his lien junior to the lender's; (2) recording the lender's trust deed before the seller's.

Both methods of giving a lender a prior lien, whether by express subordination agreement or by priority of recording, are used to obtain a quicker sale and a higher price for the land. A reading of the commentators suggests lending institutions may prefer the latter method over written subordination agreements because of the reluctance of courts to enforce express written agreements which are deemed to be unfair to the seller. This latter type of subordination situation has been referred to as "automatic subordination".

In the cases that have appeared in the California courts the automatic type of subordination has been said to be the legal problem-child. The negotiated agreement for subordination has seemingly not caused difficulty and is generally absent from the decided reports.

In the case before us, the record discloses an automatic subordination agreement in which the seller, after negotiating a sale, agreed to a subordination by recording after the lender. Differing positions have been taken by the California Appellate Courts with respect to these automatic subordination agreements made at the time of sale. Several cases have refused to recognize automatic subordination; others have accepted and enforced it. Remaining cases have applied other tests to determine whether the courts would place their stamp of approval upon the particular arrangement of the parties.

On the basis of the allegations in the complaint, the project in the case at bench would appear to be a typical automatic subordination arrangement as found in Miller v. Citizens Sav. & Loan Assn., 248

Cal.App.2d 655, 56 Cal.Rptr. 844. As we interpret the pleadings, the subordination agreement shows the parties intended to enter into an arrangement of subordination whereby the seller relied upon the responsibility of the lender to make voucher payments only for construction purposes and the reliance of the seller was known to the lender.

The basic thrust of plaintiffs' complaint is that the automatic subordination should be voided because of the misapplication of a portion of the construction loan fund, in that the lender failed to comply with the conditions which occasioned plaintiffs' agreement to subordinate. This theory is supported by a number of cases and is endorsed by certain of the text writers mentioned herein.

. . .

Respondents assert their non-liability on four grounds: (1) the lender had no duty to supervise the distribution of loan funds (Gill v. Mission Sav. & Loan Assn., 236 Cal.App.2d 753, 46 Cal.Rptr. 456); (2) there was no privity of contract between lender and seller (Matthews v. Hinton, 234 Cal.App.2d 736, 44 Cal.Rptr. 692); (3) since no "subordination agreement" was alleged, seller could have suffered no loss of priority; and (4) no public policy basis exists for imposing a duty on the lender (Gill v. Mission Sav. & Loan Assn., supra). Respondent cites two other cases in support of the asserted grounds: Weiss v. Brentwood Sav. & Loan, supra, 4 Cal.App.3d 738, 84 Cal.Rptr. 736, and Spaziani v. Millar, supra, 215 Cal.App.2d 667, 30 Cal.Rptr. 658.

In light of the facts set forth in the complaint, however, we find insufficient merit in these arguments to prevent a trial of the matter on the merits. We find compelling reasons to the contrary.

Gill involved an appeal from a judgment of dismissal upon an order sustaining a demurrer with leave to amend, no amendment having been filed. The issue was whether the lender owed a duty to the sellers to manage and supervise the distribution of loan funds so that these funds would be used solely for construction purposes. The court concluded that because of the lack of privity of contract and the fact that plaintiffs did not allege that defendant had voluntarily undertaken to supervise the distribution of the loan funds, the complaint for damages was properly demurrable.

In *Gill* the complaint was that the lender had acted negligently in failing to supervise and manage the loan funds. As stated by the court in *Gill*, "Nowhere in the first amended complaint does it appear that the defendant agreed with anyone to manage or supervise distribution of the loaned funds, assumed to do so, actually undertook such, or was required by statutory law or regulation to so manage and supervise. Nor is there any showing of a voluntarily assumed relationship between defendant and plaintiffs from which such an obligation might arise." (236 Cal.App.2d at 756–757, 46 Cal.Rptr. at 458.)

Such allegations do appear in the pleading in the case at bench. Moreover, the damage claim in the complaint in *Gill* rests on a different legal theory than the claim of loss of priority here involved. The former is grounded on traditional negligence concepts while the latter is based on principles of contract law. Underlying the latter theory, the lender's claim to priority flows from the agreement between the seller and the buyer. It is only as a result of the seller's waiver of his statutory right to a first lien that the lender achieves priority. Thus, the lender is a third party beneficiary in the seller-buyer agreement, but only to the extent that it abides by the conditions of subordination. If the lender does not comply with the seller's conditions it does not achieve priority. Since one condition to priority is the proper use of the construction loan funds, the priority of the construction loan lien does not vest until such time as the funds are applied to the construction purpose. This latter theory was not before the *Gill* court.

. . .

Lender contends since the case before us does not involve a "subordination agreement" there was no loss of priority and therefore as a matter of law plaintiffs may not have their lien declared to be prior to the construction loan lien. In support of this argument defendants rely on a treatise, Current Law of California Real Estate, Vol. 2, by Messrs. Miller and Starr. The same authors have restated their position in 13 U.C.L.A.L.Rev. 1298, 1301 to the effect that if the seller agrees in the deposit receipt agreement or the escrow instructions that the buyer may obtain a construction loan which will be recorded as a first trust deed and the seller's purchase money trust deed is made junior by virtue of the time of its recording, then a "true" subordination does not result. The problem, it is said, "... does not involve alteration of lien priority; that is, it does not involve the subordination of an earlier lien to a later lien, because by the execution of the purchase transaction the priorities are determined by the initial creation and recordation of the liens. Since the seller at no time has a 'prior' lien, he is not 'subordinating' his lien but merely agreeing to accept junior security. The problem, therefore, is primarily one of contract law between the buyer and the seller and not one of lien law between the seller and the lender." (p. 1301.)

In our view there is no justification, legal or otherwise, which would call for a different result whether the seller in a joint transaction records first and then agrees that his lien will be subordinated or whether he agrees that the lender may achieve priority through first recording. In C.E.B. California Real Estate Secured Transactions, supra, § 5.16 at 217 the author expressly disagrees with the Miller and Starr position stating:

"This author disagrees with Miller and Starr due to the prevailing policy of title companies of recording the subordinating lien before the subordinated deed of trust. [citation]. In Conley v. Fate (1964) 227 Cal.App.2d 418, 38 CR [Cal.Rptr.] 680, a seller agreed to accept a second deed of trust for a portion of the purchase price, and the

court properly referred to this as being subordinate to the construction loan, and further referred to the pertinent portion of the
deposit receipt as a subordination clause. In the event the vendor
is required to finance partially the purchase of his property,
through either a second deed of trust or a subordinated first deed of
trust, there should be no difference in his status based on the time
of recording of the two encumbrances. On some occasions the
purchase-money deed of trust held by the vendor will be reconveyed and rerecorded immediately after recordation of the subordinating encumbrance. [citation]. Therefore, if the institutional
lender is to finance a portion of the purchase price, the institutional lender should incur the same liabilities for misapplication of
funds, whether the vendor holds a second deed of trust by virtue of
reconveyance and rerecordation or a first subordinated by agreement without a change in the order of recording."

. . .

Finally, in our opinion strong public policy reasons to protect the
seller in subordination situations are set out in Handy v. Gordon, supra,
65 Cal.2d 578, 55 Cal.Rptr. 769, 422 P.2d 329:

"Although the parties to a contract of sale containing a subordination clause may delegate to the vendee or third party lenders power
to determine the details of subordinating loans, an enforceable
subordination clause must contain terms that will define and
minimize the risk that the subordinating liens will impair or
destroy the seller's security. Such terms may include limits on the
use to which the proceeds may be put to insure that their use will
improve the value of the land, maximum amounts so that the loans
will not exceed the contemplated value of the improvements they
finance, requirements that the loans do not exceed some specified
percentage of the construction cost or value of the property as
improved, specified amounts per square foot of construction, or
other limits designed to protect the security. Without some such
terms, however, the seller is forced to rely entirely on the buyer's
good faith and ability as a developer to insure that he will not lose
both his land and the purchase price.

. . .

"The contract alleged in the complaint does not afford defendants
any additional protection. Although the proceeds of the subordinating loans are to be used primarily for construction and refinancing, any funds that are not needed for these purposes may be
disbursed to plaintiff. The absence of restrictions on plaintiff's use
of these funds leaves defendants without assurance that all of the
proceeds of the loans will be used to improve the land that
represents their security. Because the limits on the loans are
expressed as absolutes, they provide no assurance that the amounts
of the loans will not exceed the value the improvements add to the

security. Moreover, the limits are maximums per lot, and plaintiff has unrestricted discretion in determining the size of each lot. Thus defendants are not assured that the total amount of the subordinating loans will be kept low enough to enable them to protect themselves by bidding on the property if the senior liens are foreclosed. Finally defendants did not receive a down payment that would effectively cushion their position, and the first payment of principal is deferred until three years after the close of escrow.

"Thus, the contract leaves defendants with nothing but plaintiff's good faith and business judgment to insure them that they will ever receive anything for conveying their land. Such a contract is not as to them 'just and reasonable' within the meaning of Civil Code, section 3391."

It has been pointed out by many courts and commentators that as between the seller and the lender, the lender is by far in the better position to control the use of the loan proceeds and thereby prevent misappropriations by the developer. The lender can require documented evidence that expenses have been incurred and can corroborate this by on-site inspections. It is common for lenders to control disbursements, since they, too, have an interest in preventing misuse of loan proceeds. If the lender loses priority as a result of improper disbursements, it remains in a position to redeem the seller's purchase money lien and foreclose on the junior construction lien and thereby own the property for a price presumably less than the market value. Also, loan proceeds would be at least partially recouped by the improvements made. The seller, on the other hand, is normally not in a position to protect himself by redemption of the larger construction lien in the event the lender were to obtain priority. After redemption, the lender can obtain a deficiency judgment against the defaulting developer whereas the seller, holding a purchase money security interest, would be barred by Code of Civil Procedure, § 580b, if he tried to recover a deficiency judgment against the developer. The lender is in a far better position to absorb any loss since such contingencies may be provided for in its profit and loss estimates. Finally, allocation of the loss to the lender would encourage the parties to provide for the various contingencies by contract.

An implied agreement in the instant case can and, in equity, should be spelled out from lender's alleged actual knowledge of the provisions of the seller's lien in general, and of the subordination therein in particular. In the superior position of a financial institution constantly engaged in professional construction lending, Southwestern had no reason to believe their trust deed conferred any lien to which the fee was subordinate other than to the extent of money spent for construction purposes. Its loan under the circumstances cannot be viewed other than as subject to the fair application of the construction funds. Accordingly, we conclude that such lien as the trust deed might have conferred on the lender should not be advanced or preferred over the seller.

Here, it is alleged the lender, with full knowledge of the subordinated lien of the seller, disbursed the funds without limitation. Its disinterest in the application of the funds not used for construction amounted to a failure to prevent the loss sustained by seller—who, in the vernacular of the market place, was "wiped out". The particular equities discussed above incline us to the conviction that the philosophy of fair dealing as expressed in Handy v. Gordon, supra, 65 Cal.2d 578, 55 Cal.Rptr. 769, 422 P.2d 329, is most appropriately invoked here.

We hold the actions of the parties here, if proved as alleged, did create a subordination agreement, and the lender's failure to protect seller's security interest gives seller a cause of action; the validity of the first, second, and third causes of action are supported by the cases.

The fourth cause of action is based on the theory seller was a third party beneficiary of the construction loan agreement between lender and the buyers. Lender, to support its demurrer, asked the court to take judicial notice of the construction loan agreement filed with certain answers to interrogatories. A provision of this agreement expressly states it is to be for the benefit of lender and buyers only. The court may take judicial notice of documents in its file when considering a demurrer. But the meaning of this agreement given the wide latitude of parol evidence admissible in interpreting a contract, is not the type of matter made judicially noticeable by Evidence Code, § 452. To go beyond notice of the existence of a document to an interpretation of its meaning constitutes improper consideration of evidentiary matters. We thus do not consider this agreement and hold the fourth cause of action to be regular on its face.

The fifth and sixth causes of action turn on lender's refusal to accept seller's tender of due principal, interest, and late charges to cure buyers' default. If the refusal was wrongful, the trustee's foreclosure sale was invalid and seller is entitled to the relief it seeks in these causes of action. The lender rejected seller's tender because it did not include the amount in excess of $50,000 which had been spent to repair and complete the apartments; plaintiffs allege defendants had no right to demand this sum because it was not stated in the notice of default. The notice need not, however, state the amounts which are in default; it need only describe the nature of the breach. Rejection of the tender thus was not wrongful and the trustee's sale was valid; sustaining the general demurrer without leave to amend was proper on the fifth and sixth causes of action.

All of seller's causes of action, as discussed herein, posit the existence of a subordination agreement and seek recovery for its breach. This amounts to an action on a contract: the punitive damages sought in the tenth cause of action are not recoverable in an action on a contract.

. . .

Thus since a subordination agreement is sufficiently alleged in the pleadings and supported in law, the first, second, third and fourth causes of action are valid and the judgment of dismissal should be reversed as to them. We hold the demurrer was properly sustained as to the fifth, sixth, and tenth causes of action. (Only the fifth, sixth, and tenth causes of action purport to state a claim against defendant Western Escrow.) The judgment of dismissal is reversed with directions to the trial court to overrule the general demurrer as to the first, second, third and fourth causes of action, and allow respondent a reasonable time within which to answer the third amended complaint.

Without ruling on the worth, if any, of the causes of action, set forth in the third amended complaint, seller should be afforded an opportunity to present the case on the merits. We do not decide, however, the valid portions of the complaint may not be subject to special demurrer, and the trial court may in its discretion require further clarification of any uncertainties or ambiguities.

The judgment is reversed in part and affirmed in part as set forth herein.

KERRIGAN, Acting P.J., and KAUFMAN, J., concur.

NOTES

1. A seller will often agree to subordinate his purchase money lien to the lien of the construction lender in the expectation that the improvements financed by the construction loan will increase the value of the land at least dollar for dollar, leaving his security intact. It was to honor this expectation that the *Middlebrook* court reached the decision it did. Yet, sellers usually have another reason to take a second position. Subordination may be the only, or at least the most rewarding, way that they can sell their property for development since institutional lenders will rarely finance on the basis of other than a first lien security.

Would the *Middlebrook* rule be applied if the construction lender did not know that the purchase money mortgage was subject to the condition that the funds be used for construction purposes only? In In re Sunset Bay Associates, 944 F.2d 1503 (9th Cir.1991), the court held that the subordination was contingent on the condition, whether or not the construction lender had actual knowledge of the condition. Does this place an unfair burden on the construction lender to discover conditions? What would a reasonable inquiry entail? Would it be more efficient if the purchase money mortgagee had the duty to give notice of the condition? How could a purchase money mortgagee give such notice? Should it matter whether subordination was achieved through a recorded subordination agreement or by order of recording as in *Middlebrook* ?

The approach taken in *Middlebrook* is by no means universal. Other states have been more generous to construction lenders, holding that, if construction loan funds are diverted to non-construction purposes, the subordinating seller can regain his first lien position only by showing collusion between the developer and the construction lender or an express agreement by the construction lender to oversee the disbursement of loan funds. See, e.g., Connecticut Bank and Trust Co. v. Carriage Lane Associates, 219 Conn. 772, 595 A.2d 334 (1991); Kennedy v. Betts, 33 Md.App. 258, 364 A.2d 74 (Spec.App.1976).

On the general issues raised in *Middlebrook,* see Korngold, Construction Loan Advances and the Subordinated Purchase Money Mortgagee: An Appraisal, A Suggested Approach, and the ULTA Perspective, 50 Fordham L.Rev. 313 (1981); Lambe, Enforceability of Subordination Agreements, 19 Real Prop., Probate & Trust J. 631 (1984); McNamara, Subordination Agreements as Viewed by Sellers, Purchasers, Construction Lenders, and Title Companies, 12 Real Est.L.J. 347 (1984); Note, Purchase Money Subordination Agreements in California: An Analysis of Conditional Subordination, 45 So.Cal.L.Rev. 1109 (1972).

Consider the use of the obligatory/optional advance rule as a means to assist the subordinated purchase money mortgagee. See pages 711–712 above.

2. *Remedies.* Should the remedy for a construction lender's failure to police the borrower's use of loan proceeds be complete subordination of the construction loan or subordination only to the extent that funds are misapplied? Say, for example, the seller subordinates a $95,000 purchase money deed of trust to the lien of a $349,500 construction loan, $323,158.70 of which was later properly disbursed and $26,341.30 of which was improperly disbursed. Miller v. Citizens Sav. & Loan Ass'n, 248 Cal.App.2d 655, 56 Cal.Rptr. 844 (1967) set the priorities as follows: a first lien to the construction lender for $323,159; a second lien to the seller for $95,000; and a third lien to the construction lender for $26,341.

What if the construction loan offends the subordinated purchase money loan not in its administration, but in its terms—for example, the interest rate exceeds the rate permitted by the subordination agreement, or the take-out commitment required by the seller as a condition to subordination was never obtained. What policies are served and disserved by a remedy that would totally reorder the priorities, placing the seller first? See Ruth v. Lytton Sav. & Loan Ass'n of Northern Cal., 266 Cal.App.2d 831, 72 Cal.Rptr. 521 (1968), modified 272 Cal. App.2d 24, 76 Cal.Rptr. 926 (1969); Jones v. Sacramento Sav. & Loan Ass'n, 248 Cal.App.2d 522, 56 Cal.Rptr. 741 (1967).

d. OTHER CONSTRUCTION LIENORS

i. Mechanics' and Materialmen's Liens

WILLIAMS & WORKS, INC. v. SPRINGFIELD CORP.

Supreme Court of Michigan, 1980.
408 Mich. 732, 293 N.W.2d 304.

WILLIAMS, Justice [For Reversal].

This case concerns the sole question whether off-site engineering services rendered before the beginning of actual, on-site construction qualify, pursuant to § 9(3) of the Michigan Mechanics' Lien Law, as "the commencement of said building or buildings, erection, structure or improvement" [1] so as to give priority to mechanics' liens over a mortgage recorded after the provision of such services but prior to the beginning of any visible, on-site construction. [2]

Long established Michigan precedent in line with that in most American jurisdictions requires a visible, on-site "commencement" for the purpose of fixing priorities under § 9(3) of the Mechanics' Lien Law. Plaintiffs in this case, however, claim the Legislature intended to change by indirection this traditional rule based on § 9(3) "commencement of said building or buildings, erection, structure or improvement" by amending the list of lienable items in § 1 [5] of the Mechanics' Lien

---

1. The paragraph of Michigan's Mechanics' Lien Law which governs the specific priority question in this case is M.C.L. § 570.9 (third); M.S.A. § 26.289 (§ 9[3] or the "priority section"). In pertinent part this section provides:

"The several liens herein provided for shall continue for 1 year after such statement or account is recorded in the office of the register of deeds, and no longer unless proceedings are begun to enforce the same as hereinafter provided, and such liens shall take priority as follows:

* * *

"Third, They shall be preferred to all other titles, liens or incumbrances which may attach to or upon such building, machinery, structure or improvement, or to or upon the land upon which they are situated, which shall either be given or recorded subsequent to the *commencement of said building or buildings, erection, structure or improvement.*" (Emphasis supplied.)

2. Appellees also contend, cursorily, that the twelve six-inch borings that were filled and staked by the engineering firm of Williams & Works prior to the recordation of the mortgage constituted a "continuing visible notice that improvements were in progress." However, this contention was essentially refuted by cross-examination of Ed Culver, a Williams & Works employee who was present while the borings were taken. Culver testified that there was no other work being performed

on the site at the time, the site being essentially a vacant lot covered with weeds. Further, Culver stated that although the soil borings were marked with a stake or flag after they were taken and filled in, the stakes and flags would tend to disappear because children would take them [Tr 160–161]. Thus, it is not certain whether these stakes were visible to a reasonable observer inspecting the premises. Further, assuming that the stakes were visible and remained upon the site, such minimal staking of the property is not activity which constitutes "commencement" of a building or improvement within M.C.L. § 570.9 (third); M.S.A. § 26.289 (third).

5. M.C.L. § 570.1; M.S.A. § 26.281 (§ 1) is an old (1891 P.A. 179) much amended section describing what is lienable. In pertinent part it provides:

"*Every person who shall,* in pursuance of any contract, express or implied, written or unwritten, existing between himself as contractor, and the owner, part owner or lessee of any interest in real estate, build, alter, improve, repair, erect, ornament or put in, survey or plat any lot or parcel of land, or portion thereof, or engineer or design any sewers, waterlines, roads, streets, highways, sidewalks, or *prepare and furnish* pursuant to such contract to such owner, part owner or lessee of any interest in real estate *any survey, plat, plat of survey or design or engineering plan, or plans,* for the *improvement of any lot or*

Law to include engineering and surveying services and by adding to the definition of "improvement" [6] found in § 1 the language, "designs or engineering plans for the improvement of any lot."

In view of the overwhelming weight of historical precedent, whose rationale and policy underpinnings remain vital today, we find that such non-visible, off-site engineering services as those rendered in the instant case, although lienable under Michigan law, do not signal the "commencement" of a building, erection, structure, or improvement for the purpose of fixing priority under Michigan's Mechanics' Lien Law. Accordingly, since the appellant mortgagee recorded its mortgage prior to any visible, on-site construction which could be said to "commence" the building, erection, structure or improvement, the trial court and Court of Appeals improperly accorded priority to the appellee mechanic lienors. We therefore reverse.

I. FACTS

Springfield Corporation ("Springfield") desired to erect a multifamily apartment building complex on certain land located in Genesee County, Michigan, and owned by LAW Development Company and appellant Kelly Mortgage and Investment Company ("Kelly"). In pursuance of this desire, Springfield contacted Williams & Works ("W & W") about May 16, 1972 in regard to using its engineering services for the contemplated development. Thereafter, on June 8, 1972, Robert Foote, President of Springfield, met two representatives of W & W at the contemplated development site for discussions and a preliminary

parcel of land not exceeding one-quarter section of land, or who shall furnish any labor or materials in or for building, altering, improving, repairing, erecting, ornamenting or putting in any house, swimming pool, building, machinery, wharf or structure, or who shall excavate, or build in whole, or in part, any foundation, cellar or basement for any such house, swimming pool, building, structure or wharf, or shall build or repair any sidewalks, sewers, sewage disposal equipment, water lines and pumping equipment or wells or shall furnish any materials therefor, or shall furnish any nursery stock, or labor in connection therewith for any property, or shall rent or lease equipment in connection therewith for any property, and every person who shall be subcontractor, laborer, or material man, perform any labor or furnish materials or shall rent or lease equipment to such original or principal contractor, or any subcontractor, in carrying forward or completing any such contract, *shall have a lien therefor * * *.*" (Emphasis supplied.)

The section goes on to describe the scope of the lien and the procedural requirements for its enforcement.

6. M.C.L. § 570.1; M.S.A. § 26.281 defines "improvement" as follows:

"*The term 'improvement'* or the plural thereof as used in this act, *shall include* the improvement, beautification or embellishment of property by the furnishing of nursery stock or the performance of labor in connection therewith or the planting thereof, or the furnishing by any registered land surveyor of any survey, plat, plat of survey of any lot or parcel of land, or the furnishing by any registered professional engineer of any engineering design or plans for the installation of any swimming pools, sewers, water lines, roads, streets, highways, sidewalks, or prepare and furnish pursuant to such contract to such owner, part owner or lessee of any interest in real estate and *other designs or engineering plans for the improvement of any lot* or parcel of land not exceeding one-quarter section of land, or the renting or leasing of any contractor's equipment for excavating, ditching, earth removal, landscaping, leveling, grading or changing the contour of any land, or the repairing, maintaining, restoring, constructing or demolition of any structure or the laying of any drains, sewers or pipelines." (Emphasis supplied.)

view of the premises. Then, near the end of June, 1972, W & W and Springfield entered into a formal written contract, under which W & W was to perform certain engineering services for the contemplated development. The contract was divided into three parts or phases with Springfield reserving the right to terminate the contract at the end of any phase. Phase I called for W & W to undertake and complete initial feasibility studies which included soil borings, drainage studies, topographical and boundary surveys, preliminary utility plans, cost estimates and plan approvals. Phase II called for W & W to finalize all plans for site development, including final drafting of the construction plans. Phase III involved the actual construction of the project and required W & W to supervise and direct parts of the construction work.

By September, 1972, Phase I was substantially completed. The only on-site work done by W & W during Phase I consisted of certain soil borings, which were taken on August 29, 1972, when two workers drilled twelve holes into the ground, each approximately 6″ in diameter.

After the completion of Phase I, W & W began Phase II and throughout the latter part of 1972, it submitted various construction specifications to Springfield. It was also established that during this period Kelly knew of W & W's work since Kelly had actually written W & W requesting that all correspondence dealing with W & W's work to date be forwarded to Kelly since it would be handling the project for Mr. Foote. In late December, 1972, after substantial completion of the Phase II drawings, Springfield decided to go forward with the construction of the apartment building project. Thereafter, on January 4, 1973, Springfield purchased the land from LAW Development and Kelly and executed a mortgage on the property to City National Bank ("CNB") which was recorded in Genesee County and which was subsequently assigned from City National Bank to Kelly. On January 9, 1973, Springfield executed a second mortgage to Kelly, which was also recorded in Genesee County. Almost one year later, Springfield conveyed its fee interest in the premises to Bristol Square Properties Group, a limited copartnership in which Mr. Foote and Springfield are the sole general partners, by deed dated December 27, 1973.

It is undisputed that building operations on the premises did not begin until February, 1973, almost one full month after the mortgages were recorded by CNB and Kelly. The initial Phase III work, consisting of staking, began on February 10, 1973 and building operations commenced sometime thereafter. The project went into default in 1974 and this mechanics' lien foreclosure action followed.

This suit was commenced on March 25, 1974, in the Genesee Circuit Court. The Complaint alleges that the plaintiff, W & W, had a mechanics' lien upon the project property and prayed for its foreclosure. Numerous other parties were joined as defendants or intervened, and several cross-claims were filed by various other contractors, alleging mechanics' liens against the property. Kelly, the mortgagee in the instant proceeding, as well as other defendants aligned in interest, answered the various mechanics' lien claims, denying the validity of the claims and asserting that the mortgage interest in the property was superior and paramount to the interest of the various mechanics' liens.

After pretrial and trial proceedings concluded, the trial court entered judgments of foreclosure against the owner of the apartment project, Bristol Square Properties Group, in favor of W & W and the instant appellee mechanics lienors (Shank, Coupland and Long, Co., PPG Industries, Inc., and Garno Brothers Heating and Cooling, Inc., all subcontractors who began supplying labor and materials while the project was owned by Springfield, and completed their work after Springfield conveyed to Bristol Square Properties Group). The trial court also ruled that all mechanics' liens were prior to the mortgage interest of Kelly in the property because it found W & W's services to have been "improvements", as that term is defined in § 1, M.C.L. § 570.1; M.S.A. § 26.281, which were "commenced" before the mortgage was recorded.

The Court of Appeals affirmed the trial court's conclusion that, in the instant case, "commencement", for purposes of priority, meant when engineering services were first performed, and not when actual construction on the site was begun.

We granted leave to appeal on March 5, 1979 limited to the issue of priority between the mortgage and the mechanics' liens under § 9(3), M.C.L. § 570.9 (third); M.S.A. § 26.289 (third).

II.   DISCUSSION

A.   *Michigan's Mechanics' Lien Law Pre-1958*

The term "commencement of a building" had a well-established meaning in most states when Michigan incorporated that term into its own mechanics' lien law. As illustrative of this meaning, and in order not to belabor the point, we quote from one such case, while citing the reader to others which preceded or were contemporaneous with Michigan's statute:

> "The commencement of a building is the doing of some act upon the ground upon which the building is to be erected, and in pursuance of a design to erect, the result of which act should make known to a person viewing the premises, *from observation alone,* that the erection of a building upon that lot or tract of land has been commenced." James v. Van Horn, 39 N.J.L. 353, 363 (1877). (Emphasis supplied.)

Accord, Brooks v. Lester, 36 Md. 65 (1872); Kansas Mortgage Co. v. Weyerhaeuser, 48 Kan. 335, 29 P. 153 (1892); Fitzgerald v. Walsh, 107 Wis. 92, 82 N.W. 717 (1900); Conrad & Ewinger v. Starr, 50 Iowa 470 (1879).

Likewise, early Michigan case law espoused this same idea of keying the concept of "commencement" in its priority section to some actual, visible work on the land such that it was apparent to all that a building was being erected or improvements were being made. In Kay v. Towsley, 113 Mich. 281, 283, 71 N.W. 490, 491 (1897), this Court, in ruling that two materialmen's liens were prior to that of a mortgagee who had recorded his mortgage prior to the furnishing of the materials but subsequent to the erection of the foundation wall, stated:

> "This provision [the priority provision in the Mechanics' Lien Law] has been passed upon frequently by the courts, and it has been uniformly held that the lien has priority over a mortgage executed upon the land or premises *after the actual commencement* of the building, though no part of the labor performed or materials furnished for which the lien is claimed was done or performed until after the execution and recording of the mortgage." (Emphasis supplied.)

One early commentator summarized the meaning of "commencement of said building" in Michigan thus:

> "In determining priorities, liens attach as of the date of the actual commencement of the building or improvement, regardless of the time when, or person by whom, particular work is done or materials furnished, for which lien is claimed. *The building is begun when the first permanent work is done on the land.*" (Emphasis supplied; citations omitted.) Wykes, The Michigan Laws of Mechanics' Liens (2d ed.), pp. 167–168, fn. 2.

"Commencement", then, as defined by early case law and commentary, required an act of such a character that it was notice to all of the existence of mechanics' liens. As Professor Thompson wrote:

> "The 'commencement of a building', within the meaning of these statutes, is the first labor done on the ground which is made the foundation of the building, and forms part of the work suitable and necessary for its construction. It is some work or labor on the ground, such as beginning to dig the foundation, which everyone can see and recognize as the commencement of a building; and the work, moreover, must be done with the intention thus formed of continuing it to completion." 8A Thompson, Commentaries on the Modern Law of Real Property (1963 Supp.), § 4427, p. 228.

In such fashion, "commencement" of a building gave constructive notice to prospective lenders or purchasers of the possible existence of liens. This visible notice was especially important since under Michigan's Mechanics' Lien Act, as well as those of other states, "commencement" fixed the date to which all mechanics' liens related back, even if other contractors started their work weeks or months later. M.C.L. § 570.9 (first); M.S.A. § 26.289 (first).[7] It was in keeping with this

---

7. M.C.L. § 570.9 (first); M.S.A. § 26.-289 (first) provides:

"As between persons claiming liens under this statute, the several liens upon the same property attaching by reason of work, labor or materials furnished in carrying forward or completing the same building or buildings, machinery, structure or im-

interpretation that this Court early held, in response to a mechanic lienor's contention, analogous to that made in the present case, that the "commencement" of a building occurred when the architect began drawing the plans and specifications for the building, that

> "[i]t is, we think, clear, that the drawing of plans for a building is not 'the commencement of said building or buildings.'" Stevens v. Garland, 198 Mich. 24, 32, 164 N.W. 516, 518 (1917).

B. *Michigan's Mechanics' Lien Law Post-1958*

In 1958 the Michigan Legislature amended § 1 of the Mechanics' Lien Law, which describes lienable services, to include engineering and surveying services. Amended § 1, further, included engineering and surveying services under the definition of the word "improvement":

> "The term 'improvement' or the plural thereof as used in this act, shall include the * * * prepar[ing] and furnish[ing] * * * designs or engineering plans for the improvement of any lot or parcel of land * * *."

The gist of appellees' argument on appeal to us is that this definition of "improvement" found in § 1 of the Mechanics' Lien Law describing liens is freely substitutable for the word "improvement" as it appears in the priority section of the lien law. The word "improvement" appears in § 9(3) in the following context:

> "Third, They [mechanics' liens] shall be preferred to all other titles, liens or incumbrances which may attach to or upon such building, machinery, structure or improvement, or to or upon the land upon which they are situated, which shall either be given or recorded subsequent to the commencement of said building or buildings, erection, structure or *improvement*." (Emphasis supplied.)

By this process of substitution, the appellees present us with a priority section which they claim, in this case, should read, in edited fashion, as follows:

> "Third, they [W & W as professional engineers] shall be preferred to all liens recorded subsequent to *the commencement of its furnishing engineering design or plans for the improvement of said lot*." (Emphasis in appellees' brief.) [Appellees' Brief, p. 6]

To safeguard their position, appellees assert that the cases requiring visible, on-site construction in order to constitute "commencement" are obsolete since they construed the Act at a time when engineering services were not lienable and that cases from other jurisdictions are of little significance since they construe statutes different from that of Michigan.

The issue for resolution, then, is whether the Legislature, by amending M.C.L. § 570.1; M.S.A. § 26.281 to expand the definition of lienable items to include engineering services, intended to effect a departure

provement, shall be deemed simultaneous mortgages."

from the requirement of visible, on-site construction which courts have traditionally required for a building or improvement to be "commenced" for purposes of the priority section. In other words, should the performance of non-visible, off-site engineering services before the recording of a mortgage, as was done in the present case, be sufficient to give all mechanics' lienors priority over the mortgagee?

We find the appellee mechanic lienors' substitution of the definition of "improvement" found in § 1 for the word "improvement" found in the priority section, although of some superficial persuasiveness, to be fundamentally unsound for several reasons. ...

Third, we think it unreasonable to believe the Legislature intended to indirectly change § 9(3), containing the traditional and well-established rule requiring a visible, on-site commencement of construction in order to establish priority, by the simple expansion of the lienable services outlined in a different section, § 1. Section 1 and § 9(3) treat of two entirely different concepts. Section 1 merely determines *what* is a lienable service in Michigan. It runs the gamut from the furnisher of labor and materials and the surveyor and engineer to the renter or lessor of equipment and the supplier of nursery stock. Section 9(3), on the other hand, deals with the determination of *when* a particular lien attaches for priority purposes. It specifically leaves the establishment of what services are lienable to another part of the act, i.e., § 1, and concerns itself primarily with the ascertainment of the priorities among the liens:

> "The several liens *herein provided for* * * * shall take priority as follows: [hereafter follow four rules for determining priorities]." (Emphasis supplied.)

Fourth, the 1958 amendment to § 1 of the mechanics' lien law was only one of successive amendments to that section expanding *what* constitutes a lienable service in Michigan. For example, the protection of this section was extended to nursery stock in 1941, to surveying and engineering services and works in 1958, to sewers, sewage disposal equipment, water lines and pumping equipment in 1960, to rented or leased equipment in 1963, and to swimming pools in 1965. See fn. 5, supra.

Fifth, in contradistinction to this constant expansion of lienable services under § 1, § 9(3), fixing priorities, has been conspicuously quiescent. Not one of the many amendments to § 1 has been accompanied by an amendment significantly affecting the priority section of the mechanics' lien law. ...

For the above reasons, we believe that the Legislature neither intended the § 1 definition of "improvement" to be freely substitutable for the word "improvement" found in § 9, nor intended to indirectly change the established interpretation of § 9(3) through an amendment of § 1. Thus, we find that while the Legislature has continually broadened the range of lienable services in Michigan, it has not chosen to effect any change in the long-established judicial interpretation of "commencement of said building or buildings, erection, structure or improvement" as that phrase has been used in the past to determine priority between a mechanics' lienor and a mortgagee. ...

We also believe that our decision, in continuing to key "commencement" into the concept of constructive notice, is based on sound public policy. Were we to adopt appellees' position and rule that the "commencement" of a building, erection, structure or improvement could be triggered by the rendering of off-site, non-visible engineering plans, mechanics' liens could relate back to a long time before any visible signs of construction existed to inform prospective lenders inspecting the premises that liens had attached. Under such circumstances, construction financing would become exceedingly difficult. It was just such a concern that compelled the California Supreme Court in *Walker,* [Walker v. Lytton Savings & Loan Ass'n of Northern California, 2 Cal.3d 152, 84 Cal.Rptr. 521, 465 P.2d 497 (1970)] to reach the same result we do today.

> "But if, despite these specific and detailed rules laid down by the Legislature, it be held for the benefit of plaintiff architects that even though, as here, an encumbrance has attached before any work has been done on the owners' property or materials delivered thereto for a planned improvement, nevertheless the work of improvement had commenced earlier when the architects began work on the plans and specifications, then the liens of all others who contributed work or materials to the work of improvement * * * would likewise relate back to the earlier date of commencement and thereby take priority over the subsequent encumbrance—whether given for a construction loan or based on some other consideration. That the Legislature intended no such result seems obvious. Additionally, under such circumstances it would appear that construction loans would shortly become next to impossible to obtain, as it is a rare construction project of any magnitude which does not require the preliminary nonvisible services of architects or engineers. But if all liens arising from the subsequent construction will relate back to the date of commencement of the nonvisible services, how many prudent businessmen would be willing to assume the risk?" *Walker,* supra, 2 Cal.3d 159–160, 84 Cal.Rptr. 526–27, 465 P.2d 502–03.

In contrast to this significant judicial authority, we have found only one jurisdiction that takes a contrary approach. See Bankers Trust Co. v. El Paso Pre-Cast Co., 192 Colo. 468, 560 P.2d 457 (1977). Appellees have cited to us no other relevant case law.

Finally, one last contention of appellees' needs to be addressed. Appellees argue that because appellant Kelly had actual notice (of which there is record support) of the identity of and services being furnished by W & W before it sold the land to Springfield and filed mortgage liens, it should not be heard to urge the adoption of a visible and actual commencement standard in this particular case. It is unclear whether this argument rests on notions of waiver or estoppel.

However, whatever the theory, actual notice is not the relevant issue in determining the priorities question in this case. The issue is the determination of when "commencement" of the building or improvement occurred. In *Walker*, supra, it was found that the holder of the deed of trust had actual knowledge that plaintiff architects had provided services. In fact Lytton, the holder of the deed of trust, had relied on plaintiffs' work in making its appraisal for loan purposes. The Court, after noting that the condition precedent to the architects' priority was the commencement of construction, stated that such knowledge alone cannot constitute waiver or estoppel. In support of this conclusion, the Court opined, quoting from Tracy Price Associates v. Habard, 266 Cal.App.2d 778, 787–788, 72 Cal.Rptr. 600 (1968), that

> " 'To hold that such knowledge constitutes waiver or estoppel would expose lenders to so many unpredictable hazards that construction financing would become extremely difficult. Although mechanic's lien laws should be liberally construed to protect those who have contributed skills, services or materials, towards the improvement of property, it has been recognized that lien laws are for the protection of owners as well as mechanic's lien claimants. * * * It may be said with equal validity that section 1188.1 * * * prescribing a rule for determining priorities was designed for the protection of those who take security interests in land as well as for the protection of mechanic's lien claimants.' " *Walker*, supra, 2 Cal.3d 158, 84 Cal.Rptr. 525–26, 465 P.2d 501–02.

We agree with the California Supreme Court that construction and purchase money loans are not made in a vacuum. Lenders often consult engineers' work in order to evaluate and minimize their risks. Thus if a lender's use of and reliance upon the plans prepared by engineers on behalf of the owner or would-be purchaser are to work a change in the statutory priority rules, the change must be sought from the Legislature and not from this Court.

III. CONCLUSION

Because we have found that the engineering services here at issue were not such as to constitute the "commencement of said building or buildings, erection, structure or improvement", the trial court erred in its ruling that the appellee mechanics' lienors had priority over the mortgage held by appellant Kelly. Accordingly, we reverse the decision of the Court of Appeals and vacate the trial court's judgment and order.

Costs to appellant.

COLEMAN, C.J., FITZGERALD, Deputy C.J., and RYAN, MOODY, LEVIN and KAVANAGH, JJ., concur.

NOTES

1. What kind of protection can, and should, be given to architects and engineers who will characteristically provide their services before

the commencement of physical improvements on the construction site? As explicated in *Williams & Works,* the purpose of the physical improvement requirement is to put the construction lender on notice that work has begun and that liens may have attached. Would this purpose be equally well served by a rule that allowed engineers and architects to record their contracts, thus giving the lender constructive notice that work has begun? Such a rule would impose no additional search burden on construction lenders who, as standard operating procedure, will search title before closing and recording their loans.

A rule that makes liens attach either from the moment that physical improvements commence or from the moment of their recording would not substantially increase construction lenders' economic risk. Having identified all lien claimants prior to recording the construction loan, the construction lender can require that they be paid off before the loan closes. As to mechanics and materialmen who provide services and supplies *after* the construction loan is recorded, but who can nonetheless take advantage of the earlier mechanics' lien priority, the construction lender can, by carefully monitoring a well-structured disbursement program, assure that no liens arise.

How would you advise an engineer or architect to protect herself in states like Michigan where her lien will virtually always be subordinated to the construction lender's lien?

After the decision in *Williams & Works,* the Michigan legislature amended its mechanics' lien statute. Mich.Comp. Laws Ann. § 570.119 provides that a "construction lien" (the new term for a mechanics' lien) takes priority over other interests recorded subsequent to the "first actual physical improvement." Section 570.1103(1) specifically provides that "actual physical improvement" does not include architectural or engineering work, even though such work can be the basis for a valid construction lien. § 570.1104(7).

The Uniform Construction Lien Act, promulgated by the National Conference of Commissioners on Uniform State Laws in 1976 and amended in 1977 takes a different approach than most statutes to the priority issue. Rather than assigning priority from the time of commencement of work (or some similar formulation), the Act requires the owner to record a "notice of commencement" prior to the beginning of work. This recording puts third parties on notice that construction liens might be filed and if a lien claimant subsequently records a lien, her priority is the date of recording of the notice of commencement. §§ 208, 209, 210, 301. It is asserted that this approach relieves the burden on construction lenders to determine before recording their mortgages whether work has begun and alleviates the need to preserve evidence that no work was done before the recording. Additionally, the Uniform Act permits architects and engineers to file construction liens on a priority with other lien claimants. §§ 102(17)(v), 209.

2. Mechanics' lien practice varies from state to state. In some states the lien attaches on the commencement of construction. In

others, it attaches when a claim for payment is first filed. In still others it attaches when the general contract is executed. Requirements may exist for perfecting the lien, such as by recording the underlying claim within a specified time after construction is completed. Once the lien is perfected, time limits are usually imposed for the commencement of foreclosure proceedings. In some states the lienor must give the owner notice of her intention to record her claim of lien. Rules on attachment, perfection and foreclosure may differ depending on whether it is the general contractor or a subcontractor who is asserting the lien. See generally, Dugan, Mechanics' Liens for Improvements on Real Property, 25 S.D.L.Rev. 238 (1980); Urban & Miles, Mechanics' Liens for the Improvement of Real Property: Recent Developments in Perfection, Enforcement and Priority, 12 Wake Forest L.Rev. 283 (1976); Goulden & Dent, More on Mechanics Liens, Stop Notices and the Like, 54 Calif.L.Rev. 179 (1966).

3. *Constitutional Issues.* In recent decades, courts have addressed the constitutionality of mechanics' lien procedures. Although most courts have taken the view that the attachment of a mechanic's lien does not materially inhibit the owner's freedom of alienation, and consequently does not violate his right to procedural due process, others see a potential clog on alienation and follow the guidelines set down by the United States Supreme Court in decisions invalidating wage garnishment and replevin statutes. For the view that mechanics' lien procedures do not give the property owner due process, see Roundhouse Const. Corp. v. Telesco Masons Supplies Co., 168 Conn. 371, 362 A.2d 778 (1975), vacated and remanded for clarification of ground for decision 423 U.S. 809, 96 S.Ct. 20, 46 L.Ed.2d 29 (1975). For the opposing view, see Ruocco v. Brinker, 380 F.Supp. 432 (S.D.Fla.1974); Spielman-Fond, Inc. v. Hanson's Inc., 379 F.Supp. 997 (D.Ariz.1973), affirmed without opinion, 417 U.S. 901, 94 S.Ct. 2596, 41 L.Ed.2d 208 (1974). For a comprehensive study of the cases and their background, see generally, Note, 26 Cath.U.L.Rev. 129 (1976).

4. *Claims Against Undisbursed Construction Funds.* Compliance with mechanics' liens procedures will be of no help to the unpaid laborer or material supplier if the security is exhausted by the claims of the construction lender or other senior encumbrancers. Equity may in these circumstances aid the supplier by attaching a lien not to the exhausted real estate security, but rather to any undisbursed construction funds. To be entitled to this equitable remedy, the supplier must show "special and peculiar equities." Crane Co. v. Fine, 221 So.2d 145, 149 (Fla.1969).

In addition to the practical requirement that there be undisbursed funds to which the equitable lien can attach, the unpaid supplier must show that she justifiably relied on the availability of the construction loan funds as a source of payment for her labor or materials, and that for the owner or lender to withhold these undisbursed funds would constitute unjust enrichment. Unjust enrichment is easiest to show if the owner or lender holds undisbursed construction funds after the project is completed. Would there be unjust enrichment if the project were unfinished and the construction lender needed to use the undisbursed funds to complete the improvement and otherwise protect its collateral? See A–1 Door & Materials Co. v. Fresno Guar. Sav. & Loan Ass'n, 61 Cal.2d 728, 40 Cal.Rptr. 85, 394 P.2d 829 (1964). To keep the issues in perspective, remember that the mechanic can always bring a contract action against the owner or contractor who agreed to pay for the labor or materials.

A similar, but more systematic, approach to undisbursed funds is offered by statutory "stop notice procedures." A lender or owner holding construction funds who fails to honor an unpaid supplier's stop notice demand that it withhold sufficient funds to satisfy the supplier's claim will be personally liable to the supplier for the amount owed. See, for example, Cal.Civ.Code § 3156 et seq.

Some courts hold that equitable liens are not permitted on the theory that the jurisdiction's mechanics' lien and stop notice statutes were intended as the exclusive remedies for unpaid laborers and suppliers. See, e.g., Nibbi Brothers, Inc. v. Home Federal Savings & Loan Association, 205 Cal.App.3d 1415, 253 Cal.Rptr. 289 (1988) (applying Cal.Civ.Code § 3264 which states that subcontractors and suppliers are limited to statutory remedies and may not assert any other equitable right); contra Embree Construction Group v. Rafcor, 330 N.C. 487, 411 S.E.2d 916 (1992).

For an extensive review of these and other theories of construction lender liability, see Reitz, Construction Lenders' Liability to Contractors, Subcontractors and Materialmen, 130 U.Pa.L.Rev. 416 (1981).

5. *Wrongly Disbursed Construction Funds.* Should mechanics and materialmen whose liens attached after the construction mortgage was recorded be given priority over the claims of a construction lender who allowed the construction loan proceeds to be diverted from the construction project? Peoples Bank & Trust Co. and Bank of Mississippi v. L & T Developers, Inc., 434 So.2d 699 (1983), judgment corrected, 437 So.2d 7 (1983), answered that they should be given priority. The Mississippi Supreme Court began by noting that the equities favored the materialmen. "If, as here, the materialmen are not paid, quite likely the construction lender will be unjustly enriched at their expense. For in this situation, if the construction lender were allowed a priority over the materialmen, it would have received the enhancement to the value of its collateral while the materialmen, without whose services the bank cannot expect the secured construction loan transaction to succeed, would as a practical matter be without security, and, most likely, with little prospect of getting paid." 434 So.2d at 705.

The court further concluded that this was "an instance in which the law follows and embodies the equities." It cited an earlier decision, Guaranty Mortgage Co. of Nashville v. Seitz, 367 So.2d 438 (Miss.1979), for the proposition that "The lien of a deed of trust securing a construction loan has priority over mechanics' and materialmen's liens only to the extent that: (a) the funds disbursed actually went into the construction, *or* (b) to the extent that the construction lender used reasonable diligence in disbursing the construction loan. 367 So.2d at 441. [Emphasis added]" 434 So.2d at 707.

The court emphasized that "the bank/construction lender is in a far better situation than is the materialman to protect itself and police the use of the construction loan funds and thereby avoid the predicament which has in fact ensued." Specifically, "construction lenders may make advances in the form of drafts or checks payable directly to materialmen or payable to materialmen and the builder jointly." 434 So.2d at 705. On much the same reasoning the court concluded that the materialmen were also entitled to priority over the landowner-purchase money mortgagee: "Wickes and Arick [the construction lienors] are parties who supplied materials and labor to the improvements on the two lots, thereby enhancing the value of these projects. Through sweat and elbow grease, these two construction lienors in a very real sense created value which previously was not there. The landowner, on the other hand, has made no similar contribution. The landowner had the far greater capacity to protect his interest, and, further, the landowner profits directly from the success of the overall construction project to which the materialmen so materially contribute." 434 So.2d at 714.

Under the reasoning of *Peoples Bank,* should the mechanics and materialmen have been given not only first priority, but also an action against the construction lenders for any part of their construction liens not satisfied by the foreclosure sale of the property? An action against the landowner-purchase money mortgagee?

Should a construction lender be under a similar duty to a mechanic who has not perfected a lien? Should the failure of the mechanic alter the balance of the equitable considerations that the court made in *Peoples Bank*? See Riley Building Supplies, Inc. v. First Citizens National Bank, 510 So.2d 506 (Miss.1987).

The obligatory/optional advance rule has also been applied to boost the priority of mechanics. See the discussion of this doctrine and various reforms at pages 711–714 above.

ii. Fixtures

KRIPKE, FIXTURES UNDER THE UNIFORM COMMERCIAL CODE

64 Columbia Law Review 44–46, 48–51 (1964).

The Uniform Commercial Code deals comprehensively with transactions and security in personal property. With minor exceptions it touches real estate only in connection with the "fixture" problem, which arises when tangible chattels acquire a permanent association with a parcel of real estate.

The fixture problem involves various types of possible conflict between persons who contend that the chattel has become part of the real estate and persons who claim that it has remained a chattel. The problem may arise in conflicts between an heir to real estate and the next of kin who receives the decedent's personal property; or between a grantee or devisee of real estate and the grantor or other person claiming the chattel as such. It may arise as a problem in procedure in determining whether a tort claim is based on an injury to real estate or on conversion of or damage to a chattel. It may arise in eminent domain in determining whether the public authority taking the real estate is obliged to pay for the chattel. But in the area covered by the Code, the problem arises between an owner of the real estate or a lender against the real estate, each of whom claims the chattel as part of the real estate, and a person claiming a security interest in the chattel under the Code. In the writer's view, the [1962] Code provisions present several difficulties and require re-examination.

To set the stage for more detailed discussion, let us take a simple case. Suppose that a furnace is sold to the owner of a home under a conditional sale contract and installed in the home, and that the owner has a pre-existing real estate mortgage on the home, or subsequently encumbers it with a real estate mortgage. Of course, both the holder of the real estate security and the holder of the chattel security may claim the furnace as against the owner. The problem arises in determining a conflict between the real estate mortgagee and the conditional vendor of the chattel. In resolving this conflict three broad approaches are possible:

1. The court might apply the maxim *quicquid plantatur solo, solo cedit*—whatever is affixed to the soil belongs to the soil—and hold that if the furnace has become part of the real estate, the chattel security is at an end and the real estate mortgagee prevails. Thus, the term "fixture," as used in the decisions in Ohio and some other states, simply announces the court's decision that the chattel has become part of the real estate and that the real estate claimant prevails. One consequence of a rule like this which gives full victory to the real estate claimant is that the court will avoid its application in hard cases by holding that the chattels involved have not become part of the real estate. This was the result in a series of Massachusetts cases and the effect has been to leave the law of that state imprecise as to when a chattel has become part of the real estate.

2. A second position is that if in the particular state conditional sales contracts are valid against third parties without filing, or if the regular filing rules have been complied with prior to affixation, the conditional sale remains valid against real estate interests. The consequence of this rule is that persons with real estate interests must not only search the real estate title but must also make a chattel search unless they are willing to risk the existence of valid chattel liens on chattels that have become part of the real estate. Again, the result of a rule that goes too far in favor of one set of interests is that the court

may avoid its consequences in some cases by holding that the chattel has become so affixed to the real estate as to lose its chattel character.

3. A third approach is to recognize that both chattel security interests and real estate interests are entitled to protection and that the problem is one of accommodation. A first step in that accommodation would be to require that security interests on chattels affixed to real estate be made a matter of public notice in the real estate records, so that persons with real estate interests could discover them by searching the real estate title. The second step would be to work out specific rules for deciding between real estate interests and chattel interests under specific concrete sets of circumstances. This is the approach of the Code, and before it of the Uniform Conditional Sales Act, and of the Pennsylvania statutes both before and after Pennsylvania's enactment of the Uniform Conditional Sales Act.

The draftsmen of the Code assumed that this approach and the specific rules embodied in Section 7 of the Uniform Conditional Sales Act (UCSA) had worked satisfactorily, with one exception to be mentioned shortly; that no fundamental reconsideration was necessary; and that, except for remedying the one deficiency to be mentioned, the problem was simply to redraft and clarify the solutions of the UCSA and to integrate them into the Code.

How wrong we were!

... The rules contained in Section 7 of the UCSA and in the Code may be summarized as follows:

1. Chattels that lose their identity by being transformed into the fabric of a building, like sand and cement into mortar and concrete, or bags and cans of ingredients into plastered and painted walls, lose their character as chattels and become no longer subject to chattel interests. There are other items, however, like the structural supporting members and crossbeams of a building, which maintain their identity but cannot be removed without substantially destroying the building. Section 7 of the UCSA excluded both groups from the rules of accommodation to be discussed below by a rule that chattels were not legally removable if they could not be removed without material injury to the freehold. In some states, however, this material injury test was interpreted to deny the removability of items far less integral a part of the real estate than structural members. A concept developed in these states of the real estate as an economic entity, so that the application of the test prevented removal of chattels that could have been removed with little or no physical injury to the land or building. The resulting diversity of state views made a supposedly uniform state statute far from uniform in practice. Accordingly, the draftsmen of the Code abandoned the material injury test and sought to achieve the same result by providing that (a) the types of chattels described above were not subject to the rules set forth in Section 9–313, and (b) with respect to other types of chattels, when under other provisions in the section the chattel interests prevailed over all real estate interests, the chattels could be

removed, regardless of material injury, but the chattel-secured party would have to reimburse any real estate claimant who is not the debtor for any physical injury caused to the real estate (injury caused by the absence of the chattels themselves being expressly excluded). It was thought that considerations of economic convenience would preclude removals that would disrupt the building too much.

2. Chattel security interests that attach before the chattel becomes affixed to the real estate are valid against prior real estate interests even without filing. This is on the theory that the addition of the chattel to the real estate is in the nature of a windfall to the party with the prior real estate interest since he did not rely on it, and that he is accordingly not entitled to protection against even an unfiled chattel security interest. This rule was a matter of judicial decision before and under the UCSA, but is express in the Code. The statutes do not make an exception in the case of chattels which replace those already subject to the real estate interests. ...

3. To protect the chattel security interest against the interests of subsequent buyers of the real estate and subsequent mortgagees of the real estate, it must be filed in the real estate records before the real estate is purchased or mortgaged.

4. It is apparent that when a construction mortgage on real estate is recorded before the chattel is affixed to the real estate, but some of the construction advances are made later, special consideration is required. The UCSA left it to the courts to hold that subsequent advances had the status of subsequent mortgages. The Code attempts to deal with the problem but with ambiguous phrasing.

5. The UCSA ignored creditors with judgment liens on the real estate, but the Code gives subsequent judgment lien creditors the same protection as subsequent mortgagees.

6. To protect the present owner of the real estate against chattel security when he is not the person who created it, the UCSA requires that the chattel security interest be filed in the real estate records before the chattel becomes affixed. The draftsmen of the Code eliminated this requirement, unconsciously it is believed, by a provision that affords no protection to a present owner.

7. The extent, if any, to which all of the foregoing rules apply to tenants' fixtures is not explicitly set forth in either the UCSA or the Code.

HOUSE v. LONG

Supreme Court of Arkansas, 1968.
244 Ark. 718, 426 S.W.2d 814.

W.B. PUTMAN, Special Justice.

This litigation involves the priority of liens among a purchase-money mortgage, a construction money mortgage, various mechanics' and materialmen's liens and a security agreement involving certain fixtures in thirteen different dwellings.

The defendant Long, a builder, had arranged for financing with Modern American Mortgage Company for approximately forty residences to be constructed primarily in Beverly Hills Addition to the City of Little Rock, Arkansas. On each lot purchased by Long, purchase-money mortgages were given in amounts varying from $2,750.00 to $3,200.00, and in addition, separate construction money mortgages in the amount of $10,000.00 were given on each lot. Both the purchase and construction money mortgages and the notes which they secured were subsequently assigned in trust to the appellant, A.F. House. Construction was not begun until these mortgages were placed of record.

On ten of the thirteen residences in question, arrangements were made to disburse the proceeds of the construction money loans through Beach Abstract and Guaranty Company. Disbursements on the other three were through Standard Title Company. The procedure established required Long to submit to the disbursing agent each week a list of the laborers, mechanics and materialmen who were entitled to payment and the amounts thereof on each house. An officer of Modern American would then inspect the premises to determine whether construction had progressed sufficiently to justify the requested disbursement. If so, funds would be sent to the disbursing agent, and Long would execute a separate note for each disbursement. Individual checks would be issued to each laborer, mechanic or materialman in the amount shown on the list and delivered to them by Long.

Cross-appellant, Arkansas Louisiana Gas Company, had entered into a separate contract with Long to sell a heating and air-conditioning unit, a cooling tower, a kitchen range and oven and to install the duct work in each house. A blanket security agreement was executed on November 30, 1964, but was never recorded. Security agreements on individual lots were also executed as the goods were delivered, but these also were not recorded. It was not until December 27, 1965, approximately two months after construction had ceased and Long's insolvency was generally known, that additional security agreements were executed and recorded.

The chancellor held that the language of the construction money mortgages did not unqualifiedly commit the mortgagee to make the advances so as to afford it priority over the mechanics' and materialmen's liens. He further held that the transaction between Arkansas Louisiana Gas Company and Long created a purchase-money security interest in collateral other than inventory which was not perfected within ten days after the debtor received possession as required by Ark.Stats. 85–9–312(4) (Repl.1961) in order to give it priority over conflicting security interests.

Accordingly, the chancellor established the priorities in the following order: (1) Purchase-money mortgage; (2) mechanics' and materialmen's liens; (3) construction money mortgage; (4) the security interest of Arkansas Louisiana Gas Company. From this decree, A.F. House, Trustee, and Arkansas Louisiana Gas Company have appealed.

The pertinent language in each of the thirteen construction money mortgages in question is as follows:

> "Grantee agrees that the acceptance and recordation of this mortgage binds grantee, its successors and assigns absolutely and unconditionally to make said loans and advances. Such advances will be made as requested by grantor as such work progresses."

It was the view of the trial court that this language was insufficient under our decisions requiring such a recitation to leave the mortgagee no option in the matter of making advances and that the conduct of the parties left it to the discretion of the lender whether to make such advances. We are unable to agree with this conclusion.

The provision plainly recites that upon acceptance and recordation of the mortgage, the grantee (mortgagee) is "absolutely" and "unconditionally" bound to make the advances. Had the recitation stopped at the end of the first sentence, we presume there would have been no quarrel with it. If, therefore, there is any deficiency in the provision, it must be created by the last sentence which provides that "such advances will be made as requested by the grantor as such work progresses." We do not believe that this language grants the mortgagee any option in the matter. On the contrary, whatever options there are rest with the mortgagor. If he causes the work to progress and requests the advances, the mortgagee has no choice other than to make them.

. . .

We hold that the language in the construction money mortgages unconditionally required Modern American to make advances to Long and that they should take priority over the mechanics' and materialmen's liens.

Arkansas Louisiana Gas Company has filed a cross-appeal asserting that the chancellor did not accord it the priority to which it is entitled. We believe this point is well taken. The trial court held that Ark.Stats. 85–9–312 (Repl.1961), dealing with priorities among conflicting security interests in the same collateral, was determinative of the rights of Arkansas Louisiana Gas Company. It was, however, stipulated that the kitchen range and oven were fixtures, and the chancellor held that the heating-air-conditioning units and cooling towers became fixtures when installed. We are of the opinion that under these circumstances, the applicable statute is 85–9–313 which is the provision of the Uniform Commercial Code designed to establish priority of security interests in fixtures. The appropriate provisions of that statute are as follows:

> "(2) A security interest which attaches to goods before they become fixtures takes priority as to the goods over the claims of all persons

who have an interest in the real estate except as stated in subsection (4).

"(4) The security interests described in subsections (2) and (3) do not take priority over

"(c) a creditor with a prior encumbrance of record on the real estate to the extent that he made subsequent advances if * * * the subsequent advance under the prior encumbrance is made or contracted for without knowledge of the security interest and before it is perfected."

Under this statute if Arkansas Louisiana's security interest in the goods, although not yet perfected, *attached* to the goods before they became fixtures, it would take priority, as to the goods only, over the prior recorded mortgages to the extent that advances were made under these mortgages before the goods were affixed to the realty.

Ark.Stat. 85–9–204(1) provides that a security interest attaches when there is an agreement that it attach and value is given and the debtor has rights in the collateral. The chancellor found that as between Arkansas Louisiana and Long, the security interest attached before the goods became fixtures.

All of the purchase money had been advanced before the goods became fixtures, and it is apparent from the record that some construction funds were advanced before and some were advanced afterward. In order to establish the extent to which Arkansas Louisiana is entitled to priority as to its goods which became fixtures, it will be necessary to determine in each case how much money had been advanced under the construction money mortgages before the goods became fixtures and how much was advanced thereafter.

It is likewise our holding that the materialmen's liens will take priority over Arkansas Louisiana's attached but unperfected security interest in the goods only to the extent that labor or material was supplied after the goods became fixtures.

It is argued that this permits a "secret lien" and results in inequities to the other lien holders. The answer to this is that there is no inequity in prohibiting a secured creditor from looking to security other than that upon which he relied when he decided to advance the money. Arkansas Louisiana's priority of security interests affects only the goods which became fixtures and not the remaining realty and improvements. Ark.Stat. 85–9–313(5) provides for the removal of the fixtures from the real estate in circumstances of this kind upon the posting of adequate security for the payment of damages resulting from the removal.

Appellant House argues, however, first: That Arkansas Louisiana's security interest attached at the time of the execution of the blanket security agreement on November 30, 1964, and that all the mortgage funds were advanced after that date; and, second: That this issue was raised by Arkansas Louisiana for the first time on appeal. We consider both of these arguments to be without merit. A security interest cannot attach under Ark.Stat. 85–9–204(1) until value is given and the debtor has rights in the collateral, and, in any event, it is important only to determine whether the security interest attached *before* the goods became fixtures. The significant time in determining the extent of priority is the time the goods were affixed to the real property, for it is only after this has been done that a prior mortgagee may be induced to make further advancements by seeing the fixtures in place.

. . .

This case must be reversed and remanded for determination of the amounts advanced under each construction money mortgage prior to and after the goods were affixed to the realty in question, for similar determinations in connection with the mechanics' and materialmen's liens, and for establishment of priorities of liens on the fixtures and on the remaining real property in accordance with this opinion.

FOGLEMAN and BYRD, JJ., disqualified.

LEROY AUTREY, Special Justice, joins in the opinion.

SCHROEDER, SECURITY INTERESTS IN FIXTURES *

1975 Arizona State Law Journal 319, 328–331.

III. FIXTURES UNDER THE NEW UCC

A. Scope

Consistent with the old [1962] version, revised [1972] section 9–313 applies only when an Article 9 security interest in fixtures conflicts with a realty interest. Like the old version, the new section does not regulate when an interest in fixtures may arise as the result of the real estate law. The new section, however, does attempt to define fixtures more precisely.

New section 9–313 makes explicit the implicit tripartite classification of property of the old Code. A security interest cannot be created in goods which are "ordinary building materials incorporated into an improvement on land." [71] Fixtures are defined as goods which "become so related to particular real estate that an interest in them arises under real estate law." [72] As under the former version, when the Article 9 security interest has priority, the chattel financer has the right to remove the goods upon reimbursement for physical injury to the property.

The new Article 9 still relies upon other law to define fixtures. The test is whether an interest in the goods arises under real estate law. The comments indicate that the relevant local law should be that

---

* Reprinted by permission of the Arizona State Law Journal, 1975, Ariz.St.L.J. 319.

71. UCC rev. § 9–313(2).

72. UCC rev. § 9–313(1)(a).

"applicable in a three-party situation, determining whether chattel financing can survive as against parties who acquire rights through the affixation of the goods to the real estate." [74]   Thus, like the old Code, new section 9–313 uses pre-Code law to define fixtures.

The new fixture section reduces some of the definitional problems by identifying certain categories of goods for special treatment. The new section introduces two new subclassifications: Readily removable factory or office machines and readily removable replacements of domestic appliances which are consumer goods. To minimize the danger that a chattel financer will be penalized by failing to perceive that these types of goods might become fixtures, priority rules are established which treat these goods like ordinary personal property.

B. Prior Realty Interests

New section 9–313 establishes, as a general rule, priority for purchase money security interests. The chattel financer who has a perfected purchase money security interest will have priority over a conflicting realty interest which arose before the goods were affixed to the real estate. Unlike the old UCC, however, the chattel financer must perfect by a fixture filing which is a filing in the real estate record. As against prior realty interests, the financer has a 10-day grace period in which to perfect.

The new UCC creates two special cases where the Article 9 purchase money financer has priority without a fixture filing. If the goods are readily removable factory or office machines or if they are readily removable replacements of domestic appliances which are consumer goods, a fixture filing is not required. The security interest may be perfected by "any method permitted" under Article 9.[80]   This means that a security interest in qualifying factory and office machines may be perfected by an ordinary Article 9 filing, and security interests in qualifying consumer goods may be perfected without any filing whatsoever. As to both of these categories of goods, however, the chattel financer will have priority only if perfection occurs before the goods become fixtures. No grace period exists under these sections. If the chattel financer fails to perfect, the party with an interest in the realty will have priority unless he has consented to the security interest in writing or the debtor has a right as against this party to remove the goods.

The new Code creates an exception for construction mortgages to the general purchase money priority rule. When a construction mortgage is recorded before the goods become fixtures, the construction mortgage is prior to all security interests created during the period of construction except perfected purchase money interests in readily removable office or factory machines. This priority also carries over to mortgages given to refinance the construction mortgage.

74. § 9–313, Comment 2.   **80.** UCC rev. § 9–313(4)(c).

C. Subsequent Real Estate Interests

The general rule for resolving conflicts between chattel interests and subsequent realty interests is priority of record. If the security interest is perfected by a fixture filing before the real estate interest is of record, the chattel financer will prevail. By the same token, realty interests arising after the goods become fixtures which are recorded before the chattel financer makes a fixture filing have priority. This rule applies even to purchase money security interests. The 10-day grace period for perfection does not apply against realty interests arising after the goods become fixtures.

This priority of record is modified to some extent by a provision allowing the holder of a realty interest to succeed to the priority position of his predecessors in title. Thus, the mortgagee with priority over a later created fixture security interest will be able to assign his mortgage to a subsequent purchaser and give that purchaser the same priority.

Under the general rule, a chattel financer must perfect with a fixture filing in order to have priority over a subsequent real estate interest. The special exceptions for readily removable factory or office machines or readily removable replacements of domestic appliances which are consumer goods modify the general rule. Perfection as to these goods may be accomplished by any method permitted by Article 9.

In addition, a major exception is carved out for conflicts between security interests in fixtures and subsequent real estate lien creditors. The chattel financer will have priority over the lien creditor if he has perfected by any method allowed under the Code.

D. Filing

The new Article 9 filing provisions require the fixture filing to be indexed with real estate mortgages under the names of the debtor, the secured party, and any owner of record of the real estate. The name of the record owner of the real estate must be shown if the debtor does not have an interest of record in the real estate. And, in alternative language, section 9–402 requires the financing statement to contain a legal description of the property. The new provisions also make it easier to consider the recording of a real estate mortgage as a financing statement for a fixture filing.

NOTE

Virtually all states now follow the 1972 version of U.C.C. § 9–313. But see Fla.Stat.Ann. § 679.313 (1991); Md.Com.Law Code Ann. § 9–313 (1991). Arkansas, in which House v. Long was decided, moved to the new version in 1973. Ark.Stats. § 85–9–313. Would House v. Long have been decided differently under the new provisions? It is easy enough to understand the rationale behind requiring a fixture filing to defeat subsequent real estate interests. But what justification is there for the requirement of a fixture filing within ten days to preserve the purchase money priority against *prior* interests?

For a comprehensive examination, see Squillante, The Law of Fixtures: Common Law and the Uniform Commercial Code, 15 Hofstra L.Rev. 191 (Part I), 535 (Part II) (1987). For commentary on the 1962 version of section 9–313, see Coogan, Security Interests in Fixtures under the Uniform Commercial Code, 75 Harv.L.Rev. 1319 (1962); Coogan, Fixtures—Uniformity in Words or in Fact? 113 U.Pa.L.Rev. 1186 (1965); Gilmore, The Purchase Money Priority, 76 Harv.L.Rev. 1333, 1388–1400 (1963); Shanker, An Integrated Financing System for Purchase Money Collateral: A Proposed Solution to the Fixture Problem Under Section 9–313 of the Uniform Commercial Code, 73 Yale L.J. 788 (1964).

For commentary on the 1972 version, see Carlson, Fixture Priorities, 4 Cardozo L.Rev. 381 (1983); Coogan, The New U.C.C. Article 9, 86 Harv.L.Rev. 477 (1973); A.B.A. Comm. on Real Estate Financing, Fixtures and Personal Property and Mortgage Transactions Under U.C.C., 9 Real Prop., Probate & Trust J. 653 (1974); Adams, Security Interests in Fixtures Under Mississippi's Uniform Commercial Code, 47 Miss.L.J. 831 (1976); Berry, Priority Conflicts Between Fixture Secured Creditors and Real Estate Claimants, 7 Mem.St.U.L.Rev. 209 (1977).

B. LEASES

---

1. THE GROUND LEASE AND LEASEHOLD MORTGAGE
G. GRENERT, GROUND LEASE PRACTICE *
7–9; 15–18 (1971).

While a ground lease is a lease of land, it is usually much more than that. It differs fundamentally from the usual lease of space for an office or store in a number of respects, including the following:

First, the improvements on the land, called leasehold improvements, generally are owned or become owned by the lessee. If the land is unimproved, the lease ordinarily contemplates improvements to be constructed by the lessee. If the land is improved, the most common arrangements call for the lessee either to demolish the improvements and construct his own or to purchase the improvements as personal property severed from the land (though in all practical respects they are to be regarded as real property).

Second, ground leases are customarily "net"; the lessee pays for the maintenance of the improvements, all property taxes, fire insurance, and practically everything required to protect the lessor's role of

---

* Reprinted from Ground Lease Practice,   by The Regents of the University of California
by Gerald T. Grenert. Copyright © 1971   fornia.

passive investor. The lessor's position is akin to that of a secured lender in many ways.

Third, long terms characterize ground leases. Seldom is the term less than 35 years, and many leases extend to the statutory limit. Anticipating that conditions may change substantially during the life of a long-term lease, the use clause must be very broad.

Fourth, the needs and requirements, both legal and practical, of the institutional lender must be anticipated by both lessor and lessee.

Fifth, a ground lease is best understood not in lease or property terms but as a financing device.

... The ground lessee's principal purpose is ordinarily to employ leverage, i.e., to hold his cash investment to a minimum in order to maximize the ratio of anticipated return to dollars invested.

Assume that an owner desires to receive all cash for improved property, e.g., a neighborhood shopping center, that he values at one million dollars. The property consists of 200,000 sq. ft. of land (5 "commercial" acres) with 50,000 sq. ft. of rentable space leased at an average of 25 cents per square foot. Conventional first trust deed financing is available for $800,000. This requires $200,000 cash from the buyer. The buyer is willing to pay the asking price of $1,000,000, but is either unwilling or unable to put up the $200,000 cash. One reason for the buyer's reluctance is that the estimated cash flow income of about $40,000 per year (item 8 on the table) would constitute a return of only 20 percent on the $200,000 investment. The buyer is willing to invest $100,000 (on which the cash flow income would constitute a return of approximately 40 percent), but 90 percent trust deed financing is unavailable.

Either party's attorney should ask whether a ground lease could be used in this situation. The buyer might find a pension fund willing to buy the land at its fair market value (let us assume $2.50 per sq. ft., totaling $500,000) and to lease it to the buyer for $40,000 per year (an 8 percent yield for the pension fund). Assuming that the improvements are worth an additional $500,000, the buyer could pay the owner $100,000 in cash, plus the proceeds of a loan for $400,000, secured by a leasehold mortgage (or a fee title mortgage, assuming that the lessor was willing to subordinate his land to the encumbrance). If the replacement cost of the improvements exceeded $500,000, the likelihood of obtaining a loan for $400,000 would be enhanced. The buyer's advantage from the use of leverage is illustrated by the following table.

	Outright purchase $200,000 cash investment * $800,000 loan, 7½% interest, 20-yr. amortization	Ground lease $100,000 cash investment † $400,000 loan, 7½% interest, 20-yr. amortization
1. Assumed gross income after operating expenses (50,000 sq. ft. × $.25 × 12)	$150,000	$150,000
2. Rent (8% yield to owner on land worth $500,000)		40,000
3. First year interest (approx.)	60,000	30,000
4. First year principal (approx.)	17,340	8,670
5. Assumed depreciation (straight line) ($500,000 cost over 40 yrs.)	12,500	12,500
6. Assumed income subject to tax (1 minus 2, 3, and 5)	77,500	67,500
7. Income tax at assumed effective rate of 44% ‡	34,100	29,700
8. "Spendable" cash flow income (1 minus 2, 3, 4, and 7) **	38,560	41,630
9. Cash flow income as percentage of cash invested	19.3%	41.6%

CHECKLIST FOR INTERVIEWING

This checklist is for interviewing purposes only. ...

1. Parties and Title

Who is lessor (individual, husband and wife, general partnership, limited partnership, corporation, trustee, executor, administrator)? What is his title?

Who is lessee?

What is lessee's financial strength?

Are there outstanding encumbrances or leases that must be cleared for the lessee to have clear title and right to possession?

If there are outstanding loans, are they to be discharged and paid off, or subordinated to the new lease? If they are to be paid off, do they provide for right to prepay? Assuming they do, where is the cash coming from to pay them off?

---

* As part of $1,000,000 purchase price.

† For purchase or construction of improvements worth $500,000.

‡ Actually, taxable income is subject to many more elements than are indicated here. See CCH US Master Tax Guide 80 (1969). Moreover, the results in the above example depend on the various facts assumed for this illustration.

** "Cash flow income" in the real estate trade usually does *not* contemplate deducting item 7, estimated income tax.

2. Premises

Is the land unimproved? Underimproved (structures to be removed by lessee)? Well improved (structures to be used by lessee)?

Are any problems presented by the site or its environment?

Does lessee have a minimum square footage requirement? What are lessee's other minimum expectations? Has a recent survey been made?

How is property described in preliminary title report? In lessor's deed?

3. Improvements

Are there buildings on the land? If so, does lessee intend to use them? Will lessee have the right to demolish them in the future?

Must lessee insure against damage? Must he reconstruct? What are the provisions for reconstruction near end of term? Does lessor have the right to approve financing for reconstruction? Can lessee avoid the lease if destruction occurs before the term begins?

Will income tax depreciation on those existing improvements belong to lessor or lessee?

Does lessee have a duty to construct new improvements on the land in the near future? If so, does lessor have a right to approve plans and specifications?

Are any new improvements constructed on the land to remain on the land at the expiration of the lease?

Can lessee remove any improvements during the middle or latter part of the lease term? If so, how is lessor to be protected against (a) liens, (b) failure to rebuild?

Can or should lessor have the right to approve size, height, design or function of new improvements?

Can or should lessor have the right to approve insurance? Is lessor protected against diversion of insurance proceeds to lender?

4. Term

Are legal requisites and limits complied with? What are lender's requirements respecting term? When is the term to begin? Possession? Does the commencement date present perpetuities problems?

How do lessor and lender view lease provisions in light of possible termination before expiration of term?

Should term be extended and reconstruction required if improvements are damaged or destroyed near end of term? Will lender acquiesce?

Shall lessee have a right to extend or renew? An option or first refusal to buy?

5. Uses and Purposes

What is to be lessee's use of premises? Does lessee have required flexibility? Is lessor protected against diminution in rent, zoning downward, reduction of market value, or impairment of security?

Is lease contingent on lessee's being able to use the property for a particular purpose? If so, has a means of clearing the contingency been discussed, i.e., an option period, escrow, etc.?

If lessee's desired use cannot be accomplished, can he terminate the lease without liability? ...

6. Zoning

Did lessor make representations to lessee concerning zoning or anything else that would affect lessee's ability to use the land? If so, what are those representations?

Assuming lessor made no such representations, does he believe that zoning variances or exceptions will be required for lessee's desired use? If so, who is to be responsible for procuring zoning variance? Who is to pay for any additional legal or other expenses required to accomplish variances?

7. Deposits, Bonuses

Is there to be a good faith deposit by lessee? If so, is deposit to be in the form of prepaid rent, bonus for lessor's entering into lease, or security for faithful performance by lessee?

Can lessor commingle the deposit with his own funds? Must he pay interest to lessee?

8. Rent and Other Payments

What are proposed monetary arrangements?

Is rent to be net to lessor, i.e., spendable by lessor after all carrying charges on the premises have been paid? Any offsets?

Is initial minimum rent based on market value and cap rate?

Does lessor have benefit of outside appraisal or opinion on the fairness of the agreed rent? On the formula for escalation?

Are there any escalation provisions regarding rent (such as cost-of-living index or an override based on percentage of gross receipts)?

At what intervals should variation in rent occur?

What other charges is lessee to pay?

9. Financing and Subordination. ...

Is terminology of subordination understood?

Has lessor agreed to subordinate his land (and lease) to the lien of a lender who will supply funds to construct or buy new improvements? If so, is lessor aware that he may lose his land if lessee defaults and lender forecloses?

If lessor has agreed to subordinate his land, has this factor been considered in the amount of rent he is to be paid or the amount of security to be posted by tenant?

Does or should lessor have the right to approve of mortgage financing in its final form if he subordinates? If he does not subordinate?

If lessor subordinates to lessee's financing at beginning of lease, should he or must he do so for future new construction (sometimes called second round)?

Is lessor protected against personal liability? Against lessee's mortgaging out? Against misapplication of loan funds?

Regardless of whether lessor subordinates, is lessee's ability to obtain financing a precondition to final consummation of lease? If not, should it be?

If financing is a contingency, what are minimum and maximum amount, interest rate, term, allowable loan points, and other charges?

Has effect of physical condition been considered?

If lessee is to construct new improvements in the near future, where is his financing to come from? Have any of the details of lessee's financing been discussed?

10. Chattel Financing

Does lessee have unrestricted rights to finance the purchase of furniture, equipment, etc.?

Does lessor, or should he, agree to subordinate his interest to the lien of any proposed chattel lender? If so, under what safeguards for lessor?

Is lessor to have an express lien on chattels regardless of whether the lien is inferior and subordinate to that of the chattel lender or leasehold mortgagee? Is this fair to lessee?

Are lender's and subtenants' requirements for lease provisions known?

11. Loss or Destruction of Improvements

What happens if the improvements (regardless of who constructed them) are destroyed?

If loss is covered by insurance?

If loss is uninsured, e.g., earthquake, flood, etc.?

12. Condemnation

What happens if there is a partial taking of the land, but not of any buildings, due to a condemnation?

What happens if there is a partial taking by condemnation which also destroys or removes some, but not all, of the improvements? Must lessee rebuild?

13. Brokers

Are there dealings with brokers or finders, and if so, is there a firm arrangement concerning their commissions or fees?

Has broker or finder or any other agent of landowner made any representations concerning the use to which the land could be put by this lessee?

14. Assignment and Subletting ...

15. Liability, Insurance

Is lessor indemnified against *all* liability for personal injury or property damage? Has insurer waived subrogation? Can policy be modified?

Is amount of coverage adequate for possible risks in future years of the term? Is insurer financially responsible?

KAHN, RENEWAL RENTALS IN LONG–TERM LEASES,* 4 Real Est.Rev. 42–44 (Summer 1974): ... A poorly drawn lease of real estate may not only grant the tenant use of the property in return for a stipulated rental, but also transfer to the tenant a substantial financial interest never contemplated by either party to the lease. This can arise because, over the term of the lease, the fair market rental value of the land can move sharply higher than the stipulated rental. Although this inequitable situation may occur at any time during either the original term of the lease or a renewal period, the likelihood of its occurrence obviously increases as the years pass.

Consequently, one of the most difficult matters facing real estate owners and tenants, and their attorneys, is the drafting of long-term ground leases (i.e., a lease of land upon which the tenant is obligated to construct a suitable improvement for its own use or for rental to others). The rental should be modified periodically to remain consistent with changes in the value of the dollar and to represent fairly the rental value of the land.

The parties to this type of transaction face many hazards and problems. Generally, the ground lease rental must be reasonably firm for an initial period of twenty to thirty years in order to make mortgage financing more readily available for new construction. This initial rental can be fixed for the entire period or provide for graduated periodic increases. Typically, these ground leases also contain one or more renewal periods for which the rental is to be fixed at the time the option to renew is exercised. It is with such rent-fixing procedures that this article is concerned. Substantial changes of rental values may have taken place, the general economy may have changed, and some measure of inflation usually can be expected to have occurred.

SHOULD APPRAISERS FIX LAND VALUE OR A FAIR RENT?

Most ground leases provide that if the parties themselves cannot agree to a new rental figure at the end of the initial lease term, the matter must be turned over to appraisers and arbitrators. The intention is to insure a fair market rental during the renewal period. Despite this intention, the lease clauses that control the appraisal function often are drafted in a way to produce numerous difficulties for those charged with reaching a decision.

In every assignment in which our office has been engaged, the reappraisal clause requires that the appraiser find land value only. A percentage of this land value, designated by the lease, is then used to produce the rental figure to be paid during the renewal period. If the appraisers find the land value to be $500,000, for example, and the rental percentage required by the lease is 6 percent, the annual rental is automatically set at $30,000. The appraiser is not fixing a fair rental; the lease prevents this from occurring. Appropriate percentage rental figures fluctuate, since they are tied to interest rates and investment rates. During the 1940s, the rate designated by leases may have been 4 percent, 5 percent, or 6 percent. During the 1970s, 1980s, and thereafter, similar property may carry land rental rates of 7 percent, 8 percent, 9 percent, or higher, or may even revert to rates prevailing in the 1940s. The appraiser can make this determination after thoroughly investigating leases currently being made in the market.

The reason for having an appraisal review after twenty or thirty years is to determine the *fair market rental value* of the land, not the land value. Why should leases not require appraisers to set land "rental" value rather than land "price" value? What the principals really want is to agree on a fair land rent, not on the value of the land. An inflexible percentage-of-land-value lease clause prevents the appraiser from fixing an objective fair market rental value. ...

Some clauses will require that the appraiser must consider the land as unimproved and ignore the fact that there is a tenanted building on the site. By contrast, other clauses may require that the land value be set to specifically apply to the present improvement. Each clause is inequitable and prevents the appraiser from producing a fair rental after careful consideration of all factors.

If he must consider the land as being unimproved, he must ignore the additional costs that a developer must incur for the site after giving consideration to the cost of making it ready for a new structure.

On the other hand, if the revaluation restriction gives consideration only to the land value under the existing structure, the appraiser is prohibited from consideration of substitute land uses. Neither may he consider an assemblage even if the lessee controls the adjacent properties.

To illustrate this problem more specifically, consider an example. The initial lease period is twenty years, and the lease provides for renewal options for an additional thirty years. Although there is a two-story commercial building on the site when the lease renewal is being negotiated, the lease states that the rental must be consistent with the current land value as if there were no building on the site. Over the twenty years of the original lease term, the location has become suitable for a commercial-office skyscraper, and the space is in high demand.

Obviously, the site has a much higher use than that provided by the current building, and the leasehold tenant can readily pay the higher land rental and erect a new building or sell his leasehold to another developer. Since it pays to demolish the small building and erect a skyscraper in this situation, the appraiser should be permitted to consider the higher-use factor. ...

A.B.A. SECTION OF REAL PROPERTY, PROBATE AND TRUST LAW, COMMITTEE ON LEASES, GROUND LEASES AND THEIR FINANCING *

4 Real Property, Probate & Trust Journal 437, 453–462 (1969).

III. LEASEHOLD MORTGAGE

A. *Nature of Leasehold Mortgage*

A lender whose security is a leasehold mortgage, that is a security interest in the interest of the tenant under a lease, has the same concerns as any lender secured by a fee or any other mortgagee would have, plus certain special concerns which are peculiar to the fact that the security is a leasehold mortgage. It is only the latter aspects which will be covered in this Section.

The principal special consideration of a lender secured by a leasehold mortgage is that the security of the lender is a defeasible estate under circumstances where the lender cannot cure all defaults. Therefore, the leasehold mortgagee must be in a position to control all contingencies which could terminate the tenant's leasehold estate and thus wipe out the lender's security. He should have notice of defaults and an opportunity to cure them.

The leasehold mortgagee is in effect a third party to the principal lease, a tenant once removed. The leasehold mortgagee must have at least all of the rights which the tenant has. A clause providing the landlord and tenant will not modify or cancel the principal lease or surrender the leased premises without the prior written consent of the leasehold mortgagee may be required by the mortgagee even in states where the mortgagee would not be bound by the action without such consent.

It is therefore desirable that the lease be drafted in contemplation of a mortgage of the leasehold estate by the tenant. An awareness by both landlord and tenant of the requirements of a proposed mortgagee is essential. If the lease is so drawn at the outset, a saving in both time and expense will result. If secondary financing will be required by the tenant, problems with respect to conceivable conflicts between encumbrances will have to be provided for.

B. *What is Security?*

The lender's security is the tenant's leasehold estate, which is essentially the right to possession of the leased premises for a stated term provided that the tenant performs the covenants and satisfies the conditions of the lease.

Prior to closing a leasehold mortgage, the leasehold mortgagee should be sure the tenant is not in default, that the lease is in full force and effect, that all conditions for effectiveness of the lease are satisfied, that the leasehold mortgagee knows what the entire lease contains, including all amendments, and that tenant's estate is not primed by prior encumbrances which are unsatisfactory to the leasehold mortgagee either because they violate statutory requirements or because they pose undue business risks. Therefore, a title search by the mortgagee and warranties by the tenant are required. In addition, the best protection for the leasehold mortgagee is to obtain an estoppel certificate from the landlord.

C. *Provisions of Lease*

1. TERM OF LEASE

The term of the lease should be as long as the term of the mortgage plus one year, if possible, but in all events a period sufficient to enable the mortgagee to foreclose its mortgage.

To be financible, a leasehold must be acceptable to the proposed mortgagee and comply with the legal investment or insurance or banking laws of the domicile of the mortgagee. In general, this means that there must be no way in which the leasehold can be cut off or terminated without a right in the mortgagee to preserve its security. For example, the insurance companies law of Massachusetts permits investment in loans ... "upon leasehold estates in improved unencumbered real property ..."[70] and the laws of New Jersey permit life insurance companies to invest in "unencumbered ... leasehold real estate ...."[71] The New Jersey law goes on to provide that an estate is not deemed encumbered by reason of certain listed encumbrances "provided that the security created by the mortgage or trust deed on such real estate or interest therein is a first lien thereon." Thus, in Massachusetts, the leasehold must be on unencumbered real estate while in New Jersey the leasehold itself must be unencumbered and the

---

70. Mass.Gen.Laws ch. 175, § 63.   **71.** N.J.Stat.Ann. 17:24–17c.

mortgage a first lien on the leasehold. Both Mark and Hyde [72] point out the distinction between the two statutes cited above—i.e., that the New Jersey type law might permit an encumbered fee with an unencumbered leasehold—and then proceed to recommend that in any event a ground lease should be superior in all respects to any mortgage on the fee.

Statutory limitations on leasehold mortgages must be considered. In addition to the statutory rules in many jurisdictions limiting the principal amount of a loan to a certain percentage of the value of the security, there are special limitations in many jurisdictions on leasehold mortgages, and requirements that the lease have a minimum term which is longer than the term of the loan. In this connection, the leasehold mortgagee should pay particular attention to clauses giving the landlord the right to terminate the lease later in the term in the event of destruction of improvements. Any such right must be limited so that the basic statutory requirement on term is not infringed. Even if there is no statutory rule on length of the term, the leasehold mortgagee would want to have a lease term longer than the life of the loan and no right in the landlord to terminate the lease by reason of destruction of improvements.

If the lease is subordinated to the fee mortgage, but the fee mortgagee executes a nondisturbance agreement, the tenant may nevertheless find that he cannot mortgage his leasehold interest. The laws of some states and the policies of the mortgagees require that the leasehold be on the "unencumbered fee." A bare nondisturbance agreement will not protect the leasehold mortgagee in case of fire or condemnation. Even if all contingencies could be covered by a properly drawn nondisturbance agreement, counsel for the tenant should not consider a subordination to a fee mortgage because, by doing so, he might limit the financibility of his client's interest under the laws or policies of some states and some mortgagees.

If financibility of the leasehold is not a significant matter to the tenant, it would be possible to permit a senior fee mortgage. The tenant desiring nevertheless to protect himself should then insist on protective provisions in a nondisturbance agreement which should, in all events, be executed by the fee mortgagee. The agreement should reserve to the tenant the proceeds of condemnation or fire insurance on the tenant's improvements so that the tenant can replace such improvements. The amount of the senior loan should be limited so that the rent reserved in the lease will be sufficient in amount to amortize the senior mortgage (i.e., the mortgage should be a direct reduction loan in such amount that equal constant payments not exceeding the rent over a term not exceeding the lease term will discharge the loan in full). The tenant should have a right to notice of any default of the landlord

---

72. Hyde, Leasehold Mortgages, XII Proc. Ass'n. Life Ins. Counsel 659, 660 (1959); Mark, Leasehold Mortgages: Practical Considerations, 14 Bus.Law. 609, 616 (1959).

under the senior mortgage, together with the right, specifically granted by the mortgage, to cure any such default and to apply the cost of such action against the rent. Even with all of the protections outlined above, a lease, being a defeasible estate, might be subject to termination by causes beyond the control of the tenant. Therefore, the protections of a traditional nondisturbance agreement remain inadequate.

The landlord should have little objection to placing the lease first. The true security is the improvement and investment to be made by the tenant. So long as the tenant will erect improvements upon the premises the landlord will have substantial security. After putting the lease first, the landlord normally retains the right to mortgage his reversion and the rent payable under the lease. If the tenant is a so-called "high credit tenant," the landlord will be enabled to obtain a substantial mortgage loan.

2. RIGHT TO ENCUMBER

In the absence of statutory or contractual restrictions, the tenant may assign, sublet or mortgage the term, and the same right is generally extended to his successors. Nevertheless, it is desirable to have express authorization in the lease for the tenant to obtain a leasehold mortgage, in part because, as will be seen below, there are certain express rights of a leasehold mortgagee which are in some cases greater than the rights a tenant would ordinarily have in a lease. On balance, in the modern world of commercial financing, it seems appropriate for a tenant to have broad rights to obtain a leasehold mortgage even if this involves some limitation on the landlord's ordinary rights under the lease.

The consent to encumber the leasehold should expressly state that such consent includes both the right of the mortgagee to foreclose and also to acquire the leasehold estate at the foreclosure sale or by the acceptance of a grant or assignment of the leasehold estate in lieu of foreclosure. Of course, the tenant's loan secured by a leasehold mortgage will be smaller than the loan the tenant could have obtained by a mortgage secured against the landlord's fee interest. However, if the landlord will not agree to allow the tenant to place a mortgage against the landlord's fee interest, or if the landlord will agree only to allow such placement for initial construction but not thereafter, obtaining a leasehold mortgage at least provides the tenant with some method of financing a substantial part of development of the property.

3. EFFECT OF OPTIONS

The lease may contain one or more options in the tenant to renew the lease, an option in the tenant to purchase the landlord's interest, or right of first refusal on the part of the tenant to purchase the landlord's interest on the same price and terms as are contained in an offer to purchase which is acceptable to the landlord. From the point of view of the leasehold mortgagee, it is desirable for all options of the tenant to be exercisable by the leasehold mortgagee as attorney-in-fact for the tenant. Further, the leasehold mortgagee may wish to have the tenant's option specifically assigned by the tenant to the leasehold mortgagee. In any event, the documents should clearly provide that any options of the tenant under the lease are security to the leasehold mortgagee for the leasehold mortgage.

Section 70b of the Bankruptcy Act gives the trustee in bankruptcy power to assume or reject executory contracts of the bankrupt, with the following limitation as to leases in the case of bankruptcy of the landlord: "Unless a lease of real property expressly otherwise provides, a rejection of the lease or any covenant therein by the trustee of the landlord does not deprive the tenant of his estate." [80]   Since it is unclear whether the options of the tenant are part of his "estate," it is desirable, from the viewpoint of the leasehold mortgagee, to have the tenant exercise all exercisable options prior to the placing of the leasehold mortgage so that these options will not be executory contracts and will thus not be subject to the possibility of being rejected by the landlord's trustee in bankruptcy. It is for this reason that mortgages require that the initial term be for the maximum term needed to amortize the loan.

If the tenant has made any deposits with the landlord, such as security deposits against the tenant's obligations to the landlord, it should be provided that these deposits are also secondary security for the leasehold mortgagee. The rights of the landlord in the security deposits are obviously prime, but, subject to those rights, the leasehold mortgagee should have rights in them. There may be no residual rights at all for the leasehold mortgagee's benefit, but there are residual rights in some cases if, for example, a deposit is to be returned before the end of the term of the lease. A security deposit during construction is another example.

4.   Freedom of Assignment

It is essential that the tenant have the unqualified right to assign the leasehold estate without the landlord's consent. This will permit the mortgagee or purchaser at the foreclosure sale to acquire the leasehold estate without the landlord's consent. This right should also apply to successive assignees or successors of the purchaser at the foreclosure sale, and grantees or assignees of the leasehold estate in lieu of foreclosure under the mortgage.

Partial restrictions on the right of the tenant to assign his leasehold estate will be acceptable to the mortgagee so long as such restrictions do not apply to the mortgagee, its assignees or any other assignees, *ad infinitum*. Such restrictions, for example, require that the assignee meet certain specified requirements of the landlord as to designated financial worth. The effect of limiting the right to assign the leasehold estate only to the immediate successor of the purchaser at the foreclosure sale is unacceptable to the mortgagee.

80. See, e.g., In re N.Y. Investors Mutual Group, 153 F.Supp. 772 (S.D.N.Y.1957), aff'd sub nom. Cohen v. East Netherland Holding Co., 258 F.2d 14 (2d Cir.1958).

The assignee of the tenant must not be required to assume the lease, and thus have personal liability. It is desirable for the leasehold mortgagee to have the right to take over the tenant's estate through a nominee. It may be satisfactory to the leasehold mortgagee to have personal liability while the lender is in possession of the premises on the doctrine of privity of estate or with the assumption agreement limited to that period.

5. RESTRICTION ON SUBLETTING

The value of the leasehold as an asset attractive to a mortgagee may depend on the strength of subleases and right to procure prime subtenants with a right in the tenant to sublease to such subtenants. The provisions permitting subletting should be as liberal as those permitting assignment.

The leasehold mortgagee has the usual interest of a lender in operating leases—credit standing of subtenant, term, rent, options, condemnation provisions, insurance, etc. With respect to the principal lease, it has been noted that the leasehold mortgagee is essentially a tenant once removed. With respect to subleases, the leasehold mortgagee is essentially a landlord once removed.

The leasehold mortgagee may require conditional assignment of subleases by the tenant to the leasehold mortgagee; that is, an assignment by this tenant of its rights under subleases which assignment is inoperative until such time as the tenant defaults on the leasehold mortgage, at which time the condition operates so that the leasehold mortgagee has the ability to come in and collect the subrent directly from the subtenant.

The leasehold mortgage may require approval by the leasehold mortgagee of all subleases and that there be no modification or cancellation of subleases, or surrender thereof, or prepayment of rent without the consent of the leasehold mortgagee. If the leasehold mortgagee forecloses upon default by the tenant, the leasehold mortgagee will be unhappy to discover that the subtenant has substantially prepaid the rent to the tenant who has gone to Mexico. Such a clause must be binding on the subtenant to be effective as a practical matter.

Since termination of the principal lease terminates subleases, if the leasehold mortgagee is relying on the subleases, the leasehold mortgagees will want an affirmative agreement by the subtenant to attorn to the leasehold mortgagee if the leasehold mortgagee or its assignee becomes the tenant under a "new lease" (see discussion below). In such event, the leasehold mortgagee should be willing to give a subtenant a nondisturbance clause.

6. ESTOPPEL CERTIFICATES

The lease should require that both the landlord and the tenant furnish estoppel certificates to the other and to the leasehold mortgagee at reasonable intervals on request so that the mortgagee, purchaser at foreclosure sale or assignee of the lease may obtain confirmation that the lease is in full force and effect and that neither party is in default.

7. TENANT'S DEFAULT—TERMINATION OF LEASE

The leasehold mortgagee's basic concern is that the lease may be terminated, thus extinguishing the tenant's leasehold estate and the leasehold mortgagee's security, without the leasehold mortgagee being able to cure the default. Therefore, the leasehold mortgagee must have all of the rights to cure defaults which the tenant has, plus protection if there is a default which the leasehold mortgagee cannot cure.

The formalities with respect to default can be quite important. It is not enough for the leasehold mortgagee to have a provision in the leasehold mortgage that the tenant must notify the leasehold mortgagee in the event of notice of default being sent to the tenant from the landlord. The tenant may fail to do so, either inadvertently or, because he does not want the leasehold mortgagee to know he is in trouble, deliberately. Accordingly, it is important to the leasehold mortgagee to have a provision in the lease that the landlord will not only give notice of default to the tenant but will also give notice of default to the leasehold mortgagee. The leasehold mortgagee prefers a provision that any notice of default by the landlord to the tenant is not effective unless a copy is sent to the leasehold mortgagee. Of course, this requirement should bind the landlord only in respect of a leasehold mortgage of which he has notice.

The leasehold mortgagee should have time to cure any default by the tenant, such time period being at least as long as the time period allowed the tenant, preferably longer, because institutions move slowly and because the leasehold mortgagee does not want to have to cure a default unless the tenant fails to cure the default.

There are essentially three types of default: default in the payment of money, default other than in the payment of money but which default is curable by the leasehold mortgagee, and default other than the payment of money which is not curable by the leasehold mortgagee.

Default by the tenant in the payment of money does not raise any special problems. The leasehold mortgagee should have the right to cure if the tenant does not. Rent escalation clauses in the principal lease which will result in an increase in rent geared to the cost of living or adjustments based on revaluation of the property during the term of the leasehold mortgages are not acceptable to the leasehold mortgagee because it cannot allow the amount of rent under the principal lease which must be paid ahead of the leasehold mortgage to escalate enormously without regard to the ability of the property to produce sufficient income both to pay the rent and to amortize the mortgage. Increases geared to the income produced by the property from subtenants should, however, be acceptable.

Defaults by the tenant, other than the payment of money, which are curable by the leasehold mortgagee, also cause no peculiar problems, although some special provisions may be necessary. The leasehold mortgagee has no problem as long as the leasehold mortgagee has the ability and time to cure. For example, if the tenant defaults on the duty to repair, the leasehold mortgagee must have the ability to gain possession of the leased premises in order to make the needed repairs. The default should not permit the landlord to terminate the lease if the mortgagee proceeds promptly to obtain possession and continues diligently thereafter to prosecute the curing of the default and if the rental and other rental amounts are paid by the mortgagee.

The third type of default is a default by the tenant which is not subject to being curable by the mortgagee, *e.g.,* bankruptcy of tenant, receivership, assignment for the benefit of creditors by the tenant, abandonment of the leased premises by the tenant and violation of state or local ordinances. The lease should expressly state that, provided the mortgagee, after receiving notice of such default and prior to the expiration of the tenant's grace period, promptly institutes foreclosure proceedings to foreclose the mortgage and proceeds with due diligence to prosecute such foreclosure proceedings to a conclusion, the landlord will not cancel the lease if, during such period, the mortgagee continues to make rental payments and discharges other monetary obligations required of the tenant by the lease.

8. NEW LEASE

As added protection to the mortgagee, the lease should require the landlord to covenant that, if the lease is terminated due to the tenant's default, or in the event of abandonment by the tenant, the landlord will enter into a new lease with the mortgagee upon the same terms and conditions as are contained in the lease with the tenant and for the balance of the term thereof. The advantage to the landlord is that he avoids becoming involved in the bankruptcy of the tenant. The new lease could even provide for the revival of rights, such as options, which may have lapsed under the old lease.

In situations where the landlord is willing to give an option to purchase his fee interest or the landlord is leasing to a tenant at a high rent under circumstances where the tenant will not execute the lease unless a particular leasehold mortgage is obtained, and the landlord is desirous of accommodating the wishes of the mortgagee, it may be possible for the mortgagee to obtain an option to purchase the fee interest of the landlord in the event of default by the tenant. The Federal Housing Administration, when it insures a loan secured by a leasehold mortgage, requires that the Secretary of Housing and Urban Development have an option to purchase the landlord's fee interest within 12 months after FHA has acquired title to the property by assignment or foreclosure. This requirement has made leasehold mortgages insured by FHA rather unattractive to borrowers.

The disadvantages to such a provision are the possibility that the new lease will be subject to intervening liens which may have attached to the fee subsequent to the closing of the leasehold mortgage, the enforceability of such a provision against the landlord's trustee in bankruptcy and the possibility that such a provision will violate the rule against perpetuities.

While a new lease provision is desirable, in order to prevent intervening encumbrances from priming the leasehold mortgage, there should be a provision that the landlord cannot terminate the lease so long as curable defaults are cured. Or, to put it another way, defaults by the tenant which are not curable by the leasehold mortgagee are not defaults as between the landlord and leasehold mortgagee.

9. INSURANCE—DAMAGE OR DESTRUCTION TO PREMISES

The lease should require the tenant to insure the improvements under a standard loss payable endorsement (such as BFU438 in California) with the insurance proceeds to be payable to the mortgagee, if it be an institutional lender or, if not, then to a named bank or title company as insurance trustee. Consideration should also be given to requiring replacement type insurance.

The proceeds are generally required to be disbursed by the trustee to the tenant as restoration work progresses upon submission to the trustee of appropriate architect's certificates, subject to a holdback with respect to each payment of ten per cent or other agreed percentage until the work of construction is completed, and the time for lien claimants to lien the property has expired.

The lease should specify that, except in case of a nominal loss in a designated amount, the mortgagee should be permitted to participate in the adjustment of the loss and in any arbitration proceedings pertaining thereto.

If the lease does not provide for rent abatement during the period of restoration (and a ground lease generally does not), the tenant should be required to maintain rent or business interruption insurance either by the lease or the mortgage.

10. CONDEMNATION

The mortgagee will want the first right to the share of the condemnation award due the tenant, and the mortgagee will want to be sure that the provisions in the lease giving the tenant a share of the award are adequate to protect the interest of the mortgagee.

If premises are taken to such an extent (i.e., a total or substantial taking) that the lease is terminated, the mortgagee should be first paid an amount sufficient to satisfy the mortgage debt. The mortgagee has no interest in how the balance of the award is apportioned between the landlord and the tenant.

In the event of a nonsubstantial taking that does not result in a termination of the lease, the total award should be paid to the mortgagee, if an institutional lender or, if not, to a trustee for restoration of buildings and improvements, with similar provisions as those provided for insurance trusts.

T. D. BICKHAM CORP. v. HEBERT

Supreme Court of Louisiana, 1983.
432 So.2d 228.

LEMMON, Justice.

The primary issue in this case is the validity of a provision in a lease contract which subordinates the lease to an unspecified future mortgage.

Defendant, a dentist, leased Suite 1717 in Elk Place Medical Plaza (EPMP) on September 1, 1976. The recorded lease provided for a ten-year primary term, with two five-year options, and a monthly rental of $3,448. The lease also contained a subordination clause, which provided:

> "This lease shall at all times be subject and *subordinate* to the lien of *any mortgage* or mortgages *now or hereafter* placed upon said 'EPMP', and to all advances made or hereafter to be made upon the security thereof. Lessee agrees to execute and deliver such further instrument or instruments, subordinating the lease to the lien of any such mortgage or mortgages, at any time same may or shall be desired by any mortgage [sic] or proposed mortgage [sic] of any Lessor." (Emphasis supplied.)

On December 22, 1977, EPMP's owner mortgaged the property in order to retire its interim debt incurred during the construction and renovation of the premises. Contemporaneously with the mortgage, EPMP's owner assigned all the leases on the property to the mortgagee. When the mortgagee foreclosed on the mortgage after the owner's subsequent default, plaintiff purchased the property at a sheriff's sale on October 27, 1980 for $8,600,000. Among the recorded leases shown on the certificate was the one to defendant. Thereafter, plaintiff notified defendant that his lease had been cancelled by the judicial sale, but that occupancy would be allowed to continue, pending renegotiation of the lease. When the parties failed to agree on new terms, plaintiff instituted this eviction proceeding.

The trial court dismissed the suit on the ground that the recorded contract of lease, of which plaintiff had knowledge, did not contemplate cancellation of the lease in the event of a judicial sale. The court of appeal affirmed, holding that the subordination provision was vague, indefinite, repugnant to the bilateral nature of the contract, and against public policy. The court also noted that the defendant was never requested to execute any further instruments specifically subordinating the lease when the mortgage was later placed on the property after his lease. We granted certiorari to review those judgments.

Generally, the lessee of immovable property, in the absence of a violation of the contract, is entitled to peaceable possession of the premises during the continuance of the lease. Even when the lessor sells the property which is subject to a recorded lease, the lessee retains the right to possession, *unless there was a contrary stipulation in the contract.* La.C.C. Art. 2733.

The court of appeal held that the subordination clause in this case was ambiguous and should not be interpreted as a "contrary" stipulation so as to deprive the lessee of his normal right to peaceable possession until the expiration of the lease. However, the pertinent provision clearly states that "[t]his lease *shall* at all times *be* subject and *subordinate to* the lien of *any mortgage* now or *hereafter placed upon*" the property. While defendant may not have realized the legal consequences of consenting to subordination of his lease to a future mortgage by the lessor, the language can hardly be characterized as unclear. Defendant may have disregarded the provision as meaningless, but he certainly could not have understood the provision to have a *different* meaning than that the lease was subject to being placed in a lower position or rank by a mortgage which is granted on the property after the lease.

The second sentence of the subordination provision is likewise unambiguous. The subordination is self-operative by the first sentence, and the second sentence *requires* the lessee to execute a separate document evidencing the subordination of the lessee if the lessor's mortgagee (or proposed mortgagee) desires such an instrument. One cannot reasonably infer from the second sentence that the parties to the lease intended that an additional contract would be necessary before the subordination became effective or that the lessee retained the right to withhold consent to subordinate the lease in the event of a future mortgage.

We therefore hold that the subordination provision contained in the lease constitutes a specific and unambiguous contrary stipulation in which the lessee surrendered his superior position to present and future mortgages.

As to the effect of the subordination provision, La.C.C.P. Art. 2372 expressly provides that property sold at a judicial sale is sold subject to any real charge or lease which is "superior to" the rights of the seizing creditor.[1] Further, La.C.C.P. Art. 2376 provides that a judicial sale results in the cancellation and release of rights which are "inferior to" the right exercised by the seizing creditor.[2] Under these two articles, a judicial sale cancels a right in property sold at a judicial sale which is inferior to the right of the seizing creditor.

---

1. Article 2372 provides:

"The property is sold subject to any real charge or lease with which it is burdened, superior to any mortgage, lien, or privilege of the seizing creditor."

2. Article 2376 provides:

"The sheriff shall give the purchaser a release from the mortgage, lien, or privilege of the seizing creditor, and from all inferior mortgages, liens, and privileges, and he shall direct the recorder of mortgages to cancel their inscriptions in so far as they affect the property sold."

Although there are no Louisiana cases dealing with provisions that subordinate a lease to a future unspecified mortgage, prior cases have consistently held that leases, which are recorded subsequent to a mortgage, are cancelled and dissolved by the judicial sale of the property pursuant to a foreclosure on the mortgage. Conversely, in the absence of the contrary stipulation in the contract, defendant's lease (which was recorded prior to the mortgage foreclosed upon) would not have been cancelled by the judicial sale. This case therefore turns upon the validity of the subordination provision.

Louisiana courts have given effect to contractual provisions altering or modifying the priority of the rights or claims otherwise established by law. See Richey v. Venture Oil and Gas Corp., 346 So.2d 875 (La.App. 4th Cir.1977), cert. denied, 350 So.2d 891, which upheld the validity of a contractual provision subordinating the mortgage to a specified (but subsequently recorded) mortgage. We see no reason in law or in public policy why an unambiguous provision in a lease between two parties with equal bargaining power cannot validly subordinate that contract to an unspecified future mortgage which is contracted in good faith.

Furthermore, a provision subordinating a lease to a future unspecified mortgage is a reasonable contractual provision which has a legitimate business purpose. The owner of an office building or shopping center frequently intends to undertake future renovation or additions and foresees that a future mortgage will be required. A subordination provision is generally included in the leases in anticipation of the requirements of institutional lenders. Because the value of a commercial building is related directly to the building's rental income, the prospective lender will frequently require that his position be superior to existing leases, so that the lender may be protected in the event of foreclosure.[3] When the owner requires a subordination provision in the leases, he protects the value of his property for purposes of obtaining future mortgages.

Of course, the lessee at the time of confection of the lease does not have to consent to a subordination provision which threatens the security of his business in the event of foreclosure. The inclusion or exclusion of such a provision is a negotiable term, just as is the rate of rental. The lessee may also control the future risks by limiting the subordination to institutional mortgagees, to first mortgages, and to specific amounts or specific purposes. (Of course, the lessee normally faces the risk of foreclosure on the mortgage *existing* at the time of execution of the lease if the owner defaults on the existing mortgage.) However, once a lessee consents to a subordination provision (perhaps in exchange for a reduced rental rate), he cannot successfully resist the

---

3. The existence of an attractive lease by a major tenant will generally induce lenders. However, a small tenant in a strategic location or a series of long-term, low-rate leases may discourage a lender who will be saddled with troublesome problems in the event of foreclosure.

termination of the lease if a subsequent mortgagee forecloses on the property through a judicial sale.

Finally, there is no suggestion in this case that the subordination provision has been utilized in bad faith or with fraudulent intent.[4] The first mortgagee foreclosed on EPMP to collect a debt in excess of $8,000,000. Plaintiff, a third party unrelated to either the prior owner or the mortgagee, purchased the building by bidding the highest price at an open judicial sale. The former owner has been forced to seek relief in the bankruptcy court and will derive no benefit from this litigation.

Accordingly, the judgments of the lower courts are reversed, and the matter is remanded to the district court to enter judgment ordering the eviction.

CALOGERO, J., concurs.

WATSON, Justice, dissenting.

When leased property is encumbered with a prior recorded mortgage and there is a foreclosure, the judicial sale dissolves the lease. However, generally, when the lease is recorded first, the lease follows the property into the hands of a buyer.

LSA–C.C. art. 2733 provides:

"If the lessor sells the thing leased, the purchaser can not turn out the tenant before his lease has expired, unless the contrary has been stipulated in the contract."

The subordination clause here does not constitute a specific contrary stipulation within the meaning of the codal article. See Republic Nat. Life Ins. v. Lorraine Realty, 279 N.W.2d 349 (Minn., 1979) where a general nonspecific subordination clause was enforced on equitable grounds because of fifteen years detrimental reliance. However, the result was not cancellation of the lease. In *Republic* the ground lessors subordinated their interest in the leased premises to future mortgages. "Their [the lessors'] interest in the lease, in particular to rent, is subordinated to, *not extinguished by* Republic's [the mortgagee's] interest." 279 N.W.2d at 357. (Emphasis added)

Subordinate is defined in *Black's Law Dictionary,* Fifth Edition, as follows:

"Placed in a lower order, class, or rank; occupying a lower position in a regular descending series; inferior in order, nature, dignity,

---

4. Defendant contends that he made substantial improvements to the leased premises in reliance on the leasing agent's (apparently incorrect) explanation of the subordination provision. The lease contract contained no reference to any obligation on the defendant or the owner as to specific improvements by defendant or to any other provision which might alert a subsequent mortgagee that the subordination provision could be called into question. Moreover, since the lessee undertook any improvements at the risk that an existing mortgagee might foreclose in the event of the owner's default, a subsequent mortgagee who examined the subordination provision would reasonably conclude that the lessee undertook the same risk as to future mortgages.

power, importance, or the like; belonging to an inferior order in classification, and having a lower position in a recognized scale; secondary, minor."

There are no Louisiana cases dealing with this type of clause in a lease and there are no provisions in the Civil Code for subordination of a lease to a future mortgage. Subordination clauses in mortgages have been given effect when the language specified the obligations to which they were subordinate.

LSA–C.C.P. art. 2372, concerning foreclosure sales, provides:

"The property is sold subject to any real charge or lease with which it is burdened, superior to any mortgage, lien, or privilege of the seizing creditor."

This lease, superior by time of recordation to the mortgage of the seizing creditor, states that it is nonetheless inferior to any future mortgage.

"According to traditional civilian notions, a contract of lease establishes personal rights only. * * * [T]he contract of lease produces all the effects of personal rights and none of the effects of real rights. * * Since a recorded lease may be asserted against third persons, the landowner may not grant a predial servitude or other real or personal right in violation of the terms of the lease without the concurrence of the lessee." 2 La.Civ.Law Treat. (Yiannopoulos) 2d at pp. 414 and 418. A fair reading of this subordination provision is in accord with the foregoing statements of Louisiana law. Dr. Hebert, the lessee, had to concur in any future mortgage placed on the leased premises by executing a specific subordination agreement as to that mortgage. It is significant that Dr. Hebert was never asked to execute a specific instrument subordinating his lease to the mortgage placed on the property by The Mutual Life Insurance Company of New York.

In other jurisdictions, subordination clauses which were uncertain and indefinite have not been enforced. Particularly pertinent here is the case of Am. Fed. Sav. & Loan Ass'n v. Orenstein, 81 Mich.App. 249, 265 N.W.2d 111 (1978). A mortgage there contained a subordination clause which provided:

"This Mortgage and Assignment of Leases and Rentals is subject and subordinate in all respects to the following: ...; and all advances, obligations and indebtedness now or hereafter incurred up to the sum of $4,125,000, exclusive of interest, and ...." 265 N.W.2d at 113.

The Michigan court held:

"The ambiguity in the instant subordination clause was so obvious as to put a prudent person on inquiry notice." 265 N.W.2d at 112.

Because of the obvious ambiguity, third persons were not entitled to rely on the publicly recorded subordination clause. The language used in the lease from E.P.M.P. to the defendant, Dr. Hebert, is more vague and ambiguous than that in the *Orenstein* case.

The subordination clause executed by Dr. Hebert is so vague and ambiguous as to put any prospective purchaser on notice that it might not be enforceable. Dr. Hebert understood that sale of the property would not cancel his lease. Nothing to the contrary is clearly specified in the lease's subordination provision or any "further instrument". Therefore, the agreement cannot be interpreted to authorize Bickham, a remote third party, to cancel the lease. There is no basis, in law or equity, to hold that T.D. Bickham Corporation is entitled to unilaterally cancel Dr. Hebert's lease of Suite 1717 in Elk Place Medical Plaza.

I respectfully dissent.

NOTES

1. Was the decision in *Bickham* correct? If Dr. Hebert's consent to subordination had appeared in a purchase money mortgage rather than in a lease, many states would have voided it on grounds of unfairness to the subordinating party. Compare Middlebrook-Anderson Co. v. Southwest Sav. & Loan Ass'n, page 753 above. Does a subordinating tenant like Hebert have more or less of a claim on judicial solicitude than a subordinating mortgagee? Is a tenant more or less likely than a mortgagee to see her investment wiped out by foreclosure of the prime mortgage? Whose interest is more likely to have appreciated during a period of rising land values?

Apparently Hebert's lease called for a flat rent and did not provide for escalators or other means to keep the rent in line with the value of money or of the land. Should *Bickham* have been decided differently if the lease had contained an escalator and thus was less of a losing proposition to the landlord?

Would the lender have lost priority in *Bickham* if the lease had not been recorded? See Ontiveros v. MBank Houston, N.A., 751 F.Supp. 128 (S.D.Tex.1990) (fee mortgagee had "constructive" notice of lease executed prior to mortgage based on tenant's possession, so foreclosure did not extinguish tenant's interest).

See generally, Halper, Planning and Construction Clauses in a Subordinated Ground Lease, 17 Real Est.L.J. 48 (1988); Kobren, Three Perspectives on Ground Lease Negotiations, 19 Real Est.L.J. 40 (1990).

2. *Escalators.* Leases, particularly long term leases, expose the landlord to the risk of decreases in the value of the dollars with which rent is paid and to the risk of increases in real property taxes and maintenance and utility costs. One solution is to provide a formula in the lease for adjusting rental payments to keep pace with changes in the value of the leased property, the tenant's business, or in the economy generally. Thus, as indicated in the excerpt from the Kahn article, rent may be adjusted on the basis of periodic reevaluation of the premises. The parties must be careful, however, to clearly specify the standards by which the property is to be reappraised. See Harris Trust

& Savings Bank v. LaSalle National Bank, 208 Ill.App.3d 447, 153 Ill.Dec. 450, 567 N.E.2d 408 (1990), appeal denied, 137 Ill.2d 665, 156 Ill.Dec. 561, 511 N.E.2d 148 (1991) (remanding for evidentiary hearing on question of whether appraiser was to consider the possibility of assemblage of lots as lease clause was ambiguous). A simpler, though less accurate mechanism for adjusting rents is the "step-up" clause, specifying the amounts and intervals by which rent will be increased. For example, the lease may provide that rent in the first year will be $1,200, to be stepped up in the second year to $1,800, and to $3,000 in the third. Obviously, step-up clauses are only as good as the landlord's and tenant's guesses about the property's future worth.

Linkage or index clauses, requiring periodic adjustments in rent based on a cost of living index such as the United States Bureau of Labor Statistics' consumer price index, operate almost as fluently as step-up clauses and offer greater certainty that rental payments will have a constant economic worth. More specific indices, oriented to the locale in which the property is situated or to the type of business conducted on the leased property, can also be used. If the landlord wants to link rent payments to the tenant's business rather than to an abstract economic index, she may propose that the rent consist in part of a percentage of the tenant's gross receipts from the property. Though most commonly used in leases with retail tenants, percentage rents can also be tailored to ground leases. For example, a ground tenant who builds and operates an office building may agree to give his landlord a percentage of the gross rentals he receives from his tenants.

For details on the theory and practice of rent escalators, see N. Hecht, Long Term Lease Planning and Drafting 39–150 (1974).

3. *Indices.* Parties who incorporate an index in their lease should also install safeguards against events outside their control, such as elimination or alteration of the chosen index. Consider the plight of a California landlord whose lease provided that renewal term rentals would float with local property taxes. At the time the lease was executed, real property taxes were based on the current appraised fair market value of real property and thus, presumably, served as an effective substitute for a more cumbersome appraisal provision in the lease. Subsequently, however, "California voters passed Proposition 13, Cal.Const. art. XIIIA, which limits tax on real property to 1% of the county assessor's valuation of the property as of 1975–1976, and allows a maximum increase in the valuation for property tax purposes of 2% per year. As a result the property taxes on the leased premises did not increase with the value of the property as the parties had expected." Indeed, using the formula, the rent to be paid by the tenant in the first renewal period decreased by 5.08%.

Nonetheless, the Ninth Circuit Court of Appeals rebuffed the landlord's claim for rescission based on frustration: "The passage of Proposition 13 did not render meaningless the entire lease. The lessors continue to receive valuable consideration in return for the use of their property." Waegemann v. Montgomery Ward & Co., Inc., 713 F.2d 452, 453–454 (9th Cir.1983).

4. *Net Lease.* Another way for landlords to reduce the effects of inflation is to shift upkeep expenses from landlord to tenant. In the jargon of the real estate market, a *gross lease* is one under which the landlord pays for repairs, maintenance, insurance and real property taxes. A *net lease* shifts some of these incidents onto the tenant. If the lease shifts all incidents to the tenant, it is a *triple net lease* (sometimes called a *bond lease* to reflect the fixed rate of return to the landlord).

Triple net leases are also attractive to investors who wish to employ the lease as a financing device under which, as landlord, they are effectively in the position of lender and the tenant is effectively in the position of borrower, paying debt service in the form of rent. Like mortgagors generally, the tenant under the net lease will bear all upkeep and tax expenses, thus assuring the landlord of a fixed, net return. For an example of the net lease used as a financing device, consider the next principal case, Frank Lyon Co. v. United States.

5. *Destruction or Condemnation.* The prospect that the leased premises will be condemned or destroyed by fire or other hazard raises several questions for landlord and tenant negotiating a long term lease. Should they provide that the lease be terminated in these circumstances? Should the rent be abated? Who should be entitled to the insurance proceeds or the condemnation award and in what proportions? Should there be an obligation to rebuild and, if so, who should bear it?

The answers reached by landlords and tenants will vary with their relative bargaining strength, the nature of the premises and improvements, and the length and other terms of the lease. One approach commonly taken is to provide that the lease will terminate in the event of complete condemnation or destruction. In the case of condemnation, the tenant will be compensated from the part of the award allocable to the value of his leasehold and the value of any improvements he constructed on the premises. The landlord will receive the rest, presumably the value of her reversionary interest. If fire or other hazard destroys the tenant's improvements, he would receive the insurance proceeds for their value.

Landlord and tenant may provide that in the event of partial condemnation or destruction, the lease can be terminated at the election of either; that rent will be abated proportionately; or that the tenant will rebuild the premises using the insurance or condemnation proceeds. These provisions often connect termination with reconstruction: the tenant may terminate after a partial condemnation or destruction if reconstruction will not be feasible in the circumstances.

Doubtless the most important party in shaping these arrangements is the fee or leasehold mortgagee whose investment in the property likely exceeds the investments of landlord and tenant combined. A mortgagee, whose security consists in part of the good credit of the tenant who will be leasing the premises, will focus carefully on partial condemnation and destruction clauses and will probably insist that the tenant not be allowed to terminate the lease if the interference with his business is insubstantial. Lenders may also require that they receive condemnation awards or insurance proceeds directly, to be used in paying off the mortgage in the event of termination, or to be disbursed by them to the tenant in the event the tenant undertakes reconstruction.

See generally, Committee on Leases, Fire Insurance and Repair Clauses in Leases, 5 Real Prop., Probate & Trust J. 532 (1970); Broadman, Providing in the Lease for the Event of Condemnation, 14 Prac. Lawyer 27 (May 1968).

6. *Federal Income Taxation.* The Internal Revenue Code's treatment of lessors and lessees, like its treatment of fee owners, offers considerable opportunity for strategically timing the incidence of income, expenses, gains and losses. Indeed, the continuing relationship between two parties, and their ability to shift tax burdens and benefits between themselves by contract, gives landlords and tenants an enviable opportunity to manipulate tax consequences with a fine hand.

Acquisition of Lease. While a landlord can take ordinary business deductions for the costs of managing her property, she must capitalize any costs specifically incurred to obtain a tenant. Thus, the landlord cannot deduct broker's commissions and title insurance premiums immediately, but must amortize them over the term of the lease. A tenant's payment of advance rent or a bonus at the time he acquires the lease is taxable as ordinary income to the landlord in the year she receives them. By contrast, receipt of a refundable security deposit to secure the tenant's performance of the lease has no tax consequence for the landlord.

If the tenant incurs costs such as broker's commissions and title premiums in acquiring the lease, he, like the landlord, cannot deduct them presently, but must amortize them over the life of the lease. While the landlord must report bonuses or advance rentals in the year she receives them, the tenant cannot deduct these payments in the year that he makes them. Rather, these outlays are treated as costs of acquiring the lease and must be amortized over the term of the lease. (If the tenant can show that the payment is allocable to a specific period, shorter than the lease term, he can amortize it over the shorter period.) Similarly, if the tenant purchased the lease from a former tenant, he may amortize his cost over the remaining term of the lease. Finally, just as payment of a true security deposit is not taxable to the landlord, it is neither deductible nor amortizable by the tenant.

Depreciation. The landlord, not the tenant, is entitled to take depreciation deductions for any improvements leased to the tenant. If, as is typically the case under a ground lease, it is the tenant who owns the improvement, then the tenant, not the landlord, can take the appropriate depreciation deductions. If the tenant's lease expires before the tenant has fully recovered the cost of the improvement through depreciation deductions, the tenant may deduct the unrecovered cost at the end of the lease.

Disposition of Lease.   On the expiration or cancellation of a lease, the landlord may face several questions.   Suppose the tenant has built a valuable improvement on the premises during the lease term.   Will it constitute income to the landlord when the lease ends?   The Internal Revenue Code expressly provides that the value of a tenant's leasehold improvements at termination of a lease is not income to the landlord. When the landlord later sells or exchanges the property she must, however, pay tax on the gain represented by the improvement since the sales price will reflect the value of the improvement while her basis would not have been stepped up by the value of the improvement. I.R.C. §§ 109, 1019.

What if tenant pays landlord to cancel the lease?   The Regulations provide that such a payment "constitutes gross income for the year in which it is received, since it is essentially a substitute for rental payments."   Treas.Reg. § 1.61–8(b).   Say it is the landlord who pays the tenant to cancel?   This is considered a capital expense, and its specific treatment is governed by the landlord's purpose in making the payment.   If the landlord's purpose in obtaining cancellation was to use the property herself, her payment will be amortized over the remainder of the original lease term.   If, instead, the landlord's motive was to free herself to enter into a new lease, the payment will be amortized over the term of the new lease.   If the landlord's reason for obtaining cancellation was to sell the property unencumbered by the lease, the payment will be added to her basis.   If the distinctions seem arbitrary, it is probably because they are.   See Note, The Tax Treatment of the Cost of Terminating a Lease, 30 Stan.L.Rev. 241 (1977); Levin, *Handlery* and the Tax Treatment of Lease Cancellation Expenditures, 9J. Real Estate Tax 371 (1981–82).   See generally, Dreier, Real Estate Leasing Transactions, 32 N.Y.U.Tax Inst. 1655, 1668–1669 (1974).

The tenant's sale or exchange of his lease is treated like the sale or exchange of any other real property.   Gain or loss will be computed by subtracting the tenant's adjusted basis from the amount realized, and will be treated as capital gain or loss, and ordinary income or loss, depending on whether the lease is characterized as section 1221, section 1231, or inventory property.   The landlord's payment to the tenant for cancellation of the lease will be treated like payments received from any other sale by the tenant.   I.R.C. § 1241.   By contrast, if the tenant pays the landlord to cancel the lease, the payment is deductible as a business expense.

For background on the taxation of landlords and tenants see, in addition to the sources cited, Robinson, Tax Consequences of the Acquisition and Disposition of Leases, 1 J.Real Est.Tax. 49 (1973); Thompson, Some Tax Problems on Mid-Stream Modifications and Terminations of Leases, 4 J.Real Est.Tax. 214 (1977); Bartlett, Tax Treatment of Replacements of Leased Property and of Leasehold Improvements Made by a Lessee, 30 Tax Law. 105 (1976).

2. THE SALE–LEASEBACK

SMITH & LUBELL, REFLECTION ON THE SALE–LEASEBACK *

7 Real Estate Review 11–13 (Winter 1978).

The sale-leaseback is a financing vehicle which enables the developer to minimize his equity investment in a property. Conventional mortgage financing is generally limited to a 75 percent loan-to-value ratio. This ratio can be exceeded by the use of a sale-leaseback in addition to, or in conjunction with, a mortgage loan. While the sale-leaseback has been employed by developers and owners for many years, its advantages were not generally recognized by institutional and other real estate investors until the period following the end of World War II. Since that time, the device has enjoyed considerable popularity, although the economic and tax factors which have motivated the investor-purchaser-lessor have changed materially from decade to decade.

When it is reduced to its barest elements, the sale-leaseback is a comparatively simple transaction. The owner of a parcel of real estate sells it to an investor and simultaneously leases it back under a long-term net lease. This lease imposes on the lessee virtually all of the obligations, and gives the lessee substantially all of the benefits, of ownership, subject, of course, to the lessor's reversionary rights in the fee. While the terms and conditions of the lease are the core of the transaction, in essence, the boiler-plate provisions of the lease are the same as those that will be found in any ground lease or other absolutely net lease. The lessee is obligated to pay rent without off-set or deduction and also to pay

Real estate taxes;

Fire, liability, and other insurance premiums;

All costs of operating, maintaining, repairing, and restoring the premises; and

All other costs relating to the premises that an owner would normally bear.

HISTORICAL BACKGROUND

During World War II, the life insurance industry invested heavily in U.S. government obligations. At the end of the war, investment officers, seeking to diversify their portfolios, began to look for investment opportunities outside of the traditional area of bonds and mortgage loans. At that time, a life insurer was not allowed to own real estate other than that which it occupied itself for the conduct of its insurance business. Recognizing the desirability of portfolio diversification, virtually all jurisdictions in the United States enacted legislation in the late 1940s that permitted life insurance companies to make direct investments in income-producing real property.

For a number of years, most life insurance company investments under the new statutory authority involved sale-leasebacks with creditworthy corporations. The lease normally called for a rent sufficient to enable the purchaser (insurance company) to recover its entire investment and to receive a satisfactory rate of return on the investment over the initial term of the lease. It contained provisions by which the creditworthy tenant guaranteed that the purchaser would come out whole under any circumstances, even in the event of total condemnation or destruction of the property. Although the entire return on the purchaser's investment was taxable income (i.e., rent), this disadvantage was offset by the purchaser's ability to depreciate the improvements.

The corporate borrower obtained the benefit of 100 percent financing. The fact that this was off-balance-sheet financing was also an important consideration.[e] The loss of the right to depreciate the improvements for income tax purposes was offset by the right to deduct rent (including rent for the land) as a business expense. Of course, the loss of use of the property at the expiration of the lease term was a disadvantage to the corporate lessee. This disadvantage began to appear important to corporations as other forms of 100 percent financing became available, particularly financing through real estate subsidiaries on the basis of a "bond type" net lease. Today, large creditworthy corporations rarely undertake direct sale-leaseback transactions with insurance company investors.

TAXES AND INFLATION

During the 1960s and early 1970s, private investors found that excellent tax shelter was to be had from depreciation and other real estate deductions available to them as owners under a sale-leaseback arrangement. The seller-lessee, which sought the private investor, was generally not a corporation seeking financing, but a developer and owner of real estate which desired to realize on its equity in a property without relinquishing control of it. In this type of sale-leaseback, the seller-lessee obtained added financing above existing mortgages, while the buyer-lessor obtained a competent operator and manager as a lessee.

---

e. The F.A.S.B. has since promulgated Statement 13, "Accounting for Leases," requiring that, if a lease meets at least one of four specified criteria, each of which points to effective fee ownership by lessee rather than lessor, the lessee must account for the lease (called a "capital lease") as an acquisition of property with a connected debt liability represented by the obligation to pay rent. Rent payments are to be treated as debt service payments, with an allocation made between principal and interest components. The new rules apply to all leases entered into on or after 1 January 1977 and, after 31 December 1980, retroactively to all leases, whenever entered into. Financial Accounting Standards Board, Statement of Financial Accounting Standards No. 13 Paragraphs 7, 10–14 (Nov. 1976). Ed.

Recent federal tax legislation has significantly reduced the incentives to private investors to enter into these transactions.

In the last two or three years, institutional investors and foreign interests have turned to sale-leaseback transactions in sound income-producing properties as inflation hedges. This hedge exists for a number of reasons:

The investor may anticipate appreciation in the market value of the investment.

Periodic increases in rent, based on appraisals or on adjustments tied to a price index, may be included in the lease.

Percentage rates, based on income derived from occupancy subtenants, may be included.

The investor may arrange to participate in a percentage of profits derived from a sale or refinancing of the leasehold estate created through the leaseback.

EQUITABLE MORTGAGES AND ADVERSE CONSEQUENCES

In many cases, the seller-lessee is unwilling to give up the reversionary interest in the property. It therefore negotiates for the right to recapture the real estate at one or more times during or at the end of the term of the lease by means of repurchase options. Unless the two parties proceed with great care, they may find that because of the repurchase options, they have so structured a transaction that the Internal Revenue Service or the courts consider it to be an equitable mortgage, rather than a true conveyance and a true lease. This is a significant exposure.

There can be substantial problems if the transaction in its entirety is an equitable mortgage and not a sale-leaseback:

If the lessee should default, the lessor will not have the option of eviction by summary proceedings. It will have to resort to the longer and generally more cumbersome and expensive remedy of foreclosure.

If the lessee becomes bankrupt or insolvent, the investor will be uncertain as to whether it is a landlord or a secured creditor. There may be consequent difficulties and delays in establishing its claim and otherwise protecting its interests.

If the transaction is deemed to be a mortgage, it may be subject to substantial mortgage and intangible taxes which were not anticipated by the parties.

The transaction may become usurious. Payments of rent are not payments of interest. If a sale-leaseback is found to be an equitable mortgage, all or a portion of the rent may be held to represent interest. If the rate of rental is high enough, the whole transaction may be tainted with usury.

The possible adversities discussed thus far are primarily of concern to the lessor. However, there are obvious tax consequences for both lessor and lessee if the IRS or the courts determine that a transaction should be treated as a mortgage, instead of a sale-leaseback. Payments made by the lessee will be regarded as debt service, and the lessee will be permitted to deduct for tax purposes only that portion of each payment that is attributable to interest. Of course, conversely, the taxable income of the investor will be only the interest portion of each payment, and not the full rent. On the other hand, any right to take depreciation on the leased premises will pass from the investor to the lessee.

SAFE REPURCHASE OPTIONS

Obviously, a change in the character of periodic payments from rent to debt service and transfers of the rights to depreciation and deductions from one party to the other can have adverse tax results for one or both parties.

It is possible to have repurchase options which will not convert an otherwise valid sale-leaseback into an equitable mortgage. The price at which the property may be reacquired should bear some reasonable relationship to its probable value at the time of repurchase. A repurchase price which reasonably attempts to estimate and take into account both the possible increase in the property value resulting from inflation and the decrease in value due to the depreciation of the improvements should be acceptable. A repurchase price equal to the original selling price, or the original selling price plus an inconsequential premium, is likely to be attacked as resembling the customary mortgage prepayment charge. A repurchase price to be fixed at the appraised value of the property as of the time of the exercise of the option is probably unquestionable.

THE FUTURE

The economic considerations that have induced people to enter into sale-leaseback transactions have varied considerably in the past and may be expected to vary considerably in the future. Tax considerations have attracted the private investor. The institutional investor probably has been more interested in sale-leasebacks as inflationary hedges. Although economic circumstances change, both tax and economic motivations should continue to make the sale-leaseback device popular.

FRANK LYON CO. v. UNITED STATES

Supreme Court of the United States, 1978.
435 U.S. 561, 98 S.Ct. 1291, 55 L.Ed.2d 550.

Mr. Justice BLACKMUN delivered the opinion of the Court.

This case concerns the federal income tax consequences of a sale-and-leaseback in which petitioner Frank Lyon Company (Lyon) took title to a building under construction by Worthen Bank & Trust Company (Worthen) of Little Rock, Ark., and simultaneously leased the building back to Worthen for long-term use as its headquarters and principal banking facility.

I

The underlying pertinent facts are undisputed. They are established by stipulations, the trial testimony, and the documentary evidence, and are reflected in the District Court's findings:

A

Lyon is a closely held Arkansas corporation engaged in the distribution of home furnishings, primarily Whirlpool and RCA electrical products. Worthen in 1965 was an Arkansas-chartered bank and a member of the Federal Reserve System. Frank Lyon was Lyon's majority shareholder and board chairman; he also served on Worthen's board. Worthen at that time began to plan the construction of a multistory bank and office building to replace its existing facility in Little Rock. About the same time Worthen's competitor, Union National Bank of Little Rock, also began to plan a new bank and office building. Adjacent sites on Capitol Avenue, separated only by Spring Street, were acquired by the two banks. It became a matter of competition, for both banking business and tenants, and prestige as to which bank would start and complete its building first.

Worthen initially hoped to finance, to build, and itself to own the proposed facility at a total cost of $9 million for the site, building, and adjoining parking deck. This was to be accomplished by selling $4 million in debentures and using the proceeds in the acquisition of the capital stock of a wholly owned real estate subsidiary. This subsidiary would have formal title and would raise the remaining $5 million by a conventional mortgage loan on the new premises. Worthen's plan, however, had to be abandoned for two significant reasons:

1. As a bank chartered under Arkansas law, Worthen legally could not pay more interest, on any debentures it might issue, than that then specified by Arkansas law. But the proposed obligations would not be marketable at that rate.

2. Applicable statutes or regulations of the Arkansas State Bank Department and the Federal Reserve System required Worthen, as a state bank subject to their supervision, to obtain prior permission for the investment in banking premises of any amount (including that placed in a real estate subsidiary) in excess of the bank's capital stock or of 40% of its capital stock and surplus. Worthen, accordingly, was advised by staff employees of the Federal Reserve System that they would not recommend approval of the plan by the System's Board of Governors.

Worthen therefore was forced to seek an alternative solution that would provide it with the use of the building, satisfy the state and federal regulators, and attract the necessary capital. In September 1967 it proposed a sale-and-leaseback arrangement. The State Bank

Department and the Federal Reserve System approved this approach, but the Department required that Worthen possess an option to purchase the leased property at the end of the 15th year of the lease at a set price, and the federal regulator required that the building be owned by an independent third party.

Detailed negotiations ensued with investors that had indicated interest, namely, Goldman, Sachs & Company, White, Weld & Co., Eastman Dillon, Union Securities & Company, and Stephens, Inc. Certain of these firms made specific proposals.

Worthen then obtained a commitment from New York Life Insurance Company to provide $7,140,000 in permanent mortgage financing on the building, conditioned upon its approval of the title holder. At this point Lyon entered the negotiations and it, too, made a proposal.

Worthen submitted a counterproposal that incorporated the best features, from its point of view, of the several offers. Lyon accepted the counterproposal, suggesting, by way of further inducement, a $21,000 reduction in the annual rent for the first five years of the building lease. Worthen selected Lyon as the investor. After further negotiations, resulting in the elimination of that rent reduction (offset, however, by higher interest Lyon was to pay Worthen on a subsequent unrelated loan), Lyon in November 1967 was approved as an acceptable borrower by First National City Bank for the construction financing, and by New York Life, as the permanent lender. In April 1968 the approvals of the state and federal regulators were received.

In the meantime, on September 15, before Lyon was selected, Worthen itself began construction.

B

In May 1968 Worthen, Lyon, City Bank, and New York Life executed complementary and interlocking agreements under which the building was sold by Worthen to Lyon as it was constructed, and Worthen leased the completed building back from Lyon:

1. Agreements between Worthen and Lyon. Worthen and Lyon executed a ground lease, a sales agreement, and a building lease.

Under the ground lease dated May 1, 1968, Worthen leased the site to Lyon for 76 years and seven months through November 30, 2044. The first 19 months comprised the estimated construction period. The ground rents payable by Lyon to Worthen were $50 for the first 26 years and seven months and thereafter in quarterly payments:

12/1/94 through 11/30/99 (five years)—$100,000 annually

12/1/99 through 11/30/04 (five years)—$150,000 annually

12/1/04 through 11/30/09 (five years)—$200,000 annually

12/1/09 through 11/30/34 (25 years)—$250,000 annually

12/1/34 through 11/30/44 (ten years)—$ 10,000 annually

Under the sales agreement dated May 19, 1968, Worthen agreed to sell the building to Lyon, and Lyon agreed to buy it, piece by piece as it was constructed, for a total price not to exceed $7,640,000, in reimbursements to Worthen for its expenditures for the construction of the building.

Under the building lease dated May 1, 1968, Lyon leased the building back to Worthen for a primary term of 25 years from December 1, 1969, with options in Worthen to extend the lease for eight additional five-year terms, a total of 65 years. During the period between the expiration of the building lease (at the latest, November 30, 2034, if fully extended) and the end of the ground lease on November 30, 2044, full ownership, use, and control of the building were Lyon's, unless, of course, the building had been repurchased by Worthen. Worthen was not obligated to pay rent under the building lease until completion of the building. For the first 11 years of the lease, that is until November 30, 1980, the stated quarterly rent was $145,-581.03 ($582,324.12 for the year). For the next 14 years, the quarterly rent was $153,289.32 ($613,157.28 for the year), and for the option periods the rent was $300,000 a year, payable quarterly.

The total rent for the building over the 25-year primary term of the lease thus was $14,989,767.24. That rent equalled the principal and interest payments that would amortize the $7,140,000 New York Life mortgage loan over the same period. When the mortgage was paid off at the end of the primary term, the annual building rent, if Worthen extended the lease, came down to the stated $300,000. Lyon's net rentals from the building would be further reduced by the increase in ground rent Worthen would receive from Lyon during the extension.[3]

The building lease was a "net lease," under which Worthen was responsible for all expenses usually associated with the maintenance of an office building, including repairs, taxes, utility charges, and insurance, and was to keep the premises in good condition, excluding, however, reasonable wear and tear.

Finally, under the lease, Worthen had the option to repurchase the building at the following times and prices:

11/30/80 (after 11 years)—$6,325,169.85

11/30/84 (after 15 years)—$5,432,607.32

11/30/89 (after 20 years)—$4,187,328.04

---

3. This, of course, is on the assumption that Worthen exercises its option to extend the building lease. If it does not, Lyon remains liable for the substantial rents prescribed by the ground lease. This possibility brings into sharp focus the fact that Lyon, in a very practical sense, is at least the ultimate owner of the building. If Worthen does not extend, the building lease expires and Lyon may do with the building as it chooses.

The Government would point out, however, that the net amounts payable by Worthen to Lyon during the building lease's extended terms, if all are claimed, would approximate the amount required to repay Lyon's $500,000 investment at 6% compound interest. Brief for United States 14.

11/30/94 (after 25 years)—$2,145,935.00

These repurchase option prices were the sum of the unpaid balance of the New York Life mortgage, Lyon's $500,000 investment, and 6% interest compounded on that investment.

2. Construction financing agreement. By agreement dated May 14, 1968, City Bank agreed to lend Lyon $7,000,000 for the construction of the building. This loan was secured by a mortgage on the building and the parking deck, executed by Worthen as well as by Lyon, and an assignment by Lyon of its interests in the building lease and in the ground lease.

3. Permanent financing agreement. By Note Purchase Agreement dated May 1, 1968, New York Life agreed to purchase Lyon's $7,140,000 6¾% 25-year secured note to be issued upon completion of the building. Under this agreement Lyon warranted that it would lease the building to Worthen for a noncancelable term of at least 25 years under a net lease at a rent at least equal to the mortgage payments on the note. Lyon agreed to make quarterly payments of principal and interest equal to the rentals payable by Worthen during the corresponding primary term of the lease. The security for the note were a First Deed of Trust and Lyon's assignment of its interests in the building lease and in the ground lease. Worthen joined in the Deed of Trust as the owner of the fee and the parking deck.

In December 1969 the building was completed and Worthen took possession. At that time Lyon received the permanent loan from New York Life, and it discharged the interim loan from City Bank. The actual cost of constructing the office building and parking complex (excluding the cost of the land) exceeded $10,000,000.

C

Lyon filed its federal income tax returns on the accrual and calendar year basis. On its 1969 return, Lyon accrued rent from Worthen for December. It asserted as deductions one month's interest to New York Life; one month's depreciation on the building; interest on the construction loan from City Bank; and sums for legal and other expenses incurred in connection with the transaction.

On audit of Lyon's 1969 return, the Commissioner of Internal Revenue determined that Lyon was "not the owner for tax purposes of any portion of the Worthen Building," and ruled that "the income and expenses related to this building are not allowable ... for Federal income tax purposes." He also added $2,298.15 to Lyon's 1969 income as "accrued interest income." This was the computed 1969 portion of a gain, considered the equivalent of interest income, the realization of which was based on the assumption that Worthen would exercise its option to buy the building after 11 years, on November 30, 1980, at the price stated in the lease, and on the additional determination that Lyon had "loaned" $500,000 to Worthen. In other words, the Commissioner determined that the sale-and-leaseback arrangement was a financing transaction in which Lyon loaned Worthen $500,000 and acted as a conduit for the transmission of principal and interest from Worthen to New York Life.

All this resulted in a total increase of $497,219.18 over Lyon's reported income for 1969, and a deficiency in Lyon's federal income tax for that year in the amount of $236,596.36. The Commissioner assessed that amount together with interest of $43,790.84, for a total of $280,-387.20.

Lyon paid the assessment and filed a timely claim for its refund. The claim was denied, and this suit, to recover the amount so paid, was instituted in the United States District Court for the Eastern District of Arkansas within the time allowed by 26 U.S.C.A. § 6532(a)(1).

After trial without a jury, the District Court, in a memorandum letter-opinion setting forth findings and conclusions, ruled in Lyon's favor and held that its claimed deductions were allowable. It concluded that the legal intent of the parties had been to create a bona fide sale-and-leaseback in accordance with the form and language of the documents evidencing the transactions. It rejected the argument that Worthen was acquiring an equity in the building through its rental payments. It found that the rents were unchallenged and were reasonable throughout the period of the lease, and that the option prices, negotiated at arm's-length between the parties, represented fair estimates of market value on the applicable dates. It rejected any negative inference from the fact that the rentals, combined with the options, were sufficient to amortize the New York Life loan and to pay Lyon a 6% return on its equity investment. It found that Worthen would acquire an equity in the building only if it exercised one of its options to purchase, and that it was highly unlikely, as a practical matter, that any purchase option would ever be exercised. It rejected any inference to be drawn from the fact that the lease was a "net lease." It found that Lyon had mixed motivations for entering into the transaction, including the need to diversify as well as the desire to have the benefits of a "tax shelter."

The United States Court of Appeals for the Eighth Circuit reversed. It held that the Commissioner correctly determined that Lyon was not the true owner of the building and therefore was not entitled to the claimed deductions. It likened ownership for tax purposes to a "bundle of sticks" and undertook its own evaluation of the facts. It concluded, in agreement with the Government's contention, that Lyon "totes an empty bundle" of ownership sticks. It stressed the following: (a) The lease agreements circumscribed Lyon's right to profit from its investment in the building by giving Worthen the option to purchase for an amount equal to Lyon's $500,000 equity plus 6% compound interest and the assumption of the unpaid balance of the New York Life mortgage. (b) The option prices did not take into account possible appreciation of the value of the building or inflation. (c) Any award realized as a result of destruction or condemnation of the building in excess of the mortgage balance and the $500,000 would be paid to Worthen and not Lyon. (d) The building rental payments during the primary term were exactly equal to the mortgage payments. (e) Worthen retained control over the ultimate disposition of the building through its various options to repurchase and to renew the lease plus its ownership of the site. (f) Worthen enjoyed all benefits and bore all burdens incident to the operation and ownership of the building so that, in the Court of Appeals' view, the only economic advantages accruing to Lyon, in the event it were considered to be the true owner of the property, were income tax savings of approximately $1.5 million during the first 11 years of the arrangement. The court concluded that the transaction was "closely akin" to that in Helvering v. Lazarus & Co., 308 U.S. 252, 60 S.Ct. 209, 84 L.Ed. 226 (1938). "In sum, the benefits, risks, and burdens which [Lyon] has incurred with respect to the Worthen building are simply too insubstantial to establish a claim to the status of owner for tax purposes. ... The vice of the present lease is that all of [its] features have been employed in the same transaction with the cumulative effect of depriving [Lyon] of any significant ownership interest."

We granted certiorari because of an indicated conflict with American Realty Trust v. United States, 498 F.2d 1194 (CA 4 1974).

II

This Court, almost 50 years ago, observed that "taxation is not so much concerned with the refinements of title as it is with actual command over the property taxed—the actual benefit for which the tax is paid." Corliss v. Bowers, 281 U.S. 376, 378, 50 S.Ct. 336, 74 L.Ed. 916 (1930). In a number of cases, the Court has refused to permit the transfer of formal legal title to shift the incidence of taxation attributable to ownership of property where the transferor continues to retain significant control over the property transferred. In applying this doctrine of substance over form, the Court has looked to the objective economic realities of a transaction rather than to the particular form the parties employed. The Court has never regarded "the simple expedient of drawing up papers," Commissioner of Internal Revenue v. Tower, 327 U.S. 280, 291, 66 S.Ct. 532, 538, 90 L.Ed. 670 (1946), as controlling for tax purposes when the objective economic realities are to the contrary. "In the field of taxation, administrators of the laws and the courts are concerned with substance and realities, and formal written documents are not rigidly binding." Helvering v. Lazarus & Co., 308 U.S. 252, 255, 60 S.Ct. 209, 210, 84 L.Ed. 226 (1939). Nor is the parties' desire to achieve a particular tax result necessarily relevant.

In the light of these general and established principles, the Government takes the position that the Worthen-Lyon transaction in its entirety should be regarded as a sham. The agreement as a whole, it is said, was only an elaborate financing scheme designed to provide economic benefits to Worthen and a guaranteed return to Lyon. The latter was but a conduit used to forward the mortgage payments, made under the guise of rent paid by Worthen to Lyon, on to New York Life as mortgagee. This, the Government claims, is the true substance of the transaction as viewed under the microscope of the tax laws. Although the arrangement was cast in sale-and-leaseback form, in substance it was only a financing transaction, and the terms of the repurchase options and lease renewals so indicate. It is said that Worthen could reacquire the building simply by satisfying the mortgage debt and paying Lyon its $500,000 advance plus interest, regardless of the fair market value of the building at the time; similarly, when the mortgage was paid off, Worthen could extend the lease at drastically reduced bargain rentals that likewise bore no relation to fair rental value but were simply calculated to pay Lyon its $500,000 plus interest over the extended term. Lyon's return on the arrangement in no event could exceed 6% compound interest (although the Government conceded it might well be less, Tr. of Oral Arg. 32). Furthermore, the favorable option and lease renewal terms made it highly unlikely that Worthen would abandon the building after it in effect had "paid off" the mortgage. The Government implies that the arrangement was one for convenience which, if accepted on its face, would enable Worthen to deduct its payments to Lyon as rent and would allow Lyon to claim a deduction for depreciation, based on the cost of construction ultimately borne by Worthen, which Lyon could offset against other income, and to deduct mortgage interest that roughly would offset the inclusion of Worthen's rental payments in Lyon's income. If, however, the Government argues, the arrangement was only a financing transaction under which Worthen was the owner of the building, Worthen's payments would be deductible only to the extent that they represented mortgage interest, and Worthen would be entitled to claim depreciation; Lyon would not be entitled to deductions for either mortgage interest or depreciation and it need not include Worthen's "rent" payments in its income because its function with respect to those payments was that of a conduit between Worthen and New York Life.

The Government places great reliance on Helvering v. Lazarus & Co., supra, and claims it to be precedent that controls this case. The taxpayer there was a department store. The legal title of its three buildings was in a bank as trustee for land-trust certificate holders. When the transfer to the trustee was made, the trustee at the same time leased the buildings back to the taxpayer for 99 years, with option to renew and purchase. The Commissioner, in stark contrast to his posture in the present case, took the position that the statutory right to depreciation followed legal title. The Board of Tax Appeals, however, concluded that the transaction between the taxpayer and the bank in reality was a mortgage loan and allowed the taxpayer depreciation on the buildings. This Court, as had the Court of Appeals, agreed with that conclusion and affirmed. It regarded the "rent" stipulated in the leaseback as a promise to pay interest on the loan, and a "depreciation fund" required by the lease as an amortization fund designed to pay off the loan in the stated period. Thus, said the Court, the Board justifiably concluded that the transaction, although in written form a transfer of ownership with a leaseback, was actually a loan secured by the property involved.

The *Lazarus* case, we feel, is to be distinguished from the present one and is not controlling here. Its transaction was one involving only two (and not multiple) parties, the taxpayer-department store and the trustee-bank. The Court looked closely at the substance of the agreement between those two parties and rightly concluded that depreciation was deductible by the taxpayer despite the nomenclature of the instrument of conveyance and the leaseback. ...

The present case, in contrast, involves three parties, Worthen, Lyon, and the finance agency. The usual simple two-party arrangement was legally unavailable to Worthen. Independent investors were interested in participating in the alternative available to Worthen and Lyon itself, also independent from Worthen, won the privilege. Despite Frank Lyon's presence on Worthen's board of directors, the transaction, as it ultimately developed, was not a familial one arranged by Worthen, but one compelled by the realities of the restrictions imposed upon the bank. Had Lyon not appeared, another interested investor would have been selected. The ultimate solution would have been essentially the same. Thus, the presence of the third party, in our view, significantly distinguishes this case from *Lazarus* and removes the latter as controlling authority.

III

... There is no simple device available to peel away the form of this transaction and to reveal its substance. The effects of the transaction on all the parties were obviously different from those that would have resulted had Worthen been able simply to make a mortgage agreement with New York Life and to receive a $500,000 loan from Lyon. Then *Lazarus* would apply. Here, however, and most significantly, it was Lyon alone, and not Worthen, who was liable on the notes, first to City Bank, and then to New York Life. Despite the facts that Worthen had agreed to pay rent and that this rent equalled the amounts due from Lyon to New York Life, should anything go awry in the later years of the lease, Lyon was primarily liable. No matter how the transaction could have been devised otherwise, it remains a fact that as the agreements were placed in final form, the obligation on the notes fell squarely on Lyon. Lyon, an ongoing enterprise, exposed its very business well-being to this real and substantial risk.

The effect of this liability on Lyon is not just the abstract possibility that something will go wrong and that Worthen will not be able to make its payments. Lyon has disclosed this liability on its balance sheet for all the world to see. Its financial position is affected substantially by the presence of this long-term debt, despite the offsetting presence of the building as an asset. To the extent that Lyon has used its capital in this transaction, it is less able to obtain financing for other business needs.

In concluding that there is this distinct element of economic reality in Lyon's assumption of liability, we are mindful that the characterization of a transaction for financial accounting purposes, on the one hand, and for tax purposes, on the other, need not necessarily be the same. Accounting methods or descriptions, without more, do not lend substance to that which has no substance. But in this case accepted accounting methods, as understood by the several parties to the respective agreements and as applied to the transaction by others, gave the transaction a meaningful character consonant with the form it was given. Worthen was not allowed to enter into the type of transaction which the Government now urges to be the true substance of the arrangement. Lyon and Worthen cannot be said to have entered into the transaction intending that the interests involved were allocated in a way other than that associated with a sale-and-leaseback.

Other factors also reveal that the transaction cannot be viewed as nothing more than a mortgage agreement between Worthen and New York Life and a loan from Lyon to Worthen. There is no legal obligation between Lyon and Worthen representing the $500,000 "loan" extended under the Government's theory. And the assumed 6% return on this putative loan—required by the audit to be recognized in the taxable year in question—will be realized only when and if Worthen exercises its options.

The Court of Appeals acknowledged that the rents alone, due after the primary term of the lease and after the mortgage has been paid, do not provide the simple 6% return which, the Government urges, Lyon is guaranteed. Thus, if Worthen chooses not to exercise its options, Lyon is gambling that the rental value of the building during the last 10 years of the ground lease, during which the ground rent is minimal, will be sufficient to recoup its investment before it must negotiate again with Worthen regarding the ground lease. There are simply too many contingencies, including variations in the value of real estate, in the cost of money, and in the capital structure of Worthen, to permit the conclusion that the parties intended to enter into the transaction as structured in the audit and according to which the Government now urges they be taxed.

It is not inappropriate to note that the Government is likely to lose little revenue, if any, as a result of the shape given the transaction by the parties. No deduction was created that is not either matched by an item of income or that would not have been available to one of the parties if the transaction had been arranged differently. While it is true that Worthen paid Lyon less to induce it to enter into the transaction because Lyon anticipated the benefit of the depreciation deductions it would have as the owner of the building, those deductions would have been equally available to Worthen had it retained title to the building. The Government so concedes. The fact that favorable tax consequences were taken into account by Lyon on entering into the transaction is no reason for disallowing those consequences.[15]   We cannot ignore the reality that the tax laws affect the shape of nearly every business transaction.   Lyon is not a corporation with no purpose other than to hold title to the bank building.   It was not created by Worthen or even financed to any degree by Worthen.

The conclusion that the transaction is not a simple sham to be ignored does not, of course, automatically compel the further conclusion that Lyon is entitled to the items claimed as deductions.   Nevertheless, on the facts, this readily follows.   As has been noted, the obligations on which Lyon paid interest were its obligations alone and it is entitled to claim deductions therefor, under § 163(a) of the 1954 Code, 26 U.S.C.A. § 163.

As is clear from the facts, none of the parties to this sale-and-leaseback was the owner of the building in any simple sense.   But it is equally clear that the facts focus upon Lyon as the one whose capital was committed to the building and as the party, therefore, that was entitled to claim depreciation for the consumption of that capital.   The Government has based its contention that Worthen should be treated as the owner on the assumption that throughout the term of the lease Worthen is acquiring an equity in the property.   In order to establish the presence of that growing equity, however, the Government is forced to speculate that one of the options will be exercised and that, if it is not, this is only because the rentals for the extended term are a bargain.   We cannot indulge in such speculation in view of the District Court's clear finding to the contrary.   We therefore conclude that it is Lyon's capital that is invested in the building according to the agreement of the parties, and it is Lyon that is entitled to depreciation deductions, under § 167 of the 1954 Code, 26 U.S.C.A. § 167.

IV

We recognize that the Government's position, and that taken by the Court of Appeals, is not without superficial appeal.   One, indeed, may theorize that Frank Lyon's presence on the Worthen board of directors; Lyon's departure from its principal corporate activity into this unusual venture; the parallel between the payments under the building lease and the amounts due from Lyon on the New York Life mortgage; the provisions relating to condemnation or destruction of the property; the nature and presence of the several options available to Worthen; and the tax benefits, such as the use of double declining balance depreciation, that accrue to Lyon during the initial years of the arrangement, form the basis of an argument that Worthen should be regarded as the

---

15. Indeed, it is not inevitable that the transaction, as treated by Lyon and Worthen, will not result in more revenues to the Government rather than less.   Lyon is gambling that in the first 11 years of the lease it will have income that will be sheltered by the depreciation deductions, and that it will be able to make sufficiently good use of the tax dollars preserved thereby to make up for the income it will recognize and pay taxes on during the last 14 years of the initial term of the lease and against which it will enjoy no sheltering deduction.

owner of the building and as the recipient of nothing more from Lyon than a $500,000 loan.

We however, as did the District Court, find this theorizing incompatible with the substance and economic realities of the transaction: the competitive situation as it existed between Worthen and Union National Bank in 1965 and the years immediately following; Worthen's undercapitalization; Worthen's consequent inability, as a matter of legal restraint, to carry its building plans into effect by a conventional mortgage and other borrowing; the additional barriers imposed by the state and federal regulators; the suggestion, forthcoming from the state regulator, that Worthen possess an option to purchase; the requirement, from the federal regulator, that the building be owned by an independent third party; the presence of several finance organizations seriously interested in participating in the transaction and in the resolution of Worthen's problem; the submission of formal proposals by several of those organizations; the bargaining process and period that ensued; the competitiveness of the bidding; the bona fide character of the negotiations; the three-party aspect of the transaction; Lyon's substantiality and its independence from Worthen; the fact that diversification was Lyon's principal motivation; Lyon's being liable alone on the successive notes to City Bank and New York Life; the reasonableness, as the District Court found, of the rentals and of the option prices; the substantiality of the purchase prices; Lyon's not being engaged generally in the business of financing; the presence of all building depreciation risks on Lyon; the risk borne by Lyon, that Worthen might default or fail, as other banks have failed; the facts that Worthen could "walk away" from the relationship at the end of the 25-year primary term, and probably would do so if the option price were more than the then current worth of the building to Worthen; the inescapable fact that if the building lease were not extended, Lyon would be the full owner of the building, free to do with it as it chose; Lyon's liability for the substantial ground rent if Worthen decides not to exercise any of its options to extend; the absence of any understanding between Lyon and Worthen that Worthen would exercise any of the purchase options; the nonfamily and nonprivate nature of the entire transaction; and the absence of any differential in tax rates and of special tax circumstances for one of the parties—all convince us that Lyon has far the better of the case.

In so concluding, we emphasize that we are not condoning manipulation by a taxpayer through arbitrary labels and dealings that have no economic significance. Such, however, has not happened in this case. In short, we hold that where, as here, there is a genuine multiple-party transaction with economic substance which is compelled or encouraged by business or regulatory realities, is imbued with tax-independent considerations, and is not shaped solely by tax avoidance features that have meaningless labels attached, the Government should honor the allocation of rights and duties effectuated by the parties. Expressed another way, so long as the lessor retains significant and genuine attributes of the traditional lessor status, the form of the transaction adopted by the parties governs for tax purposes. What those attributes are in any particular case will necessarily depend upon its facts. It suffices to say that, as here, a sale-and-leaseback, in and of itself, does not necessarily operate to deny a taxpayer's claim for deductions.

The judgment of the Court of Appeals, accordingly, is reversed.

It is so ordered.

Mr. Justice WHITE dissents and would affirm the judgment substantially for the reasons stated in the opinion in the Court of Appeals for the Eighth Circuit.

Mr. Justice STEVENS, dissenting.

In my judgment the controlling issue in this case is the economic relationship between Worthen and petitioner, and matters such as the number of parties, their reasons for structuring the transaction in a particular way, and the tax benefits which may result, are largely irrelevant. The question whether a leasehold has been created should be answered by examining the character and value of the purported lessor's reversionary estate.

For a 25-year period Worthen has the power to acquire full ownership of the bank building by simply repaying the amounts, plus interest, advanced by the New York Life Insurance Company and petitioner. During that period, the economic relationship among the parties parallels exactly the normal relationship between an owner and two lenders, one secured by a first mortgage and the other by a second mortgage. If Worthen repays both loans, it will have unencumbered ownership of the property. What the character of this relationship suggests is confirmed by the economic value that the parties themselves have placed on the reversionary interest.

All rental payments made during the original 25-year term are credited against the option repurchase price, which is exactly equal to the unamortized cost of the financing. The value of the repurchase option is thus limited to the cost of the financing, and Worthen's power to exercise the option is cost-free. Conversely, petitioner, the nominal owner of the reversionary estate, is not entitled to receive *any* value for the surrender of its supposed rights of ownership. Nor does it have any power to control Worthen's exercise of the option.

"It is fundamental that 'depreciation is not predicated upon ownership of property *but rather upon an investment in property.*' No such investment exists when payments of the purchase price in accordance with the design of the parties yield no equity to the purchaser." Estate of Franklin v. C.I.R., 544 F.2d 1045, 1049 (CA 9 1976). Here, the petitioner has, in effect, been guaranteed that it will receive its original $500,000 plus accrued interest. But that is all. It incurs neither the risk of depreciation, nor the benefit of possible appreciation. Under the terms of the sale-leaseback, it will stand in no better or worse position after the 11th year of the lease—when Worthen can first exercise its option to repurchase—whether the property has appreciated or depreciated. And this remains true throughout the rest of the 25-year period.

Petitioner has assumed only two significant risks. First, like any other lender, it assumed the risk of Worthen's insolvency. Second, it assumed the risk that Worthen might *not* exercise its option to purchase at or before the end of the original 25-year term. If Worthen should exercise that right *not* to repay, perhaps it would *then* be appropriate to characterize petitioner as the owner and Worthen as the lessee. But speculation as to what might happen in 25 years cannot justify the *present* characterization of petitioner as the owner of the building. Until Worthen has made a commitment either to exercise or not to exercise its option, I think the Government is correct in its view that petitioner is not the owner of the building for tax purposes. At present, since Worthen has the unrestricted right to control the residual value of the property for a price which does not exceed the cost of its unamortized financing, I would hold, as a matter of law, that it is the owner.

I therefore respectfully dissent.

NOTES

1. For a fascinating, critical analysis of the facts surrounding the *Frank Lyon* transaction and litigation, see Wolfman, The Supreme Court in the *Lyon's* Den: A Failure of Judicial Process, 66 Cornell L.Rev. 1075 (1981). Among the other facts disclosed in this valuable article: "early in 1981 Worthen repurchased the bank building from Lyon in exchange for cash of $500,000 and Worthen's seven percent cumulative preferred stock of an aggregate par value of $14,000,000 and that twenty years hence Lyon can put the stock to Worthen for cash redemption at par plus accrued dividends.

"Under the terms of the Worthen-Lyon sale-leaseback, Worthen was granted an option to repurchase the building first exercisable after the eleventh year of the lease, on November 30, 1980, at a price of $6,325,169.85 (the amount of the unpaid New York Life note plus Lyon's $500,000 'equity' with six percent compound interest).[130]

"For the first eleven years of the lease, Lyon's depreciation and interest deductions exceeded its rental income, providing substantial shelter for its other income. Thereafter, beginning in 1981, if it

---

130.   ... A 20 year bond with a face value of $14,000,000, paying semi-annual interest of 7% and discounted to yield an annual return of 17.69%, would have a present value of approximately $5,825,170. That sum, plus the $500,000 cash payment, equals the option price. A discount rate of 17.69% appears reasonable for early 1981. According to the attorney for Worthen and Lyon, "Because of Worthen's need to increase its capital, this was a better buy for Worthen than exercising its option on November 30, 1980 to purchase the building for $6,325,170 in cash." Letter from J. Gaston Williamson to Bernard Wolfman (October 19, 1981) (on file at *Cornell Law Review*). As the government foresaw from the beginning, as the Eighth Circuit and the dissenting Justices would understand, Lyon has received only the repayment of its $500,000 with interest at six percent.

remained the 'owner' Lyon's rental income from Worthen would exceed the deductions, producing taxable income.

"The Government had projected the repurchase as an almost inevitable event. It urged this strong probability as an important reason for treating Worthen as owner of the building from the beginning. But Lyon persuaded the district court to find:

> Because of Worthen's future capital requirements, the very substantial amounts of the option prices, the reasonableness of the net rents Worthen will be required to pay . . ., it is most unlikely that Worthen will exercise its options to purchase at the end of the first eleven years of the lease. . . .

The Supreme Court said that it could not 'indulge in . . . speculation' to the contrary in light of this 'clear finding.'" 66 Cornell L.Rev. 1101–1102.*

Frank Lyon, and tax-motivated sale-leasebacks generally, are also discussed in Weinstein & Silvers, The Sale and Leaseback Transaction After Frank Lyon & Co., 24 N.Y.L.Sch.L.Rev. 337 (1978); Fuller, Sales and Leasebacks and the *Frank Lyon* Case, 48 Geo.Wash.L.Rev. 60 (1979); Del Cotto, Sale and Leaseback: A Hollow Sound When Tapped? 37 Tax L.Rev. 1 (1981); Harmelink & Shurtz, Sale-Leaseback Transactions Involving Real Estate: A Proposal for Defined Tax Rules, 55 S.Cal.L.Rev. 833 (1982); Shurtz, A Decision Model for Lease Parties in Sale-Leasebacks of Real Estate, 23 Wm. & Mary L.Rev. 385 (1982); Milich, The Real Estate Sale-Leaseback Transaction: A View Toward the 90s, 21 Real Est.L.J. 66 (1992).

One commentator has speculated on the effect of changes in the tax law on the use and structure of sale-leaseback arrangements:

> The effects of the Tax Reform Act of 1986 remain to be seen, but the extended depreciation periods (twenty-seven and a half years for residential rental property and thirty-one and a half years for nonresidential real property), slower depreciation rates (straight-line only), reduction of capital gains treatment, extension of the at-risk rules to real estate and repeal of the investment tax credit certainly diminish the overall tax benefits of the real estate sale-leaseback. The limitations of TRA '86 on losses and credits from passive trade or business activities further restrict participation in, and the tax advantages of, many otherwise desirable sale-leaseback arrangements. Lowered tax rates will favor the party taking in income (i.e., the buyer-lessor with respect to rental income and the seller-lessee with respect to the proceeds of sale), whereas they will decrease the value of deductions to higher-bracket taxpayers. This will lessen some of the sale-leaseback's tax advantages for both the buyer-lessor (e.g., depreciation, mortgage interest, and the other expenses of property ownership it retains) and the seller-lessee (rental payments, real estate taxes,

---

* © Copyright 1981 by Cornell University. All Rights Reserved.

and the other expenses of property operation it assumes). Thus, a new balancing of tax benefits and detriments must be undertaken by prospective participants.

Maller, Structuring a Sale–Leaseback Transaction, 15 Real Est.L.J. 291, 293 (1987).*

2. *Frank Lyon and Tax Planning.* The principal difficulty in using *Frank Lyon* for guidance in real estate tax planning is that the underlying transaction was not at all typical of the standard sale-leaseback tax shelter widely used today. Only a few of the many factors that the Court said pointed to a true sale-leaseback will be found in the typical tax shelter. The "barriers imposed by the state and federal regulators" will rarely be present. A limited partnership using nonrecourse debt is the prevalent financing vehicle, and individual liability to the institutional lender will hardly ever appear. Finally, unlike Lyon, which was a substantial and diversifying business, the limited partnership will characteristically be thinly capitalized and will have the particular sale-leaseback as its single purpose.

3. *Frank Lyon and the § 1031 Pitfall.* The sale-leaseback might at first appear to be an excellent vehicle for the taxpayer who knows that her business property has declined in value, wishes to get tax recognition of this loss to set off against gains from other sources, but does not want to give up use and possession of the property which may be important to her business. The pitfall lies in the rule that a fee interest in land, and a leasehold interest in land with thirty years or more to run, are considered to be "like-kind" properties for purposes of a section 1031 tax free exchange. Treas.Reg. 1.1031(a)–(1)(c)(2). If the taxpayer takes back a lease of thirty years or more it may be held that a tax free exchange, not a sale-leaseback, has occurred and the taxpayer will be denied recognition of her loss as a result of section 1031's mandatory operation.

Leslie Co. v. Commissioner, 539 F.2d 943 (3d Cir.1976), illustrates the problem. Under an agreement with Prudential Life Ins. Co., taxpayer, Leslie, built a new office building and manufacturing plant for itself on land that it owned. Taxpayer's cost, including land, was $3,187,414. The agreement called for Prudential to purchase the land and improvement from Leslie for $2,400,000 or Leslie's actual cost, whichever was less, and simultaneously to lease the facility back to Leslie for a thirty-year term with two ten-year renewal options. In the year of sale, Leslie claimed a deductible loss of $787,414 (the difference between the $2,400,000 paid by Prudential and the land and building cost of $3,187,414). The Internal Revenue Service rejected Leslie's claimed loss, taking the position that in fact the transaction was a section 1031 like-kind exchange, so that loss was not recognizable. Under this view, the Service treated the $787,414 as Leslie's cost of acquiring the lease, and amortized this sum over the lease's initial thirty-year term.

The Tax Court took a different view, resting its decision on two specific findings of fact. First, the court found that the fair market value of the land and buildings was approximately $2,400,000. Second, it found that the rents to be paid by Leslie under the lease also approximated fair market value, so that the lease itself had no capital value and could not be considered additional consideration for Leslie's sale of the property to Prudential. From this, the Tax Court concluded that, since Leslie's only consideration for the transfer was the $2,400,-000 paid by Prudential, there was no exchange of like-kind properties, only a sale, on which of course loss could be recognized. 64 T.C. 247 (1975). The Court of Appeals for the Third Circuit affirmed. Like the Tax Court, it equated "property" with "value" and found no exchange of properties because the lease received had no value.

For a good discussion of this and other problems surrounding treatment of gain or loss on a sale-leaseback, see Morris, Sale-Leaseback Transactions of Real Property—A Proposal, 30 Tax Law. 701 (1977).

4. *Non-tax Issues.* In non-tax contexts, courts sometimes refuse to treat a sale-leaseback as creating a bona fide landlord and tenant relationship. For example, in Essex Property Services, Inc. v. Wood, 246 N.J.Super. 487, 587 A.2d 1337 (Law Div.1991), the Woods were facing foreclosure on their home. Essex entered into a sale-leaseback arrangement under which the Woods sold the house to Essex and received a one year lease and options to renew for one year and to repurchase the house. After the Woods exercised the renewal and the additional year ended, Essex sought to remove the Woods as holdover tenants. The court refused summary dispossession finding that "originally the parties contemplated that their transaction was a method of temporary refinancing and that both parties contemplated that the defendants would 're-purchase' the property. The relationship of landlord and tenant was incidental to that mutual and dominant contemplation." The court noted that "substance must control the form" and that Essex lacked "real" title to form the basis of a dispossession action. If landlord-tenant law does not control, what rights should Essex have in the property and how should it be permitted to vindicate them?

In the bankruptcy context, courts may also refuse to treat a sale-leaseback as a true lease arrangement. See Homburger & Andre, Real Estate Sale and Leaseback Transactions and the Risk of Recharacterization in Bankruptcy Proceedings, 24 Real Prop. Probate & Trust J. 95 (1989).

C. PROPERTIES IN DISTRESS

An increasing number of commercial real estate properties have fallen into trouble in recent years, yielding inadequate rental income to pay carrying charges. When default on the mortgage occurs, the lender must chose among several courses of action. Rather than immediately exercising its legal remedies, the lender often chooses to restructure the loan transaction in a way that may ultimately allow the property to become self-sufficient This restructuring is known as a "workout." The first section following this note examines the reasons for property defaults and the different options available to the lender, focusing on workouts.

The real estate lender whose borrower has defaulted on her note, the installment seller whose buyer has breached their agreement, and the landlord whose tenant has broken a leasehold covenant, will usually find that his rights and remedies are substantially confined by state law. Debtors, buyers and tenants have increasingly come under the protection of state courts and legislatures through such devices as antideficiency rules, one-action rules, statutory rights of redemption, the incorporation of debtor protection provisions into installment land contracts, and limitations on the availability and speed of summary eviction proceedings. State law also imposes restrictions on the use of deeds in lieu of foreclosure by borrowers and lenders who are attempting to avoid judicially enforced remedies. The second section below examines state law rules that shape the lender's ability to realize on its investment in the face of default.

Borrowers, buyers and tenants who breach their real property obligations will often be in financial distress. As a result, their secured creditors may also have to consult federal bankruptcy law which limits the rights and remedies of a lender, seller or landlord whose borrower, buyer or tenant has filed for liquidation under Chapter 7, or for reorganization under Chapter 11, of the Bankruptcy Code. (The purpose of a Chapter 7 liquidation is to allocate the debtor's assets equitably among his creditors and to discharge him from all further liability; the purpose of a Chapter 11 reorganization is to restructure the debtor's obligations and continue his business.) Moreover, the rights of lenders, sellers and landlords under state law will often conflict with the rights of debtors and their general creditors under bankruptcy law. State and federal rules on default and bankruptcy will also substantially influence efforts by the parties to restructure and work out their difficulties short of judicial proceedings. The third section below samples some federal bankruptcy law issues that intersect with remedies under state real estate law and that may alter a real estate transaction. This is not intended as a substitute for the bankruptcy law course but rather is designed to sensitize future real estate lawyers to some key issues that they should explore as they structure real estate transactions and advise clients on state law remedies.

Bibliography. See generally, Miller & Love, Real Estate in Bankruptcy, in Negotiating Real Estate Transactions (M. Senn ed.1988); A.B.A. Sec. Real Prop. Probate & Trust, Real Estate Loan Workouts (1991); A.L.I.–A.B.A., Real Estate Defaults, Workouts, and Reorganizations (1991); L. Cherkis, Real Estate Transactions and the Bankruptcy Code (1984); Real Estate Bankruptcies and Workouts: A Practical

Perspective (A. Kuklin & P. Roberts, eds. 1983); Andrew, Real Property Transactions and the Bankruptcy Amendments and Federal Judgeship Act of 1984, 2 Cal.Real Prop.J. 1 (Fall 1984); Anderson & Ziegler, Real Property Arrangements Under the Old and New Bankruptcy Acts, 25 Loy.L.Rev. 713 (1979).

On more specialized topics, see Countryman, Real Estate Liens in Business Rehabilitation Cases, 50 Am.Bankr.L.J. 303 (1976); Lacy, Land Sale Contracts in Bankruptcy, 21 U.C.L.A.L.Rev. 477 (1973); Siegel, Landlord's Bankruptcy: A Proposal for Treatment of the Lease by Reference to Its Component Elements, 54 B.U.L.Rev. 903 (1974); Countryman, Executory Contracts in Bankruptcy, (Pts. 1 & 2), 57 Minn.L.Rev. 439, 58 Minn.L.Rev. 479 (1973, 1974); Creedon & Zinman, Landlord's Bankruptcy: *Laissez Les Lessees,* 26 Bus.Law. 1391 (1971); Alces, Unexpired Leases in Bankruptcy: Rights of the Affected Mortgagee, 35 U.Fla.L.Rev. 656 (1983).

On counselling considerations, see Leta & Jones, Selected Bankruptcy Considerations in Drafting Real Estate Documents, 1984 Utah L.Rev. 227; Jones, Structuring the Deed in Lieu of Foreclosure Transaction, 19 Real Prop., Probate & Trust J. 58 (1984); Kahn & Huberman, Default, Foreclosure, and Strategic Renegotiation, 52 Law & Contemp. Probs. 49 (1989).

1. WORKOUTS

ROSS, REAL ESTATE WORKOUTS: A LENDER'S PRIMER*

21 Real Estate Review 16, 16–22 (No. 3, Fall 1991).

As they face an increasing number of problem loans, lenders find that they must develop skills and methodologies different from those they employed during the 1980s. This article attempts to demystify the intimidating aura that has developed around workouts and to provide guidelines for approaching and implementing a workout. The article divides the workout process into four phases. These phases may overlap and they do not necessarily progress in a linear, chronological manner. They are:

- Fact gathering;
- Analysis/planning;
- Negotiation; and
- Implementation.

FACT GATHERING PHASE

As in any transaction, the workout participant should learn as much as possible about the subject matter of the transaction. In a workout, the subject is both the property and the borrower.

Initially, the borrower may be the lender's only source of certain types of information. Examples of such information are current rent rolls, operating reports, and financial statements. If the borrower is cooperative (and borrowers usually are in the early phase of a workout), the lender needs to move quickly to gather this data.

To expedite rapid data collection a lender should have ready a standard checklist that identities information that is under the borrower's control. The checklist can, of course, be modified to address specific information for the workout property.

If the buyer is not cooperative, the lender must rely on information released by the borrower earlier (which may be outdated) and the results of its own investigations, and it may seek to obtain certain facts through legal processes. Whether or not the borrower is cooperative, the lender should seek an array of data from professional sources.

An appraisal. For several reasons, the lender should obtain a current appraisal of the property. An appraisal will almost surely be required for regulatory and accounting purposes. Moreover, knowledge of how the property's value compares to the loan amount will be important in upcoming negotiations with the borrower. If the parties know that the property is worth less than the loan, it should be easier to reach a settlement that results in the friendly transfer of the property (if that is the lender's desire). If the value of the property exceeds the debt, the borrower well may argue for restructuring the loan. When recourse debt is involved, knowledge that the property is currently worth less than the loan enables the lender to consider what additional collateral or payments it will require of the borrower in order to restructure the deal.

Finally, the value of the property relative to the amount of the debt can have significant implications under bankruptcy and creditors' rights laws (as explained below).

A new market study. A market study that quantifies the supply and demand for specific types of space in a given market is a valuable workout tool. The study should establish whether the property's problems are unique or marketwide. It helps the parties to judge whether the property is likely to appreciate or to continue to depreciate. And it helps ascertain what, if anything, can be done to enhance the property's value.

A physical inspection. A physical inspection can consist of a simple walk through the property or a detailed engineering report. The inspection gives the lender a sense of how well or poorly the property has been maintained and of the level of capital that may have to be committed to make the property a viable investment.

An environmental audit. As many articles in this publication have indicated, federal and state laws impose liability on an owner of land that is contaminated with hazardous substances.[2] A lender that suc-

---

2. The primary federal statute dealing with hazardous waste sites is the Compre- hensive Enviromental Response, Compensation and Liability Act of 1980 (CERCLA)

ceeds to ownership of contaminated property will similarly become liable, even if that lender did not play any role in the creation of the environmentally hazardous condition. Even more frightening, the lender, although not in title to the property, may incur liability if it actively participates in the management and operation of the property. Needless to say, it is imperative that a lender discover whether any environmental problems exist *before* it takes any steps that may lead to its exposure to liability. Therefore, if possible, before it engages in a workout, a lender should obtain a "phase I" environmental audit.

Title search/foreclosure certificate. A title search will verify that the borrower is the present owner of the property and reveal whether the borrower, either voluntarily or involuntarily, has encumbered the property with additional liens, judgments, or encumbrances. It will also disclose whether a foreclosure action has been initiated and if real estate taxes are in arrears. If specifically requested, a title search can determine whether the borrower has filed for, or been placed into, bankruptcy. Moreover, if the lender orders and obtains a foreclosure certificate and it subsequently decides to commence a foreclosure action, it is in a position to move quickly.

Violation and license search. A violation and license search can give a lender insight into the care with which the property has been operated. Furthermore, the existence of violations may impair the lender's legal right to operate the property. Because violations must ultimately be cured, the lender must factor into a workout analysis the expense of doing so. A search of the licenses issued in connection with the use and operation of the property (e.g., a liquor license for a hotel or a building permit for a construction project) will alert the lender to the need to transfer these licenses.

UCC search. The lender should search the applicable filing offices to ensure that it has properly perfected its security interest in the non-real estate portions of its collateral. In the event of a borrower's bankruptcy, failure to have a properly perfected security interest may turn a secured creditor, who has enhanced priority, into a general unsecured creditor. It may also limit the lender's enforcement of nonbankruptcy remedies.

Checking the borrower's insurance. Loan documents customarily require that the borrower's insurance company provide the lender with notice of any potential lapse of insurance coverage. Nonetheless, the consequences of a lapse in insurance coverage for a lender are so severe that a check of such coverage, and its adequacy, is warranted. Some loan documents do not require the borrower to maintain liability insurance. In those cases, the lender should verify that its liability coverage extends to its active control and/or ownership of the property.

(43 U.S.C. § 9601 et seq.). For a discussion of CERCLA (and other relevant federal statutes) see Paul Katcher, "Lenders' Liability for Enviromental Hazards," *Real Es-* *tate Review* 20 (Fall 1990): 72; Hugh O. Nourse and James S. Trieschman, "Managing the Risk of Enviromental Liability," *Real Estate Review* 20 (Spring 1990): 84.

Other private investigations. Because a workout is often caused by the borrower's problems as well as the property's problems, the lender should not be reticent in seeking information about the borrower's financial condition and the status of the borrower's other projects and assets. The prospects for the property may make a workout appear feasible when the property is viewed independently. However, if the borrower's other problems are so severe that he either will not be able to devote attention to the property or will eventually succumb to those problems, the lender should avoid a deal that depends on the borrower.

Thus, in certain circumstances, the lender should consider retaining a private investigating firm. This is particularly true if the borrower is personally liable for the loan. The lender needs to discover and catalogue, as quickly as possible, the size and location of the borrower's other assets.

Review of the loan documents. In addition to investigating the property and the borrower, the lender should ask legal counsel to thoroughly review the original loan papers (particularly in complex transactions). This will ensure that the lender understands the original business deal and will enable it to analyze how the loan problems developed and what restructuring may be possible.

In reviewing the loan documents, the lender and its counsel will look for a variety of things. The lender should assure itself that it has possession of the original promissory note (such possession often being a prerequisite to bringing a foreclosure action or an action on the note). Similarly, the papers should be checked for proper execution and completeness. The review of the loan documents identifies any limitations the documents may have placed on the lender's remedial actions. Additionally, the documents will alert the lender to the need to notify other parties of the borrower's problem. For example, a lender may have agreed to notify the franchisor of a hotel of the borrower/franchisee's default.

In addition to reviewing the original loan transaction, the lender should review the loan's history since the closing and the manner in which it dealt with the loan. Such conduct may have a direct impact on claims the borrower will subsequently assert.

Legal review. The lender must, of course, be familiar with the law that may govern the workout. At a minimum, this review includes the Bankruptcy Code and the laws of the jurisdictions that govern the enforcement of the lender's rights.

Each jurisdiction's laws with respect to foreclosure, enforcement of guarantees, election of remedies, and creditors' rights can be quite different and those differences can be crucial in deciding on a course of conduct. For example, New York foreclosure entails a judicial proceeding that, if contested, can easily stretch to more than eighteen months. California, on the other hand, provides for a nonjudicial foreclosure that can usually be effected within four months. The time difference can radically alter a lender's workout strategy.

The lender must also understand the federal and local tax laws that may affect the workout and their impact on both lender and borrower. A loan restructuring that gives the lender an equity position will probably have income tax consequences quite different from those of a restructuring in which the lender remains a traditional mortgagor. A workout that requires the transfer of the property by the borrower may require the borrower to recognize significant income. Faced with that prospect, a borrower may prefer a restructuring, even if it requires that he contribute significant additional cash or collateral.

State and local transfer taxes can also be quite high, and minimizing or eliminating them can become an important element in a workout that results in the transfer of the property.

THE ANALYSIS/PLANNING PHASE

Having gathered the facts, the lender next must turn to an analysis of those facts. The facts of each workout situation are unique, and the causes of problem loans are multiple. Therefore, this article does not attempt to analyze any particular problem loan but offers some general comments.

Composition of the Lender's Team

A workout is a multiparty, multidisciplinary endeavor. To obtain the facts it will now be analyzing, the lender probably had to assemble a workout team, whose members all researched their areas with some degree of independence. For analysis and planning, it is useful to bring certain team members together to consider the data jointly. The lender's core team may be in-house specialists in finance underwriting and real estate management, plus lender's counsel. For strategic planning, the team may add a local real estate consultant who is familiar with the market, a management/ leasing company, an accounting firm, and a construction manager/ general contractor.

The Borrower's Position

In all transactions, understanding the position and situation of the other side is important. In a workout, not only must the lender gather facts about the borrower, it must understand the borrower's psychological and emotional needs. The borrower has probably committed significant time, effort, and money to a project that has soured for reasons beyond his control, and may be unwilling or unable to admit that he no longer has equity in the property. Understanding the borrower's problems can aid the analysis.

The lender should encourage the borrower to offer his version of why the problem with the property developed. The borrower should also present a pro forma statement for the property. This undoubtedly optimistic forecast of the property's future will help the analysis, and it may provide a basis for measuring the borrower's performance in any eventual restructuring.

Assessing the borrower helps the lender form an opinion about why the borrower and the property now find themselves in trouble. Is the borrower a skilled developer/operator who is the victim of the market, or is he inept or dishonest? Any workout that relies on the borrower's continuing involvement assumes that the lender has answered this basic question to its own satisfaction.

General Policy and Legal Considerations

During the analytical phase, all team members should understand the lender's general policies clearly, and be familiar with the limits imposed on restructuring by the law and regulators. Some lenders may be unwilling to restructure any transaction in which the borrower does not have a minimum equity. Others may determine that because of overall internal financial considerations, restructurings are almost always preferable to ownership of property.

NEGOTIATION PHASE

Eventually, all workouts involve discussions and negotiations between the parties. This article does not discuss the internal dynamics of negotiations, although some of these are alluded to in the discussion of borrower psychology. There are certain general guidelines, however, that negotiators should bear in mind.

Lender Liability

The lender's negotiators should be familiar with the issues of "lender liability," which is the label commonly given to various defenses and claims that borrowers raise against lenders. These claims and defenses are rooted within traditional and developing concepts of law. Lender liability claims are based on one of the following legal theories: (1) fraud, (2) constructive fraud, (3) breach of contract; and (4) breach of an implied duty of good faith and fair dealing.

The lender must be aware that in the negotiation, the borrower is likely to threaten to assert a lender liability defense. However, although the lender should not ignore the potential risks of a successful lender liability claim, generally a lender that acts within the rights granted to it by the loan documents and applicable law has little cause to be concerned.

The one element that can provide a basis for lender liability is a finding that the lender acted in a fiduciary capacity to the borrower. However, fiduciary relationships are usually very difficult to demonstrate in the context of a loan transaction.

Borrowers' claims of lender liability are usually asserted to delay and discourage lender action. The assertion is often a defensive tactic intended to bring the lender to the negotiating table. Therefore, the lender should conduct itself in a manner that not only will minimize the risk of a successful claim but will also discourage the borrower from concluding that it has a colorable claim to assert.

To that end the following guidelines may be helpful:

- To avoid any claim that the borrower was unaware of his position (and to allow the running of any time periods that may be required prior to exercising remedies), a lender should, as a general matter, serve all notices of default and acceleration when permitted.

- The borrower should be represented by counsel.

- All proposals made to the borrower, and if possible, summaries of all discussions between the lender and borrower, should be furnished in writing to the borrower. All such discussions and written communications should be made without prejudice to the lender's rights.

- The lender should keep in mind that in litigation internal memos and similar documents will likely be discoverable and the borrower will be able to obtain copies. The lender should therefore, not include such memos (1) negative characterizations of the borrower (which may lead a court to conclude that the lender was not acting in good faith); and (2) language that indicates an agreement has been reached with the borrower or that the lender has waived certain rights.

- During discussions the lender should avoid promises, waivers of rights and, of course, gratuitous threats.

Workout Agreement

Many of the problems raised by these lender liability issues can be mitigated through the use of what is variously called a "workout agreement," "preworkout agreement," or "standstill agreement."

A workout agreement is a written agreement between the parties that sets forth the rules by which, during a specified period of time, they will conduct themselves and their discussions. At a minimum, the workout agreement should acknowledge that all discussions between the parties are without prejudice to their rights. Additionally, the agreement usually requires the lender to refrain from exercising, or agree to a limited exercise of, its legal remedies.

In exchange for this restraint, a lender can reasonably expect the borrower to agree to one or more of the following:

- Borrower's release of any claims of lender liability;

- Borrower's acknowledgment of (1) the facts constituting the default, (2) the amount of the debt, and (3) the validity of loan;

- Borrower's agreement to provide information to the lender; and

- Borrower's agreement (either in the workout agreement or by separate instrument) to establish a cash collateral or lockbox account (with attendant provisions for dealing with the receipts from the property).

IMPLEMENTATION PHASE

The negotiations will conclude in one of two ways. The lender may decide that the borrower should be permitted to continue to own the property in whole or in part, or the lender may conclude that it wishes to obtain title to the property.

In the first instance, the parties will try to restructure the loan. In the second instance, either the parties will agree on a friendly transfer of the property, or both will avail themselves of available legal processes.

Restructured Loan

Loans can be restructured in many different ways. Such restructuring will usually involve lower interest rates, accruals of interest, and/or extended maturity dates. In many respects, a loan restructuring is similar to underwriting and effecting a loan transaction. However, the lender must consider the genesis of the restructuring—a problem, after all, does exist. Four rules may be useful.

Recourse requirement. Although the lender may customarily lend on a nonrecourse basis, it should attempt to obtain personal recourse against the borrower (and the borrower's principals). The borrower should be subject to significant downside risk if the restructuring fails. The liability can extend to all principal and interest, or it may simply insure the proper payment of all net operating income to the lender.

Additional collateral. The borrower should seek additional collateral for the restructured loan. The additional collateral will strengthen the lender's position should enforcement of the loan obligations become necessary.

Participation. A restructuring should not only increase the borrower's downside risk, it should enhance the lender's upside potential. If the restructuring succeeds, the lender should not be in the anomalous position of having the borrower reap all of the consequent rewards. The particular mechanisms for such sharing are outside the scope of this article. However, shared appreciation mortgages or partial lender ownership of the property are possible options.

Performance criteria. A restructured loan should include strict performance criteria and controls on the borrower. The cash collateral account that was put into place during the earlier phase of the workout may be worth continuing.

Friendly Transfers of Title

If the outcome of the negotiation was a decision that the lender would obtain title to the property, and the borrower agreed to transfer title, the parties can choose from three primary ways of conveying the property:

- A deed-in-lieu of foreclosure;
- A "friendly" or "consensual" foreclosure; and

• A prepackaged bankruptcy plan.

Deed-in-lieu. A deed-in-lieu of foreclosure is simply a voluntary conveyance of the property by the borrower to the lender, or its designee. A deed-in-lieu's chief advantage is the speed by which the property can be transferred. Further, it minimizes the expense of transferring the property and avoids the uncertainties of a litigation. A voluntary conveyance of the property may eliminate much of the negative publicity and trauma involved in a foreclosure or bankruptcy.

However, there are negative aspects to a deed-in-lieu of foreclosure. Unlike a foreclosure action, a deed-in-lieu does not cut off subordinate interests in the property. If the lender chooses this course, it must make some arrangements with other lienors. There are also potential bankruptcy problems associated with a deed-in-lieu. For example, if the value of the property exceeds the debt and the borrower was insolvent, and if the borrower files a bankruptcy petition within a year of the transfer, the transfer may be voidable as a fraudulent conveyance.[6]

A deed-in-lieu will almost certainly entail the payment of any local transfer taxes. In bankruptcy such transfer taxes should and, in foreclosure, may be avoided. Finally, in certain jurisdictions it may not be possible to obtain fee title insurance following a deed-in-lieu.

If a deed-in-lieu is utilized then the transfer should be structured so as to keep alive the mortgage debt upon conveyance.[7] By keeping the debt alive, the lender retains its ability to later foreclose the mortgage and may preserve its position in the event of a later bankruptcy of the borrower.

A friendly foreclosure. A friendly foreclosure is a foreclosure action in which the borrower submits to the jurisdiction of the court, waives any right to assert defenses and claims and to appeal or collaterally attack any judgment, and otherwise agrees to cooperate with the lender in the litigation. In certain jurisdictions, such cooperation by the borrower can significantly shorten the time required to effect a foreclosure. By foreclosing, the lender has the right to cut off subordinate liens (although to expedite the proceedings, it may choose to pursue a settlement with the lienors). Additionally, a foreclosure judgment and sale is undoubtedly better protection than a deed-in-lieu in the event of a subsequent bankruptcy by the borrower.[8] The foreclosure action,

---

6. It is possible, although not probable, that the transfer could be avoided in bankruptcy as a preference, if the transfer occurred within 90 days (subject to extension in certain cases) of the filing of the bankruptcy petition, if the debtor was insolvent at the time of the transfer, and if the lender obtained through the transfer more than it would have received in a chapter 7 liquidation.

7. The lender can accomplish this by appropriate nonmerger language in the deed and/or by having the property transferred to a designee of the lender, as previously noted. For a discussion with respect to deeds-in-lieu of foreclosure, see Harvey Boneparth, "Taking a Deed in Lieu of Foreclosure: Pitfalls for the Lender." *Real Estate Law Journal* 19 (Spring 1991): 338.

8. A foreclosure sale may constitute a fraudulent transfer under Section 548 of the U.S. Bankruptcy Code. In 1984, Sec-

however, may even under the best of circumstances require appreciably more time in certain jurisdictions than a deed-in-lieu.

Prepackaged bankruptcy. In a so-called prepackaged bankruptcy, before the petition is filed the borrower agrees with all its creditors to the terms on which it will turn its assets over to its creditors in exchange for a discharge of liability. Agreeing on the ultimate plan before the petition is filed avoids postfiling disputes that can prolong the proceedings at great cost to all parties. It is impossible to estimate how long it might take to resolve a nonconsensual bankruptcy. However, a prepackaged case could conceivably be resolved in not much more than six months. If foreclosure would take longer, a prepackaged plan may be an alternative worth considering.

Involuntary Transfer of Property

Unfortunately, many workouts end with the lender and borrower unable to reach agreement. In such instances, if the lender wishes to obtain title to the property, it has little choice but to utilize the processes available at law. It must either foreclose its mortgage lien or seek to place the borrower into involuntary bankruptcy under chapters 7 and 11.

Foreclosure. Foreclosure proceedings are creatures of local law and vary widely from state to state. Certain states provide for judicial foreclosures which require the commencement of formal legal action. If the borrower contests the action, the foreclosure can be time-consuming and expensive (not to mention the damage to the property's value that delay entails). Other jurisdictions provide for a nonjudicial foreclosure that can be effected relatively quickly. Certain interim remedies are available to the lender. The most important interim remedies are the appointment of a receiver to take control of and operate the property and the right to direct the payment of rents to the lender.

Involuntary bankruptcy. The lender may wish to consider an involuntary bankruptcy if: (1) it is concerned that the borrower is wasting assets; (2) it is concerned that its management is not competent to administer the property; and (3) it can prove that the borrower is not paying its debts generally as they come due. The lender may also pursue an involuntary bankruptcy if it concludes that a voluntary bankruptcy by the borrower is likely at the end of a lengthy foreclosure proceeding. Because serious penalties may be imposed on the creditors

tion 101(54) of the Bankruptcy Code was amended to define a transfer as every mode of disposing of or parting with property or an interest in property, *including* foreclosure of the debtor's equity of redemption. A foreclosure may therefore be a fraudulent tranfer if the mortgagor is insolvent and does not receive "reasonably equivalent value" at the foreclosure sale. Compare *Durrett v. The Washington Ins. Co.,* 621 F.2d 201 (5th Cir.1980); (receipt of less than 70 percent of "fair market value" is not "reasonably equivalent value") with *Madrid v. Lawyers Title Ins. Corp.,* 725 F.2d 1197 (9th Cir.1984) (sale price obtained at a regularly conducted foreclosure sale is presumed conclusively to be the reasonably equivalent value for purposes of Section 548 of the Bankruptcy Code). See also *In re Bundles,* 856 F.2d 815 (7th Cir. 1988); cf. *In re Brown,* 119 Bankr. 413 (S.D.N.Y.1990).

who initiate an involuntary petition in bad faith, this remedy should be viewed cautiously.

Bankruptcy in general may have significant consequences for secured lenders. First, as mentioned previously, if the security interest is not perfected, the claim may be treated as a general unsecured claim. To the extent that the collateral securing the debt is worth less than the principal amount of the debt, the deficiency will be treated as an unsecured debt. Moreover, interest is not paid currently after a petition is filed unless the lender can demonstrate both that it is oversecured and that its collateral is decreasing in value. In addition, there is a high likelihood that if for some reason the debt is prepaid, prepayment charges will not be paid to the lender, especially if the lender requested prepayment.

CONCLUSION

Real estate workouts may not be fun, but they are interesting and should not be intimidating. Although each workout is unique, the broad guidelines set forth in this article should enable lenders to navigate these treacherous shoals.

2.   LENDER'S REMEDIES

LIFTON, REAL ESTATE IN TROUBLE: LENDER'S REMEDIES NEED AN OVERHAUL

31 Business Lawyer 1927, 1931–1937, 1945–1949 (1976).

I.   LENDER'S REMEDIES: STATE LAW

A. Mortgagee's Pre-Foreclosure Rights: To Physical Possession, Assignment of Rents, Appointment of Receiver

Three different conceptual approaches to the mortgage and the mortgagee's right to possession in case of default are embodied in state mortgage acts and judicial decisions. In the majority of states, even where the mortgage instrument uses language that signifies a transfer of title, the mortgagee only gets a lien or security interest in the property which can be activated by foreclosure sale. When a default occurs, unless the owner voluntarily turns over possession, the mortgagee has little hope of getting physical possession except through foreclosure proceedings.

A few title states, however, like the early common law, still treat the mortgage as a conveyance of the property to a lender to be returned to the borrower when the mortgage debt is discharged. In theory, the lender also gets the continuing right to possession which he agrees not to exercise unless there is a default. In another small group of so-called "intermediate" theory states, courts talk in terms of the right to possession being retained by the mortgagor until default, but after default automatically accruing to the mortgagee. Despite these theoretical differences, even in the title and intermediate states, modern courts are reluctant to grant a mortgagee physical possession of the property. And even where physical possession may be available, restraints on the mortgagee and the risks of possession may dissuade lenders from seeking it. In some jurisdictions, a mortgagee in possession may have minimum power over the property. It may not be compensated for its own management efforts or be able to recover money advanced for improving or maintaining the property during its possession. The mortgagee in possession also may risk having to account to the owner under stringent rules of accounting for decisions on renting and operating the property if the owner later redeems the property. As a result of these limitations, rather than seek physical possession to protect itself against the owner skimming off the income while the property deteriorates the lender will usually look to the traditional remedies granting constructive possession. These are contained in standard mortgage provisions for assignment of rents and for appointment of a receiver in case of default.

Generally, an assignment of rents can be activated in title, intermediate and some lien states by the mortgagee's serving notice on the tenants in the property to pay their rents to the mortgagee. Although an assignment of rents is of no value in a property like a hotel, restaurant or theatre with daily operating income, it may be more effective in the case of a property with monthly tenants. Frequently, however, when the mortgagee attempts to activate an assignment of rents, the tenants will react to the conflicting demands for rent from the owner and the mortgagee by not paying rent to either until the issue is resolved in court. And many courts, particularly in lien states, are unwilling to deliver the rents to the mortgagee even if such action is warranted, preferring instead to appoint an independent receiver to collect and apply the rents.

Convincing the court to appoint a receiver, though, is not always easy. In some jurisdictions a provision in the mortgage for appointment of a receiver upon the mortgagee's demand is sufficient as a matter of course to get a receiver installed. But in a few states it has been almost impossible to get a receiver appointed because of legislation enacted during the depression years to protect homeowners and farmers. In between, are those courts which require proof that the security is impaired and sometimes also that the borrower is insolvent. Courts differ considerably on what constitutes impairment and what is required to prove it. Where the court's criterion is replacement value rather than economic value, it is difficult to prove that the property is impaired unless the building is being so poorly maintained that physical inspection shows a sharp deterioration in value. Impairment may also be demonstrated where the economic values have plummeted dramatically; for example, where utilities are cut off because of nonpayment and large numbers of tenants are leaving.

The mortgagee may present expert testimony from the appraiser who made the original loan appraisal that because of the economic decline of the property—the failure to reach certain rental levels, for example—the present value of the property is less than the appraised value on which the loan was based. In the case of certain institutional lenders, the mortgagor may counter by noting that under state law the lender was prohibited from making a loan of more than 75 percent of the property's value so that the economic value of the property had to fall more than 25 percent for the loan to be impaired. It is difficult for a lender to admit what is often true—that the original loan exceeded 75 percent of value, and therefore any significant loss of value endangers its mortgage.

The struggle to have a receiver appointed can take too much time, in the face of what appears to be obvious need. In the case of one apartment hotel in Miami, for example, after defaulting on a mortgage of $7,500,000, the owner sold the property for $12,000 in cash to two out-of-state speculators. A purchase of defaulted property with a yearly gross income of $4,000,000 for a cash price that low inevitably suggests that the purchaser has in mind quickly recouping the cash portion of his purchase price from any available funds, as well as taking advantage of whatever else he can milk from the property. The buyers of this property quickly retrieved their investment and more at the expense of the creditors. They purchased three Cadillac cars for $65,000 in due bills and entered into favorable long-term leases with members of their families. Yet, it took almost two months from the time the mortgagee requested the court to appoint a receiver to get a receiver appointed.

Finally, a receiver is too often chosen by the court because of his political connections or friendship rather than his managerial ability and real estate knowhow. And the award for a receiver's fees can eat up a good part of the property's income.

B. Deed in Lieu of Foreclosure and Mortgage Foreclosure

Ultimately, the mortgagee will seek repayment of its loan by recovering and selling the underlying security. Almost every state upholds the validity of an owner's voluntary conveyance of the property to the lender by a deed in lieu of foreclosure. And a number of owners are willing to turn over defaulted property without cost or only for legal fees in order to maintain their relationship with a particular lender or their reputation in the real estate lending community—or sometimes to get off the hook of a possible deficiency judgment. At first blush, therefore, a voluntary conveyance would appear to be the quickest and least expensive way for the mortgagee to recover the property. Mortgagees are wary about taking a deed in lieu of foreclosure, however, because of the possibility that if bankruptcy is filed against the debtor within four months of the conveyance the conveyance may be set aside as a preference. They may also be concerned with the less likely possibility that in case of bankruptcy within a year the transfer may be deemed fraudulent under the Bankruptcy Act. Many title companies refuse title insurance on a deed in lieu of foreclosure until expiration of the four month preference period. In some cases they may require an independent appraisal to satisfy themselves that there is fair consideration for the transfer in order to comply with the fraudulent transfer provisions of the Act. Moreover, a voluntary conveyance from the owner does not cut off junior mortgage or mechanics' liens on the property, so that the mortgagee still must face the prospect of a foreclosure action to wipe out those liens. A final obstacle to a voluntary conveyance in some states results from the fact that the state transfer tax is calculated on the total value of the property including the mortgage rather than on the cash consideration. Such a tax might run quite high on a transfer by deed.

The usual way for the mortgagee to realize on its security is to foreclose on the property and see it sold to a third party or buy it in the foreclosure sale. The laws governing mortgage foreclosure are the outgrowth of efforts by the courts and legislatures to balance two competing claims: the secured lender's right to its security and the owner's right to whatever value the property has above the mortgage loan. ...

If real estate were traded in a ready auction market like listed securities, the foreclosure sale would have resolved the problem of the mortgagee's and owner's competing equities. The security would be sold on the market, the debt repaid to the lender and any excess returned to the owner. But real estate does not trade freely in an auction market. Most real estate buyers are not accustomed to all-cash purchases, and require the flexibility of face-to-face negotiation to tailor a transaction to meet the economic and tax needs of the parties. Under the best of circumstances it takes time and most often a knowledgeable broker to find a buyer for real property. Under the circumstances of a forced auction sale, it is almost impossible to find a buyer. As a result, in about 99 percent of public foreclosure sales the mortgagee ends up as the only bidder in the sale and buys the property in. An auction sale is particularly ineffective during periods of economic depression and collapsed real estate values. Yet, it is in periods of economic strain that large numbers of foreclosures occur and mortgagors get wiped out, eliciting the concern of voters, judges and legislators. And the courts and legislators have responded by formulating a variety of laws and procedures aimed at protecting the owner from losing his equity in the property. ...

MURRAY, DEEDS IN LIEU OF FORECLOSURE: PRACTICAL AND LEGAL CONSIDERATIONS

26 Real Property Probate & Trust Journal 459, 461–468 (1991).

II. ADVANTAGES TO LENDER AND BORROWER

From a lender's standpoint there are many advantages to accepting a voluntary conveyance of real property from a borrower. Some of the most important include:

1. The lender or its nominee becomes the owner of the property and can control its operation and obtain all its income. The lender can preserve valuable contracts and tenants can immediately take steps to maximize the economic value of the property.

2. The parties can quickly negotiate and consummate the transaction, with fee title vesting in the lender upon recordation of the deed. The lender immediately obtains marketable title.

3. The potential negative publicity, time (including redemption periods), and expense of a foreclosure action (including receivership) can be avoided. The lender's acquisition of the property makes it unnecessary to extinguish the borrower's interest through foreclosure and to wait until the end of the redemption period to acquire title.

4. If the transaction is structured and documented properly and if the equity in the property does not exceed the amount of the outstanding debt, the transaction is not likely to be set aside by a bankruptcy court or a court of equity if the borrower later files bankruptcy or attempts to rescind the transaction based on fraud or coercion.

Several advantages exist for the borrower who offers to convey to the lender real property securing a loan. These advantages include:

1. The borrower can obtain release of all or some of the personal liability under the mortgage indebtedness, whether such liability exists under the loan documents, separate guaranty agreements, personal undertakings, indemnities, or otherwise.

2. The borrower can avoid the publicity, notoriety, expense, and time involved in foreclosure litigation.

3. The lender might agree to pay all or part of the expenses of the transfer (for example, transfer taxes, title costs, delinquent taxes, debts to trade creditors, attorney's fees, or recording fees) or might agree to pay additional monetary consideration for the voluntary conveyance of the property.

4. The lender might grant certain limited possessory or other property rights to the borrower. These rights could include, for example, a lease, an option to purchase, a right of first refusal, the right to manage or lease the property, or the right to consult on certain aspects of the operation of the property.

III. OFFER TO DEED

Unless the offer of conveyance by the borrower is voluntary, there is a significant risk that the borrower may later contest the transaction. Factors that taint a transaction include undue pressure, fraud (actual or constructive), unconscionable advantage, duress, undue influence, or grossly inadequate consideration. For example, if the borrower successfully argues duress or undue influence, the entire transaction may be set aside. In the alternative, the borrower may choose to recover the value of the property, the equity of redemption, or the profits realized on resale.   Additionally, if the lender's conduct is flagrant or outrageous, courts may assess punitive damages against the lender.   Before a court will set aside a transaction, the borrower must clearly show that the lender used the borrower's necessity to drive a hard bargain and must conclusively prove wrongful conduct by the lender.

Because the right of redemption prior to foreclosure is cut off by a deed in lieu of foreclosure, the borrower may make a "clogging the equity" argument.   Based on old case law, this doctrine holds "once a mortgage, always a mortgage."   Consequently, no mortgage provision can allow the lender to obtain a "collateral advantage" or can prevent the borrower from redeeming and retaining ownership of the mortgage property prior to entry of a valid foreclosure decree upon full payment of the indebtedness.   Although the borrower, as part of the mortgage transaction, may not barter the equity of redemption, the borrower may, in the absence of fraud, undue influence, oppression or duress, convey the fee interest at a subsequent time for adequate consideration.

To ensure that courts deem a transaction voluntary, the borrower should originate the offer to deed.   The borrower or the borrower's attorney should submit a written offer to convey to the lender voluntarily offering to deed the property and stating the reasons for the offer.   By establishing the voluntary nature of the offer, the lender will not be subject to later claims by the borrower that the lender did not act in "good faith" or that the transaction should be set aside because it constitutes an "insider" transaction under the Bankruptcy Code.   After the lender receives the borrower's written offer to convey, the transaction must be closed promptly, or the lender should proceed with foreclosure to avoid delay tactics by the borrower.   The lender should send a reply letter acknowledging the offer, stating the express conditions under which it will accept a conveyance.   The letter should specify that no contractual obligation to accept the property exists until all required documentation is fully executed and all considerations are paid, delivered, or both.   A lender is under no obligation to accept a deed tendered by a borrower unless the borrower meets all conditions required by the lender.

IV. DOCUMENTATION AND CONDITIONS

All terms and conditions of the voluntary conveyance, including waivers, estoppels, warranties, representations, and express recitals of consideration, should be set forth in a written agreement between the borrower and the lender entitled the "Settlement Agreement."   The Settlement Agreement should be structured to retain the lender's rights against guarantors and any other parties secondarily liable for repayment of the loan, unless the lender intends to release such parties along with the borrower.

A.   Deed In Escrow

In general, an agreement to give a deed in lieu of foreclosure in the future if certain conditions arise should be avoided.   An example of the type of agreement is when a borrower places a deed in escrow with a third party such as a title insurance company. Courts might construe such an agreement as an equitable mortgage, and the borrower may claim that the lender must foreclose to enforce the provisions of the agreement. Courts of equity will closely scrutinize these types of transactions. In addition, title insurance companies may not provide coverage for this type of escrow arrangement.

B. Consideration

The Settlement Agreement must recite actual and adequate consideration. The amount of debt canceled and any additional cash consideration given by the lender should normally equal or exceed the fair market value of the property. To substantiate the fair market value of the property, the lender should obtain a thorough appraisal by an independent professional appraiser or by a qualified appraiser employed by the lender. In addition, the Settlement Agreement should state that both the lender and the borrower acknowledge that the current value of the property is equal to or less than the outstanding indebtedness. The lender usually should not accept a voluntary conveyance unless the appraisal indicates the property is worth no more than the amount of the outstanding debt, including delinquent interest and advances.

CUNA MORTGAGE v. AAFEDT

Supreme Court of North Dakota, 1990.
459 N.W.2d 801.

LEVINE, Justice.

This is a consolidated appeal by Dean W. and Pamela J. Aafedt from summary judgments in favor of CUNA Mortgage, also known as CUNA Mortgage Corporation [CUNA], foreclosing three real estate mortgages. We affirm.

In November 1985, the Aafedts executed three promissory notes, each in the amount of $15,150 and payable to the Williston Cooperative Credit Union, to finance the purchase of three townhouse properties. To secure the debts, the Aafedts gave the Credit Union separate short-term redemption mortgages for each of the three individual lots. The mortgages were insured by the United States Department of Housing and Urban Development [HUD]. The Credit Union subsequently assigned the notes and mortgages to CUNA. The Aafedts defaulted on the notes in February 1989.

In October 1989, CUNA commenced these actions to foreclose the mortgages. CUNA stated in the foreclosure complaints that it would not seek deficiency judgments in separate actions against the Aafedts. The Aafedts, through counsel, offered to deed the properties back to CUNA in lieu of the foreclosure actions. CUNA rejected the Aafedts' offer to deed back the properties, apparently, because HUD would not agree to that procedure and would not reimburse CUNA for the funds CUNA invested if CUNA accepted the deed. In spite of CUNA's rejection of the offer to deed back the properties, the Aafedts executed a quitclaim deed purportedly conveying all the properties to CUNA. The quitclaim deed was recorded on November 2, 1989, without the knowledge of CUNA.

The Aafedts then filed their answers in which they admitted all of the allegations in the complaints but asserted that the actions should be dismissed because they had already conveyed the properties to CUNA by quitclaim deed. The Aafedts moved for summary judgment dismissing the actions. The trial court granted summary judgments in favor of the Aafedts on December 1, 1989, on the basis that CUNA had failed to respond.

On December 11, 1989, CUNA moved for relief from the summary judgments under Rule 60(b), N.D.R.Civ.P., asserting that "a timely response to the Motion was completed and served upon the [Aafedts], but because of mistake or inadvertence, the original documents were not filed with the Court." CUNA also requested the trial court to consider its response to the Aafedts' original motion and to grant summary judgments in its favor foreclosing the mortgages.

The trial court granted CUNA's Rule 60(b) motion and vacated the December 1 summary judgments. The court concluded that the Aafedts' quitclaim deed was void, determining that "the act of deeding the property to [CUNA] was done unilaterally, without [CUNA's] consent or acceptance and not duly delivered to [CUNA]." The court also granted summary judgments in favor of CUNA foreclosing the three mortgages. These appeals followed.

. . .

The Aafedts ... assert that the trial court erred in concluding, as a matter of law, that the quitclaim deed purportedly conveying the properties to CUNA was void.

Under North Dakota law, conveyance by deed takes effect upon delivery of the deed by the grantor. *Fredrick v. Fredrick*, 178 N.W.2d 834, 837 (N.D.1970); § 47–09–06, N.D.C.C. Absent a delivery of the deed, the deed is of no effect. *First Nat'l Bank in Minot v. Bloom*, 264 N.W.2d 208, 210 (N.D.1978) [quoting *Stark County v. Koch*, 107 N.W.2d 701, 705 (N.D.1961)]. Because "an estate cannot be thrust upon a person against his will" [23 Am.Jur.2d *Deeds* § 173, at p. 195 (1983)], it is well settled that "[a]cceptance by the grantee is an essential part of a delivery." *Arnegaard v. Arnegaard*, 7 N.D.475, 75 N.W. 797, 805 (1898). *See also* 8 G. Thompson, *Commentaries on the Modern Law of Real Property* § 4252, at p. 166 (1963); 4 H. Tiffany, *The Law of Real Property* § 1055 (3d ed.1975); Annot., *What constitutes acceptance of deed by grantee*, 74 A.L.R.2d 992, 995 (1960).

In this case, a CUNA official stated by affidavit that CUNA "rejected all offers of the [Aafedts] to deed the properties back to it in lieu of foreclosure" and that "the preparation, execution and placing of record" of the quitclaim deed "were not made with the consent, knowledge or acceptance of" CUNA. The Aafedts do not dispute these statements, but assert that there was a "constructive acceptance" of the deed by CUNA because four weeks lapsed before CUNA formally voiced any resistance to the deed being placed of record. The Aafedts provide us with no authority to support this argument. We treat their "constructive acceptance" argument as an assertion that CUNA's four-week silence raised a presumption of acceptance of the quitclaim deed.

The recording of a deed may create a rebuttable presumption of its delivery to, and its acceptance by, the grantee. *Dinius v. Dinius*, 448 N.W.2d 210, 216 (N.D.1989) [quoting *Eide v. Tveter*, 143 F.Supp. 665, 671 (D.C.N.D.1956)]. A failure to renounce a deed after knowledge of its existence may also in some circumstances be sufficient to show that a grantee accepted the deed. 23 Am.Jur.2d, *supra*, § 181, at p. 200. However, presumptions of acceptance arise only when the deed is beneficial to the grantee, not when the deed places a burden on the grantee. 8 G. Thompson, *supra*, at p. 176; 4 H. Tiffany, *supra*, § 1057, at p. 460; 23 Am.Jur.2d, *supra*, § 183, at p. 200; *Arnegaard v. Arnegaard, supra*. CUNA has asserted that it would be burdened by the deed because its ability to receive insured funds from HUD "would be in jeopardy" if it accepted the quitclaim deed. The Aafedts did not present any evidence to counter this assertion. Therefore, a presumption of acceptance did not arise in this case.

Moreover, we do not believe that CUNA's four-week delay in making a formal court objection to the recorded quitclaim deed, after the Aafedts had been informed by CUNA that a deed in lieu of foreclosure would be an unacceptable alternative, is sufficient to raise a genuine issue of material fact with regard to laches, estoppel, or a presumption of acceptance. We conclude that the trial court correctly determined on these undisputed facts that the Aafedts' attempted quitclaim conveyance of the properties to CUNA is void.

The premise underlying all of the Aafedts' arguments in this case is that CUNA's insistence on pursuing the foreclosure actions is unjustified and unfair because the relief it seeks could be more easily obtained by accepting a deed to the property. According to the Aafedts, CUNA's acceptance of a deed in lieu of foreclosure would not only alleviate a burden on the courts but would spare them the adverse publicity which accompanies a foreclosure action. We recognize that an action to foreclose a mortgage is an equitable proceeding [*Federal Land Bank of St. Paul v. Overboe*, 404 N.W.2d 445, 448 (N.D.1987)], and are familiar with the maxim that "[h]e who invokes the jurisdiction of equity must come with clean hands...." *Sorum v. Schwartz*, 411 N.W.2d 652, 655 (N.D.1987).

Although the ultimate relief a mortgagee receives through a foreclosure action may often be the same as that acquired by accepting a deed in lieu of foreclosure, *i.e*, title to the property, the consequences to the mortgagor and mortgagee of using one method as opposed to the other in satisfying the mortgagee's claim can vary widely. *See* 3 R. Powell, *The Law of Real Property* ¶¶ 469.1 [practical effects] and 469.2[federal income tax effects] (1990). In this case, CUNA has asserted that, because of HUD rules and regulations,[1] it will be injured through the loss of HUD funds if it accepts the quitclaim deed in lieu of the foreclosures. The Aafedts have failed to present any evidence whatsoever to raise an inference that CUNA is pursuing the foreclosure actions in bad faith. Because the Aafedts admitted all the allegations in the foreclosure complaints, and absent any showing by the Aafedts of a bad faith refusal by CUNA to accept the deed in lieu of the foreclosure actions, we conclude that the trial court properly granted the summary judgments of foreclosure in favor of CUNA.

We conclude that the trial court did not err in granting CUNA's Rule 60(b) motion for relief from the December 1 dismissals, in declaring the quitclaim deed void, and in granting summary judgments in favor of CUNA in the foreclosure actions. Accordingly, the judgments are affirmed.

ERICKSTAD, C.J., and VANDE WALLE, GIERKE and MESCHKE, JJ., concur.

NOTE

If there were no HUD regulation affecting the parties, should the court have forced the lender in *CUNA Mortgage* to accept a deed in lieu of foreclosure? Would such a result be a legitimate expression of the trend elsewhere in the law to shift dispute resolution from the courts to the parties themselves or to other dispute resolvers? Reconsider the policies favoring nonjudicial foreclosure discussed at pages 479–495.

---

1. 24 C.F.R. § 203.357 allows mortgagees holding a mortgage insured by the FHA to accept deeds in lieu of foreclosure only under certain circumstances:

" § 203.357 *Deed in lieu of foreclosure.*

"(a) *Mortgagors owning one property.* In lieu of instituting or completing a foreclosure, the mortgagee may acquire property from one other than a corporate mortgagor by voluntary conveyance from the mortgagor who certifies that he does not own any other property subject to a mortgage insured or held by FHA. Conveyance of the property by deed in lieu of foreclosure is approved subject to the following requirements: "(1) The mortgage is in default at the time the deed is executed and delivered;

"(2) The credit instrument is cancelled and surrendered to the mortgagor;

"(3) The mortgage is satisfied of record as a part of the consideration for such conveyance;

"(4) The deed from the mortgagor contains a covenant which warrants against the acts of the grantor and all claiming by, through, or under him and conveys good marketable title;

"(5) The mortgagee transfers to the Commissioner good marketable title accompanied by satisfactory title evidence.

"(b) *Corporate mortgagors.* A mortgagee may accept a deed in lieu of foreclosure from a corporate mortgagor in compliance with the requirements of paragraph (a) of this section, if the mortgagee obtains the prior written consent of the Commissioner.

"(c) *Mortgagors owning more than one property.* The mortgagee may accept a deed in lieu of foreclosure in compliance with the provisions of paragraph (a) of this section, from an individual who owns more than one property which is subject to a mortgage insured or held by the FHA if the mortgagee obtains the prior written consent of the Commissioner."

3. BANKRUPTCY

The potential and actual bankruptcy of a party to a real estate transaction has a great effect on the other parties in the relationship. First, actions taken by creditors and other parties prior to bankruptcy may come back to haunt them in the event that bankruptcy does actually occur. Transfers by a debtor to a creditor prior to bankruptcy may ultimately be found to be a fraudulent conveyance or an avoidable preference. A creditor's behavior in dealing with a troubled borrower may lead to an equitable subordination of the lender's claim. Thus, the real estate attorney must be aware of the specter of bankruptcy in structuring transactions and advising clients in order to protect against the consequences of rearrangement of the deal should bankruptcy occur. These issues are developed in Durrett v. Washington National Insurance Co., In Re Pinetree Partners, Ltd., and the notes following those cases, at pages 857–885.

If bankruptcy does occur, the consensual arrangements of the debtor with creditors and other parties may be significantly or totally altered. For example, section 365 of the Bankruptcy Code allows the trustee in bankruptcy or debtor in possession to assume or reject executory contracts and leases. Reorganization plans may be permitted over the objections of some creditors under the "cram down" provisions. The automatic stay of actions against a debtor or her property which is imposed by the Code prevents a mortgagee from foreclosing unless an exception is granted and may also prevent a lender from taking self help, such as collecting rents under an assignment of rents by the debtor. These and related issues are discussed in notes at pages 874–885.

The first reading analyzes the reorganization provisions of the Bankruptcy Code which provide an alternative to debtors in distress.

NOTE, REAL ESTATE REORGANIZATIONS: THE NEW BANKRUPTCY CODE v. CHAPTER XII *

1980 University of Illinois Law Forum 251, 254–258 (1980).

The new Bankruptcy Code makes sweeping changes in the entire bankruptcy field, but some of the more far-reaching changes have come in the area of debtor reorganizations. The new reorganization law, codified as Chapter 11 of the new Code, is a consolidation and revision of former Bankruptcy Act Chapters X, XI, and XII. Railroad reorganizations are treated separately at the end of the new Chapter. The new Code has significantly reformed corporate reorganizations as they existed under old Chapters X and XI. The approach adopted by Congress to resolve the special problems of corporate reorganizations, however, will operate to the detriment of noncorporate real estate debtors who enjoyed a liberal reorganization law in old Chapter XII. The new Code represents a significant policy shift, granting increased protection to the secured creditor of the noncorporate real estate debtor. ...

I. A REAL ESTATE REORGANIZATION OVERVIEW

The reorganization process begins with the filing of a petition for bankruptcy with the Bankruptcy Court. Under old Chapter XII, only the debtor could file for relief; involuntary or creditor-forced reorganization was not possible. The new Code, however, provides for both voluntary and involuntary petitions. Once the petition is filed, all proceedings against the debtor are subject to an automatic stay.

After filing the petition, a party to the reorganization will file a reorganization plan with the court. In the usual voluntary case, the debtor files the plan, either simultaneously with the petition or later in the proceeding. In elaborate detail, the Code lists the provisions to be contained in an acceptable reorganization plan. The essential functions of these many provisions, however, can be reduced to three—to classify claims, to specify treatment for each class of creditors, and to provide in detail for the execution of the reorganization.

Claims are classified according to their legal character and interest in the debtor's estate, the most basic division being between secured and unsecured claims. Within each division, however, the claims may be further classified. Generally, only claims of the same legal character, of equal rank, and against the same property are placed in the same class. For secured claims, for example, two claims secured by a first mortgage on the same property are put in the same class, but a first mortgage claim and a second mortgage claim will fall into separate classes. Mechanic's lien holders are likewise separated from mortgagees. Furthermore, two claims of the same kind and rank will be separated if they are secured by different property: the first mortgage claim on the apartment phase of a real estate development, for example, will be in a class separate from the first mortgage claims on the condominium phase.

Unsecured claims, which include deficiency claims, personal notes, accounts, contract claims, and others, are generally classed together regardless of form. All claims sharing the characteristic of unsecured indebtedness, therefore, usually rank equally in the reorganization plan. If an unsecured claim has a special status which merits priority, however, it may receive classification. Both old Chapter XII and the new Code, for example, provide specifically for priority of unsecured claims such as accrued wages, contributions to employee benefit plans, and claims of governmental units.

In a typical real estate reorganization, the classes consist of one or more mortgagee classes, a lien-holder's class, classes for priority claims such as accrued wages, and an unsecured debt class. The mortgagee classes are likely to have only one creditor in each class, although the other classes may have multiple creditors.[46]

46. Real estate may be subject to several succeeding mortgages, each in a separate class. Each mortgage, however, is likely to be held by only one entity, be it a

Specifying treatment of the debts of each class is another important aspect of the plan and, in fact, is the essence of a reorganization. Original contractual obligations yield to the provisions of a judicially confirmed reorganization plan. Under the terms of a typical reorganization plan, the rights and duties of the parties are redefined in one of two ways. First, the plan may restructure the debt to provide extended payment at possibly reduced installments. In the alternative, a plan may scale down the debt, reducing the debtor's obligation to an amount less than the full claim.

Once a plan is filed, the process of soliciting acceptances for the plan begins. The proponent of the plan, usually the debtor, must transmit to each claimholder a summary of the plan and a written disclosure statement. The court must approve the disclosure statement, which must contain "adequate information" to allow the claimholder to make an informed judgment about the plan. After the creditors have received the statement, the proponent solicits acceptances from each creditor class. Under the new Code, class acceptance of a plan is conditioned upon a two-pronged vote of approval: holders of two-thirds of the total amount of claims, and a majority of the total number of claimholders, must assent to the plan.

Once the acceptances have been solicited and received, a court must analyze the terms of the proposed plan in light of the Code's list of technical prerequisites to judicial confirmation. If a plan meets these requirements, the court's confirmation will be granted to make the plan legally binding if all the credit classes have accepted the plan. Even if one or more creditor classes dissent, however, the court can confirm the plan if it meets certain statutory requirements for creditor protection. This alternative method of confirmation, commonly known as the "cram-down," will not be used on the court's own initiative; a party to the reorganization, usually the debtor, must request the cram-down.

Two sections of the old Chapter XII outlined the cram-down procedure. The first section required the debtor to provide dissenting secured classes "adequate protection" for the realization of the value of their debts. If each class, excluding those who received adequate protection, accepted the plan, the second section permitted a court to confirm the plan. Thus, a judicial finding of "adequate protection" in effect nullified a class dissent and permitted cram-down.

The new Code's cram-down is contained in a subsection of the section dealing with confirmation of the plan. The new Code no longer uses "adequate protection" concepts to preclude a class from the acceptance vote. Under the new Code, after the acceptance vote is taken, a court may confirm a plan despite a secured creditor class's dissent provided that the plan meets one of three statutory provisions designed

bank, investment house, insurance company, or individual. The real estate reorganization, therefore, differs from the corporate situation in which bonds secured by asset mortgages are likely to be held by many investors. . . .

to insure that the dissenting creditors will receive the full amount of their claims.

The availability of a cram-down is essential to keeping the debtor whole in a reorganization attempt. Without a cram-down, secured creditors could always thwart reorganization through dissent and then foreclose on the significant assets of the debtor. Cram-down is especially significant in real estate reorganizations, because the property, often heavily mortgaged to obtain maximum tax benefits, is usually the only significant asset.

The final step in reorganization is the execution of the plan. Unlike corporate reorganizations in which the issuance of securities may create problems, the execution of a real estate reorganization is relatively simple. Moreover, the court may issue any orders necessary to effectuate the provisions of the plan.

DURRETT v. WASHINGTON NATIONAL INSURANCE COMPANY

United States Court of Appeals, Fifth Circuit, 1980.
621 F.2d 201.

ORMA R. SMITH, District Judge:

This appeal concerns an action instituted in the United States District Court for the Northern District of Texas, wherein plaintiff Jack W. Durrett, Sr. (herein "Durrett"), acting as debtor in possession under Chapter XI of the Bankruptcy Act,[1] 11 U.S.C. §§ 701, et seq., seeks to set aside and vacate an alleged transfer of real property effectuated nine days prior to the filing of a Petition for an Arrangement under Chapter XI. Durrett charges that the transfer is voidable under section 67(d) of the Act, 11 U.S.C. § 107(d).[2] The district court held

---

1. The sale of the property under attack here, occurred January 4, 1977. Plaintiff filed a Petition for Arrangement Under Chapter XI of the Bankruptcy Act on January 13, 1977. Section 403(a) of Pub.L. No. 95–598, Title I (Nov. 6, 1978), 92 Stat. 2549; provides as follows:

A case commenced under the Bankruptcy Act, and all matters and proceedings in or relating to any such case, shall be conducted and determined under such Act as if this Act [Pub.L. 95–598] had not been enacted, and the substantive rights of parties in connection with any such bankruptcy case, matter, or proceeding shall continue to be governed by the law applicable to such case, matter, or proceeding as if the Act had not been enacted.

Because the acts giving rise to this litigation occurred before the effective date of the new bankruptcy act, Pub.L. 95–598, the rights of the litigants are governed by "Repealed Title 11". When reference is made

herein to the "Act" or the "Bankruptcy Act" the same shall refer to "Repealed Title 11".

2. Section 67(d) of the Act provides in pertinent part:

(1) For the purposes of, and exclusively applicable to, this subdivision: ... (e) consideration given for the property or obligation of a debtor is "fair" (1) when, in good faith, in exchange and as a fair equivalent therefor, property is transferred ....

(2) Every transfer made and every obligation incurred by a debtor within one year prior to the filing of a petition initiating a proceeding under this title by or against him is fraudulent (a) as to creditors existing at the time of such transfer or obligation, if made or incurred without fair consideration by a debtor who is or will be thereby rendered insolvent, without regard to his actual intent; ...

(6) A transfer made or an obligation incurred by a debtor adjudged a bankrupt

that the non-judicial sale involved in the litigation constituted a transfer within the meaning of section 67(d). However, the court determined that the amount paid by the purchaser at the sale conducted by a trustee in the foreclosure of a deed of trust executed by Durrett, the indebtedness which it secured being then in default, was a "fair" consideration and a "fair equivalent" within the meaning of section 67(d)(1), (e)(1) of the Act, 11 U.S.C. § 107(d)(1), (e)(1). The court denied the relief sought by Durrett and he appeals. We reverse.

A review of the record on appeal reflects the following facts. On April 7, 1969, Durrett executed a note in the amount of $180,000.00 in favor of Southern Trust and Mortgage Company (hereafter "Southern"). The note was secured by a deed of trust upon the subject real property. Southern, on April 7, 1969, assigned the trust deed and note to defendant, The Washington National Insurance Company (hereafter "Washington"). Defendant J.H. Fields, Jr. (hereafter "Fields"), was named as the trustee in the deed of trust. The deed of trust contained a provision for a public sale of the real property thereby conveyed, in case of default in payment of the indebtedness.

On December 13, 1976, Fields, in his capacity of trustee, posted the property for foreclosure sale. The sale was held on January 4, 1977. Defendant Shannon Mitchell, Sr. (hereafter "Mitchell"), appeared at the sale and bid the sum of $115,400.00 for the property. This was the only bid received by the trustee at the sale. The amount of the bid was the exact amount necessary to liquidate the indebtedness secured by the deed of trust. Upon receipt of the bid price, Fields executed and delivered to Mitchell a trustee's deed to the property. The parties agree that Mitchell did not have any actual fraudulent intent when making the purchase. He responded to the notice of sale and became the successful bidder. Mitchell and Durrett are the only parties now interested in the case.

Durrett contends that the transfer of the property, pursuant to foreclosure of the deed of trust, is voidable under the provision of section 67(d).

The district court dismissed the complaint after a non-jury trial. In its findings of fact, the court held that the fair market value of the property on January 4, 1977, the date of the foreclosure sale, was the sum of $200,000.00.

The parties do not take issue with this finding. Both agree that it is not clearly erroneous.

under this title, which is fraudulent under this subdivision against creditors of such debtor having claims provable under this title, shall be null and void against the trustee, except as to a bona fide purchaser, lienor, or obligee for a present fair equivalent value: ... *And provided further,* That such purchaser, lienor, or obligee, who without actual fraudulent intent has given a consideration less than fair, as defined in this subdivision, for such transfer, lien, or obligation, may retain the property, lien, or obligation as security for repayment. ... (Emphasis in original).

Durrett asserts, on appeal, only one assignment of error, i.e., "Is $115,400.00 payment for an asset worth $200,000.00, a 'fair equivalent' ".

In consideration of the issue of "fair equivalent", we should determine by what standard we are to judge the district court's conclusion of law that the amount paid for the property, $115,400.00, is "fair" consideration and a "fair equivalent" within the meaning of section 67(d)(1), (e)(1).

We have held that our review of conclusions of law by the district court in non-jury cases is not restricted by the "clearly erroneous" rule and will be reversed if incorrect.

The question with which we are confronted is whether the district court's conclusion of law on the "fair equivalent" issue is incorrect, when considered in light of the record made in the district court and the applicable case law.

The parties have cited a number of cases which deal with this issue. A great percentage of these, however, involve factual situations quite different from the facts which exist in this appeal. Here, there is involved only one event, i.e., one parcel of real estate sold at a foreclosure sale for a price which is approximately 57.7 percent of the fair market value of the property. Is the price paid a "fair equivalent" for the transfer of the property? We hold that it is not.

The sale of real property was involved in one of the cases cited by Durrett, Schafer v. Hammond, 456 F.2d 15 (10th Cir.1972). There the Tenth Circuit affirmed a holding by the district court that a sale of real property for approximately 50 percent of its market value was void for lack of a fair consideration. Here, Mitchell paid slightly more than 50 percent (57.7%) for the property involved. The sale, however, deprived the bankruptcy estate of an equity in the property of $84,600.00, if computed on the $200,000.00 market value fixed by the district court.

We have been unable to locate a decision of any district or appellate court dealing only with a transfer of real property as the subject of attack under section 67(d) of the Act, which has approved the transfer for less than 70 percent of the market value of the property.

Assuming, arguendo, that we should review the district court's conclusion of law as a finding of fact under the "clearly erroneous" standard, the results would be the same. We cannot affirm the district court on this issue. Our review of the entire evidence leaves us with a definite and firm conviction that the price which Mitchell paid for the property at the trustee's sale was not a "fair equivalent" for the property. Under such circumstances, it is our duty to declare the transfer voidable under section 67(d).

The defendant-appellee Mitchell seeks to sustain the final judgment of the district court on the ground that the transfer accomplished by the trustee pursuant to the power of sale provision of the deed of trust was not a transfer *made* by the debtor in possession within the contemplation of section 67(d). We find this position to be without merit.

The word "transfer" is defined in section 1 of the Act, 11 U.S.C. § 1. Section 1 provides in pertinent part:

> The words and phrases used in this title and in proceedings pursuant hereto shall, unless the same be inconsistent with the context, be construed as follows:
>
> . . .
>
> (30) "Transfer" shall include the sale and every other and different mode, direct or indirect, of disposing of or of parting with property or with an interest therein or with the possession thereof or of fixing a lien upon property or upon an interest therein, absolutely or conditionally, voluntarily or involuntarily, by or without judicial proceedings, as a conveyance, sale, assignment, payment, pledge, mortgage, lien, encumbrance, gift, security, or otherwise; the retention of a security title to property delivered to a debtor shall be deemed a transfer suffered by such debtor; . . .

The comprehensive character of this definition leads us to conclude that the transfer of title to the real property of the debtor in possession pursuant to an arrangement under Chapter XI of the Act, by a trustee on foreclosure of a deed of trust, to a purchaser at the sale constitutes a "transfer" by debtor in possession within the purview of section 67(d). The actual transfer of title was made by Durrett to Fields, as trustee, via the deed of trust, executed April 7, 1969, to secure an indebtedness then owing to Southern and thereafter assigned to Washington. Possession of the property was retained by Durrett subject to the power of the trustee to sell and deliver possession of the property, on default, at a foreclosure sale. While the actual conveyance of title by Durrett was made on April 7, 1969, possession was retained until foreclosure of the deed of trust. The "transfer" within the contemplation of the Act, was not final until the day of the foreclosure sale, January 4, 1977. This was accomplished within the one-year period provided by section 67(d)(2), 11 U.S.C. § 107(d)(2). This conclusion is supported by reliable and ample authority. See 1 Collier on Bankruptcy, § 1.30 at 130.28(2), (3) (14th ed. 1967), where it is said: "[t]he present definition covers not only alienations of title but includes surrender of possession".

For the reasons herein given, the judgment of the district court must be vacated, and the cause reversed with directions.

Upon remand, the district court shall enter judgment for plaintiff-appellant, directing the rescission of the transfer under section 67(d) of the Act, dealing with the property in such manner as will protect Mitchell's equity therein.

JUDGMENT VACATED; REMANDED WITH DIRECTIONS.

IN RE PINETREE PARTNERS, LTD.

United States Bankruptcy Court, Northern District of Ohio, 1988.
87 B.R. 481.

FINDINGS OF FACT, OPINION AND CONCLUSIONS OF LAW

JAMES H. WILLIAMS, Chief Judge.

Pinetree Partners, Ltd. (Pinetree), as debtor and debtor in possession, commenced the instant adversary proceeding against OTR and State Teachers Retirement System of Ohio (STRS)[1] wherein Pinetree seeks to subordinate or recharacterize the claims of OTR and the return of moneys paid by Pinetree to OTR. OTR denies both the factual and legal bases of Pinetree's allegations and has further alleged that Pinetree is equitably estopped by its conduct from raising these issues.

A four day trial was held at which time evidence was introduced and arguments of counsel were heard. Upon conclusion of the trial, the parties submitted to the court proposed findings of fact and conclusions of law.

FACTS

1. Pinetree, an Ohio Limited Partnership, was formed in late 1982 to acquire real property consisting of land in Albuquerque, New Mexico, upon which five office buildings, known as the Pinetree Office Park (Project), are situated.

2. CIDCO Partners One (CIDCO), an Ohio General Partnership, is the sole general partner of Pinetree. Thomas P. Slavin (Slavin) and Robert Messing (Messing) are the sole general partners of CIDCO.

3. STRS manages a retirement fund created by the Ohio state legislature for the benefit of present and former Ohio teachers. Ohio Rev.Code Section 3307.01 *et seq.* OTR is an Ohio general partnership that was formed to facilitate investments of STRS.

4. In 1981, Slavin learned of the Project and subsequently became interested in purchasing it. The Project was then owned by Banco Mortgage Company (Banco) which had purchased it out of foreclosure. Banco was willing to sell the Project for $10,850,000.00.

5. In late 1981 or early 1982, Slavin met James Sublett, then the Executive Director of STRS. Slavin eventually sought funding from OTR, and to assist OTR with its pre-commitment due-diligence, Slavin furnished OTR with cash flow forecasts for several years' operations of the Project.

---

1. The parties have stipulated that "for all purposes as relates to the within Adversary Proceeding, references, whether in the pleadings, briefs, or during the trial, to either OTR or STRS shall under the context be and mean either or both of them, despite their being separate entities." Accordingly all references to OTR hereinafter shall mean and include both and either OTR and STRS.

6. By letter dated April 14, 1982, Slavin made a proposal to OTR for it to finance the purchase of the Project. Slavin proposed "that you [OTR] serve as our mortgagee, with a 'step-up mortgage'; and secondly I am suggesting that you also serve in the capacity of land lessor."

7. On May 27, 1982, OTR delivered to Slavin a conditional letter of credit that provided, inter alia, that OTR would lend Pinetree $9,000,-000.00 at 12.5% interest for a 25–year term, subject to conversion and call provisions. The offer also called for OTR to purchase the underlying real estate from Pinetree for $900,000.00 with a lease-back provision.

8. This offer was accepted by Slavin on May 28, 1982.

9. On August 27, 1982, Banco and Slavin, as nominee for Pinetree, executed a purchase agreement for the purchase of the Project. Pinetree agreed to pay Banco $10,850,000.00.

10. On August 27, 1982, OTR delivered to Pinetree, and Pinetree accepted, a commitment in writing with respect to the then contemplated transactions. (Pinetree Commitment).

11. On September 22, 1982, Pinetree simultaneously purchased the Project from Banco and closed the transaction with OTR. The transaction between Pinetree and OTR was carried out in accordance with the Pinetree Commitment.

12. On September 22, 1982, and as part of the closings, the following documents were executed by Pinetree and OTR:

a. Pinetree's promissory note in the sum of $9,000,000.00 payable to OTR.

b. Pinetree's mortgage and security agreement wherein Pinetree is the mortgagor/debtor and OTR the mortgagee/secured party.

c. Purchase agreement for real estate wherein Pinetree sells a portion of the Project, being the land but not the five buildings situated thereon, to OTR for $900,000.00.

d. Documents captioned Agreement of Lease wherein OTR leases the land to Pinetree.

e. Memorandum of lease for purposes of recordation of the ground lease from OTR to Pinetree which was filed for record in Bernalillo County, New Mexico on September 23, 1982.

f. Memorandum of a conversion option agreement filed for record in Bernalillo County, New Mexico on or about September 23, 1982.

g. Conversion option agreement wherein Pinetree granted to OTR the option to convert under the terms set forth therein the mortgage loan from OTR to Pinetree to equity ownership in the Project.

h. Assignment of lessor's interest in leases wherein Pinetree assigned tenant leases with respect to occupants of the Project to OTR as security for the payment of the obligations of Pinetree to

OTR, filed for record in Bernalillo County, New Mexico on or about September 23, 1982.

i. Indemnification agreement wherein Pinetree undertook to guarantee perspective improvements to the Project as provided therein.

j. Special warranty deed from Pinetree to OTR, wherein Pinetree conveyed that portion of the Project consisting of the underlying land to OTR, and which was recorded in Bernalillo County, New Mexico on September 23, 1982.

k. Financing statements filed for record with the clerk and recorder of Bernalillo County, New Mexico and the New Mexico Secretary of State within a few days after September 22, 1982.

13. The $950,000.00 balance of the purchase price for the Project was provided by a portion of a $1,400,000.00 interim loan from National City Bank (NCB).

14. The NCB interim loan was not secured by any assets of Pinetree and was to be paid off out of the funds generated by the syndication of limited partnership units.

15. The working capital provided by the NCB interim loan was thought to be sufficient to cover the operating deficiencies projected for the years 1982 and 1983. For the years after 1983, cash flow from the operation was projected to be sufficient to cover Pinetree's working capital needs for the Project.

16. The parties contemplated that after the closing on September 22, 1982, Pinetree would proceed to syndicate and sell limited partnership units.

17. The syndication of limited partnership units was commenced by Pinetree in December, 1982, and a Private Placement Memorandum was prepared and used for such purposes.

18. OTR was given access to a copy of the Private Placement Memorandum and an opportunity to comment thereon prior to syndication being commenced.

19. The syndication efforts continued through the first quarter of 1983 which resulted in the sale of 35 limited partnership units at a selling price of $66,500.00 per unit for an aggregate sum of $2,327,500.00, plus a nominal additional sum to be contributed by the general partner.

20. The purchasers of the limited partnership units were to pay the purchase price in five installments as follows: $7,000.00 upon subscription, and thereafter $27,500.00, $15,000.00, $12,000.00 and $5,000.00 on April 1st of the succeeding four years.

21. At the time of the closing, the existing tenant leases at the Project were "below market." The income generated was therefore not sufficient to permit Pinetree to pay the market rate of return on the funds it borrowed from OTR. The prime interest rate as of the closing

date was approximately 13.5% per annum. The market interest rate for fixed rate return real estate loans was approximately 150 basis points (1.5%) per annum above the prime rate. Pursuant to the promissory note and ground lease, OTR was to receive a fixed return of 12.5% per annum. To induce OTR to make this below market rate loan, OTR received potential "kickers" in a "shared appreciation mortgage" so that in the event the Project was successful, OTR's return would increase.

22. Among provisions of the transaction documents between OTR and Pinetree were the following:

a. Pinetree was prohibited from engaging in any business other than the operation of the Project without the consent of OTR.

b. Pinetree was prohibited from constructing new buildings or additions to existing structures without the prior written consent of OTR.

c. Pinetree was prohibited from obtaining secondary financing or other borrowing without OTR's consent.

d. Pinetree was required to pay all closing costs and expenses plus up to $15,000.00 of OTR's legal fees.

e. OTR possessed an absolute veto power with respect to cancellation, modification, or rental adjustments to any existing tenant lease.

f. All existing and prospective leases were to be approved by OTR and assigned to OTR.

g. OTR was entitled to 12.5% fixed interest plus 50% of the difference between the fair market value of the Project and the then outstanding principal balance of the loan on final payment of the promissory note.

h. The $9,000,000.00 loan was payable in monthly installments of $98,175.00 commencing October 1, 1982.

i. Pinetree was not permitted to prepay the loan prior to the 11th year.

j. Pinetree was required to obtain OTR's consent before selling its interest in the Project.

k. Pinetree was required to obtain OTR's consent before granting to any other party any lien or interest in and to Pinetree's rights in the Project.

l. The ground lease and mortgage both contained cross defaults so that a default by Pinetree under either was a default under both.

m. Pinetree was required to deliver to OTR monthly operating statements and an annual audited financial statement. Additionally, OTR had the right at all reasonable times to inspect books, records, plans, drawings and other documents applicable to the Project.

n. OTR had the right at all reasonable times to enter into and inspect the Project.

o. The ground lease between Pinetree and OTR was for 25 years, unless sooner terminated as provided in the lease.

p. Pinetree, as lessee, had no option to extend the term of the lease. Pinetree had the right to repurchase the land from OTR upon full amortization of the mortgage. The purchase price was to be the fair market value.

q. OTR was entitled to receive additional rent of 50% of the annual cash flow. Annual cash flow was defined as gross revenues minus permitted expenditures for each lease year.

r. Pinetree was prohibited from entering into leases or other agreements which were based on income or profits.

s. OTR had the option to convert the loan, beginning in the 8th year of the loan, to a 60% interest in Pinetree, thereby completely terminating the loan.

t. If OTR did not exercise the conversion option, it was permitted to call the promissory note due and payable at the end of the 11th year after giving Pinetree 12 months' notice.

u. Upon default, OTR had the right to select and require the employment of a managing agent for the Project.

23. OTR requested that as a part of the transaction, the operations of the racquet club and health spa located in the Project be severed, as OTR was concerned the facility would adversely impact on OTR's tax exempt status.

24. OTR had prior experience with participation mortgages that had "kickers."

25. Neither Slavin nor Pinetree's counsel prior to September 22, 1982, had any experience with mortgages containing "kickers."

26. Pursuant to the Pinetree Commitment and in connection with the closing of the loan, Pinetree provided OTR with an opinion of its counsel. This opinion provided, inter alia, that the loan documents were enforceable in accordance with their terms.

27. John McCarter, Senior Vice President of AmeriTrust with 25 years' experience in commercial lending, testified that the provisions in the mortgage and lease were customary and not unusual in real estate transactions financed by insurance companies or pension funds at that time.

28. While the loan documents contained the aforesaid provisions, ... the evidence at trial showed that in practice they were of little or no significance in the dealings between Pinetree and OTR. The evidence showed:

(a) Pinetree never made any request for OTR's approval of secondary financing.

(b) OTR gave its consent to the only structural change requested. (E.F. Hutton expansion).

(c) OTR approved all leases presented by Pinetree.

(d) Pinetree made no request to sell its leasehold interest.

(e) The transaction was structured so that the health club property was not owned by Pinetree with the result that the rent under the ground lease would not be subject to unrelated business income under Section 512 of the Internal Revenue Code, 26 U.S.C. § 512.

(f) Pinetree did not seek to prepay the loan.

(g) OTR's visits to the Project were with Pinetree's knowledge and were at reasonable times.

(h) Even after default, OTR did not select a managing agent.

(i) Pinetree furnished routine financial information to OTR.

(j) OTR did not seek inspections of the books and records of Pinetree.

(k) OTR did not exercise its conversion option.

(l) OTR received no additional interest, due to the poor performance of the Project.

(m) OTR received no additional rent, due to the poor performance of the Project.

(n) The eleventh year of the loan is not until 1993. Accordingly, OTR has never had the right to call the Loan.

29. The Private Placement Memorandum issued to potential limited partners contained a tax opinion from Pinetree's prior counsel which characterized the promissory note as debt and the relationship between OTR and Pinetree as not being a joint venture or partnership.

30. The Private Placement Memorandum also contained cash flow projections of the expected income from operations at the Project for the years 1982–1991. These projections show that Pinetree expected operating deficits for the years 1982 and 1983 and positive cash flow beginning in 1984. It was expected that the initial working capital would be sufficient to fund the operating deficits.

31. Consistent with the projected cash flow deficits for 1982 and 1983 the limited partners of Pinetree would receive a return on their investment by passing through tax benefits. This is what actually occurred with the limited partners taking deductions on their individual tax returns for the losses passed through to them.

32. Pinetree has carried the loan on its financial statements and federal tax returns as a mortgage loan for each year since the loan was made. Pinetree accrued the interest arising under the promissory note on its 1982 and 1983 audited financial statements. Pinetree has deducted interest expenses from operating income on its federal tax returns in each year since its inception regardless of whether such interest was actually paid. Similarly, the lease payments made by Pinetree to OTR under the ground lease have been deducted from

Pinetree's operating income as rental expenses on its federal tax returns.

33.   From and after September 22, 1982 through March 28, 1984, there were numerous meetings and telephone conversations between Slavin and representatives of OTR.   The topic of these discussions concerned the status of syndication, tenant leases, prospective tenants, market conditions, operations and maintenance of the Project.

34.   During 1983, as a result of being "over-built" without a corresponding increase in demand for office space, the Albuquerque, New Mexico commercial real estate market began a decline that adversely affected the Project.   This decline was not expected by either party and has continued through 1987.   As the Albuquerque market declined, Pinetree was unable to generate sufficient operating income from the Project to support the debt service and lease payments to OTR.

35.   OTR was aware of the changing circumstances of the Albuquerque market which resulted in more favorable terms for tenants.

36.   In April of 1983, Pinetree informed OTR of the possible need for the financing of expansion and tenant improvements of certain spaced leased by E.F. Hutton.   OTR encouraged Pinetree to proceed with negotiations with Hutton regarding such expansion.   The expected cost of such work was approximately $200,000.00.   OTR informed Pinetree that it would consider the financing for the expansion.

37.   During the time Pinetree was negotiating with E.F. Hutton, Pinetree was consistently in default under the loan documents and did not provide OTR with acceptable terms for the curing of such defaults and the repayment of the desired financing.   Consequently, when asked by Pinetree to make an additional loan of $200,000.00 in December of 1983 for the proposed E.F. Hutton expansion, OTR refused.

38.   In December of 1983, a tenant, Plateau, Inc. (Plateau), which was going out of business, informed Pinetree of its desire to terminate its long-term lease.   Plateau and Pinetree entered into negotiations as to a buy-out by Plateau of its lease.   OTR was aware of these negotiations and was kept informed of their status.   OTR, however, did not become actively involved in these negotiations although it did have an opinion as to what would be an acceptable buy-out by Plateau.

39.   At some point in time when the Plateau negotiations were being conducted, Santa Fe Mining (Santa Fe), another tenant, was seeking to consolidate its operations at the Project.   Santa Fe had expressed some interest in the Plateau space.   Plateau did not completely vacate the Project until mid–1984, Santa Fe found alternative space at another location in Albuquerque and moved out of the Project.

40.   Even though OTR was to approve all lease agreements entered into between Pinetree and prospective tenants, OTR never informed Pinetree management as to general parameters that would be acceptable.

41. By mid-March, 1984, Pinetree was in substantial default under the promissory note and the ground lease. Payments were approximately $500,000.00 in arrears. As a result thereof, Slavin and Messing were asked to come to OTR's office in Columbus, Ohio. No disclosure was made to Slavin and Messing as to the purpose of this meeting or OTR's contemplated agenda of items to be discussed.

42. At the meeting on March 28, 1984, representatives of OTR, who were present with counsel, demanded Pinetree propose, within five days, a plan to bring current the arrearages under the promissory note and ground lease. OTR's Director of Investments, Stephen Mitchell, informed Slavin that unless satisfactory action was taken, OTR would initiate foreclosure proceedings. OTR had also prepared a deed in lieu of foreclosure which Slavin and Messing refused to sign.

43. On April 2, 1984, OTR filed a complaint against Pinetree in state court in New Mexico for foreclosure of the mortgage and security agreement. On April 9, 1984, Pinetree filed for relief under Chapter 11 of Title 11 thereby staying OTR's foreclosure proceedings.

44. Between September 22, 1982 and April 9, 1984, Pinetree paid to OTR approximately $1,625,300.00.

45. From April 10, 1984 through December 18, 1987, Pinetree paid to OTR approximately $1,386,100.00.

OPINION

A

EQUITABLE SUBORDINATION

Pinetree, based upon the facts and evidence, requests the court to subordinate the claims of OTR. It is well established that a bankruptcy court has the authority to subordinate a claim on equitable grounds. *See, Pepper v. Litton*, 308 U.S. 295, 60 S.Ct. 238, 84 L.Ed. 281 (1939). This exercise of equitable jurisdiction has been codified in 11 U.S.C. § 510(c) which provides:

> Notwithstanding subsections (a) and (b) of this section, after notice and a hearing, the court may—

> (1) under principles of equitable subordination, subordinate for purposes of distribution all or part of an allowed claim to all or part of another allowed claim or all or part of an allowed interest to all or part of another allowed interest; or

> (2) order that any lien securing such a subordinated claim be transferred to the estate.

Equitable subordination is an extraordinary remedy and certain conditions must be satisfied before the exercise of the subordination power becomes appropriate.

(i) The claimant must have engaged in some type of inequitable conduct.

(ii) The misconduct must have resulted in injury to the creditors of the bankrupt or conferred an unfair advantage on the claimant.

(iii) Equitable subordination of the claim must not be inconsistent with the provisions of the Bankruptcy Act.

In re Mobile Steel Company, 563 F.2d 692, 699–700 (5th Cir.1977) (citations omitted); *In re Bell & Beckwith*, 44 B.R. 664 (Bankr.N.D.Ohio 1984); *In re Teltronics Services, Inc.*, 29 B.R. 139 (Bankr.E.D.N.Y.1983); *In re Pacific Express*, 69 B.R. 112, 16 C.B.C.2d 286 (9th Cir.B.A.P.1986).

In applying the above tests, certain principles must be considered. First, the inequitable conduct need not have been related to the acquisition or assertion of the claim. Second, a claim should be subordinated only to the extent necessary to offset the harm which the debtor and its creditors suffered on account of the inequitable conduct. *In re Mobile Steel*, 563 F.2d at 701.

The burden is upon the objector to the claim to prove by a preponderance of the evidence that the claimant engaged in such substantial inequitable conduct to the detriment of the debtor's other creditors that subordination is warranted. *In re Teltronics*, 29 B.R. at 169; 3 Collier on Bankruptcy para. 510.05 (15th Ed.1987).

In applying equitable subordination, the creditor sought to be subordinated must: (a) have acted in a fiduciary capacity; (b) have breached a fiduciary duty; (c) that breach resulted in detriment to those claimants to whom a duty was owed; or, (d) committed an act of moral turpitude, causing damages to other creditors. *In re W.T. Grant Company*, 4 B.R. 53, 74 (Bankr.S.D.N.Y.1980) (citations omitted); affirmed 20 B.R. 186 (S.D.N.Y.); affirmed 699 F.2d 599 (2nd Cir.1983). Thus, the claims of fiduciaries, as well as those of non-fiduciaries, can be subordinated.

> The primary distinctions between subordinating the claims of insiders versus those of non-insiders lies in the severity of misconduct required to be shown, and the degree to which the court will scrutinize the claimant's actions towards the debtor or its creditors. Where the claimant is a non-insider, egregious conduct must be proven with particularity. It is insufficient for the objectant in such cases merely to establish sharp dealings; rather, he must prove that the claimant is guilty of gross misconduct tantamount to fraud, overreaching or spoliation to the detriment of others. Where the claimant is an insider, his dealings with the debtor will be subjected to more exacting scrutiny. If the objectant comes forward with sufficient substantiations of misconduct on the part of the insider claimant, the burden will shift to the insider to establish that each of his challenged transactions with the debtor had all the earmarks of an arms-length bargain.

In re Teltronics, 29 B.R. at 169. (Citations omitted).

The court, before reaching the merits of the allegations, must first determine the status of OTR. Normally, a creditor is not a fiduciary of either the debtor or other creditors of the debtor and "owes them no special obligation of fidelity in the collection of his claims." *In re Teltronics*, 29 B.R. at 169. *In re W.T. Grant*, 699 F.2d at 609–610.

As was stated by the Seventh Circuit in *In re Prima Company*, 98 F.2d 952, 965 (1938):

> Aside from the provisions of the bankruptcy law, a creditor has the right to call a loan when due and to lawfully enforce collection. He may refuse an extension for any cause which may seem proper to him, or even without any cause. The law provides certain means for the enforcement of claims by creditors. The exercise of those rights is not inherently wrongful.

This general rule that a non-insider creditor is under no fiduciary obligation to its debtor or to other creditors is not without exception. "In the rare circumstances where a creditor exercises such control over the decision-making processes of the debtor as amounts to a domination of its will, he may be held accountable for his actions under a fiduciary standard." *In re Teltronics*, 29 B.R. at 170. A "non-insider creditor will be held to a fiduciary standard only when his ability to command the debtor's obedience to his policy directives is so overwhelming that there has been, to some extent, a merger of identity. Unless the creditor has become, in effect, the *alter ego*, he will not be held to an ethical duty in excess of the morals of the market place." *In re Teltronics*, 29 B.R. at 171; *In re Ludwig Honold Manufacturing Company, Inc.*, 46 B.R. 125, 128 (Bankr.E.D.Pa.1985). "The creditor must exercise virtually complete control to be treated as a fiduciary." *In re Osborne*, 42 B.R. 988, 997 (W.D.Wis.1984).

In the instant proceeding, Pinetree asserts that OTR should be held to a fiduciary standard based on the control OTR exerted over Pinetree by virtue of: (1) the amount of financing; (2) the limitations in the loan documents; (3) the limitations in the ground lease; (4) the structure of the loan with its conversion options; and (5) the frequent meetings between Pinetree and OTR.

The court, however, does not reach this conclusion. The facts established at trial suggest that the rights OTR possessed ... were not excessive in light of the nature of the transaction and did not place OTR in control of Pinetree.

The loan agreement and related transactions between OTR and Pinetree were entered into at arms-length. Both parties were willing participants to the transaction and no coercion was applied to either Pinetree or OTR to assent to the conditions and requirements in the loan documents. The fact that no other lender was available to Pinetree does not alter this arms-length characterization.

Additionally, the rights and restrictions which OTR possessed were never utilized to a point where it could be found that OTR virtually controlled Pinetree. *In re Osborne, supra.* In fact, most of the rights and powers held by OTR were never exercised. The management of Pinetree was, at all times, in control of the debtor and made the day to day decisions necessary for the operation of the business.

As for the numerous meetings between Pinetree and OTR, the actions of OTR can only be characterized as those of a cautious lender. The failure of OTR to monitor closely a $9,000,000.00 loan would be a dereliction of its duty to its own principals and creditors.

Accordingly, OTR's relationship with Pinetree did not transcend that of debtor and creditor, and OTR will not be held to a fiduciary standard.

Having determined that OTR is not a fiduciary of Pinetree, Pinetree must therefore show that OTR engaged in gross misconduct tantamount to fraud, overreaching or spoliation to the detriment of other creditors. *In re Teltronics, supra.*

Pinetree asserts that this burden has been met and equitable subordination is appropriate based on the nature of the transaction itself and OTR's conduct after the transaction was consummated.

As the court stated earlier, the transaction was negotiated between the parties at arms-length. Further, there is undisputed testimony before the court that the terms of the loan documents were common and ordinary for loans of this type, in light of the fixed rate of return being below the then current market rate.

The fact that the loan documents contained "kickers" that enabled OTR to share in any potential good fortune of Pinetree does not in itself amount to inequitable conduct tantamount to fraud or overreaching. Additionally, the fact that OTR, through its representations, may have been a shrewd negotiator, again is not conduct amounting to fraud or overreaching.

As for OTR having access to Pinetree's books and records, requiring annual financial statements, and approval of rental leases and additional financing, these requirements can only be seen as those of a prudent lender protecting its interests. These rights possessed by OTR cannot be said to amount to gross misconduct on OTR's part.

Pinetree argued extensively at trial that it was undercapitalized at the time the transaction with OTR was entered into, and OTR knew of this undercapitalization. Consequently, it urges, OTR's knowledge and conduct supports subordination of its claims. The court, however, must find otherwise. Both Pinetree and OTR projected that the interim loan from NCB would provide enough working capital to sustain Pinetree until such time as the income from the operations would be sufficient to support the Project. Miscalculations by OTR as to the profitability of the Project is hardly conduct that can be characterized as inequitable and result in subordination. OTR, as a creditor of Pinetree, had nothing to gain by Pinetree being undercapitalized; just the opposite is true. OTR may not have thoroughly evaluated this transaction and may even have been slightly blinded by the prospects of a large return on its investment [2], but its lack of analysis as to the Project's viability cannot be characterized as egregious conduct that was detrimental to other creditors.

Pinetree also asserts that OTR's denial of an additional $200,000.00 loan to finance the construction of the E.F. Hutton extension amounts to inequitable conduct. Pinetree further asserts that OTR's lack of guidance as to a reasonable settlement with Plateau resulted in the loss of Santa Fe as a tenant.

The evidence produced at trial simply does not support either of these assertions. OTR was under no obligation to Pinetree, or other creditors, to extend additional financing. As the evidence reflected, Pinetree, at the time it requested the additional financing, was in substantial default of the original loan. OTR's refusal to extend additional money can only be construed to be cautious, not egregious, conduct.

As for settlement negotiations with Plateau, Pinetree was the appropriate party to conduct those negotiations. OTR may have been required to approve any settlement reached, but no settlement offer was communicated to OTR for which approval was requested. Additionally, if OTR had become directly involved in the settlement negotiations, this could be perceived as overreaching by a creditor.

As for the loss of Santa Fe as a tenant, besides the unexpected softening of the Albuquerque market, for which OTR was certainly not responsible, no evidence was presented to support a finding that OTR engaged in any conduct that forced Santa Fe to leave and was detrimental to other creditors of Pinetree.

Finally, Pinetree claims that because OTR met with Messrs. Slavin and Messing often and specifically demanded their presence in Columbus, Ohio, on March 28, 1984, at which meeting OTR threatened to foreclose upon its mortgage, it is guilty of "egregious conduct that is inequitable ..." The court finds, however, that such actions cannot support a claim for equitable subordination. Again, OTR's monitoring of its loan can only be seen, from the evidence presented to the court, to be that of a prudent lender. As for OTR threatening to foreclose, as previously stated, a creditor has a right to call a loan due and to lawfully enforce collection. *In re Prima, supra.*

Even if the court were to find the conduct of OTR to be egregious, no evidence has been presented by Pinetree to show that any other creditor relied to its detriment on any conduct by OTR. *In re W.T. Grant,* 4 B.R. at 74.

Accordingly, the claims of OTR are not subject to equitable subordination pursuant to Section 510(c).

2. The court uses the word investment in its "generic sense" and in no way intends for it to be read any broader or for it to appear that the court finds OTR to have an equity investment.

B

RECHARACTERIZATION

Pinetree alternatively asserts, for many of the same reasons given for its position that the claims should be subordinated, that OTR's claims should be recharacterized as an equity investment.

This issue was directly addressed in *In re Pacific Express, supra,* wherein the court held:

> Where the Code supports the court's ability to determine the amount and the allowance or disallowance of claims [11 U.S.C. § 502(a)], those provisions do not provide for the characterization of claims as equity or debt. The result achieved by such a determination, i.e. subordination, is governed by 11 U.S.C. § 510(c). Where there is a specific provision governing these determinations, it is inconsistent with the interpretation of the Bankruptcy Code to allow such determinations to be made under different standards through the use of the courts equitable powers. Although a bankruptcy court is essentially a court of equity, its broad equitable powers may only be exercised in a manner consistent with the provisions of the code.

Id. 69 B.R. 115, 16 C.B.C.2d at 290 (citations omitted).

This court agrees. The equitable powers of the court derive from the Bankruptcy Code and consequently reach no further than its provisions. Accordingly, the claims of OTR are not subject to recharacterization from debt to equity absent controlling provisions of the Bankruptcy Code. Section 510(c) *supra*.

. . .

CONCLUSIONS OF LAW

In conclusion the court finds:

(1) OTR's claims are not subject to equitable subordination pursuant to 11 U.S.C. § 510(c).

(2) OTR's claims are not subject to recharacterization by the court from debt to equity, absent controlling provisions in the Bankruptcy Code.

. . .

ORDER

For the reasons set forth in the accompanying Memorandum of Decision, the court finds the complaint to subordinate alleged claims, determine such to be contributions to capital, invalidation, avoidance, or reformation of promissory note, ground lease, real estate deed, mortgage and security agreement, assignment of leases, enforcement of conversion agreement, and to recover funds paid, filed on behalf of the plaintiff, Pinetree Partners, Ltd. against the defendants, OTR and State Teachers Retirement System of Ohio, not to be well taken.

IT IS THEREFORE ORDERED that the complaint of the plaintiff, Pinetree Partners Ltd. against defendants, OTR and State Teachers Retirement System be, and the same hereby is, DISMISSED.

IT IS FURTHER ORDERED that each party shall bear its own costs in conjunction with this action.

NOTES

1. Does *Durrett* properly align the objectives of bankruptcy law with the objectives of state foreclosure law? A year later, concern for *Durrett's* adverse impact on land finance markets prompted Judge Thomas A. Clark to dissent from a Fifth Circuit decision, Abramson v. Lakewood Bank & Trust, 647 F.2d 547 (5th Cir.1981), applying *Durrett's* holding that a foreclosure sale is a transfer within the meaning of section 67(d): "The cloud created over mortgages and trust deeds by making foreclosure sales subject to being voided by a bankruptcy trustee will naturally inhibit a purchaser other than the mortgagee from buying at foreclosure. This tends to depress further the prices of foreclosure sales and thus increase the potential size of the deficiency in each foreclosure...." 647 F.2d at 550.

Does federal bankruptcy policy dictate that *Durrett* be extended to the context of Chapter 7 liquidations, where its principal beneficiaries will be the debtor's unsecured creditors, or confined to the context of Chapter 11 reorganizations where the increased value produced on the foreclosure sale, or the return of the property in the event the sale is voided, will better advance the goals of reorganization?

Should *Durrett* be limited to nonjudicial foreclosures or should it apply to transfers following judicial foreclosures as well? *Durrett* aside, the title acquired by a buyer at a judicial foreclosure sale is far more secure than the title acquired at a nonjudicial foreclosure sale which is subject to collateral attack and, in many states, to statutory redemption. Thus, while the uncertainty created by *Durrett* may not significantly reduce the already low marketability of titles acquired at nonjudicial foreclosure sales, it may introduce a new element of uncertainty into judicial foreclosure sales. See generally, Colletti, A Title Insurer Looks at the Avoidance Provisions of the Bankruptcy Reform Act of 1978, 15 Real Prop., Probate & Trust J. 588 (1980).

What is Fair Market Value? The *Durrett* court compared the winning bid with the property's appraised fair market value and concluded that the bid was not a "fair equivalent." The flaw in this comparison is its apparent reliance for fair market value on the amount that would have been realized from a negotiated sale in which the buyer had the opportunity to arrange for the most suitable financing and for a title policy with no material exceptions, rather than the amount realized on a forced sale in which the property must be bought for all cash, within a limited time, and with no assurance that title will be free from attack. Indeed, the fact that the usual buyer at these sales is the mortgagee and the usual sales price is the mortgagee's untopped full credit bid, suggests that the land's fair market value will commonly be *less,* not more, than the amount of the outstanding debt. *Durrett* was the unusual case in which a third party, and not the mortgagee, bid the mortgage balance. And, if the property had in fact been worth more than the mortgage balance, other bidders would presumably have bid the price up further.

Appreciating the constrained economics of foreclosure sales, the Ninth Circuit Bankruptcy Appellate Panel refused "to follow *Durrett's* 70% fair market value rule for the reason that a regularly conducted sale, open to all bidders and all creditors, is itself a safeguard against the evils of private transfers to relatives and favorites." In re Madrid, 21 B.R. 424, 426–27 (9th Cir. BAP 1982), affirmed on other grounds, 725 F.2d 1197 (9th Cir.1984). Applying section 548 of the Bankruptcy Act, the successor to section 67(d) applied in *Durrett,* the panel concluded that the "law of foreclosure should be harmonized with the law of fraudulent conveyances. Compatible results can be obtained by construing the reasonably equivalent value requirement of Code § 548(a)(2) to mean the same as the consideration received at a non-collusive and regularly conducted foreclosure sale. Thus, in the absence of defects such foreclosure withstands avoidance as a fraudulent conveyance."

H.R. 5174, § 575, 130 Cong.Rec. § 6127 (Daily ed. May 21, 1984), proposed amending the Bankruptcy Act to provide that "A secured party or third party purchaser who obtains title to an interest of the debtor in property pursuant to a regularly conducted noncollusive foreclosure, power of sale, or other proceeding or provision of nonbankruptcy law permitting or providing for the realization of security upon default of the borrower under a mortgage, deed of trust, security agreement or other lien, whether before or after the date of the filing of the petition, gives reasonably equivalent value to the debtor ... if such creditor or third party bids in the full amount of the debt secured by such mortgage, deed of trust, security agreement or other lien at such foreclosure sale." This proposed change was ultimately rejected in the bill that became the 1984 Bankruptcy Amendments and Federal Judgeship Act of 1984, Pub.L. No. 98–353, 98 Stat. 333 (July 10, 1984).

When is Title Transferred? Another ground for rejecting *Durrett* is the one relied on by Judge Clark in his *Abramson* dissent: transfer of title occurs not at the foreclosure sale but, rather, upon the original execution of the deed of trust, an event that will usually occur well before the one-year period of section 67(d), 11 U.S.C.A. § 107(d), and in any event before the debtor becomes insolvent. The Ninth Circuit Court of Appeals relied exclusively on this ground in affirming the Bankruptcy Appellate Panel's decision in *Madrid.* Madrid v. Lawyers Title Insurance Corp., 725 F.2d 1197 (9th Cir.1984). Congress, however, soon appeared to repudiate this approach in the 1984 Bankruptcy Amendments and Federal Judgeship Act by amending section 101's definition of "transfer" to include "foreclosure of the debtor's equity of redemption." S. Amendment No. 3083 to H.R. 5174, 421(i), 130 Cong. Rec. S6118 (Daily ed. May 21, 1984). See In re Ehring, 900 F.2d 184

(9th Cir.1990) (questioning *Madrid* in light of statutory amendment, and finding that transfer occurs both at the initial perfection of the security interest and at foreclosure).

Should Involuntary Transfers Count? Finally *Durrett* might be rejected on the ground that because foreclosure is, from the debtor's viewpoint, an involuntary transfer in which she did not participate, it should not be considered a transfer for purposes of section 548 which permits the trustee to set aside a transfer "if the debtor ... received less than a reasonably equivalent value in exchange...." Thus, Judge Farris, concurring in the Ninth Circuit's *Madrid* decision argued that "one cannot presume fraud by the debtor in a transaction where the debtor was not a party.... I would therefore hold that only transfers where the bankrupt was a participant can be set aside for absence of 'reasonably equivalent value'." 725 F.2d 1203–4. But Congress apparently rejected this approach, too, in the 1984 Amendments by replacing the phrase in section 548(a), "if the debtor," with the phrase, "if the debtor voluntarily or involuntarily." Pub.L. 98–353, 98 Stat. 378 § 463(a)(1). See Jackson, Avoiding Powers in Bankruptcy, 36 Stan. L.Rev. 725, 777–786 (1984).

State Law. Fraudulent conveyances can be actionable outside of bankruptcy under state law. Section 512(c) of the Uniform Land Security Interest Act specifically rejects the *Durrett* approach, stating that "a regularly conducted, noncollusive transfer" under judicial or nonjudicial foreclosure to a transferee for value and in good faith is not a fraudulent conveyance even though the amount paid is less than the value of the mortgagor's interest in the land.

See generally, Alden, Gross & Borowitz, Real Property Foreclosure as a Fraudulent Conveyance: Proposals for Solving the *Durrett* Problem, 38 Bus.Law. 1605 (1983); Andrew, Real Property Transactions and the Bankruptcy Amendments and Federal Judgeship Act of 1984, 2 Cal.Real Prop.J. 1 (Fall 1984); Simpson, Real Property Foreclosures: The Fallacy of *Durrett*, 19 Real Prop., Probate & Trust J. 73 (1984); Kennedy, Involuntary Fraudulent Transfers, 9 Cardozo L.Rev. 531 (1987); Schuchman, Data on the *Durrett* Controversy, 9 Cardozo L.Rev. 605 (1987); Shanker, What Every Lawyer Should Know About the Law of Fraudulent Transfers, 31 Prac.Law. 43 (No. 8, 1985). For an analysis of the views of different courts on the *Durrett* issue, see In re Brown, 104 B.R. 609 (Bkrtcy.S.D.N.Y.1989).

2. *Pinetree Partners* illustrates how improper lender behavior can create problems for a mortgagee in the bankruptcy context. Even if bankruptcy does not result, lender liability may arise for actions taken during a workout. See Murray, Deeds In Lieu of Foreclosure: Practical and Legal Considerations, 26 Real Prop. Probate & Trust J. 459, 463 (1991); Comment, Lender Liability Under a Workout Agreement: A View Toward A More Balanced Approached, 8 No.Ill.U.L.Rev. 505 (1988). In a case involving special facts of a financially troubled mortgagor's reliance on the bank for advice, one court found that a

fiduciary relationship was created so that the bank was prohibited from foreclosing the mortgage and was assessed compensatory and punitive damages. Boatmen's Nat'l Bank of Hillsboro v. Ward, 231 Ill.App.3d 401, 172 Ill.Dec. 261, 595 N.E.2d 622 (1992). Consider how these cases fit into the pattern of lender liability, discussed at pages 218–220.

3. *Preferences.* Section 547(b) of the Bankruptcy Code permits a trustee in bankruptcy to avoid transfers of property by an insolvent debtor within 90 days of bankruptcy if the transfer was on account of antecedent debt, was for the benefit of a creditor, and would enable the creditor to get a larger share of the estate than she would have received if the transfer had not been made. Such avoidable payments are known as preferences. The purpose of the preference rule is to discourage creditors from demanding payments during a debtor's slide into bankruptcy that will dismember the business, making it less possible for the debtor to work his way out of the problem. The preference rule also helps foster equality of all treatment of creditors by preventing some from getting a disproportionate share of the debtor's assets. See H.R.Rep.No.95–595, pp. 177–178, printed in U.S.Cong. & Admin. News 1978, pp. 6137–6138.

Should monthly payments by a mortgagor to a mortgagee within 90 days of bankruptcy be subject to scrutiny as preferences? Section 547(c)(2)(B) of the Code states that transfers otherwise treated as avoidable preferences will not be considered such if they are payments "made in the ordinary course of business of financial affairs of the debtor and transferee." In Union Bank v. Wolas, ___ U.S. ___, 112 S.Ct. 527, 116 L.Ed.2d 514 (1991), the Supreme Court rejected the position of some courts of appeals (see, e.g., In re CHG International, Inc., 897 F.2d 1479 (9th Cir.1990)) which held that the payment in the ordinary course exception applies only to short term debt and not long term debt. The Court held that payments to a lender under a long term revolving credit agreement within 90 days of bankruptcy could be excepted from treatment as a voidable preference and remanded for a determination of whether the two interest payments and commitment fee payment were in the ordinary course of business.

Lenders face the risk that payments or property transfers made in a workout attempt might be attacked as preferences if bankruptcy ultimately results. See Murray, Deeds In Lieu of Foreclosure: Practical and Legal Considerations, 26 Real Prop. Probate & Trust J. 459, 476–478 (1991).

4. *The Automatic Stay.* One complaint frequently heard from real estate lenders in the discussions that led to passage of the 1978 Bankruptcy Code was that the previous act harbored several devices capable of impairing their security interests during the course of reorganization proceedings. One device, the automatic stay of foreclosure proceedings upon the filing of a petition, was particularly obnoxious. Stays can seem interminable, and possibly devastating, when real property security is daily decreasing in value because of the

borrower's distressed circumstances. Lenders were also concerned about the previous act's provisions governing trustee's certificates. There was some authority under the previous act that trustees could obtain new debt financing by issuing certificates secured by liens on the debtor's property that would become senior to liens securing loans made prior to the petition, thus unilaterally subordinating the secured lender's position. See In re St. Simon's Properties, 11 C.B.C. 729 (N.D.Ga.1976).

The Bankruptcy Code responded to these concerns modestly, modifying and refining old rules rather than introducing dramatic innovations. Automatic stays and senior or equal liens are authorized in sections 362 and 364, respectively. Their potential for impairing the lender's security is, however, limited by the requirement that the automatic stay be lifted, and the senior or equal lien be barred, if necessary for the "adequate protection" of the secured lender. Still, the lender's protection is far from complete. The measure of adequate protection is tied to the value of the collateral, and remedial steps will be triggered only by decreases in the collateral's present value. There is no assurance that the accruing *interest* obligations will be paid off in full.

Section 361 describes three ways in which adequate protection can be afforded: (1) requiring the trustee to make periodic cash payments to the lender to the extent that the stay, lien, or "use, sale, or lease [by the trustee] under section 363" results in a decrease in the value of the lender's interest in the property; (2) providing an additional or replacement lien to make up for the decrease in value; and (3) granting any other relief that will enable the lender to realize "the indubitable equivalent of [its] interest in [the] property." Section 362(d)(2) also requires that a stay of foreclosure be lifted if the debtor has no equity in the property and the property is "not necessary to an effective reorganization."

The automatic stay may also prevent a mortgagee from asserting rights under an assignment of rents executed by the mortgagor prior to the commencement of a bankruptcy action. For an excellent analysis of this issue, see Randolph, When Should Bankruptcy Courts Recognize Lenders' Rents Interests?, 23 U.C. Davis L.Rev. 833 (1990).

See generally, Kennedy, Automatic Stays Under the New Bankruptcy Law, 12 U.Mich.J.L.Ref. 3 (1978); Nimmer, Real Estate Creditors and the Automatic Stay: A Study in Behavioral Economics, 1983 Ariz.St.L.J. 281. For background on automatic stays before passage of the Reform Act, see Kennedy, The Automatic Stay in Bankruptcy, 11 U.Mich.J.L.Ref. 177 (1978); Nellis, The Mortgagor-Mortgagee Relationship in Bankruptcy: When a Stay is Not a Stay and Other Problems, 12 Real Prop., Probate & Trust J. 457 (1977).

5. *Executory Contracts.* Section 365 of the Bankruptcy Code empowers the trustee to assume or reject the executory contracts of the debtor. The Code, however, does not define the term "executory

contract." While a precise definition is difficult, many courts follow Professor Countryman's view that performance of a material obligation must remain on both sides in order for the contract to be executory. Countryman, Executory Contracts in Bankruptcy: Part II, 58 Minn. L.Rev. 479 (1974), followed in In re Speck, 798 F.2d 279 (8th Cir.1986). A mortgage note, for example, usually will not be treated as an executory contract when the only performance that remains is payment, as the other side has already fully performed. See H.R.Rep.No. 95–595, 95th Cong., 1st Sess.347 (1977), reprinted in 1978 U.S. Code Cong. & Admin. News 5787, 6303.

The courts have divided on the question of whether a land sales contract is executory. When the seller has remaining material obligations, such as delivering marketable title, and the buyer has yet to pay the price, the contract is executory. See In re Leefers, 101 B.R. 24 (C.D.Ill.1989). If, however, the land sale contract is used as a financing device, such as in Skendzel v. Marshall on p. 522, and the only obligations remaining are payment by the buyer and delivery of the deed by the seller or an escrow agent, some courts hold that the contract is not executory. See In re Bertelsen, 65 B.R. 654 (Bkrtcy.Ill. 1986). The seller thus takes the position of a secured creditor with respect to the buyer/debtor and the trustee cannot reject the contract.

Most courts, though, find land sale contracts used as financing vehicle to be executory on the theory that the seller still must deliver the deed. See, e.g., In re Coffman, 104 B.R. 958 (Bkrtcy.Ind.1988) (refusing to distinguish between situations when the seller has executed the deed and placed it in escrow and when the seller will not execute the deed until final payment by buyer).

6. *Leases in Bankruptcy.* Commercial landlords and tenants are tied to each other in an extended, complex and intimate economic relationship. As a consequence, each may find itself particularly affected by the financial distress of the other. When a tenant files for liquidation or reorganization, its landlord will probably want to remove it in order to relet the premises to another, more flourishing business. The tenant's trustee, however, may want the tenant to stay on if the leased premises are essential to the tenant's rehabilitation. If it is the landlord who files for liquidation or reorganization, the tenant may have to choose between leaving the premises and staying on without vital services such as heat, water and electricity that the landlord had originally agreed to provide. Section 365 of the Bankruptcy Code seeks to resolve these and other landlord-tenant conflicts.

Protecting the landlord. Before the 1978 Bankruptcy Code, the landlord's principal safeguard against tenant bankruptcy was the so-called "ipso facto," or bankruptcy, clause. Under this lease clause, the tenant's bankruptcy automatically terminated the lease or gave the landlord the right to terminate. In cases decided under the previous Act, courts sometimes refused to honor these clauses. The Bankruptcy Code bluntly invalidates them in bankruptcy. Notwithstanding any lease provisions to the contrary, an "unexpired lease of the debtor may not be terminated or modified ... at any time after the commencement of the case solely because of a provision in such ... lease that is conditioned on—(A) the insolvency or financial condition of the debtor at any time before the closing of the case; (B) the commencement of a case under this title; or (C) the appointment of or taking possession by a trustee in a case under this title or a custodian before such commencement." 11 U.S.C.A. § 365(e)(1). Further, section 365(f) permits, within limits, assignment of the unexpired lease to a third party even though the lease expressly prohibits or conditions assignments.

Recognizing the risk that assumptions and assignments pose for landlords, the Bankruptcy Code requires that, for the trustee to assume the lease, she must cure any outstanding defaults on leasehold obligations, other than default on the bankruptcy clause itself, and, if there has been such a default, must provide "adequate assurance of future performance." 11 U.S.C.A. § 365(b)(1).

Landlords complained that these safeguards were insufficient. For example, under section 365(d)(2), the trustee in a Chapter 11 reorganization could, absent a specific judicial order, elect to assume or reject the lease at any time before confirmation of the Chapter 11 plan. Congress responded to landlords' complaints in the 1984 Amendments, adding new subsection 365(d)(4) which deems a lease of nonresidential real property to be rejected unless it is expressly assumed within 60 days from commencement of the case, or within any additional period permitted for cause, by the court. Further, the Amendments added new subsection 365(l) providing that, if the lease is assigned, the lessor "may require a deposit or other security for the performance of the debtor's obligations under the lease substantially the same as would have been required by the landlord upon the initial leasing to a similar tenant." Pub.L. No. 98–353, § 362(a), (b), 98 Stat. 361–63 (1984).

The 1978 Bankruptcy Code also sought to tailor the requirements for assumptions and assignments to the special needs of shopping centers, where the landlord's economic returns are closely tied to the center's overall health through percentage rental clauses, and where the overall health of the center depends on maintaining the proper mix of tenants. Section 365(b)(3) provided that "adequate assurance of future performance of a lease of real property in a shopping center includes adequate assurance—

(A) of the source of rent and other consideration due under such lease;

(B) that any percentage rent due under such lease will not decline substantially;

(C) that assumption or assignment of such lease will not breach substantially any provision, such as a radius, location, use, or exclusivity provision, in any other lease, financing agreement, or master agreement relating to such shopping center; and

(D) that assumption or assignment of such lease will not disrupt substantially any tenant mix or balance in such shopping center."

The 1984 Amendments strengthened subsection 365(b)(3)(A) by requiring that "in the case of an assignment, that the financial condition and operating performance of the proposed assignee and its guarantors, if any, shall be similar to the financial condition and operating performance of the debtor and its guarantors, if any, as of the time the debtor became the lessee under the lease ..." The amendments also strengthened subsections 365(b)(3)(C) and (D) by effectively removing the qualifier, "substantially," from the prohibitions against breach or disruption and providing "that assumption or assignment of such lease is subject to all the provisions thereof ..." Pub.L. No. 98–353, § 362(a), 98 Stat. 361–63 (1984).

Protecting the tenant. If it is the landlord who files, and if its trustee rejects an unexpired lease, section 365(h)(1) allows the tenant to elect between treating the lease as terminated or remaining in possession of the leased premises for the balance of the lease term, including any renewal periods. If the tenant decides to stay on, section 365(h)(2) protects it against the trustee's rejection of leasehold obligations, such as the obligation to maintain the premises and provide utilities, by allowing the tenant to set off the expense of these services against his rental payments. Obviously, this will cause little concern to the tenant under a typical net lease arrangement. But what of the office space tenant on the forty-second floor whose elevator service ceases?

For background on the landlord-tenant relationship under the pre-1978 bankruptcy law, see Kane & Ruttenburg, The Landlord-Tenant Relationship in Bankruptcy, 12 Real Prop., Probate & Trust J. 482 (1977); Jacobson, Lessor's Bankruptcy: The Draftsman's Response to the Tenant's Plight, 1 Real Est.L.J. 152 (1972). Rules under the Reform Act are considered in Ehrlich, The Assumption and Rejection of Unexpired Real Property Leases Under the Bankruptcy Code—A New Look, 32 Buffalo L.Rev. 1 (1983); Fogel, Executory Contracts and Unexpired Leases in the Bankruptcy Code, 64 Minn.L.Rev. 341 (1980). Landlord-tenant rules under the 1984 Amendments Act are discussed in Andrew, Real Property Transactions and the Bankruptcy Amendments and Federal Judgeship Act of 1984, 2 Cal.Real Prop.J. 1 (Fall 1984).

7. *Reorganization.* The 1978 Bankruptcy Code modified the principles and procedures for business reorganization previously contained in Chapters X, XI and XII, consolidating them into Chapter 11, a single, comprehensive reorganization scheme. Of the three old chapters, Chapter XII was clearly the best-suited for reorganizing distressed real property ventures. Added to the Bankruptcy Act in 1938, it was originally designed to resolve depression-era problems created by a unique form of realty debt, Straus Bonds, then marketed mainly in Illinois. Unlike Chapter X, Chapter XII could be used by noncorporate debtors; unlike Chapter XI, it could be employed to alter the rights of secured creditors. Chapter XII soon fell into disuse, however, and,

according to its leading student, "could appropriately have been described as the forgotten provision of the Chandler Act of 1938." W. Norton, Real Property Arrangements 1 (1977). A troubled real estate market, and the special needs of noncorporate real estate ventures, led to a brief revival in the mid-1970's.

8. *Cram Down.* One of bankruptcy law's great remedial attractions is that it enables the reorganization of a debtor's business and the modification of its liabilities with less than the unanimous consent of her creditors. Under old Chapter XII, a plan of reorganization could be confirmed, and debts covered by the plan discharged, if, within each class of creditors affected by the plan, creditors holding two-thirds in dollar amount of the filed and allowed claims voted in favor of the plan.

The Bankruptcy Code, like the previous act, rejects the unanimity principle. An entire class of creditors will be deemed to have accepted a plan if the plan is accepted by creditors holding "at least two-thirds in amount and more than one-half in number of the allowed claims of such class held by creditors." With respect to each class, section 1129(a)(7)(A) requires that, if the vote to accept the plan was less than unanimous, each claim holder in the class must receive no less than he would receive if the debtor were liquidated under the straight bankruptcy provisions of Chapter 7.

Say that the consent of one or more *classes* is not obtained. Will this bar confirmation? The question is particularly important in the context of real estate reorganizations where each secured creditor— first mortgagee, second mortgagee, third mortgagee, and so on—is considered to comprise a separate class, with the result that objection from any one could stymie confirmation. Chapter XII's response to this problem was the "cram down," allowing confirmation over the objection of an entire class so long as the plan of arrangement provided "adequate protection" to the dissenting class.

The Bankruptcy Code similarly allows confirmation over the objection of one or more classes, but through a more circuitous route. The starting point is section 1129(a)(8) which requires that, for the plan to be confirmed, it must, as to each class, have been accepted by the class or not impair the class. Section 1124(3)(A) states, for example, that a class is impaired unless, with respect to each claim in the class, its holder receives cash equal to the "allowed amount" of the claim. This definition of impairment represents a particular boon to real estate lenders who will, in the workout situation, often be undersecured, with their loan secured by property whose value (say $10,000,000) is less than the face amount of the loan (say $14,000,000). Section 1111(b)(2) effectively provides in this situation that the creditor may choose to have an "allowed" and "secured claim" to the full extent of the loan's face value—$14,000,000—even though the security is worth much less—$10,000,000. Thus, in the example given, the "allowed amount of the claim" will be $14,000,000 and if the plan gives the secured creditor anything other than a cash payment of that amount, it will be deemed to be impaired.

If the nonaccepting creditor is impaired within these terms, the debtor's only remaining alternative is a cram down under section 1129(b). Section 1129(b) authorizes confirmation over the objection of an impaired class if "the plan does not discriminate unfairly, and is fair and equitable, with respect to each class of claims or interests that is impaired under, and has not accepted, the plan." The subsection further defines "fair and equitable" to include at least one of three criteria in the case of secured creditors: (i) that the creditor retain its lien and receive deferred cash payments that, in the aggregate, at least equal the allowed amount of the claim ($14,000,000 in the example above) and that, when discounted to present value as of the effective date of the plan, will equal the value of the collateral ($10,000,000 in the example); (ii) if the collateral is to be sold unencumbered by the creditor's lien, the lien must attach to the sale proceeds; or (iii) the plan must provide for the creditor's realization of "the indubitable equivalent" of his claims.

Section 1129(a)(10) requires as a condition to confirmation that at "least one class of claims ... has accepted the plan." The purpose of that requirement is to assure that there is some element of a bargain in the reorganization plan by removing the possibility that, as a consequence of subsection (a)(9)'s treatment of nonimpairment, and subsection (b)'s provision for cram downs, a plan could be accepted with no vote at all. Finally, section 1129 itemizes several substantive requirements for a plan to be confirmed. Section 1129(a)(1)–(5) essentially requires compliance with other provisions of the chapter, good faith, and full disclosure of payments and of personnel to be employed by the debtor.

For a detailed analysis of cram downs under the Bankruptcy Code, see Pachulski, The Cram Down and Valuation Under Chapter 11 of the Bankruptcy Code, 58 N.C.L.Rev. 925 (1980); Klee, All You Ever Wanted to Know About Cram Down Under the New Bankruptcy Code, 53 Bankr.L.J. 133 (1979). For a discussion of cram downs before the 1978 Bankruptcy Code, see Miller & Goldstein, Chapter XII—Real Property Arrangements: Is 'Cram Down' A Debtor's Panacea? 12 Real Prop., Probate & Trust J. 695 (1977); Dole, The Chapter XII Cram-Down Provisions, 82 Com.L.J. 197 (1977); Polk, The Chapter 13 Cramdown: New Nightmare for the Lender, 19 Real Est.L.J. 279 (1991).

9. *Federal Income Tax Consequences.* The mortgagor or mortgagee facing a default must consider the federal income tax consequences of foreclosure, of the alternatives to foreclosure, and of liquidation or reorganization.

The mortgagor. As a general rule, the Internal Revenue Code treats real property mortgage foreclosures just as it treats voluntary sales or exchanges, with capital or ordinary gain or loss treatment given accordingly. Loss or gain will be measured by the difference between the amount realized on the foreclosure sale and the taxpayer's adjusted basis in the property. If the property's fair market value exceeds the liabilities discharged, the amount of liabilities satisfied—whether recourse or nonrecourse—will be included in the amount realized. If the liabilities discharged exceed the fair market value of the property, the tax consequences will differ depending on whether the liability was recourse or nonrecourse. If the liability was recourse, the excess of liabilities over fair market value will be considered a cancellation of indebtedness and thus treated as ordinary income. See I.R.C. § 61(a)(12); Treas.Reg. § 1.1001–2(a)2 (1983). If the liability was nonrecourse, the amount realized will be treated as including the full amount of the liability; because the mortgagee has no personal action against the mortgagor, or recourse against his other assets, there is no cancellation of indebtedness income. See Treas.Reg. § 1.1001–2(a)(2) (1983); Comm'r v. Tufts, page 618, above.

The mortgagee. As a general rule, the foreclosing mortgagee is entitled to a bad debt deduction to the extent that the outstanding loan exceeds the proceeds to the mortgagee from the foreclosure sale. Special rules apply when, as often happens, it is the mortgagee who makes the winning full credit bid at the foreclosure sale. Here, the mortgagee will be entitled to deduct as a bad debt the difference between its basis in the debt and the fair market value of the property; the winning bid is presumed to represent the property's fair market value at the time of the sale. See Treas.Reg. § 1.166–6(b)(2).

Insolvency or bankruptcy. The Bankruptcy Code's reorganization provisions can soften some of the Internal Revenue Code's otherwise harsh effects for owners of distressed property. An automatic stay of foreclosure proceedings gives the taxpayer breathing space to work out an arrangement with its creditors or to time the foreclosure so that it occurs in the most advantageous year. Additionally, the 1980 Bankruptcy Tax Act amendments to the Internal Revenue Code provide that no cancellation of indebtedness income arises from the discharge of a debt in the course of bankruptcy proceedings, or while the taxpayer is insolvent; in the case of insolvency, however, the amount excluded "shall not exceed the amount by which the taxpayer is insolvent." I.R.C. § 108(a)(3). Under section 108, the bankrupt or insolvent taxpayer must pay for these exclusions from income by correspondingly reducing certain "tax attributes" (for example, the taxpayer's net operating loss in the year of discharge) or, at the taxpayer's election, reducing the basis of the taxpayer's depreciable property. I.R.C. § 108(b)(1), (2), (3), (5).

For a consideration of tax aspects of foreclosure, bankruptcy, and workouts see Onsager & Becker, The Federal Tax Consequences of Foreclosure and Repossessions, 18 J. Real Est.Tax. 291 (1991); Scheele & Ripp, Income Tax Issues Related to Distressed Commercial Real Estate, 27 Ariz.Att. 13 (Aug.-Sept.1990); Kalteyer, Real Estate Workouts—Original Issue Discount Implication of Troubled Debt Restructuring, 43 Tax Law. 579 (1990); Taggart, Workouts—Lender's Basis and

Lender's Income, 45 Tax Law. 263 (1992); Phelan, The Bankruptcy Tax Act and Other Tax Considerations Relating to Real Estate Bankruptcies, in Real Estate Bankruptcies and Workouts: A Practical Perspective 45 (A. Kuklin & P. Roberts, eds. 1983); Boris, Tax Planning in Connection with the Restructuring and Recasting of Real Estate Transactions, Moratoriums, Foreclosures, Deeds in Lieu, 35th Ann.N.Y.U.Tax Inst. 963 (1977); Rabinowitz, The Failing Real Estate Investment and the Federal Income Tax, 34th Ann.N.Y.U.Tax Inst. 357 (1976).

D. THE IMPACT OF ENVIRONMENTAL REGULATION ON REAL ESTATE TRANSACTIONS

Over the past two decades, environmental regulations have exposed participants in real estate transactions to potentially great liability. This new found source of legal risk substantially affects the way buyers, sellers, lenders, lessors, lessees, brokers, and others do business. The impact of environmental laws commands the attention of the parties and their counsel in virtually every real estate transaction today.

Of the many environmental regulations that touch real estate transactions, the key statute is the federal Comprehensive Environmental Response, Compensation and Liability Act of 1980, 42 U.S.C.A. §§ 9601–9675, commonly known as "CERCLA." "Potentially responsible parties" under CERCLA include not only landowners who themselves have discharged hazardous materials but also subsequent buyers. Negligence, intent and the comparative fault of the contributors to a hazardous waste problem are irrelevant in determining liability under CERCLA; the current owner will be strictly liable even though it had no role in the discharge, did not benefit from it, and did not own the land at the time the discharge occurred. The courts have interpreted CERCLA to impose joint and several liability, see, e.g., United States v. Monsanto Co., 858 F.2d 160 (4th Cir.1988), cert. denied, 490 U.S. 1106, 109 S.Ct. 3156, 104 L.Ed.2d 1019 (1989). The current landowner alone may be held liable for the full cost of the cleanup unless it meets the difficult burden of showing that the harm is divisible or is able to obtain contribution. See pages 908–909.

Section 9607 entitles federal, state, and local governments, as well as private parties, to recover from responsible parties the "response costs" incurred by the government or private party to remedy and remove the contamination. For example, where a landowner disposes of hazardous substances that leak into a neighbor's water well, the neighbor may recover the cost of remedying the problem. Also, the federal government may remove the hazardous materials itself or, in some situations, obtain an injunction forcing responsible parties to abate the danger of contamination. 42 U.S.C. §§ 9604, 9606. See generally, Slap & Israel, Private CERCLA Litigation: How To Avoid It? How To Handle It? 25 Real Prop. Probate & Trust J. 705 (1991); Reitze, Harrison & Palko, Cost Recovery by Private Parties Under

CERCLA: Planning a Response Action for Maximum Recovery, 27 Tulsa L.J. 365 (1992); Belthoff, Private Cost Recovery Actions Under Section 107 of CERCLA, 11 Colum.J.Envtl.L. 141 (1986).

A purchaser of contaminated land faces staggering potential liability. The purchaser stands not only to lose the value of its investment; it could also be required to dig into its pockets to clean up the land itself or pay response costs under section 9607. According to the Environmental Protection Agency, the cost of a Superfund cleanup through 1986 averaged approximately $14 million per site. See 52 Fed.Reg. 2495 (Jan. 22, 1987), discussed in Fitzsimmons & Sherwood, The Real Estate Lawyer's Primer (And More) to Superfund: The Environmental Hazards of Real Estate Transactions, 22 Real Prop. Probate & Trust J. 765, 770 (1987).

The materials that follow are intended only to introduce some of the key aspects of CERCLA affecting real estate transactions; they are not a comprehensive treatment of this very difficult and controversial statute. The materials start with liability of owners under CERCLA, then considers how this liability can be avoided, and concludes with the issue of lender liability. Consider throughout these materials how you should arrange transactions and counsel clients in light of CERCLA.

Bibliography. For an excellent analysis of the various provisions of CERCLA, see Barr, CERCLA Made Simple: An Analysis of the Cases Under the Comprehensive Environmental Response, Compensation and Liability Act of 1980, 45 Bus.Law. 923 (1990). See also R. Matthews, Superfund Claims and Litigation Manual (1990); Fitzsimmons & Sherwood, The Real Estate Lawyer's Primer (And More) to Superfund: The Environmental Hazards of Real Estate Transactions, 22 Real Prop. Probate & Trust J. 765 (1987). For excellent policy analyses of the statute, see Healy, Direct Liability For Hazardous Substance Cleanups Under CERCLA: A Comprehensive Approach, 42 Case W.Res.L.Rev. 65 (1992); Grad, A Legislative History of the Comprehensive Environmental Response, Compensation and Liability ("Superfund") Act of 1980, 8 Colum.J.Envtl.L. 1 (1982).

1. LIABILITY OF SELLERS AND BUYERS

a. THE STATUTORY SCHEME

HEALY, DIRECT LIABILITY FOR HAZARDOUS SUBSTANCE CLEANUPS UNDER CERCLA: A COMPREHENSIVE APPROACH

42 Case Western Reserve Law Review 65, 72–86, 87–88 (1992).

The CERCLA liability scheme can only be understood in the context of the statute's fundamental purpose. Congress enacted CERCLA in late 1980, after several years of legislative effort, in response to findings that more than 2,000 sites, many abandoned, had been used for the disposal of hazardous substances and posed a threat both to the public health and to the environment. CERCLA's paramount goal is to facilitate cleanup of hazardous substances through Superfund-financed and privately-financed response actions.

1. Facilitating Cleanups by Replenishing the Fund and Encouraging Private Response Actions

In view of the "tremendous" scope of the problems posed by unsound disposal of hazardous substances, the EPA had estimated that cleanup of the 1200 to 2000 most dangerous sites would cost between $13.1 billion and $22.1 billion. Indeed, more recent cost estimates are substantially higher. Congress established the Superfund to finance response actions pursued by the federal government at those sites posing the greatest threat to public health and the environment. Even though CERCLA limited the sites that the government could clean using Superfund monies, lawmakers understood at the time the Act was debated and passed that the $1.6 billion initially authorized by CERCLA would be insufficient. In 1980, CERCLA provided funding at only "the absolute minimum necessary to begin a responsible effort." [33] As a result, the CERCLA liability scheme, mandating recovery of response costs from responsible parties, was necessary to replenish the Superfund.

In addition to the replenishment effect, Congress intended that the CERCLA liability scheme encourage other parties to pursue cleanups not financed by Superfund. CERCLA allows private parties and states who proceed with cleanups to seek recovery for those response costs in actions brought under Section 107. Congress understood that its goal of ensuring the cleanup of hazardous substance facilities would depend upon response actions undertaken by private, responsible parties. Indeed, private response actions may be less costly than government cleanups and may permit the EPA to focus its efforts and resources on the facilities where releases pose the greatest threat to human health and the environment. Accordingly, proper construction of the liability provisions will have a substantial impact on the willingness of private parties to pursue cleanups on their own and will ensure that the limited sums appropriated to the Superfund are not used unnecessarily.

In sum, CERCLA's paramount objective of facilitating the cleanup of hazardous waste sites that pose a threat to public health or the environment is tied directly to the availability of funds in the Superfund and to the readiness of private parties to undertake response actions. Advancing that policy depends on the construction and application of the liability standard established by the Act.

2. Establishing a New Standard of Care for Hazardous Substance Disposal Activities

In enacting CERCLA, Congress also intended to "create a compelling incentive for those in control of hazardous substances to prevent

---

33. 126 CONG. REC. 26,346 (statement of Rep. Rostenkowski) * * *.

releases and thus protect the public from harm." [39]   Congress imposed this new, uniform standard of care on those actors most able to protect against the risks presented by inadequate disposal.   Moreover, Congress believed that, even though hazardous substance disposal involved inherent risks, much of the harm to public health and the environment could be eliminated through the use of greater care.   CERCLA's liability provision, which seeks to establish the responsibility of persons to pay the cost to remedy the harmful effects of their inadequate disposal activities, was critical to Congress' choice to implement the new, strict standard of care.   In contrast, the tax levied on chemical and petrochemical concerns to finance the Superfund would not necessarily create an incentive to observe a stricter standard of care because the tax was uniformly imposed on each enterprise in those industries without regard to specific disposal practices.

To promote this new standard of care, Congress imposed liability throughout the chain of distribution so that all waste generators who make disposal arrangements are liable for the costs of cleaning up releases, regardless of whether those parties actually disposed of the substances.   By extending liability in this manner, Congress has ensured that various actors will have an incentive to observe a high standard of care.   Congress also acted to ensure the new standard's integrity by precluding responsible parties from relying on third-party defenses; a party, such as a generator, who is involved in disposal activities, cannot avoid liability for cleanup costs by claiming that another person was contractually responsible for adequately performing the disposal.

Congress viewed the imposition of this new standard of care for hazardous substance disposal activities as warranted for several reasons.   First, Congress believed that such liability would promote the internalization of costs within business organizations so that the market price of goods would reflect the actual, total cost of their production.   In Congress' view, this policy to encourage internalization of costs would be equitable to all market participants.   Internalization is equitable because companies that have borne the costs of disposing of hazardous substances adequately will have no cleanup costs, while companies that attempted to avoid costs by disposing of hazardous substances inadequately will be liable for the expense incurred in cleaning up the improperly handled waste.   Congress also reasoned that cost internalization would be beneficial to the economy in general.[50]   Second, Congress decided to impose a higher standard of care

---

39. S. REP. No. 848, [96th Cong., 2nd Sess. 7, 34 (1980)]. . . .

50. The Senate report on CERCLA explained that the economy would "operate better" because

[s]trict liability is, in effect, a method of allocating resources through choice in the market place.

The most desirable system of loss distribution is one in which the prices of goods accurately reflect their full costs to society.   This therefore requires, first, that the cost of injuries be borne by the activities which caused them, whether or not fault is involved, because, either way, the injury is a real cost of these activities.   Second, it requires that

based on its understanding that the costs of adequate disposal are substantially less than the costs of eliminating the harms caused by inadequate disposal via cleanup. Finally, Congress believed its new liability scheme was necessary because state laws imposing liability for inadequate disposal of hazardous substances lacked uniformity and contained insufficient standards of care.

Although Congress' intent in and rationale for creating a new standard of care to govern disposal activities are plain, Congress did not elaborate on the significance of the fact that the liability scheme would effectively impose this heightened standard of care retroactively in many instances. To be sure, CERCLA has important prospective effects. For instance, it assigns liability in the case of unintentional spills, encouraging potential responsible parties to take steps aimed at reducing the likelihood of accidental releases. . . .

CERCLA's retroactive effects, however, are at least as significant as its forward looking objectives. Congress intended to apply the new liability standard to inadequate disposals which occurred in the past but which result in a present release of hazardous substances. It broadened the theory of cost internalization to support CERCLA's retrospective effects; by imposing liability upon parties who were responsible for and profited from past improper disposals that require present cleanup measures, CERCLA ensures that those parties ultimately bear the full cost of their activities. Indeed, this nexus rationale emphasizing past profit as a justification for current liability has been relied upon by courts upholding CERCLA against claims that its retroactive effects violate due process.

Congress did not relate imposition of liability for past improper disposal directly to development of a new, safer standard of care. Justifying retrospective liability as a means of encouraging modified behavior would have been inconsistent with the Supreme Court's . . . decision in *Usery v. Turner Elkhorn Mining Co.* In *Turner Elkhorn*, the Court upheld a federal statute requiring coal companies to pay benefits for black lung disease to miners who had ceased employment in the industry prior to the Act's effective date. The Court held that retrospective effects of legislation must satisfy due process requirements and concluded that it would "hesitate to approve the retrospective imposition of liability on any theory of deterrence or blameworthiness." Nonetheless, the majority found that the retroactive liability imposed by Congress was permissible because the legislation rationally spread the costs of black lung disease.

. . .

among the several parties engaged in an enterprise the loss be placed on the party which is most likely to cause the burden to be reflected in the price of whatever the enterprise sells.

S.REP. NO. 848, [96th Cong., 2nd Sess. 7, 34 (1980)]. . . .

Congress thus intended to impose a new standard of care for hazardous substance disposal activities, without addressing in detail the fact that this standard would be applied retroactively in many cases. There is *no* indication that Congress intended the scope of liability for responsible parties to differ depending on whether the liability-causing conduct pre-dated CERCLA's enactment. The only reasonable conclusion which can be drawn from the legislative history is that the uniform liability standard should be applied in a manner that prospectively promotes cost internalization as well as the new standard of care.

In applying the CERCLA liability scheme, courts have followed Congress' direction that those who profit from inadequate disposal should pay the costs resulting from releases of hazardous substances into the environment. Courts have not, however, accounted sufficiently for Congress' decisions to impose a new standard of care on all those engaged in or responsible for hazardous substance disposal activities and to ensure that those persons internalize the costs of adequate disposal. By failing to rely on these two stated congressional objectives, courts have created a body of common law which does not provide a coherent foundation for assessment of liability in future CERCLA cases.

. . .

CERCLA expressly provides that the mere ownership of a vessel or facility at which the release of a hazardous substance occurs is sufficient to create liability; it is irrelevant whether the owner actually was involved in operating the vessel or facility. Thus, Congress intended "owner and operator" liability under Section 107(a) to attach regardless of whether a person fitting that statutory description can be viewed as directly liable because of actual involvement in hazardous substance disposal activities.

Current owner liability, in particular, furthers Congress' intent that the liability scheme encourage site cleanups. Failure to hold all *current* owners liable without regard to their relationship to the property at the time of disposal would remove the incentive for prospective purchasers and lenders to complete careful environmental audits prior to executing a purchase or loan. Moreover, liability imposed on current owners of sites contaminated by hazardous substances encourages those owners to assess the environmental quality of their property and to perform the cleanup.

TANGLEWOOD EAST HOMEOWNERS
v. CHARLES–THOMAS, INC.

United States Court of Appeals, Fifth Circuit, 1988.
849 F.2d 1568.

Before POLITZ and JOHNSON, Circuit Judges, and BOYLE, District Judge.

POLITZ, Circuit Judge:

In this cause we granted an interlocutory appeal under 28 U.S.C. § 1292(b), to determine whether the district court had erred in rejecting defendants' motion to dismiss filed pursuant to Fed.R.Civ.P. 12(b)(1) and 12(b)(6). Finding no error in that ruling, for the reasons assigned we affirm.

Background

For purposes of the pending motion, we accept as true the allegations of the complaint. Appellant, First Federal Savings & Loan Association of Conroe, is a lending institution. The other defendants against whom appellees have complained are residential developers, construction companies, and real estate agents and agencies. All participated in the development of the Tanglewood East Subdivision in Montgomery County, Texas. The complainants-appellees are owners of property in that subdivision. The subdivision was built on the site upon which the United Creosoting Company operated a wood-treatment facility from 1946 to 1972. During that quarter century substantial amounts of highly- toxic waste accumulated on the property. In 1973 certain of the defendants acquired the property, filled in and graded the creosote pools, and began residential development.

In 1980, Tanglewood homeowners and residents complained to Texas authorities about toxic problems and all development ceased. In 1983 the Environmental Protection Agency placed the site on its National Priorities List for cleaning under the Comprehensive Environmental Response, Compensation and Liability Act (CERCLA), commonly known as the "Superfund Act," 42 U.S.C. §§ 9601, *et seq.* The cleanup, expected to cost millions of dollars, will require the demolition of six homes and the construction of bunkers to contain the hazardous materials.

The purchasers of the subdivision lots invoked CERCLA and the Resource Conservation and Recovery Act (RCRA), 42 U.S.C. §§ 6901, *et seq.* and sought damages, response and cleaning costs, and injunctive relief. They also sought, but have now withdrawn, claims under the Federal Water Pollution Control Act, 33 U.S.C. § 1251.

The defendants filed a joint motion to dismiss under Fed.R.Civ.P. 12(b)(1) and 12(b)(6). The district court denied the motion but certified its ruling under 28 U.S.C. § 1292(b). First Federal sought and secured our approval of an interlocutory appeal.

Standard of Review

When a motion to dismiss challenges both the court's jurisdiction, 12(b)(1), and the existence of a federal cause of action, 12(b)(6), the *Bell v. Hood* [1] standard is applied and the motion is treated "as a direct attack on the merits of the plaintiff's case." *Williamson v. Tucker*, 645 F.2d 404, 415 (5th Cir.1981). In reviewing such a 12(b)(6) motion, we accept as true all well-pled allegations, resolving all doubts in favor of

1. 327 U.S. 678, 66 S.Ct. 773, 90 L.Ed. 939 (1946).

the complainants. Such a motion will be granted only if "it appears beyond doubt that the plaintiff can prove no set of facts in support of his claim which would entitle him to relief." *Conley v. Gibson*, 355 U.S. 41, 78 S.Ct. 99, 2 L.Ed.2d 80 (1957). A motion to dismiss for failure to state a claim "is viewed with disfavor, and is rarely granted." *Sosa v. Coleman*, 646 F.2d 991, 993 (5th Cir.1981).

Analysis

A. CERCLA

Appellant contends that it and the other defendants are not covered persons under the CERCLA, which, it submits, was intended to apply only to the person responsible for introducing the toxins, in this case, the United Creosoting Company. We do not share that crabbed a reading of this statute. Although it was enacted in the waning hours of the 96th Congress, and as the product of apparent legislative compromise is not a model of clarity, the statute has an extensive legislative history.

Under 42 U.S.C. § 9607(a) (1988), CERCLA provides a private cause of action where a release or threatened release of a hazardous substance causes response costs to be incurred. The persons covered are:

(1) the owner and operator of . . . a facility,

(2) any person who at the time of disposal of any hazardous substance owned or operated any facility at which such hazardous substances were disposed of,

(3) any person who by contract, agreement, or otherwise arranged for disposal or treatment, or arranged with a transporter for transport for disposal or treatment, of hazardous substances owned or possessed by such person . . . , and

(4) any person who accepts or accepted any hazardous substances for transport to disposal or treatment facilities. . . .

1. *Present Owners*

Appellant maintains that under § 9607(a)(1), the only owner and operator who discharged hazardous materials was the United Creosoting Company, who abandoned the site in 1972. We find nothing in the wording of § 9607(a) to exclude present owners of properties previously contaminated. We join our colleagues of the Second Circuit in concluding that the structure of the statute removes any doubt. Section 9607(a)(2) expressly applies to past owners and operators who contaminate their surroundings; it is therefore manifest that § 9607(a)(1) applies to current owners of adulterated sites. See *New York v. Shore Realty Corp.*, 759 F.2d 1032 (2nd Cir.1985). We hold that § 9607(a)(1) imposes strict liability on the current owners of any facility which releases or threatens to release a toxic substance.

"Facility" is defined in § 9601(9) to include

(A) any building, structure, installation, equipment, pipe or pipe-line (including any pipe into a sewer or publicly owned treatment works), well, pit, pond, lagoon, impoundment, ditch, landfill, storage container, motor vehicle, rolling stock, or aircraft, or (B) *any site or area where a hazardous substance has been deposited, stored, disposed of, or placed, or otherwise come to be located* ; but does not include any consumer product in consumer use or any vessel. (Emphasis added.)

The statute leaves no room for doubt; the Tanglewood East development is a covered facility.

The *Shore* court held the developer-owners liable for the cleanup costs of their facility even though no construction or development had been undertaken.   A lending institution was found to be a current owner and operator under § 9607(a)(1) in *United States v. Maryland Bank & Trust Co.*, 632 F.Supp. 573 (D.Md.1986).   In that case, a bank which acquired a contaminated site by foreclosure was held accountable under CERCLA.   And courts addressing the issue have rejected the argument implicit in appellant's position, that liability may be imposed upon only those persons who both own and operate polluted property. *Artesian Water Co. v. Gov. of New Castle County*, 659 F.Supp. 1269 (D.Del.1987); *United States v. Northeastern Pharm. & Chem. Co., Inc.*, 579 F.Supp. 823 (W.D.Mo.1984).

2.   *Past Owners*

Section 9607(a)(2) applies to persons who owned or operated a facility at the time of the disposal of the toxins.   Appellant contends that the only person who qualifies under that section is United Creosoting Company.   We do not so read the statute.   Referring to 42 U.S.C. § 6903(3), we find "disposal" defined to include

the discharge, deposit, injection, dumping spilling, leaking, or placing of any solid waste or hazardous waste into or on any land or water so that such solid waste or hazardous waste or any constituent thereof may enter the environment or be emitted into the air or discharged into any waters, including ground waters.

We recognize merit in appellees' argument that this definition of disposal does not limit disposal to a one-time occurrence—there may be other disposals when hazardous materials are moved, dispersed, or released during landfill excavations and fillings.

3.   *Post Arrangers and Transporters*

Appellant next argues that defendants neither arranged for nor transported any hazardous material for disposal or treatment under § 9607(a)(3) and (4).   This argument rests on the narrow interpretation of disposal, which we reject, and a like interpretation of "treatment" which is defined by § 6903(34) as

any method, technique, or process, including neutralization, designed to change the physical, chemical, or biological character or composition of any hazardous waste so as to neutralize such waste or so as to render such waste nonhazardous, safer for transport, amenable for recovery, amenable for storage, or reduced in volume. *Such term includes any activity* or processing *designed to change the physical form* or chemical composition *of hazardous waste* so as to render it nonhazardous. (Emphasis added.)

Appellees argue that the activity of filling and grading the creosote pools constituted treatment to render the waste non-hazardous, and that those involved in that activity are covered persons under § 9607(a)(3). Furthermore, since disposal may be merely the "placing of any ... hazardous waste into or on any land....," § 6903(3), those who move the waste about the site may fall within the terms of the provision. Under these readings of the terms "disposal" and "treatment," relevant evidence under the complaint may establish that some of the defendants were arrangers for, or transporters of, the toxic materials.

Finally, appellant maintains that CERCLA was intended to cover only persons actually engaged in the chemical/hazardous materials industry and those engaged in businesses which generated such materials. It vigorously contends that the legislation was not meant to impose chilling liability on the defendants' businesses: banking, real estate, construction, and development. It cites an imposing list of cases, obviously not including *New York v. Shore Realty; United States v. Maryland Bank & Trust Co.; Artesian Water Co. v. Gov. of New Castle County;* and *United States v. Northeastern Pharm. & Chem. Co.* We are persuaded beyond peradventure that a determination of the specific businesses and activities covered by CERCLA is beyond the pale of a 12(b)(6) motion. That remains for another day.

In light of the foregoing, we are satisfied that the complaint may not be dismissed for failure to state a claim upon which relief under CERCLA may be granted. We are not prepared to rule as a matter of law that complainants-appellees can prove no set of facts in support of their claims which would entitle them to relief. The district court correctly denied the motion to dismiss the claims made under CERCLA.

. . .

C. *Remedies Under CERCLA*

Section 9607(a)(4) provides that covered persons shall be liable for

(A) all costs of removal or remedial action incurred by the United States Government or a State or an Indian Tribe not inconsistent with the national contingency plan;

(B) any other necessary costs of response incurred by any other person consistent with the national contingency plan....

Appellant contends that under this provision appellees must demonstrate that their response costs were "necessary" and "consistent with the national contingency plan." *Mardan Corp. v. C.G.C. Music, Ltd.,*

600 F.Supp. 1049, 1054 (D.Ariz.1984). Appellees have alleged that their costs are consistent with the national contingency plan. It remains for them to prove such. The issue of consistency cannot be resolved on the pleadings alone, but must await development of relevant evidence. *See Artesian Water Co. v. Gov. of New Castle County*, and authorities cited therein.

Appellant next maintains that some degree of governmental involvement is a necessary requisite for the application of § 9607. On this issue we agree with the conclusion reached by our colleagues of the Ninth Circuit in *Wickland Oil Terminals v. Asarco, Inc.*, 792 F.2d 887 (9th Cir.1986), after a careful and exhaustive analysis of the statute, regulations, and legislative history. The *Wickland* panel relied in part on EPA interpretations as reflected in the preamble to the rules revising the 1972 National Contingency Plan. 50 Fed.Reg. 5862–83 (1985); 50 Fed.Reg. 47, 912–50 (1985). The preamble states that the final rule "makes it absolutely clear that no Federal [or lead agency] approval of any kind is a prerequisite to a cost recovery...." 50 Fed.Reg. 47, 934 (1985). *See also NL Industries v. Kaplan*, 792 F.2d 896 (9th Cir.1986).

The *Wickland* court also relied on the fact that there is no procedure or mechanism by which "a private party could seek to obtain prior governmental approval of a cleanup program." 792 F.2d at 892. A subsequent panel in *Cadillac Fairview/California, Inc. v. Dow Chemical Co.*, 840 F.2d 691, 695 (9th Cir.1988), followed the same reasoning, underscoring that "there is no indication in the statute that prior approval or action by a state or local government is either necessary or desirable." We agree. We find no merit to the contention that prior governmental involvement is a prerequisite to the recouping of response costs.

Finally, as to the recovery of response costs under CERCLA, appellant maintains that the costs alleged by complainants—relocation costs, investigatory costs, and the cost of dikes and trenches—are not encompassed by the statute. We find no merit in this argument. First, relocation costs are specifically authorized. § 9601(24). And under the statute, response means "remove, removal, remedy and remedial action." § 9601(25). "Remove" or "removal" includes "such actions as may be necessary to monitor, assess, and evaluate the release or threat of release of hazardous substances...." § 9601(23). Investigatory costs fall within the ambit of this provision. *Cadillac Fairview/California, Inc. v. Dow Chemical Co.* As an analytical caboose, § 9601(24), which defines "remedy" and "remedial action," as actions "to prevent or minimize the release of hazardous substances," specifically includes the construction of dikes, trenches, or ditches among a host of other containment measures.

We find no basis for dismissing on the pleadings that part of the complaint seeking response costs under CERCLA.

. . .

The judgment of the district court is AFFIRMED.

UNITED STATES v. SERAFINI

United States District Court, Middle District of Pennsylvania, 1988.
706 F.Supp. 346.

MEMORANDUM

CALDWELL, District Judge.

Introduction

This is an action brought under the Comprehensive Environmental Response Compensation and Liability Act ("CERCLA"), 42 U.S.C. § 9601 *et seq.*, for injunctive relief and recovery of the federal government's response costs in connection with the cleanup of a hazardous waste site in Taylor, Pennsylvania. Before the court is the government's motion for partial summary judgment against defendants Serafini, Bernabei, Buttafoco and Naples, individually and trading as the Empire Contracting Company ("Empire defendants"), on the issue of liability for response costs under section 107 of CERCLA, 42 U.S.C. § 9607. For the reasons that follow the government's motion will be denied.

Background

The Taylor hazardous waste site is a tract of land consisting of approximately 125 acres located in Taylor Borough, near Scranton, Pennsylvania. In May, 1967, the Parmoff Corporation leased a portion of the site to the City of Scranton for the purpose of dumping garbage and refuse. Until at least March 31, 1968, Scranton operated a sanitary landfill and waste disposal site on the leased premises. On December 12, 1969, the Parmoff Corporation sold all but a small portion of its interest in the Taylor site to the Empire Contracting Company, a partnership wholly owned by the Empire defendants. According to the fictitious name certificate filed in February, 1966, in Lackawanna County, the Empire Contracting Company was created "[t]o buy, sell, manufacture, lease, service any and all kinds and types of real and personal property, to act as contractor, subcontractor and developer with respect to any and all kinds of work, including but not limited to buildings, improvements, roads, bridges, mining, drilling, flushing and otherwise." The Empire defendants are the current owners of a portion of the Taylor site.

Beginning in 1981, the United States Environmental Protection Agency ("EPA") and the Pennsylvania Department of Environmental Resources conducted various surveys and investigations at the Taylor site. According to the uncontested affidavit of Michael Zickler, the EPA on-scene coordinator assigned to the site, in October and November, 1983, EPA conducted an immediate removal action under section 104 of CERCLA, 42 U.S.C. § 9604. Approximately 1,141 fifty-five gallon drums were scattered across and under six separate areas of the site. Many were open, crushed, completely or partially buried, and in various stages of decay. Samples from the drums, as well as soil and water samples, were sent to the EPA laboratory in Annapolis, Maryland. Laboratory analysis revealed that 847 drums contained hazardous substances as defined in section 101(14) of CERCLA, 42 U.S.C. § 9601(14), 105 drums contained non- hazardous substances, and 189 were contaminated with residues.

The government instituted this action on November 10, 1986, seeking injunctive relief and recovery of response costs. On July 20, 1987, the court entered a consent decree negotiated between the United States and four defendants requiring the defendants to complete the remedial work at the Taylor site. On September 25, 1987, the court granted the United States' motion for partial summary judgment on liability for federal response costs against the City of Scranton. The government has filed a similar motion now against the Empire defendants.

Discussion

A.   The Summary Judgment Standard

A court shall render summary judgment only "if the pleadings, depositions, answers to interrogatories, and admissions on file, together with the affidavits, if any, show that there is no genuine issue as to any material fact and that the moving party is entitled to a judgment as a matter of law." Fed.R.Civ.P. 56(c). A material fact is one which might affect the outcome of a suit under governing law. *Anderson v. Liberty Lobby, Inc.*, 477 U.S. 242, 250, 106 S.Ct. 2505, 2510, 91 L.Ed.2d 202, 211 (1986). Factual disputes that are irrelevant or unnecessary are not to be considered. *Id.* While the materiality inquiry addresses the substantive law, it is only the substantive law's identification of which facts are critical and which facts are irrelevant that controls. Any proof or evidentiary requirements imposed by the substantive law are not germane. *Id.*

Summary judgment will not lie if the dispute as to a material fact is "genuine," that is, "if the evidence is such that a reasonable jury could return a verdict for the non-moving party." *Id.* at 249, 106 S.Ct. at 2510, 91 L.Ed.2d at 212. An adverse party opposing a properly supported motion for summary judgment "may not rest upon the mere allegations or denials of the adverse party's pleading, but the adverse party's response, by affidavits or as otherwise provided in [Rule 56], must set forth specific facts showing that there is a genuine issue for trial." Fed.R.Civ.P. 56(e).

> [T]here is no issue for trial unless there is sufficient evidence favoring the nonmoving party for a jury to return a verdict for that party. [*First National Bank v.] Cities Service [Co.]*, 391 US [253] at 288–289, 88 S Ct 1575, [1592] 20 L Ed2d 569[(1968)]. If the evidence is merely colorable, *Dombrowski v. Eastland*, 387 US 82,

87 S Ct 1425, 18 L Ed2d 577 (1967) (per curiam), or is not significantly probative, *Cities Service,* supra, [391 U.S.] at 290, 88 S Ct 1575, [1592] 20 L Ed2d 569, summary judgment may be granted.....

[T]his standard mirrors the standard for a directed verdict under Federal Rule of Civil Procedure 50(a), which is that the trial judge must direct a verdict if, under the governing law, there can be but one reasonable conclusion as to the verdict. *Brady v. Southern R. Co.,* 320 US 476, 479–80, 64 S Ct 232, [234] 88 L Ed 239, (1943). If reasonable minds could differ as to the import of the evidence, however, a verdict should not be directed. *Wilkerson v. McCarthy,* 336 US 53, 62, 69 S Ct 413, [417] 93 L Ed 497 (1949).

. . .

[T]he "genuine issue" summary judgment standard is "very close" to the "reasonable jury" directed verdict standard: "The primary difference between the two motions is procedural; summary judgment motions are usually made before trial and decided on documentary evidence, while directed verdict motions are made at trial and decided on the evidence that has been admitted." [*Bill Johnson's Restaurants, Inc. v. NLRB,* 461 US 731, 745, n 11, 103 S Ct 2161, [2171, n. 11] 76 L Ed2d 277] (1983). In essence, though, the inquiry under each is the same: whether the evidence presents a sufficient disagreement to require submission to a jury or whether it is so one-sided that one party must prevail as a matter of law.

Anderson, 477 U.S. at 249–52, 106 S.Ct. at 2511–12, 91 L.Ed.2d at 212–14. In making that determination, the court must view the facts and the inferences drawn therefrom in the light most favorable to the nonmoving party. *Matsushita Electric Industrial Co. v. Zenith Radio Corp.,* 475 U.S. 574, 587–88, 106 S.Ct. 1348, 1356–57, 89 L.Ed.2d 538, 553 (1986).

B. Prima Facie Case for Liability Under CERCLA

Congress enacted CERCLA in 1980 in response to the environmental and public health hazards posed by improper disposal of hazardous wastes. In general terms, the statute established the "Superfund," which is financed primarily through excise taxes on the oil and chemical industries.[2] The federal government is authorized to use the Superfund to finance governmental responses to hazardous waste problems, to pay claims arising from the response activities of private parties, and to compensate federal or state governmental entities for damages to natural resources, 42 U.S.C. § 9611(a). The government may then recover Superfund expenditures from those responsible for

---

2. Section 517 of the Superfund Amendments and Reauthorization Act of 1986 ("SARA"), Pub.L. 99–499, § 517, 100 Stat. 1772 (1986), established the Hazardous Substances Superfund, which is in effect a continuation of the Hazardous Substance Response Trust Fund established by section 221 of CERCLA, 42 U.S.C. § 9631 (repealed).

the generation, transportation or disposal of the hazardous substances. 42 U.S.C. § 9607(a).

Section 107(a) of CERCLA, 42 U.S.C. § 9607(a), provides, in part, as follows:

Notwithstanding any other provision or rule of law, and subject only to the defenses set forth in subsection (b) of this section—

(1) the owner and operator of a vessel or a facility,

(2) any person who at the time of disposal of any hazardous substance owned or operated any facility at which such hazardous substances were disposed of,

(3) any person who by contract, agreement, or otherwise arranged for disposal or treatment, or arranged with a transporter for transport for disposal or treatment, of hazardous substances owned or possessed by such person, by any other party or entity, at any facility or incineration vessel owned or operated by another party or entity and containing such hazardous substances, and

(4) any person who accepts or accepted any hazardous substances for transport to disposal or treatment facilities, incineration vessels or sites selected by such person, from which there is a release, or a threatened release which causes the incurrence of response costs, of a hazardous substance, shall be liable....

In construing the terms of section 107(a), the courts have uniformly imposed strict liability, subject only to the defenses set forth in section 107(b). *Artesian Water Co. v. Gov. of New Castle County*, 659 F.Supp. 1269 (D.Del.1987). Accordingly, in this case, a *prima facie* case under section 107(a) is established if the United States shows that:

1. the site is a "facility"; [3]

2. a "release" or threatened release of a "hazardous substance" from the site has occurred; [4]

3. the release or threatened release has caused the United States

---

3. 42 U.S.C. § 9601(9) defines "facility" as follows:

The term "facility" means (A) any building, structure, installation, equipment, pipe or pipeline (including any pipe into a sewer or publicly owned treatment works), well, pit, pond, lagoon, impoundment, ditch, landfill, storage container, motor vehicle, rolling stock, or aircraft, or (B) any site or area where a hazardous substance has been deposited, stored, disposed of, or placed, or otherwise come to be located; but does not include any consumer product in consumer use or any vessel.

4. 42 U.S.C. § 9601(22) defines "release" as follows:

The term "release" means any spilling, leaking, pumping, pouring, emitting, emptying, discharging, injecting, escaping, leaching, dumping, or disposing into the environment (including the abandonment or discarding of barrels, containers, and other closed receptacles containing any hazardous substance or pollutant or contaminant)....

42 U.S.C. § 9602(a) provides that the EPA shall promulgate regulations designating materials as hazardous substances. The regulations at 40 C.F.R. § 302.4 designate substances found at the Taylor site as hazardous substances.

to incur "response costs"; [5] and

4.   the defendants are "owners" of a facility.[6]

United States v. Maryland Bank & Trust Co., 632 F.Supp. 573 (D.Md. 1986).

It is clear from the materials before the court that the government has made a prima facie case. The Empire defendants admit the first three elements and challenge only the government's assertion that they are owners of a facility. Yet in their answer to the complaint, they admitted that on December 12, 1969, they purchased all but a small portion of Parmoff's interest in the Taylor site and that they have owned a portion of the site ever since. They further admitted that the land they bought from Parmoff was the parcel that Parmoff had previously leased to the City of Scranton for use as a refuse disposal area. As discussed below, the defendants' argument is aimed, not at challenging the government's prima facie case, but at establishing one of the three defenses set forth in section 107(b).

C.   Affirmative Defense to the Prima Facie Case

Section 107(b) provides as follows:

There shall be no liability under subsection (a) of this section for a person otherwise liable who can establish by a preponderance of the evidence that the release or threat of release of a hazardous substance and the damages resulting therefrom were caused solely by—

(1) an act of God;

(2) an act of war;

(3) an act of omission of a third party other than an employee or agent of the defendant, or than one whose act or omission occurs in connection with a contractual relationship, existing directly or indirectly, with the defendant (except where the sole contractual arrangement arises from a published tariff and acceptance for carriage by a common carrier by rail), if the defendant establishes by a preponderance of the evidence that (a) he exercised due care with respect to the hazardous substance concerned, taking into consideration the characteristics of such hazardous substance, in light of all relevant facts and circumstances, and (b) he took precautions against foreseeable acts or omissions of any such third party and the consequences that could foreseeably result from such acts or omissions; or

(4) any combination of the foregoing paragraphs.

---

5. "Response" means "remove, removal, remedy and remedial action," including "enforcement activities related thereto." 42 U.S.C. § 9601(25).

6. "Owner" means "in the case of an onshore facility ..., any person owning or operating such facility...."   42 U.S.C. § 9601(20). The term "person" includes an individual and a partnership.   42 U.S.C. § 9601(21).

The Empire defendants have raised the "third party" defense in paragraph 3, and under the facts of this case, must prove by a preponderance of the evidence that:

1.   the release or threat of release of a hazardous substance and the resulting damages were caused solely by an act or omission of a third party;

2.   the third party's act or omission did not occur in connection with a contractual relationship (either direct or indirect) with the defendants;

3.   the defendants exercised due care with respect to the hazardous substance; and

4.   the defendants took precautions against the third party's foreseeable acts or omissions and the foreseeable consequences resulting therefrom.

Of the four elements of the defense, the government seriously challenges only the second, and asserts that a contractual relationship existed, presumably between the Empire defendants and the Parmoff Corporation.   The defendants argue that the entry of summary judgment would be improper because there are genuine issues of fact concerning the existence of that contractual relationship, as that term is defined in CERCLA.

As originally enacted, CERCLA, or more specifically, section 107(b), was unclear as to the liability of owners of contaminated property who were innocent of any involvement with the disposal of hazardous substances.   The 1986 SARA amendments attempted to clarify section 107(b), not by amending it directly, but by adding to section 101 a lengthy new subsection defining the previously undefined term, "contractual relationship."   Section 101(35)(A) provides, in relevant part, as follows:

(35)(A) The term "contractual relationship", for the purpose of section 9607(b)(3) of this title includes, but is not limited to, land contracts, deeds or other instruments transferring title or possession, unless the real property on which the facility concerned is located was acquired by the defendant after the disposal or placement of the hazardous substance on, in, or at the facility, and ... the circumstances described in clause (i) ... is also established by the defendant by a preponderance of the evidence:

(i) At the time the defendant acquired the facility the defendant did not know and had no reason to know that any hazardous substance which is the subject of the release or threatened release was disposed of on, in, or at the facility.

The new definitional provision also specifies at section 101(35)(B):

To establish that the defendant had no reason to know, as provided in clause (i) of subparagraph (A) of this paragraph, the defendant must have undertaken, at the time of acquisition, all appropriate inquiry into the previous ownership and uses of the property consistent with good commercial or customary practice in an effort to minimize liability. For purposes of the preceding sentence the court shall take into account any specialized knowledge or experience on the part of the defendant, the relationship of the purchase price to the value of the property if uncontaminated, commonly known or reasonably ascertainable information about the property, the obviousness of the presence or likely presence of contamination at the property, and the ability to detect such contamination by appropriate inspection.

As stated earlier, the Empire defendants have admitted that they received from Parmoff title to land comprising part of the Taylor site. Furthermore, it is not disputed that they acquired the land after the disposal of the hazardous substance had already occurred. The government contends, however, that at the time they purchased the land, the Empire defendants had reason to know that hazardous substances had been deposited at the Taylor site, and thus there exists a "contractual relationship" negating the use of the innocent landowner defense. In essence, the government's position is that the Empire defendants failed to undertake, at the time of acquisition, "all appropriate inquiry into the previous ownership and uses of the property consistent with good commercial or customary practice" as required by section 101(35)(B). The government's argument is two-pronged. First, it contends that the Empire defendants had reason to know of the site's condition because at the time they purchased the land in 1969, it was obviously and visibly contaminated, and any site visit would have revealed hundreds of abandoned drums on the surface. Second, the government asserts that since defendant Serafini was the Secretary of the Parmoff Corporation at the time the Empire defendants purchased a portion of the site from Parmoff, they possessed "specialized knowledge" of the site's condition.

With respect to the government's first argument, the evidence submitted with and in response to the government's motion shows that at the time the defendants purchased the Taylor site, it was littered with drums which were visible to the naked eye. On November 17, 1982 counsel for Empire wrote to the Environmental Protection Agency, stating that the hazardous waste at the Taylor site was not Empire's responsibility because "these barrels were on the property prior to any purchase made by Empire Contracting Company.... Please note the enclosed photos, our photos, which indicate proof to this averment." Attached to Empire counsel's letter were two photographs showing drums scattered across the surface of the site. Subsequent correspondence from Empire Contracting Company on September 22, 1983 also mentioned photographs of the site "taken on October 4, 1968" as proving that the abandoned drums on the property were there prior to the Empire defendants' purchase. Furthermore, in order to obtain this and other evidence regarding the condition of the site when it was purchased in 1969, the United States served the Empire defendants with a request that they admit that "On December 12, 1969 the cylindrical metal drums present at the Site were visible to the naked eye." The Empire defendants did not respond, thereby conclusively establishing, for purposes of this litigation, that at the time they purchased the land from the Parmoff Corporation, abandoned drums were plainly visible.[7]

The Empire defendants' contend that the mere showing that the drums were visible is not enough to establish that they knew or had reason to know that hazardous substances had been deposited at the site. Their affidavits indicate that at the time of the purchase they did not conduct an on-site inspection, nor did they have any reason to do so. They assert that the purchase involved the inspection of various maps to determine the location of the 225 acres and that it was not until 1980 or 1981, when the EPA conducted its investigation, that they became aware of the existence of the 1968 photographs.

The government counters that the defendants' affidavits cannot create issues as to whether they knew or had reason to know of the presence of hazardous waste at the Taylor site because landowners cannot avail themselves of the innocent landowner defense by closing their eyes to hazardous waste problems. The government argues that the defendants had no knowledge of the clearly visible drums only because they failed to inspect the premises prior to purchasing it and they made no inquiry into the past uses of the site. The government posits that SARA's innocent landowner defense does not protect the owner who fails to inspect the land or fails to inquire into its current condition or past history.

Although the government's argument is tempting, the court cannot reach that conclusion on the record before it. Section 101(35)(B) requires a landowner to have undertaken "all appropriate inquiry ... consistent with good commercial or customary practice" and lists several factors to be considered in making that determination. After analyzing the evidence in the light of those factors, the court is unable to find that the defendants' inaction was inappropriate under the facts of this case. The government has presented no evidence from which the court can conclude that the defendants' failure to inspect or inquire was inconsistent with good commercial or customary practices.[8] Thus, there exists unresolved questions of fact as to the propriety of the defendants' conduct at the time of the purchase.

The government next argues that, beyond the apparent conditions at the site, there is additional evidence demonstrating knowledge of the

---

7. Earlier in this litigation, the court applied Federal Rule of Civil Procedure 36(b) to another party's failure to respond to requests for admissions, and held that matters as to which unanswered admissions were requested are conclusively established for purposes of this litigation. The discussion of Rule 36(b) in the court's September 25, 1987 order need not be repeated here.

8. For example, the government could have submitted affidavits from real estate developers stating that, with respect to the purchase of a 225 acre tract to be developed at a later date, it is the customary or good commercial practice to visually inspect the property before the purchase.

site's previous use. Specifically, the government asserts that since defendant Serafini acting in his capacity as the Secretary of the Parmoff Corporation, signed the lease granting the City of Scranton the right to use the land as a rubbish dump, he possessed the kind of "specialized knowledge" of the previous use of the land contemplated by section 101(35)(B). Serafini's affidavit, however, states that he was only Acting Secretary of the corporation as a convenience to the owners, and that he was neither an officer nor director. He claims he had no personal knowledge of the operation of the corporation or of the management of the corporation's real estate holdings and asserts that he executed documents only as a witness to the signatures of the corporation's officers. The copy of the lease submitted by the government supports Serafini's contention in that his signature appears on a line labeled "ATTEST." Thus the evidence before the court does not clearly show the relationship between Serafini and Parmoff. Questions still exist as to whether Serafini knew the contents of the lease or that the Taylor site was used as a landfill by the City.[9]

Conclusion

For the foregoing reasons the United State's motion for partial summary judgment on the issue of liability against defendants Serafini, Bernabei, Buttafoco and Naples will be denied. However, the court finds that the United States has established a prima facie case of liability under section 107(a) of CERCLA, 42 U.S.C. § 9607(a). The Empire defendants will have opportunity to present affirmative defenses under section 107(b), 42 U.S.C. § 9607(b), at trial.

UNITED STATES v. SERAFINI

United States District Court, Middle District of Pennsylvania, 1990.
791 F.Supp. 107.

ORDER

McCLURE, District Judge.

BACKGROUND:

This is an action for injunctive relief and recovery of response costs pursuant to Sections 106 and 107 of the Comprehensive Environmental Response, Compensation and Liability Act ("CERCLA"), 42 U.S.C. §§ 9606(a) and 9607(a), in connection with the Taylor Borough hazardous waste site located south of Scranton, Pennsylvania. The remedial action at the Taylor Borough site has been completed pursuant to a consent decree negotiated by the United States and several defendants. The United States is now seeking reimbursement of the outstanding costs it incurred in responding to the release of hazardous substances at

---

9. Having so found, we need not address the government's somewhat tenuous assertion that knowledge of the existence of a sanitary landfill gave Serafini reason to know of the existence of hazardous wastes on the premises.

the site from the remaining defendants. The instant motion concerns the current owners of the Taylor Borough site, defendants Louis Serafini, Alfred Bernabei, Ernest Buttafoco, and Michael J. Naples, Jr., individually and trading as Empire Contracting Company.

On February 19, 1988 Judge Caldwell issued an order denying the government's motion for partial summary judgment on the issue of liability. However, following a lengthy discussion of the relevant law, Judge Caldwell limited the issue of liability to whether the defendants' failure to inspect the Taylor Borough site prior to purchasing it complied with the requirement of making all appropriate inquiry into the previous ownership and uses of the property consistent with good commercial or customary practice. See 42 U.S.C. § 9601(35)(B). More specifically stated, the issue is whether the customary or good commercial practice in the Scranton, Pennsylvania area in 1969 included, at a minimum, that a prospective purchaser, or his representative, actually view land before purchasing it.

Subsequently, the government filed a supplementary motion for partial summary judgment. Along with this motion, the government filed the affidavits of two real estate experts stating that it is inconceivable that a commercial real estate purchaser in 1969 would have purchased the Taylor Borough site without inspecting it prior to purchase. The defendants responded by filing affidavits from two real estate experts stating that it was unusual for a prospective purchaser in Scranton in 1969 to traverse a large tract of land. Judge Caldwell denied the government's supplementary motion for summary judgment because of the contradictory nature of the affidavits.

During May of 1989 the government conducted depositions of the defendants and their real estate experts. Based on these depositions, on September 25, 1989 the government filed a second supplemental motion for summary judgment on the issue of liability. The depositions taken by the government establish that the customary practice in Scranton in 1969 was at least to view land before purchasing it. Therefore, the government's motion for summary judgment will be granted.

The depositions of the defendants confirm the fact that neither they nor their representatives visited, inspected or viewed the land prior to purchase. While the defendant's experts testified that it would be unusual for a prospective purchaser actually to traverse the entire acreage, based on their experience, prospective purchasers or their agents usually inspected or viewed land prior to purchase. In fact, they testified that it was their practice actually to view the land before forming an opinion to purchase, and that they always told prospective purchasers to visit and look at land prior to purchase. See John Siegle deposition at 27–33; Mary Vanston deposition at 21–24.

Therefore, by not conducting an appropriate inquiry consistent with customary or good commercial practice, the defendants cannot satisfy the statutory requirements of the innocent landowner defense. 42 U.S.C. § 9607(b)(3).

NOW, THEREFORE, IT IS ORDERED THAT:

Plaintiff's second supplemental motion for summary judgment on the issue of liability against defendants Louis Serafini, Alfred Bernabei, Ernest Buttafoco, and Michael J. Naples, Jr., individually and trading as Empire Contracting Company., filed September 25, 1989, is granted.

NOTES

1. *Who Is Liable Under CERCLA?* As *Tanglewood* and *Serafini* indicate, any number of entities can be a "responsible party" liable under the statute for hazardous substances deposited on the land in question. Examine section 9607(a) of the statute. What policies does liability under section 9607(a) serve? How do notions of fault and risk spreading play out in CERCLA?

Buyer. How does a buyer of land becomes liable under CERCLA? How are the courts reading the words "the" and "and" in the phrase "the owner and operator of . . . a facility" in section 9607(a)(1)? In United States v. Maryland Bank & Trust Co., 632 F.Supp. 573 (D.Md. 1986), the court held that based on legislative history and logic, the terms "owner" and "operator" should be read in the disjunctive not the conjunctive. According to the court, "[p]roper usage dictates that the phrase 'the owner and operator' include only those persons who are both owners and operators. But by no means does Congress always follow the rules of grammar when enacting the laws of this nation." Id. at 578.

Seller. When will a seller of land, and other past owners, be a responsible party under section 9607(a)? Compare *Tanglewood* and *Serafini* to the situation where employees of landowner *A* bury barrels of hazardous substances on *A*'s land and the barrels begin to leak. *A* then sells the land to *B*, who is unaware that the barrels continue to leak. Several years later, *B* sells the land to *C* who discovers the leaking barrels. Is *B* a "person who at the time of disposal of any hazardous substance owned" the property and thus a responsible party? The courts disagree, since the key term "disposal" invites competing interpretations.

Some courts hold that "passive" disposal—the leaking and migration of hazardous substances—is not the sort of a "disposal" within CERCLA that would make *B* a responsible party. For example, in United States v. Petersen Sand & Gravel, Inc., 806 F.Supp. 1346 (N.D.Ill.1992), the court closely examined the statute to find that passive disposals would not make an owner a responsible party. Moreover, the court ruled that passive disposal would bar the innocent landowner defense in all but the rare case where the hazardous substance remained tightly sealed underground, since any leakage after the transfer of ownership would constitute disposal by the owner herself. The court reasoned that Congress could not have intended to eviscerate the innocent landowner defense by defining "disposal" as passive. The court quoted with approval from Edward Hines Lumber Co. v. Vulcan Materials Co., 861 F.2d 155, 157 (7th Cir.1988): "We are enforcing a statute rather than modifying rules of common law.... To the point that courts could achieve 'more' of the legislative objectives by adding to the lists of those responsible, it is enough to respond that statutes have not only ends but also limits. Born of compromise, laws such as CERCLA and SARA do not pursue their ends to their logical limits. A court's job is to find and enforce stopping points no less than to implement other legislative choices." Accord Snediker Developers Ltd. Partnership v. Evans, 773 F.Supp. 984 (E.D.Mich.1991); Ecodyne Corp. v. Shah, 718 F.Supp. 1454 (N.D.Cal.1989).

Other courts would hold *B* liable for a passive disposal. In Nurad, Inc. v. William E. Hooper & Sons Co., 966 F.2d 837 (4th Cir.), cert. denied, ___ U.S. ___, 113 S.Ct. 377, 121 L.Ed.2d 288 (1992), the court criticized the insertion of an active participation requirement into such clearly passive words as "leaking" and "spilling." In the court's view, barring liability for passive disposals would interfere with CERCLA's policy to encourage hazardous waste cleanup and would clash with the strict liability scheme of the statute. Moreover, such a constrained reading would burden the owner who voluntarily begins a cleanup since it would be liable for at least a portion of the cost as a current owner while a prior owner who did nothing to stop the leaking would not be liable.

Lessors and Lessees. Like buyers and sellers, lessors and lessees may be responsible parties under CERCLA. The lessor will most likely be liable as an owner under section 9607(a)(1) or (2). Lessors cannot escape liability by claiming that "they were innocent absentee landlords unaware of and unconnected to the waste disposal activities that took place on their land." United States v. Monsanto, 858 F.2d 160, 169 (4th Cir.1988), cert. denied, 490 U.S. 1106, 109 S.Ct. 3156, 104 L.Ed.2d 1019 (1989). A lessee may be an operator within section 9607(a)(1) if it disposes of hazardous waste on the property; a lessee may also be liable under CERCLA as an owner if it controls the property and is functionally equivalent to a landowner. See United States v. South Carolina Recycling & Disposal, Inc., 653 F.Supp. 984 (D.S.C.1984), affirmed in part, vacated in part by United States v. Monsanto, 858 F.2d 160, 169 (4th Cir.1988), cert. denied, 490 U.S. 1106, 109 S.Ct. 3156, 104 L.Ed.2d 1019 (1989).

What policies are served by holding lessors and lessees liable under CERCLA? Is the innocent landowner defense discussed in *Serafini* available to a lessor when its tenant discharges hazardous substances? What risks does CERCLA create for commercial landlords? On the subject of landlord and tenant liability under CERCLA, see Feder, The Undefined Parameters of Lessee Liability Under the Comprehensive Environmental Response, Compensation, and Liability Act (CERCLA): A Trap for the Unwary Lender, 19 Envtl.L. 257 (1988); Street & Zaleha, Environmental Risks: Negotiating and Drafting Lease Agreements, 27

908 COMMERCIAL REAL ESTATE TRANSACTION Pt. 2

Idaho L.Rev. 37 (1990–1991); Larsen & Boman, Environmental Liability: Lender and Landlord–Tenant Issues, in The Impact of Environmental Regulation on Business Transactions, Practicing Law Institute 273 (1988).

Brokers. Will a broker ever be liable to a buyer for failing to discover or disclose hazardous material? Reconsider the materials on the role of the broker, pages 47–66 above. See Comment, A Toxic Nightmare On Elm Street: Negligence and the Real Estate Broker's Duty in Selling Previously Contaminated Residential Property, 15 B.C.Envtl.L.Rev. 547 (1988); Edwards, Successor Landowner and Real Estate Broker Liability in Environmental Torts: Going Beyond Property Lines, 1 Real Est.Fin.L.J. 16 (1988).

Corporate Liability. Courts and commentators have addressed the issue of the liability under CERCLA of successor, parent, and subsidiary corporations as well as shareholders and officers. See, e.g., Dent, Limited Liability in Environmental Law, 26 Wake Forest L.Rev. 151 (1991); Oswald & Schipani, CERCLA and the "Erosion" of Traditional Corporate Law Doctrine, 86 Nw.L.Rev. 259 (1992); Barr, CERCLA Made Simple: An Analysis of the Cases Under the Comprehensive Environmental Response, Compensation and Liability Act of 1980, 45 Bus.Law. 923, 979–982 (1990); Healy, Direct Liability For Hazardous Substance Cleanups Under CERCLA: A Comprehensive Approach, 42 Case W.Res. L.Rev. 65, 109–128 (1992).

2. *Apportionment of Liability.* Although CERCLA provides for joint and several liability, the statute offers two possible routes of escape.

Divisible Harm. Where the harm is divisible, courts have held that joint and several liability does not apply. But see United State v. R.W. Meyer, Inc., 889 F.2d 1497 (6th Cir.1989), cert. denied, 494 U.S. 1057, 110 S.Ct. 1527, 108 L.Ed.2d 767 (1990), where the landowner argued that it did not cause an indivisible environmental harm with its tenants, and the court affirmed the district court's determination that the harm was not divisible, even though the tenants, but not the owners, released hazardous materials on the land:

> "[A]lthough the basis for each defendant's liability differed, the harm, *i.e.*, the presence of hazardous materials at the Northernaire facility, was the same. [The owner's] liability pursuant to 42 U.S.C. § 9607 was predicated on ownership of the land, notwithstanding the fact that [the tenants], as operators of the facility, directly were responsible for the presence of the hazardous substances on [the owner's] property."

889 F.2d at 1507.

Equitable Contribution. Section 9613(f) allows a responsible party to seek contribution from other potentially responsible parties, and "the court may allocate response costs among liable parties using such equitable factors as the court determines are appropriate." A buyer of contaminated property, liable himself under section 9607(a)(1), would like the court to apply section 9613(f) to allocate a (great) portion of the response costs to the seller who actually contaminated the property. Presumably, the plaintiffs in *Tanglewood* were proceeding under this strategy.

However, the statute only permits, but does not mandate, equitable contribution. Also, the statute does not say how costs should be allocated, leaving allocation to the courts. Congress evidently intended the courts to consider the involvement of the various parties in the actual disposal of the hazardous substances. Presumably, consideration of involvement in the disposal would reduce the burden of buyers such as the home purchasers in *Tanglewood*. The courts, however, provide few guidelines for deciding equitable contribution claims, outside of making a few general (and nonbinding) statements. See United States v. Monsanto Co., 858 F.2d 160, 168 n.13 (4th Cir.1988), cert. denied, 490 U.S. 1106, 109 S.Ct. 3156, 104 L.Ed.2d 1019 (1989) ("[t]he site owners' relative degree of fault would, of course, be relevant" for applying equitable contribution); Smith Land & Improvement Corp. v. Celotex Corp., 851 F.2d 86, 90 (3d Cir.1988), cert. denied, 488 U.S. 1029, 109 S.Ct. 837, 102 L.Ed.2d 969 (1989) (the statute "expressly conditions the amount of contribution on the application of equitable considerations").

In In re Sterling Steel Treating, Inc., 94 B.R. 924 (Bkrtcy.E.D.Mich. 1989), buyers spent $8,500 to remove hazardous waste found in a trailer on land bought from the landowner's trustee in bankruptcy. The trustee did not know that the trailer contained hazardous materials, and the buyers did not inspect the land before buying. The court allocated the removal cost equally between the bankruptcy estate and the buyers, holding that equitable considerations required buyers to bear some of the cost under the principle of caveat emptor. The court held the estate liable since the trustee should have inspected, discovered and disclosed the contamination to the buyers.

How would you advise a client who is a potentially responsible party on how equitable contribution will affect its liability?

See generally, Barr, CERCLA Made Simple: An Analysis of the Cases Under the Comprehensive Environmental Response, Compensation and Liability Act of 1980, 45 Bus.Law. 923, 990–993 (1990).

3. *Innocent Landowner Defense.* Section 9607(b)'s innocent landowner defense is very difficult to establish. See, e.g., In re Sterling Steel Treating, Inc., 94 B.R. 924 (Bkrtcy.E.D.Mich.1989) (buyer who knew of prior owner's business and failed to inspect property prior to sale); State of Washington v. Time Oil Co., 687 F.Supp. 529 (W.D.Wash. 1988) (lessee failed to supervise sublessee's operations). Only a handful of reported decisions uphold the defense. United States v. Pacific Hide & Fur Depot, Inc., 716 F.Supp. 1341 (D.Idaho 1989), for example, involved the children of the founder of a corporation that ran a recycling facility who had given the children shares in the corporation. The court found that the children were innocent landowners, and not

responsible in an action to recover costs of removal of hazardous substances found on the site:

> [The] legislative history establishes a three-tier system: Commercial transactions are held to the strictest standard; private transactions are given a little more leniency; and inheritances and bequests are treated the most leniently of these three situations. [1986 U.S. Code Cong. & Admin. News] at p. 3280. The present case is actually more like an inheritance than a private transaction. Certainly these three defendants did not obtain their interest in an arms-length private sales transaction—they obtained their initial interest by familial gift and their ultimate interest by a corporate event beyond their control. All of this occurred when they were barely out of their teenage years. This is precisely the situation designed to be covered by the innocent landowner defense.

716 F.Supp. at 1348.

The case law illustrates the larger problem of the innocent landowner defense, particularly what an "appropriate inquiry" requires. What do you think of the Congressional proposal for a rebuttable presumption that "appropriate inquiry" is made upon compliance with specific steps set out in the bill, such as a review of the chain of title, certain governmental records, and physical inspection? H.R. 2787, 101st Cong., 1st Sess., § (2) (1989). See Comment, CERCLA's Innocent Landowner Defense: The Rising Standard of Environmental Due Diligence For Real Estate Transactions, 38 Buff.L.Rev. 827, 848–851 (1990); Slap & Israel, Private CERCLA Litigation: How To Avoid It? How To Handle It?, 25 Real Prop. Probate & Trust J. 705 (1991).

Serafini demonstrates the fluidity of the due diligence requirement. If the sale had taken place in 1987 rather than 1969 would the court have decided the case differently in the first opinion? What level of inquiry does "commercial practice" require?

Many environmental law practitioners believe that the "appropriate inquiry" requirement effectively disables the innocent landowner defense. They argue that if a potential buyer performs an "appropriate inquiry," it will find the hazardous substance, reject the property, and consequently never need to rely on the defense. If, however, the buyer makes an inquiry, does not find the contamination, and buys the property, the court will likely determine that the inquiry was not "appropriate" as it did not uncover the problem. See generally, Hitt, Desperately Seeking SARA: Preserving the Innocent Landowner Defense to Superfund Liability, 18 Real Est.L.J. 3 (1989); Anderson, Will The Meek Even Want The Earth?, 38 Mercer L.Rev. 535 (1987).

The due diligence necessary to claim the innocent landowner defense is often based on an environmental audit of the property conducted by the buyer before purchase or closing. See pages 935–936 below for a discussion of environmental audits and how they relate to the innocent landowner defense. For a fine examination of various aspects of the innocent landowner defense, see Comment, CERCLA's Innocent Landowner Defense: The Rising Standard of Environmental Due Diligence For Real Estate Transactions, 38 Buff.L.Rev. 827, 848–851 (1990). See also Patterson, A Buyer's Catalogue of Prepurchase Precautions to Minimize CERCLA Liability in Commercial Real Estate Transactions, 15 U. Puget Sound L.Rev. 469 (1992); Comment, The Environmental Due Diligence Defense and Contractual Protection Devices, 49 La. L.Rev. 1405 (1989); Boggs, Real Estate Environmental Damage, The Innocent Residential Purchaser, and Federal Superfund Liability, 22 Envtl.L. 977 (1992); Annotation, Third–Party Defense to Liability Under § 107 of Comprehensive Environmental Response, Compensation, and Liability Act (42 USC § 9607), 105 A.L.R.Fed. 21 (1991).

4. *CERCLA and Bankruptcy.* What if an owner of contaminated land is in bankruptcy? On one hand, CERCLA would hold landowners strictly liable in order to achieve the statutory aim of cleaning the environment and forcing owners to be careful with hazardous wastes. On the other hand, the Bankruptcy Code aims to provide debtors with a "fresh start" free from prior obligations, and empowers the bankruptcy court to discharge claims against the debtor as part of the liquidation of the estate in favor of creditors. (See pages 854–885 above.) To what extent should a bankruptcy court wipe out the liability, or potential liability, of a landowner for CERCLA response costs?

In re Chateaugay Corporation, 944 F.2d 997 (2d Cir.1991), addressed this issue in the context of the Chapter 11 reorganization of the LTV Corporation. The debtor's schedule of liabilities included 24 pages of "contingent liabilities" asserted by the federal Environmental Protection Agency and the environmental enforcement officers of all fifty states. EPA claimed $32 million in response costs incurred before the bankruptcy petition was filed for fourteen sites for which LTV was a potentially responsible party. EPA further indicated that additional response costs would be required to completely clean these fourteen sites. LTV sought a discharge of its potential environmental liability relating to conduct by LTV prior to the filing of the petition. However, the EPA maintained that response costs incurred after the bankruptcy petition were not "claims" under the Bankruptcy Code, 11 U.S.C.A. § 101(4), and thus were not subject to discharge. The court held that unincurred response costs for the debtor's pre-petition conduct causing the release or threatened release of hazardous materials before the petition were "claims" under the statute that will be discharged. The court stated:

> True, EPA does not yet know the full extent of the hazardous waste removal costs that it may one day incur and seek to impose upon LTV, and it does not yet even know the location of all the sites at which such wastes may yet be found. But the location of these sites, the determination of their coverage by CERCLA, and the incurring of response costs by EPA are all steps that may fairly be viewed, in the regulatory context, as rendering EPA's claim "con-

tingent," rather than as placing it outside the Code's definition of "claim." ...

Accepting EPA's argument in this Chapter 11 reorganization case would leave EPA without any possibility of even partial recovery against a dissolving corporation in a Chapter 7 liquidation case. Indeed, while EPA obviously prefers in this case to keep its CERCLA claim outside of bankruptcy so that it may present it, without reduction, against the reorganized company that it anticipates will emerge from bankruptcy, one may well speculate whether, if unincurred CERCLA response costs are not claims, some corporations facing substantial environmental claims will be able to reorganize at all.

Id. at 1005.

As to the conflict between bankruptcy and environmental policies:

Our point is the more limited one that in construing the Code, we need not be swayed by the arguments advanced by EPA that a narrow reading of the Code will better serve the environmental interests Congress wished to promote in enacting CERCLA. If the Code, fairly construed, creates limits on the extent of environmental cleanup efforts, the remedy is for Congress to make exceptions to the Code to achieve other objectives that Congress chooses to reach, rather than for courts to restrict the meaning of across-the-board legislation like a bankruptcy law in order to promote objectives evident in more focused statutes.

Id. at 1002.

Other courts have taken different approaches. See, for example, In re National Gypsum Co., 134 B.R. 188 (N.D.Tex.1991) (permitting discharge only of costs related to pre-petition conduct resulting in a release or threat of release that could have been "fairly contemplated" by the parties and expressly refusing to favor the "fresh start" goal of the Bankruptcy Code over CERCLA's policy to the extent adopted in *Chateaugay*).

See generally, Salerno, Ferland, & Hansen, Environmental Law and Its Impact On Bankruptcy Law—Saga of "Toxins–R–Us," 25 Real Prop. Probate & Trust J. 261 (1990); Mirsky, Conway, & Humphrey, The Interface Between Bankruptcy and Environmental Laws, 46 Bus. Law. 626 (1991); Carlson, Successor Liability in Bankruptcy: Some Unifying Themes of Intertemporal Creditor Priorities Created by Running Covenants, Products Liability, and Toxic–Waste Cleanup, 50 Law & Contemp. Probs. 119 (1987).

5. *The Lawyer's Ethical Obligation.* Richman & Bauer, Responsibilities of Lawyers and Engineers to Report Environmental Hazards and Maintain Client Confidences: Duties in Conflict, 5 Toxics Law Reporter 1458 (1991), poses the following question: if seller's attorney learns of hazardous wastes buried on the property, must he or she reveal this knowledge to the buyer or to the appropriate governmental

official?   The answer requires a difficult balancing of the attorney's duty to maintain confidentiality against the obligation to refrain from assisting the client's commission of fraudulent or criminal acts and the potential duty pursuant to statute to report environmental hazards. See Note, Attorney–Client Confidentiality: The Ethics of Toxic Dumping Disclosure, 35 Wayne L.Rev. 1157 (1989).

6. *Other Regulation.*   Federal environmental statutes other than CERCLA, may also impose liability on the owner or manager of contaminated land.   See, for example, Resource Conservation and Recovery Act of 1976 ("RCRA"), 42 U.S.C.A. § 6901 et seq., setting standards for hazardous waste treatment and disposal.   See generally, Curry, Hamula, & Rallison, The Tug–of–War Between RCRA and CERCLA at Contaminated Hazardous Waste Facilities, 23 Ariz.St.L.J. 359 (1991);   Hill, An Overview of RCRA: The "Mind–Numbing" Provisions of the Most Complicated Environmental Statute, 21 Envtl.L. Reporter 10254 (1991);   Stoll, The New RCRA Cleanup Regime: Comparisons and Contrasts With CERCLA, 44 Sw.L.J. 1299 (1991);   Melosi, Hazardous Waste and Environmental Liability: An Historical Perspective, 25 Hous.L.Rev. 741 (1988).

State Laws.   State environmental regulations also affect real estate transactions.   Some of these statutes called "baby CERCLA" acts, essentially track the federal act.   One example is the Michigan legislation discussed in Niecko v. Emro Marketing Company, appearing on pages 919–935 below.   Other state statutes require disclosure of specified environmental conditions before land is transferred.   See, e.g., Cal. Health & Safety Code §§ 25230(a)(2), 25359.7;   Pa.Stat.Ann.tit.35, § 6018.405.

New Jersey's Environmental Cleanup Responsibility Act ("ECRA"), N.J.S.A. 13:1K–6 et seq., takes a different approach, requiring that before the transfer of an "industrial establishment" (defined as any place of business used for storage, manufacture, or disposal of hazardous waste), the owner must notify the state of the proposed transfer and obtain approval of a declaration that there have been no discharges of hazardous wastes or that any discharges have been removed.   If the land still is contaminated, the owner must receive approval of a cleanup plan.   Penalties for failure to comply with ECRA include the voiding of the sale.   On ECRA, see generally, Farer, ECRA Verdict: Successes and Failures of Premier Transaction–Triggered Environmental Law, 5 Pace Envtl.L.Rev. 113 (1987);   Schmidt, New Jersey's Experience Implementing the Environmental Cleanup Responsibility Act, 38 Rutgers L.Rev. 729 (1986).

See generally, Gieser, Federal and State Environmental Law: A Trap For the Unwary Lender, 1988 B.Y.U.L.Rev. 643.

7. *"Indoor Air Pollution."*   The air inside a building may in fact be far more contaminated than the air outside.   Indoor air pollution involves contaminants, such as gases, bacteria, and chemicals, that may produce illness in the people on the premises.   For example, radon that

seeps into structures from the earth and accumulates presents a significant cancer risk. Federal legislation provides for the study of radon and assistance to the states but does not regulate radon in homes. Radon Pollution Control Act of 1988, 102 Stat. 2755 (codified at 15 U.S.C.A. §§ 2661–2671); Radon Gas and Indoor Quality Research of 1986, Title IV, 100 Stat. 1758. Federal regulation controls emissions of radon from certain facilities. 40 C.F.R. §§ 61.20–61.26, 61.220–61.225 (1991). See Locke, Promoting Radon Testing, Disclosure, and Remediation: Protecting Public Health Through the Home Mortgage Market, 20 Envtl. L. Reporter 10475 (1990); Shepard & Gaynor, Radon: A Growing Menace In Real Estate Transactions, 3 Probate & Prop. 6 (May–June 1989).

Asbestos in buildings is also regulated by federal law, see, e.g., 40 C.F.R. §§ 61.140–61.157 (1991), prohibiting installation of certain asbestos materials and setting requirements for the removal of asbestos), and state legislation, see, e.g., N.Y. Labor Law § 902 (McKinney 1988). In 3550 Stevens Creek Associates v. Barclays Bank of California, 915 F.2d 1355 (9th Cir.1990), cert. denied, ___ U.S. ___, 111 S.Ct. 2014, 114 L.Ed.2d 101 (1991), the court held that CERCLA does not apply to asbestos insulation installed in a building. Installing asbestos was not a "disposal" which would trigger CERCLA; the court held that Congress intended that CERCLA would control only when hazardous materials were waste and not while they were being put to productive use. As a result, a private party may not recover the cost of asbestos removal from a prior owner. For an excellent discussion of the asbestos issue, see Gluckstern, A Guide To Asbestos Liability For Real Property Owners, Lessors, and Managers, 5 Toxics Law Reporter 37 (1990). See also Fox, Asbestos: How To Conduct Real Estate Transactions in the Age of Asbestos Liability, 3 Prac. Real Est.Law. 59 (May 1987).

b.   AVOIDING LIABILITY

COMMENT, THE ENVIRONMENTAL DUE DILIGENCE DEFENSE AND CONTRACTUAL PROTECTION DEVICES

49 Louisiana Law Review 1405, 1422–1428 (1989).

The following discussion provides the general framework for conducting a due diligence inquiry in various types of transactions and can be used by either purchasers or lenders.

PHASE I

The first phase of the due diligence inquiry involves five basic procedures: the loan questionnaire, the chain of title search, the governmental records search, interviews of various parties, and the site inspection. With the possible exception of single family residential transactions where the lender is allowed to rely on the appraiser's investigation, the careful lender should be able to show that it conducted each of these procedures properly. Otherwise, it might not be able to show that its decision to forego the phase II environmental audit was prudent under the circumstances.

The first step a lender should take is to develop an environmental questionnaire. The questionnaire should address whether the site is vacant or developed, the nature of the borrower's business, prior activities at the site, pending environmental enforcement actions or private lawsuits, and other questions considering the wide range of environmental liabilities that affect different types of businesses. From this information, a loan officer trained in environmental hazards will assess the potential risks and conduct further investigations as required. This will allow the lender to decide the extent of the initial investigation and if the risks look particularly dangerous, whether to proceed at all.

Assuming the lender has decided to proceed with the property investigation process, the next step is the title search. CERCLA requires that the defendant conduct an "appropriate inquiry into the previous ownership" of the property.[93] Merely asking about prior ownership in the loan questionnaire would certainly not be appropriate by anyone's commercial standards. Thus the lender is required to conduct the title search.

Of course, the title search does not tell the lender anything about the condition of the property. It does, however, indicate possession of the property by known polluters, such as chemical companies. It also provides a starting point for the interview process.

The statute further requires the defendant to conduct an appropriate inquiry into previous uses of the property. A number of due diligence techniques are designed to achieve this requirement. Perhaps the most important is the governmental records search. Governmental agencies at both the local and national level accumulate information about contaminated properties, permit applications, health records, environmental compliance data, and other relevant information. Since this information is available to the general public from federal agencies under the Freedom of Information Act (F.O.I.A.), and from state agencies under state law, the courts will probably require a governmental records search under the "commonly known or reasonably ascertainable information" language of CERCLA.

At the federal level, the primary source of information should be the Environmental Protection Agency. Site-specific data should be available through the F.O.I.A., unless a valid trade secret claim can be asserted. This information should include: sites listed or targeted for listing on the National Priorities List[99] or RCRA underground storage

---

93. 42 U.S.C.A. § 9601(35)(B) (West Supp. 1988).

99. CERCLA requires that sites targeted for Superfund cleanups be listed on the National Priorities list, 42 U.S.C. § 9605 (1983).

tank registry; [100] facilities violating air, water, and hazardous waste laws; permit applications and permits issued to particular facilities; enforcement actions; computer lists of settlement actions; and other information required to be maintained by the EPA.

In addition to using the EPA as a source of information, a lender or purchaser could obtain information from the filings required to be made to the Securities Exchange Commission, such as the 10–K disclosure documents. Companies subject to registration requirements under the Securities Act of 1933 or the Securities Exchange Act of 1934 must disclose "material" information to the SEC, its shareholders, and its prospective shareholders. The extent to which environmental litigation is "material" is indicated by the SEC's Regulation S–K, which requires disclosure of environmental litigation when there is serious personal injury, property damage exceeding $50,000, a life-threatening situation, or a release of radioactive materials or "etiologic agents" (which includes a "viable microorganism, or its toxin, which causes or may cause human disease").

If the property was once used or is proposed to be used by a shipper or carrier, the Department of Transportation (DOT) should also be a source of environmental information. DOT requires shippers and carriers to notify federal authorities of "incidents" involving hazardous materials in transportation. Compliance data can also be obtained through DOT.

At the state level, records can usually be found as to the location of underground storage tanks, the locations of landfills and other waste disposal facilities, areas of radon contamination, asbestos records, discharge permits, Community Right to Know disclosures, and other helpful information.[107] There may also be a state agency which maintains "priority lists" for state funded cleanups, much like that kept by EPA. Local health agencies and sanitation departments could also assist in the search for information.

. . .

In summary, lenders and purchasers should become familiar with the type of information available within each agency and how that information may affect the property. By doing so, the loan officer will know which agency to contact for that specific information when a given problem arises. The lender, by being unaware of the availability of such information, runs the risk of having constructive knowledge of the information in the public records. Furthermore, as awareness of the environmental problems associated with real estate grows, the

---

100. RCRA requires owners of underground storage tanks storing hazardous substances to register such tanks, 42 U.S.C.A. § 6991(a) (West Supp. 1988). This program is often administered at the state level, and many tanks remain unregistered.

107. Miller and Bennett, Government Records: An Essential Element of Environmental Due Diligence, 3 Toxics L. Rep. 920, 922 (1988).

standards for inquiry will increase. It is likely, then, that review of government records will become an essential element in every real estate transaction.

Once these record searches are completed, the lender should conduct interviews with various parties connected with the property. This step is designed to fulfill the "commonly known or reasonably ascertainable information" requirement. Ideally, the lender or purchaser will have a list of names of former owners from its title search. A questionnaire should be sent to each of these former owners to ascertain the previous uses of the property. The same questionnaire should also be sent to the transferor of the property and neighbors. Additionally, these parties should be asked whether they ever leased the property to a third party, because this information is usually not discovered in the chain of title search. Next, the questionnaire should be sent to the former lessees. Specifically, the lender or purchaser should inquire about environmental compliance and past enforcement actions.

It is likely that many of the parties questioned will be reluctant to release information; they may, for example, fear liability for misleading statements in whatever information they disclose. It is important, however, that at least some attempt be made to get this information. If the questionnaire goes unanswered, perhaps a follow up phone call would be in order. All attempts to obtain this information should be documented. If there is still no response, the inference should be that the information was not reasonably ascertainable, and the lender or purchaser should be protected.

The final step of the phase I inquiry is the site inspection. This does not include expensive chemical testing as is done in the environmental audit, but rather requires only a simple visual examination of the site by a knowledgeable party. For example, if the property is a processing or manufacturing plant, the lender should have someone check for: required pollution control equipment; for stains or evidence of corrosion; for asbestos and PCB's; storage containers; fuel kept on site; pipelines; and record keeping practices. If the site is unimproved land, the terrain should be checked for discoloration, absence of vegetation, filled areas, stormwater ditches or conduits, pits or lagoons, and the presence of any wastes disposed of or stored on the site. Of course, other types of diligence techniques may alert the lender or purchaser to more specific evidence of contamination.

This does not mean that an extensive on site inspection should be conducted in every transaction. However, the statute implies that some type of inspection should be made. Section 101(35)(B) provides that the "obviousness" of the contamination and the ability to detect the contamination by an appropriate inspection must be considered by the court. ...

Phase I is completed when all of the above mentioned procedures have been done properly. Next, the lender or purchaser must evaluate the information he has received to decide whether further investigation is warranted. In reviewing documents, the lender should be especially suspicious of evidence of previous uses of the property to produce chemicals, pesticides, fertilizers, or types of manufacturing known to present environmental problems. The documents should also be reviewed to determine whether record keeping requirements have been complied with. Otherwise, there will be doubt as to the presence of wastes from undocumented activities. Prior enforcement actions should be reviewed for the severity of the releases. Finally, this information should be considered in conjunction with any problems that were discovered by the on-site inspection. In addition, the statute requires that the defendant consider the relationship of the purchase price to the value of the property if uncontaminated. It is possible that this could be the sole suspicious factor discovered during phase I, but could still be considered enough to necessitate a phase II environmental audit.

If any of the above investigations would raise suspicions in a reasonable person, considering the statutory limitations of this term, the lender or purchaser should either reject the transaction or loan, or proceed with the phase II environmental audit. If the transaction is a very large one, the parties may decide to incur the expenses of further investigation purely in the interest of caution.

PHASE II

The term "environmental audit" is loosely defined. Often it is used to describe the entire investigatory process, while other times it is used to describe any type of physical inspection of the property. For purposes of this comment, the term will be used to refer only to soil or groundwater sampling, or certain types of surface inspection or testing. The reason for this restrictive definition is the conclusion that some type of minimal visual inspection will be required in every transaction in order to fulfill the statutory requirement that the defendant conduct an "appropriate inquiry" into the "obviousness" of the presence of the contamination, and the ability to detect the contamination by appropriate inspection.[117] While the extent of the on-site inspection will vary according to each individual transaction, the fact that some type of investigation is necessary in order to claim the defense warrants the more restrictive definition. Therefore, the simple on-site inspection is considered part of the phase I inquiry, which should be conducted routinely, while the more extensive on-site inspection is part of the environmental audit conducted in Phase II.

Generally, an environmental audit is conducted by environmental experts. The sampling process must be undertaken with accepted procedures to ensure the reliability of the test, and lenders and purchasers are usually not able to properly conduct the audit themselves. The objectives are to identify the amount and types of contaminants in the soil or groundwater and to predict the rate and direction of

---

117. 42 U.S.C.A. § 101(35)(B) (West Supp. 1988).

migration of the contaminants.   If the audit refutes the suspicions raised by the phase I inquiry, the lender or purchaser may proceed with the transaction without losing his defense.   However, if the audit confirms suspicions of contamination, the lender or purchaser is considered to have actual knowledge of the contamination and may not claim the third party defense.   In addition, the parties should consider whether the contamination must be reported to the appropriate government agency.   Moreover, if title is finally taken, the purchaser must take reasonable steps to prevent harm to the public, which could include a cleanup of the property.

NIECKO v. EMRO MARKETING COMPANY

United States District Court, Eastern District of Michigan, 1991.
769 F.Supp. 973, affirmed 973 F.2d 1296 (6th Cir.1992).

OPINION AND ORDER GRANTING DEFENDANT'S
MOTION FOR SUMMARY JUDGMENT

ROSEN, District Judge.

Presently before the Court is the Defendant's Motion for Summary Judgment.   This motion was brought before the Court for hearing on May 14, 1991, at which time the Court heard the arguments of counsel for both parties.   At the May 14, 1991 hearing, the Court specifically requested the parties to file supplemental briefs addressing certain additional issues raised by the Court at the hearing.   The parties have now filed their supplemental briefs, which the Court has reviewed and considered in rendering this opinion.

FACTS:

The Plaintiffs, Walter Niecko and Thelma Niecko, husband and wife, seek to recover the $138,367 that they spent to clean up certain toxic hydrocarbons, specifically benzene, toluene, ethyl benzene, and xylene, from the soil of a certain parcel of real property located near the I–94 interstate expressway in Jackson Michigan.   The Plaintiffs purchased the property from Defendant Emro Marketing Company ("Emro") in March, 1987 for $46,000.   Emro is a subsidiary of Marathon Oil Company.

In the mid–1960s, the property was owned by Humble Oil & Refining Company which built and operated a gas station on the property at that time.   Humble eventually became a part of Exxon and Exxon operated the gas station until June, 1977.   At that time, the gas station and the real property were purchased from Exxon by Checker Oil Company.   In 1981, Checker permanently closed the gas station but retained ownership of the property.   Checker was itself subsequently purchased by Marathon Oil Company.   Marathon transferred title to the real property to Defendant Emro, its subsidiary, on January 1, 1984.   The gas station was never operated by Emro or during Emro's ownership of the property, but Emro did assume the liabilities of

Checker Oil Company, when that company was purchased by Marathon.

When Emro sold the property to the Plaintiffs in March, 1987, the purchase contract contained the following disclaimers:

> 10. It is expressly agreed that Seller makes no warranties that the subject property complies with federal, state or local governmental laws or regulations applicable to the property or its use. *Buyer has fully examined and inspected the property* and takes the property in its existing condition with no warranties of any kind concerning the condition of the property or its use.

> 11. *Buyer acknowledges that he has inspected and is familiar with the condition of the property*; that Seller has not made and makes no warranties or representations as to the condition of said property, including, but not limited to, *soil conditions*, zoning, building code violations, building line, building construction, use and occupancy restrictions (and violations of any of the foregoing), availability of utilities; and that Buyer is purchasing the same "as is"; *that he assumes all responsibility for any damages caused by the conditions on the property upon transfer of title.*

(Exhibit A to Defendant's Summary Judgment Brief, Pars. 10–11, pp. 2–3) (emphasis added).

The sale of the property from Emro to the Plaintiffs occurred in March, 1987, and the Plaintiffs took possession of the property in 1987. In 1989, McDonald's Corporation approached the Plaintiffs regarding the possible sale of the property to McDonald's for one of its restaurants. (The property was conveniently situated adjacent to I–94.) Before completing its purchase from the Plaintiffs, McDonald's conducted an environmental audit of the property, which uncovered the existence of hydrocarbons in the soil. McDonald's told the Plaintiffs about the soil contamination and conditioned its purchase of the property on the Plaintiff's removal of the contaminated soil. After the soil was removed, McDonald's purchased the property from the Plaintiffs for $110,000.

According to the Affidavit of Plaintiff Walter Niecko, Emro never disclosed to him that there were previously underground storage tanks on the property which contained gasoline and waste oil. Emro further failed to disclose that the storage tanks sat unused with gasoline and oil in them from 1981, the time the gas station was closed, until 1984, when the underground storage tanks were removed.[1] Emro also never disclosed to him that the underground pipes which connected the underground storage tanks to the individual gas pumps remained in the ground even at the time of the sale. According to Walter Niecko, when

---

1. Willis Deetz, the former operator of the gas station, testified in his deposition that the underground storage tanks were pumped dry when the station was closed in 1981.

the soil was removed at McDonald's request, the underground pipes were also dug up and were then in a state of severe corrosion.[2]

Walter Niecko's affidavit omits any claim that he was unaware that the property was previously operated as a gas station or that he was unaware that there were previously underground storage tanks on the property. Nevertheless, in their complaint, the Plaintiffs assert that "Plaintiffs would not have purchased said property from Defendant if Defendant had disclosed to them that there were leaking underground storage tanks on the property." (Complaint, Par. 21, p. 4).

In its summary judgment brief, Emro notes that the Plaintiffs admitted, in response to Emro's interrogatories, that they conducted a "surface inspection" of the property. Further, Plaintiffs admitted, in response to Emro's requests for admissions, that they were previously aware that a gas station was operated on the property.

In July, 1990, the Plaintiffs filed this action to recover the $138,367 they allegedly spent to remove and dispose of the contaminated soil. The First Amended Complaint is divided into eight distinct theories of liability. In Count I, the Plaintiffs argue that the Emro breached the purchase contract. Because the property turned out to be worth less than zero (i.e., it cost more to clean it up than it was worth even in clean condition), there was a "failure of consideration."

In Count II of the First Amended Complaint, the Plaintiffs argue that Emro committed fraud when it failed to disclose to them, prior to the purchase, that the property contained underground storage tanks and that the tanks had leaked hazardous substances into the soil.

In Count III, the Plaintiffs seek to recover the $138,367 they spent to clean up the property pursuant to the Comprehensive Environmental Response Compensation and Liability Act (CERCLA), 42 U.S.C. § 9607(a). In Count IV, the Plaintiffs seek to recover the same clean-up costs under a "contribution" theory.

. . .

In their response to the Defendant's Motion for Summary Judgment the Plaintiffs claim that they not only seek to recover the $138,367 they expended to haul away the contaminated soil on the property sold to them by Emro; they also seek to recover the alleged loss of the market value to the site and to the adjacent, vacant, 5 1/2 acre parcel which the Plaintiffs also own. However, the Plaintiffs purchased the adjacent 5 1/2 acre parcel in December, 1986 for $20,000, and sold it to McDonald's, in 1989, for $250,000. According to the affidavit of Plaintiff Walter Niecko, McDonald's now intends to sell the 5 1/2 acre parcel for $660,000.

---

2. The affidavit of the Plaintiffs' expert, Keith Gadway, indicates that the soil contamination resulted from leakage from the underground tanks and the gas pumps, not the connecting pipes.

Thus, even taking into consideration the $138,367 the Plaintiffs paid to clean up the property purchased from Emro, and the price they paid for that parcel ($46,000) and the adjacent 5 1/2 acre parcel ($20,000), the Plaintiffs ultimately gained $155,633 from their ownership of the two parcels.

DISCUSSION:

A. BREACH OF CONTRACT

Emro argues that the Plaintiffs' breach of contract claim should be dismissed because the Plaintiffs received just what they bargained for. The disclaimers in Paragraphs 10–11 make clear that the Plaintiffs voluntarily assumed the risks associated with the condition of the property, including, specifically, "soil conditions." Emro further argues that these disclaimers are fully enforceable under Michigan law, citing *Lenawee County Board of Health v. Messerly*, 417 Mich. 17, 331 N.W.2d 203 (1982); *Christy v. Glass*, 415 Mich. 684, 329 N.W.2d 748 (1982); *Dingeman v. Reffitt*, 152 Mich.App. 350, 393 N.W.2d 632 (1986); *Allied Corporation v. Frola*, 730 F.Supp. 626 (D.N.J.1990).

In response, the Plaintiffs argue that "because Defendant is strictly liable, the 'as is' clause in the contract should not be a defense to Plaintiff's action to recover cleanup costs. Therefore, Defendant's Motion for Summary Judgment as to Plaintiff's Breach of Contract Count must be denied." However, in making this argument, the Plaintiffs blur the distinction between their breach of contract cause of action (Count I of the complaint) and their statutory and common-law tort actions set forth in other counts of the First Amended Complaint. As stated by the court in *Frola* :

> Count 1 alleges that Allied breached the covenant against grantor's acts in the deed to Frola because the site was "charged and encumbered by asphalt, tars and oils containing hazardous substances and oils." Amended Counterclaim, count 1, para. 10. The deed, however, expressly states that it is "[s]ubject to covenants, easements, agreements and restrictions of record." The contract upon which the deed is based provides, in a typed addition to the printed form: "Premises are sold 'as is.' " Allied argues that the "as is" clause precludes any cause of action in contract based on implied representations as to the condition of the property. The Court agrees.

> The "as is" clause does not, however, extinguish Frola and Von Dohln's tort theories.

Frola, 730 F.Supp. pp. 629–30.

. . .

[T]he Court concludes that the "as is" disclaimer in the purchase contract protects Emro from contractual liability to the Plaintiffs. In *Messerly*, the Michigan Supreme Court held that a similar "as is" disclaimer in the purchase agreement was legally effective to insulate the sellers from liability to the purchasers on account of a defective sewerage system which rendered the property (a 3–unit apartment complex purchased for rental income) uninhabitable. The *Messerly* court stated:

> While there is no express assumption in the contract by either party of the risk of the property becoming uninhabitable, there was indeed some agreed allocation of the risk to the vendees by the incorporation of an "as is" clause into the contract which, we repeat, provided:
>
>> "Purchaser has examined this property and agrees to accept same in its present condition. There are no other or additional written or oral understandings."
>
> That is a persuasive indication that the parties considered that, as between them, such risk as related to the "present condition" of the property should lie with the purchaser. If the "as is" clause is to have any meaning at all, it must be interpreted to refer to those defects which were unknown at the time that the contract was executed. Thus, the parties themselves assigned the risk of loss to Mr. and Mrs. Pickles.
>
> We conclude that Mr. and Mrs. Pickles are not entitled to the equitable remedy of rescission and, accordingly, reverse the decision [of] the Court of Appeals.

Messerly, 331 N.W.2d, at 210–211.

The "as is" provision in the purchase contract at issue in this case is no less applicable than the one in the *Messerly* purchase contract. In the instant case, not only does the purchase contract recite that the Plaintiffs have inspected the property, it also specifically disclaims any warranties or representations "as to the condition of said property, including, but not limited to, *soil conditions* . . . ." Under these circumstances, the Court finds that the risk of unknown soil contamination has been contractually assumed by the Plaintiffs, and Emro, therefore, cannot be held liable on a breach of contract theory.

B. FRAUD

Plaintiffs argue that their claim for "fraudulent concealment" may be maintained even though Emro did not make any affirmative misrepresentations to them. In their view, Emro's failure to disclose that underground storage tanks were once located on the property, but were removed in 1984, and that the connecting pipes remained underground at the time of the sale constitutes actionable fraud under Michigan law because, "one who remains silent when fair dealing requires him to speak may be guilty of fraudulent concealment." (quoting *Nowicki v. Podgorski*, 359 Mich. 18, 101 N.W.2d 371, 378 (1960)). The Plaintiffs further rely on *Hand v. Dayton–Hudson*, 775 F.2d 757 (6th Cir.1985), and *Fred Macey Company v. Macey*, 143 Mich. 138, 153, 106 N.W. 722 (1906), for the proposition that silence can, under the right circumstances, equal fraud.

The cited cases are not dispositive here, however, since the circumstances in the instant case are not such that Emro had any duty to speak up. The thread running through the cited cases is that silence may constitute fraud where the surrounding circumstances are known and intended by the defendant to mislead the plaintiff and will mislead the plaintiff in the absence of further disclosure on the defendant's part.

. . .

In the instant case, the surrounding circumstances are not such that Emro could be said to have intended that the Plaintiffs receive a mistaken impression regarding the soil condition of the property. Instead, the purchase agreement itself was drafted specifically to *disclaim* any representations and warranties concerning the condition of the property, in general, and the soil condition, in particular. Emro did not have any actual knowledge that the soil was contaminated. Although Emro was aware that the property had previously been operated as a gas station, so did the Plaintiffs. In fact, the Plaintiffs owned the adjacent parcel. Although Emro did not inform the Plaintiffs that the underground storage tanks had been removed and the connecting pipes remained underground, neither did Emro deny these facts. Instead, the parties mutually agreed and represented to each other that the Plaintiffs would conduct their own investigation of the property. If the Plaintiffs had diligently performed this duty of inspection under the contract, it is likely that they would have discovered the true extent of the soil contamination. Indeed, McDonald's conducted an environmental audit before it agreed to purchase the property from the Plaintiffs, and McDonald's discovered the contamination.

Instead of requiring Emro to make a thorough analysis and disclosure of the condition of the property at the time of the sale, including the existence or prior removal of hidden underground storage tanks and pipes, the parties here contracted with each other to transfer this duty to the Plaintiffs. If the Plaintiffs had wanted representations and warranties from Emro concerning the condition of the property, they could have asked for them, possibly offering to Emro, in exchange, an increase in the purchase price. Having once struck what now appears to be an imprudent bargain, the Plaintiffs ask the Court to interfere with their own contracting powers for no other reason than that they made a bad deal when left to their own devices in the first instance.

The Court concludes that there is nothing in the surrounding circumstances from which the Court could infer that Emro had a duty, under Michigan law, to make further disclosures to the Plaintiffs. The Court will, therefore, dismiss the Plaintiffs' "fraudulent concealment" claim.

C. THE PLAINTIFFS' CERCLA CLAIM

[The court held that no claim could be brought under CERCLA as § 9601 excludes petroleum from the definition of "hazardous substance" under § 9607, and the contamination in question was due to petroleum.]

. . .

D. PLAINTIFFS' "CONTRIBUTION" CLAIM

. . .

In response to Emro's motion for summary judgment, the Plaintiffs assert that they are seeking contribution from Emro for having paid their potential joint liability under the Michigan Leaking Underground Storage Tank Act,[3] M.C.L. § 299.831, *et seq.*, as well as under Section 12 of Act No. 233 of the Michigan Public Acts of 1990. Accordingly, the Court will consider whether the Plaintiffs' actions in removing the contaminants from the property discharged a *potential* joint liability of the Plaintiffs with Emro such that the Plaintiffs would be entitled to bring a contribution action against Emro under Michigan law.

1. PLAINTIFFS' AND DEFENDANT'S POTENTIAL LIABILITY

The Plaintiffs argue that, under Section 12 of the Michigan Leaking Underground Storage Tank Act, M.C.L. § 299.842, the Plaintiffs and Emro are both "owners"[4] of the leaking underground storage tanks and are, therefore, jointly and severally liable to clean up the contaminated soil caused by the leaking underground storage tanks. Section 299.842 reads, in pertinent part, as follows:

299.842. Liability of owners or operators

Sec. 12.   (1) Except as otherwise provided in this section, liability imposed upon an owner and operator under this act shall be strict and without regard to fault, as applied to either or both of the following:

   (a) The obligation to carry out all corrective action requirements pursuant to this act.

---

3. This Act is commonly known, and the parties refer to it, by the acronym "LUST."

4. Emro evidently would not be an "owner" of the underground storage tanks unless the release occurred at the time Emro or Checker Oil held title to the property. M.C.L. § 299.834(2) defines "owner" for the purposes of the Leaking Underground Storage Tank Act and states, in pertinent part, as follows:

299.834. Definitions

* * *

   (2) "Owner" means a person who holds, or *at the time of release* held, a legal, equitable, or possessory interest of any kind in an underground storage

tank system, or in the property on which an underground storage tank system is located . . .

M.C.L. § 299.833 (emphasis added).

Under the facts stipulated by the parties in their proposed Joint Final Pretrial Order in this case, Emro assumed the liabilities of Checker Oil Company, which operated the gas station from 1977 through 1981, when Emro merged with Checker Oil in 1984. However, it is still not determined whether the release occurred during Checker Oil's operation of the gas station, or when the gas station was operated by Exxon.

(b) Any liability for other relief provided in section 13(1) [M.C.L. § 299.843(1)].

* * *

M.C.L. § 299.842(1).

Although this statute does not explicitly identify *to whom* the "owner and operator" shall be liable, Section 299.842(1)(b) and (by implication arising out of Section 299.842(1)(b)'s use of the term "other relief provided in section 13(1)") Section 299.842(1)(a) refer to the liability established by M.C.L. § 299.843 in favor of the Michigan attorney general, on behalf of the director of the Michigan Department of Natural Resources. Section 299.843 authorizes the Michigan Attorney General to bring a civil action to enforce the Michigan Leaking Underground Storage Tank Act....

Read together, Section 299.842(1) and Section 299.843 create potential liability on the part of owners and operators to the Michigan Department of Natural Resources ("DNR"). Thus, the Court concludes that both the Plaintiffs and Emro were potentially liable to the DNR at the time the Plaintiffs conducted the clean-up, depending, in part, on whether the release occurred when Checker Oil Company operated the gas station.

This assumes, of course, that the release was of such a nature and extent as to be subject to action under LUST, a fact not made part of the evidentiary record. However, for purposes of this opinion, the Court will assume the release in question would have been subject to corrective action.

. . .

2. EFFECT OF THE PARTIES' CONTRACTUAL PROVISIONS

At the May 14, 1991 hearing, the Court specifically requested the parties to file supplemental briefs addressing whether the provisions in Paragraphs 10 and 11 of the March 1987 purchase contract (see pp. 2–3, *infra*) are effective to release Emro from any rights to contribution the Plaintiffs may otherwise possess with respect to the Michigan Leaking Underground Storage Tank Act. This issue has now been fully briefed by the parties.

Paragraph 11 of the purchase contract explicitly states, "Buyer acknowledges that he has inspected and is familiar with the condition of the property; that Seller has not made and makes no warranties or representations as to the condition of said property, including, but not limited to, *soil conditions* ... [and] *that he assumes all responsibility for any damages caused by the conditions on the property upon transfer of title*" (emphasis added). Emro argues that this language in the parties' agreement effectively releases Emro from liability to the Plaintiffs with respect to damages incurred by the Plaintiffs as a result of the soil conditions on the property, including the presence of hazardous substances caused by oil leaking from the underground storage tanks.

In response, the Plaintiffs argue: (1) the contract language is merely a warranty disclaimer and does not purport to release Emro from its statutory liability to the Plaintiffs under the Michigan Leaking Underground Storage Tank Act; and (2) even if the contract could be construed to release Emro from the Plaintiffs' claim under the Michigan Act, the contract is nevertheless unenforceable under Section 12(6) of the Act, M.C.L. § 299.842(6).

   a.   Does the Contractual Language Release Emro from its Statutory Liability to the Plaintiffs?

In their supplemental brief, the Plaintiffs argue, first, that above-quoted provision in the purchase contract merely constitutes a warranty disclaimer and, as such, bars only the Plaintiffs' claims against Emro based upon breach of warranty. The Plaintiffs rely on *Southland Corp. v. Ashland Oil Co.*, 696 F.Supp. 994, 1000 (D.N.J.1988) and *Channel Master Satellite Systems v. JFD Electronics Corp.*, 702 F.Supp. 1229 (E.D.N.C.1988), in support of this argument.[6] However, there are significant differences between the contract language analyzed by the courts in *Southland* and *Channel Master* and the contract language at issue in the instant case.

   In *Southland*, the court stated:

   Ashland [the seller of the contaminated property] argues that because the term "as is" negates any representation on the part of the seller with regard to warranty or guarantee, this somehow conveys the idea that the purchaser assumes *all* of the associated risks. This argument is unpersuasive. As Southland correctly notes, an "as is" provision is merely a warranty disclaimer and as such precludes only claims based on breach of warranty. It does not act to shift liability from one party to an agreement to another and is inapplicable in a cause of action which is not based on breach of warranty. Therefore, *standing alone*, the "as is" clause cannot defeat Southland's CERCLA claims.

Southland, 696 F.Supp., at 1001 (emphasis added) (citations omitted).

   Similarly, the contract at issue in *Channel Master* stated, in pertinent part:

   4.4   Buyer represents that it has inspected, examined and investigated the Property and the uses thereof to its satisfaction, that it has independently investigated, analyzed, and appraised the value and the profitability thereof and that, except as expressly provided in this contract, it is purchasing the Property "as is" at the date of this contract and at the Closing.

   6. *See also Wiegmann & Rose International Corp. v. NL Industries*, 735 F.Supp.   957, 962 (N.D.Cal.1990).

Channel Master, 702 F.Supp., at 1230. With respect to the legal effect of this clause, the Channel Master court said:

> As indicated in *Southland,* the "as is" clause does not shift affirmative obligations of the parties imposed by statute independent of the contract. It is applicable only to rights arising by the dealings of the parties *inter se,* and hence is no bar to Channel Master's claim predicated upon § 107(a)(2) of CERCLA.

Id., at 1232.

In both the cited cases, it is clear that the courts were construing the legal effect of the "as is" provision standing alone. *See Southland,* 696 F.Supp., at 1001. However, in the instant case, it is not the "as is" clause standing alone which purports to release Emro. Rather, the provision in the contract that states, "Buyer acknowledges ... that he assumes all responsibility for any damages caused by the conditions on the property upon transfer of title," releases Emro from liability to the Plaintiffs under the Michigan Act. This language contemplates not only that the Plaintiffs waive their claims against Emro for damages "caused by the conditions on the property," but, further, that the Plaintiffs assume the risk of damages to third parties "caused by the conditions on the property."

In this respect, as between Emro and Plaintiffs, the *assumption* language in the instant contract is effective to encompass both damages claims brought by third parties and the Plaintiffs' claim for reimbursement of statutory clean-up costs. *FMC Corp. v. Northern Pump Co.,* 668 F.Supp. 1285, 1291 (D.Minn.1987); *United States v. South Carolina Recycling and Disposal, Inc.,* 653 F.Supp. 984, 1011, 1012 (D.S.C.1984). Therefore, the Court rejects the Plaintiffs' argument that the language in Paragraph 11 of the purchase contract purports to waive only breach of warranty claims.

b. Is the Contract Enforceable Under Michigan Law?

The Plaintiffs argue, in the alternative, that Section 12(6) of the Michigan Leaking Underground Storage Tank Act renders unenforceable Emro's attempt, in the purchase contract, to absolve itself from potential liability to the Plaintiff under the Act. Sections 12(6) and (7) (also pertinent) of the Michigan Act provide:

299.842. Liability of owners or operators

* * *

(6) No indemnification, hold harmless, or similar agreement or conveyance shall be effective to transfer from the owner or operator or from any person who may be liable for a release or threat of release under this act, to any person the liability imposed under this act. Nothing in this subsection shall bar any agreement to insure, hold harmless, or indemnify a party to such agreement for any liability under this act.

(7) This act shall not bar a cause of action that an owner or operator or any other person subject to liability under this act, or a guarantor, has or would have by reason of subrogation or otherwise against any person.

M.C.L. § 299.842(6), (7).

As noted by the parties in their supplemental briefs, this statute was enacted by the Michigan legislature effective January 19, 1989 and has not received any interpretation or construction by a Michigan or federal court. However, the parties further note that Sections 12(6) and (7) are virtually identical to, and obviously based upon, the analogous provisions contained in Sections 107(e)(1) and (2) of CERCLA, 42 U.S.C. § 9607(e)(1), (2). This statute reads in relevant part as follows:

§ 9607. Liability

* * *

e) Indemnification, hold harmless, etc., agreements or conveyances; subrogation rights

(1) No indemnification, hold harmless, or similar agreement or conveyance shall be effective to transfer from the owner or operator of any vessel or facility or from any person who may be liable for a release or threat of release under this section, to any person the liability imposed under this section. Nothing in this subsection shall bar any agreement to insure, hold harmless, or indemnify a party to such agreement for liability under this section.

(2) Nothing in this subchapter, including the provisions of paragraph (1) of this subsection, shall bar a cause of action that an owner or operator or any other person subject to liability under this section, or a guarantor, has or would have, by reason of subrogation or otherwise against any person.

42 U.S.C. § 9607(e)(1), (2).

The first rule in the construction of any statute is to begin with the language of the statute itself. *United States v. Ron Pair Enterprises, Inc.*, 489 U.S. 235, 109 S.Ct. 1026, 1030, 103 L.Ed.2d 290 (1989); *Mallard v. United States District Court for the Southern District of Iowa*, 490 U.S. 296, 109 S.Ct. 1814, 1818, 104 L.Ed.2d 318 (1989). "The plain meaning of legislation should be conclusive, except in the 'rare cases [in which] the literal application of a statute will produce a result demonstrably at odds with the intention of its drafters.' " *Ron Pair*, 109 S.Ct., at 1031 (quoting *Griffin v. Oceanic Contractors, Inc.*, 458 U.S. 564, 571, 102 S.Ct. 3245, 3250, 73 L.Ed.2d 973 (1982)); *Bradley v. Austin*, 841 F.2d 1288, 1293 (6th Cir.1988).

At first glance, the first and second sentences of Section 107(e)(1) may appear to be contradictory. Read cursorily, the first sentence seems to proscribe indemnification and hold harmless agreements, and the second sentence seems to permit them. In fact, a number of federal courts addressing this issue have found that the second sentence nullifies the first.[7] However, these courts seem to have predicated their decisions on the public policy rationale that, because CERCLA liability is far reaching, the parties should be able to distribute it as they see fit. 750 F.Supp. at 1025–26.

In interpreting this section, this Court will begin with the understanding that Congress intended that liability under CERCLA be joint and several. All parties who qualify as owners or operators are to be held liable to the claimant.[8] As noted in the legislative history,

> The Committee fully subscribes to the reasoning of the court in the seminal case of *United States v. Chem–Dyne Corporation*, 572 F.Supp. 802 (S.D.Ohio 1983), which established a uniform federal rule allowing for joint and several liability in appropriate CERCLA cases.

H.R.Rep. No 99–253(I), 99th Cong., 1st Sess. 74, reprinted in 1986 U.S.CODE CONG. & ADMIN.NEWS 2835, 2856.

The first sentence of Section 107 clearly assumes the joint and several liability of all liable parties to any party that, under the Act, has a right to demand cleanup and redress of damages, e.g., the government. It is this joint and several liability to which Congress is clearly referring when it speaks of "the liability imposed under this section" in the last words of the first sentence of the section.

With this premise firmly in mind, the first and second sentences of Section 107(e)(1) are not contradictory, but rather clear in their scope and intent. The first sentence simply voids any attempted transfer of joint and several liability to another party. Thus, assuming that Party A is the government and Party B is an owner-operator who sells property to Party C, the clear intent and effect of the first sentence is to void any attempt by Party B to contractually transfer, through indemnification or hold harmless agreements, to Party C all the liability it

---

7. As stated by the court in *Jones–Hamilton Co. v. Kopcoat, Inc.*, 750 F.Supp. 1022 (N.D.Cal.1990),

> A majority of federal courts that have considered the issue have held with minimal discussion that the second sentence of section 107(e)(1) completely negates the first sentence, thereby permitting parties to bargain over indemnification for CERCLA liability under all circumstances. *See e.g., American Nat'l Can Co. v. Kerr Glass Mfg. Corp.*, 1990 WL 125368 (N.D.Ill.1990); *Versatile Metals, Inc. v. Union Corp.*, 693 F.Supp. 1563 (E.D.Pa.1988); *Chemical Waste Management v. Armstrong World Indus., Inc.*, 669 F.Supp. 1285, 1293 (E.D.Pa.1987); *FMC Corp. v. Northern Pump Co.*, 668 F.Supp. 1285, 1289 (D.Minn.1987), appeal dismissed, 871 F.2d 1091 (8th Cir.1988).

Id. at 1025.

8. As defined in CERCLA, "claimant" is "any person who presents a claim for compensation under this chapter." 42 U.S.C. § 9601(5). In most cases, the United States government, operating through the Environmental Protection Agency, will be enforcing the statute. However, the Act also provides for recovery, under certain conditions, by private parties. *See* 42 U.S.C. § 9607(a)(4)(B); *Pennsylvania v. Union Gas Co.*, 491 U.S. 1, 109 S.Ct. 2273, 2285, 105 L.Ed.2d 1 (1989); *Amoco Oil Co. v. Borden, Inc.*, 889 F.2d 664, 667 (5th Cir. 1989).

The Michigan statute likewise assumes that the state government, i.e., the DNR, will be responsible for collecting response costs for hazardous waste cleanup. See M.C.L. § 299.843.

owes Party A. In other words, Party B cannot, by contractual indemnification, escape its obligations to Party A under the Act. Congress intended to protect the rights of the claimant against attempts by owners or operators to escape liability to claimants through private contractual devices. *See Rodenbeck v. Marathon Petroleum Co.*, 742 F.Supp. 1448, 1456 (N.D.Ind.1990).

The legislative history of CERCLA provides clear support for this interpretation. During a Senate debate, the following exchange took place between Senator Cannon and Senator Randolph, a sponsor of the bill:

> Mr. CANNON. Section 107(a)(1) prohibits transfer of liability from the owner or operator of a facility to other persons through indemnification, hold harmless, or similar agreements or conveyances. Language is also included indicating that this prohibition on the transfer of liability does not act as a bar to such agreements, in particular to insurance agreements.
>
> The net effect is to make the parties to such an agreement, which would not have been liable under this section, also liable to the degree specified in the agreement. *It is my understanding that this section is designed to eliminate situations where the owner or operator of a facility uses its economic power to force the transfer of its liability to other persons, as a cost of doing business, thus escaping its liability under the act all together [sic]*.
>
> Mr. RANDOLPH. That is correct.

126 CONG.REC. 30,984 (1980) (emphasis added). Senator Cannon makes clear that the purpose of the section is to ensure that the responsible parties will fund the cleanup. These responsible parties may enter insurance agreements to add parties who will pay for the cleanup. They may not, however, avoid liability to the claimant (usually the government) by transferring this liability.

There is nothing in the first sentence that purports to prevent liable parties under the Act from apportioning, allocating, or even shifting completely *among themselves* the liability that each party will owe the CERCLA claimant, so long as each contracting party understands that it will remain jointly and severally liable to that CERCLA claimant. An interpretation to the contrary would effectively burden all contractual exchanges involving property that may fall under CERCLA's purview. This was not Congress's intention. *See Mardan Corp. v. C.G.C. Music, Ltd.*, 804 F.2d 1454, 1460 (9th Cir.1986).[9] Rather, Con-

---

9. The *Mardan* court touched upon this issue in a CERCLA case involving facts similar to those before the Court in the instant case:

By contrast, nothing in CERCLA suggests that it was intended to offer special protection to unwary purchasers of businesses. Moreover, since CERCLA releas- es are likely to be entered into by major companies, there is little need for a special federal rule to protect releasors of CERCLA recovery rights from their own ignorance or weak bargaining power. In fashioning a statute to further a federal interest, Congress seldom if ever intends to pursue that interest at any cost.

gress passed CERCLA to ensure that the responsible parties, and not the government, would ultimately pay for waste cleanup.[10]

The second sentence of Section 107(e)(1) clarifies and reinforces the scope of the prohibition in the first sentence. It notes that the first sentence will not prohibit agreements between parties to insure, indemnify, or hold harmless: "Nothing in this subsection shall bar any agreement to insure, hold harmless, or indemnify a party to such agreement for any liability under this section." 42 U.S.C. § 9607(e). Read in conjunction with the first sentence, insurance, indemnification, or hold harmless agreements are valid so long as they do not transfer liability from an owner or operator to a third party. Thus, Party C may indemnify or insure Party B because this indemnification will not jeopardize Party A's ultimate ability to collect the costs of cleanup. The liability remains with the transferor; the transferee simply agrees to fund the cleanup on behalf of the transferor.

Section 107(e)(2) lends even further support to this interpretation. It reads in pertinent part:

> (2) Nothing in this subchapter, including the provisions of paragraph (1) of this subsection, shall bar a cause of action that an owner or operator or any other person subject to liability under this section, or a guarantor, has or would have, by reason of subrogation or otherwise against any person.

42 U.S.C. § 9607(e). This section would permit parties to bring an action to enforce their rights of subrogation (i.e., their contractual rights to indemnification or contribution) notwithstanding the provision of Section 107(e)(1). Thus, if a party that has indemnified or insured himself against liability is sued by a CERCLA claimant, that party may recover from the other party to the agreement. This language ensures that Section 107(e)(1) will not be interpreted to abrogate such contractual agreements.

In reaching this conclusion, the Court finds persuasive the analysis of Section 107 adopted by the Ninth Circuit in *Mardan Corp. v. C.G.C. Music Ltd.*, 804 F.2d 1454 (9th Cir.1986). In that case, Mardan Corporation ("Mardan") bought from Macmillan, Inc. ("Macmillan") a plant used to make musical instruments. For ten years prior to the sale, Macmillan had manufactured instruments at the plant and had deposited waste into a settled pond at the site. Prior to the sale of the plant, Macmillan filed with the EPA a Notification of Hazardous Waste Activity. Later, the parties executed an "Agreement of General Settle-

---

Rather Congress seeks to balance that interest against countervailing considerations, such as the utility of indemnification agreements, which it recognized in section 107(e)(1).

Mardan Corp. v. C.G.C. Music, Ltd., 804 F.2d 1454, 1460 (9th Cir.1986) (Footnote omitted).

10. *See* H.R.Rep. No. 99–253(I), 99th Cong., 2nd Sess. 55, *reprinted in* 1986 U.S.CODE CONG. & ADMIN.NEWS 2835, 2837 ("As a result, an underlying principle of H.R. 2817 is that Congress must facilitate cleanups of hazardous substances by the responsible parties while assuring a strong EPA oversight role with a set of tough legal enforcement standards").

ment and Release" under which Macmillan paid Mardan $995,000 in settlement of a variety of claims arising out of the purchase. The language of the settlement agreement encompassed "all actions, causes of action, suits, ... based upon, arising out of or in any way relating to the Purchase Agreement...." *Mardan*, 804 F.2d at 1456. Later, the EPA brought suit against Mardan and, pursuant to a consent agreement, Mardan agreed to clean up and close the settling pond. Mardan then brought an action under Section 107 of CERCLA seeking to recover damages for costs incurred in cleaning up the pond.

The district court granted summary judgment to Macmillan on the ground [11] that Mardan's action under Section 107 of CERCLA was barred by the terms of the release executed as part of the settlement agreement. *Mardan Corp. v. C.G.C. Music, Ltd.*, 600 F.Supp. 1049 (D.Ariz.1984). The Ninth Circuit affirmed stating:

> Contractual arrangements apportioning CERCLA liabilities between private "responsible parties" are essentially tangential to the enforcement of CERCLA's liability provisions. Such agreements cannot alter or excuse the underlying liability, but can only change who ultimately pays that liability. Moreover, regardless of how or under what law these agreements are interpreted, the result cannot prejudice the right of the government to recover cleanup or closure costs from any responsible party, including either Mardan, Macmillan, or both. CERCLA § 107(a), 42 U.S.C. § 9607(a) (1982).

Mardan, 804 F.2d at 1459.

The Ninth Circuit's interpretation of the intersection between contractual and CERCLA liability was not followed, however, by the Northern District of Ohio in *AM International, Inc. v. International Forging Equipment*, 743 F.Supp. 525 (N.D.Ohio 1990).[12] That court relied on legislative history to formulate a different interpretation of the statute. It noted that one prior draft of Section 107 read as follows:

> No indemnification, hold harmless, conveyance, or similar agreement shall be effective to transfer from the owner or operator of a facility, or from any person who may be liable for a release under this section, to any other person the liability imposed under this section: *Provided*, That this subsection shall not apply to a transfer in a bona fide conveyance of a facility or site (1) between two parties not affiliated with each other in any way, (2) where there has been an adequate disclosure in writing ... of all facts and conditions (including potential economic consequences) material to such liability, and (3) to a[transferee] who can provide assurances of financial

---

11. As an alternative ground, the court held that Mardan's action was barred by the doctrine of unclean hands.

12. The Court notes that the *AM International* decision has since been followed

by the United States District Court for the Western District of Michigan in *CPC Intern., Inc. v. Aerojet–General Corp.*, 759 F.Supp. 1269, 1282–1283 (W.D.Mich.1991).

responsibility and continuity of operation consistent with the degree and duration of risks associated with such facility or site.

S. 1480, 96th Cong., 2d Sess., 126 CONG.REC. 30,900 (1980). This draft was, however, later changed to the present version by excising the exception to the prohibition on the transfer of liability.

From this, the *AM International* court concluded that the section as now drafted precludes all attempts contractually to relieve parties of liability under the Act with a single exception "recognizing agreements that may provide for indemnity or additionally liable parties." *AM International*, 743 F.Supp. at 528–29. This Court respectfully disagrees with the interpretation of Section 107 chosen by the *AM International*. It believes that that court failed adequately to take into consideration the difference between a *transfer* of liability and an agreement for indemnification or contribution between parties otherwise liable to the government. It made the erroneous assumption that simply because Congress had prohibited the release of liability to the claimant, it had also forbade the release of liability to another liable party.

The prior draft proves only that Congress earlier considered allowing the transfer of liability under limited circumstances. With the exception of clause (2) of the draft legislation,[13] the conditions set forth in this prior draft were clearly inserted to protect the recovery rights of the principal CERCLA claimants under the Act. Clause (1) protects innocent claimants against sham transactions between insiders merely intended to insulate potential "deep pockets" from CERCLA liability. Similarly, clause (3) of the draft allows a responsible owner or operator to transfer liability only if the proposed transferee is financially capable of responding in damages to claimants. These protections were thought necessary only because Congress evidently believed that, in the absence of Section 107(e)(1), potentially responsible owners and operators would have been able to escape CERCLA liability simply by transferring the liability to others.[14]

Thus interpreted, there is nothing "internally inconsistent" or contradictory between the first and second sentences of Section 107(e)(1) which would lend ambiguity to the plain language used in the first sentence.

Consequently, this Court concludes that Section 107(e)(1), 42 U.S.C. § 9607(e)(1), and, by analogy, the identical provision of LUST, M.C.L. § 299.842(6) and (7) which are here being construed, is unambiguous.

---

13. The purpose of clause (2) seems to be directed at protecting the person who assumes liability. However, this protection was not carried forward in the version of Section 107(e)(1) that was ultimately enacted.

14. The perceived need for such protection also explains Senator Cannon's remark concerning the present version of Section 107(e)(1): "It is my understanding that this section is designed to eliminate situations where the owner or operator of a facility uses its economic power to force the transfer of its liability to other persons, as a cost of doing business, thus *escaping its liability under the act all together*." 126 Cong.Rec. 30,984 (1980) (emphasis added). *See AM International*, 743 F.Supp. at 529.

Since there is no clear legislative intent to the contrary disclosed in the legislative history, the Court will enforce the Michigan statute according to the "plain meaning" of the words chosen by the legislature. *Ron Pair*, 109 S.Ct. at 1031. In this case, this means that the terms of Paragraph 11 of the purchase contract are enforceable. Therefore, as between Emro and themselves, the Plaintiffs have released Emro from liability arising out of the condition of the property at the time of the sale, including the "soil condition," and this release bars the Plaintiffs' claim under the Michigan Leaking Underground Storage Tank Act.

. . .

CONCLUSION:

For the reasons stated herein, and the Court being otherwise fully advised in the premises;

NOW, THEREFORE;

IT IS HEREBY ORDERED, ADJUDGED, AND DECREED that the Defendant's Motion for Summary Judgment is GRANTED, and the First Amended Complaint shall be and hereby is DISMISSED WITH PREJUDICE.

LET THE JUDGMENT BE ENTERED ACCORDINGLY.

NOTES

1. *Environmental Audits.* The environmental audit serves several purposes. First, a buyer may try to cancel a contract of sale if the audit discloses contamination. (Must there be a contract condition to that effect?) Second, an environmental audit may form the basis for the innocent landowner defense under CERCLA if the buyer completes the transaction and subsequently discovers hazardous waste. (See *Serafini* and following notes on page 896 above.) A lender may require an environmental audit, to ensure that the land—its security—is not contaminated and to avoid liability as an innocent landowner in the event of foreclosure. (See pages 938–951 below).

The lack of uniformity in standards for environmental audits makes it difficult for buyers, sellers, lenders, and environmental engineers to develop a common language enabling them to reach a clear understanding of their expectations. Uniform standards would make it easier to predict what is necessary to achieve "appropriate inquiry" for the purposes of the innocent landowner defense. Professional groups such as the American Society for Testing and Materials are attempting to draft uniform standards. See note *3* on page 909 above.

For other descriptions of environmental audits, see Patterson, A Buyer's Catalogue of Prepurchase Precautions to Minimize CERCLA Liability in Commercial Real Estate Transactions, 15 U. Puget Sound L.Rev. 469, 488–491 (1992); Slap & Israel, Private CERCLA Litigation: How To Avoid It? How To Handle It?, 25 Real Prop. Probate & Trust J. 705, 715–717 (1991); Fitzsimmons & Sherwood, The Real Estate

Lawyer's Primer (And More) to Superfund: The Environmental Hazards of Real Estate Transactions, 22 Real Prop. Probate & Trust J. 765, 775–782 (1987); M. Blumenfeld, Conducting An Environmental Audit (2d ed.1989).

On the recourse a buyer may have against an environmental engineer who fails to discover existing contamination, see Note, Holding Environmental Consultants Liable For Their Negligence: A Proposal For Change, 64 S.Cal.L.Rev. 1143 (1991).

2. *Indemnification.* As Niecko v. Emro Marketing Company indicates, courts differ on the enforceability of clauses that attempt to shift CERCLA liability. Two issues control: is the contract language used by the parties adequate to show an intent to shift the cost?; does CERCLA permit the parties to shift liability? Consider how you would draft the clause if you represented buyer or seller.

See generally, Parker & Slavich, Contractual Efforts To Allocate The Risk of Environmental Liability: Is There A Way To Make Indemnities Worth More Than The Paper They Are Written On?, 44 Sw.L.J. 1349 (1991); Note, Contractual Transfers of Liability Under CERCLA Section 107(e)(1): For Enforcement of Private Risk Allocations in Real Property Transactions, 43 Case W.Res.L.Rev. 161 (1992); Note, Passing The Big Bucks: Contractual Transfers of Liability Between Potentially Responsible Parties Under CERCLA, 75 Minn.L.Rev. 1571 (1991); Note, An "As Is" Provision in a Commercial Property Contract: Should It Be Left As Is When Assessing Liability for Environmental Torts?, 51 U.Pitt.L.Rev. 995 (1990).

3. *Other Buyer Remedies.* As indicated in *Niecko*, the buyer of contaminated property may seek to hold the seller responsible under a number of state law theories explored in other contexts. See page 913 above.

Niecko discussed express warranty theory and liability for nondisclosure. Is the court's view of the disclosure obligation consistent with Thacker v. Tyree and Stambovsky v. Ackley, at pages 192–198 above? See Roberts v. Estate of Barbagallo, 366 Pa.Super. 559, 531 A.2d 1125 (1987) (permitting cause of action against seller's estate and broker for fraudulent concealment by broker of ureaformaldehyde foam insulation that presents a health risk); Westwood Pharmaceuticals, Inc. v. National Fuel Gas Distribution Corp., 737 F.Supp. 1272 (W.D.N.Y.1990), affirmed, 964 F.2d 85 (2d Cir.1992) (holding that New York's caveat emptor rule is no defense to CERCLA action by buyer against seller). See generally, Tracy, Beyond Caveat Emptor: Disclosure to Buyers of Contaminated Land, 10 Stan.Envtl.L.J. 169 (1991).

Buyers sometimes succeed, such as in tort for abnormally dangerous activities on the land, see, e.g., T & E Industries, Inc. v. Safety Light Corp., 123 N.J. 371, 587 A.2d 1249 (1991) (permitting buyer to maintain action against owner earlier in chain of title that discarded radioactive materials on the site in the course of manufacturing operations); public and private nuisance, see Westwood Pharmaceuticals, Inc. v. National

Fuel Gas Distribution Corp., 737 F.Supp. 1272 (W.D.N.Y.1990), affirmed, 964 F.2d 85 (2d Cir.1992); cf. Adkins v. Thomas Solvent Co., 440 Mich. 293, 487 N.W.2d 715 (1992) (finding no nuisance when neighboring company polluted groundwater in area but not plaintiffs' groundwater and finding negative publicity caused by that pollution was not actionable nuisance); mutual mistake, see, e.g., Garb–Ko v. Lansing–Lewis Services, Inc., 423 N.W.2d 355 (1988) (seller permitted to rescind contract where neither seller nor buyer knew of underground gasoline tanks); and builder-vendor warranty, see, Powell, Builder–Vendor Liability For Environmental Contamination in the Sale of New Residential Property, 58 Tenn.L.Rev. 231 (1991).

Buyers have enjoyed less success in claiming that the presence of hazardous materials breached promises relating to title. See, e.g., United States v. Allied Chemical Corp., 587 F.Supp. 1205 (N.D.Cal.1984) (hazardous waste was not "encumbrance" within seller's covenant that land was free from encumbrances); see Cameron v. Martin Marietta Corp., 729 F.Supp. 1529 (E.D.N.C.1990) (presence of hazardous waste did not breach provision of contract of sale that there were "no restrictions, easement, zoning or other governmental regulation" that would prevent reasonable use of the property for the purposes for which it was currently zoned since court believed buyers could maintain innocent landowner defense under CERCLA).

4. *Liability Insurance.* Landowners generally accept that pollution exclusion clauses typically inserted in their insurance policies will bar recovery from the insurer for liability arising from the hazardous substances on the property. Even if an insured could convince a court to extend coverage, a reasonable buyer will be reluctant to rely on that possibility as her protection from CERCLA liability. See Comment, Comprehensive General Liability Insurance Coverage for CERCLA Liabilities: A Recommendation for Judicial Adherence to State Canons of Insurance Contract Construction, 61 U.Colo.L.Rev. 407 (1990); Note, Insurance Coverage for Superfund Liability: A Plain Meaning Approach to The Pollution Exclusion Clause, 27 Washburn L.J. 161 (1987); see also Raskoff, Arguments Advanced By Insureds For Coverage of Environmental Claims, 22 Pac.L.J. 771 (1991). Some insurers have been offering special insurance coverage to buyers and lenders for cleanup expenses of undetected hazardous waste under CERCLA and similar state regulation. See Feder, Making a Difference; New Policy on Pollution, N.Y. Times, June 9, 1991, sec. 3, at 7 (discussing the Environmental Risk Insurance Company Group property transfer liability insurance).

For an excellent analysis of the issues of environmental insurance, see Abraham, Environmental Liability and the Limits of Insurance, 88 Colum.L.Rev. 942 (1988).

5. *Title Insurance.* The presence of hazardous materials does not breach the title insurance policy's warranties of marketability of title and freedom from encumbrances. See, e.g., Chicago Title Insurance Co.

v. Kumar, 24 Mass.App.Ct. 53, 506 N.E.2d 154 (1987); Lick Mill Creek Apartments v. Chicago Title Insurance Co., 231 Cal.App.3d 1654, 283 Cal.Rptr. 231 (1991). However, a title company may be liable on a policy if it fails to detect an environmental lien recorded before issuance of the policy. See Bozarth, Environmental Liens and Title Insurance, 23 U.Rich.L.Rev. 305 (1989).

2. LENDER LIABILITY

UNITED STATES v. FLEET FACTORS CORP.

United States Court of Appeals, Eleventh Circuit, 1990.
901 F.2d 1550, cert. denied, ___ U.S. ___, 111 S.Ct. 752, 112 L.Ed.2d 772 (1991).

Before VANCE and KRAVITCH, Circuit Judges, and LYNNE, Senior District Judge.

KRAVITCH, Circuit Judge:

Fleet Factors Corporation ("Fleet") brought an interlocutory appeal from the district court's denial of its motion for summary judgment in this suit by the United States to recover the cost of removing hazardous waste from a bankrupt textile facility. The district court denied summary judgment because it concluded that Fleet's activities at the facility might rise to the level of participation in management sufficient to impose liability under the Comprehensive Environmental Response Compensation and Liability Act ("CERCLA"), 42 U.S.C. §§ 9601–57 (1982 & West Supp.1988), despite the statutory exemption from liability for holders of a security interest. We agree with the district court that material questions of fact remain as to the extent of Fleet's participation in the management of the facility; therefore, we affirm the denial of Fleet's summary judgment motion.

FACTS

In 1976, Swainsboro Print Works ("SPW"), a cloth printing facility, entered into a "factoring" agreement with Fleet in which Fleet agreed to advance funds against the assignment of SPW's accounts receivable. As collateral for these advances, Fleet also obtained a security interest in SPW's textile facility and all of its equipment, inventory, and fixtures. In August, 1979, SPW filed for bankruptcy under Chapter 11. The factoring agreement between SPW and Fleet continued with court approval. In early 1981, Fleet ceased advancing funds to SPW because SPW's debt to Fleet exceeded Fleet's estimate of the value of SPW's accounts receivable. On February 27, 1981, SPW ceased operations and began to liquidate its inventory. Fleet continued to collect on the accounts receivable assigned to it under the Chapter 11 factoring agreement. In December 1981, SPW was adjudicated a bankrupt under Chapter 7 and a trustee assumed title and control of the facility.

In May 1982, Fleet foreclosed on its security interest in some of SPW's inventory and equipment, and contracted with Baldwin Industrial Liquidators ("Baldwin") to conduct an auction of the collateral.

Baldwin sold the material "as is" and "in place" on June 22, 1982; the removal of the items was the responsibility of the purchasers. On August 31, 1982, Fleet allegedly contracted with Nix Riggers ("Nix") to remove the unsold equipment in consideration for leaving the premises "broom clean." Nix testified in deposition that he understood that he had been given a "free hand" by Fleet or Baldwin to do whatever was necessary at the facility to remove the machinery and equipment. Nix left the facility by the end of December, 1983.

On January 20, 1984, the Environmental Protection Agency ("EPA") inspected the facility and found 700 fifty-five gallon drums containing toxic chemicals and forty-four truckloads of material containing asbestos. The EPA incurred costs of nearly $400,000 in responding to the environmental threat at SPW. On July 7, 1987, the facility was conveyed to Emanuel County, Georgia, at a foreclosure sale resulting from SPW's failure to pay state and county taxes.

The government sued Horowitz and Newton, the two principal officers and stockholders of SPW, and Fleet to recover the cost of cleaning up the hazardous waste. The district court granted the government's summary judgment motion with respect to the liability of Horowitz and Newton for the cost of removing the hazardous waste in the drums. The government's motion with respect to Fleet's liability, and the liability of Horowitz and Newton for the asbestos removal costs was denied. Fleet's motion for summary judgment was also denied. The district court, *sua sponte*, certified the summary judgment issues for interlocutory appeal and stayed the remaining proceedings in the case. Fleet subsequently brought this appeal challenging the court's denial of its motion for summary judgment.

STANDARD OF REVIEW

The district court's disposition of the summary judgment motion is reviewable de novo because it involves legal questions of statutory interpretation. *See Florida Power & Light Co. v. Allis Chalmers Corp.*, 893 F.2d 1313, 1315–16 (11th Cir.1990); *Hiram Walker & Sons v. Kirk Line, Inc.*, 877 F.2d 1508, 1513 (11th Cir.1989); *Clemens v. Dougherty County, Ga.*, 684 F.2d 1365, 1368 (11th Cir.1982). Under Fed.R.Civ.P. 56(c), summary judgment is only appropriate when "there is no genuine issue as to any material fact and ... the moving party is entitled to a judgment as a matter of law." *Allis Chalmers*, 893 F.2d at 1318. In evaluating a summary judgment motion, the burden of establishing the absence of a material dispute of fact is on the moving party; the court must view all evidence in the light most favorable to the non-movant and resolve all reasonable doubts about the facts in favor of the non-movant. *Id.; WBS–TV v. Lee*, 842 F.2d 1266, 1269 (11th Cir.1988); *Warrior Tombigbee Transportation Co. v. M/V Nan Fung*, 695 F.2d 1294, 1296 (11th Cir.1983); *Celotex Corp. v. Catrett*, 477 U.S. 317, 323, 106 S.Ct. 2548, 2552–53, 91 L.Ed.2d 265 (1986).

DISCUSSION

The Comprehensive Environmental Response Compensation and Liability Act was enacted by Congress in response to the environmental and public health hazards caused by the improper disposal of hazardous wastes. *United States v. Maryland Bank & Trust Co.*, 632 F.Supp. 573, 576 (D.Md.1986); S.Rep. No. 848, 96th Cong., 2d Sess. 2 (1980), U.S.Code Cong. & Admin.News 1980, p. 6119. The essential policy underlying CERCLA is to place the ultimate responsibility for cleaning up hazardous waste on "those responsible for problems caused by the disposal of chemical poison." *Allis Chalmers*, 893 F.2d at 1316; *United States v. Aceto Agricultural Chemicals Corp.*, 872 F.2d 1373, 1377 (8th Cir.1989); *Dedham Water Co. v. Cumberland Farms Dairy*, 805 F.2d 1074, 1081 (1st Cir.1986). Accordingly, CERCLA authorizes the federal government to clean up hazardous waste dump sites and recover the cost of the effort from certain categories of responsible parties. *Maryland Bank & Trust Co.*, 632 F.Supp. at 576.

The parties liable for costs incurred by the government in responding to an environmental hazard are: 1) the present owners and operators of a facility where hazardous wastes were released or are in danger of being released; 2) the owners or operators of a facility at the time the hazardous wastes were disposed; 3) the person or entity that arranged for the treatment or disposal of substances at the facility; and 4) the person or entity that transported the substances to the facility. *Allis Chalmers*, 893 F.2d at 1317; 42 U.S.C. § 9607(a) (1982 & West Supp.1988). The government contends that Fleet is liable for the response costs associated with the waste at the SPW facility as either a present owner and operator of the facility, *see* 42 U.S.C. § 9607(a)(1), or the owner or operator of the facility at the time the wastes were disposed, *see* 42 U.S.C. § 9607(a)(2).

The district court, as a matter of law, rejected the government's claim that Fleet was a present owner of the facility. The court, however, found a sufficient issue of fact as to whether Fleet was an owner or operator of the SPW facility at the time the wastes were disposed to warrant the denial of Fleet's motion for summary judgment. On appeal each party contests that portion of the district court's order adverse to their respective interests.

A. Fleet's Liability Under Section 9607(a)(1)

CERCLA holds the owner or operator of a facility containing hazardous waste strictly liable to the United States for expenses incurred in responding to the environmental and health hazards posed by the waste in that facility. *See* 42 U.S.C. § 9607(a)(1); S.Rep. No. 848, 96th Cong., 2d Sess. 34 (1980). This provision of the statute targets those individuals presently "owning or operating such facilit[ies]." *See* 42 U.S.C. § 9601(20)(A)(ii). In order to effectuate the goals of the statute, we will construe the present owner and operator of a facility as that individual or entity owning or operating the facility at the time the plaintiff initiated the lawsuit by filing a complaint.

On July 9, 1987, the date this litigation commenced, the owner of the SPW facility was Emanuel County, Georgia. Under CERCLA, however, a state or local government that has involuntarily acquired title to a facility is generally not held liable as the owner or operator of the facility.[4] Rather, the statute provides that

> in the case of any facility, title or control of which was conveyed due to bankruptcy, foreclosure, tax delinquency, abandonment, or similar means to a unit of State or local government, [its owner or operator is] any person who owned, operated or otherwise controlled activities at such facility immediately beforehand.

42 U.S.C. § 9601(20)(A)(iii).

Essentially, the parties disagree as to the interpretation of the phrase "immediately beforehand." The district court reasoned that Fleet could not be liable under section 9607(a)(1) because it had never foreclosed on its security interest in the facility and its agents had not been on the premises since December 1983. The government contends that the statute should be interpreted to refer liability "back to the last time that someone controlled the facility, however long ago." Appellee's Brief at 23. Thus, according to the government, the period of effective abandonment of the site by the trustee in bankruptcy (from December 1983 to the July 1987 foreclosure sale) should be ignored and liability would remain with Fleet since it was the last entity to "control" the facility.

We agree with Fleet that the plain meaning of the phrase "immediately beforehand" means without intervening ownership, operation, and control. Fleet, therefore, cannot be held liable under section 9607(a)(1) because it neither owned, operated, or controlled SPW immediately prior to Emanuel County's acquisition of the facility. It is undisputed that from December 1981, when SPW was adjudicated a bankrupt, until the July 1987 foreclosure sale, the bankrupt estate and trustee were the owners of the facility. Similarly, the evidence is clear that neither Fleet nor any of its putative agents had anything to do with the facility after December 1983. Although Fleet may have operated or controlled SPW prior to December 1983, its involvement with SPW terminated more than three years before the county assumed ownership of the facility. The fact that the bankrupt estate or trustee may not have effectively exercised their control of the facility between December 1983 and July 1987 is of no moment. It is undisputed that Fleet was not in control of the facility during this period. Although a trustee can obviously abdicate its control over a bankrupt estate, it cannot in such a manner unilaterally delegate its responsibility to a previous controlling entity. To reach back to Fleet's involvement with

---

4. CERCLA does provide that a state or local government will be liable under these circumstances when it "has caused or contributed to the release or threatened re-lease of a hazardous substance from the facility...." 42 U.S.C. § 9601(20)(D). This exception, however, is not applicable here.

the facility prior to December 1983 in order to impose liability would torture the plain statutory meaning of "immediately beforehand."[5]

B. Fleet's Liability Under Section 9607(a)(2)

CERCLA also imposes liability on "any person who at the time of disposal of any hazardous substance owned or operated any . . . facility at which such hazardous substances were disposed of. . . ." 42 U.S.C. § 9607(a)(2). CERCLA excludes from the definition of "owner or operator" any "person, who, without participating in the management of a . . . facility, holds indicia of ownership primarily to protect his security interest in the . . . facility." 42 U.S.C. § 9601(20)(A). Fleet has the burden of establishing its entitlement to this exemption. *Maryland Bank & Trust*, 632 F.Supp. at 578; *see United States v. First National Bank of Houston*, 386 U.S. 361, 366, 87 S.Ct. 1088, 1092, 18 L.Ed.2d 151 (1967). There is no dispute that Fleet held an "indicia of ownership" in the facility through its deed of trust to SPW, and that this interest was held primarily to protect its security interest in the facility. The critical issue is whether Fleet participated in management sufficiently to incur liability under the statute.[6]

The construction of the secured creditor exemption is an issue of first impression in the federal appellate courts. The government urges us to adopt a narrow and strictly literal interpretation of the exemption that excludes from its protection any secured creditor that participates in any manner in the management of a facility. We decline the government's suggestion because it would largely eviscerate the exemption Congress intended to afford to secured creditors. Secured lenders frequently have some involvement in the financial affairs of their debtors in order to insure that their interests are being adequately protected. To adopt the government's interpretation of the secured creditor exemption could expose all such lenders to CERCLA liability for engaging in their normal course of business.

Fleet, in turn, suggests that we adopt the distinction delineated by some district courts between permissible participation in the financial

---

5. This interpretation of § 9607(a)(1) is particularly appropriate in the context of the entire statutory scheme. While § 9607(a)(1) targets present owners and operators of toxic waste facilities, § 9607(a)(2) focuses on the entities that owned or operated the facility at the time the wastes were disposed. A narrow reading of this section would not, therefore, create an unintended loophole for individuals or entities to escape liability for improperly disposing hazardous waste.

6. The government correctly formulates this issue as being comprised of two distinct, but related, means of finding Fleet liable under § 9607(a)(2). First, Fleet is liable under the statute if it operated the facility within the meaning of the statute.

Alternatively, Fleet can be held liable if it had an indicia of ownership in SPW and managed the facility to the extent necessary to remove it from the secured creditor liability exemption. *See United States v. Kayser–Roth Corp.*, 724 F.Supp. 15, 20–21 (D.R.I.1989). Although we can conceive of some instances where the facts showing participation in management are different from those indicating operation, this is not such a case. The sum of the facts alleged by the government is sufficient to hold Fleet liable under either analysis. In order to avoid repetition, and because this case fits more snugly under a secured creditor analysis, we will forgo an analysis of Fleet's liability as an operator.

management of the facility and impermissible participation in the day-to-day or operational management of a facility. In *United States v. Mirabile*, the first case to suggest this interpretation, the district court granted summary judgment to the defendant creditors because their participation in the affairs of the facility was "limited to participation in financial decisions." No. 84–2280, slip op. at 3 (E.D.Pa. Sept. 6, 1985) (available on WESTLAW as 1985 WL 97). The court explained "that the participation which is critical is participation in operational, production, or waste disposal activities. Mere financial ability to control waste disposal practices ... is not ... sufficient for the imposition of liability." *Mirabile*, No. 84–2280, slip op. at 4; *accord United States v. New Castle County*, 727 F.Supp. 854, 866 (D.Del.1989); *Rockwell International v. IU International Corp.*, 702 F.Supp. 1384, 1390 (N.D.Ill. 1988); *see also Coastal Casting Service*, No. H–86–4463, slip op. at 4(complaint alleging that secured creditor's entanglement with facility's management surpassed mere financial control held sufficient). The court concluded that "before a secured creditor ... may be held liable, it must, at a minimum, participate in the day-to-day operational aspects of the site. [Here, the creditor] ... merely foreclosed on the property after all operations had ceased and thereafter took prudent and routine steps to secure the property against further depreciation." [7] *Id.* at 12; *accord United States v. Nicolet*, 712 F.Supp. 1193, 1204–05 (E.D.Pa. 1989).

The court below, relying on *Mirabile*, similarly interpreted the statutory language to permit secured creditors to

> provide financial assistance and general, and even isolated instances of specific, management advice to its debtors without risking CERCLA liability if the secured creditor does not participate in the day-to-day management of the business or facility either before or after the business ceases operation.

Fleet Factors Corp., 724 F.Supp. at 960 (S.D.Ga.1988); *accord Guidice*, at 561–62; [8] *Nicolet*, 712 F.Supp. at 1205. Applying this standard, the trial

---

7. The court permitted a secured creditor to secure a facility against vandalism by boarding up windows and changing locks, make inquiries as to the cost of disposing various drums of toxins, visit the property in order to show it to prospective purchasers, monitor its cash collateral accounts, ensure that receivables went to the proper accounts, and establish a reporting system between the facility and the bank. *Mirabile*, No. 84–2280, slip op. at 5, 8. The court suggested that activities which might bring a secured creditor outside the protection of the exemption included determining the order in which orders were filled, demanding additional sales from the facility, supervising the operations of the facility, and insisting on certain manufacturing changes and reassignment of personnel. *Id.* at 8.

8. In *Guidice*, the district court applied this analysis to exempt a bank from CERCLA liability because the bank's activities with respect to the facility were directed at protecting its security interest rather than controlling the facility's operational, production, or waste disposal activities. 732 F.Supp. at 561–62. The bank's involvement with the facility included meetings where it was informed of the status of the facility's accounts, personnel changes, and the presence of raw materials; assistance in procuring a loan from another lender; communicating with local officials to assist the facility with wastewater discharge compliance; inspecting the property after it ceased operations; efforts to restructure

judge concluded that from the inception of Fleet's relationship with SPW in 1976 to June 22, 1982, when Baldwin entered the facility, Fleet's activity did not rise to the level of participation in management sufficient to impose CERCLA liability. The court, however, determined that the facts alleged by the government with respect to Fleet's involvement after Baldwin entered the facility were sufficient to preclude the granting of summary judgment in favor of Fleet on this issue.

Although we agree with the district court's resolution of the summary judgment motion, we find its construction of the statutory exemption too permissive towards secured creditors who are involved with toxic waste facilities. In order to achieve the "overwhelmingly remedial" goal of the CERCLA statutory scheme, ambiguous statutory terms should be construed to favor liability for the costs incurred by the government in responding to the hazards at such facilities. *Allis Chalmers*, 893 F.2d at 1317; *see Maryland Bank & Trust Co.*, 632 F.Supp. at 579 (secured creditor exemption should be construed narrowly); Note, *When Security Becomes a Liability: Claims Against Lenders in Hazardous Waste Cleanup*, 38 Hastings L.J. 1261, 1285–86, 1291 (1987) (same) [hereinafter *Claims Against Lenders*]. The district court's broad interpretation of the exemption would essentially require a secured creditor to be involved in the operations of a facility in order to incur liability. This construction ignores the plain language of the exemption and essentially renders it meaningless. Individuals and entities involved in the operations of a facility are already liable as operators under the express language of section 9607(a)(2). Had Congress intended to absolve secured creditors from ownership liability, it would have done so. Instead, the statutory language chosen by Congress explicitly holds secured creditors liable if they participate in the management of a facility.

Although similar, the phrase "participating in the management" and the term "operator" are not congruent. Under the standard we adopt today, a secured creditor may incur section 9607(a)(2) liability, without being an operator, by participating in the financial management of a facility to a degree indicating a capacity to influence the corporation's treatment of hazardous wastes. It is not necessary for the secured creditor actually to involve itself in the day-to-day operations of the facility in order to be liable—although such conduct will certainly lead to the loss of the protection of the statutory exemption. Nor is it necessary for the secured creditor to participate in management decisions relating to hazardous waste. Rather, a secured creditor will be liable if its involvement with the management of the facility is sufficiently broad to support the inference that it could affect hazardous waste disposal decisions if it so chose.[11] We, therefore, specifically

the facility's loans; and an agreement to provide financing if a particular party purchased the facility at a foreclosure sale. *Id.* at 562.

11. This narrow construction of the secured creditor exemption is supported by the sparse legislative history on the subject. The Senate version of CERCLA initially lacked an exemption for secured

reject the formulation of the secured creditor exemption suggested by the district court in *Mirabile. See,* No. 84–2280, slip op. at 4.

This construction of the secured creditor exemption, while less permissive than that of the trial court, is broader than that urged by the government and, therefore, should give lenders some latitude in their dealings with debtors without exposing themselves to potential liability. Nothing in our discussion should preclude a secured creditor from monitoring any aspect of a debtor's business. Likewise, a secured creditor can become involved in occasional and discrete financial decisions relating to the protection of its security interest without incurring liability.

Our interpretation of the exemption may be challenged as creating disincentives for lenders to extend financial assistance to businesses with potential hazardous waste problems and encouraging secured creditors to distance themselves from the management actions, particularly those related to hazardous wastes, of their debtors. *See Guidice,* 732 F.Supp. at 562; Note, *Interpreting the Meaning of Lender Management Under Section 101(20)(A) of CERCLA,* 98 Yale L.J. 925, 928, 944 (1989). As a result the improper treatment of hazardous wastes could be perpetuated rather than resolved. These concerns are unfounded.

Our ruling today should encourage potential creditors to investigate thoroughly the waste treatment systems and policies of potential debtors. If the treatment systems seem inadequate, the risk of CERCLA liability will be weighed into the terms of the loan agreement. Creditors, therefore, will incur no greater risk than they bargained for and debtors, aware that inadequate hazardous waste treatment will have a significant adverse impact on their loan terms, will have powerful incentives to improve their handling of hazardous wastes.

Similarly, creditors' awareness that they are potentially liable under CERCLA will encourage them to monitor the hazardous waste treatment systems and policies of their debtors and insist upon compliance with acceptable treatment standards as a prerequisite to continued and future financial support. *Claims Against Lenders, supra* at 1294; Note,

---

creditors in its definition of "owner or operator." *See* S. 1480, 97th Cong., 2d Sess., *reprinted in* 2 Senate Comm. on Environmental and Public Works, 97th Cong., 2 Sess., 1 *A Legislative History of the CERCLA* 470 (Comm. Print 1983). Representative Harsha introduced the exemption to the bill that was finally passed stating:

This change is necessary because the original definition inadvertently subjected those who hold title to a ... facility, but do not participate in the management or operation *and are not otherwise affiliated* with the person leasing or operating the ... facility, to the liability provisions of the bill.

Remarks of Rep. Harsha, reprinted in 2 Senate Comm. on Environmental and Public Works, 97th Cong., 2d Sess., 2 *A Legislative History of the CERCLA* 945 (Comm. Print 1983) (emphasis added). The use of the word "affiliated" to describe the threshold at which a secured creditor becomes liable clearly indicates a more peripheral degree of involvement with the affairs of a facility than that necessary to be held liable as an operator. It also suggests that the interpretation of the exemption intended by Congress is more consistent with the level of secured creditor involvement described in our opinion than with the management of day-to-day operations standard set forth in *Mirabile.*

The Liability of Financial Institutions for Hazardous Waste Cleanup Costs Under CERCLA, 1988 Wis.L.Rev. 139, 185 (1988)[hereinafter *Liability of Financial Institutions*].[12] Once a secured creditor's involvement with a facility becomes sufficiently broad that it can anticipate losing its exemption from CERCLA liability, it will have a strong incentive to address hazardous waste problems at the facility rather than studiously avoiding the investigation and amelioration of the hazard.

In *Maryland Bank & Trust Co.*, the court aptly described and weighed the competing policy interests of creditors and the government in interpreting the secured creditor exemption:

> In essence, the defendant's position would convert CERCLA into an insurance scheme for financial institutions, protecting them against possible losses due to the security of loans with polluted properties. Mortgagees, however, already have the means to protect themselves, by making prudent loans. Financial institutions are in a position to investigate and discover potential problems in their secured properties. For many lending institutions, such research is routine. CERCLA will not absolve them from responsibility for their mistakes of judgment.

632 F.Supp. at 580 (citations omitted).

We agree with the court below that the government has alleged sufficient facts to hold Fleet liable under section 9607(a)(2). From 1976 until SPW ceased printing operations on February 27, 1981, Fleet's involvement with the facility was within the parameters of the secured creditor exemption to liability. During this period, Fleet regularly advanced funds to SPW against the assignment of SPW's accounts receivable, paid and arranged for security deposits for SPW's Georgia utility services, and informed SPW that it would not advance any more money when it determined that its advanced sums exceeded the value of SPW's accounts receivable.

---

12. One commentator notes that a narrow construction of the secured creditor exemption

conforms with CERCLA's implicit function of encouraging safer hazardous waste procedures. The possibility that CERCLA liability will depress the value of the security property provides economic incentive for lenders to guard against its misuse. Lending institutions are especially well-equipped for this function. They can require the borrower to submit to periodic environmental audits, either as a condition to receiving a loan or by an amendment to an existing agreement. Lenders can also require warranties from their borrowers guaranteeing that they are in full compliance with hazardous waste laws and regulations. . . . Ultimately, lenders can refuse to lend money to persons believed to be operating illegal or improper hazardous waste activities. While there is a clear risk that innocent borrowers will find it difficult to obtain credit because of the nature of their business, this result is consistent with CERCLA's general effect of spreading hazardous waste costs industry-wide.

Claims Against Lenders, supra, at 1294 (citations omitted); *see also Liability of Financial Institutions, supra*, at 183–85 (discussing lender strategies for decreasing liability risk under a narrow interpretation of the secured creditor exemption).

Fleet's involvement with SPW, according to the government, increased substantially after SPW ceased printing operations at the Georgia plant on February 27, 1981, and began to wind down its affairs. Fleet required SPW to seek its approval before shipping its goods to customers, established the price for excess inventory, dictated when and to whom the finished goods should be shipped, determined when employees should be laid off, supervised the activity of the office administrator at the site, received and processed SPW's employment and tax forms, controlled access to the facility, and contracted with Baldwin to dispose of the fixtures and equipment at SPW. These facts, if proved, are sufficient to remove Fleet from the protection of the secured creditor exemption. Fleet's involvement in the financial management of the facility was pervasive, if not complete.[13] Furthermore, the government's allegations indicate that Fleet was also involved in the operational management of the facility. Either of these allegations is sufficient as a matter of law to impose CERCLA liability on a secured creditor. The district court's finding to the contrary is erroneous.

With respect to Fleet's involvement at the facility from the time it contracted with Baldwin in May 1982 until Nix left the facility in December 1983, we share the district court's conclusion that Fleet's alleged conduct brought it outside the statutory exemption for secured creditors.[14] Indeed, Fleet's involvement would pass the threshold for operator liability under section 9607(a)(2).[15] Fleet weakly contends that

---

13. Generally, the lender's capacity to influence a debtor facility's treatment of hazardous waste will be inferred from the extent of its involvement in the facility's financial management. Here, that inference is not even necessary because there was evidence before the district court that Fleet actively asserted its control over the disposal of hazardous wastes at the site by prohibiting SPW from selling several barrels of chemicals to potential buyers. As a result, the barrels remained at the facility unattended until the EPA acted to remove the contaminants.

14. The district court summarized the government's allegations of Fleet's conduct at the facility during this period as follows:

Plaintiff alleges that Baldwin moved the barrels that allegedly contained hazardous substances before Baldwin conducted the public auction. Plaintiff contends that after the auction, Baldwin auctioned some, but not all, of the machinery and equipment as is, and in place, and permitted the purchasers to remove the equipment and machinery that they had purchased. Plaintiff asserts that after the auction Fleet signed a document that permitted Nix to have access to the facility for 180 days and to remove any remaining machinery and equipment.... Plaintiff maintains that fria-

ble asbestos was knocked loose from the pipes connected to the machinery and equipment by either the purchasers of the equipment at the auction or Nix. Plaintiff alleges that the condition of the chemicals and the asbestos in the facility after Baldwin, Nix, and the purchasers concluded their business constituted an immediate risk to public health and the environment....

Fleet Factors, 724 F.Supp. at 960–61. Fleet disputes these material facts. *Id.* at 961.

15. During oral argument, counsel for Fleet virtually conceded operator liability for its conduct with respect to the facility when he discussed Fleet's potential for liability were it to have fixed a hole in the roof of an SPW building:

JUDGE KRAVITCH: If [Fleet] finds in fixing the roof that there is some asbestos that is being dislodged can it just ignore that?

. . . .

MR. GOOD: Once it fixes the roof, once it takes over control of fixing the roof, it has opened a potential pandora's box both as to that asbestos and anything else at that facility underneath it known and unknown.

JUDGE KRAVITCH: Why isn't that analogous to what happened here?

its activity at the facility from the time of the auction was within the secured creditor exemption because it was merely protecting its security interest in the facility and foreclosing its security interest in its equipment, inventory, and fixtures. This assertion, even if true, is immaterial to our analysis. The scope of the secured creditor exemption is not determined by whether the creditor's activity was taken to protect its security interest. What is relevant is the nature and extent of the creditor's involvement with the facility, not its motive. To hold otherwise would enable secured creditors to take indifferent and irresponsible actions toward their debtors' hazardous wastes with impunity by incanting that they were protecting their security interests. Congress did not intend CERCLA to sanction such abdication of responsibility.

CONCLUSION

We agree with the district court that Fleet is not within the class of liable persons described in section 9607(a)(1). We also conclude that the court properly denied Fleet's motion for summary judgment. Although the court erred in construing the secured creditor exemption to insulate Fleet from CERCLA liability for its conduct prior to June 22, 1982, it correctly ruled that Fleet was liable under section 9607(a)(2) for its subsequent activities if the government could establish its allegations. Because there remain disputed issues of material fact, the case is remanded for further proceedings consistent with this opinion.

AFFIRMED and REMANDED.

NOTES

1. *Lender Liability.* Before *Fleet Factors*, courts held that a lender that accepted a deed in lieu of foreclosure, or purchased the mortgaged property at foreclosure sale, could be liable for hazardous waste on the property under 42 U.S.C.A. § 9607(a)(1) as a current owner. United States v. Maryland Bank & Trust Co., 632 F.Supp. 573 (D.Md.1986) held that section 9601(20)(A), which excludes from the definition of "owner" a person who holds "indicia of ownership primarily to protect his security interest" did not apply after the lender foreclosed on its security interest and acquired title at foreclosure sale.

Maryland Bank presented the prospect not just of loss security; banks also saw exposure to indeterminable CERCLA claims. Many lenders thought they could protect themselves by carefully evaluating the property before foreclosing or accepting a deed in lieu or by simply choosing not to take title to a contaminated property. *Fleet Factors* undercut these assumptions by exposing lenders to liability prior to their taking of title if the lender "participat[ed] in the financial management of a facility to a degree indication a capacity to influence the corporation's treatment of hazardous wastes."

Is the "capacity to influence" hazardous waste decisions an appropriate standard in light of the language of the statute, other evidence of legislative intent, and policy considerations? How binding and influential is *Fleet Factors* ?

Examine the language of 42 U.S.C.A. § 9601(20)(A). Does it apply to all mortgage transactions and lenders? *Maryland Bank* explained that the exemption was designed to protect lenders in jurisdictions where lenders commonly took title for the purposes of security rather than receiving a mortgage. (Reconsider the discussion of title versus lien theories of a mortgage on page 352 above.) Could a lender in a lien theory jurisdiction become liable before foreclosure as an "owner" under the language of sections 9607(a)(2) and 9601(20)(A) just as the lender became liable in *Fleet Factors* ? Is this reading of the statute consistent with the Environmental Protection Agency's interpretation described in note 3 below?

As a matter of policy, is the "capacity to influence" test desirable? Is it fair to lenders? What type of behavior will it encourage?

Not all courts follow the *Fleet Factors* "capacity to influence" approach. In In re Bergsoe Metal Corporation, 910 F.2d 668 (9th Cir.1990), the Port of St. Helens sold Bergsoe 50 acres of land for a lead recycling facility. In a series of transactions, Bergsoe conveyed the land back to the Port which then leased it back to Bergsoe in order to facilitate the issuance of bonds by the Port to finance the facility. After the recycling venture failed and Bergsoe entered involuntary bankruptcy, hazardous wastes were found on the property. Bergsoe's shareholders alleged that the Port was responsible as an "owner" for response costs since it had received a deed to the property from Bergsoe. The court found, however, that the Port was exempt under 42 U.S.C.A. § 9601(20)(A), refusing to apply the *Fleet Factors* test:

> [W]hatever the precise parameters of "participation," there must be *some* actual management of the facility before a secured creditor will fall outside the exception. Here there was none, and we therefore need not engage in line drawing.... Creditors do not give their money blindly, particularly the large sums of money needed to build industrial facilities. Lenders normally extend credit only after gathering a great deal of information about the proposed project, and only when they have some degree of confidence that the project will be successful. A secured creditor will always have some input at the planning stages of any large-scale project and, by the extension of financing, will perforce encourage those projects it feels will be successful. If this were "management," no secured creditor would ever be protected.

Id. at 672.

For excellent analyses of the secured lender issue, see Howard & Gerard, Lender Liability Under CERCLA: Sorting Out The Mixed Signals, 64 S.Cal.L.Rev. 1187 (1991); Note, Cleaning Up The Debris After *Fleet Factors* : Lender Liability and CERCLA's Security Interest Exemption, 104 Harv.L.Rev. 1249 (1991); Schmall & Tellier, Developments In Lender Liability in the Wake of *Fleet Factors*, 25 Real Prop. Probate & Trust J. 771 (1991). See also Healy, Direct Liability For Hazardous Substance Cleanups Under CERCLA: A Comprehensive Approach, 42 Case W.Res.L.Rev. 65, 128–134 (1992); Comment, Interpreting the Meaning of Lender Management Participation Under Section 101(20)(A) of CERCLA, 98 Yale L.J. 925 (1989).

2. *Avoiding Lender Liability.* As indicated in the excerpt from the Louisiana Law Review on page 914 above, lenders conduct environmental audits before making loans in order to avoid taking contaminated land as security and to also lay the groundwork for an innocent landowner defense in the event they later acquire the property at foreclosure sale or by a deed in lieu. What if the property was contaminated during the term of the loan? In Resolution Trust Corp. v. Polmar Realty, Inc., 780 F.Supp. 177 (S.D.N.Y.1991), the court held that after the commencement of a foreclosure action, the lender has a right to enter the property and conduct a Phase II environmental audit even though the mortgage only provided a right to possession to mortgagee after default and did not give a privilege to enter and conduct an environmental test.

To deal with *Fleet Factors*, lenders may redraft loan documents, that typically reserve significant powers to the lender, in order to avoid a finding that they had the "capacity to influence" the operation. Such a step should not be taken lightly since the lender needs to have some control over the borrower's affairs in order to protect the security and ensure repayment of the loan. Would a clause giving the lender the option to assume control, but not the automatic right to do so, protect it from *Fleet Factors*? See Howard & Gerard, Lender Liability Under CERCLA: Sorting Out The Mixed Signals, 64 S.Cal.L.Rev. 1187, 1218–1219 (1991); Wolf, Lender Environmental Liability Under the Federal Superfund Program, 23 Ariz.St.L.J. 531, 551–553 (1991).

3. *The EPA Lender Liability Regulations.* In response to concerns raised over the extent of lender liability and the unsettled state of the law after *Fleet Factors* and *Bergsoe*, the Environmental Protection Agency promulgated a final rule on lender liability under CERCLA. Lender Liability Under CERCLA, 57 Fed.Reg. 18,344 (April 29, 1992) (to be codified at 40 C.F.R. § 300). The rule interprets the definition of "owner or operator" in 42 U.S.C.A. § 9601(20)(A).

The rule is intricate, reflecting a long and extensive comment process. But a few highlights emerge. First, the rule construes the phrase "indicia of ownership" broadly to include a "security interest" as well as a deed. § 300.1100(a). All lenders, even those holding mortgages in lien jurisdictions, are subject to potential liability as "owners" and covered by the rule. § 300.1100(b)(1). Also, the rule addresses lender liability during three stages: before the loan is made, during the term of the loan, and during the foreclosure and post foreclosure period.

The rule focuses on lender activity. There is a general provision that the lender will be held to have participated in management before foreclosure if it exercises (a) decision making control over borrower's hazardous waste disposal or (b) overall, day-to-day management control over the operational aspects of the business (as opposed to administrative or financial management). The regulation states that participation means "actual participation in the management or operational affairs ... and does not include the mere capacity to influence, or ability to influence, or the unexercised right to control facility operations." § 300.1100(c).

Second, the rule sets out specific activities that do not constitute participation in management of the facility, including policing the loan (e.g., monitoring and inspecting the property for environmental or other problems, examination of the borrower's business and financial condition, requiring compliance with environmental laws), undertaking a financial workout for a troubled borrower, or foreclosing and preparing the property for sale or liquidation. However, despite these approved specific activities, the lender must be careful not to violate the general rule on control over hazardous waste disposal or operational aspects of the business. § 300.1100(c)(2).

Acts or omissions before taking the mortgage, such as inspecting or failure to inspect for environmental problems, do not constitute participation in management. § 300.1100(c)(2)(i). A lender who acquires title by foreclosure or deed in lieu will retain its exemption if it undertakes to "divest itself of the property in a reasonably expeditious manner, using whatever commercially reasonable means are relevant or appropriate." § 300.1100(d). The rule specifies certain actions that must be taken to qualify within that provision, such as monthly advertisements for sale and listing the property with a broker within twelve months.

Many important issues remain. While the EPA rule controls the Agency in actions against lenders, it is not clear that it binds private party actions under CERCLA. Also, the rule has been challenged by those seeking increased lender responsibility. Plaintiffs have argued that the rule exceeds EPA's authority, by going beyond interpretation of CERCLA and creating an exemption not present in the statute. See Michigan v. Environmental Protection Agency, No. 92–1312 (D.C.Cir. 7/28/92). On the other side, some lenders have called the rule inadequate and have sought legislation to increase lender protection. See Legislation Said Still Needed To Protect Secured Creditors From Liability Under CERCLA, 23 Envt. Reporter 315 (5/15/92).

See generally, Healy, Direct Liability For Hazardous Substance Cleanups Under CERCLA: A Comprehensive Approach, 42 Case W.Res. L.Rev. 65, 134–146 (1992); Howard & Gerard, Lender Liability Under CERCLA: Sorting Out The Mixed Signals, 64 S.Cal.L.Rev. 1187, 1202–1222 (1991); Schmall & Tellier, Developments In Lender Liability in the Wake of *Fleet Factors*, 25 Real Prop. Probate & Trust J. 771, 792–802 (1991).

III. BUILDING ON THE BASICS: THE SHOPPING CENTER DEVELOPMENT

Many fundamental similarities run through the assembly, finance and eventual disposition of all forms of major real estate development, from low-slung shopping centers to high-rise office buildings, from suburban subdivisions to central city apartment houses. The developer will place the site under option or contract while the engineering, design and financing details are worked out and the requisite governmental approvals are obtained. Often the seller will finance the developer's acquisition of the land, through a purchase money mortgage or deed of trust or through a ground lease subordinated to the construction financing. The construction lender will insist on close control over the project and a binding takeout commitment from the permanent lender. The permanent lender will insist on terms that require it to take out the construction lender only if all building specifications and conditions are met. Title reports and survey maps must be examined to assure that the owner's title will be clear and the lender's security unimpaired and that the site will be free of easements and other restrictions that might interfere with the development. The proposed development must wend its way through the growing maze of local, state and federal land use controls, and accommodation must be reached with neighbors and local environmental groups.

The shopping center development offers an excellent vehicle for examining the structure and practice of complex land transactions. Shopping center developments typically embody a combination of financing, investment and leasing techniques that may appear only individually in other forms of real estate development. In addition to the usual elements of construction and permanent financing, a shopping center may involve limited partnerships, groundleases and subleases, long-term leases, transfers of fee interests to major, "anchor," tenants and short-term leases to smaller, "satellite," tenants. As in other commercial land transactions, expert drafting is crucial. Space leases must be structured with care, for the shopping center is a complex organism and depends for its health on the deft coordination of use clauses, covenants not to compete and percentage rent clauses as well as reciprocal operating covenants tying the anchor stores into the life of the center. Finally, among private real estate investments, shopping centers may be unsurpassed in their contemporary social impact.

Bibliographic Note. See generally, E. Halper, Shopping Center and Store Leases (rev.ed.1991); Urban Land Institute, Dollars & Cents of

Shopping Centers: 1984 (1984); Shopping Centers: U.S.A. (G. Sternlieb & J. Hughes, eds., 1981).

A. THE CONCEPT

HARRIS, SPACED–OUT AT THE SHOPPING CENTER *
New Republic 23–26.
(December 13, 1975).

The year 1976 is an anniversary for all kinds of things besides American independence. It marks, for example, the 20th anniversary of the Southdale Shopping Center near Minneapolis, the work of Victor Gruen & Associates. Southdale has a special place in the history of the American shopping center; it marked the debut of the large, enclosed mall, and set a pattern which has been extensively imitated and adapted in the last two decades. The regional shopping center is now so ubiquitous, that it is surprising how short a history it actually possesses. All the more reason then, to survey its varieties and social implications, as they become more apparent.

Early shopping centers, like so many modern innovations, developed in California during the 1920s and '30s. Living in the first set of urban communities built entirely around the automobile, Californians quickly discovered the advantages of placing groups of stores around or within parking areas. Similar arrangements soon appeared in other parts of the country. Richard Neutra designed a small shopping center for Lexington, Kentucky; New Jersey had the Big Bear Shopping Centers, built around giant groceries, with parking space for up to 1000 cars.

In the '30s also, chain and department stores, both vital to the future centers, began to adapt their businesses to the increasingly affluent suburbs and the ever mobile automobile. Until then, retail location in large American cities had been generally a function of existing transportation lines. But as automobile usage spread, downtown location became more problematic. "The automobile emancipated the consumer but not the merchant," the *Architectural Forum* noted in 1949, and well before then firms like Macy's and Sears Roebuck had begun building in the suburbs or on the peripheries of metropolitan centers.

It was the union of department stores with the older ideal of grouping easily accessible smaller stores that produced the first regional centers. This was supplemented, of course, by the explosion of highway construction during the Eisenhower era. The years from the early '50s to the late '60s were the golden era of shopping center construction. By the end of the '60s more than 10,000 shopping centers of every size and shape had been built. The huge shift of wealth and population to the suburbs guaranteed their profits. Large department stores—like Hudson's in Detroit and Dayton's in Minneapolis—were eager to get a piece of this action. Instead of simply opening up more branches, department stores began to organize their own centers, hire architects and developers, and get mortgages from life insurance companies, whose huge supply of capital enabled them to influence the suburban landscape as powerfully as their huge downtown skyscrapers shaped the center cities.

By the middle '50s also, developers began to realize the crucial role of design planning. The department stores were the magnets, their drawing power and placement making or breaking the profits of their smaller neighbors. The straight lines of the early malls, like John Graham's Northgate in Seattle, began to yield to more informal treatments. In Chicago, whose suburbs offer a veritable encyclopedia of shopping center forms, Old Orchard in Skokie, and later Oakbrook, opened in 1962, contained several department stores and carefully landscaped courtyards, with flower beds, streams, ponds, bridges, fountains and seating areas. The rambling, informal lines of these centers, and the series of differently sized quadrangles, produced a village-like atmosphere, the large size (sometimes more than one million square feet) deliberately underplayed. At Mondawmin Shopping Center, in Baltimore, developer James Rouse used two levels to produce what contemporary critics found to be an intimate, casual setting, something like "a charming market town." By the late '50s two-level centers were increasingly popular; they cut down on the forbiddingly long walks between stores, a feature of older malls.

If the rambling, garden-like centers of the late '50s and early '60s were profitable and inviting to shoppers, the Southdale model was the wave of the future. Gruen concentrated his buildings in a two-level mall, and in his enclosed, air-conditioned structure he placed sculpture, trees, benches, so arranging the various spaces to give the impression of downtown bustle. Serenity and village charm were not Southdale's goals; instead, it sought a replication of downtown energy, exploiting the concentration that two enclosed levels, each open to the sight of the other, permitted.

Precedents existed. Glass-covered arcades like Milan's Galleria and London's Burlington Arcade were familiar to European-born designers like Gruen. A few American cities—Cleveland and Providence among them—also possessed important arcades. But even more exemplary were the courtyards and light wells of American commercial buildings constructed at the turn of the century. Department stores, for example, had courts that were cathedral-like in their boast of space, sometimes topped by stained glass domes. Aware of being surrounded by hundreds of other shoppers, customers made their way in an atmosphere of bustle and activity.

This kind of collective drama was what Southdale and many of its successors sought. Shopping centers, Gruen wrote in 1960, "can provide the need, place and opportunity for participation in modern community life that the ancient Greek Agora, the Medieval Market

Place and our own Town Squares provided in the past." The new open spaces, he continued, "must represent an essentially urban environment, be busy and colorful, exciting and stimulating, full of variety and interest."

Thus two levels quickly became standard for most centers along with ramps, escalators, broad staircases and two-level parking lots. Ramps were particularly useful for women shoppers (the vast majority of customers), who could move strollers and high heeled shoes easily up and down the undulating inclines, and catch a maximum view of other shoppers and store fronts. Even more than the verticality, it was the enclosed character of the new malls that delighted their users. Southdale was covered because of cold winters and hot summers, but areas with mild climates also sought temperature control. Marvin Richman, of Chicago's Urban Investment and Development Company, points out that the continued profitability of open centers like Oakbrook does not diminish the zeal of tenants to move into covered centers. "It is unlikely we will see any more of the large open centers constructed," he concludes.

If that is what customers want, that is what they will get. Little at the shopping centers is left to chance. Along with Disneyland they were early experimenters in the separation of pedestrian and vehicular movement, and the isolation of service activities from customers. Ingenious devices handled crowded parking lots, security problems and the normal difficulties of congestion. Logos were adopted and incorporated into shopping bags, maps and guard uniforms. Graphics and lighting experts facilitated shopping convenience. But nothing was given away, and efforts made only where they could show. Seen from the outside, from its vast acreage of parking lots, the typical shopping center looks like a pile of blocks. The elemental shapes of the center don't blend into the landscape—for there is no landscape to blend into—but they are not easily separable from it either. The streets are inside, so there is little reason to control facades which abut highways and parked cars.

But if clarity and concern are absent from the outside, the manipulation and self-consciousness become clear once the complex has been entered. Piped-in music, pavements designed to cushion noise, forced ventilation, controlled lighting, all screen the customer from distraction and aid his sense of location. The malls and arcades that lead to the main courts, writes an analyst and designer of shopping centers, Louis Redstone, "should strive for an intimate character and subdued atmosphere. The purpose is to have the shopper's eye attracted to the store displays." To encourage "shopping interest," when upper galleries are separated by large spaces, connecting bridges should promise convenient access and "give tempting views of the lower floor." Everything that goes into the center is organized to enhance the shopping act. "The typical shopper," according to one designer, "makes no thoughtful judgments concerning good or bad graphics, architecture or space design. He feels good or uncomfortable concerning buying or not buying, staying or leaving." Thus most shopping centers don't aim for good design as such; they seek an environment that will pull people in, keep them there, and encourage them to return.

If the end is unambiguous, the setting is not. The desire for variety coexists with an insistence on order; the marvel of discipline and control yields impulse buying; the natural environment is destroyed in order to produce a replanted landscape; indoors and outdoors are blurred through climate control and the conceit of street lamps, trees and occasionally, aviaries and zoos.

There are legal as well as environmental ambivalencies. In the past 15 years shopping center owners have had to fight a series of challenges that focus specifically on the public/private, or inside/outside character of their properties. The rights of freedom of speech and assembly, of picketing and distributing pamphlets, are not totally clear. The latest Supreme Court decision split 5–4, in determining that, in fact, shopping centers were not public thoroughfares but could limit activities normally permitted in public spaces. But it is probably not the last word.

The shopping center itself exemplifies how strongly boundary problems influence contemporary design and social life. One thrust of modern technology has been to permit and even to encourage acts which were once public and collective to be broken down into more private compartments. The automobile, which took the traveler out of a shared setting and allowed him to move either by himself or with selected companions, has spearheaded these changes, aided by the telephone, radio and television. The potential for social violence, the threat of crime and the nature of racial tensions have also served to limit the number of public occasions for casual mingling.

Compartmentalization, however, has inevitably produced reactions. The hunger for great, enclosed spaces that can provide dramatic settings for collective acts can be detected in the many new sports arenas, the Portman hotel interiors, the atriums and courtyards of a number of recent city skyscrapers. Substitutes for streets, which are now so pervasively associated with danger and dirt, nodes of concentration in a sprawl that does not quite satisfy the urban memories of the displaced, the shopping centers permit suburbanites to shop, eat, attend films, exhibitions, lectures, even orchestra concerts and plays.

The designers offer several options. If some suburbanites seek to recall urban glitter and excitement, planners can oblige. Real limitations exist, of course. While all cities are attempts to control chaos, their control is frequently disguised because of the lengthy period of imposition. In the shopping center, artificiality is more obvious because nothing is any older than anything else. There is nothing worn, nothing used; even the flower beds stay fresh. But when the developer aims unambiguously at an urban mood—as in Woodfield Mall, near Chicago, or Eastridge in San Jose—he produces, with hard materials and bright colors, exciting, dynamic interplays of light, texture and movement: great hanging mobiles, huge open plazas, balconies, ramps and stairways cutting with sharp angles across the empty spaces.

From dozens of vantage points the shopper can gaze across what seem
to be limitless vistas, depressing when they are empty, but exhilarating
when they are filled with active people, a landscape in perpetual
movement, assertive and ever changing.

Even cities need to recall what they once were, or are still trying to
become. Many have built their own shopping centers, in an effort to
retrieve the downtown. Chicago's new Water Tower Place, beginning
its slow unfolding this month, has carried the vertical possibilities of
center design to new extremes. The shopping center, that supports a
22-story hotel and 40 floors of expensive condominiums, has seven
levels. Seen from the outside its marble, windowless walls (which
conceal the service corridors) could be housing a warehouse or conven-
tion hall. The street is as irrelevant to it as the suburban parking lots
are to their centers. Inside, however, after customers arrive by escalators at the mezzanine, they will encounter a seven story courtyard,
bulging at the middle floors, crossed by three glass-enclosed elevators.
Powerful lights will pick out the prismatic colors of the glass, increasing the sense of movement within the center; five other small courts,
two and three-story, will be scattered through the rest of this quintes-
sentially urban setting.

The glitter and extravagance of Water Tower Place's atrium recall
another period of Chicago design, the era of John Root and his partner,
Daniel Burnham. Root provided, in the Rookery, the Masonic Temple,
the Chicago Hotel, the Mills Building in San Francisco, Kansas City's
Board of Trade and the Society for Savings in Cleveland, a series of
unforgettable light courts in glass and iron, surrounding delicately
banistered staircases and filigreed elevator wells. Passage upward in
those elevators, unlike the closed cabs of today, was an exhilarating
adventure, playing lights and shadows against one another. "Through
the constant interplay of dualities," writes Donald Hoffmann, Root's
biographer, "of solid and void, structure and space, stasis and kinesis,
opacity and transparency, darkness and light," the architect achieved a
vital resolution. With its totally artificial lighting and very different
materials it is not yet clear that Water Tower Place can approach the
achievement of 19-century masters like Root. But the effort to try to
recapture the lost glories of courtyard, stairway and elevator is a
welcome one.

Water Tower Place and Woodfield, centers that are urban in spirit
or place, form only one among many varieties. The developers of
Water Tower Place have just opened another shopping center, this one
in Aurora, Illinois. It maintains the conventions of size and enclosure,
its retail space projected at well over one million square feet; but its
very different approach to large space gives it another kind of personal-
ity. The Fox Valley Center is almost as large as Woodfield but much
less urban in feeling: its use of wood and tile—in flooring, fixtures,
railings and columns—the subdued earth colors, the controlled scale of
its courts and its lighting system, prevent this center from unleashing a
sense of overpowering size or energy. The vast distances are disguised,

and the center courts divided into two unequal parts, each a studied contrast to the other. Each department store has its own plaza, but they are or appear to be more intimate than their cubic footage suggests. The shopper can still detect the several levels, and come upon large, dramatic openings, but the wood and the foliage screen and break up the stark vistas, faintly echoing the village-like qualities of the older, open centers like Oakbrook.

Not that the "rural" centers are any "softer," to apply Robert Sommer's term, any more flexible or responsive to individual needs. These are, on the whole, hard environments, their seating and traffic patterns clearly established and permanently fixed. The shopping itself can be disappointing. Because small, individually-owned businesses do not generally have the capital to relocate here, chain stores and franchises dominate. One shopping center repeats the outlets found in another. The music, the fixtures, the forced air can all be dreadful. At certain times of day there is an inertness, a deadness about the centers which no city space ever quite descends to. They are dominated by homogeneous groups—housewives, older people or teen-agers—and thus lack the human variety of the street scene. And finally there is that single-minded devotion to the profit motive, the supervisory spirit which has outraged those critics who prefer to associate architectural innovation with more disinterested planning, and who find closed interiors to be oppressive.

But there is little evidence that many customers object to the total definition of the shopping center. There may indeed be relief at the lack of ambiguity, the limits on choice which the environment poses. All the attractions are controlled. One walks from the car to the center, and then tours the shops. Everyone seems there for a reason. Social transactions are simplified and dignified by the spatial drama of the great courts. Aware of the amphibious quality of contemporary American life, the merging of one function or activity into another, the studied informality to so many personal interchanges, developers have created integrated spaces with multiple uses that can handle anything from the most trivial errand to an evening on the town.

It is their capacity for visual surprise and contrast, and their impressive displays of technical virtuosity, that make the shopping centers stand out. The last architectural form that serviced American dreams so effectively were the movie palaces of the interwar years, and they relied on decorative detail and costly materials. Architectural fantasy today employs space and lighting rather than electric stylistic quotation. Engineering technologies permit the shopping center to expand the achievement of their true ancestors, the great railroad stations: span a void in metal and glass, and use the proportions to honor the activity within. Space and light have always been luxurious, and few have exploited them as cleverly as the center designers. Conspicuous spatial consumption brings monumental status. In joining modern pleasure in large, unadorned surfaces to an older, baroque theatricality, the best of these buying machines remind us, once again, that the commercial spirit has nutured much of our most interesting American design.

URBAN LAND INSTITUTE, COMMUNITY BUILDERS' COUNCIL, THE COMMUNITY BUILDERS HANDBOOK
265–269 (1968).

(A) TYPES OF SHOPPING CENTER

As the shopping center evolved, three *types* emerged, each distinctive in its own function: the Neighborhood, the Community, and the Regional. In all cases the shopping center's type is determined by *its major tenant* or *tenants.* Neither site area nor building area determines the type of center.

The Neighborhood Center—provides for the sale of convenience goods (foods, drugs and sundries) and personal services (laundry and dry cleaning, barbering, shoe repairing, etc.) for day-by-day living needs of the immediate neighborhood.

It is built around a supermarket as the principal tenant.

In size, the neighborhood center has an *average* gross leasable area close to 50,000 sq. ft. It may range from 30,000 sq. ft. up to as much as 100,000 sq. ft. For its site area, the neighborhood center needs from four to ten acres. It normally serves a trade area population of 5,000 to 40,000 people within six minutes driving time.

The neighborhood is the smallest type of center.

The Community Center—in addition to the convenience goods and personal services of the neighborhood center, provides a wider range of facilities for the sale of soft lines (wearing apparel for men, women, and children) and hard lines (hardware and appliances). It makes more depth of merchandise available—variety in sizes, styles, colors, and prices.

It is built around a junior department store or a variety store as the major tenant, in addition to the supermarket. It *does not* have a full-line department store, though it may have a strong specialty store.

In size, the community center has an *average* gross leasable area of about 150,000 sq. ft. but the range is between 100,000 sq. ft. and 300,000 sq. ft. For its site area, the community center needs from 10 to 30 acres or more. It normally serves a trade area population of 40,000 to 150,000 people.

This is the type of center that is most difficult to estimate for size and pulling power. Because some shopping goods are available, the shopper will compare price and style. This complicates sales volume predictions and opens the way to competition from other centers. The shopper is less predictable in her shopping habits for clothes and appliances, but she will generally go to her favorite supermarket for her household's daily needs.[5]

The community is the intermediate or "in-between" type of center.

The Regional Center—provides for general merchandise, apparel, furniture and home furnishings in *full depth* and *variety.*

It is built around a full-line department store as the major drawing power. For even greater depth and variety in comparative shopping, *two* department stores, or even three and more, are being included in the tenancy.

In size, the regional center has an *average* gross leasable area of 400,000 sq. ft. Regional centers range in area from 300,000 sq. ft. up to 1,000,000 sq. ft. or more. Normally about one-third to one-half of the total gross leasable area is devoted to department stores. The regional center needs at least a population of 150,000 to draw upon. It is generally designed to serve a trade area of 150,000 to 400,000 or more people. In site area, the average regional center needs at least 30 acres or more.[6]

The regional center provides complete comparison shopping goods in depth and variety. Because of this characteristic, its customer drawing power stems from its capacity to offer complete shopping facilities. This attraction extends its trade area by 10 or 15 miles or so, modified by the factors of competitive facilities, travel time over access highways, etc.

---

5. If population increases in the trade area can be predicted substantially, the prudent developer of a community center will plan to have adequate land available for expansion. When the growth in sales volumes warrants and the drawing power justifies additional apparel shops and services, the community center often can be enlarged to regional status by the introduction of a full-line department store.

In a metropolitan city, the community center is vulnerable to competition. It is too big to live off its immediate neighborhood trade and too weak to make a strong impact on the whole community. The development of a strong regional center, with the pulling power of its department store, can hurt the community center even though the two centers are located several miles apart.

In cities of 50,000 to 100,000 population, the community center may actually take on the aspect of a regional center because of its local dominance and pulling power even though such center's tenancy does not include a full-line department store.

6. Site areas approaching 80 acres begin to get too vast for pedestrian distances.

On such sites, other commercial land uses may be introduced—such as office buildings, medical units, motor hotels, etc.

Roy P. Drachman, Council Chairman, points out: "Regional centers often grow to a size not contemplated originally by the developer. This happening is caused generally by either (1) expanding the existing stores, most likely the department store building, or (2) adding another department store and more satellite tenants. Consequently, it is difficult to say precisely in the beginning how much land is enough to reserve for a regional shopping center." Mr. Drachman adds, "Department store executives have indicated recently their preference for being located in the shopping center with their competitors rather than to go 'down the road' to a new location. For this reason, in a strong location we are finding there can be three, four, and sometimes five full-line department stores in the same shopping center. Good examples of this technique are found at Hillsdale where Emporium has joined with Macy's and Sears; King of Prussia Center where a third department store has been added to a former array of two."

The regional is the largest type of shopping center. It comes closest to reproducing the shopping facilities and customer attractions once available only in central business districts.

Indicators for Types and Sizes in Shopping Centers *

	Neighborhood	**Community**	**Regional**
Leading Tenant (basis for definition)	Supermarket or Drug Store	Variety or Junior Department Store	One or more full-line Department Stores
Average Gross ** Leasable Area	50,000 sq. ft.	150,000 sq. ft.	400,000 sq. ft.
Ranges in GLA **	30,000–100,000 sq. ft.	100,000–300,000 sq. ft.	300,000 to over 1,000,000 sq. ft.
Usual Minimum Site Area	4 acres	10 acres	30 acres
Minimum Support	7,500 to 40,000 people	40,000 to 150,000 people	150,000 or more people

Shopping Center Composition by Tenant Classification

Average Percentage of the Centers' GLA

	Neighborhood	**Community**	**Regional**
Food and Food Service	34%	22%	9%
General Merchandise	14	32	53
Clothing and Shoes	9	12	15
Furniture	2	3	3
Other Retail and Dry Goods	20	15	10
Financial	4	3	2
Offices	3	2	1
Services	8	4	1
Other	3	4	3
Vacant	3	3	3
Total	100%	100%	100%

Source: The Dollars and Cents of Shopping Centers: 1966 Urban Land Institute

* The precise characteristics under these indicators do not hold rigidly. Often elements change because of the treatment required to make necessary adaptations or adjustments for the characteristics of the trade area, nature of competition, and variations in site location.

** These figures represent indicators only for definition purposes. It is not size, but tenant composition and the characteristics of the leading tenant that define a shopping center type.

As learned in the operation aspects of shopping centers as they exist and as reported in the study of income and expenses, The Dollars and Cents of Shopping Centers: 1966, footnote 49, shopping centers range in size as follows:

Neighborhoods:	11,700–130,000 sq. ft. GLA
Communities:	61,000–370,000 sq. ft. GLA
Regionals:	192,000–1,300,000 sq. ft. GLA

Other definitions needed for the language of shopping centers refer to areas and to parking usages. For descriptive and comparative purposes the most frequently used are:

(B) AREAS

Site area—The gross land area of the property within the property lines; expressed as that area in square feet against which real estate taxes are levied ordinarily (including not only land held in fee but also that which may be under lease).

Building area—The ground area covered by the structure or structures, including malls where covered.

Gross floor area—The total floor area of all buildings in the project, including basements, mezzanines, and upper floors. It is the figure best used for quoting building costs. Abbreviated as GFA.

Gross leasable area—The total floor area designed for tenant occupancy and exclusive use, including basements, mezzanines, and upper floors, if any; expressed in square feet and measured from the center line of joint partitions and from outside wall faces. Abbreviated as GLA.

GLA is all that area on which the tenants pay rent; it is the area producing income.

GLA lends itself readily to measurement and comparison. Because of this, GLA has been adopted by the Council as the standard for statistical comparisons in the shopping center industry. As it includes the actual *sales* area, GLA is the true indicator of traffic and parking requirements.

Sales area—The gross leasable area *minus* the tenant's storage and work areas, a variable in tenant classifications.

Common area—The total area within the shopping center that is not designed for rental to tenants and which is available for common use by all tenants or groups of tenants and their invitees. For example, parking and its appurtenances, malls, sidewalks, landscaped areas, public toilets, truck and service facilities, etc.

(C) PARKING USAGES

Parking area—The space devoted to car parking, including onsite roadways, aisles, stalls, islands, and other features incidental to parking.

Parking index—The number of car parking spaces made available per 1,000 sq. ft. of GLA. The parking index is the standard comparison to be used in indicating the relationship between the *number* of parking spaces and the gross leasable area.

Parking ratio—The relationship between the area allotted for parking and the area occupied by the building. This ratio is useful only in preliminary planning stages to indicate whether there may be sufficient on-site space allocated to parking. It is not an accurate indicator of the number of parking spaces provided for in relation to the center's tenant composition. Too many variable factors such as area assigned per car, layout and appurtenances of the parking area, differences in using GFA, GLA or sales area, etc., as the denominator, affect the comparison. Hence, the parking index is the better standard for expressing relationship between parking and the commercial structure.

Parking ratio is often calculated inaccurately on the basis of a relationship of square feet of parking as related to the square feet of GFA, and expressed as a ratio of 3 to 1, for example.

B. ASSEMBLY AND FINANCE

URBAN LAND INSTITUTE, COMMUNITY BUILDERS' COUNCIL, THE COMMUNITY BUILDERS HANDBOOK

298–299, 306–310 (1968).

With the market analysis to substantiate justification for the project, the development can move forward to its next preliminary stage— site evaluation and selection. In evaluating the suitability of a site for shopping center development, as mentioned earlier, findings from the market analysis must be tied in closely. Care must be taken to assure that the location is the best possible from all points of view. In the case where the site is already owned, the problem is to evaluate the site and to justify its use as suitable for the shopping center type and purpose.

In site selection or evaluation, whether the center is to be a small neighborhood one or a regional giant, whether you already own a site or not, *the same principles hold but in varying degrees*. The following points should be weighed:

1. SITE SELECTION FACTORS IN OUTLINE

Location and Access—a first consideration. There must be a free flow of traffic throughout the feeder area. It is essential that the site be in an impregnable economic position—at least from the standpoint of location.

Shape—a prime requirement. The property should be shaped so that the ultimate development is all in one piece, undivided by highways or important through traffic streets. A few successful centers, however, are divided by a dedicated street. Even though it is preferable for the site to be in one piece, there are factors that compensate for disadvantages of a split site—size of market, drawing power of the tenants, the size of the center, the skill of management, etc.

Size—a basic element. There must be sufficient site area for the initial development intended, with room for expansion and for buffer strips.

Topography—a factor in site layout, building design, and construction. A fairly level or gently sloping piece of ground is easily adaptable to a neighborhood center. With steep slopes, heavy grading or deep piling, an ingenious arrangement is necessary. With skill, a steeply sloping site can be adapted to provide customer access at different levels. (This solution would apply only to regional centers.) Low-lying or swampy ground conditions add to complications in construction. . . .

6. UTILITIES

Availability of utilities at or near the site is a positive factor in site selection. Long runs to reach utility connections are a development cost to be avoided. Off-site development costs usually can be adjusted with the municipality and customarily with the private utility company. To minimize time-consuming negotiations with officials, make sure the site is at least within easy reach of required water supply and sewage disposal facilities.

No precise policy for a shopping center's off-site improvements has been established even though in some cities a policy is evolving for residential development.

7. FAVORABLE ZONING

Favorable zoning is needed.

Favorable, in this sense, means zoning provisions that allow the shopping center development to go ahead. Ordinarily, suitable shopping center sites are not zoned in advance of development. Hence the developer must obtain commercial zoning.

Even though zoning provisions in some jurisdictions may not have yet been revised to provide automatically for the planned unit concept, which is what the shopping center is, the attitude on the part of zoning authorities generally is becoming sympathetic instead of antagonistic toward the shopping center as a recognized form of land use. Under the shopping center concept, retail uses are compatible with the trade area and off-street parking is provided in relation to the commercial use. Hence, site area and parking for the shopping center require acreage areas having depth and breadth, not narrow strips or lengthy ribbons. In many jurisdictions, the shopping center concept and its development have gone ahead of commercial use under standard zoning procedures. So it is important that zoning ordinances be "up-dated" to provide for "planned shopping center districts," not through map indication as arbitrary locations but through planning commission review, public hearing, and board of appeals procedure.

There are valid reasons in the public interest for favorable shopping center zoning. Shoppers like shopping centers because their varied shopping needs can be satisfied in a "one-stop shopping" area. The community-at-large is relieved of parking space and site traffic problems by the shopping center's private provision of adequate off-street parking and loading space. Rightly located, the center produces a net income to the community far in excess of land uses resulting from single-family residential zoning. Advantages to the community tax-wise and traffic-wise can overcome objections that may arise from existing business areas. But the presence of a nearby school or residential area is accounted for by the design elements of the shopping center project itself. Sometimes there may be local opposition to zoning a tract for shopping center development, particularly if the center is to be built on a site adjacent to a built-up, single-family residential subdivision.

In an atmosphere where resentment against "intrusion" by a new shopping center may prevail, the developer must sell his idea to the community and to the authorities. He must judge the local temper before he goes too far in firming his plans. In advance of a public hearing or before going to various city officials, it is well for the developer to meet with local residents and citizens' associations to explain his proposal. He should make full use of visual aids, sketches, and a model for his proposal. And if there is a tone of resentment continuing against his project even before it is started, he must be doubly sure that he meets all the criteria for good shopping center development. Where the center may be located close to existing residences, buffer planting strips, or protective screening walls or well-designed fences, and controlled night lighting within the site area are an essential requirement to insulate against any adverse effect on the adjacent residences.

Other means to overcome objections to shopping center zoning can be met through explaining the manner of shopping center operation— not a miscellaneous aggregation of stores, but a unit with integrated parking privately policed and maintained for public benefit, with controlled truck delivery arrangement, etc. Buffer or screen planting along a border street across from residences can minimize any adverse effects from night lighting and noise.

Walls, solid fences, or narrow but dense plantings of hedge or evergreen material can be introduced. Failure to insure permanent and effective physical separations between business and high quality single-family residential uses can detract from the value and desirability of the nearby houses.

8. ADJACENT LAND USE

A site too large for the immediate development that is contemplated has the advantage of holding land in reserve. Or if the zoning has been granted for commercial use over the entire tract, compatible uses such as single-tenant office buildings, medical clinics, motels, apartments, and non-competitive commercial facilities can be introduced. The shopping center can be encouraged to become a center for focus of community life and activities.

Apartment development adjacent to a shopping center site is an excellent transition between a shopping center location and a single-family residential area.

The shopping center site should not be vulnerable to adverse influence from adjacent uses outside the control of the developer. If an area across the road is open for sporadic development, it is possible for parasite business uses, such as drive-ins and discount operations, to come in and trade on the drawing power of the shopping center. As mentioned earlier, the possibility of fringe development that could offer competition must be considered in site selection.

The comprehensively planned development, particularly the regional shopping center, unquestionably increases the value of land adjacent to the center. Because the developer knows in advance the potential strength of the development he is planning, it is logical that he should benefit by the increase in value induced around the perimeter. It is important to invite development of compatible buffer uses. By buffer uses we mean development for apartments, office buildings, medical clinics, motels and other non-retail commercial uses, as mentioned above. Such buffer development will improve traffic flow to the center. It will also concentrate shopper traffic within the center rather than diverting and diluting a portion of that buying to the perimeter.

HALPER, GIANT JIGSAW: PUTTING TOGETHER A SHOPPING CENTER SITE *

1 Real Estate Review 84–88 (Summer 1971).

Multiple ownership of shopping center parcels is a perplexing but profoundly important phenomenon.

Were God to have created the world in neatly arranged, rectangular, flat, twenty-acre parcels, all lying at intersections of bustling highways, the community shopping center developer and discount store operator would find the earth a harmonious paradise. If the rectangles were somewhat rearranged and combined, the regional shopping center operator of today would be ecstatic.

Reality confronts us with the most confounding combinations of sizes, shapes and locations. It is the job of the developer and his lawyer to rearrange, combine, and subdivide, to enable the shopping center plant to exist. As if coping with farmers and land speculators when buying or leasing the land is not enough, we must satisfy the tenant who insists upon owning his own land, the tenant who insists upon leasing his own land, the tenant who wants a building built for him, and the tenant who is interested but wants to wait. Add the following to the confusion: spiraling building costs, unbelievably high interest rates, state laws restricting institutional investments in leaseholds, usury laws, a complicated income tax statute, and an inflation psychosis.

To unscramble this web requires patience.

The conditions I've listed result in three principal problems, which we will discuss in some detail below:

Assembling. We find a fabulous location, but it is divided into eight different tracts.

Staging. We would like to build a twenty-acre center today, and expand it to thirty-five acres in five years; but this property and fifty acres more is owned by one person who will sell none of it, but will lease all of it—*only* all of it.

Inducing a Tenant. We've got the right sized parcel and the owner will play ball. However, the department store tenants will allow the developer to build their buildings only if the floors are flown in from Italy and rare Aztec relics are hung every five feet at the developer's expense. And all this for a rent of $1.28 gross. Then the developer asks the department stores, "Would you consider leasing your own land and building your own building?"

ASSEMBLING

The picture of the assembled jigsaw puzzle stares at us in the shape of a skillfully drawn plot plan. What beautiful stores! What great cash flow!

Unfortunately, the fifty acres we want are divided into eight tracts. See a simplified diagram of the premises below:

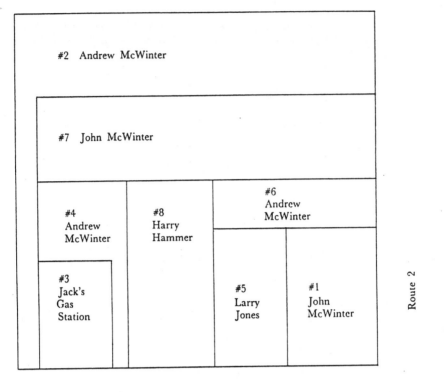

How many times have we seen this? Our land (ours still only in fantasy) was purchased in foreclosure sales from farmers and assembled in 1898 by Job McWinter, a teacher who emigrated to our town from England. He died in 1920. His executor conveyed three parcels (# 3, 5 and 8) to businessmen and the other five (# 1, 2, 4, 6 and 7) to his two sons, John and Andrew. John and Andrew hate each other, of course. Somehow it must have been an infernal plan. We can't put together anything unless *both* John and Andrew will cooperate. Andrew won't sell but he'll lease. He told us that he'll never subordinate. John will subordinate, unless you tell Andrew, and embarrass him. Jack's Gas Station won't move but might consider it if you build a new gas station at the corner of Route 2 and General Boulevard.

To tie the package of our problem site together, we will need the patience to get at least five leases or deeds executed. Because of the layout, it is really essential to deal with each of the owners of the parcels and their eccentricities. John and Andrew are most important, of course, and their refusal to cooperate can prevent any development from taking place. We must use the utmost patience and tact in dealing with them. However, we must negotiate simultaneously with Hammer, Jones and Jack's Gas Station, who have different desires. As we conduct our negotiations, we must keep the following problems in mind as well as those outlined further down below:

The parcels must be contiguous to each other.

All must be properly zoned.

Our estate in each parcel must be a legal investment and an interesting investment to a lender.

Our leases and deeds may not restrict our use to any great degree.

All must be joined together by an agreement or declaration providing for the operation of a unified shopping center, including the unimpeded flow of vehicular and pedestrian traffic.

Questions of assuring contiguity and zoning are not peculiar to land leases and we need not explore them thoroughly here.

Can we combine "unsubordinated" leasehold estates in tracts # 2, 3 and 6 with subordinated leasehold estate in tracts # 1, 7 and 8, and a fee estate in tracts # 4 and 5 as security for one loan? Of course we can. Since the owners of five parcels and the owners of six leaseholds will execute the mortgage, we have a combined leasehold and fee mortgage. Possible? Yes. Desirable? Well, that depends on the developer and his lawyer. We must, however, overcome the hurdle of convincing the lender and its attorneys that its security is safe.

Certainly it is desirable to try to keep the provisions of the leases as uniform as possible, if for no other reason than to keep the mortgagee's attorney happy. Each "unsubordinated" lease must separately meet the tests required by the lenders and their attorneys.

The pieces must tie together neatly so that the result is a functioning, integrated shopping center capable of being financed.

In an assemblage, from time to time, it will be necessary for the developer to be satisfied with diverse estates. Sometimes he will be able to purchase (and this may be his only option even if he prefers to go the leasehold route). Some owners will refuse to sell, but will lease, and some of those who will lease will also agree to execute fee mortgages (i.e., "subordinate"). There is no impediment to a loan which is secured partially by a leasehold and partially by a fee mortgage as long as statutory requirements are met for each type of security. In fact a portion of the security might well be a mortgage of an easement. Of course some lenders may balk because of the complexity of the transaction.

Tying the diverse pieces together by a clear and comprehensive easement declaration goes a long way toward creating order out of chaos and allaying the lender's fears of complexity. The declaration should not fail to include the following material:

All parcels must be operated as a unified shopping center.

The owners and lessees of each parcel must have the right to use parking, mall and other facilities in common. The lenders must be in a position to prevent common facility rights from being extinguished by the defeasance of a leasehold estate.

No fences separating parcels may be permitted.

The uninterrupted flow of traffic by foot and vehicle among the parcels and the abutting highways must be assured.

The parking areas and accessways must be constructed and maintained. Of course, provisions should be made for lighting, stripping, drainage, cleaning, repairs, insurance and snow removal.

The mall must be constructed and maintained. Provisions must be included for heating, air-conditioning, cleaning, lighting and repairing.

The covenants should run with the land in cases where the developer acquires the fee. If the developer has acquired a leasehold interest and the landlord will not burden his fee with the easement declaration, the covenants must be binding on each successor owner of the leasehold.

Arrangements should be made for easements of support in case it is necessary for a part of a building to rest on the footing or foundation of another parcel.

A party wall agreement may be necessary.

Provision should be made for easements to utility companies and municipalities in connection with bringing water, electricity, gas, telephone and other services to various parts of the premises and the discharge of sewage and drainage therefrom.

Further complications may arise with local zoning authorities where there are side-yard requirements for each parcel. The easement agreement will usually solve the problem. Where some of the parcels are not owned but leased by the developer, the zoning authorities may have their own requirements as to the length of the leases. Similar problems can come from fire codes which may, on their face, appear to make construction more expensive by insisting that fire rated walls separate different lots.

The great care necessary when integrating the parcels of an assemblage is even more apparent where the individual parcels or leaseholds thereon are mortgaged separately as security for different loans. Of course, what may occur is that provisions which will satisfy one lender may not satisfy another. The lenders themselves may argue over the appropriateness of one clause or another in the easement agreement.

If you have purchased seven parcels and are able to lease (but not purchase) an essential eighth parcel, it is not too good an idea to rely on the so-called "subordination" clauses in the lease. (If, indeed, there is one.) When you put the mortgage in front of him the landlord might not execute it. That might create quite a mess and you might be on your way to insolvency. "Subordination" is not always enforceable. Litigation in Hawaii and California indicates that the courts of these states won't enforce such a covenant unless many aspects of the loan to be secured by the fee mortgage are carefully delineated. Even if the courts in your state do enforce your particular "subordination" clause, they aren't likely to do so in the brief period between mortgage commitment and closing. So be sure that the leasehold itself is "mortgageable."

Similar problems come about in urban assemblages. In such an assemblage the developer may acquire a leasehold interest over air rights. Sometimes these leases are executed to comply with bulk requirements of zoning ordinances. In other situations the developer will construct a building on the premises demised by the lease of air rights. Additional problems to be met are in describing the demised premises as an air mass over a particular land mass, the location of easements for support of columns, and the location of an easement for staircases, pipes, wires and elevators.

STAGING

When the developer enters into a lease with an owner for a parcel larger than the developer can use all at once, he is confronted with dividing it into economically useful segments. Even where only a small parcel is leased and improved, a developer may find at a later date that an unneeded part of the parking area might be severed from the shopping center and be used for a gas station or fast food operations.

Mortgaging a leasehold is different from mortgaging real estate. If you own the fee, you can always divide it (assuming that any applicable subdivision and lot splitting ordinances are complied with). However, you can't mortgage a part of a leasehold.

What do you do? The ground lease must provide that the tenant has the option to require the landlord simultaneously to (i) cancel the lease, and (ii) execute two or more additional leases. By the new leases the demised premises are divided into as many parcels as desired and there is a separate lease for each parcel. Of course, the aggregate of all the separate parcels should equal the area of the demised premises, and all the parcels must be tied together with an easement agreement. It sounds simple, but it might not be.

What about the rent? If landlord will buy it, each of the separate leases will provide for a rent which bears the same proportion to the rent under the original lease as the area of the parcel demised by the new lease bears to the original demised premises. It is simple but the landlord will fight you like a tiger. This is a problem very similar to the familiar problem of releases from a purchase money mortgage. If the landlord permits tenant to allocate rent in proportion to area, the most valuable parts of the original demised premises may be governed by a lease with an unrealistically low and unfair rent. Since the tenant-developer cannot consent to a provision that a default under one lease constitutes a default under the others, the landlord someday might find tenant abandoning less desirable parts of the demised premises while keeping the rest.

Some problems that are common to assemblage situations and staging situations are: bringing utility services to the site; discharging sewage therefrom; and effective design of traffic patterns. Every attempt should be made to provide in the lease that landlord will subject his fee interest in the demised premises to suitable easements for the necessary lines. Frequently a municipality or other governmental authority will request that a portion of the premises be dedicated for public use as a *quid pro quo* for the issuance of a building permit. A governmental authority is not easily satisfied with a leasehold interest. They want to own the property. Therefore, the lease should require landlord to convey it to the public authority free of the lien of the lease. Under these circumstances, rent would not be reduced and landlord should receive no compensation for the conveyance.

For example, the State of New Jersey has a requirement that the state highway department demand a conveyance to it of property suitable for acceleration and deceleration lanes. This demand arises as part of the State's highway safety program. Under the highway safety program, median traffic dividers are being constructed. Of course, a median divider will prevent a left turn into the shopping center, depriving access to it by fifty percent of the available traffic. The conveyance of the acceleration and deceleration lanes is requested as consideration for the State's construction of a jughandle on the opposite side of the road, a traffic light, and a median divider. (These facilities permit a smooth left turn directly into the shopping center.) Therefore, in New Jersey and states with similar requirements, the developer must use every effort to induce the landlord to agree to dedicate a portion of his property for public facilities.

INDUCING THE TENANT

Another way diverse ownership may arise is if the developer gives or leases land to a department store. The obvious consideration for a gift of land, or cheap rent, is the department store's covenant to operate.

This relationship requires adding to the easement agreement, or declaration, such provisions dealing with:

Control over signs;

Contributions to the merchant's association;

Contributions to common area and mall maintenance;

Restrictions against competition, or undesirable uses;

Hours of operation; and

Construction of the department store.

URBAN LAND INSTITUTE, COMMUNITY BUILDERS' COUNCIL, THE COMMUNITY BUILDERS HANDBOOK

399–401, 403–404 (1968).

As noted above, shopping center finances rest heavily on the rental return anticipated. It is difficult to get financing for shopping center construction before major leases have been negotiated. There is no set formula but the requirements for obtaining a loan will vary, depending upon the lender, the borrower, the money market at the time, the strength of the project—its location, quality of planning—and the rent scale for leases negotiated up to the application for a loan, as well as the degree of protection against increasing taxes and operating costs.

Richard M. Hurd, Council member and mortgage banker, speaks of financing in this way: "Most lenders—insurance companies, banks and pension funds—are limited either by law to a maximum loan of 75 per cent of a competent appraisal of land and improvements, or stay within this limit by normal prudent practice. The appraisal relies on the future 'income stream' as demonstrated by leases with major tenants and the length of time for which such an income stream can be expected to continue. This not only takes into account the credit rating of the tenant, but the length of the lease and the so-called escalation clauses in the lease.

"The appraiser bases his capitalization rate chiefly upon these factors. For a regional center, he may often use one capitalization rate for the rent from the department and chain stores and another rate (higher) for the local tenants.

"Regional centers which may often contain two or more department stores do not necessarily need to include all the department stores within the mortgage security as often better deals can be made with a major store by either selling or leasing the ground on which the store is to be built and have the department store provide its own building. Most lenders prefer to have at least one department store within the security of the mortgage to provide a strong expected continuity of income plus a relatively high percentage of major tenants (75 to 80 percent).[93] However, it is well recognized that the local independent merchant-tenants pay the higher rents and provide the owner with his greater income proportionately to the space occupied by the 'smaller' tenants.

"A larger percentage of the cost of development can be procured if the developer is able to obtain his land through a subordinated long-term ground lease. In such a case, the value of the ground is security for the first mortgage although not paid for as a capital outlay by the

---

93. By major tenants, Mr. Hurd means those tenants with AAA–1 credit ratings, nationally and locally.

developer. This may also have income tax advantages to the developer."

In addition to Mr. Hurd's remarks just quoted, further presentation on current shopping center financing from the point of view of a mortgage lender is offered by Bruce P. Hayden:

"Except for the smallest of neighborhood centers, the shopping center developer usually is in the market for a loan of $1 million or more and, hence, normally must seek his financing from major financial institutions. In most communities the local savings bank or savings and loan will not be in a position to accommodate him.

"Unlike the financing of single-family housing or small apartment developments, which are largely dominated by the local savings institutions, shopping center financing is chiefly the specialty of the life insurance industry. Most of the larger life companies make this type of loan, doing so either through loan correspondents or through branch offices. Probably fortunately, the likes and dislikes of the life insurance lenders in this field are widely varied.

"In general, the more experienced a lender is in shopping center financing, the more flexibility he is apt to show in his approach to the developer's problems.

"The developer should start thinking about his financing at a very early stage in the development of his plans. He normally should be in contact with his likely lender before any signatures are affixed to any leases. Leasing negotiations should be brought to the stage where there seems to be a reasonable meeting of minds between developer and tenant before the developer talks with the lender, however.

"Lending institutions can be expected to review leases very carefully, to be particular not only about the rental provisions and length of term but also about such things as exclusive clauses, fire and condemnation clauses, cancellation clauses, if any, hours of operation, agreement to operate a store as distinguished from the agreement to pay rent for the store, tax escalation clauses, merchants association membership, common area maintenance agreements, etc.

"Experienced developers have long known and the study, *The Dollars and Cents of Shopping Centers,* has confirmed that, in general, the independent tenants and local chains will do more business and pay more rent than the national or Triple A chains. Despite this, most lending institutions continue to look with disfavor on shopping center financing unless a relatively high percentage of income comes from such AAA credits. Some lenders will require that such AAA credit income covers all operating costs and debt service. Some lenders will require that all operating costs, plus interest expense, be covered. The continued requirement on the part of major lenders that developers fill most of their space with the category of tenant that does the least business and pays the least rent may seem questionable to some and deplorable to others, but this continues to be the situation. It should be added that the more experienced the lender, the less true this is apt to be.

"Since, in most instances, the availability of financing to the developer is contingent upon the number and dollar amount of Triple A leases he is able to sign; and since major chains are fully aware of this fact, the developer is usually at a negotiating disadvantage in trying to work out reasonable lease terms with this type of tenant. However, more experienced lenders will generally take a dim view of financing centers wherein the developer has had to make too favorable lease terms available to his key tenants. 'Subsidy situations,' in which a key tenant does not guarantee to pay enough rent to cover the developer's cash out-of-pocket costs, are looked on with particular disfavor by some lenders.

"A hypothetical but fairly common subsidy situation might involve a 150,000 square foot department store which would agree to pay a rental of $1.25 a square foot minimum versus, say, 2 percent of sales. The tenant requires a 'turn-key job.' Here the best available cost indication is that the landlord will have to spend $18.00 a square foot in order to finish the space to the tenant's specifications. The landlord is hopeful of getting a loan of $15.00 a square foot. The lease term is for 25 years.

"In such a situation, debt service on a $15.00 per square foot loan at 8 per cent constant will amount to $1.20 a square foot a year. A minimum allowance for operating expenses and taxes might be an additional 55 cents a square foot. Thus, the developer, without any regard to return on his own investment of $3.00 a square foot, must collect $1.75 per square foot per year *cash*, simply to pay his bills. His tenant has agreed to pay $1.25. The landlord is committed to subsidizing the operation to the extent of 50 cents a square foot a year, which for 150,000 square feet is $75,000. $75,000 a year for 25 years is $1,875,000. This is the measure of the potential subsidy which the landlord must make to have this particular tenant. The strain that this subsidy puts on the financial health of the full enterprise is obvious, and more sophisticated lenders in the shopping center field usually prefer to have no part of the financing.

"There are a number of possible ways for the developer to work around a subsidy situation such as this, even in instances wherein he is unable to persuade his key tenant to pay an adequate rental. One of the most common is to give, or sell, or lease to the tenant the ground on which his store is to be located, let the tenant arrange his own financing and do his own building, but then tie the tenant back into the center for operating purposes through the operating agreements, cross easements, etc. Most major lenders today will approve of such arrangements, although they will review the collateral agreements very carefully.

"Where a high degree of financing is both needed and justified, lenders and developers have worked out patterns that may involve ownership of the land by the lending institution with a ground leaseback to the developer, and then a leasehold mortgage; or may involve ownership of the entire asset by the financing institution with a leaseback to the developer; or may involve ownership by the lender of part of the stock in the developer's corporation, etc. The general feeling on the part of lenders is that if they are expected to assume all or a good part of the equity risk, they should have a substantial interest in the equity rewards that flow from a successful enterprise. Unusual financial arrangements of this type seem to be more and more popular, both with lenders who seek an additional return and with the professional developers who find a path open to them for more liberal financing.

"Whatever the form of financing, the developer should not overlook the cost of arranging it. The correspondent or branch office of the lender will normally expect to be paid about 1 per cent for its services at the time the commitment is accepted. The borrower also bears all the costs of legal services, surveys, sometimes appraisal fees, etc. A standby fee, perhaps 0.1 per cent per month, may be charged for holding money aside for 'take-down' when construction is finished.

"While some long-term lending institutions will also handle the interim or construction financing, most prefer to see this handled by a commercial bank. Many lenders, however, like to cooperate with the borrower and with the commercial bank through early agreement on use of a single set of loan documents which can be transferred upon completion from the bank to the permanent lender, thus reducing both the cost of financing to the borrower and the risk to the bank of being stuck with the loan. Such agreements, if properly drawn, also tend to reduce the risk to the long-term lender of loss of the loan due to material change in money market conditions.

"From the developer's standpoint, the importance of the skill, experience, and reputation of both the permanent lender and the construction lender should not be underestimated. It is literally true that just as the experienced lender is normally not interested in doing business with the amateur developer, the experienced developer is normally not interested in doing business with the inexperienced financial institution. Shopping center financing, at best, is complex, time-consuming, relatively costly to arrange, and full of pitfalls. Inexperience and lack of know-how on the part of either party in the financial arrangement add materially to all these factors."

SIEGELAUB & MEISTRICH, HOW THE PROFESSIONAL SHOPPING CENTER DEVELOPER OBTAINS A MORTGAGE *

9 Real Estate Review 50–58 (Spring 1979).

Recent economic events have altered the underwriting practices of U.S. lending institutions. Lenders have become increasingly more conservative and are requiring developers to document loan applications with details previously unheard of.

This article outlines the stringent requirements of many construction and permanent lenders for information that must be included in loan applications and for closing documentation. While the items enumerated are representative of those required by many institutional lenders, they may differ from the requirements of a specific lender.

The article assumes that the borrower is building a shopping center and that he needs both construction and permanent financing. With modest changes, these six checklists will serve the developer of any investment property. These are the important document categories:

Permanent loan submissions;

Construction loan submissions;

The interim (construction) lender's closing requirements;

Construction loan documents;

The permanent lender's closing requirements; and

Permanent loan documents.

PERMANENT LOAN SUBMISSION

The request for a permanent loan should include the following items:

(1) *A description of the project and the overall development plans.* Many shopping center developments are built in phases, and initial plans are designed with an eye toward future expansion. Practical and legal complications may be created if the documentation for the later phase or phases is not submitted at the time that the developer applies for the first-phase financing. Start your loan application with a narrative of what you currently contemplate building, but also describe what may ultimately be built on the site. Clearly mark all "out parcels" on the survey which are not to be encumbered by the current loan. Alert the lender to potential problems of partial land releases, cross easement agreements, common wall agreements, use restrictions, height restrictions, etc. You will have also notified the lender that at some time in the future you may seek a loan increase, a loan modification or the financing for a future phase.

(2) *An outline of the loan terms requested, specifying each of the following:*

Loan amount;

Interest rate;

Maturity date;

Term, if different from maturity date;

Constant annual payment;

Prepayment terms;

Loan origination fees;

Holdbacks and conditions permitting the release of holdbacks.

(3) *Identification of the construction lender and of any permanent lender that may participate in the construction loan.* Many permanent lenders, attracted by the relatively high yields of construction loans, are interested in participating in a construction loan with a sophisticated construction lender. Other permanent lenders control construction funds either through real estate investment trusts or through holding companies.

(4) *Borrowers' financial statements.* Sophisticated lenders no longer accept balance sheet data typed on the developer's letterhead. Have your accountant prepare a certified balance sheet and a cash-flow analysis of your operations. Balance sheets should be prepared for each partner in the proposed development. A financial statement should also be included for the project's architect and general contractor because lenders wish to make judgments concerning the ability of these entities to complete the project.

(5) *Description of borrower's background.* Submit resume describing your development experience. List the projects in which you have been involved as owner, developer, leasing agent, or broker. Describe your firm's current projects and present construction status. Include photographs of previous and current jobs. List the lenders involved in the current projects. Each partner owning an interest in the proposed development should submit his own history.

(6) *Bank references.* Each of the borrower's principals should list the names of two officers of each financial institution from which he has borrowed funds in the last three years.

(7) *Income-expense pro forma.* The pro forma is probably the single most important component of a loan application package.

The income portion of the pro forma should include a spread sheet for *each existing or proposed tenant,* giving the following information for each:

Name of tenant;

Type of store;

Store area on which rental will be based;

Initial lease term (in years);

Renewal options (number and duration of each);

Base rent;

Rent escalation during initial term;

Rent per square foot per annum;

Rent during renewals;

Percentage rental clauses;

Tenant contributions for common area maintenance; for merchants association; for management; for mall maintenance; for parking lot maintenance; and for utilities expenses;

Details of the tax stop: when it becomes effective; the percentage of future increases absorbed by the tenant or by the landlord; the arithmetic base on which tax reimbursements are computed;

The exact status of each lease: Has it been executed? Is it out for execution? Are you negotiating or are you still soliciting tenants?

The expense portion of the pro forma should be given in great detail. *Exhibit 1* itemizes the operating categories that should appear in each pro forma.

EXHIBIT 1

**EXPENSE CATEGORIES IN PRO FORMA
SUBMITTED WITH PERMANENT
LOAN SUBMISSION**

Fixed Charges
  Real estate taxes
  Insurance
  Ground rent

Operating Expenses
  Air-conditioning
  Central utility system
  Cleaning
  Common area maintenance (subdivide into mall, common sidewalk areas, parking lot)
  Electricity
  Elevator and escalator
  Fuel
  Garbage removal
  Payroll and payroll taxes (Be specific. List each position together with contemplated weekly and annual salaries.)
  Security guards
  Supplies and materials
  Water and sewer

Building Maintenance
  Tenant alterations
  General repairs
  Landscaping
  Outside services
  Painting and decorating
  Structural repairs

General and Administrative
  Advertising and promotion
  General and administrative
  Leasing
  Legal and accounting
  Merchant's association
  Miscellaneous

---

(8) *Copies of major tenant leases and/or letters of intent.* In addition to the copies of major tenant leases, the front cover of each of the major leases should include an outline of the important components of the lease following the form of the income pro forma given in item (7).

(9) *Examination of rental and operating comparables or a feasibility study.* This market study should include a detailed analysis of competing shopping centers of any type within three miles of the proposed development. Ideally, the following information should be included:

A street map outlining the site and competing projects;

Age and physical condition of competitors;

Rental comparables;

Information on operating costs (such as real estate taxes, insurance, and maintenance);

Analysis of competitors' performance;

Demographic analysis;

Comparable land sale information;

A list of recent multifamily and industrial construction within three miles of the proposed development.

Either the appraisal or the feasibility study should include a good economic description of the neighborhood.

(10) *Site plan.* Outline the site in red, and note the number of square feet of the premises "to be mortgaged." The plan should clearly define the areas that will be encumbered; if further development is contemplated, indicate the land areas that must be released in the future.

(11) *Survey and legal description of the demised premises.* This survey, which should indicate the location of roads, easements, utility lines, etc., will alert the lender to any potential problems.

(12) *Aerial photographs of the site.* These photographs should include at least three sweep shots taken from different views showing the immediate trading area and one photo taken from a high altitude encompassing the surrounding area to a distance of three to five miles from the site.

(13) *Description of present site use and construction status.* Although the permanent lender has received the preceding identifying data, it may be unfamiliar with the site and unable to identify it when making a site inspection. Carefully describe any landmarks and indicate the proximity of the site to cross streets. The loan narrative should indicate whether or not construction has commenced.

Either the narrative or another document must indicate the month of construction start and projected completion date. Since an accurate timetable is important, be certain to build in adequate time for such contingencies as strikes, bad weather or material shortages.

(14) *Data on land cost and land acquisition date.* This data should be documented. If the land is presently controlled by an option, this fact must be revealed, and the contracted acquisition price should be specified.

(15) *Zoning statement.* State whether the land is presently zoned for the proposed use or whether zoning changes are required. Once the lender has been notified of potential zoning problems, a contingency clause can be added to the loan commitment so that if the required zoning is not obtained, the borrower need not forfeit any deposit or fee paid in advance. If the lender learns of the zoning problem after the loan has been approved, and the zoning change is subsequently denied, the lender may retain as liquidated damages any deposits or fees previously tendered.

(16) *Rendering.* A rendering should be part of the architectural package and should graphically show the appearance of the proposed project. Colored renderings are not required, but they are attractive and may therefore be helpful.

(17) *Preliminary building plans and construction specifications.* At the time that most mortgage applications are made, complete working drawings are generally not available. However, the borrower should be able to submit a plot plan, a floor plan with subdivided space and building elevations. He should include, in outline form, construction specifications describing both construction and general finish materials. If working drawings have been completed for specific major tenants, these may be submitted with the application.

(18) *List of project features and amenities.* This list should include information about the following features:

Number of available parking spaces on site;

Type of heating fuel to be used in the heating, ventilating, and air conditioning plant;

Elevators and escalators;

Special landscaping or architectural suggestions;

Special security facilities;

Storage facilities;

Basements; and

Amenities for disabled shoppers.

(19) *Projected cost breakdown.* The amounts of the following construction costs should be specified:

Direct building costs;

Land;

Site preparation (cleaning and leveling);

Paving;

Construction interest;

Real estate taxes during construction;

Architectural charges;

Engineering charges;

Legal and accounting charges;

Closing expenses;

Promotion and advertising (leasing and preopening);

Operating deficits;

Brokerage (leasing and financing);

Loan fees (to lenders);

Tenant improvements to be paid for by developer;

Contingencies;

Overhead;

Developer's profit;

Landscaping;

Insurance bonds.

(20) *Description of real estate tax computation.* Information should be submitted on how the completed property will be assessed for tax purposes, on the equalization rate used by the municipality and the proposed tax rate in mils.

(21) *Leasing brochure.* The leasing brochure for the proposed development should be included in the submission. If one is not yet available, it is useful to submit brochures that you prepared for earlier projects.

(22) *Projected month of loan closing.* Schedule the loan closing for two or three months after the expected date of construction completion. You will need this time to complete the documentation required by the permanent lender.

(23) *Unusual development problems or obstacles.* If you can anticipate problems that may arise during construction, you are wise to alert the lender. Will the balance sheet of a proposed main tenant be changed because the tenant will be acquired by another firm or because it will acquire other firms? Do you anticipate a challenge to your zoning change request from local environmentalists, even though you have received necessary environmental approvals?

You can always go back to the lender that has been alerted to these possibilities, and, in good faith, request a loan extension or modification.

CONSTRUCTION LOAN SUBMISSION

Many of the items prepared for submission to the permanent lender also meet the information needs of the interim lender. The three items listed immediately below, however, are different and must be specially prepared.

(1) *A copy of the permanent or standby commitment.*

(2) *Bank reference.* List all lenders with which you have had a relationship. Include the name of the current permanent lender, its

address, and the telephone number of the loan officer who is to handle the loan.

(3) *Architectural plans and specifications.* Submit a complete set of working drawings and detailed specifications for the proposed project.

For each of the following items, you may submit the same documents which were given to the permanent lender in the permanent loan submission package.

(1) *Borrower's financial statement.* (See "Permanent Loan Submission," item (4).)

(2) *Description of borrower's background.* (See "Permanent Loan Submission," item (5).)

(3) *Income-expense pro forma.* (See "Permanent Loan Submission," item (7) and Exhibit 1.)

(4) *Detailed projected cost breakdown.* While this cost breakdown should be similar to "Permanent Loan Submission," item (19) to the permanent lender, break out the direct building costs allocated to each construction trade.

(5) *Survey and legal description of the demised premises.* (See "Permanent Loan Submission," item (11).)

(6) *Appraisal and/or feasibility study.* If the permanent loan commitment specifies that an appraisal is required before the permanent loan can close, it is advisable to complete such an appraisal quickly so that it can also be submitted to the interim lender for review. The appraisal and feasibility study and market survey which were completed for the permanent lender should also be submitted to the interim lender. (See "Permanent Loan Submission," item (9).)

(7) *Names and financial statements of architect and general contractor.* (These documents are included among the documents of "Permanent Loan Submission," item (4).)

THE INTERIM LENDER'S CLOSING REQUIREMENTS

It might seem that after the borrowing developer has submitted to the interim lender the quantity of documents included in the preceding checklist, the borrower could expect to close the loan with a relatively small number of additional submissions. The list that follows suggests that the borrower must prepare even more voluminous submissions to meet the interim lender's closing requirements. He will, however, be rewarded by a return flow of documents from that lender.

(1) *Statement that principals have suffered no adverse change in financial condition since application.* This statement should be in the form of a letter which says that the financial statement, initially submitted by the borrower, has not substantially changed since the construction loan commitment was made. If any adverse changes have occurred, they must be described.

(2) *Evidence that the permanent lender has approved the borrower's submissions.* The borrower may have to demonstrate that the permanent lender specifically approved the following:

The site;

The signed leases and/or requested lease amendments;

The plans;

The specifications;

The appraisal;

The survey and legal description;

The title policy; and

The building permit.

(3) *Names of the general contractor and major subcontractors.* If a general contractor will be handling all minor subtrades, submit a detailed financial statement for that contractor. If you intend to act as your own general contractor, submit a list of all subcontractors with contracts in excess of $10,000. Include their names, addresses, company representatives, trade classification, size of contract, bond requirements, and financial statements.

(4) *Copies of the general contract and major subcontracts.* If these documents are not yet available, submit the standard form of these contracts.

(5) *Contractor's performance and/or payment bond.* If the contract has not yet been signed, submit the name of the bonding company and form of the bond.

(6) *General contractor's agreement to perform for construction lender.* This is a commitment by the general contractor to perform his contractual obligation for the interim lender should the latter take over the project as the result of a default or foreclosure.

(7) *Architect's contract and architect's agreement to perform for construction lender.* The agreement is a similar commitment from the architect to perform for the interim lender.

(8) *Builder's risk insurance policies and other casualty policies with endorsements naming lender as loss payee.*

(9) *Public liability and workmen's compensation policies.* The coverage insuring the developer often overlaps the coverage of the general contractor's and subcontractors' insurance. Binders or short contract forms may be sufficient evidence of insurance for many interim lenders.

(10) *Title insurance binder or commitment.* Include copies of all easements, restrictions, covenants, deeds, etc. The title insurance binder or report should be dated to the time when you took title to the property. If the land is still under option, you must obtain and submit the most recent copy of a valid title report.

(11) *Inventory of personal property.* This inventory must list all personal property (trucks, cleaning equipment, etc.) which will be part of the lender's security in the project.

(12) *Executed leases.* All tenant leases should be executed with at least four duplicate originals. One will be kept by the tenant; one should be filed or recorded; one should be set aside for the interim lender; and the last should be submitted to the permanent lender. Attach a summary to each major lease. (Use the spread sheet which is part of item (7) of the "Permanent Loan Submission Checklist.") Remember that you are often paying the lender's attorney fees. The easier you make the job of the lender's attorney, the lower these legal fees should be.

(13) *Executed lease amendments.* Any amendments to executed leases that are required by the permanent lender should be included in the package of documents submitted to the interim lender. Copies will be sufficient for preliminary review, but duplicate originals should be given to the interim lender prior to the closing of the interim loan.

(14) *Executed ground lease.* If the project is to be built on land which will be leased from a third party, a copy of the ground lease should be submitted.

(15) *Ground owner's estoppel certificate.* In this document, the ground owner affirms that, at the time of the construction loan closing, the ground lease is in full force and effect, that the rent is current, and that there are no offsets against the rent. The estoppel certificate protects the interim lender from a future claim by the ground owner that rents were in arrears or that the lease was in technical default.

(16) *Evidence that real estate taxes and assessments are current.* Copies of recent tax bills marked paid will generally be sufficient proof that the taxes are current. A letter from the local taxing authority may also be adequate.

(17) *Required legal opinions.* Before it makes a commitment, the permanent lender often requires borrower's counsel to submit opinions on certain legal questions. If any legal opinions were required and approved by the permanent lender, copies of both opinions and approvals should be submitted to the interim lender.

(18) *Restrictive covenants.* If the proposed development requires the common use of walls, parking areas, entrances and exits, etc., with adjoining owners, you must submit to the lender copies of the agreements establishing the rights or liabilities.

(19) *Subordination agreements.* If there are mortgages on the land and any existing buildings or if the seller of the land has taken back a purchase money mortgage, those mortgagees must agree to subordinate their mortgages to the interim lender's proposed first mortgage. If a mortgagee is to be repaid in full at the time of the interim lender's first advance, you must submit to the interim lender a letter from the

mortgagee stipulating the exact amount required for total (or partial) satisfaction of such mortgage.

(20) *Corporate, partnership, beneficiary documents, and consents.* Lenders require the borrowing entity to submit evidence that the transaction is legal. Your attorney must draft proper authorizations for the signatures of stockholders, partners, beneficiaries, etc.

(21) *Copies of the building permit and other permits or required variances.* The interim lender will not make the initial advance until the building permit is issued. It will wish to see not only the building permit but documents which indicate that the municipality has issued any required variances.

(22) *Copies of other governmental consents.* Approvals may be required for, but are not necessarily limited to, the following areas: health; water; sewer; air; ecology; environmental impact.

(23) *Utility availability letters.* You must submit letters from all utility suppliers and from the entities that supply sewer lines, storm drainage, and similar services that assure the interim lender that these services will be available to your tenants upon completion of construction. If utilities are not available, tenants do not normally take possession, and the permanent lender is not obligated to close the permanent loan.

(24) *Computation of closing costs and legal fees.* Prepare a proposed closing or settlement statement at least two weeks prior to the closing of the construction loan. Outline the allocation of fees and expenses which require payment at the time of closing and list all loan disbursements.

(25) *Establishing of closing date, time, and location.* The date, time, and location of the closing should be established at least two weeks before the actual event. You should inform all interested parties, including the following:

Attorneys for the borrower, interim lender, and permanent lender;

Title insurance company;

Insurance agent;

General contractor;

Land mortgagees; and

Brokers.

THE INTERIM LENDER'S CLOSING DOCUMENTS

The borrower's reward for transmitting the enormous stream of information enumerated above, is the closing itself. The following documents and forms change hands at the closing:

(1) *Construction loan commitment.* The commitment may be a one-page letter from the interim lender agreeing to make the construction loan subject to certain documentation. It will specify the interest rate,

term, maturity date, and other terms of the loan, all of which will be documented in the note and mortgage (see items (3) and (4) following).

(2) *Buy/sell agreement.* This agreement, also known as the "tripartite" or the "triparty" agreement, is signed by the borrower, the interim lender, and the permanent lender. In it, the permanent lender agrees to purchase the construction loan from the interim lender when construction is completed, and if certain other requirements are met within a specified time.

(3) *Promissory note.* This document, almost always in the interim lender's form, creates the debt obligation and describes the conditions under which the interim lender is making the loan. It also outlines the events of default and the remedies available to the lender.

(4) *Mortgage or deed of trust.* This document secures the obligation created by the promissory note and outlines the terms of the security for the note.

(5) *Collateral assignment of tenant leases, rents, and profits.* This document or group of documents assigns the tenant leases during the construction period to the interim lender so that if the lender forecloses as the result of borrower default, the lender will control these leases as the owner in possession.

(6) *Principal's guaranty of payment and/or completion.* This document creates the borrower's personal obligation to complete the project or repay the loan as a condition of the release of his personal guaranty of the loan.

(7) *Conditional assignment of construction contract.* This document is executed by the borrower, the general contractor, and the interim lender and assigns the construction contract, at the option of the interim lender, to the interim lender in the event of a default or foreclosure.

(8) *Loan requisition form.* At the closing, the interim lender will probably make available to the borrower the standard form on which it expects the borrower to make its periodic requisitions for the advance of construction funds. Borrower and lender should devote some time before the closing to a discussion of the lender's requirements for making advances and its procedures for billing interest. This is an area in which many misunderstandings occur.

THE PERMANENT LENDER'S CLOSING REQUIREMENTS

Many of the documents which the borrower must give the permanent lender at closing are similar to those prepared for the closing of the construction loan. However, they obviously must be brought up-to-date.

(1) *Statement that principals have suffered no adverse change in financial condition since application.* This statement may be identical to the letter submitted to the construction lender (item (1) of the "Interim Lender's Closing Requirements").

(2) *Certified final rental schedule.* Prior to closing the permanent loan, the borrower must present a revised tenant list dated and certified. The list should reflect executed leases, the leases out for signature, under negotiation, or proposed.

(3) *A final as-built survey.* This document should show the exact location of all building lines, property lines, easements, etc.

(4) *Appraisal.* If an appraisal was required under the terms of the permanent loan commitment, it must now be submitted.

(5) *Architect's certificate of completion.* The project or supervising architect must certify that the building has been completed in accordance with the plans and specifications submitted to and approved by the permanent lender.

(6) *Complete set of final plans and specifications.*

(7) *Final site inspection and approval from the lender.* Almost all permanent commitments require that, prior to closing, the permanent lender or its representative (or correspondent) inspect the premises and approve the project as built.

(8) *Required insurance policies with endorsements naming permanent lender as loss payee.*

(9) *Title insurance binder or commitment updated to the closing date with copies of all easements, restrictions, covenants, etc.*

(10) *Inventory of personal property.* This is a list of items that will secure the loan by a financing statement UCC–1 (see "Permanent Lender's Closing Documents," item (5)).

(11) *Mortgage insurance policy as issued to permanent lender.* At the closing, the title insurance company will issue a binder or a policy insuring the lender's loan with respect to the quality of the title.

(12) *Executed leases and amendments.* Original or duplicate original forms of the leases must be fully executed and approved by the lender. Any amendments required by the permanent lender must be approved prior to the closing.

(13) *Executed ground lease and ground owner's estoppel letter.* This is the document from the ground owner indicating that at the time of the closing of the permanent loan the ground lease is in full force and effect, that the rent is current, and that there are no offsets against the rent.

(14) *Subordination and nondisturbance agreements.* These are documents executed by the tenants wherein they state that their leases are superior (or subordinate) to the permanent mortgage. The determination as to superiority or subordination is made by the permanent lender's attorney. The subordination and nondisturbance agreements are normally drafted by the permanent lender's attorney.

(15) *Tenant estoppel letters.* These are letters from each tenant indicating that their leases, as executed (and perhaps amended), are in

full force and effect, that there are no offsets in the rentals, and that all conditions required for tenancy to begin have been met.

(16) *Evidence that real estate taxes and all assessments are current.* Copies of paid tax bills will usually suffice, although a letter from the tax assessor indicating that the taxes are current, as paid, is also generally acceptable.

(17) *Required legal opinions.* If the permanent commitment required the opinion of either the borrower's or lender's counsel as to any questions of law, these opinions should be submitted to the permanent lender.

(18) *Cross easement, common wall, ingress and egress, and other similar agreements.* If the proposed development requires common use of walls, parking areas, entrances and exits, etc., with other property, these agreements must be submitted.

(19) *Letter of construction lender and other mortgagees indicating amount required for satisfaction (or subordination agreements).* Since the permanent loan will be a first lien on the encumbered property, the interim lender must indicate the exact amount of money required to retire the interim loan. Any other lenders who are to be paid out of the proceeds of the permanent loan disbursement should also indicate the amount due to them at closing. If prior lien holders are not to be paid at the time of closing, the borrower must submit letters from them indicating that they are subordinating their liens to the lien of the permanent lender.

(20) *Corporate, partnership, or beneficiary documents and consents.* Lenders often require borrowers to submit documents which affirm the approval of the borrower's owners or partners as well as proper authorizations from stockholders, partners, beneficiaries, etc.

(21) *Certificate of occupancy and other permits or variances.* The original of the certificate of occupancy and any variances that were required should be documented by a letter from the municipality addressed to the builder.

(22) *Required governmental consents.* Approvals may be required for, but are not necessarily limited to, the following areas: health; water; sewer; air; ecology; and environmental impact.

(23) *Computation of closing costs and legal fees.* Prepare a proposed closing or settlement statement at least two weeks prior to the closing of the permanent loan. Outline the allocation of fees and expenses which require payment at the time of closing and list all loan disbursements.

(24) *Establishment of closing date, time, and location.* At least two weeks before the closing of the construction loan, establish a specific date, time, and location for the closing and inform all interested parties, including:

Attorneys for the borrower, interim lender, and permanent lender;

Title insurance company;

Insurance agent;

General contractor;

Land mortgagees; and

Brokers.

THE PERMANENT LENDER'S CLOSING DOCUMENTS

(1) *Mortgage note (or endorsement from construction lender without recourse).* This document creates the debt obligation, describes the conditions under which the permanent lender is making the loan, and outlines the terms of default and the remedies available to the lender.

(2) *Mortgage or deed of trust.* This document secures the obligation created by the promissory note and outlines the terms of the security for the note. It almost always provides that the sole recourse of the lender is to the property.

(3) *Loan agreement for continued disbursements.* If the full amount of the loan is not to be made at the time of closing, an agreement outlining the conditions under which the additional disbursements will be made must be a part of the closing documents.

(4) *Assignment of tenant leases, rents, and profits to the permanent lender.* In this document, the borrower agrees to assign to the lender his interest in the leases, rents, and profits in the event he defaults under the terms of this assignment agreement or under the terms of the mortgage note, the mortgage, or the deed of trust.

(5) *Uniform Commercial Code (UCC) security agreement and financing statement.* These agreements perfect the lender's right to possession of personal property used in connection with the operation of the real estate such as air-conditioning equipment, cars, trucks, service equipment, etc., in the event of a default under the note and mortgage. It is a universal form and is filed in a specified manner in each state.

(6) *Exculpation agreement relieving principal from personal liability.* This agreement limits the lender's recourse in a default or foreclosure action to the real estate and exculpates the borrower from personal liability.

(7) *An interest and amortization schedule.*

NOTES

1. *Lawyer's Role.* Finance, marketing and design professionals may dominate the early stages of shopping center assembly but there are also important tasks for the developer's lawyer to perform. Before an option on a site is exercised, or a contract closed, a perimeter survey must be examined and a title report reviewed. The site should be inspected for any unrecorded easements or other restrictions that might interfere with construction of the shopping center or access to it. A dirt pathway cutting across a corner of the site may indicate a neigh-

boring landowner's prescriptive right of way. A visible sewer connection may be the tip-off to an underground network of pipes, access to which is protected by an implied easement. Even express, recorded easements can require a lawyer's judgment to resolve ambiguities respecting the easement's location, extent, nature and duration. In evaluating these restrictions, the lawyer must think not only of the client developer's willingness to proceed without quitclaim deeds from the easement's holders, but also the willingness of construction and permanent lenders to accept these possible impairments to their security.

Building and occupancy permits have to be obtained. Favorable zoning for the proposed development is just the starting point. Will the zoning ordinance permit commercial uses such as movie theaters and bowling alleys that, though not presently included in the center plans, may be added at some future point? Setback, parking, sign and height variances may have to be individually negotiated unless the site is in a zone that permits shopping centers to be proposed in the more flexible, easily negotiated format of a planned unit development. In addition to negotiating with the planning department and planning commission, the architectural review board, and the maps, buildings, streets and highway departments, the developer and her lawyer may have to confront the political process more directly, in meetings and through compromises negotiated with the city council or other local legislative body, as well as with neighbors and local environmental groups. Regional shopping centers, particularly, may be a significant indirect source of automotive emissions so that compliance with federal, state, and local air quality regulations will be required.

Title insurance can absorb the risk of some legal judgments. The owner's or lender's title policy, and endorsements to them, can insure that all parcels comprising the center are contiguous and lie within the commercial zone indicated on the municipality's zoning map, that the parcels described in the deeds and title policy correspond to those outlined on the survey maps, that no structure encroaches on an easement, and that the easements and covenants in the reciprocal easement agreements between the shopping center occupants are valid and enforceable according to their terms.

2. *Permanent Lender's Role.* If anchor stores set the shopping center's tone, it is the permanent lender who dictates the center's financial structure and underlying legal arrangements. Must the developer acquire the fee or will a ground lease suffice? Will the ground lessor be required to subordinate its interest to the lender's? What terms must appear in the ground lease and in the space leases? These are all points, often deal points, for the permanent lender's decision. Inevitably, these decisions also affect the center's complexion and tone. Because anchors today so frequently own or ground lease the land they occupy in the shopping center, their land and improvements are not

part of the lender's security, so that lenders must look for added security to rent payments from satellite tenants. This added security frequently takes the form of a requirement that as many as sixty-five to seventy-five per cent of the satellite tenants be high credit firms, often national chains.

What of lender liability? In Yousef v. Trustbank Savings, F.S.B., 81 Md.App. 527, 568 A.2d 1134 (1990), appellants purchased a shopping center. The original mortgagee permitted appellants to assume the existing mortgage in exchange for a $50,000 fee. The commitment agreement provided that "Borrower shall provide Lender copies of leases representing not less than eighty-five percent (85%) of the net rentable area, which leases must be satisfactory to Lender in all respects." The seller warranted to appellants that 91% of the space was rented; the mortgagee approved the leases. When appellants discovered that some of the leases did not exist, they sued the lender claiming that it had negligently failed to inspect the leases. The court, however, rejected lender liability: "Appellants' reliance upon that provision of the Commitment Agreement, is, to put it mildly, misplaced. We point out to appellants that the provision requires the leases be satisfactory in all respects to the *lender* .... A provision such as the one relied upon by the appellants is purely and simply for the protection of the lender, it is not for the protection of the buyer." Id. at 53, 568 A.2d at 1137.

For a panoramic view of shopping center finance, see Rogers & Brown, Shopping Center Financing, 43 U.M.K.C. L.Rev. 1 (1974). See also, Halper, People and Property: The Anatomy of a Ground Lease, 3 Real Est.Rev. 9 (Fall 1973); Practising Law Institute, Business and Legal Problems of Shopping Centers 39–59 (3d ed. 1971); Minskoff, Mortgaging-Out the Regional Mall, 7 Real Est.Rev. 38 (Fall 1977).

3. *Developer's Role.* Within the conservative lending policies established by permanent lenders and those who regulate them, considerable leeway remains for the shopping center developer to achieve her own financial objectives, probably the most cherished of which is "mortgaging out" the shopping center—obtaining a nonrecourse loan for one hundred percent or more of her land and development costs. How can she achieve this object within the limits set by lender's loan-to-value ratios? One answer lies in the fact that these ratios are calculated on the basis of the center's appraised value, not its cost, so that the entrepreneur who assembles a solid group of tenants on a well-situated parcel can get an appraisal and a loan well exceeding her costs. Another answer lies in the use of component financing through which the cost of appliances such as air conditioning, electrical, and plumbing systems is directly financed by their suppliers or manufacturers who will take back a second or more subordinate lien as security.

C. LEASING AND OPERATIONS

1. COORDINATING LANDLORD AND TENANT INTERESTS

McANDREWS, OPERATING AGREEMENT—CONTROL WITHIN SHOPPING CENTER COMPLEX *

7 Real Property, Probate & Trust Journal, 812–815, 817–818 (1972).

I. INTRODUCTION

An operating agreement among owners, major tenants and/or ground lessees within a shopping center complex sets forth certain rights and benefits in favor of each of the parties, imposes certain obligations upon the parties and creates certain easements which are a burden upon or a benefit to the respective parcels. The operating agreement may be called by many names, such as "Easement, Restriction and Operating Agreement" (EROA), "Construction Operating and Reciprocal Easement Agreement" (COREA), "Reciprocal Easement Agreement" (REA), "Development and Operating Agreement" (DOA) and "Deed of Declaration" (when a single owner establishes certain rights, duties and easements before dividing the land), but, regardless of the name, its contents could be a deciding factor as to the overall success of the complex.

Because the concepts of (i) enclosed mall shopping centers generally and (ii) parcels within a shopping center complex being owned by different entities are relatively new, the legal effect and interpretation of such operating agreements have not been considered by the courts in many instances. Thus, the law is not settled as to such agreements and we may only deduce the effect that will be given to them by making an analogy between, and considering the interpretation given to, comparable provisions in occupancy leases.

The main points to be considered in an operating agreement are (a) operating covenants, (b) protective covenants, (c) reciprocal easements and (d) contribution toward costs.

II. OPERATING COVENANTS

The success of any shopping center rests to a great extent on the department stores and the major tenants (national chains). The department stores (anchor tenants or major stores, as they are often called) may be strictly occupancy tenants, leasing only the building from the developer, or, as presently the more common method, fee owners or ground lessees of a portion of the shopping center land. In the latter cases, the department store would construct its own building.

In the pure occupancy lease situation, it is a relatively simple matter to confirm and insert in the lease agreement an operating covenant which obligates the lessee to operate a department store under a certain name for a certain period of time. Needless to say, the longer the period, such as for 20 or 25 years, the better it is for the developer, but the department stores are wary of being bound to such a long operating term since no one can accurately foresee what the market area will be 20 years from the time the agreement is executed.

In the situation where the department store is the owner or ground lessee of the fee (underlying land), the operating agreement is a necessity to the developer of the mall stores, so as to have some assurance there will be "anchor stores" for its mall. The covenant to operate may be put into the basic operating agreement which will be recorded but, more often, the only reference to it is made in the operating agreement and the actual covenant is contained in a supplemental agreement to the operating agreement. The department store prefers the latter course so as to keep the term of the operating covenant confidential and to prevent other shopping center developers from learning of the agreed operating period.

While the department store will normally agree to some period of operation as a department store, it wants in return an agreement that a certain percentage of mall store space will be open and operating. It also wants certain assurances there will be a proper tenant mix; the developer usually will agree to this. The percentage of mall store space occupied or the gross leaseable area of mall store space being committed to use should not be too great. Mortgage lenders require an operating covenant, normally for 20 years or more from anchor stores, and are wary of any violation or default by developer which could result in a termination of the department store's operating covenant. In a regional shopping center, the mall stores (or satellite stores) and the department stores are meant to complement each other.

III. PROTECTIVE COVENANTS

With different owners or builders working to form a single shopping center complex, certain protection is required to maintain architectural harmony, a minimum level of maintenance, exclusive rights and parking areas.

The parties should agree upon one architect having final say with respect to the over-all appearance of the center. This is necessary when each owner or ground lessee has its own architect designing its particular store and retains its own builder for construction. To have a proper enclosed mall shopping center, all designs must dove-tail to form a harmonious whole.

The operating agreement normally limits the size of the stores to be erecte (e.g., one level, two levels), and sets the minimum and maximum gross leaseable area for each parcel, the gross area and width of the enclosed malls and location of them in relation to the various buildings, and the actual areas within each parcel where buildings may be located. For the latter items, a diagram is usually attached showing the relative sizes and locations of each.

The parties should also agree upon the areas where the buildings may be constructed and the extent to which each building may be expanded. The balance of the area, referred to as "common area," will be controlled by provisions for the number of parking spaces required (e.g., 5.5 cars per 1000 square feet of gross leaseable area on each tract) and for the use of the mall area (e.g., number of kiosks to be erected or use to which mall may be put). Each owner and ground lessee will be required to maintain the agreed upon parking ratio for the term of the agreement within its particular tract.

Construction and maintenance of the common areas, i.e., mall, parking areas, roadways, entrances and exits, and the walks and grass areas of the entire complex are normally the responsibility of the mall store developer. However, it is sometimes agreed that the mall area developer will construct or improve the common areas and thereafter each party will maintain its respective common area. The maintenance would be defined to include, among other things, paving, striping, cleaning, snow removal, lighting and parking and directional signs. With respect to the enclosed mall area, the parties ordinarily agree that the developer of the mall store area will be responsible for the lighting and maintenance and for the heating, ventilating and air conditioning (HVAC) of the mall. Provision is normally made that each party shall maintain the temperature within its store at a certain level, so as to prevent the drainage of the heat or air-conditioning from the enclosed mall.

The location, type and size of signs are usually agreed upon by the parties in order to maintain a proper over-all appearance of the center. The parties would agree to abide by certain rules and regulations, such as a prohibition of noise outside the various tenant spaces (thus, avoiding a honky-tonk atmosphere), or if music is desired, all tenants will purchase the service from the same commercial supplier. Certain business hours can be established and it can be agreed that the lighting and heating of the enclosed mall and the lighting of the common areas shall be maintained for a certain specified period after closing hours. A proper tenant mix can be agreed upon so that the mall or satellite stores will not be of one type, but such agreement should not unreasonably restrict or limit the developer in its operation of the mall.

An important item is restoration in the event of damage. If any building abutting the mall is damaged, the entire mall is unsightly unless the building is restored. It should be provided that in the event of damage or partial condemnation, the insurance proceeds or condemnation award shall be used, at least during the period the operating covenant is in effect, for restoration purposes, but if the period for required restoration has ended and the owner has decided not to restore, the debris must be removed and the premises put in a sightly condition. ...

V. RECIPROCAL EASEMENTS

Easements will be needed for ingress and egress to all public streets or highways and for parking and roadway purposes over the various parcels. This is a necessity in establishing a unified shopping center.

Without such reciprocal easements, each owner could fence in his particular parcel to the detriment of the other owners.

An easement is also needed for ingress and egress over the enclosed mall, if stores abutting the mall are under different ownership.

Easements are often needed among the mall store owners for encroaching footings, foundations, walls, roofs and roof overhangs. During the construction period, temporary easements could be required for the storage of materials on the adjoining parcels.

In many centers the utility easements for light, gas, water, telephone and sewerage circumscribe the stores' building area, and each fee owner has the right to connect its particular building to them. Since each owner is dependent upon the entire system, reciprocal easements are a necessity. Each owner has the right to use them and has the obligation of maintaining all such common reciprocal utility easements which are located within its parcel. If replacement of any of the utility lines is needed, the agreement could provide that each party shall pay its proportionate share of the costs.

In some states, a tax sale could wipe out all easements. If such be the case, each owner should be required to present receipted tax bills, or copies of the receipts, to all other parties at least once each year.

While easements for parking and for ingress and egress are only given for the term of the operating agreement, easements for a perimeter road and for utilities should be in perpetuity. Most easements are nonexclusive and should so state.

The operating agreement should provide that if any party enters upon the property of another to install or replace an underground line in the easement area, such party shall restore the surface area to its former condition and should do the work with a minimum of interference to the other owner. Also, if work is done on the property of another owner, it should be done so as to avoid any liens being filed against the other fee owner.

VI. CONTRIBUTION TOWARD COSTS

With respect to the common areas, each owner could agree to maintain the common areas on its parcel and to pay all costs relative thereto. If each owner agrees to maintain its own common areas, an inequitable burden could be imposed on one owner if most parking areas are within the particular owner's common area. In the event it is agreed that the owner of the mall area has the responsibility for the maintenance of all common areas within the center, each owner should agree to pay its proportionate share of the expenses, including applicable taxes, insurance and management fee.

The costs of maintaining, heating and air-conditioning the enclosed mall should be borne proportionately by all owners of stores abutting the mall. These costs would include the taxes, insurance and management fee allocable to the mall area.

The operating agreement could contain provisions for contributions by the respective owners for the initial installation of the various underground common utility lines, for the paving, lighting and striping of the parking areas and for sidewalks, shrubbery and other amenities within the common areas. Another item often included is contributions by the respective owners or ground lessees for off-site improvements, such as road widening, deceleration lanes and traffic lights.

AMERICAN BAR ASSOCIATION, SECTION OF REAL PROPERTY, PROBATE AND TRUST LAW, COMMITTEE ON LEASES, DRAFTING SHOPPING CENTER LEASES *

2 Real Property, Probate & Trust Journal 222, 232–242, 245–246 (1967).

V.   COVENANTS AGAINST COMPETITION

1.   Exclusives to Tenant—No Competition by Another Tenant

a.   *Overlapping Lines of Merchandise*

One of the more difficult drafting problems that faces the landlord's lawyer in a preparation of leases during the development of a shopping center project concerns the so-called "exclusive," a clause inserted at the tenant's request which limits or eliminates competition in certain lines of merchandise or prohibits the operation of a competing store by another tenant in the shopping center and possibly on other land within a specific radius of the center. However, competition among tenants is the lifeblood of the shopping center. The trend is away from requesting or granting exclusives, either for the type of store or for a specific line of merchandise. This is true for two reasons: (a) many shoppers wish to compare merchandise and values; (b) present-day methods of merchandising have led to an expansion of items carried by many chain stores, necessarily resulting in considerable overlap (supermarkets, drug stores and variety stores may compete with each other); consequently, an owner granting an exclusive is always in danger of breaching a lease covenant with one or more tenants.

Most chain tenants insist upon some protection against excessive competition. In the smaller shopping centers such protection generally consists of a complete restriction against a business which directly competes with the tenant in question. In the regional shopping centers the restriction may, for example, limit the competition to (i) not more than one additional department store or variety store, or (ii) not more than four additional shoe stores.

In view of the fact that many retail stores have consistently expanded and broadened the items and lines of merchandise, it is most important that the exclusive be limited as narrowly as possible. For example, many problems can be created for a developer if a food supermarket is given an exclusive for the sale of food for off-premises consumption in the shopping center in lieu of an exclusive for a food supermarket.

Most attorneys representing the developer will insist that the exclusive operations clause be limited to the main or principal line of business of the tenant which is specified in the use clause. In such event, items of merchandise which are sold by the tenant in question as an incidental line of merchandise are not within the purview of the exclusive operations clause and may be sold by the other tenants in the center.

b. Advantages in Recording Lease

The memorandum of lease which may be prepared for recording should contain in it any exclusives and other restrictions, although this in and for itself may not solve the problem of notice to all concerned. This is a matter which will vary from state to state and care should be taken to see that all that is necessary to be done has been done so that any exclusives will be as valid as possible. If the competitor who violates the exclusive is deemed to have had notice, injunctive relief will lie. A memorandum of the lease containing the exclusive should be recorded immediately upon execution and can be supplemented by a later one setting forth the exact commencement and expiration dates. This will help solve any notice problems that might arise under any applicable state statute. The tenant who fears that an exclusive has already been given and that he might violate it would be somewhat protected by receiving a warranty from the landlord that he takes the property subject to no liens, encumbrances or restrictions, except as specifically set forth.

c. Problems of Enforcement

If the landlord has breached the covenant as to exclusives the tenant can quit the premises, sue for damages or attempt to obtain an injunction. Loss of profits would generally be the measure of damages if they can be satisfactorily established, but the damages are often difficult to determine. If the tenant quits the premises he may use the breach as a defense in an action by the landlord for rent. If the store has not been established long enough for there to be provable damages in terms of loss of profits, the difference in rental value between the worth of the lease with the covenant and the worth of the lease without the covenant would be the damages.

Injunctive relief is available against the covenantor and against all who take the premises with notice of the covenant.

Thus with problems of enforcement it has become common to find exclusive clauses containing cancellation privileges and rent adjustments and leaving the tenant such other remedies as may be available to him.

d. Difficulty in Drafting

The literature on the subject includes several exercises in developing the form of the exclusive covenant so that it will cover the desired situation and hopefully will not be subject to varying interpretations. The area restricted by the exclusive operations clause should be clearly delineated. If it is intended that such clause is to apply (i) to only the initial stage of the shopping center and not to any enlargement thereof, or (ii) to only land which now forms a part, or may hereafter form a part of the shopping center land, such intention should be specified in the lease.

If the area set forth is unreasonably large, it may invalidate the exclusive. The problems concern after acquired land, land used for expansion of the shopping center, and whether or not land across a public street is to be considered contiguous. The draftsman should be aware also of the expansion potential of the center when he draws the covenant.

Most mortgage lenders object to an exclusive operations clause which extends beyond the confines of the shopping center for the lender may have no control over the enforcement of such a clause in an area not covered by the mortgage, except to provide that a breach thereof would constitute a default under the mortgage. In addition, if the mortgage lender becomes the owner of the shopping center by foreclosure or otherwise, and is thus bound by the exclusive operations clause, and if such mortgage lender also becomes the owner of a second shopping center within the proscribed area, the exclusive operations clause would restrict the operations of tenants in the second shopping center.

e. Enforceability when Shopping Center Consists of Separate Parcels Having Different Owners

The question has been raised, both in litigation and in thoughtful articles, as to whether or not an exclusive violates the federal anti-trust laws. Part of the question has arisen with regard to multiple ownerships, but to date there have been no cases reported which have held such exclusives in violation of any federal anti-trust law.

The question of the validity of the exclusives has also been raised unsuccessfully in a number of cases involving state anti-trust laws. Two Texas cases [62] have held restrictive covenants to be in violation of the state laws where jointly given by the landlords and owners of contiguous property. The Supreme Court of Texas has recognized as an exception a restrictive covenant given on other land owned solely by the landlord if such restriction is incidental and collateral to a lawful lease. [64]

---

62. Schnitzer v. Southwest Shoe Corp., 364 S.W.2d 373 (Tex.1963); Kroger Co. v. Weingarten, 380 S.W.2d 145 (Tex.Civ.App. 1964).

64. Schnitzer v. Southwest Shoe Corp., 364 S.W.2d 373 (Tex.1963).

Since a tenant cannot enforce an exclusive provision under the Texas rule, he should seek other remedies such as cancellation rights or a substantial lowering of his rent in the event of direct competition. A reasonable penalty such as the elimination of the minimum rent might well be a satisfactory answer.

There are a number of large shopping centers being developed today where the ownership has been divided prior to any leasing. This is of concern to a tenant who wishes an exclusive for the entire center only to be met by the response that his immediate landlord owns only the one building in which his store is located. To be assured of some protection the tenant should require a penalty to be included in the lease. The question remains open as to the enforceability of an exclusive in such a situation if granted by the owners of all of the shopping center.

2. Exclusives to Landlord—No Competition by Tenant within Defined Area

The opposite of the exclusive is the so-called "radius clause" by which the landlord receives protection against the tenant competing with itself by means of a clause wherein tenant agrees not to own or operate another store within a defined geographical area.

The theory behind such a prohibition is that when the rent to be paid by the tenant is at least in part based upon a percentage of sales, it is necessary to prevent any dilution of its sales by means of a competing business.

The two primary factors to be considered in establishing the area in which the tenant is to be restricted are the location of the shopping center and the type of business engaged in by the tenant. One should examine the already established competing business areas and the possibility and availability of new ones being established, as well as the zoning patterns present in the community. A larger radius would be appropriate in a rural area. A supermarket chain will agree to a much smaller radius restriction than a high-fashion ladies ready-to-wear store or a department store.

It would be a rare situation indeed if a radius restriction were in excess of five miles; three miles is probably more common.

A radius clause should include: (a) the persons restricted, (b) the type of business restricted, (c) the area restricted, (d) the period of time during which the restriction is to be effective, (e) a prohibition against direct or indirect competition or financial investment, and (f) any exceptions thereto. The persons restricted might include the tenant and, if a corporation, its affiliates, subsidiaries, parent and stockholders; if a partnership, all members of the partnership and their families.

The radius can be set forth as follows: "Within a radius of _____ miles in all directions from the outside boundaries of the shopping center," or "_____ miles, measured along major streets, highways and traffic arteries from the outside boundaries of the shopping center," or "A radius of _____ miles from the leased premises."

The type of business restricted must be spelled out carefully. For example, if the tenant is part of a chain that operates both high priced and popular priced shoe stores under different names, the name should be included in the restriction as well as the type of merchandise, and it should specify which of the stores is being restricted.

The exceptions to the restriction could properly be any stores in operation at the time of the execution of the lease either at their present location or at any location to which they may be moved provided the size thereof is not increased more than 10%. Another exception could properly be any stores subsequently purchased which are part of a chain at the time of purchase (which should be defined as a group of two or more stores) and where only one of such stores is located in the restricted area.

If the tenant has a store within the restricted radius, the landlord should properly request that the lease not be renewed and be allowed to expire at the termination thereof and, if this is not acceptable, that the store not be enlarged in size. The tenant's response to such a request could be an agreement to close the store provided the average amount of sales made therein for the last three years of its operation be thenceforth from the time of closing excluded from the gross sales in the leased premises on which percentage rent is to be paid. The landlord would also want a clause whereby the tenant would agree not to advertise the older store, nor to encourage the transfer of business to the old store. Another common approach is to include the sales of the store in the prohibited area in the gross sales of the tenant.

If there is doubt as to whether or not a proposed location falls within the radius restriction, a safe practice would be to obtain from the prospective landlord a surveyor's certificate certifying to the fact that the proposed location is outside of the radius. A warranty to that effect could properly be included in the new lease together with an agreement indemnifying the tenant against any loss sustained by reason of the inaccuracy of the certificate and as a result of action taken by the landlord of the prior store.

If the clause is to be effective there should be injunctive relief and an action for damages, but in an action for damages it would be necessary for the landlord to plead and prove that the parties knew of the possible future rental loss because of the tenant's breach and that such a loss was contemplated as a contingency which might follow a breach by the tenant. There has been very limited litigation in this area and the clauses appear to be enforceable. The same theories that are used to support any covenants running with the land as well as covenants against competition executed in connection with employment contracts and the sale of a business would seem to be applicable.

VI. USE

1. Necessity of Defining Use Specifically

The desirability of extreme care in defining the use to which the leased premises will be put arises not only from consideration of good tenant mix, but from the necessity of avoiding conflict with exclusives that may have been given to other tenants in the shopping center. From the landlord's point of view, for purposes of flexibility, it is desirable to avoid as much as possible the giving of exclusives. A department store or major chain will sometimes seek a clause permitting the use of the premises for any legal purpose. This will conflict with all usual exclusions. An exclusive should never be given for a specific item such as coats, hats, shoes, etc., since under normal circumstances a number of stores will be selling such items. Even an exclusive for an entire category, such as men's clothing, raises difficulties since it could be claimed that a subleased department for men's clothing in a department store violated such an exclusive.

Some shopping center developers attempt to solve potential problems of conflict by making exceptions in any provision granting an exclusive for various tenants that will be expected to sell similar items. The difficulty with this approach is the likelihood of not covering all possible present or future conflicts. Another approach offering some protection is to provide that the store in question will be the only one "primarily devoted" to a particular use.

In drafting the use clause, limiting words such as "only" and "for no other purpose" should be used so as to be as restrictive as possible. The clause should also state that any subtenant or assignee of the tenant is not excused from the restrictions contained therein, and it should provide for immediate forfeiture in case of a violating use.

Care should be taken on the part of the landlord to examine any restrictions and exclusives that have been previously given and to comply with any notice requirements contained in them. Occasionally a tenant who has received an exclusive will insist that notice of it or an extract thereof appear in all leases made thereafter in the shopping center by the landlord.

2. Requirement that Tenant Keep Store Open and Operating

There has been much litigation and much literature concerning the obligations of a tenant to keep open and continuously operate its business when it is occupying the premises under a lease agreement that provides for a percentage of its gross sales to be paid as rental, but which lease does not contain a provision calling for continuous operations by the tenant. The litigation has generally revolved about whether or not there is an implied covenant to continuously operate.

While it is difficult to establish general rules, it would be reasonable to state that where the minimum rental is considered to be adequate, no such covenant will be implied, but where there is no minimum rental or where the minimum rental is so low as to be nominal, then a covenant may be implied. The burden is on the landlord to show that the minimum rental is inadequate.

The very nature of a shopping center almost requires that all of the stores continuously remain in operation and that such a requirement be included in the lease. Aside from any percentage rental that might be lost from the closing by one tenant, the adverse effect on the remainder of the center is important; and all tenants are generally required to keep open when the major stores (big department stores) remain open for business.

Many tenants insist on the right to close during hours when other stores operated by it in the community are closed so as to avoid operational problems; other tenants insist on some type of escape clause providing that on the happening of certain events (e.g., tenant's gross sales falling below a certain minimum through no fault of tenant) tenant can terminate the lease and vacate the premises. They also request the right to cease operating a reasonable time prior to the expiration of the lease term so as to enable them to fulfill any lease obligations they might have regarding vacating the premises and delivering them back to the landlord or where unforeseen problems develop, including strikes, acts of God, etc.

Regardless of how firmly a lease provides that the tenant will keep its store operating during the lease term, courts are reluctant to grant an affirmative injunction requiring the tenant to stay in business because of the practical difficulties of enforcement. However, since the landlord has suffered real damage, which cannot be calculated with precision, it is at least possible that a court would enforce a reasonable liquidated damage provision and not characterize it as a penalty, including a requirement that the sales made in the new store be treated as sales in the leased premises.

3. Store Hours

For a shopping center to be an effective merchandising unit, it is preferable that all of the stores maintain the same business hours or at least some semblance thereof. The lease should contain general standards regarding hours of operations and require the tenant to adhere to the hours of the majority or all of the stores. It is obvious, however, that not all businesses require the same hours. Since hours that might be appropriate at the commencement of the term will in most probability fluctuate during the term and also due to seasonal variations, it would appear unwise to attempt to set forth in the lease itself the specific hours for the tenant to remain open.

One alternative is for the Merchants' Association to set the hours; another reasonable one would be to require the tenant to remain open when any store in the shopping center containing over 100,000 square feet of floor space (or in the alternative the size of the smallest department store or other key or major tenant in the center) is open for business to the public, and during any other hours when the shopping center is generally open for business as may from time to time be determined by the landlord, except to the extent the tenant may be prohibited from being open for business by any applicable law. Another approach which would be more applicable in a small shopping center would be to require the tenant to maintain the same hours as competing businesses in the same city maintain.

The necessity for careful draftsmanship in establishing the desired controls as to hours was shown in a recent case concerning a lease which provided that the tenant would keep its store open until 5:00 p.m. or longer if it so desired, and also that the tenant would abide by the rules to be thereafter promulgated by the landlord for the betterment of the shopping center.[83] A rule was promulgated more than a year after the execution of the lease to the effect that the store was to be kept open until 9:00 p.m. This rule was held not to constitute a covenant under the terms of the lease, and the noncompliance of tenant was not sufficient to bring about forfeiture of the leasehold.

VII.   RIGHTS TO CANCEL OR TERMINATE

1. Tenant's Right to Cancel

It is still the majority rule in the country that the obligations of the tenant, including the obligation to pay rent, are "independent" and are not excused by the landlord's failure to perform under the lease or by fortuitous events like destruction of the building by casualty. This concept is giving way in some jurisdictions to a recognition that the lease is also a bilateral contract with mutually dependent promises. Under the latter concept the lease is a contract by which the landlord agrees, for a valuable consideration, to allow the tenant to use the land for a definite period, and a substantial breach of a material covenant by one party excuses the other party from further performance. The change was forced on the courts by the development of the complex contractual provisions in modern business leases.

The shopping center lease is a prime example of a document that expresses a complex business relationship and numerous obligations on the part of both parties. The approach that the courts take in solving a dispute arising out of such a lease has a vital effect on the tenant for the landlord's breach, and puts the developer's mortgagee on the alert to look for lease clauses, or a lack of protective clauses, that might result in the loss of rental or of the lease itself.

The essential security for a mortgage loan on a shopping center is the income from the tenant; the value of the land and structures is of lesser importance. The mortgagee inspects with great care the leases which will be the security for his loan, and in examining them he looks first for lease provisions which would threaten the very existence of the leases, i.e., those covenants of the landlord which if breached would, in a "contract state," give the tenant the right to cancel the lease.

---

83. O'Fallon Development Co. v. Reinbold, 69 Ill.App.2d 169, 216 N.E.2d 9 (1966).

Williams [89] points out that the courts have used three theories in reaching decisions which carry out the contractual intent of the parties though often appearing to follow property concepts. One theory rests on the finding of a constructive eviction where the breach substantially deprives the tenant of the beneficial use of the premises, giving the tenant the right to remove from the premises. Another theory is that the breach of a material covenant goes to the whole consideration, and in such case the covenants are dependent and, upon the landlord's breach, the tenant is excused from further performance. The third theory is the contractual doctrine of frustration, treating a landlord's breach as the cause of the frustration of the purpose for which the premises were leased. In addition, mutual mistake of fact, fraud and misrepresentation and, in some jurisdictions, mistake of law will entitle a tenant to a cancellation or, in some cases, a reformation.

In some jurisdictions the landlord's breach of his covenant to restrict the use of his property to prevent competition with the tenant would be a ground for the tenant's cancelling the lease; the courts apply the principle of dependent covenants and say that the breach goes to the whole consideration of the lease. The breach of a covenant to repair, to share expenses, to furnish heat, water or other essential services, may give rise to the tenant's right to cancel the lease on the theory that the tenant's covenant to pay rent and the covenants of the landlord are mutually dependent.

A provision commonly found in shopping center leases, that may be dangerous for the mortgagee, at least in some jurisdictions, is one which obligates the landlord to build expanded facilities for the tenant. The landlord's breach might give rise to a number of remedies, but from the standpoint of this discussion, it might be said to frustrate the purposes of the lease and give the tenant the right to cancel it.

2. Landlord's Failure to Meet Construction Deadlines and to Solve Other Problems

Where the lease concerns a shopping center to be built in the future, it is obvious that deadlines for the commencement and for the completion of construction are needed for the protection of both parties. The deadlines are usually generous and it is the universal practice to extend both deadlines for the period of "excusable delays." If either deadline is not met each party is usually given the power to cancel the lease, without liability to the other.

In order to limit his loss to the costs of attorneys' fees and architect's fees, possibly commitments for the purchase of fixtures and inventory, and tying up working capital, a tenant might ask for deadlines for various stages of construction in order to reduce the risk that those expenses may be incurred without the shopping center's

---

89. Williams, The High Credit Lease as Security, 12 Ass'n of Life Ins. Counsel Proc. 17.

being completed. This is, of course, hard on the landlord and will not be given unless the tenant has a bargaining position.

What the rights and liabilities of the parties would be if the deadline were not met, and the lease makes no provision for such contingency, it is hard to say. In a "contract" state it seems clear that the tenant may avoid the lease. If the lease commences upon signing, as many leases do, and the deadline is not met, then in a "property" state the tenant may not have the power to cancel for the landlord's failure to complete the construction on time; he may have only an action for damages. If the term does not begin until completion and the outside date is not met, the tenant might avoid the lease even in a "property" state by contending that the completion was a condition precedent to the effectiveness of the lease.

The developer asks for the right to abandon the project without liability to the tenant if he does not succeed in obtaining the necessary zoning changes, if he cannot sign up certain major tenants or if he cannot get his mortgage financing. The lease does not ordinarily give the tenant any remedies for such failure other than the right to cancel.

3. Depletion of Shopping Center

A problem frequently raised in the negotiation of a shopping center lease is the effect on the landlord, the tenant and the mortgagee of a "depletion" of the shopping center, e.g., a loss of all or a material part of the parking space, a loss of retail store space or the discontinuance of business by one or more of the major tenants. These conditions may come about as a result of a taking by eminent domain, destruction by casualty, the right given to some major tenants to stop doing business or the fact that certain tenants stop doing business in spite of a covenant requiring them to continue. The interests of the respective parties are obviously in conflict.

a. Eminent Domain; Destruction by Casualty

In the case of the taking of a substantial part of the shopping center, the lender will likely have an award sufficient to satisfy his loan, and in such circumstances he will probably apply the award to the satisfaction of the mortgage. Most leases provide for the termination on a taking of substantially all of the shopping center.

In the case of a condemnation of the parking area, the lender will permit a clause giving the tenant the right to cancel a lease if the parking ratio is reduced below an agreed figure or if more than 20% of the area is taken, provided the developer has the right to prevent cancellation by substituting new parking facilities on conveniently located land, or by building a second parking deck on the remaining land.

In the case of a taking of part of the leased premises, the lender will consent to a clause providing that the tenant may cancel if the premises are not reasonably useable for his business, and if the lease continues as to the part not taken, a pro rata reduction in the rent.

The lender will limit the use of the condemnation award for the purpose of restoring the premises, usually to the amount of the award allocated to the taking of the structure.

In the case of a destruction by casualty, the lender will object to a cancellation of the lease and will usually permit a clause requiring the landlord to rebuild, using the insurance proceeds to cover the cost. He will also permit an abatement of rent during the period of restoration because he is covered by rent insurance. The landlord and tenant usually agree that each has the right to cancel the lease in the last three years of the term if the damage is extensive enough. The lender will not object to such a provision because the loan will likely be substantially reduced by that time. If the tenant has an option to extend his lease, the landlord may insist on the tenant's exercising the option and remaining in the shopping center.

In the case of either a condemnation or a destruction by casualty the landlord will often reserve the right to terminate all leases in the shopping center if he feels that the shopping center is no longer an economically feasible project.

b. Discontinuance of Business by Major Tenant

The lender would not object to the discontinuance of business because the major tenant continues to pay at least the minimum rent and the security is not impaired. The landlord would have preferred not giving the major tenant such an option, but he may have had no choice. Thus, the risk of this kind of depletion is thrown entirely on the small tenant. More and more the smaller tenants are asking for lease clauses which afford them some relief.

Where it is clear that the tenant made the lease in reliance on the continued presence of one or more major tenants, and the tenant is given the right to cancel the lease if that condition is breached, the tenant will be permitted to cancel if a major tenant discontinues business and closes up shop though his fixtures remain in the store and he continues to pay rent.

A clause which is often given to a small tenant is a representation that the landlord has made leases for ten years or more with certain major tenants and that these tenants will open simultaneously with the small tenant. Nothing is said about a right to cancel the lease if any of the major tenants or its business is lost to the shopping center. If the lease of a major tenant is terminated because of some fortuitous happening or if a major tenant discontinues the conduct of business though the lease remains in effect, the tenant probably would not have the right to cancel his lease. But there is an understandable sympathy for the "little fellow" and the courts may go far to find help for him. It may be that the developer already has a built-in protection in a lease form which provides that the rent will be paid "without set-off or deduction, for any reason whatsoever."

Perhaps the risks attendant upon depletion might be acceptably distributed among the parties involved if the likelihood of a cancellation of the lease were made more remote. Thus, instead of providing for an outright option to cancel the lease, the parties might provide that, if one or more major tenants cease the conduct of business, in x% or more of the aggregate of the space leased to all major tenants, the smaller tenant could then elect to limit his rent to a percentage of gross sales until the resumption of business or the replacement of the tenants; if, however, in the first lease year following the year in which the depletion occurred, the tenant attains a volume of gross sales equal to those in the lease year preceding the depletion, he must again pay the minimum rent (and restore any rent lost by the landlord during the lease year); and if he does not attain such a volume then the landlord and the tenant have the option to cancel the lease during the next ensuing lease year unless in the interim the space has been restored to use. The tenant can avoid the clause by not electing to go on a percentage basis after the occurrence of the depletion. ...

IX. MERCHANTS' ASSOCIATION

All tenants concede that a Merchants' Association in a shopping center serves a useful function. It is an organization that, in conjunction with the landlord, can solve planning, promotional and operating problems of the shopping center, such as achievement of maximum success of promotions by the coordinated efforts of all the merchants, improvement of public relations, planning for existing or potential competition, decisions regarding store hours, traffic control and employee parking. It also simplifies the landlord's relationship with his tenants.

1. Requirement of Tenant Participation

The lease should require membership in the association. There are two methods of requiring such participation:

(a) *On a Fixed Rate or Percentage of Sales.* Many shopping centers require the tenants to pay a fixed rate per month, quarter or year as dues to the Merchants' Association. The rate is not necessarily the same for all tenants but is generally the same for those of the same size or sales volume, depending upon which method of classification is used.

This fixed rate enables the tenant to know what the dues are as one of his fixed charges. The disadvantage of a fixed rate is that it does not take into account inflationary trends or extra promotion that may be necessary because of future, unforeseen competition.

(b) *Dues to be Levied by Association.* Other leases provide that the tenant must join the association and leave the amount of the assessments for the determination of the tenant members. A representative committee of the association is probably better able to make a fair annual determination of the assessment for each tenant.

Some tenants object to this, claiming they will never know what their dues will be in the future despite their voice in the association. Experience, however, has demonstrated that this method will work equitably.

2. Voting

Although the landlord can run the association and rely upon the cooperation of the members, it is advisable for the Merchants' Association to have its own corporate entity. But whether a corporation or a voluntary association is created, conflicts may develop over voting rights. The allowance of one vote to each member is unfair to the large tenants who may then be at the mercy of a group of small store owners, but voting rights based on square feet can result in placing the large number of small shops under the domination of several of the large shops. A practical answer probably lies somewhere between the two extremes.

3. Enforcement

The obligation to pay dues and assessments is a personal obligation which the courts will enforce. It is best that the breach of the tenant's covenant to maintain membership in the association constitute a default like any other default under the lease.

2.   TENANT RIGHTS AND OBLIGATIONS

a.   TENANT'S RIGHT AND OBLIGATION TO USE THE PREMISES

DAVIS v. WICKLINE

Supreme Court of Appeals of Virginia, 1964.
205 Va. 166, 135 S.E.2d 812.

WHITTLE, Justice.

Wickline filed a petition for declaratory judgment under § 8–578 of the Code of Virginia against Davis and others, lessors of a building which was to be erected for and used by Wickline as a drug store. The suit prayed for the construction of paragraph "Fourth" in the lease.

The point in issue between the parties was that Davis contended that paragraph "Fourth" of the lease "Contains a positive covenant (on the part of Wickline) to operate a drug store". Whereas, Wickline contended that the paragraph was a restrictive covenant only, restricting the use of the building to that of a drug store. This was the sole issue in the case. The paragraph reads:

"Fourth: It is covenanted and agreed between the contracting parties that during the term of this lease the premises hereby leased shall be used for the purpose of a drug store and for no other purpose— and that during the term of this lease or any renewal thereof the lessee shall operate said premises as a drug store."

It was conceded by the parties that the language in the lease was plain and that there was no necessity for oral testimony to explain its meaning.

In deciding the case in Wickline's favor the trial court said: "Reading paragraph 'fourth' as a whole, it is my opinion that during the term of the lease the premises must be used as a drug store and for no other purpose. There is no affirmative duty on the lessee [Wickline] to operate a drug store throughout the term of the lease. Aside from the payment of the rent, the duty of the lessee is that if he occupies the premises for any purpose, it must be for the purpose of operating a drug store."

After operating the drug store in the demised premises for a period of time Wickline moved his operation to a new location but continued to pay the monthly rental as agreed.

In Parrish v. Robertson, 195 Va. 794, 800, 80 S.E.2d 407, 410, the lessor entered into a written lease with the lessee whereby a building which was being constructed was leased to the lessee for a period of three years for the purpose of operating a restaurant therein. Lessee was to pay a rental of $250 per month plus 10% of the net profits derived from the operation of the business. Lessee operated a restaurant on the premises for eighteen months and then ceased operation and moved to another location. It was contended by the lessor that the lessee was required to operate a restaurant business for the full term of the lease and that the obligation was both express and implied by the covenant to pay in addition to the monthly rent 10% of the net profits.

In rejecting this contention we said: "It could hardly be contended that Parrish would have been obligated to continue the restaurant business if they were losing money. Acting in good faith, under such circumstances, they could close the business, thus limiting their obligation under the contract to the payment of the base rental of $250 per month."

What was said in the Parrish case applies with equal force to the case at bar. It can hardly be contended that Wickline intended to agree to continue to operate a drug store in this new, untried location for a period of ten years if the business was losing money. The factual posture of the case at bar is stronger for the construction adopted by the trial court than existed in Parrish, for in the instant case the rent is not tied into the profits made in the business.

In the case of Congressional Amusement Corp. v. Weltman (D.C.Mun.App.1947) 55 A.2d 95, the lessor sued for possession of the demised premises charging that the lessee had breached the lease by discontinuing the operation of a liquor store on the premises. A covenant in the lease provided in part: "That (lessee) *will use* said premises for the sale of alcoholic beverages ...". In holding that the covenant was restrictive only and did not impose an affirmative duty to operate a liquor store the court said:

"Reason and authority support the view that though the covenant unambiguously restricted the use of the premises to a liquor store, it did not require that it be used at all. When the parties sat down to draw the lease they had it in their power to make the use restrictions as mild or as strict as they desired (or could agree upon). If the lessor wished to impose upon the lessees the duty of continuing occupancy and continuing operation of a liquor store it should have adopted language to make that duty clear.

"... Very clearly [the language employed] did not prescribe that such a store must be kept open and in operation throughout the lease term. The law will not read into the covenant words of compulsion which are not there. The law does not say that by accepting the grant of premises for a particular purpose, with a prohibition against its use for any other purpose, a lessee becomes affirmatively obligated to use it continually for such purpose."

The following annotation is found in Vol. 47 A.L.R., page 1134: "... (T)he tenant is under no obligation in the absence of specific provisions therefor, to occupy or use, or continue to use the leased premises even though one of the parties, or both, expected and intended that they would be used for the particular purpose to which they seem to be adapted or constructed."

In Weil v. Ann Lewis Shops, (Tex.Civ.App.), 281 S.W.2d 651, 654, supra, it is said "Appellants contend that the written lease expressly provided that appellee should occupy and use the demised premises for a ladies' ready-to-wear store. ... They first present the provision of the lease which states that the premises are rented 'for occupation and use as Ladies', Misses' and Children's ready-to-wear and accessories and not otherwise.' Clauses similar to this one have been construed in many cases, and it has never been held to be an agreement to occupy and use the demised premises, but only to restrict the purposes for which the premises may be used."

In Dickey v. Philadelphia Minit-Man Corp., 377 Pa. 549, 105 A.2d 580, 581 the court said: "Generally speaking, a provision in a lease that the premises are to be used only for a certain prescribed purpose imports no obligation on the part of the lessee to use or continue to use the premises for that purpose; such a provision is a covenant against a noncomplying use, not a covenant to use." In addition to what has been said two well defined rules of construction mitigate against the position urged by Davis in this case: (1) a contract of lease is to be construed favorably to the lessee and against the lessor; and (2) breach of covenant to sustain forfeiture is construed strictly against forfeiture. The instrument must give the right of forfeiture in terms so clear and explicit as to leave no room for any other construction. Keeping these principles in mind an examination of paragraph "Fourth" of the lease is in order. The pertinent clauses are:

"... the premises hereby leased shall be used for the purpose of a drug store and for no other purpose."

This clause is clearly restrictive in nature, simply requiring the building to be used for no other purpose than a drug store. The remaining clause:

"and that during the term of this lease or any renewal thereof the Lessee shall operate said premises as a drug store".

This latter clause simply makes the restriction of the first clause applicable to the option to renew for a ten year term which was granted to Wickline under the lease.

If it had been intended by Davis that Wickline operate, at all costs, a drug store for ten years, such a burdensome obligation should have been spelled out in clear and explicit terms and should have included some standard of measurement by which the conduct of Wickline could have been measured.

We have been cited to no authority, nor have we found any, supporting Davis' contention in this case.

For the reasons stated the judgment of the lower court is affirmed.

Affirmed.

INGANNAMORTE v. KINGS SUPER MARKETS, INC.

Supreme Court of New Jersey, 1970.
55 N.J. 223, 260 A.2d 841.

JACOBS, J.

The Law Division directed that judgment for possession be entered in favor of the plaintiffs-landlords unless, within thirty days, the defendant-tenant resumes its supermarket operations at the leased premises. The defendant appealed and we certified while the matter was awaiting argument in the Appellate Division.

The plaintiffs own a small shopping center in the Borough of Dumont. It consists of a supermarket, which occupies about one-third of the total floor space in the center, and eleven satellite retail stores including, *inter alia,* a drugstore, a beauty salon, a delicatessen, a bakery, a confectionery and stationery store, a hardware store, a dry goods store, a children's clothing store, and a laundromat. In 1957 the plaintiffs leased the supermarket, which was then being operated by Acme Food Markets, to Dumont Valley Fair, Inc. for a term of ten years commencing February 1, 1958 with a five year renewal option. For several years Valley Fair operated the supermarket under the terms of its lease which provided, in pertinent part, that the leased store was "to be used and occupied only for a supermarket for the sale of all kinds of food, groceries, vegetables and refreshments, expressly excluding the sale of drugs, cosmetics, hardware, stationery, dishes, and on the premises bakery." The lease prohibited the landlord from letting premises in the "shopping center to other stores to be used as a butcher shop, fruit or vegetable store or fish market" and, so far as appears, this prohibition was strictly observed. It also provided that the parking area shall be maintained by the landlord and "shall be used for the benefit of all the tenants of the shopping center," and apparently this was strictly observed.

Early in 1961 there were negotiations with regard to an assignment of the supermarket lease from Valley Fair to defendant Kings Super Markets. The landlord's consent was required and there were relevant conversations between representatives of the landlord and Kings. Testimony introduced in the Law Division indicated that Mr. Bildner, president and general manager of Kings, had made site inspections, was told about the need for a fully operative supermarket with an adequate complement of food products, and was also told about the adverse economic effects on the shopping center from Valley Fair's inadequacies. Bildner deposed that he knew the Ingannamortes "wanted a supermarket as the nucleus of that particular center," and that he was told "that the merchants in the center were complaining about the operation" and that "the operation had to be improved." The Law Division found, on ample evidence, that Bildner had indicated "that Kings would conduct the type of active operation desired if Kings took the assignment." On May 31, 1961 the lease was assigned by Valley Fair to Kings with the landlord's written consent and Kings duly commenced its operation.

Kings operated the supermarket without interruption until October 8, 1966. At that time it ceased operation, closed its doors, and removed its exterior signs from the leased premises. However, it did not remove its equipment and continued to pay the monthly rental. On several occasions the Ingannamortes discussed the reopening of the supermarket with Bildner. At one point he told them that Kings was still interested in the area and was arranging for a study as to the feasibility of expansion. At another point, in April 1967, he told them that Kings was not interested in expanding but was "still contemplating the operation there." Finally, in July 1967, the Ingannamortes wrote to Kings notifying that its tenancy was being terminated because it had vacated and abandoned the premises and had neglected and refused "to occupy and conduct a super market business as set forth in said leasehold agreement. ... "

The plaintiffs refused to accept a tender of the August rent and on August 31, 1967 they instituted an action for possession. In the meantime Kings had notified the plaintiffs that it was renewing the lease for an additional five years, commencing with the termination of the original ten year term on February 1, 1968. Kings continued to make monthly tenders of rent until a stipulation was entered into on December 29, 1967 dispensing with further tenders until the determination of the plaintiffs' action. After taking testimony and considering the various legal contentions advanced before him, Judge Dalton filed an opinion in which he found that the use and occupancy clause of the lease was both restrictive and mandatory and that Kings had violated it by ceasing to actively operate a supermarket at the leased premises.

He also found that the landlord's notice of termination was technically defective but sensibly disposed of this subordinate issue in the following fashion:

"The court finds that the termination notice [dated July 1967] is defective since not in accord with paragraph No. 35 of the lease, which requires that before the landlord declares a default he must give thirty days' written notice to the tenant specifying the nature of the default in order to afford said tenant an opportunity to cure same.

"On representations of both counsel, the court has been informed that the plaintiff is, and has always been, willing to allow the defendant to continue on the premises provided they conduct an active supermarket operation thereon, but that the defendant is not now, nor will they be in the foreseeable future, able to make a decision as to the conduct of any future operation on the site in question. This being the case, it would be a useless as well as a time consuming gesture for the court to order that proper notice be given at this point in time.

"In view of the above, the court directs that judgment for possession be entered in favor of the plaintiffs to take effect thirty days from the entry of this order unless the defendants resume a fully active supermarket operation within that period."

The defendant's primary contention in support of its appeal is that the use and occupancy clause of the lease should be construed as restrictive but not mandatory. It cites cases such as McCormick v. Stephany, 57 N.J.Eq. 257, 263, 41 A. 840 (Ch.1898), modified, 61 N.J.Eq. 208, 48 A. 25 (Ch.1900) where the closing of a saloon was held not to violate a provision that the premises would not be used for any other purpose than a saloon, Hoffman v. Seidman, 101 N.J.L. 106, 109, 127 A. 199, 200 (E. & A. 1925) where a covenant not to use the premises for any other purpose than a dwelling and a hardware and paint store was said to impose "no obligation to use the premises at all," and Burns & Schaffer Amusement Co. v. Conover, 111 N.J.L. 257, 263, 168 A. 304, 307 (E. & A. 1933) where a covenant to use the leased premises only for the moving picture or theatre business was held to prohibit uses other than moving picture or theatre purposes but not to "require operation for those authorized uses." But these cases and others like them, did not involve the precise use and occupancy language in the lease before us and, much more to the point, did not involve a situation where, as here, there were interdependent economic units and the landlord had an obvious interest in the continued active operation of the leased premises far beyond the mere payment of the fixed monthly rental.

In Plassmeyer v. Brenta, 24 N.J.Super. 322, 94 A.2d 508 (App.Div. 1953) there was a twenty-year lease of premises to "be used and occupied only and for no other purpose than as a gasoline service station." The rent was fixed at a stipulated amount per month and as "additional rent" the lessee agreed to pay one cent for each gallon of gasoline delivered into the storage tanks on the premises in excess of a certain gallonage. The premises were never used as a gasoline service station and it was contended that so long as the tenant paid the monthly rent and did not engage in any other occupation on the premises, no breach of the lease arose. This contention was rejected by both the trial court and the Appellate Division. In the course of the latter's opinion the following appears:

"The trial court concluded that the language of the lease was clear and unambiguous and plainly created a duty to operate a gasoline service station. Our study of the instrument convinces us that this interpretation was correct. The language employed, particularly that dealing with the rental obligation, was prohibitive and mandatory with respect to use, and not merely restrictive, as in the cases on which appellant relies. Consequently failure to engage in that use constituted a breach."

24 N.J.Super. at 325, 94 A.2d at 510.

Plassmeyer viewed its lease as embodying an express mandate for continued operation whereas other cases have found implied mandates in comparable leases. Thus in Silverstein v. Keane, 19 N.J. 1, 115 A.2d 1 (1955), this Court referred to the many decisions which have implied mandatory operation requirements in percentage leases, and it pointed out that "[t]he implication of an obligation from the terms of the agreement considering what was written in the light of the attendant circumstances and conditions is a settled principle in New Jersey law." 19 N.J. at 12, 115 A.2d at 7. It matters not whether the court speaks of the mandate as implied or expressed for the ascertained intention of the parties is the same under either approach as is the judicial determination. Nor does it matter that the lease is not a percentage lease where there are other circumstances sufficiently evidencing the intention of the parties that the lessee will be under a mandate to operate reasonably within the terms of the lease. See Lilac Variety, Inc. v. Dallas Texas Company, 383 S.W.2d 193 (Tex.Civ.App.1964).

In *Lilac Variety*, supra, the owner of a suburban shopping center leased a retail store for fifteen years to TG & Y Stores and shortly thereafter leased the center's supermarket, as planned and as set forth in a provision of TG & Y's lease, to the A.C.F. Wrigley Stores. The supermarket was operated for a while and was then closed with Wrigley continuing to pay rent. TG & Y Stores then sought and obtained a judgment entitling it to cancel its lease because of the closing of the supermarket. The court found sufficient implication of a requirement that the supermarket would continue operation; in the course of its opinion it said:

"We think it is common knowledge that the volume of pedestrian traffic at the site of a retail merchandising business is a factor which affects the gross sales potential of the business. That being so the purpose and the importance to appellants of the lease provisions with reference to a supermarket are obvious. Plainly the parties intended that a supermarket should be in operation during the term of the lease. We find it impossible to believe that when the parties entered into this lease agreement it was intended that the particular lease provision in question would be satisfied if A.C.F. Wrigley Stores should continue to pay rent on an idle store building after discontinuing operation of the supermarket."

383 S.W.2d at 196.

The lease between the plaintiffs and Valley Fair contained enough on its face to imply an operating mandate as against its original lessee Valley Fair; and any doubt insofar as the assignee Kings was concerned was removed by the testimony and findings with respect to the negotiations between the Ingannamortes and Bildner at the time of the assignment. The lease itself disclosed that it was for a supermarket in the landlord's shopping center at Dumont; it provided that the premises were to be "used and occupied" only for a supermarket excluding, however, certain items which obviously were being sold in other stores in the center; these other stores were expressly to be prohibited from competing with the supermarket in its sale of meats, fish, fruits and vegetables; and the landlord was to maintain the common parking area for the entire center including the supermarket and the other stores. When these lease provisions are viewed in the light of the physical and geographic circumstances there would appear to remain little reason to question that the parties contemplated that the supermarket would continue to be operated as such and that mere payment of rent for an "idle store building" (*Lilac Variety,* supra) would not satisfy the purposes of the center or the landlord's execution of the lease.

The defendant asserts that the testimony as to the negotiations at the time of the assignment was inadmissible but we disagree. It clearly evidenced the intention of Kings and the Ingannamortes, when they entered into their acceptance and approval of the assignment, as well as their practical construction of the terms of the assigned lease. In recent years our courts have broadly admitted comparable evidence of intent and practical construction which fairly served to clarify the goals of the parties and the meaning of their language.

In the light of all of the above, the judgment entered below may properly be affirmed without any need for dealing with any of the collateral issues. Thus there is no occasion for considering whether the Ingannamortes would have the legal right to compel Kings to resume operations and, if so, under what terms. At oral argument, counsel for the Ingannamortes stated that the only thing they seek beyond the payment of rent due to date, which Kings acknowledges, is to have Kings either vacate the premises completely with cancellation of the lease, or to have it resume operation of the supermarket in reasonable fashion. Surely the terms of the lease and every consideration of fairness entitle them to that measure of relief. Kings still has the aforementioned option which it may exercise within thirty days from the filing of this opinion, and clearly it is in no just position to claim more.

Affirmed.

For affirmance: Justices JACOBS, FRANCIS, PROCTOR, HALL, SCHETTINO and HANEMAN—6.

For reversal: None.

PIGGLY WIGGLY SOUTHERN, INC. v. HEARD

Supreme Court of Georgia, 1991.
261 Ga. 503, 405 S.E.2d 478.

HUNT, Justice.

This case involves the construction of a shopping center store lease. Both the trial court and the Court of Appeals held the lease contained an express continued use covenant as well as an implied covenant of continued operation. *Piggly Wiggly Southern v. Heard*, 197 Ga.App. 656, 399 S.E.2d 244 (1990). We granted the writ of certiorari to determine whether the Court of Appeals was correct in its construction of the parties' lease, and reverse.

In 1963, the parties executed a lease in which appellees' predecessor agreed to construct a supermarket for appellant according to plans prepared by appellant. Appellant drafted the lease, which began in 1964 for a term of 15 years, and called for an annual base rent of $29,053.60 as well as a percentage rent of annual gross sales exceeding $2,000,000. The lease was renewed on the same terms for an additional seven years in 1979, with options to renew for two additional 3–year terms. Appellant exercised both renewal options and, after it was acquired by a new corporation, one month into the second 3–year term, closed its store, vacated the premises, and moved its grocery store operation to a nearby shopping center belonging to its new owner. While appellant continued to pay the annual base rent to appellees, it refused to sublease the vacant store, despite the interest of other supermarkets in the abandoned space. Appellees filed suit seeking damages for appellant's alleged breach of the lease.

We agree with appellant that the lease agreement between the parties does not contain an express covenant of continuous operation. Rather, the language of the agreement is plainly to the contrary, and, therefore, the trial court, the Court of Appeals, and this court are not authorized to construe it otherwise. *Heyman v. Financial Properties Developers, Inc.*, 175 Ga.App.146, 332 S.E.2d 893 (1985). The language of the agreement expressly negates a requirement of continuous operation:

> ... LESSEE'S use of the leased building and the leased property shall not be limited nor restricted to such purposes [use as a supermarket, etc.], and said building and property may be used *for any other lawful business*, without the consent of LESSOR (emphasis supplied).

See Kroger, Co., v. Bonny Corp., 134 Ga.App. 834, 216 S.E.2d 341 (1975).[1]

Nor does the lease agreement contain any provision which would create an *implied* covenant of continuous operation. Rather, the contract, read as a whole, indicates otherwise. The agreement's provision for free assignability by the tenant, without consent of the lessor, weighs strongly against a construction of the contract which would require the tenant to continue its business throughout the term of the lease. *Kroger, Co. v. Bonny Corp.,* supra at 836(1), 216 S.E.2d 341. Likewise, the existence of a substantial minimum base rent, in addition to the provision for percentage rental payments, suggests the absence of an implied covenant of continuous operation. *Id.* at 838 to 839(2), 216 S.E.2d 341. See also 38 A.L.R.2d Annot. p. 1113 et seq., Construction and Application of Provision in Lease Under Which Landlord is to Receive Percentage of Lessee's Profits or Receipts.

The parties did not agree to nor bargain for appellant's continuous operation of the premises, and we are not authorized to rewrite the contract to create such a provision. See *Coffee System of Atlanta v. Fox,* 227 Ga. 602, 182 S.E.2d 109 (1971).[2]

Judgment reversed.

SMITH, P.J., WELTNER and FLETCHER, JJ., and Judge STEPHEN E. BOSWELL, J., concur.

BELL and BENHAM, JJ., dissent.

CLARKE, C.J., not participating.

BENHAM, Justice, dissenting.

Because I disagree with the majority's assertion that the language of the lease expressly negates a requirement of continuous operation, and because I would hold that the Court of Appeals was correct in holding that there was in this case both an express covenant and an implied covenant of continuous operation, I must respectfully dissent to the majority's reversal of the judgment of the Court of Appeals.

In addition to the facts set out in the majority opinion, it should be noted that the complete text of the lease provision on which appellees rely reads as follows:

> Lessee is leasing the leased building for use as a supermarket and other parts of the leased property for parking and other uses incident to a supermarket business, but LESSEE'S use of the leased

---

1. In *Kroger, Co. v. Bonny Corp.,* the Court of Appeals rejected the contention that language in the lease agreement providing the tenant "use said premises in a lawful manner" created a covenant of continuous operation.

2. See Generally 40 A.L.R.3d Annot. p. 971 et seq., Lease of Store as Requiring Active Operation of Store, which states the general rule that

... the courts take the position that the lessee is under no obligation in the absence of a specific provision therefor, to occupy or use, or continue to use, the leased premises, even though one of the parties, or both expected and intended that they would be used for the particular purpose to which they seemed to be adapted or for which they seemed to be constructed.

Id. at 975.

building and the leased property shall not be limited nor restricted to such purposes, and said building and property may be used for any other lawful business, without the consent of LESSOR.

Although the language of this lease with regard to appellant's obligation to continue business operations in the leased premises during the term of the lease is not as clear as the language in non-abandonment clauses such as those quoted in *Kroger Co. v. Bonny Corp.*, 134 Ga.App. 834, 216 S.E.2d 341 (1975)[1], any ambiguity is dispelled by application of the rules governing the construction of contracts. One of the rules pertinent to this matter is

> that an ambiguity in a document should be construed against its draftsman. If the construction is doubtful, that which goes most strongly against the party executing the instrument or undertaking the obligation is generally to be preferred; ..." OCGA § 13-2-2(5).[*Anderson v. Southeastern Fidelity Ins. Co.*, 251 Ga. 556, 557, 307 S.E.2d 499 (1983).]

Under the authority quoted above, since the lease with which this case is concerned was drafted by appellant, it must be construed most strongly against appellant. Another applicable rule is the one expressed in OCGA § 13-2-2(4), requiring that a contract be considered in its entirety.

> [A] contract should not be torn apart and construed in pieces, but the court should look to the entire instrument and so construe it as to reconcile its different parts and reject a construction which leads to contradiction, in order to ascertain the true intention of the parties, which is the real purpose of the judicial construction of contracts. [Cits.] [*Sachs v. Jones*, 83 Ga.App. 441, 444, 63 S.E.2d 685 (1951).]

In considering the entirety of the lease contract in the present case, I note that in addition to the provision for appellant using the premises for a supermarket business or any other lawful business, the lease provides for percentage rental payments, i.e., that appellant pay as rent in addition to a stated base rent, a percentage of its revenues over a specified amount.

Considering the percentage rental provision together with the provision quoted above relating to business use, which includes a right to assignment of the lease without consent of the lessor, and construing the lease most strongly against appellant as the drafter of the lease, I conclude, as did the trial court and the Court of Appeals, that the lease contains an express covenant by appellant that it would conduct business operations in the leased premises during the entire period of the lease.

---

1. " '[L]essee agrees not to abandon or vacate leased premise during the period of this lease.' " *Id.*, 134 Ga.App. at 838, 216 S.E.2d 341.

Appellant and the majority rely on *Kroger Co. v. Bonny Corp.*, supra, for the proposition that the provision in the lease for use of the premises for a business other than operating a supermarket does not amount to an express covenant of continuous operation. There is, however, an essential difference between the language used in the lease in *Bonny* and the language used in the lease in this case. In *Bonny*, the pertinent language provided only that the tenant would "use said premises in a lawful manner." Paying the base rent and keeping the premises empty would certainly constitute using the premises "in a lawful manner." The lease in the present case, in contrast, requires that appellant use the premises for a "lawful business." Holding the premises empty cannot reasonably be construed as using the premises for a "business." That distinction in the lease language renders *Bonny* inapplicable to the present case.

The majority rejects the possibility of the existence of an implied covenant with the simplistic assertion that the base rent provided for in the lease is "substantial." What are the standards to be applied in determining whether the base rent is a "substantial" amount? Is substantiality of the base rent the only factor to be considered? These questions go unanswered in the majority opinion. A more reasoned approach than simply declaring that the base rent is substantial and that there cannot, therefore, be an implied covenant of continuous operation would be to apply the conditions enumerated by the Arizona Court of Appeals in *First American Bank & Trust Co. v. Safeway Stores, Inc.*, 729 P.2d 938, 940, 151 Ariz. 584 (1986):

> [C]ertain conditions must be satisfied before a covenant will be implied: "(1) the implication must arise from the language used; (2) it must appear from the language used that it was so clearly within the contemplation of the parties that they deemed it unnecessary to express it; (3) implied covenants can only be justified on the grounds of legal necessity; (4) a promise can be implied only where it can be rightfully assumed that it would have been made if attention had been called to it; (5) there can be no implied covenant where the subject is completely covered by the contract."

I am persuaded that adoption of those standards in this state would lead to more certainty in the drafting and interpretation of commercial leases, and that the application of those standards to the present case would result in the conclusion that there was an implied covenant of continuous operation in the lease under consideration. Since that conclusion would require affirmance of the judgment of the Court of Appeals, I must dissent to the reversal mandated by the majority.

b. Tenant's Right to Compete With Itself

KAUDER, KLOTZ & VENITT v. ROSE'S STORES, INC.

United States District Court, Eastern District of North Carolina, 1973.
359 F.Supp. 1280.

LARKINS, District Judge.

On June 3, 1953, defendant Rose's entered into a 25 year lease agreement with Marion Investment Company for four lots and a building in Morehead City, North Carolina. In 1961 plaintiff acquired the property subject to the original lease. The lease provides for a $15,000 per year minimum guaranteed rental which covered the 15,000 square foot building. In addition the lease provides for a 5% of gross sales override over $300,000 per year as additional rental. The store covered by the lease in question is at the corner of Arendell and 8th Streets in downtown Morehead City and is Rose's Store #59. It has been continuously operated since 1953, having produced sales in every year which returned additional rental to the owners from the percentage of sales override.

On or about August 1, 1971, Rose's opened a 50,000 square foot store (#200) in the Plaza Shopping Center approximately 1.9 miles west of downtown Morehead City. During the next year, gross sales in Store #59 dropped substantially resulting in the instant suit.

The plaintiff alleges in the complaint that the opening of Store #200 in the immediate vicinity of the demised premises diverted business from the demised premises and thereby substantially diminished sales and income at the demised premises, resulting in a drop in plaintiff's rental income based on gross sales. Plaintiff contends that these actions of the defendant violated express and implied conditions, covenants, and promises contained in the lease. The plaintiff further contends that the defendant's actions were done willfully with the intention of diverting business from Store #59 and thus reducing the amount of rent attributable to gross sales. Plaintiff prays for an accounting, compensatory and punitive damages, interest, and costs. Plaintiff also prays for the Court to enjoin the defendants from diverting business from the demised premises and maintaining a store in competition therewith.

The defendant admits the terms of the lease entered into in 1953 and the opening of the new store, #200, in the Plaza Shopping Center in 1971. However, defendant denies that it has violated any express or implied covenants, conditions, or terms of the lease and denies that it willfully opened the new store to intentionally divert business from the plaintiff's store.

Specifically, the defendant contends (1) that in the late 1960's Morehead City had expanded westward and that Carteret County was losing customers to other localities because of poor product selection, noncompetitive pricing, poor parking facilities, and a lack of modern stores; (2) that the opening of the new 50,000 square foot store would offer a wider selection of items at a lower cost to the consumer in a modern shopping center with ample parking; (3) that the defendant has at all times operated Store #59 as a profitable business and continues to do so; and (4) that the guaranteed minimum of $15,000 is a reasonable rental value of the property with 5% additional rent on gross income over $300,000 being a bonus to the plaintiffs in that Store #59 has done considerably better than anticipated by the parties making the lease.

This cause is now before this Court on a Rule 12(b)(6) motion to dismiss filed by the defendant and motions for summary judgment filed by both parties. A hearing was held in Trenton, North Carolina on May 23, 1973.

There is no express condition in the lease in question which prohibits the defendant from opening another store in any given area. Nor is there any term or condition of the lease which specifically prohibits competition in any fashion by the defendant. The key provision upon which the plaintiff relies is:

"1. The Tenant shall use and occupy the entire buildings on the demised premises for the sales by Tenant at retail of merchandise and for no other purpose.

Tenant shall diligently and continuously operate and conduct its retail business throughout the entire term and shall use all proper and reasonable efforts consistent with good business practice to the end that the gross sales of such business shall throughout the entire term be as large as possible."

The plaintiff claims that the above quoted provision places the burden upon the defendant to diligently and continuously operate its business and to use all proper and reasonable efforts to make gross sales as large as possible. Plaintiff further claims that the provision obligates the defendant to do nothing inconsistent with the production of maximum rent.

These allegations are sufficient to raise the issue that the defendant violated certain terms and conditions of the lease. Therefore, a valid cause of action has been stated and defendant's motion to dismiss under Rule 12(b)(6) must be denied.

Therefore, both parties having moved for summary judgment under Rule 56, and it appearing that there is no genuine issue as to any material fact, the Court, having carefully studied the pleadings, affidavits, answers to interrogatories, and other material in the record, will next consider the cross motions for summary judgment.

The language of the lease provides that the defendant has an obligation to diligently and continuously operate its business in Store #59 and to use all proper and reasonable efforts to make gross sales as large as possible. Therefore, the issue is whether, by opening Store #200 in the Plaza Shopping Center, the defendant has breached its obligation. This Court feels that it has not.

The basic law in this area is found in 52 C.J.S. Landlord and Tenant § 502(2), pp. 454 and 455.

"Where there is an implied obligation on the part of the lessee to occupy and use the demised property for the purpose expressed in the lease, he cannot, by ceasing to operate, or by changing the nature of his business, or by transferring operations to other locations, as by diverting his business to another store which he owns, or by moving some departments of the business to other premises, avoid liability for the percentage rent and pay merely the minimum amount provided for or guaranteed.

"In this connection it has been stated that the unconscionable diversion of business by the lessee from percentage-lease premises should be penalized, and, thus, where a lessee opens a like business in the immediate vicinity, resulting in loss of business on the leased property, the income from the new place may be treated as belonging to the old. *Whether a lessee under a percentage lease or rental agreement is prohibited from engaging in a competing business in the vicinity depends on the facts and circumstances of the particular case.*" (emphasis added)

First of all, the Court notes that Rose's did not open Store #200 in the "immediate vicinity" of Store #59. Store #200 is 1.9 miles from Store #59 and is in a suburban shopping center as opposed to Store #59's downtown location.

Next, the Court notes that in most cases which arise under similar circumstances the defendant has vacated the demised premises, changed the nature of the business, transferred operations to another location, or diverted his business. All of this is done in an attempt to diminish the rent paid the lessor on a percentage basis. Looking at the facts and circumstances in the instant case, it is noteworthy that Rose's is continuing to operate Store #59, has not changed the nature of the business, and is still paying a percentage on gross sales over $300,000 per year. The fact that some operations may have been transferred to Store #200 and that business may have been diverted from Store #59 does not appear to be the result of an attempt to diminish the rent payable to the plaintiffs on a percentage basis.

The Court has carefully studied the Retail Consumer Survey of Carteret County tabulated in 1970. The report found that a substantial percentage of apparel, general merchandise, and furniture sales were lost to the county. The reasons given were that the stores in the county could not offer the large volume, narrow profit margin competitive pricing available in other areas. The report concluded,

"Carteret stores are not modern, do not have satisfactory parking facilities, and have an inadequate variety of merchandise that is not competitively priced."

The defendant, faced with the accurate details of the above report, had an opportunity to locate in the new Plaza Shopping Center in the rapidly growing western part of Morehead City. They had a chance to lease a 50,000 square foot store which would enable them to offer large volume, narrow profit margin items which the public demands and which Store #59, with its space limitations, could not handle. Store #200 would offer a wide variety of competitively priced items in a modern facility with ample parking. L.H. Harvin, Jr., President of Rose's, stated in his affidavit,

"The Rose's management felt that if we did not exercise our opportunity to continue to be the lead mercantile store in the area that one of our many competitors would exercise the opportunity and we would be relegated to a secondary sales position in our old store and would be faced with materially decreasing sales and the possibility of an unprofitable operation."

It is the opinion of this Court that the opening of Store # 200 was not an attempt to diminish the rent payable to the plaintiffs but was merely a sound business venture. The defendant is engaged in a highly competitive business in a rapidly growing community. There is nothing unusual in chain stores adding to their number.

The original lease was entered into in 1953. Our country has changed greatly in the last 20 years with regard to consumer demand, the effects of inflation, and mobilization away from the city. Downtown area stores now have branches in suburban shopping centers. People do not want to fight the traffic, parking problems, and added distance to shop downtown when a one stop shopping center can meet their needs. The trend has always been to shop for convenience and economy. Today, a modern suburban shopping center fulfills this demand.

There has been a definite decrease in gross sales in Store #59 since the opening of Store #200. The first year gross sales dropped from over $1,000,000 to just over $500,000, a loss of $695,673.79 to be exact. This would be a rental loss of $34,783.69. This loss can be partially attributable to the trend away from downtown shopping. It is also logically attributable to the opening of Store #200. However, with the trend toward shopping center patronage, had defendant not opened the new store, a competitor would probably have done so, and business in Store #59 would likewise be hurt. Thus the Court concludes that the opening of Store #200, even if it did diminish gross sales in #59, was not done willfully with the intention of diverting business from Store #59.

The Court, in reaching this decision, has studied Food Fair v. Blumberg, 234 Md. 521, 200 A.2d 166, which analysed the extent of restrictions imposed upon chain store lessees. This Court, like the Maryland court, is unable to conclude that the lessees could not expand their business to the area of the new store.

This Court is also of the opinion that the minimum rent stipulation is, in itself, a fair and adequate rent and that the percentage override is more in the nature of a bonus. Mr. Harvin states in his affidavit,

"... in 1953 such a guaranteed minimum rental was reasonable and realistic and was designed to provide a realistic return on the investment in such a store. ... that sales volume in this store has, over the years of its operation since 1953, been considerably greater than was anticipated at the time of the entry into this lease ..."

This statement seems feasible when it is seen that the plaintiffs paid $265,071.00 for the property in 1961.

It has been held that where the percentage lease provides no minimum guaranteed rental or a purely nominal guarantee, the tenant is under an implied obligation to conduct the business in good faith. It has also been held that if the guaranteed rental provides the landlord an adequate return on his investment and the percentage rental feature is in the nature of a bonus, there is no obligation upon the tenant as to the manner of conducting the business not expressed in the lease.

The $15,000 annual guarantee is more than a purely nominal rental figure. But even if it were not so, the defendant has made a good faith effort to conduct the business in a proper and reasonable manner. The lease obligates the defendant to try to insure that gross sales will be as great as possible, and this is being done under the circumstances in this case. The fact plaintiffs are not receiving an extremely high rent is no reason to say the defendant has breached the lease. Should the defendant vacate the premises, a different conclusion might be reached.

The leading case in North Carolina is Jenkins v. Rose's 5, 10 and 25¢ Stores, Inc., 213 N.C. 606, 197 S.E. 174 (1938), which held:

"In the absence of specific provision in the lease contract that lessee should occupy and use the demised premises, lessee is not bound so to do, and lessors are entitled only to the minimum rent stipulated in the contract for the year in question."

In most cases of this sort, the defendant has either vacated the demised premises or opened a competing store adjacent to or close by the old store. That is not the case here. To say that by opening a new store nearly 2 miles from the demised premises is a failure to diligently use all proper and reasonable efforts consistent with good business practice to the end that gross sales be as large as possible and is a breach of the lease is to try to write a restrictive covenant against competition into the lease when none exists.

It was held in James C. Greene Company v. Kelley, 261 N.C. 166, 134 S.E.2d 166 (1964) that restrictive covenants not to engage in competitive employment are in partial restraint of trade and therefore must be in writing, supported by consideration, and reasonable as to time, territory, and terms. It is generally held that contracts in restraint of trade are to be strictly construed. To provide the relief requested in the complaint would be in effect allowing the plaintiff to restrict the defendant's trade without an express provision for this in the lease. Rose's was certainly operating consistently with good business practice by taking the opportunity to open a new store in a new shopping center outside of Morehead City. It is the conclusion of this Court that the defendant has breached no obligation imposed by the lease. Rose's is continuously operating the plaintiffs' store and is making a good faith effort to use all proper and reasonable methods to make gross sales as great as possible. The opening of Store # 200 was consistent with good business practice, and to hold Rose's liable for breaching the lease by opening this store would unduly restrict a modern chain store in an era in which the public demands cannot be met by the once popular downtown store.

Now therefore, in accordance with the foregoing, it is

Ordered, that the defendant's motion to dismiss be, and the same is, hereby Denied, and

Further Ordered, that the plaintiff's motion for summary judgment be, and the same is, hereby Denied, and

Further Ordered, that the defendant's motion for summary judgment be, and the same is, hereby Allowed, and

Further Ordered, that the Clerk shall serve copies of this Order upon Counsel of Record.

Let this Order be entered forthwith.

c. Tenant's Right to Assign

ROWE v. GREAT ATLANTIC & PACIFIC TEA CO., INC.

Court of Appeals of New York, 1978.
46 N.Y.2d 62, 412 N.Y.S.2d 827, 385 N.E.2d 566.

GABRIELLI, Judge.

We are called upon to determine whether a certain real property lease agreement contains an implied covenant limiting the lessee's power to assign the lease. The property subject to the lease is located in Sag Harbor, New York. In 1964, petitioner, Robert Rowe, an experienced attorney and businessman and the owner of the land involved herein, leased the property to respondent Great Atlantic & Pacific Tea Co. (A&P) for use as a "general merchandise business". The agreement required Rowe to erect a building on the property, and provided for a yearly rental of $14,000 for a 10-year term. It also granted A&P options to renew for two additional seven-year periods, at a slightly lower rental. The lease contained no restrictions on assignment of the lease by A&P. Rowe constructed the building as agreed, and A&P took possession and utilized the premises for a supermarket.

Some years later, both parties sought to renegotiate the agreement. Rowe desired a higher rental because of increases in taxes and other expenses, while A&P wished to have the building enlarged. Following protracted negotiations, a new lease was executed in 1971, in which it was provided that Rowe would expand the building by an additional 6,313 square feet, and that the base rental would be increased to

$34,420 per year. This figure was reached by estimating the cost to Rowe of the improvements to the building and then computing a rate of return agreed to by the parties and adding that to the old rental. The new lease was for a period of 15 years, and provided A&P with with the option to renew for three additional seven-year periods at the same rental. In addition to the base rental, the new lease provided that Rowe was to receive $1\frac{1}{2}\%$ of the store's annual gross receipts in excess of $2,294,666 and less than $5,000,000. In other words, unless gross receipts reached the $2,294,666 mark, the percentage clause would be inoperable. There was no warranty, stipulation or promise by A&P that sales would climb to the minimum necessary to trigger the percentage clause. The lease contained no restriction on the lessee's right to assign the lease. Nor did it make any reference to assignability other than providing that the lease would bind the heirs and assigns of the parties.

Unfortunately for all concerned, the new store did not fare as well as had been hoped. Indeed, A&P entered into a period of retrenchment in which it decided to close several of its less profitable stores, and the Sag Harbor store was one of those selected. Following months of discussion with Rowe and others, and over Rowe's objections, A&P in 1975 shut down its operation in Sag Harbor and assigned the lease of the premises to respondent Southland Corp., which operates a chain of supermarkets under the name Gristede Brothers. Rowe then commenced this proceeding seeking to recover possession of the premises as well as money damages. His claim is premised on the theory that A&P breached an implied covenant against assignment without consent of the lessor.

Following a nonjury trial, Supreme Court dismissed the petition on the merits, concluding that in the absence of bad faith, which was not shown, A&P had the unqualified right to assign the lease since there existed no provision limiting that right. With respect to Rowe's claim that the lease contained an implied covenant limiting A&P's right to assign, the court concluded that he had not met his burden of proof on this issue in that he had failed to prove that no reasonable landlord would have entered into this lease without an implicit understanding that the lessee could not freely assign the lease. The court reasoned that in order to show the existence of such an implicit covenant, the lessor would first be required to prove that without the percentage rent clause, which was the only factor indicating that there might actually exist such an implied agreement, the lease would have been unconscionable.

Petitioner appealed and the Appellate Division reversed, stating that the trial court had placed too heavy a burden upon petitioner. Noting that the courts will find the existence of an implied covenant limiting the right to assign if the lease is such that the landlord entered into it in reliance upon the special ability or characteristics of the lessee, the court reasoned that the existence of a percentage clause in a lease is a strong indication of such reliance. Although the existence of a base rental in addition to the percentage rental would be some evidence to the contrary, the Appellate Division concluded that in this case that was not true because in the court's judgment the base rental was not substantial.   Accordingly, the Appellate Division reversed Supreme Court and ruled in favor of petitioner. We cannot agree with that determination.

   . . .

   It has long been the law that covenants seeking to limit the right to assign a lease are "restraints which courts do not favor.   They are construed with the utmost jealousy, and very easy modes have always been countenanced for defeating them" (Riggs v. Pursell, 66 N.Y. 193, 201.)   This is so because they are restraints on the free alienation of land, and as such they tend to prevent full utilization of the land, which is contrary to the best interests of society.   Since such covenants are to be construed strictly even if expressly stated, it follows that a court should not recognize the existence of an implied limitation upon assignment unless the situation is such that the failure to do so would be to deprive a party of the benefit of his bargain.

   In the case presently before us petitioner Rowe has failed to prove the existence of an implied covenant limiting the lessee's right to assign the lease.   Such a covenant is to be recognized only if it is clear that a reasonable landlord would not have entered into the lease without such an understanding, for it is only in such a situation that it can be said with the requisite certainty that to refuse to recognize such a covenant would be to deprive the landlord of the fruits of his bargain.   This is not such a case.

   An implied covenant limiting the right to assign will often be found in those situations in which it is evident that the landlord entered into the lease in reliance upon some special skill or ability of the lessee which will have a material effect upon the fulfillment of the landlord's reasonable contractual expectations.   In the typical lease in which the landlord is assured of a set monthly rent, and has not placed any unusual restrictions upon the use of the premises, there is no occasion to find an implied covenant precluding or limiting assignment.   This is so because the only reasonable expectation of the landlord is that the rent will be paid and the premises not abused, and thus the identity of the tenant is not material to the landlord's expectations under the lease.   If, however, the expectations of the landlord are substantially dependent upon some special skill or trait of the lessee, the lack of which might endanger the lessor's legitimate contractual expectations, then it may be appropriate to find the existence of an implied covenant limiting the right to assign, for in such circumstances no reasonable person would enter into the contract without assurance that the tenant could not be replaced by an assignee lacking the requisite skills or character traits.   Even in such a case, however, the implied restrictions must of course be limited to the extent possible without destroying the landlord's legitimate interests.

The type of situation in which a court may properly find that there exists a covenant limiting the right to assign is illustrated by the factual pattern which confronted the court in Nassau Hotel Co. v. Barnett & Barse Corp., 212 N.Y. 568, 106 N.E. 1036, affg. on opn. at 162 App.Div. 381, 147 N.Y.S. 283. There, the owner of a hotel had leased the hotel and all its appurtenances to two men, one of whom was an experienced hotel manager. The lease granted them " 'the exclusive possession, control and management' " of the hotel, and they not only became responsible " 'for the operation ... and maintenance' " of the hotel, but also promised that they would operate it " 'at all times in a first-class, business-like manner' " (162 App.Div. at p. 382, 147 N.Y.S. at p. 284). In lieu of any set rental, the owner was to receive 19% of the gross receipts of the hotel. Subsequently, the lessees assigned the lease to a corporation and the landlord sued to recover the premises. The courts concluded that the lease could not be assigned without the owner's consent, even though the lease did not contain a provision limiting the lessees' power to assign, because the entire agreement indicated conclusively that a fundamental premise of the agreement was that the two original lessees would operate the hotel. This was so in part because the landlord had agreed to accept a percentage of the receipts in place of rent, and thus his legitimate expectations were completely dependent on the ability and honesty of the two individual lessees. To deprive him of the right to depend on the fact that the hotel was being operated by the individuals with whom he had contracted would have been to deprive him of a substantial element of his reasonable and legitimate contractual expectations.

Although the existence of the percentage clause was a significant factor in that decision, it alone was not dispositive. Rather, the court properly considered the entire agreement, with its emphasis on the operation of the hotel and the implicit dependence of the landlord upon the identity of the operators of the hotel. Thus, while a percentage clause in a lease is some sign of an implied agreement to limit the lessee's power to assign the lease, its significance will vary with the other terms of the lease, the surrounding circumstances, the nature of the business conducted upon the premises, and the identities and expectations of the parties.

Although the lease we are called upon to interpret today does contain a percentage clause, it is a far cry from that involved in *Nassau Hotel*. There, the percentage of gross receipts to be received by the landlord was the only value the landlord was to receive from the agreement, for there was no set rental. Here, in contradistinction, the landlord is provided with an annual rental of some $34,420 in addition to whatever amount he might receive pursuant to the percentage clause. We would also emphasize that the percentage clause does not result in any additional income to the landlord until and unless the store first attains sales of over $2,294,666 in a particular year. Of some interest is the fact that this figure is considerably higher than the previous record gross sales at the Sag Harbor store at the time the lease was entered into. It is thus evident that the percentage clause, although doubtless of considerable interest to the landlord as a hedge against inflation and as a means of sharing in the hoped for success of the store, was not a material part of the lessor's fundamental expectations under the lease. Hence, it cannot be said that the lease was entered into in sole reliance upon the skill, expertise, and reputation of A&P, and thus there is no reason to find an implied covenant limiting the lessee's right to assign the lease.

This conclusion is buttressed by consideration of the circumstances surrounding and preceding the making of the new lease in 1971. It should not be forgotten that at that time the landlord was bound by a long-term lease which provided substantially less rent per square foot of store space than does the current lease, taking into account the expansion in size of the store. Indeed, examination of the two leases indicates that even absent the percentage clause, the new lease was an improvement over the old from the landlord's point of view. Moreover, comparison with other supermarket leases indicates that the base rental in the new lease is not out of line with the rentals reserved in other leases. Thus we cannot agree with the Appellate Division that it is "not substantial."

Of additional interest is the identity of the parties to this agreement. Petitioner is an experienced attorney and businessman knowledgeable in real estate transactions. A&P is, of course, a national firm presumably represented by capable agents. The negotiations which resulted in the new lease were long and exhaustive, dealing with a variety of topics, and the lease itself is obviously the result of a process of give and take. Although A&P might well have agreed to include a provision limiting its right to assign the lease had petitioner insisted upon such a clause, we may safely assume that petitioner would have had to pay a price for that concession. In these circumstances, the courts should be extremely reluctant to interpret an agreement as impliedly stating something which the parties have neglected to specifically include. As we have previously declared in a similar context, "such lack of foresight does not create rights or obligations" (Mutual Life Ins. Co. of N.Y. v. Tailored Woman, 309 N.Y. 248, 253, 128 N.E.2d 401, 403).

Finally, although not necessary to our disposition of this appeal, we would note that even were the circumstances such as to support the conclusion that the lease contains a provision limiting the lessee's right to assign the lease, that finding alone would not justify judgment in favor of petitioner. It would then be necessary to further consider whether that implied restriction would in fact be violated by assignment of the lease to another supermarket chain in light of all the facts and circumstances.

Accordingly, the order appealed from should be reversed, with costs, and the judgment of Supreme Court, Suffolk County, reinstated.

BREITEL, C.J., and JASEN, JONES, WACHTLER, FUCHSBERG and COOKE, JJ., concur.

Order reversed, etc.

NOTES

1. Would *Wickline* have been decided differently if the lease had provided for a percentage rental in addition to base rent? If Wickline had been an anchor tenant in a shopping center? Would the *Piggly Wiggly* court have decided *Ingannamorte* differently? Would *Rowe* have been decided differently if A & P had been an anchor tenant in a shopping center? Would the *Ingannamorte* court have decided *Rowe* differently on its facts? After the decision in *Rowe*, would A & P be free to set up a new store within one or two miles of the old site? Would the result in any of the principal cases have been different if the action had been brought not by the landlord but by another tenant? Cf. Lilac Variety, Inc. v. Dallas Texas Co., 383 S.W.2d 193 (Tex.Civ.App. 1964). What damages are recoverable for breach of a continuous operation clause? See Hornwood v. Smith's Food King No. 1, 105 Nev.188, 772 P.2d 1284 (1989).

Representing tenant or landlord, what lease language would you have proposed to avoid the problems that arose in each of the principal cases? What does *Piggly Wiggly* tell you about the need for precision in drafting?

For an excellent discussion of continuous operation covenants, see Comment, Commercial Leasing: Implied Covenants of Operation in Shopping Center Leases, 95 Dick.L.Rev. 383 (1991). See generally, Kratovil, The Declaration of Restrictions, Easements, Liens, and Covenants: An Overview of An Important Document, 22 John Marshall L.Rev. 69 (1988); Thigpen, Good Faith Performance Under Percentage Leases, 51 Miss.L.J. 315 (1980–1981); Terkel, Reciprocal Agreements in Shopping Center Developments, 14 St. Mary's L.J. 541 (1983).

2. *Counselling Tenants.* To convince their construction and permanent lenders that the center is more than a will o' the wisp, shopping center developers will often ask prospective tenants to sign their leases well before construction on the center begins. If financing turns out to be unavailable, if other leases do not materialize, if construction costs are too high, or local planning officials too reluctant in giving the necessary approvals, the center will not open. The tenant, his expectations dashed, will find little solace in the courts. Even if the tenant can show that the developer breached an obligation, damages will be hard to prove and specific performance hard to enforce. One solution, other than dealing with a developer with a known track record, is to provide for some form of liquidated damages in the event the center does not open.

The tenant's problems do not disappear once the center is built. The location of his unit may be an issue. The tenant will want to pinpoint his location at the time he signs the lease in order to assure good exposure and access to pedestrian traffic between the parking lot and the anchor tenants. The landlord, however, will want the discretion to locate the unit where it will best meet demands later posed by other tenants, local planning officials and the center's architects and engineers. The tenant will also want to condition his performance on the presence of specified anchor tenants. If the landlord represented that certain, named anchor tenants would be in the center, the tenant's easiest expedient would be to condition his performance upon the continuing presence of these anchor tenants from the beginning of the lease term. Obviously the landlord will try to avoid this straitjacket, describing the anchors not by name but by objective criteria such as sales volume, type of operation and credit rating.

Finally, landlord and tenant must at the outset agree on the architectural and construction specifications for the tenant's yet unbuilt unit. Time will usually not permit the tenant to draft a set of plans to be attached as an exhibit to the lease unless the tenant is a chain operation that employs virtually identical specifications for all of its units. The lease can, however, provide for certain basic functional specifications (floor space and height, and lighting, air conditioning and wall covering requirements). Yet another approach is for the landlord to provide the tenant with a shell—four walls, a roof, floor and utility connections—leaving it to the tenant to construct the facilities to its own taste, sometimes with a cash allowance from the landlord. Representing a tenant whose lease calls for a shell, rather than a completed turn-key facility, what specific protections would you seek for your client? What added tax consequences would you consider? How can the client finance these leasehold improvements?

For a good introduction to pre-occupancy problems and their solutions, see Williams, Before the Shopping Center Opens: A Survival Manual for Developer and Tenant, 2 Real Est.Rev. 15 (Summer 1972).

3. *Inflation-Proofing Leases.* Shopping center landlords have increasingly sought to make their space leases inflation proof. Triple net terms are now the rule rather than the exception, with space tenants paying for their own utilities and insurance and for their proportionate share of the center's overall maintenance costs. Landlords protect themselves against skyrocketing property taxes through clauses (called "tax stops") requiring their tenants to bear a proportionate share of any increases in real estate taxes levied on the center after a specified initial period, typically the first year of operations.

The landlord's most durable inflation fighter has been the percentage rental. Although rent may be based exclusively on a percentage of the tenant's sales, most percentage leases call for a minimum fixed rental plus a percentage of the tenant's gross income over a specified level. Percentages vary by region and by type of tenant. High volume tenants, like department stores, supermarkets and drug stores pay lower percentages—typically one to two percent. Low volume, specialty tenants like gift shops, restaurants, beauty shops and stationery and jewelry stores pay in a higher range—typically five to ten percent. Candy stores may pay as much as twelve percent and motion picture theaters as much as fifteen percent. For a comparison of percentage ranges for virtually all types of retail tenants over a period of several years, see Schloss, Inflation Proofing Retail Investments with Percentage Leases, 7 Real Est.Rev. 36 (Winter 1978).

Problems in administering percentage clauses usually stem from imprecision in the lease's definition of the gross income that forms the rental base. Did the parties intend to include gross income from incidental operations (a popcorn stand, say) in the gross income of the main business (a movie theater)? Does "gross receipts" include only the fee paid to the tenant by concessionaires, or does it include the concessionaire's gross revenues? Are sales generated on the premises, but concluded off-premises, to be counted? Do returned items, excise taxes and coupons count? Can charge account expenses, employee discounts and trading stamps be deducted? See generally, Note, Resolving Disputes Under Percentage Leases, 51 Minn.L.Rev. 1139 (1967).

4. *Use Clause.* Use clauses, particularly in long-term leases, are often the object of intense negotiations. The landlord will want uses to be specified narrowly so that she can control the overall mix of goods and services in the center and honor exclusive use clauses that may appear in other leases. The tenant wants a broadly worded clause that will enable him to expand into new product or service lines, and drop old ones, to meet changing consumer tastes. A major tenant under a financeable long-term lease will be under particular pressure from his prospective mortgagee to obtain a virtually boundless use clause.

Even when they reach agreement in principle, landlord and tenant will face the difficult task of putting their agreement into words. Belvidere South Towne Center, Inc. v. One Stop Pacemaker, Inc., 54 Ill.App.3d 958, 12 Ill.Dec. 626, 370 N.E.2d 249 (2d Dist.1977), suggests the problem. Plaintiff, a shopping center landlord, sought a judgment declaring that Paragraph 10 of its lease barred its tenant, Nabors, from selling food items. The paragraph provided that "tenant will use and operate the demised building for the purpose of a Drug Store ...." Nabors' unit was immediately adjacent to an earlier tenant, One Stop Pacemaker, which operated a supermarket and package liquor store. Finding Nabors in violation of Paragraph 10, the trial court enjoined him from

> selling on or from the premises of Belvidere South Towne Center, Boone County, Illinois, any of the following items: meats of any kind, dairy products, including, but not limited to milk, cheese and ice cream, bread and bakery goods, fresh fruit and vegetables, breakfast foods, canned goods, soft drinks, frozen foods, or any other grocery products except those of a dietary nature, or candy and gum.

The appellate court affirmed. After briefly sampling dictionary definitions and judicial elaborations of the word, "drug store," the court concluded that the central issue was not "what the common usage or legal definition of a drug store is, or what a drug store may sell," but rather what the landlord and tenant had intended when they had used the term. The particular context of the center and Nabors' place in it, bore heavily on intent:

> We believe it is clear that the clause in the instant case, "tenant will use and operate the demised building for the purpose of a Drug Store", was intended by the parties to mean that Nabors would operate a drug store and would not compete in the sale of food products with Pacemaker, the adjoining tenant. ... To interpret this clause in the manner in which Nabors requests would confer an unfair advantage on Nabors over Pacemaker, the first tenant in the shopping center and the only tenant selling food products from 1966 until 1974, when Nabors began selling food products.

Though affirming the trial court order, the Court remanded for clarification "as to what specific dietetic and sugar-free dairy and food products Nabors is allowed to sell as part of his operation as a drug store."

Does a use clause in a 1957 lease calling for a "service restaurant, Automat restaurant-cafeteria, counter and stool restaurant, retail shop for the sale of baked goods and other items usually sold in Horn & Hardart retail sales" cover a fast-food, Burger King operation almost twenty years later? Looking strictly at the language of the lease, and without the benefit of the contextual evidence that proved decisive in *One Stop Pacemaker,* the New York Court of Appeals concluded that the two uses were not the same: "It cannot be said that the changes which concededly have occurred in recent years in manner and style of restaurant and food service have destroyed completely the difference between cafeterias and short order, limited menu food service primarily for off-premises consumption." Horn & Hardart Co. v. Junior Bldg., Inc., 40 N.Y.2d 927, 389 N.Y.S.2d 831, 358 N.E.2d 514, 515 (1976).

5. *Exclusive Right to Sell Clause.* Exclusive right to sell clauses are closely connected to use clauses. Indeed, the tenant whose landlord proposes a tightly confined set of uses can plausibly counter by conditioning his acceptance of the use limitation on the grant of exclusive rights to the restricted uses within the shopping center.

As noted in the principal excerpt from the Report of the A.B.A. Committee on Leases, exclusive use clauses are being employed less frequently today than formerly. Marketing studies show that consumers are drawn to centers in which several shops, as well as anchors, offer competing goods. Also, with the trend to large, regional centers, it has become virtually impossible to give exclusives to each of fifty, sixty or more tenants. Finally, the Federal Trade Commission and the courts have curtailed the use of exclusives because of their anticompetitive effects. See note 7, below.

Notwithstanding these inroads, exclusive sales clauses still appear in shopping center leases, primarily in the leases of specialty tenants in smaller shopping centers. The question these clauses most frequently raise is whether the tenant, secured against competition within the shopping center originally contemplated, will continue to enjoy its monopoly when the center is subsequently expanded.   In Slice v. Carozza Properties, Inc., 215 Md. 357, 137 A.2d 687 (1958), tenant had been given the exclusive right to sell "Beer, wine and liquor for off-the-premises consumption in the Hillcrest Heights Shopping Center ..." situated on "Block M".   About three years later, the landlord built and leased several additional stores in Block M, fifty-four feet from the original stores.   One of the new tenants sold beer and wine for off-premises consumption, violating a lease provision that restricted it to the sale of wine and beer for on-premises consumption.   The court of appeals overturned the trial court's ruling that the new and old groups of stores formed two separate shopping centers and that the new group was thus unaffected by the plaintiff's exclusive.   The court observed that, to hold otherwise "would ignore the obvious business fact that two adjacent portions of a shopping center built at different times on different portions of the same tract owned and managed by the same owner, constitute a single shopping center."   215 Md. at 367, 137 A.2d at 692.   The issue was complicated by the fact that a plan of the center, referred to in the lease as an exhibit, had never been attached to the lease.

Should the new, competing tenant be enjoined if his unit is on a second parcel, acquired by the landlord after the first unit has been leased? Will tenants in the new center have any reason to search title to the old, and be on constructive notice of restrictions appearing in leases on the first parcel?   Should the landlord be held for damages, if these later tenants cannot be enjoined?

6. *Radius Clause.*   Say that landlord and tenant in *Kauder, Klotz & Venitt* had expressly provided that Rose's Stores could not operate another store within a 1.9 mile radius.   Would the court have enforced the clause?   The tenant in *Kauder, Klotz & Vennitt* was paying a percentage rental.   Can you think of any circumstance in which a landlord would seek a radius clause, and a court would enforce it, if the tenant was not obligated on a percentage rental?

7. *Antitrust.*   Use clauses, exclusive use clauses and radius clauses each inhibit competition within or between shopping centers.   Although these clauses, and clauses giving anchor tenants the right to veto the entry and dictate the location of other tenants, produce possibly unlawful restraints of trade, they have been attacked only sporadically under state and federal antitrust laws.   One reason for the spotty record of federal enforcement may be the belief that shopping center activities and effects are strictly intrastate and thus jurisdictionally beyond the federal antitrust laws.   See, for example, St. Anthony-Minneapolis, Inc. v. Red Owl Stores, Inc., 316 F.Supp. 1045 (D.Minn. 1970).

The Federal Trade Commission has leveled the most sustained attack on anticompetitive practices among major shopping center tenants through several consent orders and one litigated case, Tyson's

Corner Regional Shopping Center, 85 F.T.C. 970, mod. 86 F.T.C. 921 (1975). Consent orders have prohibited major tenants from exacting radius restrictions and use clauses that limit stores in the price or quality of goods they can carry. See, for example, Sears, Roebuck & Co., 89 F.T.C. 240 (1977); Strawbridge & Clothier, 87 F.T.C. 593 (1976). One consent order prohibited a major tenant from obtaining exclusive use commitments in shopping centers of 200,000 or more square feet. Peoples Drug Stores, Inc., 87 F.T.C. 1 (1976). Presumably, exclusives will still be available to smaller, specialty tenants and in smaller centers.

The Commission's views on other restrictive shopping center practices can be gleaned from the much-discussed consent order in Gimbel Brothers, Inc., 83 F.T.C. 1320 (1974). The order prohibits Gimbels, as a shopping center tenant, from exacting agreements giving it the right to disapprove another retailer's entry into the center, or to determine the amount or location of the retailer's floor space. Also barred are agreements prohibiting the entry of any particular retailer or class of retailers, or limiting the types or brands of merchandise that another retailer can offer. Gimbels was, however, allowed to make agreements aimed at maintaining the quality image of its stores: it can limit the selection of tenants who will be proximate to Gimbel's stores, require the landlord to maintain reasonable standards of appearance in the center, and prohibit occupancy by "clearly objectionable types of tenants" such as pornography shops.

Earlier F.T.C. plans to promulgate a trade regulation rule governing restrictive shopping center practices have apparently been dropped. F.T.C.: Watch 17 (No. 69, April 6, 1979). The Commission has since undertaken a survey of shopping center landlords and tenants inquiring into existing restrictive practices to determine the effect, if any, of its 1975 *Tyson's Corner* decision. F.T.C. News Release, July 5, 1979.

For background on the state and federal antitrust implications of shopping center practices, see Schear & Sheehan, Restrictive Lease Clauses and the Exclusion of Discounters from Regional Shopping Centers, 25 Emory L.J. 609 (1976); Note, The Antitrust Implications of Restrictive Covenants in Shopping Center Leases, 86 Harv.L.Rev. 1201 (1973); Halper, The Antitrust Laws Visit Shopping Center "Use Restrictions," 4 Real Est.L.J. 3 (1975). On radius clauses, see Marsh, The Federal Antitrust Laws and Radius Clauses in Shopping Center Leases, 32 Hastings L.J. 839 (1981); Lentzner, The Antitrust Implications of Radius Clauses in Shopping Center Leases, 55 J.Urb.L. 1 (1977); Comment, The Shopping Center Radius Clause: Candidate for Antitrust? 32 Sw.L.J. 825 (1978).

8. *Common Areas.* The Report of the A.B.A. Committee on Leases, excerpted above, touches on several other areas of concern to tenants negotiating space leases in shopping centers. One of the more important issues involves the tenant's rights and obligations respecting common areas. The Report recommends that the space lease contain a

legal description of the entire center together with a site plan identifying the location of the leased premises and the common areas such as parking areas, sidewalks, loading areas, escalators, elevators and rest rooms. The lease should expressly give the tenant a nonexclusive easement to use all of the common areas for its own benefit and for the benefit of its employees, customers and suppliers. The lease agreement should also specify the percentage of common area that must be completed before the tenant's obligations under the lease commence and, once completed, the landlord's obligation to maintain the common areas.

9. *The Tenant and the Permanent Lender.* Space tenants, particularly those who execute and record their leases before the landlord obtains its financing, should anticipate requests from the landlord aimed at satisfying its lender. Because the lender will probably need to secure its loan with a first lien, the landlord can be expected to ask the tenant to agree to subordinate his lease to the lender's mortgage or deed of trust. Lenders will also typically want assurance that, upon foreclosure, the tenants will continue to abide by their lease obligations. Since foreclosure terminates any subordinated leases, lenders will require landlords to obtain their tenants' agreement to attorn to the lender or to any buyer on a foreclosure sale. In return for their agreement to subordinate and attorn, tenants usually request a nondisturbance covenant from the lender to the effect that the tenant will be allowed to continue its possession under its lease after foreclosure and sale.

*

INDEX

References are to Pages

1039

†

1-56662-064-3

90000